INTRODUCTION TO
AMERICAN
GOVERNMENT

Ogg and Ray's

INTRODUCTION TO AMERICAN GOVERNMENT

By William H. Young

UNIVERSITY OF WISCONSIN

13TH EDITION

New York

APPLETON-CENTURY-CROFTS

DIVISION OF MEREDITH PUBLISHING COMPANY

PREFACE

It is a pleasure to present this thirteenth edition of the *Introduction to American Government* and in so doing to continue to commemorate its original authors and particularly my former colleague, Frederic A. Ogg. In this edition I have largely rewritten the first chapter to include more modern material on the American society and belief system. I have also redesigned the chapter on *The Federal System* in order to try to make this difficult concept more meaningful to present-day students. In doing so, I have assigned most of the material on interstate relations to the chapters on the *Role of the State* and that on national limitations on state power to the chapter on *State Legislatures*. The chapter on *Citizenship and Immigration* has been abandoned in order to make room for the growing body of experience in the field of Civil Rights and the widening national activity in Foreign Affairs. A note on citizenship will be found in the chapter on *Voting* and a summary of our immigration policy in chapter one. I have added a new chapter, *Government and the Economy,* in which are considered the general policies and procedures of the government in maintaining or restoring prosperity. I have tried to notice all of the major achievements of that fantastically productive Congress of 1965 and to bring the material throughout up to February 1, 1966.

I should like here to acknowledge my debt to the many users of this text whose helpful suggestions have removed many of its imperfections.

W.II.Y.

University of Wisconsin

CONTENTS

C. FINANCES

Part III. State Government

Part IV. Local Government and Administration

ILLUSTRATIONS

Part I

THE FOUNDATIONS OF GOVERNMENT

IN THE UNITED STATES

A. THE CONSTITUTIONAL BASIS

★ 1 ★

The Setting

THE AMERICAN SYSTEM OF GOVERNMENT is now nearly two hundred years old. It has outlived virtually all the systems of popular government in the recorded history of this planet. Conceived as a great experiment in self-rule, it has survived a terrible ordeal by combat, progressively widened its popular base, deployed its strength about the globe as a world power of the first rank, and now stands as leader of the free world and model for many heretofore subject peoples striving for self-expression and self-rule. We might, therefore, be justified in taking its future for granted.

The great experiment

The history of political systems suggests, however, that popularly-based government is one of the most fragile of all. Whereas two or three generations ago the ultimate triumph of democratic government was considered by enlightened Westerners to be merely a matter of time and education, the rise of continental and Asiatic dictatorships, red and black, the prolonged economic stagnation of the thirties, the ever-mounting pace of technological change, and the determined rejection of Western tutelage by the masses of Asia and Africa, have combined to cloud the future and shake our optimism. In the present posture of world affairs, the American nation has undertaken staggering commitments to preserve Western society. It has equipped itself and witnessed the equipment of its leading rival with explosive power capable of devastating most of the earth's surface and the peoples who live upon it. For these new responsibilities, it is ill-prepared. Can our system survive the stresses of racial conflict and cold war uncertainty? Can it bear the frustrations of guarding the lid of Pandora's box of nuclear explosives? Can it stand a prolonged period of huge defense expenditures? What would happen to our economy if disarmament could actually be achieved? Is it capable of promoting creativity amidst the pressure for conformity? Depending as it does on an enlightened populace can it be subverted by the irrational, the tension-hounded, the spectator-oriented? No one can be certain.

Can our system survive the tests?

The American governmental system is neither simple to understand nor easy to operate. We have come to call it a democracy but this only in this century and not because it altogether resembles the classical model. It is, in truth, a mixture of elements from constitutional models as well as democratic

A mixture of democracy and constitutionalism

3

ones. From the constitutional traditions of Western, mainly English, civilization, it has incorporated the concepts of limited public authority, divided power, regional and local autonomy, and respect for legality. It has adapted from this same tradition, the institutions of civil rights, due process of law, representative legislatures, and separated and mutually antagonistic institutions of political power. From the democratic ideal it has gathered esteem for the individual, granting to him the dignity and worth of the Christian tradition and the equality of spirit and the freedom of thought, utterance, and conscience consistent with this faith. To the democratic spirit it also owes its respect for majorities and their right to govern and it has embodied these ideals in its institutions of voting, political parties, organized associations of interests, and its deference to public opinion. Each of these great ideals—democracy and constitutionalism—has influenced the development of the American system and each has reacted to and influenced the other in such a way as to produce the unique blend which we know and cherish as our governmental system.

American pluralism

Government is, we believe, but one aspect of a larger whole—the American society or the American nation. It is, perhaps, the major institutional embodiment of that larger entity but it is expected—in large part because of our constitutional tradition—to share influence with the family, the church, and various economic, fraternal, charitable, educational, recreational, and cultural associations of which the society is composed. Ours is thus a pluralistic society with many centers of influence, prestige, and validly exercised authority. The government we regard as the servant of the people and of their interests as manifested by the other associations through which they pursue happiness. It is entirely fitting, therefore, to begin the study of the American government with an analysis of the people by whom and for whom it is operated and of the society which it is intended to serve.

THE AMERICAN PEOPLE

The population of the U.S.

There are 195 million American residents of a continental and island area of 3.6 million square miles endowed with an abundance of natural advantages unmatched by any area of comparable size. These people are responsible for the lives and fortunes of another 2.6 million people in 4.5 thousand square miles of island and other territorial areas over which flies the American flag. The attempt to practice self-government over an area so vast and among so numerous a people is without parallel in history. In fact, many of the wisest minds of Western culture had supposed it to be impossible. It has probably been the revolution in the technology of transportation and communication that has accompanied the rise of the American nation and the spread throughout it of democratic processes that has made it possible to unite such an area in a single system of popular political institutions. Even so the centrifugal pull of regional and local interests and ambitions has

U.S. POPULATION GROWTH, ACTUAL AND PROJECTED 1790-1980

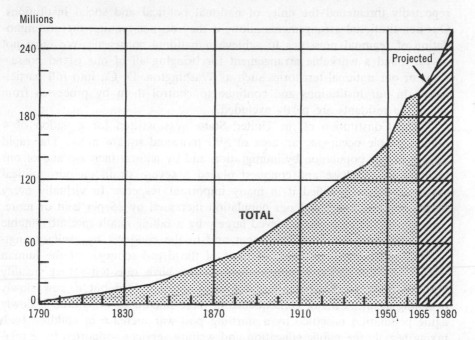

THE IMMIGRATION PICTURE, 1820-1963

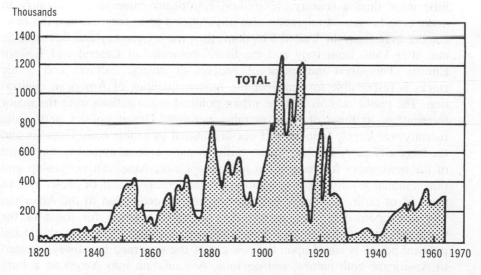

repeatedly threatened the unity of national political and social institutions. Our constitutional arrangements allow, if they do not require, the accommodation of regional pressures to achieve a national consensus. We have not as yet found a workable arrangement for bringing all of our island possessions or our national territories such as Washington, D. C., into full participation in our institutions and continue to control them by processes from which the residents are partly excluded.

Population growth

The Constitution of the United States was written for a nation of 4 million people occupying an area of 890 thousand square miles. The rapid growth of our population by immigration and by natural increase and of our territory by purchase and conquest placed a severe strain on our political system and has modified it in many important respects. In virtually every decade until World War I our population increased by 25 per cent or more. The natural increase was achieved largely by a falling death rate attributable to an abundant natural environment and to the conquest by sanitary engineering and modern medicine of most of the dread scourges of the human species. As the nation became urbanized the birth rate fell rather steadily until World War II. Thereafter, it took a sharp upturn but is now slowly declining again. A major consequence of these fluctuations has been a slowly aging population unsettled by a startling post-war increase in children both taxing heavily the public education and welfare services supported by a relatively smaller productive population.

Immigration

Until 1920 a major factor in population growth was immigration. In a little more than a century, 40 million Europeans came to this country to make their homes—a migration also unparalleled in history. At first the newcomers were from the United Kingdom, then from Germany and Scandinavia and after 1880 from Italy and the Slavic countries of Central and Eastern Europe. This great movement of peoples of diverse cultures and ethnic stocks is responsible for many of the unique qualities of American civilization. The public schools and the urban political organizations were the major transmitters to them of the American heritage. Urban politics until quite recently was largely influenced if not dominated by ethnic considerations and the large city party machines were built, in part, around appeal to the desire of the newcomers for recognition and acceptance. American citizenship and thus national loyalty was for a nation of immigrants an act of choice not an accident of birth. As such it has aroused intense dedication to the American way accompanied by misunderstanding of and contempt for those of the world whose national loyalty was otherwise acquired. The idea that valid political power is based upon the consent of the governed has always seemed to Americans both natural and obvious. Assimilation into American culture through the public schools was achieved by the children at the expense, typically, of repudiating their parents; peer group rather than familial tradition set the standards of conduct and fashioned the goals by which achieve-

ANNUAL IMMIGRATION QUOTAS OF SELECTED NATIONS
AUTHORIZED BY ACT OF 1952

Austria	1,405	Italy	5,645
Belgium	1,297	Japan	185
China	100	Korea	100
Czechoslovakia	2,859	Netherlands	3,136
Denmark	1,175	Norway	2,364
Egypt	100	Palestine	100
France	3,069	Philippines	100
Germany	25,814	Poland	6,488
Great Britain, North Ireland	65,361	Spain	250
India	100	Sweden	3,295
Ireland	17,756	U.S.S.R.	2,697

ment has been measured. Many experts believe that the permissiveness of child raising, the pressures for conformity, and the mother-oriented family style of American life may be traced directly to the influence of the immigrant.

"Give me your tired, your poor, your huddled masses," was the American policy until 1921. The closing of the land frontier in the 1890's, the rise of organized labor, the antipathy toward central Europeans aroused by the spread of communism among them, all contributed to the closing of America's front door. When various restrictions against paupers, contract laborers, criminals, orientals, and others failed markedly to reduce the tide, a quota system was instituted. It remained until 1965 the basis of our admissions policy as set forth in The Immigration and Nationality (McCarran-Walter) Act of 1952. Under it, 156,000 migrants from Europe, Asia, and Africa are authorized annually on the basis of quotas allotted to each nation or group of peoples in accordance with the relative contribution of that nation or people to our national population as it stood in 1920. The ostensible purpose of this program is to admit a group of persons each year ethnically equivalent to those already here. In practice the total quota is never used because there is no longer any important migration from Great Britain and Ireland whose peoples have a large share of the quota allotments. Most of the average annual influx of 270,000 represents migrants from this hemisphere, Canada and Mexico mainly, to whom the quota system does not apply. Some relaxation of the quota system was authorized in the period 1948-1958 in behalf of European refugees from Nazi and later Communist tyranny, many of whom had been gathered by the Allies and the new governments of Western Europe into displaced persons camps. Pressure to open the doors a little wider and to abandon the preferential treatment of Northern Europeans built in to the

The door is closed

quota system brought Congress to refashion the policy, abandon the ethnic bias, and improve the procedure.[1]

Of the 4 million who founded the nation more than 90 percent were farmers. The philosophy of the self-reliant, free-holder expressed so compellingly by Thomas Jefferson dominated the nation for generations. It still has a strong hold upon the outlook and affections of large numbers of our people. Today, however, more than 90 percent of our people live in cities, villages, or small towns; fewer than 7 percent live on farms and this percentage is declining. More than 60 percent live in the central cities or the suburbs of the 222 major metropolitan areas of the country. We are now a preponderantly urban people, dependent, huddled-together, insecure and more highly dependent upon governmental services for our comfort as well as our survival than ever before in our history.

The growth of the modern pervasive state may be traced directly to the industrialization and urbanization of our society. It is the urbanite who requires the ever-widening concern of the government in his daily life to shield him from germs, loss of wages, and the consequences of aging, and to provide him with education, recreation, and congestion-ameliorating services. Compared to that of rural and even small-town society, urban culture is

dynamic, competitive, and anonymous. The rural and small-town outlook, however, yields grudgingly to the demands of the so-called "mass society." Legislative apportionment systems, the federal character of the United States Senate, the organizational arrangements of county, town and village governments all combine to accord it a larger influence than strict majoritarianism warrants. To many spokesmen for the rural-small town point of view, the great city stands as it did for Jefferson for wickedness, greed, corruption, charismatic leadership and decadence. Somewhere in many of the major political controversies of modern America in the Congress, the state capitols, the party apparatus and the huge interest groups, the conflicts of outlook of the large city and small town may be found. The constitutional fabric of American government was designed for a rural people; the processes of democracy support the growing influence of the urban masses. Adjusting the one to the other has and will continue to require the highest order of statesmanship.

The first census of the American people (1790) revealed that among the 4 million inhabitants were 757,000 Negroes, more than 90 percent of whom were slaves. According to the census of 1960 there are now more than 18.5 million Negroes in the United States. Assimilating the African slave into

---

[1] President Johnson early in 1965 recommended to the Congress a change in the immigration laws which would: (1) eliminate the "national origins" quota system; (2) make certain the total annual quota would, in fact, be used; (3) abandon the discriminatory practices against Asian peoples. Late in 1965, these proposals were mainly approved by Congress and a limit of 170,000 established annually for Europe and Asia and 120,000 for the Western Hemisphere.

American democratic culture has proved one of the most difficult of all national problems and Negroes are still far from achieving a place consistent with their numbers or with the democratic ideals of the nation. For some decades before and after freedom, the Negro was largely an adjunct to the Southern plantation system of agricultural production. In this century and especially during the World Wars, the Negroes have been moving in large numbers to the large metropolitan centers of the North and Middle West. Here, like other streams of immigrants before them, they have sought recognition through political participation and have become active and assertive members of the big urban party organizations. From this vantage point they have pressed their claims for greater governmental exertion on behalf of themselves and their Southern brethren. Since World War II colored peoples everywhere in the world have been casting off the chains of white colonialism and demanding recognition of their own aspirations. The combination of these domestic and international challenges to "white supremacy" has thrust the race question more vigorously into our national politics than at any time since the crusade of the abolitionists and has and will test our faith in equality, our pretensions to democratic forms, and our commitments to self-determination.

Elsewhere—in the Southwest and on the Pacific coast—the Mexicans and the Chinese and Japanese resident minorities present similar if not quite such dramatic challenges to the political and cultural handicaps long imposed upon them. There were, in fact, 1.6 million members of other nonwhite races in our national population in 1960.

The virtual cessation of immigration from outside this continent has not meant a halt to the constant ebb and flow of people within our continental area. Our population is probably the most mobile in the world. Internal migration continues at a spectacular rate and is of three kinds: (1) from the east to the west; (2) from the farm to the small town to the city; and (3) from the central city to the suburbs. California, for example, is now the most populous state in the Union whereas only 50 years ago it ranked twelfth. The center of population has moved steadily westward and is now (1960) located in south-central Illinois. Despite the rapid urbanization of the nation, the central cities of Chicago, Cleveland, Detroit, Minneapolis-St. Paul, New York, Philadelphia, Pittsburgh, St. Louis, San Francisco, Washington, D. C., and many others actually lost population from 1950-1960 while the suburban areas of these same cities recorded huge gains. Mobility on this scale has many political as well as social consequences. A vast portion of our people at any time have no real attachment to the local communities in which they reside. Roots in local traditions and self-conscious community loyalties are not easily formed nor very durable. In every election, further, people are disqualified from voting because of their too recent settlement in the state and voting district. Appeals to local sentiment, state pride, and regional autonomy are relatively ineffectual to those on the move.

A mobile people

AMERICAN SOCIETY

*The
family*

Under the impact of urbanization, industrialization, and migration the American family has been undergoing a thorough reconstruction. In the family farm culture of yesteryear the family was a major unit of production. Each member contributed important and specialized labor and children could become economic assets almost as soon as they could walk and talk. Patriarchal in organization, the rural family was held together by the strong claims of the soil and the job of wresting food and fiber from it. In urban culture, the family is a consuming unit not a producing one; children are an economic liability until well into their teens and the high cost of housing, the congestion of living areas, the demands of factory and office all exert unremitting pressure on the traditional family relationships. The first shock of urban environment is revealed in falling birth rates, rising crime rates, rising divorce rates, rising emotional disturbances among the newest recruits to the cities. The father is torn between the demands of his home and those of his work. The mother takes charge of the children's moral education, and the school becomes the chief transmitter of the cultural heritage. The urban family is small, isolated from the relatives of the parents, consumption-oriented, and fragile. The immigrant family has suffered the most painful dislocation—the father's authority repudiated, schoolmates fixing the goals for dress, taste, and achievement. More recently, the flight to the suburbs of middle-class families, the spread of public housing for lower-income groups, the recapture of open space for recreation, the decline in the work-week, the increase in job security, the transfer of entertainment from cinema to home television are all recreating a new family environment. The birth rate took, at least for a time, a sharp upward turn: home-ownership is increasing. Status is now acquired more by standards of consumption than by position. Although the divorce rate continues high and women continue to enter the labor market in large numbers, the family is nevertheless recapturing some of the functions it had lost. Signs of renewed vigor are appearing first in the middle classes but may spread. Concern is still widely manifested, however, for the permissive, cooperative, nonauthoritarian and success-oriented, child-rearing practice of the American urban family. The pressure for higher and higher consumption standards takes a heavy toll of the breadwinners; the demand for more and more education for the children is placing great strains on all systems of higher education in the land; the rise in unemployed, in some cases unemployable, youth—high school dropouts—is giving city authorities constant concern.

*Religous
affiliations*

In the main this nation is composed of Protestant Christians. Approximately 60 percent of all those who profess some religious faith are members of one of the Protestant sects. About 30 percent are Roman Catholics. We are thus inheritors largely of the spirit of the Reformation—individualistic and anti-authoritarian. Religious exercises, on the whole, occupy a declining

PROPORTIONS OF RURAL AND URBAN POPULATION
1860-1960

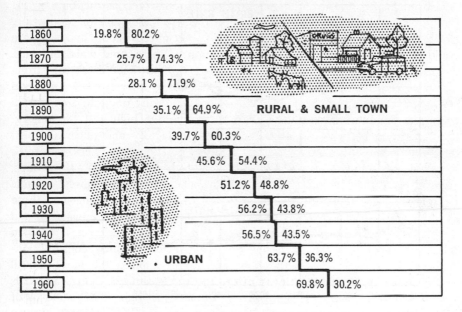

1860	19.8%	80.2%	
1870	25.7%	74.3%	
1880	28.1%	71.9%	
1890	35.1%	64.9%	RURAL & SMALL TOWN
1900	39.7%	60.3%	
1910	45.6%	54.4%	
1920	51.2%	48.8%	
1930	56.2%	43.8%	
1940	56.5%	43.5%	
1950	63.7%	36.3%	
1960	69.8%	30.2%	

URBAN

SOURCE: U. S. Bureau of the Census. Since 1910 the Census Bureau has broken down the category rural into farm and nonfarm.

place in our national culture. The separation of church and state to which our constitutional tradition binds us and the pervasive influence of the rigidly nonsectarian public-school system make the family the chief transmitter of religious beliefs. We have observed that the modern urban family is changing its character. It may not, therefore, be as effective as the patriarchal, agricultural family in inculcating strong religious feelings. The school system continues to be the arena of struggle among the faiths for influence over the young.

The modern American enjoys a standard of living not rivaled nor even closely approximated in the modern world. This has been achieved by a combination of rich natural resources, widely shared technical facility and willingness to experiment with new methods, and a strong preference for privately-owned and -operated economic institutions. While our achievements *Economic* in art, literature, music, and fundamental science have not perhaps been *system* outstanding, our technology of production of all sorts of material goods is unsurpassed. The preferred method of organizing production is the joint-stock corporation characterized, at present, by widely distributed stock ownership (20 million stockholders in 1965) and small tightly knit directorates.

BIRTH AND DEATH RATES IN THE UNITED STATES, 1915-1963

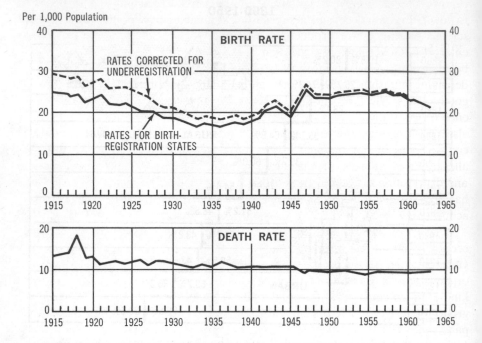

Per 1,000 Population

Some of our corporations have grown to such size, wealth, and power that they overshadow many of our local and regional institutions of government. Our economic system is characterized by a high degree of competition and great deference to the market place as the determinant of corporate effectiveness. The competition, however, is rather closely managed in many sectors of production and rarely extends to prices charged. The economic and political power of corporate management has been challenged for the past two generations by the spread of labor unions among the factory workers. Twenty-two percent of those gainfully employed are now members of some labor organization and the labor of several key industries (e.g. steel, automotive, transportation) is unionized throughout the nation. However, the increasing application of technology to productive processes and the substitution of capital for manpower is reducing the demand for semiskilled and unskilled factory hands, contributing to the rise of unemployment and to the demand for more technically-trained operatives, and, perhaps, limiting the growth potential of the industrial labor unions. American productive capacity is stimulated and supported by a huge enterprise for which there is nothing quite comparable elsewhere in the world: advertising. Symbolized by Madison Avenue, New York City, American advertising persuades the consumer to want what the American factories can produce.

Not pure capitalism   Although the American economy is predominantly a private enterprise economy, it is by no means a pure system of capitalism of the nineteenth-century model. Every variation of governmental intervention has been or is now being practiced and a substantial amount of public enterprise (postal service, electric power production, credit supply) exists alongside of private enterprise. Governmental regulation of the private sector of the economy has been steadily growing in scope and impact. More importantly, the huge defense establishment, the efforts to penetrate outer space, and the use of goods and services in our diplomacy have important, if not decisive, influence on substantial areas of private enterprise. The corporate income tax is also a prime regulator of corporate conduct. Many of the major political controversies of our national history have stemmed from efforts to mitigate alleged disadvantages of unrestrained private decisions in the production and distribution of wealth. In no other modern industrial nation, nevertheless, has the society allowed such free play to private initiative and personal acquisitiveness.

Much of the stimulus to political controversy in America is provided by economic groups—corporate, union, or agricultural—as each seeks to advance its interests in the political arena. Our system gives free play to the organization of interests of all types and rewards concerted efforts of this kind with influence over governmental and political decisions. The clash of group interests, notably but not exclusively economic interests, is a very large part, some would say all, of the dynamics of American politics. One of the major lessons of the American experience is that separate individuals are relatively ineffectual in giving direction to the machinery of government unless they associate together to promote common aims. Our democratic processes combined with constitutional separation of decisive authority invites organizations of many kinds to struggle for advantage. *Groups in American life*

American society has been free almost from its origin from the rigid class distinctions of our European ancestors. The Southern plantation aristocracy fell before the free-farmer and the factory owner and operator. The great appeal of the Marxist ideology to the proletariat, enthusiastically received by many European workers, has fallen largely on deaf ears in America. More than 80 per cent of our people think of themselves as members of the middle class. Sociologists perceive that our society is in truth divided into classes on the basis of living style, attitudes, and belief systems but not very rigidly, and that it is characterized by a considerable degree of upward-and-downward-mobility. The very rich and the very poor seem to be the most class-conscious members of American society and together they are a distinct minority of the population. Our productive genius, further, can turn out cars, clothes, homes, appliances, and food in such volume and at such costs that the ordinary family lacks little except servants that the rich family can afford. The difference between going on horseback and going on foot was after all, a whole world, while that between a Cadillac and a second-hand Ford is but a few feet. *Absence of class distinction*

The
urban
style of
life

Perhaps the most significant difference of social organization in America is that between urban society and small town already alluded to. Urban society is diffuse, hectic, competitive, bureaucratic, consumption-dominated, anonymous, noisy, overstimulated, and highly dependent. The small town is neighborly, compact, unadventurous, closed, immobile, and where intimately related to the countryside, relatively independent. Since, however, urban culture dominates the mass media of communication and volume production supported by nation-wide advertising is the predominant system of supplying consumer wants, the independent or family farm and the small town are slowly but surely giving way to the tastes, styles, and distribution systems of the cities. The automobile allows the urbanite to penetrate ever deeper into the hinterland for living space as well as recreation. Furthermore, the farm and village are constantly exporting their ablest youth to the cities. It seems virtually certain that the subculture of rural America will soon be swallowed up in the mass culture of the metropolis.

The
American
belief
system

Debate continues as to whether it is divine benediction, superior ethnic origins, the frontier, economic abundance, the absence of aggressive neighbors, the religious convictions of the early settlers, the small freehold farm system of land tenure, the assimilation of the immigrant, the addiction to private enterprise, or some other factor which has molded the American character and given it a unique stamp among the peoples of the earth. There is a considerable, although not perfect, agreement, however, that there is a uniquely American belief system and that it is compounded largely of individualism, equalitarianism, anti-authoritarianism, and materialism and that our political system to a large degree reflects these attitudes. The American is an individualist in the sense that he believes in the worth of each separate soul. Man is entitled to respect, to pursue his salvation, and to make such contribution as he is able because he is a man not because he is a member of some larger entity—the folk, the chosen tribe, or the proletariat. The heroes of much of the greatest American imaginative literature are lonely adventurers, alienated from society, fighting their desperate struggles for redemption unaided and uncomforted. Americans are the most optimistic people on earth in their belief in rejuvenation by self-will. We bedevil ourselves constantly with improving instruction and exhortation designed to strengthen the will to succeed. We do not, on the whole, believe that men are or should be perfectly equal in intelligence, wealth, ability, or influence but we do aspire to equality of opportunity. Man should have the chance to move upward, to improve upon the situation into which he was born. The most popular programs of public benefit are likely to be those aimed at improving a man's chances to compete successfully. This attitude, of course, requires that men accept the responsibility for their own situations. Since most of us do not achieve all that we hope for and many stumble and falter on the path, this is a hard and a tension-inducing faith. It drives men to despair as well as to high achievement. The roots of the American's distrust and dislike for author-

LIFE EXPECTANCY AND ITS EFFECT ON POPULATION

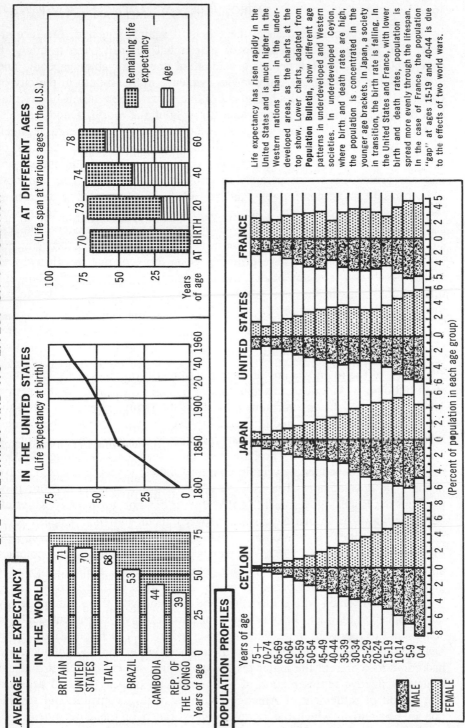

AVERAGE LIFE EXPECTANCY
IN THE WORLD

BRITAIN	71
UNITED STATES	70
ITALY	68
BRAZIL	53
CAMBODIA	44
REP. OF THE CONGO	39

Years of age: 0   25   50   75

IN THE UNITED STATES
(Life expectancy at birth)

75 — 50 — 25 — 0

1800   1850   1900   '20 '40 1960

AT DIFFERENT AGES
(Life span at various ages in the U.S.)

Remaining life expectancy

Age

100 — 75 — 50 — 25

70   73   74   78

Years of age: AT BIRTH   20   40   60

POPULATION PROFILES

Years of age: 75+, 70-74, 65-69, 60-64, 55-59, 50-54, 45-49, 40-44, 35-39, 30-34, 25-29, 20-24, 15-19, 10-14, 5-9, 0-4

CEYLON   JAPAN   UNITED STATES   FRANCE

MALE

FEMALE

(Percent of population in each age group)

Life expectancy has risen rapidly in the United States and is much higher in the Western nations than in the under-developed areas, as the charts at the top show. Lower charts, adapted from **Population Bulletin**, show different age patterns in underdeveloped and Western societies. In underdeveloped Ceylon, where birth and death rates are high, the population is concentrated in the younger age brackets. In Japan, a society in transition, the birth rate is falling. In the United States and France, with lower birth and death rates, population is spread more evenly through the lifespan. In the case of France, the population "gap" at ages 15-19 and 40-44 is due to the effects of two world wars.

ity are deep. Puritan conscience, the rebellion against England, the second-generation immigrant's repudiation of patriarchal authority, the frontier, all have contributed. We are neither a deferential nor a law-abiding people and are capable of exploding in more lawless violence in one month in the city of Chicago than the people of all England in one year. The materialistic orientation of American culture is notorious throughout the world. Goods, goods, and more goods, we produce and we consume. Success is measured as much by what we consume as by what we produce and money is the yardstick of accomplishment. Appliances rather than abstractions excite our enthusiasm and our pride. We are desperately determined to make life here and now more pleasant, more comfortable, and more hygienic. For this, by the rest of the world, we are occasionally despised, frequently patronized, and universally envied. And yet this is not the whole story. About our material possessions we are not miserly, owning them satisfies our desire for esteem but not hoarding. As a people we have probably given more of our wealth away at home and abroad than any other. And paradoxically, we frequently state our international aims in the most idealistic terms—"making the world safe for democracy."

OUR ENGLISH POLITICAL HERITAGE

English experience dominates our political inheritance

Each of the main streams of migrants from Europe has made important contributions to American life and together those who came in the period 1840-1920 have had an enormous impact on the family, economy, and politics of urban society. Our main lineage, however, is undoubtedly English and it is to the English traditions that we owe the basic forms and concepts of our system of government. The fathers of the American Constitution and of the War for Independence were inseparably linked to centuries of English institutional development. The triumph of the Revolution separated our people from the English government of that day; it did not, fortunately, sever all ties of memory or shared experience between them and their English forebears. Our political institutions did not emerge suddenly and in complete form in 1776 nor yet in 1787, but had been long abuilding in the colonies and in the mother country as well. Our people lived in the British Empire for almost as long before independence as they have lived outside of it since.

1. The idea and practice of representative government

The Englishmen who settled this land brought with them, among many other concepts, the idea that the powerful parts of any government ought in some sense to represent those who are governed by it. The English Parliament had been in existence for several centuries when this nation was founded and had come to represent the major classes of English society even if it had not achieved effective representation of the great mass of peasants and artisans. The period of settlement of America coincided with a constitutional revolution in England in which the representative branch of the government successfully wrested power from the despotic or monarchical branch. Although settlers sympathetic to both sides came to America, those favorable to Parliament were especially influential throughout New England.

The colonies were established under various auspices—private proprietors, trading companies, and monarchical endowment—but whatever their origin, a representative assembly was established sooner or later in every one of them to share power with, occasionally to dominate, the executive agents of the sponsors. The members of these legislatures were everywhere elected by vote of a limited number of their fellow citizens (property owners or taxpayers mainly) under much more systematic schemes of representation than in the mother country. There was no need in America to represent an almost nonexistent landed aristocracy in an upper house, for example. These colonial legislatures proved the training grounds for colonial politicians and provided this nation with more than a century of experience with elected representative assemblies before we struck off the ties with the English crown.

In our long colonial history something very like the contest between Crown and Parliament occurred. These representative bodies proved their ability time and again to keep the imported English executives under close control. The idea that the legislature ought to represent the people—or at least the better (richer) part of them—that it ought to control the public treasury and determine major public policy was, therefore, firmly established in practice when the constitutions for a new nation were written. It should also be added that most of the colonial assemblies formed the lower house of a two-house legislature, the upper house being a governor's council. The practice of bicameralism was thus well established in America before 1776.

The essence of constitutional government is that power is limited by law and these limits are enforced upon rulers by established procedures. Our English forefathers, for the most part, brought with them a firm attachment to the idea that this kind of government is both wise and practicable. The citizens of a nation, they believed, had certain rights which were beyond the power of any government to impair. As Englishmen, they claimed a sphere of personal freedom and asserted that fair procedures must be observed by executive officials. These conceptions linked them with hundreds of years of English constitutional development. The English settler brought tangible records—some old like the Magna Charta and some new like the Petition of Right—to support and illuminate these assertions. In the contest with the mother country, the colonists repeatedly claimed that the English government was trampling upon their rights as Englishmen. There is no more lucid statement in the literature of Western civilization of this English idea of human rights than the opening paragraphs of the Declaration of Independence. Every constitution written for the newly organized states during the Revolutionary period contained guarantees of individual liberty and requirements for fair procedure. In at least seven of these charters these safeguards against undue power were grouped in bills of rights.

That the ultimate source of all legitimate public authority is the people

2. The idea of limited government

3. The idea of popular sovereignty

themselves is an idea which our forefathers took for granted. To most of them government came into being by agreement of the governed (social contract), found its justification in protecting their liberties, and received only so much authority as the people felt it necessary to grant. The great English philosopher John Locke, who in the late seventeenth century formulated these views for all time, was speaking for the Englishmen in America as well as for those in his own country. The practice of colonial America—illustrated by the Mayflower Compact, the self-written charters of Connecticut and Rhode Island, and the state constitutions drafted by the colonists at the time of separation—more nearly approached the theory than did any experience of European or English history. When the colonists became their own masters they conferred power upon their own governments in the most grudging and distrustful manner. Frequent elections, short terms of office, and specific limitations on power characterized every one of the first state constitutions. It should not be assumed, however, that the idea that power rested upon consent included the notion that all or even most of the governed were qualified by merit or by right to participate in the processes of selection or decision. The right to vote was not one which either practice or theory attributed to all adult citizens. In other words, our English political heritage was constitutional government, not democratic government; and popular sovereignty was a theory about the origin of power, not about its exercise or its organization. Coupled with the tradition of human rights, however, this theory of government by consent laid the foundation for the ultimate triumph of democratic ideals.

4. The common law   Perhaps the most complete institutional transfer from England to the New World was that of the English system of jurisprudence. From the beginning of our history to the present day, the English common law has been the basis of our legal system.[2] Deeply imbedded in it at the time of its transportation were conceptions like "due process," "trial by jury," "freedom from arrest except for demonstrable cause," "equity," and many others which constituted important and specific elements in American bills of rights and in our ideas of limited governmental authority. The common law is largely judge-made law, built up over centuries by the application of traditional legal doctrines (precedents) to new situations. The slow and deliberate adjustment of the laws to the changing fabric of life, which adherence to the common law of England encourages, has been and is now one of the major conservative influences in our national life.

5. The institutions of local government   English institutions of local government, evolved over centuries, were also transplanted almost intact to America. The county was established in 1634 in Virginia and in 1643 in Massachusetts. The town dates almost from the landing of the Pilgrims; the chartered municipal corporation from 1686.[3] The borough took root, however, only in the middle colonies like Pennsyl-

[2] Except in Louisiana where the French legal system is the basis.
[3] From 1653 if the Dutch charter for New York City is counted.

vania. Local officials like the sheriff and the justice of the peace continue to this day to remind us that the history of our political institutions reaches backward without interruption into Anglo-Saxon England. The states of the new nation made no important modifications in these agencies of local government.

Upon this heritage of English ideas and institutions the American system of government was established. Overlaid, one must add, by a strong belief especially among the Puritans in the wickedness of man and the corroding effects of power. To the stock of English political wisdom with which our ancestors launched this nation as an independent unit in the world of nation-states, the American contributions have been: (1) the democratization of the entire system; (2) the practice of written constitutions and the ultimate interpretation of their meaning by an independent judiciary; (3) the practice of separation of powers among the principal branches of the state and national governments; and, most important of all, (4) the achievement of federal union of the 13 independent states.

Since studies of contemporary public attitudes suggest that the great mass of Americans do not understand very clearly nor appreciate very deeply the lineaments of our political heritage or the modifications made in it by our own experience, it might be concluded that the concepts and institutions outlined above have been submerged in the changing fashions in ideas. Similar studies, however, reveal that the politically active citizens who staff our parties, occupy public offices, and articulate views on public policy, although a minority of the population, are the keepers and transmitters of our political culture. In the main, they understand and appreciate the institutional and ideological bases of our system and so long as they are entrusted by the mass of citizens with the keys to power are likely to operate within the framework of constitutional democracy for which these concepts provide the foundation.

References

A. H. Kelly and W. A. Harbison, *The American Constitution: Its Origins and Development* (New York, 1948), Chaps. I-IV.

R. G. Adams, *The Political Ideas of the American Revolution* (Durham, N.C., 1922).

A. Nevins, *The American States During and After the Revolution, 1775-1789* (New York, 1924).

C. Becker, *The Declaration of Independence: A Study in the History of Political Ideas* (New York, 1922).

P. Olson (ed). *America As a Mass Society* (New York, 1963).

D. M. Potter, *People of Plenty: Economic Abundance and the American Character* (Chicago, 1954).

G. Gorer, *The American People: A Study in National Character* (New York, 1964).

M. Mead, *And Keep Your Powder Dry* (New York, 1942).

R. Hofstadler, *The American Political Tradition and the Men Who Made It* (New York, 1949).

A. J. Vidich and J. Bensman, *Small Town in Mass Society* (Princeton, N.J., 1958).

Bureau of the Census, *Historical Statistics and the United States: Colonial Times to 1957* (Washington, 1960).

———, *Statistical Abstract of the United States* (Washington, Annually).

J. F. Durhurst and Associates, *America's Needs and Resources* (New York, 1955).

A. Barach, *U.S.A. and Its Economic Future* (New York, 1964). Based on *America's Needs and Resources.*

A. A. Berle, *The American Economic Republic* (New York, 1963).

S. M. Lipset, *The First New Nation: the United States in Historical and Comparative Perspective* (New York, 1964).

H. R. Isaacs, *The New World of Negro Americans* (New York, 1963).

C. M. Green, *The Rise of Urban America* (New York, 1965).

L. Killian and C. Grigg, *Racial Crisis in America* (Englewood Cliffs, N.J., 1964).

M. L. King, Jr., *Why We Can't Wait* (New York, 1964).

G. Myrdal, *An American Dilemma,* revised ed. (New York, 1963).

W. Brink and L. Harris, *The Negro Revolution in America* (New York, 1964).

★ 2 ★

The Constitution of the United States

THE ACHIEVEMENT OF FEDERAL UNION

ALTHOUGH STRUNG ALONG A SEABOARD almost 1300 miles in length, nothing more hostile than wooded hills and swift rivers separated the English colonists from one another. The great majority were English-speaking Protestants. Founded under different auspices, however, they seemed more aware of their dissimilarities than of their resemblances—more concerned about achieving their own destinies than about working toward common goals. Fearful of the consequences of concerted colonial action, the English government never gave ideas of unity much encouragement. Scattered proposals like Franklin's Albany Plan and experiments like the New England Confederation (1643-83), looking to solidarity, had captured little loyalty. Growing controversy with the mother country, after the defeat of the French in North America removed the compelling need for English support, stimulated the idea of union, and events after 1770 gave the idea of co-operation new impetus. Even yet, there was slowness to act. With the colonies involving themselves ever more deeply in bold and hazardous resistance to English authority, the creation of at least some intercolonial consultative and directing machinery became a matter of the most obvious common sense, and in the autumn of 1774 the First Continental Congress assembled in Philadelphia. It brought together irregularly chosen delegates from every colony except Georgia. For seven weeks the Congress devoted itself to considering the common peril, planning co-operation, adopting a "declaration of rights," and formulating resolutions for consideration by the colonial legislatures. It concluded with a call for a similar congress to meet the following year unless in the meantime the emergency became war. When the Second Continental Congress convened in May, 1775, it found itself obliged, in the absence of any other common authority, to step into the breach, take measures for raising armies and funds, and in effect transform itself into a government. Moving from place to place as the exigencies of hostilities required, this body served as the country's sole organ of national authority until March, 1781.

Without some such unifying medium as the Continental Congress, the

The Continental Congress

Need for a stronger government

21

War for Independence could hardly have been carried to a successful conclusion. As an agency of government, however, the body left much to be desired. Starting as a voluntary intercolonial conference, it remained to the end a revolutionary assembly, resting on no basis of law and exercising powers only by virtue of having assumed them with the tacit consent of the governments and peoples of the newly established states. To meet a temporary emergency, makeshift arrangements such as these might, and did, serve. But the war gave promise of lasting many weary years; if successful, it would leave the country confronted with the problem of a permanent national government. In any event, finance, commerce, and foreign relations, to say nothing of military and naval operations, called for management by a government resting on some regular basis, endowed with definite powers, and assured of some degree of permanence. Out of this practical necessity and the deep commitment of the revolutionary leaders to government by consent arose the idea of a genuine and enduring union of the states under a written national constitution that found expression in the Articles of Confederation, and then in the Constitution of 1789.

The Articles of Confederation

The first constitution for a union of states originated in a resolution offered to the Continental Congress in 1776 by Richard Henry Lee of Virginia, at the same time that he moved for a declaration of colonial independence. A committee appointed by the Congress quickly drafted a plan of union. It was not, however, approved by the Congress until November 15, 1777, and was not approved by every participating state until 1781. When this new form of government finally was put into operation, the war that had evoked it was nearly at an end.

Sovereignty of the states

Under the Articles,[1] the United States at last achieved a government resting on a written constitution and with functions and powers defined therein—a government which, it must in fairness be remembered, was considerably superior to the extralegal Continental Congress, even though it in turn eventually was replaced. Three main features characterized it. The first was the recognition of the practice under the Continental Congress of state sovereignty, expressly asserted in the document's second "article." The states, it is true, relinquished important powers to the new central establishment, but on the whole the union remained a loose confederation or league. In this respect as in others it closely resembles the General Assembly of the modern United Nations.

A congress of delegates

A second feature was the concentration of all national powers in a Congress of one house, meeting annually and composed of delegates appointed in each state for a single year as the state legislature might direct. Each state paid its own delegates and could recall them and appoint others at any time; and no person might serve more than three years out of any six. Voting was

---

[1] The complete text may be found in *Documents Illustrative of the Formation of the Union of the American States,* 69th Congress, 1st session. House Document No. 398, Government Printing Office, 27-37 (Washington, 1927).

by states, and each state had a single vote regardless of the number of delegates it sent. Committees might, of course, be set up and subordinate officers appointed. There was no separate executive branch [2] and no national system of courts.

In the third place, powers and functions conferred on the national government were few and severely restricted. Far from being a general lawmaking authority like our present Congress, the Congress of the Confederation was only a grand committee of the states charged with executive and managerial functions, such as looking after foreign relations, declaring and conducting war on land and sea, building and equipping a navy, carrying on dealings with the Indian tribes, borrowing money, issuing bills of credit, regulating weights and measures, and making requisitions upon the states for soldiers and for funds. It could not reach down past the state governments to control the people in any effective way. It could adopt resolutions and issue commands, but it had only limited means of enforcing them—none at all through judicial process except by resort to the courts of the states. And some of the most important powers entrusted to it—for example, making treaties and coining and borrowing money—could be exercised only if the delegations of as many as nine states concurred.

Powers and limitations

Even before the Articles took effect, several leading statesmen of the new nation—Washington, Hamilton, Madison, Jay, among others—felt that the power of the central government was inadequate to its tasks. The Confederation period was thus marked from the outset by controversy over the fundamental law itself, and as the years passed the controversy grew in intensity and scope. On the one side were the nationalists—including many of the officers of the Revolutionary army, the merchants, the holders of certificates of public debt, and the manufacturers—who felt the new union cut but a sorry figure internationally, inviting abuse if not invasion by the boastful and aggressive nations of Europe. Only a strong central government could muster cash, soldiers, and armaments sufficient to compel respect abroad. This group was skeptical of the competence and disillusioned by the behavior of the state legislatures which were the centers of political power in the nation. Distrustful of democracy, they disdained the frequent elections, short terms of office, and the agrarian biases of the state lawmakers. Only a central authority, they argued, could establish the public credit, restrain state imposition on trade, deal with foreign nations, and stimulate the development of national rather than regional loyalties and ambitions. On the other side there was a numerous group, largely of freehold farmers and without the brilliant leadership of the nationalists, who supported confederation and opposed granting any more power to the central government. Central governments are far removed from the immediate problems of domestic life and are apt to be despotic, they said. We have not thrown off the chains of a transoceanic

Controversy over the Articles

---

[2] The functions of Congress were, in fact, almost wholly executive in character and thus it might be more accurate to say there was no *legislative* branch.

monarch only to fetter ourselves to a home-grown one. The states are the important units for the exercise of power. Their governments under new constitutions are everywhere close to "the people" and sensitive to their needs. In this way did one of the enduring issues in American politics originate. These two conceptions ultimately contributed to the formation of political parties and even under the new Constitution of 1787 continued to clash for generations thereafter.

Achievements under the Articles

The extreme claims of the talented nationalists have obscured many significant achievements under the Articles. A new national domain was created by the cession to the central government of the claims of the states to lands west of the Alleghenies. In a series of acts culminating in the famous Northwest Ordinance of 1787, the Confederation Congress laid the foundation for the development of five republican institutions in this vast area and their ultimate admission to the Union as states. Executive departments were created and staffed with a permanent bureaucracy: the Post Office, Treasury, War, and Foreign Affairs agencies were created under individuals designated by Congress. The vast debt created by the war was brought into manageable form by the settlement of accounts and was substantially reduced. New loans were rather readily negotiated with Dutch bankers. The country successfully weathered the economic depression following victory, and signs of recovery were everywhere apparent at the end of the Confederation period.[3]

Weaknesses of the Articles

The nationalists were, however, able to point to the lack of an independent income and the inability of the Confederation government to meet all of its fiscal responsibilities, either to foreign or domestic creditors, as a serious flaw in the United States government. Without dependable income, the government could not meet its past obligations and it could not prepare the nation to defend itself from hostile European powers. The nation could do little to compel obedience to its mandates; it was wholly dependent upon the states for execution as well as for income.

The immediate impetus to reform of the Confederation was interstate controversy over commerce. Successful negotiations between Virginia and Maryland, held under the auspices of George Washington, led to another conference on the rising interstate tariff barriers to which Virginia, at the suggestion of Washington and Madison, invited other interested states. To the convention in Annapolis in 1786 came representatives of only five states, but among them were Madison and Hamilton, leaders of the nationalist cause. They induced the delegates to invite all the states to send delegates to a new convention in 1787 in Philadelphia at which all of the defects of the Confederation could be considered, together with proposals for the reform of the Articles. Congress added its weight by formally "calling" the conference, specifying that it be held for

---

[3] For a detailed account of the Confederation's achievements as well as its failures see M. Jensen, *The New Nation: A History of the United States During the Confederation* (New York, 1950).

. . . The sole and express purpose of revising the Articles of Confederation and reporting to Congress and the several state legislatures such alterations and provisions therein as shall, when agreed to in Congress and confirmed by the states, render the federal constitution adequate to the exigencies of government and the preservation of the Union.

The nationalist leaders threw their full influence behind the conference, and out of it came the Constitution of the United States.

THE CONVENTION OF 1787

The convention was announced to meet on the second Monday of May. *Member-* When that day arrived, however, only a few delegates had reached Philadel- *ship* phia; and since it was useless to start until a majority of the states were represented, the opening session did not take place until May 25. Though characterized by Jefferson as "an assembly of demigods," the convention contained men of widely differing temperaments, abilities, and aptitudes. There were members of great personal force and political sagacity: Washington and Madison of Virginia, Franklin and Wilson of Pennsylvania, Alexander Hamilton of New York, John Dickinson of Delaware.[4] There were delegates of fair, but not exceptional, ability: Rufus King of Massachusetts, Roger Sherman and Oliver Ellsworth of Connecticut, Gouverneur Morris of Pennsylvania, William Paterson of New Jersey, George Mason and Edmund Randolph of Virginia, John Rutledge and Charles Pinckney of South Carolina. And there were a few members of narrow vision and limited constructive talent: Lansing and Yates of New York, Elbridge Gerry of Massachusetts, and Luther Martin of Maryland. Lawyers predominated, and several of the delegates were reasonably well acquainted not only with the history of English law and politics but with the governmental systems of continental Europe. About half were college graduates. Most had been active in the government and politics of their respective states. Many had helped frame constitutions, sat as members of legislatures, or held executive or judicial offices. Thirty-one had served in Congress. Men of age and maturity were included, notably Franklin, who was almost 82. But a large proportion of the most active and influential delegates were comparatively young: Madison, the master-builder, was 36, Gouverneur Morris 35, Hamilton 30, Charles Pinckney 29.

Furthermore, the men who now held the country's political destinies in *Conserva-* their hands were not ardent supporters of the Confederation. Many of the *tive* revolutionary leaders were absent. Patrick Henry "smelt a rat," and refused *temper* to attend. John Hancock was not there; nor were Richard Henry Lee, Samuel Adams, and Thomas Paine. Almost to a man, the delegates were drawn from the professional and propertied classes, chiefly in the tidewater areas

---

[4] Jefferson and John Adams were on diplomatic missions in Europe; otherwise they undoubtedly would have been members.

where such wealth as existed was largely concentrated. Not one was a frontiersman or a wage earner, and only one had a small farmer background. Few were as conservative as Hamilton, who wanted to see a highly centralized and more or less aristocratic political system set up. But few, also, sprang from the small-propertied or propertyless elements of the population.[5]

Common objective

Plenty of disagreements were bound to arise, once the delegates had started their discussions. Upon the objective chiefly to be aimed at, however, there was, first and last, little difference of opinion—namely, a government of sufficient strength not only to take care of national defense and to discharge national obligations, but to withstand agrarian-debtor agitation typified by Shays's Rebellion in Massachusetts, and preserve social order. And although the resulting Constitution provided for a more popular plan of government than could at that time have been found in any other important country in the world, it is not surprising that, motivated as it was, it should have been purposely shaped—by means of checks and balances, indirect elections, perpetuation of suffrage limitations in the states and presidential veto —to prevent majoritarian elements from capturing control of affairs. It did not, however, close the doors against more democracy later on, and therein lay one of its principal merits.

Organization and procedure

The convention's sessions were held in the old brick State House in Philadelphia, probably in a room directly above that in which the Declaration of Independence was signed. Seventy-four delegates in all were appointed,[6] but only 55 ever attended; of these, some were present only part of the time, and the average attendance seems not to have exceeded 30 or 35. At the opening meeting, Washington was unanimously chosen to preside, and this prevented him from taking an active part in the debates. Indeed, so far as is known, he addressed the convention only twice, on the opening and closing days. With the possible exception of Franklin, he, however, was less dependent on speech-making than any other delegate. He performed his duties as moderator in a manner to allay strife; in private conversation and informal conference, his opinions and advice were always to be had; and it is doubtful whether, on the whole, any member exerted greater influence.

[5] The members of the convention are characterized briefly, one by one, in M. Farrand, *The Framing of the Constitution* (New Haven, 1913), Chap. II; and the correlation between their economic interests and their political ideas and aims is discussed illuminatingly in C. A. Beard, *An Economic Interpretation of the Constitution of the United States* (new ed., New York, 1935), 74-149, 189-216. Beard's famous thesis has been subjected to much recent critical analysis. See, for example, R. E. Brown, *Charles Beard and the Constitution: A Critical Analysis of "An Economic Interpretation of the Constitution"* (Princeton, N. J., 1956). A somewhat facetious "Who's Who" of the members of the convention, written by one of the delegates—William Pierce of Georgia—is reprinted in J. Butzner [comp.], *Constitutional Chaff* (New York, 1941), and in *Amer. Hist. Rev.*, III, 310-334 (Jan., 1898); and a good deal of information about them (including their careers subsequent to the convention) will be found in H. Lyon, *The Constitution and the Men Who Made It* (Boston, 1936), especially Chap. XVII.

[6] From 12 states; Rhode Island, dominated by inflationists suspicious of the undertaking, was at no time represented.

Having full power to make its own rules, the convention early decided that each state, regardless of number of delegates, should have one vote, as in the contemporary Congress. In order to enable the members to speak freely and plainly and to protect them against outside criticism and pressure, the convention further decided that the sittings should be behind closed doors, and that nothing should be put into print or otherwise made public until the work was finished. This injunction of secrecy was observed with remarkable fidelity. A secretary was appointed and a journal kept. When, however, in 1819, this official record was printed by order of Congress, in the hope that it would throw light on the way in which various provisions of the Constitution then in controversy should be interpreted, it proved to be a bare and not wholly accurate enumeration of formal motions and of votes by states.[7] Happily, Madison, one of the most vigilant and efficient delegates, sensing the importance of what was being done, kept a record of his own. Fragmentary memoranda were left by a few other members, and something can be learned from letters written by certain delegates to their friends. But what we know today about the convention's discussions, as distinguished from its formal actions, comes mainly from the clear and candid *Notes* laboriously compiled —sometimes to the extent of three or four thousand words a day (though of course not a verbatim record)—by the learned and methodical Virginian.[8]

THE CONSTITUTION FRAMED

We, the people of the United States, in order to form a more perfect union, establish justice, insure domestic tranquility, provide for the common defense, promote the general welfare, and secure the blessings of liberty to ourselves and our posterity, do ordain and establish this Constitution for the United States of America. PREAMBLE TO THE CONSTITUTION

Deliberations had not gone far before the delegates were brought face to face with a truly challenging question. Should they merely revise the Articles of Confederation, or should they make a new constitution? There was no getting away from the fact that their instructions looked only to revision, or

The convention's main problem

[7] For the official journal, printed directly from manuscript, see *Documentary History of the Constitution, 1786-1870* (Washington, 1894-1905), I, 48-308.

[8] This was in addition to his exacting labors as, in effect, convention "floor leader." Madison's papers were purchased by the national government after his death in 1836, and those containing the *Notes* were first published in 1840. Of several editions, the best are: G. Hunt [ed.], *Writings of James Madison* (New York, 1900-10), III-IV; G. Hunt and J. B. Scott [eds.], *The Debates in the Federal Convention of 1787 Which Framed the Constitution of the United States of America* (New York, 1920). The *Notes* and all other contemporary materials relating to the work of the convention are conveniently assembled in M. Farrand [ed.], *The Records of the Federal Convention*, cited at the end of this chapter.

from the suspicion that the proposal for a convention never would have prevailed if the people of the states had supposed that anything more drastic would be undertaken. On the other hand, many thoughtful persons agreed with Washington when he confessed the hope that the convention would "adopt no temporizing expedients," but would "probe the defects of the constitution [i.e., the Articles] to the bottom and provide a radical cure, whether they are agreed to or not." Both points of view were strongly represented in the convention, and a plan based on each was quickly presented for consideration.

The Virginia plan

The first scheme to appear came logically from the state that had taken the initiative in bringing the convention about, that is, Virginia. Governor Edmund Randolph presented it, although Madison was its principal author. It embodied the best thought of the convention's ablest student of political, and especially federal, institutions. The plan did not explicitly repudiate the Articles. But it looked to a general reconstruction of the system of government existing under them; and after it was submitted the fiction that a mere revision was intended was soon dropped. A national executive was to be established; also a national judiciary; and, finally, a legislature, with a lower house elected directly by the people and an upper one chosen by the lower from persons nominated by the state legislatures. Thus reconstructed, the national government was to have greatly increased powers, among them those of levying taxes, vetoing state legislation when considered contrary to the national constitution or to a treaty, and calling forth the militia against any member of the union "failing to fulfill its duty." Presented on May 29, in the form of 15 resolutions, this plan gave the convention something to go to work on at once. For two weeks the delegates, sitting in committee of the whole, discussed it zealously.

The New Jersey plan

One feature of the plan strongly objected to by members particularly sensitive about the "rights" of their states was the proposal to substitute for the existing equal voting power of the states in Congress an arrangement under which, in both branches, such power should be apportioned in accordance with numbers of free inhabitants or perhaps contributions to the national treasury. To forestall such an innovation, a group of delegates from the less populous states decided to present a counterplan based on a "purely federal" principle. Cast in the form of nine resolutions, this alternative scheme was laid before the convention on June 15 by William Paterson of New Jersey. It went far toward meeting the demands of the delegates for a drastic change. It allowed Congress power to raise money from duties on imports and from stamp taxes, and to regulate commerce, and it invested acts of Congress with the character of "supreme law of the respective states." It even envisaged a national executive in the form of a council chosen by Congress and a national judiciary composed of a "supreme tribunal." Congress, however, was still to consist of but a single house, with all states retaining an equal voice.

Compromise the only solution

Advocated ably by Paterson and other interested members, the New

Jersey plan enlisted the support of the delegates of about half of the states. Its introduction, indeed, split the convention sharply into two factions or groups: one representing the nationalist view, the other the federationist view. One wanted political power proportioned to the ability of the states to aid in bearing the public burdens; the other wanted the states to retain the full equality they had enjoyed since independence, and argued that on any other basis the less populous ones would be placed at grave, and even ruinous, disadvantage. Happily, it was not necessary that either element have its way completely. The delegates were, after all, not dogmatic theorists and were accustomed in their business relations and in their state politics to the saving principle of give and take. They expressed their widely differing views freely, sometimes acrimoniously. Having done so, most of them were not averse to compromise. The constitution upon which they finally agreed became, clause after clause, a product of mutual concession.

Fortunately, however, a majority of the delegates were essentially united on matters of decidedly larger significance than those on which they differed; and compromise was resorted to only after certain vital decisions had been reached. The most important of these was to cast aside the Articles and to establish a government resting on a more truly national basis. Some delegates were of the opinion that the instructions given by the states were binding literally, and that if the convention wanted to do more than merely revise the Articles, its members ought to go back to their states and ask for appropriate authority. But the majority were, as Randolph later put it, "not scrupulous on the point of power," and felt, as he further testified, that "when the salvation of the republic was at stake it would be treason to our trust not to propose what we found necessary." Within five days after the convention began work, a resolution was adopted in committee of the whole "that a national government ought to be established consisting of a supreme legislative, executive, and judiciary." Madison, Hamilton, and other delegates made it perfectly clear that this meant a government embodying one supreme power, with "complete and compulsive operation." The federationists protested, saying at first that they would have no part in such a union; the nationalist delegates declared they would accept nothing less. The federationists, as we have seen, brought forward the New Jersey plan, yet at the final test only three states voted for it. From first to last—sometimes at grave risk of driving the convention on the rocks—the initial determination was wisely adhered to. The time for compromise had not yet come.

From this key decision flowed certain great corollaries: (1) the powers of the national government should be sharply increased; (2) the machinery of government should be expanded, as indeed was proposed in all of the plans offered; (3) the national government, equally with the state governments, should operate directly on the people, through its own laws, administrative officers, and courts; and (4) the new constitution should be the "supreme law of the land," enforceable in the courts like any other law and

Decision in favor of a strong national government

paramount over all other constitutions, laws, and official actions, national or state.

A national government resting upon the people

Adoption of the third principle, in particular, meant that the national government was to be put on a wholly new basis. Instead of resting only upon semi-independent states, and having little control over the people except through the medium of state authorities, it was thenceforth to be a government of a single body politic, with power to levy and collect taxes and to make and enforce laws by its own direct action. Thereafter, as James Wilson explained, over each citizen were to be two governments, both "derived from the people," both "meant for the people," and both operating by an independent authority upon the people. And, as Madison subsequently wrote to Jefferson, in adopting such an arrangement the convention deftly divested itself of one of its most delicate problems. If the experience of the Confederation indicated anything, it was that states might fail to live up to their obligations; and every plan thus far presented to the convention had embraced or assumed some arrangement for coercing states proving delinquent. The nature and method of such coercion would, however, have stirred grave differences of opinion; and members must have been relieved to find that in providing for a national government endowed with power to enforce its authority directly upon *people,* they had made the coercion of *states* unnecessary.

The great compromises:

These fundamentals settled, the nationalist forces were ready to make concessions; and the first and most notable one related to voting power in Congress. The nationalists wanted representation, and with it voting power, proportioned to population; the federationists wanted voting power to be equal; delegates on both sides threatened more than once to withdraw unless their demands were met. At a very critical point in the proceedings, the delegates from Connecticut—a middle-sized state firmly attached to the idea of a stronger union—brought forward a proposal for equal representation in the upper house, combined with representation in the lower house in proportion to numbers; and after heated debate the deadlock was broken and the compromise adopted. This eminently sensible disposition of the matter was casually suggested quite early in the deliberations and did not originate with the Connecticut delegation. Franklin, indeed, was probably its actual author. Dr. Johnson and his colleagues deserve credit, however, for putting it formally before the convention with an array of unanswerable arguments; and the agreement has ever since been known as the "Connecticut compromise." It removed the greatest single obstacle to harmony.

1. The Connecticut compromise

2. The three-fifths clause

The decision in favor of proportioned representation in the lower house, however, made it necessary to determine how population should be computed; and difficulty at this point was produced by the existence of slavery. Should slaves be regarded as persons or as chattels? If the former, they ought to be counted in; if the latter, they ought to be left out. With a view to increasing their quotas in Congress, the southern states wanted slaves included;

the northern and middle states, having few slaves, wanted them disregarded. A possible solution was, however, already in men's minds when the convention met. When asking the states for additional funds in 1783, Congress had proposed changing the basis of requisitions from land values to numbers of population, so computed as to include three-fifths of all slaves. This "federal ratio" was early incorporated in the Virginia plan as an amendment; it found a place also in the New Jersey scheme; and, notwithstanding initial differences of opinion, it was ultimately adopted by the convention as being, in the words of Rufus King, "the language of all America." There was no defense for it in logic. But it represented the closest approach to a generally satisfactory arrangement that a body of practical-minded men could discover. The slave states received less representation than they thought their due. They found compensation, however, in a provision that direct taxes laid by Congress should be apportioned on the same reduced basis as representation— although, in point of fact, direct taxes were actually imposed by the national government only four times before slavery was abolished.

Still another compromise pertained to the powers of Congress over commerce. The delegates north of the Potomac were keenly interested in commerce and wanted Congress to have full power to regulate trade and navigation. The four states farther south, however, were agricultural, and their delegates feared that Congress would levy export duties on southern products and in other ways discriminate against the noncommercial section. Furthermore, there was the question of the slave trade. The northern states would have been willing to see the traffic abolished immediately, and Maryland and Virginia, being well stocked, had no great interest in it. But Georgia and the Carolinas wanted it to continue, and the convention was told firmly that these states would never accept the new plan "unless their right to import slaves be untouched." The outcome was an agreement which pacified all elements. Congress was to have broad powers to regulate navigation and foreign trade, including power to lay duties on imports. But national taxes on exports were forbidden, and the importation of slaves might not be interfered with by the national government (except to the extent of a head-tax not exceeding $10) prior to the year 1808.

3. Commerce and the slave trade

Many other important matters claimed the attention of the delegates through the sultry midsummer days during which the convention patiently pursued its labors. The nature and powers, and especially the mode of selection, of the executive absorbed much time and thought, the more by reason of the fact that plans gradually took form for a chief executive different from any the world had ever known. The manner of electing Senators— whether by the people, by the state legislatures, or by some agency especially devised for the purpose—proved difficult to decide. The appointment and status of the national judiciary provoked ardent discussion. The broadened powers to be vested in Congress, the mode of admitting new states, the con-

The Constitution completed

trol of the national government over state militia, the manner of amending the new constitution—these and a score of other topics required painstaking consideration; and the convention, as Franklin testified, spent a great deal of time "sawing boards to make them fit." From first to last, the Virginia plan, as progressively amplified, formed the main basis of discussion. First, the essentions of this plan, embodied in the Randolph resolutions, were thrashed out in committee of the whole. Then, after being reported back to the convention considerably altered, they were again debated in full. Next, the growing document was turned over, after a couple of months, to a committee of detail which worked it into a balanced constitutional text. The convention spent upwards of six weeks more in discussing this draft. Finally, Gouverneur Morris, aided by his fellow Pennsylvanian, James Wilson, wrote out with his own hand the completed fundamental law, putting it into the lucid English for which it has ever since been notable among great documents; and on September 17, 39 delegates, representing 12 states, signed it.

The great Franklin, in his closing plea to the delegates, stated exactly the political wisdom which for almost two centuries has sustained this Constitution and the American system:

> "I confess," [he said], "that there are several parts of this Constitution which I do not at present approve, but I am not sure that I shall never approve them. For having lived long, I have experienced many instances of being obliged by better information or fuller consideration to change opinions even on important subjects, which I once thought right, but found to be otherwise . . . the older I grow, the more apt I am to doubt my own judgment, and to pay more respect to the judgment of others.
>
> In these sentiments, [he continued], I agree to this Constitution with all its faults, if they are such; because I think a general government necessary for us . . . I doubt whether any other Convention we can obtain may be able to make a better constitution . . . Thus, I consent, Sir . . . because I expect no better and because I am not sure that it is not the best. The opinion I have had of its errors, I sacrifice to the public good . . ."

The test ahead   While the signatures were being affixed the venerable Doctor further remarked that "often and often" during the session he had looked at a sun painted on the president's chair without being able to tell whether it was rising or setting. "Now, at length," he added hopefully, "I have the happiness to know that it is a rising, and not a setting sun." The actual test, however, was yet to come. The convention had ignored the instructions given most of its members and, instead of patching up the Articles, had prepared a new and very different frame of government. Would the people of the states approve what it had done? Few, if any of the delegates, were entirely satisfied. Three of those present when the document was signed refused to put their names to it. Of thirteen who were absent, at least four are known to have been critical if not actually hostile.

THE CONTEST OVER RATIFICATION

A decade earlier, adoption of the Articles had been held up for three and *Procedures*
one-half years awaiting ratification by every one of the states. To ease matters
this time, the Constitution provided in its closing article that it should take
effect when ratified by nine states. To give it a more popular basis, action
was required to be taken in each state not by the legislature, as in the case of
the Articles, but by a convention chosen for the purpose by the voters.[9] Assenting to both procedures, Congress, on September 28, formally transmitted
the proposed instrument to the states without recommendation or other
comment.

The controversies that had stirred the convention were now transferred *Objections*
to the country at large. From New England to Georgia, the new frame of *to the new*
government was circulated and discussed, dissected, explained, praised, de- *plan*
nounced. Objections arose in many quarters; scarcely a feature of the plan,
indeed, escaped attack. There were men who, like Patrick Henry and Samuel
Adams, were so imbued with the Revolutionary concepts of liberty that they
took instant offense at any proposal looking toward a centralization of authority.[10] On the other hand, some people thought that the new plan did not provide for as much centralization as was needed. The debtor elements were
aroused by the clause which forbade the states to issue bills of credit. Many
northerners considered that too much was conceded to the slave-holding interests; many southerners felt that these interests had been dealt with unfairly.
Large inland elements—small farmers, backwoodsmen, pioneers—feared the
effects of the commercial powers given to Congress; men of property, although generally favorable, wondered how freely the new taxing powers
would be used. Everywhere the complaint was voiced that the document failed to take any notice of numerous fundamental rights and liberties,
e.g., freedom of speech, freedom of the press, freedom of assembly, right of
petition, and religious liberty, so carefully guaranteed in the bills of rights
prefixed to a majority of the state constitutions, and likely to need protection
even more, popular elements thought, against a strong central government.
In most states the various hostile elements tended to merge into an oposition
extremely difficult to convert or overcome.

In the Philadelphia convention, the interests hardest to satisfy were *Ratifica-*
those anxious to preserve state equality and a measure of independence. The *tion by*
conclusions arrived at were, however, on the whole favorable to those inter- *nine*
ests, which accordingly became the first to ratify. In Massachusetts, Virginia, *states*
New York, and other states, time was required to rally support. There was
grave danger lest some state indispensable to the proposed union because of

[9] In addition, it seems to have been believed that newly-elected conventions would
be more likely to act favorably than existing legislatures.
[10] "I look on that paper" (the proposed constitution), said Patrick Henry, "as the
most fatal plan that could possibly be conceived to enslave a free people."

its location or general importance should remain obdurate. By cleverly appeasing Samuel Adams and John Hancock, to whom the "Anti-Federalists" of the interior looked for leadership, the supporters of the pending plan won in Massachusetts by a close vote, and only after agreeing to a series of suggested amendments aimed at reducing the power of the central government. Ratification in New Hampshire after a hard contest brought the number to the required nine. But no one supposed that the new government could be launched successfully on this minimum basis. Even after Virginia gave a favorable decision, following an exceptionally bitter fight, the battle was not yet won. New York was still outside, without it the union would be a mere caricature.

Ratification in New York: The Federalist

Moreover, the opposition in New York, especially in the rural sections, was very formidable; and, realizing this, the friends of the Constitution made every effort before the state convention met at Poughkeepsie to convince the people that the proposed plan of government was moderate, safe, and workable. Most active in this was Hamilton, who, after having been "praised by everybody but supported by none" at Philadelphia, now came into his own as a leader in the campaign for ratification. He it was who conceived the idea of printing in the leading newspapers of the state a systematic explanation and defense of the Constitution in the form of a series of brief public letters, associating with himself for the purpose another able New Yorker, John Jay, and also the most convincing expounder outside of New York, Madison. The result was the remarkable group of papers, 85 in number, appearing over the pen-name "Publius," but known ever since to students of American history as *The Federalist*. The letters were prepared in haste and published in New York City newspapers at the rate of three or four a week, as campaign documents.[11] But their authors—all young and vigorous—were full of their subject and knew how to write. Taken as a group, the papers, though frankly propagandist and presenting only one side, have never been surpassed as examples of direct, lucid, and convincing exposition. Completed by six papers first appearing in book form, and constituting one of the world's great treatises on government, the full collection has passed through more than 30 editions. Better than anything else—unless possibly Madison's *Notes*—it shows what the Constitution meant to the men who made it.

The Constitution put into effect

Either won over by Hamilton and his collaborators or unwilling to see the state remain outside of the Union after all but two of the others had joined, the New York convention finally ratified on July 26, although by a margin of only three votes. Meanwhile, on July 2, it was officially announced in Congress that the ninth state had ratified, and attention was turned to preparations for putting the new government into operation. The states were

[11] Hamilton alone wrote 51 of them. Madison contributed some 26 and Jay five. Three were prepared by Hamilton and Madison jointly. See D. Adair, "The Authorship of the Disputed Federalist Papers," *William and Mary Quarterly*, 3rd Ser., I (April-July, 1944).

RATIFICATION OF THE CONSTITUTION OF 1787

State	Date	Vote
Delaware	Dec. 7, 1787	Unanimous
Pennsylvania	Dec. 12, 1787	46-23
New Jersey	Dec. 19, 1787	Unanimous
Georgia	Jan. 2, 1788	Unanimous
Connecticut	Jan. 9, 1788	128-40
Massachusetts	Feb. 6, 1788	187-168
Maryland	April 28, 1788	63-11
South Carolina	May 23, 1788	149-73
New Hampshire	June 21, 1788	57-46
Virginia	June 25, 1788	89-79
New York	July 26, 1788	30-27
North Carolina	Nov. 21, 1789	184-77
Rhode Island	May 29, 1790	34-32

instructed to choose presidential electors, Senators, and Representatives, and New York City was fixed as the temporary seat of government.[12] Then the old Congress, already incapacitated by lack of a quorum, disappeared, leaving the field clear for its successor. The new House of Representatives was organized on April 2, 1789; the Senate came together three days later; and on April 30, Washington took the oath of office as President. Seven months afterwards, North Carolina, appeased by a decision of Congress to submit a series of constitutional amendments guaranteeing civil liberties, and threatened with being treated commercially as though a foreign country, ratified the new fundamental law; and similar action by Rhode Island in the spring of 1790 made the union complete.

THE CONSTITUTION'S CHARACTERISTICS AND SOURCES

"This paper," wrote Gouverneur Morris in commending the Constitution to a friend, "has been the subject of infinite investigation, disputation, and declamation. While some have boasted it as a work from Heaven, others have given it a less righteous origin. I have many reasons to believe that it is the work of plain honest men, and such, I think, it will appear." Herein lies the reason why the instrument, once adopted, succeeded and survived beyond the hopes of its most ardent advocates. As constitutions go, it is a brief and simple document. Even with the later amendments, its approximately 6000 words fill only 12 or 15 pages of print; one can read it through in leisurely fashion in half an hour. Its contents are organized according to a clear and logical pattern. Following a brief preamble (significant as a statement of general purpose, but having no legal force), three main articles are devoted

The Constitution as a document

[12] In 1790, however, Philadelphia once more became the "capital," serving as such until 1800.

to the legislative, executive, and judicial branches, respectively. Four shorter articles deal, in order, with the position of the states, the modes of amendment, the supremacy of national power, and ratification. Finally come the amendments, appended at the end and numbered serially. Thanks to the committee of detail, and especially to Gouverneur Morris, the document's language is clear, direct, and concise; there is not an unnecessary word or an intentionally ambiguous phrase. To be sure, some clauses, for example, those touching citizenship, or that authorizing Congress to "provide for . . . the general welfare of the United States," lend themselves to more than one interpretation; and the conflicts and decisions arising out of resulting differences of opinion make up a considerable part of the country's constitutional history in the past 177 years. Nevertheless, our greatest constitutional controversies are traceable rather to omissions than to provisions of doubtful meaning.

Significance of its omissions

It is its omissions, at least as truly as its actual provisions, that stamp the document as "the work of plain honest men." If theorists had written it, it would have been filled with high-sounding phrases out of touch with reality. Even "practical" men might well have made the mistake of overloading it with details. Instead of merely authorizing Congress to regulate interstate commerce, they might have undertaken to define "regulate" and "commerce." Instead of simply empowering Congress to lay and collect taxes to provide for the general welfare, they might have undertaken to specify the kinds of taxes to be employed and even to indicate what they meant by "general welfare." If they had done such things, however, they would at once have tied the hands of the new government, and would either have forced a long line of later amendments or permanently thwarted the freedom of interpretation, experiment, and decision that has been the very lifeblood of the nation in later days. What the framers wisely undertook was simply to apply practical remedies to the defects of an existing political system. In doing this, they did not hold back from strong measures. Aware, however, that their judgment and foresight were not infallible, they deliberately omitted from the resulting basic law everything that could safely be supplied by generations faced with new problems and blessed with even richer experience.

Its sources

It follows that the framers did not go out of their way to invent political forms. Nor did they borrow far afield. Some of them were students of Vattel, Montesquieu, and other continental writers; some had read history and could cite the failures of ancient confederacies or draw illustrations from the experiences of France and other continental states. But, as an earlier writer has remarked, this knowledge taught them rather what to avoid than what to adopt; and insofar as they drew upon European sources at all, such sources were the common law, the principles of Magna Carta and the Bill of Rights, the writings of Locke and Blackstone, and other characteristic products of their English motherland. In the main, however, this monumental heritage had passed to America far back in colonial days, and, at the time when the national Constitution took form, was already deeply embedded in the constitutions, laws, and usages of the states. In a very true and literal sense, therefore, the new instrument grew out of the political life of Americans themselves in the colonial and Revolutionary periods. "Experience," said John Dickinson, "must be our guide; reason may mislead us." Fortunately, our forefathers had accumulated enough political experience by 1787 to serve as a rich and adequate resource.

All of the great ideas and institutions of our English heritage were embodied in the Constitution as adopted in 1788 and amended by the First Congress and the states. The government established by it was limited in power, representative in character, and based upon the people. By leaving the prescription of voting qualifications to the states it opened the door to the spread of the voting privilege throughout adult America, and thus paved the way for the democratization of American government which has so strikingly modified the entire machinery provided in 1787. By providing a written instrument self-designated as the "supreme law of the land," the framers stimulated the innovation of judicial review, that is, the ultimate and authoritative interpretation of its provisions by an independent national judiciary. The system of separation of powers and of checks and balances which it contains, although directly traceable to colonial and state experience, marks one of the major departures from both the tradition and evolving practice of the British government. The greatest achievement of the framers, however, was unquestionably the federal union—the creation of a strong national government side by side with strong and effective state governments. This feature will be developed more fully in the next chapter. The Constitution, finally, provides for orderly change, and by legislation, custom, executive action, judicial interpretation, and formal amendment it has proved adaptable to the revolutionary changes in the life of our people since it was adopted. Despite all of the modifications and adaptations, the great principles of the Constitution have endured.

Great principles embodied

THE PROCESSES OF CONSTITUTIONAL DEVELOPMENT

The Congress, whenever two-thirds of both houses shall deem it necessary, shall propose amendments to this Constitution, or, on the application of the legislatures of two-thirds of the several States, shall call a convention for proposing amendments, which in either case shall be valid to all intents and purposes as part of this Constitution, when ratified by the legislatures of three-fourths of the several States, or by conventions in three-fourths thereof, as the one or the other mode of ratification may be proposed by the Congress, provided that no State, without its consent, shall be deprived of its equal suffrage in the Senate. ART. V

Actual Constitution is more than a document

The moment the new instrument became effective, executive officers, congressmen, and judges began to interpret and apply its provisions and thus to build up year by year in accumulating practice and precedent the flesh of government that covers the skeleton. The constitutional system of our own times, therefore, embraces the whole fabric of document, practices, and conceptions, and hundreds of pages are required to expound its operations. It is appropriate that we examine the ways in which the Constitution, thus conceived, expands and adjusts itself to the never-ending flux of American society. The first method to be considered is that of formal amendment.

Stages in the amending process

Two methods of initiating amendments to the Constitution and two methods of ratifying them are provided. All thus far adopted have been proposed in the same way: by joint resolution of the two branches of Congress. All except the Twenty-first (repealing national Prohibition) have likewise been ratified in the same manner: by action of the state legislatures. Any amendment receiving a two-thirds vote of those present in both House and Senate is transmitted by the head (administrator) of the General Services Administration to the governors of the several states, to be laid before legislatures or conventions. The President can interpose no veto.[13]

1. Initiation

The national convention an unused device

This does not mean that there have been no attempts to launch amendment proposals by the alternative method of a national convention. In fact, at one time or another the legislatures of considerably more than two-thirds of the states have called upon Congress to convoke a convention for the purpose. For the past few years a concerted drive has been underway, sponsored by the Council of State Governments, to get the requisite number of state legislatures to petition Congress to call a convention to consider amendments aimed at reducing the power of the Supreme Court in matters of legislative apportionment and strengthening the position of the states. One of these would change the amending process itself and would, if adopted, authorize an amendment to be initiated by the legislatures of two-thirds of the states without Congressional approval. Petitions designed to convoke a convention for a broad reconstruction of the Constitution were especially numerous at the time of the nullification controversy of 1832 and again in 1859-60 when civil war was imminent. The opinion has sometimes been advanced that every request for a convention made at any time by a state is to be regarded as pending indefinitely, and that whenever two-thirds of the states are found to have made such a request (a situation that has long existed, although not in support of any particular amendment or amendment program), Congress ought forthwith to call a convention. This "cumulative" view, however, is not generally accepted. Even though there never has been any official determination of the length of time a request from a state shall be regarded as remaining "alive," it is hardly conceivable that Congress would call a convention unless petitions were received from the necessary number of states within a

---

[13] Hollingsworth *et al. v.* Virginia, 3 Dallas 378 (1798). In submitting an amendment, said the Court, Congress is not legislating and, therefore, the President has no part in the process. Neither is a state legislature doing so when ratifying—with the result that the governor has no veto on ratifications.

84TH CONGRESS
1ST SESSION

H. J. RES. 214

IN THE HOUSE OF REPRESENTATIVES

FEBRUARY 14, ____

Mr. JOHNSON of California introduced the following joint resolution; which was
referred to the Committee on the Judiciary

JOINT RESOLUTION

Proposing an amendment to the Constitution of the United States
providing for the election of President and Vice President.

1   *Resolved by the Senate and House of Representatives*

2   *of the United States of America in Congress assembled,*

3   *(two-thirds of each House concurring therein),* That an

4   amendment is hereby proposed to the Constitution of the

5   United States which shall be valid to all intents and purposes

6   as part of the Constitution when ratified by three-fourths

7   of the legislatures of the several States. Said amendment

8   shall be as follows:

THE BEGINNING OF AN AMENDMENT TO THE CONSTITUTION

sufficiently limited period to create an appearance of concerted demand. Before that point was reached, Congress itself would quite likely have put the desired amendment before the states by its own direct action, as happened in the case of Prohibition repeal. If a convention were once convoked, it presumably could go as far as it liked in proposing amendments, and might even put before the country a completely rewritten fundamental law.

Whether a given amendment shall be acted upon by state legislatures or by conventions especially chosen for the purpose is determined entirely by Congress. Although the original Constitution was ratified by conventions, the

2. Ratification

legislative method was adhered to uniformly for amendments until the Twenty-first was submitted in 1933. Conventions, although more costly, are likely to give quicker results, and they have the further advantage of being chosen by the people with reference solely to the proposal upon which they are to act. Although ratified by legislatures, the Eighteenth (Prohibition) Amendment came to be looked upon as more appropriate for action by conventions, which therefore were employed in repealing it. Whichever plan is used, reports of actions taken are sent by the governors to the General Services Administration, which, if the necessary three-fourths majority is attained, proclaims the amendment effective as part of the Constitution.[14] Until fairly recently, a proposal failing to get the requisite majority was never officially announced as rejected, and accordingly was looked upon as remaining before the states indefinitely. By their own terms, however, four out of the last six amendments were to become operative only if ratified by the necessary three-fourths within seven years. How long an amendment with no time limit shall be considered pending is, the Supreme Court has said, a political question and therefore one for Congress alone to decide.[15] No decision on the matter has ever been made; and a child labor amendment submitted in 1924 is regarded by some as still "alive." If the requisite number of ratifications were secured, Congress might have to rule on the point. Already, however, Congress has gone so far as to decree that while a state which has rejected an amendment may change its mind and ratify, a state, once having ratified, cannot reverse its action.[16] Finally, under judicial interpretation of Article V, ratification must be literally by state legislatures or conventions, as Congress may ordain, and not by the people acting directly. In 1918, Ohio amended her state constitution to provide that after her legislature should have ratified an amendment the voters should be given an opportunity through a referendum to confirm or reverse the decision. A test case being brought, the United States Supreme Court held that the term *legislature* as employed in Article V means literally an elected representative body, and not the people acting directly.[17]

Number of amendments proposed and adopted

The states were not yet safely gathered under the "new roof," as the Constitution was popularly termed in early days, before proposals began to be made for "extensions of the eaves." In all, no fewer than 5000 drafted amendments (many of them duplicates, of course, or relating to the same

14 In Dillon *v.* Gloss, 256 U. S. 368 (1921), the Supreme Court ruled that an amendment becomes effective the moment when the last of the required number of states ratifies.

15 Coleman *v.* Miller, 307 U. S. 443 (1939). The view is logical, since it is Congress that submits the amendment in the first place.

16 Sustained by the Supreme Court in Coleman *v.* Miller, cited above.

17 Hawke *v.* Smith, 253 U. S. 221 (1920). There is no constitutional obstacle to an "advisory referendum" on a proposed amendment before the legislature votes; and such a test of public opinion has been made in a number of states. Official decision, however, must be by legislature or convention.

matters) were introduced in Congress from 1789 to 1965.[18] Nowadays, anywhere from 40 to 60 proposals are presented in the House or Senate (or both) during an average session, referred to the appropriate judiciary committee, filed, and mostly forgotten. The total number of amendments actually endorsed by the two houses from 1789 is, however, only 30, and the number ratified by the states only 24. Indeed, it would hardly be erroneous to say that the Constitution really has been amended only 14 times, because the first ten amendments were, to all intents and purposes, part of the original plan promised to many state ratifying bodies.

THE AMENDMENTS

The successful use of the amending process has been episodic; a few years of intense effort separated by long periods of quiescence. In the first twenty years of its life, 12 amendments were added to the Constitution: ten as a result of promises given to ratifying conventions and two as a result of unforeseen difficulties in applying certain provisions.

The first ten amendments comprise the Bill of Rights, the absence of which from the original document was widely criticized in the contest over ratification. Hamilton, in *The Federalist,* had contended that most of the state constitutions contained guarantees of certain rights and in the light of the restricted powers of the national government none were really needed.[19] Madison, however, gave certain assurances that the defect would be remedied and in the first Congress he prepared a series of amendments aimed to fulfill the commitment. Of 17 amendments voted by the House, 12 were endorsed by the Senate and ten ratified by the states.

The Bill of Rights

The eleventh amendment reversed a highly unpopular decision of the Supreme Court [20] and provided that thereafter a state could not be sued in the national courts by a citizen of another state or nation. The election of 1800, dominated as it had been by party activities, ended in an electoral vote tie, between Jefferson and his running mate Aaron Burr. The Federalist

18 The proposals between 1789 and 1889 are classified in H. V. Ames "The Proposed Amendments to the Constitution of the United States During the First Century of Its History," *Annual Report of the American Historical Association* (Washington, 1896); those between 1889 and 1929 are similarly classified in M. A. Musmanno, "Proposed Amendments to the Constitution," *70th Cong., 2nd Sess., House Doc. 551* (1929); and the 740 introduced between 1926 and 1941 are listed in E. H. Halsey, *Proposed Amendments to the Constitution of the United States Introduced in Congress December 6, 1926-January 3, 1941* (Washington, 1941), carried to 1947 in C. A. Loeffler, *Proposed Amendments to the Constitution of the United States Introduced in Congress from the 69th Congress, 2nd Session through the 79th Congress, Dec. 6, 1926, to Jan. 3, 1947* (Washington, 1947). Amendments proposed from year to year will be found listed in the appropriate volumes of the *U.S. Statutes at Large.*
19 In the convention in Philadelphia a motion to appoint a committee to draft a federal bill of rights had been rejected by 10 states out of 12 represented.
20 Chisholm v. Georgia, 2 Dallas 419 (1793). In this case, Georgia had been sued to pay its debts.

partisans in the "lame-duck" Congress conspired for a time to throw the election to Burr contrary to the widely understood popular intent. Cooler heads prevailed but the Jeffersonian partisans were sufficiently alarmed that they supported a new amendment (1803-04, Twelfth). Henceforth, the electors were required to cast separate ballots for President and Vice-President.

Civil War Amendments

Not until the Reconstruction era after the Civil War was the Constitution again formally changed despite numerous efforts to resolve, postpone, or mitigate the impending crisis by constitutional modification. The Republican majority, after victory, attempted to protect and define the rights of the emancipated Negroes by three amendments aimed at prohibiting slavery (Thirteenth), preventing discriminatory state action against the freedmen (Fourteenth), and at forbidding the denial of the vote to them on the grounds of race, color, or previous condition of servitude (Fifteenth). The Southern states were required, as a condition of their readmission to the Union on equal terms, to approve these amendments.

Wilson Era Amendments

The next reform era coincided with the administration of Woodrow Wilson and represented the culmination of years of agitation. The nation had enjoyed and suffered a period of great and rapid national growth and industrialization. Controversy over the proper relation of the government to the economy was widespread and deeply maintained. The most far-reaching of the Wilson-era changes—perhaps the most important of all the amendments—was that (Sixteenth) authorizing national taxation of incomes without apportionment. Relying upon the precedent set during the Civil War, the Congress had levied an income tax in 1894 only to have the Supreme Court [21] declare it a direct tax and, therefore, one that must be apportioned among the states according to population. The amendment was to overcome this decision. Two others aimed at increasing the democratic aspects of our system and thus presumably reducing the special position of certain interests in our society provided for the popular election of Senators (Seventeenth) and the elimination of barriers to female suffrage (Nineteenth). The fourth passed in a wartime mood of dedication embodied the ill-fated effort to prohibit the manufacture and sale of intoxicating liquor (Eighteenth).

New Deal Era changes

The reformist New Deal of Franklin Roosevelt achieved most of its goals by procedures other than formal constitutional change. However, during this era the old constitutional calendar was modernized: the traditional "lame-duck" session of the old Congress which met from December to March, after a new one had been elected was eliminated (Twentieth). The effort to achieve national Prohibition by law was abandoned and the amendment supporting it was repealed by the Twenty-First Amendment. As an aftermath of the New Deal era and the long, tradition-shattering tenure of Roosevelt, the Constitution was again changed in 1951 (Twenty-Second) to limit Presidential tenure to two terms.

New amendments spread democracy

The most recent uses of the amending process stem from continued

21 Pollock *v.* Farmers' Loan and Trust Co., 158 U. S. 601 (1895).

efforts to spread democracy through our system and are a product of lively and continuing agitation over human rights. The Twenty-third proclaimed in 1961 grants to residents of the national capitol the right to vote in Presidential elections. The Twenty-fourth, adopted in 1964, is aimed at tax-paying qualifications for voting in national elections and was primarily intended to get rid of the poll-tax requirements then extant in five Southern states.

A pending Twenty-fifth Amendment approved by the Congress in 1965 and now before the states is a product of the assassination of President Kennedy and is intended to fill a long-standing deficiency in the constitutional arrangements for determining Presidential disability and for filling vacancies in the office of Vice-President.

Looking over the 24 adopted amendments as a group several observations are appropriate. (1) In the main, they deny powers rather than confer new powers. Sometimes (as in the first eight) it is only or chiefly the national government that is restrained; sometimes (as in the Civil War group) it is only or chiefly the state governments. But in any event, most of the number are restrictive rather than otherwise. (2) The amendments are to only a slight extent responsible for the remarkable growth of governmental functions and activities in the last few decades. The phenomenal extensions of national power associated with the New Deal and World War II came without any change whatsoever in the written fundamental law. From a somewhat earlier amendment, it is true, the central government derived the exceedingly important power to tax incomes and this has been an important factor in financing the new programs. If it be asked how so much could happen without more resort to amendments, the answer arises immediately that there has been frequent, indeed ceaseless, resort to fresh and broadened interpretations of words, phrases, and clauses happily chosen a century and a half ago to allow precisely such flexibility. (3) While, however, the amendments have not conferred many express powers on the national government, they have imposed enough restrictions upon the states to have augmented national supremacy indirectly, and hence may be said to have had a nationalizing tendency. Finally, (4) the amendments while introducing relatively few changes in governmental machinery and procedures, have contributed materially to the advancement of democracy. The first eight defined and guaranteed civil liberties; the Fifteenth, Nineteenth, Twenty-third, and Twenty-fourth removed barriers to universal suffrage; the Sixteenth shifted the burden of government costs in the direction of the well-to-do; the Seventeenth definitely placed the election of Senators in the hands of the people.

Observations on the amendments as a group

Of proposing new changes in the Constitution there is, of course, no end. And in recent years Congress has repeatedly been urged to adopt amendment resolutions: (1) granting equal rights to women; (2) changing the method of counting the electoral vote in Presidential elections; (3) straightening out the tangle of marriage and divorce laws in the 50 states; (4) forbidding national intervention in systems of state legislative apportionment;

Proposed amendments

(5) limiting the amount of income that may be taken by taxation; (6) changing the treaty-making procedure by making it easier to ratify treaties, by increasing Congressional control of executive agreements, and by limiting the subjects on which treaties might be negotiated; and (7) creating a new Court of the Union made up of the chief justices of the 50 states and empowered to review on appeal certain decisions of the Supreme Court.

Criticism
of the
amending
process:
1. On the
grounds
that it
is too
difficult

Madison believed that the modes of amendment agreed upon by the framers guarded "equally against that extreme facility which would render the Constitution too mutable and that extreme difficulty which might perpetuate discovered faults." On the whole, history has sustained his judgment. Chief Justice Marshall, however, characterized the amending machinery as "unwieldy and cumbrous." During the long periods between effective use of the process, notably those from 1870-1913 and 1920-1933, reformers have strongly attacked the process as unnecessarily difficult. Several proposals for lowering the vote in Congress necessary for initiation and for reducing the number of state approvals required for ratification have been made in these periods.

2. On the
grounds
that it is
too easy

Hamilton devoted almost an entire number (85) of *The Federalist* to arguing that the amending process could not have been made any easier without inviting constitutional instability. The speedy ratification of the Eighteenth Amendment by legislatures of states in which, both before and after the advent of national Prohibition, the people in state-wide referenda voted against the plan led many people to believe that in point of fact the amending process was easier than it ought to be. For some years (1920-29), therefore, proposed changes looked chiefly in the direction of making it more difficult. However, people who were disturbed because of the ease with which the Eighteenth Amendment swept through the state legislatures were elated over the equal facility with which the amendment repealing it was carried.

3. On the
grounds
that
Congress
controls
the process

The most recent criticism is on quite different grounds from any of these. Congress, the President, and the Supreme Court, acting together or separately, may and do conspire to enhance the power of the central government at the expense of the states, say the critics—mostly state officials. Unless the states can protect themselves through constitutional guarantees they may be devoured. The national authorities are even now, say the critics, subverting the federal system, and must be halted by authorizing states to initiate as well as ratify amendments without reference to Congress. This view has as yet been endorsed by fewer than a dozen state legislatures.

Change
unlikely

Any change in the amending procedure is highly improbable. We have found that it is workable but usually only in great emergency or after prolonged agitation. More than this, we have found that by other procedures the Constitution can be subtly accommodated to changing conditions without the necessity for formal amendment. The so-called "undemocratic" features of the process are part of the whole scheme of American government and will not lightly be thrust aside. Finally, it seems unlikely that Congress will consent to eliminate itself from the amending process.

OTHER METHODS OF CONSTITUTIONAL ELABORATION

The secret of the endurance of the Constitution will be found not in the formal amending process but in the other processes of constitutional elaboration: legislation, executive action, judicial interpretation, and custom. Illustrations of each of these are found throughout this volume, but a general comment is here appropriate.

Desirous of avoiding what one of them called "a too minutious wisdom," *Legislation* the framers of the Constitution outlined clearly enough the general framework and functions of the new government, but wisely left a multitude of matters to be taken care of, as need might arise, by Congress, and even at certain points by the state legislatures. For example, they provided for a Vice-President to take over the duties of the Presidency in case of necessity, but said nothing about what should happen if there was no Vice-President; and Congress later supplied the deficiency. They assumed the existence of executive departments, and twice referred in the Constitution to the heads of such establishments; yet left Congress to create the departments and to determine what should be their functions and interrelations. The composition of the two houses of Congress was prescribed carefully, but the times, places, and manner of electing both Senators and Representatives were left to be fixed by the state legislatures, subject to control by Congress itself. In a somewhat belated statute of 1842 on the election of Representatives, and another of 1866 on the election of Senators, Congress amplified the constitutional law of this subject in much detail. Again, the judicial power of the United States was vested in "one Supreme Court, and in such inferior courts as Congress may from time to time ordain and establish." Aside from the Supreme Court, therefore, the entire national judicial establishment—the names, numbers, grades, and jurisdictions of the courts, together with their procedures—rests upon acts passed from time to time by Congress.

Congress defines commerce and creates agencies like the Interstate Commerce Commission and the Federal Communications Commission to regulate it. The means and methods of governing territories are provided by Congress. And so one could go on. Every time, in fact that Congress enacts a law it, in effect, starts with some express or implied constitutional provision, interprets it, and applies it, perchance in some new area or in some new manner, thereby projecting the Constitution into a new field or extending its meaning in an old one. In doing these things, Congress, of course, does not have a completely free hand; its constitutional interpretations may be challenged, and the courts *Executive* may overrule them. In the great majority of instances they stand; and legisla- *and* tion thus becomes one of the principal means by which the Constitution grows. *adminis-*
trative
It is not Congress alone that interprets and applies and adds. Within *action*

their spheres, the other two great branches of government, executive and judicial, do the same thing. On the executive side, the power starts with the President, who not only is as much entitled to construe the constitutional provisions as is Congress, but is equally entitled to make decisions and perform acts in accordance with his interpretations—subject to similar check from the courts. In the exercise of their powers, many Presidents have taken and maintained positions virtually settling constitutional questions previously considered open, or even giving the Constitution some meaning and application never before attributed to it. Moreover, from the White House this function of constitutional interpretation and adaptation filters down through the various levels of administration. Confronted almost daily with the necessity of making decisions, heads of departments, and even inferiors within their proper spheres, adopt positions, perform acts, or give orders resting, however remotely, upon some interpretation of a constitutional provision, and perhaps stretching the provision's meaning. When such actions escape successful challenge and establish themselves as precedents, the Constitution may be found to have undergone permanent extension, in however limited a particular.

Judicial interpretation   Then there is the significant matter of constitutional expansion at the hands of the courts. How this comes about must already be apparent. Congress, or a state legislature, passes a law, or a national or state official performs an act, which some person or group of persons affected adversely challenges as exceeding proper authority. A case is brought in the courts and the law or action is attacked as being unconstitutional; whereupon the judges must decide whether the charge is well founded—in other words, whether the measure is or is not in conformity with constitutional provision or reasonable construction. To do this, it is, of course, necessary to determine what the pertinent constitutional clauses mean. This opens wide opportunity to make them mean something different from, and probably more than, they previously had been supposed to mean, with the result of giving the Constitution a new twist or slant. The process operates cumulatively. A disputed phrase is so interpreted as to give it new scope and content. This, in turn, furnishes a point of departure for a further extension when the next similar case comes up. The most important single reason why the Constitution has not been amended more frequently is that from an early stage in the nation's history the Supreme Court has sat (in Woodrow Wilson's words) as "a kind of continuous constitutional convention," interpreting, developing, and expanding the basic law. One might say that every time the Court hands down one of its weekly batches of decisions, we have a constitution in some respects new.

Usage or custom   "Time and habit," remarked Washington, "are at least as necessary to fix the true character of governments as of other human institutions"; and so it comes about that still another mode by which our Constitution expands and develops is usage or custom. This method of change attracts less attention than the others; it does not—at all events at the outset—result in amendments, laws, or judicial decisions. Superimposed, nevertheless, upon the instrument of 1787 and its formal amendments, upon the laws that amplify and the decisions that extend it, is a broad and steadily developing "unwritten constitution," consisting of usages determining actual governmental practice quite as truly as do the provisions of written law. Plenty of illustrations will be encountered as we proceed; for the present, it must suffice merely to call to mind the manner in which the electoral college functions in choosing the President, the assembling of department heads in the advisory body known as the Cabinet, the frequent use of "executive agreements" in lieu of treaties, the caucus and committee systems in Congress, the introduction of all appropriation bills in the House of Representatives, the custom requiring members of the House of Representatives to be residents of the districts in which they are elected, and virtually all of the apparatus—caucuses, conventions, committees, platforms, funds—of political parties.

The general theme need not be elaborated farther. The upshot of all that has been suggested is that the bare outline of a governmental system contained in the Constitution as it came from the hands of the framers, and as it still can be read in the books, has been amplified and filled in—by amendment, executive action, statute, judicial construction, usage—until it has come to be one of the most elaborate and complicated plans of political organization and procedure known to history. And the process goes on unceasingly. The actual Constitution at any time is what citizens, lawmakers, administrators, and judges think it is. If a time should come when the fundamental law no longer grows and changes, the nation it serves will have vanished.

"The living word and deed of living men"

References

1. GENERAL WORKS ON CONSTITUTIONAL HISTORY

A. C. McLaughlin, *A Constitutional History of the United States* (New York, 1935).

H. C. Hockett, *The Constitutional History of the United States* (New York, 1939).

C. B. Swisher, *American Constitutional Development* (2nd ed., Cambridge, Mass., 1954).

A. H. Kelly and W. A. Harbison, *The American Constitution: Its Origins and Development* (New York, 1948).

B. F. Wright, *The Growth of Constitutional Power in the United States* (Chicago, 1947).

B. Schwartz, *The Reins of Power: A Constitutional History of the United States* (New York, 1963).

2. SPECIALIZED WORKS

A. Achievement of Federal Union

E. C. Burnett, *The Continental Congress* (New York, 1941).

A. C. McLaughlin, *The Confederation and the Constitution* (New York, 1905).

M. Jensen, *The Articles of Confederation: An Interpretation of the Social and Constitutional History of the American Revolution* (2nd ed., Madison, Wis., 1948).

————, *New Nation: A History of the United States During the Confederation, 1781-1789* (New York, 1952).

————, *The American Union: Its Interpretation and Its Historic Origins* (Oxford, 1950).

B. The Convention of 1787 and the Framing of the Constitution

A. N. Holcombe, *Our More Perfect Union: From Eighteenth-Century Principles to Twentieth-Century Practice* (Cambridge, Mass., 1950).

C. Van Doren, *The Great Rehearsal: The Story of the Making and Ratifying of the Constitution of the United States* (New York, 1948).

H. Lyon, *The Constitution and the Men Who Wrote It; the Story of the Constitutional Convention, 1787* (Boston, 1936).

C. A. Beard, *An Economic Interpretation of the Constitution of the United States* (new ed., New York, 1935).

C. Warren, *The Making of the Constitution* (Boston, 1928). An attack on Beard's economic interpretation.

R. E. Brown, *Charles Beard and the Constitution: A Critical Analysis of An Economic Interpretation of the Constitution* (Princeton, N.J., 1956).

I. Brant, *James Madison: Father of the Constitution, 1787-1800* (Indianapolis, 1950). The third volume of a full biography.

G. Hunt and J. B. Scott (eds.), *The Debates in the Federal Convention of 1787 Which Framed the Constitution of the United States of America* (New York, 1920).

M. Farrand (ed.), *The Records of the Federal Convention* (rev. ed., 4 vols., New Haven, 1937).

————, *The Framing of the Constitution* (New Haven, Conn., 1913).

J. P. Roche, "The Founding Fathers: A Reform Caucus in Action," *Amer. Polit. Sci. Rev.,* LV, No. 4, Dec. 1961.

C. The Contest Over Ratification

A. J. Beveridge, *The Life of John Marshall* (Boston, 1916), Vol. I, Chaps. IX-XII.

S. B. Harding, *The Contest Over the Ratification of the Federal Constitution in the State of Massachusetts* (New York, 1896).

C. E. Miner, *The Ratification of the Constitution by the State of New York* (New York, 1921).

J. Elliott (comp.), *Debates in the Several State Conventions on the Adoption of the Federal Constitution,* 5 vols. (2nd ed., Washington, 1854).

The Federalist, edited by J. E. Cooke (Middletown, Conn., 1958).

O. G. Libby, *Geographical Distribution of the Vote of the Thirteen States on the Federal Constitution* (Madison, Wis., 1894).

D. Processes of Constitutional Development

D. P. Myers, *The Process of Constitutional Amendment* (76th Cong., 3rd Sess., Sen. Doc. #314, 1940).

L. B. Orfield, *The Amending of the Federal Constitution* (Ann Arbor, Mich., 1942).

N. B. Lasson, "The History and Development of the Fourth Amendment to the United States Constitution," *Johns Hopkins Univ. Studies in Hist. and Polit. Sci.,* Vol. LV, pp. 223-360 (1937).

H. E. Flack, "The Adoption of the Fourteenth Amendment," *ibid.,* Extra Vol. XXVI (1908).

J. M. Mathews, "Legislative and Judicial History of the Fifteenth Amendment," *ibid.,* Vol. XXVII, Nos. 6-7 (1909).

E. K. Ketcham, *The Sixteenth Amendment* (Urbana, Ill., 1926).

E. S. Brown, *Ratification of the Twenty-first Amendment of the Constitution of the United States: State Convention Records and Laws* (Ann Arbor, Mich., 1938).

J. P. James, *The Framing of the Fourteenth Amendment* (Urbana, Ill., 1956).

J. A. Garraty (ed.). *Quarrels That Have Shaped the Constitution* (New York, 1964).

E. Documents

Documents Illustrative of the Formation of the Union of the American States, 69th Congress, 1st Session, House Doc. #398 (Washington, D.C., 1927).

The Constitution of the United States of America: Analysis and Interpretation, 88th Congress, 1st Session, Senate Doc. #39 (Washington, 1964).

★ 3 ★

The Federal System

The powers not delegated to the United States by the Constitution nor prohibited by it to the States, are reserved to the States respectively, or to the people. TENTH AMENDMENT

The system established by the framers

THE CONSTITUTION ESTABLISHED OVER THE AMERICAN PEOPLE a new central government, strikingly independent of the existing state governments, and endowed it with authority to deal with virtually all those transactions carried on across state lines or beyond the national boundaries. In general, the valid powers of this new agency were to be exercised directly on the people and not through intermediate authorities. The existing governmental institutions in the 13 separate states were left largely undisturbed, except that by express limitation and by fair implication their potential powers were somewhat curtailed. The division of responsibilities between the two levels of authority was achieved by the specific enumeration of the powers of the central government, the denial of certain powers to the states and by the reservation of all the unspecified residue to the states and the people. This arrangement is called a federal system. It may be distinguished from a centralized or unitary system on the one hand in which all valid power is entrusted to the central government and from a league or confederation on the other in which the central government is a creature of the regional governments and exercises power only on their sufferance.

American federal system is unique

Some members of the constitutional convention were familiar with other federal systems in ancient Greece and contemporary Switzerland and with the theoretical literature about such systems. The actual assignment of powers, however, was not based on some preconceived formula but rather on the felt needs of the times. The framers were primarily preoccupied with establishing a stronger central government and with giving it as much authority as they believed would be acceptable to informed public opinion.[1] They went no further than absolutely necessary in charting the dividing line between national and state power. As with other aspects of the new charter, they left

---

[1] In fact, to them, the word "federal" meant the same as confederation or league and they described their creation as a mixture of federal and national systems. M. Diamond, "What the Framers Meant by Federalism," *A Nation of States: Essays on the American Federal System* ed. by R. A. Goldwin (Chicago, 1964).

to future statesmen the resolution of many problems—existent and unforeseen. Much of the political history of our nation has revolved around the problems of national-state powers and responsibilities and the federal system today is quite unlike that established in 1789.[2]

THE STRUGGLE FOR NATIONAL SUPREMACY

The Constitution, and the Laws of the United States which shall be made in pursuance thereof; and all treaties made, or which shall be made, under the authority of the United States, shall be the supreme law of the land; and the judges in every State shall be bound thereby, anything in the Constitution or laws of any State to the contrary notwithstanding. ART. VI, Cl. 2

To many people today the major problem of the federal system is to preserve an important sphere of independent authority for the states and their local units in view of the advancing might of the national authority and its ever deeper penetration into the fabric of American society. To the framers and the statesmen of early America, however, the problem was to protect and preserve the ability of those in command of national power to make national policy effective throughout the nation against the opposition or obstruction of regional interests. Most of the governing in America throughout the nineteenth and well into the present century was done by the states and local units. During peacetime, national expenditures, national public employment, and the range of national services and controls, were considerably narrower than those of the states and their subdivisions. Although regional differences threatened national unity in the controversies about the War of 1812, slavery, and tariff policy, over the years national power became more firmly established and now is universally acknowledged to be supreme wherever validly exercised.

The slow growth of national authority

The achievement of effective national authority throughout the land and across the seas into insular possessions may in great part be attributed to the economic, technological, and social development of the American population from an agricultural, frontier, immigrant, individualist and isolated people to

Growth of industrialism promotes national authority

[2] The advantages and disadvantages of federalism are considered at some length in J. W. Garner, *Political Science and Government* (New York, 1932), 346-356, 412-422, and J. Bryce, *The American Commonwealth* (4th ed., New York, 1910), Chaps. XXVII-XXVIII. Canada, Australia, Switzerland, Brazil, Argentina, and Mexico have federal systems; although outside the United States, the most interesting federal arrangements are perhaps those prevailing in the U.S.S.R. Some excellent modern books devoted specifically to federalism are K. C. Wheare, *Federal Government* (rev. ed.) (London and New York, 1951); R. R. Bowie and C. J. Friedrich (eds.), *Studies in Federalism* (Boston, 1954); A. W. MacMahon (ed.), *Federalism Mature and Emergent* (New York, 1955); W. S. Livingston, *Federalism and Constitutional Change* (London, 1956); R. A. Goldwin (ed.), *A Nation of States: Essays on the American Federal System* (Chicago, 1964); and, H. G. Shaffer, *The Soviet System in Theory and Practice* (New York, 1964).

an interdependent, urban, industrial, mobile, and highly inter-related society. Local authority is largely ineffective in regulating and protecting such a society. It may also be attributed to the establishment, growth and acceptance of patterns of politics and law and of constitutional arrangements which facilitated the development of as well as responded to the pressures of modern society.

Judicial review and national supremacy

The Constitution itself made a major contribution to the establishment of effective national supremacy through the "supremacy of the law" clause which stands at the head of this section.[3] After much discussion, the framers had abandoned a provision authorizing Congress to disallow state legislation in favor of this provision intended to require state courts to invalidate state and local actions conflicting with declared national policy. To be effective, however, an arrangement for reviewing, overriding if necessary, state decisions was clearly required and this was provided by the Congress. In the first judiciary act passed in 1789, authority was conferred upon the Supreme Court of the United States to hear on appeal decisions of state courts in which a state law or official action was upheld although alleged to be in conflict with the Constitution, a national law, or a treaty. Under the vigorous leadership of nationalist, John Marshall, the court from 1801 began to exercise this review power and from thence forth numerous state laws have been rendered unenforceable by judicial determination.[4] The practice by the courts of enforcing the constitutional assignment of powers upon the various levels of governments as well as upon the various branches of a particular level is known as judicial review. It is a distinctive American contribution to the art and science of constitutional government.

The fact that the arbiter of disputes over the boundaries separating state and national authority has been the national Supreme Court, an institution organized and staffed by national authority, has not been a minor factor in the achievement of national supremacy. In the words of a writer of an earlier generation, the Supreme Court has throughout our history been "as impartial an umpire in national-state disputes as one of the members of two contending teams could be expected to be." [5] There is, therefore, no limitation on national as against state authority which Congress, the President, and the Court acting concurrently could not, in theory at least, override. Among these

[3] "This clause," observes a distinguished historian, "may be called the central clause of the Constitution, because without it the whole system would be unwieldy, if not impracticable. Draw out this particular bolt (other writers have called it the linchpin) and the machinery falls to pieces. In these words the Constitution is plainly made not merely a declaration, a manifesto, dependent for its life and usefulness on the passing will of statesmen or of people, but a fundamental law, enforceable like any other law on courts." A. C. McLaughlin, *The Confederation and the Constitution* (New York, 1950), 247.

[4] The first Supreme Court decision holding a state law unconstitutional was Fletcher *v*. Peck. 6 Branch 87 (1810).

[5] O. P. Field, "States versus Nation, and the Supreme Court." *Amer. Polit. Sci. Rev.* XXVII. 233 (April, 1934).

national agencies over the years have been discovered large areas of unsuspected national power and undoubtedly others will be found in the future.

Standing alone, with no enforcing agents, no national political apparatus, and against the determined opposition not only of many states but of Congress or perhaps even the President, the Supreme Court can, however, be relatively helpless. Some problems have been so deeply divisive and so bitterly disputed that judicial fiat could not resolve them. Congress, and the President, have also made important and lasting contributions to the achievement of national supremacy. When Jefferson captured the Presidency in 1800, the first major challenge to national authority was happily abandoned. While out of power nationally, he and his followers had fashioned and promoted the first state effort (Virginia and Kentucky Resolutions) to veto national policy by state legislative resolution. In this case the target was the Alien and Sedition Acts of 1798, sharply curtailing freedom of speech. The doctrine of state "interposition" was concocted to frustrate national enforcement. These acts expired during Jefferson's Presidency and the state efforts were thus obviated. Several New England states considered resistance to national authority in 1814 at Hartford in a desperate attempt to change the course of national trade policy. Peace with England brought these efforts to an end without further incident. South Carolina mounted a similar offensive in 1832 against national tariff policy, even threatening secession if its nullification efforts were ignored. President Jackson firmly resisted and threatened military measures if necessary to uphold national law. Many and diverse efforts were made in the 1850's in Massachusetts, Wisconsin, Vermont, and other northern states to frustrate enforcement of the national fugitive slave law but in the major judicial test of their efforts the Supreme Court gave little comfort to state pretensions.[6] It was the Civil War, however, which finally and firmly established the doctrine that this is an indestructible union and that those in possession of national power may and will use it, if challenged, to enforce national policy throughout the land. Upon defeat, the Southern states were not only occupied for some years by armies of the national government but were readmitted to the Union only upon terms prescribed in Washington. The passage at the end of this bloody struggle of the Fourteenth Amendment laid the basis for the ultimate extension of national authority into areas not theretofore regarded as of proper national concern and also endowed the national courts with new powers to review state actions and force them into line with nationally ordained standards.

The Civil War also removed most of the remaining barriers to the rapid industrialization and urbanization of the nation. Incident to these developments came new challenges to national power. The national courts struck down several efforts by states to mitigate the disadvantages of rapid industrialization by economic regulation. Several attempts to prevent railroad rate extortion and to safeguard workingmen were disallowed. President Cleve-

Contribution of Congress and the President

National-state disputes over industrial regulations

6 Ableman v. Booth, 21 Howard 206 (1859).

into the Union without prior territorial status and five states (Vermont, Kentucky, Tennessee, Maine, and West Virginia) were formed by separation from other states.

Congres-
sional
review at
time of
admission

The Constitution confers on Congress general power to admit new states subject to two restrictions: (1) No state may be erected within the jurisdiction of any other state except with the consent of the legislature of the latter; (2) No state may be formed by the union of two or more states except with the approval of the legislatures of the states concerned. Congress, traditionally, has authorized the steps for admission of a particular territory and the establishment of a convention to draft a constitution for the new state. It has, also, insisted on reviewing the new constitution before recognizing a new member. Although, legally, a state once admitted becomes the equal of the other states, the admission process has provided national officials with an opportunity to insist upon certain conditions as a price of admission. Ohio, for example, was required in 1802 to agree not to tax for five years public lands within its borders sold by the national government; Nevada, in 1864, to agree never to deny the vote to colored persons; Utah, in 1896, to write into its constitution a prohibition of polygamy; Oklahoma, in 1907, to promise not to move the state capitol from Guthrie before 1913; Arizona, in 1910, to eliminate a provision in its constitution authorizing the recall of judges; Alaska, in 1959, to allow the administration of fish and wildlife regulations to remain under the Secretary of the Interior until he should certify to Congress that the Alaskan legislature had made adequate provision for state administration. In general, only those conditions, usually of a contractual nature, which appear not to compromise the political freedom of the state have been held to be enforceable upon the states after admission.[8]

Admission
of Hawaii
and Alaska

The newest members of the Union, Hawaii and Alaska, were admitted after submitting constitutions prepared by them without express Congressional authorization and after Congressionally-required public referenda on

[8] The capital of Oklahoma, for example, was moved to Oklahoma City by legislative act in 1910; and when challenged, the Supreme Court (in Coyle v. Oklahoma, 221 U. S. 559, 1911) ruled that while Congress is free to impose any conditions initially that it chooses, once a state is admitted, there is no way of compelling fulfillment of them if they are of such a nature as to compromise the independence of the state in managing its own internal affairs.

When, in 1910, the people of Arizona, yielding to the objections of President Taft and many members of Congress, voted to eliminate recall of judges from their proposed constitution, it was locally understood that the surrender was to be only temporary. In his very first message, the governor of the new state recommended a constitutional amendment restoring the recall; and forthwith such an amendment was adopted by the legislature and approved by the voters. Arizona has had recall of judges ever since. On the other hand, a requirement that the state of Minnesota impose no tax on lands belonging to the United States, and no higher tax on nonresident proprietors than on residents, was upheld in 1900 (Stearns v. Minnesota, 179 U. S. 223) on the ground that it was a contractual agreement concerning a matter of property and did not affect the state's political freedom. In the same way, New Mexico was balked in 1919 (Ervien v. United States, 251 U. S. 41) in an attempt to use proceeds of the sale of public lands in a manner different from that specified in the terms of the state's admission.

the question of admission. The overwhelming public endorsement in the two territories of immediate statehood and the election of Congressional delegations set the stage for Presidential admission by proclamation: Alaska on January 3, 1959 and Hawaii on August 21, 1959.

NATIONAL REVIEW OF STATE POLITICAL INSTITUTIONS

A third constitutional contribution to national supremacy is the authority invested in Washington to review and approve certain state political institutions. The Constitution, for example, obliges the national government to guarantee to every state a republican form of government. In fixing terms for the readmission of the Southern states after the Civil War, the Congress required them to adopt suffrage and other arrangements which the Republican majority professed to regard as essential to a republican form of government. In general, however, neither Congress nor the courts have relied extensively on this provision to support national power. In the single instance prior to the Civil War, in which the guaranty clause was invoked, the Dorr Rebellion in Rhode Island in 1841-42, President Tyler recognized the established government of the state and aided it against the rival government set up by Dorr. According to the court, the fact that Congress continued to receive the state's elected Representatives and Senators constituted valid and final recognition of the republican form of government of Rhode Island. Furthermore, the Court in this situation declared the question to be primarily a political one to be settled by Congress not a justiciable one to be resolved in a law suit.[9] These views prevailed also when Oregon's popular initiative and referendum was challenged in the courts as direct rather than republican government[10] and when an Ohio law was attacked as an unrepublican delegation of legislative power to an administrative agency.[11]

The guarantee of a republican government

The Fourteenth Amendment and to a lesser extent the Fifteenth Amendment provide the legal basis for the more significant national review of state institutions. Under the provision that no state may deny to any person within its jurisdiction the equal protection of the laws, the modern Supreme Court has held that state efforts to exclude Negroes from participation in the Democratic primary are invalid.[12] It has also invalidated a rearrangement of the municipal boundary lines in Tuskegee, Alabama, designed to exclude most of the Negro population of that city from participating in municipal politics.[13] And, in a most significant reversal of earlier judicial policy, it has quite recently asserted that apportionment systems for state legislatures are review-

Judicial review of legislative districting systems

[9] Luther v. Borden. 7 Howard 1 (1849).
[10] Pacific States Tel. and Tel. v. Oregon. 223 U. S. 118 (1912).
[11] Ohio ex rel. Bryant v. Akron Metropolitan Park District, 281 U. S. 74 (1930).
[12] Nixon v. Herndon, 273 U. S. 526 (1927) and Nixon v. Condon, 286 U. S. 73 (1932).
[13] Gomillion v. Lightfoot, 364 U. S. 339 (1960).

able by the courts and will be held as denying equal protection if the districts in both houses are not substantially equal in population.[14] These decisions claim for the national courts the most sweeping power to overturn long-established state political arrangements many of which are expressly sanctioned by state constitutions. Critics are now mounting a strong offensive to obtain a constitutional amendment authorizing states to apportion at least one house on a basis other than population.

Review of discrimina-tory administra-tion of state programs

Under the Civil Rights of 1964 (Title VI), the national administration is now also endowed with authority to require drastic changes in the practices, policies, and institutional arrangements of the states. "No person . . . shall . . . be subjected to discrimination under any program or activity receiving federal financial assistance," says the Act. Armed with the power to cut off grants-in-aid, administrative officials are now reviewing state educational, welfare, health, housing, conservation, highway and other programs receiving aids to determine whether changes are or will be required in states and in many instances are demanding and getting cooperation which had been denied to the courts and the United States attorneys.

GROWING PERVASIVENESS OF THE NATIONAL GOVERNMENT

Expanded national activities and powers

The establishment of effective national authority is, perhaps, one aspect of the greatly increased scope of national activities which characterize the modern federal system. The rise of urban industrialism, the extension of American influence throughout the world, and the growth of the huge establishment for national defense have all paved the way for the tremendous expansion of the national government which is characteristic of twentieth-century America. With one exception, these developments have rested on no change in the basic constitutional assignments of power. The Fourteenth Amendment supplied the authority for increased national concern with civil rights and racial discrimination. It has been evolving interpretations of national power by Congress, the President, and the courts which have kept these developments firmly anchored to the constitutional language.

The doctrine of implied powers

One of the most useful tools of constitutional politics favoring the growth of national power was provided early in our history: the doctrine of implied powers.

Arguments for

Lively controversies about the limits of national power arose before the new system had been in operation a year. In 1790, Hamilton, as Secretary of the Treasury, proposed the establishment of a national bank. People who considered that centralization had already been carried far enough at once objected that the Constitution, in enumerating the powers of Congress, said nothing about a bank; they could show, indeed, that its authors had deliberately refused to give Congress even limited power to create corporations.

[14] Baker *v.* Carr, 369 U. S. 186 (1962) and Reynolds *v.* Sims, 377 U. S. 364 (1964).

Hamilton and others who supported his project replied that while the Constitution truly enough did not authorize Congress in so many words to create a bank, the power to do so could easily be deduced from certain grants of authority about which there could be no question—in particular, those relating to currency and other aspects of national finance, backed by the "sweeping clause," with which the Constitution's enumeration of the powers of Congress concludes, in which the two houses are authorized "to make all laws which shall be necessary and proper for carrying into execution the foregoing powers, and all other powers vested by this Constitution in the government of the United States, or in any department or officer thereof." The Hamiltonian view prevailed, and the bank was established by Congress.

Led by Jefferson, "strict" constructionists argued that the national government had no powers except such as were expressly conferred upon it in the Constitution, or, at most such as could be shown to be indispensably involved in the exercise of these delegated powers. To take a single step beyond the boundaries "specially drawn" around the powers of Congress by the Tenth Amendment, urged the Virginian,[15] "is to take possession of a boundless field of power, no longer susceptible of any definition." Hamilton replied that the national government had all powers which could by any reasonable interpretation be regarded as implied in the letter of the granted powers, and also that it had a right to choose the manner and means of performing its functions, even though involving the employment of agencies not necessarily *indispensable* for its purposes. *Arguments against*

In the course of time, the question reached the Supreme Court; and in a memorable series of nationalizing decisions between 1809 and 1835, that tribunal—while acknowledging limits beyond which powers could not properly be inferred—lent the Hamiltonian doctrine the full weight of its authority. Classic expression was given the Court's views by Chief Justice Marshall in the case of McCulloch *v.* Maryland, in 1819 as follows: [16] *The Court decides*

> This government is acknowledged by all to be one of enumerated powers. The principle that it can exercise only the powers granted to it is now universally admitted. But the question respecting the extent of the powers actually granted is perpetually arising and will probably continue to arise as long as our system shall exist. . . . The powers of the government are limited, and its powers are not to be transcended. But we think the sound construction of the Constitution must allow to the national legislature that discretion with respect to the means by which the powers it confers are to be carried into execution, which will enable that body to perform the high duties assigned to it in a manner most beneficial to the people. Let the end be legitimate, let it be within the scope of the Constitution, and all means which are appropriate, which are plainly adapted

---

[15] In a letter in which he gave Washington his views on the constitutionality of a proposed bank.

[16] 4 Wheaton 316.

to that end, which are not prohibited but consist with the letter and spirit of the Constitution, are constitutional.

The principles here laid down gained general acceptance and are today firmly embedded in our constitutional law. Even the Jeffersonians, after they gained control of the government in 1801, found themselves invoking it to support the annexation of Louisiana in 1803 and the embargo placed on foreign trade in 1807. Time and again Congress has devised programs, created agencies, and established national regulations on the basis of a chain of inference from the most meager phrases of the constitutional text and the courts have followed along usually but not invariably acceding to the Congressional will.

The expanding definition of interstate commerce

The ability of the national government to aid a growing industrial economy by subsidy and service was, as we shall see, never sharply contested but its authority to minimize some of the worst disadvantages of entreprenurial aggressiveness and to provide national remedies for economic depressions was confined for many decades by narrow definitions of power over interstate commerce. Although the national authorities progressively widened the meaning of commerce to embrace the new technologies of transportation (railroads, aeroplanes, motor cars) and of communication (telephone, telegraph, cable, radio, television) and almost from the beginning had interpreted commerce to mean the movement of people and services as well as goods, until the late 1930's the courts had insisted that mining and manufacturing regardless of the source of raw materials or the destinations of the finished products were not commerce. Meanwhile mass production, national advertising, and business consolidation had created a national economy in which transportation was but one facet. More than this, certain state efforts to protect workers and consumers were nullified by the national judiciary under a wonderfully ingenious interpretation of the due process clause of the Fourteenth Amendment. The national power, thus defined, to curtail monopoly, forbid child labor, establish minimum wages, and promote collective bargaining reached but a small segment of the industrial system. Confronted with the depression of the thirties the President and Congress found themselves relatively powerless to curb practices which many felt were unjust and economically repressive. The judicial revolution of 1936-37 established the principle that the production and distribution of goods and services constituted a more or less completely integrated series of transactions, every one of which depended upon every other and the national authority over interstate commerce could be effective only if it extended to the entire process of manufacture and sale.[17] In this way, and after several decades of the liveliest agitation, was the present vast sweep of national authority over the economy supported. In consequence, there are today relatively few economic transac-

[17] National Labor Relations Board *v.* Jones Laughlin Steel Corp., 301 U. S. (1937) and U. S. *v.* Darby Lumber Co., 312 U. S. 100 (1941)

tions which are not within the reach of Congressional power. The area of state action has been progressively contracting as more and more businesses serve regional, national and international needs. Congress and the courts have left some small freedom to the states to deal with business, transportation, or communication within their boundaries in their own ways under the following circumstances: (1) if the enterprise or activity is wholly and exclusively intrastate and does not substantially affect interstate commerce; (2) if Congress has not seen fit to exercise the power it possesses, provided that the courts find that state regulation in these circumstances either is authorized by the Congress or is not inconsistent with the courts' view of national needs; (3) if a state regulation in the interests of public health and safety imposes only an incidental and insignificant burden on interstate commerce; and (4) if a state regulation is not inconsistent with a national government action and deals with a matter not held to be pre-empted by national action.

Speaking broadly, this great expansion of national power has now been generally accepted. In fact, Congress has not yet exercised all of the authority the courts have authorized. Around one aspect, however, controversy continues and that is whether Congress intended to pre-empt a particular subject and thus to bar all state action in it.[18] Most of the traditional controversy over the "pre-emption doctrine" centered on the commerce clause and much of it still does, especially in the matter of national-state authority in labor relations.[19] However, the use of the doctrine to strike down a state act regulating subversive activities against the United States has caused most of the recent stir.[20] *The pre-emption controversy*

The third aspect of increasing national power is the gradual emergence of a system of nationally guaranteed civil rights. For several generations after its adoption the provisions of the Fourteenth Amendment were narrowly construed and added little, if anything, to national power to control state official behavior in this field. Beginning in the twenties, in connection with state curtailment of free speech, the court has progressively expanded the application of the Amendment to include religious practices, censorship, racial dis- *Emergence of a national system of civil rights*

[18] See, for example, *The Report of the Committee on Federal-State Relationships Affected by Judicial Decision Adopted by The Conference of Chief Justices* distributed by The Virginia Commission on Constitutional Government (Richmond, Va., 1959), and the reply given by W. B. Lockhard, Dean of the University of Minnesota Law School reprinted in *Congressional Record,* 6076-6077 (April 27, 1959). Detailed studies prepared for the Conference of Chief Justices of various aspects of the federal pre-emption question may be found in *Special Supplement #1—University of Chicago Law School Record VIII,* No. 1, Dec., 1958). Several bills have been introduced into recent Congresses designed to express the intent of Congress that none of its acts shall be construed as invalidating state acts in similar fields unless the act expressly states that this is the intention. None of these has been passed.

[19] Several recent labor law cases involving pre-emption are: DeVeau *v.* Braisted, 363 U. S. 144 (1960); Hill *v.* Florida, 325 U. S. 538 (1945); Textile Union *v.* Lincoln Mills, 353 U. S. 448 (1957); San Diego Building Trades Council *v.* Garmon, 359 U. S. 236 (1959).

[20] Penna. *v.* Nelson, 350 U. S. 497 (1956).

crimination in housing, public facilities, and schools, and criminal justice, and allegedly unequal systems of legislative apportionment. All of this, followed as it has been by various national legislative and administrative activities, has introduced national authority into areas of social relations and administrative behavior heretofore dominated by states and localities. It has also provoked the strongest criticism and the most energetic efforts to reduce national power of any of the developments of this century.

GRANTS-IN-AID TO THE STATES

National financing of state and local programs

The most powerful engine in this century for reshaping national-state relations has been the "grant-in-aid" system of national financing of state and local activities. Grants by the national government to the states are no novelty; on the contrary, they go back almost to the beginning of our national history. Starting in Ohio in 1802, Congress made a regular practice of bestowing on newly admitted states public land within their boundaries equivalent to one section in every township, to be used for the development of permanent school funds—in fact, two sections after 1848, and even four in the cases of Utah, Arizona, and New Mexico. In the famous Land Grant College (Morrill) Act of 1862, it set aside still more land for the benefit of the states, specifying that the proceeds should be used by each in endowing and maintaining one or more colleges devoted primarily, although not exclusively, to instruction in "such branches of learning as are related to agriculture and the mechanic arts." Funds derived from this source help support many of our "land-grant" colleges. Not only land but also money (in periods of surplus revenues) was bestowed in earlier times; and not only for education but likewise for roads and canals.

The conditional grant-in-aid system

In recent decades, a new form of conditional grant has been devised and used widely, and it is this new form that has enlarged national power. Referred to commonly as a "grant-in-aid," its cardinal principle is that Congress will appropriate money for a specified service or activity to be carried out by the states, apportioning the sum for any given purpose among the whole number of states on some fixed basis, but permitting a state to share in the subvention only, as a rule, on four conditions: (1) that the state shall spend the national money only for the exact purpose indicated and under whatever conditions may have been laid down; (2) that the state itself, or its subdivisions, shall make concurrent appropriations for the purpose (usually in amounts at least equal to its share of the national grant, but sometimes more, sometimes less, and occasionally none at all); (3) that the state shall maintain a suitable administrative agency—highway commission, extension director, vocational education board, or whatever it may be—with which the national government can deal in connection with the activity to be carried on; and (4), that in return for the assistance received, the state shall recognize the national government's right (with suitable regard for local conditions) to approve plans and policies, interpose regulations, fix minimum standards, and inspect results. Often, of course, it has been necessary for states to enact new legislation in order to qualify for sharing in a given grant. Usually administrative machinery has been reconstructed so as to open a way for supervision by national officers over activities that previously—if undertaken at all—were entirely in that state's own hands. Ostensibly, no compulsion is exercised. A state may, if it likes, decline to meet the conditions imposed in which event it simply does not participate in the subsidy. This voluntary aspect of the plan has been of great help to the courts in getting around the constitutional difficulties which some of the legislation dealing with matters far out on the rim of national authority presents. Compliance by the states is, however, less voluntary than appears. For the national funds represent the proceeds of taxes paid by the people of the entire country, and if any state refuses to go into a given arrangement, it thereby cuts itself off from the benefits which its taxpayers are helping to bestow on the states that participate. Typically, the state has been reluctant to do this; and the same considerations that initially induce a state to accept its share of a grant commonly impel it to live up to the standards and specifications required rather than run the risk of having its subvention withheld. Virtually all existing forms of grants-in-aid are shared in by all of the states.

Beginning in 1887 with cash grants for the maintenance of agricultural experiment stations in the states, the modern grant-in-aid program has steadily reached out to embrace ever larger areas of state and local action. Forestry was added to agricultural research and education as an object of grant-in-aid in 1911, highways in 1916, vocational education in 1917, health in 1918, social welfare in 1935, low-cost housing in 1937, airports and hospitals in 1946, urban renewal in 1949, soil conservation in 1954, libraries in 1956, civil defense in 1958, educational television in 1962, higher education facilities in 1963, urban mass transportation in 1964, and general education in 1965. From 1895, with the requirement of national audit of state expenditures under the agricultural experiment station program, the amount and character of national administrative supervision of state agencies has also steadily expanded. Under the social-welfare aid legislation of 1935 even the personnel policies of state agencies spending national funds have come under national review and under the Civil Rights Act of 1964, their policies with regard to racial discrimination in education, welfare, housing, and other aided public services must be adapted to national requirements. Furthermore, the dependence of the state governments upon income from this source to finance their operations has progressively become greater. In 1965, the national payments averaged more than 23 per cent of total state receipts from all sources. Finally, the total demands on the national budget made by the grant-in-aid programs have risen from $33 million in 1920 to more than $10 billion in 1965. The end of this period of expansion in national financing of state and local functions is not yet in sight. The national government in 1965 has just

The evolution of national supervision of subsidized programs

GROWTH OF NATIONAL GRANTS-IN-AID TO STATES AND LOCALITIES
1902-1964

(Excludes Shared Revenues, Loans, Special Payments for Impacted School Districts, Research and Demonstration Projects, Emergency Grants, Veterans Aids, and Expenditures for Military Programs)

Program	1902	1912	1920	1930	1940	1954	1964
Agricultural Exp. Stations	786	1,593	1,440	4,335	6,848	13,426	39,388
Agricultural Extension	—	—	4,472	7,540	18,448	31,772	75,149
Agricultural Colleges	1,200	2,500	2,500	2,550	5,030	5,051	14,500
Highways	—	—	20,306	77,891	153,379	521,637	3,644,174
Airports	—	—	—	—	—	17,482	65,248
Vocational Education	—	—	2,107	7,385	19,299	25,332	41,076
Vocational Rehabilitation	—	—	—	736	2,125	22,997	87,573
Public Health & Hospitals	—	—	1,759	—	13,689	72,716	335,446
School Lunch & Food Distribution	—	—	—	—	—	83,498	786,779
Child Welfare & Mothers Care	—	—	—	10	9,545	29,380	113,776
Public Assistance	—	—	—	—	279,181	1,388,967	2,981,492
Unemployment Comp. & Public Employment Service Adminis.	—	—	—	—	61,702	202,837	557,156
Public Housing, Urban Renewal	—	—	—	—	—	44,474	676,261
Forestry & Conservation	—	—	—	1,318	2,212	9,800	308,919
Manpower Dev.	—	—	—	—	—	—	89,031
Misc.*	1,015	1,162	1,302	725	2,200	21,389	41,503
Total	3,001	5,255	33,886	102,490	573,658	2,539,277	9,777,541

* Includes Library Services, Educational T.V., Veterans Homes, Civil Defense, and Marine Schools.
SOURCE: Figures 1902-1940 from Council of State Governments, *Federal Grants-in-Aid* (Chicago, 1960), p. 32. Figures 1954-1964 from *Budget of the United States, 1956* and *1965*.

begun a program of financing of general public education which is certain to grow.

The grant-in-aid procedure has, furthermore, reached beyond the states down into the local units of government. Direct fiscal and administrative relations have been established between the national government and cities and counties in such programs as housing, airport construction, urban renewal, youth job opportunity promotion, and mass transportation. For a time during the depression, local relief and public works programs were also supported by national funds. In these programs the state government has been by-passed to link national and local units of government together.

National-local relations established

The result of this twentieth-century development has been to cast the states and their local units into a new relationship of subordination to the national government. The states are today, for those programs involving national financing, largely administrative subdivisions of the national government. Although they are subdivisions of a novel kind—a good deal of autonomy of method and objective is tolerated—nevertheless they are more dependent upon national money and more susceptible to national control than ever before in our history.

These developments have not been universally approved. The South, however, which has strongly opposed national intervention in race relations has been a major beneficiary of the grant-in-aid system and its leaders, therefore, are ambivalent. Critics of the aid system tend to come from those "overprivileged" states and interests which help to subsidize the "underprivileged." Republican Party leaders have been especially critical of what they call national "give-away" policies. In 1953, when they gained control of the national government, they authorized the creation of a Commission on Intergovernmental Relations to evaluate the system and, it was hoped, recommend its curtailment. However, the report of this Commission delivered in 1955 contained no proposals for drastic changes in the present system but rather accepted the aid system as fundamentally sound and recommended changes of a relatively minor nature.[21] Returning to the attack in 1957, President Eisenhower named a committee of his administrative officers to work with a committee of governors to study what national functions and what revenue sources might wisely be returned to the states. This Joint Federal-State Action Committee proposed that the national government abandon the excise on telephone service and the responsibility for vocational education, disaster relief and other programs. The Congress has not, as yet, implemented any of these suggestions.[22] In 1959, Congress created, in part at Eisenhower's suggestion, a permanent Advisory Commission on Intergovernmental Relations

Attack on and defense of the aid system

[21] *Report of the Commission on Intergovernmental Relations* (Washington, 1955). This report, together with the staff studies of the various subcommittees, is the most comprehensive account of contemporary national-state relations now available. It contains a balanced and fair appraisal of virtually every aid program now in operation together with an excellent statement of the development of the federal system.

[22] The committee's suggestions may be found in *The New York Times*, Dec. 6, 1957.

to keep a constant eye on the pattern of grants-in-aid and on national-state relations generally.

Despite these various efforts, the aid system was actually expanded during Eisenhower's Presidency and with his blessing. In fact, no national administration since 1932 has really attempted to abandon any of the aid programs and it is doubtful if Congress would concur if it did. Usually, the aid system has been resorted to only after other expedients have failed and only after a substantial segment of informed opinion has demanded action. In some cases the aid program has served to prevent complete national administration of a service.[23]

THE OUTLOOK FOR THE FEDERAL SYSTEM

Coopera-
tive versus
competitive
federalism

There are many who view modern federalism with dismay. Some feel that there is a finite and certain amount of political power and, therefore, that power gains by one level of government must necessarily be at the expense of the other. The states and the nation are rivals in a deadly competition and the balance swinging as it has been to the nation has and will lead to the ultimate destruction of the states. For perhaps 100 years (1830's-1930's) the tenor of court decisions and national political debate served to support this view and it is still maintained by many self-styled conservatives. Citing the Jeffersonian tradition, they deplore the trend to national authority, talk of keeping government close to the people, despair of managing the giant of the Potomac, and regret the inducements to fiscal irresponsibility of a system in which money raised at one level is spent at another.[24] Others suggest that the proper perspective on the federal system is that the various levels are partners not rivals. Every major domestic problem, they suggest, requires the cooperative effort of all levels of government. There is enough for each to do. For the states to attempt solutions to what are national difficulties will lead only to frustration and lack of public confidence in self-government. The people are not really as interested in or as aware of the behavior of their local and state officials as they are of what is happening in Washington. This cooperative concept of federalism seems to be supported by the modern Supreme Court and by many Congressmen and several presidents.[25]

[23] For a detailed analysis of the modern grant-in-aid system, consult Council of State Governments, *Federal Grants-in-Aid* (Chicago, 1947), Commission on Intergovernmental Relations, *Report to the President* (Washington, 1955); W. B. Graves, *American Intergovernmental Relations* (New York, 1964), Chaps. XIV-XVI, and Advisory Commission on Intergovernmental Relations, *The Role of Equalization in Federal Grants* (Washington, 1964).

[24] Cf. Russell Kirk, "The Prospects for Territorial Democracy in America," in *A Nation of States,* ed. by R. A. Goldwin (Chicago, 1963).

[25] cf. W. Anderson, *The Nation and the States: Rivals or Partners?* (Minneapolis, 1955) and Nelson A. Rockefeller, *The Future of Federalism* (Cambridge, Mass., 1962).

What then is the future of the states? Are they to be completely over-borne by the advancing might of the national government? Have they become but provinces in a great centralized colossus of governmental power? In the first place, it must not be overlooked that the states too within their boundaries are more pervasive than once they were. They perform more services, employ more staff, spend more money, and have a greater impact on the lives of their citizens than they ever have done. They are not dying but are growing and expanding. All talk of the weakness, helplessness, and moribund character of state governments is at odds with the facts. There are, it is true, several of our most pressing problems—economic security, international peace, and military preparedness—with which the states as such cannot cope. As public interest has centered in them much of the time recently, the activities of the states may have been forgotten or ignored by many of us. In the second place, the states, as we shall presently observe in more detail, are vital parts of our system of political parties. Our great national parties are not highly centralized but are more nearly federations of state party organizations. In the states, the parties practice their tactical exercises; leaders are trained in the ways of democratic statecraft; workers energize the electorate into participation in the processes of self-government. The states, furthermore, continue to provide testing grounds for embryonic statesmen. Many Congressmen gained their experience of popular lawmaking in state legislatures; the governor's offices have frequently tested candidates for the Presidency; the state courts supply recruits for the national judiciary. The states too are laboratories for experimenting with new ways by which the government can serve and enrich the lives of our people. From their experience, the nation has saved itself numerous failures and heavy additional costs. The states even today assume the heaviest responsibilities for the leadership, the costs, and the day-to-day services in education, law enforcement, rehabilitation of criminals, care of the mentally ill, construction and maintenance of our far-flung system of highways, protection of wildlife, regulation and supervision of the entire election process, and many other areas of public concern. The states of the United States have a useful and important life ahead of them.

The future of the states

References

The Federalist, Nos. XLI-XLVI

W. S. Livingston, *Federalism and Constitutional Change,* (London, 1956).

M. S. C. Vile, *The Structure of American Federalism* (Oxford, 1962).

D. J. Elazar, *The American Partnership: Intergovernmental Cooperation in the Nineteenth Century United States* (Chicago, 1963).

B. Schwartz, *The Powers of Government: Vol. I. Federal and State Powers* (New York, 1963).

W. B. Graves, *American Intergovernmental Relations* (New York, 1964).

J. P. Clark, *The Rise of a New Federalism: Federal-State Cooperation in the United States* (New York, 1938).

S. Seabury, *The New Federalism* (New York, 1950).

G. S. C. Benson, *The New Centralization: A Study of Intergovernmental Relationships in the United States* (New York, 1941).

W. Anderson, *The Nation and the State, Rivals or Partners?* (Minneapolis, 1955).

R. A. Goldwin (ed.), *A Nation of States: Essays on the American Federal System* (Chicago, 1961).

N. A. Rockefeller, *The Future of Federalism* (Cambridge, Mass.).

A. W. Macmahon (ed.), *Federalism: Mature and Emergent* (New York, 1955).

J. A. Maxwell, *The Fiscal Impact of Federalism in the United States* (Cambridge, Mass., 1946).

D. Fellman, "Federalism," *Amer. Pol. Sci. Rev.* XLI (Dec. 1947).

J. R. Schmidhauser, *The Supreme Court as Final Arbiter in Federal-State Relations, 1789-1957* (Chapel Hill, N.C., 1958).

Council of State Governments, *Federal Grants-in-Aid* (Chicago, 1949).

Commission on Intergovernmental Relations, *Report to the President* (Washington, 1955).

Advisory Commission on Intergovernmental Relations, *The Role of Equalization in Federal Grants* (Washington, 1964).

———, *Statutory and Administrative Controls Associated with Federal Grants for Public Assistance* (Washington, 1964).

The Constitution of the United States: Analysis and Interpretation (88th Congress, 1st Session, Senate Doc. #39, Washington, 1964).

★ 4 ★

Civil Rights and How They Are Protected

> We hold these truths to be self-evident, that all men are created equal, that they are endowed by their Creator with certain unalienable Rights, that among these are Life, Liberty, and the Pursuit of Happiness.
>
> That to secure these rights, Governments are instituted among men, deriving their just powers from the consent of the governed. DECLARATION OF INDEPENDENCE

NOTHING QUITE SO APPROPRIATELY characterizes the deep ideological gulf separating the leading members of the Atlantic community from the Iron Curtain states or from the totalitarian aggressors of World War II as their various conceptions of the proper relation between the individual and his government. Emphasizing the dignity and worth of the individual, the people of Great Britain, France, the United States, and other Western nations regard government as resting on the consent of the governed and ascribe to even the humblest of citizens a sphere of personal liberty which no state authority, however organized, can impair. Everything that is valuable in this earthly realm, they assert, is created by individual effort and this creativeness requires a large measure of freedom in order to bear fruit. The state they regard as the traditional enemy of individual self-government and hold tightly to the conviction that its power over individuals must be confined by effective constitutional machinery and fair and workable legal procedures. The Communists and authoritarians of other shades practice, if they do not subscribe to, the conception that it is enough for the state to serve man. It is neither necessary nor desirable that he possess any right to develop in his own way. The individual has neither right nor destiny apart from that of the group of which he is a member. He must and should conform his behavior and his thoughts to what his rulers have determined group welfare requires. To be an effective instrument of group welfare, the state must not be restricted in any significant way.[1]

Two opposing theories of government

[1] For a time after World War II had brought disaster to the more strident dictatorships of Europe and Asia it seemed as if the Western nations might bring much of the world to accept their ideas of human dignity. In Article 55, the United Nations Charter

69

American ideals not easily reconciled

Each of the Western democracies has developed its own institutional arrangements to embody these great ideals of freedom. In the United States, we place our faith in the democratic process by which our officials are chosen and in the social recognition and constitutional protection of civil rights. It is, however, necessary to point out that these two facets of the American system are not easily harmonized. The democratic process is predicated upon the idea of the determination of the scope and direction of governmental effort by majority rule in which each participant is equal to every other one. The constitutional system of civil rights is predicated upon the idea that there are some personal liberties which even majorities may not infringe and that a semi-independent and politically irresponsible judiciary is essential to enforce these limitations. It is hard for the American people to conceive of genuine citizen participation in the processes of government without freedom publicly to criticize, explore, and discuss the problems of the day. For the exercise of free speech, they are nevertheless dependent upon a legal rather than an electoral procedure. Another area of conflict between the two notions concerns the rights of property. In the late nineteenth and early twentieth centuries, one of the major battlegrounds of American politics concerned the question of whether property rights were, equally with personal rights, immune from governmental infringement. A strong and vigorous argument in behalf of property rights issued from those who maintained that the practice of personal freedom depended upon the sanctity of property and an equally insistent claim for governmental regulation from those who maintained that personal freedom was enhanced by restrictions on property. In this conflict judicial restraints upon governmental efforts to regulate property came into disrepute with those who claimed the most progressive democratic ideals.

Contemporary interest in civil rights

The rise of continental dictatorships both red and black in the thirties and the spread of Communist domination after World War II accompanied by suppression of personal freedom and the use of police-state methods stimulated a renewed appreciation in America of the importance of civil rights. The rise after the war of subject peoples in Africa, Asia, and the Middle East and the increasingly insistent demands for equality of the racial minorities in our own country have contributed to the liveliest agitation on the subject since the Reconstruction Era. As the United States assumed the leadership

---

proclaimed the principle of "universal respect for and observance of human rights and fundamental freedom for all without distinction of race, sex, language, or religion." The United Nations General Assembly in Paris in 1948 adopted a Universal Declaration of Human Rights and an International Covenant of Human Rights was prepared several months thereafter and submitted to the General Assembly for ultimate transmission to the member states as a treaty. Since that time the matter has more or less languished. The ardor of the West has cooled especially as the underdeveloped areas pressed for the inclusion of economic and social rights as well as civil and political ones. In the United States, a strong contingent of Senators has repeatedly evidenced hostility to American ratification of any such convenant.

of the "Free World," it was perforce brought to face the question of whether its own practice corresponded to the ideals it professed. Furthermore, along with a growing insistence on a better and more broadly conceived application of the traditional *restrictions upon government* in the interest of personal liberty there has developed, notably in the area of enforced segregation of the races, a mounting demand for *positive governmental* exertion to achieve a more adequate realization of the ideals of human worth, dignity, and equality.

Enlarge-ment of scope of civil rights programs

As early as 1941, President Franklin Roosevelt, in a message to Congress, sought to redefine prevailing concepts, bracketing Freedom from Want and Freedom from Fear with the traditional Freedoms of Speech and Religion as rights to which men everywhere are entitled. Both major parties began in 1944 to write civil rights planks into their national platforms, promising increased activity in this field, especially in improving the situation of racial minorities. Early in 1947, President Truman, responding to growing public concern, set up a Committee on Civil Rights, the report of which— "To Secure These Rights"—is rated as one of the great public documents of our time. On the basis of this report, Mr. Truman early in 1948 transmitted to Congress a strongly-worded message affording a blueprint for bringing our civil rights system into better accord with our professions. Included in the President's program were a number of proposals calling for governmental action to promote the enjoyment of rights, thus going far beyond the traditional view that governmental action poses the chief threat to such rights.[2] Repeated urgings by Truman, then by Eisenhower [3] and the adoption of increasingly vigorous platform language bore no significant legislative fruit until 1957 when the first national civil rights legislation since Reconstruction days was passed. This was followed by a second act in 1960 and finally by the momentous and sweeping Civil Rights Act of 1964. All of this legislation was passed by a bipartisan coalition of Northern and Western Democrats and Republicans. The Act of 1964 had been strongly urged by President Kennedy and was vigorously pushed by President Johnson.

The Civil Rights Acts 1957-64

The first acts dealt almost exclusively with Negro suffrage in the South and conferred some rather modest powers on the Department of Justice to intercede in behalf of Negroes illegally denied voting privileges. The Act of

[2] For the text of this message, see *New York Times,* Feb. 2, 1948. The President proposed laws involving: (1) fair employment practices, barring discrimination on grounds of race, color, and the like; (2) national protection for the right to vote, with poll-tax requirements abolished; (3) national protection against lynching; (4) end of discrimination in interstate transportation facilities; (5) home rule and presidential suffrage for residents of the District of Columbia; and (6) statehood for Hawaii and Alaska.

[3] President Eisenhower in 1956 and in 1957 recommended the establishment of a bipartisan commission to examine charges of denials of voting privileges and of economic pressures. He also asked for a Civil Rights Division in the Department of Justice. He proposed additional legislation in 1959 and 1960.

1957 also created a Civil Rights Commission in the national executive branch empowered to investigate and appraise discriminatory practices which deprive citizens of their rights or of their voting privileges. This Commission, the life of which was repeatedly extended, provided much of the evidence upon which the law of 1964 was based. The Act of 1964 greatly expanded national power to enfranchise Negroes, and this power was further enhanced by the Voting Rights Act of 1965. It also added to the power of the Department of Justice and of the Office of Education authority to intervene in school desegregation controversies or to aid those seeking effective solutions to racial problems in public schools. It also forbade discrimination by private owners or operators of many types of public accommodations (hotels, motels, cafeterias, restaurants, theatres, sports arenas, etc.) where the discrimination is supported by state law or where the goods, travelers, or entertainment move in interstate commerce. An Equal Employment Opportunity Commission was created to enforce prohibitions of discrimination in employment or in union membership and a Community Relations Service was created to assist localities in handling disputes arising from racial problems. In sum, the Civil Rights Act of 1964 went a long way toward the goal outlined by President Kennedy of providing a legal remedy for every deprivation of right. It also embraced the modern conception that governmental power and prestige must be used to bar private discrimination.

Judicial, executive, and state progress in civil rights

Although Congress was brought to act in these matters slowly and after a great deal of public agitation, much meanwhile was being achieved by the other branches and other levels of government. The national courts struck down one state-supported form of racial segregation after another, broadened the guarantees of free speech, further enforced a separation of church and state and redefined and elaborated the standards of judicial and executive fairness to those caught in the grip of criminal prosecution. A large number of states and many cities enacted laws against discrimination in employment and in places of public accommodation including, in some cases, apartment rentals and sales or leases of private homes. The national executive desegregated the armed forces and sought to eliminate job discrimination in firms contracting with the government.[4]

Demonstrations: violent and peaceful

In view of the explosive character of racial tensions and the deep-seated animosities and fears involved, it is perhaps not surprising that civil rights agitation has been heated and in too many cases violent. Race riots swept sections of several Northern cities in the summer of 1964 and again in 1965, and bombings, beatings and murders have occurred in the South. However, while the Civil Rights Act was before the Congress in mid-1963, more than 200,000 supporters marched upon Washington, staged a huge rally at the Lincoln Memorial and dispersed without serious incident. Hundreds of mass

---

[4] President Kennedy appointed the first Negro to high executive office, Robert C. Weaver, head of the Housing and Home Finance Agency. He became the first Negro Cabinet officer in 1966 by appointment of President Johnson.

meetings, picketing demonstrations, and "sit-ins" [5] have also occurred without personal injury or property damage.

GENERAL CHARACTERISTICS OF THE AMERICAN SYSTEM OF CIVIL RIGHTS

Full enumeration of rights impossible

Traditionally, rights to which Americans can lay valid claim have been set forth in bills of rights found in the constitutions of the 50 states and in the Constitution of the United States. These have been enlarged or redefined by amendments, statutes, and judicial interpretations and are constantly being reappraised, challenged, and restated in the light of changing conditions. The dynamic character of our system of rights makes it impossible therefore to compile a complete and definitive list. If we turn to the national Constitution, for example, we discover a long and impressive list—chiefly in the first eight amendments, but also in Sections IX and X of Article I—followed, however, by the baffling provision that "the enumeration—of certain rights shall not be construed to deny or disparage others retained by the people" (Ninth Amendment). What others? In all the state constitutions also are lists but nowhere are these claimed to be exhaustive. In the Slaughterhouse Cases of 1873,[6] the Supreme Court after considering the matter in some detail said that interpretation of our system of rights must be "a gradual process of judicial inclusion and exclusion."

Rights are not absolute

Liberty is not license; rights are relative, not absolute. After all, one of the main purposes of government is to prevent the safety and well-being of the many from being jeopardized by the few. Freedom of speech and press does not carry with it any right to utter or publish slander or libel or to incite persons to crime or panic; freedom of assembly does not entitle any group to interfere with public order and safety. To be validly claimed, a right must be exercised so as to cause no impairment of the same or any other right possessed by others. The attempt to apply this principle, however, catapults us immediately into all of the major controversies of civil rights. If it is carried to extremes, it spells the end of any rights at all.[7]

Civil rights in war

The history of the United States suggests that the emphasis on public order and safety is likely to grow with a concomitant reduction in the area of

[5] "Sit-ins" were used by Negroes mainly to compel service at segregated lunch counters in various chain and drug stores. Efforts to prosecute the "sitters" have, in many cases, been frustrated by the Supreme Court's refusal to sustain convictions.

[6] 16 Wallace 36

[7] "The liberty of the individual to do as he pleases, even in innocent matters," said the Supreme Court in Adkins v. Children's Hospital, 261 U. S. 525 (1923), "is not absolute. It must frequently yield to the common good; and the line beyond which the power of interference may not be pressed is neither definite nor unalterable, but may be made to move within limits not well defined, with changing need and circumstance." "Neither property rights nor contract rights," said the Court again, in the case of Nebbia v. New York, 291 U. S. 502 (1934), "are absolute . . . Equally fundamental with the private right is that of the public to regulate it in the common interest."

allowable individual liberty, especially freedom of expression and of association, when the nation is engaged in or feels itself threatened by war. Although,
legally speaking, constitutional rights are not created or suspended by "national emergency," they are, in practice, sharply curtailed and, typically, with
both electoral and judicial consent.[8] Since 1939-40 this nation has been living
through a period of real or supposed emergency. Although technically at
peace since 1953, and from 1945-50, concern for the spread of Communist
influence has mounted to such intensity that restrictions have been piled upon
restrictions until the sum total of prohibitions of various kinds of expressions
and activities is probably as great as has existed at any time since 1917. Happily there has been some relaxation of efforts at "thought control" in the last
few years.

The
federal
system
and
civil rights

Constitutionally recognized civil rights are not identical throughout the
length and breadth of the nation. Our federal system not only complicates
but introduces variation in the pattern of rights. There are rights—for example, "the privileges and immunities of citizens of the United States"—that
can validly be claimed only by national citizens. There are others which are
assigned only to state citizens—by state laws and constitutions. There are
still others to which all "persons"—natural or artificial (corporation), citizen
or alien—are entitled. Some rights may be properly invoked only against the
national government; others may be invoked against the states; and still
others against both. Of those which may be claimed against state action, some
are based on the prescriptions of the national constitution, others on the provisions of state constitutions, and still others on the absence of any express
or implied grant of authority to any government.

Rights
national-
ized

The variations in state constitutional prescriptions, especially since the
Civil War, have been declining in importance. In fact, there has been an
unmistakable trend toward centralizing the guarantees of many civil rights
in the national government. During the first half-century of our national history the Bill of Rights embodied in the first 10 amendments to the Constitution was construed (as plainly had been its intent) as restricting the national
government only. The states enjoyed a good deal of latitude for establishing
slavery, restricting freedom of religion, speech, and press, tolerating judicial
processes now generally discarded, and imposing other restraints forbidden
only to the national government. Not only was there a dual system of civil
rights, but a very wide divergence between rights that were national and
those that were state. The Civil War amendments mark the change in this
policy—the Thirteenth making it impossible for a state to legalize slavery,
and the Fourteenth going much further by forbidding a state (1) to make or

---

[8] For an excellent survey of the country's earlier experience with wartime civil
liberties, see C. B. Swisher, "Civil Liberties in Wartime," *Polit. Sci. Quar.*, LV, 321-347
(Sept. 1940), and for a full study of the impact of World War II, E. S. Corwin, *Total
War and the Constitution* (New York, 1947), Chap. III.

enforce any law abridging the privileges or immunities of citizens of the United States, (2) to deprive any person of life, liberty, or property without due process of law, or (3) to deny to any person within its jurisdiction the equal protection of the laws. The broadening of national concern in guaranteeing civil rights which these amendments made possible was, however, realized but slowly. For almost half a century, the Supreme Court construed the Fourteenth Amendment's mandates so narrowly that no great changes resulted. In the 1920's, however, at a time when state legislatures were attempting restrictions upon freedom of speech, press, and teaching, the Court began "discovering" the Amendment and declaring its full impact upon the states. In 1925 it affirmed freedom of speech and of the press, protected by the First Amendment from abridgment by Congress, to be "among the fundamental personal rights and liberties protected by the due process clause of the Fourteenth Amendment from impairment by the states." [9] When in later decisions the same view was asserted of religious liberty, freedom of assembly, and freedom of association there arose a single system of rights in these major areas of human freedom uniformly guaranteed throughout the land. There are still numerous variations of state practices in regard to jury trials, grand juries, and other guarantees of procedural fairness. Even in this area, however, the right of an accused person to counsel has been recognized as a nationally protected one, state enforcement officers have been required to obey national standards of "reasonableness" in searches and seizures and the right of a person to be protected from self-incrimination has been extended to state proceedings.

As we have suggested the rights claimed by and on behalf of Americans have not reached final and definitive enumeration. We hear much nowadays of rights to equality of opportunity, to privacy, to vote, to work, to employment security. All of these represent aspirations of various segments of our population that thus far have not achieved legal, as distinguished from political, recognition. The effort to improve the lot of the Negro in America has to some degree shifted the rights struggle from the judicial to the legislative arena and has emphasized that some types of rights must be achieved, if at all, by positive public effort rather than by restraint on governmental agents and activities. This shift is an important one in both theory and practice and its success depends heavily on popular understanding of and commitment to the ideas of human rights. Studies of popular attitudes in America indicate that our politicians, judges, and opinion leaders are far more dedicated to the freedoms of the type protected by bills of rights than are the rank and file of the American voters.[10]

The public attitude toward rights

[9] Gitlow v. New York, 268 U. S. 652
[10] cf. S. A. Stouffer, *Communism, Conformity, and Civil Liberties* (New York, 1955).

SPECIFIC AMERICAN RIGHTS:

A. Rights of Personal Liberty

Neither slavery nor involuntary servitude, except as a punishment for crime whereof the party shall have been duly convicted, shall exist within the United States or any place subject to their jurisdiction. THIRTEENTH AMENDMENT

1. Right to personal security

"Freedom can exist," said the President's Committee on Civil Rights, "only where the citizen is assured that his person is secure against bondage, lawless violence and arbitrary arrest and punishment." [11] No general immunity from personal servitude was legally recognized in the United States until the adoption of the Thirteenth Amendment in 1865. Since that time, slavery in all of its forms has been eliminated. This amendment has been interpreted to mean that a laborer cannot be compelled to work out a debt in his employer's service.[12] National statutes as well as several state constitutions and statutes forbid peonage in this or any other form, and several state constitutions also prohibit imprisonment for debt. Persons may, however, validly be held to the completion of terms of service for which they have contracted (sailors, for example) and may also be conscripted for military, police, jury, or highway laboring duty. These latter are considered appropriate exercises of governmental power and do not, therefore, involve "servitude."

Efforts to halt lynching and intimidation

The deprivation of personal liberty by mob violence (lynching) has posed a very different problem of civil rights. For a time after the Civil War, the Congress felt that positive action in the form of national statutes was necessary to assure the Negroes of the South the new status which the Civil War amendments sought to give them. In a series of civil rights acts passed between 1866 and 1875, national authority was invoked to prevent intimidation of or violent assault upon American citizens. The Supreme Court,[13] later the Congress, took the view, however, that the Fourteenth Amendment did not intend to authorize the national government to regulate the behavior of citizens nor to replace local or state law enforcement. The demand for positive national action to guarantee personal security against coercion or violence has been voiced with new vigor in the past three decades. Congress has repeatedly been urged, unsuccessfully, to enact laws against lynching and

---

[11] *To Secure These Rights* (Washington, 1947)

[12] Laws of Georgia, Alabama, and Florida permitting this form of compulsion were invalidated by the Supreme Court as recently as 1942 and 1944. Peonage cases occasionally cropping up elsewhere further indicate that involuntary servitude still tends to persist locally—a situation of which the President's Committee on Civil Rights took due notice. A Workers Defense League devotes itself to ferreting out instances of the kind.

[13] Civil Rights Cases, 109 U. S. 3 (1883)

to strengthen the remnants of the old civil rights acts. The pressure for national legislation on the subject subsided until the effort to mix the races in the schools followed by the vigorous campaign to end discrimination in places of public accommodation was accompanied by a renewal of violence and new demands for stronger national efforts to protect those attempting to exercise their rights. Although the Civil Rights Act of 1957 repealed an old (1866) statute authorizing the President to employ troops to enforce or to prevent violation of civil rights legislation, the national executive has intervened with troops, with marshals or with the FBI in situations where: (1) a national court order was defied (Little Rock, Ark., and Oxford, Miss.); (2) interstate movement of persons was being obstructed (Montgomery, Ala.); and, (3) when invited by local or state officials to help preserve order (Clinton, Tenn., and Selma, Ala.).

An illustration of the lengths to which curtailment of the rights of personal security will be tolerated in a wartime atmosphere is provided by the wholesale, compulsory relocation of 110,000 Japanese-Americans (citizens as well as aliens) from the West Coast in 1942 by Congressional and executive authority with the approval of the Supreme Court and without trial.

Congress shall make no law respecting an establishment of religion, or prohibiting the free exercise thereof . . . FIRST AMENDMENT

Freedom of religious worship is guaranteed against national legislative impairment by the First Amendment and against state impairment by the prevailing interpretation of the Fourteenth Amendment. It is also guaranteed against state restriction by the constitutions of the states, although not always in identical terms. By these guarantees individuals are, in general, free to cherish such religious convictions as they please, to declare them publicly, to seek converts to them, and to engage in whatever forms of worship they prefer. These guarantees do not, however, confer any exemption from the criminal laws of the land, for example, to practice polygamy [14] or to extract fees from the gullible for occult cures.[15] *2. Right to religious freedom*

Religious beliefs, on occasion, come into conflict with norms of conduct cherished by some members of society as well as with governmentally ordained principles of safety and order. In recent years the vigorously nonconformist sect known as Jehovah's Witnesses has repeatedly tested the contours of the constitutional guarantees. This sect attracted national attention several years ago when it denounced the practice in some public schools of saluting the American Flag. This, they said, was idolatry and they refused to allow their children to join in the ceremony. Attempts by local school *Jehovah's Witnesses*

[14] Reynolds *v.* United States, 98 U. S. 145 (1878); Church of Jesus Christ *v.* United States 136 U. S. (1890).
[15] United States *v.* Ballard, 322 U. S. 78 (1944).

boards to exclude their children were at first sustained.[16] Later, regulations requiring their expulsion were declared invalid [17] by the Supreme Court. The strident anti-Roman Catholic tenor of their literature and preaching, coupled with their penchant for street-corner and house-to-house solicitation, have stimulated a number of communities to attempt to curtail the Witnesses by local ordinances or police regulations. A number of such efforts have been brought to the courts with varying results.[18] On the whole, religious canvassers have been given a rather wide latitude to proselytize without licensure or payment of fees so long as they are careful to keep the streets free and to observe other local regulations governing public meetings in public parks or on public thoroughfares.

Subsidization of parochial schools

The right of religious bodies to establish and maintain their own schools and thus to avoid compulsory public school attendance has long been recognized.[19] In recent years, the related problem of subsidizing religious schools from the public treasury has come increasingly into prominence. In a number of states (Wisconsin, for example) the state constitution forbids subsidy of any kind (books, transportation, buildings, etc.), but in some (New Jersey, for example) the practice is expressly sanctioned by law or constitutional prescription. Several years ago the Supreme Court of the United States was invited to declare state subsidy of parochial school pupil transportation a violation of the religious freedom guarantees of the Constitution. In a close and vigorously contested decision, the Court ruled that states could validly subsidize private schooling if they wished to do so.[20] The question of religious freedom was not involved but rather one of public benefit, said the Court majority. On the other hand, the Court has refused to review a Vermont decision holding subsidization of parochial schools to be contrary to the constitution of that state. One of the troublesome issues in the debate on a national grant-in-aid program for public education has been the question of the validity of providing aid for parochial schools. The aid program finally adopted in 1965 attempts to sidestep this issue by gearing the aid to "needy" pupils, a method used earlier in the school-lunch aid program. This issue has not as yet been resolved in the courts.

[16] Minersville School District *v.* Gobitis, 310 U. S. 586 (1940).

[17] West Virginia State Board of Education *v.* Barnette, 319 U. S. 624 (1943).

[18] See, for example, Murdock *v.* Pennsylvania, 319 U. S. 105 (1943). On this interesting chapter in our civil-rights experience, see V. Rotnem and F. G. Folsom, Jr., "Recent Restrictions upon Religious Liberty," *Amer. Polit. Sci. Rev.*, XXXVL, 1053-1068 (Dec., 1942); H. W. Barber, "Religious Liberty *v.* the Police Power: Jehovah's Witnesses," *ibid.*, XLI, 226-247 (Apr., 1947); and comments by R. E. Cushman, ibid., XXXVII, 278-280 (Apr., 1943), and XXXVIII, 277-284 (Apr., 1944). Cf. O. K. Fraenkel, *Our Civil Liberties* (New York, 1944), Chap. VI; H. Stroup, *The Jehovah's Witnesses* (New York, 1945).

[19] An Oregon law undertaking to suppress all private schools for children between the ages of 8 and 16 was promptly invalidated in 1925. Pierce *v.* Society of Sisters of Holy Names, 268 U. S. 510 (1925).

[20] Everson *v.* Board of Education of Ewing Township, 330 U. S. 1 (1947). In point of fact, 19 states now permit transportation of parochial pupils at public expense.

Religious education in the public schools, long a sensitive nerve in the anatomy of free public education, has repeatedly been touched in recent years by controversy. A sharp jar to widely accepted practices came in 1948 when the Supreme Court declared that an Illinois practice of offering religious instruction to willing children by various denominations in the school buildings on time "released" for the purpose by the school authorities was inconsistent with the principle of separation of church and state embedded in the Constitution.[21] This decision spread consternation among the hundreds of communities then using this or a similar procedure and started several new cases to the courts to discover if any extant practice could be accepted. The Court, in 1952, set at rest much of the uneasiness created by its 1948 decision by approving a New York City procedure in which denominational religious instruction was provided to those who wanted it on released time outside the public school buildings.[22] "Government may not finance religious groups nor undertake religious instruction nor blend secular and sectarian education nor use secular institutions to force one or some religion on any person," said Justice Douglas for the Court. "It may not make a religious observance compulsory. It may not coerce anyone to attend church, to observe a religious holiday, or to take religious instruction. But it can close its doors or suspend its operation as to those who want to repair to their religious sanctuary for worship or instruction." The Court, in 1962, further held that official prayers, even if denominationally neutral, may not be recited in public schools [23] and, in 1963, that states may not require the reading of selections from the Bible nor the recitation of the Lord's Prayer in the public schools.[24] Critics of these decisions are proposing a constitutional amendment to reverse them.

By way of further definition of allowable state conduct, the modern Supreme Court has also held that state constitutions and laws may not require officeholders to declare a belief in God as part of the oath of office. "Neither a state nor the Federal Government can constitutionally force a person to profess a belief or disbelief in any religion," said Justice Black.[25] The Court has refused, however, to strike down "blue" laws, restricting the sale of goods and services on Sundays, now found in many states. The Court said that the essential purpose of these laws today is social and recreational, not religious.[26]

Positive governmental assertion of the value of religious freedom has

[21] Illinois *ex rel* McCollum *v.* Board of Education, 333 U. S. 203 (1948).

[22] Zorach *v.* Clauson, 343 U. S. 306 (1952). See also F. J. Sorauf, "Zorach *v.* Clauson: The Impact of a Supreme Court Decision," *Am. Pol. Sci. Rev.,* LIII, 777-791 (Sept., 1959).

[23] Engel *v.* Vitale, 370 U. S. 421, 430 (1962).

[24] Abington School Dist. (Pa.) *v.* Schempp and Murray *v.* Curlett, 374 U. S. 203 (1963).

[25] Torcaso *v.* Watkins, 367 U. S. 488 (1961).

[26] Two Guys *v.* McGinley, 366 U. S. 582 and McGowan *v.* Maryland, 366 U. S. 420 (1961).

occurred under trying circumstances in both world wars of this century and during the life of the modern system of military conscription. The Congress, as an act of grace, has authorized draft boards to exempt "conscientious objectors," those with bona fide religious scruples [27] against military service, or to call them only for noncombatant service or for service in other public programs not operated by the armed services (park improvement, conservation, care of the ill).[28]

> Congress shall make no law . . . abridging the freedom of speech or of the press . . . FIRST AMENDMENT

3. Right to speak and write freely

Freedom of speech almost never involves the right to say or to print things that a majority of the people already believe. It is the right to say unpopular, unorthodox, or unconventional things which is really at issue. Further an untrammeled right to say anything one pleases has never been recognized by any nation. And in the United States from the beginning, speaking and writing have been confined by prevailing standards of decency of language and subject and of slanderousness of intention as well as by certain imprecise requirements of public peace and safety. Although standards and tastes in these matters have changed from generation to generation, even the most ardent exponents of unfettered communication recognize the wisdom and necessity of some limitation. In our day, as in many prior epochs of our history, the major problems of speech and press arise from the determination of a large number of our people to use the authority and prestige of the government to suppress opinions which they detest and which they believe tend to undermine our scheme of social values, our system of constitutional government, or our national independence. This determination, now as in earlier years, gains added vigor when applied to utterances which betray or seem to betray or can be made to appear to betray an affinity for some foreign state or imported ideology. When, as in the case of England in 1776, France in 1798, Germany in 1917 and 1941, and Russia since 1947, this foreign state is an actual or potential enemy the determination becomes well-nigh irresistible. Under these circumstances, restrictions on freedom of communication have gone and do now go far beyond the suppression of alleged seditious, subversive, or alien ideas. They embrace positive injunctions to loyal behavior and speech. Even criticism of those in power, essential as it is to the conduct of a democratic state, tends to be regarded as seditious and disloyal, and on the other hand, extremists charge even those in power with treasonable intention or subversive association because public officials are obliged to deal with the communist nations and their leaders. The modern

---

[27] The Supreme Court has recently construed "religious" to mean also philosophical or ethical. U. S. *v.* Seeger et al., 85 S. Ct. 850 (1965).

[28] For an extensive study of the treatment of "conscientious objectors" see M. Q. Sibley and P. E. Jacob, *Conscription of Conscience: The American State and the Conscientious Objector,* 1940-1947 (Ithaca, N. Y., 1952).

problem is further complicated by the fact that the opinions and movements which the prevailing restrictions are aimed at suppressing, communism and totalitarianism, are themselves hostile to freedom of expression. Should democratic tolerance be accorded to those who do not believe in it and would not practice it if they had the opportunity?

The long history of national legislative and executive efforts to restrict speech and publication in the interests of national safety begins with the Alien and Sedition Acts of 1798, which among other things forbade the uttering of defamatory remarks about the President or the Congress or the inciting of the hatred of the people against them. These acts when applied by zealous partisans to their opponents aroused a storm of protest, figured importantly in Jefferson's elevation to the Presidency and were allowed to expire when he achieved office. In the Civil War period, the President took the initiative in suppressing pro-Southern expressions in the North. Congress passed no general limitations on speech, although it did later ratify some of the executive actions. In World War I, the Congress dealt with seditious writing and talking by sweeping restrictions on expressions critical of the government or its wartime policies. In each epoch the courts have, with very few exceptions, sustained these types of laws and their application to individuals. *National legislation restricting speech*

Out of the post-World War I efforts to curb Socialist, Communist, and Syndicalist movements in the United States by state legislation, the Supreme Court gradually evolved one of its most significant doctrines in the field of free speech: the clear and present danger test. As enunciated by Justice Holmes in the Schenck case [29] and in several dissenting opinions thereafter, this theory holds that restrictions on freedom of expression in the interest of public safety can be validly applied only when the statements and the circumstances in which they are uttered involve a clear and present danger of evils which the government has a right to prevent. By 1940, the Court had fully adopted this theory as controlling in such matters,[30] and had, in doing so, considerably broadened its previous theories of the amount of freedom of speech and of press which would be tolerated. *"Clear and present danger" doctrine*

A new wave of restrictive legislation and executive action set in about this time. The first peacetime sedition act since 1798 was passed in 1940 (Alien Registration or Smith Act), aimed at advocates of the violent overthrow of the United States. This was followed in 1950 by the Internal Security Act designed to force Communist-dominated organizations to reveal themselves as such and to place their activities under rigid surveillance.[31] A Com- *Contemporary restrictions aimed at Communists*

[29] Schenck v. United States, 249 U. S. 47 (1919).

[30] See Thornhill v. Alabama, 310 U. S. 88 (1940).

[31] The Internal Security Act was passed over a strongly worded veto by President Truman alleging that it was unworkable and would put the government in the "thought-control business." The Act requires Communist-action and Communist-front organizations to register with the Attorney General of the United States and to reveal their financial and membership records. It further requires such organizations to give public notice in connection with their propaganda that they are Communist-dominated and finally it places restrictions on the employment and travel of members of registered organizations.

munist Control Act in 1954 withdrew from the Communist Party or any of its offspring the rights, privileges, and immunities of legal bodies in the United States or in any state. By these and other statutes governing public employment, Communists or individuals found to have advocated forceful revolution are denied positions on the public payroll, in the armed services, or in defense plants. Congressional committees in this period lashed out at suspected subversives, questioned scores of people about their associations, and demanded executive action against those in public life. In this atmosphere, the clear and present danger doctrine lost ground. After a long trial, eleven of the top leaders of the Communist movement in America were convicted in 1951 of violating the Act of 1940. In sustaining this conviction, the Supreme Court held that the Communist Party did advocate the violent overthrow of the government and that Congress had the power to prohibit such advocacy.[32] Chief Justice Vinson, speaking for the Court, said, "An attempt to overthrow the government by force even though doomed from the outset because of inadequate numbers or power of the revolutionists, is a sufficient evil for Congress to prevent." The clear and present danger doctrine, he observed, should not be applied or construed to force the government to wait for a violent uprising before it can act.

Gradually the furor against subversives abated. Senator McCarthy, a prime mover in the agitation, was repudiated by the Senate. As more cases against Communists were brought before the courts, it became clear that the Supreme Court was not willing to abandon completely the tests of clear and present danger or to set aside other legal protections even for Communists. Advocacy of violent revolution, it was held, must be more than just discussion of an abstract right or doctrine.[33] Organizing a conspiracy to overthrow the government must be in the present not in some past protected by the statute of limitations.[34] A member of the Communist Party to be convicted must be shown to have a specific design or intention to overthrow the government and must be an "active" member of the party.[35] Individuals may not be convicted of violating state laws forbidding advocacy of violent overthrow of the national government since the national act of 1940 pre-empts the field.[36] Reliance by a state on the Attorney General's list of "subversive" organizations as a basis for proceeding against members of listed organizations was invalidated because it did not constitute judicial proof of subversion.[37] Al-

[32] Dennis et al v. U. S., 341 U. S. 494 (1951).

[33] Yates v. U. S. 354 U. S. 298 (1957).

[34] Ibid. After this decision, the Act of 1940 was amended to define organizing in such a way as to embrace continuing activities such as recruitment.

[35] Scales v. U. S. 376 U. S. 203 (1961).

[36] Penna. v. Nelson, 350 U. S. 497 (1956). This case aroused the most severe attacks on the Court of any of the communist cases. Critics accused the Court of making policy contrary to the wishes of Congress. Congress had not expressly indicated that the Act of 1940 was to supersede all state laws on the subject.

[37] Dombrowski v. Pfister, 85 S. Ct. 1116 (1965).

though the registration requirements of the Internal Security Act of 1950 are valid as applied to the Communist Party,[38] no party official or member can be required to register for the party since in doing so he would risk self-incrimination under the act of 1940.[39]

In general, the efforts to rid the public service of Communists or other subversives have been upheld even though the accused was not always able to confront the evidence [40] but mere invocation of the Fifth Amendment before an investigating body cannot be made grounds for summary dismissal.[41]

Not satisfied with prohibitions of seditious or subversive behavior and with denials of certain employment opportunities to Communists or totalitarians, public executives and legislatures by law and by the activities of investigating agencies have sought positive declarations of loyalty or at least of freedom from subversive associations from public employees, military men, school teachers, beneficiaries of national research grants, loans, or fellowships and others. These loyalty-oath requirements have been upheld in some cases.[42] Several have been invalidated as too vague and uncertain in application or too sweeping in scope.[43] An effort by California to require a loyalty affidavit from those who claimed property tax exemption was declared to be invalid as placing the burden of proof on the taxpayer rather than the state.[44] Also an attempt by Congress to demand such oaths from tenants of public, low-rent housing projects has been set aside by several state courts and the national administration ceased, in 1956, any effort to enforce the rule.

Loyalty oaths

One final word on these efforts to root out "subversive" influences in American life. There is a great deal of disagreement on what constitutes subversion. Many of the state and national statutes, executive orders and legislative committee fiats, are loosely worded and imprecisely aimed. There

[38] Communist Party *v.* Subversive Activities Control Board, 367 U. S. 1, (1961).

[39] Communist Party *v.* U. S., 331 F. 2d 807 (1963). The Supreme Court refused to review this decision. In a new case to test the rule, Albertson *v.* Sub. Act. Control Bd., 15 L ed 2d 165 (1965), the Court took the same position.

[40] Garner *v.* Los Angeles Board, 341 U. S. 716 (1951); Bailey *v.* Richardson, 341 U. S. 918 (1951); Adler *v.* Board of Education, 342 U. S. 485 (1952).

[41] Slochower *v.* Board of Higher Education of New York, 350 U. S. 557 (1956). However, the dismissal of an employee for refusal to answer questions on subversion without invoking the Fifth Amendment and where refusal is forbidden under state law has been upheld. Malone *v.* County of Los Angeles, 362 U. S. 1 (1960).

[42] Garner *v.* Los Angeles Board, 341 U. S. 716 (1951); Bailey *v.* Richardson, 341 U. S. 918 (1915); Adler *v.* Board of Education, 342 U. S. 485 (1952).

[43] An Oklahoma law imposing an oath on faculties of state educational institutions was overturned because membership in a subversive organization disqualified a person whether he knew of the real character of the organization or not. Wiemann *v.* Updegraff, 344 U. S. 183 (1952). A Florida oath requirement of all public employees and a Washington one for public employees and another for teachers were all nullified. Cramp *v.* Board of Orange County, Florida, 386 U. S. 278 (1961); Baggett *v.* Bullet, 377 U. S. 360 (1964).

[44] Speiser *v.* Randall, 357 U. S. 513 (1958). First Unitarian Church *v.* Los Angeles, 357 U. S. 545 (1958).

is some danger that in rooting out the Communists we may also be intimidating every type of unconventional opinion. There are far too many in the land ready to stamp out any kind of opposition to those in power on the grounds that any criticism of the existing policies or institutions of our society gives aid and comfort to our enemies.[45]

Censorship   In the age-old conflict between freedom of speech and press and standards of public decency, courts and public have been developing a broader tolerance. Books, films, plays, and periodicals deal with sex, religion, and evolutionary biology in a more uninhibited fashion than would have been tolerated in any other period of our history. Although the Supreme Court has refused to disallow censorship and has even supported the requirement of film censorship in advance of public showing,[46] it has nevertheless overturned numerous decisions by censorial agencies. Local bans have been invalidated on such films as "The Miracle," "Pinky" and "The Lovers." [47] Laws which when applied had the effect of forbidding material to adults which was alleged to be corrupting to children have been disapproved.[48] Book sellers have been exempted from local prosecution for the sale of obscene literature if they could show ignorance of the contents of the book in question.[49] The Postmaster General's efforts to stop the circulation of nudist magazines, or those catering to homosexuals, or the book *Lady Chatterly's Lover"* have all been halted. All of this does not mean that obscenity is permissible but only that broader conceptions of what is obscene are being applied.[50]

Nuisance   The widespread use of sound trucks and public address systems for capturing the mind and attention has confronted defenders of free speech with the problem of reconciling it with public nuisance. Although the courts have invalidated efforts to restrain religious broadcasting in public places [51]

[45] For detailed appraisals of the current problems of subversion, see, for example, J. L. O'Brian, *National Security and Individual Freedom* (Cambridge, Mass., 1955); M. Grodzins, *The Loyal and the Disloyal: Social Boundaries of Patriotism and Treason* (Chicago, 1956); J. S. Commager, *Freedom, Loyalty, Dissent* (New York, 1954); S. A. Stouffer, *Communism, Conformity, and Civil Liberties: A Cross-section of the Nation Speaks its Mind* (New York, 1955); G. R. Taylor (ed.). *Communism, the Courts, and the Constitution* (New York, 1964).

[46] Times Film Corp. *v.* Chicago, 365 U. S. (1961). However, the procedure for censoring must place the burden of proof on the censor not on the exhibitor. The state systems of Maryland (Friedman *v.* Maryland, 85 S. Ct. 734) and New York (Trans-Lux Corp. *v.* Regents of N. Y. (*per Curiam*) 85 S. Ct.) were both overturned in 1965 because of their failure to meet this requirement. This leaves only Kansas and Virginia with state film censors and these state programs are under attack.

[47] Burstyn *v.* Wilson, 343 U. S. 495 (1952); Texas *v.* Gilling, 343 U. S. 960 (1952); and Jacobellis *v.* Ohio, 378 U. S. 184 (1964).

[48] Butler *v.* Michigan, 352 U. S. 380 (1957).

[49] Smith *v.* California, 361 U. S. 147 (1959).

[50] The definition of obscenity is discussed rather fully in Roth *v.* U. S. 354 U. S. 476 (1957) and the question of national vis-a-vis community standards of obscenity in Jacobellis *v.* Ohio, 373 U. S. 184.

[51] Saia *v.* U. S. 334 U. S. 558 (1949).

and have sustained the power of public transportation companies to bombard unwilling passengers,[52] they have also sustained the right of regulation of sound equipment on the public thoroughfares.[53]

The ability of the national government to restrain the circulation of undesirable opinions or materials is greatly aided by its operation of the mails. Congress has authorized the postal authorities to exclude from postal privileges indecent, fraudulent, and seditious materials and has conferred rather wide discretion on these authorities to decide what falls within the prohibition.[54] The licensing of radio and television broadcasting also places the national government in a strategic position from which to exclude by administrative determination similar materials from the air waves. The Federal Communications Commission, although denying censorship, nevertheless does in fact exercise it both directly and indirectly. In wartime, the government is obliged to introduce rigid and stern controls on the flow of news on the conduct of military operations. Frequently, however, these have gone far beyond the strict requirements of military security. The post-World War II period of international tensions, Korean and Vietnam police actions, and huge armaments has stimulated the continuation of many types of restrictions on free communication to the press and public by executive departments and agencies. The most recent controversy in this field has concerned the security regulations issued by President Truman, continued by Presidents Eisenhower, Kennedy, and Johnson. The newspapers, in particular, have been campaigning nationally against what they regard as a growing and unwarranted suppression of information by government agencies. Scientists too have joined the attack, claiming that important research is being hampered by the secrecy surrounding governmental scientific programs.

National censorship

> Congress shall make no law . . . abridging the right of the people peaceably to assemble, and to petition the government for a redress of grievances. FIRST AMENDMENT

The right to peaceable assembly is regarded by the Court as equally fundamental with those of free speech, press, and religion and, therefore, as guaranteed against state encroachment by the Fourteenth Amendment.[55] The right of petition has the same status. It also includes the right to demand positive actions by government as well as a redress of grievances. It does not, however, include a right to have the government take action on the request. For a time (1840-45), the lower house of Congress refused to receive peti-

4. Right to peaceable assembly and to petition

---

52 P.U.C. *v.* Pollak, 343 U. S. 451 (1952).

53 Kovacs *v.* Cooper, 336 U. S. 77 (1949).

54 However, the law requiring persons to whom is addressed Communist political propaganda from abroad to make a special request to the Post Office to obtain it was declared an unconstitutional infringement of free speech. Lamont *v.* Postmaster General, 85 S. Ct. 1493 (1965).

55 De Jonge *v.* Oregon, 299 U. S. 353 (1937).

tions on the subject of the abolition of slavery. John Quincy Adams, in one of his last great efforts in the House of Representatives, paved the way for a repeal of this rule. Petitions now, as for many years, are regularly delivered by any member of Congress to the clerk for entrance on the records of Congress. Many of these are referred to the appropriate committee. Most are never heard of again. The regulating of public assembly has presented the Court with more difficulties than the preservation of the right of petition. In 1937, the Court struck down a Jersey City ordinance under which the city officials had been prohibiting many types of meetings by "leftist" organizations.[56] In general, the courts have sustained regulations where the major purpose has been to keep streets and thoroughfares free of obstruction and where licensure is used without discrimination among groups seeking authority to hold meetings in public places.

A well regulated Militia being necessary to the security of a free state, the right of the people to keep and bear Arms shall not be infringed. SECOND AMENDMENT

5. Right to keep and bear arms

Provisions similar to that above may be found in many of the state constitutions. The arms referred to are those of the soldier; and it is not only the right, but also the duty, of every citizen, if called upon, to bear such arms in the service of his country. Under the police power, the "bearing" of arms intended for private use, however, may be regulated and restricted by both the national government and the states. There are many laws forbidding the carrying of concealed weapons (pistols, revolvers, dirks, bowie-knives, sword-canes, etc.) and the sale, possession, or use of sawed-off shotguns and other weapons not employed for military purposes but habitually used by criminals.[57]

6. Right to freedom of association

One of the by-products of the developing program to eliminate racial discrimination from most aspects of American life—a program to be described shortly and one which has been conducted under the civil rights banners—has been the unequivocal assertion by the Court of the right of freedom of association as one protected by the due process clause of the Fifth and Fourteenth Amendments. Several Southern states and cities sought to force the National Association for the Advancement of the Colored People (NAACP)—a leader in the efforts to halt discrimination—into the open by requiring registration and submission to the authorities of membership lists. In cases [58] from Alabama and later from Little Rock turning on the refusal of the NAACP to comply, the Court held the regulations invalid. "It

[56] Hague v. CIO, 307 U. S. 496 (1939).
[57] See United States v. Miller, 307 U. S. 174 (1939), for a Supreme Court decision upholding the constitutionality of the National Firearms Act of 1934. Cf. G. I. Haight, "The Right to Keep and Bear Arms," *Bill of Rights Rev.*, II, 31-42 (Fall, 1941).
[58] NAACP v. Alabama, 357 U. S. 449 (1958); Bates v. City of Little Rock, 361 U. S. 576 (1960).

is beyond debate that freedom to engage in association for the advancement of beliefs and ideas is an inseparable aspect of the liberty assured by the due process clause of the Fourteenth Amendment," stated Justice Harlan for the Court.[59]

Although, as yet, no general legal recognition has been accorded to privacy as a fundamental but unspecified civil right, the courts have increasingly been urged to recognize such a right. The invalidation in 1965 of a Connecticut statute on the use of and dissemination of information about birth-control devices was largely based on the idea that such a right exists.[60]

7. Right to privacy

RACIAL DISCRIMINATION

No state shall . . . deny to any person within its jurisdiction the equal protection of the laws. FOURTEENTH AMENDMENT

The most controversial frontier of civil rights today is racial discrimination. The key constitutional stipulation on this question is the "equal protection" clause of the Fourteenth Amendment. Originally intended to protect the emancipated Negroes from discriminatory treatment at the hands of officials of the Southern states, it largely failed of this objective until the middle of the present century. Rather, the clause provided the basis for judicial reconsideration of numerous state regulatory and tax programs aimed at real or alleged abuses of business enterprises. During the latter part of the last century it developed into a general guarantee against "arbitrary" or "unreasonable" classification of enterprises for tax or regulatory purposes. After the withdrawal of the troops from the defeated states (1877), a system of race relations was established based upon state-ordained segregation in public schools, public facilities, and places of public accommodation. This pattern developed also in the border states to some extent. When challenged, late in the century, "Jim Crowism" was found by the highest court to be compatible with the Fourteenth Amendment provided the separated facilities were substantially equal.[61] As the Negroes migrated out of the South in larger and larger numbers to the great industrial areas of North and Midwest, patterns of segregation developed there also, although normally not under the cover of law but rather on the basis of private decision.

8. Right to equal protection of the laws

The increasingly vigorous demands of the Negroes for fair and equal treatment and their denunciation of segregated enterprises have finally led to a complete restatement of the "equal protection" guarantees and to the outlawry of virtually all governmentally ordained segregation. Through many generations, however, the freed Negro had been segregated and discriminated against by most of American society, North and South, without the con-

[59] See also D. Fellman, *The Constitutional Right of Association* (Chicago, 1963).
[60] Griswold *et al v*. Connecticut, 85 S. Ct. 1678 (1965).
[61] Plessy *v*. Ferguson, 163 U. S. 537 (1896).

straints of public ordinance. In housing, employment, department stores, theaters, night clubs, sports arenas, hotels, and all manner of commercial, industrial, professional, academic, religious, and fraternal enterprises and activities, racial segregation was widely practiced. The negative restraints of the constitutional system of civil rights are, of course, not aimed at nor effective in removing private prejudice. Thus, the opponents of racial discrimination have also sought the support of legislation and executive action to penalize discrimination and to forbid its practice. In this, they have helped redefine our conceptions of civil rights and the duties men owe to one another.

Housing　　　In the great industrial and commercial cities of the North and Midwest, newly established Negro communities were segregated by various official and unofficial devices into "ghettos," usually slums and overcrowded neighborhoods. One of the favorite devices of the twenties and thirties for enforcing the racial "purity" of certain neighborhoods and thus keeping out Negroes —Jews, Poles, Italians also, in some cases—was restrictive real estate covenants upheld by state courts at various times in at least 19 states. The first great victory of the modern era for the cause of racial equality and the first effort to re-establish the importance of the "equal protection" clause occurred in 1948 when the Supreme Court declared that states could not use their judicial machinery to enforce such real estate covenants.[62] Furthermore, said the Court in a later case, state courts may not even entertain suits for damages by owner-residents against another who sold in violation of the covenant.[63] The Negro leaders now turned their fire on the nationally supported public-housing programs which had, until this time, conformed to community practice in the matter of racial segregation. After more than a dozen states (including New York, Illinois, Massachusetts, Michigan, Pennsylvania, Indiana, New Jersey, and Connecticut) and several cities forbade discrimination in publicly supported housing, and after several unsuccessful efforts to get Congress to change the national public housing laws, President Kennedy in 1962 by executive order forbade racial discrimination in the sale or rental of housing supported in whole or in part by public funds including housing provided through loans insured or guaranteed by a national agency. In 1963, New York became one of the first states to enact a sweeping prohibition of racial discrimination in all types of private housing except owner-occupied one-or-two family dwellings. A few other states followed and the demand for such legislation spread rapidly. In a state-wide referendum in California in connection with the Presidential election of 1964, however, such a housing law already on the books was repudiated.

Employ-　　　The Negroes have for years smarted under various open and subtle
ment　　 forms of discrimination in employment and in labor union membership and have felt that they have been denied access to the better-paying part of the

---

[62] Shelley *v*. Kraemer, 334 U. S. 1 (1948).
[63] Barrows *v*. Jackson, 346 U. S. 249 (1958).

labor market. This problem is not a constitutional one, solvable in the judicial forum, but a political one solvable, if at all, in the legislative arena. New York State pioneered in 1945 by enacting a "Fair Employment" law outlawing discrimination on the basis of race, religion, etc., in hiring and firing or in admission to union membership. More than twenty states, including most of the industrial ones, and several cities followed this lead. A few states enacted laws based on consultative rather than compulsive techniques. President Truman strongly urged national legislation on this subject as did the Democratic platform of 1948.[64] Although Congress successfully opposed action until 1964, the executive branch, by order, struck at discrimination in civil service employment, in the armed forces, and in the hiring practices of government contractors. As part of the sweeping legislation of 1964, a national program to eradicate discrimination in private employment was established. An Equal Employment Opportunity Commission was created, clothed, however, with largely investigatory and educational authority.[65] Local enforcement machinery where existent was endorsed and, in some cases, given a preference in handling disputes and small employers were included only on a gradual basis over a period of five years, but by this Act the government of the United States became the avowed enemy of employment practices based on race, color, religion, sex, or national origin.

One of the reasons frequently advanced by the Negro for his relative *Education* failure in the job market has been the inadequate quantity and quality of his education in the facilities offered under the segregated system of public education practiced in the South, in the border states, and even in Northern cities where Negroes are segregated geographically. In the effort to enlarge educational opportunities, these systems were brought under vigorous attack. In a series of cases [66] between 1948 and 1954 several states were ordered to admit Negroes to state-supported collegiate and professional institutions. Finally in 1954, the Supreme Court ordered the abandonment of all segregation in publicly supported educational institutions at all levels everywhere and specifically reversed the traditional doctrine. "Separate educational facilities are inherently unequal," said Chief Justice Warren for the Court. "Segregation (itself) is a denial of equal protection." [67] Recognizing that such a drastic change in the practices and attitudes of many decades invited cau-

---

[64] The split in the party in 1948 resulting in the walkout of several Southern delegations and the formation of a "Dixiecrat" Party was on this question.

[65] The Commission replaced an Equal Employment Opportunity Committee created by executive order and charged with enforcing "fair" employment practices among government contractors.

[66] For example, Sipuel v. Board of Regents of the University of Oklahoma, 332 U. S. 631 (1948); McLaurin v. Oklahoma State Regents et al., 339 U. S. 637 (1950); and Sweatt v. Painter et al., 339 U. S. 629 (1950).

[67] Brown v. Board of Education of Topeka, 347 U. S. 483 (1953). In the same set of controversies the Court also ruled that the national government was bound to respect the equal protection doctrine as part of the "due process" clause of the Fifth Amendment Bolling v. Sharpe, 347 U. S. 497 (1954).

tion, the Court delayed the execution of its judgment pending further review and invited the states affected to submit recommendations at a later date. Early in 1955 the Court heard arguments on how best to carry out its decision. Florida, North Carolina, Arkansas, Oklahoma, Maryland, and Texas took part in the proceedings, but Virginia, South Carolina, Georgia, Mississippi, and Alabama did not. The Court then ordered (June, 1955) the lower national courts to determine in each case how best to end segregation in the schools. The lower courts were instructed to allow time for the necessary readjustments but to insist on reasonable efforts at compliance. In all cases the burden of proof was placed on the local authorities to show why they could not move faster and that they had a plan to end segregation.

Southern resistance to desegregation in education

Although in several of the border states the integration of races in the public schools has steadily advanced and largely by voluntary methods since the famous decision, in the deeper South resistance has been widespread, continuous, and determined and for the most part, the conversions have thus far been few and difficult. The Congressmen of these states in 1956 signed a resolution pledging themselves to "use all lawful means to bring about a reversal of this decision . . . and to prevent the use of force in its implementation." State legislatures and governors have declared the decision an unwarranted and unconstitutional invasion of their reserved powers and several have invoked the old nullification doctrine of "interposition" to justify disobedience to the court's orders. Laws and state constitutional amendments have been adopted authorizing: the closing of any school ordered to desegregate; the use of public funds to support private schools; the withdrawal of authority over school affairs from local to state officials. New and ingenious procedures for the assignment of pupils have been devised.[68] Violence has erupted in Little Rock, Arkansas; Clinton, Tennessee; Oxford, Mississippi; Birmingham, Alabama. A very threatening situation also arose in Tuscaloosa. Troops were ordered into active duty at Little Rock, Oxford, and Birmingham, and the National Guards of Arkansas, Mississippi, and Alabama were at various times called into national service to prevent their being used by the governors to obstruct court-ordered integration. The schools of Prince Edward County, Virginia, were closed from 1959 to 1964 to avoid integration and money was paid to private organizations to provide schooling to white children of that county. The Supreme Court, meanwhile, steadfastly adhered to its position. Invited to stay the execution of a desegregation order for Central High School in Little Rock in order to avoid violence, it enjoined Governor Faubus (Ark.) from intervening, denounced state support of segregation "through any arrangement, management, funds, or property" and

[68] Shuttlesworth *v.* Birmingham Board of Education, 358 U. S. 101 (1958). The Supreme Court concurred in a lower court decision holding an Alabama pupil-assignment law as not invalid on its face. It carefully reserved the right, however, to determine if its application was illegal.

dismissed the "interposition" resolutions and assertions as, in John Marshall's words, making a "solemn mockery" of the Constitution.[69]

Throughout the years since the school decision, the executive branch has been relatively powerless to intervene in a positive way to expedite integration. Only when a court order was defied or violence occurred which threatened the lives or safety of national agents or services or when invited by the local officials to help (this occurred only in Clinton, Tenn.) has the executive branch been able to move. Attorney General Robert Kennedy did, in 1961, enter the suit involving the Prince Edward County schools on behalf of the government and did participate in the settlement of that controversy in 1964.[70] Efforts to strengthen the enforcement powers of the executive in school desegregation questions were successfully resisted by the Southern Congressmen in the civil rights debates of 1957 and 1960. Finally, by the Act of 1964, the Attorney General is authorized to file suit for the desegregation of a public school on the basis of a complaint if he certifies that the complainant is unable to initiate proceedings and that such an action would "materially further" orderly school desegregation. The Office of Education is authorized to offer technical and financial assistance to local school officials planning desegregation or actually achieving it. Most important of all racial discrimination is outlawed in all programs supported financially by the national government. While opposition to racial integration in education continues in much of the South, gradually public schools in the urban South (Atlanta, Tuskegee, New Orleans, Birmingham) are being opened to both races. The Office of Education has now (1965) set the fall of 1967 as the deadline for school districts to be completely integrated or face the loss of federal aids.[71]

The racial segregation in living accommodations which has been characteristic of many cities has resulted in "de facto" segregation in neighborhood public schools in those cities. Encouraged by the effectiveness of their protests, Northern Negro leaders are now demanding that Northern and Midwestern educational officials develop systems of transporting some Negroes out of the Negro neighborhoods to "white" schools and some whites into Negro schools.[72] New York City amidst bitter demonstrations by white

School problems of Northern cities

69 Cooper v. Aaron, 358 U. S. 1 (1958).

70 Kennedy entered the suit as a plaintiff attacking the closing of the schools and asking the Court to prevent Virginia from spending money on any schools so long as these remain closed. Previously, the government had entered desegregation suits only on Court invitation and as a friend of the Court.

71 A good review of the cases, laws, and problems of desegregation is H. H. Humphrey (ed.), *School Desegregation: Documents and Commentaries* (New York, 1964).

72 The civil rights act of 1964 explicitly does not authorize a U. S. official or court to order transportation of children to achieve racial balance. The Supreme Court also has let stand a lower court ruling (Bell v. City of Gary, Ind., 324 F. 2d 209, 1963) that school boards have no constitutional duty to end racial imbalance resulting from housing patterns.

parents has made the first major effort to accommodate this new demand. Many supporters of racial equality have been chagrined to be reminded by these agitations of the extent of segregation outside the South.

Public facilities and places of accommodation The final area of racial controversy to be considered concerns segregation in public facilities and places of public accommodation. This battle like the others has been waged in the judicial arena insofar as publicly ordained segregation is concerned and in the legislature insofar as the practices of private firms and persons are concerned. In 1946 the Supreme Court held invalid a Virginia "Jim Crow" law segregating the races in buses on the grounds of inconvenience to interstate carriers rather than on the question of equal protection.[73] In a later case against the Southern Railway turning on its refusal to seat a Negro in the dining car, the Court, in effect, invalidated all forms of discrimination on railroad trains and the laws on which they rest.[74] The Interstate Commerce Commission followed this decision by a sweeping order in 1955 ending segregation in all interstate trains and buses. The next step was a decision in 1956 outlawing an Alabama law and a Montgomery City ordinance requiring segregation on intrastate buses.[75] This decision came in the midst of a boycott of city buses by the Negroes of Montgomery. Ultimately segregation in buses in a number of large Southern cities was ended by the bus companies. Using the "sit-in" system the Negroes then attacked segregation in restaurants, terminals, and large chain stores. The Court when asked outlawed segregation in the terminals as well as in the bus or train.[76] Attorney General Kennedy in 1961 urged the ICC to order an end to discrimination in all terminals and in restaurants in terminals and this it did. In other areas of concern, the Court has swept away enforced segregation in public parks, playgrounds, golf courses, and bathing beaches.[77] A provision of the national hospital-aid legislation authorizing aid for segregated facilities was declared invalid in 1964.[78]

In 30 northern, western, and midwestern states, meanwhile, legislation was enacted forbidding discrimination by private persons operating hotels, restaurants, and resorts. Human-rights agencies were established to direct the campaign against discriminatory practices. After years of debate the Congress was finally brought into the struggle against segregation in privately owned places of public accommodation by the Civil Rights Act of 1964. Discrimination is, by it, outlawed in all such places (restaurants, motels,

---

[73] Morgan *v.* Virginia, 328 U. S. 373 (1946).

[74] Henderson *v.* United States, 339 U. S. 816 (1950).

[75] Gayle *v.* Browder, 352 U. S. 903 (1956).

[76] Boynton *v.* Virginia, 364 U. S. 454 (1960).

[77] Mayor and Council of Baltimore *v.* Dawson, 350 U. S. 877 (1955); Holmes *v.* Atlanta, 350 U. S. 879 (1955). In Watson *v.* Memphis 373 U. S. 526 (1963) the Court further held that delay in desegregating such public facilities would not be tolerated and that the gradual system of desegregation was applicable only to public schools.

[78] Simkins *v.* Cone Memorial Hospital, 323 F. 2d 959 (1963). The Supreme Court refused to review the decision.

hotels, theaters, sport arenas, stadiums, lunch rooms, cinema) except owner-occupied units with five or fewer rooms for rent [79] and where the segregation is based upon state laws or official action or where it can be shown that the customers, goods, or entertainment move in interstate commerce. A Community Relations Service, established by the Act, handles complaints and seeks voluntary compliance before legal action may be sought by the Attorney General. Locally established agencies where they exist are given preference in resolving disputes which might arise.

ONE MAN—ONE VOTE

The equal protection clause has quite recently been injected into another highly controversial field of American politics: the apportionment of seats in state legislatures. In a series of decisions, the Court has cast aside its traditional position that apportionment systems were not reviewable because of the apparent lack of judicial power to correct legislative error and has held that such systems for both houses of state legislatures may be reviewed by the national courts under the equal-protection clause and may, if found to depart sharply from equal representation according to population, be invalidated,[80] regardless of state constitutional specifications requiring that attention be given area or governmental unit as well as population in designing districts for one or both houses. Other state political arrangements aimed at maintaining rural or white domination of politics such as the county-unit systems for counting the vote for state-wide elective offices in Georgia [81] and Maryland and the redrawing of the boundary lines of Tuskegee, Alabama, so as to place most of the Negro population outside the municipal limits have also been invalidated.[82]

9. Right to equal representation in legislature

B. RIGHT TO FAIRNESS IN GOVERNMENTAL PROCEDURES

It is an axiom of Anglo-American jurisprudence that a person suspected or accused of illegal behavior is entitled to a fair trial, by humane procedures, and with the burden of proof resting on his accusers. This conception sharply differentiates the English-speaking world from that of the modern authoritarians with their secret police, torture chambers, and stealthy apprehension. The constitutions of the United States and of the several states, in pursuance of our traditional ideas, surround the entire process of criminal justice with restrictions aimed at protecting the individual against tyrannical, arbitrary, or

[79] Places also not expressly covered are: barbershops, retail stores, bars, bowling alleys. Private clubs are exempted.
[80] Baker *v.* Carr, 369 U. S. 186 (1962) and Reynolds *v.* Simms, 377 U. S. 533 (1964).
[81] Gray *v.* Sanders, 372 U. S. 368 (1963).
[82] Gomillion *v.* Lightfoot, 364 U. S. 329 (1960).

capricious administration of the laws. And while the guilty occasionally escape conviction by hiding behind the ancient guarantees, the innocent usually find refuge in the shelter of their time-tested rights.

No person shall be held to answer for a capital or other infamous crime, unless on a presentment or indictment of a grand jury . . . FIFTH AMENDMENT

1. Indictment by grand jury

    The grand jury is an institution of ancient origin, consisting of 12 to 23 citizens who hear the public prosecutor make accusations of crime and then determine if there is sufficient evidence to require the suspects to be held for trial. It was designed to prevent frivolous or capricious prosecutions by public officials. The procedure, however, is cumbersome and many states, especially western ones, have abandoned it in favor of indictment by "information" of the district attorney. Even the national government authorizes the use of the information procedure in major but noncapital offenses when the defendant agrees and in minor offenses at the discretion of the prosecution. The Supreme Court has accepted these procedures as within the spirit of the constitutional guarantees.[83] When the grand jury is used, however, it must be constituted so as not to discriminate among races.[84]

The privilege of the writ of habeas corpus shall not be suspended, unless when in cases of rebellion or invasion the public safety may require it. ART. 1, Sec. IX, Cl. 2

2. Writ of habeas corpus

    The most revered of the great safeguards of personal security is the privilege of the write of habeas corpus. This writ is a court order, addressed to any officer having custody of a prisoner, directing that the petitioner be brought before the court that the court may inquire if he is being properly detained. President's Lincoln's suspension of the privilege in certain areas of the North during the Civil War evoked considerable legal controversy over the question of which branch of the government has this power. The general conclusion from this debate is that the function belongs to Congress but may be exercised by the President if authorized by statute.[85] The state governments are similarly bound by provisions in state constitutions, although some of them have forbidden the suspension of the privilege under any circumstances. The uses of the writ have been steadily expanding over many centuries and the law surrounding its use is still developing. One of its growing uses is to test compliance of state authorities with proper constitutional pro-

---

    [83] In Hurtado *v.* California, 110 U. S. 516 (1884), the Court held that the "due process" clause of the Fourteenth Amendment did not require grand-jury indictment by the states, and in Duke *v.* United States, 301 U. S. 492 (1937) that the national government could indict by information in minor offenses.

    [84] Norris *v.* Alabama, 294 U. S. 587 (1935); Reece *v.* Georgia, 350 U.S. 85 (1955); and Eubanks *v.* Louisiana, 356 U. S. 584 (1958).

    [85] *Ex parte* Milligan, 4 Wallace 2 (1866).

cedures and it is frequently sought in national courts by those held in custody in the states.[86]

The trial of all crimes . . . shall be by jury. ART. III, Sec. II, Cl. 3

In all criminal prosecutions the accused shall enjoy the right to a speedy and public trial by an impartial jury of the State and district wherein the crime shall have been committed . . . SIXTH AMENDMENT

Like indictment by grand jury, trial by jury passed into American usage with the English Common Law. The Constitution provides for it in several places and no state constitution fails to ordain it also. It is, however, by common law that a jury must consist of 12 persons and must arrive at its verdict by unanimous vote. It is also by common law that the right of jury trial does not apply to cases in courts of equity, to cases in contempt of court, and to petty offenses or misdemeanors punishable only by small fines. Formerly it was supposed that wherever applicable under constitutional provision or common law, jury trial must prevail. The Supreme Court has now held, however, that since the device is intended fundamentally for the accused's protection, he may, if he considers it to his interest to do so, waive the right in national proceedings; and many states allow the same discretion.[87] The Court, has also held on many occasions that a jury trial is not required in cases of criminal contempt of a national court—a position which it recently reaffirmed when the defendants were the governor and lt. governor of the state of Mississippi [88] charged with violating a court order in the matter of the admission of a Negro to the state university in 1962. The Court, moreover, has ruled that where juries are employed, they must not be made up deliberately to exclude workingmen, Negroes, or any other particular class of persons—although there still are states in which women are debarred.[89] State civil procedures that modify the old common law jury requirements have, typically,

3. Trial by jury

[86] See the discussion by Justice Black of the developing use of the writ in Johnson v. Zerbst, 304 U. S. 458 (1938).

[87] Patton v. United States, 281 U. S. 276 (1930). Cf. J. A. C. Grant, "Felony Trials Without a Jury," *Amer. Polit. Sci. Rev.*, XXV, 980-995 (Nov., 1931). The defendant may not, however, demand a trial without a jury in a national court, if the government wants one. Singer v. U. S. 85 S. Ct. 783 (1965).

[88] U. S. v. Barnett et al., 376 U. S. 681 (1964). The plea for a jury trial in this case was denied by closely divided court and in terms which implied that absence of a jury could be supported only if the punishment was relatively mild. The two defendants were, however, later cleared of the charges by the Court of Appeals.

[89] Among cases, see Thiel v. Southern Pacific Co., 328 U. S. 217 (1946). The Court has held repeatedly that a Negro is constitutionally entitled to be indicted and tried by juries from which Negroes have not been excluded on grounds of race—Norris v. Alabama, 294 U. S. 587 (1935); Hill v. Texas, 316 U. S. 400 (1942). In 1947, also, it ordered a new trial of a Mississippi Negro condemned to the electric chair, on the ground that in a county where Negroes composed more than one-third of the population, no Negro name had appeared on grand- and petit-jury lists in more than 30 years. See Patton v. Mississippi, 332 U. S. 463 (1947).

been upheld by the Court as in compliance with the Fourteenth Amendment.

Military
law

Trial by jury is, of course, replaced by court-martial proceedings for all those subject to military discipline. The Uniform Code of Military Justice enacted in 1950 is an effort precisely and uniformly (for all services) to prescribe the use of courts-martial and the possibilities of appeal to civilian tribunals. The Supreme Court in determining rights under the Code has held that contrary to the Code a person discharged from the Service cannot later be tried by court-martial for an offense committed while in the Service.[90] Civilians who accompany the army abroad are also not subject to court-martial procedure in time of peace for offenses committed abroad even if this procedure is sanctioned by an agreement with the country involved.[91]

The right of the people to be secure in their persons, houses, papers, and effects against unreasonable searches and seizures shall not be violated . . . FOURTH AMENDMENT

4. Security
in the
house

Another treasured inheritance from English Common Law is grounded upon the ancient maxim that every man's house is his castle. The language employed in the Fourth Amendment suggests that there are searches and seizures which are reasonable and defines them as being such as are conducted on the basis of warrants (1) issued "upon probable cause, supported by oath or affirmation" and (2) "particularly describing the place to be searched and the persons or things to be seized." The Supreme Court has, however, recognized situations in which the police may legitimately make searches and seizures without a warrant. Thus, if it is known or thought probable that a person guilty of a felony or breach of the peace has taken refuge in a certain house, officers of the law may go in after him without waiting for written authority. Likewise, if a search is to be made of a boat, automobile, airplane, or other vehicle which could take advantage of delay in order to escape, a warrant is not needed. In general these rules are also imposed on the states by their constitutions or by the "due-process" clause of the Fourteenth Amendment as now construed by the Supreme Court.[92] The possibility under our federal system of state and national jurisdiction over certain offenses has surrounded this ancient right with a number of the most complex questions concerning the use of evidence obtained illegally —by wiretapping, for example—by one enforcement level or the other. The modern Court has been imposing what many describe as increasingly strict standards on state enforcement officers and has forbidden them to use wiretapped evidence whether obtained by the local police or by federal agents

[90] U. S. *ex rel.* Toth *v.* Quarles, 350 U. S. 11 (1955).
[91] Reid *v.* Covert, 354 U. S. 1 (1957).
[92] In Kerr *v.* California, 374 U. S. 23 (1963) and Aquilar *v.* Texas 378 U. S. 108 (1964) the Court held that the standard of reasonableness for obtaining a warrant is the same under the 14th as under the Fifth Amendment.

and has insisted upon national standards for "reasonableness" as against many local variations heretofore tolerated by local and state judges or endorsed by legislatures in codes of criminal procedure.[93]

No person . . . shall be compelled in any criminal case to be a witness against himself. . . . FIFTH AMENDMENT

The frequent invocation of the "Fifth Amendment" by witnesses in widely publicized hearings into subversion by Congressional committees in the last fifteen years has brought into great prominence the ancient guarantees against self-incrimination contained therein. This old English rule, developed largely to prevent persons from being tortured to extract admissions of guilt, has come down to us as a well-tested protection against inquisition in most any form. It may be claimed by witnesses as well as by those accused and be pled as an excuse for not giving evidence even if that evidence only lends support to a charge of crime. Courts have repeatedly lashed out at those who assert that anyone who claims protection of this rule is obviously guilty,[94] and in most courts in the land it is not permissible for the judge or the prosecutor to comment to the jury on the failure of a defendant to testify in his own behalf. Recently the Supreme Court modifying an earlier ruling held that under the "due-process" clause of the Fourteenth Amendment the states may not infringe this privilege.[95]

5. Protection against self-incrimination

There are a large number of national and state laws authorizing the granting of immunity from prosecution in order to extract testimony from reluctant witnesses. The National Immunity Act of 1954 was designed to assist the committees of Congress in ferreting out subversive behavior. Our federal system complicates the immunity problem since a state cannot protect

Immunity authorization

[93] See Harris v. United States, 331 U. S. 145 (1947). See also McNabb v. United States, 316 U. S. 41 (1943) on use of illegally obtained evidence in national court; Rea v. United States, 350 U. S. 214 (1956) on use of illegal evidence by a federal agent in a state case; Elkins v. United States, 364 U. S. 206 (1960) on use of wire tapped evidence in state court; and Mapp v. Ohio 367 U. S. 643 (1961) which held that all evidence obtained by unconstitutional searches and seizures is inadmissible in state courts. See also Rochim v. California, 342 U. S. 165 (1953) and Breithaupt v. Abram, 352 U. S. 432 (1957) for use of evidence taken from a person against his will; Frank v. Maryland, 359 U. S. 360 (1959) on the inspection of private premises by health inspectors without a warrant; Ohio ex rel. Eaton v. Price, 360 U. S. 246 (1959) on entry by a housing inspector.

[94] The Supreme Court took a strong stand on this matter in Slochower v. Board of Education of New York City, 350 U. S. 551 (1956) when it ruled that the dismissal of a public-college professor for invoking the Fifth Amendment violated "due process." In a similar case in 1960, however, the Court upheld the dismissal of employees of Los Angeles County on the grounds that they had been directed by law and by their superiors to answer questions about subversion. Nelson v. County of Los Angeles, 362 U. S. 1 (1960). The Court most recently threw out a California murder conviction because of the comments by the trial judge and the prosecutor on the failure of the accused to testify. Griffin v. California 85 S. Ct. 1229 (1965).

[95] Malloy v. Hogan, 378 U. S. 1 (1964).

a person to whom it has granted immunity from national prosecution if he has also transgressed a national law. For some years there was a kind of double standard in this matter but the Supreme Court in 1964 declared that one jurisdiction in the federal system may not compel a witness to give testimony which might tend to incriminate him under the laws of another jurisdiction unless both jurisdictions have waived prosecution.[96]

6. Miscellaneous procedural guarantees

Under the Constitution, in matters involving national offenses and officers of the national government, a person accused of crime is further guaranteed a speedy trial by an impartial jury of the district in which the crime was committed. He has a right to confront his accusers, to have counsel in making his defense, to compel the attendance of witnesses in his behalf. He may not be subjected to cruel and unusual punishment or required to pay excessive fines or offer unreasonable bail. He may not be twice put in jeopardy of life or limb for the same offense.[97] The state constitutions generally contain the same guarantees as against state actions and the Supreme Court has held that the Fourteenth Amendment also imposes most of these on states.

7. Right to due process of law

The broadest of all guarantees of governmental fairness is the Constitution's requirement that neither the nation (Fifth Amendment) nor the states (Fourteenth Amendment) may deprive any person (individual or corporation) of "life, liberty, or property" without "due process of law," a guarantee which is also contained in all of the state constitutions. The term has never been fully and conclusively defined. Broadly equivalent to the "law of the land" as guaranteed in *Magna Carta* and to the "rule of law" upon which English jurists have traditionally placed the utmost stress, it has, like those phrases, been subject to steadily broadening and deepening interpretation.

"Due process" and fair procedure

As applied to the national government, the "due-process" clause supplements the more specific guarantees of the other amendments dealing with fair procedure. It imposes on national authorities the duty of providing "persons" with a *fair* trial before a proper agency—court or administrative agency. They must be given proper notice, be allowed to present evidence and be permitted, ordinarily, an appeal to a court of law to assert their rights. Throughout this discussion, we have noted how the Supreme Court has applied the clause to the states so as to impose upon them the duty in civil and criminal cases to provide a regular proceeding before a proper court with a *fair* hearing for both parties. While it does not guarantee a jury trial nor an indictment by grand jury, it does outlaw the use of evidence or confession obtained by force or fraud, demand that the accused be confronted with the

---

[96] Murphy *et al. v.* Waterfront Commission of New York Harbor, 378 U. S. 52 (1964). Justice Goldberg in his opinion discusses the development of the law on immunity.

[97] He may be tried once by the state and once by the nation, however, for an offense which is a crime against both. For a recent case, see Bartkus *v.* Illinois, 356 U. S. 121 (1959).

witnesses against him,[98] forbid the televising or broadcasting of the trial,[99] and require the state to respect the rights of the accused to legal counsel, and even requires the state to make counsel available to poor people.[100]

Although the "due-process" guarantee is one of the major constitutional supports of proper governmental procedure, it would claim much less interest and attract very much less litigation if this were all it involved. Toward the end of the last century the Supreme Court gave the phrase a new meaning and a new direction which represented a sharp departure from the traditional view. Industrialization and urbanization of the nation were at that time revealing some of their less benevolent aspects and state governments were attempting by various types of remedial legislation to mitigate the evils of rapid expansion. The Court, repeatedly invited to upset state efforts at regulating the economy, finally yielded to the idea that the "due-process clause" conferred upon it the power to review legislation to determine if it contemplated an *arbitrary* or *unreasonable* limitation on property rights. The problem was not whether the judicial or administrative procedures used by the state or prescribed by the law were fair but rather whether the legislation or regulation was itself proper. This use is usually referred to as *substantive due process* to distinguish it from the procedural due process already described. The Court in a series of decisions [101] proceeded to invalidate state laws regulating industry, hours of labor, wages, rate-fixing for utilities if not based on proper evaluation of economic factors, and other aspects of the economic relations of individuals and groups. It also discovered new limits on the statutory authority of Congress arising from the Fifth Amendment's "due-process" clause. The Court was charged, even by some of its own members, with interpreting the clause as if it prescribed the economic tenets of Adam Smith and made them the law of the land. Thus, it found efforts to equalize the power of workers in dealing with corporations as unduly interfering with the freedom of contract of both parties. In doing this, the Court necessarily defined the power of the states to promote the health, safety, and welfare of its citizens (police power) in very narrow terms. In adopting this interpretation of the "due-process" clause, the Court further found that the word *person* was meant to include corporation. This view allowed it to consider any legislation which might be shown to threaten corporate property. The result of the attitude and theory of the Court was to plunge it into the middle of bitter political controversy and to earn for it the scorn of those determined to bring the economy under public control and the applause of those striving

"Substantive due process" in economic matters

[98] Pointer *v.* Texas, 85 S. Ct. 1065 (1965).

[99] Estes *v.* Texas, 85 S. Ct. 1628 (1965).

[100] Gideon *v.* Wainwright, 372 U. S. 335 (1963). An excellent story by Anthony Lewis of this case, its background, and significance appeared in *The New Yorker* magazine, April 25, May 2 and May 9, 1964.

[101] The best known are Lochner *v.* New York, 198 U. S. 45 (1905); Smith *v.* Ames, 169 U. S. 466 (1898); Coppage *v.* Kansas, 236 U. S. 1 (1915); Stettler *v.* O'Hara, 243 U. S. 629 (1917); Adkins *v.* Children's Hospital, 261 U. S. 525 (1923).

to stave off public regulation. The depression of the 1930's brought a new appreciation to the vast majority of the nation of the necessities of energetic governmental action in the economic field and, after some political maneuvering by President Roosevelt, it brought a new view to the Supreme Court. From its first reversal of precedent in 1937 when it sustained a state law regulating the wages of women and children,[102] the Court has steadily broadened its view of allowable interference by the government in the economic relations of our society. "We have returned to the original constitutional proposition," said Justice Black in 1963, "that courts do not substitute their social and economic beliefs for the judgment of legislative bodies who are elected to pass laws." "The doctrine—that due process authorizes courts to hold laws unconstitutional when they believe the legislature has acted unwisely—has long since been discarded." [103]

PROPERTY RIGHTS

The reversal of judicial attitude on the protection to corporate property against governmental regulation embraced in "due process" does not mean that property is no longer entitled to protection against the state. In general, private property may not be taken for public use without proper procedure and reasonable justification and when it is taken just compensation must be rendered. The right of eminent domain (to take private property for public use) is, of course, one which every government has to have. In our society this power has also been conferred upon public utilities upon certain conditions. Nevertheless, rights to "just" compensation, to be deprived only for a public purpose, to a fair hearing and determination of value are all property rights which can be asserted in our courts.

References

1. GENERAL

C. B. Swisher, *The Growth of Constitutional Power in the United States* (Chicago, 1947), Chap. VII.

Learned Hand, *The Bill of Rights* (Cambridge, Mass., 1958).

[102] West Coast Hotel Co. *v.* Parish, 300 U. S. 379 (1937). Only the year before the Court had declared a similar law unconstitutional. Morehead *v.* New York, 298 U. S. 587 (1936).

[103] Ferguson *v.* Skrupa, 372 U. S. 726 (1963). See also R. J. Harris, "Due Process of Law," *Amer.-Polit. Sci. Rev.,* XLII, 32-42 (Feb., 1948), reviewing developments particularly during the decade 1937-47.

W. Gellhorn, *Individual Freedom and Governmental Restraints* (Baton Rouge, La., 1956).

T. I. Emerson and D. Haber, *Political and Civil Rights in the United States* (2nd ed., Buffalo, 1958).

W. J. Brennan, Jr., *The Bill of Rights and the States* (Santa Barbara, Calif., 1961).

D. Fellman, *The Limits of Freedom* (New Brunswick, N.J., 1959).

R. K. Carr, *The Federal Protection of Civil Rights; Quest for a Sword* (Ithaca, N.Y., 1947).

C. H. Pritchett, *Civil Liberties and the Vinson Court* (Chicago, 1944).

H. D. Lasswell, *National Security and Individual Freedom* (New York, 1950).

E. Cahn (ed.), *The Great Rights* (New York, 1963).

A. P. Grimes, *Equality in America: Religion, Race, and the Urban Majority* (New York, 1964).

P. G. Kaufer, *Civil Liberties and the Constitution* (Ann Arbor, Mich., 1962).

C. J. Friedrich, "Rights, Liberties, Freedoms: A Reappraisal" *Amer. Pol. Sci. Rev.* LVII, No. 4 (Dec. 1963).

The Constitution of the United States of America; Analysis and Interpretation. Annotated to June 30, 1964 (88th Cong., 1st Sess., Sen. Doc. 39).

2. FREEDOM OF SPEECH, PRESS, RELIGION, AND ASSEMBLY

Z. Chafee, *Free Speech in the United States* (Cambridge, Mass., 1941).

――――, *Three Human Rights in the Constitution of 1787* (Lawrence, Kan., 1956).

A. Meiklejohn, *Free Speech and Its Relation to Self-Government* (New York, 1948).

Commission on the Freedom of the Press, *A Free and Responsible Press; A General Report on Mass Communications* (Chicago, 1947).

M. L. Ernst, *The First Freedom* (New York, 1946). Speech, press, radio, etc.

―――― and A. U. Schwartz, *Censorship: The Search for the Obscene* (New York, 1964).

W. G. Torpey, *Judicial Doctrines of Religious Rights in America* (Chapel Hill, N.C., 1948).

M. R. Konvitz, *Fundamental Liberties of a Free People* (Ithaca, N.Y., 1957).

C. H. Pritchett, *The Political Offender and the Warren Court* (Boston, 1957).

A. W. Johnson and F. H. Yost, *Separation of Church and State in the United States* (Minneapolis, 1948).

R. E. Cushman, "Public Support of Religious Education in American Constitutional Law," *Ill. Law Rev.* (of Northwestern University) XLV, 333-356 (July-Aug., 1950).

W. Parsons, *The First Freedom; Considerations of Church and State in the United States* (New York, 1948).

H. W. Barber, "Religious Liberty *v.* The Police Power: Jehovah's Witnesses," *Amer. Pol. Sci. Rev.,* XLI, 226-247 (Apr., 1947).

L. Pfeffer, *Church, State, and Freedom* (Boston, 1953).

R. McKeon, R. K. Merton, W. Gellhorn, *Freedom to Read: Perspective and Program* (New York, 1957).

W. Berns, *Freedom, Virtue, and the First Amendment* (Baton Rouge, La., 1957).

"Internal Security and Civil Rights," *The Annals of the American Academy of Political and Social Science,* Vol. CCC (July, 1955).

A. K. Stokes and L. Pfeffer, *Church and State in the United States* (New York, 1965). A revised one-volume edition of the Stokes work.

H. M. Hyman, *To Try Men's Souls: Loyalty Tests in American History* (Berkeley, Calif., 1960).

D. Fellman, *The Censorship of Books* (Madison, Wis., 1957).

————, "Separation of Church and State in the United States; A Summary View," *Wis. Law Rev.,* 1950 vol., 427-478 (May, 1950).

W. W. Van Alstyne, "Constitutional Separation of Church and State: The Quest for a Coherent Position," *Amer. Pol. Sci. Rev.* LVII, No. 4 (Dec. 1963).

P. B. Kurland, *Religion and the Laws: of Church and State and The Supreme Court* (Chicago, 1962).

D. E. Boles, *The Bible, Religion, and the Public Schools* (Ames, Iowa, 1961).

R. F. Drinan, *Religion, the Courts, and Public Policy* (New York, 1963).

D. R. Manwaring, *Render Unto Caesar: The Flag Salute Controversy* (Chicago, 1962).

A. Guttmann and B. Ziegler, (eds.) *Communism, the Courts, and the Constittuion* (New York, 1964).

3. RACIAL DISCRIMINATION

R. A. Goldwin (ed.), *One Hundred Years of Emancipation* (Chicago, 1964).

M. Grodzins, *American Betrayed: Politics and the Japanese Evacuation* (Chicago, 1949).

To Secure These Rights; Report of the President's Committee on Civil Rights (Washington, 1947).

M. R. Konvitz, *The Constitution and Civil Rights* (New York, 1947).

B. Muse, *Virginia's Massive Resistance* (Bloomington, Ind., 1961).

————, *Ten Years of Prelude: The Story of Integration Since the Supreme Court's 1954 Decision* (New York, 1964).

A. P. Blaustein and C. C. Ferguson, Jr., *Desegregation and the Law* (New Brunswick, N.J., 1957).

J. Greenberg, *Race Relations and American Law* (New York, 1960).

D. Shoemaker (ed.), *With All Deliberate Speed: Segregation—Desegregation in Southern Schools* (New York, 1957).

C. E. Vose, *Caucasians Only: The Supreme Court, the NAACP, and the Covenant Cases* (Berkeley, Calif., 1961).

D. McEntire, *Residence and Race: Final Report to the Commission on Race and Housing* (Berkeley, Calif., 1961).

R. J. Harris, *The Quest for Equality* (Baton Rouge, La., 1960).

C. Vann Woodward, *The Strange Career of Jim Crow* (New York, 1955).

J. W. Peltason, *Fifty-eight Lonely Men: Southern Federal Judges and School Desegregation* (New York, 1961).

S. S. Ulmer, "Supreme Court Behavior in Racial Exclusion Cases: 1935-1960," *Amer. Pol. Sci. Rev.,* LVI, No. 2 (June, 1962).

O. Handlin, *Fire-Bell in the Night: the Crisis in Civil Rights* (Boston, 1964).

U.S. Commission on Civil Rights, *Reports* (Washington, 1958-1964).

C. H. Pritchett, "Equal Protection and the Urban Majority," *Amer. Pol. Sci. Rev.,* LVIII, No. 4 (Dec. 1964).

J. Tussman, *The Supreme Court on Racial Discrimination* (New York, 1963).

4. PROCEDURAL RIGHTS

D. Fellman, *The Defendant's Rights* (New York, 1958).

———, "Cruel and Unusual Punishments," *The Journal of Politics,* Vol. 19, 1947, pp. 34-45.

S. H. Hofstadter, *The Fifth Amendment and the Immunity Act of 1954* (New York, 1956).

E. N. Griswold, *The Fifth Amendment Today* (Cambridge, Mass., 1955).

W. M. Beaney, *The Right of Counsel in American Courts* (Ann Arbor, Mich., 1955).

A. R. Beisel, Jr., *Control Over Illegal Enforcement of the Criminal Law: Role of the Supreme Court* (Boston, 1955).

R. A. Watson, "Federalism v. Individual Rights: the Legal Squeeze on Self-Incrimination," *Am. Pol. Sci. Rev.,* XIV, No. 4 (Dec., 1960).

A. S. Trebach, *The Rationing of Justice: Constitutional Rights and the Criminal Process* (New Brunswick, N.J., 1964).

A. Barth, *The Price of Liberty* (New York, 1961).

5. PROPERTY RIGHTS

B. Schwartz, *A Commentary on the Constitution of the United States: Part II: The Rights of Property* (New York, 1965).

B. THE DEMOCRATIC PROCESS

★ 5 ★

Voting and Elections

THE SPREAD OF DEMOCRACY

Democracy the second element in the American system

THROUGHOUT MOST OF ITS HISTORY, the American system of government has been described and analyzed largely in terms of the constitutional assignment of powers among the several levels and branches of which it is composed. During the past half century, however, increasing stress has been placed upon the spread of democracy throughout the land and the modifications in our constitutional arrangements which have resulted. Today we could with good reason, begin a description of our policy with the voter, the elaborate arrangement of interest groups, the parties, elections, and processes of communication through which he seeks to influence the determination of public policy or, as some would say, the allocation of the resources of our society. The modern American government is in fact a dynamic mixture of constitutional and democratic elements. The demand of various groups to play a greater role will continue to challenge any institutional arrangements which safeguard entrenched interests. The majoritarian democrat sees little validity in power assignments which cannot be modified by popular will. The constitutionalist, however, sees lawlessness and popular tyranny as consequences of serious modifications in the nicely calculated prohibitions of our legal tradition. We have in the previous chapters indicated the major elements of our constitutional system and we must now seek an understanding of its democratic aspects.

Self-government: myth or reality?

Government to many of us is some remote *they* who make decisions which affect us but for which we have no direct responsibility. We read about *them* in our newspapers, criticize *their* bungling, speculate about *their* motives and objectives. *We* feel no direct connection with them. We like to think that we believe in something called democracy, a noble conception by which men, or a large part of them, govern themselves. Only occasionally do many of us identify our own parts in this great dream. On election day, for example, thousands of us troop to the polls moved by some deep feeling that what we do on that day will in some way determine the course of national destiny. It is when we come to consider how, in fact, the people govern themselves that we begin to realize the complexities and subtleties of this system of government and also to feel any strong sense of personal identification with it.

There are many ways open to most every adult citizen to participate in governing these United States. He may vote on election days for nominees and then for candidates for the positions of power and influence. He may join one or more organizations a major purpose of which is to express to those in positions of power the views of the members on questions of public policy. He may contest a governmental order before the courts. He may seek public office himself. He may join a political party, work for it and contribute money to its support. He may entreat public officials for or against a contemplated or accomplished act of public policy. He may speak out formally or informally on the conduct of public affairs. He may, of course, decide not to do any of these and thus leave the job of governing America to others. *How citizens may participate in public affairs*

Throughout its short history democracy has meant to its proponents as well as its critics a very high degree of participation by the populace in decision-making. Certainly, most of us have been brought up to believe that an enlightened, interested, and civic-minded citizenry is necessary to successful self-government. There have been disagreements, to be sure, about the legitimacy, as well as the efficacy, of the various methods by which people do participate in public affairs, but little doubt, that it is the duty of the citizen to pay attention to his government. It is, therefore, with some dismay that we confront the facts now being revealed by survey research techniques that the level of participation in America is after all not very high. From one-fifth to one-third of the adult population are almost completely indifferent to politics —they rarely even vote. About 60 per cent vote but participate in no other important way. About 5 to 10 per cent are activists who work for or contribute to parties, join interest groups, speak to or attend rallies, and in other ways described above seek to influence public policy.[1] *Participation in America*

It would appear that either our system of civic education is woefully inadequate or that our understanding of the possibilities of the democratic system is incomplete. Students of this subject are energetically reviewing and reappraising the older concepts of what democracy entails. On one proposition at least most of the modern analysts join hands with the philosophers of yesterday and that is that popular election of those who hold the reins of the state is fundamental to a democratic society. It is appropriate, therefore, to begin our analysis of the American democratic system by a consideration of voting. The other methods of participation or lack of it, we shall consider in subsequent chapters.

[1] L. W. Milbrath, "Political Participation in the States," *Politics in the American States,* edited by H. Jacob and K. Vines (Boston, 1965). See also the same author's *Political Participation* (Chicago, 1965) for a summary of the research on this subject.

THE NATURE AND HISTORY OF THE "SUFFRAGE"

. . . the electors (of the House of Representatives) in each state shall have the qualifications requisite for electors of the most numerous branch of the state legislature. ART. I, Sec. II, Cl. 1

Constitu-
tional
basis

Every democratic system defines those who are entitled to vote for the officers of the government. In every system known to history this definition has excluded some persons (aliens and children most commonly). It is obviously of great consequence who makes this definition and on what basis, since if any great numbers are excluded, especially if any particular class, race, or religious group is excluded, to that extent the system is not genuinely based on the great body of citizens. In the United States, this determination has up to now been made by each of the 50 states. Each state has been left largely free to determine for itself who might vote for national as well as for state and local officers. The states are restricted by the Constitution only to the extent that they may not deny the right to vote to those otherwise qualified because of their race, color, previous condition of servitude (Fifteenth Amendment), sex (Nineteenth Amendment), or failure to pay a tax (Twenty-fourth Amendment), nor may they deny to any person the equal protection of their laws (Fourteenth Amendment). They are restricted by national statutes only in matters relating to racial discrimination. The national *electorate* (all those entitled to vote) is, therefore, the sum of separate electorates determined largely by state constitutions and laws.

The
"right"
to vote

It might well be asked at this point, How can any person be denied the right to vote? Is this not a natural right similar to the right of religious freedom which cannot validly be withheld? The answer to this in American constitutional theory and practice is that it is not a natural right of the type called civil rights. It is a *legal* right and belongs only to those who have been properly endowed with it. The Constitution does not guarantee to anyone the right to vote as it does guarantee that freedom of speech may not be infringed by the Congress or due process of law denied to anyone by the states. The Constitution may and has been invoked, as we shall see, to prevent discriminatory state regulations which effectively deny the vote to certain classes of citizens contrary to its provisions. It does not, however, confer the voting privilege on anyone.

Expansion
of the
suffrage

The legal theory and practice in determining who may vote may, perhaps, be best understood in the light of the history of the suffrage. When the Constitution of the United States was adopted it could hardly be said to have established a system of government as democratic as it is today. Although it recognized the idea of popular participation as the basis of just government and although, in fact, a larger number of people were authorized to and did participate in the processes of government than in most major nations of the world at that time, nevertheless, the suffrage was restricted to white, male, property-owners. Probably three-fourths of the adult males did not vote in the elections for the ratifying conventions—whether from disfranchisement or indifference is difficult to ascertain.[2] Since that time, and especially since 1810, one after another of the restrictive qualifications has been abandoned and the suffrage progressively widened to embrace nearly the whole of the adult population of this country.

The main battle against property or taxpaying qualifications for voting occurred in the older states along the Atlantic seaboard in the period 1810-50. The frontier states had no such economic distinctions and virtually all of them entered the Union without property qualifications of any kind. It was partly the political strength and example of the newer states which forced the older ones to extend the vote to the "common" people. Antipathy to Irish-Catholic immigrants induced Connecticut in 1855 and Massachusetts in 1857 to require reading and writing tests designed to disqualify the illiterate foreign-born, but by 1860, the nation had substantially achieved universal, adult, white, male suffrage. *Elimination of property qualifications*

Since 1860, the suffrage has been broadened to include Negroes and women. A few Negroes were authorized to vote in a few states (mainly in New England) before 1860. General enfranchisement of the Negroes came in the Northern states, however, only in the Civil War period. In the South, the Negro was enfranchised as a result of the pressure of the radical Republican majority in Congress during the Reconstruction era. The Fourteenth [3] and Fifteenth Amendments were added to the Constitution by the victorious Northern forces in an attempt, largely unsuccessful, to guarantee Negro suffrage in the South for all time. In many of the Southern states, the Negroes were effectively disfranchised as soon as possible after the Union troops were withdrawn in 1877. Outside the South few barriers have been erected to Negro voting and they may and do vote in large numbers. In the South the battle to regain the vote for them is still under way and the number of registered Negro voters is increasing. *Enfranchisement of the Negro*

Demand for the enfranchisement of women was heard as early as the Jacksonian era. It was pressed rather vigorously in some states during the later stages of the Abolition movement, but no legislature or constitutional convention in this period gave serious attention to the petitions presented on the subject. After the Civil War, the situation changed. The first major triumph of the cause was in Wyoming, where in 1869 women were given the privilege of voting for territorial officers on the same terms as men.[4] On being *Enfranchisement of women*

2 See R. E. Brown, *Charles Beard and the Constitution* (Princeton, N. J., 1956) for a reasoned argument that the suffrage in 1788-89 was more widespread than has usually been supposed.

3 A clause of the Fourteenth Amendment penalizing the states for abridging the suffrage except for participation in rebellion or other crime is relevant, but has never been enforced.

4 Kentucky in 1838 and Kansas in 1861 began permitting women to vote in school elections. Other states gradually took similar action, and in 1887 Kansas conferred full municipal suffrage.

admitted to the Union in 1890, this territory preserved its woman suffrage arrangements. Before the close of the century, Colorado, Idaho, and Utah also became equal suffrage states, and in the next fifteen years Washington, California, Arizona, Kansas, Oregon, Montana, Nevada, and Illinois joined the list. The suffragists then turned to the larger objective of a general nation-wide enfranchisement and finally backed the "Susan B. Anthony Amendment" (first brought forward in 1869) forbidding the United States or any state to withhold the ballot on account of sex. A few years of vigorous agitation (dramatized at one stage by picketing the White House because President Wilson continued to favor state action only, though in the end he changed his position) brought complete success. The Nineteenth Amendment was adopted by Congress in 1919 and became effective in time for the national and state elections of November, 1920. Victory for the feminists in the struggle for the ballot was part of a larger movement for feminine independence in the home, in industry, and in society. As such, it both celebrated their newly won position and contributed to it.

Contraction of the suffrage

Together with the wide extension of the voting privilege in the last century there were also a few contractions in addition to the disfranchisement of the Southern Negro. The addition of the requirement of registration,[5] the development of more rigid residence requirements, the imposition of literacy tests in some states and the addition of numerous grounds for disqualification all have served to reduce the number of persons eligible to participate in any particular election.

VOTING QUALIFICATIONS TODAY

General qualifications:

Although the qualifications for voting vary in details from state to state, at the present time there are some types of qualifications which are universally imposed and others which are employed only in certain states.[6] In the first category are age, citizenship, and residence.

1. Citizenship

Western states used to bid for settlers by offering voting privileges to aliens who had taken out "first papers." Since 1926, when Arkansas at last fell into line, every state has required of its voters that they be American citizens.[7] A few states require a person to have been a citizen for at least 90 days.

[5] Registration is not strictly speaking a qualification for voting but rather a means of identifying qualified voters. As such it will be discussed later on in this chapter in connection with election administration. The effect of the requirement, however, has been to make a larger number of "qualified" persons ineligible to cast a ballot on election day.

[6] For a table of voting qualifications state by state see Council of State Governments, *Book of the States, 1964-65* (Chicago, 1964), 24-25.

[7] For many years in the United States the laws of citizenship also varied from state to state. The Civil War finally ended this confusion with the adoption of the Fourteenth Amendment. From that time to the present all persons born in the United States are citizens regardless of the status of their parents. Children born to American parents abroad are enabled to retain citizenship under national statutes.

The legal voting age in every state but four is 21. Georgia in 1943 and   *2. Age*
Kentucky in 1955 lowered the required age to 18. Alaska entered the Union
with the age fixed at 19, and Hawaii with it fixed at 20. In inaugurating the
movement for a lower voting age, the Governor of Georgia (Ellis Arnall)
declared that the "fresh viewpoint of youth" was needed in politics and that
the young people would benefit from acquiring political experience at an early
age. Elsewhere the argument most widely pressed was that if young men and
women were old enough for military service they were old enough to vote. In
a large number of states the matter was considered at that time and rejected.[8]
Interest then subsided until it was revived by President Eisenhower. He proposed in 1954 and again in 1955 that the Congress submit a constitutional
amendment to the states authorizing citizens 18 and older to vote. The Congress on both occasions failed to respond. Southern members, generally, led
the opposition and argued for state determination of voting qualifications. A
large number of states once again considered the matter and in all except
Kentucky it has thus far been disapproved.

The typical requirement relating to residence is that the voter shall have   *3. Resi-*
lived in the state at least one year, some specified portion of which (frequently   *dence*
three or six months) must have been spent in the county, and some briefer
portion (often 30 days) in the district in which one's ballot is to be cast. No
one may vote in a given election in more than one place; and this place must
be the voter's legal residence, however little of his time he may actually spend
there. Such requirements tend to prevent importations of "floaters" at election time, but operate also temporarily to disfranchise many thousands of
adults who have moved since the last election. In view of the mobility of our
population, the numbers thus made ineligible are quite large.[9]

The payment of taxes as a qualification for voting has at one time or   *Special*
another been a requirement by 19 states. Its major modern use, however, has   *quali-*
                                                                              fications:

American citizenship may also be acquired by naturalization. Collective naturalization is, typically, accomplished by an act or treaty extending citizenship to the inhabitants
of an area acquired by purchase or conquest. Individual naturalization is accomplished
by a judicial procedure initiated by the resident alien applicant. This possibility is open
only to those who have reached 18, have resided here at least five years, can read, write
and speak English and are not associated with criminal or subversive enterprises. The
process usually takes several months and includes investigation by the Naturalization
Service.

[8] In 1946, the Democrats of South Carolina made 18 the age for voting in their
primaries; but the rule was rescinded after two years.

[9] One of the most troublesome questions raised by residence requirements is that
of the right of students attending a college or university to vote in the town or city in
which the institution is located. The crux of the matter is, of course, whether they are
legal residents. But this may be difficult to determine. If 21 years of age, continuously
resident beyond the period required by law, and especially if self-supporting, the presumption may be in the affirmative. There is, however, no hard and fast rule. Most students
regard their residence as their parents' home. Thus, they must vote at home or by mail.
For an Illinois supreme court decision on the subject, see Anderson *v.* Pifer, 315 Ill. 164,
168 (1925).

1. Payment
of taxes

been in the form of poll taxes required in Southern states as part of a system to bar Negroes.[10] After several years of agitation had succeeded in eliminating the tax requirement in all but five states,[11] it was finally outlawed by Constitutional amendment everywhere in so far as national elections are concerned. Four states (Alabama, Mississippi, Texas, and Virginia) now have the poll-tax requirement for voting in state and local elections but it is under heavy attack. The Congress has been urged to outlaw it entirely [12] and the Supreme Court has consented to reconsider its constitutionality.[13]

In six states (Michigan, Montana, Nevada, New Mexico, Texas and Utah) some kind of property tax payment is required for those voting on local bond issues or special assessments.

2. Literacy

The imposition of educational or "literacy" qualifications for voting began in Connecticut in 1855 and spread from there to Massachusetts and to New York and other New England states. In these states it was aimed at immigrants. The device was borrowed in the 1890's by most of the Southern states to keep Negroes and "poor whites" from voting and was copied by a few Western states to exclude Orientals. Nineteen states (including four in New England, four in the West, and six in the South) now have this requirement in some form.[14] In a few states the test is confined to ability to read English. In most, however, the ability to write in English is also required —though in some the ability to write one's name is adequate. A few Southern states employ an alternative test in the form of demonstrating to an election board (of white members) ability to "understand and give a reasonable interpretation" of a selected passage from the national or state constitution. The test is ordinarily conducted at the time of registration, and in the South at least, wide latitude in administering it is conferred on the local election officials. One of the fairer systems is that adopted by New York in 1921 in which a test of reading and writing designed by experts is administered by the state educational department annually for those who have not successfully com-

[10] The original poll-tax states with the dates of adoption were: Georgia (before 1860); Florida (1889); Mississippi and Tennessee (1890); Arkansas (1892), South Carolina (1895), Louisiana (1898), North Carolina (1900), Alabama and Virginia (1901), and Texas (1902).

[11] Alabama, Arkansas, Mississippi, Texas, Virginia.

[12] The issue of outlawing the poll tax by national statute in state and local elections was vigorously contested in the debate on the Voting Rights Act of 1965. The Johnson administration opposed the inclusion of such a ban on the grounds that it might not be valid. A compromise was finally worked out in which the Attorney General was directed to institute court proceedings against the levies.

[13] In Harman v. Forssenius, 85 S. Ct. 1117 (1965) the Supreme Court invalidated a Virginia requirement that in lieu of a poll tax receipt a prospective voter had to file a notarized certificate of residence to vote in national elections. The Court in this case did not pronounce on the validity of the requirement in state and local elections but agreed to hear arguments in the term beginning in October, 1965.

[14] The 19 states referred to include South Carolina, where literacy is not an absolute qualification but rather an alternative to ownership of property and Louisiana where an alternative method of qualification is permitted.

pleted the sixth grade in public school.[15] Where fairly administered, there is much to be said for this type of requirement but it has been and is widely used mainly to keep Negroes from voting. To curb abuses, the Congress finally in the Civil Rights Act of 1964 has imposed certain standards for its use in national elections: the test, if used, must be administered in writing and the candidate must be entitled to see his paper. Further, the Act stipulates that evidence of the successful completion of sixth grade of elementary schooling constitutes a rebuttable presumption of literacy. After some experience revealed that the tests were still being used adversely to the Negroes' hopes, President Johnson in 1965 asked Congress to outlaw the tests entirely in certain states. In the Voting Rights Act of 1965, the Congress did exactly that. Under the terms of the Act such tests are to be waived in any state or county that had them in force on November 1, 1964, and in which fewer than 50 per cent of the voting age population was registered at that time or voted in the election.

Certain categories of persons are almost universally disqualified from voting: inmates of prisons or asylums; violators of certain election laws, for example, those forbidding bribery; malfeasants in office; vagrants.[16]

THE PROBLEM OF ENFRANCHISING THE SOUTHERN NEGRO

The right of citizens of the United States to vote shall not be denied or abridged by the United States or by any State on account of race, color, or previous condition of servitude.

The Congress shall have power to enforce this article by appropriate legislation. FIFTEENTH AMENDMENT

The Southern states, as we have noted, were compelled to give Negroes the vote if they wished to be restored to partnership in the Union. For more than a decade the armies of the central government occupied the South to insure compliance with these commitments. The results of the Northern poli

---

[15] Only those first voters are required to submit themselves to examination (by designated school teachers, and in school buildings) who cannot present as proof of literacy a diploma showing completion of the eighth grade of a public or private school or, in lieu of that, a certificate from the school superintendent indicating completion of the sixth grade in a school (or second year in an evening school) in which English is the language of instruction. For all purposes of the law, "literacy" means ability to read a paragraph or two of fairly simple English and to answer in writing questions designed to show some comprehension of what has been read, the whole procedure occupying about five minutes. Introduction of the literacy test greatly stimulated the interest of the foreign-born in evening-school instruction. When under the Voting Rights Act of 1965 a sixth-grade education under the American flag in a language other than English was made acceptable as a standard of literacy, the New York requirement was modified accordingly.

[16] The Council of State Governments is authority for the assertion that, in one state or another, the privilege of voting can be denied for "any one of 50 or more reasons," with an average of six or seven per state.

cies were disastrous from the Southern point of view, and the Reconstruction Era has always been for them a black page in the nation's history. Gullible freedman led by Northern "carpet baggers" depleted their treasuries and mocked their cultural and social traditions. The Southern whites resorted to violence and intimidation through the Ku Klux Klan to regain control of their governments and, when the troops were withdrawn (in 1877), firmly and vigorously re-established white supremacy, partly by these methods. Fearful that national intervention might again be attempted, unhappy over the demoralizing effects of forceful methods, and anxious to legitimatize white dominion, the Southern statesmen cast about for "respectable" methods for surmounting the plain requirements of the Fifteenth Amendment.[17] Agrarian discontent in the 1880's further stimulated certain groups to find methods for weakening the power of the share-cropper and the small farmer—white or black.

The Mississippi plan

In 1890, Mississippi pointed the way for her sister states by writing into her constitution clauses under which, in order to vote, one not only must have lived two years in the state and one year in the election district, but must have paid all taxes assessed against him (including a poll tax of $2), and must be able either to read any section of the state constitution or to give a reasonable interpretation of it when read to him. None of these was aimed on its face at the Negro. The lengthy period of residence, however, barred large numbers of Negroes accustomed to drift from plantation to plantation. The poll tax was artfully required to be paid a year before election time. Few Mississippi Negroes could read, and still fewer could give an interpretation of a craftily selected passage from the state constitution likely to be accepted as "reasonable" by a white official with a strong predisposition against Negro voting. If, too, in replying to searching personal questions a candidate for registration was detected deviating an iota from the truth, he became guilty of perjury, for which also he could be disfranchised. When the Supreme Court scrutinized these provisions in a test case, it was unable to find that they in any manner violated the Fifteenth Amendment.[18] Clauses of similar purport accordingly found their way into the constitutions of most other Southern states—all going to show how ingenious men can become when trying to find a way around nationally ordained requirements not supported by local or regional public sentiment.

"Grandfather clauses"

There was, however, one drawback: while a secondary object of the tests was in some instances to curb the political effects or radical (chiefly Populist) inclinations among poor whites, the restrictions operated to debar too many whites along with Negroes. But for this, also, a remedy was found —in the so-called "grandfather clauses" adopted at one time or another, as temporary constitutional amendments, in as many as seven different states.

17 See V. O. Key, *Southern Politics in State and Nation* (New York, 1949, Chap. 25).

18 Williams *v.* Mississippi, 170 U. S. 213 (1898).

SOUTHERN NEGRO VOTER STATISTICS BY STATE
March, 1965

STATE	Total Negro Voters as of 11/1/64[1] (1)	Increase Since 4/1/62 (2)	% of Eligible Negroes Registered (3)	% of Eligible Whites Registered (4)	% Negro of Total Registered (5)	% Negro of Voting Age Population (6)	Unregistered Negroes of Voting Age (7)
ALA.	111,000	42,700	23.0	70.7	10.4	26.2	370,000
ARK.[1]	105,000	36,000	54.4	71.7	14.6	18.4	88,000
FLA.	300,000	117,500	63.7	84.0	12.0	15.2	170,000
GA.[2]	270,000	94,500	44.0	74.5	16.8	25.4	343,000
LA.	164,700	13,000	32.0	80.4	13.7	28.5	350,000
MISS.	28,500	4,500	6.7	70.1	5.2	36.0	394,000
N.C.	258,000	47,500	46.8	92.5	11.7	21.5	293,000
S.C.	144,000	53,100	38.8	78.5	17.0	29.3	227,000
TENN.	218,000	67,100	69.4	72.9	14.4	14.9	96,000
TEXAS	375,000	133,000	57.7	53.2	12.5	11.7	275,000
VA.	200,000	59,900	45.7	55.9	16.0	18.8	237,000
TOTAL[1]	2,174,200	698,000	43.3	73.2	13.0	22.4	2,843,000

[1] Arkansas figures are as of Jan. 1, 1965.
[2] Voting age 18.
SOURCE: Voter Education Project of the Southern Regional Council. Copyright, 1965, *Congressional Quarterly, Inc.*

The clauses differed in details, but their general purport was to open a way by which any man otherwise qualified could avoid the tax and literacy requirements and become a permanently registered voter if either he or a lineal ancestor had been a voter on January 1, 1867. The significance of this date is that it preceded by two months the first act of Congress prohibiting the disfranchisement of freedom. No Negro could get on a voters' list under the new provisions, but the poorest and most illiterate white could do so because of being the son or grandson of a voter of 1867. All of the clauses were for a duration of only a few years, or even a few months; and most had served their purpose and expired before the Supreme Court, in 1915, got around, in an Oklahoma case, to pronouncing them discriminatory, contrary to the Fifteenth Amendment, and therefore unconstitutional.[19] Contrary to a common misunderstanding, grandfather clauses disfranchised nobody. They did help bolster the principle of white supremacy.

Negro disfranchisement becomes general in the South

Thus, constitutional and statutory disfranchisement of the Southern Negro was accomplished with one barrier rising behind another in massive array. First of all, there was the poll tax, so obviously designed to trip up the Negro that in many places little or no effort was made to collect the tax at all from whites, and in any event payable only (whether by Negroes or whites) in election years—in effect, therefore, simply a fee for the privilege of voting. If that were surmounted, there was the literacy test, and sometimes an "understanding" test so administered that even instructors in Negro colleges often failed it. Beyond this might lie a "character" test under which a Negro aspiring to vote must produce "evidence of good character," backed by testimony from as many as ten or a dozen registered voters, and satisfactory to white registration officials disposed to be incredulous. And crowning all this was exclusion, by constitutional provision, statute, or party regulation, from participation in the only significant electoral contests in the one-party South: the Democratic primaries.

It should be understood that the Negro was not kept from voting solely by these devices. Much evidence exists to show that the Negro had been "persuaded" to stay away from the polls before these laws were enacted. The laws tended to insure that intimidation would be unnecessary in the future. The result of the persuasion, followed by the laws, however, was that Negro voting in the Southern states fell to insignificant proportion. The border states of West Virginia, Kentucky, Tennessee, and Arkansas tended, however, to have larger Negro participation than the states of the Deep South.

The attack on the poll tax

Gradually these suffrage policies of the South became part of the ac-

[19] Guinn *v.* United States, 238 U. S. 347 (1915). The Oklahoma legislature followed up this decision with a statute of 1916 requiring electoral registrars to enroll as voters only persons who were voters in 1914 (when few, if any, Negroes were on the lists), together with such others as should apply for registration during a specified 12-day period; but, on the ground that the registration period was inadequate and the measure as a whole designed to perpetuate the old discriminations, the Supreme Court eventually nullified the effort, in Lane *v.* Wilson, 307 U. S. 268 (1939).

cepted pattern of American politics. The acrimonious attacks of the late nineteenth century abated. In 1912, the Republican Party stopped writing in its
platform its traditional denunciation of Southern practices. In the past three
decades, however, the issue has exploded into national politics with as much
force as before. The two world wars of this century were accompanied by
heavy migration of the Negroes into Northern and Midwestern industrial centers. Here they have become increasingly articulate participants in party organizations, inspiring sympathetic attention to their demands on behalf of
their Southern brethren. Also as part of a general movement to eradicate
racial discrimination in all its forms from the American scene, many groups
are seeking to give the vote back to the Southern Negro. The first major
target of the urban leaders was the poll tax. As recently as 1937, however,
the Supreme Court was unable to see that, in the absence of prohibitive
national legislation, the tax requirement was invalid.[20] Congress was then
called upon to outlaw taxpaying qualifications for voting in national primaries and elections. President Truman (1948-50) strongly urged such legislation. Finally, after many states had either abandoned the requirement or
granted so many exemptions as to weaken it, the Congress in 1962 agreed
to constitutional amendment and the requisite ratifications were procured in
1964.

The next attack was on the "white primary" rules of several Southern
states. Efforts to exclude Negroes as such from Democratic Party primaries
had been successfully challenged in the courts in those instances where the
exclusion rested on express statutory or constitutional provision.[21] The Supreme Court in 1935, however, could find nothing wrong with a white primary rule uttered by a party convention and not required by state law.[22] The
problem, in part, was whether a primary was in fact an election and when
the Supreme Court held that it was,[23] the opponents of the primary renewed
their assault and persuaded the Court to reverse its earlier position.[24] If the
state, by statute, said the Court, entrusts the selection of candidates to political parties then the process by which the selection is made is part of the election and the party is acting as an agency of the state. Several expedients to
evade the consequences of this decision were also invalidated.[25] The Southern
states then fell back upon discriminatory administration of their numerous
qualifications and applied most of them to the primaries. With the demise
of the "white primary," Negro voting in the South increased sharply but by
1950 probably did not yet exceed 20 per cent of the adult Negro population
and in some states was below 10 per cent.

The "white primary" is abolished

[20] Breedlove v. Suttles, 302 U. S. 277 (1937).
[21] Nixon v. Herndon, 273 U. S. 536 (1927); Nixon v. Condon, 286 U. S. 73 (1932).
[22] Grovey v. Townsend, 295 U. S. 45 (1935).
[23] U. S. v. Classic, 313 U. S. 299 (1941).
[24] Smith v. Allwright, 321 U. S. 649 (1944).
[25] Rice v. Elmore, 165 F 2d, 387 (1947); Certiorari denied 333 U. S. 875 (1948);
Baskin v. Brown, 145 F 2d, 391 (1944). Terry v. Adams, 345 U. S. 461 (1953).

A new assault on the Southern practices occurred in the mid-fifties. Republican leaders began to join the Northern urban Democrats in pushing for electoral reform. President Eisenhower and Republican leaders in the Congress sought legislation authorizing national intervention in behalf of eligible Negro voters. As part of the first civil rights legislation of this century, pushed through Congress against strong Southern opposition by a Republican-Democratic coalition, the Attorney General was authorized to seek injunctive relief in a national court to prevent threatened intimidation or coercion designed to prevent any person from voting for national officials.[26]

National intervention

The Civil Rights Commission created by the law and authorized to inquire into deprivation of voting privileges held a series of inquiries in several Southern cities on voting practices.[27] As a result of the investigations it proposed certain changes in the law including the requirement that registration and voting records should be retained at least five years and that the President should be authorized to appoint a federal registrar to enroll voters in national elections where it can be shown that the state registrars have refused voter registration in a discriminatory way. These became the major issues in the debates in 1959 and 1960 as the coalition returned to the attack.

Civil Rights Act of 1960

The Civil Rights Act of 1960, as finally passed, enlarged the powers of inquiry of the Civil Rights Commission (the life of this Commission had been extended in 1959 and again in 1961) required that voting records and registration papers in national elections including primaries must be preserved for 22 months, and provided that when the Attorney General won a civil suit in a case of deprivation of voting privileges he might then ask the Supreme Court to make a finding that there was a "pattern or practice" of deprivation in the area. If the Court found that such existed, then a Negro in this area could apply to the Court for an order declaring him eligible to vote.[28] Voting referees might be appointed by the court to hear requests for registration orders from deprived Negroes.

Civil Rights Act of 1964

Under these laws the Department of Justice started numerous suits aimed at discriminatory administration of voting requirements but the judicial process is a slow one and Southern resistance was vigorous and stubborn. In 1961, the Civil Rights Commission issued a new report—*The Right to Vote* —summarizing months of intensive investigation and alleging that in about 100 counties in 8 states there was reasonable grounds to believe that large

---

[26] Civil Rights Act of 1957. The original version of this Act as proposed by the President would have allowed courts to punish summarily for contempt any person violating the injunction. After prolonged debate a compromise was agreed to that requires a jury trial in contempt cases arising under this provision when the summary conviction has resulted in a fine of $300 or imprisonment in excess of 45 days.

[27] The Commission's procedures were attacked in the courts and sustained in Hannah *v.* Larche, 363 U. S. 420 (1960).

[28] In order for the Negro to sustain the application in court, he was required to show that he was qualified under state law, that he had tried to register after the "pattern or practice" finding, and that he had been refused by someone acting under the color of law.

numbers of Negro citizens are denied the vote largely by the discriminatory way in which the requirements are administered by white election officials. President Kennedy called repeatedly and unsuccessfully for more national action. Through 1963 amidst mounting violence, rioting, and determined demonstrations the Congress resisted until, stung by Kennedy's assassination and spurred by one of its own sons, now President, Lyndon Johnson, it finally passed the sweeping Civil Rights Act of 1964. Once again a coalition of Republican and Northern-Western Democrats provided the legislative muscle great enough to break the Southern filibuster in the Senate and thus make passage possible. The voting rights section was, however, considerably weakened in the process. The new law: forbids disqualification from voting in national elections because of minor technical errors of omission or commission in registering or applying to register; makes it illegal to apply different standards to or require different procedures for individuals seeking to vote in the same district. It surrounds the literacy test with certain safeguards already described. After passage, the Negro leaders mounted new offensives to get their followers on the voting rolls and selected Selma, Alabama (in the heart of the "Black Belt"), as test area for demonstrations against the continued difficulties placed in the way of registration. Met with violence in a proposed march to Montgomery, the capital, to petition the governor, the National Guard had finally to be called into national service to protect them. President Johnson then called upon Congress to pass even more sweeping legislation to get the Negro the vote. His proposals submitted in March, 1964, sought *Voting* federal registrars, suspension of the literacy test, and enhanced authority for *Rights* the Attorney General to intervene in behalf of the Negro, especially in areas *Act of* or districts where fewer than 50 per cent of the persons of voting age are *1965* registered and where fewer than 50 per cent actually voted in the elections of November, 1964. The Congress approved these recommendations in 1965 and national registrars appointed by the Civil Service Commission were immediately dispatched to the counties and states determined by the Census Bureau to be eligible for them. Included in the new law were not only bans on the literacy tests but also on tests of moral character, of educational achievement, of understanding, and also on requirements that a person be certified by other eligible voters. New voting laws enacted by affected states to avoid the consequences of the new law were required to be approved by the Attorney General or the national courts before they could take effect.

The Supreme Court, in the meantime, had not been idle. It had outlawed a Louisiana literacy and "constitutional-understanding" requirement [29]

---

[29] Louisiana v. U. S. 85 S. Ct. 817 (1965). The Supreme Court also invalidated a Virginia law requiring separate voting, property, and tax records for Negroes and whites, (Virginia State Board of Elections v. Hunter, 230 F. Supp. 156, 33 U. S. Law Week, 3153, Docket #412) a Louisiana law requiring that the candidate's color be listed on the ballot, Anderson v. Martin, 375 U. S. 399 (1964), and a lower federal court had ordered the polls integrated in a Georgia county (see *New York Times*, June 3, 1962).

and had opened the way for the Attorney General to proceed against a whole state to enforce the civil rights laws [30] instead of the slower district by district method used heretofore. It may take a few years but clearly the Southern Negro is going to get the vote.

PARTICIPATION BY THE VOTER

The Southern Negro is desperately determined to get the vote. Thousands have and will risk grave injury and death to place their names on the polling lists and cast ballots on election day. And yet millions of their fellow citizens who could vote never do so. In the Presidential election of 1964, 45,000,000 (39.3%) adults of voting age did not vote. In fact, since 1916 the turnout for a Presidential contest has never exceeded 65 per cent of the potentially eligible adult population and on two occasions (1920 and 1924) *Small voting turnout* was below 50 per cent. In mid-term elections for Congress and many state offices, the turnout in the past 50 years has never exceeded half the potential and on three occasions (1922, 1926, and 1942) was smaller than one-third. Local elections and primaries show even smaller rates of participation. Despite the spread of public education and the growing impact of political decisions on the lives of our people, their performance in this regard is much poorer than that of their grandfathers. Several elections in the period 1870-1920 attracted more than 75 per cent of the potentially eligible adult population and in some more than 80 per cent. Most European democracies have much higher ratios of participation.

Institutional obstacles to voting A part of the problem is legal and institutional. In view of the variations in state requirements and state practice, in every election some number of adult citizens are technically ineligible to participate. Until 1964, for example, residents of the District of Columbia could not vote in national elections and even now are not directly represented in Congress and thus may vote only for the chief executive. Estimates vary, but as of 1965, there were still 2,000,000-2,500,000 adult Southern Negroes as yet not registered for the reasons and by the means already described. The mobility of our population operates to deprive several million adults of their voting privileges because they cannot satisfy residence requirements.[31] Of the 3 million aliens, more than half are of voting age but many are not yet able to satisfy residence requirements to become citizens. A large number of adults are traveling on business on election day, are in military service, or are bedridden. Procedures for absentee voting are still cumbersome and inconvenient in 15 or 20 states. Of course, adult inmates of prisons and asylums are disqualified.[32]

[30] U. S. *v.* Mississippi, 85 S. Ct. 808 (1965).

[31] The President's Commission on Registration and Voting Participation estimated that 4 million adults were disfranchised by residence requirements in 1950, 5 million in 1954, and 8 million in 1960. See *Report,* (Washington, 1964).

[32] See *Congressional Quarterly Weekly Report,* Sept. 18, 1964, page 2178-2180. A survey by the American Heritage Foundation in connection with the election, Nov. 6, 1956, estimated that of the 40 million adults who did not vote at that time 17 million could be accounted for as follows: insufficient residence in voting district—6,000,000;

POPULATION OF VOTING AGE
AND
VOTE CAST FOR PRESIDENTIAL ELECTORS AND MEMBERS
OF U.S. HOUSE OF REPRESENTATIVES
1920-1964

Year	Estimated Population of Voting Age (000)	Vote for Presidential Electors		Vote for Representatives	
		No.	%	No.	%
1920	60,581	26,748	44.2	25,080	41.4
1922	62,984	—	—	20,409	32.4
1924	65,597	29,086	44.3	26,884	41.0
1926	67,912	—	—	20,435	30.1
1928	70,362	36,812	52.3	33,906	48.2
1930	72,602	—	—	24,777	34.1
1932	75,048	39,732	52.9	37,657	50.2
1934	77,215	—	—	32,256	41.8
1936	79,375	45,643	57.5	42,886	54.0
1938	81,514	—	—	36,236	44.5
1940	83,512	49,891	59.7	46,951	56.2
1942	85,759	—	—	28,074	32.7
1944	89,517	47,969	53.6	45,103	50.4
1946	91,497	—	—	34,398	37.6
1948	94,470	48,691	51.5	45,933	48.6
1950	96,992	—	—	40,342	41.6
1952	99,016	61,551	62.2	57,571	58.1
1954	101,097	—	—	42,589	42.1
1956	103,625	62,027	59.9	58,426	56.4
1958	106,083	—	—	45,818	43.2
1960	107,949	68,839	63.8	64,133	59.4
1962	110,266	—	—	51,264	46.5
1964	113,931	69,007	60.6		

SOURCE: *Statistical Abstract of the U.S., 1964.*

Much effort is currently being expended to eliminate these legal and procedural impediments to greater participation.[33] We have already described

travelling on business—2,600,000; illness—5,000,000; noncitizens—2,500,000; unable to meet literacy requirements—800,000; residence in the District of Columbia—500,000; contrary to religious beliefs—115,000. *The New York Times,* Nov. 28, 1956.

[33] A few states have flirted with the idea of compelling those eligible to vote by some sort of fine. Massachusetts and North Dakota have constitutional provisions authorizing legislation of this type but neither has used it. In a few states, e.g., California and Oregon, compulsory voting measures have been rejected by the electorate. In 1896, the Missouri Supreme Court held unconstitutional a home-rule charter of Kansas City imposing a poll tax on males over 21 but exempting all who voted. Kansas City v. Whipple, 136 Mo. 475.

the irrepressible determination to give the vote to the Southern Negroes. A movement to allow newcomers in the state to vote in Presidential elections gained its first victories in 1953-54 in Wisconsin and Connecticut and has since spread to thirteen other states. Seven states also permit former residents who have not acquired residence in their new homes to vote in Presidential elections.[34] Absentee voting has increased substantially in the past few elections as procedures have been made more convenient.[35] President Kennedy in 1963 appointed a Commission on Registration and Voting Participation to suggest further steps to increase turnout. In a report delivered later the same year, the Commission proposed: (1) reducing residence requirements everywhere to six months; (2) easier procedures for absentee voting and broader grounds for permitting it; (3) proclaiming election (national) day a national holiday; (4) elimination of literacy tests and poll taxes as voting requirements; and (5) numerous other minor changes in state election laws.[36] A judicial challenge to state residence requirements for participation in Presidential elections on the grounds that they bore no reasonable relation to the election process was rejected by the Supreme Court.[37]

Efforts to remove obstacles

The major aspect of the problem of nonparticipation, however, is not legal and technical but psychological and social. Modern studies [38] of voting behavior indicate that almost one-third of adult America is apathetic to politics. The political dimension of modern life is outside the world of these citizens. They are uninformed and uninterested. They see little connection between political decision-making and the forces that shape their lives. On those rare occasions when some of them can be brought to the polls, their knowledge of candidates is scanty and of issues nil and their motivations confused. They identify with no political party and get no effective stimulation from family, friends, school, church, or campaign. The uneducated and undereducated, the unskilled and semiskilled young people, the Negroes, the dwellers in rural areas, and women contribute disproportionately to the ranks of the nonvoters.[39] Some, perhaps, are alienated or cynical [40] but there is much yet to be learned about personality and electoral behavior. Why is the

Political indiffer- ence

[34] Connecticut, Wyoming, Wisconsin, Vermont, New Jersey, Maryland, Arizona.

[35] Absentee voting is forbidden to civilians in only 3 states (New Mexico, South Carolina, and Mississippi) but in 16 states some justification for the absence is required. See *Report of President's Commission on Registration,* cited below.

[36] President's Commission on Registration and Voting Participation *Report* (Washington, 1963).

[37] Drueding *et al. v.* Devlin, 274 F. Supp. 721 affirmed 85 S. Ct. (1965). The Court did, however, hold invalid a Texas constitutional provision that any member of the armed services who moves his home to Texas during his military duty is barred from voting in that state so long as he remains in the Army. Carrington *v.* Rash, 85 S. Ct. 775 (1965).

[38] These studies are expertly summarized in L. W. Milbrath, *Political Participation,* (Chicago, 1965).

[39] See Campbell, Converse, Miller, and Stokes, *The American Voter* (New York, 1960) Chap. V. The most comprehensive study of American voting behavior.

[40] See E. Litt, "Political Cynicism and Political Futility," *The Journal of Politics,* Vol. XXV (May 1963).

POPULAR VOTE FOR PRESIDENTIAL ELECTORS, 1912-1964

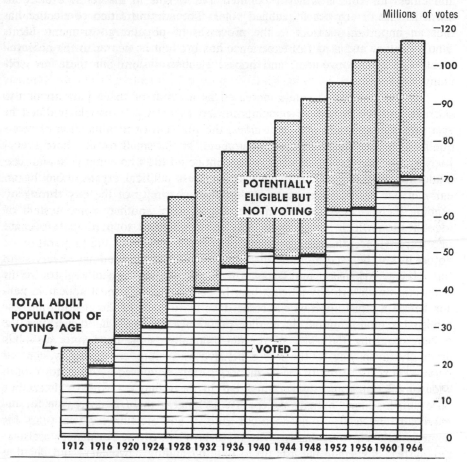

Millions of votes

POTENTIALLY
ELIGIBLE BUT
NOT VOTING

TOTAL ADULT
POPULATION OF
VOTING AGE

VOTED

1912 1916 1920 1924 1928 1932 1936 1940 1944 1948 1952 1956 1960 1964

SOURCE: U. S. Bureau of the Census.

record of this century so much poorer than that of the last? Was rural and small-town America more civic-minded than metropolitan America? [41] Is it better for democracy to get these people to the polls anyhow, anyway? Until they are adequately motivated and interested may it not do more harm than good to pry them loose from their apathy?

THE CONDUCT OF ELECTIONS

The intentions of the voter are not completely realized unless he can record them in secret, on a ballot which provides him with a choice, in a

Importance of election administration

[41] Cf. W. D. Burnham, "The Changing Shape of the American Political Universe," *Amer. Pol. Sci. Rev.* LIX, No. 1 (Mar. 1965) for some interesting suggestions on this subject.

place which he can get to, under circumstances which are not oppressive, and unless his vote is honestly counted and weighs in the result exactly as much as that of any other qualified voter. The administration of elections is thus an important element in the processes of popular government. More than a century and a half of experience has brought us nearer to the achievement of a fair, convenient, and honest election system but there are still many weaknesses.

Registration

As the number of voters increased as a result of the expansion of the suffrage and the growth of population, and especially as people huddled in ever larger numbers in our great cities, the problem of identification of those qualified to vote became increasingly acute. In the small town, where everybody knows everybody, almost any resident could tell who could vote and who could not. In the great cities, however, ruthless political organizations began early in our national history to exploit the anonymity of the city throng by sending their lackeys to vote in one district after another. Some system of identification which would allow only those qualified to participate became necessary. Hence, the rise of systems of registration and of the preparation of voting lists to be used by those directing the election proceedings. Every state but Alaska, Arkansas, and Texas now requires some type of registration in connection with virtually all elections. In general, a voter must appear in person before a registration official some days in advance of the election and establish his qualifications. An earlier preference for *periodic* registration—a system requiring the voter to register annually or at fixed intervals—has gradually given way to the less expensive and more convenient system of *permanent* registration. In the permanent system now used by 43 states (statewide in 32 states and for certain areas in the others) a voter registers but once and his name remains on the list as long as there is no reason for removing it. Typically, if he does not vote in any election for two years his name is stricken from the list. The main problem of the permanent registration system is keeping the lists up to date by adding newcomers and deleting those who have died or moved away. Sluggish and partisan administration of the system opens the door for the "cemetery" and the "vacant house" vote.[42]

Creation of precincts

In order for each voter to be able to get to the polls and to cast his ballot in the same day it is, of course, necessary that cities and counties be divided into polling districts. These districts are called precincts and are laid out by city or county officials. Typically, a precinct is designed to contain

[42] A very complete analysis of the registration systems of all states will be found in Council of State Governments, *Registration for Voting in the United States* (rev. ed., Chicago, 1946). The pricipal work on the subject is J. P. Harris, *Registration of Voters in the United States* (Washington, 1929) and his *Model Voter Registration System,* National Municipal League (New York, 1957). Cf. J. B. Johnson, *Registration for Voting in the United States* (rev. ed., Chicago, 1945), and J. K. Pollock, *Permanent Registration of Voters in Michigan* (Ann Arbor, Mich., 1937). Studies of Southern practice are: O. H. Shadgett, *Voter Registration in Georgia* (Athens, Ga., 1955) and D. S. Stray, *Registration of Voters in Alabama* (University, Ala., 1956).

Democratic Ticket

DEM.	For United States Senator **ALEX M. CAMPBELL**
DEM.	For Secretary of State **CHARLES F. FLEMING**
DEM.	For Auditor of State **JAMES M. PROPST**
DEM.	For Treasurer of State **F. SHIRLEY WILCOX**

Republican Ticket

REP.	For United States Senator **HOMER E. CAPEHART**
REP.	For Secretary of State **LELAND L. SMITH**
REP.	For Auditor of State **FRANK T. MILLIS**
REP.	For Treasurer of State **WILLIAM L. FORTUNE**

Prohibition Ticket

PROHI.	For United States Senator **LESTER N. ABEL**
PROHI.	For Secretary of State **J. RALSTON MILLER**
PROHI.	For Auditor of State **GARNETT JEWELL**
PROHI.	For Treasurer of State **HORACE N. SMITH**

PARTY COLUMN BALLOT FORM

To vote for a Person, mark a Cross X in the Square at the right of the Party Name or Political Designation. **X**

GOVERNOR — Vote for ONE
- PAUL A. DEVER - of Cambridge — Democratic
- ARTHUR W. COOLIDGE - of Reading — Republican
- HORACE I. HILLIS - of Saugus — Socialist Labor
- MARK R. SHAW - of Melrose — Prohibition

LIEUTENANT GOVERNOR — Vote for ONE
- CHARLES F. JEFF SULLIVAN - of Worcester — Democratic
- LAURENCE CURTIS - of Boston — Republican
- LAWRENCE GILFEDDER - of Boston — Socialist Labor

SECRETARY — Vote for ONE
- EDWARD J. CRONIN - of Chelsea — Democratic
- RUSSELL A. WOOD - of Cambridge — Republican
- ELLSWORTH J. M. DICKSON - of Needham — Prohibition
- FRED M. INGERSOLL - of Lynn — Socialist Labor

To vote for a Person, mark a Cross X In the Square at the right of the Party Name or Political Designation. **X**

CONGRESSMAN — Fifth District — Vote for ONE
- EDITH NOURSE ROGERS - of Lowell — Republican
- CLEMENT GREGORY McDONOUGH - of Lowell — Democratic

COUNCILLOR — Third District — Vote for ONE
- OTIS M. WHITNEY - of Concord — Republican
- JOHN A. DOLAN - of Boston — Democratic

SENATOR — Fifth Middlesex District — Vote for ONE
- RICHARD I. FURBUSH - of Waltham — Republican
- JAMES J. VAHEY - of Watertown — Democratic

OFFICE BLOCK BALLOT FORM

from 350 to 1000 voters and is a subdivision of a city ward or a rural township. Each precinct contains a polling place where the voting occurs. In general, school houses, fire stations, or other public buildings are now used for this purpose but in some areas private quarters (stores usually) are rented by the local officials.

Election officials

The next stage in preparing for elections is the designation—on a temporary basis—of a large number of election officials to preside over the polls on election day, to count the ballots and to decide disputes. These officials are selected most everywhere on a partisan basis, with the leaders of each party designating their choices for each precinct to the city, county or state officials charged with the selection. Most state laws require that some from each party serve in each district. The theory that bipartisan selection will prevent fraud in the polling place is only partly supported by the facts. Typically, five officials preside at the polls: an inspector, in charge; two judges to help decide disputes; and, two clerks who keep the voters lists, check off the citizens as they vote, and issue ballots or attend the voting machines.[43] In an effort to improve the quality of polling officials, Milwaukee in 1936 and Minnesota in 1940 authorized the use of qualifying examinations. Printed instructions are now quite generally used to inform the officials of their duties in advance. There is still much room for improvement, however, in the quality and, in some places, in the honesty of the officials.

Casting the ballots

When, on election day, the voter enters the polling place, he takes his turn in identifying himself to the clerks, carries a blank ballot to a screened compartment, or "booth," marks the ballot according to his preferences, folds the ballot, and emerging, deposits it in the ballot-box, and is duly checked off as having voted. Under only one circumstance may his privacy in the voting booth be invaded: if on account of blindness, illiteracy, or other handicap, he asks for assistance, one clerk of each party may, under normal arrangements in most states, enter the booth to give it.

Voting machines

Paper ballots are gradually disappearing. It has been estimated that about half of all the votes cast in 1964 were on voting machines. These machines are now authorized in all but a handful of states. Where such machines are employed, the voter identifies himself at the polls in the usual way, but instead of receiving a printed ballot, is directed to a curtained space in which stands the machine showing on its face the candidates' list which the ballot would contain if one were used, and where he votes by merely pulling levers—a single master lever (in states providing it) if voting a straight ticket, otherwise individual levers for particular candidates. Automatically recording votes, and simultaneously adding them up, the voting machine has the great advantages of complete secrecy, economy of time, elimination of defective votes, and full tabulation of results the moment the

---

[43] Recognized party organizations, and even individual candidates, are allowed to be represented by "watchers" or challengers entitled to observe everything done by the election authorities in connection with both the casting and the counting of ballots.

polls are closed. Aside from hesitancy to adopt new ways, and perhaps in some cases the lukewarmness of politicians toward a device that cannot be easily manipulated, the main obstacle to wider employment of voting machines is the cost of the machines themselves—something like $1700 apiece, besides transportation and upkeep. A few districts are now experimenting with electronic tallying systems [44] and perhaps in the future, punch-cards and computers may be used.

Not all voters are so situated at a given election as to be able to present themselves at the polls. The number who cannot do so is, of course, particularly large in wartime; and as far back as the Civil War, provision (although not very effective) was made for soldiers to cast their ballots *in absentia*. In addition to soldiers and sailors, there are, however, the ill and the disabled, students in attendance at distant colleges and universities, migrant workers, people away from home on business trips, and many other persons "unavoidably" or "necessarily" absent (as the laws put it) from their voting precincts at election time. Considering it unjust that people so situated should be compelled to lose their votes, Vermont led off in 1896 with a statute making general provision for absentee voting; and today all states except New Mexico [45] have laws on the subject, although in some instances applying only to certain (e.g., Presidential) elections rather than to all, and in Maryland, Mississippi, and South Carolina only to persons in the armed services. Procedures vary in detail, but in general the voter concerned makes application to the proper home official for the privilege of voting in absentia, receives a ballot directly or through an official in charge of elections where the voter is, and—after validating himself before a notary or other official—marks his ballot and mails it to the proper home authority. The Congress in 1955 recommended to the states the adoption of uniform procedures for absentee voting by members of the armed forces, sailors of the merchant marine, and civilian employees serving outside the country. In the same legislation, national officials were directed to facilitate voting by persons under their jurisdictions.

Absentee voting

When the polls close, the results are tabulated by the election officials and entered upon an official "return" which is sent to the county or city election board to be consolidated with those from other precincts. In a state-wide or national election these city or country returns are then forwarded to a state canvassing authority. All of this, of course, takes some time and it is usually several days after the election before the official canvass is completed and the results formally recorded. Meanwhile, however, the totals from each precinct are phoned into the newspapers, the city clerk, the police or the party

Counting and reporting the results

[44] The Coleman electronic vote tally system was used in one California county as early as 1962.

[45] The legislature of New Mexico in 1955 enacted legislation on the subject but its operation was made contingent upon the adoption of a constitutional amendment authorizing absentee voting and this failed to be approved.

FULL VIEW OF A MODERN VOTING MACHINE

DETAIL OF A VOTING MACHINE

headquarters where they are totalled, and these unofficial returns are announced hour by hour through the night so that the public is informed how the election is coming out.

The task of the precinct officials is completed when they return to their superiors all of the ballots (used, spoiled, and unused), poll-books, voters lists, and tally sheets which had been issued to them. When paper ballots are used, all are deposited in a sealed ballot box where they are kept for a specified period. Dishonest counting, stolen ballot boxes, stuffed ballot boxes, and mutilated voting machines appear to be a diminishing characteristic of this phase of election administration. In the past these practices were all too common in virtually every large city.

Disputed
elections

The final stage in the process is the issuance of a certificate of election to each person declared elected by the official county (county clerk) or state (secretary of state) canvassing authority. This certificate is *prima facie* evidence of legal right to hold the office. It is not, however, conclusive. All state laws make provision for disputed elections. Such cases are commonly settled in the courts except that legislative bodies, national, state, and local, invariably have the power to settle all such contests involving their own membership. Most states also make some provision for a "recount" in disputed cases. Many such laws require the candidate making the protest to pay all or part of the costs.

BALLOT FORMS

The Aus-
tralian
ballot
in
general
use

It took about a century for the American voter universally to achieve secrecy in casting his vote. Votes for many decades were cast orally and in public with untold pressures and irregularities surrounding the process. Then, for a time, each party printed its own ballots, frequently on colored paper so that watchers could tell how any person voted. Since 1888, however, the "Australian" ballot has been adopted by every state. The essence of the Australian system is that the only ballots allowed to be used at the polls are prepared by responsible public officials at public expense in accordance with forms prescribed by law and hence can be cast without possibility of detection of the ticket or person for whom one has voted. The ballot is normally in blanket form, that is, bearing on a single sheet the complete list of offices to be filled and of candidates; although when national, state and city elections are held simultaneously, the names of candidates for Presidential elector, and also of candidates for municipal offices, are sometimes printed on separate sheets. Where voting machines are used, these are prepared by public officials in accordance with state laws and are identical for all voters in the same constituency.

Ballot
forms

The arrangement of names on the ballot or machine varies from state to state but, in general, tends to conform to one or the other of two plans. In the party-column ballot, introduced in Indiana in 1889, the names of the

candidates for the various offices are ·listed in vertical columns under the *a. Party-*
name and symbol of the party with which they are identified. Typically, there *column*
is a box at the top of the column in which the voter by making a cross (or
pulling one lever in the voting machine) may vote for the entire slate of
candidates for that party. This type of ballot arrangement is designed to facilitate "straight-ticket" voting and is highly favored by professional politicians.
Some variation of the party-column ballot is now used by 33 states.[46] The
other ballot arrangement is the "office-group" ballot and was introduced in *b. Office-*
Massachusetts in 1888. On this type of ballot, the names of the candidates *group*
of all parties are grouped under the offices for which they are contesting.
Designed to place more emphasis on the office than on the party and to discourage "straight-ticket" voting, this system is less popular with the politicians. It is now used in some form in 17 states. In nine states, a separate
ballot is provided for the Presidential vote.

RECALL ELECTIONS

Normally, elections are held only when officers' terms are about to *Purpose*
expire, or occasionally to fill a vacancy arising from the death or resignation
of an incumbent. Elections are sometimes held in reverse, aimed at "recalling" an official in the midst of his term. In the early part of the present century, with a tide of "direct" popular government running strong, many people
became enamored of the idea that the voters ought to be in a position to
oust an elected official in the midst of his term if they were displeased with
him. The idea took hold to such an extent that a dozen states adopted some
form of recall procedure for use against state and local officers (usually
elective ones only).[47]

Except for the manner in which it is initiated, a recall election does not *Procedure*
differ greatly from any other one. When a movement to oust a given official
gets underway, a paper setting forth the charges against him, and known as
a "petition," is circulated in a quest for signatures. If the requisite number
(usually about 25 per cent of the electorate of the area concerned) is obtained, the city clerk or other official with whom it is filed sets a date for a
recall election (unless a regular election is about to take place). If the official
whose recall is sought chooses not to face the issue, he may simply resign.
If, however, he prefers to fight for vindication, his name is placed on the
ballot along with the names of any other persons nominated (usually by
petition) to succeed him. The voters then render the verdict. If the incumbent
polls the largest number of votes, he continues in office. But if one of his

[46] In six of these states, however, a "straight-ticket" vote is not authorized.
[47] Oregon (1908), California (1911), Washington, Colorado, Idaho, Nevada, and
Arizona (1912), Michigan (1913), Louisiana and Kansas (1914), North Dakota (1920),
and Wisconsin (1926). In only eight of these states does the recall apply to judges. The
device made its first appearance in a municipal charter of Los Angeles in 1903.

opponents outstrips him, the victor forthwith assumes the office and fills out the remainder of the term.[48]

Results

In practice, the recall has proved a very modest addition to our electoral usages. There is, it is true, no way of measuring its moral effect upon office-holders, but one can hardly believe that the comparatively few instances in which the device has been successfully invoked by dissatisfied voters represent all of the situations in which officials deserved to be ousted. A goodly number of local officers, including a mayor of Los Angeles, have been recalled in California [49]—a mayor also in Seattle and one in Detroit. But in only two instances have officials chosen by the voters of an entire state been reached.[50] It is significant that there have been no new state adoptions of the plan in more than 30 years. The terms of most public officers are short enough that dissatisfaction can readily be registered in the regular election.

CRITICISM OF THE ELECTORAL SYSTEM

The task of the electorate

Although much remains to be done, especially in our larger cities, to insure a fairer, less expensive, more convenient, and more honest system for casting and counting the votes, the improvements of the past half-century in all these respects have been substantial. The most persistent and thoughtful criticism of our electoral process is that it heaps too large a task on the voter. He is called upon to vote too frequently on too many offices and propositions. Not only is there an election of some kind in many states every year but, if primaries are included, there are two and even three a year. It is not easy for the average citizen to keep up an intelligent interest and to take an active part in so many electoral contests. More serious than this, when he does go to the polls he is confronted with a long ballot filled with scores of names and dozens of offices.[51] He cannot easily be familiar with the duties of so many offices or the qualifications of all of the candidates for them. The length and complexity of the typical ballot may be accounted for: (1) by the fact that in many states national, state, and local elections occur at the same time; (2)

[48] Under some systems, however, the first vote is on the question of recall only, with a separate election following if a vacancy results.

[49] More than 200 recall movements in California, directed almost exclusively at municipal, county, and irrigation-district officials, and resulting in 155 petitions or resignations, with 72 actual "recalls," are summarized in F. L. Bird and F. M. Ryan, *The Recall of Public Officers; Study of the Operation of the Recall in California* (New York, 1930). No such record has been established in any other state.

[50] In 1921, the governor, attorney general, and commissioner of agriculture in North Dakota were recalled because of their connection with developments growing out of the Non-Partisan League movement; and the next year, two members of the state public utility commission of Oregon (one elected by the entire state and one from a district) were recalled because of popular dissatisfaction with certain rate increases which the commission had authorized.

[51] An unusual illustration of this occurred in Illinois in 1964. Failure to apportion the state legislature resulted in all members being elected at-large and the ballot listing all the names was several feet long.

by the use of popular referenda in many states which require the voter to express his views on proposed constitutional amendments, municipal charter changes, pieces of legislation or bond issues; (3) by the large number of state and local offices that are filled by election. A great many voters start off well by voting for President, Governor, Senator, and perhaps members of the House of Representatives but then succumb to "voter's fatigue" or "fall off" and never reach members of the state legislature, the elected state officers, local officers, or referred propositions. The vote on constitutional amendments, for example, is rarely more than 75 per cent of the vote for Governor or Senator. Politicians with a small but solid block of votes to be cast for local officials can frequently determine the outcome of these minor contests. Few voters trooping to the polls to select a President of the United States will be even mildly informed on the candidates for coroner when they reach that office on the ballot.

The movement for reform is commonly called the "short-ballot" movement. One of the remedies proposed is to hold state and local elections at a different time from national elections. This simplifies the ballot in any given election and also has the merit of focusing attention on state and local issues. This is now being done in a number of states. Another remedy is sharply to reduce the number of elective officers. Only the President and members of Congress among our national officials are elected. If the same policy were adopted in state, county, and municipal government, the ballot would be much simpler. There is no excuse, say the critics, for electing essentially administrative or judicial officers. Provision should be made for appointing judges, sheriffs, coroners, district attorney, state treasurers, and all of the other offices of this type which clutter up the ballot and confuse and irritate the voter. Promoters of these reforms, however, find a deep resentment among many voters against proposals that appear to be taking away the power of the people.

The short ballot

References

V. O. Key, Jr., *Politics, Parties, and Pressure Groups* (5th ed., New York, 1963).

————, *Southern Politics in State and Nation* (New York, 1949), Chaps. XXI, XXIII-XXXI.

D. O. McGovney, *The American Suffrage Medley; The Need for a National Uniform Suffrage* (Chicago, 1949).

K. H. Porter, *History of Suffrage in the United States* (Chicago, 1918).

H. F. Gosnell, *Democracy: The Threshold of Freedom* (New York, 1948).

————, *Getting Out the Vote; An Experiment in the Stimulation of Voting* (Chicago, 1927).

E. H. Litchfield, *Voting Behavior in a Metropolitan Area* (Detroit) (Ann Arbor, Mich., 1941).

D. Anderson and P. E. Davidson, *Ballots and Democratic Class Struggle; A Study in the Background of Political Education* (Stanford University, 1943).

B. H. Nelson, *The Fourteenth Amendment and the Negro in the United States* (Washington, 1946).

J. M. Mathews, "Legislative and Judicial History of the Fifteenth Amendment," *John Hopkins Univ. Studies in Hist. and Polit. Sci.* XXVII (Nov. 6-7, 1909).

G. Myrdal, *An American Dilemma; The Negro Problem and Modern Democracy* 2 vols. (New York, 1944), especially I, Chaps. XX-XXIII.

P. F. Lazarsfeld, "Votes in the Making," *Scientific American*, CLXXXIII, No. 5 (Nov., 1950).

E. Burdick and A. J. Brodbeck, *American Voting Behavior* (Glencoe, Ill., 1959).

G. S. Blair, *Cumulative Voting* (Urbana, Ill., 1960).

A. Campbell, P. Converse, W. Miller, and D. Stokes, *The American Voter* (New York, 1960).

R. Scammon, ed., *America Votes: A Handbook of Contemporary American Election Statistics,* 5 vols. (Pittsburgh, Pa.), covers 1952-1964.

J. W. Anderson, *Eisenhower, Brownell, and the Congress: The Tangled Origins of the Civil Rights Bill of 1956-57.* (Tuscaloosa, Ala., 1964).

L. W. Milbrath, *Political Participation* (Chicago, 1965).

D. Wallace, *First Tuesday* (New York, 1964) a voting study of Westport, Conn., in four successive elections.

B. R. Berelson, P. F. Lazarsfeld, W. N. McPhee, *Voting; A Study of Opinion Formation in a Presidential Campaign* (Chicago, 1954).

E. Flexner, *Century of Struggle: The Woman's Rights Movement in the United States* (Cambridge, Mass., 1959).

L. H. Holland, *The Direct Primary in Georgia* (Urbana, Ill., 1949).

C. C. Catt, *Woman Suffrage by Constitutional Amendment* (New York, 1917).

─────── and N. R. Shuler, *Woman Suffrage and Politics* (2nd ed., New York, 1926).

E. C. Stanton, S. B. Anthony, and M. J. Gage (eds.), *History of Woman Suffrage,* 6 vols. (New York, 1887-1922).

J. P. Harris, *The Registration of Voters in the United States* (Washington, 1929).

───────, *Election Administration in the United States* (Washington, 1934).

───────, "New Primary System," *State Government,* XXI, 140-143, 153 (July, 1948).

S. D. Albright, *Ballot Analysis and Ballot Changes Since 1930* (Chicago, 1940).

───────, *The American Ballot* (Washington, 1942).

C. O. Smith, *A Book of Ballots; Representative Facsimile Ballots of Local, State, and National Governments* (Detroit, 1938).

Committee on Election Administration, National Municipal League, "A Model

Election Administration System," *Nat. Mun. Rev.,* Supp. XIX, 625-671 (Sept., 1930).

A. Heard and D. S. Strong, *Southern Primaries and Elections,* 1920-1949 (Univ. of Ala., 1950). A full statistical picture, with annotations, for 10 states.

C. A. M. Ewing, *Congressional Elections, 1896-1944; The Sectional Basis of Political Democracy in the House of Representatives* (Norman, Okla., 1947).

W. R. Yates, "The Functions of Residency Requirements for Voting," *The Western Pol. Quart.* Vol. XV, No. 3 (Sept. 1962).

U.S. Bureau of the Census, *Elective Offices of State and County Governments* (Washington, 1946).

Council of State Governments, *Book of the States,* biennially, articles and tables on election laws, voter qualifications, etc.

Presidents Commission on Registration and Voter Participation, *Report* (Washington, 1963).

★ 6 ★

Public-Opinion and Political-Interest Groups

Voting is not the whole of democracy

THE SOLITARY CITIZEN in the privacy of the polling booth, casting his vote for those who will direct his government, is a stirring dramatization of the processes of democracy. In this great drama each player, the humble and the proud, the rich and the poor, the intellectual and the workingman is equal to every other player. It is easy, however, to mistake election day for the whole of government by the people. The people of the Soviet Union also vote and in very large numbers. With them, however, voting is a testimonial to the virtue of their rulers; it is not a process for giving them direction. A democratic system must offer the voter a choice among competing programs or policies. The victor in the contest must emerge with some sense of what he is to do with his victory. Furthermore, the governors of the nation should, as we believe, be made rather persistently aware of the desires of the governed. We expect our officials to resolve the conflicts in society, and this requires that they know what these conflicts are and who and what is involved.

Group basis of politics

Influencing public policy is a far more complex task than selecting persons to hold office. Electing persons committed to the policies that we desire is but one way in which this is done. A great deal more than voting is involved even in making sure that the persons who stand for office are committed to some policies. In this aspect of democratic government the individual, as such, is relatively powerless and ineffectual. By associating himself with others of similar persuasion he mobilizes and articulates his interests and desires and places himself in a position to give direction to the government. The constituent elements of society are not solely atomic individuals or even families but also groups of many kinds. It is through the group that the individual participates in and reacts to society. It is in terms of the group that the individual very largely defines the "public good" or the "general welfare." It is as members of a group that individuals realize their personal or familial ambitions. Group activity is as much a part of the processes of government as individual behavior. Not all groups, of course, have political implications. A great many of them are formed to advance the interest—religious, economic, social, fraternal, racial—of the individuals who compose them. Advancing the interest of a group, especially the economic interest, commonly involves participation in the political process. The state with its vast power and its traditional prestige is in a position to advance benevolently or to curtail harshly the interest of any segment of society.

Groups which seek to advance the interest of their members in the political arena may be called *political-interest groups* to distinguish them from groups with other objectives. Some authors refer to these groups as *pressure groups,* which is rather a designation of one of their typical methods than a description of their general orientation. It is through such groups, however named, that citizens seek to influence the policies of government. *Political-interest groups*

One of the outstanding characteristics of the American system of government is the great multiplicity and diversity of political-interest groups which operate within it. The ease of formation, the intensity and scope of activities undertaken, and the political concern of these groups in our society exceeds that in any other in the modern world. This may be attributed in part to the tremendous technological development in the United States in the last century, accompanied as it has been by increasing specialization of function, by increasing interdependence, and by increasing ease of communication over wide distances. The rapidity of technological change has stimulated the formation of groups to soften the hardships associated with such rapid change. To put it another way, groups spring into being as a result of maladjustment in social or economic relations and seek to order anew, relationships which have been shattered by technological change. The labor union, for example, is a response to the factory system, accompanied by the removal of the management from daily face-to-face contact with the laborer. The second factor contributing to the growth and activity of political-interest groups in American society is the tolerance of our laws and customs. Freedom of association is a cherished cornerstone of the American way and is protected against undue governmental restriction.[1] Some observers assert that we are a nation of "joiners"; the necessity for group identification is a characteristic of the American individual. However this may be, it certainly is demonstrable that our society comprises more political-interest groups than any other today. *Interest groups in American society*

The interests of some groups are very frequently served only at the expense of the interests of others. The clash of such interests is the very essence of political dynamics. From the beginning of our national life the activities of economic interest groups have been regarded by many as sordid, unpatriotic, and dangerous to social unity and political stability. Sensational exposés of the "behind-the-scenes" activities of the "interests" in the legislative halls or the administrative offices still shock segments of the American populace and fill them with a sense of the futility of democratic government and the treach- *The clash of interests*

---

[1] The Supreme Court has recently held that "freedom of association" is protected by the "due-process" clause of the Fourteenth Amendment. Bates *v.* City of Little Rock, 361 U. S. 516 (1960) and NAACP *v.* Alabama, 347 U. S. 449 (1958). See also B. Smith, *A Dangerous Freedom* (New York, 1954).

ery of their officials. Group interest, in this view, is opposed to "national" or "public" interest. It is unkind but just to point out that the interest groups whose conduct revolts us and whose machinations we distrust are not the groups to which we belong. James Madison, in the most frequently quoted of the Federalist papers (No. 10), revealed his keen understanding of the role of interest groups in society and of the place of the government in respect to them:

> A landed interest, a manufacturing interest, a mercantile interest, a moneyed interest, with many lesser interests, grow up of necessity in civilized nations and divide them into different classes, actuated by different sentiments and views. The regulation of these various and interfering interests forms the principal task of modern legislation, and involves the spirit of party and faction in the necessary and ordinary operations of the government.

In the same essay Madison took some pains to show that the constitutional arrangements of 1787 were designed to prevent any one group from ever getting the upper hand. Whether regarded as signs of illness or of health in the body politic, the activities of interest groups are an essential part of the American scheme of democratic government.[2] It is impossible to understand the behavior of political leaders, legislators, executives, judges, or even the voters themselves except in terms of the groups with which they tend to identify themselves or from which they expect support.[3]

American system and interest groups   One other characteristic feature of our governmental system influences not only the number but the activities of the interest groups of our society. The federal system, the division of power among three branches of government at the various levels, and the two-party system provide an unusually large number of points of access to power and influence. Interest groups thus may aspire to influence by working at a number of entrances, and each of the doors is likely to be well attended by numerous and conflicting groups. No single door leads certainly and inexorably to domination of the nation.[4]

POLITICAL-INTEREST GROUPS IN ACTION

Numbers of groups   How many political-interest groups are active on the American scene no one can say with accuracy. At least 500 maintain permanent headquarters

[2] The American public is apparently ambivalent on interest-group activities. There is a feeling that it is effective for others but improper for oneself. See L. W. Milbrath, "Interest Groups in the States," in H. Jacob and K. Vines, *Politics in the American States* (Boston, 1965).

[3] For detailed analyses of the influence of group membership on voting see A. Campbell, P. E. Converse, W. E. Miller, and D. E. Stokes, *The American Voter* (Ann Arbor, Mich., 1960) sec. IV.

[4] For balanced and comprehensive treatments of the role of interest groups in American government consult D. B. Truman, *The Governmental Process* (New York, 1951) and A. F. Bentley, *The Process of Government* (New York, 1908). This section is very largely based upon these two works.

in the national capital but this is only a small portion of those that are politically active at some level of government. The Department of Commerce in 1949 listed 4000 national trade, professional, civic, and other associations.[5] If account is taken of local branches, chapters, affiliated units and independent local groups, there are perhaps 150,000 groups more or less active in politics.[6] The number swells or recedes daily as new groups are formed and old ones languish. Most of these groups and associations have interests other than political ones and the intensity of their political activity varies widely from one year to the next and among themselves. All of them are at least potentially political forces. Even among those that are regularly active politically there is great diversity. Some number only a handful of adherents; others have memberships running into the millions. Some have little money to spend; others have a great deal. Some have more or less elaborate headquarters and secretariat; others engage the attention of one part-time employee. It is possible here to describe only a few of the more important ones.

One of the largest spokesmen for the "business community" is the *Business* Chamber of Commerce of the United States. The Chamber is essentially a *groups* federation of local Chambers of Commerce and these include firms as well as individuals and typically embrace the merchants, manufacturing establishments, and financial and service institutions in each substantial community. It is thus a cross-section of the "business" interests of the country and cannot and does not commit itself to political issues about which the business community is sharply divided. In the national scene it can regularly be found attacking governmental regulation of prices or wages, supporting reductions in the tax rates on profit or investment, advocating rigid economy in government—except in the public works fields where many of its local chapters are strong pleaders for new post offices, river and highway improvements, maintenance of government installations, and defense contracts—and assailing any government protection for labor unions. The national headquarters produces and publishes material for the members, for Congress, and for Congressional committees, urging its point of view on matters in which it is interested. In *Nation's Business* it presents its views to the public. Its position in national questions is frequently determined by the results of a referendum of its constituent groups.[7]

Close to the Chamber in size and even more aggressively belligerent in behalf of the interests of industrialists is the National Association of Manufacturers (NAM) organized in the 1890's. Composed of firms engaged in every type of manufacturing, its chief focus throughout this century has been

---

[5] U. S. Department of Commerce, *National Associations of the United States* (Washington, 1949).

[6] A very high proportion of these groups are "business" groups and have memberships of fewer than 100 persons.

[7] Consult the annual *Policy Declarations of the Chambers of Commerce of the United States* for its current position on national issues.

to counteract the power and influence of organized labor.[8] Since 1933, when it was reorganized, it has been more or less dominated by the large corporations. It can be relied upon to support private enterprise, governmental curbing of labor unions, economy in government, low taxes (on profits, incomes, or manufacturing), and similar views on which industry as a whole is agreed. It maintains friendly, and in some cases paternal, relations with the thousands of trade associations organized in the last three or four decades to promote the interests of particular industries, such as the Cotton Manufacturers Association, Newspaper Publishers Association, Iron and Steel Institute, Automobile Manufacturers Association. For years the NAM was a staunch advocate of the protective tariff, but its policy today is not quite so clear, as many industrialists have shifted their views.[9]

Labor groups   The outstanding pleaders for the interests of organized labor are the American Federation of Labor and Congress of Industrial Organizations (AFL-CIO), and the railroad brotherhoods. The AFL-CIO, like the Chamber of Commerce, is a federation, in this case of unions and represents a merger of the AFL with the CIO. Many of the older AFL unions are organized on the craft basis (carpenters, plumbers, etc.) while many of the CIO unions are organized on the industrial basis (auto workers, steel workers, etc.). The federation is importantly concerned with achieving peaceful relations among these unions and with representing the unions' point of view to the public and to the government. Traditionally, the AFL had opposed governmental restriction on the freedom of labor to use its customary methods in dealing with employers. It had also opposed the use of governmental power in regulating many aspects of the economy. It has been gradually modifying these attitudes to one more sympathetic to governmental intervention in behalf of workingmen. And now it will usually be found with its partner supporting minimum wage legislation, unemployment insurance, public housing, and many public welfare programs. The CIO had been more disposed to governmental action from its origin than its parent, the AFL. Its representatives could usually be found supporting emergency price controls, wage and hour regulation, social insurance, expanded public educational programs and many other policies aimed at benefiting the laboring man.[10] The merger of these two great federations late in 1955 produced what has been described as the most formidable interest group in American politics. Since merger, however, one of the largest unions, the Teamsters, has withdrawn amidst charges of corruption and dictatorship in its organization. The railroad brotherhoods are the most conservative of the union organizations. They

---

[8] For a study of its earlier activities see A. G. Taylor, *Labor Policies of the National Association of Manufacturers* (Urbana, Ill., 1928).

[9] See *Industry Believes,* annual statement of the NAM for its current positions.

[10] The position of labor can be found in the AFL-CIO News, a weekly publication and in the pamphlets and newsletters prepared by the political arm of the federation, COPE (Committee on Political Education).

direct a large share of their political energies to those special programs of government dealing with the railroad industry.

The most powerful organization representing the farmers' interests is the American Farm Bureau Federation. A product of agrarian discontent in this century, it is a federation of county farm bureaus organized around the county extension program of the United States Department of Agriculture.[11] Although its membership blankets the nation, it is especially strong in the Midwest and South and is sometimes described by its critics as an alliance of cotton and corn. Clearly it represents the more successful farmers. The Bureau speaks with a strong, and frequently compelling, voice on such subjects as price supports, parity, increased agricultural research and extension and against high property taxes, governmental production controls, and trade regulation.[12] The National Grange dates from the agrarian upheavals of the 1870's and at one time was one of the most belligerent of all farm organizations. Its membership and strength are now largely confined to New England and the Middle Atlantic states and it reflects the conservatism of the farmers of those areas. It is a strong supporter of the family farm against the large commercial farm, an enemy of organized labor, and an eloquent advocate of the spiritual superiority of rural life.[13]

Farm groups

The National Farmer's Union is the most reform-minded of the great farm groups and represents the marginal farmers of the Plains. Its strength is centered in Oklahoma, Nebraska, Colorado, and the Dakotas. It has been a strong supporter of high, rigid price supports, the cooperative movement and has been consistently friendly to organized labor. The newest and most militant of the farm organizations is the National Farmers Organization which has organized a number of strikes against processors of farm products in the last few years.

This is but a small sample of the active and influential groups identified with the sectors of the economy. Every sector has its groups. The professions are all organized. In fact, the American Medical Association is one of the most generously financed and politically active groups in the country. It has been among the top spenders on lobbying as it has opposed government-supported medical care in connection with old-age insurance. The explosive race questions of modern American politics are agitated by many groups: White Citizens Council and Ku Klux Klan on the one hand and National Association for the Advancement of Colored People, Committee on Racial Equality,

Other groups

[11] The tie between the Farm Bureau Federation and the Agriculture Extension Service was formally severed under Secretary Benson. See W. J. Block, *The Separation of the Farm Bureau and the Extension Service; Political Issue in a Federal System* (Urbana, Ill., 1960).

[12] See O. M. Kile, *The Farm Bureau Federation Through Three Decades* (Baltimore, 1948). For an extensive bibliography on agricultural politics see C. M. Campbell, *The Farm Bureau and the New Deal* (Urbana, Ill., 1962).

[13] See C. M. Gardner, *The Grange—Friend of the Farmer* (Washington, 1949).

Christian Leadership Conference, Student Non-Violent Coordinating Committee on the other. Veterans groups—the American Legion, the Veterans of Foreign Wars—have been especially active in pressing the claims of ex-servicemen upon the government at all levels and also promoting patriotism, and attacking unorthodoxy of many kinds. The promotion of political ideologies, particularly of the extreme right, has stimulated the organization of the John Birch Society, Christian Anti-Communist Crusade, and many "Constitutional" societies of various descriptions. To the left of center is the Americans for Democratic Action—a militant non-Communist movement aimed at capturing the reform leadership from the Marxists. We could extend the list for several pages for it is hard to imagine an interest, feminist, child, preacher, teacher, censor, consumer that has no group speaking for it.

Group organization   Effectiveness in advancing the interests of the group in the political arena is generally held to depend in large part on organization. A treasury, a permanent staff, a headquarters, an annual convention, a news organ, these are regarded as minimal needs for group success. Many groups are organized in the most casual way with little money and no staff. The group interests, however, which persist and which command attention and enjoy influence are, typically, highly organized. Commonly, the group is supported by dues or contributions from the members supplemented by gifts from affluent supporters. Several of the groups operate profitable enterprises (publishing, insuring, loaning) as a source of part of their fiscal requirements. Many groups which lay claim to large membership and substantial popular sympathy are entirely supported by a few large contributors whose backing is not apparent. Many of the groups operating in national politics are federations of local or state groups which are active at those levels. These groups are likely to exhibit less cohesion and to have more internal disagreements on policy than the groups with unitary-type organizations. Some groups are directed and controlled by elections and referenda and periodic conventions in which a large part of the membership participates. Most groups, however, are dominated and directed by a small portion of the total membership. Some are controlled completely by one man. Some groups make no pretense to democratic procedures for determining the group position on public issues. In recent years, however, most groups have claimed to be democratic. Almost every group operates on the basis of a formal constitution approved by the members at some stage in its organization. The permanent staff is likely to be especially influential in most group activities and decisions, regardless of how it may be selected. In some groups the entire staff spend all their time promoting group political interests. In others, with broader scope, this phase of the group interest is assigned to a special bureau, committee, or person.

Methods employed: How do these organized groups go about the business of promoting group interest in the politics of the nation? The best-known method is lobbying before the legislature. This method, as we shall describe later in more detail, takes many forms but may be summarized as presenting the group point of view to individual legislators or before legislative committees. Urging the peculiar claims of one interest group upon public officials is not confined to the legislative halls. In modern American government, wide discretion to benefit or to harm certain interests is conferred on administrative agencies and individual administrators, and increasingly the spokesmen of interest groups seek out those concerned in the executive branch to make timely representations on behalf of their members. Even the courts are not immune to these representations.[14] A substantial amount of litigation, contesting legislative or administrative decisions, is carried before the judiciary by interest groups rather than by individuals in their own interests. The smaller, less affluent groups are likely to hire skilled pleaders to present their views before the various governmental agencies; the larger groups make this the business of their permanent staffs. Not all of the special pleading before the government is done by or in behalf of interest groups. Some corporations and individuals make representations on behalf of their own interests. Much of their representation is, of course, done by members of the bar.

1. With the government

Interest groups seek to influence the policies and personnel of political parties as well as of the state. Claims on behalf of these groups are frequently urged upon party platform committees at all levels of government and upon individual members of important party committees and conventions. Although many of the groups prefer, and some practice, a kind of neutrality as between parties or among candidates, several of them seek to promote the candidacy of individuals favorably disposed to their claims and to assist one or the other of the major parties to victory.[15] Influence in party circles is sought, and sometimes achieved, in many ways: by contribution to campaign chests, by grants of publicity or office space, by loans of skilled personnel to candidates or parties. Some avowed spokesmen of large interest groups stand for office as candidates in their own right.

2. With the parties

In modern times, interest groups have more and more sought to go beyond the traditional methods of dealing with a few important statesmen or party leaders on a private and personal basis and by propaganda to cultivate a favorable attitude on the part of the great mass of citizens not members of the group. In other words, they have tried to build a broadly-based support, a favorable climate of opinion, which legislators and executives will be obliged to respect. Every known medium of communication with the public is used by one or more interest groups: newspaper releases, radio broadcasts, periodicals, television programs, leaflets, brochures, speeches, advertisements. Much of this publicity is so artfully contrived and so skillfully inserted in the stream of daily communication that its source is not apparent and its bias not

3. With the public

14 See for example, C. E. Vose, "Litigation as a Form of Pressure Group Activity," *The Annals of the American Academy of Political and Social Science.* Vol. 319 (Sept., 1958).

15 See N. A. Masters, "The Politics of Union Endorsement of Candidates in the Detroit Area," *Midwest Journ. of Pol. Sci.,* Vol. 2 (Aug., 1957).

disclosed. Much of it, of course, bears the imprimatur of the group which has sponsored it. A direct method for appealing to the public is the demonstration: picketing, "sit-in," march. Used occasionally in the past by labor unions, suffragettes, pacifists, the unemployed, and others, this technique has been and is being extensively used in the civil rights movement of today. It has been particularly effective where the participants have been capable of rigid self-discipline but it can easily lead to violence and has done so on numerous occasions. It is also a system with which it is hard to reason or to compromise.

LIMITATIONS ON INTEREST-GROUP EFFECTIVENESS

Interest-group politics not all of democracy

Having been exposed for the first time to the activities, especially the successes, of economic interest groups in our governmental system, young citizens are apt to be disillusioned. The idyllic view of the unselfish, responsible citizen majestically casting his ballot in behalf of what is good for the public and not necessarily for himself, and by this process electing statesmen who take the same attitude, is an easy one to puncture. Unfortunately, many citizens never grow in understanding beyond the sophomoric conception that all of the processes of democracy in America can be summarized in the selfish, ruthless, immoral, and deceitful behavior of certain interest groups and their representatives. It is as easy to mistake interest-group operation for the whole of American democracy as it is to mistake voting for the whole of it. What saves us from a polity dominated wholly at each level by the stronger or the wilier interest group or groups at that level?

Conflicting loyalties of group members

In the first place, many citizens identify themselves with a number of interest groups. It is quite possible for a person to be a member of the Retail Grocers' Association, a member of the American Legion, a Republican, a Lutheran, a member of the Parent Teachers Association, and a member of the Chamber of Commerce all at the same time. These groups may frequently be found urging mutually contradictory policies upon the government. His Grocers' Association may be attacking a sales tax which his Chamber of Commerce is supporting. His veterans organization may be demanding preference for veterans in teaching positions which his educational association is opposing. His party may require his support of a candidate who is wholly obnoxious to his Legion Post. No group can fairly represent the whole of a citizen's public views. No group can make the politician's job of balancing and reconciling conflicting views unnecessary. When group conflict occurs where overlapping membership is common, the group spokesman cannot command the effective loyalty of the whole membership and cannot, therefore, swing it behind the group program either at the ballot box or before the officers of the government. The larger the group, the more likely it is that most of its members will have other loyalties which may at any time conflict with loyalty to that group.

In any group there is usually only a hard core of members who react to all political issues as members of that group.

In the second place, members of the same group frequently disagree on policies which affect the group. The larger the group, the more unlikely it is that it can reach agreement on anything. The huge federations like the Chamber of Commerce or the AFL-CIO find that the numerical strength which makes them formidable makes them soft. The "business" community is to some extent a myth. Individual men and firms have decided differences on what is good national policy. A high tariff may be a fine thing for the watch-making industry; it may be a bad thing for the automobile industry. What stand can the NAM or the Chamber of Commerce take on the tariff issue and still hold their members' loyalty? Furthermore, there is a tendency for the permanent staff to act as if it were the whole group, to arrogate to itself power to make policies which the group does not in fact support. Balloting has frequently revealed that the members do not act like the leaders say they are going to do. The point is that if the group leaders cannot punish on election day the politicians who have opposed the group interests, they have, to that extent, made it less necessary for the politicians to please them. A politician will, typically, be more responsive to interest-group pressure if he feels that the group can hurt him. Parenthetically, the representation of group interests informs the politician of possible repercussions to policy decisions which he is contemplating. Lobbying, thus, serves the valuable purpose of a barometer of the political weather in the politician's district. *Lack of internal cohesion in groups*

In the third place, most citizens and perhaps even most members of any particular group are not aware of the group's activity or its program. We have observed in the previous chapter that political activism is a role chosen by a very small minority of our people. While the typical American may well be a member of some organization,[16] the number of members who actively participate in the group deliberations or identify with its program is quite small, probably below 10 percent. It is, therefore, most unlikely that the inactive and indifferent multitude can be relied upon to behave politically as the group leadership would like it to do. *Indifference of most members*

Finally, there are a large number of genuine and deeply felt interests in society which are rarely expressed and are almost never organized. There is a great deal of loyalty among our citizens to the traditions of American government as they understand them and to ethical conceptions like the Golden Rule or the Ten Commandments—to the "rules of the game" in a phrase. An organized group interest which flouts any of these traditions is likely to lose the loyalty of many of its members. What is more serious, it is likely to arouse *The unorganized interests*

---

[16] Almond and Veba in their studies of civil cultures found 57 percent of their American respondents were members of some organization but only half of them believed the organization had any political interest. Quoted in L. W. Milbrath, "Interest Groups in the States" in H. Jacob and K. Vines, *Politics in the American States* (Boston, 1965), 105.

these deep-seated interests on the part of the public, that is, the nonmembers of that group. It is easy to underestimate the force of these unorganized interests in our society simply because they are not organized and ordinarily have no spokesman. When any of these interests are threatened, however, they come vigorously to the surface of the political sea and assail those who endanger them. The best example of the role of the unorganized interest is the attack on corruption in government. There are interest groups that promote their own advantage by coarse methods: bribery, entertainment of officials, expensive presents. When exposed to public view, these methods frequently stimulate the expression of the unorganized interest in honesty in government. When corruption is rife, this interest in preserving honesty in government is likely to become organized and mobilized to "throw the rascals out." Many politicians and interest-group leaders have found to their sorrow that there is a limit beyond which they cannot go without arousing this slumbering interest in clean and honest government. Loyalty to interests like those in maintaining the separation of powers, respect for the individual, fair play in governmental procedures, and the federal system may seem to be weak and ineffectual in everyday life, but let a group, a party, or an individual attempt or seem to attempt to undermine or destroy them and these interests arise quickly to the surface of political consciousness of many of our citizens. Loyalty to the rules of the game is quite as strong, even if latent, as loyalty to an interest group.

PUBLIC OPINION

Party orators and interest group propagandists usually try to pose as upholders of the traditions of our society. In seeking popular approval they tend to identify their policy or program with the latent or unorganized interests in democracy of constitutional government. While such appeals are testimonials to the belief that our society is dedicated to these ideals, they are also witnesses to the view that public opinion is important and influential in the conduct of public affairs. The spread of equalitarian ideas, the achievement of literacy among the masses, and the development of an elaborate network of communication have all aided in placing our governors under the strong, if not decisive, influence of public opinion. "The voice of the people is the voice of God," is the trite way this view is usually declaimed.

Democracy and public opinion: (a) Myth

Every form of government in the modern world seeks mass approval of its policies and fear of public hostility is by no means confined to the democratic states. And yet the democratic system is built upon popular consent and therefore peculiarly dependent upon public views. Apologists for the democratic ideal—its critics too—have postulated a direct correlation between majority will and public policy. Some see the government in a democratic society, for good or ill, as under the constant and decisive influence of the concerted and more or less spontaneously developed will of the masses.

The ballot box is the most concrete and most important vehicle for the expression of this will but it is not the only one. Individuals are expected to be alert to the tides of affairs and to speak out from time to time on the issues of the day, either alone or in concert with others. In democracies, at least, these views if widely enough held are expected to be controlling.

New knowledge and bitter experience have combined to challenge the validity, the feasibility, and the wisdom of these cherished postulates. Psychologists probing the subconscious have shown that attitudes and opinions can be and are influenced by nonrational experience and that skillful manipulation of the stimuli can evoke desired response. Thoughtful men everywhere have taken alarm at the brutal and unreasoning aberrations of great masses of supposedly educated people as exhibited in Nazi Germany, for example. The extent of public ignorance even with the achievement of literacy has shocked others. On many issues in which some are deeply concerned, a vast majority know little, understand little, and care little about the matter in controversy. Opinion which emerges in these cases is actually that of a small minority with high stakes in the outcome. Even the ballot box speaks in equivocal language. Electoral triumph may depend on "image" carefully contrived—rather than commitment to program or policy.

(b) Reality

Heretofore the problems of empirical verification of the nature, content, and direction of public opinion have been formidable. What can validly be accepted as demonstrating a popular attitude? Do statesmen pay any attention to the various and frequently contradictory expressions of opinion? Is not all of this apparent deference to the public merely a ritual designed to give the appearance of legitimacy to the actions of the few rulers? Cannot skilled modern sophists manufacture opinions to specification? Is there any relation between the opinions a person holds on public affairs and the way he votes or the party with which he identifies himself? Should greater stress be placed on civic education or should we quit trying to badger the "man-in-the-street" into taking an interest in something for which he is poorly equipped?

Testing the assumptions

The invention of and the continued improvement in the technique of sample-interviewing for testing public attitudes have in the past few decades offered an opportunity to probe the nature and influence of citizen opinion. Many of the best minds in sociology, psychology, and political science are now studying these questions and striving for light in this cave-like world. The validity of modern inquiries is, of course, dependent upon the validity of the sampling technique. Capturing and recording and analyzing the attitudes of a substantial majority of the American people is manifestly impossible. If some small number (500-5000) could be taken to represent the whole, then intensive and repeated interviewing of these could reveal many things about opinion that students and statesmen need to know. The polling system may, as in earlier studies, assume that attitudes on public matters are influenced by economic, religious, ethnic, geographical, and similar factors and use

Survey-research

these as the basis for constructing a sample of the body politic, or, as in more modern techniques, it may select its sample at random on a geographic basis.

The sampling technique first achieved wide and impressive popularity when it was used in 1936 to predict the outcome of the Presidential election and scored astonishing success, especially when compared with the straw-vote system used for several years by the *Literary Digest* magazine. Until 1948, the pre-election polls conducted by the American Institute of Public Opinion, Elmor Roper and others gained increasing prestige and respectability but the forecast in that year of a Dewey victory brought them under a cloud from which their cautious forecasts of 1952 and 1960 and more accurate predictions of 1956 and 1964 have not completely removed them.[17] Whatever public confidence they may or may not elicit, however, there is no question that the parties and the candidates are placing greater and greater reliance upon polling in planning campaign strategy and in determining issues to emphasize. Each party in 1960 and in 1964 had its own private polling experts and huge sums were expended by aspirants and candidates for detailed polls of voter attitudes.[18]

*Polling
on issues* The sample-interview or polling system is also used widely to measure sentiment on questions of public policy as they arise in the course of events. In fact, some of the leading pollsters assert that they are valuable, if not essential, additions to the democratic process. They not only tell public officials how the people feel about proposed courses of action—and in a democracy officials should know this—but also reveal areas of ignorance and indifference which should aid those involved in planning programs of civic education. The value of the election-poll and of the issue polls is still widely debated. Many people feel that predictions cannot be validly made and the effort should be abandoned; others that the consequences of publishing results

[17] See F. Mosteller *et al., The Pre-election Polls of 1948* (New York, 1949), for a thorough study of the failure of 1948 in the light of previous polling experience. In 1952, the final Roper poll showed Eisenhower 49 percent, Stevenson 37 percent, and undecided 14 percent and the final result was Eisenhower 55 percent and Stevenson 44 percent. The Gallup Poll also showed Eisenhower leading Stevenson but with a decisive undecided vote. However, the polling organizations made no flat predictions and claimed the election was too close for a definite forecast. In 1956, Roper made no outright prediction; Gallup forecast an Eisenhower victory. In 1960, Roper's final poll showed Nixon 49 percent and Kennedy 47 percent. Gallup's final poll gave Kennedy 49 percent and Nixon 48 percent. All pollers qualified their final predictions to allow victory for either candidate. In 1964, Gallup's final poll showed Johnson 64 percent and Goldwater 36 percent. The Louis Harris Poll showed the same split. In both cases the undecided vote has been allocated.

A very good explanation of the sampling procedures used by both Gallup and Roper and a defense of their value may be found in replies each sent to a long set of questions posed by Senator Gore (Tenn.). See *Congressional Record, Senate* (Feb. 11, 1960), pp. 2203-2205.

[18] See T. H. White, *The Making of the President, 1960* (New York, 1961) and *The Making of the President, 1964* (New York, 1965) for accounts of the use of various polling experts, notably the Louis J. Harris organization, by Kennedy and Johnson and of others by Nixon, Goldwater, Rockefeller and the party headquarters.

are unfortunate—creating band-wagon effects or showing the woefully inadequate state of public understanding.[19]

Whatever the merits of this controversy, the controlled, objective, and *Polling*
increasingly knowledgeable use of the sampling technique by scholars has *and*
provided us with much new knowledge about political behavior and public *opinion*
attitude.[20] It has also suggested vast areas of ignorance about the practices *studies*
and professions of democracy. We have already noted that these studies indicate that a very small proportion of the adult population is active politically
and that the large mass of people is characterized by varying degrees of indifference, misunderstanding, ignorance, and docility. There is some evidence,
that within the large mass is some vague sort of consensus about the nature
of and their expectations from government.[21] Among the activists, however,
is a deeper appreciation and wider attachment to the rules of American government and they normally operate within this framework. The activists probably are too numerous to form a self-conscious power elite but are certainly
too few to justify any very extravagant claims for the majoritarian basis of
public policy.

Among the major influences on the formation of public attitudes are *The*
the family, school, the group, the party, the mass media of communication. *formation*
Party loyalty, for example, appears to be strongly influenced by family tradi- *of*
tion and party identification is likely to be acquired before almost any other *opinion*
type of political awareness. The disposition to political activism seems also to
be influenced by familial behavior. The school provides the setting for peer-
group influences to operate and the materials for transmitting the cultural
heritage including political concepts. The group provides pressure for conformity to group norms and also articulates more precise positions on public
policy. Leaders who are liked or trusted are likely to aid their followers in
crystallizing and channeling their views.

As sources of information and influence the mass media of communica- *The mass*
tion play a significant role in the American democratic process. Mass media *media and*
opinion is likely to be accepted as public opinion. When politicians talk about *opinion*
what the public is thinking they frequently base their statements on what the
mass media are saying. Many citizens learn what they know about the conduct of affairs from the news reports and broadcasts. Most politicians cultivate a favorable media "image" as diligently as a manufacturer promotes the

[19] See L. Rogers, *The Pollsters; Public Opinion, Politics, and Democratic Leadership*
(New York, 1949).

[20] The Survey Research Center of the University of Michigan has probably the most
complete collection of data and has produced one of the most important bodies of
research in the field. *The American Voter* previously referred to contains the most complete statements of the findings of the Center.

[21] Cf. H. McCloskey, "Consensus and Ideology in American Politics," *Amer. Pol.
Sci. Rev.*, Vol. LVIII (June, 1964); V. O. Key, *Public Opinion and American Democracy*
(New York, 1961). Chap. 2 raises some doubts about a consensus on principles of
government; R. E. Lane, *Political Ideology; Why the American Common Man Believes
What he Does* (New York, 1962).

*Limitation
on news-
papers as
media of
communi-
cation*
sale of his product. The primary function of news reporting, according to journalists, is to inform public opinion. This is admittedly difficult without also influencing or molding attitudes. Facts are hard to handle meaningfully and interestingly. Which facts are to be reported? There is not space or time for all. Which will be read? However factual or dispassionate the story, if not read, it will inform no one. What significance is to be attached to the "facts"? Reporting happenings without background and statements without context is meaningless. Some, however, place primary emphasis on the molding and attach only secondary importance to the informing.

On the whole, ours is probably the best-informed citizenry in the world today. Nevertheless, our media are not perfect vehicles of public communication: (1) They have become large-scale enterprises and thus cautious, semi-monopolistic, and dependent upon maintaining a wide reader-interest; (2) they labor under a great shortage of time for reflection and review—they must publish each day; (3) the people who write the news cannot possibly know enough properly to evaluate everything they must report; (4) news must, therefore, be presented dramatically, usually as conflict or controversy, and highly personalized. These attributes of the modern metropolitan daily newspaper, the great news telecasts, and the weekly magazines reflect to a large extent the social environment in which they operate. Circulation or listening audience is the key to business success. Getting and keeping readers consists in serving them what they want to read. Mass circulation means mass appeal and this means sensationalism, comics, department store advertising, advice to the lovelorn, sports, and glamor. In spite of their obvious limitations, it is easy to overestimate the direct influences of newspapers. For 20 years—from 1932 to 1952—the overwhelming majority of American newspapers were unsympathetic, if not openly hostile, to the party and its leaders repeatedly returned to power by a majority of the voters.

About all of this, however, we have much yet to learn. What are the elements of the consensus? How is wide agreement on the rules of humanitarian democracy produced? How much influence do the various elements of our society exert. How can basic predispositions be modified? What links private and personal attitude to public decision? [22]

References

1. POLITICAL INTEREST GROUPS

D. D. McKean, *Party and Pressure Politics* (Boston, 1949), Chaps. XVIII-XXIX.

H. A. Bone, *American Politics and the Party System* (New York, 1965).

[22] An excellent summary of the state of present knowledge as of 1960 is V. O. Key, *Public Opinion and American Democracy* (New York, 1961). Another stimulating synthesis is R. E. Lane and D. O. Sears, *Public Opinion* (Englewood Cliffs, N. J., 1964).

R. H. Penniman, *Sait's American Parties and Elections* (5th ed., New York, 1952).

V. O. Key, Jr., *Politics, Parties, and Pressure Groups* (5th ed., New York, 1963).

S. Chase, *Democracy Under Pressure; Special Interests vs. The Public Welfare* (New York, 1945).

P. H. Odegard, *Pressure Politics: The Story of the Anti-Saloon League* (New York, 1928).

B. Zeller, *Pressure Politics in New York* (New York, 1937).

D. D. McKean, *Pressures on the Legislature of New Jersey* (New York, 1938).

W. McCune, *The Farm Bloc* (New York, 1943).

E. E. Schattschneider, *Politics, Pressures, and the Tariff* (New York, 1935).

K. Crawford, *The Pressure Boys* (New York, 1939).

D. B. Truman, *The Governmental Process* (New York, 1951).

A. F. Bentley, *The Process of Government* (New York, 1908).

B. Smith, *A Dangerous Freedom* (New York, 1954).

R. E. Dowling, "Pressure Group Theory: Its Methodological Range," *Amer. Pol. Sci. Rev.,* LIV No. 4 (Dec., 1960).

H. McClosky and H. E. Dahlgren, "Primary Group Influence in Party Loyalty," *Amer. Pol. Sci. Rev.,* LIII No. 3 (Sept., 1959).

H. Zeigler, *Interest Groups in American Society* (Englewood Cliffs, N.J., 1964).

D. Blaisdell, *American Democracy Under Pressure* (New York, 1957).

A. Hacker, "Pressure Politics in Pennsylvania: The Truckers *vs.* the Railroads" in A. F. Westin (ed.). *The Uses of Power: 7 Cases in American Politics* (New York, 1962).

A. Forster and B. R. Epstein; *Danger on the Right* (New York, 1964).

J. Monsen and M. W. Cannon, *The Makers of Public Policy; American Power Groups and Their Ideologies* (New York, 1965).

2. PUBLIC OPINION

F. C. Irion, *Public Opinion and Propaganda* (New York, 1950).

M. B. Ogle, Jr., *Public Opinion and Political Dynamics* (Boston, 1950).

G. Gallup, *Public Opinion in a Democracy* (Princeton, N.J., 1939).

———, *A Guide to Public Opinion Polls* (Princeton, N.J., 1944).

H. Cantril, *Gauging Public Opinion* (Princeton, N.J., 1944).

L. W. Doob, *Public Opinion and Propaganda* (New York, 1948).

W. Lippmann, *Public Opinion* (New York, 1930).

N. J. Powell, *Anatomy of Public Opinion* (New York, 1951).

G. L. Bird and F. E. Merwin, *The Press and Society* (New York, 1951).

S. Kelley, Jr., *Professional Public Relations and Political Power* (Baltimore, 1956).

D. Cater, *The Fourth Branch of Government* (Boston, 1959).

C. Schettler, *Public Opinion in American Society* (New York, 1957).

H. L. Childs, *Public Opinion—Nature, Formation* (New York, 1965).

J. T. Klaffer, *The Effects of Mass Communication* (New York, 1960).

V. O. Key, *Public Opinion and American Democracy* (New York, 1961).

R. G. Lane and D. O. Sears, *Public Opinion* (Englewood Cliffs, N.J., 1964).

R. E. Lane, *Political Ideology* (New York, 1962).

Dan D. Nimmo, *Newsgathering in Washington: A Study in Political Communication* (New York, 1964).

The Public Opinion Quarterly. Published quarterly at Princeton, N.J., by the National Office of Public Opinion.

★ 7 ★

Political Parties

thus far described by which individual citizens participate in directing the government would be wholly effective without political parties. Unless candidates for office stand for something, voting is likely not to be successful in giving direction to the machine of state. Unless the range of choice is narrowed down, the electorate is likely to be divided among numerous claimants with no single claimant representing more than a small portion of the total. No political-interest group can claim the loyalty of more than a minority of the voters and cannot, therefore, itself dominate and direct public policy. The results would be tragic if it could, for it might push its own claims to the exclusion of those of other groups and so divide our society that rebellion or revolution would ensue. None of the methods for voicing or recording opinions on the questions of the day makes certain that the opinions will be influential. Although for decades there were grave doubts about the usefulness or the necessity of political parties and even today there are lingering suspicions, it is now generally conceded that strong parties are essential to the practice of democratic government.

Parties are essential to democratic government

THE NATURE OF A POLITICAL PARTY

In a sense a political party is a kind of political-interest group. It is a group of voters consciously bound together to contest elections and with a shared interest in promoting some kind of public policy and a shared adherence to some sort of traditional values. A party differs rather strikingly, however, from all other political-interest groups or associations in that it seeks to capture the power of the state. It is not content merely to persuade those in power to follow a particular policy. The party offers candidates for office and is willing to assume the responsibility for running the government. Although devoted to some kind of program, the major aim of an American party is power and, within certain broad limits, it will shift its program to attain it. The ordinary political-interest group is much more rigidly dedicated to a program of governmental benevolence to its own members than is any party. Strong parties are likely to be much larger than any other type of interest group and to embrace members of many different groups. Of course, parties may be large or small, national or local, highly organized or loosely

Nature of a party

151

built. The major parties of American experience, however, have operated on a national scale and have permeated all levels of government.

Party member-ship

American parties are loose and amorphous associations. Membership in a party is a vague and elusive matter. How does one join a party? A few minor parties have regular enrollment, the members subscribe to a body of doctrine and, in many instances, pay dues. The major parties, however, have nothing so clear cut. There is no enrollment, except that arising in several states from preprimary registration of party affiliation. There are no dues, although many efforts have been made to institute regular contributions. There are no rules of behavior for members and no effective sanctions for improper conduct. In common with the large interest groups, there is at the center of each party a hard core of party officials and workers surrounded by a steadfast band of supporters who contribute money and time and influence, if they have it, to promote the success of the party. Close to this core, but not always part of it, are the officeholders whom the party has helped elect. There is the party in Congress and the party in state legislatures and in city and county councils and commissions and the party in the executive branch at all levels. These groups are closely identified with the party hierarchy, may even be part of it, but in view of official positions have responsibilities and loyalties which transcend party status. At any particular time, a segment of the party in office may be at odds with the party hierarchy. Beyond the hierarchy and the officeholders are the office-seekers and others who aspire to influence in the party and in the government. Then there are the myriad hosts of those who regularly support the party at election time, occasionally work for it, usually talk for it in their own circles, and sometimes contribute to its treasury. Beyond this group are a large number of persons who usually support the party but cannot be depended on to do so and who are rather quick to change their loyalties and support another party or candidates. Finally, there are on election day all of those who vote for the party's candidates. Many of these, however, are not members in any sense save this one and for this short period.[1]

The use-fulness of parties in American govern-ment

How can a group whose membership is so hard to determine and whose character is so difficult to define be so useful to democratic society? No better agency for mobilizing the electoral power of large numbers of people and channeling it to drive the wheels of government has been found in almost 200 years of experimentation. No other agency assumes for its chief task the formation of a majority so that officials can assume office with the knowledge that they may speak and act for their fellow citizens. No other agency so persistently or so successfully stimulates citizen interest and participation in the processes of self-government. No other agency is quite so responsive to the feelings of the people. No other agency is in a position effectively to harness the multiple seats of power provided by our federal and tripartite constitutional system and drive them toward an agreed goal. Finally, no other agency

[1] On the general subject see C. A. Birdahl, "Party Membership in the United States," *Amer. Pol. Sci. Rev.*, XXXVI (Feb. and Apr., 1942).

has, at the same time that it has promoted political division, also promoted national unity. Only the political party reaches across sectional boundaries, economic distinctions, interest-group competitions, religious differences, and racial antagonisms and softens the conflicts, bridges the gulfs, and helps to cement together a divergent, mobile, and aggressive people.

One of the distinguishing characteristics of genuinely democratic government everywhere in the world is the free competition of political parties. The ruling cliques in some authoritarian governments also call themselves parties largely because of their origins in differently organized regimes. In the democratic sense the Communist Party in the Soviet Union, for example, is not a political party at all and the system is not a party system. Parties, to correspond to our definition and to function as they do in democratic states, must be free to compete openly for public support and to critize freely those in charge of the state. *Parties in authoritarian states*

THE DEVELOPMENT OF THE AMERICAN PARTY SYSTEM

The disposition of the American electorate to divide into major groups identified with particular governmental policies or conceptions and personalized by particular statesmen extends back to the very beginnings of our national government. The movement for separation from England sharply divided the people of the colonies, with the Loyalists or Tories opposing the revolutionaries. Achievement of independence was accompanied by a general suppression of Loyalist sentiments. The attempt to replace the Articles of Confederation with a new constitution providing a stronger central government evoked a loose union of its sponsors into Federalists and of its opponents into anti-Federalists. The Federalists drew their chief strength from the commercial, financial, industrial, and plantation interests, their opponents from the small farmers and frontiersmen. These loose coalitions more or less dissolved with the establishment of the new government, only to reappear in slightly different array during the late phases of Washington's Presidency. The commercial, financial, and industrial elements of New England and the Middle States retained their party label of Federalist and, led by Hamilton and Adams, sponsored new national programs for the benefit of these sections and interests. Their policies in regard to national debt, a protective tariff, and the role of the national government, however, stimulated Jefferson and Madison to rally the planters along with the small farmers and artisans into a new party—the Jeffersonian Republicans. Jefferson's skill as a party leader, continued expansion of the frontier, quarreling among the opposition leaders, the War of 1812, and other factors too complex for easy summary brought such sweeping victories to this party that by 1816 the Federalist Party was driven from the field. Renamed Democrats, the party of rural America held the field unchallenged nationally until 1832. The Jacksonian Democracy of 1828, however, was a coalition different from Jeffersonian Republicanism. *The history of party cleavage in America*

Jackson's appeal to the artisans of the city and the farmers of the frontier was much stronger than his appeal to the Southern plantation aristocracy. Many of the slave-holders were driven into an alliance with Northern manufacturing, commerce, and finance in the National Republican or Whig Party organized about 1832 and contesting national offices with the Democracy from 1832 to 1856. The slavery controversy rended the Democratic Party still further and created an unbridgeable gulf finally between Southern and Northern agriculture. The Whig Party, too, disintegrated under the fires of abolitionism and secession, its Southern wing joining hands with the slave-holding Democrats and its Northern industrial wing forming the chief sinews of the new Republican Party which emerged in 1860. Lincoln's party successfully united the Northern industrial and financial groups with the Midwestern free farmers in a coalition for union, against the spread of slavery, and for tariffs. The shades of rebellion hung over the Democracy for decades after the Civil War, but farm depression, rigid credit controls, high tariffs and industrial exploitation drove more and more Northern workingmen and farmers to embrace the Democratic standard. Deep distress in American agriculture in the 1920's, followed by an unparalleled depression in industry in the 1930's, cemented a powerful new farmer, laborer, Southern plantation coalition which is the basis of the modern Democratic Party. The Republican Party continues to receive the support of the manufacturing, commercial, and financial interests of the North and Midwest and of the more prosperous farmers of these regions. The Democratic Party can thus trace its ancestry back to Jeffersonian Republicans and the Republican Party to Hamiltonian Federalists. Each, thus, draws upon traditions and conceptions reaching far back into the past.[2]

Economic and sectional interests not sole determinants of party cleavage

This characterization of American major parties as based largely upon economic and sectional interests has only rough validity. There have been many cross-currents of interests, religious and social, for example, which influenced party affiliation at every epoch of our national history. No party ever enlisted the undivided support of any economic interest or section. Family tradition has proved capable of maintaining party loyalties long after any direct economic attachment is discernible. Regional devotion too has been a strong contributor to party loyalty. The South, for example, for generations shunned the Republican Party as the author of its defeat and the despoiler of its culture. The older a party becomes, the more likely is habit to be a large factor in the devotion of its followers.

A two-party system

This capsule history of the American party battle does show, however, that certain great economic and sectional interests have persistently sought political expression through the vehicle of a party. Some of them, industry, for example, have been consistent supporters of a particular party. Most significant of all, however, the history of American parties reveals the deep attachment of the American voter to one or the other of two major parties.

[2] A good account of the history of American parties can be found in W. E. Binkley, *American Political Parties; Their Natural History* (New York, 1944).

In sharp contrast with continental practitioners of democratic government, English-speaking peoples generally seem to prefer a two-party alignment to a multiparty one. Despite the great diversities of sections, economic groups, and religious loyalties, which in France, Italy, Germany, Belgium, Holland, and the Scandinavian countries have promoted numerous parties contending for power, the American people have tended to coalesce into two great combinations of such interests. American experience contrasts also with that of many of the newly developing nations. In many of these, India for example, one party dominates the national elections.

A number of explanations have been offered for bipartisanship in American politics. On the one hand, some have ventured the belief that the two-party system is more natural than any other. People "naturally" tend either to conservatism or reformism by temperament, upbringing, and disposition. A conservative party and a reform party are, therefore, in keeping with human nature. This explanation is not very satisfying. Human nature is not so simply catalogued; few of us are consistently conservative or consistently reformist throughout all of the phases and facets of our lives. Some find the explanation in American constitutional history. They find that there have usually been but two main attitudes toward our constitutional arrangements: a strict constructionist, states'-rights attitude; and a loose constructionist, nationalist attitude. This explanation fails to reckon with the fact that the party in power in the national government has usually been nationalist while it was in power—whether Democrat, Whig or Republican—while the party out of power nationally has typically been in favor of states' rights. The Republican devotion to state's rights of the last two decades would sound strange to the supporters of Lincoln. Elihu Root felt that the two-party system was the product of longer practical experience of self-government than the continental peoples had enjoyed. Contemporary students believe that the following factors are more important than any thus far mentioned: (1) the single-member district system for electing legislators—plurality election in each district invites if it does not compel coalition of interests in order to achieve a decision at the polls; (2) the popular election of the President—this contributes a powerful impetus to unite groups across state, sectional, and economic lines in order to make the voting decisive. Perhaps most important of all, these constitutional considerations operate within a society not split by class or ideological divisions. The two-party system also has become entrenched psychologically and legally.

Why we have a two-party system

Not all Americans have been content with the two-party division. Dissident elements in the electorate have periodically launched independent or "third-party" movements. One of the first of them was the Anti-Masons, appearing in 1826 and spreading over New England, New York, and Pennsylvania. It made a lasting contribution to American politics in the national convention system for nominating Presidential candidates. It also formed part of the basis of the opposition to Jackson which later became the Whig Party.

Minor parties in America

The equivocation of the major parties on the slavery question stimulated the formation of the Liberty Party about 1840, dedicated to abolition, and of the Free Soil Party, active in the campaign of 1848 and determined to sustain the Wilmot Proviso. Antipathy to immigrants, especially Irish Catholics, led to the formation of the Native-American or "Know-Nothing" Party which flourished in the fifties. The Republican Party, itself, began as a third party in 1854-56. Agrarian discontent on the Plains and in the South after 1870 was largely responsible for the Greenback party of the seventies and the People's or "Populist" party of the nineties. Urban industrial capitalism was the target of the Socialist Party organized in the late nineties and of the Communist and Socialist-Labor parties organized after World War I. In this century the National Progressive Party of 1912 embodied the Presidential aspirations of Theodore Roosevelt, the Progressive Party of 1924, those of the elder LaFollette and the Progressive Party of 1948, those of Henry Wallace. The LaFollette tradition was embraced in a new Progressive Party in Wisconsin in the years 1934 to 1946. A Farmer-Labor Party in Minnesota joined with the Democratic Party in 1944 after several years of independent existence. Southern resistance to Northern pressure in behalf of the Negro, especially within the Democratic Party, has produced States Rights or "Dixiecrat" parties in each election since 1948. A Conservative Party made its appearance in New York in 1964. New York City continues to be the home of a vigorous labor party, the Liberal Party.[3]

Their strength and role   Some of these parties momentarily attained sufficient strength, especially in pivotal states, to affect the results of a Presidential election.[4] One—the Republican—grew into a major party. In only two elections in this century (1912 and 1924) has the combined vote of all minor parties exceeded 6 percent of the total vote cast, and since 1932 it has exceeded 4 percent only once (1948). In fact, third parties have been steadily declining in importance since that time. The Progressive parties which did so well in 1912 and in 1924 were

[3] A brief account of the history of minor parties together with a bibliography of the principal works can be found in W. B. Hesseltine, *The Rise and Fall of Third Parties* (Washington, 1948).

[4] The political history of New York affords several examples. In 1844, the Liberty Party's poll in that state was sufficient to throw the state's electoral vote to James K. Polk, the Democratic candidate, and so to insure his election over the Whig candidate, Henry Clay; in 1848 the Free Soil Party drew away so many votes from Cass, the Democratic nominee, that the Whig candidate, General Taylor, carried the state; in 1884, the Republicans held the Prohibitionists responsible for loss of the state and for the resulting election of Grover Cleveland; and in 1944 the American Labor Party and its offshoot, the Liberal Party, both supporting the Democratic candidate, President Franklin D. Roosevelt, gave him the margin of victory in the state. In 1912, the National Progressive Party, a Republican seceding element supporting Theodore Roosevelt, and in 1924 the Progressive Party supporting Senator LaFollette, sharply split the bulk of the popular vote throughout the country (with 35 percent and 17.1 percent polled, respectively), but without deflecting the eventual result from what certainly it would have been in 1924, and probably in 1912, in any case. In 1948, the substantial popular vote polled by the (Wallace) Progressive Party and the "Dixiecrat" State Rights' Party operated merely to reduce the Truman majority in the electoral college.

both short-lived. These minor parties—free to cultivate ideas rather than worry about power—have found their importance mainly in revealing and crystallizing dissenting opinion (usually on economic and social matters). As threats to the rather evenly balanced major parties, third parties have impelled them, whether they liked it or not, to bid for support by taking up issues sponsored by these minority groups. A large proportion, indeed, of leading party issues in the past several decades—the income tax, the regulation of railroads and other corporations, the use of injunctions in labor disputes, woman suffrage, prohibition, farm relief, and others—were "borrowed" from third-party platforms. Except for occasional "one-purpose" parties like the Prohibitionist, minor parties are typically more radical (to the right or left) than the old-line organizations. The internal heterogeneity and lack of cohesion of our major parties are more than matched by the rigid and doctrinaire character of minor parties.

MINOR PARTIES IN THE PRESIDENTIAL ELECTION
1964

		Party	Candidate	Vote
Democrats	(60.6)	Liberal (N.Y.)	Johnson	342,432
42,786,586		Conservative (N.Y.)	Goldwater	284,646
		Ind. Dem. Electors	unpledged	210,732
		Socialist Labor	Haas	45,186
		Socialist Worker	DeBerry	32,705
Republicans	(38.0)	Prohibition	Munn	23,267
26,892,227		National States Rights	Kasper	6,953
		Constitution	Lightburn	5,060
		Other		12,762
		Total		963,743

THE TWO MAJOR PARTIES TODAY

The two major parties of today are notoriously composite and disunited. In order to capture the loyalty of great numbers of voters scattered throughout the nation, they must stand for many different things and not too rigidly for any one thing. To a foreign observer, especially one accustomed to the doctrinaire parties of Europe, it must seem that the Republican and Democratic parties are identical. James Bryce 75 years ago described them as two bottles carefully labeled but empty. Many observers since his time have been baffled by the excitement engendered in an American political campaign when the contestants seem to be so much alike. This is really not so surprising in a society where there is such wide agreement on fundamental concepts of politics.

Two parties hard to distinguish

*The
Democratic
Party*

The watershed of modern politics is the great depression of the 1930's and the modern Democratic Party was forged in those desperate economic times. It is a coalition of urban workers, urban minority groups and the Southern white agricultural leadership to which a large number of the less prosperous farmers of the Plains and ranchers and miners of the Mountain States have also given their allegiance. Stated another way, it is a coalition of the dominant white Southern politicians and the highly organized political apparatus of the large cities of the nation. In this coalition, the urban groups have been increasingly influential in Presidential politics. The party has carried virtually every large city in the country in every election since 1932 except the Eisenhower ones of 1952 and 1956. Numerous studies of voter preference show that the party has a strong appeal to laboring men and women and to lower-income groups everywhere. The uneasy partner has been the white South. After a few successes by Hoover, Eisenhower, and Nixon in states like Florida, Tennessee, and Virginia, the Republicans with Goldwater finally carried much of the deep South in 1964 on the civil rights issue. The victory, however, on these terms cost them the allegiance of the Southern Negroes who until that time had no reason to ally with the white Democratic leadership. Prior to 1964, Dixiecrat movements of various kinds had eroded Democratic strength in the elections of 1948 and 1960.

*A
majority
party*

In general the modern Democratic Party is the preferred party of a majority of American adults. Repeated surveys in the last several years have indicated that 50 percent-55 percent of American adults think of themselves as Democrats, 32 percent-38 percent as Republicans and the rest as independent or indifferent.[5] The Democratic majority, however, contains a considerable share of those who are least likely to vote and it is hard for the party to deliver its full strength at the polls. The orientation of the party is indicated further by the kinds of programs it has sponsored. In general the Democrats have been more willing than the Republicans to control the economy in the interest of the workers, to sponsor programs of public succor for the poor, the underprivileged, the unfortunate, to promote public housing and public power, to favor lower tariffs and to undertake more extensive international political and military commitments.

*The
Republican
Party*

The sectional strongholds of the modern Republican Party are New England (except Massachusetts and Rhode Island) and the Northern Great Plains (Kansas, Iowa, Nebraska, and the Dakotas). The small towns and the rural areas of the Midwest and Middle Atlantic regions (Wisconsin, Illinois, Indiana, Ohio, Michigan, Pennsylvania, and New York) have also been strongly in the Republican camp for many decades, although the Democrats did attract a large number of Midwestern and Plains farmers in the period

[5] Surveys by the Survey Research Center, University of Michigan, reported in *The American Voter,* abridged edition (New York, 1964) 69 and in F. I. Greenstein, *The American Party System and the American People* (Englewood Cliffs, N. J., 1963) 32.

1930-50. The manufacturing and financial interests have been especially influential in the party as have upper-income groups everywhere but in the Deep South. Everywhere the party cadres are particularly filled with white, Anglo-Saxon, Protestants. In contrast to the Democrats, the Republicans have been less sympathetic to governmental restriction on private industrial management and have tended to emphasize individual initiative and free enterprise as against governmental benevolence and economic security. In international affairs, the Republican Party contains a much higher proportion than the Democratic Party of those who are critical of international commitments, who favor high tariffs on imports and more vigorous military measures to resist Communists.

It should not be inferred from these thumbnail portraits of the two parties that there are no wealthy Democrats nor poor Republicans, that there are no Republican laborers and no small-town Democrats. There are some of every kind of class, race, religion, and sectional patriot in each party. Each party is furthermore sharply divided within itself. Its unity is assailed by factional contests of the bitterest kind. The conservative Southern leaders of the Democratic Party are staunch foes of the demands of Northern urban leaders for an end to racial discrimination and for stronger governmental protection for labor unions. Agrarian Democrats in the Middle West are likely to find Southern preferences for cotton and tobacco do not square easily with their own aspirations in regard to dairy products, corn, and hogs. Eastern Republicans committed to international trade and the support of friendly nations in Europe find themselves vigorously assailed by isolationist Republicans of the Plains and Middle West and by "Asia-firsters" on the West Coast. New England farmers do not easily support the agricultural programs sponsored by the Republican corn farmers of Iowa and Illinois. These intraparty squabbles are often as animated as are the contests between the two parties. Each party does, however, have a center or gravity in particular sections and interests which is different from that of its chief rival. Neither of the central blocs is powerful enough to win elections unaided. The Democrats must hold their supporters and what is more difficult get them out to the polls. The Republicans must appeal to other sections and interests to gain victory at the polls.

Composite character of both major parties

Although both major parties and most minor parties offer candidates for national office and campaign on national issues over the whole nation, the real strength of the parties is in their state apparatus. The major political parties of America are federally organized in much the same way as the government. In the case of the government, however, the national level is more powerful in relation to the state level than in the case of the parties. Party activity in state and local government resembles that in the national government. Candidates are sponsored for state and local offices; platforms are written. dealing with city and state problems; campaigns are conducted for governor, legislator, mayor, councilman, sheriff, district attorney, and all

The parties and the states

other offices filled by election. In these contests for local and state power the parties prepare themselves for the national contests. It is here that the skills of the politician are learned and that political leaders are developed. Here the professional politician finds his livelihood in public office and puts himself in position to participate in national campaigns. Here party organization attains its maximum of effectiveness and detail. Each of the major parties has arisen from devastating defeat in national election to contest vigorously the next election with its rival because it still holds place and power in numerous localities and states from which to strike out anew. No party can hope for success nationally unless it is strong in many states and dominant in some. Confronted with imminent defeat nationally, local and state leaders will bend every effort to stay on top in their own states and cities. They have been known even to sabotage their own national ticket if they thought by so doing they could salvage local victory. In 1964, for example, Republican gubernatorial and Senatorial candidates in New York, Michigan, Ohio, Illinois, Pennsylvania did everything possible to avoid outright identification with the Republican Presidential ticket.

One-party states   The states are not perfect miniatures of the nation in party matters. For decades a goodly number of states have not had genuine two-party competition of the national variety. The Deep South has been solidly Democratic since the Civil War, and most of the Plains, New England and, until the 1930's, the Mid-Atlantic have been predominantly Republican. In these one-party states, factions within the party tend to develop and to offer candidates, contest nominations, and promote controversial policies. These factional competitions resemble bipartisan conflicts but take many peculiar local forms. The nominating procedure is likely to be the chief battleground in one-party states and the elections less significant. Two-party competition has, however, been increasing in the past few years and there are fewer one-party states today than at any time since 1865.[6]

Non-partisan state and local elections   The cooperative union of national, state, and local politicians in the American party pattern is widely believed to promote a similar cooperative union of national, state, and local government. It helps to overcome the centrifugal tendencies in the federal system. To some, however, the mixture of national issues into state and local campaigns which necessarily accompanies the federated party organization is a monstrous evil. Only misgovernment locally results from confusing the voter by injecting national party positions on war, taxes, or international affairs into municipal campaigns, they argue. For a generation (1900-1920) the stock remedy for this alleged illness was the nonpartisan ballot (one having no party emblems or identification).

[6] Austin Ranney, "Parties in State Politics," *Politics in the American States,* ed. by H. Jacob and K. N. Vines, (Boston, 1965) identifies 25 states as two-party states, 8 states as one-party Democratic, 9 states as modified one-party Democratic states, and 8 states as modified one-party Republican states as of 1964. See also V. O. Key, *Politics, Parties, and Pressure Groups,* 5th ed. (New York, 1964), and P. T. David, *The Changing Party Pattern* (Washington, 1956).

And a number of states adopted such ballots for municipal officials, judges, and state administrative officials. Two states, Minnesota and Nebraska, select the members of their legislatures in a nonpartisan election and somewhat more than half of all the members of city councils in municipalities with more than 5000 population are selected in this way.[7] This method has not completely eliminated partisan campaigning but it has certainly reduced it. It has also weakened the influence of city officials in state and national politics. The separation of national, state, and local elections is another way which has been widely adopted for getting at the same problem. This procedure strengthens the state position of a party not in command in Washington. Little is heard any more of reforms of this type aimed at weakening the party apparatus. Most students are seeking ways to strengthen the party.

REGULATION OF PARTIES

Political parties are as much a part of the American system of government as the Congress of the United States. They are the most important vehicles for translating individual will into public policy. And yet they have developed almost wholly outside the law. The national and most state constitutions are completely silent about them. Even the statutes were relatively indifferent to their existence for 100 years. Congress passed its first laws touching them directly in 1907,[8] and state laws dealing with their machinery and operations are, typically, of more recent origin. Legally speaking, parties are voluntary nonprofit associations with no personality apart from the individuals who compose them. Over the recent decades, however, national and state regulation has invested them with a public status without, however, making them organs of the government.[9]

Parties as voluntary associations

Under constitutional authority to regulate national elections including primaries—an authority which in practice would tend to extend also to state and local elections not separately held—Congress might control party machinery and operations. This, however, it has not chosen to do, except with respect to campaign finances. Accordingly, the task is left largely to the states. Congress has, however, closed party competition to the Communist Party. By an act of 1954, the Communist Party was specifically outlawed and all political privileges withdrawn from it or its successors.

The development of public regulations: 1. National

The old situation in which parties determined their own form of organization, made their own rules, nominated their candidates, and raised their funds with no external controls, was gradually brought to an end in most

2. State

---

[7] A recent study suggests that nonpartisan elections are considerably influenced by partisan considerations. O. P. Williams and C. R. Adrian, "The Insulation of Local Politics Under the Non-Partisan Ballot," *Amer. Pol. Sci. Rev.,* LIII, No. 4 (Dec., 1959).

[8] An act chiefly forbidding corporations to contribute to campaign funds in national elections.

[9] J. R. Starr, "The Legal Status of American Political Parties," *Amer. Polit. Sci. Rev.,* XXXIV, 429-455, 685-699 (June and Aug., 1940).

states by demand that abuses be halted and party activities be recognized as a matter of public concern. Regulations (following no single pattern) are now found in nearly every state covering: (1) definition of what constitutes a party, with the privilege of a place on the ballot,[10] (2) composition and powers of party committees and conventions; (3) manner of making nominations; (4) dates for holding primaries; (5) membership tests for voting in primaries; (6) settlement of disputes in connection with nominations; (7) campaign contributions and expenditures, and other aspects of party finances; (8) corrupt and illegal electoral practices, financial or otherwise; (9) outlawry (in many states) of parties advocating totalitarianism, overthrow of the government by violence, or other "subversive" doctrines or objectives; [11] (10) protection for parties against impostors as candidates in primaries, against misleading and unauthorized use of party names (including adoption of them by separate organizations), and against appropriation of party emblems duly adopted and recorded.

Not infrequently, cases involving party matters get into the courts. In addition to sustaining a great deal of statutory regulation when questioned the courts have, at various times and places, ruled (1) that a political party has no right to limit the suffrage at a general election or a primary; (2) that it has no authority to add to qualifications for voting specified in state constitutions or statutes; and (3) that it has no authority over eligibility to public office, nor any right to make binding decisions on questions relating thereto.[12]

PARTY ORGANIZATION—STATE AND LOCAL

*Charac-
teristics
of party
organiza-
tion*

Every successful party has elaborate organizational machinery to hold its members together, stir them to action, raise funds, carry on propaganda, recruit new members and supporters, and guide the party effort in primaries

[10] The criterion most commonly employed is the polling of a specified percentage of the state's entire vote at the last general election, occasionally as low as one or two percent, but usually higher. In upwards of half of the states, however, a minor party may get on the ballot also by means of a petition signed by some specified proportion of the voters, e.g., in Pennsylvania one-half of 1 percent and in California 5 percent. In general, laws of this type clearly favor the major parties and make it very difficult for minor parties to compete in elections.

[11] Laws of this nature vary considerably. In Texas and Illinois, Communist, Fascist, and Nazi parties are expressly named; in other states (as also indeed in Illinois) the language employed is broad enough to cover any party charged with cherishing "un-American principles"—unfortunately broad enough, in fact, to open ways for possible discrimination by the major parties against new or other minor groups merely because of being dissenters or "radicals." The 12 states having "outlawry" statutes are Arkansas, California, Illinois, Indiana, Kansas, Oklahoma, Ohio, Oregon, Pennsylvania, Texas, Wisconsin and Wyoming. For summaries of laws see *Cong. Rec.,* Apr. 1, 1947, pp. A1479ff. All of these state acts are now partially superseded by the national act of 1954 outlawing the Communist Party.

[12] For a summary of state regulation of parties see L. R. Gaitskill, *State Regulation of Political Parties,* Legislative Research Commission (Frankfort, Ky., 1962).

and elections. This machinery in each of the two major parties enlists more than 150,000 men and women who make a profession or at least a major vocation of their party work. Although there are many local variations, the pattern of party organization is fairly uniform throughout the country. Its characteristic feature is a pyramid of committees ranging upward from the city or county to the national level but with cooperative rather than authoritative relations among the levels. Wherever, in fact, there are offices to be contested there are likely to be committees to contest them. Although in earlier times parties were free to contrive their own organizational arrangements, increasing public control of electoral processes has brought with it public regulation of party machinery. Almost everywhere the structure and mode of election of party committee members is regulated by state law. Typically, they are elected by the voters in connection with a direct primary election of candidates for public office.

During the rapid rise of urban, industrial America, the most highly organized party apparatus was in the great cities and the urban machine is still in some sense a model of detailed party organization. Built block by block with workers responsible to a precinct captain or committeeman and he in turn to a ward leader presiding over a ward committee and he to the chairman of the city committee, the party kept in close and year-round contact with a high proportion of its registered affiliates. Fueled by specific rewards—job finding, ticket fixing, poor relief, intercession with police, courts, inspectors—the organization was little interested in national issues and greatly interested in assimilation of ethnic minorities into American society. The key piece was likely to be the precinct leader who might occupy a public job (by patronage appointment) the duties of which were such that he could spend most of his time in his precinct and who cultivated his flock with "favors" and "friendship" in return for loyalty to his ticket on election day. At the top of the structure a city or county "boss" dealt with the leaders of other cities and counties in state and national conclaves for determining party candidates and allocating the "spoils." Little was left to chance in such an organization, voter's canvasses based on lists of registered voters gave the leadership highly accurate knowledge of the ebb and flow of public opinion. The leadership could and did give firm commitments on official attitudes toward utilities, municipal housekeeping services, and vice. This was the politics of "boodle," graft, and spoils but it was also a highly effective mechanism for bringing the immigrant into the American system and for overcoming the frustrations of divided power at the local level. Several developments in the last half century have seriously modified and in some cases destroyed this machinery. The restrictive immigration policy has halted the flow of Europeans to the city. The inauguration of huge programs of poor relief, social security, and public employment offices has eliminated much of the value and need for party benevolence. The outward flow of urbanites to the suburbs has changed the character of the central cities. Radio and television have

The urban "machine"

brought national issues and political personalities into the homes of the voters in ways that overshadow the messages and friendship of the local party worker. A few of the "old-style" organizations like that in Chicago have been able to adapt. The Negroes moving in large numbers into the cities have found the party apparatus useful to accommodate their ambitions. The effectiveness of the organization in getting people registered and then to the polls on election day has made their continuance a matter of great importance to party leadership. Nevertheless, the modern urban party organization is likely to be more issue-oriented, less dependent upon specific rewards, less dominated by ethnic considerations and less hierarchial than it used to be.[13]

Local party committees

Urban America continues to provide the setting for the most completely organized local party apparatus, with its precinct leaders, ward committees and leaders and city-wide committees. In some cases, there are also intermediate committees organized around state legislative districts. By contrast in rural and small-town America the party apparatus is likely to be most informal and to center around the county courthouse. The most powerful leader is likely to be the chairman of the county committee. This committee is composed typically of township, city and village representatives. As with the urban ward, legislative-district, and city committees, the county committees are importantly concerned in raising money, directing local campaigns, selecting candidates for the various offices at these levels and uniting party support for these candidates, preparing and distributing literature, holding rallies and performing other party chores.

District organization

Intermediate between the county and the state organization, various types of district committees may usually be found. Congressional and state legislative districts are apt to be formed of several counties and the parties frequently make some effort to create a campaign organization to support their candidates for these posts. A district committee made up of representatives of the county committees in the district is the most common. Rarely do these district organizations hold together between elections. They function during a campaign and in many areas have only a shadowy existence.

State organization:

In earlier days, the supreme party authority in a state was a state convention whose members were elected, in counties or other areas, by the party voters directly or in local conventions. In a decision of 1935, validating (for the time being) Texas' white primary system, the Supreme Court recognized a convention as the highest authority of a party. For most practical purposes, however, the state convention has now lost its importance. Supreme party authority on the state level is now centered almost completely in a state central committee and its chairman. State committees vary greatly in size, and

[13] There are many good studies of the old-fashioned machine. One of the best is W. Riordan, *Plunkett of Tammany Hall* (New York, 1948). See also H. Zink, *City Bosses in the United States* (Durham, N. C., 1930); H. Gosnell, *Machine Politics: Chicago Model* (Chicago, 1947); S. Forthal, *Cogwheels of Democracy: A Study of the Precinct Captain* (New York, 1946); J. T. Salter, *Boss Rule: Portraits of City Politics* (New York, 1935).

their members are chosen in different ways. Occasionally they consist simply of all county chairmen in the state. Usually they are elected directly or indirectly by the voters in counties or other units of representation, with the trend strongly toward direct choice through primaries, and often with men and women elected in equal numbers. Their functions include maintaining effective organization throughout the state, adjusting dissensions, promoting the election of party candidates (in cooperation with the national committee in Presidential years, with Congressional committees when members of Congress are being chosen, and at all times with county and other local committees), raising funds, occasionally nominating candidates for certain minor offices, sometimes preparing the party platform, and in some states selecting the state delegation to the national nominating convention. Committee membership is often far too large to permit effective collective action, and tasks tend to fall into the hands of a smaller executive committee and especially to such officers as the chairman and treasurer.

1. State convention

2. State central committee

The state chairmanship is a post much sought after by politicians and often bitterly fought over by rival party leaders or factions. The state central committee commonly elects the chairman. In doing so, however, it may merely ratify a choice already made by the party nominee for governor or even by a powerful party leader who prefers not to occupy the titular post. In many cases, the United States Senator is likely to be influential in selecting the chairman. The party leadership, in any case, is often shared with the governor or a senator. Whether the real leader of his party or a member of the top party team, the chairman, presumably working with the state committee, is the principal director of state-wide party campaigns. He usually is influential in making up state wide slates and, in the event of party victory, is importantly involved in dispensing patronage, both state and national.

3. State chairman

Throughout our experience of organized political parties the apparatus has evoked much criticism. During the time when party posts were filled by local caucuses or city, county, or state conventions, the party organization fell rather easily under the domination of a few ruthless and unprincipled leaders who solidified their position by carefully contrived organization and bolstered it by corruption, graft, and spoils. This was notably true in the large cities and the scandals of the Tweed Ring and of Tammany Hall in New York City, of the Penrose and Vare machines in Philadelphia, of the Pendergast machine of Kansas City, of the Kelly-Nash machine in Chicago, and of many others during the past decades—blackened the reputations of party organizations everywhere. The word *machine,* used to characterize a highly organized and tightly controlled party apparatus, is still an epithet connoting corruption and oligarchy. "Boss," as the leader of the "machine" is still called, is also a term of opprobrium. The system of filling party office by election was widely adopted in the period 1900-15 to make oligarchic or dictatorial control of the party organization more difficult. It was supposed by the reformers that the voters disapproved of machine politics and if given an opportunity would destroy it.

Criticism of party organization

"Bossism"

State regulation of party organization involving the prescription of party offices and the methods of filling them has not been as effective as some had hoped. The fundamental difficulty, if it be one, is that only a small percentage of the electorate are really interested in party organization or in party work. Elections of party officials ordinarily attract a very light vote. Further, it does no good to elect to party office persons who are neither fitted for nor interested in working at the job. The small band of party enthusiasts who do the party's chores and, of course, enjoy the party's rewards are indispensable to strong parties. Since they are a small minority, they can always be criticized as an oligarchy. Even the most dictatorially managed party organization, however, depends in the final analysis on the public support. It cannot survive repeated repudiation of its candidates at the polls. The voters in any area have today and have always had it in their power to destroy a machine or a boss. Wherever they continue to exist, and they still do in some places, it is a fair assumption that a majority of those voting approve of what they do.

Development of informal party organization

One unintended result of state regulation of party organization has been the development of informal or "voluntary" party organization outside the legally-constituted party organization. In Wisconsin, for example, the elected "statutory" party committees are relatively unimportant parts of the party apparatus and real power has shifted to party committees and groups which have grown up outside the law. These groups use the old caucus and convention procedures for selecting officials and candidates just as was done in the last century. "Reform" has brought us full circle.

PARTY ORGANIZATION—NATIONAL

Although much of the strength and vitality of our major political parties is in their state and local organizations, they also are organized nationally to conduct campaigns for the Presidency and for members of Congress. In general, however, the national machinery of the parties is a federation of state organizations and lacks the powerful central direction characteristic of a few state and many local organizations.

1. Senatorial and congressional campaign committees

Pursuing the ascending order thus far followed, one finds first among national agencies two committees of which as a rule the public hears little— (1) a Senatorial campaign committee, composed usually of six or seven United States Senators chosen by the party group in the upper branch and charged with promoting the election or re-election of the party's Senatorial candidates in the biennial contests; and (2) a corresponding Congressional campaign committee consisting in the case of the Republicans of one member of the House of Representatives from each state having a Republican delegation, and in that of the Democrats, of one member from each state having a Democratic delegation, plus also a woman member from each state insofar as the chairman chooses to designate such. In a Presidential contest, these two committees, typically, place their resources at the disposal of the national committee (with which, however, they have no organic connection) and become its close allies. Elections tend to follow the fortunes of the contest for the Presidency. In "off years" the committees (which now maintain permanent working staffs) tend to play an independent role. Relying, of course, upon the cooperation of national, state, and local committees, they provide central coordination of the Senatorial and Congressional campaigns. In meeting this responsibility they distribute political literature and film strips, maintain a speakers' bureau, raise and disburse money (giving special attention to marginal states or districts), offer technical aid on radio and television appearances, and often intervene to smooth out local factional differences. Despite much duplication of effort with the national committee, the Congressmen jealously guard the independence of their own campaign committees.

Although on the lower levels party conventions have largely been displaced, the supreme organ of the national party is still the national convention. It not only nominates candidates for the highest offices and formulates a platform but formally at least controls the party organization and "constitution." This convention which meets every four years will be discussed in some detail shortly. At this point we need only to discuss the two major arms of the convention: the national committee and the national chairman.

2. The national convention and its agencies:

The national committee of the Democratic Party consists of two party members—a man and a woman—from each state and territory. The Republican Party, since 1952, has in addition to two from each state, the state party chairman from each state which was carried by the party in the preceding Presidential election or in which the governor or a majority of the members of Congress are Republicans. The two traditional state members of the committee of each party are formally designated by the conventions on the nominations of the respective state delegations. In at least 30 states, however, the real selection is made at primaries or at state conventions and the national delegation simply confirms the local selections. The national committee is most active during a Presidential campaign year. It decides where and when the nominating convention will be held and makes all the necessary local arrangements. It issues the call to the state party organizations, compiles the temporary roll of delegates who may attend and selects the temporary officers of the convention. Both of the latter decisions are subject to review at the convention. The committee also makes recommendations to the convention for changes in the rules governing the national organization. The convention selects a new national committee which then bears a heavy responsibility for conducting the national campaign. In between campaign years, the committee is not nearly so active. Its continuing responsibilities for "off-year" campaigning and for mobilizing sentiment nationally for the party and its leaders are discharged largely by the permanent staff which each major party maintains in Washington, D. C. These staffs supply material for local and state use, recruit speakers, assist in arranging the campaign itinerary of the President, if he is to be active, or of the chief party spokesman—usually the

a. The national committee

defeated Presidential candidate—gather and distribute funds, and generally
try to coordinate state party effort throughout the nation.

The chairman of the national committee is the active campaign manager
of the Presidential candidate of the party. He is ordinarily selected by the
candidate and formally invested with office by the committee. When the
campaign is over, the defeated candidate's manager ordinarily does not stay
in the job until a new candidate is selected four years hence. Under these
circumstances, the committee picks a chairman to serve until a candidate for
President is named. If the campaign is successful, the chairman traditionally
moves into the new President's cabinet or onto his personal staff,[14] and the
President, in consultation with the committee selects a new chairman. The
tasks of the chairman are many and difficult and only the most skillful politicians of long experience are ordinarily selected for this post.[15] In the party,
he ranks second only to the President himself as the director of its operations.[16]

PARTY FINANCES

To maintain party organization, carry on propagandist and other activities
and wage campaigns requires money, and usually a great deal of it. There have
been instances in which use of large sums backfired against a candidate or a
party, but no party management ever thinks it has money enough or relaxes its
efforts to get more. The first, and often the principal, task of many of the party
committees is to raise funds. As a rule, the burden devolves primarily upon the
treasurer of the committee concerned, although in states and localities it may
be assigned to a director of finance. Such officials commonly leave no stone unturned in their search for the "sinews of war," appeals going not only to people
of wealth, but to any and all party adherents. Money is only one factor in
winning elections, but it is important enough to tip the scales when two parties
or two candidates are rather evenly matched. Some amount of money is essential just to get the candidate's name before the voters.

Recent
levels of
expendi-
ture in
presiden-
tial cam-
paigns

If they are to remain going concerns, parties must spend money all of the
time to support the permanent headquarters and the organizational work which

[14] For more than 100 years, the practice was to appoint the chairman to the post
of Postmaster General. In recent years this practice has not been followed. Robert
Kennedy was made Attorney General; Bailey remained as chairman after Johnson's
election in 1964. See D. G. Fowler, *The Cabinet Politician: The Postmaster-General
1829-1909* (New York, 1943).

[15] Associated with the chairman will normally be one or more vice-chairmen, a
secretary and assistant secretary, a treasurer, and an executive committee with members
serving as staff officers and advisers during the campaign; and for carrying on different
branches of campaign work, a dozen or more bureaus, departments, or divisions
are likely to be set up, such as a speakers' bureau, a publicity department, a research
division, a foreign-language division, and a farm division, with others as needed.

[16] A current account of the work of the various party committees operating na-
tionally will be found in H. A. Bone, *Party Committees and National Politics* (Seattle,
Wash., 1958) and in C. P. Cotter and B. G. Hennessy, *Politics Without Power: The
National Party Committees* (New York, 1964).

is always going on.[17] Their outlays are highest and attract the most attention in connection with campaigns. It would be interesting if figures could be compiled showing precisely what such outlays are. Few accurate records are kept, however, and it is impossible to discover with exactness what is spent in campaigning in the United States. There are, it is true, certain published figures. Party organizations engaging in national campaigns are required by law not only to stay within a specified maximum, but to make full reports on their financial operations, both intake and outgo. Various states also require reports. However, the regular channel for party expenditure on a campaign— the party's national, state, or local committee—is by no means the only one through which money is spent. All sorts of voluntary, unofficial committees and organizations raise and spend large sums. With possibly three times as much actually spent as reported by the committee, Republican outlays on the Presidential (and Congressional) campaigns of 1928 to 1936 inclusive reached a high of $14.2 million, and Democratic outlays, of $9.2 million (both in 1936). In 1939, an Act (Hatch) was passed limiting a national committee's outlay in any calendar year to $3 million. The committees have, of course, reported spending less than this in each national campaign since that time, but the reported expenditures of auxiliary organizations (citizens groups, labor unions, etc.) and the unreported expenditures of informal, voluntary, and state groups have far exceeded the reported totals. The costs of campaigning since 1940 have increased the same as other costs. Estimates of the total expenditures in the campaign of 1952 vary from a low of $35 million to a high of $140 million. The parties and other participating national groups reported spending $23 million. An exhaustive study by the Senate Subcommittee on Privileges and Elections of the expenditures in 1956, placed the national total at $33 million ($21 million by Republicans, $12 million by Democrats and labor). Reported national expenditures in 1960 were $28 million (Republicans, $15 million; Democrats, $13 million).[18] In 1964, the totals were $36 million ($19 million Republican and $17 million Democratic and Labor) and $9 million more by the Congressional Campaign Committee. It has been estimated, for example, that the total for election-day workers alone (watchers, challengers,

---

[17] The headquarters staff of the Republican National Committee spends more than $1 million annually in "off" years and that of the Democratic Committee more than $750 thousand.

[18] Reported campaign expenditures for 1960 are summarized in *Congressional Quarterly,* Special Report No. 26 (June 30, 1961). The report of the Senate Subcommittee on Privileges and Elections in the 1956 campaign will be found in *Congressional Record, Senate,* 5003-5022 (April 12, 1957). Expenditures for 1952 may be found in *Congressional Quarterly Almanac,* 40-56 (1953). Information on the 1948 election will be found in *Congressional Quarterly,* VII, No. 3 (Jan. 21, 1949). For an analysis of national campaign expenditures in all presidential elections from 1932 to 1944 inclusive, see articles by L. Overacker in *Amer. Polit. Sci. Rev., XXVII,* 769-783 (Oct., 1933), XXXI, 473-498 (June, 1937), XXXV, 701-727 (Aug., 1941), and XXXIX, 899-925 (Oct., 1945); also the same author's *Presidential Campaign Funds* (Boston, 1946). The reported 1964 expenditures are summarized *Special Report,* Jan. 21, 1966, by Congressional Quarterly Series.

people transporting voters to the polls, and the like) is not less than $17.5 million in Presidential years.

*Why ex-
penditures
are so
large*
Many people contemplate such outlays with apprehension, wondering whether money in politics has not become a menace to our democratic institutions. Rival party organizations or candidates, especially if blessed with less ample resources, habitually take advantage of this popular concern and loudly denounce the "slush funds" of their opponents. It is, however, possible to spend very large sums of money in perfectly legitimate ways. It is true that a good deal of party work is done without pay. Only a small proportion of committee members or other party officials receive any salary or other stipend from the party. The general public pays for some, perhaps without realizing it, when public officials take time off from their regular work to make speeches, collect funds, and otherwise serve their party, especially during campaigns. But even in off years all this is far from enough. There are publicity men, research workers—even clerks and stenographers—to be paid. There is office space (sometimes entire buildings) to be rented, often at high cost in large cities; there are office supplies to be provided; there are heavy demands for postage and travel; telephone and telegraph charges mount up; printing takes its toll, along with many forms of advertising, including banners, buttons, and the like; radio and television time is essential and both major parties pour money into party periodicals such as the *Democratic Digest* (1953-1961) and the *Republican News*. All in all, a party, if alive and vigorous, must spend a great deal, and all of the time, merely to keep itself going. The public knows little of all this and probably cares less. Criticism centers chiefly about the spectacular outlays, especially on Presidential campaigns.

Any fair-minded person, however, who will look into the facts will find that in a nation-wide political effort it takes only a few items of a perfectly legitimate nature to account for outlays running into the millions. Like other forms of publicity and salesmanship, campaigning has come to be tremendously expensive. One reason is the size of the electorate. If we allow nine or ten cents for stationery, printing or typing, and postage, more than $10 million would be required merely to prepare and mail one circular letter addressed to all registered voters. A nation-wide campaign necessarily involves the expenditure of millions of dollars, in the aggregate, for the rental of headquarters and places for holding political meetings, for printing and distributing campaign literature, for the traveling expenses of speakers and higher party officials, for an army of organizers, canvassers, clerks, copyists, typists, tabulators, and addressers, to say nothing of the towering cost of advertising in newspapers, in magazines, on billboards, and by radio. The largest item in the cost of modern campaigning is television time and the two parties reported in 1956 having spent over $9 million, in 1960 over $15 million, and in 1964 over $24 million on this item alone from Sept. 1-Nov. 6. When all of these entirely proper objects of expenditure are duly listed and footed up, it will not be difficult to understand why, in spite of protracted and searching investigations by special Senate committees in connection with the big outlays in every Presidential campaign from 1920 to 1956 inclusive, almost no evidence has come to light justifying suspicion of extensive corruption in the national politics of recent years. This is perhaps the price we pay for stirring interest and getting our citizens to do their civic duty. If we remember that tobacco companies will spend many millions in one year to advertise their products, expenditures for electing our national officers may not seem excessive.

Whence come the funds with which to meet party outlays on the present generous scale? Speaking broadly, from anybody who can be induced (or coerced) to give. Raising money in humdrum times between elections is a thankless task. Party officers charged with the responsibility do what they can; but normally—at least in the case of the major parties—nearly all is gathered in at campaign time, and for immediate use. To begin with, candidates are almost invariably expected to dig into their pockets to take care of part of their own campaign expenses. Party members already in public office, whether or not up for re-election, are likewise counted on for contributions, frequently in terms of some fixed percentage of salary received. Especially are public officers or employees, national, state, or local, who get their jobs by partisan appointment expected to contribute to the party. Close friends and associates of the candidates are pressed and clubs are organized with regular dues. *Sources of party funds*

All of these sources, however, would not carry a major party far toward the vast sums required. By and large, the money for national, and to some extent for state, campaigns comes rather from businessmen, bankers, government contractors, labor unions, and other private citizens who have, or think they have, something at stake in the success or defeat of a given party. These chiefly are the "prospects" on whom the party treasurers and members of finance committees work in their money-raising drives. Corporations are forbidden by law to contribute. This does not stand in the way of gifts by officers, directors, stockholders, acting as individuals. The list, especially of Republican contributors, is filled with the names of the executives of large corporations. Since 1943, labor unions also have been forbidden to contribute to campaign funds, but this has not prevented the AFL-CIO from aiding the campaigns chiefly of Democratic candidates through auxiliary agencies, notably the Committee on Political Education. Although the number of very large gifts to either party is small, the bulk of the contributions come from a comparatively few persons. The six top party committees in 1952 reported 55 percent of their contributions were received from 2407 gifts of $1000 or more and the figures in 1956 and 1960 showed about the same thing. Both parties have tried energetically in the past few campaigns to increase the number of small donors. Undoubtedly they feel that the small gift ties the giver more strongly than otherwise to the party. An increasingly popular device for this purpose is the $50- to $100-plate dinners invented by the Democrats but now used also by the Republicans. These efforts have been highly successful. A Salute to Eisenhower dinner in January, 1958, featuring closed circuit television to 37 *Contributions at campaign time* separate banquet halls netted over $4 million. Furthermore, the number of givers has been strikingly increased by these devices. The number of contributors is estimated at 8 million in 1956 and 10 million in 1960. The Michigan Survey Research Center reports about 10 percent of the adults surveyed reported making a contribution in the 1956 campaign.[19]

REGULATION OF CONTRIBUTIONS AND EXPENDITURES

The need for regulation

The high cost of modern campaigning and the resultant pressure on the party organization to raise huge sums of money raise a number of difficult problems. In the first place, the candidate in modest circumstances who cannot afford a large outlay on his own behalf is either unable to compete or is completely dependent upon the party organization to support him. In the second place, some of the contributions are not wholly disinterested. Some contributors expect personal favors from a successful party or candidate in the form of an appointment to office—as ambassador, for example—or of benevolent governmental policies toward the enterprise or group with which they are identified. The political-interest group, for example, is likely to want legislation or administration favorable to the group in return for campaign aid. Concern over the excessive domination of candidates or parties by a few wealthy persons or special interests has induced national and state governments to attempt to regulate political contributions and expenditures by laws known as "corrupt-practice acts."

State regulation

The corrupt-practices legislation of the 47 states that attempt to regulate party finance varies widely and only a brief summary is possible. Typically, it prohibits such patently corrupt behavior as bribery, treating, intimidation or impersonation of voters, ballot-box stuffing, and tampering with voting machines. It also outlaws many practices not in themselves corrupt and extends to both giving and spending party funds. About three-fourths of the states, for example, forbid contributions by banks and other corporations—although not by the officers or directors as individuals. About one-fourth of the states forbid levies on officeholders. Nearly all the state laws attempt to place a ceiling on expenditures by or on behalf of candidates either as a flat sum or as a percentage of salary of the office sought or as a multiple of the number of voters in the constituency.[20] A few states place a limit on the total expenditures of a state committee. Few of these regulations are effective anywhere. If the law limits the party committee or the candidate, expenditures can be made by unofficial committees or by friends of the candidate. If assessments of officeholders are forbidden, contributions by officeholders rarely are. A more effective

---

[19] The whole subject of campaign costs and contributions is treated extensively in A. Heard, *The Costs of Democracy* (Chapel Hill, N. C. 1960).

[20] One of the newest of the state acts, that of Florida of 1951, makes no attempt to limit expenditures but places most emphasis on reporting and on limiting contributions. See E. E. Roady, "Florida's New Campaign Expense Law and the 1952 Democratic Gubernatorial Primaries," *Amer. Pol. Sci. Rev.*, XLVIII (June, 1954).

part of most state corrupt-practice laws is that requiring publicity of receipts and disbursements. About three-fourths of the states require candidates and parties to file reports of their finances either before or after election or at both times. Publicity after the election is usually not effective, however, and that before the election is incomplete.

Congress, on its part, has also attempted to regulate campaign financing in connection with the election of national officers. The Congressional efforts have been little more effective than those of the state legislatures. They may be summarized under four heads.   *National regulation*

1. *Limitations on the raising of money.* Under civil-service law, persons on the national payroll may not be solicited for contributions for political purposes by any officer or employee of the government or by anyone in a government office building. An act of 1907 forbids any national bank or other corporation organized under national law to contribute to any campaign fund whatsoever, and makes it unlawful for any corporation organized under state law to contribute to such a fund in connection with the election of national officials. A clause in the War Labor Disputes (Smith-Connally) Act of 1943 extended these restrictions to labor unions. The Labor-Management Relations (Taft-Hartley) Act of 1947 replaced the expired act of 1943 and prohibited, under severe penalties, contributions *or expenditures* by labor unions or other organizations (equally with banks and corporations) in connection with national elections and all primaries, caucuses, and conventions held in connection therewith.[21] Finally, under the Political Activities Act (Hatch) of 1939 as amended in 1940 no contributions from relief workers (when such exist) may be received, and no individual, committee, or association may donate more than $5000 in any calendar year to the campaign of any candidate for a national office, exclusive of any contribution to a state or local committee.

2. *Restrictions on amounts that may be spent.* The Federal Corrupt Practices Act of 1925 limits the expenditures of a candidate for the Senate to $10,000 and of a candidate for the House to $2500, unless a lower maximum is fixed by law of the candidate's state, in which case that law governs. A candidate has a right, however, to the benefit of an alternative rule under which he may spend up to three cents per vote cast for all candidates for the given office in the last preceding general election, with a maximum of $25,000 for a Senatorial candidate and $5000 for a candidate for the House. One other restriction, found in the amending Political Activities Act of 1940, is that no "political committee" operating nationally may receive or expend more than $3 million in any calendar year.

3. *Limitations on the purposes for which money may be spent.* State laws

[21] The Supreme Court has thus far avoided ruling on the question of whether infringement of free speech or press is involved in these regulations although two cases have been before them involving political expenditures by C.I.O. unions. See United States *v.* C.I.O. 355 U. S. 106 (1948) and United States *v.* U.A.W.-C.I.O., 352 U. S. 567 (1957).

on this subject are usually quite ample. National restriction does not extend much beyond prohibition of the more obvious types of corrupt practice; indeed, in limiting the amount of expenditure as indicated above, the law expressly exempts outlays of candidates on travel, subsistence, stationery, postage, circulars, telegraph and telephone service, and for "personal" items.

4. *Requirement of publicity.* This takes two main forms. First, every candidate for the Senate or House is required to file with the secretary of the Senate or the clerk of the House, both before and after election, a full report of all contributions received in support of his candidacy and an itemized statement of expenditures. Second, all party committees (and likewise all other committees, organizations, and associations which receive donations or spend money for political purposes in two or more states) must under oath make full periodic reports of their financial operations. Thus, pre-election reports are due September 1-10, October 17-22, and October 27, and must include the names of all donors of $100 or more (in the case of national organizations, $10 or more).

Weaknesses:

As a writer on American politics once remarked, there is no law on the subject of campaign expenditures without loopholes large enough to "drive a four-horse team" through.[22] A brief analysis of the national regulations will show why they do not achieve their apparent objectives.

1. Excludes primaries

At the time the Corrupt Practices Act of 1925 was passed, it was widely supposed that Congress could not constitutionally regulate primary elections preceding national elections. Although the Supreme Court now holds the primaries to be subject to Congressional regulation, the Congress has never extended the act to include expenditures in primaries. Not infrequently, especially in one-party states, primary campaign expenditures are larger than those in the election campaign. Secondly, a candidate need not report as expenditure any sums paid out for his travel, subsistence, stationery, postage, printing, or personal services. A larger loophole is that there is no restriction or even any reporting required of amounts spent on behalf of candidates by friends or associates or local or state party groups, whether such expenditures are with the knowledge and consent of the candidate or not. The attempt to limit national committee expenditures to $3 million a year has the same weakness. All sorts of new clubs, associations, and informal committees have grown up alongside the national committee as vehicles for additional expenditures, for example, Citizens for Eisenhower, Associated Willkie Clubs of 1940, Citizens for Kennedy-Johnson. The prohibition of labor union or corporation expenditures does not apply to auxiliary organizations which may be supported by union or corporate funds. As for individuals having contributed the legal maximum of $5000 to a national committee, they are not prevented from making further contributions to auxiliary organizations and to state and local committees.

2. Excludes personal expense

3. Excludes indirect expenditure

4. Excludes auxiliary organizations

5. Excludes loans

In their desperate campaign-time search for funds, party authorities not only seek gifts but sometimes contract loans, usually from affluent well-wishers.

[22] F. R. Kent, *The Great Game of Politics* (Garden City, N. Y., 1923), 217.

Whether originally so intended by the lenders, such loans often turn into actual contributions, though at campaign time are unaccounted for as such. Parties sometimes emerge from campaigns with sizable deficits and may raise the money to meet them long after the accounting for the year's expenditures has been made. Publicity requirements of both national and state statutes are very imperfectly met, and accounts are often so poorly kept and reports so carelessly prepared as to be almost unintelligible. In a single recent campaign year, 122 candidates for the House of Representatives completely failed to turn in any reports—and apparently nothing happened. Such looseness and obscurity balk anyone trying to find out what actually goes on and, of course, defeat the purpose of well-meant legislation. Finally—and it is now hardly necessary to add this—the entire system (apart, at least, from the main reports of the two national committees) suffers from inadequate enforcement. In fact, there is no proper and permanent enforcing machinery at all. A candidate alleged to have overspent in his campaign may be haled into court or before a Congressional committee by a rival contesting his seat; and after each quadrennial campaign, special Congressional committees on campaign expenditures dig through such records as they can lay hold of and issue voluminous reports. By and large, however, it is only occasionally, and often largely by accident, that anything is done really to put teeth into the laws.

6. Deficits

7. Publicity

8. Enforcement

The problem of regulating campaign finances is clearly one of great difficulty and complexity. Parties must have money and lots of it. Only a small proportion of the electorate are willing to contribute. Under the circumstances, it is not surprising that great influence in party affairs and in the government accrues to those who are willing and able to give or to those who although unable to give are willing to work at the chores of democracy. Although the results of corrupt-practices legislation have been disappointing to some, nevertheless there has been a great deal of genuine improvement over the years in the ethics of political competition. There is little outright bribery, vote buying, and ballot-box stuffing today, and there was a great deal 75 years ago. Party leaders are not quite so anxious to throw money around, callously indifferent to public reaction, as they used to be. On the other hand, campaigning is more expensive than it used to be. Voters will no longer attend the old-fashioned rallies which are relatively inexpensive; they want to sit at home and be reached by radio and television. In 1961, President Kennedy appointed a Commission to look at the subject of campaign costs after a complete revision of the Federal Corrupt Practices Act had passed the Senate the year before and failed even to clear the committee in the House.[23] This Commission recommended that the ceilings on national committees' expenditures be repealed as well as those on individual contributions, that more careful and more complete reporting of expenditures be required, that more

The problem of improvement

[23] The Senate bill based largely on the studies of Senator Gore (Tenn.) would have raised the ceilings on expenditures to more realistic limits and would have extended regulation to primaries.

effective enforcement machinery be created and that a limited tax credit be allowed for political contributions.[24]

Public
financing
of cam-
paigns
In order to reduce the influence of wealth in the democratic process and to equalize party and candidate competition, it has been repeatedly suggested that some or all campaign expenses should be appropriated from the public treasury. In justification it is pleaded that these are necessary costs of our system of government. President Theodore Roosevelt advanced this idea in 1907. In 1910, Colorado undertook an experiment in this direction but the law was declared unconstitutional on the grounds that as drafted it was unfair to minor parties and to new parties. Former Senator Hatch, author of the national legislation in 1939 and 1940, suggested limiting the expenditures of each party in a national campaign to $1 million, with the government giving this amount to each party. In Oregon at present and in four other states at various times brochures on the candidates and party platforms have been prepared and distributed for each campaign at state expense. These "publicity" pamphlets are intended to relieve the candidates and parties of some of the costs of getting their names before the voters. In general, the reaction to these schemes for public financing of campaigns has been unfavorable. Many people regard this as a private, not a public, problem. A large proportion of the voters are not deeply interested. It would be very difficult to draft a system of public financing which would consider legitimate costs realistically, would be fair to all candidates and parties, and would eliminate competition for additional funds.[25] Minnesota now allows a very modest income-tax credit for political contributions and this method of encouraging contributions and wider participation is attracting a great deal of favorable attention.

References

H. A. Bone, *American Politics and the Party System* (3rd ed., New York, 1965).

———— and A. Ranney, *Politics and Voters* (New York, 1963).

M. Duverger, *Political Parties: Their Organization and Activity in the Modern State,* trans. by B. and R. North (New York, 1963).

R. R. Alford, *Party and Society: The Anglo-American Democracies* (Chicago, 1963).

J. M. Burns, *The Deadlock of Democracy; Four-Party Politics in America* (Englewood Cliffs, N.J., 1963).

[24] *New York Times,* April 19, 1962, for full text of report.

[25] Puerto Rico in 1957 adopted a system of public financing of campaigns and party activities. Major parties could draw up to $75,000 a year in off years and up to $150,000 in election years. See H. Wells, *Government Financing of Political Parties in Puerto Rico* (Princeton, N. J., 1961).

D. D. McKean, *Party and Pressure Politics* (Boston, 1949), Chaps. I-II, IV-V, IX-XIV, XVI-XVII.

V. O. Key, Jr., *Politics, Parties, and Pressure Groups* (5th ed., New York, 1963). Chaps. VII-XVIII.

W. Goodman, *The Two Party System in the United States* (New York, 1960).

E. P. Herring, *The Politics of Democracy: American Parties in Action* (New York, 1940), Chaps. III-IV, VII-VIII, XIII-XV, XXV.

W. E. Binkley, *American Political Parties; Their Natural History* (New York, 1943).

A. N. Holcombe, *Our More Perfect Union; From Eighteenth-Century Principles to Twentieth-Century Practice* (Cambridge, Mass., 1950), Chaps. IV-V.

————, *The Middle Classes in American Politics* (Cambridge, Mass., 1940).

J. R. Starr, "The Legal Status of American Political Parties," XXXIV, 439-455, 685-699 (June and Aug., 1940).

Anon., "The Right to Form a Party," *Ill. Law Rev.*, XLIII, 832-846 (Jan.-Feb., 1949).

Committee on Political Parties, American Political Science Association, *Toward a More Responsible Two-Party System* (New York, 1950).

M. Moos, *The Republicans: A History of Their Party* (New York, 1956).

D. L. Cohen, *The Fabulous Democrats: A History of the Democratic Party* (New York, 1956).

W. B. Hesseltine, *The Rise and Fall of Third Parties; From Anti-Masonry to Wallace* (Washington, 1948).

W. Moscow, *Politics in the Empire State* (New York, 1948).

M. S. and S. W. Stedman, *Discontent at the Polls; A Study of Farmer and Labor Parties, 1827-1948* (New York, 1950).

F. I. Greenstein, *The American Party System and the American People* (Englewood Cliffs, N.J., 1963).

C. P. Cotter and B. C. Hennessy, *Politics Without Power: the National Party Committees* (New York, 1964).

B. C. Hennessy, *Dollars for Democrats, 1959*, Eagleton Institute Cases in Practical Politics (New York, 1900).

R. V. Peel, *The Political Clubs of New York City* (New York, 1935).

E. E. Schattschneider, *Party Government* (New York, 1942).

————, *The Struggle for Party Government* (College Park, Md., 1948).

D. Acheson, *A Democrat Looks at His Party* (New York, 1955).

A. Leiserson, *Parties and Politics: An Institutional and Behavioral Approach* (New York, 1958).

S. A. Mitchell, *Elm St. Politics* (New York, 1959).

A. Ranney and W. Kendall, "The American Party Systems," *Amer. Pol. Sci. Rev.*, XLVIII (June, 1954).

H. A. Bone, *Party Committees and National Politics* (Seattle, Wash., 1958).

P. T. David, *The Changing Party Pattern* (Washington, 1956).

H. N. Megill (comp.), *Federal Corrupt Practices Act and the Hatch Political Activity Act* (Washington, 1948).

L. Overacker, *Money in Elections* (New York, 1932).

————, *Presidential Campaign Funds* (Boston, 1946).

A. Campbell, G. Gurin, and W. E. Miller, *The Voter Decides* (Evanston, Ill., 1954).

A. Heard, *The Costs of Democracy* (Chapel Hill, N.C., 1960).

N. E. Alexander, *Money, Politics, and Public Reporting* (Princeton, N.J., 1960).

J. R. White and J. R. Owens, *Parties, Group Interests and Campaign Finance: Michigan 1956* (Princeton, N.J., 1960).

R. E. Lane, *Political Life: Why People Get Involved in Politics* (New York, 1959).

F. J. Sorauf, "Patronage and Party," *Midwest Jour. of Pol. Sci.*, III (May, 1959).

————, *Political Parties in the American System* (Boston, 1964).

H. McClosky and H. E. Dahlgren, "Primary Group Influence on Party Loyalty," *Amer. Pol. Sci. Rev.*, Vol. LIII, Sept. 1959.

J. G. Grumm, "Theories of Electoral Systems," *Midwest Journal of Pol. Sci.*, (Nov., 1958).

President's Commission on Campaign Costs, *Report* (Washington, 1962).

C. E. Schutz, "Bureaucratic Party Organization Through Professional Political Staffing," *Midwest Journal of Pol. Sci.*, Vol. VIII, No. 2 (May, 1964).

S. J. Elderserld, *Political Parties: A Behavioral Analysis* (Chicago, 1964).

★ 8 ★

Nominations

AMONG THE MANY USEFUL purposes in the American system of government served by political parties, none is more fundamental than the designation of candidates to stand for public office. In sifting out the many aspirants for power and place in the vast constituencies of American politics, the parties reduce the alternatives available and thus facilitate majority decision. Without this sifting process the power of the electorate would be scattered among numerous choices, no one of which might command the support of more than a small handful of the voters. Although party efforts do not universally produce majority decisions, they do tend to prevent domination of the electoral process by one or two groups.

Impor-tance of nomination procedure: 1. Facili-tates majority rule

The grip of the party organizations on the nomination process has been loosened but not shattered by the introduction of direct participation by the voters in the selection of party candidates. The primary election systems have made the nominating of candidates an integral part of the election process. An understanding of nominating procedure is indispensable, therefore, to a proper appreciation of the meaning and nature of the power of the voter in American democracy.

2. Has become a part of elections

In many communities and in several states, where one political party so far overshadows any others that its nominees are virtually assured of election, the nominating procedure is the main point at which real influence can be exerted by the average citizen. In the Democratic South, Republican New England and the Plains, and cities such as Chicago and New York, dominated by entrenched political organizations, the nominating process is frequently more influential in determining the policies of the governments of those areas than is the election.

3. Re-places election in one-party areas

THE EVOLUTION OF NOMINATING PROCEDURES

Contemporary nominating procedures are the product of many decades of political experience. They have evolved through successive forms—caucus, convention, primary—each of which has broadened the amount of popular participation over its predecessor but none of which has ever been wholly abandoned. Before we embark, however, on a survey of this development it may be useful to digress a moment and to point out that candidates do not

Nomina-tion by petition

have to be nominated in order to be elected. A qualified person may, legally at least, be elected to almost any office in the nation without ever having been nominated in any formal sense. Aspirants for public office in nearly every state may have their names appear on the ballot on election day by filing a petition supported by some specified number of qualified voters. Such aspirants are

"Write-in" can-didates not, however, entitled to bear the label of a major political party. They must run as independents or as representatives of a party which cannot or will not participate in the regular nominating process. Moreover, candidates may be selected to office whose names do not appear on the ballot at all. Virtually every ballot (or voting machine) in America makes provision for a voter to "write-in" for any office within his choice the name of an individual whom he wishes to support. Few persons, however, ever attain office either as "independents" or as "write-in" candidates. Occasionally, in small constituencies and for local offices, such candidates are swept into office by their fellow citizens. In the state and the nation, however, election is normally achieved only by those who have been nominated by a party.

Caucus The earliest known nominating procedure in American experience appeared in pre-Revolutionary days in connection with election to city councils or colonial assemblies and came to be called the *caucus*. This method is quite informal and is simply a meeting of party or faction or community leaders at which they agree to support, and to propose that their fellow citizens support, some individual or slate of individuals to the office or offices presently to be filled by election. The caucus sprang up and flourished spontaneously without legal prescription or party rule, and until the Jacksonian era no other nominating procedure was used to any extent. As party organization became more formalized, caucuses also became more formalized and spread upwards to state and national politics much as the hierarchy of party committees reached across city, county, and state lines. Gradually the caucuses at the local (ward, town, city), level began to designate representatives to meet with those from other districts to form county and state bodies which coordinated the selection of party standard bearers for state and Congressional offices. As they enlarged their scope they became formalized into county, state, and ultimately national conventions of representatives from local caucuses, and thus the convention system of nominations came into being.

The legis-lative caucus Side-by-side with the development of the caucus system for local nominations, a special form of caucus came into being at the state and national levels: the legislative caucus. In the absence of state-wide or national machinery for designating party candidates for Governor and President, the party members in the state legislatures and in the Congress took it upon themselves to meet in caucus to agree on candidates for these high offices to be presented in behalf of the party to the voters. This procedure united the legislative and executive branches of the government more firmly than they have ever been since it disappeared. But it united them under circumstances which enlarged the legislative influence over the executive. Its abandonment paved the way for the gradual emergence of a more powerful and more dominating executive in both state and national government. The legislative caucus fell into disfavor and gradually disappeared in the decade after 1820. The attack upon it sprang from the fact that it was not representative—it contained no members to speak for the party in states or districts represented at the moment by members of the other party. And also from the fact that it promoted executive dependence upon the legislature which was out of keeping not only with the aspirations of ambitious executives but with the spirit of the "Founding Fathers" as well. On the national scene, the Congressional Democratic caucus made the "fatal" mistake of not nominating Andrew Jackson in 1824 and then followed this "blunder" by refusing to support him when the electoral vote was so split that the decision fell to the House of Representatives. By 1835, the legislative caucus as a nominating device for executive office had virtually disappeared from the American scene.

The predominant mode of designating candidates from 1825 to 1910 was the party convention. Caucuses continued to function as devices for selecting delegates from precincts, wards, or towns to city, county, or state conventions. The national, state, and local conventions became more and more regularized institutions for naming party candidates. Apportionment systems were developed for determining the number of delegates to which each precinct, ward, or election district was entitled. Party rules were adopted, providing for such delegate apportionment and for the methods for selecting delegates. Typically, delegates were chosen from precincts for city or county conventions, from city or county conventions to state conventions and to Congressional district conventions, and from state conventions to national conventions. This method, it was asserted, transmitted the wishes of the party voters from the precinct upward to the national conclave by an unbroken chain. The conventions also came to serve many other partisan functions. They provided rallying places for energizing the party apparatus and enthusing the party workers. They provided a useful facility for the adoption and promulgation of local, state, and national platforms. They served as testing grounds for party orators and for influential party leaders from other areas of the nation. The convention, although characterized by noise, confusion, and drama, nevertheless provided a means through which party leaders could weigh and balance the qualifications of the candidates. Tickets could be properly balanced; sections, interest groups, racial and religious minorities could all be considered and, if possible, placated. Behind the scenes of the conventions, a few leaders continued as before to meet in caucus and propose slates which the rank-and-file delegates might accept. With this difference, however: a larger and more representative segment of the party members had the opportunity to ratify or veto the leaders' choices.

Toward the end of the nineteenth century, the convention fell increasingly into disrepute. The delegate selection procedures, irregular at best, fell periodically under the domination of ruthless leaders who packed local caucuses and

Convention

Criticism of convention

frustrated genuine representation of local party sentiment. By the time that attempts to regulate such matters by law became general, the convention system was disappearing. The delegates, frequently an undistinguished group, were too often bought and sold or traded by bosses who callously disregarded public sentiment. In the state and national conventions, several stages removed from popular participation, opponents of the leaders found it especially difficult to make headway, although frequently they enjoyed wide public support. The Civil War, too, had left a large number of one-party states (Democrats in the South and Republican in New England and the Midwest) in which the nominating procedure was of major importance. The continued surge of the democratic ideal, interpreted in this situation as demanding more voter participation, also contributed to the downfall of the convention system.[1]

Direct primary

After 1900, the convention system was gradually discarded as a nominating device. It survives today only for Presidential nominations and for statewide offices in a few states (notably New York, Connecticut, Delaware, and Indiana).[2] In its place the direct primary system for making nominations has been adopted in some form in every state. The essence of the direct primary is the selection of the candidates by direct action of the voters themselves. The procedures employed are so similar to those used in the final elections that the primary becomes, in effect, a preliminary intraparty election, and often in earlier days was called a *direct primary election*. Primaries of the different parties are commonly held on the same day and at the places where the regular elections are held later; they are administered by the regular election officials, with all costs met out of the public treasury; the ballots are like those used in regular elections; and the same corrupt-practice laws and other safeguards apply.[3] Persons seeking nomination to an office may get their names on a primary ballot simply by self-announcement and perhaps payment of a fee; or they may have been picked at some sort of caucus or preprimary convention. The common method, however, is to file a petition signed by some specified proportion of the voters in the area, the proportion being gauged

[1] For fuller discussion of the rise and defects of the caucus-convention system, see M. Ostrogorski, *Democracy and the Party System* (New York, 1910), Chaps. II-V; E. C. Meyer, *Nominating Systems* (New York, 1902), Pt. 1, Chap. V; and F. W. Dallinger, *Nominations for Elective Offices in the United States* (New York, 1897).

[2] In six Southern states, however, parties are permitted to employ conventions if they choose; and in Iowa a convention is employed for nominating a party candidate for any office, state or local, for which no person has received as much as 35 percent of the primary vote, with South Dakota following the same plan in connection with the offices of Governor, United States Senator, and Representative in Congress.

With a view to meeting the charge that large nominating conventions are "rigged" and organization-controlled, Indiana in 1948 introduced a plan under which, instead of voting on candidates orally from the floor, delegates register their choices secretly on voting machines. At the first test results evidenced unusual independence.

[3] Exceptions, however, appear in southern states, where only Democratic primaries are held, and where, in some states, e.g., Texas, the costs are borne by the party or the candidate.

roughly in accordance with the importance of the office, and varying all the way from one-half of 1 percent to as high as 5 or even 10 percent.[4] A number of states require the petition to be accompanied by a filing fee. Ordinarily, a candidate receiving the largest number of votes for a given office is declared the party nominee for that office, even though, with often three or four persons seeking the same nomination, the victor may win by virtue of a plurality. All Southern states except Virginia [5] and Tennessee, however, require (as did Utah until 1947) a majority; and if at the first balloting no candidate for a given position receives the requisite vote, a second or "runoff" primary is held, with the voters choosing between the two candidates standing highest at the first test.[6] In any event, winners in the respective party primaries automatically get their names on the ballots placed in the voters' hands at the regular elections.

"Run off" primary

Following local experiments in Pennsylvania and other states, Wisconsin, in 1903, adopted the first mandatory state-wide direct primary law. With reaction against convention nominations sweeping the country in a period of developing progressivism, every state but four, by 1917, enacted similar legislation covering all state offices and in many cases local offices as well (although New York and Indiana, reverted later to the convention system for certain principal offices). The movement went on until the primary became the sole or main mode of nomination the country over and not only for state offices, but for those of the great majority of counties and cities, and also for members of Congress. Connecticut was the last state to fall into line and in 1955 authorized a primary for most public offices when convention choices were chal-

Spread of the system

---

[4] California, in 1927, simplified the plan by substituting for petitions signed by a large number of voters declarations signed by "sponsors," the number ranging from 10 to 20 for the lowest offices up to from 60 to 100 in the case of the highest. A few states have experimented with "preprimary" conventions composed of delegates chosen in preliminary primaries and designed to agree upon lists of persons to be placed on the subsequent regular nominating-primary ballots. Nebraska, Minnesota, and South Dakota have abandoned such a plan. But Utah adopted it in 1947, Massachusetts also adopted one in 1953 and New Mexico, after abandoning the plan in 1955, adopted it again in 1963; Colorado adheres to a similar one, preferring, however, the term *preprimary assembly.* Some sort of preprimary conference or convention has the genuine advantage of offsetting a fundamental weakness of the primary system, i.e., the assumption that satisfactory candidates will always spontaneously seek office and provide the voters with good choices. Connecticut retains the convention system, but if convention nominations are challenged, a primary may be held.

[5] Virginia in 1952 adopted a second or run-off primary if requested by the second-highest candidate within five days of the announcement of the official result.

[6] In order to approximate majority nominations, a number of other states have tried the preferential system of voting, under which each voter is given an opportunity to express his first, second, and sometimes his third, choices among the candidates, with second, and even third, choices added to firsts, if necessary, in order to find a majority for some candidate. Cf. O. D. Weeks, "Summary of the History and Present Status of Preferential Voting in State Direct Primary Systems," *Southwestern Soc. Sci. Quar.,* XVIII, 64-67 (June, 1937).

lenged. In addition, the primary has come to be employed in many states as the occasion for selecting candidates for party offices and committee posts and for service as national convention delegates.

Partisan and non-partisan primaries

The direct primary presupposes elections on a party basis, and consequently is itself partisan. Persons seeking nomination do so as Republicans or Democrats and are so listed on the ballots used. Where, however, nonpartisan elections have been introduced (as for legislative members in Minnesota and Nebraska, and for local offices in many cities and some counties), they usually are preceded by a single nonpartisan primary conducted in all respects like an ordinary party primary, except that the ballots carry no indication of the party affiliations of the persons to be voted for, and that no question as to the voters' own affiliations is raised at the polls. Partisan and nonpartisan primaries, for different offices, may indeed be held at the same time and place, with separate ballots employed for the two. In any event, the two candidates on a nonpartisan ticket polling the highest and next highest number of votes for each office get their names on the nonpartisan ballot used at the ensuing election, the primary thus becoming "a sort of qualifying heat which eliminates the weaker contestants from the final race" and at the same time assuring ultimate election by majority rather than mere plurality. Primaries of this nature may, however, be considerably less nonpartisan than appears; for not only are the contestants likely to be known to the voters as Republicans or Democrats (and voted for accordingly), but they may actually have a good deal of more or less undercover party backing. Even so, the system tends to decrease the role of party organizations in the election and the dependence of candidates on party labels to win support. It has gained most acceptance in judicial elections and those for school officials.

"Closed" and "open" primaries

Partisan primaries may be classified as "closed" or "open," on the basis of the conditions laid down for participating in them. The closed primary is one in which participation is confined to bona fide members of the given party. The intention is to prevent members of the opposition party from helping to select the party's candidate. Two methods of guarding against this "raiding" are employed. One—required by law in most of the closed-primary states (including New York, Pennsylvania, and California)—is an advance enrollment of the party affiliations of all voters. This party registration is shown on the voter lists supplied to polling officials on primary election day and enables them to give to each voter only the ballot or voting machine of the party with which he has claimed affiliation. The other method, employed in most of the remaining closed-primary states, involves a procedure for challenging voters who call at the polls for the ballot of a party with which they are not known to be identified. Such voters may, for example, be asked to state whether they supported that party at the last election, or at all events half of its candidates, or perchance whether it is their expectation to adhere to it in the future. Either of the two procedures can be flouted by persons of easy conscience if there is sufficient motive; the second is particularly weak. By and large, however, a closed primary of a given party is participated in only by more or less habitual adherents of that party.[7]

Some voters, however, have no strong and abiding party allegiance and others believe this is a personal affair. Eight states frankly accept the fact and maintain "open" primaries in which there is no attempt to put the voters' party preferences on record.[8] Instead of asking for and being handed a Republican or a Democratic ballot when he presents himself at the polls, a voter in any one of those states is given either a blanket ballot listing the candidates of the respective parties in separate columns (*one* only to be voted) or a sheaf of ballots containing one for each party. In any event, he votes the ticket of his choice, with no one the wiser. Republicans may take a hand in Democratic nominations, and vice versa; and something of the kind often happens. Some states ostensibly having the closed form of primary really have the open form in disguise, since the tests which they prescribe notoriously fail to prevent voters from shifting their adherence from one party to the other.[9] Professional politicians and strong partisans generally favor the closed primary on the theory that the primary is really a party affair and should not be open to "independents," nonpartisans, or members of some other party. The secrecy of the open primary has a compelling appeal to many voters.

The primary is a nominating device and serves none of the other purposes which conventions had come to serve. There is no room in the primary itself, for example, for preparing a party platform for the coming election. In the few states still using the convention system for state-wide purposes this is no problem. In the exclusively direct primary states, however, some other provisions must be made for platform preparation. In 14 states, some form of party conference is recognized by law as the platform-drafting agency. The Wisconsin system illustrates this procedure. After the primary, the nominees

The primary and the platform

[7] To the general rule that a voter may take part in only one primary at a time, Washington offers the only exception. In that state, since 1935 candidates of all parties have been grouped on a single primary ballot according to the offices sought, and the voter may vote for one candidate for each office regardless of party—thus, if he likes, really participating in the primaries of two or more parties. C. O. Johnson, "The Washington Blanket Primary," *Pacific Northwest Quar.*, XXXIII, 27-39 (Jan., 1942); D. M. Ogden, "Parties Survive Cross-Voting," *Nat. Mun. Rev.*, XXXIX, 237-241 (May, 1950).

[8] Idaho, Minnesota, Montana, North Dakota, Utah, Washington, Wisconsin, and Alaska. Arizona, Colorado, Massachusetts, Missouri, and Nebraska abandoned the open system and in Oregon it was declared unconstitutional.

[9] Several states tacitly permit a member of one party to "cross-file," i.e., to run in the primary of a different party, although a winner of two nominations may usually accept only one. California until 1959 permitted acceptance of two nominations only if one of them came from the candidate's own party. An earlier attempt to repeal "cross-filing" in California in 1952 was narrowly defeated in a state-wide referendum—for the repeal, 2,150,073; against, 2,153,727. In New York, the constitutionality of a (Wilson-Pakula) law of 1947 prohibiting a candidate from entering the primary of a party in which he is not enrolled without permission of the appropriate party committee has been upheld by the state court of appeals. The measure was aimed at Vito Marcantonio, a county chairman of the American Labor party, who had kept himself in the national House of Representatives by running on the tickets of other parties.

of the party for the state legislature and for the state executive posts and the hold-over party members of the state senate are directed by law to assemble and prepare a platform upon which presumably they will collectively campaign.

Critique of the primary

The direct primary unquestionably gives the rank and file voter a larger share in the nominating process than either of its predecessors. It has not, however, eliminated the need for organization to achieve electoral success nor, consequently, the need for some agreement among party leaders on candidates that ought to be offered for the approval of the public. Thus the caucus of party leaders continues to function in many, if not in most, constituencies. With the primary, however, the party voters have to ratify the leaders' choices and minority groups may contest the leaders' slate. Although there is probably less outright vote-buying today than in the heyday of the convention, the cost of getting elected has probably been increased, not decreased, by the primary. With the primary system a candidate has to run twice. Important public office is farther out of the reach of candidates without private means and unsupported by an organization than ever before. The primary system also tends to weaken party organization and party responsibility. The party apparatus may well find itself obliged to support candidates who are distasteful to it and opposed to its ideology but who have captured the sympathy of the voters. The National Municipal League in its Model Direct Primary Elections System recommends that the party organization by conference or caucus ought to be allowed to place a slate on the primary ballot. In the home of the state-wide primary, Wisconsin, both major parties have gone outside of the legally prescribed party machinery and created unofficial and unregulated party organs (called voluntary committees) to breathe new ideological homogeneity and a sense of party responsibility into their operations.[10] This has taken them back to the convention system; and the Republican Party, at least, meeting in unofficial convention endorses candidates for state-wide offices and for United States Senator to the rank and file of its members. This endorsement carries with it the support of the treasury and of the organization of the extralegal committee. Party organizations by these and other methods are gradually adjusting themselves to the primary system, but it has been a painful and difficult process for many of them. They are still not proof against a strong upsurge of popular feeling sweeping away their most cherished tenets of public policy. In considering the results of the direct primary system, it must also be remembered that state law and practice vary in many details from one state to another. No two systems are identical in every respect. There is, finally, no concerted effort of consequence to abolish the primary and return to any earlier nominating process.[11]

[10] F. J. Sorauf, "The Voluntary Committee in Wisconsin," *Amer. Polit. Sci. Rev.,* XLVIII, 692-705 (Sept., 1954).

[11] The standard treatise on the general subject, with full consideration of the question of merits, is C. E. Merriam and L. Overacker, *Primary Elections* (New York, 1928); and much information will be found in C. A. Berdahl, "Party Membership in the United States," II, *Amer. Polit. Sci. Rev.,* XXXVI, 241-262 (Apr., 1942).

REGULATION OF THE NOMINATING PROCESS

Like other activities of political parties, nominations are regulated mainly *By the* by the states. The history of regulation of the nominating process parallels *states* very closely that of party organization already described. The attempt to curb abuses in party procedures for naming candidates accompanied the growing dissatisfaction with the convention system. California in 1866 attempted to bring its party conventions under state law. The movement for state regulation never, however, caught up with the movement for abolishing the conventions. Comprehensive state regulation of the nominating process really accompanied the introduction of the direct primary system. Virtually every state now has constitutional or statutory provisions governing the naming of candidates at all levels. Furthermore, where the convention system survives it is, typically, closely controlled by state laws governing its composition, organization, and procedures. State regulation in practice embraces the nomination as well as the election of national officials as well as of state and local ones.

State regulation of nominations is, however, subject to national modifica- *By the* tion. A constitutional power rests with the Congress, when it cares to exercise *national* it, to regulate the time, places, and manners of electing Senators and Repre- *govern-* sentatives. The Supreme Court has declared that the primary is an integral *ment* part of the election process and is, therefore, subject to the guarantees of the Civil War amendments. Negroes, thus, may not validly be denied the right by any extant procedure to participate in the primaries of any party. The power of Congress to regulate spending and other aspects of national election and campaign procedures conceivably under the modern interpretation extends to the primaries for these elections as well. Congress has not, however, seen fit to occupy this field except to achieve Negro participation, and the state regulations continue to be the only effective ones.

References

C. A. Berdahl, "Party Membership in the United States," *Amer. Polit. Sci. Rev.,* XXXVI, 16-50, 241-262 (Feb. and Apr., 1942).

C. E. Merriam and L. Overacker, *Primary Elections* (New York, 1928).

J. K. Pollock, *The Direct Primary in Michigan* (Ann Arbor, Mich., 1943).

L. M. Holland, *The Direct Primary in Georgia* (Urbana, Ill., 1949).

P. Beckett and W. L. McNutt, *The Direct Primary in New Mexico* (Albuquerque, N.M., 1947).

B. A. Martin, *The Direct Primary in Idaho* (Stanford Univ., 1947).

R. N. Ballard, *The Primary Convention System of Utah* (Salt Lake City, 1947).

National Municipal League, *A Model Direct Primary System* (New York, 1951).

C. Ewing, *Primary Elections in the South* (Norman, Okla., 1953).

J. E. Holmes, *Problems Relating to Various Nominating Procedures in New Mexico* (Santa Fé, N.M., 1955).

D. Lockard, *Connecticut's Challenge Primary: A Study in Legislative Politics* (New York, 1959).

A. Hacker, "Does a Divisive Primary Harm a Candidate's Elective Chances?," *Amer. Pol. Sci. Rev.,* Vol. LIX, No. 1, (Mar. 1965).

L. Row, *Preprimary Endorsements in California Politics* (Berkeley, Cal., 1961).

See also the works cited at the end of Chapters 6 and 8.

★ 9 ★

Nominating and Electing
a President

THE DEMOCRATIC PROCESS realizes its most significant fruit in the quadrennial selection of the nation's chief magistrate. All of the elements of the process coalesce in this unique and dramatic spectacle. The political parties reach their maximum effectiveness; the nomination process, involving caucuses, conventions, and primaries, captures the interest and enthusiasm of the people as at no other time. Every medium of communication—radio, television, newspapers, magazines, books, pamphlets, leaflets—swamps the public with fact, argument, and exhortation on the affairs of the nation and of those who seek to run it. Political-interest groups strive for places in the sun of each candidate's appreciation. The voters troop out to the polls on election day in larger numbers than on any other occasion. A vast radio and television audience intensely follows the tabulation of the returns. The pageant of an American Presidential election is the most remarkable exhibition of popular government anywhere in the world. No other election quite equals it in drama, suspense, oratory, participation in electioneering, carnival atmosphere, ink spilled, or money spent. *The pageant of a Presidential election*

It is impossible to fix a precise time at which this great spectacle begins to unfold. In one sense it is going on all the time, for hardly has a new chief executive settled into the White House before some plans are afoot for the next campaign. Late in the year preceding an election year, however, "available" candidates begin to utter declarations or make decisions which convey their willingness to make the run. Organizations then begin to form, "booms" are launched, personal and party groups spar for advantage in the press, in the Congress, in state capitals, city halls, and courthouses throughout the land. Voter participation in the nominating process begins in March of a Presidential year and continues sporadically through April, May, and June. In July or August the great and tumultuous national conventions assemble to select their standard bearers. A pause follows while the campaign apparatus of the parties is geared and oiled for the great effort. Then from September until election day in early November, the drama moves from scene to scene, mounting in intensity, noise, and enthusiasm. At length the vote is cast, the *The timetable of a Presidential election*

189

decision made by 70 million people. It is a stirring demonstration of American democracy in action.

THE OPENING OF THE CAMPAIGN 1960

THE KENNEDY STATEMENT

Following is the text of Senator John F. Kennedy's Statement announcing his candidacy for the 1960 Democratic Presidential nomination:

I am announcing today my candidacy for the Presidency of the United States.

The Presidency is the most powerful office in the free world. Through its leadership can come a more vital life for our people. In it are centered the hopes of the globe around us for freedom and a more secure life. For it is in the Executive Branch that the most crucial decisions of this century must be made in the next four years.

How to end or alter the burdensome arms race, where Soviet gains already threaten our very existence; how to maintain freedom and order in the newly emerging nations; how to rebuild the stature of American science and education; how to prevent the collapse of our farm economy and the decay of our cities; how to achieve, without further inflation or unemployment, expanded economic growth benefiting all Americans, and how to give direction to our traditional moral purpose, awakening every American to the dangers and opportunities that confront us.

These are among the real issues of 1960. And it is on the basis of these issues that the American people must make their fateful choice for their future.

"I CAN WIN"

In the past forty months, I have toured every state in the Union and I have talked to Democrats in all walks of life. My candidacy is therefore based on the conviction that I can win both the nomination and the election.

I believe that any Democratic aspirant to this important nomination should be willing to submit to the voters his views, record and competence in a series of primary contests. I am therefore announcing my intention of filing in the New Hampshire primary and I shall announce my plans with respect to the other primaries as their filing dates approach.

I believe that the Democratic party has a historic function to perform in the winning of the 1960 election, comparable to its role in 1932. I intend to do my utmost to see that that victory is won.

For eighteen years I have been in the service of the United States, first as a naval officer in the Pacific during World War II and for the past fourteen years as a member of the Congress. In the last twenty years, I have traveled in nearly every continent and country—from Leningrad to Saigon, from Bucharest to Lima. From all of this, I have developed an image of America as fulfilling a noble and historic role as the defender of freedom in a time of maximum peril—and of the American people as confident, courageous and persevering.

It is with this image that I begin this campaign.

SOURCE: *The New York Times,* Jan. 3, 1960.

THE OPENING OF THE CAMPAIGN OF 1964

THE GOLDWATER STATEMENT

Jan. 3, 1964

Following is the transcript of Senator Barry Goldwater's news conference yesterday in Paradise City, Ariz.

Ever since the last Republican convention, thousands of Americans have asked me to seek the Republican Presidential nomination in 1964. Now I've withheld a decision until now not to be politically coy, but because I've been giving every aspect of such a decision the most serious consideration.

Today, here at our home in a state that I love, with my family and with the people whose friendship and political interest have placed me where I am, I want to tell you two things.

First, I want to tell you that I will seek the Republican Presidential nomination. And I have decided to do this because of the principles in which I believe and because I'm convinced that millions of Americans share my belief in those principles.

I've decided to do this also because I have not heard from any announced Republican candidate a declaration of conscience or of political position that could possibly offer to the American people a clear choice in the next Presidential election.

Now one of the great attributes of our American two-party system has always been the reflected differences in principle.

As a general rule, one party has emphasized individual liberty and the other has favored the extension of Government power.

I am convinced that today a majority in the Republican party believes in the essential emphasis on individual liberty.

WON'T ALTER BELIEFS

Now I've been spelling out my position for 10 years in the Senate and for years before that here in my own state. Now I'll spell it out even further in the months to come.

Back—back in the first Senatorial campaign that I engaged in I was asked by a very prominent member of the press in this state what kind of a Republican are you? And I replied that I was not a me-too Republican and this still holds.

I won't change my beliefs to win votes. I will offer a choice, not an echo. This will not be an engagement of personalities. It will be an engagement of principles.

I've always stood for Government that is limited and balanced and against ever-increasing concentrations of authority in Washington.

I've always stood for individual responsibility and against regimentation. I believe we must now make a choice in this land and not continue drifting endlessly down toward a time when all of us, all of our lives, our property, our hopes and even our prayers will become just cogs in a vast Government machine.

I believe that we can win victory for freedom both at home and abroad. And I believe that we can be strong enough and determined enough to win those victories without war.

CALLS 1964 YEAR OF CHOICE

And I believe that appeasement and weakness can only bring war. I have asked and I will continue to ask across this country: Why not victory—why not victory for sound constitutional principles in government? Why not victory over the evils of Communism?

I am convinced that in this year of 1964 we must face up to our conscience and make a definite choice. We must decide what sort of people we are and what sort of a world we want—now and for our children.

My candidacy is pledged to a victory for principle and to presenting an opportunity for the American people to choose.

Let there be a choice right now and in clear understandable terms. And I ask all those who feel and believe as I do to join with me in assuring both the choice and the victory.

SOURCE: *The New York Times,* Jan. 4, 1964.

THE CONSTITUTIONAL ELECTORAL SYSTEM

The plan originally adopted

This is not at all the sort of thing that the makers of our Constitution had in view. They did not want the President elected by Congress, because then he would not be sufficiently independent. Neither did they want him elected by the people, because the voters, scattered thinly over what already seemed a large country, would not know enough about the qualifications of available men to be able to make wise decisions. The matter troubled the convention considerably, and 30 different votes on it were taken. At last, however, a plan of indirect election was agreed upon under which: (1) each state should have as many "Presidential electors" as Senators and Representatives in Congress; (2) these electors should be chosen in the several states in whatever manner the state legislatures should specify; (3) each elector, at the proper time, should cast a ballot for two persons for the Presidency; and (4) the persons receiving the highest and next highest votes, respectively, should be President and Vice-President. The entire procedure was to be quiet, dignified, and deliberate, with presumably the best qualified men emerging from the sifting. During the struggle over ratification, the plan proved one of the few features of the new Constitution that did not have to be defended. This system produced two Presidents: Washington and Adams. By 1800, it had been modified almost beyond recognition.

In 1788, and again in 1792, every elector wrote the name of Washington *Effect of* on his ballot, with second names scattered. In 1796, with Washington bent *the rise of* on retiring, 13 different persons received electoral votes, John Adams stand- *political* ing first and Jefferson second. In 1800, however, every elector except one, the *parties* country over, wrote on his ballot the names of either Jefferson and Burr or Adams and Pinckney. In the meantime two political parties—Federalist and Republican—had organized to capture the Presidency. Each had taken steps in advance of the elections in the states to agree upon particular "candidates" (nominally for the Presidency, but actually for the Presidency and Vice-Presi- dency), and to put before the voters and legislatures making the choices lists of men who would, if chosen, cast their electoral ballots in all cases for the persons supported by the party to which they belonged. With the rise of na- tional political parties, Presidential elections from that time assumed an en- tirely different aspect from that planned. The way was thus opened for partisan, popular Presidential campaigns to develop the "tumultuous" characteristics which the framers would have deplored. The Presidential electors became the mere "row of ciphers," which we know today, with President and Vice-Presi- dent to all intents and purposes chosen by the people. No better illustration can be found of how the actual working Constitution changes without a hand being laid on the written fundamental law.

In the new situation, a tie between the two candidates of a winning party *The* was inevitable unless anticipated beforehand. Jefferson and Burr, in fact, re- *Twelfth* ceived the highest, and the same number of votes. The Constitution, it is true, *Amend-* provided that a tie was to be broken by the House of Representatives, voting *ment* by states; and in this manner Jefferson finally was elected. The Federalist op- *(1804)* position, however, were strongly tempted to thwart the intention of the victors by maneuvering Burr into the highest office; and before the next election came around any repetition of the difficulty was made impossible by an amendment to the Constitution specifying that thereafter electors should in all cases "name in their ballots the person voted for as President, and in distinct ballots the person voted for as Vice-President." Thenceforth the issue between Presiden- tial candidates would have to be settled between them alone, and similarly that between Vice-Presidential candidates—although, of course, an election still might be thrown into the House of Representatives. With the Vice-President thereafter being separately selected, the character of that office underwent a decided change. Thenceforth, the second place on the ticket was awarded largely without regard to the individual's capacity to be President.

MACHINERY FOR NOMINATING CANDIDATES— THE NATIONAL CONVENTION

The next significant development had to do with a matter for which the *Nomina-* framers of the Constitution made no provision, that is, the nomination of *tions* candidates. The original electoral system did not contemplate "candidates" *become* at all. The main object of the national political parties came to be to capture *a necessity* the Presidency. To do this, they had to concentrate their support at election time upon a given individual, which, in turn, they could do only if such individual, or candidate, were agreed upon in advance. Thus arose the need for machinery for making the selection in advance of the regular election.

From Congressional caucus to national convention

The first device hit upon was the caucus composed of the (national) Senators and Representatives of a given party; and it was employed steadily from 1800 to 1824. There were, however, serious objections to it. The caucus acted only by assumed authority; it provided little or no voice for party members in states and districts in which the party was in a minority; and it gave members of the legislative branch an influence in selecting the chief executive which they clearly were not intended to have. The caucus fell from favor when in 1824 it refused to endorse Andrew Jackson, later the plurality winner of the popular vote. In 1831, both the National Republican and Anti-Masonic parties turned to popularly-chosen nominating conventions, already employed usefully in many state elections. The Democrats fell into line with a convention of their own in 1832. Many political leaders, including Webster and Calhoun, opposed the new method on the ground that it gave too much power in party matters to the rank and file. Nevertheless, by 1840 the national convention became the generally accepted means of putting both candidates and platforms before the voters; and such it has remained.

Arrangements for conventions: time and place

The national conventions of the two major parties today, and likewise of such minor parties as have built up durable organizations, are held on call of the national party committee. A year or more preceding a Presidential election, the committee meets, decides upon the place and date of the coming convention, and authorizes the party organizations in the states and territories to see that delegates and alternates are chosen in accordance with an apportionment set forth in the call. Typically, the Republicans meet first and the Democrats several days or even weeks later. In 1956, and 1960, however, the Democrats met first. A serious effort was made to shorten the campaign in 1956 by holding the conventions in August instead of late June or early July, and although in 1960 both parties returned to July meetings, in 1964, the Democrats again met in August. The national committees are strongly pressured by business interests of many of the large cities to select their cities as convention sites. Eager for the advertising and certain of large sales to delegates and visitors, the city representatives typically offer substantial contributions to the party treasuries to win approval. The national committees are, however, concerned about more than donations. They must keep an eye on the adequacy of hotel and convention facilities and they seek to gain any partisan advantage they can by selecting cities where the convention enthusiasm will assist the party or a particular candidate. Chicago and Philadelphia have been the most popular convention sites but St. Louis, Cleveland, and Baltimore also ordinarily receive consideration. The West Coast has grown in popularity recently; the Republicans met in San Francisco in 1956 and 1964 and the Democrats in Los Angeles in 1960. Each party determines for itself how its convention will be constituted. Thus far, there are no national laws regulating the matter.

The first national conventions had no regular plan of membership but it was soon learned that without a plan partisans from nearby states and cities would swamp the convention. The earliest plan was quite simple: each state was assigned as many delegates as it was entitled to electoral votes (one for each member of both houses of Congress). In 1852, the Democrats doubled the number assigned to each state, probably to allow more persons to participate in the choice. The Republicans followed the same plan in 1860. This remained the plan of both parties until modified in this century. *Conven-tion member-ship: 1. Earlier arrange-ments*

Weaknesses in the traditional system for apportioning delegates were revealed most clearly in the Republican Party. The states of the Solid South repeatedly sent to Republican national conventions delegates who really represented no consequential party strength. In 1912, for example, Alabama, Louisiana, Mississippi, and South Carolina were represented by 82 delegates, although the combined Republican vote of those states in 1908 had been only 42,592. The 745,779 Republican voters of Pennsylvania were represented at the same meeting by only 72 delegates. The Republican delegates from the South were, in practice, representative of a small group of national officeholders appointed by Republican Presidents. A Republican President could, therefore, and did, usually, control these patronage-delegates and thus was able to wield a powerful influence in the convention. Theodore Roosevelt certainly used these delegates to help bring about Taft's nomination in 1908. When, however, Taft used the same device in 1912 to achieve his own renomination, the party was badly split. Roosevelt, now a strong contender and the clear choice of many rank-and-file Republicans where they had any say in the delegate selection, denounced the system by which Taft controlled the convention and took his followers out of the party into a new Progressive Party. This move cost the Republicans the election and convinced many of the leaders that something would have to be done about the Southern delegations. Beginning with the convention of 1916, the Republicans began paring down the relative strength of the Southern delegations with some paring occurring as recently as 1952. The method used by the Republicans has been to make the number of district delegates contingent upon a minimum Republican voting strength and to grant bonus state delegates to Republican states. *2. Weak-nesses* *3. Re-publican modifica-tion*

The system as it stood for the 1964 convention provides:

STATE DELEGATES (at-large)

1. Four from each state.
2. Two additional for each Congressman-at-large (if any).
3. Six additional from each state casting a majority of its votes for the Republican nominee at the last Presidential election or electing then or in the intervening election a Republican Senator or Governor.

4. Present apportion-ment systems: a. Repub-lican

4. Nine from the District of Columbia, five from Puerto Rico and three from the Virgin Islands.

DISTRICT DELEGATES

1. One from each Congressional district casting 2000 or more votes last time for the Republican Presidential candidate or for the Republican Congressional candidate in the intervening election.
2. One additional from each district casting 10,000 votes or more for the Republican candidates in either election.

b. Demo-crat

The Democrats, with party strength more evenly distributed throughout the country, were able to operate until 1940 without too much friction. In this party, however, the Southern Democrats were underrepresented compared to those in New England. In the convention of 1936 when the rule requiring a two-thirds vote for nomination was repealed, the Northern supporters of the repeal agreed to reward solidly Democratic states by instituting the system of bonus delegates. The repeal of the two-thirds rule greatly weakened the control of the South on the Democratic nomination and the bonus system was introduced partially to offset this. The Democrats seem, also, to be under continuing pressure to increase the number of those attending conventions. A modest provision of two bonus delegates was begun in 1944 and then increased to four in 1948, but in 1952 the rules were modified to protect any state from loss as a result of Congressional reapportionment. Then in 1956 every state was authorized as many delegates as it had in 1952 plus four more if the state had gone Democratic for President or in the interim for Senator or Governor. For 1960, a complex plan was devised granting two and one-half delegate votes for each Representative and Senator and one-half vote for each national committee member but providing that no state might have fewer votes than it had in 1956. Then in 1964 an even more complex system was devised giving each state three votes for each Senator and Representative and one vote for every 100,000 votes cast for the national ticket in 1960 and 10 bonus votes if the state went Democratic in 1960. All of these moves aimed not only at increasing attendance but at increasing the strength of state organizations that had been effective in 1960. The Democrats have also awarded delegates to the territories including the Canal Zone and Guam.

5. Num-bers

Speaking strictly, the composition of a national convention is defined in terms of votes, rather than of delegates. In Republican usage, the distinction has been one without a difference, each delegate having one vote. A rule adopted in 1944 now expressly forbids more delegates from any state or territory than the number of convention votes allotted for it. In Democratic usage, however, many states and territories send delegates in excess of their quota of votes, each delegate in such case casting only a fractional vote. In later days the practice, motivated usually by desire to provide good conven-

HOW THE REPUBLICAN APPORTIONMENT
SYSTEM WORKS

Delegations from Selected States

1964

State	Total Delegates	Delegates at-Large	District Delegates
Alabama	20	4	16
California	86	10	76
Illinois	58	10	48
Mississippi	13	4	9
New York	92	10	82
South Carolina	16	4	12
West Virginia	14	4	10

HOW THE DEMOCRATIC APPORTIONMENT
SYSTEM WORKS

Delegate Votes from Selected States

1964

State	Total Votes	Maximum No. of Delegates
Alabama	38	58
California	154	162
Illinois	114	138
Mississippi	24	46
New York	179	228
South Carolina	38	42
West Virginia	37	50

tion seats for the "boys from home," developed into a serious abuse. To the Democratic convention of 1940 at Chicago, one Mississippi district sent 54 delegates to cast its two votes (each delegate shouldering responsibility for $\frac{1}{27}$ of a vote!), and the state of Texas sent 132 delegates to cast a total of 46 votes; all told 1844 delegates appeared to cast only 1100 votes. On complaint of officials in charge of seating arrangements, the 1940 convention decreed that thereafter no state might send delegates in excess of twice its quota of votes; and delegate attendance fell sharply. In 1952, the convention in violation of its own rules seated oversize delegations from six states, and the total roll was 1643 delegates to cast 1230 votes. In 1960, 3042 delegates were authorized to cast 1521 votes and in 1964, 2944 delegates were authorized to cast 2316 votes. The Republicans in 1964 had 1308 delegates and votes. With one alternate standing ready to fill in for each delegate, the two national conventions are obviously not of "deliberative" size.

SELECTION OF THE DELEGATES

Rise of Presidential primaries

The delegates to the national convention were, in the formative years, chosen in a variety of ways—by mass meetings, by caucuses, by district and state conventions, and by party committees. Gradually each party settled upon a fairly standard system. The Democrats, giving great emphasis to the state as the basic unit of representation and expecting the delegations from many of the states to act as units in the proceeding, usually selected their delegations by means of a state convention or a state central committee. The Republicans, much less concerned about state solidarity, preferred to select district delegates in Congressional district conventions and state-wide delegates in state conventions. By rules adopted in 1884 and 1888 the Republican national convention made this selection procedure mandatory. When, however, the direct primary began sweeping the country, the application of this procedure to delegate and Presidential candidate selection became an important public issue. The first effort to select delegates to the national conventions by direct popular vote in a primary election was made in Wisconsin in 1905. Thereafter the idea spread rapidly and by 1916 more than half of the delegates of the major parties were designated at primary elections by direct vote of the people. In 1912, the Republican convention undertook to withhold seats from delegates chosen in this way on the grounds that the primary procedure was contrary to the party rule requiring convention selection. This position did not prevail against the state laws requiring primary selection.

The spread of Presidential preference primaries

The application of the primary method to the designation of Presidential candidates proved somewhat more complex and it was not until 1910 that Oregon first provided on the primary ballot an opportunity to the voters to express their preferences among Presidential aspirants. The Democratic platform of 1912 urged every state to adopt a *Presidential preference primary* and the Progressive platform urged a constitutional amendment which would make it compulsory. President Wilson in his first message to Congress asked for legislation which would allow Presidential and Vice-Presidential candidates to be nominated by direct vote of the people and would thus relegate the conventions to platform-making agencies after the candidates had been selected. The Presidential preference primary in this period became linked to the national-convention delegate primary (Presidential primary) and shared in its rapid spread over the nation. After 1916, the movement, however, lost momentum and several states which had adopted either or both of the primary procedures abandoned one or the other. The primary in either form has made few important gains since that time.[1]

In the conventions held in 1964 fewer than half of the delegates were selected in some form of primary or were committed by some popular vote

[1] Florida adopted a new preference primary system in 1956; Minnesota abandoned its system in 1959 as did Montana.

on Presidential aspirants. These delegates came from 18 states and the District of Columbia. The systems by which delegates were elected and preferences expressed may be classified as follows: [2]

1. Direct election of unpledged delegates and no popular vote on aspirants—New York (district delegates only), Alabama (Democratic delegates only).

2. Direct election of unpledged delegates and a separate nonbinding vote on aspirants—Illinois (district delegates only), Pennsylvania (district delegates only), District of Columbia, West Virginia, Nebraska (district delegates only). *Present primary system*

3. Direct election of delegates who may be pledged to a particular aspirant and a separate nonbinding vote on aspirants—New Hampshire, New Jersey, Massachusetts.

4. Direct election of delegates who, typically are pledged to a particular aspirant and no separate vote on aspirants—Florida, South Dakota, Ohio, Wisconsin, California.

5. Direct election of delegates who may be pledged to a particular aspirant and a separate binding vote on aspirants—Oregon.

6. Direct vote on aspirants which is binding on delegates but no vote on delegates—Maryland, Indiana.

7. Direct vote on aspirants which is not binding on delegates—Texas (Republican Party only).

Most of the state delegates to the two conventions in 1964 were selected by party procedures which did not include any type of general, public, primary election. In most of these states, the delegates were selected by district or state conventions or both; in a few states, the delegates were selected by the state party committee. In many of the convention states, popular participation in selecting the delegates to the local or state conventions was widespread. In several, there was little real opportunity for rank-and-file participation. The nonprimary selection procedures differ as widely from state to state as do the primaries. *Selection by party organizations*

Recent campaigns have awakened a new interest in the Presidential preference primary, stimulated discussion of its value in many parts of the country, and led to several proposals for strengthening and extending it. It is

[2] For a complete account of the procedure for selecting delegates in 1952 and the variations in system from state to state see P. T. David, M. Moos, and R. M. Goldman, *Presidential Nominating Politics in 1952* (Baltimore, 1954). This work incorporates the results of a cooperative project sponsored by the American Political Science Association with the assistance of the Brookings Institution and represents the most comprehensive study ever made of the make-up and character of the national conventions of the two parties. For the 1956 and 1960 conventions see P. T. David, R. M. Moos, R. M. Goldman, and R. C. Bain, *The Politics of National Party Conventions* (Washington, 1960). For the 1964 conventions see Congressional Quarterly Service, *Weekly Report* (July 16, 1964 and Aug. 28, 1964).

appropriate, therefore, to review the successes and failures of the primary system as applied to delegates and Presidential candidates. Despite the apparent lack of enthusiasm by state lawmakers since 1916 for the primary procedure in delegate selection, it is still vigorously defended in the states where it exists. State party leaders tend to prefer the convention method of selection because it is more of a party operation than a public one and thus party leaders are likely to be more influential in determining the result. The advantages of convention selection are perhaps best exhibited in states like New York and Illinois where both methods are used. The convention selection of the state-wide delegates in these states makes it possible to provide places in the delegation for important party leaders—the governors, for example—who do not wish to contest such places in a public election. The primary in which delegates are selected and which offers no opportunity to vote on Presidential candidates does not, it is argued, attract voter interest to the same degree as the Presidential contest.

Future of the primary system

The real controversy concerns the desirability of giving the voters an opportunity to participate directly in the selection of the Presidential nominees of the parties. A secondary controversy concerns the best method for voter participation: the election of delegates pledged to a particular aspirant or a direct vote on the aspirant. The fear of those who strongly oppose direct voter participation is that the voters are in no position to assess the abilities of candidates to unite the party and to make a broad appeal to the nation. Voter sentiment is likely to be divided among many regional candidates, local "favorite sons," and representatives of large interest groups. Only a convention, runs the argument, can reconcile conflicting interests and select a candidate who will unite the party. Experience indicates that such a candidate may not be a willing one and may not, therefore, be in active contention for primary endorsement. Neither of the candidates in 1952 was an active or a willing seeker of public support in every major sector of the nation. Where preference primaries are now used, not all of the candidates compete. In general, candidates enter state contests only when they think they can win and stay out of contests where they might lose. Thus the voters in many primary states are not able to select among all of the aspirants. The preference primary system is best suited to advance the fortunes of avowed candidates and these, say the critics, are not always the ones that the nation needs or wants. On the other hand, the popular preference system opens the door to candidacies which might otherwise be impossible. President Kennedy certainly won his way to the nomination in 1960 in great part because of his successes in the primaries. Harold Stassen in 1948 and Estes Kefauver in 1956 showed how candidates without strong party backing can nevertheless make an impressive showing. If the system of pledged delegates is used as a vehicle for voter participation, the convention may find that no candidate has a majority and no delegate can change his vote. The costs in money and energy for a nation-wide primary campaign for Presidential aspirants is forbidding. The Presidency is already difficult

Controversy over the preference primary

enough without requiring nine or ten months of arduous campaigning to reach it.[3] None of the present primary systems make any provision for the selection of the Vice-Presidential candidates or for writing a party platform.

The supporters of preference primaries argue that if the primary system is good for all other state and national offices it is good for the Presidency. Popular participation will tend to prevent boss-dominated conventions and will open the Presidential contest to the "fresh-air" of public opinion. There is nothing deliberative about the conventions, say the critics. They are too big, too noisy, too expensive, and too tumultuous to do as adequate a job of selection as their supporters pretend. Although variation of procedure from state to state has some advantages, the nation ought to stipulate, say the supporters of the primary, a minimal procedure which will allow the voters to express their wishes in the matter of candidates in every state.[4] There does not appear, at present, any vigorous effort to push a national law or constitutional amendment on this subject.

THE NATIONAL CONVENTION AT WORK

By whatever method selected, the delegates to the major party national conventions are largely professional politicians. Most of them are holders of public office or of party post. Included in the delegations are many of the most prominent state leaders—Governors, Senators, Representatives, Mayors, state legislators, and county leaders.[5] The convention meets in a large hall capable of seating more than 15,000 people, with the delegates seated by states on the main floor and the alternates directly behind them. The press is accorded, typically, a very large section to the right and left of the speaker's platform and the galleries accommodate the interested public. Radio and television carry the proceedings to virtually every corner of the nation.[6] The atmosphere of a convention is noisy and hectic. The hall is ordinarily jammed, making it

Surroundings

[3] An excellent account of the burden on the candidate entailed by the primary systems is given in T. H. White, *The Making of the President—1960* (New York, 1961), and T. H. White, *The Making of the President—1964* (New York, 1965).

[4] See *Presidential Nominating Politics in 1952* (Vol. I), and the *Politics of National Party Conventions* already referred to for detailed analyses of the relative merits of the various primary systems. See also an older study by L. Overacker, The *Presidential Primary* (New York, 1926).

[5] Formerly, the delegates often included a large number of postmasters, revenue collectors, and other national officeholders. The Hatch Act, prohibiting political activity on the part of such officeholders (except the relatively few having to do with framing policy), now operates to debar them from serving. The Constitution (Art. II, Sec. 1, cl. 2) forbids members of Congress to act as Presidential electors; but, they take part freely in selecting Presidential candidates—which has come to be a far more important matter than serving as an elector.

[6] Radio broadcasting first assumed importance in the conventions of 1924. The Republican convention of 1940 was signalized by the earliest use of television on such an occasion, although the service was available only in a restricted area. Both major conventions in Philadelphia were more widely telecast in 1948 and virtually all of the proceedings were telecast in 1952, 1956, 1960, and 1964.

difficult to move about. There is a buzz of conversation in the air except during major speeches and at tense moments in the procedure. Every interval of the official program is filled with music by band, organ, or vocalist. Demonstrations in behalf of various candidates interrupt the proceedings periodically —especially during the nominating speeches—and hired noisemakers and cheer leaders whip the delegates and galleries into frenzied outbursts of movement and noise. The whole proceedings get entirely out of control of the presiding officers at times and sometimes for an hour or more at a stretch. The aisles, restrooms, snack-bars, and lobbies are frequently crowded with caucuses as leaders negotiate and compromise and reconcile conflicting views. There is nothing in the outward show that resembles deliberation. All of the real issues are usually threshed out behind the scenes, in hotel rooms, restaurants, headquarters suites, and anywhere men can hold private conferences. The convention city also acquires the frantic air of the hall. The hotels housing the delegates and the headquarters of the parties and candidates are seething masses of people. Banners, music, streamers, and noisemakers of all types fill the lobby and corridors with noise and confusion. At the candidates' headquarters, skilled persuaders hand out their wares to public, press, and politicians. Soundtrucks, bands, balloons, and entertainers fill the streets and stimulate flagging emotions. Hundreds of thousands of dollars are poured out in an effort to exhibit the candidates as personifications of the American way and as certain winners in the election contest. Appeals are made to every level of emotion and reason. It is easy to mistake all of this froth for the real decision-making process. The delegates are more or less immune to such frenzied appeals and they sort and weigh chances and choices usually with the calm sagacity of skilled players of the great American game.

Temporary organization   Ordinarily the conventions last four or five days—a few have dragged on for more than a week. On the first day, the meeting is called to order by the chairman of the national committee who, after the prayer and the reading of the official call for the convention, announces to the delegates the temporary convention officers agreed upon by the national committee. This slate of officers is virtually always accepted by the convention. The temporary chairman then takes the rostrum, perhaps after a recess for some oratorical warmups, and delivers the "keynote" address to the delegates and to the world. The keynote speech is a cry to close ranks and prepare for battle and for ultimate triumph. A recitation of the record of the party and of its great leaders past and present warms the delegates to the tasks ahead and of the despicable record and potentiality of the opposite party puts the convention in fighting trim. The rules of the previous convention are then adopted temporarily and the convention committees are organized.

The committees   During the next day or perhaps two days the convention marks time with oratory and music while the committees do their work. Both national conventions assign certain functions to four great committees. These are (1) credentials; (2) permanent organization; (3) rules and order of business;

and, (4) platform and resolutions. Each is composed of one delegate from each delegation (named by the delegation) except the fourth which has two delegates (one man and one woman) from each state. Typically, the chairman of the delegation supplies the names to the convention officers. The committees are obliged to report to the convention at the conclusion of their deliberations and the next major order of business is to receive these reports. The committee on rules submits a set of rules governing the convention procedure, delegate apportionment and selection, and the composition and powers of the national committee. Typically, these are the same rules as have previously been in effect, but from time to time changes will be proposed. The report is usually approved with little or no debate. The committee on permanent organization submits a slate of officers to direct the convention for the remainder of the sessions. This too is usually accepted, although there have been contests on this question as the managers of rival candidates have sought to place in the chair officers sympathetic to their candidates. The permanent chairman can wield great power in close contests by his rulings on points of order and by his recognition of those who may speak to the convention. The credentials committee prepares a permanent roll of delegates entitled to sit in the convention. For most delegates at most conventions there is no problem of determining who may rightfully participate, but every convention has some contested seats. The Republican convention, especially, has been troubled for several decades by credentials contests in the Southern delegations. The party is so small, its organization so fluid, and the selection procedures so informal in the Deep South that contests are almost unavoidable. In 1952, for example, rival delegations appeared from Texas, Louisiana, Mississippi, Georgia, and Florida. The fight over these delegations was the highlight of the convention and the success of the Eisenhower forces in seating their delegates as against those of Senator Taft influenced the result of the convention.[7] In 1952, as in some previous years, the recommendations of the credentials committee were not wholly accepted by the convention. Usually, however, the committee report is approved without debate and without a call of the roll. The Democrats experienced a unique credentials contest in 1964 when a delegation of Negroes challenged the white Mississippi delegation on the grounds that it had been improperly elected under laws which denied the vote to Negroes. The challenge was rejected by the committee but only on the basis of: (1) forcing the duly-elected delegation to pledge loyalty to the nominees (which most delegates refused to do); (2) admitting two of the claimants to the convention as delegates at-large; and, (3) establishing a bar to discrimination in the selection of delegations to future conventions.

[7] One consequence of the fight of the Eisenhower forces on the seating of certain delegations was a new rule for the Republican convention which under certain circumstances prevents delegates holding contested seats from voting on matters before the convention pending the settlement of the controversies. The rules, therefore, had authorized the delegates enrolled on the national committee temporary roster to participate as accredited delegates pending the report of the credentials committee.

Platform
adoption

When the permanent officers are installed the permanent chairman customarily delivers an addre.s of the keynote type but usually more restrained. The convention is then ready to receive the proposed party platform from the platform committee.[8] Typically, a small drafting committee designated by the national committee from among prospective members of the platform committee has been at work for some days before the convention assembled preparing a draft of a platform. Hearings have been held to allow interest groups to urge their programs and the leading candidates have been solicited for their views. Working day and night in the first few days of the convention the committee will then whip into final shape a platform to be read to the convention. Platform writers are skilled craftsmen of the "glittering generality" and the "emotion-filled symbol," and most controversies within the party are resolved in favor of platitudinous noncommitment. Much labor, however, is poured into the exact platform language on controversial subjects. The convention almost invariably accepts the committee's proposals, although occasionally it has done so only after heated debate.[9] As approved by the convention, the platform of a major party is likely to be about 10 pages long and cover a large number of subjects of national policy. On some matters the platform will be relatively clear and specific; on others it will be general and vague. The words *sound, stable, peace, prosperity, reasonable, fair, just,* will be used over and over again. The party's vast achievements will be extolled and those of the other party indicted. The platform is not so much an outline of proposals as a bid for support. It is invariably overshadowed by the announced views of the Presidential candidates and is read in its entirety by very few people. Rightly viewed, it is but one of the less important guides to what this party or its candidates will do if entrusted with power.[10]

Nomina-
tion of
candidates

At last, by the third day, the convention arrives at its main objective, the nomination of candidates. The secretary calls the roll of states, beginning with Alabama, and each delegation, in its turn, has an opportunity to place a "favorite son" or other person in nomination. If the delegates of a state which

[8] Prior to 1932, the Democrats customarily nominated candidates before adopting their platform. Since then they have adopted their platform first, as the Republicans have long done.

[9] One of the exceptional occurrences in recent years was a fight in the Democratic convention of 1948, provoked by a minority report of the platform committee and led by Congressman Andrew J. Biemiller of Wisconsin and Senator Hubert H. Humphrey of Minnesota, to strengthen a civil-rights plank in the platform as reported on the floor. The effort succeeded, but at the cost of a walkout by the 35 delegates from Alabama and Mississippi, followed by the formation of a new States' Rights or "Dixiecrat," Party.

Governor Rockefeller (New York), Republican, threatened for a time in 1960 to carry his criticisms of the tentative platform to the floor of the convention. Eventually, however, he worked out a compromise with Vice-President Nixon, the party's standard bearer.

A platform fight developed in the 1964 Republican convention when the opponents of Senator Goldwater sought from the floor to amend the platform on the issues of Civil Rights and extremism. The convention refused to support them.

[10] The platforms of the major parties may be found in K. H. Porter and D. B. Johnson, *National Party Platforms, 1840-1960* (Urbana, Ill., 1961).

stands near the top of the list choose to do so, they may yield to a delegation which under alphabetical order would not be called until later. This opportunity to get a candidate's name officially before the convention in advance of others, and to touch off a demonstration in his behalf, is believed by some managers to be advantageous. From two or three to upwards of a dozen names may be presented, each in a vigorous, eulogistic, and sometimes flamboyant nominating speech followed by briefer seconding speeches by delegates carefully picked to give an impression of widely distributed support.[11] No effort is spared by either the orators or the delegates and spectators favoring a given candidate to whip up enthusiasm for him. At the proper psychological moment, delegates and alternates may break forth with all manner of vocal and mechanical noise, seize flags and standards and start parading around the hall, and plunge the assemblage into pandemonium from which it can be extricated only when the enthusiasts have reached a state of exhaustion an hour or more later. Rarely are such demonstrations genuinely spontaneous. They are staged according to careful prearrangement and usually fail in their presumed purpose of sweeping the convention off its feet.[12]

When, finally, all of the names have been presented, the convention proceeds to ballot.[13] The roll of states is called again, and each delegation, through its chairman, announces its vote. In both parties, votes as reported may be unanimous for a given candidate or may be divided among two or more. Republican tradition favors full freedom for delegations to divide and to have their vote so recorded, except only as limited by instructions received in Presidential primaries. Democratic tradition, however, has been different. Reflecting the states'-rights antecedents of the party, and yielding the practical advantage of greater power and importance for a state in a convention proceedings, a "unit rule" has been favored under which a state convention may require a delegation to cast its votes in a block for a single candidate. Even if no such requirement is imposed, a delegation may itself, by majority vote, determine how the votes of all of its members shall be recorded. This practice is not imposed by the national convention; state conventions or delegations may invoke it or not as they choose. The national convention will, however, recognize and enforce it when ordained by a proper state party authority. It is usually employed by some states, especially Southern ones.[14]

Voting on the candidates

The Democratic "unit rule"

[11] There have been instances in which convention oratory rose to the level of genuine eloquence. Senator McCarthy's (Minnesota) nomination of Adlai Stevenson in 1960 is a good example. The Republicans now restrict nominating speeches to 30 minutes and the Democrats to 20, with four seconding speeches allowed by the Republicans and any number by the Democrats, but limited in both cases to five minutes.

[12] Sometimes, however, the spectators themselves become demonstrative, as notably in behalf of Wendell L. Willkie during the Republican convention of 1940, and in behalf of Adlai Stevenson in the Democratic convention in 1960.

[13] No printed or written ballots are employed; all voting is oral. In convention usage, however, a roll call for votes is termed a "ballot."

[14] In the convention of 1960 the following state delegations reported themselves as operating under the "unit rule": Alaska, Arizona, Delaware, Mississippi, Missouri, North Dakota, Oklahoma, and Virginia. There were no roll call votes in the convention of 1964.

The
Democratic
"two-
thirds"
rule
abandoned

Until fairly recently, another important difference between Republican and Democratic procedure was that whereas a simple majority of all votes cast was sufficient to nominate in a Republican convention, the Democrats (from as far back as 1836) required two-thirds. This latter rule frequently was responsible for convention deadlocks, and sometimes—as in 1924—prevented the party's strongest candidate from receiving nomination. In 1936, when President Roosevelt was about to be renominated at Philadelphia without opposition and thus no candidate's chance would be in any way affected, the historic two-thirds requirement was rescinded, with nominations—for both the Presidency and Vice-Presidency—thenceforth to be by simple majority. This change in Democratic practice amounted to a sharp reduction in the influence of the Southern wing of the party over the nominations. Under the old "two-thirds rule" the South had exercised a veto over candidate selection. Since the death of President Roosevelt, the power struggle between the Northern and Southern wings of the party has repeatedly broken out into the open at the national convention. In 1948, a portion of the Southern Democrats seceded and founded the Dixiecrat Party, and in 1952 formal unity was preserved only by the skillful maneuvering of the presiding officer. In 1956 and 1960, rival candidates were offered in several Southern states, and in 1964 an unpledged slate of Democratic electors was offered in Alabama in place of a slate pledged to the convention nominee. The South has sought to gain bargaining power by offering a Southern candidate and by threatening to bolt.[15]

The
balloting

After the votes of all of the states have been recorded and counted, the result is announced. Sometimes—especially when a President is being renominated—a single ballot suffices. But often the votes are so divided among a number of candidates that no one obtains the requisite majority and additional ballots must be taken. These usually follow in quick succession as the leaders try to force a decision. Sometimes, however, a recess is called between ballots to allow the candidates' managers more time to maneuver. Typically,

[15] In 1948, the Mississippi delegation had been admitted by a majority vote to the convention although bearing credentials which limited the power of the delegation to bind the state party to accept the results of the convention. With this precedent several Southern state delegations bore credentials of this type in 1952. The Northern wing of the party in 1952 attempted to reduce the Southern bargaining power by making it impossible for them to help select the nominees and then to bolt if they were dissatisfied. A "loyalty pledge" was introduced and accepted and had it been applied as conceived it would have required delegates as a condition of their participation in the convention to pledge themselves to support the candidates approved by the convention. After much confusion, delegates unwilling to sign the pledge in a form acceptable to the credentials committee were nevertheless allowed to participate in the convention. In 1956 and 1960, a loyalty rule was adopted requiring the state party organization to "assure" that voters in the state will have a chance to vote for the Democratic nominee and for "electors pledged formally or in good conscience" to his election. Meanwhile, six Southern states had adopted laws to prevent the national convention from legally binding their state parties to the convention nominee. In 1964, in a contest with an all-Negro delegation from Mississippi the "regular" delegates were required to take a loyalty pledge if they wished to participate. This most of them refused to do.

the favorite sons drop out early in the balloting and the contest centers around two or three strong candidates. During these hours, the managers work tirelessly dickering with the leaders of delegations, making promises, and bringing outside pressure to bear in an effort to capture a majority. Eventually some one of the contestants (or perchance a "dark horse" agreed upon behind the scenes) emerges a victor. Sometimes the balloting (and bartering) is very prolonged, the record being the nomination of John W. Davis by the Democrats in 1924 on the 103rd ballot, after a deadlock lasting nine days. With a Democratic candidate, however, no longer obliged to muster a two-thirds vote in order to win, there hardly will be another experience so trying.

The nomination for the Presidency having been made, the weary delegates hurry their labors to an anticlimactic conclusion. A candidate for the Vice-Presidency is still to be named; and the same procedure—roll call, nominating and seconding speeches, and balloting—is followed. But the contest usually is not very keen, and a decisive vote is soon reached.[16] As a rule, the grounds on which the nomination is made (usually by the Presidential nominee and always with his assent) leave a good deal to be desired. The prize—such as it is—may be used to placate an important element in the party that has lost in the fight over the Presidential nomination or over the platform, or to reward a favorite son who has thrown his support to the winning Presidential candidate, or to enhance the chances of capturing a pivotal state. It will usually be bestowed also with a view to balancing the ticket: an Eastern Presidential nominee commonly calls for a Western Vice-Presidential nominee; a dyed-in-the-wool conservative ordinarily must be counterbalanced with a man of known liberal views, or vice versa. Every sort of consideration, indeed, may contribute to the decision except one, the qualifications of the person nominated to become President if anything should happen to the President.

Nomination for the Vice-Presidency

One more task, purely formal yet necessary, remains: the party's national committee must be elected, consisting of a man and woman from each state and territory,[17] and charged with carrying on the coming election, looking after party interests during the ensuing four years, and arranging for the next national convention. With all members designated (in theory "nominated") either by state conventions or primaries, by state committees, or by state delegations, election by the national convention, however, is a mere gesture. The secretary reads the list of names proposed by the states, some one offers a motion that the persons named be elected, and the motion usually carries unanimously by *viva voce* vote. In earlier times, it was customary also to choose two committees, each consisting of one representative from each state

The convention's closing acts

[16] The most spirited contests over the Vice-Presidency in recent years occurred in 1944 in the Democratic convention (Wallace *v.* Truman) and in 1956 again in the Democratic convention (Kennedy *v.* Kefauver).

[17] The Republican Committee by rule adopted in 1952 also now includes as ex officio members the state chairman of the party in each state which has a Republican governor or a Republican majority of the states' members in both houses of Congress, or which cast its electoral vote for a Republican President at the last election.

and territory, to "notify" the respective candidates of their nomination, usually at large public gatherings planned for the purpose. Since Franklin D. Roosevelt got his first campaign off to a dramatic start in 1932 by climbing into an airplane at Albany and a few hours later ascending the convention rostrum at Chicago to accept his nomination, old-style notification ceremonies have gradually been dispensed with by both major parties. Successful candidates now signify their acceptance in an address at the convention itself. The convention thus ends on a new call to battle and an eloquent statement of faith by the candidate.

THE PRESIDENTIAL CAMPAIGN

Machinery   Although the conduct of a national campaign involves thousands of party workers, central direction is ordinarily provided by the national committees. Shortly after the conventions, the new committees meet and organize for the great effort ahead. A chairman is selected to manage the campaign, nominally by the committee but actually by the Presidential candidate. Headquarters are established or enlarged to house the hundreds of employees added temporarily and, frequently, regional offices are established in key cities. Subcommittees are created to coordinate publicity, fund-raising, speaker activities, and the like. Individuals are assigned to direct all of these processes in collaboration with the committee or under the immediate direction of the chairman. Campaign biographies of the candidate are prepared; "textbooks" are compiled for ready reference by local and state party workers, containing the platform, important speeches, statistics, speech material organized by subject to support the party position on the issues of the campaign, and biographical data on the party candidates; leaflets and brochures of many kinds are prepared, and slogans and mottoes are manufactured for the occasion. Arrangements are also made to coordinate campaigns for state and local offices with the Congressional and Presidential campaign. Since the limitation on total spending of a national campaign committee was enacted in 1940, more and more use is being made of auxiliary and semi-independent committees to supplement the work of the national committee and to serve as vehicles for the expenditure of funds beyond the ceiling established for any national committee. Auxiliary organizations are used also to reach voters and financial supporters that the regular party organizations do not reach: women, for example, "independents," supporters from the opposite party, ethnic groups, professional people, laboring men, even intellectuals.

Funds   The combined costs of all the campaign activities of a single party in a national election certainly exceed $25 million and probably exceed $50 million. Raising this money is one of the most trying and most difficult of tasks for the campaign organization, and a great deal of effort must be put into it right down to the closing hours of the campaign. In fact, the fund-raising frequently goes on after the election to pay off deficits piled up during the enthusiasm of the campaign. Experience suggests that both parties rely upon the substantial gifts of a relatively small proportion of their supporters. As has been suggested earlier, attempts to limit expenditures in campaigns have been uniformly unsuccessful as have attempts to limit the amount any person may contribute. The amount of money involved, however, and the small number of persons who give it open the way for allegations of undue influence by such givers and the interests which many of them represent.

A considerable portion of the money now spent goes for the purchase of radio and television broadcasting time and for the preparation and distribution of party literature. The amount spent for broadcasting has been increasing relatively and absolutely in recent years and there are many indications that television, in particular, will be the major campaign vehicle in the future. The quality and character of the literature and the broadcasts vary widely. Party money is spent on everything from one-minute spot announcements to the televising of a formal oration by the candidate and from windshield stickers to full-length book biographies. More and more, parties are relying upon the cumulative impact of advertising through every medium and less and less upon elaborate, formal, and hortatory speech-making. The use of television also tends to reduce the relative amount of formal speech-making. They are also relying on the expert services of Madison Avenue (advertising and public relations firms) to design campaign publicity. Much of the campaign "literature" reaches the voter only through his favorite newspaper or from his receiving set. One other trend deserves notice, and that is that the cost of campaigning is increasing and will continue to do so as more and more reliance is placed on broadcasting and on the services of experts in communication techniques. *"Literature" and broadcasts*

Through the years professional politicians and seasoned campaigners have developed an elaborate folklore on the art and strategy of campaigning. Little of this has ever been verified scientifically and much of it perhaps never will be. Experts in the matter are usually much more certain after the election is over than while the campaign is in progress. The character of a national campaign, however, can hardly be understood except in terms of those "rules of the game" which the campaigners follow. In most campaigns, in the first place, great stress is placed on the personality of the candidates, and this usually far overshadows the issues of public policy which may be involved. The voters, it is believed, choose more easily and more readily among personalities than among programs. Each side attempts to build a picture in the eyes of the public of a personality which coincides with the supposed inner wishes of the electorate. This picture will, of course, vary with the times. In 1932, the Democrats were anxious to depict their candidate as daring, aggressive, and uninhibited by respect for tradition. More frequently, the candidate is cast in the role of the defender of the best traditions of the American past, as a man who knows the value of his American heritage. Until quite recently, Horatio Alger had probably done more to set the style of the "people's *Strategy and tactics:* *1. The candidate* choice" than any other American: the self-made hero, product of a harsh rural or small-town environment, a boyhood close to the soil and a manhood of successful achievement in competition with the sophisticated city "slickers." As the country has become more urban, a city background is no longer considered disabling. The candidate's personality must also, however, symbolize an approach to the issues of the day: "normalcy," New England shrewdness, engineering efficiency, champion of the forgotten man, eager fighter for honest government, popular military genius. The real personality of the candidate is invariably swallowed up by the mythical hero which the publicists have carefully constructed for the campaign.

2. The issues
  Much thought and effort is given by the campaigners to the selection of the issues or themes of the campaign. What in the record should be played up, and what ignored? Of the many evidences of dissatisfaction in the electorate, which are the deeper and more decisive? In recent years, the strategists have paid close attention to the results of public-opinion sampling polls in determining what impresses the electorate. In 1952, the Republicans felt that their best issues were the Korean stalemate, Communists in government, and corruption. In 1956 and 1960, the Republicans stood on the slogan, "peace and prosperity." In 1956 and 1960, the Democrats cried out against complacency, demanded that the people rise to the challenge of the times. As the campaign proceeded in 1964, it became increasingly clear that the Democrat's best issue was public fear of the war-like postures of Senator Goldwater.

3. Offense or defense?
  One of the perennial campaign questions is how to treat the opposition: attack them or ignore them. Franklin Roosevelt was a master of pretending complete indifference to his opponent and Lyndon Johnson in 1964 imitated him skillfully. Dewey tried this in 1948 and failed with it. Eisenhower generally ignored his opponents and was successful. Usually the "outs" are forced to more aggressive attacks than the "ins." An incumbent President can frequently ignore his opposition more successfully than they can ignore him. A common device is to appoint a lesser party figure to debate the opposition and to answer their charges, and thus keep the Presidential candidates above the debate. A great many politicians believe, however, that you can never catch up with your opponent's charges, and therefore the best thing to do is to make no attempt to answer but rather to charge him with something else.

4. The strategy of superior place*
  The dream of every campaign manager is to make his candidate the center of the campaign. He would rather have a lot of campaign oratory directed against his candidate than to have him ignored. An ideal situation from this point of view was one achieved briefly by Woodrow Wilson in 1912 when Taft and Roosevelt were both attacking him and he was presenting his program to the people. Every candidate was thus discussing Wilson. How to achieve this goal is another question and on this the campaigners differ sharply among themselves. They all agree, however, that the candidate must act and talk as if he were confident of winning. No doubts on this score must

ever be allowed to appear in the literature or in the words or actions of the
candidate. Presumably, however, with the increased use of polling, the candidate who is the underdog is aware of it; and, in 1964, it was virtually impossible for the Republicans to pretend that they would win. The statistical
experts in the party headquarters, however, supply the press and public with
a great deal of "scientific" data which proves their assertions of victory.
Jim Farley's accurate forecast of the 1936 election result—that the Democrats would carry every state except Maine and Vermont—remains up to this
time, however, the only occasion in which the scientific extravagance of partisan forecasts was sustained by the voters.

5. The illusion of victory

The electoral college method of counting the vote for President and
Vice-President has considerable influence in campaign planning and execution. Presidential campaign efforts are usually concentrated in "doubtful
states" and in states with a consequential electoral vote. President Eisenhower
and Vice-President Nixon made a few forays into the South and Senator
Goldwater campaigned there extensively and successfully. Usually the Republicans as well as the Democrats limit their efforts in the one-party states.
In the unusual campaign of 1964, President Johnson campaigned extensively
in Republican New England and was rewarded by resounding majorities in
all the Northeastern states. By far the largest effort in money, organization,
and candidate speaking appearances is ordinarily made in New York, Indiana, Ohio, Illinois, Michigan, California, New Jersey, and in recent years, in
Pennsylvania and Texas.

6. Con-centration in doubtful states

The campaign of 1960 introduced a new dimension into campaigning
with four great televised debates between the two candidates. Although extensive use was made of television in the campaigns of 1952 and 1956, all
of the programs had been offered under partisan direction on time purchased
at great cost for the purpose. The broadcasters, under some fire because of
their alleged indifference to concepts of public service, offered to stage these
programs free provided Congress would waive the rule of the Federal Communications Commission requiring them to offer equal time to the 14 other
minor party candidates for the Presidency. Congress by statute suspended
the rule for the campaign of 1960. Representatives of the broadcasters and
the candidates then negotiated the terms under which the programs would be
presented. Generally, the candidates were allowed a few minutes for set
speeches and then were questioned by representatives of the press under
carefully controlled time-limits for their answers. Each candidate was permitted to comment on the answers of the other. The time thus donated by
the broadcasters would have cost the two parties about $2 million if pur-
chased in the traditional way. The best estimates place the audience for one
or all of the debates at 115 to 120 million persons, the greatest listening audience ever assembled for any program of any type. Many analysts and opinion
surveyors believe that Kennedy's showing was an important factor in his final

The televised debates of 1960

POPULAR AND ELECTORAL VOTE FOR PRESIDENT

1964

Major Party Candidates

| State | POPULAR | | ELECTORAL | |
	Johnson	Goldwater	Johnson	Goldwater
Ala.	—*	479,085	—	10
Alaska	44,329	22,930	3	—
Ariz.	237,753	242,535	—	5
Ark.	314,197	243,264	6	—
Calif.	4,171,877	2,879,108	40	—
Colo.	476,024	296,767	6	—
Conn.	826,269	390,996	8	—
Del.	122,704	78,078	3	—
Fla.	948,540	905,941	14	—
Ga.	522,557	616,584	—	12
Hawaii	163,249	44,022	4	—
Idaho	148,920	143,557	4	—
Ill.	2,796,833	1,905,946	26	—
Ind.	1,170,848	911,118	13	—
Iowa	733,030	449,148	9	—
Kan.	464,028	386,579	7	—
Ky.	669,659	372,977	9	—
La.	387,068	509,225	—	10
Maine	262,264	118,701	4	—
Md.	730,912	385,495	10	—
Mass.	1,786,422	549,727	14	—
Mich.	2,136,615	1,060,152	21	—
Minn.	991,117	559,624	10	—
Miss.	52,618	356,528	—	7
Mo.	1,164,344	653,535	12	—
Mont.	164,246	113,032	4	—
Neb.	307,307	276,847	5	—
Nev.	79,339	56,094	3	—
N. H.	182,065	104,029	4	—
N. J.	1,867,671	963,843	17	—
N. M.	194,017	131,838	4	—
N. Y.	4,913,156	2,243,559	43	—
No. Car.	800,139	624,844	13	—
No. Dak.	149,784	108,207	4	—
Ohio	2,498,331	1,470,865	26	—
Okla.	519,834	412,665	8	—
Ore.	501,017	282,779	6	—
Penna.	3,130,228	1,457,336	29	—
R. I.	315,463	74,615	4	—
So. Car.	215,700	309,048	—	8

POPULAR AND ELECTORAL VOTE FOR PRESIDENT

1964

Major Party Candidates

| | POPULAR | | ELECTORAL | |
State	Johnson	Goldwater	Johnson	Goldwater
So. Dak.	163,010	130,108	4	—
Tenn.	635,047	508,965	11	—
Texas	1,663,185	958,566	25	—
Utah	219,628	180,682	4	—
Vt.	108,127	54,942	3	—
Va.	558,038	481,334	12	—
Wash.	779,699	470,366	9	—
W. Vir.	538,087	253,953	7	—
Wis.	1,050,424	638,495	12	—
Wyo.	80,718	61,998	3	—
D of C	169,796	28,801	3	—
	43,126,233	27,174,989	486	52

* Democratic electors were not pledged to Johnson.

victory.[18] It can hardly be said that the debates did much to clarify the issues of the campaign. The rigid time limits made thoughtful responses on complex questions, such as farm policy, Quemoy and Matsu, civil rights, etc., impossible. They did project to the voters the personalities of the two candidates and showed their behavior under great stress.

Assured by all the available polling data of a sweeping victory and with the party treasury in good shape, President Johnson chose not to share his audience with the Republican challenger in 1964. The bill to suspend the equal time rule was not approved by the Senate and the debates were not repeated despite the offers to do so of the broadcasters and the Republicans.

For all of the planning, thought, money, time, and energy given to a national campaign, there is a growing body of evidence suggesting that it changes very few votes. A vast majority of American voters—perhaps as many as 80 percent—cast their votes in November exactly as they would have cast them in June or July before the campaign got under way.[19] If true, does this

Value of campaign

[18] Elmer Roper in a survey conducted for CBS estimated that four million persons believed the debates were decisive in their own choice between the candidates and that of these, 26 percent voted for Nixon and 72 percent for Kennedy. See T. H. White, *The Making of the President, 1960* (New York, 1961) 294.

[19] See, for example, P. F. Lazarsfeld, *The People's Choice* (New York, 1945); A. Campbell, P. E. Converse, W. E. Miller and D. E. Stokes, *The American Voter* (New York, 1960); and B. R. Berelson, P. F. Lazarsfeld and W. N. McPhee, *Voting* (Chicago, 1954).

mean that campaigns are useless? Not at all, say the politicians. Elections are always decided by a relatively small percentage of the voters. Furthermore, one of the tasks of a campaign is to infuse the supporters of a party with enough enthusiasm to bring them out to the polls on election day. Apathy is the dread disease of the body politic and especially of the traditional supporters of a party. Only the intense excitement of a campaign will bring to the polls the 68 million voters who came out in 1960 or the 70 million in 1964. Furthermore, the campaign stimulates the party organization, infuses it with a renewed sense of purpose, tests the merit of its functionaries, and attracts to it new blood and talent without which it would soon wither and decay. Strong parties are essential to our system, it is argued, and campaigns make strong parties.

CASTING AND COUNTING THE ELECTORAL VOTES

Presidential electors

What happens after the last local "spellbinder" has descended from the rostrum, the last national "hookup" has brought the leading candidates' appeals to the voter at his fireside, and the last rosy forecast has been given out by an at least outwardly confident party chairman? Early in the campaign, party conventions, primaries, or committees (as determined by the legislature) in each state made up the respective "slates" of Presidential electors. Each party designates as many electors as the state is entitled to, that is, one for each Senator and for each Representative in Congress. It is for these men and women that the voters actually cast their ballots on election day, although they may think of themselves as voting for the President and Vice-President. This is true legally even though the voters may not know the names of the electors for whom they are voting, and though in a majority of states their names do not even appear on the ballot. Regardless of the formalities, the results are tabulated and announced on election night much as if the people had on that day chosen the chief magistrate. Certain it is that their voting does determine the result.

Choice by legislatures gives way to choice by the people

To many persons it would come as a surprise to be told that Presidential electors were not always chosen exclusively, or even mainly, by popular vote. A national law of 1845 requires that they be elected in all cases on the Tuesday following the first Monday in November; but as for the mode of selection, there never has been any nationwide rule except a simple constitutional provision that each state shall determine the matter for itself by action of its legislature. At the outset, the legislature itself elected in a majority of states, and the people took no direct part at all. As democratic sentiment grew, however, popular election was substituted in one state after another, with the result that after 1832 the legislature elected only in South Carolina, and there only until the Civil War.[20] Furthermore, in states in which the electors were first chosen by popular vote, it was not unusual for most of the electors to be chosen by

[20] In Florida in 1868 and Colorado in 1876 electors were chosen by the legislature.

Congressional districts. Under this system, of course, a state's electoral vote might be split among two or more candidates. Party politicians came to prefer the general or statewide system, and it gradually replaced the district arrangement. By 1832, only four states retained the district system and they soon abandoned it. Michigan reverted to it in 1891 but only temporarily. Today, in every state, the voter casts his ballot for as many electors as his state is entitled to and the winner of the state contest captures the entire electoral vote to that state.

A majority of electoral votes is necessary to victory—unless achieved through election by the House. But this does not prevent us from having "minority" Presidents, that is, Presidents who (speaking strictly, the electors who chose them) received fewer than half of the total popular votes cast. As a matter of fact, we have had 11 such—two of them at two different times each. Lincoln, in 1860, obtained more popular votes than did any one of his competitors, but nevertheless polled half a million less than a majority. Wilson, in 1912, received 2 million more popular votes than did his nearest competitor, Theodore Roosevelt, yet only 42 percent of the total. In both of these cases, the opposition was divided. President Kennedy received 49.7 percent of the popular vote in 1960. The same thing can happen even if there are only two major tickets in the field. Hayes was elected over Tilden in 1876, although his popular vote was about 300,000 smaller; and Harrison triumphed over Cleveland in 1888, although with 100,000 fewer votes. All that a candidate needs in order to obtain the full electoral vote of a state is a plurality of the popular vote. An opposing candidate may have swept the states which he carried by heavy pluralities and thus gained a larger number of popular votes. But, lacking the requisite number of electoral votes, he nevertheless goes down to defeat. _{"Minority" presidents}

This circumstance accounts for the fact, previously alluded to, that campaign managers are likely to concentrate their efforts in large "doubtful" or "pivotal" states. Party managers are not likely soon to forget that Kennedy, although he lost virtually the whole West, Plains, and Mountain States, won because he captured the electoral vote of Illinois (27) by only 10,000 votes, of New Jersey (16) by only 22,000 votes and of Texas (24) by only 46,000 votes.

The theory of the Constitution is that the electors are officers of their respective states, and it was on this account that the states were left free to determine how they should be chosen. The place where each group meets within its state is fixed by the legislature thereof (normally, the state capital); and if the electors receive any remuneration, it must come out of the state treasury. A national statute of 1934, however, requires that they meet in the respective states and cast their ballots on the first Monday after the second Wednesday in December following their election. And the Twelfth Amendment enjoins that the voting be by ballot; that Presidential and Vice-Presidential candidates be voted for separately; that distinct lists be made up showing all persons supported for either office, with the number of votes received by each; and that these lists, signed and sealed in duplicate, be sent to the president of the Senate (nowadays actually to the head of the General Services Administration for transmission to the Senate's presiding officer) at the seat of the national government. As evidence of their power to act, the electors must transmit in addition their certificates of election, bearing the signature of the Governor.

The count of electoral votes

The vagueness of the constitutional provisions on counting the electoral vote created no real difficulties until 1876. In the Hayes-Tilden contest of that year, two conflicting sets of electoral certificates were received in Washington from South Carolina, Florida, and Louisiana and one vote from Oregon was also disputed. The outcome of the contest awaited the determination of the 21 disputed electoral votes. After much wrangling, an electoral commission of 15 members (five Senators, five Representatives, and five members of the Supreme Court) was created and the Congress agreed to accept its rulings on the disputed certificates. The commission (split eight Republicans to seven Democrats) awarded all of the disputed votes to Hayes and he was declared elected by 185 votes to 184 for Tilden.[21]

The Electoral Count Act (1887)

When the excitement died down, public-spirited men of both parties began looking for some way of preventing similar trouble in the future, but a decade passed before any agreement could be reached. Finally, in 1887, an Electoral Count Act supplied at least a partial solution. Recognizing that Presidential electors are state officers whose right to act is certified by the Governor, and who meet and perform their sole task within the state boundaries and under state authority, the new law placed responsibility for settling disputes as far as possible upon the states themselves. Manifestly, however, the authorities of a state might fail to reach a settlement and conflicting returns still make their appearance at Washington. In such event, the two houses of Congress, acting separately, were to decide which certificates should be accepted. If the Houses could not agree, any returns having the advantage of being certified by the Governor of the state should be honored. If none came with such endorsement, and the Houses still could not agree, the state concerned should lose its vote in that particular election. To this day only a few states have provided by law for handling this type of controversy.

The electoral count as now carried out

With rare exceptions, of course, the counting of the electoral votes is a mere formality; the country knows two months in advance precisely what the figures will be. On the day fixed by law—formerly the second Wednesday in February, but now the sixth day of January—the members of the two Houses gather in the hall of the House of Representatives, with the president (or president *pro tempore*) of the Senate in the chair, and with four previously designated tellers—a Democrat and a Republican from each House—ready

[21] A. C. McLaughlin, *A Constitutional History of the United States* (New York, 1935), Chap. XLVIII; P. L. Haworth, *The Hayes-Tilden Disputed Presidential Election of 1876* (New York, 1906); C. V. Woodward, *Reunion and Reaction* (New York, 1952).

to tabulate and count. Starting with Alabama, and proceeding in alphabetical order, the presiding officer opens the certificates transmitted by the several electoral bodies and hands them one by one to the tellers; the latter read the contents aloud and set down the numbers of votes. The presiding officer announces the totals, which in due time are entered, with a list of the votes by states, in the journals of the two Houses. The person receiving the largest number of votes for President, provided the number is a majority of the whole number of electors chosen, is declared elected; and similarly in the case of the Vice-Presidency.

In the event that no candidate for President receives a majority, the election is, of course, thrown into the House of Representatives, where each state has one vote, bestowed as the majority of the state delegation determines. Until 1804, the choice of the House in such a contingency was to be made between the candidates who were tied, or among those highest on the list (up to five) if there was simply lack of a majority. The Twelfth Amendment, however, provided for selection among "the persons having the highest numbers not exceeding three." Since Jefferson was so elected in 1801, the President has been chosen by the House only once, in 1825 when John Quincy Adams emerged victor over Jackson, Crawford, and Clay. If no candidate for the Vice-Presidency obtains a majority of the electoral vote, the Senate—the members voting as individuals—chooses from the highest two, the victor being required to receive the votes of a majority of the whole number of Senators. Vice-President Richard M. Johnson was elected in this way in 1837. *Provision in case of lack of a majority*

Notwithstanding all the constitutional and statutory regulations on the subject, it still is possible for the country to come up to the expiration of a Presidential term with no President-elect ready to be inaugurated. Not only may the choice itself still be hanging fire, but a person duly elected may have died before the inauguration date, or may have failed to qualify (as, for example, by refusing to serve). Providing belatedly for such contingencies, the Twentieth Amendment, adopted in 1933, specifies (1) that in case of the death of a President-elect, the Vice-President-elect shall become President, and (2) that if at the time for inauguration a President-elect has not been chosen or has failed to qualify, the Vice-President-elect "shall *act as President* until a President shall have qualified." Conceivably, however, the same situations might arise as to both President-elect and Vice-President-elect; and for this contingency the amendment authorized Congress to make provision by law—which, in a Presidential Succession Act of 1947, it has done. *Some recent safe-guards*

PROPOSED CHANGES IN ELECTORAL COLLEGE

More than once, the mode of electing the President and Vice-President has been pronounced a weak point in our American system of government. Over the years, it is true, improvements have been introduced by the Twelfth and Twentieth Amendments, by statutes like the Electoral Count Act, by state legislation such as that removing the names of electors from the ballot (Presidential short ballot), and by party regulations like those now governing the apportionment of delegates to the national conventions. Passing over faults of the nominating process, one finds the plan of election criticized on several grounds. (1) The electoral college no longer serves the sifting purposes for which it was designed, and as a mere recording machine has become useless. (2) The unit system under which a candidate captures all of the state's electoral votes merely by polling a state-wide popular plurality is unfair to sections of a state carried by a different party. (3) Occasionally, a candidate wins election with only minority popular backing. (4) The present system exaggerates the electoral importance of the large cities in the pivotal states and, therefore, of disciplined pressure-group blocs. (5) In the absence of state laws so requiring (and these exist only in a few states, such as California, and Oregon), there is no iron-clad guarantee that electors chosen in the states will vote for the Presidential and Vice-Presidential candidates receiving the largest popular vote in their states.[22] Formerly, this last situation was not a matter of much concern; in over a century and a quarter, only two electors chosen to vote for the candidates of a given party ever ignored their mandate and actually voted for different ones.[23] The confused position of the South in the election of 1948, however, marked by legislation in Virginia empowering a state convention to instruct the state's electors *not* to vote for the regular party nominees, by an unsuccessful attempt in Alabama to compel the state's 11 electors, chosen to support the States' Rights candidates, to switch to Truman and Barkley, and by the persistence of one Tennessee elector in voting contrary to the state popular vote, brought this previously neglected angle of the electoral system sharply to the fore. In the election of 1960, one elector in Oklahoma, elected on the Nixon slate, cast his vote for Byrd, and in Alabama, a mixed slate of electors was presented to the voters. Then in 1964 no slate of electors pledged to Johnson-Humphrey was on the ticket in Alabama. Congress has repeatedly considered, since that time, several constitutional amendments on the subject. President Johnson in connection with his proposal to resolve the problem of Presidential inability discussed later also proposed in 1965 that electors be required to vote in accordance with the popular mandate.

Proposals for betterment have been many. Some of them start from the premise that the people should elect directly, with no intervention of either personal electors or electoral votes, and from this advance to the suggestion either (1) that the country be thrown into a single grand constituency, with the people in the mass electing directly, by plurality or majority, without

---

[22] The Supreme Court, however, has held that an elector may pledge his vote to candidates for President and Vice-President in advance of the election and that a party is not violating the Constitution when it requires such a pledge. Ray *v.* Blair, 343 U. S. 214 (1952).
[23] One in 1824 and one in 1912.

reference to state lines, most recently supported by Senators Morse (Ore.), Smith (Me.), and Mansfield (Mont.) or (2) that voting continue on a state basis, but with election by popular pluralities in a majority of states. The first suggestion ignores all considerations of state interest and pride, and would increase the need for a uniform national suffrage and election law which could not easily be obtained. The second, opening a way for a number of smaller states to swing an election by means of only a minority (perhaps very small) of the nationwide popular vote, is palpably objectionable. Every plan now receiving serious attention presumes the retention of ultimate choice by electoral rather than popular votes, the only questions being as to how such votes shall be allotted and whether they shall literally be "cast" by actual persons or be only abstractions mathematically calculated from the popular vote. Three main propositions in this vein have been made. (1) Abolish the electoral college and simply translate state-wide popular plurality votes into state quotas of electoral votes, all going in each state (as now) to the plurality candidates. Long advocated by Senator George W. Norris of Nebraska, a constitutional amendment of this purport twice narrowly failed to secure the necessary two-thirds vote in the Senate in 1934. Except for dropping out the electors, this plan would merely write into the Constitution what we already have, without touching the heart of the controversy, that is, getting away from a candidate's securing all of the electoral votes of a state simply by polling a state-wide popular plurality. To accomplish this major purpose (along with others), we have had two principal proposals, differing chiefly in the manner of proportioning electoral votes to popular votes. (2) Continue choosing one elector at large in each state, by plurality, for each Senator and for each Representative-at-large (if any), but choose all others—as was the common practice in early days—district by district, so as to make possible (and in most cases probable) a division of a state's electoral votes among different candidates. This plan has been supported recently by Senators Mundt (S. Dak.), Morton (Ky.), and Thurmond (S. C.).[24] (3) Discard electors, let the people vote directly for President and Vice-President, translate popular votes into electoral votes, and allot a state's electoral quota among the candidates in proportion to the statewide popular votes polled. This plan has been supported by Senators Lodge (Mass.), Kefauver (Tenn.), and Daniel (Texas).

The major arguments raised against the district system of electing Presidential electors are: (1) district lines are easy to gerrymander; (2) campaigning might be concentrated in a few marginal districts; (3) splinter parties by concentrating effort in a few districts might swing the election into the House of Representatives. Those raised against the plan of allocating electoral votes in each state on the basis of popular vote are: (1) a "minority" President would still be possible; (2) it would weaken the two-party systems by allowing

[24] A strong argument for the district plan is made by L. Wilmerding, Jr., *The Electoral College* (New Brunswick, N. J., 1958).

small parties to gain electoral votes and thus prestige. Many persons also say that the present system has served us well and there is no necessity for changing it.[25]

Any state might now, if it chose, institute the district plan, or indeed any other plan for proportioning popular to electoral votes—so long as electors were retained. The states already, therefore, have it in their power to solve, at least in piecemeal fashion, the main problem involved in the whole matter. The same considerations of interest and pride (chiefly the increased political weight accruing from an undivided block of electoral votes) which originally induced one after another of them to give up the earlier district plan may be counted upon to frustrate any attempt within their own boundaries to revive it or anything resembling it.

RESULTS OF THE PRESENT SYSTEM IN TERMS OF PRESIDENTIAL FITNESS

Thirty-five different men have attained the Presidency—27 by being elected directly to the office and eight by succeeding a deceased chief executive. In exercising their electoral function, what sort of a record have the people achieved? How do the Presidents that they have chosen measure up in terms of capacity, vision, diligence, and other qualities of statesmanship?

Some 75 years ago, Lord Bryce included in his classic treatise, *The American Commonwealth,* a chapter entitled "Why Great Men Are Not Chosen President." [26] He did not mean to imply that none such is ever chosen. But, looking back over a line of 20 Presidents who had served the nation in its first 100 years, our friendly English critic could not see that the people had shown any consistent disposition to elevate even their strongest men (leaving aside the somewhat elusive quality of "greatness") to the highest office in their power to bestow. Through a century and a half, American Presidents, another foreign observer affirms, have for the most part been mediocre when compared, for example, with British Prime Ministers during the same period.[27] The judgment seems severe. There have been inferior Prime Ministers and able Presidents. It is true, however, that many of the ablest American statesmen have never been elevated to the Presidency and have witnessed this high office bestowed on inferior colleagues. Hamilton, Gallatin, Marshall, Clay, Webster, Calhoun, Burton, Sumner, Hay, Blaine, Root, Sherman, and Robert Taft, to select a few giants of the past, although dominant in their parties were passed by in favor, typically, of less influential and, in many cases, of less able men.

It is useless to wonder whether the original plan of the Constitution

[25] A good review of pending proposals for change may be found in *Congressional Quarterly Weekly Report,* 279-289 (Feb. 17, 1961).

[26] Vol. I, Chap. VIII.

[27] H. J. Laski, *Parliamentary Government in England* (New York, 1938), 243. In another book published shortly afterwards, however, this writer conceded 11 of 31 presidents to that time to have been "extraordinary men." *The American Presidency* (New York, 1940), 8. Cf. A. M. Schlesinger, *Paths to the Present* (New York, 1949), Chap. V, "A Yardstick for Presidents."

would have produced better results. The rise of the party system and the spread of democracy doomed the arrangement almost from its inception. It is to the exigencies of party politics that we must look to discover why and how Presidents are selected. The voters in November can pick among two or three candidates, but the party organizations screen the field to narrow the choice. This is not to say that if a big democracy is going to have an elective chief executive at all, there is any better method of choosing him; nor certainly to imply that it would be practicable for choices of such magnitude to be made in any way other than through the instrumentality of parties. It is merely to state a basic fact: that the few persons who ever have a chance under our system to become President get it only when, and because, parties give it to them.

The considerations and circumstances making a man "available"—the "logical choice"—as a party candidate, and thereby narrowing the field of contenders, are not always such as to guarantee that he will be a strong President. There is, of course, no single formula, or pattern, for Presidential timber; the same person might be wholly acceptable to a party under one set of conditions and not at all so under another; everything depends on the character of the times, the prevailing public temper, and many other things. Experience indicates, however, that certain qualities or characteristics are likely to play a major role in making a candidate available. (1) He should have demonstrated capacity for getting the voters to vote for him, that is, he should have run successfully for an important public office. (2) He should have attained his electoral successes preferably in a "pivotal" or "doubtful" state or section, especially one which the party must almost certainly carry to win the election (this rules out the statesmen of the South, and the Plains, and Republican New England). (3) He must be sufficiently regular in his party affiliation to be regarded as reliable on party matters by the leaders. (4) He must be well enough known nationally to have some following outside his own state and yet not be identified with a particular region, cause, or program which is offensive to some other area (this rules out many important Congressmen who have been obliged to vote on controversial issues). (5) He must have a group of loyal, devoted, and able supporters who can manage his campaign for him and carry on negotiations with other leaders which he, personally, can never do. (6) He might well have had military experience (12 of our Presidents have had military titles). (7) It is best if he has a normal family situation and belongs to a recognized church.[28]

Some factors in "availability"

---

[28] Until 1960 Al Smith was the one Catholic candidate in our history and his poor showing has been widely blamed on religious prejudice. Cf. R. Silva, *Rum, Religion, and Votes: 1928 Re-examined* (State College, Pa., 1962). Adlai Stevenson is the first candidate who had divorced his wife and his party's leaders feared this might hurt his chances. President Kennedy may well have ended the fear of a Catholic President although because of the closeness of the election and the great amount of religious feeling it aroused, it is not clear whether his Catholicism made him President or held down his popular vote. Rockefeller's divorce and remarriage certainly hurt his candidacy in 1965.

The best route to the Presidency until World War II was from the Governor's chair in New York, Ohio, Illinois, or other populous states where party strength was evenly divided between the two major parties. As foreign affairs has become increasingly important in the modern era, the Senate has been proving a more important source of candidates than previously. As yet the House has not; its members ordinarily suffer from their small districts and the long period of apprenticeship required to reach a position of power and prestige in that body. Luck is also an important factor in President-making. Strong candidates emerging at the same time in the same party have on several occasions battled one another out of the race at the convention and opened the door for a "dark horse" less well known than either—Lowden and Wood in the Republican convention of 1920 paved the way for Harding and McAdoo and Smith prepared the path for Davis as the Democratic nominee in 1924. Coolidge happened to be Governor of Massachusetts when the Boston police strike occurred, which gained him national publicity. If Smith had been Governor of New York in 1932 instead of 1928 he, almost certainly, would have been President. These are the factors which have brought to the Presidency men of mediocre talent and have kept out of it their abler compatriots. Nevertheless, a system which has produced Washington, Jefferson, Jackson, Polk, Lincoln, Cleveland, Theodore Roosevelt, Wilson, and Franklin Roosevelt cannot be written off as a hopeless failure. It certainly works as well as the participants (the voters) have any right to expect.

One final word is necessary. The office of President, with its awesome responsibilities and its solitary dignity, has accumulated a tradition and a prestige through the years that lift the men who fill it beyond their realized talents. Men try to live up to the marks set by their illustrious predecessors. The ambition of thousands of politicians, although attained by few, its influence raises all to loftier conceptions of the public good.

References

The Federalist, No. LXVIII.

E. S. Corwin, The President: Office and Powers; History and Analysis of Practice and Opinion (4th ed., New York, 1957), Chap. II.

V. O. Key, Jr., Politics, Parties, and Pressure Groups (5th ed., New York, 1963), Chaps. XV-XVI.

H. W. Horwill, The Usages of the American Constitution (London, 1925), Chap. II.

L. Overacker, The Presidential Primary (New York, 1926).

S. Lorant, The Presidency: A Pictorial History of Presidential Elections (New York, 1952).

E. Stanwood, A History of the Presidency from 1897 to 1916 (New York, 1928).

C. Becker, "The Unit Rule in National Nominating Conventions," *Amer. Hist., Rev.,* V, 64-82 (Oct., 1899).

C. A. M. Ewing, *Presidential Elections* (Norman, Okla., 1940).

H. Agar, *The People's Choice* (Boston, 1933).

S. Hyman, *The American President* (New York, 1954).

D. B. Johnson, *The Republican Party and Wendell Wilkie* (Urbana, Ill., 1960).

H. L. Stoddard, *Presidential Sweepstakes* (New York, 1948).

E. E. Schattschneider, *The Struggle for Party Government* (College Park, Md., 1948).

R. V. Peel and T. C. Donnelly, *The 1928 Campaign; An Analysis* (New York, 1931).

——, *The 1932 Campaign: An Analysis* (New York, 1935).

E. E. Robinson, *The Presidential Vote, 1896-1932* (Stanford Univ., 1934).

——, *The Presidential Vote, 1936* (Stanford Univ., 1940).

——, *They Voted for Roosevelt: The Presidential Vote, 1932-1944* (Stanford Univ., 1947).

L. H. Bean, *Ballot Behavior: A Study of Presidential Elections* (Washington, 1940).

P. F. Lazarsfeld, B. Berelson, and H. Gaudet, *The People's Choice: How the Voter Makes Up His Mind in a Presidential Campaign* (New York, 1945).

S. Lubell, *Revolt of the Moderates* (New York, 1956).

G. J. Shulz, *Election of the President of the United States by the House of Representatives,* 68th Cong., 2nd Sess., Sen. Doc. No. 227 (1925).

P. David, M. Moos, R. Goldman, *Presidential Nominating Politics in 1952* (Baltimore, 1954).

P. David and R. Goldman, *Presidential Nominating Patterns* (Washington, 1955).

P. David, R. M. Goldman, R. C. Bain, *The Politics of National Party Conventions* (Washington, 1960).

R. C. Bain, *Convention Decisions and Voting Records* (Washington, 1961).

E. N. Roseboom, *A History of Presidential Elections* (New York, 1957).

C. A. H. Thompson and F. N. Shattuck, *The 1956 Presidential Campaign* (Washington, 1959).

W. D. Burnham, *Presidential Ballots, 1836-1892* (Baltimore, 1956).

T. H. White, *The Making of the President—1960* (New York, 1961).

——, *The Making of the President—1964* (New York, 1965).

G. Pumper, *Nominating the President: The Politics of Convention Choice* (Evanston, Ill., 1963).

S. Peterson, *A Statistical History of the American Presidential Elections* (New York, 1963).

Official Report of the Proceedings of the Republican National Convention, Issued quadrennially; *ibid.,* Democratic National Convention.

Part II

THE NATIONAL GOVERNMENT

A. ORGANIZATION, POWERS, AND PROCEDURES

★ 10 ★

The Structure and Organization of Congress

HAVING CONCLUDED A SURVEY of the constitutional basis of the American system of government and the democratic processes by which it is operated, we turn now to a consideration of the organizational structure through which legitimate power is exercised by our national government. It is appropriate to begin our discussion with the Congress. Not only is the legislature provided for first in our Constitution, but it may be said to have a certain primacy in any republican form of government. It can claim with some color of truth to be closest to the people and it is the major repository of power to make and declare public policy and to provide the means for its achievement. Its power of decision making, however, it shares with the President and to some degree also with the executive branch agencies, the great interest groups, and the apparatus of our two major political parties.

THE BICAMERAL PATTERN

All legislative powers herein granted shall be vested in a Congress of the United States, which shall consist of a Senate and House of Representatives. ART. I, Sec. 1

With the exception of the Continental and Confederation Congresses and the legislatures briefly established by Vermont and Pennsylvania, the entire political experience of England and of colonial and revolutionary America confirmed the view that a legislature ought to consist of two Houses. If a popular assembly were to be provided, a second chamber representing sectional or substantial vested interests ought to review its deliberations. The framers of our Constitution made this decision early in their deliberations and never seriously considered changing it. The compromise by which the federationists were mollified by representing states as such in one House and

Why two houses were established

227

the nationalists by representing people in the other merely confirmed the wisdom of an arrangement already regarded as indispensable and provided a convenient basis for organizing the two Houses upon different principles. In this way, the framers could be assured of some antagonism between the two bodies which would result in mutual restraint as well as accommodation.

General acceptance of the two-house system

The arrangement, although never entirely free of criticism, has become an accepted and approved part of the American system. Most of the criticism has come from those who decry the deadlocks, delays, duplications, and diffusion of responsibility which two equal and independent authorities tend to induce. All levels of government at one time or another imitated the national legislature but virtually all cities and one state, Nebraska, have abandoned the bicameral plan and gone over to the one-House legislature, partly as a result of the frustrations alluded to by these critics. Some criticism has come also from those who deplore any organizational arrangements which mitigate or obstruct the clear will of a numerical majority of the electorate as expressed by their representatives. The Senate, in which a majority of the membership does not necessarily coincide with a majority of the voters, is regarded as an obstacle to driving the popular will to the statute book. The adoption of popular election of Senators early in this century lessened somewhat the criticisms of that body as being essentially undemocratic. In any event, there are now few serious suggestions to abandon the two-House system in the Congress. A great many competent authorities see it as a positive source of strength to our republic, making possible the acceptance of national authority over an area as vast, as varied, and as populous as that of the United States.

Both houses represent states as states

Broadly speaking, the House of Representatives is based upon population regardless of area and the Senate upon area regardless of population. However, all of the 435 seats in the House are assigned to states as states, and area considerations are not absent from its structure, as we shall presently observe.

REPRESENTATION IN THE HOUSE—THE DISTRICT SYSTEM

Representatives . . . shall be apportioned among the several States . . . according to their respective numbers, counting the whole number of persons in each State, excluding Indians not taxed.[1] The actual enumeration shall be made . . . within every term of ten years, in such manner as they shall by law direct. The number of representatives shall not exceed one for every thirty thousand, but each State shall have at least one representative. ART. I, Sec. 2, cl. 3 as amended by ART. XIV

Reapportionment and increasing the size of the House

Although the Constitution does not expressly require a redistribution of the seats in the House of Representatives to accommodate that body to changes in population revealed by the decennial census, that is clearly what

[1] The Supreme Court having held (Superintendent v. Commissioner, 295 U. S. 418, 1935) that all Indians are subject to national taxation, all were included in the population basis for the apportionments of 1941, 1951, and 1961.

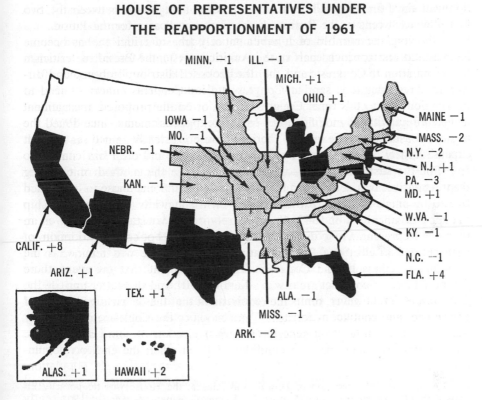

CHANGES IN REPRESENTATION IN THE
HOUSE OF REPRESENTATIVES UNDER
THE REAPPORTIONMENT OF 1961

MINN. −1   ILL. −1
MICH. +1
OHIO +1
IOWA −1   MAINE −1
MO. −1   MASS. −2
NEBR. −1   N.Y. −2
                                 N.J. +1
KAN. −1   PA. −3
                                 MD. +1
                                 W.VA. −1
                                 KY. −1
CALIF. +8
                                 N.C. −1
ARIZ. +1   FLA. +4
TEX. +1   ALA. −1
MISS. −1
ARK. −2
ALAS. +1   HAWAII +2

was intended. Until 1920, the Congress never failed to readjust its membership each decade. The actual statute typically reflected some pulling and hauling of sectional interests, but the resultant distribution roughly approximated the population shifts which had occurred. With the exception of that of 1842, every decennial readjustment up to World War I had been achieved, however, only by substantial increase in the total number of Representatives. By the turn of the century, apprehension was gaining that the House was becoming too large for effective deliberation. Given the great mobility of our people, if a limit on the size of the House is to be achieved, some states and, of course, some Representatives would have to give up seats. This the state delegations in both Houses were understandably reluctant to do. Unable to agree either to increase the size of the House or to take seats away from some states, the Congress after 1920 did nothing for several years.

Before a census would reveal exactly which states might gain or lose and how much, the Congress in 1929 provided for a "permanent" [2] system of re-

Present method of reappor- tionment

[2] A Congress, however, cannot bind its successors; hence, notwithstanding its declared "permanency," it is not to be regarded as necessarily final.

apportionment which would discourage any further growth in its own member-ship and would obviate the necessity for any further Congressional action on the subject. This act, as amended in 1941, has served as the basis of reappor-tionment since that time. Under it, (1) the size of the House is fixed at 435; [3] (2) after each census, the Bureau of the Census prepares for the President a table showing the number of inhabitants of each state and the number of Representatives to which each state is entitled; [4] (3) the President transmits the information to Congress; and, (4) the proposed distribution becomes effec-tive 15 days after it is sent to Congress unless Congress enacts a different distribution. Up to this time, Congress has allowed the proposed arrangement to take effect without modification.[5] In the reapportionments since 1929, the western coastal states, Texas and Florida, have consistently gained seats at the expense largely of New York, Pennsylvania, Illinois, and the Plains states.

The single-member district system

For the first half-century of our national life the method of choosing Representatives was determined by state legislatures. Some chose to have them elected by single-member districts, others on a statewide (at-large) basis. In the apportionment act of 1842, Congress required every state entitled to more than one Representative to divide the state into districts of contiguous territory, each entitled to elect one Representative. This language was retained in all subsequent actions by the Congress. The requirement that the districts be composed also of compact areas was added in 1901 and thereafter until 1929. The present act, however, omits the requirement that the districts be composed of compact and contiguous territory [6] and modifies the single-member district requirement by authorizing general (at-large) election of some or all of the Representatives under specified conditions.[7] Even when the earlier rules ap-

[3] At the time of admission of Hawaii and Alaska, the House was temporarily in-creased to 437, but reverted to 435 after the decennial reapportionment of 1961.

[4] Until 1941, the Bureau of the Census made the distribution on the basis of the "major fractions" formula used also in 1911 which measures the differences in terms of representation per million of inhabitants and which involves comparing the discrep-ancies by simple subtraction of the representatives per million of one state from those of another. In 1941, the law was amended to require the Bureau to use the method of "equal proportions" which involves comparison of the population of the average district for each state as well as of the number of representatives per million of inhabitants. The problem, of course, is how to handle the fractional population left after division of a state's population by the population quota for representatives. This matter is discussed in detail in L. F. Schmeckebier, *Congressional Apportionment* (Washington, 1941).

[5] The pressure to increase the size of the House after the 1960 census was greater than in any recent decade but firmness by the leadership halted any change.

[6] It was held for a time that the omission was inadvertent, but the Supreme Court held that the failure to repeat these requirements had, in effect, repealed them. Woods v. Broom, 287 U. S. 1 (1932). A bill restoring the compact and contiguous rule passed the House in 1965 and is pending before the Senate. The same bill also prohibits at-large election in any state with more than one House seat.

[7] These conditions are: (1) if a state gains seats by a reapportionment and the state legislature fails to redraw the district lines, the added members are elected at-large; (2) if the state loses seats and the state legislature fails to redraw the lines, all repre-sentatives for the state are elected at-large.

plied, however, Congress made no effort seriously to enforce them upon the states.

A bill restoring the compact and contiguous rule passed the House in 1965 and is pending before the Senate. The same bill also prohibits at-large election in any state with more than one House seat.

In spite of the qualifications and modifications mentioned, the single-member district system is predominant in practice and is firmly fixed in the American system of government. No one seriously expects that it will soon be abandoned. Unless some form of voting is used which will guarantee minority representation in connection with the state-wide form of representation,[8] the single-member district system is decidedly the better of the two systems. It tends to assure representation to a wider variety of groups and interests, and thus to strengthen the representative character of the lower house. The district system as it now operates, however, is not without its difficulties, and the House of Representatives elected by this system has been far from a perfect reflection of the national population for which it speaks. *Superiority of the district system*

The major problems of the present system spring from the great difficulties—political, emotional, and geographical—of drawing the district boundaries, a job which is assigned to the state legislatures. There are two kinds of impulses that color the views of state legislators on this subject: (1) the hope of partisan advantage from drawing the lines in a particular way; and (2) the fear, by rural and small-town legislators, of granting to the rapidly growing urban areas the representative strength to which their numbers entitle them. Obviously, it is not possible to have districts which are perfectly equal in population and which also pay some regard to local governmental boundaries. Thus inequality will occur to some extent in the most objective and impersonal efforts to draw the lines. State legislators typically, have no strong impulse to be either objective or impersonal when drawing the boundary lines of the Congressional districts. *Problems of redistricting*

The practice of drawing district boundary lines with a view to partisan or factional advantage is known as gerrymandering.[9] The method is to spread the known support for your party or faction over as many districts as possible and to concentrate the known support for the other party into as few districts as possible. Few redistricting laws have been passed by state legislatures which do not bear evidence of some manipulation of lines for partisan purposes. Some episodes, however, have been much more flagrant than others. *Gerrymandering*

Virtually every census for the past century has revealed the continuing movement of the American people from East to West, farm to city, and city to *Effect of urbanization on redistricting*

[8] Where the general-ticket or at-large scheme has been used, the party or group which polled a plurality of the state vote has captured the entire state delegation in the House of Representatives.

[9] The name is derived from Governor Elbridge Gerry of Massachusetts who allegedly inspired, or at least condoned, a notorious piece of partisan districting in 1812. The name was coined by an opposition editor and has become a part of the American vocabulary of politics.

suburb. Every state legislature has, therefore, been repeatedly confronted with the necessity, if districts are to be kept reasonably equal, of increasing the number of seats in the urban and suburban areas and, since 1929, of decreasing the number in the rural and small-town areas. In most of our state legislatures the rural and small-town areas are grossly overrepresented in terms of population and the rural legislators have been and are now reluctant to augment the strength of the urban contingent in Congress. Frequently this cleavage has been aggravated by the fact that one party, usually the Democrats, has been predominant in the large cities and another party, the Republicans, in the countryside. This reluctance has produced redistricting in which the districts were still quite unequal in size, partial redistricting only, and, in some cases, no redistricting at all for several decades. Rural and small-town America has been, in consequence, somewhat overrepresented in the House of Representatives. Rural overrepresentation also stems from the constitutional requirement that each state have at least one Representative. Thus Nevada and Alaska with total populations under 300,000 are entitled to a Representative each, although the average district contains 410,000.

Judicial compulsion of equal representation   In connection with the reapportionment of 1951, President Truman recommended that the Congress attempt to improve state districting practice by restoring the "compact and contiguous" rule and by specifying that no district in any state should deviate from the average population of Representative districts by more than 50,000 either way. Several urban Congressmen repeatedly and unsuccessfully urged similar action. Then in 1964, the Supreme Court reversing a precedent of long standing held that the Constitution requires that Representative districts be as nearly equal in population as practicable.[10] The command that "Representatives be chosen by the people of the several states means," said the Court, "that as nearly as practicable one man's vote in a Congressional election is to be worth as much as another's." Although the case applied to Georgia, the districting systems of several states were placed in jeopardy by the decision. New district lines have been drawn under Court pressure not only in Georgia but in Utah, Indiana, South Dakota, Michigan, Connecticut, Alabama, Colorado, Texas, Ohio, Idaho, Kansas, Maryland, and Arkansas. Many wide disparities in districts have thus been eliminated or reduced and those still extant in Arizona, Florida, and a few other states are under attack.[11] In an effort to wrest initiative from the courts,

---

[10] Wesbury v. Sanders, 376 U. S. 1 (1964). In Colegrove v. Green, 328 U. S. 549 (1947) the Court had refused to accept jurisdiction in a contested apportionment of House districts in Illinois.

[11] For data on the Congressional districts—size, population characteristics, election returns, etc., see Congressional Quarterly Service; *C.Q. Census Analysis: Congressional Districts of the United States* (Washington, 1964); Congressional Quarterly Service Special Report, *Congressional Districting* (Washington, 1962), Bureau of the Census; *Congressional District Data Book* (Washington, 1963). On the problem of districting see A. Hacker, *Congressional Districting: The Issue of Equal Representation* (Washington, 1963).

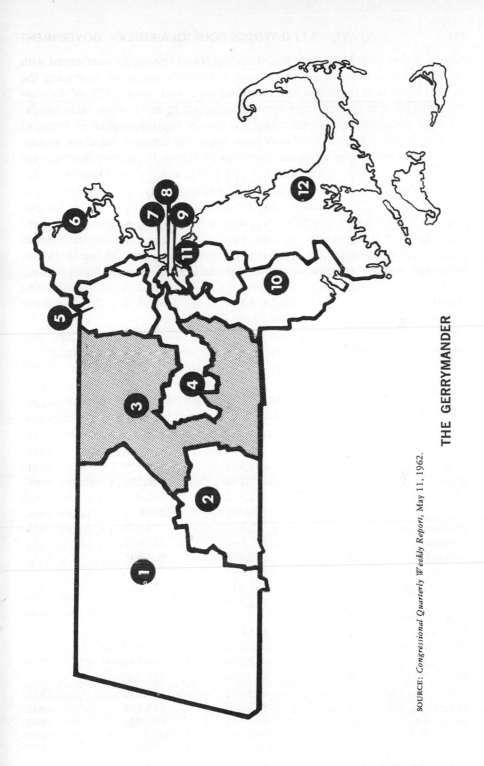

THE GERRYMANDER

SOURCE: *Congressional Quarterly Weekly Report*, May 11, 1962.

	No. of Dist.	POPULATION		Date of Apport.
		Largest Dist.	Smallest Dist.	
Alabama	8	440,538	383,625	1965
Alaska	1	226,167	—	—
Arizona	3	663,510	198,236	1947
Arkansas	4	453,567	443,892	1965
California	38	588,933	301,872	1961
Colorado	4	493,887	405,899	1964
Conn.	6	482,135	404,201	1964
Delaware	1	446,292	—	—
Florida	12	660,345	237,235	1961
Georgia	10	455,575	329,738	1964
Hawaii	2	Both at-large		1959
Idaho	2	364,984	302,207	1965
Illinois	24	552,582	278,703	1961
Indiana	11	454,208	369,663	1965
Iowa	7	442,406	353,156	1961
Kansas	5	472,522	394,056	1965
Kentucky	9	453,298	341,468	1965
Louisiana	8	536,029	263,850	1962
Maine	2	505,465	463,800	1961
Maryland	8	443,331	329,826	1965
Mass.	12	478,962	376,336	1961
Mich.	19	417,174	403,263	1964
Minn.	8	482,872	375,475	1961
Miss.	5	608,441	295,072	1962
Missouri	10	506,854	378,499	1961
Montana	2	347,748	327,019	1965
Nebraska	3	530,507	404,695	1961
Nevada	1	285,278	—	—
New Hamp.	2	331,818	275,103	1881
New J.	15	555,555	255,165	1961
New Mexico	2	Both at-large		1911
New York	41	471,001	350,186	1961
No. Car.	11	487,159	277,861	1961
No. Dak.	2	333,290	299,156	1960
Ohio	24	457,774	351,760	1965
Okla.	6	552,863	227,692	1951
Oregon	4	522,813	265,164	1941
Penna.	27	553,154	303,026	1962

STATE DELEGATIONS AND DISTRICTS

HOUSE OF REPRESENTATIVES

1965

	No. of Dist.	POPULATION		Date of Apport.
		Largest Dist.	Smallest Dist.	
R. I.	2	459,706	399,782	1931
So. Car.	6	531,555	272,220	1932
So. Dak.	2	351,901	328,613	1965
Tenn.	9	453,298	341,468	1965
Texas	23	457,092	376,200	1965
Utah	2	451,864	438,763	1965
Vermont	1	389,881	—	—
Virginia	10	419,642	377,511	1965
Wash.	7	510,512	342,540	1957
W. Va.	5	422,046	303,098	1961
Wis.	10	408,677	381,830	1963
Wyo.	1	330,066	—	—

the House in 1965 passed a bill which is pending in the Senate to bar any district which deviates by more than 15 percent from the average for the state's districts and to forbid at-large representation in states with more than one Representative.[12]

REPRESENTATION IN THE SENATE—STATE EQUALITY

The Senate of the United States shall be composed of two Senators from each State, elected by the people thereof, for six years; and each Senator shall have one vote. ART. I, Sec. 3, Cl. 1, as amended by SEVENTEENTH AMENDMENT

The Senate is not troubled by the problems of the district system. Representation in it is not and was never intended to be in any sense related to population. Every state, large or small, populous or not, rich or poor, industrial or agricultural, is entitled to two Senators. And it may not be deprived of its equality with the others except with its own consent. The Senate is a federal institution. It is not a democratic one, at least insofar as democratic principles require an equality of representation for people as people. Until the Constitution was amended in 1913 to provide for the popular election of Senators, it was not democratic in any respect. The tide of democracy which

Undemocratic character of the Senate

[12] As of July 1, 1965, 127 districts in 29 states deviate by more than 15 percent and Hawaii and New Mexico are currently electing their two Representatives at-large.

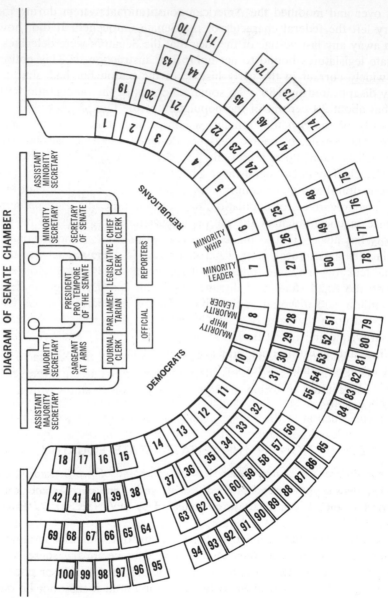

DIAGRAM OF SENATE CHAMBER

swept over and modified the American constitutional system during the last century left the federal character of the Senate untouched. It did, however, sweep away any last vestige of the idea that the Senators were delegates from the state legislatures bound to act upon their instructions.[13] This notion had been widely current in the early history of the nation but had almost completely disappeared by 1865. To some adherents of the democratic faith, the fact that about 20 percent of the population of the United States can control a majority of the Senators remains a conspicuous failure of the American system. The Senate, of course, was not designed by democrats but by constitutionalists intent upon preserving and strengthening the American Union.

Political significance

The chief political significance of the structure of the Senate has been that agricultural and other nonurban interests which are predominant in many states have, regardless of population, had a profound and even a predominant influence in one branch of the national legislature. The will of the popular majority has always had to make its peace with sectional and regional interests, largely agricultural, if it were to prevail in the national capital. The original fear that the large states would engage in deadly and prolonged combat with the small states and disrupt the Union has proved groundless, just as Hamilton said it would at the time. Cleavage in the Senate has rarely if ever rested upon the basis of size. The fears of others that the Senate would necessarily and inevitably be the stronghold of political and economic conservatism and constitutional fundamentalism has also not been borne out. The sparsely populated states have sent radicals and reformers to the Senate about as frequently as the urban states have sent them.

No likelihood of change

There is no substantial element in the United States which now advocates reconstruction of the Senate. It may be doubted if major reconstruction could be achieved peacefully and by constitutional methods.

THE MEMBERS OF CONGRESS: A. SELECTION

Regulated by state law

The manner of electing Senators and Representatives is largely regulated by state law and thus varies in many details from state to state. Experience in this matter has been little different from that of electing all types of public officers in the United States, and at the present time the predominant mode is nomination by direct primary and election by secret, partisan ballot at the same time as many other public officials are chosen. Congress has exercised its constitutional authority to regulate the election of its members by requiring: (1) the single-member district system for Representatives (1842); (2) the secret ballot (1872); [14] (3) the election everywhere to take place on the Tuesday after the first Monday in November of any even-numbered year.[15] The

---

[13] W. H. Riker, "The Senate and American Federalism," *Amer. Pol. Sci. Rev.,* Vol. XLIX, No. 2 (June, 1955).

[14] This, of course, does not preclude the use of voting machines.

[15] Unless the constitution of a state fixes a different date, as was the case in Maine until a few years ago.

Congress has also enacted regulations governing campaign expenditures in national elections. The qualifications for voting in these Congressional elections are established by state law also, but the Supreme Court has held that the right to vote for members of Congress is not conferred by the states but rather is one of the "privileges and immunities" of citizens of the United States protected by the Fourteenth Amendment.[16]

The adoption of popular election of senators

The most important changes in the method of selecting members of Congress were the widespread introduction of the direct primary system for making nominations (1905-1920) and the adoption in 1913 of direct popular election of Senators in place of selection by state legislatures, which had been the practice up to that time. Whatever may have been the advantages which characterized legislative selection, toward the end of the last century it fell increasingly into disrepute. Recurring deadlocks left some seats vacant for several years; the preoccupation of state legislators with the selection of Senators interfered with the discharge of their state and local responsibilities; concern by the voters for the legislature's selection led to election of state legislators on no other basis except their promised support of a particular candidate. The Senate was widely charged with being filled with the minions of powerful (and at the moment unpopular) interests which browbeat, bribed, and intimidated state legislators into choosing rich men who were not really representative of the state. The swelling enthusiasm for democratic processes instilled in many the conviction that legislative election was undemocratic and ought to be abandoned. Political parties endorsed the idea in their platforms; two-thirds of the state legislatures went on record in favor of it; the House of Representatives repeatedly (five times between 1893 and 1912) passed resolutions proposing constitutional amendments to accomplish it. In 29 states by 1912 some form of advisory primary in which the voters indicated their preferences for Senators to the legislature were being held. The Senate finally, though reluctantly, concurred and the Seventeenth Amendment was added to the Constitution.

The primary and Congressional elections

In the same period the direct primary replaced district conventions for nominating candidates to the House and then was applied after 1913 to nominations for the Senate. The primary, as we have noted, tended to weaken the hold of the regular party organization on the selection of candidates. In the case of Congressmen, the primary system has tended to maintain and perhaps to strengthen the local influences at work in his designation. The formal party apparatus—national and state—is more or less obliged to stay out of the primary and the candidate is on his own until the general election campaign at which time he may receive national, Congressional, or state campaign committee help. In considering the relative lack of party discipline over the members of Congress and the problem of producing more responsible party behavior, it is important to bear in mind that Representatives and Senators are nominated by processes which are mainly local in emphasis. Furthermore, in a large number of districts (perhaps two-thirds, in the period of

[16] *Ex parte Yarbrough,* 110 U. S. 651 (1884).

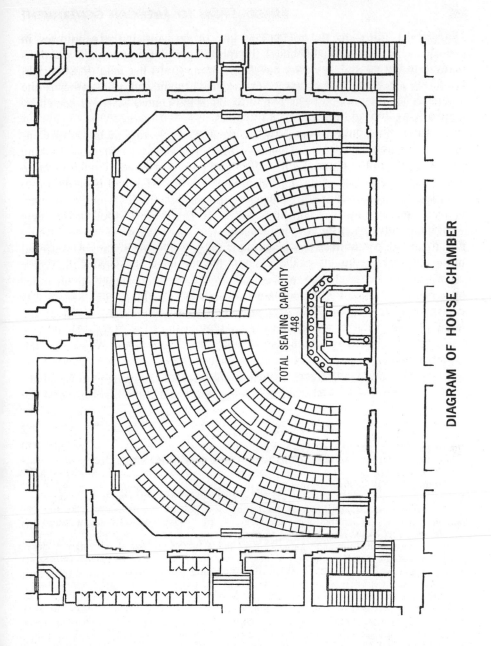

TOTAL SEATING CAPACITY
448

DIAGRAM OF HOUSE CHAMBER

1945-1965) and some states (perhaps half in the same period) the election contests have been one-sided and, therefore, perhaps less demanding than many primary contests in these same districts. Candidates for Congress also are not to any important degree recruited or designated by the national party leadership as they are to some extent in the highly disciplined parties of the United Kingdom and the European democracies. It should, therefore, not be surprising if the Congressman is frequently more responsive to pressures from his constituency than from his national party leaders.[17]

Results of popular election
The effect of popular election of Senators also cannot easily be measured. The expectation of its sponsors that money would play a less important role in elections has certainly not been realized. Legitimate expenditures for individuals campaigning over an entire state are probably greatly in excess of what might have been spent to influence a state legislature. Excessive, perhaps illegitimate, expenditures have been made on several occasions.[18] The change in the character or quality of the Senators has not been appreciable. Certainly there was no abrupt change in personnel. Virtually every Senator who might have been continued by the legislature was elected by the voters. Contrary to expectations, re-elections have been more numerous than under the old system. Some observers detect a decline in party regularity in the Senate of the past half-century. They allege that Senators today have less patience with party government and cross party lines more frequently than before. State legislatures have clearly been made freer to concentrate on the tasks of state government than they were before and deadlocks have become impossible.[19] If under the

[17] See W. J. Keefe and M. S. Ogul, *The American Legislative Process* (Englewood Cliffs, N. J., 1964), Chap. 4; L. A. Froman, Jr., *Congressmen and Their Constituencies* (Chicago, 1963); and, H. D. Price, "The Electoral Arena," D. B. Truman (ed), *The Congress and America's Future* (Englewood Cliffs, N. J., 1965).

[18] In winning a senatorial seat in Michigan in 1918, Truman H. Newberry spent something like $195,000—an amount far in excess of that recognized by Michigan law as a legitimate electoral outlay, i.e. $1875, as also by the national statute of 1910, which fixed the figure at $10,000. Most of the amount was poured out in securing the nomination in a primary in competition with Henry Ford. Convicted under the national law in a lower court, Newberry appealed to the national Supreme Court, which in 1921 set aside the conviction, four of the nine Justices being of the opinion that Congress lacked power to regulate nominations and a fifth concurring for a different reason (Newberry v. United States, 256 U. S. 232). When finally seating the defendant by a close vote in 1922, the Senate passed a resolution declaring his outlay in quest of his nomination excessive, contrary to sound policy, and dangerous to free government; and in the end, Newberry decided that his seat would not be comfortable and resigned. A full account of the affair will be found in S. Erwin, *Henry Ford* vs. *Truman H. Newberry* (New York, 1935). In 1928, the Senate refused to seat William S. Vare and Frank L. Smith of Pennsylvania and Illinois, respectively, on charges of receiving and spending too much money in securing nomination and election; and prolonged subsequent investigations and controversies failed to bring a reversal of the decisions. See C. H. Wooddy, *The Case of Frank L. Smith; A Study in Representative Government* (Chicago, 1931).

[19] It should be noted that if a vacancy arises under the present system due to the death, resignation, or expulsion of a Senator, most states authorize the governor to appoint a member to serve until an election can conveniently be held to fill the remainder of the term.

old system an occasional plutocrat bought his way into the Senate to satisfy purely personal ambition, under the new one the demagogue and the windbag probably get in more readily than before. If, however, our Senators today are not demonstrably better than they once were, they are not demonstrably worse as the opponents of popular election predicted. Taft, Johnson, Fulbright, Millikin, Russell, among recent Senators, are probably as able and as honest as any that the Senate of the past century can show.

Disputed elections of members of Congress are ultimately decided by the House or the Senate. A candidate has the right to carry his case to the body concerned regardless of state regulations and to have it heard by an appropriate committee. In 1961, for example, the election in the 5th District of Indiana was so close that the case was carried to the House and only after weeks of investigation, recounting, and analysis was a decision reached. Partisan considerations may, and sometimes do, color the decisions of the Congressmen on these matters and this has led some persons to suggest that we adopt the English system and have such questions decided by a board of judges.[20] *Disputed elections*

THE MEMBERS OF CONGRESS: B. TERM

The term of Senators is six years and of Representatives two years. Each Senator is thus able to devote himself for several years to his Senatorial responsibilities without constant anxiety about re-election. He serves through several sessions of Congress and is able to acquire a great deal of understanding and experience before he is obliged to stand before the voters of his state and ask for a vote of confidence. Many Senators serve more than one term and periods of service extending to 18 or even 24 years are not uncommon. Continuity of personnel is obtained by the constitutional arrangement for the election of only one-third of the membership every two years.[21] *Term*

In his State of the Union message in early 1966, President Johnson proposed that the term of Representatives be extended to four years. Members of the House could render better service to the nation if campaigns were less frequent, he argued.

THE MEMBERS OF CONGRESS: C. QUALIFICATIONS

No person shall be a Representative who shall not have attained to the age of twenty-five years, and been seven years a citizen of the United States and

[20] In "Contested Congressional Elections in Recent Years," *Polit. Sci. Quar.*, LIV, 187-214 (June, 1939), V. M. Barnett, Jr., however, shows the record in the House to have been commendable on this point during the period studied, i.e., 1918-37.

[21] The original Senators were divided into three classes, with terms expiring in two, four, and six years, respectively. In no case were both Senators of a state placed in the same class, and the Senators of states admitted later were always assigned, by lot, to different classes. Hence, barring vacancies arising from death or resignation, only one Senator is elected in a state in any given year.

who shall not, when elected, be an inhabitant of that State in which he shall be chosen. ART. I, Sec. 2, Cl. 2

No person shall be a Senator who shall not have attained to the age of thirty years, and been nine years a citizen of the United States and who shall not, when elected, be an inhabitant of that State for which he shall be chosen. ART. I, Sec. 3, Cl. 3

To be seated in either branch of Congress, a duly elected person must meet the three requirements imposed by the Constitution. He need not, however, attain the required age until the time to be sworn in. In addition to these qualifications, the Constitution forbids members of Congress when sworn in, or at any time during their tenure, to hold any "office under the United States." This provision represents a rather sharp departure from the English tradition of our ancestors, for according to custom Great Britain requires ministers to be also members of Parliament. The prohibition includes military as well as civil officers but does not preclude the service by members of Congress as temporary representatives of this nation in international conferences. An officer of the government may be elected to Congress but must resign the office when he takes his seat. Members of Congress may be appointed to national office but they must resign their seats when appointed.

Qualifi-
cations
added by
usage
Many decades of political experience have resulted in the addition by custom and usage to the bare constitutional requirements. It is virtually a universal requirement that Representatives be residents of the district for which they sit as well as of the state in which it is located.[22] In some sections of the country, it is almost indispensable that an individual be a Republican and in others that he be a Democrat in order to seek election with any hope of success. Every district has by this time a large number of unwritten qualifications which constitute "availability" in a candidate for the national legislature. These are so varied, however, that no safe generalization is possible. Suffice it to say that simple compliance with the age, citizenship, and residence requirements does not "qualify" a person for Congress.

Qualifi-
cations
imposed by
the two
houses
The two houses of Congress, furthermore, have each chosen to exercise their prerogative of judging the qualifications of those who present themselves for membership by excluding individuals on grounds unrelated to the constitutional specifications. The House in 1900 refused to seat Brigham H.

[22] In 1964 two unusual candidacies raised questions about the meaning of the Constitutional provision. Pierre Salinger, President Kennedy's press secretary and a voting resident of Virginia from 1955 to that time resigned to run for the Senate from California, his native state prior to 1955. His interim appointment by Governor Brown in August on the death of Senator Engel was challenged in the Senate but he was seated after a spirited debate. He was later defeated in the November election. Attorney General Kennedy, brother of the President and a resident for many years of Massachusetts, resigned in 1964 to run for the Senate from New York—he had maintained an apartment in New York City. Despite efforts to discredit him as a nonresident, he was successful in the election.

Roberts of Utah on the grounds that he was a polygamist. Victor L. Berger of Wisconsin was excluded in 1919 because he had been judicially convicted of obstructing the war effort.[23] In both instances there were members of the House who argued that this procedure was unconstitutional and the proper course was to seat such individuals and then, if they were deemed unfit for membership, expel them.[24] It takes only a majority vote to exclude and a two-thirds vote to expel, and the critics of the two individuals preferred, and successfully persuaded the House to prefer, the easier method.[25] The Senate, on its part, has accepted "questionable" members after some debate on the grounds that the constitutional method is expulsion. Reed Smoot of Utah (1903)[26] and William Langer of North Dakota (1941)[27] were both seated although under attack. On the other hand, in 1928 it refused to seat Frank L. Smith of Illinois and William S. Vare of Pennsylvania on the grounds that they had exceeded by a great deal the legal limit on campaign expenditures in their contests for election. Grave doubts still exist among members of Congress and students of the propriety and legality of the imposition by the two houses of additional qualifications.

THE MEMBERS OF CONGRESS:
D. PRIVILEGES, IMMUNITIES, AND PAY

The Senators and Representatives shall receive a compensation for their services, to be ascertained by law and paid out of the Treasury of the United States. They shall, in all cases except treason, felony, and breach of the peace, be privileged from arrest during their attendance at the session of their re-

---

[23] He was later cleared by the Supreme Court and, after being elected a third time, was seated.

[24] A Senator or Representative may be expelled for any cause. Not, however, being regarded as a civil officer of the United States in the meaning of the Constitution, neither is subject to impeachment.

[25] The House in 1965 refused to bar Representative Richard L. Ottinger of New York when he was attacked by a constituent for excessive campaign expenditures. The House majority held that his election could be challenged on these grounds only by his defeated rival. In another unusual contest, the House in 1965 also refused to bar the Mississippi delegation. It had been challenged by the Mississippi Freedom Democratic party on the grounds that Negroes had been systematically excluded from the electoral process by which the delegation had been chosen.

[26] The charge against Smoot was that he was an adherent of the Mormon Church, although not a polygamist himself.

[27] The charge against Langer was that, when attorney general and later governor of his state, he had allowed his official actions to be influenced by his interest in various business deals. The Senate committee on elections (as then existing) recommended that he be unseated, but the recommendation did not finally prevail. In January, 1947, a recently re-elected Senator, Theodore G. Bilbo of Mississippi, was not officially denied his seat, but confirmation of his right to sit was held up pending his recovery from an operation. Various charges had been brought against him relating to improper dealings with war contractors and inciting racial hatred in his primary campaign. During the following summer he died and the matter was dropped.

spective houses, and in going to and returning from the same; and for any speech or debate in either house they shall not be questioned in any other place. ART. I, Sec. 6, Cl. 1

Congressional immunity

The privileges and immunities of members of Congress, while taken for granted now, are protections designed to assure freedom of attendance, debate, and voting which were won by English legislators in a long and historic struggle with the Crown. The meaning of the constitutional guarantees is that members enjoy no particular exemptions from the requirements of the criminal law,[28] but may not be subpoenaed or otherwise compelled to testify or to serve on a jury and may not be served with any type of legal process in civil action. Freedom of debate includes protection against libel or slander suits for anything said orally or in writing before committees or other agencies of the Congress as well as in debate on the floor.[29] Congressmen are, of course, not protected against criticism of their remarks or conduct.

Pay and perquisites

Until 1855, the members of Congress awarded themselves a small per diem allowance ($6-$8), but at that time an annual salary of $3000 was authorized. This allowance was raised to $5000 in 1865, to $7500 in 1907, to $10,000 in 1925, to $12,500 in 1946, to $22,500 in 1955, and to $30,000 in 1964. In addition to salary, each member of Congress receives: (1) a mileage allowance of 20 cents per mile for five round trips between his home and Washington, D.C., each session, (2) an allowance for secretarial and clerical help in his office, for Representatives about $50,000 annually and for Senators, from $40,000 to $140,000 depending upon the size of the state and including for each Senator one administrative assistant to be paid $16,-000; (3) the privilege of using the mails without postage charges (the annual cost of franking privileges is about $4 million); (4) an allowance for telephone and telegraph service out of his office; (5) an allowance for stationery, office supplies and equipment; and (6) a retirement allowance under the national retirement system based upon contributions and length of service. The floor leaders have somewhat larger allowances and the presiding officers receive higher salaries as well as larger expense allowances. Despite what at first glance appears to be rather generous provision for our lawmakers, many Congressmen complain that they are hard put to make ends meet. If one considers the cost of modern campaigning, the added cost as well as inconvenience associated with trying to maintain two homes, the cost of returning frequently to their home constituencies, and the necessity they are under to make gen-

[28] Williamson *v.* United States, 207 U. S. 425 (1908). An extensive discussion of the power of the courts to subpoena a senator may be found in *Congressional Record,* Senate, 3709-3718 (1957).

[29] If, however, a Congressman repeats or publishes his affirmations outside of the House, the immunity ceases to apply. In 1964, a lower court conviction of a former Congressman (Thomas F. Johnson) was set aside on the grounds that a court could not try a member for charges arising out of a speech on the floor. See *The New York Times,* Sept. 17, 1964.

erous contributions to every worthy cause and to entertain visiting constituents, it is easy to appreciate their dissatisfaction.

THE MEMBERS OF CONGRESS: E. DISCIPLINE

Each house may . . . punish its members for disorderly behavior, and with the concurrence of two-thirds, expel a member. ART. I, Sec. 5, Cl. 2

Although the Constitution clothes the Congress with power to discipline its members for improper conduct, in comparison with other democratic legislative bodies, the Congress of the United States has been unusually tolerant of its members. The misuse of a government railway ticket under extenuating circumstances resulted in the resignation and disgrace a few years ago of a member of the British House of Commons. The Congress has failed to take action against its own members even when they have been under indictment for criminal offenses. Our Congress has never felt any embarrassment over the fact that legislators with direct financial interests participate in deliberations and vote on questions concerning those interests and yet the American bar expects a judge to disqualify himself if he has any direct or even indirect personal or financial interest in the outcome of a case before him. Recent Congresses have been quick to criticize employees and officers of the executive branch for their laxness and tolerance of shady dealings. As soon as rumor or gossip points to any member of the legislature, the others seem to gather round to protect him from the same justice they dispense so sternly to the "bureaucrats." [30]

Laxness of Congressional self-discipline

This is not to say that Congress has more than its share of dishonesty or sharp practice, nor even that its leaders are more cynical or more indifferent to the proprieties than those of other institutions of our society. It is that habits of mutual tolerance of long standing have drawn the attention of Congress away from its own sinners. It has never successfully formulated a code of ethics for its members. Jefferson's *Manual* is strangely silent in these matters. The thoughtful members, in recent years at least, have probably dreaded doing anything to cast any more discredit on the institution which they regard as the heart and soul of the democratic process and which has suffered throughout history in the popular mind in comparison with the other two branches. Several recent efforts, notably those of Senator Douglas of Illinois and of the subcommittee of the Senate Committee on Labor and Public Welfare which he headed,[31] have urged the Congress, but very tenderly, along the road to more effective and more rigorous self-discipline. There is a growing sentiment that members of Congress should make a rather complete

Ethical standards

[30] See H. H. Wilson, *Congress: Corruption and Compromise* (New York, 1951) for a series of case studies of Congressional tolerance of the behavior of its own members.

[31] P. H. Douglas, *Ethical Standards in Government* (Cambridge, Mass., 1952).

disclosure of their own finances at regular intervals and several Congressmen have done so. In lieu of more stringent regulations, the Senate in 1965 finally established (it had been authorized in 1964) a special bipartisan committee to investigate allegations of improper conduct against its own members or employees.

The disciplinary procedures of the two houses have been invoked most frequently to curb statements and actions of members which reflect upon other members. Some members have been officially censured, usually for intemperate statements about the motives or character of other Congressmen.[32] Expulsions have been rare.[33] As noted previously, the Congress has preferred, where it could, to deny "undesirables" admission rather than to drive them out of the chambers.

THE MEMBERS OF CONGRESS: F. CHARACTERISTICS

The typical Congress-man

What kinds of men and women are our lawmakers in Washington? They are not "average" Americans in most respects, but rather well above the average in terms of education, age, and means. A study [34] of the membership of the 89th Congress revealed that: (1) the average age of our Representatives is 51 and of Senators 58, well above the average of the population generally; (2) the lawmakers are well rooted in the districts which they represent by birth and long residence; (3) they are affiliated with one or another of the major religious faiths in about the same proportion as the people generally; (4) there are 12 women and 6 Negroes; (5) many of them had substantial prior political experience in state and local government as legislators, governors, mayors, district attorneys; (6) more than two-thirds attended college; and, (7) a majority are lawyers. In addition to the law, the other professions had some representation as did the world of business and finance. Few members were themselves farmers and only one was a skilled laborer.

This summary indicates clearly that our legislators come largely from the upper middle class economically and socially. The typical legislator is a county-seat lawyer, serving his third or fourth term, comfortable but not rich, a church member, a leader in his community and region, but not well known

[32] Only four members of the Senate have been rebuked in its entire history: Senators McLaurin and Tillman of South Carolina in 1902, Senator Bingham of Connecticut in 1929, and Senator McCarthy of Wisconsin in 1954.

[33] Senators and Representatives from the seceding states were expelled at the beginning of the Civil War. Senator Paterson (New Hampshire) was recommended for expulsion in 1873 because of his role in the Crédit Mobilier scandal. His term expired shortly thereafter and no action was taken. In 1862, Senators Simmons (Rhode Island) and Roach (No. Dakota) resigned before action could be taken as did Representative Whittemore (South Carolina) in 1870. Senator Bright (Indiana) was expelled in 1862 for a statement construed by his colleagues as favorable to President Davis of the Confederacy.

[34] Congressional Quarterly Service, *Weekly Report* (Jan. 1, 1965), 25.

outside it, a member of one of the fraternal orders, and, more and more frequently, a veteran.[35]

THE ORGANIZATION OF CONGRESS

The House of Representatives shall choose their Speaker and other officers. . . . ART. I, Sec. 2, Cl. 5

The Senate shall choose their other officers, and also a president pro tempore in the absence of the Vice President. . . . ART. I, Sec. 3, Cl. 5

Each house may determine the rules of its proceedings. . . . ART. I, Sec. 5, Cl. 2

Promptly at noon on January 4, 1965, the 89th Congress [36] of the United States assembled in the Capitol at Washington for its first session.[37] The Senate was called to order in its north wing chamber by the president *pro tempore* of the Senate there being on this occasion no Vice-President until January 20. After a short prayer, the certificates of election from the various governors were presented for the newly elected or re-elected Senators and the oath of office was administered to these members in groups of four. Over in the south wing the clerk of the 88th Congress called the House of Representatives to order and after prayer called the roll of Representatives-elect based upon the certificates of election received by his office from each state for each member.[38] The two houses then proceeded to elect their respective leaders.

A new Congress organizes for business

At this stage of the opening-day proceedings Congress reveals that it is a political institution, split by partisanship, and that its floor proceedings

[35] For a biography of an imaginary typical Congressman, see J. M. Burns, *Congress on Trial* (New York, 1949), Chap. 1.

[36] Congresses exist for two years, the term of Representatives. The first Congress assembled in 1789 and they have been numbered consecutively since that time.

[37] Congress is required to assemble at least once each year and hence every Congress has two regular sessions. It may be called, in addition, into extraordinary or special session by the President. While either house may be convoked without the other, there has never been any occasion to call the House of Representatives into session alone. The Senate, on the other hand, has been convened to act on executive appointments or treaties. A special session of the Senate is, of course, not a session of Congress. Unlike many state legislatures which, when called into special session by the governor, may act only on matters specified in the governor's call, the Congress once convened possesses its full constitutional authority.

[38] If it should appear that any seat was claimed by a person not named in the certificate, the matter is referred to the standing committee on House administration for investigation and report. Meanwhile, the person named in the certificate is presumed elected and takes his seat and participates in the work of the House. The normal procedure in the Senate also is to refer contested elections to the appropriate committee and seat the individual named in the certificate. However, there have been several lively debates at this stage and some members have been denied seats at this point as we have already described.

are frequently but formal ratifications of decisions taken in private by the leaders after many consultations and conferences. In the particular Congress under consideration, the Democratic Party had control of both houses by large majorities and in the election which had produced this result, the voters had returned a Democratic President with an overwhelming popular majority (61 percent). The strength of the American tradition and the character of the American political system is revealed by the fact that the minority was nevertheless accorded all of the usual privileges despite its reduced strength.

Senate elects its officers

The Senate, having established its roll and admitted the new members and debated a few days about the rules, proceeded to elect Senator Hayden, Democrat of Arizona, as its president *pro tempore*. This official presides over the Senate in the absence of the Vice-President and inherits all of the powers of the Vice-President in case of his death, resignation, or achievement of the Presidency. Senator Hayden was the only candidate presented by the Democratic floor leader in behalf of his party, indicating clearly that the party had agreed beforehand on its choice. Of course, the newspapers had been carrying stories for some time that Hayden had been selected. The minority Republican Party nominated Senator Dirksen of Illinois to the post, but only as a gesture, and the election of Hayden was by voice vote. In quick succession, by the same procedure, and with a similar result, the Senate elected a secretary, a sergeant-at-arms, and a doorkeeper. A secretary to the minority party was elected on the recommendation of the minority party leader.[39]

House elects its officers

Over in the House of Representatives, at about the same time, a Democratic Congressman arose, indicated he was acting at the direction of the Democratic caucus, and nominated Representative McCormack of Massachusetts to be speaker. A Republican Congressman then arose and nominated Representative Ford of Michigan to the same post, indicating that he also was acting at the direction of his party conference. No other nominations were made; none were expected. Both men had been the chosen leaders of their parties. A roll call of the Representatives assigned 290 votes for McCormack to 139 votes for Ford. By a "curious coincidence" there had been 290 Democrats and 139 Republicans voting on the question. Occasionally, the selection of speaker has not gone so smoothly; intraparty strife or a close balance of political forces has evoked deadlock and delay extending over several days. The speakership is a very powerful office, as we shall see, much more so than the president *pro tempore* of the Senate, and thus the competition for it is unusually keen. Typically, however, the issue has been settled as easily and as certainly as it was in 1965.[40]

[39] None of these officials, except the president *pro tempore*, is typically a member of the Senate. In the House, only the speaker is traditionally a Representative.

[40] One other officer is the parliamentarian of the House. His principal function being, however, to aid the speaker in interpreting the rules and deciding points of order, he is selected by that official and has more or less permanent tenure.

Ordinarily a speaker may expect to be re-elected at the beginning of each successive Congress as long as he remains a member and his party continues in control. If the

The speaker was escorted to the chair by his defeated rival; each addressed the membership briefly in a spirit of good will, mutual respect, and promises of fair dealing. The new speaker then administered the oath of office to all the certified Representatives,[41] the chairmen of the two-party conferences announced to the members the party selections for floor leaders, and the House then proceeded to elect a new clerk, sergeant-at-arms, doorkeeper, postmaster, and chaplain. Each party presented only one slate for all the offices; there was no debate. The Democratic slate was adopted by voice vote.

The next order of business (excluding the adoption of certain formal resolutions of notification to the other house and to the President) was the adoption of the rules. The Senate, which is a continuing body,[42] is under no necessity to adopt its rule anew with each Congress, but the House ceases to exist with each Congress and is reconstituted by the procedure we are describing. Representative Albert, Democrat of Oklahoma and majority floor leader offered a resolution that the rules of the House be adopted as set forth with an amendment. The rules offered by the Congressman were those under which the House had been operating for many years with two changes aimed at reducing the power of the Rules Committee.[43] This is the only stage of proceedings in the House when it is possible to get any important change in the rules. Once the rules are adopted, any amendments must be approved by the Rules Committee, and this is most unlikely. At the time of original adoption, the rules have on several occasions, notably in 1910 and 1949, been

---

party balance is overturned, the incoming majority is likely to elevate to the post the man who previously was minority floor leader. The death of a speaker during his period of service is usually followed by an election carried out without a contest, as when Speaker William B. Bankhead was chosen in 1936, Speaker Sam Rayburn in 1940, and Speaker John McCormack in 1962.

[41] Having once taken the oath, a representative can be separated from the House before the expiration of his term only by death, resignation, or expulsion. The latter requires a two-thirds vote.

[42] The question of whether the Senate is a continuing body was vigorously argued at the opening of the sessions in 1953, 1955, 1957, and 1959. Several Senators who wished to change the rules governing filibusters took this way as the most likely to be effective. On each occasion and after some debate, the Senate rejected the contention, although in 1959, the Vice-President in an advisory opinion stated that Rule XXII (the filibuster rule) was unconstitutional in so far as it exempted from closure debates to change the Senate rules. In 1959, however, Rule XXII was amended to declare that the rules of the Senate shall continue from one Congress to the next. Nevertheless spirited efforts to change the filibuster rule at the opening session were made in 1961, 1963, and 1965, presumably on the assumption that the change could be made then by a single majority vote. Every skirmish has ended thus far with the filibuster rule unchanged.

[43] One of the changes adopted in 1965 authorized the speaker to recognize a committee chairman for the purpose of bringing a measure before the House if it had been before the Rules Committee for 21 days without being granted clearance. Another authorized the speaker to recognize a member to offer a motion to send a bill to conference and the motion could be approved by a majority without requiring unanimous consent or suspension of the rules. A third change deprived a member of the right to demand an engraved copy of a bill before final passage. This had been a delaying tactic.

amended in important respects. The rules as amended were adopted, as they usually are, but on this occasion with some debate and with a roll-call vote.

With the election of the members of the standing committees, a step which occurred a few days later, the two houses were organized and ready to deal with the multitude of problems, foreign and domestic, which confronted them.

PARTY GOVERNMENT IN THE HOUSE AND SENATE

Parties and the Congress

It should be quite clear from what has been said that some form of leadership was already at work and manifesting its influence over the conduct of the Congress before the formal institutions of leadership contemplated by the Constitution and the rules of the two houses had been established. This direction is provided by the political parties. It has developed outside the Constitution, was not intended by the framers of that instrument, and is largely unknown to the laws of the nation. It is impossible to understand the character or the conduct of our national legislature without a realization of its importance. All but a small handful of the nation's legislators come to Congress bearing the label of one or the other of the two great parties and with varying but substantial ties with the state and district party organizations and to a lesser degree with the national headquarters. Elected under the sign of the elephant or the donkey, the members profess a certain loyalty to these two great political organizations and to their aims and programs enunciated during the campaign. One of the two parties will normally command the support of a majority of the members of each house and will take possession of the formal positions of authority and leadership; the other, although a minority and therefore not obliged to assume any responsibility for what is done by the Congress, is nevertheless by usage and tradition entitled to certain rights and privileges. Loyalty to these party organizations and to the leadership identified with them is a necessary requisite to the achievement of position, influence, and prestige in the legislative process, and this loyalty provides the only consequential bond which unites the party members and fuels the machine of party government.

The party conference or caucus

The font of authority for the agencies of party government is the party caucus or conference.[44] All of the members of each party in each house comprise the party caucuses of the two parties in the House and Senate. Thus all of the Republican members of the House of Representatives comprise the Republican conference of the House. The party conferences always assemble prior to the convening of each new Congress and elect the officers and functionaries of the parties for the Congress and also agree on the party candidates for the major posts to be determined by the legislature. Thus, the House conferences will designate their choices for speaker, clerk, and so on, and the

[44] The Democratic members of the House of Representatives refer to their organization as the Democratic caucus; the Republican members of the House and Senate and the Democratic members of the Senate refer to their organizations as conferences.

MAJOR PARTY STRENGTH IN CONGRESS, 1932-1964

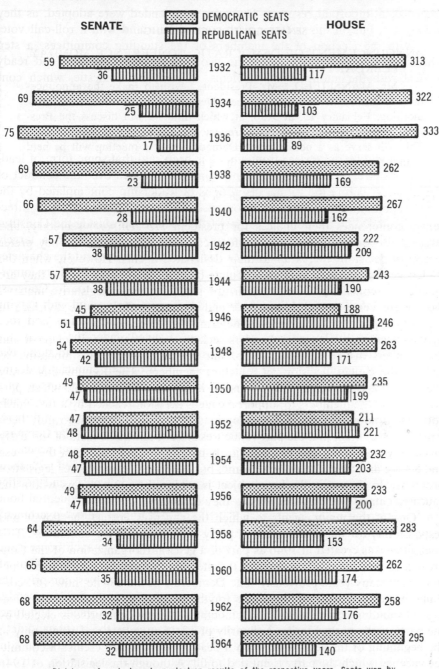

SENATE | DEMOCRATIC SEATS / REPUBLICAN SEATS | **HOUSE**

Year	Senate Dem	Senate Rep	House Dem	House Rep
1932	59	36	313	117
1934	69	25	322	103
1936	75	17	333	89
1938	69	23	262	169
1940	66	28	267	162
1942	57	38	222	209
1944	57	38	243	190
1946	45	51	188	246
1948	54	42	263	171
1950	49	47	235	199
1952	47	48	211	221
1954	48	47	232	203
1956	49	47	233	200
1958	64	34	283	153
1960	65	35	262	174
1962	68	32	258	176
1964	68	32	295	140

Divisions of seats based on electron results of the respective years. Seats won by minor parties account for the fact that figures do not always total the full membership of the Senate and the House.

SENATE CONFERENCE MEETING

ANNOUNCEMENT OF DEMOCRATIC CONFERENCE MONDAY,
FEBRUARY 15, 1960

Mr. MANSFIELD. Mr. President, I wish to make the announcement to the Senate that there will be a Democratic conference on Monday
morning, February 15, at 9:30, at which time we will discuss the President's budget, the joint economic report, and the matter of interest rates.
This will serve as a notice to the Democrats that a meeting will be held
at that time on that date to cover these particular subjects.

SOURCE: *Congressional Record, Senate* Feb. 9, 1960, 2327.

Senate conferences their choices for president *pro tempore,* secretary, and
sergeant. Beyond this, the party conferences meet infrequently.[45] They prefer
to entrust decisions thereafter to their designated agents. However, when the
leaders get out of touch with an articulate block of members or when they are
unable to reconcile differences within the group on major legislative matters,
the conferences may and do assemble and try to smooth over the divisions in
the party apparatus. The practice of determining a party position on legislation
by the caucus is a last resort. Leaders seek to avoid it at almost any cost and
the members dislike it intensely. For one reason, it is next to impossible to
enforce the caucus decision on reluctant members. The Republicans rarely
even try. The Democrats, in the House at least, have a caucus rule which purports to bind the members to support a caucus decision reached by a two-thirds
vote. The rule admits of certain exceptions, and enforcement has rarely been
strict. We see, then, that the party caucuses select both the leaders of the party
machinery and, in the case of the majority party, the chief officers of the House
and Senate and they also exercise some, but not much, control over legislative
programs. In the main, the latter object is achieved by the leaders whom the
caucuses entrust with such powers as they command.

Agents
of the
caucus:
One of the major agents to which the caucuses entrust the power and
responsibility for the achievement of party goals is the policy committee. This
committee was created in 1946 as part of a general reorganization of the Congress and was intended to replace the steering committee which had functioned for many years previously. The Democrats in the Senate, however, continue to use their steering committee for the purpose of assigning their members to standing committees. The Democratic steering committee is elected by
the party conference, consists ordinarily of 12-15 members and meets only at
the beginning of the session or when a death or resignation creates a committee vacancy which the party is entitled to fill. Although the legislation of 1946

[45] Criticism by several Senators in 1959 of the absence of meetings of the Democratic conference in the Senate has led to an increase in the number of such meetings
in the last few sessions.

creating the Senate policy committees fixed the membership at seven, neither party has hewed to the letter of the law. The Republican Policy Committee now includes 14 Senators and the Democratic Policy Committee nine. The members are selected in each case by the party conferences. Each party makes an effort to represent the major regions of the nation and the major factions in the party, although not necessarily in proportion to voting strength in the Senate or to population or party vote in the region. Typically, these committees have been composed of the most respected and experienced legislators in the two parties. These two committees meet frequently and, in the case of the majority committee, select bills to be given floor consideration, decide the time when they might be taken up, and in general, formulate positions on some measures which they hope and believe their party colleagues will support. Neither committee has ever really determined policy or formulated a legislative program for the party.[46] Their major importance has been in the staff assistance they make available to the leadership.

1. The steering and policy committees

The House of Representatives has never formally created any policy committees. In 1949, the Republicans converted their steering committee, but this was unofficial and no staff and no funds were at first provided. This committee is composed of 10 members selected by the committee on committees, four ex officio members (the floor leader, whip, conference chairman, and chairman of the Congressional campaign committee), and the Republican members of the rules committee and is now aided by a small staff. The Democratic Steering Committee, created in 1933 and allowed to atrophy from 1940 through 1960 was re-established in 1962 to give "liberals" a larger voice in leadership decisions. It is composed of 18 members representing a similar number of geographical regions and six ex officio members. Each of the 18 area Representatives is selected by the Democratic Representatives from that area. The Republicans have used their policy committee with some frequency in the last few years, not really to lay down a policy for the party but rather to prepare position papers and staff studies which the members may use if they wish to do so. The Democrat leadership has not relied on the steering committee to any degree.

The party conferences in each House designate floor leaders to direct the legislative programs of the two parties. In the House of Representatives, the majority leader plans the business of the House, offers necessary motions and resolutions to keep his party's bills moving through the legislative process, announces the intentions of his group toward future legislative business, speaks frequently in debate on behalf of his party and often on behalf of the national administration. He is, after the speaker, the second in command of his party's legislative campaign. His favorable opinion is almost indispensable to the passage of important legislation. His power and influence over the operations of the lower chamber is exceeded only by that of the speaker, and he may expect

2. The floor leaders

[46] See H. A. Bone, "An Introduction to the Senate Policy Committee," *Amer. Pol. Sci. Rev.*, L, No. 3 (June, 1956).

to succeed to the speakership upon the death or resignation of the incumbent whenever his party possesses a majority of the House.

THE SENATE FLOOR LEADER AT WORK

LEGISLATIVE PROGRAM

Mr. DIRKSEN. Mr. President, I wish to ask the distinguished majority leader whether he can acquaint us with the program for the remainder of the evening and for tomorrow, and what he contemplates will occur next week.

Mr. MANSFIELD. Mr. President, it is the hope that we can finish consideration of the Federal aid highway bill tonight. It is my understanding that the Senator from Indiana does not anticipate a yea-and-nay vote on his amendment. It is my further understanding that the manager of the bill likewise does not anticipate a yea-and-nay vote.

If we can complete our work within a reasonable time—say by 8 o'clock—we shall consider adjourning until 12 o'clock tomorrow. Then there will be no controversy of any kind. Several Senators wish to make speeches upon very important subjects. We might consider the measures on the calendar to which there is no objection.

In other words, there will be a short session, with no votes, and then the Senate will adjourn from Friday until Tuesday, at which time we shall consider the proposed reorganization plan, as already agreed to; the Department of Agriculture appropriation bill; and other measures which might be ready for action at that time.

SOURCE: *Congressional Record, Senate,* June 15, 1961, p. 9826.

The majority floor leader of the Senate occupies a position similar in most respects to his counterpart in the House. His functions and responsibilities are identical but, he exercises stronger control over the daily agenda of the Senate than does the House leader in the other body. Further, he has neither a powerful presiding officer nor a powerful rules committee with which he must share some of his power. He does, however, use the policy committee, of which he is a member, a little more often than his counterparts in the House and of course his colleagues are less easily regimented. The Republican Party in the Senate assigns different Senators to preside over the party conference, to be floor leader, and to head the policy committee. The Democrats expect their floor leader to serve in the other posts also.[47]

The minority leaders of the two houses have nothing like the responsi-

[47] For an excellent account of the work of the majority leader of the Senate and his role in the legislative process, see R. K. Huitt, "Democratic Party Leadership in the Senate," *Amer. Pol. Sci. Rev.* LV, No. 2 (June, 1961).

THE FLOOR LEADER OF THE HOUSE AT WORK

LEGISLATIVE PROGRAM FOR THE BALANCE OF THE WEEK AND FOR NEXT WEEK

Mr. GERALD R. FORD. Mr. Speaker, I have asked for this time for the purpose of asking the distinguished majority leader the program for the remainder of the week and the schedule for next week.

Mr. ALBERT. Mr. Speaker, will the distinguished gentleman yield?

Mr. GERALD R. FORD. I do.

Mr. ALBERT. Mr. Speaker, in response to the inquiry of the minority leader, we have completed the legislative program for this week and will ask to go over until Monday, subsequent to the announcement of the program for next week, which is as follows:

Monday is Consent Calendar day.

There are two suspensions:

H.R. 8989, Federal Metal and Non-metallic Mine Safety Act.

H.R. 6790, emergency highway relief.

Also on Monday, H.R. 9075, Uniformed Services Pay Act of 1965, under an open rule with 3 hours of general debate.

Also on Monday there will be eulogies for our late friend and colleague T. Ashton Thompson following the legislative program.

Tuesday and the balance of the week:

Tuesday will be the call of the Private Calendar.

H.R. 8283, Economic Opportunity Amendments of 1965, under an open rule with 5 hours of general debate.

H.R. 8856, amendment to section 271 of the Atomic Energy Act of 1954, which will be considered under an open rule with 2 hours of debate.

Mr. Speaker, I make the usual reservation that conference reports may be brought up at any time and that any further program may be announced later.

SOURCE: *Congressional Record, House of Representatives* (July 15, 1965), 16423.

bility of the majority leaders. Their party cannot expect to have a legislative program in any positive sense. As leaders of the opposition, they direct the floor strategy of their followers, attacking, criticizing, delaying the majority's program, or at least those parts of it which they are unwilling to support. In frequent conferences with the majority leaders, they seek to gain appropriate representation in parliamentary institutions and adequate time for the minority to present its views in debate. They also strive, usually successfully, to obtain from the majority leaders commitments as to the ensuing course of legislative business so they can advise their members and plan their tactics. When the party majority shifts in either or both houses, of course, the minority leaders may expect to succeed to the speakership in the House and to the majority floor leadership or presidency *pro tempore* in the Senate.

3. The whips

The floor leaders for each party in each house have been aided, since about 1900, by assistant floor leaders usually called whips. These individuals are selected by the party conferences, typically on the recommendation of the floor leaders. These whips act for the floor leaders when the latter are obliged to be absent from the chambers. The major duty of the whip is to canvass the views of the members of his party on issues before the Congress and to advise the floor leader how many votes he can count on, on any given item of legislative business. Another duty of the whip is to see that the voting strength of his party is fully brought to bear on every significant legislative decision. In the House, the whip ordinarily appoints several assistants to aid him in canvassing opinion and in mustering the members to important roll calls. The secretaries to the policy committees in the Senate perform many of the functions of assistant whips.[48]

4. The committee on committees

One final and very important agent of the caucus is the committee on committees. This group performs the difficult and delicate task of selecting the party membership for each of the standing committees. The House Republican Committee on Committees consists of one Representative from each state having Republican representation. Each state Republican delegation selects its own member. Each member of the committee has as many votes as there are Republican Representatives from his state. The House Democratic Committee on Committees is the Democratic delegation on the Ways and Means Committee and this is designated by the caucus. The Senate Republican Committee on Committees ordinarily consists of from six to nine Senators appointed by the chairman of the Republican conference. The Senate Democratic Steering Committee serves as its committee on committees with the floor leader presiding over its meetings.

THE SPEAKER OF THE HOUSE OF REPRESENTATIVES

From presiding officer to director

Of the formal institutions of leadership provided by the Constitution and by the rules of the two houses, by far the most important is the speaker of the House of Representatives. This office had had a long history in the English House of Commons before it was transported to the colonial legislatures and from there to the legislatures of the states and of the nation.[49] The powers adhering to the post were never very precisely defined, and almost two centuries of experience have made of the speakership a very different office from its con-

[48] See R. B. Ripley, "The Party Whip Organizations in the United States House of Representatives," *Amer. Pol. Sci. Rev.* LVIII, No. 3 (Sept. 1964) and Congressional Quarterly Service *Weekly Report* (June 17, 1961), 992-996.

[49] See P. Laundy, *The Office of Speaker* (London, 1964) for an authoritative account of the development of the office in England, in the Commonwealth, and in the United States.

temporary counterpart in the British Parliament. The speaker is the most powerful single individual in the House of Representatives in determining the legislative product of that body; whereas in England the speaker is simply an impartial presiding officer and has little or no influence on legislation. The power and influence of the speakership in the American system is the product of the rapid expansion of the size of the House, the continuous increase in the complexity of its business and the growth in influence and importance of the informal party government. All of these created a demand for leadership and direction. The speaker, with his party majority behind him and from his strategic post of presiding officer, gradually gathered to himself the powers of direction, some have said of dictation. The ascendancy of the speaker was further aided by the occupancy of that office by several daring, imperious, confident, and able individuals at critical periods in the history of the House: Henry Clay, 1811-14, 1815-20, and 1823-25; Thomas B. Reed, 1889-91 and 1895-99; Joseph Cannon, 1903-10 and Sam Rayburn 1940-47, 1949-53, 1955-61. By Cannon's day, the speaker had become the autocrat of the House, without whose assent virtually nothing of consequence could be done. The major instruments of speaker dominance had been achieved gradually, but by 1910 had collectively constituted a formidable array. In the first place, the speaker appointed the members of all standing committees as well as of all special or select committees of the House. The fate of legislation in the lower house was, and still is, so completely determined by the standing committees that the power to determine the membership of these committees is probably the most important authority in the Congress. Originally the committees had been staffed by vote of the whole house, but the power had slipped gradually into the sole hands of the presiding officer. Secondly, the speaker was chairman of the most powerful of the standing committees, the rules committee. This small committee, consisting at the time of only five men, completely dominated the progress of legislative business on the floor of the House. In the next place, the speaker successfully asserted and exercised the power to refuse to put motions offered by members which he considered dilatory or obstructive. Finally, the rules endowed the speaker with complete control over floor participation of individual members through his right to "recognize" members and their inability to address the House unless recognized.

The dominion of Speaker Cannon was so complete and his own policies so at variance with that of many of the members even of his own party that a long-simmering revolt against "the system" boiled over in 1910, and a coalition of insurgent Republicans with the Democratic minority succeeded in capturing control of the House long enough to deal the speakership a heavy blow. The speaker was removed from membership on the rules committee.[50] In 1911, the power to appoint standing committees was vested in the whole House by the same coalition. These actions deprived the office of two of its

The attack on the speakership in 1910-191

[50] C. R. Atkinson, *The Committee on Rules and the Overthrow of Speaker Cannon* (New York, 1911).

most important weapons, and the speaker has never been quite so powerful since.

Although weakened by the changes of 1910-11, the speaker is still the most important and most powerful member of the House. He presides over all sittings of the House, appoints those who take his place when he must be absent, preserves order and decorum, "recognizes" members desiring to speak, signs all acts, resolutions, writs, warrants or subpoenas ordered by the House, interprets and applies the rules, decides points of order (questions of parliamentary procedure raised by members), puts questions to a vote, determines the outcome of most unrecorded voting, appoints all special, select, and conference committees, and assigns bills to the various standing committees.[51] As a member of the House, he may speak in debate and vote on all questions before the House. He is not, however, required to vote except in case of a tie or when the House is voting by ballot.

Among this imposing array of powers and responsibilities the power of recognition may be used to illustrate the role of the speaker in directing the lower house. Under the rules of the House, any member desiring to speak for any purpose must address the chair and be recognized by it. The speaker has the sole authority to accord the necessary recognition.[52] Under Cannon, for a member to be recognized he had first to obtain an interview with the speaker and gain his approval in advance. It still is the practice to notify the speaker before proposing requests which deviate from the normal course of business.[53] By his refusal to recognize a member seeking the floor, the speaker can influence the course of business. If he knows that a member is seeking the floor to offer motions which might delay or sidetrack business which the speaker wants pushed forward, he refuses to "see" him when he rises. It should not be inferred that the speaker will ignore the minority. Ordinarily, he allots to their adherents a fair share of the debating time, but he is under no obligation to allow them to interfere with the majority program. The speaker is also able to inquire the purpose for which members seek the floor and thus cannot easily be caught off guard by an unanticipated parliamentary maneuver. Debate on legislative measures is customarily controlled by the chairman and senior minority member of the standing committee to which a bill was referred and these men apportion the time for each side. The speaker customarily accepts these arrangements and by rule the two leaders must be allowed the floor. In summary, through the power of recognition the speaker can influence the course of legislative business but is not free to dominate debate.

The speaker is now accorded by the rules the powers asserted earlier by

[51] These powers will be found in House Rule I, Secs. 1-7. The Speaker's powers were enlarged somewhat by the rules changes adopted in 1965 and referred to previously.

[52] The Senate rules, by contrast, give no such latitude to the presiding officer of that body. They require that he recognize the Senator who first addresses him. The House rules say "the speaker shall name the member who is first to speak."

[53] F. M. Riddick, *The United States Congress: Organization and Procedure* (Washington, 1949), 69.

Speaker Reed to refuse to put dilatory motions and to count as present all members who, in fact, are present whether they answer to their names or not.[54] Both of these grew out of minority tactics to delay and obstruct majority legislative action.

The major characteristic of the speakership which distinguishes it from that office in the House of Commons is its partisanship.[55] The House of Representatives has come to expect that the speaker will use his enormous power and influence to aid his party. Although the speaker is expected to preside in a judicial manner and to be as fair as the rules permit to the minority, he is an important leader of the majority party and is expected to use his influence in behalf of its legislative program. We have already observed that the speaker, although formally elected by the whole House, is actually the leader of the majority party and is designated for his high office by the members of the party in caucus. In his office, the formal leadership and the informal party leadership are combined. It is because he has his party behind him that he is able to exercise the influence over the proceedings that he does.

Partisanship

Neither the Constitution nor the rules establish any qualifications for the office of speaker. He does not even have to be a member of the House. Every speaker, however, has been a Representative. Furthermore, every speaker, at least for the past half century, has been a member of long service. The average service of the members who have become speakers since 1896 has been more than 22 years.[56] Seniority is not rigidly adhered to in the selection, and the speaker has not always or even typically been the member of longest service. He has, however, been one of the most experienced members of the House and, from this fact alone, has stemmed a considerable part of his influence. Like the chairmen of the standing committees, the speaker is likely to come from a "safe" district and, therefore, to emerge from a political environment quite different from that which produces the President.

Qualifications of the speaker

THE PRESIDING OFFICERS OF THE SENATE

There is no counterpart in the Senate to the speaker of the House of Representatives. The regular presiding officer of the Senate is the Vice-President of the United States. He is not a leader emerging from the operations of the Senate and, therefore, has not typically enjoyed either the power or the influence of the speaker. He has all of the normal powers of presiding officers, but he is not designated by the majority caucus. He is not a member able to take the floor and argue for his party's program. He does not ordinarily bring to the post many years of continuous service in that body. The rules of the Senate are not designed to enhance the powers of its leaders. A Vice-President is in-

The Vice-President

54 House Rule XVI, Sec. 10, and House Rule XV, Sec. 3.

55 On the English speakership see M. McDonough, *The Speaker of the House* (London, 1914).

56 F. M. Riddick, *op. cit.,* 61.

fluential in the deliberations of the Senate, and some have been, only if he personally can by his experience and ability command such influence.

The president pro tempore

The president *pro tempore,* with whom the Vice-President shares his presiding functions and who is selected by the Senate itself, comes a little closer to the speaker. Even he, however, is ordinarily overshadowed by the majority floor leader and typically exercises nothing like the speaker's influence. Only since 1890 has the post been a continuing one, and only in part of the period since then has it been an influential one. The reasons for the relative weakness of this post lie in the smaller numerical size of the chamber and the added stature that this gives to each Senator. Senators are apt to be exceedingly jealous of their prerogatives. They are not easily led and on many occasions will not be led at all, even by someone of their own choosing. The president *pro tempore* is but one of several leaders of the majority party in the Senate. His is nevertheless an office of considerable power, prestige, and perquisites and it is vigorously sought after. Like the speakership, it is a partisan office and is used to forward the program of the majority party.

THE COMMITTEE SYSTEM OF THE HOUSE AND SENATE

Development of the committee system

Legislative bodies the world over achieve more careful review of proposed legislation and save the time of the members by referring most matters brought before them to committees for study and report. Nowhere, however, do these committees play such a dominant part in shaping the legislative product as in the American Congress, and especially in the House of Representatives. The development of an elaborate system of standing committees to which are referred almost every piece of legislative business took several decades. The House started by attempting to deal with most legislation in a committee of the whole House. It was hoped that the informal rules and adaptable procedures of such a committee would save sufficient time to allow all members to participate effectively in all kinds of legislative business. The business of the House and its membership quickly outgrew this device, although it is still used effectively on certain kinds of measures but not until most of the preliminary work has been done by a standing committee. Special or select committees which came into existence for a particular task and disappeared once it was performed were then tried and used extensively for a number of years. Gradually the practice grew of referring matters to regular standing committees, and these were multiplied until virtually every possible piece of legislative business fell under the jurisdiction of one of them. By the latter part of the last century it had also become customary to assign each member of the House and Senate to one or more of the standing committees at the beginning of each new Congress.

Types of committees

In addition to the standing committees, we have noted that the House still makes use of committees of the whole. It also continues, as does the Senate, to make some use of special and select committees. At present each house, for example, has a select committee on small business. At one time investigations were undertaken very largely by special committees, but since the reorganization of 1946 which sought to make special committees unnecessary this has not been true. The Congress has occasionally created special or select committees which include representatives of both houses. These are called joint committees and may be established by resolution or by statute. Typically, they are entrusted with a mission which it is felt cannot or will not be carried out effectively by the standing committees. Sometimes they are charged with investigations, occasionally with supervising some aspect of Congressional business, such as printing or the Library of Congress. Some statutes, which have sought closer co-ordination between the legislative branch and the executive branch in a particular field of national affairs, have provided for a joint committee for this purpose, for example, the Joint Committee on Atomic Energy and the Joint Committee on the Economic Report (of the President). Another type of Congressional committee is the conference committee, about which more will be said in the next chapter. All of these special, select, joint, or conference committees are appointed by the presiding officers of the two houses. While they may, and do on occasion, achieve great prominence, their influence ordinarily is minor compared with that of the standing committees.

The pressure of increasing legislative business and of members for greater recognition and perquisites tends to multiply the number of standing committees, and this multiplication tends to produce overlapping and duplication of committee jurisdictions. Periodically, the Congress has had to reduce the number and clarify the missions of its standing committees. In 1927, for example, it reduced the number in the House from 61 to 47. The most substantial effort in this direction was made by the Congressional Reorganization Act of 1946. This act is the basis of the committee system of the present Congress. In the House, the number of committees was reduced from 48 to 19, and in the Senate from 33 to 15. The jurisdiction of each of the committees was carefully delineated in order to eliminate as much overlapping as possible, to divide the legislative business somewhat more equitably, and to assign to each committee a reasonably coherent and logical area of national affairs. The membership of each committee was also modified to make the committees of more nearly uniform size. One new committee on space exploration has been created in each house since that time. *Standing committees:*

1. Number and size

In the unreorganized Congress, most members of the two houses served on several committees. In the House, however, only a few members had more than one major assignment. On occasion, therefore, a few members in each house might have influential positions on two or three committees and thus possess unusual personal power. The reduction in committees was accompanied by an attempt, largely successful, to limit each member in the House *2. Assignments per member*

STANDING COMMITTEES, 89th CONGRESS, 1965

House of Representatives		*Senate*	
Agriculture	35	Aeronautical and Space Sciences	16
Appropriations	50	Agriculture and Forestry	15
Armed Services	37	Appropriations	27
Banking and Currency	33	Armed Services	17
District of Columbia	25	Banking and Currency	14
Education and Labor	31	District of Columbia	7
Foreign Affairs	36	Finance	17
Government Operations	34	Foreign Relations	19
House Administration	25	Government Operations	14
Interior and Insular Affairs	33	Interior and Insular Affairs	16
Interstate and Foreign Commerce	33	Interstate and Foreign Commerce	18
Judiciary	35	Judiciary	16
Merchant Marine and Fisheries	31	Labor and Public Welfare	16
Post Office and Civil Service	25	Post Office and Civil Service	12
Public Works	34	Public Works	17
Rules	15	Rules and Administration	9
Science and Astronautics	31		
Un-American Activities	9		
Veterans Affairs	25		
Ways and Means	25		

to but one committee.[57] Senators are generally restricted, under the new scheme, to service on not more than two committees.[58] The result has been a more even distribution of the work load among members of the two houses.

3. Selection of committee members

Although members of Congress are formally elected to the standing committees by vote of the house to which they belong, actually this vote is but a ratification of the selections made in private conference by the Committee on Committees of each of the two parties in each house. The rivalry for committee posts is intense and the distribution of committee seats is one of the most difficult chores in the Congress. In the House of Representatives especially, the power, influence, and legislative success of each member is largely determined by his committee assignment. Almost his entire participation in the legislative process will stem from his committee work. Therefore, members are all keenly anxious to obtain posts on the more important committees and particularly on those which handle the problems of greatest concern to the district which they represent. Many years of experience in the troublesome field

[57] Representatives assigned to the Committee on the District of Columbia or to the Committee on Un-American Activities and members of the majority party assigned to the Committee on Government Operations or to the Committee on House Administration may in each case serve on one other standing committee.

[58] Majority party Senators serving on the District of Columbia or Government Operations Committees may serve on three committees as may other senators in a few cases.

of committee assignments have induced the two houses to evolve a very rigid but unwritten code to govern the process. Major weight is assigned to length of continuous service. Once assigned to a particular committee a legislator may confidently expect to advance up the ladder of precedence as long as he continues to be elected by the voters. The only major exception to this rule involves members who are willing to sacrifice seniority on minor committees to gain seats on major committees.[59] The job of the selecting agencies thus resolves itself into: (1) determining the number of posts to be filled on each committee; (2) assigning newly elected members to the committees; (3) taking care of as many of those who have already served on each committee as the total party membership on the committee permits; and (4) accommodating as many as feasible of those who are interested in or are obliged to shift from one committee to another.[60]

Party strength on committees

The number of seats to be assigned to each party on each committee is worked out by the majority party leaders, usually in consultation with the minority leaders. Traditionally, the posts on all but one or two key committees are assigned to each party in proportion to the relative strength of that party in the chamber concerned. Thus, if the Republicans have 55 percent of the representatives they will take 55 percent of the posts on most of the committees of the House and assign 45 percent to the Democrats. The majority party usually insists, however, that it have a disproportionate representation on the Committees on Rules, Ways and Means, and Appropriations. This is to enable it so to control these committees that a coalition of minority party and insurgents from the majority which might throttle the majority program would be hard to form. Independents and members of third parties fare poorly in committee assignments. If they are taken care of at all, it is usually by the majority party.[61]

4. Committee chairmen:

The most coveted post on each standing committee is the chairmanship. This post, although formally filled by vote of the House or Senate, goes automatically to the majority member of longest continuous service on that com-

---

[59] Senator (now President) Johnson (Texas) as Majority leader, introduced a new practice in assignments aimed at giving new Senators better posts. His position was that no Senator of his party could have a second top committee seat until every Senator had at least one. See G. Goodwin, Jr., "The Seniority System in Congress," *Amer. Pol. Sci. Rev.*, LIII, No. 2 (June, 1959).

[60] See N. A. Masters, "Committee Assignments in the House of Representatives," *Amer. Pol. Sci. Rev.*, LV, No. 2 (Mar., 1961).

[61] The resignation of Senator Morse of Oregon from the Republican Party during the campaign of 1952 led to much discussion in the Senate in 1953 as to who was responsible for his committee assignments. The minority said the majority should take care of him and the majority said he had resigned from their party. The upshot of the matter was that he lost his post and rank on the committees on which he had served and was given posts on two relatively unimportant committees. See *Congressional Record* of the 83rd Cong., 1st sess., 1953, 334-357. When he later entered the Democratic party he was rewarded with good assignments. See R. K. Huitt, "The Morse Committee Assignment Controversy: A Study in Senate Norms," *Amer. Pol. Sci. Rev.*, LI, No. 3 (June, 1957).

a. selection

mittee. Only a major failure by a member to support his party, in a Presidential campaign, for example, or in voting to organize the House of Representatives, is likely to induce the party selection committees to pass over him in designating the chairman.[62]

b. power

The power of the chairmen of the committees is so great that it has allowed them repeatedly to defy their own leaders with impunity and to stifle programs demanded by the White House and by the floor leaders. It is not easy to account for their influence, for it is compounded of many bits of power. The chairman, in the first place, can reward and punish the members of his committee. He appoints the subcommittees and these have become more numerous and more important over the years.[63] He designates those who will participate in the debate for the committee majority. The chairman can usually prevent a meeting of the committee if he doesn't want one and can invariably control the agenda when the committee does meet. He normally heads conference committees for his house and he controls the dispersal of committee funds. Much of his power stems from tradition rather than rule, but it is a tradition that most Congressmen support, presumably in anticipation of the day when they will be chairmen and entitled to the privileges of these offices. The chairmen have, of course, attained their relatively great power and influence largely since 1911, when appointment by the speaker was abolished and the method of election instituted under cover of which the seniority system became so firmly entrenched.

Criticisms of the seniority system

The developing power of the committee chairman and the method by which they are selected has given rise to an increasing volume of criticism of the system. There is no demonstrable correlation between seniority and competence, say the critics. There is a demonstrable correlation between seniority and a "safe" constituency. Those districts or states dominated by one party or by one strong interest are likely to return the same Congressmen again and again. Those districts where the party battle is intense and the interests divided are likely to change Congressmen frequently. Thus, their Representatives and Senators never achieve seniority. The close districts, say the critics, are the more decisive in national campaigns. The self-determined leaders of Congress may be, and frequently are, the critics allege, out of step with the main currents of public opinion in the nation. Young, able, and ambitious legislators are not given opportunity fully to utilize their talents and grow restive in the grip of seniority. In this way, legislative talent is wasted and

---

[62] The Southern statesmen who bolted the Democratic ticket in 1948 or supported unpledged electors in 1960 were not generally deprived of their committee posts in Congress. However, two Southern Representatives who supported Goldwater in the campaign of 1964 were stripped of their seniority by the Democratic caucus. One of them then resigned and ran successfully in a special election as a Republican and was assigned to committee by that party.

[63] See C. O. Jones, "The Role of the Congressional Subcommittee," *Midwest Journ. of Pol. Sci.*, VI, No. 4 (Nov. 1962) and G. Goodwin, Jr., "Subcommittees: the Miniature Legislatures of Congress," *Amer. Pol. Sci. Rev.* LVI, No. 3 (Sept., 1962).

discouraged. Of course, if the chairmen were not so powerful, the problem would not be so acute.

The answers to these criticisms put forth by defenders of the existing arrangements are: (1) they have served the nation well, that is, there is no real breakdown of the legislative process; (2) they guarantee that the Congress will be dominated by men of experience; (3) they provide an impersonal and objective standard for determining precedence and one that avoids personalities, bitterness, and manipulation, all of which would destroy the loyalty and cooperation which make legislation possible; and (4) no one, not even the Joint Committee on the Organization of Congress which labored so manfully at the problem of improving the Congress, has yet suggested a better plan that is acceptable to most Congressmen.[64]

Defense of the system

Each of the standing committees has a commodious office with a secretarial and clerical staff, more or less elaborate files, and occasionally a library. One of the more widely heralded reforms of the Reorganization Act of 1946 was the provision of a professional staff for each of the committees. It was anticipated that each committee might employ, on a nonpartisan basis, from two to four "experts" in one or more of the fields of public policy within the purview of the committee. These persons would be able, it was felt, to collect and interpret data for the committee and to analyze the problems presented for its consideration. While nonpartisanship has not been as conspicuous in the employment of experts as some had hoped, and the change in party domination of the committees has been accompanied by shifts in staff, nevertheless a great deal more continuity and expert assistance has been brought to the aid of committee deliberations than previously. The chairmen fairly well dominate the selection and assignment of the staff.

5. Committee staffs

One of the products of the reduction in the number of committees and the increase in size of several of them has been the use of large numbers of subcommittees for particular legislation. The major committees, such as Appropriations in the House, make extensive use of subcommittees to hold hearings and develop legislation. In fact, little is done through the committee as a whole. There are more than 110 continuing subcommittees in the House alone and much of the major legislation of the modern era has been put in shape by subcommittees. Subcommittees were used widely but somewhat less extensively before the reorganization of 1946. Most of the committees meet regularly at fixed times, most commonly in the morning before the two houses assemble. Special leave is required, although it is typically granted freely, for

6. Use of subcommittees and meetings

---

[64] For fuller statements of the pros and cons of the question, see R. Young, *This Is Congress* (New York, 1943), 108-114, and G. B. Galloway, *Congress at the Crossroads* (New York, 1946), Chap. VI; and a thoughtful defense of the seniority principle, J. K. Pollock, "The Seniority Rule in Congress," *No. Amer. Rev.*, CCXXII, 235-245 (Dec., 1925-Feb., 1926). See also the article by G. Goodwin, "The Seniority System in Congress," *op. cit.* and Congressional Quarterly Service, *Congressional Reform*, Washington, 1963). The plan is followed in the Senate as in the House, and with the same advantages and disadvantages.

any committee except that on rules, to sit while the House or the Senate is in session.

RULES COMMITTEE OF THE HOUSE

How the
Rules
Committee
controls
debate
in the
House

The impressive powers of direction of the speaker and the majority floor leader of the House of Representatives are shared with the Committee on Rules. Although this committee is concerned primarily with legislative procedure, it has become so influential in determining the way in which the time of the House will be spent that in this way it is able to influence what finally is passed. From 1789 until 1880, the Rules Committee was a select rather than a standing committee, and for most of this period its chief function was to report a system of rules for the approval of the House at the time of organization. Gradually, by rulings of speakers and orders of the House, the committee was invested with substantial powers. In 1841, for example, the speaker held that a resolution from the Committee on Rules which changed temporarily the established rules could be adopted by a simple majority vote. Thus with the consent of that committee the rules, in effect, could be suspended without the normal requirement of a two-thirds majority. In 1853, the committee was authorized to report at any time and this opened the door for it to intervene in the regular process almost at will. The committee became a regular standing committee in 1880 with jurisdiction over all actions touching on the rules. In 1893, it was authorized to sit while the House was in session. In the last quarter of the past century the practice of proposing special orders to govern the course of floor debate on a piece of legislation took its present form. This practice constitutes the most important of its present repertoire of privileges and responsibilities. Most of the important bills emanating from the other standing committees must now go to the Rules Committee for clearance if time is to be found for their consideration. The Rules Committee, if it approves, may clear the way for floor consideration by bringing in a special order. If adopted by the House, the order, in the form of a resolution, establishes the time for debate and allots a share of it to the majority and one to the minority. Without the aid of a special order, legislation of many types, even though approved by the standing committee which considered it, is likely to languish on the calendar and never be taken up at all. The competition for place on the calendars is so intense, there are so many more bills received than can be debated, that the power to provide for the immediate consideration of a bill regardless of its order on the docket is of great importance. Through this procedure, the committee can demand changes in a bill as a condition for bringing it to debate, can even insist on a whole new bill, and can effectively stop consideration of a bill of which it does not approve. It can also limit floor debate, prevent amendments except those offered by the committee in charge of the bill and can set aside points of order which might be raised. It also has considerable influence over whether and when a bill in dispute between the two houses goes to a conference committee.

The Rules Committee has grown so powerful in controlling the deliberations of the House that it has increasingly become the target of determined and vigorous critics, especially among the so-called "liberal" Democrats. Under the domination of extremely conservative Howard Smith of Virginia the committee for several years impeded most civil rights and aid-to-education legislation.[65] From 1949-1951, as a result of a combination of dissident elements from both parties the powers of the committee were slightly weakened by the adoption of a rule making it possible, though difficult, for a

Special Order of the Rules Committee

EXCISE TAX REDUCTION ACT OF 1965

Mr. DELANEY. Mr. Speaker, by direction of the Committee on Rules I call up House Resolution 404 and ask for its immediate consideration.

The Clerk read the resolution, as follows:

H. RES. 404

Resolved, That upon the adoption of this resolution it shall be in order to move that the House resolve itself into the Committee of the Whole House on the State of the Union for the consideration of the bill (H.R. 8371) to reduce excise taxes, and for other purposes, and all points of order against said bill are hereby waived. After general debate, which shall be confined to the bill and shall continue not to exceed four hours, to be equally divided and controlled by the chairman and ranking minority member of the Committee on Ways and Means, the bill shall be considered as having been read for amendment. No amendment shall be in order to said bill except amendments offered by direction of the Committee on Ways and Means. Amendments offered by direction of the Committee on Ways and Means may be offered to any section of the bill at the conclusion of the general debate, but said amendments shall not be subject to amendment. At the conclusion of the consideration of the bill for amendment, the Committee shall rise and report the bill to the House with such amendments as may have been adopted, and the previous question shall be considered as ordered on the bill and amendments thereto to final passage without intervening motion, except one motion to recommit.

SOURCE: *Congressional Record,* House of Representatives (June 2, 1965), 11869.

[65] Cf. H. D. Price, "Race, Religion and the Rules Committee: the Kennedy-Aid-to-Education Bill," A. F. Westin (ed). *The Uses of Power: 7 Cases in American Politics* (N. Y., 1962).

standing committee chairman to bring a bill to the floor despite Rules Committee opposition.[66] When the rule was repealed in 1951 new efforts to reinstate it were launched at the beginning of each new Congress thereafter until 1965 when a new version of the rule was adopted.[67] At this time, the power of the committee in relation to sending a bill to conference was also weakened. Another successful attack on Smith's committee was led by Speaker Rayburn in 1961 to enlarge its membership from 12 to 15 in order that some members more sympathetic to President Kennedy's program might be added.[68]

The Senate has no counterpart for the Rules Committee. The time of the Senate is very largely determined by the floor leaders on the basis of wide agreement among the members; debate is thus freer and more extensive. The Senate leadership is not able to exercise the dominion over procedure that the House leaders enjoy.

CONGRESSMEN AND THE INSTITUTIONS OF LEADERSHIP

It must be a great shock to a new member of the House of Representatives who comes to Washington, frequently from a position of influence in his small state legislature, to find how insignificant he is in the Congress. He ranks at the bottom of any committee, even a minor one, to which he may be assigned. He is rarely allowed to address the House. In fact, he usually can speak, and even then briefly, only when a bill from his committee is before the House and when he has been assigned a role in the debate by his chairman. On many of the major questions of the day he gains his knowledge, like any ordinary citizen, by reading the newspapers. Only after he has served a few terms is he recognized as a lawmaker by Washington society, administrative agencies, and the nation's press. And only after he has served several terms is he able to assume a position of influence.[69]

---

[66] The rule adopted in 1949 and repealed in 1951 provided that a bill reported to the rules committee as approved by the standing committee and for which no order or an adverse report was brought in by the rules group within 21 days, might be taken before the House by the chairman of the standing committee on the second or fourth Mondays of each month. The speaker was required to recognize the chairman on these days for this purpose. The House could then vote to receive the bill or not and to debate it or not as it pleased.

[67] The rule adopted in 1965 authorized the speaker to recognize a chairman desirous of presenting a bill approved by his committee but for which no special order had been granted by the Rules Committee although it had been before them for 21 days. The rule was used for the first time in 1965 to secure House action on the repeal of the right-to-work provision (14-b) of the Labor-Management Relations Act (Taft-Hartley) of 1947.

[68] See J. A. Robinson, *The House Rules Committee* (New York, 1963) for a study of the Committee's operations. It should be noted that there is another way to bring a bill out of a reluctant Rules Committee: a discharge petition signed by 218 members. This is virtually unworkable and will be discussed in the next chapter.

[69] See C. L. Clapp, *The Congressan: His Work as He Sees It* (New York, 1964), for an excellent discussion of the relations of Congressmen to the institutions.

About 30 or 40 men normally dominate the activities of the House of
Representatives, firmly directing the proceedings, controlling the debate, and
determining the extent and character of the participation of the other 400
members. This handful of leaders are invariably men of long experience in
the processes of the lower house. Ordinarily they command the support of
their majority party colleagues. Periodically, however, the leaders, partly
because they tend to represent "safe" districts, lose touch with the sentiment
of the nation and of many of their fellow representatives. Revolts against the
leaders and the institutions of leadership have occurred and these have provoked sharp criticisms of the House "machine" as repressive, arbitrary, and
essentially undemocratic.[70] No system of leadership comparable to the ministry in parliamentary democracies is provided by the American Constitution.
The President, although frequently giving important direction to the Congress
especially on large matters of grave import, is outside the legislature and not
in a position to provide intimate direction of its processes. Self-developed institutions of leadership have arisen in response to imperative needs, but according to no preconceived plan and largely as the exigencies of party politics
have determined. Over the years, as the size of the House has grown and the
complexities of legislative problems increased, the power of the leadership has
become more and more firmly seated. To the President, however, and to the
party leaders as well, their inability to deliver the full party vote on many
issues, the rivalry among the leaders, and the independent satrapies of the
committee chairmen all seem to spell weakness rather than domination of
the membership.

At no time has the present interlocking system of party and formal
leadership which confers so much power upon such a small group of men
lacked defenders. Leadership in a body the size of the House is essential if
anything except talk is to be achieved. All of the institutions of control are
firmly anchored to a majority vote of the members. A dissatisfied bloc which
is able to persuade 218 Representatives can overturn the leadership at almost
any time. Special orders of the rules committee can always be rejected by a
majority vote. The rulings of the speaker can be rejected in the same way.
No one requires the parties to have caucuses or floor leaders or steering committees. The system as it stands must, therefore, reflect the will of the membership and, by inference, of the electorate.

The argument is not quite as plausible as it appears. The decisive majority is frequently not a majority at all but a majority of the majority party.
The power of reward and punishment traditionally vested in the leaders is so
great and the legislative success of a Representative so dependent upon his
gaining their favor that he is not as free to vote his convictions on questions
of procedure and leadership as the defenders imply. A Representative, it may

[70] A recent example is Rep. Richard Bolling, *House Out of Order* (New York,
1965) and on the Senate side, Senator Joseph S. Clark, *The Senate Establishment* (New
York, 1964).

be argued, has a duty to his constituents to achieve legislative recognition of their needs and aspirations. To do this he must gain a favorable committee assignment and opportunity to bring his proposals before the House for debate and disposition. If he rebels against the institutions of leadership or against the leaders, he is unlikely to be effective in either case. The most serious flaw, however, in the defense of the House apparatus is the seniority rule by which so many of the seats of the mighty are filled. Seniority is a guarantee of experience but not of either competence or representativeness of the nation as a whole. The evidence is the other way on the latter issue. Many of those who achieve power from long service come from districts that are not decisive in national elections. The central problem is perhaps the great and continuing difficulty in reconciling the constituency interest and local orientation of the member arising from the method of recruitment and selection and the programatic goals of the national party leaders—President, Cabinet, and Congressional leaders.

The situation in the Senate   At the other end of the Capitol, in the Senate, the situation is quite different. The institutions of leadership, although impressive, sit more lightly on the backs of the Senators. The business proceeds at a more leisurely pace, debate is more spontaneous and also more discursive, and program and procedural decisions are based on consensus among a fairly large portion of the members. The traditions and the rules of the Senate are sensitive to the position and perquisites of the individual Senator and of the minority. Whereas the House, typically, disposes of a major piece of legislative business in about five or six hours of floor discussion, the Senate will require several days. Every Senator that wants to usually can make his contribution to the debate. If the House is widely criticized because of its cursory dispostion of significant bills, the Senate is condemned for the opposite. A determined minority can bring the legislative process almost to a complete halt in the upper house. The final product of Senatorial deliberations is much more likely than that of the House to bear the stamp of a large number of members representing many different points of view. A Senator is simply not easily dominated.

The difference explained   The sharp differences between the two houses in respect to the matters under discussion may be explained by (1) the smaller size of the Senate; (2) the longer terms of the Senators; and, (3) the fact that the Senators are likely to be important party leaders in their home states.

References

G. B. Galloway, *Congress at the Crossroads* (New York, 1946), Chap. IV.

———, *The Legislative Process in Congress* (New York, 1953). Chaps. XII, XIII, XIV, XVII, XXIII.

J. P. Chamberlain, *Legislative Processes; National and State* (New York, 1936), Chap. V.

F. M. Riddick, *The United States Congress: Organization and Procedure* (Washington, 1949).

D. S. Alexander, *History and Procedure of the House of Representatives* (Boston, 1916), Chaps. II-VII, X, XII.

E. Kefauver and J. Levin, *A Twentieth-Century Congress* (New York, 1947), 114-142.

B. D. Gross, *The Legislative Struggle* (New York, 1953).

Committee on Political Parties, American Political Science Association, *Toward a More Responsible Two-Party System* (New York, 1950), Pt. 11 § 8.

M. P. Follett, *The Speaker of the House of Representatives* (New York, 1904).

C. W. Chiu, *The Speaker of the House of Representatives Since 1896* (New York, 1928).

G. H. Haynes, *The Senate of the United States: Its History and Practice* (Boston, 1938), I, Chaps. V-VII.

R. Luce, *Congress—An Explanation* (Cambridge, Mass., 1926), Chap. IV.

————, *Legislative Assemblies* (Boston, 1924).

D. B. Truman, *The Congressional Party* (New York, 1959).

R. Young, *The American Congress* (New York, 1958).

W. S. White, *Citadel: The Story of the U. S. Senate* (New York, 1957).

————, *Home Place: The Story of the U. S. House of Representatives* (New York, 1965).

N. MacNeil, *Forge of Democracy—the House of Representatives* (New York, 1963).

E. C. Griffith, *The Rise and Development of the Gerrymander* (Chicago, 1907).

————, *Congress: Its Contemporary Role* (New York, 1951).

C. A. Berdahl, "Some Notes on Party Membership in Congress," *Amer. Polit. Sci. Rev.*, XLIII, 309-321, 492-508, 721-734 (Apr., June, and Aug., 1949).

A. C. Hinds, "The Speaker of the House of Representatives," *ibid.*, 111, 155-167 (May, 1909).

C. R. Atkinson and C. A. Beard, "The Syndication of the Speakership," *Polit. Sci. Quar.*, XXVI, 381-414 (Sept., 1911).

L. C. Busbey, *Uncle Joe Cannon* (New York, 1927). An autobiography recorded by a private secretary.

W. A. Robinson, *Thomas B. Reed, Parliamentarian* (New York, 1930).

L. G. McConachie, *Congressional Committees* (New York, 1898).

B. L. French, "Sub-Committees of Congress," *Amer. Polit. Sci. Rev.*, IX, 68-92 (Feb., 1915).

E. E. Denison, *The Senate Foreign Relations Committee* (Stanford Univ., 1942).

A. C. F. Westphal, *The House Committee on Foreign Affairs* (New York, 1942), *Official Congressional Directory* (Washington), published annually.

C. L. Clapp, *The Congressman: His Work as He Sees It* (Washington, 1963).

D. R. Matthews, *U. S. Senators and Their World* (Chapel Hill, N.C., 1960).

L. A. Froman, Jr., *Congressmen and their Constituencies* (Chicago, 1963).

R. L. Peabody and N. W. Polsby (ed.). *New Prospectives on the House of Representatives* (Chicago, 1963).

"Congressional Reform," June 7, 1963.

Congressional Quarterly Weekly Report (Washington).

Congressional Quarterly Special Reports (Washington).

"Congressional Redistricting," Sept. 28, 1962.

★ 11 ★

The Legislative Process

CONGRESS AT WORK is typically engaged in making law. Although it performs some other important functions, the enactment of legislation is its primary task.

The grist of the legislative process may take at least five different forms: (1) *bills,* which are instruments of general legislation effective when properly passed (passed in the same form by both houses and signed by the President) upon all those individuals to whom applicable and of which there are two major kinds: (*a*) *private* bills for the benefit of a particular person, place, or institution; (*b*) *public* bills dealing with individuals or situations by classes or groups; (2) *joint resolutions,* which resemble bills in almost every respect except that they are commonly used only for the guidance of those charged with administering the laws and contain unusual or subordinate legislation; [1] (3) *concurrent resolutions,* which are not submitted to the President and are not laws, therefore, in the sense that they have no application outside of Congress and which are used to express attitudes, opinion, or intentions that the two houses share; [2] (4) *simple resolutions,* which deal with the affairs of one house only and have no effect beyond the halls of that chamber and which typically express some purpose, policy, or attitude of that house; and, (5) *orders,* which embody the commands or requests of one house typically on procedural matters and which, like simple and concurrent resolutions, are not submitted to the President.

Forms of legislative action

A *bill* is introduced into either house for consideration and when passed by either house becomes an *act.* If both houses enact it and the President signs it, it then becomes a *law* or a *statute.* Some of the bills which the Congress considers are designed to make or declare new law; others, to amend, supplement, clarify, revise, codify, consolidate, or repeal existing provisions of law; and still others not at all to make or modify the law which governs us

Types of laws

---

[1] Joint resolutions are also used for proposing amendments to the Constitution and in this case are not submitted to the President for his approval or rejection.

[2] In recent years Congress has attempted to provide for the repeal of certain laws by concurrent resolution in order to evade Presidential veto of the repealer. It has also used this type of legislative action to give its required consent to certain types of executive orders, e.g., those involved in the Administrative Reorganization Acts of 1939 and 1949. Whether this is a proper use of this device or an invasion of Presidential prerogatives remains to be determined by the courts. See Howard White, "The Concurrent Resolution in Congress," *Amer. Polit. Sci. Rev.,* XXV, 886-889 (Oct., 1941).

but to appropriate money, assign duties, or give directions to executive, judicial, or legislative agencies.

Except that there are important differences in the way private bills are handled, essentially the same procedures are used to deal with all of the different forms and types of legislative action. Therefore, an adequate grasp of the legislative activity of a Congress may be obtained by tracing the main steps which a bill takes on its path to the law books.

Before we begin the discussion of legislative procedure it is desirable to recall that the power of the Congress to make laws is not unlimited. Unlike the legislatures of many other democratic states, our national assembly is restricted to the subjects especially entrusted to it by the Constitution. Every measure which it can validly enact must be based upon some authorization, express or implied, in the Constitution. Furthermore, the fact that Congress has been invested with authority to legislate on a given subject does not of itself exclude the states from acting on the same subject. Some powers are expressly denied to the states and others by their natures or by court interpretation tend to preclude state action but between these two extremes is a vast field of authority which is or may be occupied both by the nation and the states. Most of the authority conferred upon Congress may be exercised or not at the discretion of that body. The Constitution intends, however, that some actions are mandatory although how failure to act might be remedied by court action is not altogether clear.

Many programs in the recent past aimed at combating depression or the external enemies of the nation, have been popularly described as stemming from the "emergency powers" of Congress. Legally there are no such powers. The Constitution makes no distinction between "normal" and "emergency" situations in its grant of power to Congress. The Supreme Court has said that "emergency does not create power." [3] Nevertheless, the periods of profound national crisis of our history have repeatedly called forth the exercise of powers not normally exercised, or the exercise of long-used powers in novel ways. Emergencies thus stimulate new Congressional activities and conceptions, but legally these, to be valid, must all be traced to the constitutional powers of the Congress.

Although the Constitution vests legislative power in the Congress, it also vests legislative power of a sort, for example, the veto, in the President. Despite the language of Article I, therefore, legislative power is not exclusively entrusted to but one branch of the government. The question of whether any legislative power not specifically mentioned can constitutionally be entrusted to the executive branch has cropped up repeatedly in our history. Can the Congress delegate its authority to some agency of the executive branch? It has seemed wise on many occasions for the Congress to vest legislative duties in independent regulatory commissions (e.g., in the Interstate Commerce Commission to fix railroad rates), in executive departments (e.g., in the Secretary

[3] Home Building and Loan Association *v.* Blaisdell, 290 U. S. 398 (1934).

Union Calendar No. 16

84TH CONGRESS
1ST SESSION

H. R. 1

[Report No. 50]

IN THE HOUSE OF REPRESENTATIVES

JANUARY 5, 1955

Mr. COOPER introduced the following bill; which was referred to the Committee on Ways and Means

FEBRUARY 14, 1955

Reported with amendments, committed to the Committee of the Whole House on the State of the Union, and ordered to be printed

[Omit the part struck through and insert the part printed in italic]

A BILL

To extend the authority of the President to enter into trade agreements under section 350 of the Tariff Act of 1930, as amended, and for other purposes.

84TH CONGRESS
1ST SESSION

H. RES. 170

IN THE HOUSE OF REPRESENTATIVES

MARCH 10, 1955

Mr. PATMAN submitted the following resolution; which was referred to the Committee on Armed Services

RESOLUTION

1 *Resolved,* That the House of Representatives does not
2 favor sale of the facilities as recommended in the report of
3 the Rubber Producing Facilities Disposal Commission.

84TH CONGRESS
1ST SESSION

H. CON. RES. 72

IN THE HOUSE OF REPRESENTATIVES

FEBRUARY 8, 1955

Mr. HOLIFIELD submitted the following concurrent resolution; which was referred to the Committee on Foreign Affairs

CONCURRENT RESOLUTION

Whereas the preservation of democratic institutions everywhere
demands united action by the world's leading democracies;
and

Whereas the North Atlantic Treaty has already committed its
members to "contribute toward the further development of
peaceful and friendly international relations by strengthening their free institutions", and to "encourage economic
collaboration between any or all of them"; and

Calendar No. 8

84TH CONGRESS
1ST SESSION

H. J. RES. 159

IN THE SENATE OF THE UNITED STATES

JANUARY 28, 1955

Ordered to be placed on the calendar

JOINT RESOLUTION

Authorizing the President to employ the Armed Forces of the
United States for protecting the security of Formosa, the
Pescadores and related positions and territories of that area.

FORMS OF LEGISLATIVE ACTION

of Agriculture to fix standards for grain exchanges), and in the President (e.g., to fix customs duty by reciprocal trade agreements with foreign nations). Are there any limits to such delegation? The law on this matter is confused and contradictory and no simple generalization is possible. The Supreme Court has certainly indicated that there are some limits. It struck down the National Industrial Recovery Act of 1933 on the grounds that it was an invalid delegation of legislative power to an executive agency.[4] This act, said the courts, did not contain clear standards to guide its administration and thus conferred large legislative discretion upon the agency entrusted with its enforcement. Congress alone, the Court has held, is competent to determine general policies and it may delegate only the function of making detailed applications of law, the guideposts for which have been clearly marked out in the statute. It is hard to see how the statutory standards which guide the Interstate Commerce Commission in rate-fixing ("fair and reasonable"), and those which limit the Federal Communications Commission in granting broadcasting licenses ("public interest, convenience, and necessity"), are sufficiently precise to provide any real limits upon administrative discretion. However, the courts have found nothing wrong with these particular delegations. One can only conclude, up to the present, that some kinds of delegation have been sustained and some kinds have been denied on the basis of no very clear cut or consistent theory.

Rules of procedure   We need at the outset also to pay some regard to the rules which regulate legislative traffic. The procedures of the houses of Congress are carefully delineated and elaborately controlled by a highly complex body of rules. These rules are the distillations of many centuries of legislative experience. Our own chambers have built upon, refined, and adjusted to American needs the rules of parliamentary practice of the English legislature of the eighteenth century. *The Manual of Parliamentary Practice* [5] prepared by Thomas Jefferson when he presided over the Senate provided the basic formulation of the rules of the two houses. Jefferson's prescriptions have been amended and interpreted through the years so that each of the standing rules of the House of Representatives (there are now 43) and of the Senate (now 40) has been elaborately overlaid and encrusted with decisions of speakers and determinations of rules committees and of committee chairmen in much the same way that our Constitution has been interpreted by courts and Congresses and Presidents through the years.[6] Today the rules of the House of Representatives are the

---

[4] Schecter Poultry Corp. *v.* United States, 295 U. S. 495 (1935).

[5] Jefferson's *Manual,* based largely on English practice, is printed in 80th Cong., 2nd Sess., House Doc. No. 766 (1949), and in various editions of the *House Rules and Manual* and of the *Senate Manual,* e.g., in the 1949 edition of the latter at pp. 303-409. The standing rules and orders of the House have developed to a point where it seldom is necessary to invoke the *Manual.*

[6] The rules of the House of Representatives will be found in successive editions of a volume entitled *Constitution, Jefferson's Manual, and Rules of the House of Representatives of the United States* (Washington). This is always kept strictly up to date. A convenient guide to House procedure in all of its aspects is *Cannon's Procedure in the House of Representatives* (4th ed.), 80th Cong., 2nd Sess., House Doc. No. 731 (1948).

The rules of the Senate will be found in the *Senate Manual* issued for each Congress.

most highly technical, elaborate, and complicated of those of any legislature in the world, and few members ever succeed in mastering them completely.

It would not be easy to overstate the importance of proper procedure in our national legislature. In the first place, procedural questions can easily and do frequently consume a heavy share of legislative time which is already inadequate to the great responsibilities which rest upon the Congress. Secondly, much of the debate and discussion over matters of considerable import turns on proper procedure. Thirdly, the rights of minorities to speak, to criticize, to propose alternative courses of action, rights which are essential to representative democracy, find their chief protection in the rules of procedure. Finally, the power of the majority to act, to deal decisively with the problems of the day, is supported and protected by the rules. A perfect balance between the power of the majority to act and the right of the minority to speak is rarely achieved at any time by any set of rules. In the Congress, the rules of the House lean a little heavily to the support of the power of the majority and those of the Senate to the support of the rights of the minority. *Importance of the rules of procedure*

INTRODUCTION OF BILLS

It is amazingly simple to introduce a bill into Congress. In the House of Representatives a member inscribes his name on a copy of it and deposits it in a box ("the hopper") on the clerk's desk. In the Senate, a member must first be recognized by the presiding officer, typically during the period when routine business is transacted (the "morning hour"), then announce the introduction of the bill, sometimes with a statement of explanation, and finally send it to the desk of the secretary. Any bill may begin its legislative career in either house except that bills raising revenue are required by the Constitution to begin in the lower house.[7] Once introduced, a bill continues "alive" during the life of the existing Congress or until sooner disposed of. In a subsequent Congress the bill, to be considered, must be reintroduced. *How bills are introduced*

Because bills are introduced by members of the Congress and bear their names, it should not be supposed that these members conceived the ideas set forth in the bills or drafted them in the proper legal terminology. Congress is "not to any material extent an originating body." [8] In the first place, a very *Authorship of bills:*

The complete body of parliamentary law governing the House will be found in the eight volumes of text and three volumes of index-digest ordinarily referred to as Hinds and Cannon's *Precedents*.

[7] Since the Senate may amend revenue bills even to the point of substituting a whole new bill for the House version, this constitutional requirement is of little real significance.

[8] R. Luce, *Congress—An Explanation* (Cambridge, Mass., 1926), 3. In his *The President, Congress, and Legislation* (New York, 1946), L. H. Chamberlain assigns somewhat greater weight to congressional initiative and leadership in the legislative process.

large and increasing proportion of the major public bills introduced originate
1. The
executive
branch
in the executive branch, most of them with the approval of the President. Frequently these "administration" bills are in fully drafted form. The fact that no
member of the administration can, as in parliamentary democracies, directly
introduce measures has proved no serious obstacle to executive initiative in the
American system, since a Representative or Senator can always be found to
sponsor the introduction. Typically, the bill is given for introduction to the
appropriate standing committee and introduced through it. It should be added
that many bills are prepared by the administration at the request of a member
or of a standing committee.

2. Private
interests
    In the second place, bills originate with persons or organizations entirely
outside national governmental circles. There are literally thousands of groups
and individuals who aspire to change the laws of the land benevolently to their
interests or to the objectives of their group. Many of these persons and groups
are served by legal counsel or legislative representatives (lobbyists) who cast
their desires in the form of a bill or bills and offer them to friendly legislators
for introduction. Since introduction is so easy and the legislative sponsor assumes no particular responsibility for the contents of the measure, every year
thousands upon thousands of such bills are introduced into Congress. Members
of Congress ordinarily are willing to accommodate their constituents who have
pet bills by introducing them. Frequently, the Congressman will write "by
request" on the bill to emphasize that he assumes no personal responsibility
for the measure. In a large number of cases, one must hasten to add, the
Congressman and his colleagues have no intention of passing or even of
seriously considering measures of this type. Of course, the more powerful
interest groups are able, in many cases, to procure consideration of their bills
and sometimes even passage. The largest share of these bills of private origin
are private bills for the benefit of particular persons, places, or organizations,
although the volume of this type has been reduced as a result of the changes
in handling certain matters enacted in the Legislative Reorganization Act of
1946. The large numbers of measures introduced, however, clutter up the
committee dockets and the calendars of the two houses and contribute mightily
to the time and expense of the legislative process.

    At the present time about 10,000-15,000 bills and resolutions are intro-
duced into a session of Congress of which perhaps 500-1000 are enacted in
some form.

Drafting
bills
    Casting legislative ideas into statutory language is a difficult and highly
technical undertaking. Few members of Congress or private individuals are
able to perform this task without competent advice. Each house provides bill-
drafting service for its members through an Office of the Legislative Counsel.
These offices are staffed with technically trained bill writers, many of whom
are specialists in some branch of the law, and their services are available to
any member who wishes to use them. The directors of these offices are appointed by the speaker and the president *pro tempore* of the Senate, and each

director nominates his own staff, subject to the approval of the two presiding officers.

COMMITTEE CONSIDERATION

Upon introduction, all bills are given a number (e.g., H.R. 144 or S. 177), printed, distributed to the members, made available to the interested public, and referred to one of the standing committees. In the case of private bills, the sponsoring Senator or Representative indicates on the bill the committee to which it should be referred and these instructions are frequently observed in both houses. Public bills are assigned under the direction of the presiding officer in each house, typically by the parliamentarian. In view of the fact that the subject-matter jurisdictions of the several committees still overlap somewhat and the fact that long and complex bills may involve subjects pertinent to several committees, the discretion of the presiding officer is occasionally exercised personally. Rarely is a bill sent to more than one committee or divided among two or more. The membership of either house possesses ultimate authority by majority vote to change the assignment made by the presiding officer and occasionally will direct the withdrawal of a bill from one committee and send it to a different committee. The committee to which a bill is assigned may be sympathetic or it may be hostile, and thus the discretion of the presiding officer and the occasional directions from the chamber sometimes determine the fate of the measure.

Referral to a standing committee

Both houses have come to expect that the committees will give thorough study to every "deserving" proposal and will then recommend to the parent chamber what should be done. Although there has been a great increase in this century in executive influence in legislative matters, the standing committees are the most important devices by which the legislators stamp their own imprint on legislation. The committees actually go much further than just to stamp it with their approval or disapproval. They mold or cast the bill into a form which they believe will be acceptable. Certainly, most of the thoughtful and detailed analysis which is given to legislative proposals is given to them by the standing committees. And if the spectator in the gallery, especially of the House of Representatives, is disillusioned by the poorly-attended, superficial and perfunctory debate in the chamber, he needs to remind himself that the Congress performs its central legislative duties in the committee rooms.[9] In the Senate, the committee work does not so completely overshadow the general consideration of measures by the entire membership, but even in the upper house it is a rare thing for a committee recommendation to be rejected. The character of the legislative product is determined as much, perhaps more, by what the committees reject as by what they accept or modify.

Importance of the committees

9 Woodrow Wilson described this situation very aptly 80 years ago in his classical study, *Congressional Government* (Boston, 1885).

Of the thousands of bills introduced and of the scores, even hundreds, referred to any major committee, only a few are given any serious study. Most bills end their legislative careers in the "inactive" files of a standing committee; the committees are under no obligation to report on every matter referred to them and they never do.

Sources of information:

Upon receiving a measure which is deemed worthy of consideration by the chairman or, in some cases, by a majority of the committee, the committee has then to decide what to do with it. Commonly, at present, such a measure is referred to a subcommittee for study and recommendation, and the whole committee does not hear of it again or participate in the deliberations upon it until the subcommittee reports and recommends a course of action to the whole committee. Whether in fact considered by a subcommittee or by the whole committee, the first requisite for thoughtful analysis is information on the subject covered by the measure. Under the influence of the legal profession, from which a majority of Congressmen are drawn, the committees have tended in the past to rely heavily on one or more public hearings to elicit the necessary data. Lawyers are habituated to the idea that justice is best served by public trial in which each of the contestants seeks by every ethical means to present his side in the best light. Out of this combat a skillful judge or attentive jury are supposed to sift the essential facts. Thus, it has been supposed, if facts are needed on a pending bill, one should announce to the public that arguments will be entertained from its proponents and opponents on such and such a day and then each side will present its case to the committee and the "truth" will emerge. Of late, however, the defects in the hearing system for eliciting information have become more and more apparent, and the committees are not using the hearing for this purpose but rather to influence public opinion or executive action or to discover the nature of public attitudes on the measure, especially of those most directly affected.[10] The weaknesses of the hearing system are that all of the needed data is not necessarily made available and that frequently only the proponents of the measure ever appear. The opponents expect the Congressmen to protect their interests. Public hearings are still used extensively by the committees and are valuable legislative aids but not solely, or even mainly, to supply necessary information.[11]

1. Public hearing

2. Lobbyists

Much valuable data and opinion are supplied to the committee members by lobbyists, or legislative representatives as they prefer to be called, representing those who are in favor of or opposed to the particular measure. Some of this is done through carefully prepared statements and exhibits offered during

[10] See Ralph K. Huitt, "The Congressional Committee: A Case Study," *Amer. Polit. Sci. Rev.,* XLVIII, 340-365 (June, 1954).

[11] The testimony of most of these hearings is recorded and is a matter of public record. Every session of Congress produces thousands of pages of such testimony in connection with most of its major bills. Students can get an illuminating view of the character of legislative business by perusing the records of the hearings on an important bill.

the public hearing on the measure. Much of it, however, is done in private conversations with committee members. It is hard to imagine how committees and Congressmen would carry on without the lobbyist. There are many kinds of information about the conduct of particular types of business enterprises or labor unions or professions for which no data comparable to that which they can supply is readily available. A great deal of the data they give Congress is accurate, reliable, and useful. It is also, of course, onesided. This is not necessarily harmful if the other sides are also supplying data.

A very great part of the information upon which Congressional committees base their decisions has always been supplied to them by the executive branch of the government. From the first reports of Alexander Hamilton, as Secretary of the Treasury, on public credit and on manufacturing to the most recent report of the Defense Department to the Armed Services Committees, the executive branch has made its great store of information and experience available to Congressional agencies, usually but not necessarily at the request of a committee. In these days, in which complete legislative programs may be drafted by the executive and sent to Congress, the executive departments are at great pains to see that the committee considering these programs is amply supplied with the data necessary to reach the "proper" conclusions. The interest of the executive in the result of legislative activity has, however, repeatedly aroused the suspicion of many Congressmen that they cannot rely entirely on the executive departments as their major or especially as their single source of information. Where else, however, might they turn for data on such subjects as national defense?

3. Executive agencies

Many pieces of legislation reach the Congress as a product of a more or less thorough investigation conducted by the Congress itself through a special or standing committee, by the Congress and the executive jointly, or by the executive branch alone. Ordinarily these investigations are reported fully and the legislative measures arrive in the committee accompanied by elaborate charts, exhibits, tables, and explanatory material. In these situations, little more data is really required. The Social Security Act of 1935, for example, was the result of the recommendations of a committee on economic security named a year earlier by President Franklin D. Roosevelt.

4. Investigations

Through the years many Congressmen have felt the need for sources of information of their own independent of the executive branch, independent of the lobbyists, and not limited by the hearing procedure. It was for this reason that the Legislative Reference Service was established in the Library of Congress in 1914. Its program has slowly developed and in 1946 it achieved statutory recognition and substantial expansion. This Service consists of a professional staff of recognized experts in a large number of fields of legislative interest whose knowledge and research skill and experience are available to supply Congressmen and committees with data in which they have expressed an interest. In excess of 51,000 inquiries are now received from Congress and handled annually by the Service. Legislators and com-

5. "Expert" assistants

mittees ask it for everything from a detailed memorandum on the contents of a bill to a chart showing the trend in the production of cotton.

The Legislative Reorganization Act of 1946, which provided the expansion in the Legislative Reference Service, did not stop with that in its effort to supply the need for disinterested data. As we have noted in an earlier chapter, it provided for "expert" assistants for each of the standing committees to aid them in reviewing the proposals submitted for their consideration. This particular action virtually ended a previous committee practice of borrowing experts for this purpose from executive agencies. Since the Act of 1946, staffs have grown rapidly and there are now (1965) more than 1000 committee employees. The hope of the sponsors of this program that the experts would be nonpartisan has not been completely realized. The Republicans, at least, have charged on several occasions that the minority is inadequately served.[12]

Executive sessions

Legislative measures are considered in detail by the committee or subcommittee in executive ("secret") session. Records are ordinarily kept, however, of the votes in these sessions and of the formal actions taken. Although this secrecy has been criticized, most Congressmen feel that the members make greater contributions in private than they might in public sessions. Furthermore, alert newspapermen are usually able to discover and report the occurrences in the secret sessions.

Alternative forms of committee action

In these private sessions, the committee has several alternative courses of action it may elect to follow. It may approve the bill as it stands and recommend its adoption by the chamber. This is very unusual. It may propose a number of amendments which change portions of the measure before it and then recommend the measure for passage with the amendments added. It may rewrite the bill completely, preserving only the number and title, and present the rewritten measure as a substitute. Finally it may reject the bill. In the latter case, ordinarily the committee takes no further action. But if it approves the bill with or without amendments or in substitution form, it then prepares a report to this effect and seeks an opportunity to acquaint the whole membership with its recommendations. The chairmen of the committees, since 1946, are under obligation to report any approved bills "promptly." [13]

Forcing a bill out of committee

The ease with which a committee can kill a bill simply by not reporting it has been a subject of considerable controversy in the Congress. It is easy to see how, given the method of selecting committee members, a committee decision on some measure might not reflect the desires of a large portion of the membership in either house. One of the changes made in the House in

[12] For a review of the effectiveness of the attempts to provide Congress with its own source of information see G. B. Galloway, *The Legislative Process in Congress* (New York, 1953), Chaps. 17 and 23. See also K. Kofmehl, *Professional Staffs of Congress* (Lafayette, Ind., 1962). The Republican case is set forth in Congressional Quarterly, *Weekly Report*, May 4, 1962, 764-765 and Mar. 1963, 239-240.

[13] The purpose of this rule of 1946 was to preclude the chairman from killing a bill which he personally opposed, although his committee favored it, by neglecting to report it.

1910 coincident with the attack on the speaker was the establishment of a procedure by which the House itself might pry a bill out of a hostile committee. This "discharge rule" has gone through various changes since its enactment, but as it now stands a committee may be discharged from further consideration after it has had the bill at least 30 days and by a discharge motion signed by 218 members.[14] This motion for discharge must be on the calendar at least seven days and is in order only on certain days of each month but it is privileged business and must be disposed of. The "seven-day" period is to allow the committee an opportunity to report the bill out on the floor if it cares to do so. The discharge procedure, although it depends primarily on the wishes of a majority of the members, is difficult to operate and is rarely used.[15] Most members of Congress are apparently reluctant to upset the prerogatives of the standing committees and the desires of the leaders. It, therefore, remains true that the committees have virtually the power of life or death over every legislative measure.

MOTION TO DISCHARGE COMMITTEE

MAY 21, 1956.

TO THE CLERK OF THE HOUSE OF REPRESENTATIVES

Pursuant to clause 4 of rule XXVII, I, Hon. WRIGHT PATMAN, move to discharge the Committee on Rules from the consideration of the resolution, House Resolution 414, entitled "A resolution providing for the consideration of H. R. 11, a bill to reaffirm the national public policy and purposes of Congress in the laws against unlawful restraints and monopolies, and for other purposes," which was referred to said committee February 28, 1956, in support of which motion the undersigned Members of the House of Representatives affix their signatures, to wit:

SOURCE: *Congressional Record, House* (May 21, 1956), 7734.

CONSIDERATION OF BILLS BY THE HOUSE OF REPRESENTATIVES [16]

A House standing committee reports a bill which it has considered favorably by returning it with its report to the clerk of the House. The clerk lists it

The calendars

[14] From 1931-35 a discharge petition required only 145 signatures. The Democrats who adopted this easy rule soon restored the old requirement because of dislike of minority pressure on the committees.

[15] From 1910-64, only 22 bills were taken from committees by this procedure; and 18 were then passed by the House, only two (Fair Labor Standards Act of 1938 and the federal pay bill of 1960) ever became law. Congressional Quarterly Service, *Congress and the Nation;* 1945-1964 (Washington, 1965), 1425.

[16] From this point on in the discussion of legislative procedure it will be necessary to treat the procedure in each house separately. The discussion of Senate procedure will, however, merely emphasize the important differences from House procedure.

on one of three "calendars" depending on its nature. Revenue and appropriation bills are placed on the Union Calendar; public bills not involving taxation or expenditure are placed on the House Calendar; private bills are placed on the Private Calendar.[17] Bills are placed on these lists in the order in which they are reported and once on the list remain there throughout the two years of a Congress unless they are taken up and acted upon. The original purpose of these calendars was to regulate the order in which the House would consider the measures which its committees recommended to it. And on certain days as well as at certain times during the daily session the business on one of the calendars is appropriately considered.[18] However, the volume of legislative business has become so great and the calendars consequently so congested that the order is never rigidly adhered to and the House usually adjourns with a lot of unconsidered measures still on the calendars. Revenue and appropriation bills can be taken up at almost any time if the member wishing to get them before the House can gain recognition, but the bills on the House Calendar ordinarily can get before the House only with the aid of a special order from the Rules Committee. The chairmen of committees wishing to report these "controversial" and unprivileged bills,[19] and apart from the appropriation bills these are the major bills of the session, try to get the Rules Committee to accept them and intercede on their behalf by special order. It is from this situation that the Rules Committee derives its important influence on legislation. The House Calendar listing is thus a polite fiction and provides in most instances only a basis for negotiation, not an unassailable position. Conferences and negotiations among the leaders really determine which bills will be taken up and when. It should be added that on certain days (the first and third Mondays of each month) it is in order to suspend all House rules by a two-thirds vote and the House may rove at will among the calendars picking up what it pleases to consider. The speaker, however, has got to recognize the individual for the purpose of making such a motion and thus his consent has to be obtained.

Committee of the whole

An important share of the legislative business of the House of Representatives is conducted by means of the device of Committee of the Whole. The Union Calendar [20] is made up of bills which are considered by this committee

[17] There are, in addition, two "special" calendars on which measures may be listed by transfer from the regular calendars. On one—a Consent Calendar—are placed bills (usually minor and unopposed) which can be called up and disposed of under unanimous consent; on the other—a Discharge Calendar—are listed motions to discharge a committee from further consideration of a bill.

[18] For example, the Private Calendar is ordinarily considered on Fridays; the Consent Calendar on the first and third Mondays of each month.

[19] They are called "controversial" because if there were no objections to them they could be placed on the Consent Calendar and handled on the proper days and unprivileged to distinguish them from the bills on the Union Calendar for which a motion to bring them before the House is normally in order.

[20] The name Union Calendar is a short title for Calendar of the Whole House on the State of the Union. Technically speaking, there are two Committees of the Whole, one for private bills and one for public bills; but the private bill committee is no longer used. The House itself processes private bills on the Private Calendar, however, under the general rules which govern the committee of the whole.

(revenue and appropriation measures) before they are considered, technically speaking, by the House of Representatives. The Committee of the Whole is simply the entire membership of the House sitting as a committee; but as a committee it operates under simpler, less rigid, and less demanding rules than does the House itself. Only 100 members constitute a quorum (the minimum number necessarily present to transact business) in place of the 218 in the House. Debate is governed by a rule which allows only five minutes to each speaker. There can be no time-consuming roll calls, since voting is always orally or by rising or by tellers, and there are no records kept of how any member voted. Certain types of dilatory motions, such as one to refer the matter back to the committee or to postpone consideration of it, are not allowed. At the conclusion of the debate the committee "rises," reports through its chairman back to the House, and then the House acts on the committee's actions. This device, the motion to create which is ordinarily in order, enables all fiscal measures to be considered line by line for amendment by the entire membership under circumstances which allow maximum participation and critical debate. The House in Committee of the Whole reveals itself in its best light with many members participating, short and pointed speeches, and quick decisions.

It is customary to describe Anglo-American legislative procedure as involving three formal readings for each legislative proposition. This is an accurate description only in a very loose sense. The first reading occurs upon introduction and is not a "reading" at all. The title is simply entered in the records. When the bill emerges from the standing committee it is given its second reading, either in Committee of the Whole or in the House itself. This may be and occasionally is an actual reading of the bill line by line with opportunity for discussion and for amendments to be offered. If, however, the bill is being considered under a "closed" special order of the Committee on Rules, it may not be amended from the floor. Ordinarily these closed orders are used for complex tax bills. The conclusion of this stage of legislative consideration is a vote on the question "Shall the bill be engrossed (i.e., reprinted as amended) and read a third time?" If the vote is favorable, the bill is then brought before the House again and is given its third reading. This reading is by title only, no further amendments are in order, and the debate, if any, is only on the whole bill as it stands. The conclusion of this phase is a vote on final passage. If the vote is favorable, the bill is signed by the speaker and sent to the Senate or, if it has already been passed by the Senate, to the President. This formal order of procedure here outlined may, of course, be rudely set aside by unanimous consent, by special order of the Rules Committee, or by suspension of the rules. *The three readings*

The chief contrast between the procedure in the House of Representatives and that in the Senate is the limitation upon debate in the House. Normally debate occurs in the House only during the second reading and even this debate is sharply curtailed. Over the years the House has evolved a number of devices which restrict debate, and the most important of these are: (*a*) special *Limits on debate in the House* orders of the Rules Committee which fix the total time for consideration of the bill and allot it between the proponents and opponents; and (b) the "previous question" rule which since 1811 has authorized a motion for the previous question to be made at any time during debate (except in Committee of the Whole) and which if adopted requires the House to vote immediately on whatever is pending.[21] The motion itself is not debatable and may not be laid on the table. Debate in Committee of the Whole is limited by the five-minute rule and in the House it is limited by the rule that no member may speak longer than one hour. Typically, the time of debate is fixed in advance by the leaders and either by special order or by "gentleman's agreement" an equal amount of time is given to each side. The chairman of the standing committee reporting the bill ordinarily controls the time of the majority and designates the members of his committee who will speak for the proponents. The ranking minority member opposing the bill usually controls the time of the opponents. Tables placed about half-way up the aisle on either side of the chamber are used by the two teams to assemble their papers and documents for the debate. If any time remains after the two teams have made their respective contributions, members of the House who are not members of the committee may participate. This is unusual. The effect of all of these rules and customs is to make dilatory and obstructive tactics by the minority very difficult. About the only dilatory devices which are readily available are "quorum calls," [22] roll-call votes, and demands that the clerk (in Committee of the Whole) actually read every word of a long bill.

Methods of voting

Votes are taken in the House of Representatives by four methods: (a) *viva voce,* a test by the sound of voices; (b) if any member is dissatisfied with the speaker's determination of the result he may call for *a rising vote* (division) whereupon the supporters of each side stand and are counted; (c) if one-fifth of a quorum demand it, a vote is taken *by tellers* who stand in front of the speaker's desk and the members voting "Aye" pass between them and are counted and then the members voting "No"; and, (d) by *roll call* in the House, though not in Committee on the Whole, if one-fifth of those present demand it. The clerk calls each member by name and his vote is officially entered in the records of the House.[23]

[21] If no debate has as yet occurred 40 minutes of debate is allowed after the adoption of a previous question motion.

[22] Quorum calls are points of order made to the speaker that there are not enough members in the chamber to transact business and require, if the speaker cannot count enough, that the roll be called to ascertain whether a quorum is in fact present. It takes 45 minutes to call the roll of the House and thus each roll call constitutes an important delay of the proceedings.

[23] Under existing regulations, the House has no way of protecting itself against waste of time in this manner; by express constitutional provision, not only must the yeas and nays be taken when the question is one of passing a measure over presidential veto (Art. I, Sec. 7, cl. 2), but one-fifth of the members present may demand a yea-and-nay vote at any time—and for any reason—they see fit (Art. I, Sec. 5, cl. 3). With a roll call consuming 45 minutes, it is estimated that in a recent session the 347 roll calls on de-

CONSIDERATION OF BILLS BY THE SENATE

After a bill is passed the House, it is certified by the clerk and delivered to the Senate. There it begins a journey which is quite similar to that it has already traversed in the lower house and to that traveled by a bill which originates in the Senate. There are, however, some striking differences in the procedures of the two houses when the bill emerges from the standing committee. The Senate uses only two calendars: the Calendar of Business on which are placed all bills and resolutions in the order in which they are reported; and the Executive Calendar on which are placed nominations and treaties. The Senate no longer uses Committee of the Whole except for the consideration of treaties. Furthermore, the Senate has few special devices for moving bills off the calendar onto the floor. There is in the Senate no powerful Rules Committee to step in with a special order bringing a bill before the chamber. The calendar listings are followed fairly closely, therefore, except that by unanimous consent measures may be taken out of order. The most notable difference in the two houses, however, is the relative freedom of debate in the Senate. By custom, supported in part by rule, debate in the Senate is virtually unlimited. There is no time limit on speeches; there has been no "previous question" procedure since 1806. There is no requirement that the speaker must talk on the question. As long as any member has anything to say on the matter before the chamber, whether pertinent or not, debate cannot easily be halted.

Differences between House and Senate procedure

The great freedom of the individual Senator to participate in the discussion on the floor of the chamber has provided minorities with one of their most potent weapons: the filibuster. When legislative time is precious, for example, when adjournment is near or when appropriation authority is expiring and money bills must be voted, a handful of members can get the floor and by spelling one another (yielding the floor to each other) can halt legislative business until their terms are met. There is no rule like that in the House requiring the Senators to speak to the question and these talkathons sometimes range over the whole field of human endeavor. Prior to the adoption of the "Lame Duck" Amendment (20th) in 1933, the Senate was most vulnerable to this tactic in the closing days of the short session. The Senate had to adjourn by March 4, for its life would then expire. The absence of a binding adjournment date since that time has strengthened the procedure against filibustering but has not made it impervious. There have been at least 12 significant filibusters in the Senate since 1933.[24] This surrender of command of

Filibustering

---

mand for the yeas and nays, together with the 528 to determine the presence of a quorum, used up a total of at least four months of working time. Many people have suggested the installation of a system of electrical voting now used in many states to save time. See, for example, E. Kefauver and J. Levin, *A Twentieth-Century Congress* (New York, 1947), Chap. V.

[24] For a list of filibusters from 1841 to 1951, see *Congressional Record,* 83rd Cong., 1st Sess., January 7, 1953, 216-217. For those since 1952 see Congressional Quarterly Service, *Weekly Report,* April 27, 1962, 661.

the Senate to a few Senators at critical times in various sessions has provoked sharp criticism of the Senate rules. This is government by minority, charge the critics, and sometimes a small minority at that. Surely the majority should be allowed to act after a decent amount of debate. The major, although not exclusive, use of the filibuster in the past decade has been by Southern Senators to defeat various types of proposed legislation aimed at discriminatory practices against Negroes.[25]

The closure rule

The device most widely considered as a remedy for this alleged defect in Senatorial procedure is some form of closure rule. In 1917, as a result of a successful filibuster against President Wilson's proposed legislation for arming America's merchant vessels against German submarines, Wilson induced the Senate to adopt the current rule which can be used to limit debate. This rule (XXII) authorizes 16 Senators to submit a motion for closing debate on any matter pending before the Senate and, after two calendar days, this motion must be put by the presiding officer and a vote taken on the question: "Is it the sense of the Senate that the debate shall be brought to a close?" If two-thirds [26] of the Senators present vote for closing the debate, each Senator is thereafter entitled to speak one hour and then the debate ends. This is obviously a very mild form of closure. It had been invoked successfully only four times and had been tried at all only 19 times prior to 1949. Amendments to the rule in 1949, while eliminating many dilatory motions (e.g., to approve the Senate journal), nevertheless made the closure motion itself debatable and thus subject to filibuster. Closure motions have been offered on twelve occasions from 1950 to 1965. Four have been successful.[27] The most significant success in the application of the rule occurred in 1964 when for the first time in history closure was applied to a civil rights debate paving the way for the ultimate passage of the Civil Rights Act of 1964. This success was followed by a similar triumph in 1965 on the voting rights bill then pending.

Present controversy on the rule

Demands for modification of the Senate closure rule have been strongly urged for several years. The recent use of the filibuster to frustrate attempts to legislate nationally on racial discrimination has stimulated many groups with whom this legislation is popular to a concern over the Senate rules. The

[25] Southern senators successfully filibustered for 29 days in January and February, 1938 against a bill to strengthen national authority against lynching. In 1942, 1944, 1946, and 1948 they filibustered successfully against a proposed national law to outlaw the poll tax as a voting requirement in national elections. In 1946, and in 1950 they successfully prevented consideration of a proposed fair employment practice bill by filibusters. In 1962, a proposed national standard for literacy tests was stalled by filibuster. In every case the closure rule proved ineffective. See H. E. Shuman, "Senate Rules and the Civil Rights Bill: A Case Study," *Amer. Pol. Sci. Rev.,* LI, No. 4 (Dec., 1957).

[26] Originally the rule provided for an affirmative vote by two-thirds of those present, but it was amended in 1949 to require a vote by two-thirds of the whole membership. Then it was amended back to the original version in 1959. It was also amended in 1959 to apply to debates on changes in rules. These amendments halted the effort of that year to change the rules on the Senate's opening day.

[27] For a list of closure motions from 1919 to 1965 see Congressional Quarterly Service, *Weekly Report,* Sept. 11, 1964, 2123.

relatively new use of the filibuster technique to embrace even motions to take up a bill or to close debate has provoked great concern among some members of the Senate itself. The Democratic Party, whose leaders include both Southerners and the dominant figures in the large-city political organizations where antidiscrimination legislation is popular, has been torn by bitter dissension on this issue. The city faction in the national convention of 1952 insisted that the platform include a promise to amend the Senate rules so as to restrict filibustering, and the platform did contain a rather vague promise to do something about majority rule in the Senate. Thus far, despite vigorous efforts at the opening session of the Senate in each of the last few Congresses, the Senate has been unwilling seriously to modify its rules on the subject of freedom of debate. On the contrary, many of the Senate leaders contend that despite the time consumed by filibuster the Senate does as well as the House in getting through its legislative agenda—in five recent Congresses, for example, it passed more bills and resolutions than the House—and that the frequently used device of "unanimous consent," by which the members agree in advance to limit speeches and vote at a certain time, serves every desirable need of the Senate. Finally, the protagonists argue that opposition to filibustering by some Senators is largely insincere, since they do not hesitate to use the device when their own interests are threatened.[28] The successful closures of 1964 and 1965 in the civil rights area has weakened but not halted the thrust for revision of the rules.

CONFERENCE COMMITTEES

A bill which passes both branches of Congress in identical form is sent to the President for signature. The Senate may, however, amend a House bill, the House may amend a Senate bill, and each of these actions occurs frequently. Unless one house will recede from its position and concur with the changes made by the other, a deadlock occurs which somehow must be broken. The device by which disagreements between the two houses on specific pieces of legislation are reconciled is the "Committee of Conference," appointed for each legislative measure in dispute. So frequent are these disagreements, especially on major legislative proposals, that the Conference Committee is a standard fixture of the national legislative process. From one-third to one-half of all the public bills, including virtually all of the important ones, have in recent years been referred to Conference Committees at the appropriate stage of their legislative careers.

Resolving conflicts between the two houses

[28] In the session of Congress in 1953, for example, a number of advocates of changing the closure rule talked for several days, in what they claimed was not a filibuster, against the bill to return title to off-shore, oil-rich lands to the states. In this debate, Senator Morse of Oregon, an ardent supporter of a stronger closure rule, set a new record by talking steadily for 22 hours. A filibuster by a similar group against the Communication Satellite Bill occurred in 1962. On this occasion the closure rule was successfully invoked.

The rejection by one house of the views of the other house on certain items in a bill or resolution under consideration is almost invariably accompanied by a request for conference. The request having been agreed to—and it is never refused—the presiding officer of each house names from three to nine members of his house to meet with those named by the other to attempt to reconcile the differences. By custom, the presiding officers name the chairman and ranking minority member of the standing committee which considered the bill, plus others from each side who have figured prominently in the debate and who, typically, are also members of the same standing committee. The views of the majority of the chamber are always represented by a majority of the "managers" named to represent that house in the conference. The minority view, however, is always accorded some representation. The two sets of managers then meet and discuss the points at issue, seeking by compromise to arrive at something acceptable to both houses. Agreement must be reached under the rules by a majority of each group voting separately, so that the fact that one house occasionally names more managers than the other is of no consequence. Sometimes the task of reconciliation is easy and is performed in a few hours; sometimes it is difficult and requires days, weeks, even months to reach agreement.[29] If no agreement can be reached, the bill fails or a new committee may be named to try again. Generally, agreement is reached and the proposals of the committee are accepted by both houses. It must be added that the rules and the customs of the two houses confer upon these Conference Committees an unexpected amount of power to determine the final form of legislation. The reports of Conference Committees are highly privileged in both houses and thus have the right of way over most other forms of legislative traffic. The reports of the committees must be accepted or rejected as a whole. They may not be further amended. Each house has got to take the dose compounded by the conference or go without any medicine. The deliberations of the Conference Committees are secret and unrecorded. They ordinarily hold no hearings and listen to no outside testimony. Finally, the bill—or those parts of the bill in dispute—which emerges from the deliberations of the committee may not resemble the view of either house and may, in fact, contain matters never before considered exactly in that form by either house. The Conference Committee is also an arena of continuous struggle between the two houses for legislative supremacy. The customary assumption that the Senate is predominate in conferences is not borne out by studies of these committees.[30]

The power of the Conference Committee thus partially to remake a legislative proposal and then to thrust it upon the two houses in an environment of "take this or nothing," with no opportunity for amendment, has attracted

[29] In the 81st Congress, for example, the Army civil functions appropriation bill was tied up in conference from June 1 to October 3, 1949.

[30] See G. Y. Steiner, *The Congressional Conference Committee, Seventieth to Eightieth Congresses* (Urbana, Ill., 1951).

to this necessary device a great deal of criticism. Senator George Norris once characterized the Conference Committees as a third house of the Congress. The members of this "house," he said, are not elected by the people, keep no record of their work, and perform entirely in secret—but their product must always be accepted. Many Senators in recent years have also criticized the method of selection of the Senate members. They assert that the views of the majority are not always vigorously upheld.[31] Several changes in the rules governing selection have been proposed, but thus far, none have been adopted. Efforts to confine Conference Committees rigidly to the exact points in disagreement and only to those points have been made repeatedly but never with complete success. Recent revision of the rules, partly encompassed in the Legislative Reorganization Act of 1946, have made it easier to raise points of order against Conference Committee reports that go beyond the matters in dispute; but the committees, in practice, have much latitude. Another suggested method for reducing the influence of the Conference Committee is greater use of joint-standing committees of the two houses in considering legislation. This is on the theory that it is better to prevent differences from arising than to reconcile them after the bills have passed both houses.

PRIVATE BILL PROCEDURE

More than 60 percent of all the laws enacted by the eighty-sixth Congress were private laws. Although the Legislative Reorganization Act of 1946 took a long step in reducing the volume of this type of legislation, much still remains. The Act of 1946 banned bills for individual pensions, for building bridges across navigable streams, and for the correction of military records. In each case, administrative procedures were established to care for these matters. The Federal Tort Claims Act of 1946 also provided for judicial settlement of a number of types of individual claims theretofore processed by Congress. However, three main categories of private bills are still authorized and enter the Congress in great numbers: (*a*) claim bills not covered by the Federal Tort Claims Act; (*b*) immigration and naturalization bills dealing with specific individuals; and (*c*) land bills providing for issuing titles to individuals. The vast bulk of these private bills are handled in the House by two standing subcommittees of the Judiciary Committee: one handles claims, the other immigration and naturalization bills. The committee will not consider a claims bill until it is requested to do so by the sponsor and he supplies it with proper supporting evidence, nor until the government department concerned has filed its report. Claims bills approved by the subcommittee are referred to the full committee and then to official objectors appointed by the speaker to review the committee's findings. They are then placed on the

Private bills still consume much time of the House

---

[31] Senator Fulbright (Ark.) has been a modern critic as has Senator Clark (Pa.) on the grounds stated.

Private Calendar and are disposed of on the days when that calendar is in order. A similar but not identical procedure is followed in the Senate.

THE PROBLEM OF LOBBYING

The in-crease in interest-group activities

Interest groups and their legislative representatives have become an established feature of the American political landscape. Providing a kind of functional representation to the electorate, supplying the legislature with much necessary data, initiating countless proposals for public consideration, these groups undoubtedly render a unique service to democratic government. Their activities on the national scene are not, however, an unmixed blessing. Their information tends to be one-sided; their objective is usually economic gain; their methods are occasionally devious; and their influence disproportionate to their numbers. Statesmen and students alike have been troubled by the problems of special-interest representation in the legislative process as the scope and scale of their operations has multiplied. Today more than 400 national organizations maintain more than 1000 paid agents in the national capital and spend uncounted millions of dollars to influence the course of legislation and the public attitudes which lie behind the legislation.[32] In spite of numerous attempts to make the lobbyist a respected and indispensable adjunct to democratic lawmaking, the name is still an epithet and connotes some kind of wrongdoing. At least six major investigations of lobbying have been conducted in this century by American legislatures in an effort to deal with the real or alleged problems associated with the growth of interest-group activities.[33] About three-fourths of the states have enacted laws designed to curb their operations and to disclose their objectives. None of these efforts has been wholly successful and few of them have achieved anything substantial. In Washington, the matter has received intermittent attention over several decades, but the House of Representatives has typically stifled efforts at regulation initiated by the Senate. The two houses did finally compel utility lobbyists to register in 1925 and agents of foreign interests in 1928, and in 1926 compelled agents of shipping interests to record the objects of their activities. Not until 1946, in connection with the general reorganization of the Congress, were the two houses able to agree on a procedure for dealing with lobbying.

The Regulation of Lobbying Act of 1946

The system finally adopted by the Congress is based very largely on the practice of several of the states. The fundamental premise of the Regulation of Lobbying Act is that undesirable behavior by interest groups, and their agents can best be controlled by publicity rather than by prohibition. Lobbyists, as defined in the law,[34] are required to register with the clerk of the

[32] The reported spending by lobbying agencies in the past decade has been about $4.2 million annually. See Congressional Quarterly Service. *Congress and the Nation: 1945-1964* (Washington, 1965). 1586.

[33] See G. B. Galloway, *The Legislative Process in Congress* (New York, 1953), 498.

[34] "Any person who shall engage himself for pay or for any consideration for the purpose of attempting to influence . . . any legislation by the Congress . . ."

House and the secretary of the Senate and to disclose in their registration the association or individual by whom employed and how much paid. Quarterly thereafter each registered lobbyist is required to file a statement of receipts and expenditures, including the purposes for which the sums were expended. Tabulations of these reports are published in the *Congressional Record* to apprise all interested persons of the facts. Furthermore, the law requires any organization which solicits or receives contributions to support its legislative activities to give annual public accounting of these contributions and the expenditures made from them. Failure to comply with the law may result in fine, imprisonment, or suspension of the privilege of lobbying.

In practice, the registering and reporting provisions of this law have *Results* supplied the public with more significant information about the extent and scope of lobbying than has ever before been available. The enforcement of the law has, however, been embarrassed from the beginning by the uncertainties and obscurities in the law itself. In an effort to exclude organizations who lobby rarely or only incidentally to the regular and major purposes of the organization, the law covers only those whose "principal purpose" is to influence legislation. Many of the most energetic and extensive national organizations operating in Washington claim that the law does not apply to them because lobbying is not their principal purpose. Further, the Supreme Court has held that the law applies only to direct dealings with members of Congress and does not require reports on funds expended on propaganda directed at the voters.[35] The law, of course, does not in fact regulate lobbying and certainly has not and was not intended to curb it. It merely brings certain types of information about lobbying out into the open where the public can, it it wishes, scrutinize it.[36] In general the members of Congress believe lobbying to be helpful and, on the whole, ethical and straightforward. Close students of the subject consider it impossible to buy or steal a decision in Washington today because of the numbers of persons involved and the publicity surrounding governmental functions.[37]

THE LEGISLATIVE INVESTIGATION

As an important, some would say indispensable, adjunct of its responsi- *Increase* bilities for the conduct of the national administration and the development of *in investigating activities*

[35] As interpreted the Lobbying Act was declared constitutional by a majority of the Court in U. S. *v.* Harriss, 347 U. S., 612 (1954).

[36] For a discussion of the operations of the Lobbying Act thus far, see G. B. Galloway, *The Legislative Process in Congress* (New York, 1953), 502-503, and *Report and Recommendations on Federal Lobbying Act,* a report of the House Select Committee on Lobbying Activities (The Buchanan Committee). 81st Cong., 2nd Sess., House Report No. 3239 (Washington, 1951) and, Congressional Quarterly Service, *Congress and the Nation, 1945-64* (Washington, 1964), Chap. 14.

[37] One of the best analyses is L. W. Milbrath, *The Washington Lobbyists* (Chicago, 1963).

legislation, the Congress relies extensively on the legislative investigation. In the past the investigative procedure has been widely used for the development of data and the revelation of opinion on national problems for the purpose of propounding a legislative solution. Its major use, in the past two decades at least, has been to bring to light the conduct of public employees and administrative agencies. The investigation has become one of the major ways by which the committees of Congress hold the administration accountable to the Congress and to the public for its conduct of affairs. In time, energy, expense, and publicity, the investigating activities of the last eight Congresses have rivaled their legislative activities. Investigations of administrative behavior have been conducted by both the regular standing committees and by special committees designated for the purpose. The Legislative Reorganization Act of 1946 contemplated the use of regular standing committees, and since its enactment, special committees have been used sparingly.[38] In early days, committees of the House conducted most of the investigations; more recently the Senate committees have been equally active. Several notable inquiries have been directed by joint committees of the two houses and, in a few cases, members of the executive branch and representatives of the public have been invited to serve with the legislators.

The use of the investigative procedure

Of the more than 800 investigations conducted in our national history, several have been outstanding in bringing to light and correcting egregious misconduct within the administration. Both the Teapot Dome oil reserve scandal of the Harding era and the income-tax administration scandal of the Truman regime, to select two of this century, have been aired by this method. In the broader uses of the investigative power to inform legislative policy, there have also been many of lofty purposes and far-reaching accomplishment: the studies of immigration, lobbying, stock exchange operations, conservation, monopoly in industry, the organization of Congress, and the organization of the executive branch of the government are examples from this century which come readily to mind. The investigative function, however, has not uniformly achieved its maximum potentiality. Although many, perhaps most, have been well intentioned and seriously pursued, some have had only personal or partisan malice as their stimulus and campaign ammunition or personal aggrandizement as their object. As the Congress has relied more heavily upon investigation in an attempt to redress the balance of power lost to the

---

[38] The Legislative Reorganization Act of 1946 especially charged the committees with this mission. In the Full Employment Act of 1946, the Labor-Management Relations (Taft-Hartley) Act of 1947, and the Atomic Energy Act of 1947, joint committees of the two houses were established to observe the administration of these programs.

Some observers are beginning to question the wisdom of this "reform" since it seems to encourage more investigating and since it clothes so many committees with subpoena powers. Early in 1955, the rules committee of the House of Representatives announced its determination to examine projected investigations by the standing committees with great care and to offer budgetary support only for those which could be justified at a special hearing before the rules committee itself.

executive branch during this century, the difficulties and criticisms have increased.[39]

In the first place, the field of inquiry has extended in recent years to the political sentiments and loyalties of numerous individuals and groups in American society, including teachers, preachers, writers, movie stars, labor union executives, and others. One standing committee of the Congress—the House Un-American Activities Committee—has no other major function.[40] In many cases, these inquiries have borne no apparent relevance to contemplated legislation or to administrative indiscretion. They have had as their apparent major purpose the enlightenment of the public, and as a subsidiary purpose the discrediting of certain opinions and of those who hold them. Many persons have argued that the scope of Congressional investigation is, or ought to be, confined to the legislative and administrative responsibilities of that body and that committees have no right to invade personal privacy except under the impetus of grave policy-making enterprises. The courts have increasingly been urged by reluctant witnesses to declare some limits on the scope of these inquiries and on the procedures by which they have been conducted. It is now generally conceded that the powers of investigation are not unlimited. The Supreme Court summarized the matter thus in a recent case: [41]

Problems arising from use of investigative function:

a. Scope of the inquiries

> The power of the Congress to conduct investigations is inherent in the legis-
> lative power. That power is broad. It encompasses inquiries concerning the ad-
> ministration of existing laws as well as proposed or possibly needed statutes.
> It includes surveys of defects in our social, economic, or political system for
> the purpose of enabling the Congress to remedy them. . . . But broad as is
> this power of inquiry, it is not unlimited. There is no general authority to
> expose the private affairs of individuals without justification in terms of the
> functions of the Congress.

[39] From 1789 to 1950, approximately 550 investigations had been conducted by Congress; the eighty-second Congress alone undertook 225 separate inquiries and expended more than $4,500,000 upon them and the expenditures have increased sharply since that time.

See A. Barth, *Government by Investigation* (New York, 1955), and T. Taylor, *Grand Inquest* (New York, 1955), for critical appraisals of the investigative function of Congress.

[40] Established as a select committee in 1938, the House Committee on Un-American Activities was made a permanent standing committee in 1946. Its mission is to investigate: (1) "The extent, character, and objects of un-American propaganda activities in the United States; (2) the diffusion within the United States of subversive and un-American propaganda that is instigated from foreign countries or of a domestic origin and attacks the principle of the form of government as guaranteed by our Constitution, and (3) all other questions in relation thereto that would aid Congress in any necessary remedial legislation."

[41] Watkins *v.* United States, 354 U. S. 178 (1957). The decision in this case contains a review of the history of the investigative power. A good review of the application of First Amendment guarantees to investigating authority will be found in Marvin Summers, "The First Amendment As a Restraint on the Power of Congress to Investigate," *Marquette Law Review*, XLIII, No. 4, 459-482 (Spring, 1960).

In the same case the Court condemned the mission assigned by the rules of the House of Representatives to the Committee on Un-American Activities as ambiguous. "No one could reasonably deduce from the charter the kind of investigation the committee was directed to make," said the Court. After a change in personnel, however, the Court in later cases [42] agreed that the investigation of Communist activities was a legitimate and authorized purpose of the committee and that if the questionee is explicitly told the relevance of the questions he is being asked to the Communist activity under investigation and the questions are relevant to such an inquest, then the investigation is legitimate and witnesses may not properly refuse to answer. The Court continues, however, to scrutinize the conduct of the committee with great care.[43] The Court has also suggested that serious questions of free speech might be raised by investigations into propaganda activities under the guise of inquiring into lobbying.[44]

b. Televising of committee hearings

Secondly, the Congressional investigating process during the early 50's took place amidst an inordinate amount of publicity. Newsreel and television cameras and radio microphones, not to mention crowded spectator areas, became the standard environment for many of the hearings. The opportunity that this provided for political adventure by those who direct the inquiries stimulated competition among legislators for strategic posts from which to launch personal campaigns and created concern for the abuse of the hearing process to serve these personal ambitions.[45] Criticism of the practice of making spectacles of these inquiries had mounted to the point that Speaker Rayburn early in 1952 and again in 1955 and from then, as long as he was speaker, ruled that meetings of the committees of the House of Representatives could not be broadcast, televised, tape-recorded, or photographed by moving picture cameras unless and until the rules of the House were changed specifically to authorize these practices.[46] Speaker McCormack has continued the ban.

[42] Barenblatt *v.* United States, 360 U. S. 109 (1959) and Wilkinson *v.* United States, 365 U. S. 399 (1961). In both these cases strong dissents based on the Watkins case were filed by four justices.

[43] In mid-1961, for example, it freed another witness on the grounds that the questions were not relevant to the stated purpose of the inquiry. Deutch *v.* United States, 367 U. S. 456 (1961).

[44] See United States *v.* Rumely, 345 U. S. 41 (1953). The Court did not in fact rule on the free speech question in this case. It held merely that the Lobbying Law did not require reports on money spent to influence public opinion.

[45] At least one Presidential candidacy in 1952 and in 1956 (Senator Kefauver) could be traced in part to the popularity gained by the televising of investigating committee hearings, and a comparative unknown successfully achieved high public office in New York City as a result of the fame achieved from participation in these same proceedings (Rudolph Halley). Although not attended by the same amount of publicity, the popularity of the Truman Investigating Committee of the Senate during World War II contributed importantly to Truman's nomination as Vice-President in 1944.

[46] An effort to authorize broadcasts of House proceedings was defeated early in 1961 by the Rules committees.

One hearing in 1957 was televised in defiance of the Rayburn ruling. It was held in San Francisco by Representative Walter of the Un-American Activities Committee.

Speaker Martin (1953-55) allowed each committee to decide the matter for itself.

The third problem that has arisen in connection with recent inquiries and the publicity surrounding them concerns the status and rights of persons who appear before the committees. Traditionally, Congressional committees have admitted many kinds of testimony under a variety of conditions. They have not been bound, nor have they wished to be bound, by the rules of the judicial branch in these matters. Many legislators have felt that judicial procedures which include elaborate rules on hearsay evidence, accreditation of witnesses, admissibility of evidence, and rights of the accused are too restrictive for the type of information which committees hope to elicit. Concern for a "fair" trial and for the position of the "accused" is out of place in legislative halls, they would argue. We are not trying anyone; we can invoke no criminal penalities against anyone, save to compel testimony or to initiate proceedings against perjury. The labeling of individuals as subversive, the identification of them with unpopular and unorthodox opinions, or the recounting of their youthful indiscretions, argue those who are concerned for the witnesses, is or may be more damaging to them individually and socially than conviction of a crime. Their reputations can be placed under a cloud and their employment prospects seriously curtailed. Under these circumstances, say the critics, a more judicial attitude ought to be introduced and rules of procedures adopted [47] which will prevent hearsay evidence, which will allow a person to confront and question those who assail him, and which will provide an opportunity for those who are attacked to appear and answer the attack. Several committees (really subcommittees conducting inquiries) have actually modified their rules to take account of these criticisms. Despite the urging of several Senators and the unanimous recommendation in 1955 of the Subcommittee on Rules, the Senate has not as yet seen fit to adopt any general code of this type for all of its committees. The House of Representatives, however, early in 1955 amended its rules to provide more uniform procedures for its investigating committees, to abolish one-man hearings, and to afford greater protection for individuals called to testify. The Rules Committee of the House since 1955 has also been reviewing projected investigations.

c. Fair procedures for witnesses

The fourth problem relates to the extraction of testimony from unwilling witnesses. Persons from whom information is sought are not always disposed to cooperate. Gradually, however, the Congress, with the support of the judi-

d. Compulsion of testimony from private citizens

Walter subsequently acknowledged his error. Shortly after Speaker Rayburn's death in 1961 and before the selection of a new speaker, another hearing was televised in Boston.

[47] For proposed codes for the conduct of committee hearings, see L. Rogers, "Congressional Investigations; The Problem and Its Solution," 18 *University of Chicago Law Review,* 464 (1951); R. K. Carr, "How to Improve Congressional Inquiries," *New York Times Magazine* (August 29, 1948), 5; G. Galloway, "Congressional Investigations: Proposed Reforms," 18 *University of Chicago Law Review,* 478 (1951).

ciary, has gathered authority to employ compulsion. Any duly constituted committee now has power to subpoena witnesses and administer oaths, to require the production of books, papers, correspondence, contracts, or other records deemed relevant, and to invoke judicial aid, if necessary, to obtain them. Persons refusing to answer questions properly put to them or refusing to produce records or papers may be cited by either house for "contempt of Congress." During the period 1945-64, for example, 270 persons were cited for contempt, 160 of them witnesses before the House Un-American Activities Committee.[48] Testimony before Congressional committees may lead to prosecution by the Department of Justice for perjury as well as for contempt. The celebrated case of Alger Hiss, former official of the Department of State, convicted of perjury arising out of testimony before the House Un-American Activities Committee, is an example of this type of action.[49]

With more and more frequency, witnesses before Congressional committees have been claiming the protection of the Fifth Amendment and refusing to respond to questions which, if answered, they plead, might tend to incriminate them.[50] So frequently has this plea been raised that Congress in 1954 enacted a law granting to its committees the authority to grant immunity from prosecution to a reluctant witness to compel him to testify. This law requires, however, the notification of the attorney general and the approval of a District Court and also stipulates that such grant must be requested by a two-thirds vote of the full committee membership.[51]

e. Compulsion of testimony from public officials

Thus far our discussion has centered about the problem of obtaining information from a balky or uncooperative private individual. A very different kind of problem arises out of the various attempts by committees of Congress to obtain papers and documents or testimony from the executive agencies or officials of the government. On the one hand, there is no doubt about the

[48] Fewer than half of these were ultimately found guilty by the courts. If found guilty, a person cited for contempt may be fined $100 and required to serve one year in jail. For a review of the law, see C. Beck, *Contempt of Congress* (New Orleans, La., 1959).

[49] Owen Lattimore, professor at Johns Hopkins University, was also prosecuted by the Department of Justice for perjury arising from testimony before a Senate committee. The District Court before which the charges were presented dismissed most of the indictments as "too vague." After a second effort failed, the Department of Justice announced in 1955 it had abandoned efforts to convict Lattimore.

[50] The courts have held that a person may refuse to answer the question of whether he or she is a member of the Communist party. The act of Congress which makes it illegal to advocate the forceful overthrow of the government and the decision of the Supreme Court upholding a lower court conviction of Communists for such advocacy justify the fear of the incriminating character of such an admission. Blau *v.* United States, 340 U. S. 159 (1950) and United States *v.* Bryan, 339 U. S. 323 (1950). This accounts for the failure of the Department of Justice to obtain conviction in many of the contempt cases.

[51] It should be noted that Congress can now grant immunity from state prosecution under certain circumstances.

This law was upheld by the Supreme Court in 1956—Ullman *v.* United States, 350 U. S. 422.

constitutional right of Congress to inform itself on the conduct of the executive branch. On the other hand, Presidents, beginning with Washington, have regarded themselves as entitled to refuse to open their personal files for Congressional inspection and even to throw the cloak of immunity around any department or agency if they believed that the public interest would be served by so doing. Thus far, at least, the President has successfully asserted the powers claimed. Jefferson disregarded a subpoena of Chief Justice Marshall in connection with the trial of Aaron Burr and refused to allow executive officials to testify. Several times during World War II, Congressional requests for information from the FBI were refused with Presidential approval. President Truman denied to Congress access not only to FBI files, but to the personal loyalty-investigation files of the executive departments. A special committee appointed by the Senate in 1953 to review the personal files of Ambassador Bohlen in connection with his confirmation, confined its review to a summary or digest of the FBI files prepared by the agency. The Chairman of the House Committee on Un-American Activities attempted to subpoena ex-President Truman in 1953. Mr. Truman refused to recognize the committee's power and the matter was not pushed. President Kennedy in 1962 ordered Secretary of Defense McNamara not to disclose to a Senate committee the names of those in his department who reviewed and censored particular speeches by military personnel. The legal rights of the two branches have never been fully adjudicated. The Congress has in every case stopped short of citing for contempt any official who has refused on executive order to honor a subpoena. The net legislative result of a prolonged inquiry in 1958 into government secrecy by a House Special Subcommittee on Government Information was the amendment of an ancient statute conferring power on department heads to control the custody, use, and preservation of records. The amendment simply declared that the act of 1789 could not be cited as authorization for withholding information.[52]

THE NONLEGISLATIVE FUNCTIONS OF CONGRESS

Enacting laws, while perhaps the most important, is not the sole function of the Congress of the United States. Several other important tasks make heavy demands on the time and energy of our lawmakers. The several nonlegislative functions reveal the extent to which the framers of our Constitution departed from any rigid theory of separation of powers but rather linked the various organs of government together in such a way that they cannot easily be fit into the categories of power recognized in theoretical political science.

We have in earlier chapters referred to the essential role of Congress in amending the Constitution and to the part it plays in electing the President and

1. Constituent

[52] A good statement of the issues and problems involved may be found in F. D. Rourke, "Administrative Secrecy: A Congressional Dilemma," *Amer. Pol. Sci. Rev.* LIV, No. 3 (Sept., 1960).

2. Elec-
toral

3. Execu-
tive

4. Judicial

a. Im-
peachment

Vice-President. We shall in a later chapter discuss the executive functions of treaty-making and appointments which the Senate shares with the President. It is appropriate here, however, to enlarge upon the judicial function of removal of civil officers.

In order to furnish the legislative branch with a shield to protect itself and the people against treasonable and criminal officials who might by some mischance make their way into the highest offices of the nation, the framers endowed the Representatives with the historic power of impeachment and the Senators with the power to try those thus accused. The House of Commons had for some centuries exercised the power of impeachment and, while it had fallen into disuse during the Tudor period, it had been revived under the Stuarts and was a potent weapon in the Parliament's struggle with the Crown. Under the Constitution, the President, Vice-President, and all civil [53] officers of the United States are made subject to impeachment and removal. The grounds upon which such action may validly be taken are restricted, however, to grave criminal offenses. This is not a procedure to be invoked because of political disagreements, incompetence, or unethical conduct. Any member or group of members of the House of Representatives may prefer charges against an official. These are referred either to the Judiciary Committee or to a special investigating committee. The committee reports its findings to the House; and, if the majority votes to impeach, "articles of impeachment" setting forth the grounds for removal are drafted. Managers are appointed to represent the House in presenting the case against the official in the Senate.

b. Trial

The Senate has no choice, once the procedure has gone this far, but to hear the case. A day is appointed for the hearing, the accused is furnished with the articles upon which he is to be tried, and when the appointed time arrives the Senate converts itself into a court to determine the fate of the accused. The chief justice of the United States presides over the trial of a President. For all other officials the regular presiding officer of the Senate directs the proceedings. The accused is allowed counsel, and testimony, his as well as that of witnesses for or against him, may be heard. At the close of the case, the Senate votes on the charges. A two-thirds vote is necessary for conviction. Anything short of this is acquittal. The penalty is removal from office, to which may be added disqualification forever in the future from holding "any office of honor, trust, or profit under the United States." Once removed from office, the individual may be tried and convicted in an ordinary court if he has committed an indictable offense. The President's pardoning power does not extend to Senatorial removals in impeachment procedure.

Whatever may have been the experience of our English ancestors, the impeachment and removal powers of Congress have not proved very formidable in dealing with the executive branch. Only 12 officers, most of these judges,

---

[53] Civil officers do not include military officers or legislators. The latter are not considered "officers" in the constitutional sense.

have been impeached in our national history and only four of these convicted.[54] President Johnson, however, escaped removal by a single vote. The difficulty with the impeachment process is that it is designed only for grave offenses, and few of our national officials, happily, have been flagrant offenders against the laws of the land.

Although the immediate direction of and the major responsibility for the conduct of the huge administrative organization of the national government rests with the President, Congress participates in both direction and supervision. It creates most of the agencies of administration and authorizes those it does not create directly. It specifies in more or less detail how these agencies are to be organized, defines their powers and functions, prescribes many of the procedures by which they operate, fixes objectives and standards for them, and provides the money for carrying on their activities. All of this necessarily involves the Congress in continuous concern for the way in which the agencies perform. It receives from them a large volume of annual and special reports and, typically at budget sessions, hears the principal officers of each agency explain and defend the conduct of their organizations. Congressional admonitions and exhortations are frequently addressed to officials and agencies, occasionally by resolution, commonly by verbal exchanges at hearings, sometimes by the curtailment of function, and, on occasion, by the complete deprivation of funds.[55] The inability of Congress to devote the time and energy to this great task that its effective performance requires has led on the one hand to repeated pleas that the President be given greater authority to rearrange the organizational structure of the national administration and on the other that Congressional standing committees exercise greater vigilance over the enforcement of programs falling in their respective jurisdictions. The tremendous growth of recent decades in the size and complexity of the administrative machinery of the national government has not been accompanied by changes in Congressional processes or outlook corresponding to the magnitude of the task.

5. Directive and supervisory

Of all of the nonlegislative functions of the Congress none is more burdensome nor more time-consuming than the function of representing individuals and groups before the government at Washington and informing them about its operations. Every day brings to each Congressman scores of letters, dozens of phone calls and telegrams, and several callers from the home district or state. Many, perhaps most, Congressmen spend more working time running

6. Representing constituents before the executive branch

[54] The cases involving judges are discussed in the chapter on the Judiciary; the others involved Senator William Blount (1798), President Andrew Johnson (1868), and Secretary of War William W. Belknap (1876). Secretary Belknap sought to evade impeachment proceedings by resigning his office, but the Senate was not thus deterred from hearing the case.

[55] It was in this way, for example, that two important depression-time agencies—the Civilian Conservation Corps and the National Youth Administration—were brought to an end in 1943 and 1944, respectively; also the National Resources Planning Board in 1943.

errands for their constituents, explaining the meaning of governmental requirements or policies to them, and adjusting conflicting interests between constituents and administrative agencies than they do in discharging their legislative responsibilities. As our government has grown larger, more complex, and more pervasive, this part of a Congressman's job has become more demanding. Many lawmakers complain bitterly that they are unable to grapple intelligently with the great and forbidding questions of our times because they have to give so much of their energy to this "errand boy" work.

The demands upon a member of Congress for special and benevolent intercession with the executive agencies are numerous indeed. In a small portion of the cases they are highly improper. Although most are routine requests for information or pleas of unnecessary hardship, some are for undeserved privileges or favors. Few Congressmen are in a position fairly to weigh the merits of the petitioner's claims and equitable administrative behavior is not well served by the sporadic and irresponsible intervention of legislators. Every administrative agency of any size has to maintain a sizable staff just to process Congressional inquiries. Congressmen, furthermore, are in a position to punish by deprivation of funds administrative indifference or resistance to their importunings. On the credit side it may be observed that Congressmen act on these matters as humanizers of the vast impersonal machinery of government. If some of them ask for favors that are undeserved, all of them do much to obtain favorable acceptance of administrative activities by explaining to their people the need for the rules or regulations under which they are fretting. The representative duties of Congressmen also have a healthy influence on administrative behavior, bringing to the attention of top executives callous, arbitrary, or capricious decisions by their subordinates and revealing the sources and character of popular discontent with their agencies. The legislative activities of the Congress are strengthened by the revelations of defects in existing programs which come in a Congressman's mail. The typical Congressman feels that he can neglect this function only if he is willing to give up his chances of re-election.[56]

References

J. P. Chamberlain, *Legislative Processes; National and State* (New York, 1936), Chaps. VI-IX, XIII.

H. Walker, *The Legislative Process* (New York, 1948), Chaps. X, XII-XVII.

F. M. Riddick, *The United States Congress; Organization and Procedure* (Washington, 1949), Chaps. IX-XI.

[56] See C. L. Clapp, *The Congressman: His Work as He Sees It* (Washington, 1963), Chap. II for a discussion of this problem from the point of view of a representative.

D. Acheson, *A Citizen Looks at Congress* (New York, 1957).

J. M. Burns, *Congress on Trial; The Legislative Process and the Administrative State* (New York, 1949), Chaps. IV-V.

G. B. Galloway, *Congress at the Crossroads* (New York, 1946), Chaps. VI-VIII.

———, *Limitation of Debate in the United States Senate* (Washington, 1948).

———, *The Legislative Process in Congress* (New York, 1953).

———, *Congressional Reorganization Revisited* (College Park, Md., 1956).

———, *History of the House of Representatives* (New York, 1962), 11-28.

J. C. Wahlke, H. Eulau, W. Buchanan, and L. C. Ferguson, *The Legislative System: Explorations in Legislative Behavior* (New York, 1962).

B. D. Gross, *The Legislative Struggle* (New York, 1953).

W. Wilson, *Congressional Government* (Boston, 1885), Chaps. II-IV.

R. Luce, *Congress—An Explanation* (Cambridge, Mass., 1926), Chaps. IV-V.

———, *Legislative Procedure* (Boston, 1922).

G. H. Haynes, *The Senate of the United States; Its History and Practice,* 2 vols. (Boston, 1938).

J. Q. Tilson, *Parliamentary Law and Procedure* (Washington, 1935).

R. Young, *The American Congress* (New York, 1958).

T. V. Smith, *The Legislative Way of Life* (Chicago, 1940).

J. Voorhis, *Confessions of a Congressman* (Garden City, N.Y., 1947). A vivid account of 10 years' service in the House of Representatives.

S. K. Bailey, *Congress Makes a Law: The Story Behind the Employment Act of 1946* (New York, 1949).

W. J. Keefe and M. S. Ogul, *The American Legislative Process: Congress and the States* (Englewood Cliffs, N.J., 1964).

D. Berman, *In Congress Assembled: The Legislative Process in the National Government* (New York, 1965).

A. W. Macmahon, "Congressional Oversight of Administration; The Power of the Purse," *Polit. Sci. Quar.,* LVIII, 161-190, 380-414 (June and Sept. 1943).

M. N. McGeary, *The Development of Congressional Investigative Power* (New York, 1940).

———, "The Congressional Power of Investigation," *Neb. Law Rev.,* XXVIII, 516-529 (May, 1949).

"The 150th Anniversary of the U. S. Congress" (Symposium), *Cong. Digest,* XVIII, 97-128 (Apr., 1939).

S. Scher, "Congressional Committee Members as Independent Agency Overseers: A Case Study," *Amer. Pol. Sci. Rev.,* LIV, No. 4 (Dec., 1960).

M. E. Dimock, "Congressional Investigating Committees," *Johns Hopkins Univ. Studies in Hist. and Polit. Sci.,* XLVII, 1-182 (1929).

P. Wittenburg, ed., *The Lamont Case: History of a Congressional Investigation* (New York, 1957).

T. W. Cousens, "The Delegation of Federal Legislative Power to Executive Officials," *Mich. Law Rev.*, XXXIII, 512-544 (Feb., 1935).

L. L. Jaffee, "An Essay on Delegation of Legislative Power," *Columbia Law Rev.*, XLVII, 359-376, 561-593 (Apr. and May, 1947).

A. Simpson, Jr., *A Treatise on Federal Impeachments* (New York, 1917).

————, "Federal Impeachments," *Univ. of Pa. Law Rev.* LXIV, 651-695, 803-830 (May and June, 1916).

Extracts from the Journal of the U. S. Senate in All Cases of Impeachment—1789-1904, 62nd Cong., 2nd Sess., Sen. Doc. No. 876 (1912).

A. C. McCown, *The Congressional Conference Committee* (New York, 1927).

F. L. Burdette, *Filibustering in the Senate* (Princeton, N.J., 1940).

————, *Lobbyists in Action* (Washington, 1950).

D. C. Blaisdell, *Government Under Pressure*, Pub. Affairs Pamphlets, No. 67 (New York, 1942).

S. Chase, *Democracy Under Pressure: Special Interests vs. the Public Welfare* (New York, 1945).

K. Schriftgiesser, *The Lobbyists* (New York, 1951).

R. Heller, *Strengthening the Congress* (Washington, 1945).

B. Zeller, "The Federal Regulation of Lobbying Act," *Amer. Polit. Sci. Rev.*, XLII, 239-271 (Apr., 1948).

"Economic Power and Political Pressure," Temporary National Economic Committee Monograph No. 26 (Washington, 1941).

Committee on Congress, American Political Science Association, *The Reorganization of Congress* (Washington, 1945).

Joint Committee on the Organization of Congress, *Organization of the Congress*, 79th Cong., 2nd Sess., Sen. Rep. No. 1011 (1946).

J. P. Harris, "The Reorganization of Congress," *Pub. Admin. Rev.*, VI, 267-282 (Summer, 1946). Discounts and criticizes the Legislative Reorganization Act of 1946.

E. D. Thomas, "How Congress Functions Under Its Reorganization Act," *Amer. Polit. Sci. Rev.*, XLIII, 1179-1189 (Dec., 1949).

L. W. Milbrath, *The Washington Lobbyists* (Chicago, 1963).

C. L. Clapp, *The Congressman: His Work as He Sees It* (Washington, 1963).

N. C. Thomas and K. A. Laub, *Congress: Politics and Practice* (New York, 1964).

D. R. Matthews, *U. S. Senators and Their World* (New York, 1960).

J. A. Robinson, *The House Rules Committee* (New York, 1963).

L. A. Froman, Jr., *Congressmen and Their Constituencies* (Chicago, 1963).

D. B. Truman (ed.), *The Congress and America's Future* (Englewood Cliffs, N.J., 1965).

R. L. Peabody and N. W. Polsby (ed.), *New Perspectives on the House of Representatives* (Chicago, 1963).

D. H. Riddle, *The Truman Committee: A Study in Congressional Responsibility* (New Brunswick, N.J., 1964).

Congressional Record. Published daily during sessions by the Government Printing Office at Washington (obtainable through members of Congress or by subscription through the Superintendent of Documents).

Congressional Quarterly Service, *Weekly Report* (Washington). Published since 1945 and presenting very comprehensive and trustworthy information on all aspects of the session.

———, *Congress and the Nation; 1945-1964* (Washington, 1965). See especially Chap. 1, 11, 14, and 17.

———, *Special Report: Congressional Reform* (Washington, 1963).

★ 12 ★

The President and Congress

THE MOST STRIKING DIFFERENCE between the government of the United States and that of most other democratic nations in the world is the relation between the executive and the legislature. In the parliamentary democracies (Britain, Canada, Italy, Sweden, etc.) the executive is inseparably yoked to the legislature. Prolonged disagreement or conflict between the two is impossible. The ministry or cabinet is drawn entirely or very largely from the legislature and remains in possession of the effective executive authority only so long as it commands the confidence of that body. Substantial disagreement results either in a new ministry or a new legislature. The parliamentary system is intentionally designed to guarantee harmony of the two central agencies of democratic government and to fix responsibility for the conduct of the government clearly and firmly upon the majority party if there is one or on a coalition of parties. The American Presidential system, on the other hand, with its independently elected executive serving a fixed term and without power to dissolve the legislature, deliberately creates a gulf between the two branches, disperses responsibility for the conduct of national affairs and invites, if it does not encourage, mutual antagonism and the need for accommodation. The American system suffers under these disadvantages in their most acute form when, as on numerous occasions in our history, the Congress has come under the domination of a party or a faction espousing a program quite at variance with that of the President or his party. Many students of comparative democratic institutions have, for these reasons, urged the greater merit of the parliamentary system. The parliamentary system, on the other hand, suffers from a weak and unstable executive when no party is able to capture a clear majority. France and Germany have consequently felt it desirable to strengthen their elected presidents and have made them independent of a transient parliamentary majority. Democracies established in the world since 1787 have not made their executives quite as independent of the legislatures as does the American system. Many American students and statesmen, past and present, have recommended the adoption in this country of those features of the parliamentary system which tend to promote harmony between the executive and the legislature and to fix responsibility for public policy more clearly on the majority party.

The framers of the American Constitution would have made little sense out of the arguments of the twentieth century on the proper legislative role of *Develop-* the President. Steeped in the theories of Locke and Montesquieu, familiar *ment of* with the colonial and state experience of gubernatorial-legislative dealings, *Presidency* frightened by the excesses of the state legislatures, these statesmen contrived a chief magistracy which they hoped would be above the factionalism of Rep- *1. The* resentatives and equipped to deal firmly with their ambitions. The modern *view of* form of cabinet responsibility to the parliament had not yet clearly emerged *framers* even in the British constitution. Parties in their modern form were unknown, and factional politics, the eighteenth-century equivalent of modern party politics, was reprehended. It was not executive domination or direction of the legislature that the framers anticipated, but legislative domination of the executive.

For a few years after the establishment of the national government it *2. Wash-* seemed as if the relations between executive and Congress would evolve in *ington to* about the same way as in England, where the modern cabinet system was tak- *Jackson* ing shape. Alexander Hamilton, from his post as Secretary of the Treasury, strove skillfully to make himself first minister, Washington a sort of constitutional monarch, and the Congress a reviewing body for policies and measures formulated by the Cabinet. This development was halted by the emergence of organized political parties. Hamilton's opponents rallied around Jefferson and Madison and, operating from the Congress, asserted the independence of the legislative branch and eventually wrested control even of the executive away from the Hamilton group. Jefferson as President maintained the appearance of legislative autonomy, although achieving executive direction in fact by intrigue and manipulation of his partisans in the Congress. When the Presidency came into less skillful hands, Presidential initiative in legislation subsided. Congressional dominance of policy formulation was strengthened also by the assumption by the legislature of practical control over the selection of the chief executive.

The development of the modern Presidency begins with the Jacksonian *3. Jackson* era in which was swept away legislative control of Presidential nominations *to* and out of which emerged the modern nominating convention. This action *Johnson* removed the last obstacle to genuinely popular selection of our chief magistrate. The Jeffersonians and Federalists had already stultified the electoral college system by their organization of broadly national political parties. The election of the President by popular and partisan processes paved the way for his emergence as a "tribune of the people" and encouraged him to assert his position as representative of the whole people against the sectional and local Representatives of the Congress. Almost a century, however, was required to realize the contemporary Presidential position. The pull toward Presidential leadership in the field of legislation, although erratic in force, has been persistent in direction. Chief executives learned that they and they alone were held accountable for the redemption of campaign pledges and for the realization in public policy of the programs to which they and their party had committed themselves. The fulfillment of these responsibilities demanded that the chief executive attempt to influence the Congress. Although Congress had meanwhile developed its own institutions of leadership, none of these sufficed to overcome its sectional and centrifugal tendencies. None of its institutional arrangements, further, achieved real coordination of the two houses. Furthermore, its preference for seniority as the major determinant of leadership tended to increase the likelihood that its leaders could not rightly interpret the will of the nation. As Woodrow Wilson wrote in 1908: [1]

> The nation as a whole has chosen him [the President], and is conscious that it has no other political spokesman. His is the only national voice in affairs. Let him once win the admiration and confidence of the country, and no other single force can withstand him, no combination of forces will easily overpower him. His position takes the imagination of the country. He is the representative of no constituency, but of the whole people. When he speaks in his true character, he speaks for no special interest. If he rightly interprets the national thought and boldly insists upon it, he is irresistible, and the country never feels the zest of action so much as when its President is of such insight and caliber. Its instinct is for unified action, and it craves a single leader.

Wilson's views remind us that the White House has also been occupied in this century by Theodore and Franklin Roosevelt, both of whom interpreted their responsibilities as did Wilson. All three of these men left an indelible impression on the office of President of the United States. To theirs must be joined the names of Abraham Lincoln and Grover Cleveland who, in their own ways and in an earlier age, added to the groundwork laid down by Andrew Jackson. Today, national policy as expressed in legislation is a joint product of President and Congress. The chief executive has become also chief legislator.

Criticism of the modern Presidency   The historical tendencies which produced the legislative position of the modern president have not been universally admired. Plenty of people now and in the past have not liked what was happening. The charge of dictator has been hurled at every one of the Presidents who sought to direct the legislative process. And it certainly must be admitted that, whatever view the framers may have taken of the ultimate position of the President, there is little in the Constitution that foreshadows his contemporary role. Experience confirms also the view that much of what has been said about the President's legislative position depends, in fact, on the personality and ability of the individual who occupies the office. Presidents have achieved influence over the legislative process when they were able as well as willing to do so. Presidents have varied also in the vigor with which they have sought Congressional support. Several Presidents since Jackson have been content to defer to the Congress. There is a partisan complexion to this debate. Since the Civil War,

[1] *Constitutional Government in the United States* (New York, 1908), 68.

the Republican Party seems to have preferred for the highest office men who were likely to respect the prerogatives and autonomy of the Congress. The Democrats have tended to support avowed protagonists of the view that it is the duty of the President by every fair means to influence, if not to direct, the legislative process.

It seems clear that the relations between the President and Congress have not achieved their final form. The balance between the two is shifting and unstable and subject to the accidents of personality. The trend toward executive leadership in legislation has been persistent and unmistakable, but it has been achieved largely outside the formal constitutional arrangements and at the expense of traditional conceptions of separation of powers and checks and balances. American constitutional democracy has yet to resolve the problems of achieving proper coordination between these two great branches of our government.

Executive-legislative relations not finally fixed

CONSTITUTIONAL BASIS OF THE PRESIDENT'S LEGISLATIVE ROLE

He shall from time to time give to the Congress information of the state of the Union, and recommend to their consideration such measures as he shall judge necessary and expedient; he may on extraordinary occasions, convene both houses, or either of them, and in case of disagreement between them, with respect to the time of adjournment, he may adjourn them to such time as he shall think proper. . . . ART. II, Sec. 3

The Congress and the President, although constitutionally separated, are not completely isolated one from the other. Despite the general injunction that "all legislative powers" are vested in the Congress, the President is expressly assigned several important powers and responsibilities in connection with the formulation and enactment of legislation.

The Constitution confers a modest and relatively inconsequential power on the President to control the sessions of the national legislature. The power to adjourn sessions in case of disagreement has never been exercised and the power to call either or both houses into "extraordinary" or "special" session is rapidly falling into disuse. Prior to 1933, when the regular session of Congress ended on March 4 and a President inaugurated at that time would have to wait until the following December for the next regular session, it was not unusual for the President to call special sessions of the Congress to consider his proposals and particularly to call the Senate into such sessions to act upon his appointments. The Twentieth Amendment, however, obviated the need for such sessions by changing the Congressional calendar so that the Congress would be in session ready to receive the program and to act upon the appointments of a newly-elected chief executive. Almost the only present need for a special session would be a serious domestic or international crisis requiring

1. Control over sessions of Congress

immediate legislative action and arising in the fall or early winter after mid-
summer adjournment of a regular session.

2. Mes-
sages
to the
Congress:

The constitutional directive to the President to inform the Congress on
the state of the nation and to recommend measures for its consideration is a
duty rather than a power, but it has proved over the years to be of some consequence in influencing legislative behavior. The time, place, and manner of
fulfilling this responsibility is, of course, discretionary with each President. It
long ago became customary, however, for the President to transmit at the
opening of each session of Congress a comprehensive statement of his views
on all matters requiring legislative attention and on the kind of legislation
which it ought to enact to meet each situation. Washington and John Adams
appeared personally before joint sessions of the two houses to deliver their
important messages. This practice, abandoned by Jefferson and his successors,

a. "State
of the
Union"
message

was revived by Woodrow Wilson, and since Franklin Roosevelt has become
standard procedure. The increasing utilization of radio and television broadcasting in our political life has enhanced the importance of these annual addresses. Today the "State of the Union" message of the President is an address
to the people of America and of the world as well as to the Congress of the
United States. It is a solemn occasion of state, and modern Presidents have
grasped the advantages that the spectacle offers for dramatizing their aims and
policies. This appeal to the people is, in fact, a procedure of increasing usefulness and importance in gaining Congressional sympathy and support for the
President's recommendations. The changing tone of the messages reflects these
developments: as presented in 1900 the messages were collections of proposals
from the various departments strung together with conjunctions; today they
are carefully written to emphasize one or more themes and are likely to contain fewer but more significant suggestions.

b. Other
messages

In recent times the State of the Union message is followed in quick
succession by the President's Annual Budget message—required by the Budget
and Accounting Act of 1921—and by the Economic Report of the President—
required by the Employment Act of 1946. Both of these messages, probably
because of the statistical character of their contents, are invariably delivered
in writing rather than in person. In such cases, the messages are actually
read (usually in a monotone) to the houses by their clerks and consequently
do not capture national attention in anything like the degree that those delivered in person do. In addition to these, every modern President has sent
numerous special messages to Congress at various times in any session. Ordinarily, these deal each with some special subject and are designed and timed
to push some item on the President's legislative agenda a little nearer final
passage. Sometimes these messages accompany reports embodying extensive
investigations or studies by or on behalf of the executive branch. On unusual
occasions the President will deliver a special message in person. This is especially true if the subject is of overwhelming importance or if the need for
immediate Congressional action is imperative. President Eisenhower, for ex-

ample, delivered in person in 1957 his message on the troubled situation in the Near East even before his annual message. Presidents Eisenhower and Kennedy on occasion delivered in person mid-session reviews of legislative progress.

The effect of the messages of the President upon national legislation is hard to measure. Congress is under no legal obligation to follow the President's lead. It is free to act or not to act and, if it acts, to act in accord with or directly opposite to the President's stated wishes. The objective of the President himself is not always immediate legislative action in the form suggested. He may be using the message to stimulate public interest without desiring immediate action. He may, in fact, be willing to accept a more moderate form of action than he has outlined. He may be warning a foreign nation of possible American reaction to its prospective behavior. He may be interpreting or summarizing American views for the benefit of the rest of the world or of some important part of it. Whether the President succeeds in any or all of his stated or intended purposes depends on a number of factors unrelated to the messages. The constitutional duty to inform the Congress of his views has become an opportunity to convince both Congress and people of his wise leadership, but we must continue our analysis of the relations between President and Congress if we are to discover how or why he succeeds or fails in getting the Congress to adopt his suggestions.

Effects of the messages

The Constitution directs the President to recommend specific measures for the consideration of the Congress. This might be construed as an invitation to the President to assume leadership of the legislative process. Not all of our chief magistrates have so regarded it, however, and the pattern of executive leadership established by Washington through Hamilton and by Jefferson was followed only by Jackson, Polk, Lincoln, and Cleveland in the last century and not completely even by them. In this century, however, Theodore Roosevelt, Woodrow Wilson, Franklin Roosevelt, Harry Truman, John Kennedy and Lyndon Johnson have all aspired energetically to enhance the influence of the Presidency. A large proportion of the major bills which crowd the calendars of a modern Congress originate in the executive branch. More and more commonly, messages are accompanied by or are shortly followed by bills designed exactly to achieve the President's desires. Although the Congress freely edits, amends, and modifies these measures, nevertheless at final passage many of them still carry numerous marks of their origin. It may be pleaded that this has been, thus far, a century of crises calling forth unusual Presidential energies and that when more "normal" times return Presidential initiative will subside. However this may be, our chief executives now believe that they are expected to devote their major energies to devising the laws which Congress ought to pass and then trying to get Congress to pass them. When the time for a public reckoning occurs, every modern President has been anxious to exhibit an impressive record of legislative achievement.

3. Proposal of legislative measures

Among the many areas of Congressional concern, the national finances

bring the President and Congress into the most intimate and mutually dependent relations. The Congress has never developed an effective agency of its own
for attaining cooperation between the two houses or for formulating fiscal
policy for the government as a whole. It has come, therefore, to depend almost
entirely upon the initiative of the President in this field, typified by the annual
budget message.

THE VETO POWER

Every bill which shall have passed the House of Representatives and the
Senate shall, before it becomes a law, be presented to the President of the
United States; if he approves he shall sign it, but if not he shall return it, with
his objections, to that house in which it shall have originated, who shall enter
the objections at large on their journal and proceed to reconsider it. If after
such reconsideration two thirds of that house shall agree to pass the bill, it
shall be sent, together with the objections, to the other house, by which it
shall likewise be reconsidered, and if approved by two thirds of that house
it shall become a law. But in all such cases the votes of both houses shall be
determined by yeas and nays, and the names of the persons voting for and
against the bill shall be entered on the journal of each house respectively.
If any bill shall not be returned by the President within ten days (Sundays
excepted) after it shall have been presented to him, the same shall be a law,
in like manner as if he had signed it, unless the Congress by their adjournment prevent its return, in which case it shall not be a law.

Every order, resolution, or vote to which the concurrence of the Senate and
House of Representatives may be necessary (except on a question of adjournment) shall be presented to the President of the United States; and before the
same shall take effect, shall be approved by him, or being disapproved by
him, shall be repassed by two thirds of the Senate and House of Representatives, according to the rules and limitations prescribed in the case of a bill.
ART. I, Sec. 7

The veto   Largely as a reaction against the unrestrained concentration of power in
the legislatures of the revolutionary state governments, the authors of our
Constitution endowed the President with one of his most impressive legislative
powers: the power to veto bills and resolutions of the Congress. Although the
President must proceed indirectly by suggestion and innuendo to obtain the
approval of the Congress for what he wants, he is equipped to deal firmly and
forthrightly with what he does not want. Despite the broad language of the
constitutional grant, embracing as it does even resolutions and orders, the Congress through the years has carved out a small sphere of legislative authority
free from Presidential oversight by the use of the concurrent resolution de-

scribed in the previous chapter.[2] At the same time, the Congress has probably surrendered more than it needed to by its own dilatory and complex procedures which expose a large share of its measures (those passed in the last few days of a session) to the absolute veto provided in cases where adjournment prevents reconsideration by the Congress of a vetoed measure.

THE VETO

DISASTER RELIEF—VETO MESSAGE FROM THE PRESIDENT (S. DOC. NO. 34)

To The Senate of the United States:

I return herewith, without my approval S. 327, "To provide assistance to the States of California, Oregon, Washington, Nevada, and Idaho for the reconstruction of areas damaged by recent floods and high waters."

This bill authorizes additional funds and other special assistance to aid in the reconstruction and repair of damage caused in the Pacific Northwest by the devastating floods of last winter. I am in complete sympathy with the purpose of this legislation. However, in spite of the bill's general desirability, section 5 seriously violates the spirit of the division of powers between the legislative and executive branches. Despite my strong support for the substantive relief, I must withhold approval until this unwise and objectionable provision is deleted.

The provision is contained in that part of section 5(a) stipulating that:

The President, acting through the Office of Emergency Planning is authorized to perform all or any part of the recommended work determined to be in the public interest and to reimburse any common carrier for any of such recommended work performed by such carrier, but no appropriation shall be made for any such work which has not been approved before June 30, 1966, by resolution adopted by the Committees on Public Works of the Senate and House of Representatives, respectively.

The Attorney General advises me that this provision is clearly a "coming into agreement" with a congressional committee requirement. This device requires an executive official to obtain the approval of a

---

[2] Strict application of the language of the Constitution would undoubtedly be impossible since it seems to require every vote to be submitted for approval. A Senate committee in 1897 interpreted the clause to mean that the President's approval is necessary if the order, resolution, or vote is to have the force of law and that this meant only joint resolutions. It should be noted further that joint resolutions proposing amendments to the constitution are exempted from Presidential consideration. See Hollingsworth *v.* Virginia, 3 Dallas 378 (1798).

DISASTER RELIEF—VETO MESSAGE FROM THE PRESIDENT
(S. DOC. NO. 34)—Continued

To The Senate of the United States:

committee or other unit of Congress before taking an executive action. It is not only an undesirable and improper encroachment by the Congress and its committees into the area of executive responsibilities—it also leads to inefficient administration. The executive branch is given, by the Constitution, the responsibility to implement all laws—a specific and exclusive responsibility which cannot properly be shared with a committee of Congress.

The proper separation of powers and division of responsibilities between Congress and the executive branch is a matter of continuing concern to me. I must oppose the tendency to use any device to involve congressional committees in the administration of programs and the implementation of laws. I have spoken out against this before. Less than a year ago, in a signing statement on the Water Resources Research Act of 1964, I requested deletion of a provision much the same as the one in S. 327.

Although I am unable to approve S. 327 in its present form for the reasons stated, I am anxious that the relief to the States involved be made available as quickly as possible. Accordingly, I will approve S. 327 immediately when the Congress has eliminated the provision in section 5 which infringes upon the responsibilities of the executive branch. I see no reason why this cannot be accomplished in a few days and have directed the executive branch to cooperate fully with the Congress to this end.

LYNDON B. JOHNSON.

THE WHITE HOUSE, *June 5, 1965.*

SOURCE: *Congressional Record* (June 7, 1965), 12,216.

How the veto works

When confronted by a bill or joint resolution, the President may constitutionally take any of four courses of action. (1) He may sign it, and it then becomes a law. (2) He may hold it for the prescribed time (10 days) and, if Congress is still sitting, it will become law without his signature.[3] This is an unusual course for a President to adopt and it rarely occurs. But occasions have arisen when a President was unable or unwilling to make up his mind about a measure in the period. Some Presidents have also used this procedure

[3] The 10-day period allowed for Presidential consideration is reckoned from the time the bill is actually presented to the President regardless of the time that it in fact passed the second house of Congress. In 1959, Senator Keating (N. Y.) challenged the practice of not counting the 10 days until the bill is actually presented to the President. He asserted that the 10 days should run from the time the bill is sent to the White House. A suit making such a claim was unsuccessfully pushed in court. The Supreme Court refused in 1965 to review the matter.

when they disliked certain measures but felt that a veto would be useless or unwise politically. (3) If Congress should adjourn during the 10-day period, the President may by inaction veto the measure.[4] This "pocket veto" is absolute; it cannot be overridden by the Congress. Furthermore, it does not require the President to make any explanation of his disapproval. Although some Presidents, notably Franklin Roosevelt, have offered explanations of their decisions to the public or to the Congress, most Presidents have welcomed the opportunity offered by the pocket-veto procedure quietly to kill a measure without explanations which may be embarrassing politically. Many bills are halted on their path to the statute books by this procedure, as a result, especially, of the habit of Congress of passing a disproportionate number of its enactments during the closing days of the session. (4) The President may veto the bill outright and return it to the proper house of Congress with his statement of reasons for disapproval.[5] Such a course of action requires the Congress to reconsider its position on the measure in question and, if the required support of two-thirds of the members of each house can be mustered behind the measure, it may be repassed and become law without Presidential signature.

Hamilton in *The Federalist* [6] predicted that the veto would be employed cautiously and infrequently and that most Presidents would use it too little rather than too much. He proved a good prophet, especially for the period prior to 1865. Since that time the veto has been used with increasing frequency and vigor. Not until Andrew Johnson did a President resort to the veto in defense of his constitutional authority and on only a dozen occasions in our entire history has it been used for this purpose. The turbulent era of Reconstruction, accompanied as it was by bitter dissension between the President and Congress, witnessed the first really vigorous exercise of the veto power, if one excepts the administration of Andrew Jackson. Jackson, however, while he achieved a great deal of notoriety from his vetoes, actually vetoed only 12 acts of Congress during his eight years as chief executive. The number of vetoes in recent decades has averaged 15 to 25 a year. Grover Cleveland with 584, Franklin Roosevelt with 631, and Harry Truman with 250 account for more than three-fourths of all Presidential vetoes in the history of the nation.

More important than the increase in mere numbers of vetoes has been the change in Presidential attitude on the scope of the veto power. Until Jackson, the veto power was used not to express Presidential disapproval of the merit or wisdom of an enactment, but to question the constitutionality of

The use of the veto power:

1. Frequency

2. Scope

---

[4] For many years it was believed that a bill might not be signed after the Congress adjourned. President Wilson in 1920, however, with the support of his attorney general asserted his right to sign bills within the 10-day period even though Congress had adjourned and his action in so doing was unanimously upheld by the Supreme Court. Edwards *v.* United States, 286 U. S. 482 (1932).

[5] On one occasion (1935), a President (Roosevelt) appeared before a joint session of Congress and delivered his veto message personally. No other president before or since has elected to dramatize his differences with the Congress in quite this way.

[6] No. LXXIII (Lodge's ed.) 458.

THE USE OF THE VETO 1789-1965

President	Total Vetoes	Regular	Pocket	Vetoes Overridden
Washington	2	2	0	0
Madison	7	5	2	0
Monroe	1	1	0	0
Jackson	12	5	7	0
Tyler	10	6	4	1
Polk	3	2	1	0
Pierce	9	9	0	5
Buchanan	7	4	3	0
Lincoln	6	2	4	0
Johnson	28	21	7	15
Grant	92	44	48	4
Hayes	13	12	1	1
Arthur	12	4	8	1
Cleveland	414	304	110	2
Harrison, B.	44	19	25	1
Cleveland	170	42	128	5
McKinley	42	6	36	0
Roosevelt, T.	82	42	40	1
Taft	39	30	9	1
Wilson	44	33	11	6
Harding	6	5	1	0
Coolidge	50	20	30	4
Hoover	37	21	16	3
Roosevelt, F.	631	371	260	9
Truman	250	180	70	12
Eisenhower	181	79	102	2
Kennedy	25	14	11	0
Johnson	9	5	4	0

it or to halt it because of technical errors. Jackson, however, employed the veto to stifle measures which he felt were unwise, even though he conceded they were constitutional and were properly drawn.[7] Since 1865, our Presidents have

[7] He also claimed and exercised the right to veto bills which he thought unconstitutional notwithstanding that the Supreme Court had ruled to the contrary. The best illustration is the veto, in 1832, of the bill to renew the charter of the second United States Bank—a veto, however, like others of Jacksonian days and since, with a strong tinge of partisan politics. There can be no doubt that in his broader interpretation and use of the veto power Jackson was entirely within his rights. The Constitution says simply that if the President "approves" a bill he shall sign it, and if not he shall return it. "No better word," former President Taft once observed, "could be found in the language to embrace the idea of passing on the merits of the bill." *Our Chief Magistrate and His Powers* (New York, 1916), 16.

tended to follow Jackson rather than Washington, Jefferson, Polk, and the others. It is now generally conceded that the veto is properly used to express disapproval of any kind and to any degree of policy or legality, of technicality or of procedure, on major issues and on minor ones. President Eisenhower vetoed the Natural Gas Act of 1956, for example, because he did not like the lobbying activities accompanying its passage, although he approved of the substance of the bill. The result has been to make the President a more potent factor in legislation than he was during the greater part of the past century.

This should not be taken to mean that in recent decades the veto has been employed loosely and without adequate grounds. On the contrary, it is typically employed reluctantly and only after considerable reflection. It means that Presidents have come to rely more certainly on their own views of the needs and aspirations of the people. Furthermore, the output of the Congress has increased markedly in the past several decades and thus more bills and resolutions come under Presidential scrutiny. Many Presidential vetoes have been widely popular and few Presidents have suffered serious election reverses because of them. Furthermore, relatively few Presidential vetoes have been overturned by the Congress. Not until President Tyler's administration did any bill receive the necessary support to pass it over the President's objection. Presidents Truman and Andrew Johnson suffered more reversals of this kind than any other Presidents and they were overruled in only a small number of cases. In practice, therefore, even the regular veto tends to become very nearly absolute.

3. Influence

Periods of acute tension between the President and Congress have produced criticism of the Presidential veto. Some have proposed that the veto power be weakened by requiring only a simple majority to repass a vetoed measure and others have proposed strengthening the power by requiring the support of two-thirds of the entire membership, rather than of those present, to repass a measure over Presidential objection. Neither of these suggestions is currently receiving any serious attention. The most serious contemporary criticism of the veto power is that it does not extend to items or parts of bills, especially appropriation bills, but embraces only the whole measures. Most states have equipped their governors with item-veto power in reviewing appropriation measures in an effort to achieve more responsibility and sobriety in the spending of public funds. Their experience has commended this reform to many observers of and participants in the national scene. As matters stand, the President has no effective veto power over appropriations. Confronted with one of the major annual appropriation bills passed by the Congress, the President must accept it or risk exposing one whole program of public services to extinction for lack of funds. Since he has to have appropriation authority to conduct the government or any part of it, he ordinarily must accept whatever Congress sends to him. His discretion is reduced further by the fact that such bills ordinarily reach him quite late in the session, sometimes after Congress

Reform of the veto power

The item veto

has adjourned, and thus there is no opportunity to repass a necessary appropriation, even one more nearly in line with the President's desires. Congress is, therefore, free to add sums to the appropriations suggested by the President without on many occasions adding to the national tax program to meet the obligation thus incurred. In addition, the argument runs, Congress has repeatedly added sections to appropriation bills which dealt with other aspects of public policy or administration and which it knew the President would disapprove if presented to him in any other way. These "riders" have been condemned by almost every President as an attempt to evade the constitutional system of checks and balances. Presidents Franklin Roosevelt and Harry Truman both asked the Congress to grant to them the item veto possessed by most governors, largely on the grounds that they should be allowed to strike down these "riders."

Opposition to the item veto   The reasons offered by the opponents for their refusal to accede to Presidential requests have been: (1) That such a grant would add greatly to the President's legislative power, allowing him, for example, to discriminate among the appropriations to favor his friends and punish his enemies, and that the balance of power has already been tipped too far in the Presidential direction; (2) that experience in some states indicates that the effect of such a veto might well be to increase rather than to decrease legislative irresponsibility, that is, legislators would fall into the easy habit of pleasing everyone by voting extravagant sums, knowing that the executive would veto them, and thus transferring to him the onus for so doing; (3) that, in view of the fact that the President already has the power to recommend the budget, if he could veto Congressional additions to his suggested program, then Congress would be completely powerless in the field of national finance.

One of the difficulties in the debate over the Presidential item veto is the continuing disagreement among statesmen and scholars alike as to the best way to accomplish this reform. Some, including the two Presidents who recommended it, have held that an item veto could be conferred by the Congress by writing the pertinent language into each appropriation bill. Others, including several Senators, have held that a constitutional amendment is the only valid way to achieve the change. President Eisenhower in 1955 selected a novel way of handling the rider problem. He announced in signing a major appropriation bill that the department needed the funds but that he intended to ignore certain provisions of the bill which he held to be unconstitutional.[8] President Johnson followed the same procedure in signing a public works appropriation act in 1964 and another in 1965.[9] A final observation on the item-veto debate: it seems quite unlikely that the Congress would enact the appropriations in their present form if the President's veto power were extended to items. The proponents of an appropriation which might draw Presidential censure would

[8] See *New York Times,* July 14, 1955.
[9] *New York Times,* Jan. 1, 1964. *Weekly Compilation of Presidential Documents* (Nov. 1, 1965), p. 3.

certainly be sagacious enough to combine it with an item that the President could not or would not veto.

EXTRACONSTITUTIONAL DEVICES TO ACHIEVE PRESIDENTIAL INFLUENCE IN LEGISLATION

The role of the President as a lawmaker is by no means confined to the powers and duties specifically mentioned in the Constitution. If one is to gain a real appreciation of the power and influence of the American Presidency, it is necessary to consider the numerous practices devised by energetic Presidents outside the Constitution and now accepted parts of the repertoire of our chief magistrate.

Influence may be exerted not only by using the veto power but by threatening to use it. If a President allows Congressional leaders to believe that he will veto a particular measure if it is presented to him in the form contemplated, he may be able to achieve changes before final passage and thus influence the final form of the measure. By indicating that he will veto a given measure in any form, he may be able to prevent its passage and even its introduction. Theodore Roosevelt, in many respects the father of the modern Presidency, was the first President who admitted using this technique extensively and also the first to proclaim its use publicly. Although he was roundly abused by many for thus "vetoing" measures in advance, no one could or can argue that there is anything illegal about the procedure. Since Roosevelt, the threat of veto has become a familiar tool of Presidential intervention. No chief executive in modern times has employed it as extensively as Harry Truman. It is necessary to add that on several occasions, notably in the Truman era, the threat only succeeded in stiffening the resolution of the Congress to proceed on its intended course regardless of Presidential hostility. *1. Threat of veto*

Every president has at his disposal a very large number of favors which he may dispense to legislators and their friends and supporters. The discriminating distribution of these favors is perhaps the chief behind-the-scenes source of Presidential influence in Congress. These favors range from administrative benevolence toward certain interests in the home district of the Congressman to the appointment to national office of persons recommended by members of Congress. The distribution of public offices in this way is ordinarily referred to as "patronage," although in the broad sense the word may be used to embrace any type of favor granted for political or partisan advantage. Although the extension of the civil service merit system of appointment to the national public service has gradually reduced the number of positions which any President may fill by partisan methods, there are still several thousand posts which change occupants with each change in the political character of the national administration.[10] Virtually all of these positions require Senatorial confirma- *2. Use of patronage*

[10] *Congressional Quarterly Service Weekly Report,* Jun. 20, 1961, p. 80, estimated the number of posts available to the Kennedy administration potentially for patronage purposes at 6,000.

tion and it is this procedure which encourages Congressmen to urge the claims of their friends to posts in their own states or districts. By withholding such appointments from fellow partisans in Congress, the President is in a strong position to bargain for their support of his legislative policies. These matters are rarely handled by overt threats or definite bargains,[11] but members of Congress are rarely indifferent to the advantages which accompany the position of supporters of Presidential policies. We have the word of a former President that the control over legislation arising from the President's appointing power is great.[12] This particular extraconstitutional device is obviously most effective in the first months of a term of a new President. Once most of the posts are filled by a new administration the President's bargaining power is reduced. The fact that Presidents have typically experienced a declining influence on the Congress as their term has progressed partially reflects this. Presidents have customarily striven to get as much of their program as possible out of the first Congress that they deal with and before all of the job plums have been distributed. Jobs for friends, however, are only one kind of Presidential favor which can ease the political life of a legislator. In fact, they appear to be among the lesser rewards available to a "cooperative" Congressman. Public installations, defense contracts, special national programs are more important benefits bestowed by the modern executive branch. Furthermore, constituent pressure brings every member of Congress into daily communication with agencies of the executive branch. The Presidential blessing opens the doors of powerful administrators to Congressional importuning much more readily than might otherwise be the case. At any rate, a legislator who incurs outright executive hostility is likely to find many obstacles in the way of serving his and his constituents' interests the way he would like to serve them. A Congressman, on his own, has relatively few favors to bestow.

3. Personal conference and persuasion

Still another source of Presidential influence is personal conference. While it is true that in our system the President does not appear on the floor of either house of Congress or participate in the debate, this does not prevent him from achieving the same objective privately in consultation with members of the Congress. Every modern President's visiting list has contained the names of numerous legislators, and he has felt bound to spend a fair portion of his working hours persuading, cajoling, threatening, and pleading with legislators for support. From early in his first administration, Franklin Roosevelt made systematic use of a Monday morning conference with the leaders of his party in the Congress. This practice of a regular weekly session has been continued by his successors. At these meetings the President receives reports on the status of legislative business and of his measures in particular and indicates his wishes concerning the matters pending before the Congress. Presidents also call into conference the influential members of a committee which is consider-

---

[11] An historic case is President Cleveland's direct, open, and effective threat to withdraw patronage from Democratic Senators failing to support the repeal of the Sherman Silver Purchase Act in 1893.

[12] W. H. Taft, *Our Chief Magistrate and His Powers* (New York, 1916), 27.

ing one of their measures and by whatever arts of persuasion they can command try to get the committee to act favorably on their requests. It is not at all unusual for members of Congress during the course of debate to indicate that they have recently discussed the pending issue with the President and to indicate to their colleagues what the executive's views are. And these views, so reported, are likely to be influential.

The President does not have to carry the immense burden of dealing with Congress and Congressmen alone. He has under his direction what is sometimes called "the most powerful lobby in Washington." A large share of the work of persuading and of explaining administration policies and programs is, in fact, carried on by his subordinates in the executive departments and agencies. Virtually every one of these great organizations maintains close and continuing relations with the Congress. The secretaries, bureau chiefs, and other top administrators spend much time appearing before committees, conferring with party leaders, and interpreting their programs to individual members of the legislature. Each of the great departments and many of the independent agencies have a staff of officials who do little else than coordinate departmental or agency relations with the Congress. The President himself ordinarily assigns one of his own administrative assistants to keeping track of his dealings with the Congress, and in the Bureau of the Budget another group of officers undertakes to review all bills emanating from the executive branch and to screen out those not consistent with current Presidential policy. In the last decade, the President's chief legislative aide has exercised strong and continuing leadership over the chief legislative aides of the larger departments and agencies in an effort to achieve a coordinated approach to Congress from the executive branch. All of this activity is clearly indispensable to the effective operation of our national government but it is also widely criticized as an abuse of administrative discretion, especially when views are urged upon the Congress that the Congress or the critic is reluctant to adopt.

4. The "Presidential lobby"

None of the devices thus far described is probably quite so useful to the President as energetic and articulate public support. Members of Congress are most sensitive to the views of their constituents, and if the President is strong with the voters he is likely to be successful with the Congress. Realizing this, Presidents court public approval in every way they can. Some, of course, are much more adept at it than others. All have unequaled opportunities for publicity. We have noted how the messages and addresses to Congress are more and more commonly directed beyond the Congress to the people who support it. To these may be added the many addresses that Presidents are called upon to give on occasions of state and to various influential groups throughout the nation, the consultations which are held with influential leaders of opinion, letters addressed to private individuals but intended for public consumption, "fireside chats" on the radio, and carefully prepared television programs. All of these are and can be used to build and maintain a public opinion that Congress dare not ignore. The attention lavished on the President by newsmen is, perhaps, unequalled elsewhere in the world. His every movement and utterance

5. Cultivation of popular support

is reported. A crowd of reporters follow him wherever he goes and no aspect of his personal life escapes attention. Much of this is not by his design but the result is that his personality more fully dominates the news on public affairs than in any other nation in the world and his ability to use this publicity for constructive ends is unmatched by Congress.

"The White House," said Theodore Roosevelt, "is a bully pulpit." The "gospel" as there expounded is carried to the nation largely by means of the press, the radio and television. Special mention is therefore appropriate of the use of these media by the President to achieve the support he needs. The Presidential press conference is one of the most effecive contemporary devices of Presidential politics. The practice of meeting regularly with the representatives of the press and submitting to their direct questioning was initiated by Woodrow Wilson. He abandoned it for the prepared release when the United States entered World War I. President Harding revived it but became dissatisfied with the procedure and required the advance submission of all questions in writing. This practice reduced the publicity value of the conference but it was continued by Coolidge and Hoover. President Roosevelt cast the conference in its modern guise. He had a shrewd sense of publicity and achieved the maximum in public sympathy and understanding through his semiweekly conferences. Presidents Truman and Eisenhower attempted to continue the Roosevelt practice but each of them met with the press less regularly and less frequently. With both Truman and Eisenhower, the conference became more wide-ranging in coverage. Neither liked to close off a line of questioning by saying "no comment." Eisenhower, further, opened his conference to news and television cameramen. President Kennedy followed most of the Eisenhower practices and the conference more nearly resembled a staged performance than a spontaneous exchange between the reporters and the President. President Johnson has tried several different formats without as yet clearly settling on any one of them. Franklin Roosevelt also pioneered in using the radio to reach the American people, largely through his famous "fireside chats," and proved one of the most skillful of modern practitioners of radio broadcasting. Truman and Eisenhower attempted to follow the Roosevelt pattern but neither was as effective. Presidents Eisenhower, Kennedy, and Johnson cultivated public support by carefully contrived television addresses.[13]

THE PRESIDENT AS PARTY LEADER

The relations of the President with the Congress and the effective employment by him of the constitutional and customary forms and techniques described are colored and influenced by the fact that the President is the leader

[13] For analyses of the press conference, see J. E. Pollard, *The Presidents and the Press* (New York, 1947), D. Cater, *The Fourth Branch of Government* (Boston, 1959), and E. Cornwell, Jr., *Presidential Leadership of Public Opinion* (Bloomington, Ind., 1965).

of his party. The emergence of the President as a party leader, contrary to the intentions of the founding fathers, has been one of the major contributing factors to the contemporary legislative role of the chief executive. Chosen as a party candidate to head a government operated under a party system, the President surrounds himself with advisers of his own party, consults chiefly with the leaders of his party in Congress, unites to his the interests of his fellow partisans in the legislature through patronage, and depends primarily on the loyalty and support of the members of his party in Congress for the realization of his legislative program. The President represents his party throughout the nation as his colleagues in Congress cannot. The country looks to him, much more than to the Congress, to fulfill the pledges made by his party. Under these circumstances, he is bound to claim, ordinarily successfully, direction of the party's national machinery. He selects, while still a candidate, the chairman of the national committee and frequently reviews the appointments of other dignitaries in the party apparatus. He suggests and sometimes even dictates planks in the national platform on which he expects to campaign. He is consulted and his views may be decisive on all important questions of national party policy.

As leader of his party, the President derives an additional lever to pry his program out of the Congress. He succeeds to a very great extralegal power to reward and to punish individual legislators of his party. He can exert great influence in such party decisions as the distribution of campaign funds among the states and Representative-districts, the issues that will be played up in the campaign, the local and state leaders who will be aided and encouraged. As the chief campaigner of his party, the President can take the stump or not in aid of his Congressional colleagues. He can endorse the Congressman to the voters of his district or withhold his approval. All of these courses of action are likely to influence the election prospects of a member of the legislature. A few Presidents, notably Franklin Roosevelt, have even gone so far as to campaign openly against hostile legislators of their own party. However, many professional politicians believe that a President dare not go this far. He is more likely to hurt himself than his opponent, for the voters tend to resent the intrusion of outsiders into local campaigns. In any event, this procedure has rarely accomplished the desired object. In sum, most Congressmen are keenly aware of the great advantages to be gained politically from supporting Presidential measures. *Influence on Congress from party leadership*

It should be apparent from this discussion that the President's relations with the Congress, including his influence on legislation, depend upon the party situation in the Congress. Confronted with a Congress dominated by the opposite party, few of the techniques of partisan leadership are likely to prove effective in winning Congressional support. In these circumstances, and they have been all too frequent, the President's role as party leader is rather an embarrassment than an aid to his legislative aspirations. The Presidency is the best prize of the American party struggle and the Congressional leaders of the rival party are always strongly tempted to resist Presidential advice in order *Party complexion of the Congress influences presidential success* that by discrediting his influence they can capture his office. The most favorable situation for Presidential influence is for the White House to be newly occupied after an impressive election triumph which includes a strong majority in both houses of Congress. Midterm Congressional elections have normally diminished Presidential influence. Commonly, the President's party loses ground in these elections [14] and even when his party retains control, its legislative members do not feel quite so keenly the ties with a chief executive who has not been in the campaign himself. Furthermore, as we have noted, the job patronage will be all dispensed. The lowest point in the ebb and flow of Presidential leadership is when it becomes clear that the President will not seek re-election. Both party and Congressional leaders then seek identification with a new leader.

CONTROL OVER THE PRESIDENT BY CONGRESS

Constitu-
tional
controls

The continuing gain in the influence of the President upon the Congress and the impressive array of constitutional and customary devices for making this influence effective should not be interpreted to mean that, as between the two branches, influence flows only in one direction. Congress in its turn is capable of bringing powerful influences to bear upon the President. Few of the powers of the President can be exercised without money, and for every dollar of executive branch expenditure, the President must depend on the Congress. If the President shares the legislative power of the Congress, the Congress, as we have seen, shares the executive and administrative power of the President. He and his deputies are ordinarily obliged to make an accounting of their stewardship in connection with the annual review of appropriation requests and his departments and agencies are periodically brought under critical scrutiny by the investigating arms of the Congress. The organization of the executive departments and commissions, the powers entrusted to them, and the procedures used by them are all dictated in more or less detail by Congressional enactments. Except in the field of foreign affairs, the President must rely upon Congress for virtually every major change in public service, program, or policy. Even in the field of foreign affairs, the President must get Senatorial approval of his treaties, Congressional assent to war, and Congressional approval of any financial support required for any international understanding. Finally, in extreme circumstances, the President can be impeached and removed from office by the Congress.

Extra-
constitu-
tional
controls

Congress is not powerless either in those day-to-day dealings between the

[14] The strengthened position of the Roosevelt administration as a result of the sweeping Democratic victory in the elections of 1934 stands out as a notable exception. The elections of 1938, 1942, and 1950, however, yielding heavy Republican gains, ran true to form; and the elections of 1946 put both houses under control of the opposition. Again in 1954 the Republicans lost control of the Congress. The unique modern election was that of 1956 in which the Republicans captured the White House but not the Congress. Even so, in 1958, the Democrats added substantially to their majorities in both houses and then lost some ground in 1960 while capturing the Presidency.

two branches which have developed outside the formal constitutional specifications. If Senatorial confirmation of his appointments gives the President an opportunity to reward his Congressional supporters, it also results in Congressional selection of the incumbents in many executive branch posts. If the position of party leader endows the President with substantial influence upon the electoral success of his party members in Congress, it also requires him, more often than not, to accept and even to support members of his party whom he may find personally obnoxious and who may very well be working to accomplish the defeat of his most cherished ambitions. If he can cultivate popular support by the press, radio, and television, Congressional committees have shown themselves quite adept at capturing national attention with these devices, commonly when they are investigating the national administration. Furthermore, Congress is so organized that even if the President achieves great influence over the rank and file of his party, a few hostile leaders can still defy him with impunity and effectively frustrate legislative action.

In sum, directing our national government is jointly the responsibility of the President and the Congress. Neither is in a postion completely to dominate the other. The realization of public opinion in national action requires genuine co-operation between the two.

PROPOSALS FOR IMPROVING LEGISLATIVE-EXECUTIVE RELATIONS

The boldest way of seeking greater harmony and unity between Congress and the President would be to abandon our historic principle of separation of powers and frankly go over to the British parliamentary system. The President would then become a titular chief executive with only formal and ceremonial functions like the British king. The actual executive would be a cabinet drawn from the majority party in Congress and directing both legislation and administration. Congress would then serve a fixed term only if the Cabinet so decreed, for the executive would have to be able to dissolve the legislature in case of disagreement and call for a new election. The Senate would have to be radically reconstructed and demoted to a subordinate and largely suspensive role. One needs only to recite the major changes involved in copying the British system to reveal how visionary and impractical any such proposal is. Not only are the American people wholly unprepared for anything so drastic, but the size and complexity of our society and the sectional character of our political parties make it unlikely that the system would really serve our needs.[15]

Adoption of the parliamentary system

[15] Such a change was ably advocated recently by H. Hazlitt in *A New Constitution Now* (New York, 1942) and a generation ago by W. MacDonald in *A New Constitution for a New America* (New York, 1921). A modified version of this reform including an elected President and Cabinet as a single slate and containing members of the Congress at the time of the election with a four-year term for all and also for members of Congress but without Congressional power to dissolve the executive is vigorously put forth by H. Finer in *The Presidency: Crisis and Regeneration* (Chicago, 1960).

Most of the admirers of the parliamentary solution to the problem of legislative-executive relations have sought rather to modify the American Presidential system by grafting on to it some of the features of cabinet government that might be most readily assimilated. Perhaps the mildest suggestion is that the heads of executive departments be extended the privilege of the floor in both houses of Congress for the purpose of giving information, answering questions, and engaging in debate but not voting. This would allow, it is argued, the administration to defend itself directly and before the entire membership and would obviate the back-door procedures which are now used to accomplish the same end. The position of the administration and the reasons therefore could be stated openly and forthrightly and need not be relayed second-hand to the Congress. Much of the current investigating activity of Congressional committees might be obviated if the legislators could ask questions directly of the department heads. It is hard to see, however, how a cabinet member could say anything that had not been cleared with the President beforehand and, therefore, there would be little spontaneity of discussion. Both houses are now empowered to admit persons to the floor and thus the only action required would be to amend the rules.[16]

Presidents Taft and Wilson favored a plan under which, when selecting department heads, the chief executive should take most or all of them from among Senators and Representatives, the persons chosen retaining their seats and positions in the Congress. This would bring the two branches much closer together than the more modest proposal of giving the Cabinet floor privileges. It would still, of course, leave the President outside of the legislature and free as now to accept or reject the advice of his counselors. A constitutional difficulty to this proposal is the specification that civil officers of the United States are ineligible to membership in Congress. This is probably not, however, an insurmountable barrier.[17] Another difficulty in this suggestion would arise when the President and Congress are of opposite parties.

[16] This proposal has been made by a number of publicists and statesmen in our history, including Alexander Hamilton and President Garfield. The principal contemporary advocate until his death was Senator Estes Kefauver of Tennessee, who introduced the appropriate enabling legislation periodically from 1943 to 1963. See E. Kefauver, "The Need for Better Executive-Legislative Teamwork in the National Government," *Amer. Polit. Sci. Rev.*, XXXVIII, 317-325 (Apr., 1944) and E. Kefauver and J. Levin, *A Twentieth-Century Congress* (New York, 1947), Chap. VI. The most recent proposal was made in 1965 by a group of Republicans led by Representative Lindsay of New York.

In the first Congress, department heads not only appeared on the floor of both houses in a few instances, but took part in debate. They, however, were not very hospitably received, Hamilton finally being instructed, against his desire, to present his reports in writing rather than orally; and the practice died out. A history of efforts to revive it will be found in 63rd Cong., Spec. Sess. of Senate, Sen. Doc. No. 4, *Privilege of the Floor to Cabinet Members; Reports Made to the Congress of the United States* (1913).

[17] See E. S. Corwin, *The President: Office and Powers* (4th ed., New York, 1957), 297-298.

One school of thought holds that the real key to harmony in the cabinet system is the power of dissolution of the legislature possessed by the ministry. Believing that the most critical juncture of Presidential-Congressional relations is when the Congress rejects all or most of the President's program, these analysts recommend that the President be empowered to call a new Congressional election. The people would then decide the controversy by their votes.[18] The logic of this view is that if the voters returned a Congress still opposed to the President's policies, the President should resign. Some writers and statesmen have recommended that if a midterm election goes against his party and his program, the President ought to resign in any event.[19] It is hard to see how the dissolution power could be integrated to the staggered terms of the Senators. Another suggestion is that all members of Congress be elected for the same term and at the same time as the President. This would virtually guarantee that the same party would dominate both branches at any given time.

Presidential power of dissolution

Several students of the problem suggest that the wisest course is to disturb the existing institutional arrangements as little as possible but regularize and formalize the relations between the leaders of the Congress and the President and his advisers. One proposal along this line would organize the chairmen of a reduced number of standing committees into a legislative council or cabinet to meet frequently with the President to coordinate legislative programs.[20] Another proposal would organize a council of eleven members of each house and three members named by the President to screen all proposed legislation and to consult directly with the President.[21] The combination of legislative council of committee chairmen and President's cabinet into a grand council for formulating public policy is yet another suggestion.[22] The joint committee on the organization of Congress suggested four policy committees, one for each party in each house, which would formulate the legislative programs of the respective houses and parties. The two majority party policy commit-

A legislative-executive council

[18] See, for example, W. Y. Elliot, *The Need for Constitutional Reform* (New York, 1936) and H. Finer, *The Presidency: Crisis and Regeneration* (Chicago, 1960).

[19] Senator Fulbright of Arkansas, for example, recommended that President Truman resign in the middle of his term and allow Republican Speaker Martin (under the revised Presidential Succession Act) to succeed to the Presidency when in 1946 the voters elected a Republican Congress. The people, he said, were entitled to an executive who could act in harmony with the new Congress. Mr. Truman did not receive this proposal kindly.

[20] R. Young, *This Is Congress* (New York, 1943), Chap. VIII.

[21] A. Hehmeyer, *Time For Change* (New York, 1943), Chap. IX. The suggested council would bear a good deal of resemblance to legislative councils developed in Kansas and numerous other states.

[22] T. K. Finletter, *Can Representative Government Do the Job?* (New York, 1945), Chap. XI; and cf. E. S. Corwin, *The President: Office and Powers* (3rd ed.), 361-364. An interesting momentary step in the direction indicated was taken early in 1944, when, at the suggestion of Secretary Hull, an informal committee on foreign policy, linking the Department of State and the Foreign Affairs Committees of the two houses of Congress, was instituted.

tees would meet regularly with the President.[23] The failure of the House of
Representatives formally to create the contemplated committees and the great
difference between how these committees in the Senate actually work and how
they were expected to work has not made these reforms fruitful.

Priority for
adminis-
tration
measures

One school of thought feels that the role of the executive branch as the
major initiator of legislation ought to be recognized and accepted. Change the
rules of the two houses, these men argue, and assure clear priority to administration measures. In fact, when the President has a working majority of his
party in both houses, something very like this happens anyway. When he does
not, no amount of priority could probably get his program accepted.

Although the prospects for immediate adoption of any of these proposals
are not bright, the very existence of so many suggestions reveals a wide-spread
notion that further improvement of our constitutional arrangements is both
possible and necessary. The root of the problem is now widely held to be the
difference in constituency between the leaders of Congress and the President
and his entourage. Most of the reform proposals are not aimed at this aspect.
Meanwhile, the incumbents of the Presidency have been attempting to establish on an informal basis the type of consultation and cooperation in executive-
legislative relations which will more nearly achieve the desired goals.

References

F. M. Riddick, *The United States Congress: Organization and Procedure* (Washington, 1949), Chaps. XII.

J. M. Burns, *Congress on Trial: The Legislative Process and the Administrative
State* (New York, 1949), Chaps. XII, IX-X.

A. N. Holcombe, *Our More Perfect Union: From Eighteenth-Century Principles
to Twentieth-Century Practice* (Cambridge, Mass., 1950), Chap. VIII.

W. Wilson, *Constitutional Government in the United States* (New York, 1908),
Chap. III.

———, *Congressional Government* (Boston, 1885), Chap. V.

H. L. McBain, *The Living Constitution* (New York, 1927), Chap. IV.

G. B. Galloway, *Congress at the Crossroads* (New York, 1946), Chap. VII.

G. Cleveland, *Presidential Problems* (New York, 1940), pp. 3-78.

[23] "Fourteen members of Congress," says a principal author of this last suggestion,
"would sit around the council table with the President and his ten Cabinet members.
Cabinet members for the first time would have an opportunity to participate directly in
the discussion of a unified legislative program. Legislative leaders could avoid head-on
clashes with the President over much legislation if a better understanding were secured
of the point of view of the executive branch, and *vice versa*." Ex-Senator R. M. LaFollette, Jr., in *Amer. Polit. Sci. Rev.*, XLI, 64 (Feb., 1947).

E. S. Corwin, *The President, Office and Powers: History and Analysis of Practice and Opinion* (4th ed., New York, 1957), Chap. VII.

H. J. Laski, *The American Presidency* (New York, 1940), Chap. III.

H. Finer, *The Presidency: Crisis and Regeneration* (Chicago, 1960).

S. Hyman, *The American President* (New York, 1954).

D. Rossiter, *The American Presidency* (New York, 1956).

C. P. Patterson, *Presidential Government in the United States: The Unwritten Constitution* (Chapel Hill, N.C., 1947), Chaps. VI-VII, X.

R. Young, *This Is Congress* (New York, 1943), Chap. II.

E. P. Herring, *Presidential Leadership: The Political Relations of Congress and the Chief Executive* (New York, 1940), Chaps. II-IV, VII.

————, "Executive-Legislative Responsibilities," *Amer. Polit. Sci. Rev.*, XXXVIII, 1153-1165 (Dec., 1944).

L. H. Chamberlain, *The President, Congress, and Legislation* (New York, 1946); also article on the same subject in *Polit. Sci. Quar.*, LXI, 42-60 (Mar., 1946).

A. J. Zurcher, "The Presidency, Congress, and Separation of Powers: A Reappraisal," *Western Polit. Quar.*, III, 75-97 (Mar., 1950).

R. S. Rankin (ed.), *The Presidency in Transition* (Gainesville, Fla., 1949).

W. E. Binkley, *President and Congress* (New York, 1947).

G. F. Milton, *The Use of Presidential Power, 1789-1943* (Boston, 1944).

J. E. Johnsen (comp.), *Increasing the President's Power* (New York, 1934).

E. C. Mason, *The Veto Power* (New York, 1891).

K. A. Towle, "The Presidential Veto Since 1889," *Amer. Polit. Sci. Rev.*, XXXI, 51-56 (Feb., 1937).

C. A. Berdahl, "The President's Veto of Private Bills," *Polit. Sci. Quar.*, LII, 505-531 (Dec., 1937).

R. E. Neustadt, "Presidency and Legislation: Planning the President's Program," *Amer. Polit. Sci. Rev.*, XLIX, No. 4 (Dec., 1955).

————, "Presidency and Legislation: the Growth of Central Clearance," *Amer. Polit. Sci. Rev.*, XLVIII, No. 3 (Sept., 1954).

E. Cornwell, Jr., *Presidential Leadership of Public Opinion* (Bloomington, Ind., 1965).

R. Hillsman, "Congressional-Executive Relations and the Foreign Policy Consensus," *Amer. Polit. Sci. Rev.*, LII, No. 3 (Sept., 1958).

W. Kendall, "The Two Majorities," *Midwest Jour. of Polit. Sci.*, IV, No. 4 (Nov., 1960).

R. Egger and J. P. Harris, *The President and Congress* (New York, 1963).

J. Burnham, *Congress and the American Tradition* (Chicago, 1959).

S. Horn, *The Cabinet and Congress* (New York, 1961).

★ 13 ★

The Presidency

The executive power shall be vested in a President of the United States of America. He shall hold his office during a term of four years. . . . ART. II, Sec. 1

The President the most powerful elected executive in the world

THE PRESIDENT OF THE UNITED STATES of America is, without question, the most powerful elected executive in the world. He is at once the chief formulator of public policy as embodied in legislation, leader of a major political party boasting thousands of functionaries and millions of adherents, chief architect of American foreign policy and spokesman for this nation before the world, director of one of the most gigantic administrative machines ever created, numbering over 2,000,000 civilian employees organized into 75 separate jurisdictions and expending more than $100 billion annually, commander-in-chief of more than 3,000,000 men in uniform equipped with the latest weapons of offense and defense, and ceremonial head of the government of the United States. And his power and responsibility are increasing. It may seem ironic that a nation so mistrustful of officialdom and so certain of the corrosive effects of political power should construct such an office. However, the President falls heir to these powers by the peaceful suffrages of his countrymen and he holds them for but a short time.

The Constitution a poor guide to present office

Given the great apprehension of American revolutionary leaders of executive power, it is difficult to believe that the modern Presidency is a deliberate creation of the founding fathers. The major decision of the Constitution-makers was that we should have a single executive. The remaining characteristics of the office are largely the product of practical political experience. Like the British cabinet system, it is not to the sagacity of a few solons but to the pragmatic adjustments to time and circumstance by ordinary statesmen that we owe the institution of the American chief executive. To no part of our American system is the Constitution so poor a guide. Custom and usage have wrought the office far more than constitutional prescription. The development of the Presidential office has, nevertheless, remained firmly anchored to the provisions of the Constitution.

The constitutional convention and the Presidency

The principal designer of the constitutional President was James Wilson, who argued skillfully and frequently for a single executive, independent of the legislature. No problem bothered the framers quite so much as the executive;

they repeatedly postponed action when firm decisions were impossible and reversed decisions already made. Not until the closing days of the convention did the Presidency finally take its ultimate form, and only after a majority vote had been recorded and rescinded for legislative election and after the proponents of a plural executive, or at least of an executive council to assist the President and share his powers, were beaten down for the last time. In fact, so preoccupied were the framers with these two questions and with the question of eligibility for re-election that the powers and duties of the executive office were inadequately debated and summarily handled. What is meant by "executive power"? Why were some "executive powers" listed in Article II and others omitted? What should be the role of the "officers in each of the executive departments"? The debates in the constitutional convention throw little light on the framers' intentions. Only experience has yielded answers to these questions.

THE OFFICE OF PRESIDENT

The decision of the constitutional convention for a four-year term with no limitation on the number of terms any individual might serve, in preference to a single seven-year term, turned out to be largely unacceptable to many of our nation's leaders. The first President was willing to serve only two terms, although he probably could have been re-elected. The third President, Jefferson, declined to serve more than eight years as a matter of principle. He steadily opposed indefinite re-eligibility of the chief executive. Madison and Monroe both bowed out after eight years and Jackson, who undoubtedly could have been re-elected, vigorously supported Jefferson's precedent. Thus an "anti-third-term tradition" was established which lasted until 1940. The tradition had been questioned by Grant and some of his supporters and actually assailed by Theodore Roosevelt, but never set aside until Franklin Roosevelt successfully sought a third term in 1940 and then a fourth term in 1944. Franklin Roosevelt's departure from tradition called down upon his head a great storm of criticism and abuse and encouraged his opponents staunchly to reassert the tradition. Soon after his death and following a Republican victory in the Congressional elections of 1946, an amendment to the Constitution limiting Presidential tenure was laid before the states. Aided by growing antipathy toward President Truman, then serving his second term, the forces pushing the amendment finally achieved ratification by the thirty-sixth state (Nevada) early in 1951. The Twenty-second Amendment makes it hereafter impossible for any person to serve as President of the United States for more than two terms.[1]

At the time that an individual assumes the office of President, he must, according to the Constitution, be at least 35 years of age, have lived in the

The third-term problem resolved

Presidential qualifications

[1] Unless he succeeded to less than half of a term for which some other person had actually been elected, in which case he may serve two terms plus the half-term.

United States 14 years,[2] and be a "natural born" citizen of this country. In accordance with the Twelfth Amendment, the Vice-President must also have these three qualifications. Here again, the constitutional specifications are practically of small importance in determining Presidential eligibility. All of those qualities which make up what we have described earlier as "availability" in a potential candidate are the decisive determinants.

Salary and allowances

Although Benjamin Franklin argued eloquently on the corrupting allure of wealth and against any Presidential emoluments, the President has been paid a generous salary from the beginning of our national life. The Constitution expressly protects him from Congressional attack or embrace through his pocketbook—a favorite colonial device for dealing with recalcitrant British governors—by providing that his salary may be neither increased nor diminished during his term of office. He is also forbidden to receive any other emolument from the United States or from any state. This has not, however, prevented his being supplied with an executive mansion, a suite of offices, a secretariat, a yacht, an airplane, a private Pullman Car, a fleet of automobiles and special entertainment and expense funds. George Washington's salary was fixed by the first Congress at $25,000. In 1873, the salary was increased to $50,000; in 1909 to $75,000; and in 1949 to $100,000. The total annual cost of the Presidential establishment, including the White House office and the care of the White House itself, now exceeds $3 million.

THE POWERS AND DUTIES OF THE PRESIDENT: A GENERAL VIEW

Constitution not clear on executive powers

Exactly what powers the Constitution confers or the framers intended to confer upon the President is anything but clear. Controversy has buzzed around this subject throughout our national life and the clamor has by no means abated. Demonstrably, the framers wanted firmness and vigor in the executive without autocratic domination. These are qualities imparted to an office by an individual, however; not to the individual by the office. To make the executive the servant and not the master of the subjects has ever been the goal of constitution builders, and the history of tyranny testifies to the almost insuperable difficulties in the road of such endeavors. Perhaps the framers were content to allow time and experience to decide the major contours of executive authority in the American system. Perhaps this would have happened in any event, no matter in what language they had finally depicted the Presidential power. They did, however, fall below the high standard of lucidity and consistency which characterizes most of our Constitution when they came to describe this high office. On the one hand, *the* executive power (not the power *herein granted* as in Article I) is conferred upon the President; and on the other, spe-

---

[2] The 14 years' residence need not be those immediately preceding his election, as illustrated by the case of President Hoover.

cific powers of an executive character—to appoint officers of the United States, to be commander-in-chief, to grant pardons, to make treaties, to take care that the laws be faithfully executed—are also conferred. Furthermore, the Congress is endowed with the power to make "all laws which shall be necessary and proper for carrying into *execution*" the powers granted to it. Does the Constitution mean that the President has some executive powers in addition to those specifically mentioned? Does it mean that the President must look to Congress to provide not only the means but the authority to act when, for example, rebellion, industrial violence, depression, national catastrophe or war threatens the stability of our institutions and the happiness and security of our people?

If we allow for variations in detail, two broad and competing conceptions *Two* of Presidential power emerge from the debates engendered by circumstance, *concep-* personalities, and constitutional obscurity. Hamilton, Madison (before he be- *tions of* came President), Jefferson (while he was President), Jackson, Polk, Lincoln, *executive* Cleveland, Theodore Roosevelt, Wilson, Franklin Roosevelt, Truman and *power:* Kennedy [3] have supported the view that Presidential power is broader than the specific items enumerated, that it is not completely dependent upon express *1. Broad* Congressional authorization, and that, although it should be carefully confined *view* normally, the existence of a critical or emergency situation justifies the most vigorous and independent exercise of all of the force and authority that the chief magistrate can command. In this view, the Congress, the courts, and the people of the time have generally concurred. Theodore Roosevelt best expressed this view when he labeled the President "the steward of the people" and insisted that it was not only his right but his duty to do anything that the national welfare required unless it was expressly prohibited by the Constitution or the laws.[4]

President Taft, in *Our Chief Magistrate and His Powers*,[5] sums up the *2. Limited* opposite view: *view*

> The true view of the executive function is, as I conceive it, that the President can exercise no power which cannot be reasonably and fairly traced to some specific grant of power or justly implied or included within such express grant as necessary and proper to its exercise. Such specific grant must be either in the Constitution or in an act of Congress passed in pursuance thereof. There is no undefined residuum of power which he can exercise because it seems to him to be in the public interest.

[3] President (then Senator) Kennedy's views on the powers and responsibilities of the President were set forth ably in a speech January 14, 1960 before the National Press Club in Washington, D. C. He clearly aligned himself with those who took the broad view of Presidential power. "He (the President) must be prepared," he said, "to exercise the fullest powers of his office—all that are specified and some that are not." *The New York Times*, Jan. 15, 1960.

[4] *Autobiography* (New York, 1913), 388-389.

[5] (New York, 1916). 139-140.

To this view, many of our chief executives, for example, Buchanan, Grant, Harding, and Coolidge, the Congress occasionally and the courts in several cases have subscribed.

*Precedents
for the
broad
view of
Presiden-
tial power*
The exponents of the broad, rather than the limited, view of Presidential authority largely molded the office of the Presidency as it stands today. They established most of the significant precedents. They defined the functions. They inspired their successors. They also stimulated the vigorous assertion of the opposite view and invited reaction and retreat when they thrust too far beyond the ground already occupied. The landmarks in the evolution of Presidential power are: Washington's proclamation of neutrality in the Franco-British war; Jefferson's decision to acquire the Louisiana territory, although he believed there was no constitutional authority for such an acquisition; Jackson's relegation of the Cabinet to a second-rate position among the institutions of Presidential leadership, his resolute annihilation of the Bank of the United States despite its strong Congressional support, and his strong determination to prevent the secession of South Carolina; Lincoln's assumption of virtually plenary power to deal with the Southern "rebellion" with or without Congressional authorization, in consequence of which and without express grant of Congress he raised armies of volunteers, appropriated money from the Treasury, suspended the execution of the writ of habeas corpus, issued the Emancipation Proclamation, and restored states occupied by the Union armies (many of his actions were, to be sure, later validated by the Congress); Grover Cleveland's determination to repress industrial disorder with national troops in the Pullman Strike despite the opposition of the governor of the state concerned; the decision of the United States Supreme Court in the Neagle [6] case, in which it defined "executive power" to embrace power not specifically granted by statute or expressly mentioned in the Constitution; Theodore Roosevelt's dramatic intervention in the coal strike of 1902 and his assertion of the "stewardship" conception of the Presidential office; Wilson's successful assertion of the President's complete responsibility for direction of American participation in World War I, although he acted on the basis of Congressional assignment of power; the Supreme Court's decision in the Meyers case supporting the view that the President's removal power is unrestricted; Congressional delegation to Franklin Roosevelt of great powers to deal with economic depression and to direct the American effort in World War II; Truman's assignment of American forces to battle in Korea under the United Nations without express Congres-

---

[6] *In re Neagle*, 135 U. S. 1 (1890). See W. H. Taft, *Our Chief Magistrate and His Powers*, 88-91. In the Neagle case—turning on the question of whether the President had any right to assign Neagle as a national deputy marshal to protect a national judge who had been threatened—the Court defined the executive power as including not only the enforcement of statutes and treaties, but the protection (without need for express constitutional or statutory authorization) of all rights, duties, and obligations growing out of the constitution or out of our international relations—in short, the extension of "all protection implied by the nature of the government under the Constitution."

sional authorization; the movement of national troops into Little Rock, by Eisenhower against the wishes of the Governor (Faubus) of the state; the imposition of a naval blockade of Cuba by Kennedy without express Congressional authority and aimed at forcing the removal of Soviet missiles; and, the retaliatory strikes by ships and planes against North Vietnam ordered by Johnson followed by sharp increases in American armed forces aiding the government of South Vietnam.

The Congress and the courts have provided most of the precedents for the more limited view of Presidential power. The Senate by resolution denounced Andrew Jackson's actions against the Bank of the United States as unconstitutional—a resolution which it later expunged. Lincoln's "dictatorship" was bitterly assailed from Capitol Hill and so were the actions of the Roosevelts and Wilson without, however, any official action. Andrew Johnson's attempt to assert Lincoln's powers without Lincoln's skill brought him within one vote of removal from office. The Supreme Court has declared against Presidential assumption of power on several occasions. Lincoln's suspension of the writ of habeas corpus was held to be beyond the Presidential power when the Court could find no "actual and present" necessity for its suspension in Indiana in 1864.[7] The most recent occasion for Court declaration on this weighty subject represents a rebuff to Presidential claims. President Truman in 1952, in an effort to halt a threatened steel strike which he claimed would jeopardize our national defense effort, ordered the Secretary of Commerce to seize the steel factories and to operate them. The President based his order on his power as commander-in-chief of the armed forces and the "executive power" of the President, admitting that no Congressional authority for such an action could be found. When the steel companies sought to prevent the seizing of their properties, the Court held that in the absence of Congressional authorization and in view of the fact that Congress had clearly intended not to grant such authority, the constitutional provisions governing executive power and power as commander-in-chief conferred no such power on the President.[8] The lawmaking power, said the Court, is entrusted to the Congress alone in "both good and bad times." What the steel seizure decision is a precedent for, however, is beclouded by the fact that the judgment of the Court was supported by six separate opinions, each of which took a little different ground than the others.[9]

If the President's authority and responsibility have increased strikingly in the history of our political system, to the incumbent they usually fall far short of allowing him to achieve his goals by command. President Truman

Precedents for the limited-power concept

Steel seizure case

[7] *Ex parte Milligan,* 4 Wallace 2 (1866).
[8] Youngstown Co. *v.* Sawyer, 343 U. S. 579 (1952).
[9] There was also a vigorous dissenting opinion, filed by the Chief Justice (Vinson) and supported by two other members of the Court. The dissenters took particular note of the message by the President to Congress after the seizure inviting them to reject his action if they deemed it unwise. No such rejection was registered.

once observed that what the power of the President amounts to is the ability to persuade people to do things they ought to do without persuasion.[10]

The reality of Presidential power

The powers of the President depend, in practice, upon the skill, imagination, energy, outlook, and resources of those who occupy this high office and on their understanding of the techniques by which in our democratic system they may achieve the policies to which thcy are dedicated.[11] Ordering things done is frequently a last resort and is not certainly decisive. The development of the office as outlined has meant that we expect more of our chief executives and that they are also acting on a greater stage before a larger audience than ever before. It is helpful in considering the scope of Presidential activity if we look next at the various constitutional assignments of responsibility.

POWER AND RESPONSIBILITY TO ENFORCE THE LAWS

. . . he shall take care that the laws be faithfully executed, . . . ART. II, Sec. 3

Law-enforcement power

The Presidential oath of office obligates him to protect and defend the Constitution and the Constitution itself solemnly enjoins him to enforce all national laws (by implication this includes treaties and ordinances). A great many of the laws of Congress expressly confer upon the President or upon his subordinates in the executive branch specific powers of enforcement. Some laws confer powers which may be exercised at his discretion or at the discretion of his subordinates. The sum of these constitutional and statutory grants is the potential enforcement power of the Presidency at any given time.

Presidential assistance in law enforcement

For discharging this lofty responsibility the President has virtually the entire facilities of the executive branch, including the thousands of officials and employees working in the numerous agencies of which it is constituted. One particular agency, the Department of Justice, is charged with the general responsibility for law enforcement, notably of those criminal laws the enforcement of which is not specifically assigned by the Congress to some other national agency. As an alternative to the use of troops, agents of the Department have also been used to halt violence. Attorney General Kennedy ordered a large number of U. S. marshals into Birmingham, Alabama in 1961 to "assist" local law enforcement officers in preventing attacks on the bus loads of "Freedom Riders" then touring the South in the interests of desegregation. The Governor (Patterson) of the state did not request this assistance and the Congressional delegation vigorously protested the procedure.

Suppression of disorder

The President has also under his command the armed forces of the nation

[10] H. W. Koenig, *The Chief Executive* (New York, 1964). 10.
[11] See R. E. Neustadt, *Presidential Power: The Politics of Leadership* (New York, 1960).

and even those of the states if and when called into national service.[12] The
President's power to employ military force in the enforcement of national laws
has steadily increased through the years as a result of Congressional action and
of Presidential initiative. It now seems clear that such power is not wholly
dependent on Congressional authorization nor, in cases of internal disorder, on
the invitation of the governor or legislature of any of the states. If the President
can validly assert that the disorder threatens the performance of any national
function, the safety of national property, or the flow of interstate commerce,
he can intervene with force to restore order whether the governor or the state
legislature wants him to do so or not.[13] In its famous decision supporting this
view, the Supreme Court said, "The entire strength of the nation may be used
to enforce in any part of the land the full and free exercise of all national
powers and the security of all rights entrusted to its care." [14] The use of troops
in Little Rock in 1957, in Oxford, Mississippi in 1962, in Birmingham and
Tuscaloosa, Alabama in 1963, and in Selma, Alabama in 1965, are recent
actions illustrating the scope of Presidential authority. In the first case, a reluctant President felt compelled to intervene with force when the Governor
of Arkansas (Faubus) called out the state militia to prevent compliance with
a national court order to desegregate Central High School in accordance
with a plan for admitting Negroes carefully worked out by the local school
authorities. The President asserted that "the powers of a state governor may
not be used to defeat a valid order" of a national court. In the second, the
Governor of Mississippi (Barnett) attempted to obstruct the court-ordered
admission of a Negro to the University of Mississippi. Even while rioting was
in progress, President Kennedy pled for obedience but made it clear that his
obligation was to implement national court orders with whatever means are
necessary. In Birmingham, the Governor of Alabama (Wallace) expressly
requested that the situation be left to the local authorities and later he attempted personally to obstruct the entrance of a Negro to the University of
Alabama. In Selma, the same Governor informed President Johnson that he
could not be responsible for the safety of a group of demonstrators (mostly
Negroes) proposing to march to the Capitol and present a civil rights petition to the Governor.

[12] To supply any authority at this point that otherwise might have been lacking,
Congress has passed numerous measures, beginning with (1) a Militia Act of 1792
empowering the President to call forth the militia whenever execution of the national
laws is obstructed by combinations too powerful to be suppressed through the ordinary
course of judicial proceedings, and (2) an act of 1807 authorizing use of the Army
and Navy under similar circumstances.

[13] The landmark decision on this point came during Grover Cleveland's second term
when, over the protests of Governor Altgeld of Illinois, he sent national troops to "protect the mails" against the violence associated with the Pullman Strikes of 1894. President Hayes, under similar circumstances, had supplied arms from national arsenals to
state authorities without formal invitation and had stationed national troops near the
scenes of industrial disorder.

[14] *In re Debs,* 158 U. S. 564 (1895).

Limitations on enforcement power

As awesome as the President's responsibility for law enforcement may be and as broad as some Presidents and courts have found this power to be, in practice there are numerous restraints, legal and political, upon his ability to fulfill such responsibilities or to exercise such powers. Whatever reservoir of enforcement power may be found from time to time to exist in the constitutional mandates unsupported by specific statutory authorization, normally the President must look to Congress to prescribe his exact authority to enforce any given law, for the procedures by which such enforcement is to be achieved, and for the penalties which may be invoked against transgressors. Whether or not he is dependent upon Congress for the power, he is certainly dependent upon it for the personnel and supplies, that is, the money, to do the job. The President is also dependent upon the quality of the national public service, most members of which he did not hire and, in practice, cannot fire. His appointment and his removal powers are circumscribed in many ways, as we shall observe in the next section of this chapter. The lieutenants upon whom the President must largely depend for the enforcement of any law are not, in every case, bound to him and to him alone by an unbroken chain either of authority or of communication. The President inherits not only most of the people upon whom he must depend, but the organization of these people into bureaus and departments with all the institutional traditions that these organizations have accumulated through the years. Most Presidents have found that they are supporting these institutions and the men who occupy them much more often than these are supporting the President.

Executive rule- making powers and its limits

The power of enforcement necessarily entails large powers of discretion. In applying general laws to particular circumstances it is essential that enforcement agencies decide what the law means in these varying circumstances. From this necessity has flowed an increasingly broad stream of Presidential direction in the form of executive orders, ordinances, rules, and regulations which are in plain fact laws made by the executive. Congress has repeatedly, especially in the last half-century, established national policy in very broad terms and assigned to the executive the power to achieve these broadly stated objectives by uttering detailed rules and regulations. This discretionary power, essential as it is to effective law enforcement, is limited by Congressional power to recall the delegation or to spell out the details, contrary to Presidential policy. On the other hand, the Presidential directives frequently come under the scrutiny of the courts. And when called upon in law enforcement, the courts have the final say as to what the law is.

Law enforcement and public opinion

The effectiveness of law enforcement depends in the final analysis on the attitude of the public toward the law in question. The many futile attempts to enforce the Volstead Act of 1919 (the law designed to give effect to the Prohibition Amendment) illustrate the great difficulties in the path of Presidential fulfillment of his constitutional duties in the face of a hostile or lethargic public opinion. Furthermore, a great and growing number of national policies set forth by Congress and President cannot really be achieved by enforcement in the sense of seeking out and punishing violators. They can be achieved only by methods which are essentially educational and noncoercive. The needy aged, for example, cannot be properly cared for by a program based mainly upon uncovering those wrongfully receiving public support. The "enforcement" responsibilities of the President in these types of programs can be fulfilled only with adequate public understanding and support.

POWER TO APPOINT AND REMOVE PUBLIC OFFICERS

. . . he shall nominate, and by and with the advice and consent of the Senate, shall appoint ambassadors, other public ministers and consuls, judges of the Supreme Court, and all other officers of the United States, whose appointments are not herein otherwise provided for, and which shall be established by law; but the Congress may by law vest the appointment of such inferior officers, as they think proper, in the president alone, in the courts of law, or in the heads of departments. ART. II, Sec. 2, Cl. 2

That the President is solely responsible in law and in the polling booth for the conduct of the far-flung national administrative machinery is a truism of American law and politics. His ability actually to direct the administration is dependent upon a variety of personal, political, and legal conditions. Not the least of these is the scope of his power, legally and practically, to hire and fire the individuals who compose the national civil service and the cadre of national officers who guide them. The Constitution clearly circumscribes the President's appointing authority of individuals in the executive branch in several ways. Except for members of the diplomatic service and judges of the Supreme Court, the offices to which Presidential appointment may extend must be created by the Congress. The authority to create an office carries with it the power to establish the duties of the office and the qualifications of any individual who may occupy it. Congress has, in practice, set forth such qualifications of many kinds, geographical, political, personal, and professional. Congress, furthermore, may vest the appointment of "inferior" officers—and, by and large, the Congress has decided which are "inferior" offices—in department heads as well as in the President. In fact, the Congress has assigned the appointment of more than 85 percent of the 2,000,000 civilian employees of the executive branch to department and agency heads and has limited the freedom of the department heads by the requirements of the merit system. The direct appointing power of the President now extends to about 25 thousand national officials. However, any particular incoming President may be able to fill only about 6,000 of these. The 6,000, however, include virtually all of the top-ranking posts in the official hierarchy—secretaries, assistant secretaries, some bureau chiefs, commissioners, agency directors. The President's hand does, therefore, reach those who appoint the others and who give them their orders and assign them their duties. Many students of the American sys-

Scope of the President's appointing power

tem, it is necessary to add, feel that the President's appointing power is still too extensive and that if he were confined to appointing only two or three hundred of the major executives this would be ample for the purpose of achieving the kind of directional authority which he ought to have. Presidents for years past have complained bitterly about the unconscionable burden of appointments cast upon them. This was especially the case before the extension of the merit system throughout the civil service.

Senate participation in appointments

One of the most important limitations of Presidential authority is the prescription that the Senate must be consulted on his selections.[15] Except in those few cases (there are about 375 such posts) where Congress has vested the power in the President alone (e.g., the officers of his own immediate staff), all Presidential nominations must be confirmed by majority vote of the Senate before appointment may be made.[16] The purpose of associating the Senate with the appointment process was, according to Hamilton, to curb favoritism of a geographical, familial, or personal character.[17] In practice, the Senate has tended to divide Presidential appointments into two classes with respect to the character of its participation. It has been customary for the Senate to approve, almost as a matter of course, the President's choices for the highest positions in the executive branch. It has come to be recognized that the heads of the great departments and agencies are the principal advisers of the President— the departmental heads compose his Cabinet—and that he bears direct responsibility for all of their acts and relies upon them to direct the agencies in keeping with his policies. He should, therefore, have the widest range of freedom in selecting them. Although there has been serious opposition on several occasions to the President's choices, only nine nominees for Cabinet posts have ever been rejected.[18] The President's designees for subordinate executive posts, for Supreme Court judgeships, and for diplomatic posts are contested somewhat more frequently, but even these are normally not seriously challenged.

Recess appointments

In skirmishes with the Senate over executive posts, the President is fortified by his power to make recess appointments without Senatorial approval. A few Presidents have used this procedure to keep men in office of whom the Senate disapproved.[19] Of course, the Senate is more likely to be sympathetic to Presidential wishes when his party is in the majority.

[15] For a full discussion of this subject see J. P. Harris, *The Advice and Consent of the Senate* (Berkeley, 1953).

[16] Confirmation or rejection must be absolute, without any conditions attached.

[17] *The Federalist,* No. LXXVI (Lodge's ed., 474).

[18] R. B. Taney, for Secretary of the Treasury, in 1834; Caleb Cushing and James A. Green for Secretary of the Treasury, in 1843 and 1844, respectively; David Henshaw, for Secretary of the Navy, in 1844; J. M. Porter, for Secretary of War, in 1844; Henry Stanberry, for Attorney General, in 1868; Alexander Stewart, for Secretary of the Treasury, in 1869; Charles B. Warren, for Attorney General (rejected twice), in 1925; and Lewis L. Straus, for Secretary of Commerce, in 1959. Occasionally, however, nominees are confirmed only over considerable opposition.

[19] Theodore Roosevelt, for example, in this way kept a Negro in the office of collector of customs at Charleston, S. C., from 1902 to 1904 despite persistent Senate opposition. At the present time, however, if the Senate is in session when the vacancy exists, a recess appointee to that vacancy ordinarily may draw no salary until confirmed.

There is another class of Presidential appointment, however, about which "Senatorial
courtesy" the Senate is not nearly so deferential. Several thousands of the posts filled by Presidential appointment are not major executive posts at all and are for positions in the field service (regional offices outside Washington, D. C.). These include certain positions in government corporations, U. S. district attorneys and marshals, and judges and court functionaries of the lower federal courts.[20] The appointment process for these positions is normally dominated by partisan considerations and the sum of these posts constitutes the job patronage of any given administration. Senatorial confirmation operates in this category of Presidential appointment to enforce upon the President the nominees of his fellow partisans in Congress. For those posts located in states where at least one of the Senators is of the same party as the President, that Senator's approval of the appointment is almost mandatory. The Senate has a deeply rooted tradition that it will rally to the support of any Senator in the circumstances described and reject any nominee not acceptable to him. This tradition is called "Senatorial courtesy" and is typically invoked by a Senator declaring that the nominee is personally obnoxious to him.[21] For posts which are located in Congressional districts, the members of the House of Representatives of the President's party expect to be consulted and this practice too may be enforced upon the President by the Senators. In states not represented by a Senator of the President's party, the President is obliged for party reasons and by tradition to rely on suggestions from the state party leaders, typically the national committeeman. In sum, the President has not much real freedom in making appointments to the vast majority of posts which he is entitled by law to fill. The actual selections are made by party supporters in the House and Senate and by party leaders in the state where the jobs are located. We have already described how, by the skillful use of this patronage, the President may gain support for his legislative program from the Congress and thus compensate in a sense for the restrictions upon his appointing power.

The ability of the President to get the vast national administrative service The President's
removal
power to march to his tune is strongly influenced by the scope of his power to dismiss those who disobey his orders, impair the efficiency of the service, resist his program, or neglect their responsibilities. Obviously the constitutional im-

---

[20] Of the 46,000 postmasterships in the national service, 23,000 require Senatorial confirmation. While appointees to these posts must take examinations and tenure, once appointed, is for good behavior, nevertheless partisan considerations do play some role in the selection. At any given time perhaps 3,000 of these posts may be occupied on a temporary basis and these persons could be replaced.

[21] There are occasional exceptions. In 1947, Senator O'Daniel of Texas objected to a nominee for a district judgeship in his state as "personally obnoxious to me," but nevertheless the nomination was confirmed.

Another form of Senatorial courtesy, working in reverse, comes into view when, the President having nominated a *Senator* to an office, the Senate confirms the nomination immediately and as a matter of course, without referring it in the usual way to a committee. Departure from this practice in the case of the nomination of Hugo L. Black to a Supreme Court associate justiceship in 1937 stirred much interest. See K. Cole, "Mr. Justice Black and Senatorial Courtesy," *Amer. Polit. Sci. Rev.*, XXXI, 1113-1115 (Dec., 1937).

peachment process is not designed for this purpose. It is to deal with criminal conduct by public officers. Since the Constitution is otherwise silent on the dismissal of government officers, does the President have this power or does the Senate share responsibility for dismissal as it does for appointment? Can the Congress by law prescribe the procedure for firing employees and officers of the national government? This problem arose early in the life of the Constitution and while many of the framers were still alive. Madison persuaded his fellow statesmen of the time that the removal power, insofar as officials in the executive branch are concerned, was part of the executive power and of the power to enforce the laws which the Constitution entrusted to the President alone. On another occasion, however, Madison did say that Congress might create certain types of offices—not wholly executive in character—for which some different removal procedure might be established. Until 1867, the Madison doctrine of Presidential removal authority was generally accepted in law

The Myers Case

and practice. In that year, however, and as an incident to the acrimonious contest between Congress and President Johnson, the Congress passed over his veto a Tenure of Office Act which provided that the President could not remove without the concurrence of the Senate any official whose appointment the Senate had confirmed.[22] This measure was partially repealed in 1869 and wholly expunged in 1887, but another act passed in 1876 established the same principle for postmaster appointments. Several decades later, President Wilson, probably deliberately, violated the Postmaster Act and called the constitutionality of the limitations into question. The postmaster—later his estate—carried the matter to court and in 1926 the Supreme Court, through the mouth of Chief Justice (former President) Taft, declared in favor of the Madison doctrine that the removal power belonged to the President and could not validly be restricted by the Congress in the manner described.[23]

The case of the independent commission

The decision of the Court in the Myers case, because of its sweeping assertion of Presidential power, caused immediate concern for the tenure of

[22] The President's refusal to be bound by the terms of the act, and particularly his removal of Secretary of War Stanton in open defiance of them, was a main reason for his impeachment.

[23] Myers v. United States, 272 U. S. 52 (1926). The Supreme Court had previously always succeeded in side-stepping any ruling on the nature and location of the removal power. In the course of its decision, too, it vindicated President Johnson's veto (though not his violation) of the statute of 1867 by pronouncing that measure unconstitutional *post mortem*. Incidentally, the Myers case marked the first time in history that the national government, through the Department of Justice, appeared in the Supreme Court to attack the constitutionality of an act of Congress.

E. S. Corwin, "Tenure of Office and the Removal Power Under the Constitution," *Columbia Law Rev.,* XXVII, 353-399 (Apr., 1927); H. L. McBain, "Consequences of the President's Unlimited Power of Removal," *Polit. Sci. Quar.,* XLI, 596-603 (Dec., 1926); J. Hart, "The Bearing of Myers v. U. S. upon the Independence of Federal Administrative Tribunals," *Amer. Polit. Sci. Rev.,* XXIII, 657-673 (Aug., 1929), and reply by A. Langeluttig, *ibid.,* XXIV, 57-66 (Feb., 1930). The briefs, oral arguments of counsel, and opinions of the Court in the Myers case will be found in 69th Cong., 2nd Sess., Sen. Doc. No. 174 (1936).

officials appointed to commissions, such as the Interstate Commerce Commission, which Congress had endeavored to exempt from direct Presidential domination. This aspect of the problem was brought to the court for judgment about a decade later when, in 1933, President Franklin D. Roosevelt dismissed William S. Humphrey, a Republican member of the Federal Trade Commission, whose policies did not agree with those of the President. In doing so, the President made no pretense about adhering to the statutory requirements concerning the tenure of members of the "independent commission." In this case, the Court went back and picked up the other part of the Madison doctrine and held that Congress had the power to establish agencies in the executive branch which were not exactly executive in function and that it could clothe these with a certain immunity from Presidential direction.[24] The independent regulatory commissions are of this type, said the Court, and Congress was acting within its power when it specified the terms ("inefficiency, neglect of duty, or malfeasance in office") upon which commissioners may be removed.[25] Even if Congress does not expressly provide for removal, if the nature of the agency is such that it was clearly intended to be exempt from Presidential direction, the President may not remove an incumbent.[26]

The power of the Congress to prescribe dismissal procedures for the "inferior officers" has long been recognized. Since 1883, Congress has gradually extended the protections of merit system tenure to these offices, and thus for all practical purposes the President's power to dismiss merit system employees is sharply restricted. In the absence of legislative provision, however, the President may remove inferior officers at his discretion. *Removal of "inferior officers"*

Congress has frequently and by a variety of methods attempted to remove or to force the President to remove officers of the executive establishment, and these efforts suggest that the President's authority in removal must be viewed also from a different vantage point: the role of Congress in removals. In 1924, the Senate by resolution called upon President Coolidge to request the resignation of his Secretary of the Navy in consequence of his relation to the naval oil *Congressional removal power?*

[24] Rathbun (Humphrey's executor) v. United States, 295 U. S. 602 (1935).

[25] Professor E. S. Corwin sums up the situation since 1935 as follows: "(1) as to agents of his own powers, the president's removal power is illimitable; (2) as to agents of Congress's constitutional powers, Congress may confine it to removal for cause, which implies the further right to require a hearing as a part of the procedure of the removal." *The President: Office and Powers* (3rd ed.), 114. For full discussion of the Humphrey case, see W. J. Donovan and R. R. Irvine, "The President's Power to Remove Members of Administrative Agencies," *Cornell Law Quar.*, XXI, 215-248 (Feb., 1936). In 1937, President Roosevelt sponsored a reorganization measure which would have given the chief executive full power to make such removals as that attempted in the case of Humphrey, but Congress refused to approve it.

[26] Wiener v. United States, 357 U. S. 349 (1958). This case involved the attempted removal by President Eisenhower of a Truman appointee to the War Claims Commission. This Commission had been created in 1948 with service for its members for the life of the agency and without specification about removal. The reason for the removal assigned by the President was that he regarded it in the national interest to staff the agency with personnel of his own selection.

reserve scandal. The President strongly repelled the notion that this was any of the Senate's concern and took no official recognition of the request. By statutory provision, one officer of the government, the Comptroller General of the United States, may be removed from office before the end of his term only by joint resolution of the two houses of Congress. The rationale of this law, as set forth in an act of 1945, is that this officer is peculiarly a subordinate of the legislature. President Wilson vetoed the first act creating the office on the grounds that such a provision was unconstitutional, but it was passed again during Harding's term. The easiest and least debatable procedure available to the Congress for ousting administrative officers is to abolish their positions. In 1952, for example, the Truman Wage Stabilization Board was abolished because of Congressional disapproval of its findings in the steel-labor controversy and a new board with similar functions created. Another method tried by the Congress is to specify qualifications for positions which the incumbents do not possess.[27] The Congress has also tried, unsuccessfully, to deny salaries to particular administrators of whom it disapproves.[28] Finally, the Senate has sought, also unsuccessfully, to recall confirmations of appointments of officials.[29]

[27] In 1949, a rider attached to an appropriation bill required the commissioner of reclamation and his various regional directors to be engineers of five years' standing, the object being to force from office Michael W. Straus, commissioner, and Richard L. Boke, a director, who were not engineers, and whose policies were distasteful to elements in Congress. President Truman voiced strong objections; the two officials were continued in service, with salaries withheld; the rider did not reappear in the next year's appropriation bill; and the two men weathered the storm, even recovering back pay.

[28] In 1943, Congress sought to remove three officials (Robert M. Lovett, secretary of the Virgin Islands, and Goodwin B. Watson and William E. Dodd, Jr., of the Foreign Broadcast Intelligence Service of the Federal Communications Commission) by a rider to a deficiency appropriation bill specifying that the three, charged with subversive activities as affiliates of Communist organizations, should not continue on the national payroll beyond a given date unless in the meantime renominated by the President and reconfirmed by the Senate. President Roosevelt dared not veto the measure, but in approving it he condemned the rider as being to all intents and purposes a bill of attainder and therefore unconstitutional, as well as an encroachment upon the executive branch of the government. See F. L. Schuman, "Bill of Attainder in the Seventy-eighth Congress," *Amer. Polit. Sci. Rev.*, XXXVII, 819-829 (Oct., 1943). In a suit for back pay brought by the three men (who had continued in their posts), the Supreme Court later concurred with the President, pronouncing the rider a bill of attainder and therefore void. United States v. Lovett, 328 U. S. 303 (1946). For a full account of the affair, see R. E. Cushman, "The Purge of Federal Employees Accused of Disloyalty," *Pub. Admin. Rev.*, III, 297-316 (Autumn, 1943).

[29] In 1931, the Senate after confirming three persons nominated by the President for membership in the reorganized Federal Power Commission, changed its mind and attempted to recall the confirmations. President Hoover took the position that the confirmations represented completed acts, that the commissioners were duly in office, and that the only way—aside from removal by the President—in which they could be ousted was by impeachment. "I cannot admit the power of the Senate," he asserted, "to encroach upon the executive function by removal of a duly appointed executive officer under the guise of reconsideration of his nomination." The Senate's answer was to order the names restored to the executive calendar; and although when the question of confirmation was brought up again, two of the three were endorsed by narrow margins, the

POWER AS COMMANDER-IN-CHIEF OF THE ARMED FORCES

The President shall be commander-in-chief of the Army and the Navy of the United States and of the militia of the several States, when called into the actual service of the United States. ART. II, Sec. 2, Cl. 1

Among the many factors which have contributed to the aggrandizement of the office of President, none is more important than his military and diplomatic responsibilities.[30] The three Presidents—Lincoln, Wilson, Franklin D. Roosevelt—who piloted this nation through its major wars extended the scope of Presidential authority beyond any other holders of the office. In this century especially, wars both hot and cold have centered responsibility for the peace and safety of the nation more firmly in the Presidency than has been true in any other era save that of the Civil War. The security of this nation depends in great measure upon the maintenance of a firm military posture of readiness and upon the skillful operation of our diplomacy abroad. In both of these areas of governmental activity, the President is uniquely in the focal position. The country looks to him rather than to Congress or courts to save the day. *Effect of military responsibilities on the office of President*

The constitutional basis for the President's military authority is the assignment to him of the position of commander-in-chief of the forces. If to this be added his constitutional responsibility for law enforcement, we have virtually the entire legal framework upon which has been erected the towering structure of what Lincoln called the "war powers" of the President. Until Lincoln's day, it was quite generally assumed that the duty of commander-in-chief vested the President with purely military powers, such as to deploy the armed forces, to order their internal management, and to appoint and dismiss their officers. It was recognized that the President could, if he chose, take active, direct, and personal command of the troops in the field, but it was hoped by many that he would never be tempted to do this. Lincoln regarded his constitutional duties as including far more than this. He was obliged, he said, to save the nation and to suppress insurrection and as commander-in- *"War powers" of the President*

---

third, George Otis Smith, was rejected. Backed by the President, Smith was already at work as chairman, and the Senate's next move took the form of *quo warranto* proceedings to test his right to continue. The outcome was a decision of the Supreme Court unanimously upholding the President's contention and denying the Senate's right to recall the confirmation of a nominee, once the latter's commission has been issued by the President. United States *v.* Smith, 286 U. S. 6 (1932). In 1939, President Franklin D. Roosevelt refused to yield to a request of the Senate that he return its resolution assenting to a given appointment to a district judgeship in Tennessee. On the other hand, a President is not obliged to go through with an appointment simply because the Senate has assented to it; and the Senate has no legal means of compelling the President to make any appointment.

[30] The diplomatic power and functions of the President will be discussed in a later chapter.

chief he must do whatever was required to serve those ends.[31] Lincoln did ask the Congress subsequently to ratify most of his acts, which Congress did. However, he acted upon the view that the initiative and responsibility were his and that as commander-in-chief he was peculiarly responsible for preserving public order and combating insurrection. The Presidents charged with the conduct of the two world wars of this century have assumed that Lincoln's view of Presidential power to deal with rebellion is also applicable when the country is fighting a foreign enemy. Franklin D. Roosevelt, for example, in a message to Congress in 1942 dealing with the Emergency Price Control Act, invited the Congress to take action to stabilize wages and prices but, he said, "in the event that the Congress should fail to act, and act adequately, I shall accept the responsibility and I will act." "The President," he went on to say, "has the powers, under the Constitution and under Congressional acts, to take measures necessary to avert a disaster which would interfere with the winning of the war." President Roosevelt also created numerous emergency agencies by executive order and without express Congressional sanction. Under the color of his power as commander-in-chief he also ordered the wholesale detention and relocation of Japanese residents (citizens and aliens) of certain western states.

The "cold war" and Presidential authority   The "cold war" of the present era has stimulated the application of the Lincolnian doctrines to hostile situations where no war has been formally declared, as in Korea. Our obligations under the United Nations charter can, of course, be cited as adequate legal grounds for assignment of American troops to Korea without express Congressional approval. The deployment of American troops as "technical assistants" to the French-native forces in Indo-China was a Presidential decision unsupported by United Nations resolution or specific Congressional enactment. The Steel Seizure case alluded to above represents a setback for the most sweeping assertion of the authority of the commander-in-chief, but the power of the commander to deploy American troops anywhere in the world (Berlin, for example, where President Kennedy strengthened our troop deployments in 1961) is still widely accepted. President Eisenhower, however, usually tried to associate Congress with any major decision to commit American forces abroad as in the Formosa crises of 1955 and 1958 and the Mid-East crisis of 1957. In the Cuban crisis of 1962, President Kennedy imposed the naval blockade to halt arms shipments to the islands and to force the removal of missiles and jet bombers largely on his own authority. President Johnson in 1965 increased the amount and character of American military support for South Vietnam on the basis of his own estimates. He also sent troops into Santo Domingo in the same way. In these cases, however, Congressional resolutions on the subject had been adopted but not declarations of war. In summary, the extent of the power of a President

[31] In the Prize Cases of 1863 (2 B.L. 635) involving the validity of the blockade of the Southern ports when war had not formally been declared by the Congress, the Supreme Court largely supported Lincoln's assertions.

when acting as commander-in-chief is mainly undefined, but that it is considerable no one now doubts.[32]

THE PARDONING POWER OF THE PRESIDENT

. . . and he shall have power to grant reprieves and pardons for offenses against the United States, except in cases of impeachment. ART. II, Sec. 2, Cl. 1

The power to exempt individuals from the punishment ordained for the offenses of which they have been convicted [33] is one which has been associated with the chief executive in Anglo-American law for many centuries. The framers of our Constitution simply borrowed the practice from England. It should be noted that the President's power extends only to individuals convicted of national crimes and that it may not be used to veto Congressional convictions resulting from impeachment. The pardoning power has come to embrace the power to diminish the punishment, for example, by commutation of sentence, or to delay its application by reprieve, as well as to cancel it entirely. Although the Supreme Court at one time said that the effect of a full pardon is to make the offender, in the eye of the law, "as innocent as if he had never committed the offense," [34] the power is now regarded as not quite so sweeping, and judicial cognizance may be taken of a conviction even though the individual was pardoned.[35] *Scope of the pardoning power*

At present, about 1600 applications for Presidential clemency are made annually. Typically, each application is reviewed by a pardon attorney in the Department of Justice and, usually after consultation with the prosecuting attorney and the district judge concerned in the conviction, a recommendation is made to the President by the attorney general. In rare cases, the President himself may hear the individuals pressing for relief.

A special form of pardon, *amnesty,* is a sort of blanket pardon extended to numbers of persons who, without necessarily having been convicted individually, are widely believed to have violated national law. Amnesties may be declared under certain circumstances by act of Congress but the usual method is by Presidential proclamation. Such proclamations have been made *Amnesty*

---

[32] The way our presidents have fulfilled their responsibilities as commanders-in-chief is discussed by various authors in E. R. May, ed., *The Ultimate Decision: The President as Commander-In-Chief* (New York, 1960).

[33] A pardon may be (but rarely is) granted before conviction as well as after. The framers of the Constitution left this option open as a possible means of obtaining the testimony of accomplices.

[34] *Ex parte* Garland, 4 Wallace 333, 380 (1867).

[35] See E. S. Corwin, *The President: Office and Powers: History and Analysis of Practice and Opinion* (4th ed., New York, 1957), 166. The pardon does not have the effect of restoring money paid as a fine or property that has been forfeited, or an office that has been vacated. H. Wichofen, "The Effect of a Pardon," *Univ. of Pa. Law Rev.,* LXXXVIII, 177-193 (Dec., 1939).

by Washington in 1795, by Adams in 1800, by Madison in 1815, by Lincoln in 1863, by Johnson in 1865, 1867, and 1868, and by Theodore Roosevelt in 1902. President Johnson, for example, extended amnesty to most people who had supported secession in the Civil War.[36]

INSTITUTIONS OF PRESIDENTIAL LEADERSHIP: THE CABINET

Need for Presidential assistance

The sum total of the powers and responsibilities of the President of the United States, when added to the aspirations of those who occupy the position, is a crushing burden of work and care. It is almost too big a job for any mortal being. Two of the last eight Presidents (Harding and Franklin D. Roosevelt) have succumbed under the tremendous strain while still in office, a third (Kennedy) was felled by an assassin, and a fourth (Wilson) was stricken with paralysis and emerged from the Presidency broken in body and spirit. The life of a fifth (Coolidge) was undoubtedly shortened by his Presidential anxieties. Twice during his service, a sixth (Eisenhower) was felled by serious heart attacks. Strange as it may be that men willingly seek such an office, it is stranger still that they are able to bear up under the stresses and worries of it and to perform in it as well as they have done.

It should be obvious to any thoughtful student that the President cannot do all the things he is supposed to do or carry all the weight of affairs he is required to carry without help. However solitary and self-contained the office of President may seem to be in law and in the eyes of the throng, the President, himself, is quite dependent upon his assistants, high and low, for the effective discharge of his responsibilities. It is not too much to say that the quality of Presidential assistance and the organizational arrangements through which it is brought to the aid of Presidential decision are major determinants of Presidential success. More than this, they make it possible for one human being somehow to fill the Presidency.

Origin of the cabinet

Among the institutional arrangements for Presidential assistance none is more interesting or less helpful than the Cabinet. The office of President was designed by the fathers of the American Constitution with great misgiving that any man could be found to whom could safely be entrusted such power and responsibility. Many proposals were made to share Presidential burdens with a council of some kind. In fact, there had been proposals for an executive council of the heads of the four national executive agencies during the confederation period. None of these proposals was ever adopted. The Cabinet, as we know it, grew up outside the Constitution and unknown to the law.

---

[36] Because of the numbers involved, and because based on recommendations of a special "amnesty board," President Truman's "Christmas gift" pardon in 1947 of 1500 persons who had evaded or otherwise violated the Selective Service Act of 1940 was sometimes referred to as an amnesty. It nevertheless was rather a series of pardons of persons individually convicted, and selected from a total of ten times the number.

President Washington looked first to the Senate to share some of his burdens and to offer him timely advice and then to the Supreme Court. He was rebuffed by each of them in turn. And, finally, when the House of Representatives discouraged the appearance of his departmental heads in the midst of their deliberations, he was forced to turn in upon the resources of the executive branch. Washington came to rely entirely on his own subordinates, the heads of the four executive departments, for advice and assistance and thus the Cabinet was born.[37] Hamilton's effort to model the institution into an agency of collective responsibility somewhat like the later British model was unsuccessful. Throughout the decades the Cabinet has remained a purely advisory body.

As the years have passed, the traditions and customs of the Cabinet have become more and more settled. These settled traditions, however, concern the membership, the relative rank of the members, and the formalities of meeting. Few decisive traditions have been established regarding the purpose of the Cabinet, the subjects of its deliberations, or the regard which must be given to its decisions. Cabinets have been and are now whatever the President chooses to make of them. Some Presidents, Pierce, Buchanan, and Harding, for example, consulted their Cabinets at every turn and ordinarily acted upon their recommendations. Eisenhower relied on his Cabinet a good deal more than his immediate predecessors and during his illnesses it came very close to being an agency of collective responsibility. Others have ignored their Cabinets. Jackson, preferring to lean upon personal friends and political aides, discontinued Cabinet meetings altogether. Lincoln is reported to have polled his Cabinet on a critical issue of the day and finding all opposed to his own opinion, nevertheless decided in favor of his own proposal. Wilson, Franklin D. Roosevelt, and John Kennedy leaned lightly on their Cabinets; they rarely submitted any major policy questions to the meetings. The following passage from the most recent and most comprehensive study of the operation of the executive branch ever made states rather exactly the modern position—or lack of it—of the Cabinet: [38]

The Cabinet is what the President makes it

> The members of the Cabinet are the primary advisers to the President. He is free to select them, to decide the subjects on which he wishes advice, and to follow their advice or not as he sees fit. The Cabinet as a body, however, is not an effective council of advisers to the President and it does not have a collective responsibility for administration policies. That responsibility rests upon the President. The Cabinet members, being chosen to direct great specialized operating departments, are not all fitted to advise him on every subject.

[37] The beginnings of the cabinet are described fully in H. B. Learned, *The President's Cabinet* (New Haven, 1912), Chap. V.

[38] *Report to the Congress by the Commission on Organization of the Executive Branch of the Government,* "General Management of the Executive Branch" (Washington, 1949), 17-18. One cannot repress the notion that this passage was written by the chairman of the commission, former President Herbert Hoover.

Meetings   Cabinet meetings are ordinarily held once or twice a week in a special room in the White House expressly designed for the purpose. The President and the heads of the eleven executive departments sit around a large oval table, the President in the middle and the others flanking him in order of rank. The Vice-President is commonly in attendance, as on many occasions are heads of some of the large agencies which do not have departmental status. Proceedings are informal; there are no rules of debate; no minutes are kept; and, rarely are any votes taken. Under President Eisenhower, however, a regular agenda was prepared in advance for the meetings, a secretary to the Cabinet was established, and decisions taken were noted and efforts made to see that they were properly implemented. Few of these practices were continud by Kennedy. Traditionally, the matters discussed were those introduced by the President and very commonly included party and campaign problems as well as problems of a legislative, executive, or administrative character.[39] These discussions, at best, bring out useful information and opinions, clarify the issues, and promote morale among the top executives of the administration. Almost never do they culminate in decisions on policy by mere show of hands.

Influences on Cabinet appointments   It might well be asked why the Cabinet has developed the way it has. Surely a President could only strengthen his position and lighten his cares by sharing some of his responsibility with the Cabinet, by leaning on them for advice and guidance, and by utilizing more fully the very considerable administrative and political talents which every Cabinet contains. Furthermore, the Senatorial power of confirmation provides no great barrier to Cabinet unity and loyalty. The Senate has, as we have noted, accorded unusual freedom to the President to make his own selections. The answer to the question appears to be that, although the Senate has left the President largely free to make his own appointments, the political traditions of the nation have not left him free to gather around him a group of advisors upon which he can certainly depend for loyal support. When a modern President comes to choose his Cabinet he is obliged to take account of many factors other than personal loyalty and dependability. Most Presidents have felt that the Cabinet must be an instrument of party harmony and that, therefore, the various factions and regions which are influential in party councils must be represented in it. The men and groups over whom the President climbed on his way to the nomination have got to be placated in the interests of presenting a united front to the people and a strong

[39] The above description holds true generally, but actually the atmosphere of Cabinet meetings differs under different Presidents. Under Franklin D. Roosevelt, meetings were long and leisurely, sometimes lasting two hours, with everyone given plenty of time to say what was on his mind—though with the President sometimes more or less monopolizing the conversation, and often largely with stories of the past. Under Truman, meetings were short and crisp, rarely lasting more than an hour, and with the President obviously watching the clock. Eisenhower's meetings more and more took the form of presentations by one member of a substantial program developed in his department and for which advice and concurrence by other members and by the President was sought.

claim upon the party's followers in Congress. In some instances, the managers of the successful candidate have even promised Cabinet appointments to some men in order to win their support in the party convention. Lincoln's Cabinet contained his chief rivals for the Republican nomination—Seward and Chase; Wilson felt obliged to make Bryan his Secretary of State because of his influence with a large wing of the Democratic Party; Harding appointed Hughes, the party standard bearer in 1916, to the same position; Franklin D. Roosevelt's first Cabinet had strong representatives of the Southern wing of his party. Only on rare occasions have Presidents stepped outside their parties to name men of slight political influence or men identified with the other party.[40]

Each President has tried to make his Cabinet as broadly representative as he can, with someone from the West (usually to head the Department of the Interior); someone from the South; someone from the group he is trying to detach from the other party (Eisenhower's appointment of Martin Durkin, the Democrat leader of an AFL union, for example); someone from labor, from agriculture, and from industry. The aspirations of almost every major group in the body politic are recognized in some way by the Cabinet selections. Under these circumstances, a President is surrounding himself with men and women whose loyalty to him and enthusiasm for his program is not always whole-hearted. Secretary Chase, in Lincoln's Cabinet, spent much of his time trying to unseat Lincoln and capture the Presidency for himself. Bryan was never really sympathetic to Wilson's pro-Allied foreign policy. Hoover rose to the Presidency from a Cabinet post under circumstances which did not endear him to Coolidge. A Cabinet seat (the Postmaster Generalship), furthermore, is customarily reserved for the chairman of the party's national committee. Thus, we see that when a President calls his Cabinet together for the first time he will discover as he looks around the table, men whom he did not know at all until a few days or weeks ago, men whom he has every reason to distrust, men with whom he will never be able to agree on any matter of fundamental policy. Only here and there will a familiar face of a true friend and well-wisher appear. It is for these reasons that many Presidents have preferred to seek advice elsewhere and to confine Cabinet discussion to questions of party policy or to anecdotes and trivia.

It should not be supposed from what has been said that Presidents are utterly indifferent to the competence, administrative or technical, of the individuals appointed to Cabinet position. The Attorney General is always a lawyer; the Secretary of the Treasury is frequently a financier; the Secretary of

Cabinet not fitted to share Presidential burdens

Cabinet qualifications

[40] Cleveland appointed Walter Q. Gresham, a prospective Republican Presidential candidate, to be his Secretary of State, but Gresham had supported Cleveland in the campaign. McKinley appointed a "gold" Democrat, Secretary of the Treasury. Theodore Roosevelt and Taft each appointed a Democrat as Secretary of War; Hoover made a Democrat Attorney General and Franklin Roosevelt appointed two Republicans, Henry S. Stimson and Frank Knox, to his Cabinet when he wanted to build bipartisan support for his foreign policy. In virtually every case, some political advantage was expected to accrue to the President's party by these appointments.

Agriculture is a member of some agricultural organization. Perhaps an increasing proportion of individuals are selected for their special knowledge and experience of the matters with which their departments deal. In the main, however, these qualifications are secondary in importance to the ones already discussed.[41]

THE EXECUTIVE OFFICE OF THE PRESIDENT

The most effective institutional arrangement for lightening the President's load and helping him to get through his daily chores is a product of the last three decades. It is the staff assistance provided through the Executive Office of the President. This institution is a product of the first of the two great studies of this generation of the operation of the executive branch of the national government: the Report of the President's Committee on Administrative Management (1937).[42]

The creation of the Executive Office of the President

Until well into this century, the President relied almost entirely on the departments for bringing to him timely reports, carefully conceived recommendations, answers to the questions propounded by his visitors, his correspondents, and his legislative colleagues, and estimations of the future. His own staff included only a private secretary to handle his visiting list, his mail, and his directions, some assistants to help in processing the mail, and an executive clerk to direct the various employees of the White House. Through personal contacts, Cabinet meetings, and directives, the President tried desperately to coordinate and give direction to the movements of the growing complex of agencies which comprise the executive branch. This responsibility added to his other cares impelled him to labor far beyond the powers of most persons. The first major device for equipping the President to take a broad, superdepartmental view of his responsibilities was the Bureau of the Budget, created in 1921. Although placed at first in the Treasury Department, this Bureau nevertheless became a tool of Presidential direction and its director the major financial adviser to the President. In 1928, the number of secretaries to the President was increased to three and the work of his office compartmentalized into correspondence, reception of visitors, economic research, legislative matters, and press relations. His purely ceremonial military aides were replaced at this time by distinguished officers able to advise the President on grave military questions. The tremendous expansion of governmental services and staff incident to combatting the depression engulfed the President in a new flood of papers, people, and programs demanding his personal attention. "The President needs

[41] An excellent discussion of the development and role of the modern Cabinet will be found in R. F. Fenno, Jr., *The President's Cabinet* (Cambridge, Mass., 1959).

[42] The Report of this committee is entitled *Administrative Management in the Government of the United States* (Washington, 1937). The other study is that by the Hoover Commission and its recommendations may be found in *The Hoover Commission Report on Organization of the Executive Branch of the Government* (New York, 1949).

help," said the Committee on Administrative Management in 1937. The President should have at his command a staff of assistants who can be his eyes and ears and bring to him the data necessary to inform his judgment. This staff, said the Committee, should consist of men "in whom the President has personal confidence and whose character and attitude is such that they would not attempt to exercise power on their own account." Furthermore, the Bureau of the Budget should be brought directly into the Presidential entourage and with it the major personnel agency of the government, the Civil Service Commission, and the major planning agency at that time, the National Resources Board.

Pursuant to these recommendations and to the Reorganization Act of 1939, the modern Executive Office of the President was created by Executive Order in 1939.[43] Under the roof of the Executive Office was established the White House office, embracing the personal secretaries and newly created assistants to the President and their staffs. Under President Johnson, the White House office now consists of approximately 300 employees, the most important of whom are a press secretary; a correspondence secretary; an appointment (calendar) secretary; a special legal counsel; military aides from the three armed services; an executive clerk; special assistants dealing with legislative relations, speech writing, "cold war" planning, trade negotiations, race relations, national security. President Eisenhower had a chief-of-staff directing the activities of all of the others in the office but Presidents Kennedy and Johnson abandoned this practice. President Truman made a practice of holding daily conferences with his chief lieutenants in the White House office at which time the day's duties were reviewed. The President gave directions to each man and received from each advice on the upcoming matters of the day. President Eisenhower relied heavily on his chief-of-staff to co-ordinate all of his aides of the White House staff. These men, in all recent administrations, have been the Presidents' own selections and have had a compelling influence on what and who are brought to the attention of the "boss." All except the most influential men in national life who set out to capture the President's ear end up by seeing one of his assistants.

Components of the Executive Office: 1. The White House office

The Bureau of the Budget was transferred from the Treasury Department to the Executive Office by executive order and its functions expanded to embrace not only fiscal policy but general administrative management in the executive branch. Its function of screening all departmental and agency proposals for legislation was broadened and strengthened at the same time. The present Bureau, with its 1000 employees, is the key planning agency for the nation's finances, and because of its proximity to the chief executive himself is able to exercise a profound influence on all departmental programs and policies, as these must be supported by adequate financing.

2. Bureau of the Budget

In lieu of the reorganization of the Civil Service Commission into a single-headed personnel agency and its transfer to the Executive Office as

[43] Executive Order 8248, Sept. 10, 1939.

proposed by the committee, a Liaison Office for Personnel Management was created in the Executive Office. This has never functioned effectively, however, and is now moribund. The National Resources Board, retitled the National Resources Planning Board, was also transferred to the Executive Office. After an energetic but controversial history it was killed by the Congress in 1946.

3. Council of Economic Advisers

The Employment Act of 1946 added a new unit to the President's office when it created the three-man Council of Economic Advisers. This agency was and is charged with keeping its fingers on the pulse of the American economy, advising the President on the state of the nation's economic health, and preparing periodic reports for him to submit to the Congress on the subject.[44]

4. National Security Council

As an outgrowth of the struggle for unified direction of the defense forces and of the strategy of the nation, two important Cabinet committees were created and practically, although not formally, made a part of the executive establishment. The National Security Council and the National Security Resources Board, established in 1947, were designed to improve the ability of the President to coordinate military and diplomatic policies and military mobilization policies and industrial and resources programs.[45] The staff of the National Security Council is part of the Executive Office of the President.

5. Office of Emergency Planning

The chairman and staff of the National Security Resources Board were, in 1953, consolidated with the director of defense mobilization into the Office of Defense Mobilization. In 1958, it became the Office of Civil and Defense Mobilization and in 1961 with the transfer of civil defense functions to the Department of Defense, it was retitled the Office of Emergency Planning. The present office now serves as the principal planning agency for all matters relating to current and future efforts to prepare the American economy for war.

6. National Aeronautics and Space Council

Controversy over the proper direction and the assignment of the responsibilities for American efforts in space precipitated by the Russian Sputnik led to the creation in 1958 of the National Aeronautic and Space Council. This is essentially a Cabinet committee headed by the Vice-President but the staff is part of the Executive Office.

7. Office of Science and Technology

The rapid growth of the research efforts of the national government contributed to the formation in 1962 of the Office of Science and Technology. The Director is the science adviser to the President and coordinates scientific programs with the economic, welfare, diplomatic, and defense needs of the nation.

44 The Hoover Commission recommendation that the Council of Economic Advisers be reorganized into a one-man adviser to the President on economic matters has thus far not been accepted.

45 From 1957 to 1961, an Operations Coordinating Board functioned in close connection with the Council to follow up on decisions and make certain of coordinated implementation. President Kennedy in abolishing the Board indicated that he expected the Secretary of State to play a greater role in implementing Council decisions.

To administer the war on poverty proposed by President Johnson and *8. Office* approved by Congress in 1964, an Office of Economic Opportunity was cre- *of Eco-* ated in the Executive Office. The director is responsible for developing plans *nomic Oppor-* for the youth training, job corps, community action programs, business aids *tunity* and other devices contemplated by the law for eliminating poverty in America.

During World War II, an Office for Emergency Management created in the Executive Office proved an invaluable framework for the operation of the temporary civilian war agencies charged with control of production, man-power, prices, and wages.

The new Executive Office has seemed so exactly to fit the needs of the *Executive* times that it has grown steadily in importance and utility in the past twenty- *Office* five years. Surrounding the President, as it does, with a "palace guard" of *grows in* devoted servants and multiplying by several-fold his ability to breast the *usefulness* waves of reports, orders, problems, and advice rising from the bureaus, offices, and agencies of the vast administrative sea, it provides the most effective support to the President of the United States. This was perhaps most clearly revealed by the way the office functioned during Eisenhower's illness. The Presidency has thus become not a man but an institution. Its occupant reads a very small portion of all the written matter he receives; he writes an insig-nificant number of the papers he signs; he prepares almost none of the mes-sages and speeches he delivers; he sees a fraction of those who would consult with him. Only thus can a mere man today "execute the office of Pres-ident." [46]

Despite the impressive successes of the Executive Office, few statesmen *Continued* or students are wholly satisfied that the Presidency is still within human *efforts to* capacity and that the American genius for organization has yet solved the *aid the* problems of coordinating the efforts of the huge executive establishment. Each *President* year brings a new spate of proposals for improvement. Ex-President Hoover believed we need a second Vice-President, appointed by the President and responsible to him to whom might be delegated a large part of the routine chores.[47] Governor Rockefeller (New York) has proposed a deputy Presi-dent. President Eisenhower, father of the chief-of-staff system in the White House, is believed to favor a First-Secretary above the Cabinet and below the President. Ex-President Truman and a subcommittee of the Senate, headed by Senator Jackson (Wash.), opposed these solutions.[48] A recent study also

[46] Presidential labors have been somewhat lightened by an act of Congress in 1950 authorizing the chief executive, under proper safeguards, to delegate to heads of depart-ments or agencies the performance of functions vested in him by law or previously requiring his personal attention when performed by others.

[47] He advanced this proposal in 1956 to a subcommittee of the Senate headed by Senator (later President) Kennedy. See *The New York Times,* Jan. 17, 1956 and Dec. 12, 1955.

[48] A review of a staff report for the sub-committee expressing this view may be found in *The New York Times,* Nov. 22, 1960. Mr. Truman's letter on the Hoover proposal is in the *New York Times,* Jan. 16, 1956.

undertaken for the Jackson group suggests the need for a national research organization to undertake the long-range studies of foreign and military policies and a planning staff in the Executive Office to evaluate programs and policies for the President.[49]

THE VICE-PRESIDENCY AND PRESIDENTIAL SUCCESSION

Office of Vice-President

The Vice-President of the United States has no constitutional function except to preside over the Senate and to assume the office of President in the case of the death, resignation, removal, or disability of the incumbent.[50] As presiding officer of the Senate he is not a member of that body, has no vote except when a tie occurs, and participates in the deliberations only informally, if at all. As heir-apparent to the Presidency, he is an executive officer of the government potentially rather than actually. Since 1836, the only occasions upon which the Vice-President has succeeded to the office of President have been the result of the death of the President. Eight Presidents have died in office [51] and a like number of Vice-Presidents have assumed the Presidency. No President has resigned; none has been removed. No President has been incapacitated to such an extent and for so long a period as to lead to the assumption of his duties by the Vice-President. Such a transfer was, however, seriously discussed when Garfield lay dying for two months, stricken by an assassin's bullet, when Wilson suffered a paralytic stroke which held him in bed for weeks, and when Eisenhower had a heart attack in the fall of 1955 and a mild "stroke" in the fall of 1957. Eisenhower's illness, followed by Kennedy's assassination, precipitated a considerable effort to find a statutory or constitutional remedy for the present situation in which the President alone is really the sole judge of his own disability. President Eisenhower in 1958, President Kennedy in 1961, and President Johnson in 1963 and in 1965 entered into agreements with their respective Vice-Presidents by the terms of which the Vice-President is to become "acting" President in case of Presidential disability until the disability is ended. If the President is unable to communicate

[49] See *The New York Times,* Mar. 13, 1960.

[50] Under the language of the original Constitution, the Vice-President succeeds only to the "powers and duties" of the office, not to the office itself, and hence in 1927 it was argued that another term for Calvin Coolidge would not be a third term as *President.* From the time, however, when John Tyler, succeeding the deceased William Henry Harrison, insisted upon being regarded and addressed as *President,* we have had (in such situations) only Presidents, not "acting Presidents." Certainly no one thought of Harry S. Truman, when entering the White House in 1945, as anything other than President. The Twentieth Amendment, moreover, says that if a President-elect dies before taking office, the Vice-President-elect "shall become President."

[51] Harrison, Taylor, Lincoln, Garfield, McKinley, Harding, F. D. Roosevelt, and John Kennedy, Adams, Jefferson, Van Buren and Johnson served as Vice-Presidents and were later elevated to the Presidency by the voters. P. L. Levin, *Seven by Chance* (New York, 1948). In point of fact, seven Vice-Presidents, too, have died in office, but luckily not one, as it has turned out, who would have been called upon to assume the duties of a deceased President. In all, the Presidency or Vice-Presidency has fallen vacant in mid-term 15 times in the country's history.

then the Vice-President may make the determination of disability himself after "appropriate consultation." [52] Finally, in 1965, the two houses of Congress approved and sent to the states a constitutional amendment on this subject under the terms of which if a President is unable or unwilling to declare his own disability, the Vice-President with the assent of a majority of the principal officers of the executive department—or of some other body which Congress may hereafter designate for the purpose—may assume the duties and may hold them against a Presidential assertion that the disability is ended if Congress by a two-thirds vote supports the Vice-President's assertion.[53]

The rise of the party system, the passage of the Twelfth Amendment providing separate voting for President and Vice-President and the rarity with which Presidents have dropped the reins of power combined to reduce the office of Vice-President to comparative insignificance. The result has been that candidates for this office are not selected with the same care as Presidential candidates. Many worthy and experienced statesmen have, in fact, refused to be considered for the nomination. The candidates are in practice selected by the Presidential candidate himself usually to balance the ticket, that is, to appeal to regions and interests with whom the Presidential candidate is not identified. The Vice-President has, in consequence, proved hard to fit into the chain of command or the framework of responsibility in the executive branch. Although it would appear reasonable that the Vice-President be kept informed of the policies and plans of the administration, Calvin Coolidge was the first Vice-President regularly to attend Cabinet meetings. This custom has by now become fairly well established. The Cabinet meeting, however, is not the most effective institutional device for keeping the Vice-President informed. A succession of Vice-Presidents, Garner, Truman, Barkley, Nixon, Johnson, and Humphrey selected from the Senate, have uncovered new uses of the office. These men proved valuable intermediaries between the President and the Congress. Nixon, Johnson, and Humphrey have also played roles in foreign affairs and served the President as special emissaries abroad on several occasions. When, in November 22, 1963, President Kennedy was cruelly murdered, the country was indeed fortunate that the Vice President, Lyndon B. Johnson, could bring to his accession to the Presidency long and highly responsible service on Capitol Hill and a knowledge of the inner workings of the administration unmatched by any previous Vice-President. The tragedy also stimulated much concern with the selection of Vice-Presidential candidates in the campaign of 1964. Perhaps the Vice-Presidency is at last coming to share some of the burdens of the President.[54]

There is no assurance at any given moment that there will be a Vice-

The role of the Vice-President

Arrangements for Presidential succession

[52] For the text of the Kennedy-Johnson compact used also by Johnson with Speaker McCormack and with Vice-President Humphrey. See *The New York Times*, Aug. 11, 1961.

[53] The full text of the proposed amendment will be found in the Appendix.

[54] See E. G. Williams, *The Rise of the Vice-Presidency* (Washington, 1956), and E. W. Waugh, *Second Consul: The Vice President, Our Greatest Political Problem* (New York, 1956).

President to assume the Presidential duties. Vice-Presidents may also die, resign, be removed, or become incapacitated. The Constitution authorizes Congress to provide for this contingency by "declaring what officer shall then act as President." The first legislation on this subject in 1792 provided that the president *pro tempore* of the Senate should next succeed to the Presidency and after him the speaker of the House of Representatives. In 1881, the death of President Garfield some weeks before a newly-elected Congress was to convene, and thus with neither a speaker nor a President *pro tempore* in office, brought the weaknesses of this act freshly to the country's attention. A new Presidential Succession Act of 1886 withdrew the Congressional officers from the succession and substituted for them, after the Vice-President, the heads of the departments in specified order beginning with the Secretary of State, due regard being paid to the constitutional qualifications of age, citizenship, and residence. In 1945, President Truman became disturbed over the fact that he would be naming his own successor when he selected the Secretary of State. He began urging the Congress to modify the Act of 1886 so that an elective officer and not an appointed one might succeed. A Republican election victory in 1946 which gave them control of the selection of the leaders of the two houses stimulated affirmative action on the President's suggestion. A new act in 1947 provided that next after the Vice-President shall be the speaker of the House, after him the president *pro tempore* of the Senate,[55] and then the department heads in the old order. The wisdom of the Act of 1947 was called into grave question in 1963. The elevation of Johnson to the Presidency placed in direct succession Speaker McCormack in his mid-seventies and then Senator Hayden—in his eighties. After the election of 1964 filled the office of Vice-President and this change would not reflect directly on either of these powerful solons, the matter was reviewed along with Presidential disability. Under the terms of the amendment now pending before the states, the President is empowered to fill a vacancy in the office of

[55] A speaker or president *pro tempore* succeeding to the Presidency fills out the unexpired term, but a Cabinet officer elevated to the office serves only until a speaker or president *pro tempore* becomes available. Any one (except a Vice-President) succeeding to the post is, under the new legislation, merely "acting President."

Back in 1792, James Madison objected to the legislation then enacted on the ground that the speaker and president *pro tempore* were not "constitutional officers," both being (as members of Congress) not national but state officers; and constitutional lawyers in the Senate found the same fault with the legislation of 1947. The point was made also that the main reason for repealing the original statute in 1886 was the belief of Congress at that time that the speaker and president *pro tempore*, not being officers of the United States, were ineligible to the succession. For a summary of the arguments, see "The Question of Amending the Presidential Succession Act; Pro and Con" (symposium), *Cong. Digest*, XXV, 67-96 (Mar., 1946).

For fuller discussions, see J. E. Kallenbach, "The New Presidential Succession Act," *Amer. Polit. Sci. Rev.*, XLI, 931-940 (Oct., 1947); R. S. Rankin, "Presidential Succession in the United States," *Jour. of Politics*, VIII, 44-56 (Feb., 1946); and R. C. Silva, "The Presidential Succession Act of 1947," *Mich. Law Rev.*, XLVII, 451-476 (Feb., 1949).

Vice-President by nomination subject to the confirmation of a majority of both houses of Congress. Should this change be approved the Act of 1947 will be largely obviated.

References

The Federalist, Nos. LXXI-LXXII, LXXVI-LXXVII.

W. H. Taft, *Our Chief Magistrate and His Powers* (New York, 1916), Chaps. III-V.

E. S. Corwin, *The President: Office and Powers: History and Analysis of Practice and Opinion* (4th ed., New York, 1957), Chaps. II, III-IV.

————, *The President's Removal Power Under the Constitution* (New York, 1927).

C. P. Patterson, *Presidential Government in the United States; The Unwritten Constitution* (Chapel Hill, N.C., 1947), Chap. VIII.

H. J. Laski, *The American Presidency* (New York, 1940), Chaps. I, II, IV.

G. F. Milton, *The Use of Presidential Power, 1789-1943* (Boston, 1944).

W. E. Binkley, *The Man in the White House: His Powers and Duties* (Baltimore, 1959).

L. M. Salmon, "History of the Appointing Power of the President," *Amer. Hist. Assoc. Papers,* I, No. 5 (Washington, 1886).

C. E. Morganston, *The Appointing and Removal Power of the President of the United States,* 70th Cong., 2nd Sess., Sen. Doc. No. 172 (1929).

A. W. Macmahon, "Senatorial Confirmation," *Pub. Admin. Rev.,* III, 281-296 (Autumn, 1943).

J. Hart, *Tenure of Office Under the Constitution* (Baltimore, 1930).

————, *The Ordinance-Making Powers of the President of the United States* (Baltimore, 1925).

————, *The American Presidency in Action: 1789: A Study in Constitutional History* (New York, 1948).

G. A. Schumbert, Jr., *The Presidency in the Courts* (Minneapolis, 1957).

L. L. Henry, *Presidential Transitions* (Washington, 1960).

J. Bell, *The Splendid Misery: The Story of the Presidency and Power Politics at Close Range* (New York, 1960).

R. G. Tugwell, *The Enlargement of the Presidency* (New York, 1960).

C. Rossiter, *The American Presidency* (New York, 1956).

D. C. Coyle, *Ordeal of the Presidency* (Washington, 1960).

R. E. Neustadt, *Presidential Power: The Politics of Leadership* (New York, 1960).

W. Johnson, *1600 Pennsylvania Avenue: Presidents and the People 1929-1959* (Boston, 1960).

N. D. Grundstein, *Presidential Delegation of Authority in Wartime* (Pittsburgh, 1961).

E. H. Hobbs, *Behind the President: A Study of Executive Office Agencies* (Washington, 1954).

W. H. Humbert, *The Pardoning Power of the President* (Washington, 1941).

B. M. Rich, *The Presidents and Civil Disorder* (Washington, 1941).

A. L. Sturm, *Presidential Power and National Emergencies* (New York, 1941).

C. D. Waldo and W. Pincus, "The Statutory Obligations of the President: Executive Necessity and Presidential Burden," *Pub. Admin. Rev.*, VI, 339-347 (Autumn, 1946).

N. J. Small, *Some Presidential Interpretations of the Presidency* (Baltimore, 1932).

C. C. Thach, "The Creation of the Presidency, 1775-1789," *Johns Hopkins Univ. Studies in Hist. and Polit. Sci.*, XL, 415-596 (Baltimore, 1922).

L. Brownlow, *The President and the Presidency* (Chicago, 1949).

L. W. Koenig, *The Chief Executive* (New York, 1964).

L. C. Hatch, *A History of the Vice-Presidency of the United States*, rev. and ed. by E. L. Shoup (New York, 1934).

H. B. Learned, *The President's Cabinet* (New Haven, 1912).

M. L. Hinsdale, *History of the President's Cabinet* (Ann Arbor, Mich., 1911).

W. H. Smith, *History of the Cabinet of the United States* (Baltimore, 1925).

L. Brownlow *et al.*, "The Executive Office of the President: A Symposium," *Pub. Admin. Rev.*, I, 101-140 (Winter, 1941).

F. Morstein Marx, *The President and His Staff Services* (Chicago, 1947).

T. C. Sorenson, *Decision-Making in the White House* (New York, 1963).

I. G. Williams, *The American Vice-Presidency: New Look* (New York, 1954).

R. F. Fenno, *The President's Cabinet: An Analysis in the Period from Wilson to Eisenhower* (New York, 1959).

President's Committee on Administrative Management in the Government of the United States, *Report, with Special Studies* (Washington, 1937).

★ 14 ★

The Organization and Procedures of the Executive Branch

THE NATURE AND IMPORTANCE OF ADMINISTRATION

JUST AS THE CHARACTERISTIC ACTIVITY of the Congress is legislation, that of the executive branch is administration. Governmental administration is the attempt to realize in practice the policies established by Congress and the President. The spirit of the American system of government is that public policies will be determined by elected representatives of the people, although it may be necessary to employ nonpolitical technicians to carry them out. However, the line which separates policy determination from policy execution is neither precise nor stable. Many laws and executive orders leave a great deal of discretion to the technicians; many technicians are able to exert powerful influence upon the formulation of the laws and orders. The chief of the national administration faces both ways—in collaboration with Congress he is policy determiner, and in collaboration with the executive agencies he is policy executor. The Congress on its part does not confine its attention to policy alone; it is constantly involved in administration. Thus, in practice, there is a large twilight zone between the two spheres of governmental activity in which administration and legislation are inseparably intertwined. That policy in our system of government should be determined by politically responsible officials who must account to the voters for their conduct represents, therefore, both an aspiration which must be earnestly sought and an achievement which has largely been realized.

The importance of administration in the vitality of the American system of government has only recently thrust itself upon the awareness of the American people. As a people we have tended to assume that legislation is the prime corrective of all ills of the body politic. We have a greater penchant for passing laws about things than almost any other people on earth. Only in the past half-century have we been gradually brought to the realization that passing wise

Administration and the American system

Importance of administration

GROWTH OF THE NATIONAL GOVERNMENT
1790-1964

Date	No. of Civilian Employees	Expenditures
1790	350	$4,269,027
1801	2,100	9,394,582
1816	6,327	30,586,691
1831	19,800	15,247,651
1861	49,200	66,546,645
1881	107,000	260,712,888
1901	256,000	524,616,925
1921	562,252	5,115,927,690
1941	1,370,110	12,710,629,824
1951	2,879,000	44,632,822,000
1961	2,300,000	78,900,000,000
1964	2,469,235	97,700,000,000

Improvement in administration has not kept pace with the problem

laws, as difficult as that is, is easier than having them economically and effectively administered. Many of us still do not appreciate that the laws are no better than their administration. What is more, there are many problems, foreign and domestic, that cannot be solved by laws, and some type of administrative procedure is the only method available to the government to deal with them. During much of the nineteenth century, administration was regarded as the legitimate booty of political party struggles and its aim to sustain the victors in their triumph. Almost any citizen of mature age and average mentality could administer virtually any program decided upon by the policy determiners, it was thought. Woodrow Wilson pioneered in directing the attention of the American people and their leaders to the importance of good administration.[1] Interest gradually increased, and since about 1920 administration at all levels of government has become the subject of extensive research, writing, and experimentation.[2] The result of this interest has been increased understanding, and this, in turn, has produced a remarkable improvement in the administration of governments of all kinds.

As rapidly as administrative reform has followed administrative reform in the past decades, it is doubtful if improvement has kept pace with the problem. Like the swelling mushroom of an atomic explosion which soon dwarfs

---

[1] "The Study of Administration," *Polit. Sci. Quar.*, II, 197-222 (June, 1887).

[2] Growing recognition in this country of the importance of administration was reflected in the formation, in 1939, of an American Society for Public Administration, whose quarterly journal, the *Public Administration Review*, should be known to all students of the subject. Cf. F. Morstein Marx [ed.], *Elements of Public Administration* (New York, 1946), Chap. II (by A. Leiserson) on "The Study of Public Administration."

all other features of the horizon, national administration has burgeoned into a swelling cloud of money and employees by comparison with which Congress and the courts are but specks on the national landscape. None of the changes through the years in the government of the United States is quite so startling or quite so consequential as the tremendous growth of the executive branch. In point of cost, volume of activities, and numbers of people employed, the "big government" of which so much is heard these days is really "big administration." Can an enterprise of this magnitude be managed by ordinary human beings? Can it effectively deliver the services and solve the problems which are expected of it? Can it somehow be paid for without exhausting the resources and the economic health of the nation? Can its technical skills and organizational energies be harnessed to the cart of constitutional democracy? Can the people's representatives really hold the reins? These are the more important of the problems raised by the growth of this young giant.

THE STRUCTURE OF THE EXECUTIVE BRANCH

One of the determinants of whether the vast array of officials and employees who comprise the executive branch can, in fact, be brought under the directing will of the President and his aides and under the general supervision of the Congress is the way in which they are organized to perform the tasks assigned to them. The need for organization is, of course, a product of the size and complexity of the operation, and the importance of proper organization tends to increase directly with growth. Direction of the modern executive branch of the national government would be unthinkable unless the individuals who comprise it were grouped into units on the basis of some rational pattern. Skillful administrative organization aims at assigning duties to groups of employees in such a way that each group has a clear and consistent mission and that the group commander can be held for the performance of that mission. It seeks to bring all units into due subordination through an unbroken chain of command to the chief executive. It strives to relate the size of the unit and the resources at its command to the size of the task assigned to it. Failure to observe any one of these precepts of good organization may well frustrate the intention of President or Congress. However, faithful adherence to these precepts will not of itself produce good management, for an organization can be no better than the people who serve in it.

Importance of proper organization

The traditional organizational unit of the executive branch is a single-headed department to which has been assigned a more or less homogeneous group of programs aimed at a major section of national governmental responsibility. The directing head is commonly called Secretary and is, typically, a member of the President's Cabinet. This organizational pattern was established by the Confederation Congress and its continuance was assumed by the framers

The department

of the Constitution.[3] Three such departments—State, War, Treasury—were established by the first Congress under the Constitution together with two offices—Attorney General and Postmaster General—each of which was later organized as a department.[4] The Navy Department was created in 1798, the Department of the Interior in 1849, the Department of Agriculture in 1889. A Department of Commerce and Labor was established in 1903 from which the Department of Labor was carved out and separately established in 1913. A new Department of the Air Force was joined with the Departments of War and Navy in 1947 to form the National Defense Establishment which became the present Department of Defense in 1949. Its three departmental components were at the same time reduced in rank but not in title. The Department of Health, Education, and Welfare was organized in 1953 and the Department of Housing and Urban Development in 1965. Each of the departments created after the original three was built around organizational units already in existence at the time of its establishment. Prior to 1870, the Congress showed little disposition to assign new executive functions to any other type of agency; each new or enlarged responsibility was customarily assigned to one of the existing departments. This attitude has been modified in the years since 1870, but there is still a strong tendency to find a home for any newly established operation in one of the departments. Those charged with administering programs in nondepartmental agencies rather persistently strive for departmental status. There is an aura of permanence and maturity about the department form of organization which makes it the model in an ideal as well as in a historical sense of executive branch organization.

*Charac-
teristics of
depart-
mental
organiza-
tion:
1. Political
direction*

The 14 departments (11 of Cabinet rank) of the contemporary executive branch exhibit numerous variations in structure and operation. There are, however, enough common characteristics to allow useful generalizations. In the first place, the top management of all of the departments consists largely of partisan politicians, appointed for political reasons ordinarily from the ranks of the President's party. This politically oriented management staff includes the Secretary, the Under-Secretary, the assistant secretaries, the legal counsel, the director of public relations, some of the bureau, office, or division chiefs and the more important aides of each. Experience has convinced most Presidents and members of Congress that the enforcement of responsibility to the voters upon the permanent staffs of the departments requires not only a politically responsible Secretary but a cadre of political assistants commanding all of

[3] The Constitution does not provide in so many words for such departments, nor, of course, say how many there shall be or what they shall be called. In authorizing the President, however, to "require the opinion, in writing, of the principal officer in each of the executive departments," and in empowering Congress to "vest the appointment of inferior officers in the heads of departments," it plainly assumes that departments will exist.

[4] The Post Office Department was established in 1829; the Department of Justice in 1870.

the main channels to him of information and authority. To some politicians, however, the chief virtue of this cadre is the opportunity it provides for rewarding the party faithful.

On the whole, authority and responsibility for departmental management are concentrated in the office of the department head.[5] Each department head is subject to the general direction of the President and holds most of his power subject to that direction. Within his domain, however, he is a miniature President. The authority of the department head typically includes: (1) the power to appoint subordinate officials [6] and employees, virtually all of them in accordance with the practices of the civil service merit system; (2) the power to remove subordinates appointed by himself, again subject to the tenure provisions of the merit system; (3) the power to issue binding rules and regulations for the conduct of departmental business and, in many instances, for the purpose of supplementing legislation administered by the department; (4) the power to decide appeals from the decisions of departmental subordinates not only on departmental matters, but, in many instances, in matters affecting private citizens; (5) the power to issue formal or informal orders to all of the component units of the department governing the work performed by each. Together with this authority is complete responsibility to the President, the Congress, and the public for the conduct of the department. The department head is expected to represent the views and interests of the institution he directs before the President, the Cabinet, and the Congress. He is also expected to represent to the department the policies and desires of the President. He is expected finally to support the President and his party on all occasions.

2. Centralization of authority in the department head

The component organizational units of each department are, typically, arranged in hierarchical pattern by virtue of which the authority of the department executive permeates throughout the organization in a more or less unbroken chain of command.[7] There is no standard nomenclature for designating the major organizational units in a department, but the most frequent title is bureau. To each bureau is assigned a more or less homogeneous group of department functions and services. The head of each bureau ranks next below the top-management staff already described. A substantial and increasing proportion of these bureau executives are career civil servants protected by the merit system. In many cases, furthermore, they hold a position of

3. Hierarchical arrangement of subordinate organizational units

[5] This concentration is not nearly so complete as many experts believe desirable. Congress has on many occasions assigned unreviewable authority directly to bureau chiefs and division heads. See "Departmental Management," *Report of the Commission on Organization of the Executive Branch of the Government* (Washington, 1949), Appendix E.

[6] Appointments to the political directorate are, of course, made by the President with the advice and consent of the Senate. The department head, however, is ordinarily consulted on these appointments.

[7] There are many deviations from this in practice. See "General Management of the Executive Branch," *The Report of the Commission on Organization of the Executive Branch of the Government* (Washington, 1949).

considerable independence of the department directory for historical, personal, or political reasons.[8]

The bureaus, in their turn, are subdivided into divisions, branches, and sections, proceeding down the ladder of administrative authority.

4. Congressional control of departmental organization

The organization of the typical executive department, including the names, numbers, and functions of the bureaus is largely determined by statute. Department executives are not free to arrange the pieces to suit their own estimate of departmental needs. Many of the bureaus, in fact, had legal status and traditions long before the departments of which they now are parts were established.

Other single-headed agencies

Outside the 14 executive departments are a number of single-headed organizations directly under the President called agencies or administrations. They possess every characteristic of departments save one: the head is not traditionally a member of the President's Cabinet. In recent years, however, the major agency heads have in fact attended Cabinet sessions. The precedent for this type of executive agency was set with the establishment by the first Congress of the Postmaster General's office in 1789. And from time to time since that date Congress has elected to house a new function in an agency of this kind because it has not wished to increase the size of the Cabinet or because it has hoped that the function would not become a permanent one or because it has felt that it was not sufficiently important to justify departmental status. Contemporary examples of this type of agency are the Veterans Administration, the Housing and Home Finance Agency, the National Aeronautics and Space Agency, and the General Services Administration. Every one of these, curiously enough, is larger than the Department of Labor and the Veterans Administration is larger than most of the regular departments.

The "independent" regulatory commission

The third type of executive agency, the "independent" regulatory commission, is a product of the last 75 years and is an incident to the increasing governmental intervention in the economy which has characterized that period. The prototype of this new form of organization is the Interstate Commerce Commission created in 1887.[9] The typical commission is a plural body of from 5 to 11 members appointed by the President for overlapping terms of from five to nine years. Typically, no more than a majority may be members of one party and the members are not subject to the unrestrained removal power of the President. Subordinate to the commission itself is a staff of career civil servants who assist it in the performance of its duties. The commission is, therefore, the executive head of the agency directing by order and by regulation the work of numerous subordinates. It is also a rule-making agency, just as are many of the department heads. However, a large portion of its rules, much larger than those of the typical department, are binding upon that part

[8] Good examples of independent bureaus are the Federal Bureau of Investigation, the Forest Service, the Public Health Service.

[9] The Civil Service Commission created in 1883 is largely a management device rather than an economic regulatory one.

of the public which comes under its regulatory authority. Finally, the commission is an appellate tribunal, hearing and determining a large number of cases arising from the decisions of referees or trial-examiners who are, at least nominally, its subordinates. These cases involve, typically, the application of commission-made rules to private firms. To such an agency, typically, has been entrusted the regulation of some private enterprise sector of the national economy which Congress has determined to bring under detailed government scrutiny. The power to regulate has ordinarily been entrusted to these commissions in the broadest possible terms and has extended, for many private economic institutions, to the prices charged the consumer and to the profits of the owners. Because of the singular power over these economic institutions entrusted to commissions, Congress deliberately sought to protect them from the kind of partisan political direction which the single-headed department or agency is designed to facilitate. The combination of legislative (rule-making), executive, and judicial powers which the commissions possess also suggested that the powers should be exercised in a relatively nonpartisan environment. The procedures which Congress has directed to be used to accomplish the desired regulation, furthermore, tend to make these commissions more directly responsible to the courts than to either the President or to the Congress. The location of these agencies in the executive branch, however, has meant in practice that they have not wholly escaped the influence of Presidential direction. It should also be observed that neither their powers nor procedures are unique —they can be found also in departments. In other words, the Congress has not adhered to a consistent pattern in assigning responsibilities among the various types of executive branch organizations. There are always many factors, personal as well as political, which color any legislative decision as to the proper agency to entrust with any particular function.

The executive branch also houses a number of boards and commissions which have no consequential regulatory responsibilities. There are numerous reasons, in addition to those discussed, for using multimembered agency directorates to preside over national programs or services. In some cases, it is highly desirable to ensure representation of various sections, economic interests, or social groups in the composition of the directing body. This is particularly true where the functions are largely advisory, as in the case of the Tariff Commission. It is also true where the functions are investigative, as in the Commission on Organization of the Executive Branch of the Government. Another compelling reason for the use of boards is the desire to avoid one-man responsibility and to insure that decisions will be taken only after various views have been canvassed. The most important nonregulatory commission at present is the Atomic Energy Commission and the principal purpose in creating this type of agency to develop atomic and thermonuclear weapons and power generators was to place this program on a nonpartisan footing as far as possible.

The two world wars of this century, the expansion of American national

Nonregulatory commission

Corporation: 1. Development

interests in foreign countries, and the depression of the thirties stimulated governmental programs essentially similar to those which have been or were being performed by privately owned business concerns. In order to provide a "businesslike" atmosphere for the administration of these programs and to provide somewhat greater flexibility in their fiscal administration than the traditional government bureau possessed, the corporate form of organization was established in the executive branch. Although a corporation was first used by the Congress in 1791 to provide a United States Bank, the modern government corporation is a product of the twentieth century. There are now more than 80 of these corporations in existence and their combined assets are somewhat more than $30 billion. Several of them are now in process of liquidation, including the largest and probably the most influential of all, the Reconstruction Finance Corporation. The principal government service now provided through the corporation device is the supply of credit to small businesses, farmers, and home owners. However, they are also used to manufacture and distribute electric power (Tennessee Valley Authority), construct and operate navigation facilities (St. Lawrence Seaway Development Corporation); operate railroads (Panama R. R. Co.), purchase farm surpluses (Commodity Credit Corporation), insure bank deposits (Federal Deposit Insurance Corporation), construct, purchase, and sell ships (Maritime Administration), and for scores of other purposes. Most government corporations are, at least nominally, attached to one of the departments or agencies. The extent of the control over their activities which the department head derives from this attachment is uncertain and ill-defined. A few of the corporations, notably the Tennessee Valley Authority, are independent establishments in name and in fact. Many of these corporations were created by Presidential directive rather than Congressional enactment, and all of them enjoyed for a time a great measure of real autonomy over the spending of the earnings arising from the sale of their services. All of them are, however, arms of the government. It owns them, supplies most of their capital, defines their functions, and regulates their procedures. Like business corporations, virtually all of the government corporations have boards of directors and under them general managers.[10]

2. Control   Growing criticism of these agencies for their alleged independence of Congressional and even of Presidential direction led the Congress in 1945 to bring them under more systematic scrutiny. The Government Corporation Control Act of 1945 provides that only Congress may create them in the future,

----

[10] For brief discussions of government corporations in general, see F. Morstein Marx [ed.], *Elements of Public Administration* (New York, 1946), Chap. XI, and M. Fainsod and L. Gordon, *Government and the American Economy* (rev. ed., New York, 1948), Chap. XIX. A full treatise is J. McDiarmid, *Government Corporations and Federal Funds* (Chicago, 1938); and cf. C. H. Pritchett, "The Government Corporation Control Act of 1945," *Amer. Polit. Sci. Rev.*, XL, 495-509 (June, 1946), and M. E. Dimock, "Government Corporations; A Focus of Policy and Administration," *ibid.*, XLIII, 899-921, 1145-1165 (Oct. and Dec., 1949). See also a lengthy Hoover Commission report entitled *Federal Business Enterprises* (Washington, 1949).

subjects their finances to scrutiny by the Bureau of the Budget and the General Accounting Office, and requires them to administer their personnel more nearly in accordance with civil-service merit system procedures.

THE CONTINUING NEED FOR REORGANIZATION

The proper and effective organization of the executive branch is not something that can be achieved with finality. The public, through the Congress and the President, constantly demands new services or expansions in older ones. Emphasis shifts from one function to another as changes occur in domestic or international conditions. Presidents, department heads, commissioners, and bureau chiefs change and each subtly molds his organization to suit his own interests, ambitions, and conceptions. Like any other institution built of human hopes and fears, the organization of the executive branch is a dynamic, not a static thing. It will be different tomorrow than it is today. The consequence of these factors is that the organization of the executive branch is in constant need of attention if the purposes of the government are to be realized and its principles observed.

As our nation became increasingly aware of the importance of administration, criticism began to be heard from Congressmen, journalists, administrators, students, and taxpayers that the organization of the executive branch was not adequate to its tasks. Congress, which dictates the structure of the executive branch, could be brought to act but slowly despite the prodding of Presidents Taft, Wilson, and Hoover. It became clear that only the President had both the will and the information to achieve effective organization of the executive branch and to keep the organization in tune with changing circumstances. President Franklin D. Roosevelt was the first modern President entrusted by Congress with organizational authority over his own domain. This was in 1933 under an act signed by Hoover a few days before his term ended. A few changes were made by executive order before the power expired in 1934 but the new President was unable to give the matter real attention for some years. Then in 1936, after dozens of new agencies had been created to combat depression and promote human welfare and the executive branch was more topsy-turvy than ever, and after the President had been firmly established in his second term by a tremendous popular plurality, he named a Committee on Administrative Management to survey the organization of his branch of the government. The report of this Committee, a landmark of its kind in the annals of government, reached the Congress when it had been stirred to its foundation by the President's plan for reorganizing the Supreme Court.[11] Two years later

Growing criticism of executive organization

Committee on Administrative Management

[11] The report proper was published under the title of *Administrative Management in the Government of the United States* (Washington, 1937); the report, together with various supporting studies, under the title of *Report of the Committee* [on administrative management], *with Studies of Administrative Management in the Federal Government* (Washington, 1937).

the Congress finally passed one of the major recommendations of the committee that the President be assigned by law the power to achieve a reorganization of the executive branch. The power was, however, granted only for two years and several agencies of the executive were exempted from its provision.[12] The President used his authority to achieve several significant changes through plans submitted to Congress for review. The reconstruction of the President's own office as described in a previous chapter was the most important of these changes. A new grant of power was voted to the President in 1941 for the duration of the war emergency, but this grant was restricted to changes associated with the conduct of the war. Late in 1945 Congress responded to an urgent request by President Truman for new reorganization power to enable him to readjust the war-swollen executive branch to conditions of peace. Several plans were submitted under this act, most of which were allowed to become effective by the Congress. In spite of all these changes, many observers felt that there was much still to be accomplished.

Hoover Commission

The triumph of the Republican Party in the Congressional election of 1946 ushered in a new era of administrative reform under the auspices of a party bent upon cutting the executive branch down to more "manageable" size. The Congress this time took the initiative and created and generously financed a Commission on Organization of the Executive Branch of the Government.[13] This body, headed by ex-President Hoover, prepared and submitted to the Congress and to the President in 1949 the most comprehensive analysis and report on the subject in our history.[14] It would be impossible even to summarize the 288 separate recommendations made by the Commission. Like its predecessors, this group insisted that authority to reorganize the executive branch must be vested in the President, and Hoover took the stand to support the broadest possible grant of such power to President Truman. With this impressive support the Congress in 1949 voted the most sweeping reorganizing power ever granted to a President. No agencies were exempted from the President's

The Reorganization Act of 1949

12 Under the legislation's terms, no change might be made in the names or number of the executive departments, and the principal regulatory commissions, together with certain other independent establishments, were to be left untouched.

13 With 12 members in all (6 from each of the two leading parties), the Commission consisted of 4 persons appointed by the President, four by the president *pro tempore* of the Senate, and four by the speaker of the House of Representatives, under instructions resulting in two members being drawn from the Senate, two from the House, two from the executive branch of the government, and six from private life. On the Commission, its task, and its methods of work, see F. Heady, "A New Approach to Federal Executive Reorganization," *Amer. Polit. Sci. Rev.*, XLI, 1118-1126 (Dec., 1947), and "The Operation of a Mixed Commission," *ibid.*, XLIII, 940-952 (Oct., 1949).

14 Criticisms and recommendations on various matters are indicated at appropriate points in other chapters. All reports and most task-force reports were issued early in 1949 by the Superintendent of Documents, Washington, in pamphlet form, and the Commission's own reports will be found in consolidated form in a single volume, *The Hoover Commission Report on Organization of the Executive Branch of the Government* (New York, 1949). Much miscellaneous material assembled, however, remains unpublished.

authority as had been the case in all previous acts. However, the Congress insisted that the power must be limited as to time and provided for the expiration of such power on April 1, 1953. Congress also insisted that it must retain a veto on all Presidential proposals as it had done in previous acts. In most previous acts, a Presidential proposal could be killed by a concurrent resolution of disapproval passed by both houses within a specified time limit. In the act of 1949, a Presidential plan could be nullified by a resolution of disapproval passed by a majority of the membership of either house within 60 days of its submission.[15] President Truman during his term of office submitted plans to Congress and took other actions within his power to achieve about half of the Commission's recommendations. It remained for President Eisenhower to take up where Truman had finished. He got the Congress to extend the deadline several times, the last date set being 1959. He then sent to the Congress from 1953 to 1959 several reorganization plans, most of which were approved. The most important of these was that creating the Department of Health, Welfare, and Education.[16] In 1953, he successfully persuaded the Congress to establish another Commission on organization of the Executive Branch to begin anew the Hoover Commission studies and called upon Hoover once again to direct the survey.

The new Commission in 1955 made a new series of proposals dealing with budgeting, paperwork, business enterprises, water resources, electric power, civil service, overseas economic operations and many other subjects. The new studies, however, were deeply concerned with the policies of the government as well as with its administrative practices and drew the fire of the Democrats, now in a majority in the Congress. The Second Hoover Commission proved for this and other reasons not to be so effective as the first.[17] The major reorganization accomplished since 1953 concerned the Department of Defense and occurred in 1958. *The Second Hoover Commission*

President Kennedy, shortly after he assumed office, asked the Congress once again for reorganizing power and this was granted to him until 1963 on substantially the same terms as it had been granted to President Eisenhower.

[15] In the end, this measure had the extraordinary experience of being passed unanimously in both houses.

[16] It is not practicable to enumerate or describe here the changes thus far resulting from Hoover Commission recommendations. A few already have been indicated, and others will be touched upon at appropriate later points. Standing out most conspicuously are: (1) increase of the top management responsibility of most heads of executive departments and of several chairmen of regulatory commissions; (2) transfer of the National Security Council and the National Security Resources Board to the Executive Office of the President; (3) reconstruction of the form of the national budget; (4) concentration of the scattered procurement services of the government in a new General Services Administration; (5) partial reorganization of the Department of State; (6) conversion of the National Military Establishment into a Department of Defense; (7) considerable rebuilding of a greatly weakened Department of Labor; and (8) extensive salary readjustments in the higher levels of the government service.

[17] The reports of the Commission were issued in pamphlet form under various titles and usually with accompanying task force reports during the first half of 1955.

He thereupon sought to reorganize a number of the regulatory commissions so as to place more power in the chairmen and to expedite the processing of cases. Most of his proposals were rejected by the Congress.[18] He also attempted unsuccessfully to create a new department of Urban Affairs.

In 1963, the President's authority to reorganize ended temporarily when the Senate refused to approve an extension of the Act of 1949. However, with the succession of Lyndon Johnson the power was extended in 1964 largely on the old terms until mid-1965 and then to mid-1968. One new reservation was imposed: a new executive department could not be created by a reorganization order. Johnson's major use of the power, thus far, has been to reorganize the customs service and place the district officials under the merit system.

The task of adjusting the organization of the executive branch is never completed. Although Congress has up to now insisted on placing time limits on the power of the President in this matter, it may well become by regular extension a normal attribute of Presidential authority.[19]

THE GROWTH OF MANAGEMENT SERVICES

The difference between line functions and management services

Another consequence of the tremendous growth in the size of the executive branch has been the growth of those parts that facilitate management and provide services for the rest of the organization. Students and administrators customarily distinguish among the functions of an organization those that have directly to do with the purpose of the organization—called *line* functions— from those that serve purely internal needs—called variously *staff, overhead, auxiliary, housekeeping,* or *management service* functions. The men who work in the local post office sorting and delivering the mail, the soldiers in a combat division, the social workers calling upon the disabled, all of these are engaged in line functions. Those who keep the accounts of the Post Office Department, or administer the personnel procurement program, or handle the publicity of the department are engaged in management services. Some entire agencies and many bureaus are, in the modern executive branch, engaged in management service rather than line functions, and every agency has a substantial portion of its employees engaged in such functions.

Specialization and the growth of management services

Specialization of function and the development of techniques for each

[18] The President's concern with the commissions stemmed largely from an investigation of the Federal Communications Commission and the Civil Aeronautics Board and others undertaken by the House Special Subcommittee on Legislative Oversight between 1958 and 1960 that revealed a good deal of imprudence on the part of commission members. The President asked James M. Landis to study Commission organization and procedure and make recommendations and Landis strongly urged increasing the chairman's powers. See *The New York Times,* Dec. 27, 1960.

[19] President Kennedy's Budget Director, and later President Johnson, in fact, asked the Congress to make the power permanent.

specialty are widely regarded as important keys to American industrial efficiency. Carried over into public administration, this conception has contributed to the growth of the managerial services. Fiscal administration, purchasing, personnel administration, legal advisement, public relations direction, space allocation, statistical analysis, procedures analysis, program planning, among others, are now considered the proper domain of technicians especially skilled in these functions and are separately and centrally organized in many of the large organizational units of the executive branch. The top executive staff of each department, agency, or administration, and of many bureaus and divisions includes these specialties and provides them to the rest of the organization.

Although most of the expert practitioners of these managerial service functions profess the conception that these functions and processes are subservient to the line responsibilities of the organization, in practice these management assistants frequently influence and occasionally dominate the agency. These service functions are almost universally practiced quite near the seat of authority, whereas the line functions are often largely discharged at some field station or office miles from headquarters. Although it is undoubtedly true that the effective management of the executive branch would be impossible without central controls over and standard procedures for accounting, personnel transactions, and supply procurement, the growth of these functions in size, importance, and influence has created new difficulties in communicating the aspirations of the Congress and the President for effective public service throughout a large and far-flung organization. This growth has also reduced the proportion of the tax dollar which goes directly into alleviating distress, defending the nation, protecting the lives and property of our citizens, and husbanding our natural resources.

The control exercised through the service functions

It is but just to add at this point that the American people are themselves partly responsible for the controls exercised by the administrators of management services. Through Congress and the President, they have insisted that line administrators should not be allowed to hire and fire freely but should be required to observe the rules of the civil-service merit system. They have also sought to achieve a higher standard of honesty of public officials by requiring that certain procedures (public bidding, for example) be observed whenever supplies or equipment are purchased by government agencies. They have insisted that the most rigorous audit be made of fiscal transactions and that unrelenting vigilance be exercised by corps of accountants on the expenditure of public funds. All of these requirements and many others enacted into law by Congress or imposed by executive order have contributed to the growth in numbers and influence of those officials who administer these laws and orders in the executive branch. Nowhere in our system of government is the public distrust of officialdom so patent and its consequences so clear. A large portion of the executive branch is expected to spend a good deal of time and money checking up on the rest of the branch.

The public demand for internal controls over administration

ADMINISTRATIVE PROCEDURES

The procedures used by the executive branch to accomplish its objectives are as varied as the trees of the forest. They do not as readily lend themselves to classification and explication as those used by the courts or by the Congress. The success of any public program may well depend, however, on the procedure used to achieve it.

1. Detection and prosecution of law violators

It is convenient as well as instructive to regard executive branch methods from the vantage point of the amount of coercive authority or sanction associated with them. Throughout history, government has been closely identified, in the eyes of the governed, with coercive power. Traditionally, the method of public executives is arrest and the vehicle the police. The enforcement of law everywhere has had as its ultimate sanction fine, imprisonment, corporal punishment, death, or banishment. The detection and prosecution of law violators remains to this day one of the primary methods of executive government. Many governments, however, and particularly modern democratic ones, have tended to lay increasing stress on the prevention of antisocial behavior rather than the punishment of those found guilty of it. This objective requires far more complex and subtle methods of administration than does the traditional method of arrest. Furthermore, in the American system of government the state and local authorities, rather than the national executive, deal with most offenders against the traditional criminal laws. The Treasury Department's Secret Service and Coast Guard, the FBI and the military police in the armed services, are almost the only real police forces in the national executive establishment. The Department of Justice through the district attorney in each judicial district is the chief prosecutor of offenders against national laws brought in by the various police officers of the executive branch.

2. Litigation

The offices of the courts are used extensively by the executive branch in civil litigation as well as criminal prosecution. The sanctions associated with litigation are impressive and include the assessment of costs, damages, and the expenses of the litigation itself. They are not so drastic, however, as those associated with criminal prosecution. Litigation is used by the government to collect money owed it by taxpayers or by contractors or for purchases of its services. It has also been relied upon heavily, although with indifferent success, to curb the development of monopoly in industrial organization and to enforce administratively determined orders upon business or labor organizations. Most administrators avoid litigation like the plague because of the expense of and the time consumed in judicial processes.

3. Adjudication

A third coercive method widely used by the modern executive branch is adjudication. This is essentially a judicial procedure developed within the executive branch in order to achieve specialization of interest and greater flexibility than the regular court procedures provide. The independent regulatory commissions are the major, although not the exclusive, practitioners of adjudication. Typically, the process consists of advocates for the regulatory

authority on the one hand and defenders of the regulatee on the other presenting their diverse views on the proper rates or services of the enterprises in
question before a plural body which adjudges the case and issues appropriate
orders. Most of the decisions thus reached by executive branch adjudicators
are reviewable by the national courts. The process is similar but not identical
to administrative legislation which is also practiced by these same agencies and
consists in supplementing broad statutory policies by specific rules binding
upon the regulated enterprises. Adjudication is applying these rules to specific
individual situations.

Inspection accompanied in many instances by licensure is a fourth coercive method used extensively by the national executive. This is a genteel police
method which frequently has as its purpose the achievement of proper conduct by the inspectee rather than his punishment for improper behavior. Government inspectors are used extensively to achieve proper working conditions
in factories subject to national regulation, safety on board ship and in interstate transportation, safe and sanitary meat and food products and control of
drugs moving in interstate commerce, safety in mines, and numerous other
public purposes. The requirement of a license for the operation of or practice
of some profession, vocation, or business enterprise adds the convenient sanction that, without criminal proceedings, the license may be revoked for violation of the laws governing the matter. In virtually all situations where licensure
and inspection are used, the government has determined a minimum standard
of conduct, cleanliness, health, or safety which it seeks to achieve throughout
the nation. The inspectors attempt to make certain that the standard is observed.

*4. Inspec-
tion and
licensure*

The change in the functions of the executive branch associated with the
industrialization of the nation and with the attempt to insure a fairer distribution of the products of the national economy have accentuated those executive
activities which are not coercive and which do not rely in the last analysis on
the power of the government to punish transgressors. A high standard of public
health, for example, can be achieved only if individuals voluntarily change
their habits and customs. The improvement of agricultural production in which
the government has played such a conspicuous role has been achieved largely
without coercion of any kind. Education and exhortation rather than compulsion are coming more and more to be major methods of the national administration. They constitute its chief procedures as it seeks positively to improve
the environment both physical and social for the welfare of its citizens. Education as here used is a broad term involving every type of persuasion from publishing brochures to operating demonstration farms and includes: official
exhortation; visitation by expert consultants, such as public health nurses,
county agricultural agents, or social workers; operation of experimental laboratories; development of voluntary codes of business or advertising practice;
organization of scientific conferences, and thousands of other similar activities
not excluding the instruction of young people in classrooms. The teacher must

*5. Edu-
cation*

thus be placed beside the policeman as the great executive agent of modern American government. Not only are educational procedures the major reliance of agencies like the Department of Agriculture and the Public Health Service, they are also more and more widely used to supplement, if not to replace, the methods of prosecution, litigation, adjudication, and inspection. The railroads of the United States are directed almost as much by informal nonlitigious conferences between railroad operators and ICC agents as by the formal procedures for which that commission is so well known. It is fair to add that the educational methods seem to work best when accompanied by the power ultimately to invoke sanctions against those who do not respond to persuasion.

6. Research

The executive branch of the government is not only engaged in transmitting information and urging individuals to better practice; it is also heavily engaged in discovering information. Research has become a large concern of the national administration. The conquest of disease, the improvement of our military striking power, the conquest of outer space, the expansion of agricultural productivity are but a few of the continuing objects of research by scientists under the direction of the national executive. The national government is today the leading research institution in our country and in the world. It supports and directs more than two-thirds of all the research activity in the United States and performs a considerable portion of it with its own scientists and in its own laboratories.

7. Negotiation

War is the only compulsive method for conducting the foreign relations of any nation. Eschewing this, it must rely on the noncoercive method of negotiation to serve its interests beyond its shores. The practice of diplomacy accompanied the rise of the national state and has been a traditional function of states for several centuries. The method of negotiation, while practiced extensively by the Department of State, is by no means confined to it. The Departments of Defense, Commerce, and Agriculture, for example, are extensively involved in our foreign relations as are the agencies administering foreign aid, propaganda, and espionage. The processes of negotiation, which are essentially the dealing across the table of equals, are also used in internal matters, for example, to achieve peaceful settlement of labor disputes, to purchase land for public use, and to determine state-national responsibilities in connection with grant-in-aid programs.

This brief catalogue by no means exhausts the repertoire of executive agencies in attempting to realize public policies. It does, however, point up the fact that the executive is not only an enforcement agent and that new government functions require new methods for their successful administration.[20]

THE ENFORCEMENT OF RESPONSIBILITY

The American system of government is built upon an abiding hatred for bureaucracy and a deep-seated distrust of officialdom. It is not surprising,

[20] For a more complete discussion of administrative methods see J. C. Charlesworth, *Government Administration* (New York, 1951), Pt. 7.

therefore, that the growth of the national executive has been viewed with concern in many quarters. Is it possible, the critics ask, for such an army of public officials with such a large share of the national income at their disposal to submit to direction from the voters and their representatives? Will they not rather seek to dominate the Congress by favors and the public by propaganda? How can the executive agencies, manned as they are largely by persons with permanent tenure, be made responsible to the elected officials and responsive to public opinion?

The principal safeguard against the rise of an irresponsible bureaucracy built into the executive branch itself is the position of the President. The elected Presidency is essentially a political office responsible to the voters and vested by the Constitution with the executive power. By custom of long standing, Presidential direction of the executive agencies is supported by a cadre of his political lieutenants at the helm of each agency and in command of the major channels of authority and communication. The top management of each agency changes office with each change in the national administration and thus, fresh from an election triumph, can be said to enjoy the confidence of the public. Only the independent commissions are insulated against this kind of direction. The authority of the political managers of the executive branch is weakened in practice by their inexperience and by their lack of technical competence. They must perforce rely upon the experienced technicians of their agencies for guidance. Traditionally, this guidance is supplied fully and freely regardless of the political views held by either individual. For this too is part of the American tradition, that the professional civil servant will serve any master placed over him by vote of the people. Nevertheless, the political executive is likely to be the creature rather than the master of an enterprise of long standing, with established traditions, procedures and policies, typically with an alert and interested clientele, and with a large contingent of employees of all grades who grew up, so to speak, in that enterprise. *Presidential direction*

The second great safeguard against government by technicians (bureaucracy) is the constitutional and customary powers of the Congress. Money may not be spent by executive agencies except on the basis of Congressional appropriation. Each year the administration must pray Congress to grant the funds necessary for its programs and each year must, in consequence, account to the Congress for its conduct. This great power of Congress is weakened in practice by the enormous complexity of the financial structure of the national government and, in consequence, by the fact that few Congressmen are familiar with more than a small portion of the total appropriations. It is nevertheless quite an impressive power in molding executive agency policy. The Congress prescribes not only the programs and policies which the administration will pursue but also the organizational structure and the procedures for pursuing them. Many practices of Congress in exercising this power have tended to weaken Presidential direction of his own branch and tend to diffuse responsibility for performance. The Congressmen have encouraged employees who disagree with their superiors to report to them on *Congressional oversight* matters of agency policy. Committees have sought, many times successfully, to obtain veto power over agency decisions such as where to create an installation or whether and when to close one.[21] As we earlier noted, Congressmen spend many hours negotiating in behalf of constituents with executive agencies. The Senate, as we have seen, participates in the appointment of numerous officers in the executive branch. Through the power of investigation the Congress may review the conduct of any executive agency in which it is interested. No legislative process is held in such great fear by the executive branch as the investigating one. None has been so abused by the Congress nor been so effectual in cleaning out a corrupt or incompetent agency.

Judicial review

There is an impressive body of opinion in the United States, held mainly by members of the legal profesison, that the principal safeguard against the rise of an irresponsible bureaucracy is the power of the national courts to review the acts and decisions of officials of the executive branch. Under the American system of jurisprudence most of the actions, threatened or accomplished, of administrators are reviewable by ordinary courts of law. This review customarily extends to the validity of the law on which the action is based as well as to the action itself. This type of control over administrative behavior is designed to assure conformity to constitutional prescriptions regarding personal and property rights and regarding the allocation of governmental powers between the nation and the states and among the several branches of the government. Judicial review is a device for assuring not responsiveness to democratic processes but obedience to the Constitution. It is intended to make men subservient to laws, not necessarily to other men who happen to enjoy public confidence.

The practice of judicial review of administrative decisions is much less clear cut than the principle. Congress has from time to time endowed administrative agencies, notably the independent regulatory commissions, with powers of a judicial character (referred to by the lawyers as *quasijudicial*). It has also attempted to limit the power of the courts to review certain types of administrative actions. It has conferred lawmaking power on many agencies confined only by the most general standards.

The Administrative Procedure Act of 1946

A swelling tide of criticism arose during the administration of Franklin D. Roosevelt of alleged usurpation of judicial functions by the executive branch and of widespread disregard by the executive of established legal conceptions of proper procedure. In general, it was felt, especially by lawyers, that private rights and interests received fairer consideration in the courts than in the executive branch. The American Bar Association sponsored a reform bill which

[21] See J. P. Harris, *Congressional Control of Administration* (Washington, 1964) and special studies such as H. L. Nieburg, "The Eisenhower AEC and Congress; A Study In Executive-Legislative Relations," *Midwest Journ. of Pol. Sci.,* VI No. 2 (May, 1962); M. Brown, "The Demise of State Department Public Opinion Polls: A Study of Legislative Oversight," *Midwest Jour. of Pol. Sci.,* Vol. No. 1 (Feb. 1961); and S. Scher, "Congressional Committee Members as Independent Agency Overseers: A Case Study," *Amer. Pol. Sci. Rev.* LIV, No. 4. (Dec. 1960).

was passed by the Congress in 1940 but vetoed by the President that would have greatly enlarged the scope of judicial review of executive decision.[22] The return of the Republican Party to power in the Congress in 1946 opened the way for a more sympathetic consideration of these criticisms of the executive branch and a bill worked out in conjunction with the attorney general was finally passed in that year.[23] This act, the Administrative Procedure Act of 1946, provides that every executive agency action for which no adequate court remedy is provided, shall be subject to review by an appropriate national court. The court may set aside any agency action, finding, or conclusion discovered to be arbitrary, or entailing abuse of discretion, or in excess of statutory or constitutional authority, or based upon improper proceedings or unwarranted by the facts—insofar as the facts are reviewable by the court. What these provisions added to the existing law is still a matter of dispute among experts. More clearly, the act of 1946 attempts to provide more uniform procedures in executive agencies by requiring: (1) that every executive agency give full publicity to its formal procedures so interested persons may know how to use its facilities; (2) that ample notice of the contemplated adoption of rules be given, personally or through the *Federal Register,* to interested individuals or corporations so that they may have time to protest; (3) that officials (trial examiners) holding preliminary hearings be given semi-independent status in the agencies with which they are identified; (4) that employees or officials engaged in investigating and presenting cases for adjudication have no part in deciding them; (5) that insofar as orderly procedure will permit, any interested person be allowed to appear before any agency for presentation of any issue, request, petition, or controversy; and (6) that persons compelled to appear be permitted counsel.[24]

References

L. D. White, *Introduction to the Study of Public Administration* (4th ed., New York, 1955), Chaps. I-XII.

———, *The Federalists; A Study in Administrative History* (New York, 1948).

———, *The Jeffersonians; A Study in Administrative History* (New York, 1951).

[22] The Logan-Walter Bill. See also the report of the Committee on Administrative Law of the American Bar Association, *Legislative Proposals on Federal Administration Procedure* (Chicago, 1944).

[23] The bill was based in large part on the *Final Report* of the Attorney General's Committee on Administrative Procedure (Washington, 1941). The minority report of the committee was, however, followed by the Congress in several significant matters.

[24] For a more complete analysis of the Act of 1946 see Foster H. Sherwood, "The Federal Administrative Procedure Act," *Amer. Polit. Sci. Rev.* (April, 1947), 271-281, and Nathaniel L. Nathanson, "Central Issues of American Administrative Laws" (June, 1951), 348-385.

————, *The Jacksonians; A Study in Administrative History* (New York, 1955).

————, *The Republican Era, 1869-1901: A Study in Administrative History* (New York, 1958).

W. B. Graves, *Public Administration in a Democratic Society* (Boston, 1950), Chaps. I-IV.

J. C. Charlesworth, *Governmental Administration* (New York, 1951).

L. M. Short, *Development of National Administrative Organization in the United States* (Baltimore, 1923), Chaps. II-XIX, XXIII.

A. Lepawsky, *Administration; The Art and Science of Organization and Management* (New York, 1950).

P. Appleby, *Big Democracy* (New York, 1945).

————, *Policy and Administration* (Univ. of Alabama, 1949).

A. W. Macmahon and J. D. Millett, *Federal Administrators: A Biographical Approach to the Problem of Departmental Management* (New York, 1939).

E. P. Herring, *Federal Commissioners: A Study of Their Careers and Qualifications* (Cambridge, Mass., 1936).

————, *Public Administration and the Public Interest* (New York, 1936).

S. Wallace, *Federal Departmentalization* (New York, 1941).

D. B. Truman, *Administrative Decentralization* (Chicago, 1940).

R. E. Cushman, *The Independent Regulatory Commissions* (New York, 1941).

E. Latham, *The Federal Field Service* (Chicago, 1947).

J. M. Gaus, L. D. White, and M. E. Dimock, *Frontiers of Public Administration* (Chicago, 1936).

J. D. Millett, *Management in the Public Service* (New York, 1954).

————, *Government and Public Administration: the Quest for Responsible Performance* (New York, 1959).

J. W. Fesler, "Administration Literature and the Second Hoover Commission Reports," *Amer. Pol. Sci. Rev.,* LI, No. 1 (Mar., 1957).

J. M. Pfiffner and R. V. Presthus, *Public Administration*, 4th ed. (New York, 1960).

M. H. Bernstein, *The Job of the Federal Executive* (Washington, 1958).

P. Woll, *American Bureaucracy* (New York, 1963).

F. A. Nigro, *Modern Public Administration* (New York, 1962).

M. E. Dimock, *Administrative Vitality; The Conflict with Bureaucracy* (New York, 1959).

F. M. Marx, *The Administrative State: An Introduction to Bureaucracy* (Chicago, 1957).

J. M. Gaus, *Reflections on Public Administration* (Univ. of Alabama, 1947).

F. F. Blachly and M. E. Oatman, *Administrative Legislation and Adjudication* (Washington, 1934).

————, *Federal Regulatory Action and Control* (Washington, 1940).

J. P. Chamberlain, N. T. Dowling, and P. R. Hays, *The Judicial Function in Federal Administrative Agencies* (New York, 1942).

G. Warren [ed.], *The Federal Administrative Procedure Act and the Administrative Agencies* (New York, 1947).

V. M. Barnette, Jr., "The Federal Administrative Procedure Act and the Administrative Agencies," *Pub. Admin. Rev.*, VII, 126-133 (Spring, 1948).

L. W. Koenig [ed.], "The Hoover Commission: A Symposium," *Amer. Polit. Sci. Rev.*, XLIII, 933-1000 (Oct., 1949).

B. D. Nash and C. Lynde, *A Hook in Leviathan: A Critical Interpretation of the Hoover Commission Report* (New York, 1950).

F. Heady, "The Reorganization Act of 1949," *Pub. Admin. Rev.*, IX, 165-174 (Summer, 1949).

H. Emmerich, *Essays on Federal Reorganization* (Univ. of Alabama, 1950).

President's Committee on Administrative Management, *Report of the Committee, with studies of Administrative Management in the Federal Government* (Washington, 1937).

Commission on Organization of the Executive Branch of the Government, *Reports to Congress* and *Task Force Reports* (Washington, 1955), published separately.

Commission on Organization of the Executive Branch of the Government, *Reports to Congress,* and *Task Force Reports* issued as appendices (Washington, 1949), published separately.

The Hoover Commission Report on Organization of the Executive Branch of the Government (New York, 1949). Contains in a single volume the text of all reports and recommendations, but with dissenting statements omitted.

★ 15 ★

Personnel Administration in the Executive Branch

*Impor-
tance of
proper
personnel
selection*

THE QUALITY OF ADMINISTRATION of the national government depends in the last analysis on the quality of the officers and employees of the executive departments and agencies. Effective organization, appropriate procedures, and suitable authority are secondary to the ability of the individuals who comprise this vast institution. The survival of the American system of government may well depend upon its ability to attract and to hold the ablest members of our society. No system of administrative audits, no amount of Congressional investigation, no inspirational leadership from the President could quite compensate for mediocre, unimaginative, or time-serving public employees. Certainly a decisive determinant of the responsiveness of the executive department to the principles of the American system of constitutional democracy is the character and ability of the men and women who comprise it.

THE RISE OF THE SPOILS SYSTEM

*Appoint-
ment
policy,
1789-1829*

For a generation or more after the national government was organized under the Constitution, the selection and appointment of officers and employees left little to be desired. Washington placed the matter on a high plane by announcing his intention to "nominate such persons alone to offices . . . as shall be the best qualified." Adams, Jefferson, Madison, on the whole, followed Washington's example. The rise of political parties, however, in the last years of Washington's tenure brought influences to bear upon the selection process which began subtly to modify it. Both Hamilton and Jefferson were able to introduce into their respective departments persons sympathetic to their separate views. Adams staffed an enlarged judiciary with Federalists; Jefferson, as president, tried to overcome the Federalist balance in the government service by replacing his subordinates as they retired or resigned with members of his own party. The collapse of the Federalist Party removed the pressure for partisan appointments for several years. In 1820, however, the Congress passed a Tenure of Office Act which fixed an automatic termination of office after four years for district attorneys, collectors of customs, and other specified groups of executive employees. This act made it possible for a new President to appoint new persons to these posts without the awkward necessity for finding some reason for dismissing the incumbents. The development during this same period of the practice of partisan appointment (patronage) in several states and cities [1] contributed to the institution of that system nationally.

The inauguration of Andrew Jackson in 1829 marks the real turning point in national personnel policy. Jackson, representing the forces of frontier democracy beyond the Alleghenies, determined to sweep out every vestige of the "Virginia dynasty" in the executive branch. He held the conviction that any man of average ability and industry could master the duties of any public office and that rotation in office is a good thing for the people, since "more is lost by the long continuance of men in office than is generally to be gained by their experience." His supporters in large numbers were anxious to taste the benefits of public pay. The followers of Jackson were not of a leisured class that could afford to play at the game of politics. They had to be supported if they were to continue their electioneering. Under these circumstances, the policy of rewarding faithful party service by appointment to national office— the spoils system [2]—became the announced policy of the executive branch to which the Congress readily subscribed. Jackson never carried his policy to the extremes which his supporters requested, but he removed 700 employees during his first year in office and virtually all of his appointments were of men of his party. Van Buren, his successor, was probably the most accomplished user of appointments for patronage purposes of any President up to that time. Polk, Fillmore, Pierce, and Buchanan made sweeping replacements in the executive departments and filled the posts with partisan sympathizers. Lincoln, heading a new party, indulged in patronage appointments to an unprecedented degree. In fact, Lincoln's first term might well be designated the high tide of the spoils system. From Grant's administration onward the system has been slowly but certainly losing ground to the nonpartisan merit system.

The era of patronage, 1829-1870

The spoils system of personnel administration, despite its palpable weakness in bringing into the executive department employees whose qualifications for office were minimal, has never lacked intelligent supporters. Spoils appointments, the defenders argue, are necessary to the party system. Few persons can afford to do the day-to-day work of electioneering, and the rewards of office are the best inducement to energetic party work. Parties are essential to our system of government to coordinate the legislative and executive powers and to join national, state, and local energies in a unified program. The second argument is that the President is elected to fulfill a popular mandate, and

Defense of the spoils system

[1] Notably New York and Pennsylvania. See H. L. McBain, "DeWitt Clinton and the Origins of the Spoils System," *Columbia Univ. Studies in Hist., Econ., and Pub. Law,* XXVIII (New York, 1907).

[2] The term *spoils system* derives from the statement of a Jacksonian Democrat, Senator William L. Marcy of New York, who in 1832 in a discussion of partisan appointments remarked, "To the victor belong the spoils."

unless he can staff his branch with persons loyal to his party and his program he cannot successfully redeem his pledges. If his chief political lieutenants must work with unsympathetic or uncooperative subordinates, his hold upon the executive branch is tenuous. Rotation in office, furthermore, guarantees periodic infusion of new blood and prevents administrative hardening of the arteries.[3]

THE DEVELOPMENT OF THE MERIT SYSTEM

Criticism of the spoils system

Despite the strong defense which its supporters made, the spoils system attracted, especially after 1850, increasingly vigorous criticism. The President was harassed beyond endurance by place-seekers and their friends. Lincoln, for example, could steal but a few precious hours during his first months in office to devote to the grave problem of secession which confronted him, because his days were filled with the importunings of Republican office-seekers. Every change in administration witnessed an almost complete breakdown of executive branch services as those familiar with their operations were replaced wholesale by men and women unlettered in the laws and practices of the departments. The lines of administrative authority were rudely shattered; employees gave their first loyalty to those who had gotten them the jobs and who alone could discharge them. The executive branch became increasingly corroded with the loose morals of the political hack. Graft, favoritism, and influence-peddling were rife.

Civil service reform

The first feeble steps at reform were taken in 1853 and in 1855 by the Congress when it prescribed the classification of several thousand clerkships in Washington and required that candidates for these posts pass examinations administered by the heads of the departments concerned. Reform of the civil service [4] was agitated extensively in 1867 and played a part in the campaign of 1868. In 1870, Great Britain gave a strong impetus to the cause of reform by installing a comprehensive system of merit appointment. Grant finally persuaded the Congress in 1871 to give him the power to regulate the admission of persons to the executive civil service and under this act established the first central personnel agency (Advisory Board of the Civil Service). The Board prescribed the first competitive examination for admission to office. The Congress, still unconvinced of the failure of the spoils system, starved Grant's

---

[3] For a vigorous defense of this idea, see J. Fischer, "Let's Go Back to the Spoils System," *Harper's Mag.,* CXCI, 262-368 (Oct., 1945); and cf. K. Cole, "The 'Merit System' Again," *Amer. Polit. Sci. Rev.,* XXXI, 695-698 (Aug., 1937); W. F. Davies, "Why I Believe in the Patronage System," *Nat. Mun. Rev.,* XIX, 18-21 (Jan., 1930); and W. Turn (a political boss), "In Defense of Patronage," *Annals of Amer. Acad. of Polit. and Soc. Sci.,* CLXXXIX, 22-28 (Jan., 1937). A straight-from-the-shoulder defender of spoils was a Tammany district leader by the name of George Washington Plunkitt, at the turn of the century. For his picturesquely phrased ideas, see W. L. Riordan, *Plunkitt of Tammany Hall* (New York, 1905).

[4] Technically, the words *civil service* refer to all of the nonmilitary employees and officers of the executive branch of the government.

COMPETITIVE CIVIL SERVICE JOBS IN THE NATIONAL GOVERNMENT

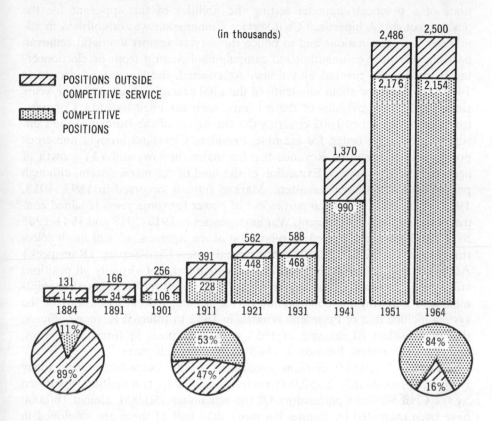

(in thousands)

ZZZ POSITIONS OUTSIDE
COMPETITIVE SERVICE

::::::: COMPETITIVE
POSITIONS

Board for funds and the examinations were abolished in 1875. The reformers, by now organized into national and state associations, redoubled their efforts.[5] *Harper's Weekly* and *The Nation* took up the cudgels. The assassination of President Garfield in 1881 by a disappointed office-seeker electrified the nation, and in 1882 the voters returned a Congress willing and able to act. Supported by President Arthur (to the consternation of his patronage-loving friends), a comprehensive civil service reform law (The Pendleton Act) was passed in 1883. This act, although modified in many details over the years, is still the basis of the personnel system of the executive branch.

[5] Notably the National Civil Service Reform League, founded in 1881, renamed in 1945 the National Civil Service League, and today one of the most vigilant and influential agencies for promoting the application of merit principles in national, state, and local civil services. On the League and its work during the period covered, see F. M. Stewart, *The National Civil Service Reform League* (Austin, Tex., 1929).

The Civil Service Act of 1883 provided that admission to certain positions would henceforth be solely on the basis of open, competitive examinations of a practical character testing the abilities of the applicant for the position sought. A bipartisan Civil Service Commission was established to administer the examinations and to police the service against wrongful removal, partisan selection, or unauthorized campaign solicitation from or electioneering by employees covered by the law. As enacted, the law extended only to 14,000 positions or about one-tenth of the total executive branch. In the years since 1883, the provisions of the act have been extended by: (1) Congress, for example, an act of 1902 covering the employees of the Bureau of the Census; (2) executive order, for example, President Cleveland brought numerous positions in the Internal Revenue Service under the law; and (3) growth of agencies already covered. Expansion of the hold of the merit system, although persistent, has not been consistent. Marked retreats occurred in 1897, 1913, 1921, 1933, and 1953 when parties out of power for some years regained control of the national government. War emergencies in 1917-1918 and 1941-1945 have also been accompanied by relaxation of the rigorous rules of merit selection. However, the Congress in 1940 passed a new Civil Service (Ramspeck) Act which authorized the inclusion by executive order of virtually all positions still outside the reach of the system except those filled by Presidential appointment and requiring the confirmation of the Senate. Recent extensions of the system include that of President Truman in 1952 to Internal Revenue officers, that of President Eisenhower in 1954 to 41,000 posts in foreign countries, and that of President Johnson in 1965 to customs collectors.

Of the 2,500,000 civilians employed by the executive branch today (1965), approximately 2,150,000 are in posts filled by competition supervised by the Civil Service Commission. Of the remaining 350,000, almost 160,000 have been exempted by statute, but more than half of these are employed in agencies like the Atomic Energy Commission, the Tennessee Valley Authority, the Federal Bureau of Investigation, the Central Intelligence Agency, and the Foreign Service of the State Department which have merit systems of their own. Somewhat more than 100,000 are in the classified service but have been exempted from competition by the Commission.[6] An additional 70,000 are overseas posts, also exempted by the Commission. The major groups of positions regularly filled at present by patronage appointees are United States marshals, district attorneys, substitute rural mail carriers, employees of several government corporations—notably the Federal Housing Administration, lawyers in many of the departments, and so-called "policy-making" posts.

---

[6] Commission exemptions are classed under Schedule A which includes a miscellaneous group of parttime or seasonal positions, Schedule B which includes, e.g., intelligence positions and which does require a noncompetitive exam, and Schedule C which includes policy determining posts and those of a confidential character (private secretary). The latter schedule was enlarged by the Eisenhower administration to cover so-called "policy-making" posts which it felt ought to be staffed by persons "sympathetic" to the President's party program.

Many of these posts require Senatorial confirmation of Presidential appointees. Postmasters might also be included in this list since those in the first three classes must still be confirmed by the Senate although they are required to take examinations and appointments must normally be made from among the top three persons qualifying.

ATTRACTING ABLE PUBLIC EMPLOYEES

The primary object of the Civil Service Act of 1883 and the later amend- *Recruit-* ments, executive orders, and new statutes extending its provisions throughout *ment* the executive branch has been to promote appointment on the basis of tested *procedures* capacity and to assure those thus appointed reasonable security of tenure during proper performance of their duties. During the long struggle with the spoils system, however, primary emphasis was placed by personnel administrators on the removal of partisan, political influences in appointment and removal. The triumph of the merit system in this century has created a more favorable climate for a searching analysis of its actual operation by friends of the merit principle. Keeping unqualified people out of office does not of itself attract well-qualified people into it, say the critics. There still remains the positive task of procuring the services of the best qualified. Is the present personnel system of the national government adequately performing its mission?

For a great many years the standard procedure of the Civil Service Commission in announcing the availability of government employment has been to post placards in post offices and public buildings throughout the nation—occasionally next to the pictures of wanted criminals—on the expectation that the interested public would be thus stimulated to apply. This method, still widely used, has been tolerably effective during periods of widespread unemployment and for unskilled and semiskilled laborers and clerks. It has never been effective in enlisting the interest of successful executives, scientists, or professionally trained persons. In recent years, stimulated by manpower shortages and prodded by dissatisfied department heads, the Commission and agency personnel officers have undertaken more aggressive programs of searching out talented persons and inducing them to apply. This they have done by newspaper publicity, radio talks, attendance at meetings of professional societies, advertisements in professional and scientific journals, participation in collegiate vocational guidance exercises, and by numerous other devices. Admittedly, the Commission still does not do as much in this respect as it would like to do and what it does do still falls far short of the mark.[7]

The most effective recruitment procedure which the Commission might *Obstacles* devise would not itself remove all roadblocks to a more competent public *to effective recruitment*

[7] See J. D. Kingsley, chairman, *Recruiting Applicants for the Public Service,* a report submitted to the Civil Service assembly by the Committee on Recruiting Applicants for the Public Service (Chicago, 1942). See also *The Civil Service Recruiter,* a periodical news sheet issued by the U.S. Civil Service Commission.

service. In the first place, many years of spoils appointment brought the national service to a low level of public esteem. Many citizens regarded it as the last refuge for the incompetent. Ambitious youth was encouraged to seek satisfaction in other walks of life. The energetic attacks of the government on the depression of the thirties, the satisfactions of those in service in two great wars have partially, but not completely, dispelled this attitude among the American people. The pay in government service, furthermore, is less than in private employment for professional, executive, and scientific skills. Many people continue to believe, further, that public employment is still largely controlled by partisan politics. More serious than any of these attitudes is the requirement that examinations be practical in their character and related to the positions for which applications are sought. Herein our American system differs sharply from the British on which otherwise it was modeled.

Contrast of American and British systems

In Great Britain, the competitive principle operates more consistently in the higher levels of the official hierarchy than with us. Public service is looked upon to a greater extent as a profession and even a career. The main object of examinations is to recruit (especially in the middle and higher levels) from young men and women who expect to spend their lives in public employment, and whose education and native ability make it probable that they will rise from one grade to another and steadily grow in usefulness as administrators. Hence British examinations are framed mainly with a view to testing broadly the candidate's general attainments and capacity. Mathematics, history, philosophy, the classics, natural science—these and other branches of higher learning receive much emphasis. Even the examinations for positions of a clerical nature are framed similarly, although confined to more elementary subjects. Under the American plan, the object, in the majority of cases, is not primarily to test general attainments and capacity; rather it is to ascertain the applicant's immediate fitness for the kind of work that he seeks. And since there is a great variety of jobs, the Commission is under the necessity of providing an equally great variety of different examinations—no fewer than 1700 when a count was made some years ago.

> There is something to be said, of course, for both systems. The American is probably more democratic; it exacts little of the beginner in the way of general knowledge, and it affords a haven for men and women of all ages who are attracted by its pecuniary rewards, modest though they are. This, however, is about all that can be said for it. The British system attracts to the public service men and women who, on the average, not only are younger and more energetic than American appointees, but better fitted by education, and probably native capacity as well, to become increasingly able, useful, and responsible officials.[8]

We are now more strongly moving in the direction of the English system. The Civil Service Commission, beginning in 1934, set up limited "registers"

[8] F. A. Ogg, *English Government and Politics* (2nd ed., New York, 1926), 231-232.

(e.g., for junior professional assistants, and later junior management assistants and junior agricultural assistants) with examinations of general rather than specific nature and open only to graduates of colleges and universities. At present, the Federal Service Entrance Examinations administered annually to prospective college graduates are used for this purpose and have become a major method for recruiting management talents. Similarly, broad examinations are being used to recruit those with scientific and technical skills. Our system, however, still suffers from attracting recruits who have crammed up on the requirements for some particular job, without regard for the mental attainments and capacities that would fit a candidate, once appointed, to go on to larger responsibilities.

The character of the examinations designed to test merit may thus be a strong deterrent to recruiting able men and women into the service. The American system, it should be added, relies extensively, although not solely, on examinations for selecting the best qualified among those who apply. All of these examinations are not, however, pencil-and-paper tests. Many are designed to test manual skills in typing, machine operating, bricklaying, and so on. Some take the form of personal interviews. For a large number of positions in the competitive civil service, especially those for professional and scientific posts, no examinations are given. The experience and training of the applicants are rated competitively on the basis of oral interviews and testimony. The Commission supervises the preparation and administration of all tests for admission to the "competitive classified service." [9] A great deal of time and money has been spent by the Commission over the years developing, with the aid of experts, valid and reliable testing devices for determining capacity for the thousands of different positions in the executive branch. None of the testing devices thus far developed, however, has proved a reliable guide to the honesty, industry, friendliness, or ambition of the applicants. This limitation of the examining process was recognized from the beginning by giving some discretion to the appointing officers and by requiring a probationary period before full tenure is acquired.

Examinations

On the registers of the Commission, at Washington and in the offices of the regional directors, are kept the names of all persons who have passed the various examinations with a grade of 70 or above, classified by types of position. Since 1939 the list itself, however many names of persons in waiting may remain on it, lapses at the end of a year—unless the Commission decides to prolong its life another year rather than order a new examination. When a

Appointment

[9] There is much popular confusion on the meaning of the various services in the executive branch. The *civil service,* as has been seen, includes every civilian position in the executive branch however filled. The *classified service* includes only those positions within the purview of the Civil Service Commission which have been classified for admission purposes. Even some of the classified positions are not filled by competition, however. The Commission may exempt some jobs from competitive appointment and thus the *competitive classified service* is that to which admission may be gained only by some form of testing.

clerk or stenographer or other employee in the classified service is needed by an agency, the Commission or now the departmental personnel office supplies the appointing officer with the names of three persons who stand highest in the appropriate list of eligibles. The officer normally appoints one of the three, and the other two resume their places at the top of the waiting list.[10] If no one of the three is appointed, the officer must be prepared to assign some good reason when asking for more names. Every appointee is placed on probation for a period typically of one year. During this time, he can be removed by his superior summarily, with no reason assigned except that his work is unsatisfactory. If retained longer, however, he gains "civil service status," with all the security of tenure for which the law provides. The probationary period has not proved an effective screening device, for removals at this stage are extremely few.

Restrictions on eligibility for appointment:
1. Citizenship
2. Apportionment according to population

The opportunity to compete for appointment is circumscribed by law in several ways not necessarily related to merit. In the first place, only citizens of the United States are eligible to enter the service.[11] In the second place, "as nearly as the conditions of good administration warrant" appointments are to be apportioned among the states and territories on the basis of population. This requirement of the original Civil Service Act has been observed in practice largely by administering the examinations through the regional offices of the Commission located throughout the country. From Civil War days, honorably discharged veterans have been granted preferential treatment in competing for civil service positions and various Civil Service Acts have required that special treatment be continued even for positions in the competitive service. The matter is now controlled by the Veteran Preference Act of 1944 which grants to any persons who have served honorably in the armed services at any time a monopoly of certain specified minor civil service jobs (as guards, messengers, etc.). The act also provides for: (1) adding 10 points to the

[10] The "rule of three," making it possible for the candidate highest on the list to be passed over in favor of the second or third, is characteristic of the American system. In Great Britain, only one name is submitted and the candidate standing highest can be sure of appointment, barring very unusual circumstances. Our Civil Service Commission has said that the rule of three should be retained for routine jobs only, with a rule of five substituted for positions on intermediate levels and "wide discretion" on higher ones. Apparently entertaining a doubt (with which many college students will sympathize) as to whether a candidate with an arbitrary rating of 90 is necessarily any better than one with 89, the Hoover Commission in 1949 recommended abandonment of numerical grading in favor of a system under which persons emerging successfully from examinations would be grouped simply as "outstanding," "well qualified," and "qualified," with appointing officers free to choose at random from the first category or from a lower one if those above were exhausted.

[11] Formerly, aliens who had declared their intention to be naturalized were permitted to take examinations, and occasionally to receive appointments. Examinations nowadays, however, are open only to citizens, save in the rare event of a lack of citizen applicants. Except in the case of scientific, technical, and professional positions, no one, under civil service law, may be debarred from taking an examination because of any lack of educational qualifications; and enough obviously unfit persons try their luck to add considerably to the work and expense. No fee is charged any applicant.

earned examination ratings of disabled honorably discharged ex-servicemen and unmarried widows of ex-servicemen; [12] (2) placing all such persons whose earned rating plus preference is above 70 at the top of the appropriate registers ahead of all other eligibles, except in the case of professional and scientific positions with entrance salary of over $3000 a year; (3) adding five points to the earned examination ratings of honorably discharged ex-servicemen and women not disabled, and giving such persons preference in appointments over all others rating equally high; [13] and (4) giving to all veteran incumbents preferential treatment when staff reductions must be made. That the nation should suitably compensate those who have risked their lives in its defense, and should take care of those who have incurred physical or mental injury in doing so, is hardly debatable. It is, however, unfortunate that we have fallen into the habit of discharging this obligation, not alone by pensions, "bonuses," hospitalization, and the like, but by setting aside the merit principle in civil service selection in such a way that the nonveteran, however well qualified, is placed at a striking disadvantage in seeking public employment. The service promises in future, nevertheless, to be very heavily manned (actually over 50 percent in 1962) with veteran-preference appointees, capable and otherwise.[14]

3. Veteran preference

Within the last two decades a new requirement for public servants has been added to the list: "loyalty" to the American system of government. Mounting public apprehension over the activities of fascistic and communistic groups and the loyalty which they seemed to exhibit to foreign governments, and charges by certain Congressional committees of executive indifference to the problem, induced the Congress in 1939 to forbid employees in the national government to belong to any organization that advocates the forceful overthrow of our constitutional government. Appropriation acts for various agencies began in the same year to carry provisions forbidding payment of salaries to persons who advocated or who belonged to organizations which advocated the overthrow of the government by force and violence. The Commission set up procedures to screen incumbent employees and to check on new applicants. The beginning of the "cold war" with Russia stimulated anew Congressional critics of administrative laxness in employing persons of ques-

4. Loyalty requirement

---

[12] Amendments in 1953 require that the veteran have at least 10% of complete disability to be classed as disabled.

[13] The 1953 changes also require the veteran to earn a passing grade before he becomes the beneficiary of the extra points.

[14] The principles and problems involved in veteran preference are discussed at length by J. F. Miller in C. J. Friedrich *et al., Problems of the American Public Service* (New York, 1935), 243-334; and a highly unfavorable view is presented in F. C. Cahn, *Federal Employees in War and Peace* (Washington, 1949). Conceding that veteran preference is "an integral part of our civil service system," the Hoover Commission in 1949 proposed changes in line with its suggested new scheme of examination ratings, two rather startling recommendations being (1) that veterans, wives, and widows entitled to 10 percent preference, and rating in the "qualified" group, be jumped ahead of other candidates not only in that group but in the two higher ones as well; and (2) that within each group veterans (even the able-bodied) be systematically placed ahead of nonveterans.

tionable loyalty. In anticipation of more vigorous Congressional attack on the executive branch, President Truman in 1947 established by executive order a new program for rooting "disloyalty" out of the government and preventing it from growing new roots.[15] Pursuant to this order, as subsequently amended by President Eisenhower,[16] and to Congressional enactment, every new employee of the national government must be investigated by the Civil Service Commission, and if any derogatory material is uncovered a full investigation must be made of his or her life history. Applicants for positions designated by the heads of agencies as "sensitive" must be fully investigated in every case.[17] Wide discretion is conferred on the Commission and on the employing department to reject any applicant believed "tainted" by subversive views or associations. The rejected applicant has little or no recourse from such decisions.

The net effect of all of these restrictions on admission to the civil service is sharply to reduce the field from which able applicants may be drawn.

MAINTAINING EMPLOYEE EFFICIENCY AND POLITICAL NEUTRALITY

*Impor-
tance of
discipline*

The attack upon the spoils system which led to the adoption of the merit system was concerned not only with the qualifications of those who gained admission to public jobs but also with protecting those already at work from dismissal for partisan reasons. Great and continuing emphasis has thus been placed in public personnel administration on security of tenure for employees of the government. Critics of the merit system have contended almost from the beginning that it has tended to protect careless, indifferent, and incompetent employees. Defenders of the system have usually responded that security against capricious or partisan disciplining is essential to competent and effective performance. The vigorous character of this continuing debate indicates that the practices of the national executive with regard to employee discipline are at least as important in maintaining a competent public service as its practices in regard to appointment.

Removal

Every member of the national civil service is liable to disciplinary action at the hands of some superior authority. Such action may include reprimand, reduction in pay or position, suspension (not to exceed 70 days), or outright dismissal. In general, the power of removal or of administering any lesser punishment accompanies the power to appoint and is formally lodged in the head of the department or agency (although in practice ordinarily exercised by a subordinate). The freedom of the department head to deal with his employees as he sees fit is limited, however, by statutory requirement that "like penalties shall be imposed for like offenses and no discrimination shall be exercised for political or religious reasons" and that removal may be only for "such cause as will promote the efficiency of the service." Furthermore, the

---

[15] Executive order 9835, March 21, 1947 (12 *Fed. Reg.*, 1935).
[16] Executive order 10450, April 29, 1953.
[17] In some cases by the F.B.I.

employee in virtually all disciplinary actions is entitled to a written statement of the charges against him and to an opportunity to answer them. No legal right to judicial review of the decision of the appointing officer is granted generally to employees nor is any right to a public hearing.[18] Despite the considerable freedom of the department head and the apparent simplicity of the rules governing the matter, disciplinary actions are relatively few. The reasons which are usually cited for this are: (1) the process is distasteful, cumbersome, and time-consuming; (2) supervisors at all levels are reluctant to antagonize their subordinates or to embarrass their superiors; (3) the departmental heads are persuaded by the traditions of the service that the system is unusable; and (4) the Civil Service Commission has tended to use other powers (such as its control over classification) to compel departmental adherence to more rigorous requirements than the law specifically provides.[19]

Until 1939, dismissal from the competitive service could not be based on political opinions. As we have already noted, in that year Congress began to require the dismissal of employees holding "disloyal" opinions. Dissatisfaction (largely Congressional) with the progress made by the departments in discharging alleged communists or communist-sympathizers led to the Truman Loyalty order of 1947. This order required the screening of all civil servants in the executive branch of the government and the dismissal of all those concerning whom "reasonable grounds exist for belief" [20] in their disloyalty. Each department and agency was directed to establish a board to review charges brought against any employee as a result of FBI or departmental investigation. Each employee charged with disloyalty was granted the right to a hearing before the departmental board and to an appeal from the departmental board to a Loyalty Review Board in the Civil Service Commission.[21] The attorney general was directed to prepare a list of subversive organizations association

Disloyalty as a grounds for dismissal

---

[18] Special protection in the form of an appeal to the Civil Service Commission is granted to those enjoying veteran preference and this includes half of all civil servants. The nonveteran employee's rights were placed on a similar basis by executive order (10988) in 1962. See H. C. Westwood, "The 'Right' of an Employee of the United States Against Arbitrary Discharge," *Geo. Washington Law Rev.*, VII, 212-232 (Dec., 1938).

[19] See Hoover Commission reports, *Personnel Management* (Washington, 1949), 33-40; *Personnel and Civil Service* (Washington, 1955); and the Task-Force report on *Federal Personnel*, 62-66; J. D. Kingsley, W. E. Mosher, O. G. Stahl, *Public Personnel Administration* (New York, 1950), 487-489.

[20] This provision was tightened by President Truman in 1951 to "reasonable doubt as to the loyalty" of the employee. Administrative amendments of this type and Congressional modifications of the type of the Internal Security Act of 1950 meant that the same cases had to be reviewed again and again.

[21] Under the Truman Loyalty program, by January, 1952, nearly 4,000,000 persons employed or seeking employment had been checked. Of this number "derogatory information" had been found concerning 17,343 and these had been fully investigated by the FBI. Of these, 1935 left the service voluntarily during the investigation. An additional 1878 persons left the service while agency loyalty board reviews were being made. The departmental loyalty boards approved the dismissal of 570 of the 15,408 cases referred to them. The Loyalty Review Board sustained the dismissal of 315 of these. T. I. Emerson and D. Haber, *Political and Civil Rights in the United States* (Buffalo, 1952), 563.

with any of which by an employee would bring his loyalty into question. The procedures used by the various agencies presented many problems and attracted much criticism. Chief of these was the difficulty, in many cases the impossibility, of confronting the employee with his detractors and with the evidence against him without disclosing the informants whose anonymity the FBI was anxious to protect. The Supreme Court reviewed this question in 1951 and sustained the power of the government to dismiss an employee for disloyalty although she had not been allowed to confront her accuser.[22]

The investigation and review procedure established by President Truman for purging the service of "disloyalty" did not satisfy several of the most critical Congressmen, and the charge of tenderness to Communist sympathizers on the part of the Truman administration played a substantial role in the 1952 campaign. The accession of President Eisenhower was soon followed by a new executive order [23] broadening still more the grounds for dismissal for "security" reasons,[24] sweeping away the entire system of loyalty boards, and conferring complete responsibility upon the heads of the agencies for ridding them of questionable employees. The Civil Service Commission was granted, however, the primary responsibility for the investigation of persons in the competitive service.[25]

Disloyalty dismissal in certain "sensitive agencies"
The various procedures for purging disloyal employees established by Presidents Truman and Eisenhower have been supplemented from time to time by statutes which confer upon certain "sensitive" agencies—notably the Department of State, Atomic Energy Commission, Department of Defense, and the Central Intelligence Agency—the power summarily to dismiss any employee regarded by the heads of such an agency as a "poor security risk." Growing criticism of the excessive zeal of administrators in removing so-called "security risks" and the loss of prestige of the leading Congressional spokesmen demanding ruthless purges led the Congress in 1955 to create a Commission on Government Security to reconsider the whole question of "loyalty" dismissals. In its report in 1957, the Commission proposed: (1) the creation of a new Central Security Office in the executive branch to conduct hearings on loyalty, to review agency procedures, and to advise agency heads in all security cases; (2) the confrontation of accused by accusers wherever this could be done without endangering national security; (3) a change in rules to allow transfer to nonsensitive positions of "security" risks who were not disloyal.[26]

[22] Bailey *v*. Richardson, 341 U. S. 918 (1951). An equally divided Supreme Court in this case sustained the decision of the Court of Appeals.

[23] Executive order 10450, April 29, 1953.

[24] The grounds were broadened by another order in Oct. 1953 making invocation of the Fifth Amendment before a Congressional committee grounds for dismissal.

[25] Under the Eisenhower program, in a little more than a year 8006 employees were dismissed or resigned while under investigation. However, many of them were not disloyal but were adjudged "poor risks" for other reasons. *The New York Times,* Jan. 4, 1955.

[26] *Report of the Commission on Government Security* (Washington, 1957).

The ferocity of the attack on the national service abated after 1954. Thus amidst a somewhat less hysterical atmosphere numerous cases of aggrieved employees began to reach the Supreme Court. Although the Court never retracted its position that dismissal for security reasons was a legitimate exercise of power even though the employee could not always be aware of the nature and source of the evidence against him, nevertheless it found in several cases that the dismissals had been in error. The most significant decision in this vein held that employees could be summarily (without hearing) dismissed as security risks only if they held sensitive positions related to national security.[27]

Most government agencies have been quietly modifying their security dismissal procedures in the light of the Court decisions and the recommendations of the Commission. No substantial legislative action, however, has been taken on the Commission's proposals.[28]

One of the objectives of the merit system from its inception has been to prevent civil servants from being required to engage in partisan political activity. The original Civil Service Act forbids the dismissal or disciplining of any classified employee because of his failure to make a contribution to a campaign chest. Further, no classified employee may be solicited for funds by any Congressman or officeholder or by anyone while on duty in a government building.[29] On their parts, employees of the classified service are forbidden to engage in partisan politics. They may vote, attend rallies as spectators, and privately voice [30] their opinions, but they may not (since 1907) take any active part in political campaigns. To do so is grounds for dismissal. Until 1939, these prohibitions extended only to the classified service. A Political Activities (Hatch) Act of that year forbids all officers and employees of the executive

Restrictions upon partisan activities

[27] Cole v. Young, 351 U. S. 536 (1956). In another related case, the Court held that in the dismissal of Dr. John Peters of Yale the Loyalty Review Board had exceeded its authority, Peters v. Hobby, 349 U. S. 341 (1955). In Harmon v. Bruckner, 355 U. S. 579 (1958), the Court ruled that the Army had no authority to grant a soldier who had performed faithfully an other than honorable discharge because of some of his activities before he was inducted into the Army. In Vitarelli v. Seaton, 359 U. S. 535 (1959), the Court held that if a department attempted to remove an employee by its security procedures, it had to live up to its rules even though the employee was not entitled to the protections of the civil service laws.

[28] On the loyalty program, see E. S. Corwin, *The Presidency: Office and Powers*, pp. 100-110 (4th ed., New York, 1957); R. E. Cushman, "The President's Loyalty Purge," *Survey Graphic*, XXXVI, pp. 283-287 (May, 1947); R. S. Abbott, "The Federal Loyalty Program: Background and Problems," *Amer. Polit. Sci. Rev.*, XLII, pp. 486-499 (June, 1948); and for full critical treatment, W. Gellhorn, *Security, Loyalty, and Science* (Ithaca, N. Y., 1950), and E. Bontecou, *The Federal Loyalty-Security Program* (Ithaca, N. Y., 1953); D. Fellman, "The Loyalty Defendants," *Wisconsin Law Review*, 1957, No. 1 (Jan., 1957); C. P. Curtis, *The Oppenheimer Case; The Trial of the Security System* (New York, 1955).

[29] There is nothing in the law, however, to prevent solicitation by nonofficeholders at the homes of employees.

[30] The law does not say "privately" and purports to allow public expression, but the rules of the Civil Service Commission do not allow much latitude for avowedly partisan utterance. See D. H. Nelson, "Political Expression Under the Hatch Act and the Problem of Statutory Ambiguity," *Midwest Jour. of Pol. Sci.*, II, No. 1 (Feb., 1958).

branch, except those in "policy-determining" positions, from taking an active part in the management of party affairs or in political campaigns.[31] Nor may they use their official positions in any way to influence the election of any candidate to national office. Officials in the unclassified service may, however, publicly voice their opinions on issues or candidates if they do not do so as "part of an organized campaign." In 1940 a new (Hatch) Act extended similar but not identical restrictions to state and local governmental employees working in programs which are wholly or partially financed from the national treasury. The intention of these recent laws to reduce the influence of the executive branch in party matters has been only partially realized. Enforcement has never been vigorous among patronage appointees.[32]

Lobbying not restricted

It is ironic but understandable that national civil servants are forbidden to engage in the type of political activities which are generally approved by the public but are allowed to lobby in their own behalf, individually or through their organizations, before Congress. An attempt by President Theodore Roosevelt to prevent employees from appealing to Congress over the heads of their superiors was squelched by the Congress in an (Lloyd-LaFollette) Act of 1912 which guarantees the right of employees to petition Congress against impairment by executive order.

Promotion and transfer

Maintaining a competent staff is not solely, perhaps not even mainly, a problem of effective punishment. It is also one of appropriate reward. In the business and professional world it is recognized that nothing contributes more to the efficiency and morale of a staff than reasonable assurance of advancement on the basis of meritorious service. The same holds true in public administration. Few problems of our American civil service (national, state, and local) have proved more difficult. Upon what qualities or attainments of the civil servant should promotion be based? How are these qualities or attainments to be measured? Should promotion be by formal examination or simply on the basis of someone's judgment? Should higher positions in a given branch of the service be filled only by promotion, or also by initial appointment from the outside? In the Civil Service Act of 1883 we read that no classified officer or employee shall be promoted "until he has passed an examination," or is shown to be specially exempted from such examination; and a long-standing rule promulgated by the President enjoins that "competitive tests or examinations shall, as far as practicable and useful, be established to test fitness for promotion in the classified service." Both regulations obviously recognize the

[31] This law has been construed to bar civil servants from becoming candidates for *any* elective office if campaigning is involved.

[32] In February, 1947, the Supreme Court handed down two simultaneous decisions holding the Hatch legislation constitutional. See United Public Workers of America *et al.* v. Mitchell *et al.* (330 U. S. 75), and Oklahoma v. United States Civil Service Commission (330 U. S. 127); and for comment, F. Heady, "The Hatch Act Decisions," *Amer. Polit. Sci. Rev.*, XLI, 687-699 (Aug., 1947). A fuller analysis of the Hatch legislation and some of the questions arising under it will be found in L. V. Howard, "Federal Restrictions on the Political Activity of Government Employees," *ibid.*, XXXV, 470-489 (June, 1941).

possibility of promotions without examination. Until recently, the selection of persons for advancement, in the staffs at Washington as well as throughout the country, was commonly at the discretion of administrative chiefs, guided somewhat by such measures of efficiency as might be available. An executive order of President Franklin D. Roosevelt in 1938, however, tightened up the procedure considerably. The Civil Service Commission was instructed to work out and put into operation a general service-wide promotion system. Since that time the Commission itself has been conducting promotion examinations for positions common to more than one department or establishment, and individual departments have been stimulated to use better procedures. All agencies were required to make promotions in the competitive service only on the basis of promotion procedures approved by the commission under a program inaugurated in 1959. The Commission's own examinations open avenues not only for direct promotions but also for transfers (often amounting to promotion) from one branch of the service to another.

One of the keys to a usable system of promotion and pay rises is the *Efficiency* development of objective methods of measuring employee performance. A *ratings* uniform system of efficiency ratings throughout the classified service was tried by the national executive beginning about 1942. This was replaced in 1950 [33] by a system of departmentally-developed, commission-approved performance ratings which places more emphasis on the improvement of employee performance than upon the use of the ratings for promotion purposes. Neither the old nor the new procedure, however, has provided reliable data for informing the discretion of the appointing authority. The absence of widely accepted standards for measuring performance has meant, in practice, that heavy reliance is placed upon seniority.

In sum, the national civil service merit program has not completely achieved a system of personnel administration in which able and ambitious young people may enter upon a distinguished career certain of continuing advance and of increasing responsibility depending solely upon competent performance.

MAINTAINING EMPLOYEE MORALE

Studies of human behavior in industry and government reveal that performance on the job is influenced by many other factors than the method of hiring, firing, and promoting. The conditions under which the work is performed, the attitudes of fellow employees, the treatment accorded grievances, the relative levels of pay, the amount of vacation, and many other factors are impressive determinants of employee morale and efficiency.

During the first forty years of the merit system, one of the greatest deter- *Classifica-* rents to effective performance was the fact that employees doing substantially *tion of* the same work were treated differently in different agencies. Standards for *positions*

[33] The Performance Rating Act of 1950.

admission, examination, and pay were not coordinated throughout the classified service. In 1923, the Congress in the Salary Classification Act—one of the great landmarks in the development of the merit system—provided for the grouping of similar positions in the service in Washington, and for the assignment of appropriate salaries, examinations, and admission standards for each class of positions. In 1940, this requirement was extended to the service outside the national capital. The Civil Service Commission has, since 1923, been charged with the responsibility for assigning positions in the classified service to appropriate classes and for determining the proper standards for admission to each of the classes. Since the classification assigned to any position is the major (although not the sole) determinant of the pay of any person holding such position, the classification power of the Commission is an important one. Departmental executives eager for favorable consideration of their requests for "upgrading" employees are, therefore, obliged to maintain good relations with the Commission.[34] As a result of recommendations by the Hoover Commission, a Classification Act of 1949 gave more authority to the departments and agencies actually to place positions in the established classes, subject to a general review by the Commission. The new act also simplified the class structure. Five classes (services) established under the Act of 1923 were reduced to two, and the subdivisions (grades) of each class made more numerous. The present system has, in consequence, somewhat greater flexibility than the old one. A General Schedule is divided into eighteen grades (GS-1, GS-2, etc.) on the basis of the difficulty of, responsibility of, and training required for the position. These grades embrace all professional, scientific, executive, administrative, fiscal, and clerical (white collar) positions in the classified service. A Crafts, Protective, and Custodial Schedule of ten grades (CPC-1, CPC-2, etc.) embraces all skilled, semiskilled, and unskilled laborers' (blue collar) positions.

Pay   On the recommendation of the Commission, the Congress, traditionally, establishes a range of pay for each grade in each schedule of the classification system. For each grade (e.g., GS-4), a minimum and a maximum pay are established with steps between by which an individual may move from the beginning pay to the highest pay for that grade. Once the top pay for the grade is reached, however, the individual can earn no more unless he is promoted to another post or the post he holds is reclassified to a higher grade or the Congress grants a general pay increase. After a series of pay increases beginning in 1955—the most recent being in 1964—the executive branch, at present, holds a distinct edge in pay over private employment for most laboring and clerical positions. It suffers by comparison largely in the upper group of executive, professional, and scientific positions. It should be added here that, in general, the standard work week for civil servants is 40 hours with additional compensation for overtime.

---

[34] Reclassification of positions to higher classifications—"up-grading"—has for some years been a practical method for increasing the pay of incumbents.

Personnel practices in the national government have frequently been influenced by the theory that the government should be a "model employer" and should establish conditions of employment for its own employees which would tend to set a standard for the nation. Nowhere in the present personnel system has this policy been so influential as in the provision of what are now called "fringe benefits" for its employees. A retirement system established in 1920 provides retirement and disability benefits for employees on a compulsory basis, financed by employee contributions (deducted monthly from pay) to which the government adds interest. Paid vacations have been a feature of executive branch employment under laws dating back at least to 1896. Vacation allowances are presently controlled by the Annual and Sick Leave Act of 1951, as amended, which authorizes paid vacations ranging from 13 days a year for persons with fewer than three years' service to 26 days for persons with 15 years' service. Paid absence during illness is also authorized at the rate of 13 days per year, and if unused this may be accumulated to take care of protracted absence due to ill-health. Employees of the national government also receive the benefit of a larger number of legal holidays than most private establishments observe. Since 1916, national employees have been protected against loss due to death or injury while on duty by a system of workmen's compensation. In 1954, a joint-contributory system of group life insurance was established by Congress for national employees which provides insurance protection approximately in the amount of annual compensation. A system of joint-contributory medical care insurance was added to the other benefits by the Congress in 1959. In total, the fringe benefits associated with civil service employment are among the most generous in the country and go far toward making such employment attractive.

"Fringe benefits"

UNIONIZATION OF CIVIL SERVANTS

As the country's largest employer, the national government encounters questions of labor organization and labor policy not unlike those confronting private industry. Organizations of national employees started in the postal service some 75 years ago as a protest against long working hours and low pay. After considerable controversy, including attempts by the executive branch to frustrate organization, the Congress in 1912 fixed the government's policy with respect to all parts of the civil establishment from that time to this by unequivocally recognizing the right of employees to petition Congress or any member thereof, by guaranteeing that membership in employee organizations designed to improve working conditions should not be made a reason for dismissal or demotion, and by conceding the full right of the organizations to affiliate with labor unions outside of the public service, so long as not entailing any "obligation or duty . . . to engage in any strike or . . . to assist . . . in any strike against the United States."

The right to organize conceded

Thereafter, and especially in the thirties, the unionizing of national em-

Existing unions and federations

ployees went forward fairly rapidly. (1) Nine different groups of postal workers now have their own separate nation-wide organizations (five affiliated with
the AFL and four unaffiliated), enlisting in some instances as much as nine-
tenths of their potential strength.[35] (2) A National Federation of Federal
Employees, dating from 1917, wholly independent, and recognized as unusually conservative, links up some 1100 local unions of civil service employees
composed of persons engaged in various services outside of the separately
organized postal branch. (3) An American Federation of Government Employees originating in a secession from the National Federation in 1932 and
affiliated with the AFL has grown rapidly, especially among employees of
agencies of New Deal antecedents. (4) A United Public Workers of America
(with which a United Federal Workers of America has been merged), formerly affiliated with the CIO but now expelled because (according to report)
of its leftist leanings, is now in decline. And, (5) thousands of employees
engaged in mechanical trades, for example, printers, carpenters, and plumbers,
belong to the regular unions maintained by their privately employed fellow-
craftsmen.

*Pros and
cons of
employee
organi-
zation*

    The employee associations are concerned first of all with salary scales,
hours, retirement rights, grievance procedures, and other matters relating to
the status of their own members. Undoubtedly they have helped secure better
working conditions for many groups of employees, the National Federation
contributing heavily, for example, to the adoption of the Retirement Act of
1920 and the Classification Act of 1923. The demands which they make
sometimes stir resentment. Many people, indeed, fear that they will grow
powerful enough to hold a club over the government, threatening paralysis
of its activities unless they get what they want. They have, however, generally
exhibited strong interest not only in promoting the general efficiency of the
service to which they belong but in keeping the public favorably disposed. As
a rule they support merit principles, promote employee morale, and help raise
the quality of work performed by their members. The things for which they
are most frequently criticized are their lobbying activities in Washington, their
relations with labor organizations outside of the service, and the possibility
that they might strike. In fairness it must be added that the no-strike pledge
contained in the constitutions of most of the number has been kept faithfully,
with the result that the government almost wholly escapes defiance of its
authority by its own regular employees such as has at times seriously embarrassed the governments of France, Italy, and other European countries.
The Labor Management Act of 1947 as amended in 1955, expresses the contemporary view of the Congress on the strike question. It makes it unlawful
"for any individual employed by the United States or any agency (including
any government corporation) thereof . . . to participate in any strike" and
provides immediate dismissal for violation.

    [35] Two of the largest unions of post office clerks merged in 1961: the National
Federation of Post Office Clerks (AFL-CIO) and the United National Association of
Post Office Craftsmen. The new union affiliated with the AFL-CIO.

ORGANIZATION OF PERSONNEL ADMINISTRATION

The main agency charged with the administration of the merit system throughout the executive branch is the Civil Service Commission. This agency of three members, appointed for indefinite terms by the President with the approval of the Senate, has been in existence since 1883. Administratively the Commission is directly under the President. From modest beginnings the Commission has grown to its present size and complexity. It now employs almost 4500 persons and spends almost $25 million annually through its central office and its regional offices in 14 major cities. The board form of organization for the central personnel agency in the executive branch has been sharply criticized in recent years on the grounds that it tends to emphasize its negative and reviewing function and that an energetic and positive program of attracting ability into the public service requires a single, forceful-executive-type organization.[36] It has survived most of the attacks largely unchanged, except that in 1949 as part of a reorganization plan more administrative authority was concentrated in the hands of the chairman.

The Civil Service Commission

Serious criticisms of Commission operation have also come from the operating establishments which have pleaded for more and more authority to handle their own personnel transactions. The larger departments have for many years felt the necessity of having rather substantial personnel agencies of their own to handle pay, records, promotions, and other matters. In 1938 an executive order required all departments and all of the major independent agencies to establish such offices. Since that time, personnel work has been increasingly decentralized from the Commission to the departments with the result that the Commission has gradually become more of a policy and an auditing agency than one concerned in the day-to-day administration of personnel. We have noted, for example, how classification responsibilities have been decentralized. There is also much pressure to decentralize examination administration. The Hoover Commission found that in 1949 more than $76 million was being spent for personnel administration in the executive branch and that 23,430 employees were engaged in this work, indicating that the departmental agencies were in the aggregate far larger than the Commission itself.

Departmental personnel agencies

PREPARING FOR A CAREER IN THE PUBLIC SERVICE

At one time, George Washington dreamed of a national university that would train young men for the national service, and often afterwards an institution was suggested that would do for the civil service what the academies at West Point, Annapolis, and Colorado Springs do for the Army, Navy, and

Civil service training

[36] The President's Committee on Administrative Management in 1937 made this point very strongly. The Hoover Commission made generally the same comment but did not go so far as to recommend the abolition of the Commission.

Air Force. Nothing of the kind has been provided; in the days of the spoils system, neither the politicians nor the people for whom they got jobs would have had any interest in such facilities. With the service as large as it is nowadays, and its activities as varied as they have come to be, no single training establishment could go far toward serving the purpose. Under a merit system, the need for training nonetheless is fully recognized; and fortunately it is met today, in considerable measure, by the opportunities provided in colleges and universities (besides many professional and other more or less specialized schools) in every part of the land. The most basic preparation thus afforded commonly takes the form of courses on the principles and practices of the American system of government and on the techniques of public administration in general. In preparation for the Federal Service Entrance Examination, a good knowledge of history, economics, and world affairs is essential. It is also very important to acquire a skill in a particular area, such as accounting, statistics, taxation, public health, forestry, some branch of law or of engineering, and the like. Happily in a lengthening list of institutions special programs for public service training have been organized and facilities provided.

In many branches of the national service, too, one's systematic training need not stop upon appointment. Just as many large private establishments provide their employees with opportunities for continued training, with a view to increasing their efficiency and preparing them to assume larger responsibilities, so extensive facilities have been developed in Washington for "in-service" training for personnel officers, income-tax officials, and other groups in various departments (notably Agriculture) and agencies. And for serious-minded persons weighing the pros and cons of entering upon a civil service career, the prospect of having opportunity, after entrance, to obtain training is often an added inducement. The available training was endorsed by Congress and officially expanded by the Government Employees Training Act of 1958.

References

L. D. White, *Introduction to the Study of Public Administration* (4th ed., New York, 1955), Chaps. xxi-xxx.

———, *Government Career Service* (Chicago, 1933).

——— [ed.], *Civil Service in Wartime* (Chicago, 1945).

C. S. Hyneman, *Bureaucracy in a Democracy* (New York, 1950), Chaps. v-x, xix.

O. G. Stahl, *Public Personnel Administration* (5th ed., New York, 1962).

P. P. Van Riper, *History of the United States Civil Service* (White Plains, N. Y., 1958).

F. T. Cahn, *Federal Employees in War and Peace; Selection, Placement, and Removal* (Washington, 1949).

Commission of Inquiry on Public Service Personnel, *Better Government Personnel* (New York, 1935).

P. T. David and R. Pollock, *Executives for Government: Central Issues of Federal Personnel Administration* (Washington, 1957).

N. J. Powell, *Personnel Administration in Government* (New York, 1958).

American Assembly, *The Federal Government Service: Its Character, Prestige, and Problems* (New York, 1954).

D. T. Stanley, *The Higher Civil Service* (Washington, 1964).

J. McDiarmid, "The Changing Role of the U. S. Civil Service Commission," *Amer. Polit. Sci. Rev.*, XL, 1067-1096 (Dec., 1946).

C. R. Fish, *The Civil Service and the Patronage* (New York, 1904).

W. D. Foulke, *Fighting the Spoilsmen; Reminiscences of the Civil Service Reform Movement* (New York, 1919).

O. P. Field, *Civil Service Law* (Minneapolis, 1939).

M. R. Godine, *The Labor Problem in the Public Service* (Cambridge, Mass., 1950).

W. G. Toepey, *Public Personnel Management* (New York, 1953).

G. R. Clapp, *et al., Employee Relations in the Public Service; A Report Submitted to the Civil Service Assembly of the United States and Canada* (Chicago, 1942).

S. D. Spero, *Government as Employer* (New York, 1948).

[Hoover] Commission on Organization of the Executive Branch of the Government, *Personnel Management* (Washington, 1949) and *Personal and Civil Service* (Washington, 1955).

W. Gellhorn, *Security, Loyalty, and Science* (Ithaca, N. Y., 1950).

Annual Reports of U. S. Civil Service Commission (Washington, 1883 ff.).

U. S. Civil Service Commission, *A Brief History of the United States Civil Service* (Washington, 1933).

The Federal Employee (Washington, 1916—). Published monthly by the National Federation of Federal Employees.

Public Personnel Review (Chicago, 1940—). Published quarterly by the Civil Service Assembly of the United States and Canada.

★ 16 ★

The National Judiciary

> The judicial power of the United States shall be vested in one Supreme Court and in such inferior courts as the Congress may from time to time ordain and establish. ART. III, Sec. 1

A separate national system of courts

THE CROWNING DEFECT of the Articles of Confederation, declared Alexander Hamilton in *The Federalist,* was "the want of a judicial power"; [1] and in planning a "more perfect union" the framers of the Constitution asserted in the preamble their purpose to "establish justice" and went on in Article III to place full judicial power alongside of executive and legislative power as one of the three main pillars of the national authority. In so doing they prepared the way for the establishment of a system of national courts, separate from the state courts, and deriving its existence and jurisdiction solely from the Constitution. When to these provisions the framers added (Art. VI) that this Constitution and the laws and treaties made under it were to be the "supreme law" of the land, binding judges in state courts, regardless of the provisions of state laws or constitutions, they laid the foundation for a national court system superior to all other courts and obliged to interpret and apply the supreme law in a uniform manner throughout the nation. The framers hoped to achieve not only uniformity of interpretation but escape from the local and sectional prejudices which would certainly influence the views of state judges, especially in controversies between states and between citizens of different states. Although some of the framers hoped to achieve these results by a single supreme court which would hear appeals from state courts, others, led by Madison, insisted that the new central government must have a full complement of courts of its own. A compromise was finally agreed to which left the matter to the Congress. Madison's view prevailed and the first Congress set up two grades of lower courts in addition to the Supreme Court for which the Constitution made express provision. [2]

SCOPE OF THE NATIONAL JUDICIAL POWER

Nature of "judicial power"

Judicial power has been defined as "the power to decide 'cases' and 'controversies' in conformity with law and by the methods established by the

[1] No. XXII (Lodge's ed., 132).
[2] The Judiciary Act of 1789 established 13 district courts, each with one judge, and 3 circuit courts, each comprised of one district and two Supreme Court judges.

404

usages and principles of law." [3] The important words in this definition are *cases* and *controversies*. Unlike the President and the Congress, courts do not initiate actions; they dispose of matters brought before them on the initiative of outsiders. They are powerless to influence the conduct of government except as they rule for or against the executive branch when it is one of the parties to a contest or as they construe the laws and orders uttered by the other branches as an incident to determining the relative merits of the claims of the litigants. In a system of government based upon a written constitution, however, the ultimate power to declare what the constitution means in any given situation is a very important power indeed whether it is exercised incidentally to the discharge of some other function or not.

The nature of the judicial function was determined early in our national history when the Supreme Court decided that it could not give legal advice either to the President or to Congress. Its only function was to decide lawsuits properly brought before it.[4] In deciding lawsuits, the courts must say what the law is that must be applied to any controversy before them and this obligation requires that they interpret statutes, treaties, executive orders, constitutions, and judicial precedents. The other branches of the government are constitutionally obliged to defer to the views of the courts. Under our system, a court is entitled to have its decisions reviewed and perhaps reversed only by a *higher court*. Judicial power has also come to embrace the authority to support valid findings of administrative agencies with orders which can be ignored only at the peril of fine or imprisonment for "contempt of court." The national courts have, however, acquiesced in allowing what they regard as questions of "fact" to be determined in some situations by agencies of the executive branch and questions which are "political" to be determined with finality by either or both of the other two co-ordinate branches of the government.

It would be quite wrong to suppose on the basis of what has been said that national judges have no other function save presiding over legal contests. Our national courts have become increasingly the managers of important business enterprises through their power in bankruptcy proceedings, for example, to appoint receivers responsible to them for the management of assets pending the outcome of litigation. Many judges thus find themselves engaged in the operation of railroads, mines, and factories and obliged to deal with all the problems of these enterprises which harass business executives. The rehabilita-

Marginal judicial activities

[3] E. S. Corwin, *The Constitution and What It Means Today* (10th ed., Princeton, N. J., 1948), 117. For the Supreme Court's elaboration of this definition, see Prentis v. Atl. Coast Line Co., 211 U. S. 210 (1908).

[4] The national courts since 1934 have been empowered by Congress to render "declaratory judgments," i.e., decisions construing the rights or status of persons or government agents in given situations and in advance of any actual damage inflicted which would provide the basis of a lawsuit. The court in these cases merely construes rights. It does not at the conclusion of the case issue a binding order of execution. The courts insist, however, that an actual controversy exist which could be settled through the normal channels of judicial procedure and the power has been used sparingly. State courts typically make much more use of this procedure than do national courts.

tion and correctional programs of the Federal Bureau of Prisons involve the judges in the affairs of prisoners sometimes for many years after trial and conviction. The national judges, like their counterparts in the states, marry and naturalize individuals as well as perform many other functions which are called judicial but are not necessarily litigious.

Basis of national jurisdiction:

It should be clear at this stage of our study that the national government created by the Constitution has only enumerated powers. This is true of the national courts as well as of the legislature. Jurisdiction, the power to hear and to determine, is conferred upon the courts only over certain kinds of cases and controversies. The state courts have jurisdiction over all others and even over some that the national courts may try. The national judicial authority is extended by the Constitution to certain classes of cases on the basis of the subject matter of the controversy and to other classes on the basis of the status of the parties concerned. The first class includes (1) all cases in law and equity arising under the Constitution, laws, and treaties of the United States; and (2) all cases of admiralty and maritime jurisdiction. Whenever in any law suit a legal right is asserted which is based upon some provision of the Constitution, national laws, or treaties, the case may be tried in the courts of the United States. Admiralty and maritime jurisdiction has to do with offenses committed on shipboard and with contracts which must be executed on the high seas or on navigable waters of the United States. Prize cases are also included in the scope of national judicial power.

1. Nature of the controversy

2. Status of the parties

The category of cases assigned to the courts of the United States because of the status of the parties includes: (1) all cases affecting ambassadors and other public ministers and consuls;[5] (2) controversies to which the United States is a party; (3) controversies between two or more states; (4) controversies between citizens of different states; and (5) controversies between a state, or the citizens thereof, and foreign states, citizens, or subjects where the state is the party plaintiff.[6]

Congressional power over jurisdiction

The assignment of certain classes of cases to the courts of the United States by the Constitution does not of itself confer power over all of these matters. Rather the Constitution specifies the limits beyond which power may not be conferred, and Congress may or may not endow the courts with all of the power within the constitutional limits. Congress thus possesses the authority to limit the jurisdiction of the courts.[7] Congress originally conferred only a portion of the jurisdiction. Throughout most of the last century Congress

---

[5] Under international law, however, diplomatic representatives of foreign governments are generally immune from prosecution in the courts of the country to which they are accredited. They may be sent home or their recall requested but are exempt from legal proceedings.

[6] The original Constitution made no such distinction as the last clause implies. This was added by the Eleventh Amendment after the Supreme Court had entertained a suit by a citizen of South Carolina against the state of Georgia. Chisholm v. State of Georgia, 2 Dallas 419 (1793).

[7] An exception to this statement is that the original jurisdiction of the Supreme Court does not depend upon any act of Congress and may not be enlarged or reduced except by constitutional amendment. Marbury v. Madison, 1 Cranch 137 (1803).

gradually added to the jurisdiction until it had conferred all that the Constitution contemplated. In this century the jurisdiction has been somewhat contracted. In several types of cases which may also be tried in state courts, for example, Congress has prescribed that the amount in controversy must exceed a certain sum before the litigants may use the national courts.

Jurisdiction shared with state courts

Much of the jurisdiction which has been conferred by the Congress is shared with state courts. The national courts, in other words, do not have exclusive authority over it. In general, only in cases in which the United States or a state is a party (unless the action is between a state and one of its own citizens), or which involve the representatives of foreign governments, a crime against the United States, or admiralty, maritime, patent, copyright, or bankruptcy laws, do the courts of the United States have complete and exclusive jurisdiction. In virtually all other types of cases to which the judicial power extends, the plaintiff may begin his case in either a state or a national court.

How cases get into the courts of the United States:

Cases get into the courts of the United States in at least three different ways. Many cases begin and end there because no other court has any authority to deal with them. Some cases may be transferred to the national courts which have been entered in state courts. The removal of a case from a state court is permissible only (1) when the District Courts of the United States have original jurisdiction over it; (2) before the case has actually come to trial in the state court, and (3) when the request is made by the defendant. Cases which involve a "federal question," that is, some right or immunity claimed under the Constitution, laws, or treaties, may be removed regardless of the residence of the parties. In cases in which the disputants are citizens of different states, the defendants may not remove the case if they are citizens of the state in the courts of which the action is brought. The purpose of this transfer power is clearly to protect a defendant against local prejudice. The third way in which cases get into the national courts is by appeal from the decisions of the highest court of the state in which the action was started.[8] If in deciding a case involving a conflict between a state law and the Constitution, laws, or treaties of the United States, the highest state court declares in favor of the validity of the state law, the case may be carried directly on appeal to the Supreme Court of the United States. This is also true of any case in which a treaty or law of the United States is held invalid. In virtually all other types of cases involving "federal questions" the defeated party has no *right* of appeal. His case may be carried to the Supreme Court of the United States only if that court is willing to hear it, by a legal process known as certiorari.[9]

[8] In view of the somewhat ambiguous language in the Constitution concerning the appellate jurisdiction of the Supreme Court, many lawyers have at one time or another argued that the Supreme Court has no jurisdiction over appeals from state courts. The Congress has from the beginning, however, thought otherwise and the Supreme Court has agreed with them. See Martin v. Hunter's Lessee, 1 Wheaton 304 (1815), Cohens v. Virginia, 6 Wheaton 264 (1821), and Ableman v. Booth, 21 Howard 506 (1859).

[9] Certiorari is a form of writ or order by which a higher court calls upon a lower one to "certify" or turn over the record in a given case to it. A litigant may petition the higher court to take such action but that court has full discretion as to whether it will hear the case or not.

KINDS OF CASES TRIED

The types of actions brought in the courts of the United States fall into the two broad categories, civil and criminal, into which are classified the actions brought in the state courts as well. With a few unusual exceptions, the same courts and judges handle both types of cases.

1. Criminal actions in the courts of the United States

The criminal actions brought in the national courts represent a small proportion of the total number of criminal prosecutions in this country. The vast majority of all criminal offenses are state offenses and the offenders are brought to the bar by state and local enforcement officers and are tried by state judges. The only concern of the national courts with these cases is to enforce upon state courts the guarantee of a fair trial which has been construed to be required by the Fourteenth Amendment. Authority to try criminal actions in the first instance is lodged in the courts of the United States only for offenses against the United States or against the laws of the United States as defined by Congress and the Constitution. The Constitution mentions only piracy, counterfeiting, treason, violation of international law, and offenses in the territories and dependencies of the United States. Congress, however, typically prescribes penalties for violation of the laws it enacts and thus the United States Code [10] includes, among others, such crimes as mail fraud, smuggling, sabotage, and election fraud, which are clearly incidental to its powers to establish post offices, regulate imports, wage war, and regulate national elections.

2. Civil actions:

The most numerous category of actions tried in the national courts are civil actions, usually between two private parties but frequently with the United States government as one of the parties. Civil actions ordinarily arise out of civil wrongs, called torts, and breaches of contract. Torts include such wrongful actions as trespass, property damage, negligence, libel, and assault.

a. At law

In settling civil disputes the national courts apply state law as well as national law. Cases which get into the national courts because of the diversity of the citizenship of the parties, for example, may involve only the application of state law. This state law may be either statutory (enacted by a state or local legislative body) or common law (the system of judge-made law brought to America from England and modified here by the decisions of American judges and by legislation).[11]

[10] The Criminal Code of the United States is Title 18 of the United States Code. It was completely revised and clarified by the 80th Congress in 1948.

[11] The question of whether the national courts are bound to apply state law as construed by the state involved, to cases brought before them which do not involve a "federal question" has been the subject of much controversy in the history of the national courts. From 1842 to 1938 the basic rule was that uttered in Swift v. Tyson, 16 Peters 1 (1842), that the national courts were bound only by state statutory law. When decisions depended upon common law principles the courts could apply their own conception of these rules regardless of the interpretation of the courts in the state concerned. In Erie Railroad Co. v. Tompkins, 304 U. S. 64 (1938), however, the Supreme Court specifically overruled the precedents of the past century and declared that the law to be applied in such cases was the law—whether statutory or judge-made—applied by the highest court of the state.

The national courts also have equity jurisdiction, the power to interpret *b. In* and apply the law of equity to appropriate civil actions. Equity is a branch of *equity* Anglo-American jurisprudence which developed side by side with the common law and as a supplement to it, designed to provide substantial justice in a large number of situations to which the strict application of the forms of action and procedures of the common law would result in unnecessary hardship. The typical redress, for example, available under common and statutory law is money damages and it is granted only after the wrongful action has transpired and the injured party can show his "wounds." Equity jurisdiction provides legal remedies for many situations in which money damages are not appropriate or come too late to be helpful. Thus the court of equity may issue orders (writs of injunction) which forbid certain actions which would cause immeasurable or irreparable damage if committed. The court of equity may issue decrees of "specific performance" requiring a party to a contract to live up to his bargain, for example, by delivering the race horse he promised when the other party is willing to pay the money and thus a damage award would be useless. To the ordinary citizen the distinction between law and equity is of no major consequence; both are administered in the same courtroom by the same judge, sometimes on the same day. Lawyers, however, frequently prefer equity to civil law procedures because there is no jury in equity and because the procedures are less hedged about by technical formalities.

We have noted that the national courts administer statutory law, the *c. In* common law, and the law of equity. They also administer international law— *international* the law among nations based upon treaties, agreements, and other types of *tional law* international understandings—and admiralty law—the law of the high seas *d. In ad-* and navigable waters of the United States based upon the technical rules of *miralty* an admiralty code developed over many centuries by English and American *law* legislatures, courts, and administrative agencies.

The procedure used by the national courts in trying all of these different *Legal* types of cases is largely devised by the courts themselves. The Constitution, *procedure* as we have seen, prescribes a number of requirements for criminal actions *for trying* designed to protect individuals from unfair or unwarranted prosecution and *cases* conviction. The Congress has from time to time regulated the procedure by statute and many of the present rules are incorporated in the United States Code. The power to make rules governing civil procedure in the courts of the United States has repeatedly, however, been delegated to the Supreme Court, and in 1940 a similar power over criminal procedure was delegated to this body. In formulating its rules, the Court relies heavily on advisory committees representing both bench and bar.

STRUCTURE OF THE NATIONAL JUDICIAL SYSTEM

The national judiciary comprises three levels of tribunals. All of these have been established by Congress and none except the Supreme Court is specifically mentioned in the Constitution.

The lowest level of courts is the district or trial courts. The 50 states are divided into 86 districts for the purpose of providing a trial court within easy reach of litigants.[12] Each state embraces at least one district. Each of these courts is manned by from one to 24 judges, depending mainly on the volume of litigation but also, of course, on the pleasure of Congress.[13] Whatever the

CASES COMMENCED IN THE DISTRICT COURTS OF THE UNITED STATES

July 1, 1963—June 30, 1964

CIVIL CASES		66.930
United States a party	22.268	
Private		
Diversity or Citizenship	20.174	
Federal Questions	18.651	
Local Juris. (D.C. and Terr.)	5.837	
BANKRUPTCY PETITIONS		171.719
LAND CONDEMNATIONS		2.350
CRIMINAL CASES		29.944
Immigration Law Viol.	2770	
Liquor—Intern. Revenue	3529	
Forgery & Counterfeiting	3868	
Fraud	3112	
Auto Theft	4195	
Fed. Statutory Off.	3059	
HABEAS CORPUS PETITIONS		
State and Local Prisoners		3.694

SOURCE: *Annual Report of Administrative Office of United States Courts 1964*

number of judges, each holds court separately, except for certain unusual occasions, and the chief justice of the United States may (since 1922) transfer judges temporarily from one district to another to assist in relieving accumulated backlogs of cases. Virtually every judge is aided by a law clerk in reviewing the legal problems presented for his consideration and the staff of the court also, typically, includes clerks who preside over the records and calendars; reporters who take the proceedings; criers; and other functionaries. Attached to each district is a district attorney who, under the direction of the Department of Justice, conducts criminal prosecutions, a marshal who executes the

[12] A trial court of comparable jurisdiction also exists in Puerto Rico, and one in the District of Columbia and thus the statutes refer to 88 District Courts of the United States. There are also similar but not identical courts in Guam, the Virgin Islands, and the Panama Canal Zone.

[13] There were 301 district judges in 1965 in the states, 15 in the District of Columbia, and 5 in the territories.

orders and serves the papers of the court, one or more of referees in bankruptcy and commissioners who hold preliminary hearings in criminal cases.

The volume of business brought to the district courts is large; approxi-   *Jurisdic-*
mately 100,000 cases are handled yearly. All offenses against the laws of the *tion*
United States are tried there. These criminal cases are given priority by the
courts and the dockets are normally up-to-date.[14] All civil actions arising
under the Constitution, laws, or treaties of the United States ("federal questions") may originate in the district courts as may all cases based upon the
"diversity of citizenship" of the parties, but in both types of cases the amount
in controversy must exceed $10,000 for the national courts to have jurisdic-
tion.[15] The original jurisdiction of the district courts extends also to a variety
of civil actions regardless of the amount involved, for example, cases in admiralty, bankruptcy proceedings, patents, copyrights, postal laws, and nationally protected civil rights. Despite the addition of a large number of new
judges in 1949, in 1953, and in 1961 the disposition of civil actions in the
district courts is seriously delayed. For some time these courts have been about
a year behind in their dockets.[16] Most cases begun in the district court also end
there. But appeals may be taken from their decisions to the courts of appeals
and in a few cases, for example, where the district court has held an act of
Congress unconstitutional, directly to the Supreme Court. The district courts,
themselves, have no appellate jurisdiction. Cases appealed from the decisions
of state high courts go directly to the Supreme Court; they do not start all
over again at the bottom of the national hierarchy.

The intermediate courts of appeals which today handle the great bulk   *2. Courts*
of appellate work in the national judicial system did not achieve their present *of appeals*
status until 1911. For most of the past century, circuit courts shared original
jurisdiction with the district courts and handled some appeals. Originally one

[14] Between 35,000 and 40,000 criminal cases are disposed of each year. Almost one-
third of these in recent years have involved illegal entry into the United States.

[15] Of the 50,000-60,000 civil cases tried yearly by the district courts about 25 percent
are "diversity of citizenship" cases of which about 30 percent have been removed from
state courts by the defendants under circumstances previously described.

This large volume of "diversity of citizenship" cases has crowded the court dockets
for many years. Congress has on several occasions, most recently in 1958, increased the
minimum amount of damages involved in order to use the national courts. It has also
forbidden jurisdiction in such cases involving taxation or rate-making by state utility
commissions where a remedy is available in the state concerned. Also in 1958 the
Congress provided that for purposes of entering the national courts corporations shall
be deemed citizens of the state where they have their principal place of business as well
as of the state in which they were incorporated. Civil action arising under state workmen's compensation laws also may no longer be removed to a national court. All of
these rules are designed to reduce the use of the district courts.

[16] A study made by the Senate Appropriations Committee in 1959 suggested that in
the Eastern District of New York it takes nearly four years to get a case to trial. See
The New York Times, May 17, 1959. Chief Justice Warren in a speech to the American
Law Institute in May, 1965, expressed alarm that the new judgeships created in 1961 had
not prevented further increases in the backlog of cases. See *The New York Times,* May
19, 1965.

justice of the Supreme Court was assigned to each circuit into which the nation was divided, and together with the district judges held circuit court. The rapidly mounting dockets of the Supreme Court gradually made this duty of the judges more and more impractical and the confusion of having two courts of original jurisdiction led the Congress finally in 1891 to create nine circuit courts of appeals. These new courts divided the appellate work with the Supreme Court. In 1911 the circuit courts were at long last abolished, leaving the district courts virtually all of the original jurisdiction of the national judiciary. Since 1948, the intermediate courts created in 1891 have been designated simply "courts of appeals." The nation is now divided into eleven judicial circuits, including one for the District of Columbia, with a court of appeals in each. Each court is composed of from three to nine judges and at least two are required to consider any case.[17]

Functions
With every form of original hearing excluded, the work of the courts of appeals consists in hearing appeals from the decisions of the district courts within the respective circuits and of enforcing the determinations of national regulating agencies such as the Federal Trade Commission and the National Labor Relations Board. Appeals are carried to these courts from the district courts as a matter of right and the judges have little or no discretion in the matter.[18] In keeping with the long-term trend of relieving the Supreme Court of much of the burden of appellate work, the decisions of the courts of appeals are final in the vast majority of the cases brought to them. Review of the decisions of courts of appeals by the Supreme Court is largely at the discretion of the latter and occurs in few cases. Only in cases in which the appeals court holds a state statute contrary to the Constitution, laws, or treaties of the United States does appeal lie to the Supreme Court as a matter of right.[19] In all others appeal is at the pleasure of the Supreme Court by certiorari procedure already described.

*3. The
Supreme
Court:*
At the top of the system stands our most august tribunal, the Supreme Court of the United States. In its infancy this tribunal showed little or no promise of becoming the powerful institution it now is. President Washington found it difficult to keep the six judgeships filled with able men.[20] Under Chief Justice Marshall (1801-35), however, the power and prestige of the Court grew by giant strides. His great decisions establishing judicial review and enlarging the authority of the central government over the states provided the basis of the centralizing tendencies which have characterized our system ever

*a. Devel-
opment*
since. Under his guiding hand the Court not only served notice on the states

[17] In 1965 there were 78 judges in the courts of appeals.

[18] That a small proportion of district court cases are so appealed is revealed by the fact that the courts of appeals handle about 6000 cases a year compared to the 100,000 of the district courts.

[19] The court of appeals may also certify a question of law to the Supreme Court on which it desires instruction and the Supreme Court may in such cases call up the whole case and decide it or it may issue binding instructions to the requesting court.

[20] Chief Justice John Jay resigned to run for governor of New York.

of its determination to strike down every local obstruction to the achievement of union but informed the other two branches of the national government of its intention to hold them to their proper functions. Through many periods of weakness as well as strength, the Court has developed into our most independent agency of power, the one most removed from popular influence, the "most venerated if least understood of all our political institutions." [21] The President, said Hamilton, "holds the sword of the community"; Congress "commands the purse." But not even Hamilton anticipated that the Court would become the great stabilizing force in the government, keeping all branches and all levels within the constitutional framework, with nothing at its command except some documents and law books.

Originally, the Court was composed of a chief justice and five associate justices. The total number, as fixed by Congress, has since been as high as 10, although for about a century now it has been nine.[22] The justices are paid $39,500 per year. All who have served at least 10 years may retire on full salary at age 70. Although receiving slightly more pay ($40,000), the chief justice has no more legal weight or influence in deciding cases than any of his associates. He presides over the sessions of the Court, assigns to his associates the task of writing the Court's opinions, and writes many of them himself. He appoints members to serve on committees which revise the rules of procedure and has many administrative duties in connection with the whole judicial system. Altogether, fourteen chief justices have presided over the Court since its creation.[23] John Marshall towers above the others in significance. His decisions earned for him the title of "the second father of the Constitution." Of the more than 85 associate justices who have served since 1789, there have also been several whose influence upon our constitutional history has been impressive: James Wilson (1789-98), Joseph Story (1811-45), Stephen J. Field (1863-97), John M. Harlan (1879-1911), and Oliver Wendell Holmes (1902-32).

b. Membership

Regular and public "terms," or sessions, of the Court are held annually in the Supreme Court building adjacent to the Capitol, beginning on the first Monday in October and ending at the close of the following May or June. Six justices must be present at the argument of a case, and any decision must be concurred in by a majority of those hearing the matter—in other words, by at least four justices. If a majority cannot be obtained for a decision, a rehearing may be ordered, but an evenly divided court on a question of reversing a

c. Sessions and quorum

[21] A. B. Tourtellot, *The Anatomy of American Politics* (Indianapolis, 1950), 115.
[22] Reduced to five in 1801, the total was increased to seven in 1807, to nine in 1837, to ten in 1863, reduced to seven in 1866, and increased to nine in 1869.
[23] In order they are: John Jay, 1789-95; John Rutledge, 1795-96 (rejected by the Senate after he had taken his seat); Oliver Ellsworth, 1796-1800; John Marshall, 1801-35; Roger B. Taney, 1836-64; Salmon P. Chase, 1864-73; Morrison R. White, 1874-88; Melville W. Fuller, 1889-1910; Edward D. White, 1910-21; William H. Taft, 1921-30; Charles E. Hughes, 1930-41; Harlan F. Stone, 1941-46; Fred M. Vinson, 1946-54, and Earl W. Warren, since 1954. Curiously, only five had previous judicial experience.

lower court has the effect of upholding the earlier decision.[24] During a typical term of court, about 2500 cases are considered [25]—a vast change from the days of John Marshall who found only ten cases on the docket and no room to hold court when he assumed the chief justiceship.

d. How the Court works

Americans commonly think of their government as built on plain republican principles and as lacking the pomp and circumstance of European sovereigns. A view of the Supreme Court in operation will quickly dispel this myth. Ensconced in its Greek temple, the Court marches daily to its task at 10:00 A.M., announced to the standing audience by cries of acclaim. Seated in high-backed chairs at an enormous elevated "bench," behind them marble columns and red velour drapes, the black-robed justices hear the polite and honorific diction of learned pleaders. These counselors, dressed in morning clothes, supplement their elaborately printed briefs with oral arguments from a central lectern well below the level of the seated dignitaries. Occasionally the worshipful attention of the ten score of spectators is aroused as a justice addresses a question or two to the earnest pleader. A century ago the chamber of the Court rang with the orotund and interminable rhetoric of Webster and Calhoun, who argued and pleaded with the Court not for hours but for days. The press of business, however, has compelled counsel to put more in the brief and less in the delivery, and oral argument is now limited to one hour. Arguments are heard on a series of cases and then the Court recesses for research and reflection.[26] Conferences of the justices are held on Fridays and it is at these meetings that the Court arrives at its decisions. When a point of view is finally agreed to by the requisite majority, the Chief Justice if he agrees with the majority designates some member of this group to write the opinion of the Court. After review by others, the opinion is read at an ensuing sitting of the Court, traditionally on Monday but since early 1965 on any day of the session, and becomes a part of the documentary history of the American system of government.

e. Concurring and dissenting opinions

The opinion of the Court ordinarily sets forth the line of reasoning by

[24] From 1789 to 1863, a minimum of five justices, constituting a majority, sufficed for hearing a case. With the Court's membership raised to 10, the majority principle was preserved by increasing the "quorum" to six. When, however, the total again became nine, the quorum rule was (inadvertently it seems) left unchanged. Situations have arisen in which the Court could not take jurisidiction of a case because as many as four justices were disqualified to participate by former connection with the Department of Justice or some other circumstance; and bills have been introduced in Congress to restore the quorum to a simple majority of five. See H. E. Cunningham, "The Problem of the Supreme Court Quorum," *Geo. Washington Law Rev.*, XII, 175-189 (Feb., 1944).

[25] However, the Court in recent years has rarely issued more than 100 written opinions and 100 memorandum opinions in a term.

[26] Except that a case involving only settled points of law on which the justices can readily agree is ordinarily not argued orally the resulting decision being designated as *per curiam.*

Any lawyer who has practiced before the highest court of his state may be admitted to practice before the Supreme Court by being presented by a sponsor and paying a small fee.

which the justices arrived at the conclusion. One or more members of the majority may have arrived at the same decision by a different line of argument and may be impelled to present a "concurring" opinion which supports the decision but offers different grounds. The minority, if any, has the privilege of presenting its views to the public in one or more "dissenting" opinions. Occasionally these have stimulated more concern than the majority opinion and, in some cases, the Court has swung around to accepting as decisive the arguments of the dissenters.[27] All of the opinions are a part of the record and are published by the government in a series of volumes called *United States Reports,* prepared under the supervision of a Court reporter.[28]

Cases come before the Supreme Court in one of three ways: (1) by original suit; (2) by appeal from the decision of a lower court; and (3) by certiorari or discretionary review of a lower court decision. The three are of very unequal importance. By far the largest share of cases get before the Court by certiorari. The original jurisdiction of the Supreme Court is set forth in the Constitution and includes cases affecting the representatives of foreign governments and cases in which a state is a party. Its jurisdiction is exclusive, however, only in controversies between two or more states and in actions against representatives of foreign states. It also has original but not exclusive jurisdiction in actions brought by ministers of foreign states, in controversies between the United States and a state, and in actions by a state against aliens or against citizens of another state. This jurisdiction may be regulated and has been by Congress as to its exclusive character but, as we have noted, it may not be validly enlarged except by constitutional amendment. The only part of this original jurisdiction which has proved significant is that involving suits by one state against another. *f. Jurisdiction*

The right of appeal to the Supreme Court is sharply limited [29] and extends only to those few categories of cases already mentioned which have been decided by the highest state courts, the courts of appeals, and the district courts of the United States. Even in these cases the right of appeal is not absolute, for the Court may dismiss an appeal if the question involved is "insubstantial." With increasing frequency the Court has been doing just that. Most cases are brought to the Court by certiorari procedure. The history of *Certiorari procedure*

---

[27] This is the more true because sometimes dissents represent the views of as many as four of the nine justices and therefore have fallen short of controlling the decision by only the narrowest of margins. A famous dissenting opinion was that of Mr. Justice Holmes in Hammer *v.* Dagenhart in 1918, becoming in United States *v.* Darby, in 1941, the majority opinion of the Court.

[28] Reports of Supreme Court decisions before 1882 are usually cited by the name of the reporter who prepared them for publication, as follows: Dallas, 4 vols., 1790-1800; Cranch, 9 vols., 1801-15; Wheaton, 12 vols., 1816-27; Peters, 16 vols., 1828-42; Howard, 24 vols., 1843-60; Black, 2 vols., 1861-62; Wallace, 23 vols., 1863-74; and Otto, 17 vols., 1875-82. Since 1882, the *Reports* have been designated by serial number only, beginning with Volume 108 and cited as 108 U. S., etc.

[29] It will be remembered that *all* of the Court's appellate power comes to it from acts of Congress, which therefore can freely expand or contract it.

this aspect of the judicial system has been one of progressive expansion of the Court's certiorari or discretionary jurisdiction and contraction of its "obligatory" jurisdiction. The rules of the Supreme Court indicate that review of lower court decisions by certiorari procedures is to be granted only when there are special or important reasons for it. Some of the circumstances which induce the Court to review are: (1) that the case involves an important principle of constitutional or statutory construction; (2) that the case involves a conflict of interpretation of law among the courts of appeals; (3) that a state high court has decided a "federal question" of substance not before determined by the Supreme Court and probably contrary to the tenor of Supreme Court decisions. In general, the Supreme Court is thus relatively free to select from among all of the cases urged upon it only those cases upon which it wishes to pronounce. Typically, it now rejects from 70 to 85 percent of all requests for review by certiorari, frequently without any explanation of its reasons. Despite assertion of the judges that denial of certiorari means only that fewer than four judges thought the case ought to be heard, many members of bar, bench, and public interpret denial as support of the lower court's decision. Thus even the negative aspects of the work of the Court may have far-reaching implications. The figures already cited indicate that even with its crowded docket the Court decides a small proportion of the total number of cases which enter the courts of the United States or which might arise from the high courts of the states.

JUDICIAL INDEPENDENCE AND ITS LIMITATIONS

Compensation and tenure
    While deliberately interlocking the executive and legislative branches of the government by numerous checks and balances, the Constitution's framers designed the judicial branch to enjoy a high degree of independence. It is most unlikely that our national courts could have successfully asserted the power to review the actions of the other branches had they not occupied a position from which they were hard to control. The constitutional cornerstones of judicial freedom are: (1) that all national judges "hold their offices during good behavior," and (2) that their compensation may "not be diminished during their continuance in office." The latter provision, intended to protect them from a hostile Congress, has always been observed to the letter. The life tenure provisions has normally been observed also. Early in our history, however, when the followers of Jefferson abolished 16 judicial offices created by the Adams administration and staffed by Federalists, the individuals concerned were left without posts. When, in later days, Congress determined to reduce the number of judgeships, it carefully provided for the incumbents by transferring them to comparable positions in the judicial branch.

    Courts gain independence also from the fact that the Congress has always had a large complement of lawyers among its members. Lawyers by training are accustomed to defer to the pronouncements of judges. Our people, too, have approved the freedom accorded our courts as is demonstrated by the strong disposition of the voters to return judges to office again and again when, as in the states, they have the opportunity of electing them. The successful assertion of the power authoritatively to construe the Constitution, and thus to prescribe the limits on the powers of the other branches of government, has provided the courts with a potent weapon to resist any aggressive thrusts in their direction by Congress or the President. At the same time, no valid power is lodged in any other branch to construe or limit the power of the courts. None of its decisions can be appealed; none of its members can be easily intimidated by threats of removal. The late Chief Justice Stone once remarked that the only check on the Supreme Court is the judges' own "sense of self-restraint."

The courts are not, however, perfectly free. There are some important limitations on the actual and potential power of the national judiciary. In the first place, it is possible to remove a judge from office. He may be impeached for and convicted of "treason, bribery, or other high crimes and misdemeanors." In other words, a national judge is subject to the same procedure as other national civil officers. Although the constitutional impeachment procedure is largely unworkable except for the most flagrant cases of official wrong-doing, nevertheless it has been used against judges more than against any other officials. In all, nine members of the judiciary have been impeached and four convicted.[30]

Limitations:
1. Impeachment

In the second place, Congress has relatively large powers to create courts, determine the number of judges, fix their salaries, and establish the range of their jurisdictions. This means that Congress can abolish courts (except the Supreme Court), reduce the number of judges, and curtail the number and kinds of cases they may hear. In practice, Congress has influenced or attempted to influence the decision of the Supreme Court by increasing the number of judges on that bench in order that enough "right-minded" new ones might be appointed to alter the anticipated decision. It has also deprived the Supreme Court of its appellate jurisdiction in a given class of cases because it anticipated a "bad" decision on an issue it regarded as vital. Both of these things occurred during the Civil War-Reconstruction period and, of course, are not typical of the relations between the two branches. They are illustrative, however, of what an aroused Congress, presumably supported by public opinion, can do.[31] The creation in 1801 of a large number of new judgeships and

2. Congressional control over the structure of the courts

[30] The successful proceedings were those against John Pickering (1803-04); West H. Humphreys (1862); Robert W. Archbald (1912-13); and Halstead L. Ritter (1936). Unsuccessful actions were those against Samuel Chase (1804-05); James H. Peck (1830-31); Charles Swayne (1904-05); and Harold Louderback (1933). In April, 1926, the House of Representatives adopted articles of impeachment against George W. English, judge of the district court for the Eastern District of Illinois; but on the eve of the trial Judge English resigned, and the proceedings were discontinued. A few other judges also have escaped impeachment by resigning when proceedings seemed imminent.

[31] In the period 1957-1959, the Supreme Court weathered the most severe attack on its jurisdiction since New Deal days. Angered by decisions which favored certain persons and groups accused of subversive activities, Congress seriously considered a

then the appointment of partisan Federalists to them in order to ensure continuing control over at least one branch of the government by a party which had been repudiated at the polls, and the subsequent abolition of most of these posts by the Jeffersonians, is an illustration from our earlier history of Congressional and executive attempts to influence the judiciary for partisan purposes.[32] Most of the recent changes in the structure of the court system have been relatively free of this type of motivation. The attempt by President Roosevelt and his followers in Congress in 1937 to achieve a more "sympathetic" Supreme Court by legislative reconstruction was defeated by the Congress. The remarkable change in the outlook of the Supreme Court which accompanied the controversy has, however, usually been regarded as a victory for the President in the real war despite the loss of the battle in the Congress.[33]

3. Partisan considerations in appointments   The major influence of the political and responsive branches of the government over the judiciary stems from the method of selection of judges. The Constitution provides that national judges are to be appointed by the President, by and with the advice and consent of the Senate. From the first development of factions in our government, Presidents have been strongly motivated to select men of their own faction or party to serve on the national bench. Many of our chief executives have also been deeply concerned not only with the political affiliation of their nominees but with their constitutional philosophies. It should be clear to the student of our institutions that the Constitution does not always speak for itself in clear and unmistakable language and even our wisest statesmen have differed about what it means. Presidents appear to de-

---

number of bills aimed at depriving the Court of jurisdiction in similar cases or at changing the law so as to reverse the effect of the decisions. The chief targets of the Congressional critics were the decisions discussed elsewhere in this volume—in the Nelson, Yates, Cole, and Watkins cases. Several of the bills passed the House—some on more than one occasion; all were finally killed in the Senate, but the margin of victory, especially in 1958, was very slight. See Symposium, "Moves in Congress to Curb the United States Supreme Court," *Congressional Digest,* XXXVII (May, 1958).

[32] M. Farrand, "The Judiciary Act of 1801," *Amer. Hist. Rev.,* V, 682-686 (July, 1900); W. S. Carpenter, "Repeal of the Judiciary Act of 1801," *Amer. Polit. Sci. Rev.,* IX, 519-528 (Aug., 1915).

[33] This controversy arose from the invalidation by the Supreme Court of a number of Roosevelt's "New Deal" measures and, especially, from the apparent determination of five of the nine members of the Court to resist all major efforts by the national government to regulate the national economy benevolently to the interests of the laboring classes. The Court at the time was composed of elderly statesmen (the youngest 61 and the oldest 80) appointed mainly by Republican Presidents. The President sought to change the attitude of the judiciary by adding to each bench one additional judge for each incumbent who, having served 10 years and having reached the age of 70, did not elect to retire within six months, with a maximum membership of the Supreme Court fixed at 15. After many days of tense and bitter debate in which the whole nature of our constitutional system was canvassed, the Congress rejected the President's plan. Meanwhile, the Supreme Court in a case before it reversed its attitude on the validity of minimum-wage legislation (by the shift of Justice Roberts) and followed this by a series of decisions sustaining as valid regulations of interstate commerce, the National Labor Relations Act, the Railway Labor Act, and the Social Security Act, all "key" New Deal measures.

sire that their appointees to the bench agree with them on fundamentals. There have, of course, been exceptions and Presidents have on occasion, willingly or unwillingly, elevated to judgeships illustrious men of the opposite party or of contrary constitutional views. These are exceptions, however, not the rule. It is interesting to note that prior judicial experience has rarely been considered an essential qualification for appointment.[34]

There are two important considerations which mitigate the effectiveness of Presidential influence over the judiciary. Once appointed, as many Presidents have learned to their chagrin, the judge obtains life tenure and thus safe from Presidential ire, may change his mind about some of the issues. Secondly, few Presidents get an opportunity to appoint as many as a majority of the members of the Supreme Court. Furthermore, the Senate has got to be considered in the appointment process. The dominant party in the Senate is probably as interested as is the President in naming "right-thinking" judges to the bench. It occasionally happens that the President and the Senate do not agree.[35] The President has to select an individual who will also be acceptable to the leaders of the Senate. In the lower courts of the United States, the President is narrowly confined in his appointing prerogatives by the practice of "Senatorial courtesy." National judgeships are now customarily regarded as patronage for the Senator or other state party leader in whose state the court is located. Under these conditions, new appointments to the lower and intermediate courts of the United States are invariably made from loyal supporters of the party in control in Washington. It goes without saying that the fitness of the individual for judicial office will not always be weighed as carefully as it might be. It is curious to note that despite the political and even partisan influences on the selection of judges, our courts are still widely supposed to be free of the taint of partisanship. A committee of the American Bar Association for some years has assisted the Senate Judiciary Committee in appraising Presidential nominees to the bench and in the last several years, it has also worked with the Department of Justice in screening prospective nominees.[36]

The Senate and the Judiciary

We have already explained that the courts must rely on others to bring them the business that they get. The executive branch, for example, brings all criminal cases and a large number of civil actions. More important, however, is the fact that the courts have no substantial enforcing agency even for their own decisions. They must rely on the executive branch to back up their orders

4. Enforcement of court processes

[34] Justice Frankfurter, in an address delivered in Philadelphia in March, 1957, reviewed the qualifications of justices throughout the Court's history, and observing that more than one-third had never had a single day's prior experience as judges, asserted that there was no correlation between such experience and fitness to serve on the Court. This address is summarized by Arthur Krock in *The New York Times,* May 7, 1957. See also J. R. Schmidhauser, "The Justices of the Supreme Court: A Collective Portrait," *Midwest Jour. of Pol. Sci.,* III, No. 1 (Feb., 1959).

[35] Nine Presidential nominees to the Supreme Court have been directly rejected by the Senate and 12 others have been rejected by inaction.

[36] J. B. Grossman, "Federal Judicial Selection: the Work of the ABA Committee," *Midwest Jour. of Pol. Sci.,* VIII, No. 3 (August, 1964).

if the recipients are unwilling to respect the commands of the United States marshals who serve the courts' papers. An uncooperative President has been able on a few occasions to frustrate the authority of the Court by refusing to be diligent in enforcing its decisions. The most famous example of this was the refusal of President Jackson to enforce against a recalcitrant officialdom of the State of Georgia (1831-32) a decision of the Supreme Court abrogating an attempt by the state to ignore its treaty obligations to the Cherokee Indians.[37] A good illustration from modern times of the great difficulties in the way of enforcing a controversial decision is the effort to achieve desegregation of races in the public schools discussed earlier in this volume. The prestige and independence of the judiciary may thus be compromised by executive inaction or indifference or by Congressional or local opposition.

THE SUPREME COURT AND JUDICIAL REVIEW

In deciding cases and controversies, all courts are obliged to consider whether the legal claims at issue are based upon laws which are consistent with relevant constitutional provisions. It thus becomes the most important and distinctive function of the Supreme Court of the United States and the lower national courts as well to pass finally on the constitutional validity of state laws, state constitutions, laws of Congress, and executive actions. In performing this function these stand as the guardian of the boundaries which separate the legitimate powers of the three branches of the national government as well as those which separate the powers of the national government as a whole from those of the states and of the people. The origin and importance of this function of judicial review and its importance in strengthening the national government in relation to the state have already been discussed. We have noted that the Constitution itself does not expressly confer this power on the Court and there have always been those who regarded its exercise as sheer usurpation. But from John Marshall's day to this it has become a settled part of the American system of government and most statesmen throughout our history have regarded it as not only a desirable but a necessary concomitant of a written constitution and a scheme of limited government with divided powers. Our people have also largely accepted it and even have acclaimed it. It is one of the unique contributions of the people of the United States to the art of constitutional self-government.

Judicial review of state action

Since the jurisdiction of the Supreme Court has come to be largely discretionary, the great majority of cases which the Court now hears involve the constitutionality of some action by some branch of the national or a state government. The review of state action stands upon a somewhat different

[37] Cherokee Nation *v.* Georgia, 5 Peters 1 (1831), and Worcester *v.* Georgia, 6 Peters 515 (1832). This was the occasion on which Jackson is reported to have said: "John Marshall has made his decision; now let him enforce it."

basis, insofar as its effect upon our constitutional system is concerned, than the review of national actions. In earlier days this was the form which judicial review customarily took, and long lists of state laws and even some state constitutional provisions have been struck down by the Supreme Court as contrary to the Constitution of the United States. It is hard to imagine how any major principle of government could be uniformly applied throughout the United States unless some national agency performed this function. Furthermore, the fact that the Supreme Court is a national agency has meant that the states'-rights doctrine has never received consistent support from it. Finally, in exercising a review of state action, the Court has been able to thwart encroachment by the state legislatures and executives on the national authority. This was one of the major problems of the first half-century of our national life.

Review of national laws and acts

The review by the Supreme Court of Congressional and Presidential actions is of a different magnitude. In these cases, the Court is dealing with allegedly coordinate branches of government. Its determination to hold these as well as the states to their proper spheres of power may, and occasionally has, brought it into conflict with those who claim the right resulting from election to give effect to popular demands. The other branches, it may be added, can assert also the duty to interpret the Constitution themselves. The other two branches are equipped by the Constitution, as we have already seen, to influence considerably the character and methods of the Court. For these and other reasons, the Supreme Court has been much more reluctant to declare Congressional statutes and Presidential actions contrary to the Constitution than it has state actions. Until 1865, the Supreme Court declared only two acts of Congress unconstitutional; since that time it has upset several dozen more, but still a small number compared to the number of state laws it has overturned.[38]

How judicial review operates

Perhaps a more vivid conception of how judicial review operates can be gained by some concrete illustrations. In 1897, the legislature of New York passed a law limiting employment in bakeries to 60 hours a week and 10 hours a day, presumably on the theory that baking was a kind of industry in which longer employment was unhealthful and the products might be thus made more dangerous to the consumer. After several years, an employer, Lochner, was accused of and indicted for violating this law. He was convicted of the offense in the state trial court and his conviction was upheld by the highest state court, despite the pleas of his attorneys that the law in question violated the Constitution of the United States. He appealed his case to the Supreme Court of the United States on the basis of this plea and as a matter of right since the state court had found the law valid. Five of the nine justices of the

---

[38] The acts of Congress declared invalid are also insignificant in number compared with the thousands of acts which have been passed. However, the importance of the ones overturned has been greater than their quantity. The laws questioned have in some cases been passed in the midst of bitter and profound controversy.

Supreme Court held that this law deprived bakery employees of their freedom (to contract their labor as they pleased) guaranteed against state deprivation without "due process of law" by the Fourteenth Amendment.[39] Four justices held that the state law was valid and that the "due process" clause contained no such guarantees as the majority inferred. Thus, Lochner was relieved of any penalty; the Court declared, in effect, that it would not punish anyone brought before it for violation of this particular New York law, and the law thus became unenforceable. This was done on the basis of five justices finding something in the Constitution that the other four could not find.

In 1943, the Congress adopted as a provision in an appropriation act that no funds available under any act of Congress should be used to pay the salaries of three individuals named unless before November 15, 1943, the President should procure Senatorial confirmation of their appointments. The three named men had been the subject of attack by the House Committee on Un-American Activities and had been accused of subversive activities against the United States. They were serving as "recess" appointees and the effect of the language of the act was to force their removal from office. The three men instituted action in the United States Court of Claims to recover salary they alleged was due them because of wrongful dismissal. The court ruled in their favor and the case was certified to the Supreme Court. A majority of the Court held that the section of the appropriation act in question constituted a bill of attainder, which they defined as a legislative act which inflicts punishment without trial, and therefore violated the constitutional prohibition of such bills (Art. I Sec. 9).[40] Two justices held that the men were entitled to back salary but that the Congressional action was not a bill of attainder, since it did not adjudge the men guilty of any offense. In this decision, the three men won back pay and the Court, in effect, said to Congress, you cannot remove officials whom you dislike from national office by this procedure.

Effect of a decision invalidating a law   It will be noted in these examples that the Court did not veto or annul either the New York statute or the act of Congress. It declared, rather, that in situations like those which confronted it, it would not enforce the laws against persons who rightfully sought its protection. State and national authorities make their own inferences from these decisions as to how the Court might regard similar laws or actions. Furthermore, the Court's action may come many years after the law was originally passed, although the logic of the Court's pronouncement is that the law was never valid at all.[41] The legal doctrine in the matter of validity is that every law is presumed to be constitutional

[39] Lochner v. New York, 198 U. S. 45 (1905). The majority held, in addition, that the law was not a legitimate exercise of the police power.

[40] United States v. Lovett, 328 U. S. 303 (1946).

[41] The Court has tended to abandon the position that an unconstitutional law was never a law at all. Such a doctrine cannot always be applied as a practical matter. For a thorough discussion of the legal and practical effect of decisions of this type, consult O. P. Field, *The Effect of an Unconstitutional Statute* (Minneapolis, 1935).

until otherwise declared by a court in a proper case and that the burden of proof is on those who question its constitutionality.[42]

It should not be surprising to the observer of our political institutions that on numerous occasions the decisions of the Supreme Court have been unpopular and have attracted wide criticism.[43] Abraham Lincoln campaigned for United States Senator and, in part, for President on his assertion that a Supreme Court decision (Dred Scott's Case) was unwise, illogical, politically motivated, and ought to be overturned. Critics of the Court have frequently asserted that the judges are deliberately frustrating popular will on the basis of their own personal and partisan views, that the judges are ignoring underlying technological, economic, and social changes in our society which have changed the meaning and importance of legal or political conceptions, and that despite the presumption of validity a majority of one on the Court can and does overturn laws which their colleagues believe to be reasonable.[44] The judges themselves habitually disclaim any disposition to do anything but apply impersonal and objective legal principles to the problems presented to them. Thus Mr. Justice Roberts said: [45]

Attacks on and defense of judicial review

> It is sometimes said that the Court assumes a power to overrule or control the action of the people's representatives. This is a misconception. The Constitution is the supreme law of the land ordained and established by the people. All legislation must conform to the principles it lays down. When an act of Congress is appropriately challenged in the courts as not conforming to the constitutional mandate, the judicial branch of the government has only one duty—to lay the articles of the Constitution which is involved beside the statute which is challenged and to decide whether the latter squares with the former. All the Court does, or can do, is to announce its considered judgment upon the question. . . . This Court neither approves nor condemns any legislative policy. Its difficult and delicate task is to ascertain and declare whether the legislation is in accordance with, or in contravention of, the provisions of the Constitution, and having done that its duty ends.

Few students of the activities of the national judiciary accept the Justice's statement as a wholly satisfactory explanation or defense. If the matter were so simple, they argue, few cases would ever be brought. The Constitution is

[42] The Supreme Court has, on occasion, notably in Thomas v. Collins, 323 U. S. 516 (1944), expressed the doctrine that in cases involving laws which on their faces are restrictions of basic civil liberties the burden of proof is on those who support the validity of the restriction.

[43] Theodore Roosevelt and Robert LaFollette advocated in their day that the Constitution ought to be amended to permit the Congress to re-enact by a vote of two-thirds of both houses any measure invalidated by the Supreme Court.

[44] Those who advance the latter criticism have suggested in past years that the rules of the Court ought to be changed so that the concurrence of at least six justices would be necessary to invalidate an act of Congress.

[45] United States v. Butler, 297 U. S. 1 (1936), p. 62.

ambiguous in many places and the judges necessarily bring to the task of clarifying the unclear a great many preconceptions as to the "real" nature of our political system. A large number of the constitutional controversies concern matters on which the Constitution is silent and toward which the framers could have had no intention since they could not possibly have foreseen the problem. In order to perceive an intention where none exists, it is necessary for the viewer to bring a great deal of mental and emotional equipment to the task. Many members of the Court itself have never subscribed to the Roberts' theory. Justice Holmes, in the Lochner case already described, said:

> This case is decided upon an *economic* theory which a large part of the country does not entertain. If it were a question of whether I agreed with that theory, I should desire to study it further and long before making up my mind. But I do not conceive that to be my duty, because I strongly believe that my agreement or disagreement has nothing to do with the right of the majority to embody their opinion in law. . . . The Fourteenth Amendment does not enact Mr. Herbert Spencer's Social Statics. . . . A constitution is not intended to embody a particular economic theory, whether of paternalism . . . or of *laissez-faire*.

The modern Supreme Court is not too sympathetic with the Roberts' doctrine; many of its more recent decisions contain references to social and economic facts and opinions which are quite outside the more traditional concern for precedents and legal authorities.[46] Times change and so do justices. The Court is not infallible and its views of constitutional questions may be and have been altered. But that it is a maker of law and not merely a discoverer of it, and that it exercises a profound influence upon public policy few would now dispute. However this may be, it has retained its hold upon the loyalty of the American people as a whole. They believe that it ought to exercise the powers that it does exercise and they, and their elected deputies, defer to its opinions and respect its detachment. Its critics of yesteryear, when it was smashing attempts to regulate business, are its friends of today when it is striking sledge-hammer blows against all forms of discrimination in defense of its conception of the civil liberties of the American people.

IMPROVED ADMINISTRATION OF THE NATIONAL JUDICIAL SYSTEM

The Federal Judicial Conference

Until some 40 years ago, the district courts, and likewise the then circuit courts of appeals, were virtually independent units, without a supervising or unifying head. When dockets grew congested and work fell behind in one

[46] C. B. Swisher, *The Growth of Constitutional Power in the United States* (Chicago, 1947), Chap. IX, "New Horizons for the Judiciary"; C. P. Curtis, *Lions Under the Throne* (Boston, 1947), Chaps. XI-XIII; R. E. Cushman, "What's Happening to Our Constitution?" *Pub. Affairs Pamphlets,* No. 70 (New York, 1942).

district or circuit, the usual remedy was for Congress to create a new judgeship or two, although there might be a dozen judges in other districts or circuits with comparatively little to do. In 1922, however, largely through the efforts of Chief Justice Taft, legislation was enacted opening the way for long-needed unification and equalization of court work. The chief justice of the United States became in some degree a supervising and directing head of the entire national judicial system, and provision was made for a Federal Judicial Conference, or council, convoked annually, presided over by the chief justice, and composed of all senior appellate court judges of the eleven circuits, with usually also representatives of the Department of Justice and of the judiciary committees of the two branches of Congress sitting by invitation. To this Conference it has since fallen: (1) to make comprehensive surveys of business in the national courts; (2) to prepare plans for assignment and transfer of judges to or from circuits and districts as circumstances make desirable; (3) to submit suggestions to the various courts "in the interest of uniformity and expedition of business"; (4) to set up committees to study and report on various matters; and (5) to recommend remedial measures to Congress. A degree of unity and flexibility long lacking has been supplied; and the courts have been made better able to cope with the ever mounting burden of interpreting and applying the complicated legislation of our day.

After a decade of experience, still further improvement seemed possible; and in his message of February 5, 1937, relating to judicial reorganization, President Franklin D. Roosevelt recommended that the Supreme Court be authorized to appoint a proctor, or manager, to assist the Court in supervising the conduct of business in the lower tribunals. No action resulted at once. But in 1939 Congress set up an Administrative Office of United States Courts, under a director appointed by the Supreme Court, and supervised by the Judicial Conference. Within this establishment a division of business administration now looks after the housekeeping needs of the lower courts (equipment, supplies, clerical service, and the like) and helps generally in the management of their routine affairs, while a division of procedural studies and statistics furnishes the Supreme Court with information concerning the state of judicial business and makes recommendations looking to increased efficiency and speed.[47]

The Administrative Office of United States Courts

The pattern of the Judicial Conference, too, has been carried farther down the scale. In addition to attending this conference, the senior court of appeals judge in each circuit holds, at least twice each year, a council composed of all the appeals judges of the circuit. This council considers plans for the effective and expeditious transaction of business in the district courts—plans which it becomes the duty of every district judge to help carry out. In addition, a conference of both appeals and district judges is held annually to review the state

Other conferences and councils

[47] H. P. Chandler, "The Place of the Administrative Office in the Federal Court System," *Council Law Quar.*, XXVII, 364-373 (Apr., 1942); J. J. Parker, "The Integration of the Federal Judiciary," *Harvard Law Rev.*, LVI, 563-575 (Jan., 1943).

of business in their courts and to discuss means of improving the conduct of their work; and since practicing lawyers, as well as judges, are vitally concerned with such matters, the law wisely permits a limited number of members of the bar to sit with the judicial members of this conference.[48] The national courts by these advances have achieved a more integrated system than most of the states.

SPECIAL AND LEGISLATIVE COURTS

"Constitutional" and "legislative" courts

The courts of the United States thus far described are the principal repositories of the judicial power conferred by the Constitution. They have been established by Congress under Article III of the Constitution and are the closest approximation which the national government has to courts of general jurisdiction. In establishing them Congress has been controlled by the provisions of the Constitution relating to judicial tenure and compensation. Congress has, however, created a number of other courts, some incidentally to certain of its enumerated powers. These are special courts and most of them are referred to as "legislative" courts by virtue of the relative freedom of Congress in creating them to prescribe terms of office for the judges [49] and to endow them with nonjudicial functions.

Court of Claims

At least two of these special courts have, however, been specifically designated as constitutional courts by the Congress. The Court of Claims was created in 1855 under the power to appropriate money to pay the debts of the United States. It was authorized to hear and adjudicate claims of private persons against the government and to report its findings to Congress or to the department concerned. Since 1887 it has also heard suits against the United States for breaches of contract and since 1946 (Federal Tort Claims Act) suits for injuries caused by negligent or wrongful behavior of a government employee. In order to clarify the confused status of this court, the Congress in 1953 declared it to be a court established under Article III of the Constitution.

Court of Customs and Patent Appeals

The Court of Customs and Patent Appeals—created in 1910 under the power to regulate commerce and to regulate patents and authorized to decide questions arising under the customs, patent, and trade-mark laws largely through the review of decisions of the Customs Court, the Patent Office, and the Tariff Commission—was declared a constitutional court in 1958.

Customs Court

Court of Military Appeals

The "legislative courts" now include (1) the Customs Court, created in 1926 out of the Board of United States General Appraisers under the power to regulate commerce, and authorized to review decisions of customs collectors and appraisals of imported merchandise; (2) the Court of Military Appeals, created in 1950 under the power to make rules for the government of the armed

[48] F. W. Morse, "Federal Judicial Conferences and Councils; Their Creation and Reports," *Cornell Law Quar.*, XXVII, 347-363 (Apr., 1942).

[49] For example, the judges of the territorial courts of Puerto Rico and the Canal Zone serve 8-year terms.

forces and authorized to review decisions of courts-martial; and (3) territorial courts, created on various occasions under the power to administer the territories of the United States and including district courts in Guam, Puerto Rico, the Virgin Islands, the Canal Zone, and the District of Columbia. All of these territorial district courts except that in Puerto Rico have, in addition to regular national jurisdiction, jurisdiction over all those matters which in the states belong to state courts. *Territorial courts*

All of these legislative courts, except those in the territories, may be accurately labeled also as administrative courts dealing as they do with questions between private persons and government agencies. In this sense they are an exception to the general rule of Anglo-American jurisprudence that cases arising out of the administration of laws shall be adjudicated by the regular courts.[50] *Administrative courts*

LAW ENFORCEMENT—THE DEPARTMENT OF JUSTICE

The judicial establishment provides a relatively impartial forum before which private individuals, corporations, and associations may bring their controversies and may expect to have them settled on the basis of established principles of law. The courts also are vital agencies in the achievement of public or governmental policies which require the enforcement of certain rules of conduct upon the members of society. Many of these rules, laid down by acts of Congress or orders of the President, are not self-enforcing. Agents of the government have got to observe conduct and to seek out and correct indifference or disobedience. In so doing they bring to the bar offenders against the law, those who are in debt to the government, those who do not pay the taxes determined to be due, and many others whose conduct the government desires to punish or to correct. All criminal cases are of this type as are many civil actions. Through their power to determine the outcome of the government's efforts, the national courts are a vital part of the entire machinery of law enforcement. *The courts and law enforcement*

The major responsibility for the enforcement of the laws of the national government rests, however, with the President. He is charged with seeing to it that the laws are "faithfully executed." Every subordinate agency of the execu- *The President and law enforcement*

[50] In 1936, a committee of the American Bar Association brought forward a plan for an integrated national administrative court with general jurisdiction over business of the kind mentioned; but no action has resulted. See L. G. Caldwell, "A Federal Administrative Court," *Univ. of Pa. Law Rev.*, LXXXIV, 966-990 (June, 1936); R. M. Cooper, "The Proposed United States Administrative Court," *Mich. Law Rev.*, XXXV, 193-252 (Dec., 1936). In 1955, the second Hoover Commission also recommended the creation of an Administrative Court with three sections (Tax, Trade, and Labor) to handle some of the judicial roles of the present Tax Court, Federal Trade Commission, Interstate Commerce Commission, Civil Aeronautics Board, Federal Reserve Board, Tariff Commission, the Departments of Interior and Agriculture, and the National Labor Relations Board. See Report of the Hoover Commission, *Legal Services and Procedure* (Washington, 1955).

tive branch, with a very few exceptions, assists him to discharge this responsibility. The Post Office, through its postal inspectors, tries to discover and apprehend offenders against the postal laws and regulations; the Treasury Department has a Secret Service to uncover counterfeiting and to protect the President personally; the Bureau of Customs has a force to prevent smuggling. The list could be extended for several pages. There is one agency which has law enforcement as its major responsibility, the Department of Justice.

The Department of Justice   Until 1870, the responsibility for enforcement of national laws was largely scattered among the various agencies of the government, as much of it still is; it was also scattered territorially among the dozens of district attorneys and marshals of the United States who were not clearly responsible to any department. An attorney general to advise the President on legal matters and to represent the government in certain judicial proceedings had existed since President Washington's time. The general law-enforcement function, including the supervision of the district attorneys and marshals, and the legal-advisory function were gathered together in 1870 in a new Department of Justice. This department was charged generally with enforcing the laws of the United States which were not the responsibility of a particular agency and with representing the United States in virtually all litigation brought by or against it. It has been charged, for example, with nearly the whole responsibility for enforcement of the Civil Rights Acts, the Sherman Antitrust Law, corrupt-practices acts, the national prohibition laws, the kidnapping law, and many others since its creation.[51] It also provides prosecuting services to many of the other agencies of government which discover offenders in the course of their duties. It conducts all suits on behalf of the United States before the Supreme Court and most of the suits involving the United States in the lower national courts. It continues to give expert legal advice not only to the President but to the other executive departments and agencies.[52] Through the famous Federal Bureau of Investigation the department extends its services in criminal identification and apprehension even to state and local governments.

The present Department of Justice embraces, in addition to the attorney general: the solicitor general of the United States who represents the government before the Supreme Court; a number of assistant attorneys general who

[51] Attorney General Kennedy promoted an expansion of the criminal laws of the United States in order to allow his department to move against organized or syndicated crime. Several bills were considered by the Congress and five were passed. See *Congressional Quarterly Weekly Report*, 1034-1039 (June 23, 1961) and 1465-1466 (Aug. 25, 1961).

[52] In many instances, such opinions prove final and conclusive, and hence determine the law on a given matter; sometimes, too, they profoundly influence the political, as distinguished from the purely legal, policies of the government. The "Opinions of the Attorney General" are published, after the manner of judicial decisions, and acquire weight as precedents in a similar way. Opinions are not furnished, however, to Congress or its committees, but only to the executive authorities. Executive orders are invariably scanned before being issued; but mere departmental regulations are not scrutinized, nor are abstract or hypothetical questions answered.

direct the divisions for antitrust matters, taxes, claims, public lands, criminal actions, alien property, customs, and executive adjudications; a deputy attorney general; and a chief administrative officer. In addition to the Federal Bureau of Investigation, the department includes the Bureau of Prisons [53] which directs the custody and rehabilitation of about 20,000 offenders confined in national prisons and penitentiaries, and about 25,000 probationers and parolees who receive extramural supervision. The Immigration and Naturalization Service is also a part of the Department of Justice, as we have already observed. A parole board in the department grants or revokes paroles of national prisoners. The department is the chief advisor to the President in the exercise of executive clemency.

Much of the burden of general law enforcement, especially criminal law, continues as in the past to fall upon the district attorneys and marshals in the various judicial districts of the United States. These positions have for years been outside the civil service merit system and are filled on the basis of patronage. Increased efforts by the department to achieve more uniformity of policy, more energy in enforcement, and more competence in litigation have all fallen short of creating a first-class organization for law enforcement.[54]

References

1. THE JUDICIAL SYSTEM

B. F. Wright, *The Growth of American Constitutional Law* (Boston and New York, 1942), Chaps. VII, IX, XI.

J. W. Peltason, *Federal Courts in the Political Process* (New York, 1955).

C. B. Swisher, *The Growth of Constitutional Power in the United States* (Chicago, 1947), Chap. IX.

A. N. Holcombe, *Our More Perfect Union; From Eighteenth-Century Principles to Twentieth-Century Practice* (Cambridge, Mass., 1950), Chaps. IX-XI.

A. B. Tourtellot, *The Anatomy of American Politics; Innovation versus Conservatism* (Indianapolis, 1950), Chap. IV.

[53] Offenders against national laws apprehended by national officials were, until the last years of the nineteenth century, confined in state and local jails and prisons on a per capita fee basis. H. Cummings and C. McFarland, *Federal Justice* (New York, 1937), Chap. XVIII. The bureau now operates 26 institutions and the Public Health Service two institutions for the confinement and rehabilitation of offenders.

[54] Attorney General Brownell in 1953 inaugurated several reforms in the Department: (1) the imposition of a requirement that all lawyers in the department abandon private practice on the side; (2) the establishment of an executive office for United States attorneys to supervise and coordinate their work; (3) the establishment of a training program to instruct United States attorneys in their duties and in departmental policies. *The New York Times,* July 1, 1953.

J. W. Hurst, *The Growth of American Law; The Lawmakers* (Boston, 1950), Chaps. IV, VI-VII.

M. Wendell, *Relations Between the Federal and State Courts* (New York, 1949).

J. P. Frank et al., "The Federal Courts," *Law and Contemporary Problems*, XIII, 3-243 (Winter, 1948).

J. J. Parker, "The Federal Judiciary," *Tulane Law Rev.*, XXII, 569-584 (June, 1948).

R. J. Harris, *The Judicial Power of the United States* (Baton Rouge, La., 1940).

C. Bunn, *A Brief Survey of the Jurisdiction and Practice of the Courts of the United States* (St. Paul, Minn., 1949).

H. J. Abraham, *Courts and Judges: An Introduction to the Judicial Process* (New York, 1959).

L. Mayers, *The American Legal Systems: The Administration of Justice in the United States by Judicial, Administrative, Military and Arbitral Tribunals* (New York, 1958).

H. G. Fins, *Federal Jurisdiction and Procedure* (Indianapolis, Ind., 1960).

2. The Supreme Court

C. E. Hughes, *The Supreme Court of the United States; Its Foundation, Methods, and Achievements* (New York, 1928).

R. E. Cushman, *The Supreme Court and the Constitution* (New York, 1938).

———, "What's Happening to Our Constitution?" *Pub. Affairs Pamphlets*, No. 70 (New York, 1942).

———, (ed.), "Ten Years of the Supreme Court: 1937-1947," *Amer. Polit. Sci. Rev.*, XLI, 1142-1181 (Dec., 1947), XLII, 32-67 (Feb., 1948).

C. A. Beard, *The Supreme Court and the Constitution* (New York, 1912).

C. G. Haines, *The American Doctrine of Judicial Supremacy* (2nd ed., Berkeley, Calif., 1932).

———, *The Role of the Supreme Court in American Government and Politics, 1789-1835* (Berkeley, Calif., 1944).

———, and F. H. Sherwood, *The Role of the Supreme Court in American Government and Politics, 1835-1864* (Berkeley, Calif., 1957).

E. S. Corwin, *The Doctrine of Judicial Review* (Princeton, N.J., 1914).

———, *Court Over Constitution; A Study of Judicial Review as an Instrument of Popular Government* (Princeton, N.J., 1938).

———, *The Twilight of the Supreme Court: A History of Our Constitutional Theory* (New Haven, Conn., 1934).

P. T. Freund, *On Understanding the Supreme Court* (Boston, 1949).

C. H. Pritchett, *The Roosevelt Court; A Study in Judicial Politics and Values, 1937-1947* (New York, 1948).

————, *Congress v. The Supreme Court,* 1957-1960 (Minneapolis, 1961).

————, "The Supreme Court Today: Constitutional Interpretation and Judicial Self-Restraint," *South Dak. Law Rev.,* Vol. 3 (Spring, 1958).

C. Warren, *The Supreme Court in United States History,* 3 vols. (Boston, 1922).

A. T. Mason, *The Supreme Court from Taft to Warren* (Baton Rouge, La., 1958).

K. N. Vines, "The Role of the Circuit Courts of Appeal in the Federal Judicial Process: A Case Study," *Midwest Jour. of Pol. Sci.,* VII, No. 4, (Nov. 1963).

B. Schwartz, *The Supreme Court: Constitutional Revolution in Retrospect* (New York, 1957).

A. A. Mavrinac, "From Lochner to Brown v. Topeka: The Court and Conflicting Concepts of the Political Process," *Amer. Pol. Sci. Rev.,* LII (Sept., 1958).

C. Warren, *Congress, the Constitution, and the Supreme Court* (Boston, 1925).

R. K. Carr, *The Supreme Court and Judicial Review* (New York, 1942).

J. R. Schmidhauser, *The Supreme Court as Final Arbiter in Federal-State Relations* (Chapel Hill, N.C., 1958).

A. T. Mason and W. M. Beaney, *The Supreme Court in a Free Society* (New York, 1960).

C. L. Black, Jr., *The People and the Court: Judicial Review in a Democracy* (New York, 1960).

G. A. Schubert, *Constitutional Politics; The Political Behavior of Supreme Court Justices and the Constitutional Policies that They Make* (New York, 1960).

R. G. McCloskey, *The American Supreme Court* (Chicago, 1961).

A. F. Westin, *The Anatomy of a Constitutional Law Case* (New York, 1958).

R. H. Jackson, *The Supreme Court in the American System of Government* (Cambridge, Mass., 1955).

R. Rodell, *Nine Men: A Political History of the Supreme Court from 1790 to 1955* (New York, 1955).

H. J. Spaeth, *An Introduction to Supreme Court Decision Making* (San Francisco, 1965).

J. E. Clayton, *The Making of Justice: the Supreme Court in Action* (New York, 1964).

D. J. Danelski, *A Supreme Court Justice is Appointed* (New York, 1965). The selection by Harding of Pierce Butler.

C. S. Hyneman, *The Supreme Court on Trial* (New York, 1963).

A. M. Bickel, *The Least Dangerous Branch: The Supreme Court at the Bar of Politics* (New York, 1962).

E. V. Rostow, *The Sovereign Prerogative: the Supreme Court and the Quest for Law* (New Haven, 1962).

R. L. Stern and E. Grassman, *Supreme Court Practice* (Washington, 1962).

3. THE DEPARTMENT OF JUSTICE

H. B. Learned, *The President's Cabinet* (New Haven, 1912), Chap. VII.

A. Langeluttig, *The Department of Justice of the United States* (Baltimore, 1927).

H. S. Cummings and C. McFarland, *Federal Justice* (New York, 1937).

A. C. Millspaugh, *Crime Control by the National Government* (Washington, 1937).

J. E. Hoover, *Persons in Hiding* (New York, 1938).

F. L. Collins, *The F. B. I. in Peace and War* (New York, 1943).

M. Lowenthal, *The Federal Bureau of Investigation* (New York, 1950).

Annual reports of the Department of Justice and of the director of the Administrative Office of United States Courts.

B. FUNCTIONS AND SERVICES

★ 17 ★

Government and the

National Economy

THE PURPOSE OF GOVERNMENT in the American ideology is to serve the people over whom it presides. The state is not an end in itself with a purpose and a destiny distinct from that of the persons who comprise it, as many European thinkers have held and rulers have practiced. The American believes the state is an agency for fostering the safety and welfare of individuals and has no other object. It is fitting, therefore, that we now turn from how the government is organized to what it does. In its programs we find the justification for its existence and a basis for determining its effectiveness.

Among the vast array of national programs, past and present, none has commanded more widespread interest nor more persistent attention than maintaining a high level of economic well-being among our people.

There has never been a time when the government was indifferent to the health of the economy. Policies or programs appropriate to one stage of our economic development have not necessarily been useful or acceptable at other stages but once begun are hard to stop. Opinions have differed widely through the years on how best to achieve economic health and the great interests of our society have each sought governmental aid and have urged mutually contradictory programs upon those in power. The result is that the government has never followed a wholly consistent theory of political economy and does not do so today. It is, nevertheless, possible to discern major changes in economic policies over the years and to appreciate that the scope of governmental concern today as well as the tools of public economic activity and the general tone of opinion on the proper role of government are all different than they were in the past.

Government and the maintenance of prosperity

THE DEVELOPMENT OF NATIONAL RESPONSIBILITY

The Constitution itself and the policies of the first administration under it were intended to and did improve the position of the business and financial

Economic policies of the past

community. Impediments to interstate trade were eliminated, a sound monetary system established, the national credit placed on a secure basis, and manufacturing encouraged. In fact, so favorable to these interests were the earliest national economic policies that they stimulated the organization of the agricultural interests and the expression through Jefferson's party of policies more popular among farmers: easier access to the public domain, purchase of Louisiana, exploration of the West. Jacksonianism brought new policies: annihilation of the Bank of the United States, freer access to public employment, greater protection to the frontiersman, continued additions to the national domain. The business community responded through the Whigs and pressed for higher protective tariffs and better arteries of transportation (canals, turnpikes, river and harbor improvements). The Civil War paved the way for the establishment of policies—promotion of the railroads, provision of free land, maintenance of high tariffs on manufactured goods—for the rapid industrialization and urbanization of the nation. The rise of the factory system and of huge corporate combinations to control the supply or processing of commodities over the whole nation produced the highly interdependent economy of the present century. It also stimulated reaction and the articulation of demands for government regulation and for intervention to protect working people, farmers and small businessmen from the consequences. Gradually, the government swept its mighty arm over certain sectors of the economy, fixing conditions of competition, regulating prices and profits and services and placing floors below which standards for working conditions might not sink. Nevertheless, in the first quarter of this century the prevailing tone of public discussion of the political economy was that governmental intervention was untypical, limited in aim, and in many situations of dubious effectiveness.

Change in policy in the thirties

    Complacency about the American system of predominantly private enterprise and limited governmental responsibility was shattered by the Great Depression of the thirties. As factories closed, unemployment mounted from 5 to 10 to 13 million and paralysis spread through the system with untold suffering and waste of precious human resources. The New Deal determined to halt the downward spiral, to start the wheels turning again, and to relieve want tried numerous experiments. What was not adequately achieved by public works and poor relief was finally achieved by World War II; prosperity with full employment. During the war it became necessary for the government to take almost complete control of the economy—regulating access to and rationing raw materials, fixing prices, allocating consumer goods, dominating transportation, and promoting increased agricultural production. At its end, many contemplated the return to the situation of 1939 or of 1929 with deep misgivings. It was widely believed that a deep industrial depression would follow disarmament, demobilization and the shift to consumer goods production and even more serious dislocation in agriculture would result as European and Asiatic fields were put back into cultivation. So deeply had the bitter experience of the thirties etched its message on American society that few, indeed, were the voices raised for a return to laissez-faire: Most statesmen were convinced that the government must keep its hand on the economic pulse of the nation ready to administer stimulating medicine whenever it appeared to flag or falter.

The controversies of the modern era, in consequence, have been about what the government ought to do not whether it might do anything. Every modern President has proposed measures aimed at preserving and improving our economic well-being. The differences have been about means and about the nature of the illness. Furthermore, the rising commitments to friendly and developing nations abroad, the maintenance and enhancement of a vast defense establishment, and the attempts to conquer outer space have all added new dimensions to the public economy. The continued revolution in technology on the farms and in the factory has flooded the nation with more and more goods turned out in most cases with fewer and fewer workers. Thus unemployment, wasted resources, and surplus commodities continue to plague a nation which otherwise has enjoyed unrivalled prosperity over almost the whole of the postwar epoch. *Contro-versies today over how, not whether!*

The contemporary commitment of the government of the United States to preserving economic well-being is contained in the Employment Act of 1946 in the following language: *Government responsibility fully endorsed*

> The Congress hereby declares that it is the continuing policy and responsibility of the Federal Government to use all practicable means consistent with the needs and obligations and other essential considerations of national policy with the assistance and cooperation of industry, agriculture, labor, and state and local governments, to coordinate and utilize all its plans, functions, and resources for the purpose of creating and maintaining, in a manner calculated to foster and promote free competitive enterprise and the general welfare, conditions under which there will be afforded useful employment, for those able, willing, and seeking to work, and to promote maximum employment, production, and purchasing power.

This awkward and tortuous passage was the product of months of controversy and numerous compromises. It represents what a majority of the Congress at that time were willing to agree upon as the duty of the national government. It is the upshot of an effort begun under President Roosevelt, through the National Resources Planning Board [1] to encourage the government to undertake a substantial program of economic planning, public works, and social security designed to guarantee full employment. The act in which it is found was, in fact, developed and introduced by a Senate committee which had been studying the problems of economic adjustment in the postwar period.[2] Certain members became convinced that only a determined effort at *Signs of economic ill health:*

---

[1] In its report, *Security, Work, and Relief Policies* (Washington, 1943).

[2] The origin of the act and the modifications made in the course of its progress through the Congress are ably reported in S. K. Bailey, *Congress Makes a Law* (New York, 1950).

public economic planning backed by a willingness to use the vast resources of the national treasury would enable us to avoid a disastrous postwar depression. The significance of the act is that it created the Council of Economic Advisors in the executive office of the President and thus provided the chief executive for the first time with the means of appraising the state of the economy and required him to report annually on his findings together with remedial proposals if he found them necessary. The act also shows that despite the growing feeling that more governmental control of economic decision-making was both desirable and inevitable, the preservation of a competitive, free enterprise system was earnestly sought. Furthermore, the act highlighted what had been its original aim: the achievement of full employment, as the major goal of a healthy economy.

1. Inflation

Postwar experience emphasized the danger to economic health of inflation and reminded our people of the bitter experience of other nations, notably Germany in the twenties, with this problem. The removal of governmental controls over the civilian economy and the pressure of pent-up consumer demand sent commodity prices into a sharp upward spiral followed by pressure on wages and salaries and then frequently when these were allayed by new rises in the price level. Those with fixed incomes were caught in this squeeze as well as those dependent upon a stable monetary and credit system. Many public policies especially of the fifties were intended to halt pressure on prices or wages and to hold the cost of living as steady as possible.

2. Outflow of gold

Rising prices and wages combined with heavy American aid to allied and developing nations contributed to a relative fall in our trade balance and soon stimulated a heavy outflow of gold reserves. These developments of the late fifties and early sixties added a new dimension to the definition of economic health—preservation of the soundness of the dollar in the international market. A new set of policies were fashioned to cope with this new threat.

3. Unemployment

Four times the general expansion of the economy from 1946 to the present (1965) has been interrupted by recession: 1947-48—11 months, 1953-54—13 months; 1957-58—9 months; and, 1960-61—9 months. Each of these has been accompanied by falling industrial production and rising unemployment. After each of these until 1965, the unemployment rate never quite returned to what it had been. It rose from 3 percent in 1951 to 4 percent in 1955 to 5 percent in 1959 and to nearly 7 percent in 1961. It finally fell below 4 percent again only in 1965. In each case the cushions against disaster built in the thirties—unemployment insurance, for example—helped to prevent more suffering but did not completely allay concern. Again and again the national policy-makers have sought to reduce the rate of unemployment by special programs aimed at depressed areas and undertrained laboring forces.

4. Slow growth in GNP

Modern economic analysis has concentrated much of the attention of students, statesmen, and leaders of the various sectors of the economy on the total goods and services produced by the economic system, called the gross national product (GNP). Many analysts regard the rate of growth of this prod-

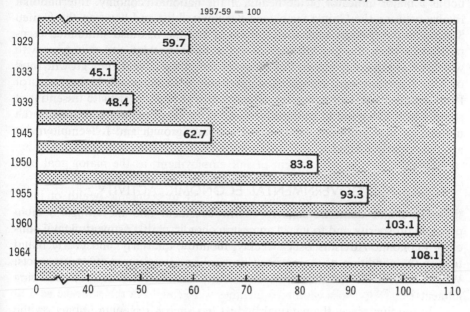

CONSUMER PRICE INDEX FOR CITY WAGE EARNERS, 1929-1964

1957-59 = 100

Year	Index
1929	59.7
1933	45.1
1939	48.4
1945	62.7
1950	83.8
1955	93.3
1960	103.1
1964	108.1

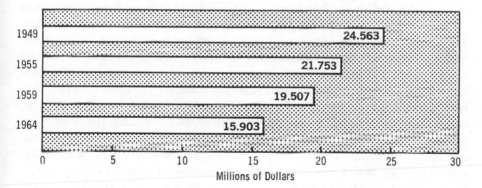

U.S. GOLD STOCK, 1949-1964

Year	Value
1949	24.563
1955	21.753
1959	19.507
1964	15.903

Millions of Dollars

uct as a major indicator of the health of the national economy. International rivalry between the United States and the Soviet bloc and between the United States and the friendly industrial nations of Europe has also stimulated comparison between the growth rates of the various systems and countries with which we are in competition. For many of the postwar years our growth rates of 2 to 3 percent were compared unfavorably with the much higher rates of France and West Germany, for example. Economic growth is essential if standards of living are to be improved and if the labor market is to absorb the millions of new additions each year. Economic growth and full employment are thus closely related.

TOOLS FOR GOVERNMENTAL ECONOMIC ACTIVITY

The major domestic concern of the President and the Congress is to promote prosperity and to guard against economic maladjustment. The Council of Economic Advisors issues weekly, monthly, quarterly, and yearly bulletins on the condition of the national economy and estimates of its prospects. What medicine do the national leaders keep on hand for new or recurring ailments?

Impact of budget decisions
In the first place, the national budget has such a sweeping impact on the whole economy that the decisions taken annually by the President and Congress about it are increasingly taken in the light of their economic consequences. The national government is the largest single employer; one person of 14 in the employed labor force is either a civilian or military employee of the government. It is also the largest single purchaser of goods and services. The annual total outlay of more than $110 billion is in itself a major determiner of economic activity. Within the total, the amount allocated to defense contracts, space technology, and atomic energy developments are all of critical importance to those regions, industries, and workers engaged. A sharp cutback, for example in our defense program would send shock waves through the entire economy. Heavy annual subsidies to farmers to maintain commodity prices also have a strong bearing upon the rural economy. Then there are the questions of tax and debt policy. Deficit spending is inflationary to some degree. The government must borrow to pay its bills and the borrowing creates the possibility of creating more currency unrelated to other changes in commodity production or consumption. Many leaders, especially of the business and financial community, regard a balanced national budget as the major determinant of economic health. The amount taken by the government in taxes is in itself of major importance and the Kennedy-Johnson administrations fought for and achieved a major cut in national taxes in 1964-1965 unrelated to a cut in expenditures and presumably for the purpose of stimulating a flagging consumer demand. The immediate spurt in production incident to the cut makes it almost certain that cuts in taxes will be considered, in fact strongly urged, the minute the economy falters again. These decisions on tax levels,

LABOR FORCE AND UNEMPLOYMENT
Selected Years, 1929-1964
(In Thousands)

Year	Total Labor Force Incl. Armed Forces	Unemployment	% of Civilian Labor Force
1929	49,440	1,550	3.2
1933	51,840	12,830	24.9
1939	55,600	9,480	17.2
1945	65,300	1,040	1.9
1950	64,749	3,351	5.3
1955	68,896	2,904	4.4
1958	71,284	4,681	6.8
1961	74,175	4,806	6.7
1964	76,567	3,466	4.7

SOURCE: *Economic Report of the President,* January, 1965

GROSS NATIONAL PRODUCT
Selected Years, 1929-1964
(in billions of Dollars)

Year	At Current Prices	At 1964 Prices
1929	$104.4	$217.8
1933	56.0	153.0
1939	91.1	227.3
1945	213.6	392.9
1949	258.1	351.8
1955	397.5	473.4
1959	482.7	518.1
1964	622.3	622.3

SOURCE: *Economic Report of the President,* January, 1965

spending levels, debt incurrence and the governmental programs to be expanded or contracted are all made today with at least one eye on their anticipated economic consequences.

In addition to the recurring decisions on the national budget, the authorities in Washington have another set of medicines to counteract a downswing in the business cycle. The vast program of unemployment insurance established in 1935 and described in more detail in a later chapter provides a first buffer. It makes possible the continuance of wage payments, although at a lower level, to workers laid off by falling demand. These payments help support a higher level of consumer purchasing than would otherwise be possible but, of course,

Unemployment Insurance

are of relatively short duration. In the recessions of 1957-1958 and 1960-1961, Congress authorized a temporary extension of the number of weeks for which benefits would be paid. In the areas hardest hit by rising unemployment the available funds were exhausted fairly rapidly but clearly many workers were helped by the weekly payments. To replenish the reserves against future demands, the payroll taxes which support the system were temporarily increased in 1962 and 1963.

Public works expenditures
The favorite remedy of many, dating from New Deal days, is to increase public works expenditures in order to increase demands for capital goods and to increase the supply of available jobs. Widely practiced in the 1930's the pump-priming system is likely to be one of the first things suggested when economic trouble appears. In each postwar recession, Congress and the President have: stepped up the works program already planned and authorized; speeded up government spending for supplies and equipment; increased the authorization for various kinds of domestic public construction. There has been also much pressure on agencies to have available stand-by programs of construction—the blueprints for which can be hauled out and dusted off on very short notice. In 1962, President Kennedy requested and Congress approved—on a reduced basis—a Public Works Acceleration Act which gave the President authority to allocate funds for job-creating public works to communities and areas with heavy unemployment. The act also gave the President standby authority for more projects if he found them to be necessary. To be effective, the public works must be financed by deficit spending. If taxes are raised to pay for the construction, then there is no net gain in economic activity. New Deal experience suggests a number of problems with the public works remedy. In the first place, the amount of governmental activity must be quite large. It was a $100 billion annual expenditure for waging war that finally brought full employment, not the $2 to $4 billion annually of the thirties. With governmental expenditures already massive, small increments will hardly be felt. The public works programs, furthermore, are not easily put together and accomplished rapidly. There is not extant a huge drawer of plans that can be opened, let out for bids, and work started rapidly enough to halt or reverse a downward swing in the economy. There are, of course, many who still urge that a balanced budget is more desirable in encouraging expanded private investment in capital replacement or expansion than the inflationary consequences of government deficits. Those who are eager to incur deficits to halt recession find a great deal of resistance in good times to achieving surpluses in order to reduce the deficit.

Money and credit controls
The Federal Reserve Board has been endowed for many years with power to influence the supply of money, the interest rates, and the supply of credit. There is some sentiment that these tools are or can be especially useful in countering recession as well as inflation. In general, the monetary policies of the board were geared in the late forties to helping the Treasury finance the public debt by fixing government bond prices and keeping interest rates low.

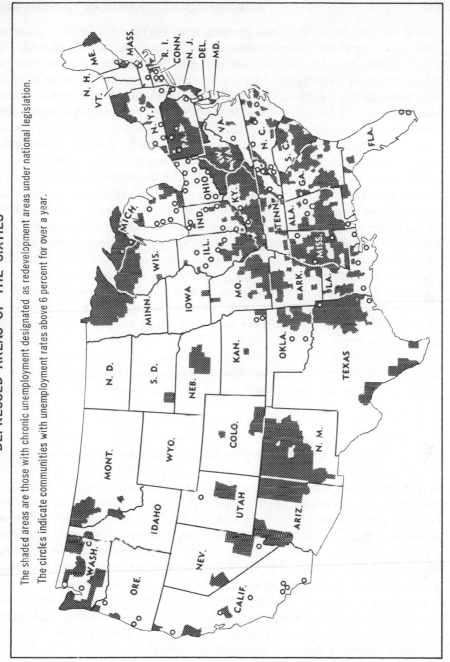

DEPRESSED AREAS OF THE SIXTIES

The shaded areas are those with chronic unemployment designated as redevelopment areas under national legislation.

The circles indicate communities with unemployment rates above 6 percent for over a year.

During the mid-fifties, after an agreement with the Treasury in 1951 gave the board more flexibility, interest rates were raised and the board generally followed tight-money policies. The main object of these policies was, however, to counter inflation rather than to stimulate economic growth. Faced with recession, however, the board has, for example in 1961, authorized banks to loan more money by reducing the reserve requirements and has encouraged borrowing by reducing interest rates. Usually, these policies have been followed by raising the rates once recovery seems apparent but in 1962 the board eased requirements again. Late in 1965, the Board sharply raised the interest rates to halt rapid credit expansion. The difficulties with the monetary and credit policies as methods to combat recession are: (1) the board is not directly controlled by and, therefore, not completely amenable to influence by the President or the Congress; (2) changes in monetary arrangements, interest rates, etc., have to be judged also in the light of their international consequences and for a number of years recently the loss of gold reserves has been sufficiently serious to justify separate consideration; (3) exclusive reliance on monetary controls was badly discredited in the early thirties when the traditional monetary remedies for recession failed to work; (4) expansion in the private sector of the economy is influenced by many factors of which the price of hiring credit and its ready availability is only one.

Aid to depressed areas

Because of the incredible complexity of the economy and the numerous factors involved, there are many who are skeptical of the generalized treatments of the type described. Certain sectors of the economy suffer from continuous malnutrition, they argue. While generalized medication may be useful, perhaps indispensable, we should deal directly and specifically with the diseased parts. In surveying the postwar national economy, it is apparent that certain groups, regions, and industries have been chronically depressed: cotton textile manufacturing, staple crop farming, coal mining and processing, railroading. These activities and the regions, cities, and workers dependent upon them have been especially affected. The first legislative accomplishment of the Kennedy administration was the passage of an Area Development Act aimed at areas of high chronic unemployment. The Congress had on two previous occasions fashioned similar legislation only to have it vetoed by President Eisenhower. The Act of 1961 provided cheap credit for industrial facilities development, technical assistance, and cash grants for public facilities to areas qualifying as depressed.[3] The Department of Commerce has been responsible for working with local communities in developing projects looking toward economic rehabilitation. President Johnson in 1964 and 1965 recommended and Congress supported the continuation of this program.

[3] Eligible areas were declared to be those where the current rate of unemployment is at least 6 per cent and where it has been this high at least three out of the preceding four years and where it has been above the national average rate of unemployment by various amounts in the past.

POVERTY IN THE UNITED STATES
Families with incomes of less than $3,000 a year at 1962 prices
Selected Years, 1947-1963

Year	No. of Families (millions)	Median Income 1963 Prices	No. of Poor Families (millions)	%
1947	37.2	$4.117	11.9	32
1950	39.9	4.188	12.6	32
1955	42.8	5.004	10.6	25
1959	45.1	5.631	9.7	22
1961	46.3	5.820	9.8	21
1963	47.4	6.175	9.0	19

A special form of aid for depressed areas was proposed by President *Aid to* Johnson and approved in 1965 by Congress: Aid to Appalachia. The eastern *Appalachia* mountain range running from Pennsylvania to Alabama has been an area of chronic unemployment for several years. Its economy has been particularly influenced by the subsidence of coal mining. Based in part upon a program urged by the governors of the states of the region, the Act of 1965 provides a varied program of aid including special funds for road building, vocational schools, reclamation of mining areas, and for the development of timber and water resources. An Appalachian Regional Commission is established to co-ordinate projects and to develop an economic program for the 360 counties of the area.

There is yet another way of looking at the problem of a healthy economy *Aid to* and that is to pay attention to those who are not successful. Some sink to the *under-* bottom or begin there and never rise for lack of opportunity or for crippling *privileged* illness or some other reason and while it is important to support industrial *people* expansion, consumer demands, chronically depressed areas and farmers, it is necessary to improve our human resources. In this spirit, President Johnson in 1964 launched an all-out war on poverty and the Congress responded with the important Economic Opportunity Act of that year giving to the govern-ment still another group of procedures for improving the American economy.

The programs launched in 1964 and 1965, aimed first at youth—school dropouts—whose economic future is particularly bleak. These may enlist in a Job Corps and receive special training in conservation camps and vocational training centers. Each of the 40,000 potential recruits receives basic education and special vocational training in a new environment. On-the-job training pro-grams are also established in the home communities to support young men and women who wish to resume their education and special help is provided for needy college students. Communities are also encouraged by the act to

APPALACHIA
1964

develop active programs aimed at the poor in the community and financial aid and technical assistance is provided by the national government. Volunteers are invited to aid in helping the poor through special training, welfare, and counselling services. Training in new skills is made available for adults on relief. Governors of the various states are made parties of the community action programs for each project must be referred to the chief executive for his comments. Special programs aimed at rural areas, migrant workers, and small business are also authorized.

In summary, the available tools for maintaining and improving the American economy are numerous, wide-ranging, and based upon several not wholly consistent theories as to the proper and effective role of the national government. A modern President is expected to look to our prosperity and to take timely action to prevent another economic catastrophe.

Closely related to the general economic policies and practices described are numerous special programs aimed at various sectors of the economy and at particular problems of social justice as well as of affluence. We must now, therefore, turn our attention to a more detailed consideration of the relations of government and business, labor, and agriculture, if we are to gain a full appreciation of the involvement of national officials in economic decisions.

References

E. S. Redford and C. B. Hagan, *American Government and the Economy* (New York, 1965), Parts I and VII.

S. E. Harris, *The Economics of the Political Parties* (New York, 1962).

C. B. Hoover, *The Economy, Liberty, and the State* (New York, 1959).

H. P. Miller, *Rich Man, Poor Man* (New York, 1964).

S. K. Bailey, *Congress Makes a Law: The Story Behind the Employment Act of 1946* (New York, 1950).

G. Soule, *Men, Wages, and Employment in the Modern U. S. Economy* (New York, 1954).

Congressional Quarterly Service, *Congress and the Nation, 1945-1964* (Washington, 1965), Chaps. 4 and 8.

A. R. Barach, *U.S.A. and Its Economic Future* (New York, 1964).

Economic Report of the President (Washington, Annually).

★ 18 ★

Government and Business

A general view of govern- ment business relations

FROM THE EARLIEST DAYS, there has been a great deal of sentiment in this country that the way to maintain a sturdy economy is to aid business in part by direct assistance but largely by maintaining a climate of opinion and practice favorable to investments and profits. The business interests have, furthermore, on many occasions been powerful enough and persuasive enough that Presidents and Congresses have responded favorably to their urgings. In fact, most of the time during the first century and a half of our history the government's only policies toward business enterprise were to encourage it and assist it. However, the rise of the factory system with its cruel use of labor power and of monopolistic corporations with the annihilation of competitors and the growing dependence of the staple farmer on transportation all combined to invite counter-pressures from farmers, laboring men, and small businesses. Ultimately, the government was pressed to halt abuses, to regulate certain business activities and forbid others and then to protect laboring men from the worst aspects of the factory system. Its modern relations with the business community are, therefore, a mixture of benevolence and regulation.

Govern- ment- business relations follow no fixed theory

It has become, furthermore, impossible to characterize the entire field of government relations with business by any simple rubric like laissez-faire or socialism. The picture is far too complex for that. Intermingled throughout our economy are at least four patterns: (1) private ownership and private operation, illustrated by the railroads and most other utilities, most banking, oil production, steel and textile manufacturing, and most life and fire insurance; (2) public ownership and public operation, illustrated by the postal service and by a long list of government corporations like the Commodity Credit Corporation, the Inland Waterways Corporation, and the Tennessee Valley Authority; (3) private ownership and government operation, as seen in the federal reserve system; and (4) public ownership and private operation, less common but illustrated by publicly built and owned munitions plants operated by private companies during World War II. While public ownership and operation have been on the increase sufficiently to cause many people to worry over a trend toward socialism, there is far more private and far less public economic enterprise than in any other major country. In particular, the American system contrasts with not only (a) the totalitarian U.S.S.R. with its collectivization of virtually all industry and business, but even with (b)

ECONOMIC INDICATORS

	Latest Week	Prior Week	1965
Commodity index	112.6	111.2	102.5
*Money in circulation	$41,963,000	$42,039,000	$38,927,000
*Coml, indl, agric loans	$52,437,000	$52,245,000	$43,522,000
Steel operating rate	71.5†	67.5	85.5
Steel production (tons)	2,312,000	2,185,000	2,670,000
Motor vehicle production ..	216,092	195,719	209,323
Daily oil production (bbls) .	9,613,000	9,569,000	7,829,260
Freight car loadings	508,282	458,444	538,856
*Elec power output, kw-hr .	21,558,000	20,100,000	20,435,000
Business failures	230	203	281

Statistics for commercial-agricultural loans, carloadings, steel, oil, electric power and business failures are for the preceding week and latest available. *000 omitted.

MONTHLY COMPARISONS

	December†	Prior Month	1964
Employed	72,749,000	72,837,000	70,375,000
Unemployed	2,888,000	2,966,000	3,466,000

	November†	Prior Month	1964
Industrial production	145.5	144.5	135.4
*Personal Income	$545,600,000	$541,200,000	$502,000,000
*Money supply	$165,700,000	$165,600,000	$159,100,000
Consumers' Price Index	110.6	110.4	108.7
*Construction contracts	$3,745,336	$4,358,900	$3,757,124
*Manufacturers' inventories .	$67,079,000	$66,642,000	$62,287,000

	October†	Prior Month	1964
*Exports	$2,348,600	$2,297,700	$2,134,300
*Imports	$2,002,000	$1,786,800	$1,550,700

† Figures shown are subject to revision by source.   * Omitted.

Commodity index, based on 1957-59 = 100, and the consumers' price index, based on 1957-59 = 100, are compiled by the Bureau of Labor Statistics. Industrial production is Federal Reserve Board's adjusted index of 1957-59 = 100. Imports and exports as well as employment are compiled by the Bureau of Census of the Department of Commerce. Money supply is total currency outside banks and demand deposits adjusted as reported by Federal Reserve Board. Business failures compiled by Dun & Bradstreet, Inc. Construction contracts are compiled by the F. W. Dodge Corporation.

SOURCE: *The New York Times*, Jan. 16, 1966

democratic Great Britain, which under a socialist Labour government from 1945-51 has seen the coal, transportation, gas and electric, and other top industries "nationalized," and with (c) equally democratic Scandinavian countries with their mixed, "middle-way" economies in which the governments have a controlling interest in most major economic enterprises. Finally, our penchant for private ownership and management has stimulated our heavy reliance upon governmental regulation of privately owned and operated business organizations and procedures. Broadly, public ownership and operation is the European way, private ownership and operation, with public regulation, the American way. In a country like Great Britain, there is comparatively little regulation of private enterprise (outside of minor rules on sanitation and the like); here, business and industry are confronted with public regulation—of rates, services, finances, pensions, hours, business practices—at almost every turn.

Business Interest: competition or solidarity
In reviewing governmental policies and programs aiding and controlling business, we must also bear in mind that the business community in its turn exerts a powerful influence on the government. One cannot say precisely how many people in this country are now engaged in business. The number has been estimated at between 6 and 8 million, depending upon what is considered "business." But in any case the gamut runs all the way from the independent corner grocery to the industrial or financial colossus like the du Pont Company or General Motors counting its assets in billions of dollars. At first glance, there is little unity in the picture. Small business contends with big business; independent dealers fight the chains, railroads do battle with bus and air lines; high-cost producers seek political protection against low-cost producers; some manufacturers want protective tariffs, importers want none; New England textile interests combat newer interests of the kind in the South; competition is intense within industries and between industries; scores of trade associations do whatever they can to get favors and advantages for their own industries, localities, or regions.

There is, nevertheless, more solidarity than appears. Business interests, large and small, have, as is often said, a "businessman's point of view"; large overall organizations like the National Association of Manufacturers and the United States Chamber of Commerce encourage and express this point of view, consolidating sentiment and speaking for the business community as a whole. Although often rivals, textile interests, iron and steel interests, transportation interests—each with its own trade association, or perhaps several such—have common ground and may work together for common purposes. At many points, big business pulls little business along with it; interlocking directorates and financial relationships blur the pattern of dispersion and harmonize conflicting interests and objectives. Representatives of "big business"—bankers, insurance men, railroad presidents, other corporation executives, newspaper publishers, and the like—"have their internecine battles and rivalries, but on the larger issues of public policy they form a solid phalanx of opinion. Intimately knit together by social and financial ties, sitting on the same boards, exercising the same general responsibilities, they easily develop a common point of view and a common outlook. Differences there may be on details of tactics and strategy, but on ultimate objectives there is a natural and understandable consensus." [1] And solidarity of opinion does not stop here. Big bankers influence lesser ones, and they still lesser ones within their radius of contact. So, too, with corporations and industries of other sorts—influence radiating downwards, indeed, through all levels, and certainly not excluding the millions of people who, having investments in General Motors or the Pennsylvania Railroad or any one of hundreds of other enterprises, large or small, instinctively incline toward the viewpoints of those bearing responsibility for operating the business. Notwithstanding incessant internal clashes of interest and policy, therefore, the American business world on a great many issues presents a common front of immense prestige and potentiality.

Furthermore, this common front is utilized powerfully for political ends. *Business in* Back of it stand millions of voters. While we hear less of the business vote *politics:* than of the labor or farm vote, no one can fail to perceive that at every Presidential and Congressional election it is thrown heavily to some particular party —normally the Republican Party—and Presidential candidate, or to the Congressional candidates of one party, as against the rest— on some occasions impressively so, as in favor of the gold-standard McKinley in 1896 or against Franklin D. Roosevelt and his New Deal in 1936. But it is not alone through nominations and elections that business seeks to mold and guide national policy. There are also broad avenues for influence upon the President by advice and persuasion, upon department heads in their work of planning and administration, upon the great regulatory commissions, and upon Congress in connection with legislation. Here we enter, of course, the labyrinth of interest-group activities, including lobbying; and the fact already has been stressed that among the scores of groups and interests assiduously endeavoring to influence Senators and Representatives to support or oppose given tax, tariff, currency, labor, farm, and other proposals, a prominent place must always be given business organizations and groups, from the National Association of Manufacturers down. Of course, business interests do not always see eye to eye; one may be found pressing for a piece of legislation strongly opposed by others. Representatives of the coal industry hardly can be expected to cooperate with the oil and gas interests in promoting pipeline transportation. All in all, however, there is a good deal of concerted effort, with even diverse and independent efforts contributing to the development of an attitude or atmosphere favorable to the business point of view in general. Furthermore, one of the major lessons which business has learned in the past generations is the folly of ignoring or defying public sentiment—the wisdom, indeed, of cultivating such sentiment in every possible way.

[1] M. Fainsod, L. Gordon, and J. C. Palamountain, Jr., *Government and the American Economy* (3rd ed., New York, 1959), 24-25.

NATIONAL ASSISTANCE TO BUSINESS

Almost everything the national government does affects business, most of the time benevolently. The maintenance of friendly intercourse abroad fosters trade across national frontiers, the defense of the nation not only preserves the plants and facilities of the business world against destruction or capture but also provides an immense market for the sale of privately manufactured armaments of all types. The preservation of law and order guarantees ownership against theft and depredation and facilitates the free movement of goods and services over a vast continental area. Assistance to the aged, the infirm, the sick, the veteran, and many others insures a market for many types of consumer goods; and granting of economic and military aid to friendly foreign powers in recent years has assured a market abroad for many types of American commodities. There are, however, many forms of assistance aimed particularly or exclusively at the business community or at segments of it. These programs are summarized and illustrated in the following paragraphs.

1. Subsidies   Throughout the country's history, business has profited immensely from subsidies from the national treasury; and some branches of it still do so. Most conspicuous among beneficiaries has been the railway industry, on which more than $1.25 billion, chiefly in public lands, has been bestowed. But transportation by air, sea, and highway have also been subsidized: contracts with air carriers for transporting mail are frankly drawn to subsidize a young industry and airport facilities are extensively supported by national, state, and local expenditures; the trucking industry has been subsidized by immense national, as well as state and local, expenditures on highways which are its roadbed; the newspaper, magazine, book publishing and direct-mail advertising industries are sustained by mail service charges which are admittedly below cost and the differential must be made up by appropriations from tax funds; during both world wars of this century armament manufacturers have been supported in plant expansions by direct grants, favorable laws, tax advantages, and public construction of facilities for private operation. The modern defense establishment supports a huge industrial complex of missile, aircraft, weapons, and ship manufacturers. One of the special recipients of Treasury largesse has been the American shipping industry. The efforts of the government to stimulate trading in American vessels have included tonnage tax advantages and subsidies to private operators by lucrative mail contracts, by government construction of vessels which are then leased to private operators, by payment of the difference in cost of operation between American-owned and foreign-owned vessels. The list of subsidies might be extended for several paragraphs. All told the business community has been the direct beneficiary of billions of dollars of national expenditure and a substantial share of the national budget currently is allocated for this purpose. Contrary to some of the pronouncements of its associations, the business community has never opposed public subsidies as such. What it opposes are subsidies to other sectors of the national economy.

The most important concealed subsidy received by business throughout most of our history has been that arising from protective tariffs. A protective tariff is a duty on imports fixed high enough to offset any price advantage which foreign goods might enjoy in the American market in competition with home-produced articles. Every tariff act from 1789 to 1930 had as one of its purposes, and often the main one, to give American products (chiefly manufactures, until eventually agricultural products were added) a competitive advantage over foreign products in our markets. The peak of such favoritism was reached under the Tariff (Hawley-Smoot) Act of 1930. In fact, tariffs had in general been rising throughout our history except for two periods: 1832-1860 and from 1913-1922. The pros and cons of this policy have been argued warmly for 160 years. Producers of raw materials such as cotton have usually opposed tariffs on manufactured goods. Manufacturers have usually argued the benefits to be derived from fostering the development of home industry and the advantages accruing to American labor by being protected against lower European or Asiatic wage scales. The point is that business has at all stages been the beneficiary of what amounts to a tax, in the form of higher prices, on the country's consumers. Since 1934 the nation has retreated from the extreme protectionist position of 1930. More and more business interests feel able to survive foreign competition and are especially anxious to enlarge their export markets, expecting that tariff reduction at home will stimulate reciprocity abroad. Other devices for controlling foreign trade-embargoes, quotas, import controls—have since the thirties largely supplanted tariffs in importance in many of the tightly controlled economies of the world. There has been a change also since 1934 in the procedure by which tariffs are fixed. Dissatisfaction with Congressional tariff-making increased steadily in this century. General tariff bills had by 1910 become such labyrinths of facts and figures that even the most conscientious legislator could inform himself on only a small portion of the duties. The influence of special interests in promoting high rates on particular goods were enormous. Fluctuations in economic conditions at home and abroad made any set of rates soon out of date.

2. Tariff protection

The first reform efforts accompanied a desire to reduce tariffs generally and led to the creation in 1916 of the United States Tariff Commission. This agency, directed by six members appointed on a bipartisan basis, was charged with continuous review of the tariffs in relation to costs of manufacture at home and abroad and with keeping both the President and Congress fully informed. The commission has never been authorized to make changes in the laws or their administration on its own. Originally it had no authority even to make recommendations except in very general terms. The Tariff (Fordney-McCumber) Act of 1922, however, charged it with the duty of investigating differences in the cost of production between the protected domestic commod-

Flexible tariff introduced

U.S. TARIFF HISTORY, 1821-1963

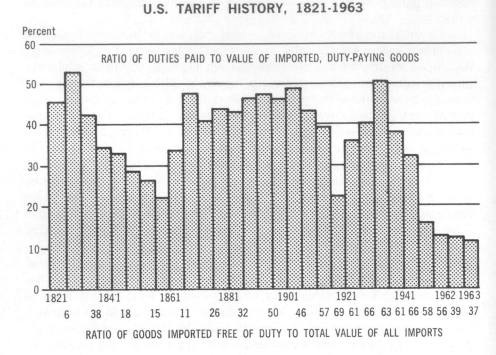

Percent

RATIO OF DUTIES PAID TO VALUE OF IMPORTED, DUTY-PAYING GOODS

1821 1841 1861 1881 1901 1921 1941 1962 1963

6   38   18   15   11   26   32   50   46   57 69 61 66 63 61 66 58 56 39 37

RATIO OF GOODS IMPORTED FREE OF DUTY TO TOTAL VALUE OF ALL IMPORTS

ity and its foreign counterpart and required it to recommend to the President specific increases or decreases in tariff rates based upon its studies. The President, in turn, was authorized to change rates by as much as 50 percent up or down. The result was our first flexible tariff.

Trade agreement system

The amount of tariff revision accomplished by this procedure was more than offset by the new high rates of the Tariff Act of 1930. The commission's procedures were slow and cumbersome and its recommendations could apply only to specific articles. A new Democratic administration, determined to stimulate international trade and to improve the tariff procedure, persuaded Congress in 1934 to inaugurate a broad new tariff program. The Reciprocal Trade Agreement Act of 1934 [2] empowered the President to bargain with foreign countries for mutually advantageous tariff concessions and to lower the tariffs by as much as 50 percent without further Congressional approval in so doing. Articles on the dutiable list might not be transferred to the free list or vice versa, and the "most-favored-nation" [3] principle had to be preserved. The President's power was to expire after three years. Succeeding Congresses have renewed the grant of power to the President up to 1967. The most recent exten-

[2] The measure was an amendment to the Tariff Act of 1930 leaving most of the base rates as they stood in that act.

[3] This principle is that concessions made to one country will be extended to all others with whom we have treaties promising such reciprocity.

sion was granted by the Congress in 1962 at the request of President Kennedy. In the fifties, however, the renewals came grudgingly and in some cases for shorted periods, especially from Republican Congresses. In the last few extensions, the role of the Tariff Commission has been enhanced so that the President must await their studies before concluding agreements and they are directed to lay before him and before Congress any evidence of injury to domestic interests from the extant duties. The Trade Agreements Extensions Act of 1958 provided further that Congress could by a two-thirds vote veto any Presidential tariff orders in those instances where the President had rejected the advice of the Tariff Commission.

The most recent extension, The Trade Expansion Act of 1962, considerably broadened Presidential authority to negotiate in particular with the European Economic Community (Common Market). He could under certain circumstances actually cancel duties on certain classes of goods and in general could agree to reduce duties by as much as 50 percent of the level of July, 1962. The Congressional veto was, however, retained and strengthened by the provision that if the President did not implement a recommendation of the Tariff Commission his refusal to do so could be overridden by a majority vote of both houses through a concurrent resolution. The act also removed Poland and Yugoslavia from the benefits of the most-favored-nation principle. The "protectionist" interests were somewhat mollified by the provision of a new program of adjustment assistance under which industries injured by tariff reductions could receive technical aid, loans, and tax concessions and the workers could get special unemployment benefits and vocational retraining where appropriate.

Trade Expansion Act of 1962

Since 1948, most of the tariff agreements have been negotiated multilaterally through the 44 countries that are signatories of the General Agreement on Tariffs and Trade (GATT) entered into at that time. GATT is regarded by the national administration as an executive agreement negotiated under the general authority of the Reciprocal Trade Agreements Acts. It has never been submitted to Congress and never expressly approved by it. Legislation authorizing American participation in the Organization for Trade Cooperation, an agency set up to implement GATT has been proposed on several occasions to Congress but has not as yet been adopted. The latest round (Kennedy Round) of negotiations under the authority of the Act of 1962 began in Geneva under GATT auspices in May, 1964. At about the same time the first United Nations Conference on Trade and Development was being staged in Geneva. Dominated by the developing nations this conference sought to improve their position relative to the industrial nations by trade concessions. This conference ended in June, 1964 after approving the establishment of a permanent organization under the UN to continue efforts to improve world trade. The Kennedy round negotiations are still (1965) going on.

GATT

Shift of negotiations from State Department to White House

Because of the numerous criticisms in Congress of the anonymity of the responsible negotiators in the trade treaty diplomacy of the State Department an office of special Representatives for Trade Negotiations was created in the executive office of the President in 1963 and has been charged with handling all trade negotiations under the reciprocal agreements program.

The result of the reciprocal agreements program to date has been a very substantial reduction in tariff levels. Average duties are now about 11 percent as compared to 53 percent in the early thirties. Agreements are now in effect with 43 countries.[4] Tariff making has to a considerable degree been removed from the legislative arena to the administrative one, although Congress can and has revised some of the base rates of the Tariff Act of 1930. Each recent extension of the President's power to make agreements has been vigorously contested but protectionist pressure although intensive seems to be abating and the 1962 Act was passed with large majorities. In the past few years the trade program has, however, been complicated by heavy outflow of gold due to investment abroad and foreign aid. Fear of exclusion from the Common Market has perhaps stimulated wider business support for tariff reduction. The program, therefore, commands wide "administration" and commercial and industrial support and is an important item of our contemporary foreign policy. It will not be easily cast aside.

3. Lending operations   Until World War I, business commonly depended for credit upon banks and other private financial institutions. A War Finance Corporation was then set up, however, to make government loans mainly to industries requiring them for increased war production. While that agency eventually disappeared, its place was taken during the depression by the Reconstruction Finance Corporation (RFC), charged with rescuing embarrassed railroads, banks, trust companies, insurance companies, and other businesses, both large and small. During World War II, through the RFC and other agencies, the government again expanded its loan functions to stimulate the manufacture of war goods. By 1950, the national government had developed into the country's largest banker, with its lending operations extending to agriculture, housing, foreign trade (e.g., through the Export-Import Bank of Washington) as well as to business of almost every variety. In 1951 and 1952, the RFC was sharply criticized in Congress. Investigation by a Senate committee revealed both partisan and personal favoritism in its operations. When the Eisenhower Administration took office pledged to reduce governmental business operations, the RFC was one of its prime targets and the agency was liquidated by act of Congress.[5] The same Congress, however, created a new Small Business Administration (SBA) and authorized it not only to assist small businesses to obtain government contracts but also to loan money to such businesses for plant

---

[4] All tariff concessions were withdrawn, however, from Russia and her satellite countries beginning in 1951.

[5] The Reconstruction Finance Corporation Liquidation Act of 1953. It is necessary to add that the RFC loaned $13 billion during its litetime on nondefense programs with a loss of only 1.3 percent offset completely by a loan reserve and that it paid over $1 billion into the U. S. Treasury as a profit on its operations.

expansion, modernization of equipment, and similar purposes.[6] In 1965, more than $31.6 billion of direct loans were outstanding on the government's books for housing, rural electrification, farm purchase and improvement, commodity support, and business development. An additional $91.7 billion of private loans were insured or guaranteed by the government for these same general purposes.

One of the great defects of the Articles of Confederation from the point of view of the business community was the freedom it allowed to debtor-controlled state legislatures to multiply the amount of money in circulation by various kinds of "cheap money" expedients. The authors of the Constitution were virtually unanimous on the need for a sound and uniform system of "hard" currency. Congress was endowed with specific authority to "coin money [and] regulate the value thereof" and the states were forbidden to "coin money, emit bills of credit, or make anything but gold and silver coin legal tender in the payment of debts." From that day to this, one of the important functions of the national government in serving business has been to provide a monetary system which will facilitate domestic and foreign commerce and will remain fairly stable as a storehouse of economic values. Although occasionally the Congress has fallen under the influence of debtor—usually agricultural—interests and has sought to "ease" the plight of the "downtrodden" by multiplying the amount of currency in circulation, in general, national management of the currency has been dominated by "sound" money policies.

4. Provision of a monetary mechanism

In 1792, when Congress provided a uniform system of currency, it wisely discarded the cumbersome English pattern in favor of the simpler decimal plan with its eagles, dollars, dimes, and cents. With both gold and silver to be employed, Congress fixed the content of the silver dollar at 371.25 grains and of the gold dollar at 24.75 grains, a ratio of 15 to 1 reflecting the current market value of the two metals. And for 100 years questions relating to changes in the ratio, in terms of the amount of gold and silver to be contained in dollars of the two varieties, furnished fuel for political controversy. After the exciting struggle of 1896 over the relations of the two metals a Republican Congress settled matters for several years by placing on the statute book a Gold Standard Act making the gold dollar the unit of value and requiring that all other money be maintained on a parity with gold.

Earlier experience with a national coinage —the gold standard

So strong was debtor pressure during the depression years 1933-1934, that the New Deal Congress and President abandoned the gold standard. All holders of gold coin, gold bullion, and gold certificates issued by the Federal Reserve banks were required to turn them over to the national government, receiving in exchange various forms of paper currency. Other forms of legal tender—even though with values still defined in terms of gold—could no longer be converted into gold. Under the Gold Reserve Act of 1932, and with a view

The system revolutionized in 1933-34

[6] The SBA was made a permanent agency in 1958 and its powers extended to include disaster loans and loans for venture capital to investment companies serving small businesses.

to accumulating a stock of gold ample to serve as a metallic base for a huge paper currency, the government was authorized to buy all gold remaining in possession of the Federal Reserve banks, and also to buy abroad. As a result of this "nationalizing" policy some $15 billion worth of bullion (about half of the world's supply) has been acquired and stored, principally in vaults buried deep in the ground at Ft. Knox, Kentucky. No longer is gold coined or circulated. In general, the object of all of these depression-time measures was a "managed" currency which would tend to raise the price level of commodities. Since these measures were adopted the business community has adjusted itself to, and largely accepted, a system of managed currency in which the amount of money in circulation is determined by other factors than the amount of gold or silver bullion in reserve. Gold is now used, apart from certain special industrial and artistic purposes, largely to adjust international trade balances and thus to strengthen the position of the dollar abroad. It is precisely this aspect of monetary policy that has caused most concern in recent years with the steady outflow of treasure (gold or dollar credits) because of foreign aid, military commitments, and investments abroad.

Problem of inter- national deficit payments

Since 1949, the United States has had deficits in the annual balance of international payments. These mounted to $3.7 billion in 1959 and have remained close to $3 billion yearly since that time. Unlike the smaller deficits of 1949-1958, those more recently have been accompanied by heavy gold shipments and the gold reserve of $22.9 billion in 1957 has shrunk to $15 billion in 1965, smaller than the total dollar credits held abroad. Presidents Eisenhower, Kennedy, and Johnson have all urged the reducing of the deficits, including discouragement of investment abroad, pressure on overseas military expenditures, and sharp limits on American tourist duty-free import privileges. The deficits seem to be coming under control but have not as yet disappeared.

Paper money introduced

Most money, as we see and use it today, is paper, with gold and silver merely held in reserve as security. The Constitution speaks only of *coining* money, without a word about paper currency—except to forbid the states to issue it. Such currency, nevertheless, was in circulation after 1789 as before. The first and second Bank of the United States issued notes, and so did state banks, even though their issues often were of shifting and uncertain value.[7] Even before the Civil War, there was some demand that responsibility for paper money be centralized in the national government; and when difficulty was encountered in floating loans for carrying on that conflict, Congress took the momentous steps of (1) authorizing, in 1863, the national government itself to issue paper currency (later known popularly as "greenbacks"), and (2) instituting our modern system of national banks, with power to issue

[7] While clearly barred from *directly* issuing notes designed to circulate as money, states freely chartered banks empowered to issue them—and with the Supreme Court's approval. Briscoe v. Kentucky, 11 Peters 257 (1837). To stop the practice, Congress in 1865 imposed a 10 per cent tax on such notes, making it unprofitable to issue them; and in Veazie Bank v. Fenno, 8 Wallace 533 (1869), the Supreme Court sustained the tax and its purpose.

notes up to 90 percent of their holdings of United States bonds. Although not redeemable in gold or silver, greenbacks were declared legal tender for every use, public and private, except payment of customs duties and of interest on government bonds. The right of Congress to authorize such currency, and, particularly, to make it legal tender for private debts, was sharply challenged —especially since the greenbacks depreciated sharply in terms of "hard money." At the first test, the Supreme Court upheld a private citizen in refusing to accept such dubious currency in discharge of a debt.[8] But, with membership somewhat altered, and after hearing two pending cases reargued, the tribunal, in 1871 (although by a slender margin), pronounced the "legal tender acts" an exercise of constitutional authority properly to be implied from the power to borrow money.[9] In so doing it threw wide open the door for national issues of and control over paper currency.

As an outcome of its rather tortuous history, the modern American currency system is more complicated than some of those abroad. Nevertheless, with gold coins and gold certificates eliminated and national bank notes nearly all called in, it is simpler than it used to be. Since 1933, all forms have been legal tender and on a parity with one another, so that no one need hesitate to accept payment for goods or services in whatever type of lawful currency is offered. By far the most important type of paper currency now in circulation is *Federal Reserve notes*. These are issued by Federal Reserve banks and are secured by deposits with the Federal Reserve Board of discounted commercial paper and government bonds. The commercial paper security tends to adjust the amount of such money in circulation to the volume of certain types of business transactions. The power of the Federal Reserve Board—discussed later in this chapter—to determine the discount rate on such paper and the size of reserves necessary to support issuances of currency form a fundamental part of its influence over the amount of currency available and thus over the national economy.

Present forms of currency

The management of the currency is largely vested in the Department of the Treasury; management of monetary policy is largely vested in the Federal Reserve Board. Coins are manufactured by the Bureau of the Mint; paper money (along with postage stamps, savings bonds, revenue stamps, etc.) is produced by the Bureau of Printing and Engraving. The comptroller of the currency controls the issuance of Federal Reserve notes and the Secret Service protects the currency against counterfeiting. The Secretary of the Treasury, in addition to giving general direction to these subordinate agencies, controls the gold and silver purchase programs and many of the programs aimed at maintaining the value of the dollar in foreign exchange.

Currency management in the Treasury Department

One of the most useful services performed by the national government in support of nation-wide markets for manufactured goods, foodstuffs, and fibers

5. Provision of uniform standards of weights and measures

[8] Hepburn *v.* Griswold, 8 Wallace 603 (1870).
[9] Knox *v.* Lee, Parker *v.* Davis, 12 Wallace 457 (1871). Cf. Julliard *v.* Greenman, 110 U. S. 421 (1884).

is the establishment of uniform standards of weights and measures. The authority given Congress to "fix the standard of weights and measures" is so broad that it can be, and has been, exercised in connection with all manner of measurements—length, weight, volume, temperature, strength, quality, and others. One of the great landmarks in this field and one of the numerous benefactions to this nation by the Adams family is the report in 1821 by John Quincy Adams on a system of uniform measures. To aid in determining such standards, the Bureau of Standards is maintained in the Department of Commerce. Along with the familiar units taken over from old English usage—the pound, yard, gallon, bushel, and so on (with their derivatives), the metric system employed in Continental countries, and having conspicuous advantages, has been given official status, even though as yet but little actual use is made of it outside of scientific circles. As developed to the present time, the function of the national government is merely to "fix" standards, keep models in the Bureau of Standards, and furnish models or copies to the states, leaving it to state and local governments, in the interest of honesty and regularity, to require compliance with the appropriate standards in business and other transactions. Congress might not only *fix* standards, but set up machinery for enforcing them nationally. This, however, it has never done.

6. Scientific research and the provision of useful data

The business community is under a heavy and growing obligation to the national government for the collection and dissemination of useful data on trade, markets, foreign exchange, labor supply, cost of living, consumer income, investment opportunities and thousands of other subjects reflecting in great detail the condition of the economy of the nation and of the world. Monthly periodicals like the *Survey of Current Business* and *Economic Indicators* keep business supplied with timely information on the state of the economy. An elaborate network of observation posts and reporting installations supplies daily and weekly data on the weather. Less extensive but no less elaborate data is also developed on minerals, water, and other resources. The government is, however, not solely a statistical collecting agency; it is also pushing the frontiers of scientific knowledge. Through such agencies as the Bureau of Standards, the Atomic Energy Commission, the National Science Foundation, and the Department of Defense, new data, much of it of great practical utility to industry, is being discovered and made available. If one includes the research program in agriculture and that in public health, it is not too much to say that the national government has beome the greatest research institution in modern America.[10]

7. Protection of copyrights and patents

From its inception the national government has sought to promote the progress of science and the useful arts "by securing to authors and inventors" the exclusive right to their respective writings and discoveries. The exclusive right conferred is by way of exception to the common-law rule against monopolies, the purpose being, of course, to reward talent and encourage creative

[10] For a thoughtful appraisal of the government's growing role in science see D. K. Price, *Government and Science* (New York, 1954).

effort. The privilege of copyright extends not only to books, but to periodicals, paintings, charts, maps, dramatic and musical composition, cartoons, lectures, sermons, motion pictures, and photographs. The period covered is 28 years, with in most cases option of one renewal for an equal length of time. Included is the exclusive privilege of translating, dramatizing, and presenting a work, and in the case of a musical composition, the right also to perform it publicly for profit and to exact a royalty for any reproduction of it by mechanical instruments. A grant of copyright is made (after publication) to everyone seeking it and depositing two copies of his work in the Library of Congress, with payment of a fee; copyright, too, is property and transferable as such. On the other hand, the Copyright Office in the Library of Congress, which administers the law, makes no effort to ascertain whether any infringement, that is, unauthorized use, of a previously copyrighted publication or production is involved; if such is alleged, the party considering himself injured can seek redress only through a suit for damages, or injunction proceedings, in a national court.[11]

Through a Patent Office in the Department of Commerce, a patent may be granted to any person who has invented or discovered "any new and useful art, machine, manufacture, or composition of matter, or any new and useful improvements thereof, not known or used by others in this country . . . and not patented or described in any printed publication in this or any foreign country . . . and not in public use or on sale in this country for more than one year" prior to the filing of the application.[12] As suggested by this phraseology, patents are not granted to everyone who applies; on the contrary, the Patent Office is supposed to do its best to find out whether the machine, device, or process for which a patent is sought is actually new and whether a patent for it would infringe rights under some patent previously granted. The period for which a patent runs is 17 years, with in general no right of renewal. Appeals against decisions of the patent examiners in the Patent Office may be taken to a board of patent appeals in the office, and thence to the Court of Customs and Patent Appeals or to a national district court. Moreover, while in general the monopolistic rights carried by a patent are not legally challengeable, the uses made of patents, especially by large industries, singly or in com-

---

[11] In order to receive the protection of our copyright laws, books printed in the English language must, with a few exceptions, be type-set in the United States. On the general subject, see Z. Chaffee, Jr., "Reflections on the Law of Copyright," *Columbia Law Rev.*, XLV, 503-529, 719-738 (July and Sept., 1945). On the many complicated aspects of international copyright, see M. M. Kampelman, "The United States and International Copyright," *Amer. Jour. of Internat. Law,* XLI, 406-429 (Apr., 1947). In 1946, a significant convention for uniform copyright protection was signed at Washington by representatives of the American republics.

[12] To promote seed-breeding and afford agriculture the same opportunity to participate in the benefits of the patent system, Congress in 1930 enacted a Plant Patent Act under which any person who has "invented or discovered and asexually reproduced any distinct and new variety of plant, other than a tuber-propagated plant," may receive a patent.

bination, sometimes bring the holders into conflict with the laws prohibiting contracts in restraint of trade. Such uses also raise the question of whether anything can or should be done to overcome the economic and social effects of concentration of sometimes hundreds, and even thousands, of patents in the hands of a single big business enterprise.[13] Slightly over 100 years ago, a Commissioner of Patents soberly recommended to Congress that his office be abolished because "everything had been invented." How far wrong he was is indicated by the fact that from 25,000 to 50,000 patents are granted every year.[14] In fact the 3 millionth patent was awarded, amidst much publicity, in September of 1961.

8. Provision of uniform bankruptcy procedures

The credit structure upon which so much of modern business enterprise depends is protected and strengthened by the provision of uniform procedures for discharging unpaid obligations through bankruptcy. Under the Constitution, bankruptcy is one of the matters over which the national and state governments have concurrent legislative power. For more than 100 years (except for three brief intervals) it was left entirely to state control. In 1898, however, Congress passed a general bankruptcy act; and thereupon former state laws on the subject either were repealed or fell into a condition of suspended animation. It still is permissible for a state to legislate on bankruptcy. The national law, however, takes precedence and this law is so comprehensive that little need for state action survives. Proceedings in bankruptcy cases, started either by the bankrupt himself or by his creditors, fall under the equity jurisdiction of the district court of the district in which the bankrupt resides; and after a bankrupt's assets have been inventoried and equitably distributed among his creditors, the judge enters a decree discharging him from all further legal liability for debts incurred prior to the commencement of proceedings.[15]

During the depression the Congress provided similar but not identical judicial relief for debt-burdened farmers, municipalities, and other types of corporations. The whole system of bankruptcy and debtor relief was coordinated and unified in 1938 and 1946.[16]

The Department of Commerce

Responsibility for assistance to the business community is spread through a large number of executive departments and agencies. One department, the

---

[13] O. R. Barnett, *Patent Property and the Anti-Monopoly Laws* (Indianapolis, 1943); W. T. Kelley, "Restraints of Trade and the Patent Law," *Georgetown Law Journ.,* XXXII, 213-233 (Mar., 1944); and A. M. Smith, "Recent Developments in Patent Law." *Mich. Law Rev.,* XLIV, 899-922 (June, 1946).

[14] In addition to granting patents, the Patent Office registers trademarks and labels for use on goods distributed through channels of interstate and foreign commerce. Registration, formerly for 20 years but indefinitely renewable, is now without time limit and can be protected through appeal to the courts. A new and more adequate trademark law (the Lanham Act) was enacted in 1946. See H. Bennett, *Trade Marks* (New York, 1948).

[15] Most of the details of bankruptcy proceedings are attended to by a referee in bankruptcy, appointed by the judge and reporting to him from time to time.

[16] Cf. E. A. Lewis [comp.], *Bankruptcy Laws of the United States* (Washington, 1946).

Department of Commerce, however, has as its major assignment serving business and representing its needs in the cabinet and to the Congress. This department was organized in 1913 by splitting the Department of Commerce and Labor which had been established in 1903. In 1965, this department employed more than 33,000 people and its annual expenditures were $735 million. Its principal divisions include: the Weather Bureau; the Patent Office; the Area Redevelopment Administration; the Bureau of the Census; the National Bureau of Standards; the Bureau of Public Roads which administers the national highway aid program; the Maritime Administration which administers subsidies to the shipping industry; the Bureau of Foreign Commerce which collects and disseminates data on foreign trade and promotes the interests of American business abroad; the Coast and Geodetic Survey which assists mariners by mapping coastlines, waterways, and currents.

NATIONAL REGULATION OF BUSINESS—AUTHORITY

The Congress shall have power to . . . regulate Commerce with foreign nations, and among the several States, and with the Indian tribes. ART. I, Sec, 8, cl. 3

The power of Congress to promote business interests by subsidies, loans, and services is sufficiently broad to encompass almost any conceivable program of this type. Few limitations of consequence have ever been discovered or enunciated by the courts to the spending power of the national government. So long as Congress declares with some reason that the object of the expenditure lies within the broad conception of public welfare, the courts appear willing to accept its power to make outlays. Specifically, the courts have rejected the notion, once argued vigorously by Jefferson, that the spending power is confined to objects embraced by the other enumerated powers of the Congress.[17] The power of Congress, however, to regulate business activities, that is, to penalize certain types of conduct and forbid others and to place limits upon the freedom of decision of the owners, stands on a very different constitutional footing. It is subject to a number of constitutional restraints. The most important of these are: (1) that the regulatory authority of the Congress is largely confined to interstate and foreign commerce; and, (2) that the power must be exercised so as not to deprive any entrepreneur, partner, or corporation of "due process of law." *The power to regulate*

All of the economic activities which are embraced in the concept of "business" are not historically included in the word *commerce* and all of those which are included are not interstate or international in character. The limitations on the power of Congress to regulate business, which are based upon the protection to property in the due process clause of the Fifth Amendment, have already been discussed in an earlier chapter. Suffice it to say here that

[17] United States v. Butler, 297 U. S. 1 (1936).

the modern Court has found few limits in this clause compared to its predecessors.

The history of the constitutional meaning of interstate commerce is one
of progressive expansion by statute and judicial interpretation so as to embrace not only the great technological changes in the fields of transportation
and communication but also to embrace more and more forms of business
activity. The floodgates for expansion were first opened in 1824, when, in
delivering a Supreme Court opinion in the famous case of Gibbons *v.* Ogden,[18]
Chief Justice Marshall not only affirmed the full authority of Congress to
maintain the free flow of interstate and foreign commerce within the individual
states, but declared commerce to consist not only of *traffic* (buying, selling,
and transporting commodities), but of *intercourse* as well, thereby giving it
a very broad content. The name of Marshall is associated with many nationalizing decisions of this period, but hardly with any of greater potential significance than this. Immediately, the carrying of persons (not simply goods) from
one state to another, or to a foreign country, became "commerce," subject to
Congressional regulation. As forms and methods of intercourse later multiplied, the field for control correspondingly expanded. In time came the steamboat; then the railroad; then the telegraph; then the telephone; then the motor
vehicle; then "wireless"; then radio broadcasting; then the airplane; finally
television (with doubtless other facilities yet to arise from the use of atomic
energy). And to all of these the regulative authority of Congress was progressively extended, with the Supreme Court coming close behind with decisions validating most of the powers asserted and sometimes hinting at even
broader ones that might be assumed.

Since 1937, the Court has found even broader meanings of commerce.
Two examples may be cited. On many earlier occasions, the question had
arisen as to whether Congress had authority to legislate concerning conditions
under which manufacturing and mining were carried on when such conditions
were more or less related to interstate commerce. For a long time, the Court
replied emphatically in the negative, saying that manufacturing and commerce
were two quite distinct things, and that under the Constitution national regulative authority extended only to commerce, or at most to activities affecting
commerce *directly*. When, for example, in 1916, Congress passed the first
child labor law, forbidding shipment in interstate commerce of products of
any factory, shop, or mine employing children, the Court—although narrowly
divided, and with Mr. Justice Holmes registering a celebrated dissent—over-

threw the measure as being aimed primarily at regulating, not commerce,
but manufacturing and mining, and therefore transcending proper Congres-

---

[18] 9 Wheaton 1 (1824). The case turned on the right of Robert R. Livingston and
Robert Fulton (inventor of the steamboat), holding from New York a monopoly of
navigation in waters of the state adjacent to New York City, to exclude from navigating
those waters a certain Thomas Gibbons, holding a coastal navigation license from the
national government.

sional authority.[19] Against growing dissatisfaction with so rigid an interpretation, the Court held its ground for another quarter of a century. Then, however, came a change. Beginning in 1933, numerous statutes enacted to promote national recovery proceeded from the bold assumption that, properly construed, the commerce clause gives Congress authority to regulate substantially the entire business structure of the country, including wages, hours, and other working conditions (incidentally child labor), prices, volume of production, the buying and selling of securities—in short, anything that affects interstate commerce *directly or indirectly*. Most of the earlier acts in the series were overthrown judicially on the ground of being too free in their delegations of power or pushing the commerce power to unjustifiable lengths, or both. In 1937, however, a majority of the Court swung around to the opinion that, nearly all manufacturing and other production being, under present-day conditions, carried on with a view to the interstate or national, or even the international, market, the commerce clause may properly be construed to permit Congress to regulate as commerce any business transactions or operations resulting in or otherwise associated with interstate or foreign commerce, however indirectly.[20] From this seminal concept, it was but a step to holding, more specifically, that all manufacturing, mining, lumbering, and other productive enterprises in which raw materials or finished products, or both, are carried in interstate commerce are inseparable from such commerce, and are, therefore, within the scope of Congressional regulative power. It was on this basis that the National Labor Relations Act of 1935 and the Fair Labor Standards ("Wages and Hours") Act of 1938—both relating primarily to industry, both gaining judicial acceptance because of their commercial implications—were sustained in 1937 and 1941, respectively.

Another illustration is supplied by recent extension of the sphere of Congressional control to include the business of insurance. In 1869, the Supreme Court held private insurance companies not to be engaged in interstate commerce, even when most of their business was carried on across state lines;[21] and on this understanding, such companies and their business were from then on regulated solely by the states. In 1943, however, some 200 private fire insurance companies and over a score of individuals identified with the South-Eastern Underwriters Association were indicted collectively for violating the Sherman Antitrust Act by conspiring to fix arbitrary and noncompetitive premium rates and to maintain monopolistic controls by boycotts and other means. When the case was argued before the Supreme Court, four

2. Insurance

---

[19] Hammer *v.* Dagenhart, 247 U. S. 251 (1918).

[20] This newer view was developed and discussed (a good while before the Court itself adopted it) in E. S. Corwin, "Congress's Power to Prohibit Commerce: A Crucial Constitutional Issue," *Cornell Law Quar.*, XVIII, 477-506 (June, 1933), and "Some Probable Repercussions of 'Nira' on Our Constitutional System," *Annals of Amer. Acad. of Polit. and Soc. Sci.*, CLXXII, 139-144 (Mar., 1934).

[21] Paul *v.* Virginia, 8 Wallace 168 (1869). There were other early decisions of similar purport.

of the seven justices then sitting refused to be bound by the decision of 75 years earlier and, on the contrary, held interstate insurance operations to be interstate commerce.[22] It was shown that when the only regulation to be feared was from the states, insurance companies had themselves sought to evade such regulation by maintaining that their business was interstate; and the decision reached, in brief, was: "No enterprise of any kind which conducts its activities across state lines has been held to be wholly beyond the regulatory power of Congress under the commerce clause. We cannot make an exception of the business of insurance." [23]

Present scope of congressional power

Under the prevailing theories of the power of Congress over interstate and foreign commerce, therefore, only the most parochial of business activities are exempted from national authority. Such business transactions must begin and end within the confines of a single state and must have no demonstrable effect upon or relevance to transactions which go beyond the state borders. This does not mean, however, that the states are wholly denied the power to regulate business activities which come within the scope of national power. They may be authorized by Congress or by the courts to exercise regulatory authority if not inconsistent with national policies or with judicially determined national needs. The states, therefore, continue to regulate many types of business transactions and institutions, even some which have interstate aspects. For the most part, however, their regulations must be consistent with national statutes or regulations or with judicial decisions on the scope of national power.

Regulation includes prohibition

The power to regulate, it must be added, includes also the power to prohibit. Embargoes on foreign commerce, for example, have been imposed several times in our history (e.g., in 1794, in 1812, and in 1917-1918) suspending trade completely with some countries or in some commodities. The slave trade was halted after the constitutional prohibition had expired. Congress has prohibited the transportation across state lines of lottery tickets, stolen goods, prostitutes, "filled" milk, liquor if being taken into "dry" states, and prison-made goods if in violation of state laws. The Supreme Court in

[22] United States *v.* South-Eastern Underwriters Association, 322 U. S. 533 (1944).

[23] The decision's effect was twofold: (1) to make the defendants liable to prosecution under the Sherman Act, and (2) to open the way for Congress to take over from the states, partly or wholly, the regulation of all private insurance business having an interstate aspect. The interests affected pressed earnestly for a chance to redeem themselves, declaring continued state regulation to be in the public interest; and the upshot was an act of Congress in 1945 making the business temporarily immune from prosecution under the antitrust laws, and postponing national regulation indefinitely, with a view to enabling the companies to mend their ways and also to giving the states an opportunity to take care of the situation if they could by making their own regulations more effective. Many states have since enacted remedial legislation on the subject— based in some instances on model bills drawn up by the insurance industry itself. See Council of State Governments, *Revision of State Systems for Insurance Regulation* (Chicago, 1946). The point to the episode for present purposes is, however, the extension of Congressional regulating authority (however little it may actually ever be exercised) to the insurance business by a Court not above changing its mind.

1925 declared that, "Congress can certainly regulate interstate commerce to the extent of forbidding and punishing the use of such commerce as an agency to promote immorality, dishonesty, or the spread of any evil or harm to the people of other states from the state of origin." [24]

Regulatory authority over foreign commerce is broader than over interstate. The exclusive and virtually unrestricted jurisdiction of the national government over our relations abroad applies to commerce no less than to everything else and, this adds materially to the regulative power conferred in the commerce clause—in addition to opening up methods of dealing with commerce otherwise than by Congressional act, for example, by treaty. Authority to regulate foreign commerce, furthermore, extends to every act of transportation or communication cutting across our national boundaries, no matter how deep in the country's interior may be the point of beginning or ending. A cablegram to England sent from Chicago is foreign commerce from the time it is first placed on the wires; a consignment of ladies' gowns from Paris to Cleveland is foreign commerce not simply until it is unloaded from a ship or airplane at New York, nor even simply until it reaches Cleveland, but until the importer has sold the original package or at least broken it for the purpose of selling its contents. Only (ruled the Supreme Court more than 100 years ago) when imports—the original package or its contents—have "come to rest," and are commingled with the general property of the people of a state, does the controlling authority of Congress end and that of the state begin.[25]

Authority over foreign commerce broader than over interstate commerce

Despite the broad sweep of authority now believed to reside in the Congress to regulate business, the Congress has not seen fit to bring the entire business community under detailed scrutiny of the national administration. The amount and character of national regulation vary widely from one type of business activity to another and from one epoch of time to another. In World War II, for example, the national government regulated businesses of all types in more minute detail than it had before or than it has since. In general, the regulatory power has been exercised more completely in those fields of business where monopolistic conditions actual or potential have threatened a weakening of the supposed regulatory effect of competition in free market. The Congress has also sought to safeguard the position of employees against exploitation by powerful corporate combinations. This type of restraint upon business we shall consider in the chapter on labor.

REGULATION OF BUSINESS—TRANSPORTATION

A discussion of the practices of business regulation must necessarily begin with the railroads, for these were the first major objects of concern. In the long struggle to bring the owners and managers of these great instrumentalities of

[24] Brooks *v.* United States, 257 U. S. 432 (1925).
[25] Brown *v.* Maryland, 12 Wheaton 419 (1827).

commerce under the control of the government there was established a pattern of regulatory theory and procedure which has been closely followed when other forms of business activities have been brought under public control.

Transportation development

It is hardly too much to say that the United States, as a nation of continental dimensions, has been made by transportation. Certainly growth in territory, population, wealth, and power not only has paralleled the sequence of horse and rider, stage coach, steamboat, railroad, automobile, and airplane but would not have been possible without it. When the Erie Canal was opened in 1825 and the first railroad (a section of the Baltimore and Ohio) in 1829, the stage was set for a long rivalry of water and rail transportation, with waterways more important at the outset, railroads gaining dominance in the second half of the nineteenth century, water transportation reviving sharply in the period of World War I, and competition continuing to this day—so heightened by the challenges of motor transport on the highways, of aircraft, and of pipelines that, while the railway system (a total of 396,000 miles) far surpasses any other in the world, the plight to which it has been reduced by increasing spread between costs and returns from operation has become one of the nation's major problems. By and large, transportation development has been one of the great achievements of our boasted free private enterprise. At the same time, it never could have taken place without a great deal of government aid.

1. Railroads: Federal regulation becomes necessary

Until long after the Civil War—and after most of the great expansion in the West and Southwest had taken place—regulation of railroad financing, operations, and procedures was left entirely to the states. As roads extended their networks through many states, and vast country-wide systems were built up, the situation got out of hand. By the later seventies and the eighties, railroad management and operation had become "big business," with formidable financial and other economic powers involved, with intense rivalries engendering ruthless policies, and with fabulous profits at stake. The railroad magnates took full advantage of the lack of effective competition. More than this, they used their great power by rebates and preferential rates to force monopoly into other segments of the business community. Abuses calling for remedy were many and glaring. Railroad stocks and bonds, often issued without adequate security, fluctuated wildly in the money markets; bankruptcies engineered by speculators involved honest investors in disaster; passenger and freight rates were pushed to the highest levels that the traffic would bear; altogether, the business was carried on with little responsibility to the public, and with plenty of dubious, if not definitely fraudulent, practices. The states attempted at first to correct matters insofar as they could. But their spheres were restricted; railroad magnates and lobbyists often dominated their legislatures. In several western states, however, agrarian revolt forced a round of "Granger" laws regulating rates and imposing other restrictions. These proved ineffectual in dealing with an interstate problem. In a series of decisions in so-called Granger cases, the Supreme Court unequivocally affirmed the right of government to regulate railroads as economic enterprises "affected with a public interest." [26] And at one time it indicated that in the case of a railroad doing both a state and an interstate business, a state was entitled to impose regulations in its own interest even if infringing upon interstate operations. Eventually (in 1886), however, it denied any authority in a state to control fares and charges in interstate commerce.[27] This left only one recourse: regulation by the national government itself.

The upshot of all this experience and of continued popular dissatisfaction and protest among western farmers and eastern small businessmen, was the passage by Congress in 1887 of an Act to Regulate Commerce, forbidding excessive charges, discriminations, and other unfair practices, and creating a special agency—the Interstate Commerce Commission—to administer and enforce the principles and rules laid down. Much additional legislation was required later, as railroad transportation raised new problems and as regulation was extended to other and newer forms of transportation. There were an Elkins Act of 1903, a Hepburn Act of 1906, a Transportation (Esch-Cummins) Act of 1920, a Motor Carrier Act of 1935, a Transportation Act of 1940, an Interstate Commerce Act of 1942 and a Transportation Act of 1958. Moreover, all of the laws underwent amendment and expansion; and of course much was added by administrative and judicial interpretation. The heart of the vast regulatory system built up over two full generations remains, however, the pioneer act of 1887. Under it and the laws and decisions supplementing it is now regulated all interstate transportation of persons and commodities carried on by railroads, by common carriers by water (both inland and coastal), by express companies, by sleeping-car and other private-car companies, by freight forwarders, by motor-bus companies, and by pipelines except those for the transportation of gas and water. Bridges, ferries, car-floats, and lighters, and indeed terminal and other facilities of whatsoever character when used in the interstate transportation of persons or goods are also regulated. Until 1934, the act applied also to instrumentalities and facilities used for the transmission of intelligence by means of electricity, such as telegraph, telephone, cable, and wireless systems. *The Interstate Commerce Act (1887) and its expansion*

Upon railroads—and, so far as applicable, upon all other instrumentalities of public service subject to the basic law—are imposed numerous restrictions each prompted by some earlier abuse. Thus, (1) rates for the transportation of persons and freight must be just and reasonable, and calculated to yield merely a "fair return" on the value of the property employed; (2) charging a higher rate for a short haul than for a long one over the same line in the same direction is forbidden, except when authorized in special instances by the Interstate Commerce Commission; (3) rebating, directly or indirectly, and undue discrimination or preference among persons, corpora- *Restrictions imposed*

[26] E.g., Peik v. Chicago and Northwestern Ry. Co., 94 U. S. 164 (1877).
[27] Wabash, St. Louis, and Pacific Ry. Co. v. People of the State of Illinois, 118 U. S. 557 (1886).

tions, or localities are prohibited; (4) free transportation may be granted only to narrowly restricted classes of persons; (5) railroads are forbidden, except in a few special cases, to operate, own, or control, or to have any interest in, any competing carrier by water; (6) except under strict supervision of the Commission, competing lines may not combine, merge their receipts, and apportion resulting profits; [28] (7) carriers may not transport commodities

RISE AND DECLINE OF THE AMERICAN RAILROAD SYSTEM

Date	No. of Locomotives	No. of Freight Cars	No. of Miles of Track
1880	17,949	539,255	115,647
1890	31,812	1,061,952	208,152
1900	37,663	1,365,531	258,784
1910	60,019	2,148,478	351,767
1920	68,942	2,388,424	406,580
1930	60,189	2,322,267	429,883
1940	44,333	1,684,171	405,975
1950	42,951	1,745,778	396,380
1960	31,178	1,690,396	381,745
1962	30,701	1,581,213	376,290

SOURCE: *Statistical Abstract of the United States, 1964.*

(except timber and its products) in which they have a direct property interest; and (8) they may issue long-term securities, purchase or build additional lines, or abandon old lines, only with the Commission's consent.

Duties prescribed   In addition, numerous positive duties are prescribed. For example, (1) printed schedules of rates must be kept open for public inspection, and changes in them may be made only with consent of the Interstate Commerce Commission; (2) full and complete annual reports must be made to the Commission, covering such matters, and arranged in such form, as the Commission may require; (3) all accounts must be kept according to a uniform system authorized by the Commission; (4) in case of injury to any of its employees while on duty, a carrier must grant pecuniary compensation, unless the accident was caused by willful act or negligence of the injured party; (5) the standard or basic work day for railway employees engaged in the operation of trains is eight hours, and carriers must conform their wage schedules to it and grant

[28] A long-pending Interstate Commerce Act Amendment (Reed-Bulwinkle) Act of 1948, passed over a presidential veto, nevertheless gives competing railroads freedom to proceed in concert in matters relating to rates and in effect exempts them from antitrust proceedings so long as the Interstate Commerce Commission approves what they do. Imminent court decisions in two antitrust proceedings brought against groups of roads by the antitrust division of the Department of Justice were forestalled by the legislation, which was regarded by the railroads as a signal victory but deplored by elements favoring vigorous regulation.

overtime pay; (6) all trains engaged in interstate commerce must be equipped
with automatic safety appliances; and (7) all railway companies so engaged
must maintain compulsory retirement and pension systems for their superannuated employees.[29]

The Interstate Commerce Commission (ICC)—charged with enforcing
the regulations outlined above and many lesser ones as well—consists of 11
persons appointed by the President and confirmed by the Senate for seven-
year terms, and has a staff of some 1800 clerks, attorneys, examiners, statis-
ticians, investigators, and technical experts, organized in 9 distinct bureaus,
each with a director or chief reporting to one of the commissioners. The
commissioners themselves work almost entirely in panels or divisions of three
members each; and a decision of a panel has the same force and effect as a
decision of the Commission itself—subject to the entire Commission granting
a rehearing. Any person, corporation, municipality, or other private or public
group may lodge with the Commission a complaint concerning any alleged
infraction of the interstate commerce laws. The Commission, acting ordinarily
through one of its panels, must institute an inquiry. If preliminary investigation
discloses that the complaint may be well founded, a hearing follows, of a sort
not unlike those to be observed in a court of justice: plaintiff and defendant
are represented by attorneys; books, papers, and other materials (which the
Commission has full power to order produced) are placed in evidence; witnesses are examined; and at the end the Commission, that is, in most instances
the appropriate panel, embodies its conclusion or finding in an order enforceable in the courts, although also with right of appeal to those courts by the
party affected adversely. Orders may relate to rates, quality or conditions of
service, or any one of literally scores of other things falling within the scope of
the laws; and disobedience renders the offender liable to prosecution.

The Interstate Commerce Commission

Under the original law, the Commission did not have power to make or
revise rates, either on its own initiative or on complaint of shippers that existing rates were unreasonable. Ultimately, however—although only after a
vigorous campaign of popular education, and in the face of persistent opposition from the carriers—the necessity of conferring extensive rate-making
power was brought home to the public. Under the transportation acts of 1906

Control over rates

[29] A Railroad Retirement Act of 1934, requiring railroads to contribute to a pension
fund for superannuated employees, was invalidated by the Supreme Court in 1935 as
"in no proper sense a regulation of interstate transportation." R. R. Retirement Board *v.*
Alton Ry., 295 U. S. 330. Eventually, under encouragement from President Franklin D.
Roosevelt, the roads and their organized employees themselves worked out a retirement
plan under which both are taxed to create a fund in the national treasury from which
the latter receive annuities, death benefits, and unemployment compensation; and laws
of 1935 and 1938 embodying the arrangements were never challenged judicially. Employees of common carriers other than railroads are not covered, but instead come under
the old-age and survivors provisions of the general Social Security system. Railroad
employers and employees have to pay higher payroll taxes than do employers and employees under the old-age and survivors system, but the benefits paid are substantially
larger. See L. Meriam, *Relief and Social Security* (Washington, 1946), 141-163.

and 1920, the Commission (as agent of Congress for the purpose) is authorized, on complaint and after hearing, not only to fix "just and reasonable"
rates, regulations, and practices, but also to prescribe definite maximum or
minimum charges. The Commission finds itself in consequence of this heavy
responsibility, perpetually under crossfire from shippers and other interests
clamoring for lower charges, and, on the other hand, carriers insisting that
rising operating costs or other factors call for rate increases.[30] On the ground
that to compel even property "affected with a public interest" to be used
without suitable compensation would amount to confiscation, the Court has
declared that rates should be such as to insure a "fair return" on the "value"
of the property involved.[31] But upon what constitutes "fair return," especially
as to how "value" is to be determined, there can be, and is, a great variety of
opinion. The matter is too involved to be discussed here, but it may be observed that, whereas for years the Supreme Court was inclined to support
valuation based (for example, in the case of a railroad) on what it would cost
currently to reproduce the road and its facilities, less an allowance for depreciation, the present tendency is rather to favor valuation in terms of the
more stable and manageable criterion of the amount of money actually put
into constructing and developing the road from its beginning, again of course
with a deduction for depreciation.[32]

The
pattern of
regulation

The pattern of government regulation which emerges from the efforts to
control the railroads is: (1) that the regulating agency be an independent
commission removed by legislative intent from the direct oversight of the
President and exercising its powers in a more or less judicial atmosphere; (2)
that the regulatory authority be granted by Congress in the broadest terms—
"just and reasonable rates"—with the agency authorized to specify in particular
how the authority will be discharged; (3) that the actions of the agency will be
carefully scrutinized by the courts on appeal and that such court scrutiny will
emphasize the protection of property rights against administrative impairment;
(4) that competition will be encouraged as a "natural" regulator until it is

[30] In its rate-making power, the Commission manifestly holds the power of life and
death over the railroads, with the charges that they are allowed to impose perhaps
spelling the difference between solvency and bankruptcy, and at the same time over industries, farmers, and other producers, who may be able to make profits only if enabled
to get their commodities to consumers at moderate cost. By the same token, the welfare
of the consumer himself is heavily at stake. It is not surprising, therefore, that when a
new member of the Commission is to be appointed, interest and activity are likely to
be stirred both in Congress and outside; or that Congressmen, and even the President,
may be placed under pressure to intercede with commissioners for or against a given
course of policy or action. For a full study of the methods employed by special interests
to influence the Commission's attitudes and findings, see P. Herring, "Special Interests
and the Interstate Commerce Commission," *Amer. Polit. Sci. Rev.,* XVII, 738-751, 899-
917 (Oct. and Dec., 1933).

[31] Smyth *v.* Ames, 169 U. S. 466 (1898).

[32] In Federal Power Commission *v.* Natural Gas Pipeline Co., 315 U. S. 575 (1942),
and Federal Power Commission *v.* Hope Natural Gas Co., 320 U. S. 591 (1944), the
Court in effect overthrew the rate-making formula laid down in Smyth *v.* Ames, while
nevertheless virtually conceding the matter to be one for the regulatory agency to
determine for itself.

CHANGING PATTERN OF PASSENGER TRAFFIC
1946-1962

Type	PASSENGER MILES (Billions)			
	1946	% of Total	1962	% of Total
Railroads	66.3	18.7	20.2	2.5
Buses	26.9	7.6	21.3	2.6
Waterways	2.3	.6	2.7	.3
Air Carriers	5.9	1.7	37.5	4.6
Private Auto	253.6	71.4	719.7	90.0

SOURCE: *Statistical Abstract of the United States, 1964*

THE CHANGING PATTERN OF U.S. FREIGHT TRAFFIC
(Percent of total ton miles)

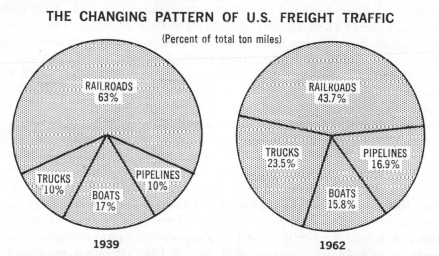

1939   **1962**

demonstrably obvious that the effort to inject competition is either impractical or unwise; [33] (5) that, although the original grant of regulatory power may extend only to certain aspects of the business under consideration, the power is likely to be broadened subsequently to bring under scrutiny more and more facets of the enterprise.

After almost 80 years of railroad regulation by the procedures and under the policies outlined, a few observations are in order. In consequence of vast and rapid technological change, more and more goods are now being moved by highway and air and more and more people are traveling by private motor

Results of regulation

[33] The Transportation Act of 1920 assumed that competition was impractical in the railroad industry and should not be encouraged and this was and has been the ICC policy. However in 1955 a Presidential Advisory Committee on Transport Policy and Organization appointed by President Eisenhower recommended that the government resume reliance on competition among railroads, trucks, and aircraft as the main regulator of rates and sharply curtail the powers of the ICC. President Kennedy in his message to Congress in 1962 on transportation policy made a similar suggestion.

car. The once proud and truculent railroad industry is sick unto death. Whatever monopoly it once could claim has nearly vanished. Its great stations are falling into disrepair and its small stations disappearing. Each of its chief competitors receives subsidy and benevolent supervision. The continuance of commuter service in our large cities probably depends on subsidies and tax advantages and in Washington pleas for financial help, advanced in every Congress received a little support in the Transportation Act of 1958 and a great deal in the Urban Mass Transportation Act of 1964. The detailed, case-by-case method of insuring fair rates and reasonable service under a bipartisan and judicial commission seems peculiarly ill-adapted to the problems of the day. How by these procedures can the relative claims of highway, air, and rail be fairly weighed? Faced by organized labor's demand for higher wages how can higher rates be promised? How relevant is the case law on "fair return" to either of these questions? How can terminals, yards, switching and sorting facilities be consolidated and moved to cheaper land to save taxes, labor costs, and transit time? There are no easy answers to these questions. The commission system, however, has not conclusively demonstrated that it can accommodate itself readily to a fast changing world.[34]

2. Water transportation

Historically, the regulation of interstate transportation has, until this century, been largely a matter of regulating railroads. A good deal of such commerce, however, has always been water-borne—in vessels plying the coastal waters of the country or its rivers and lakes. For most of our history, national attention to this type of commerce took the form almost entirely of expenditure for the improvement of rivers and harbors. Over the years billions of dollars have been spent for this purpose, sometimes legitimately and wisely, but often only on the basis of Congressional log-rolling. River and harbor bills have traditionally been a favorite source of Congressional "pork." Only when the railroads began to complain that they suffered unfairly from the competition of unregulated water traffic did the Congress attempt to bring such traffic under control. In the Transportation Act of 1940, Congress prescribed a system of regulation of rates, services, and management of water shipping under the purview of the ICC.[35] The Act of 1940, however, made numerous

---

[34] For more detailed study of the need and prospects for a unified national transportation policy see: National Resources Planning Board, *Transportation and National Policy* (Washington, 1942); Secretary of Commerce, *Issues Involved in a Unified and Coordinated Federal Program for Transportation* (Washington, 1950); Report of the Presidential Advisory Committee on Transport Policy and Organization, *Revision of Transportation Policy* (Washington, 1955).

[35] All commerce on inland waters, as well as all coastwise trade, is, by act of Congress, restricted to American vessels—except in occasional instances where such waters are used by foreign shipping merely in transit between foreign ports. In an effort to stimulate fuller use of facilities on which the nation had spent lavishly, the Inland Waterways Corporation in the Department of Commerce was created, as a fully-owned government corporation, in 1924. It operated a common carrier barge service on the Mississippi, Missouri, and Illinois rivers and along the coast of the Gulf of Mexico until it was sold to a private firm in 1953. Under the government it lost money.

exemptions and perhaps 90 percent of the tonnage of domestic carriers is unregulated.

Shipping engaged in foreign commerce and commerce between the continental United States and the island territories is regulated by a Federal Maritime Board, now located in the Department of Commerce. The Board also works in close association with the Maritime Administration in that department which administers the various programs of governmental subsidy and assistance to the shipping industry engaged in foreign trade.

Meanwhile, however, the jurisdiction of the ICC had been enormously *3. Motor* extended in another direction. The automobile had been introduced, and trucks *transpor-* and buses had come into use. For a good while, distances covered were usually *tation* limited and no regulation was deemed necessary beyond state or local provisions concerning licensing and safety. As truck and bus business developed, however, on something approaching its present huge scale, serious difficulties and abuses arose—cut-throat competition between companies and especially between them and the regulated railroads, underpayment of employees, laxity about accident insurance, dubious financing. Although remedial measures were instituted by some states, it became apparent that the business had so largely assumed an interstate character that, as the Interstate Commerce Commission long urged, the problem was fundamentally one for the national government. In 1935, therefore, Congress passed a Motor Carrier Act,[36] bringing all interstate truck and bus lines within the pale of national law and making the ICC the regulating authority. If it intends to operate across state boundaries, a truck or bus company must initially secure a certificate of convenience and necessity from the Commission. Thereupon, its financing, rates, accounts, records, hours of labor, safety appliances, and general level of service become subject to that body's supervision substantially as in the case of railroads.[37]

It might be supposed that regulations thus applied to trucks and buses would make possible a coordinated policy for land transport within the ICC. However, wholly outside the purview of the Commission is the huge highway program of the national government, laying at public expense the roadbed for the automotive industry and providing a key determinant of costs. Furthermore, a large portion of highway hauling is unregulated, except for safety and labor protection rules, since trucks wholly owned by shippers (private carriers) are exempted. The ICC estimates that its controls reach fewer than 20 percent of the motor carriers.[38]

Shortly after World War I (which imparted a considerable impetus to *4. Avia-* aviation), a standing interstate conference having as its object the promotion *tion* of uniformity in state legislation brought forward a uniform state law for

[36] W. H. Wagner, *A Legislative History of the Motor Carrier Act of 1935* (Washington, 1935).

[37] Excepted from provisions of the law are individually owned motor cars, school and hotel buses, trucks carrying newspapers, those belonging to farmers' co-operative associations, and taxicabs.

[38] ICC *Annual Report, 1956* (Washington, 1957).

aeronautics; and numerous states adopted it. As time went on, however, much, if not most, flying became interstate; and in 1926 Congress passed an Air Commerce Act applying to all interstate aviation and giving a Bureau of Air Commerce in the Department of Commerce power to fix standards of safety, to test and license aviators, and to make rules governing air traffic. This agency has since been superseded. A Civil Aeronautics Act passed in 1938 laid the basis for the present system and a Federal Aviation Act of 1958 reorganized the existing arrangements. At present two main agencies function in this field: a Federal Aviation Agency and a Civil Aeronautics Board. The former concerns itself principally with mapping, lighting, and marking interstate airways, providing regular and emergency landing fields, licensing planes and pilots, operating a national system of air traffic control, administering grants-in-aid for airport construction, devising and administering safety programs, and fostering aviation research. The latter is concerned principally with the regulatory functions of controlling rates and services for the interstate transportation of passengers, mail, and goods, reviewing accident findings and promulgating rules on safety, issuing certificates to airlines, suspending or revoking licenses, and generally controlling the economics of air transport. In a domain in which strict uniformity of rules and practices is peculiarly desirable, the states have in most instances risen to the need by incorporating all national regulations into their own aviation codes. As in the cases of rail, water, and road transportation, the government has participated heavily by expenditures for facilities. Since 1946, appropriations have been made to states and local units for airport and terminal construction. The airlines have also been aided by mail and other subsidies.[39]

5. Pipe-
lines

For a good while, crude oil and various petroleum products have been transported from the great southwestern oil fields to the North and East not only by rail and water but also by pipeline. World War II saw a considerable expansion of this form of interstate commerce. By its nature, natural gas definitely requires this method of transportation; and one of the most extraordinary developments in the transportation field since the recent war has been the multiplication and extension of transmission lines linking gas-producing areas from Kansas to Louisiana with principal cities and many smaller ones throughout more than half of the country. Under appropriate conditions, rates and services are now regulated, with the Interstate Commerce Commission functioning in the case of petroleum and the Federal Power Commission in that of gas.[40]

[39] See E. S. Redford, "A Case Analysis of Congressional Activity: Civil Aviation, 1957-58," Journal of Politics, XX (1960) for a good study of Congressional consideration of the Federal Aviation Act of 1958.

[40] For the past few years there has been a sharp controversy over the power of the Federal Power Commission to regulate the price of gas which enters the pipeline. The Supreme Court has said that the Commission has the power and the Commission has denied it. The Congress has debated the matter fiercely and several bills denying the Commission this power have been considered. A bill was finally passed in 1956 but was

REGULATION OF BUSINESS—COMMUNICATION

As illustrated by motor and air transport and indeed, by the steamship and the railroad, science and technology are responsible for many new modes of transportation, progressively expanding the instrumentalities of "commerce" and augmenting the task of regulation. In the field of communications, even more revolutionary developments have occurred in the techniques of producing and distributing newspapers, the methods of handling the mails, and especially the harnessing of electrical energy. In most European countries, facilities for electrical communication—telegraph, telephone, radio and television—are government-owned and -operated, directly or through auxiliary corporations. Apart from some limited ownership and operation of facilities for its own use by the national government, all of these instrumentalities in the United States, on the other hand, have been developed and, speaking broadly, are owned and operated privately. Since all more important ones necessarily are interstate, and in some instances international, substantially all fall within the range of Congressional control over commerce.

When first developed, intrastate wire communications were regulated, rather ineffectively, by the states, and interstate communications not at all. And this continued to be the situation even after Congress, in 1910, gave the Interstate Commerce Commission jurisdiction over telegraph, telephone, and cable companies operating in interstate and foreign commerce. Preoccupied with railway problems, the Commission paid but little attention to its new task. Partly on this account, and partly because of unsatisfactory experience with the first machinery set up for regulating radio, Congress in 1934 concentrated all responsibility for both wire and wireless communications in a new independent regulatory body, the present Federal Communications Commission (FCC), consisting of seven members appointed by the President and confirmed by the Senate for seven-year terms. Here again the impetus to effective national regulation was the existence in practice of monopolistic conditions. It is neither wise nor practical to have competing telephone or cable systems. Withdrawal of its functions in this field from the ICC marked the only instance in over 60 years of its jurisdiction being narrowed. Over numerous small, local telephone companies and the local and regional services they offer, state utility commissions continue to retain control as to rates and services. The American Telephone and Telegraph Company (actually confined to telephone service save for providing the wire circuits for Western Union), however, now covers the entire country with its facilities. Since the merger of

1. Telegraph, telephone, and cable

---

vetoed by President Eisenhower because of the widely publicized pressures on Congress associated with its passage. After proceeding for several years on a company by company basis, the Commission finally in 1965 established a price on an area basis for gas entering the pipeline.

the Postal Telegraph Company with the Western Union Company in 1943, there are no telegraph competitors of any importance. Therefore, virtually all telegraph and all long-distance telephone services are now under national regulation, as of course, for obvious reasons, are all cable lines. Submarine cables may be licensed only by the President, who also is responsible for seeing that reasonable rates and services are maintained. The FCC controls the actual transmission of messages. The telegraph and telephone lines are "common carriers"; their services must be adequate; their rates must be just and reasonable, authorized by the Commission, publicly advertised, and changed only with notice given the Commission and public; no discriminations may be practiced; new lines may be constructed and existing ones extended only with the Commission's consent; and full reports must be rendered, with access by the Commission to all records and accounts. Decisions, which are numerous, can be appealed to courts.

The basic problem of the telegraph industry is the same as that of the railroads. It is in decline and its functions largely shifted to long-distance telephone, teletype machinery, and air mail. In the telephone industry, a different set of problems plague the regulators. The powers of the FCC do not extend to certain major subsidiaries of the Bell and A. T. and T. systems such as Western Electric from which virtually all equipment was purchased. Most of the rates and services of the system are controlled by state regulatory commissions under various procedures and formulas.

2. Radio   Radio broadcasting had its actual beginning in 1920, and seven years later Congress belatedly recognized a need for regulation. Nature imposed the monopoly here by making it impossible for listeners to hear two broadcasts on the same wavelength. The first act assigned the function to a Federal Radio Commission of five members, and charged it with licensing stations, assigning wavelengths, and exercising other supervision. The arrangement did not work well, and in 1934 the Commission was abolished and its functions vested in the new Federal Communications Commission. Radio and now television broadcasting—on the theory that airwaves may cross state boundaries—has been from the beginning under *exclusive* national control; and, subject to the ultimate authority of Congress, all power over it is in the FCC. The number of channels being limited by nature, the first and largest problem is that of choosing among large numbers of applicants for the privilege of operating a station those persons (citizens only) who shall be given licenses, and deciding what frequencies they shall be assigned. The criterion required by law is "public interest, convenience, and necessity"; which, as in the other regulatory laws, leaves almost complete discretion to the Commission.

Unlike regulation of transportation systems, the regulation of broadcasting has never involved control of rates or profits. Broadcasting companies are not "common carriers" in the eyes of the law and are, therefore, not required to offer services to customers on a carefully regulated basis. Although the major control exercised over them by the FCC stems from the assignment of wavelengths and frequencies, it is by no means confined to this and includes the practices of the broadcasters in what is put out over the air.

From the beginning the task of the FCC has been extremely difficult. What standards should be considered in designating those few among many applicants who are to receive the privilege of operating a lucrative enterprise? Among the distinct interests—those of the manufacturers of receiving sets, those of the operators of broadcasting stations, those of the great networks (three in television and seven in radio), those of the advertisers and their clients, those of the receiving public—which are to be favored and to what extent? Are there other uses of broadcasting facilities than commercial ones —education, for example, that ought to be encouraged and facilitated? Is competition desirable between broadcasters or between broadcasting and other media of communication or is it better to regulate a few large concerns than many small ones? In the interests of decency, political competition, civic education and community morality what control, if any, should be exercised over program content?

In determining policies for the assignment of broadcast channels, the Commission seems to have been guided by: (1) priority—*i.e.,* those already in the business because of their huge investment in facilities are likely to be preferred to newcomers; (2) technical adequacy—*i.e.,* is the quality of the equipment and the engineering personnel such as to justify licensing; (3) financial responsibility—*i.e.,* is there adequate proof of strong backing by the users of time and by the owners of the company; (4) public service—*i.e.,* is the program content merely propaganda or are the listeners assured of reasonably well-rounded programs aimed at popular taste. All of these, however, especially the last one, are difficult to measure and judgments about them differ widely. From the beginning the Commission has been expressly forbidden to exercise censorship but it certainly must interest itself in the character and quality of the programs being offered. Required from the start also, to provide equal time to all candidates for office, it has found it difficult to encourage the use of broadcasting for civic educational purposes. The waiver of this requirement in the Presidential campaign of 1960 remains as yet an exception to the requirement rather than a permanent modification of it.

In view of all the uncertainties of the situation, the deep and abiding differences of view about proper public policy, and the great value of the privilege which the Commission can confer, it is not surprising that the FCC has been caught up in controversy almost from its inception and has suffered through several periods of obloquy. In the most recent of these—1958-1960 —the Commission was investigated by a committee of the House, many questionable practices were revealed and one commissioner was forced out of office. A scandal in network broadcasting also came to light during this period. Quiz shows of various kinds were shown to be "rigged" and record companies were shown to have encouraged the promotion of their records by various broadcasters through gifts of cash and other items of value.[41] Most of these practices were outlawed by the Communications Act Amendments of 1960. The troublesome problem of mixing UHF and VHF television broadcasting facilities in the same community was resolved in 1962 by the requirement that henceforth all TV sets shipped in interstate commerce must be designed to receive both types of channels.

REGULATION OF BUSINESS COMBINATIONS

Corpora-
tions,
trusts, and
holding
companies

Business in this country attained its present immense proportions mainly through the growth of corporations and the pyramiding of such corporations, in turn, into combinations of still greater size and power. Public, or "government," corporations obtain their charters from Congress. Private corporations may do so likewise, but usually get them rather from a state (Delaware being a favorite because of the easy terms permitted), with legal rights ostensibly restricted to the state of incorporation, but in practice extended to other states as well by simple formalities of registration. Their owners are the people who hold shares of stock; capital is obtained also from those who lend them money, receiving certificates of indebtedness in the form of bonds. The officers and directors who operate them are largely immune from personal responsibility, with the organizations, as such, also sustaining only limited liability at law. Eighty years ago, corporations began forming associations or alliances aimed at combinations based upon agreements fixing prices, dividing sales territory, limiting production, and sharing profits. Presently there appeared also trusts, in which stocks of a group of corporate units were gathered largely or wholly into the hands of a single company acting as trustee, with of course control over all of the affiliates. In time, too, arose holding companies, with assets consisting solely of stocks of operating companies whose affairs they controlled, and developed particularly in the field of gas, electric, and other public utilities.[42] And on such a scale did these various developments take place that by 1933 our 100 largest industrial units (corporations, trusts, holding companies, and other combinations), with assets aggregating almost $100 billion controlled not only nearly half of the country's industrial wealth, but one-fifth of the entire national wealth.

The prob-
lem of
monopoly

From such concentration of economic power, evils long ago began to flow—overcapitalization, "watered" stock, and the like, but chiefly monopoly,

[41] For the investigation of the FCC see *Hearings* of the House Committee on Interstate and Foreign Commerce, Subcommittee on Legislative Oversight, 85th Congress, 2nd sess. (1958). See also the summary of recommendations of the committee in *The New York Times,* Feb. 7, 1960, and the text of the report of the Attorney General on deceptive practices in broadcasting in *The New York Times,* Jan. 1, 1960.

[42] The largest earlier holding company organized was, however, the Standard Oil Company, starting as a trust in 1879 but reorganized as a holding company in 1899. The United States Steel Corporation followed shortly (1901).

with its attendant strangulation of smaller competitive enterprises, its complete domination of an economic function or group of functions, its independent and irresponsible control over services and prices. Manifestly, in certain fields monopoly is hardly to be avoided. Speaking generally, it is not practicable for two or three gas or electric companies to operate in the same city; and in such cases public regulation has been widely introduced. From England, however, America inherited a deep seated antipathy to monopoly in general, and the common law as brought across the Atlantic (and still basic to our legal system) made unlawful any monopolistic powers and practices unreasonably obstructing trade—in other words, interfering with the freedom of competing businesses, large and small, to organize and operate on equal terms. And this free scope for individual initiative and enterprise, leaving the way open for failure and disaster, but also for opportunity and achievement, and insuring the consuming public the benefits of quality and price flowing from a competitive quest for markets and profits, has always been highly prized by the American people. By the same token, the protection of this conception—in other words, the curbing of monopolistic abuses—has been, and remains a major public concern.

For more than 100 years, in part because of the limited definition given to commerce by courts and Congress, the states were left to deal with monopolistic and other practices interfering with the free flow of trade. The correctives they brought to bear rested either upon the old common-law principle that all combinations operating to restrain trade *unreasonably* were illegal, or upon statutes defining or modifying that principle's applications. In the era of big business, state regulation proved almost wholly ineffectual. *State regulation proves inadequate*

In 1890, therefore, Congress, taking a novel view of its commerce power risked judicial disapproval by passing a vigorous measure—the Sherman Antitrust Act—aimed at protecting trade and commerce "against unlawful restraints, and monopolies," and to that end declaring in sweeping terms, every contract, combination, or conspiracy in restraint of trade or commerce among the several states or with foreign nations to be illegal, and providing heavy penalties for violations. Congress, however, left enforcement to the Department of Justice, with no special machinery and hardly any funds provided; busy with other things that Department showed little zeal for action. When it did finally bring action against the Sugar Trust in 1895, a Supreme Court decision [43] severely narrowed the scope of the law by ruling that although the defendant produced all but 2 percent of the sugar used in the United States, its business was primarily *manufacturing* rather than *commerce,* and therefore subject to regulation only by the states. For another decade virtually nothing happened—with most of the really huge industrial "trusts" of later days meanwhile getting their start. *National control introduced —the Sherman Act (1890)*

"Trust-busting" was one of President Theodore Roosevelt's prime interests, and successful prosecution in 1904 of a prominent holding company *The "rule of reason"*

[43] United States *v.* E. C. Knight Co., 156 U. S. 1 (1895).

charged with monopoly in the railway field (the Northern Securities Co.[44]) gave him fresh impetus. Notwithstanding government victories in other cases, however, the Supreme Court in 1911 again weakened the law by setting up a distinction between combinations which, in the Court's opinion, involved only a "reasonable," and those which amounted to an "unreasonable," restraint of interstate or foreign trade.[45] The effect was virtually to overrule not only the probable intent of Congress, but earlier decisions in which the Court had held that *all* such combinations in restraint of interstate trade came within the limits of the statute.

Further legislation required

Experience of this sort suggested that if the law applied only to unreasonable combinations, some means should be provided by which well-intentioned combinations might know whether they would be regarded by the government as reasonable, and therefore lawful, without first being subjected to a criminal prosecution to determine the matter. Demand arose, too, for clarification as to the kinds of arrangements that the government would look upon as unreasonable restraints of trade, and as to the corporate practices that it would regard as constituting unfair competitive methods. The outcome was (1) the passage, in 1914, of the Clayton Antitrust Act to reinforce and supplement the Sherman Act of 1890, and (2) the simultaneous creation of the Federal Trade Commission as an agency to cooperate with the Department of Justice in the enforcement of antitrust laws, new and old, and especially to curb unfair competitive practices in the conduct of business.

The Clayton Antitrust Act (1914)

Earnestly sponsored by President Wilson as a "new law" to meet "conditions that menace our civilization," though opposed with equal vigor by business interests, the Clayton Act (1) forbade price-cutting to drive out competitors, granting rebates, making false assertions about competitors, limiting the freedom of purchasers to deal in the products of competing manufacturers, and a long list of other abuses, discriminations, and restraints of trade; (2) forbade corporations to acquire stock in competing concerns, if the effect would be to lessen competition, and outlawed interlocking directorates in the case of larger banks, industrial corporations, and common carriers; (3) made officers of corporations personally liable for violations of the act; (4) made it easier for injured parties in cases arising under either this act or the original antitrust law to prosecute their suits and, (5) declared labor organizations not to be considered as illegal conspiracies in restraint of trade.[46]

---

[44] United States *v.* Northern Securities Co., 193 U. S. 197 (1904).

[45] United States *v.* American Tobacco Co., 221 U. S. 106 and Standard Oil Co. of New Jersey *v.* United States, 221 U. S. 1 (1911).

[46] Labor had been disturbed because in certain antitrust cases, notably the Danbury Hatters case of 1908 (Loewe *v.* Lawlor, 208 U. S. 274) the Supreme Court had taken the position that boycotts instituted by labor unions obstructed the flow of commerce among the states and therefore were under the ban of the Sherman Act. To meet this situation, the Clayton Act specified that nothing in the antitrust laws should "be construed to forbid the existence and operation of labor . . . organizations . . . or to forbid or restrain the individual members of such organizations from carrying out the legitimate objects thereof; nor [should] such organizations, or the members thereof, be

The object of the new legislation of 1914 was to close the gaps in the *A quarter-*
Sherman Act, and President Wilson hailed it as supplying "clear and suffi- *century of*
cient law to check and destroy the noxious growth (of monopoly) in its *irregular*
infancy." Notoriously, however, it proved less effective than had been hoped. *enforce-*
Congress failed to provide adequate funds for properly staffing the antitrust *ment*
division of the Department of Justice, leaving it possible to prosecute only
the most flagrant cases in a few large industries. In interpreting "unfair methods of competition," the courts grew increasingly tolerant. To a deadweight of
opposition from large business interests was added honest doubt of disinterested persons, including some officials, as to whether the entire program was
practicable, or even desirable, and especially as to whether corrective regulation of trusts and other combinations was not preferable to attempts to break
them up completely. Efforts, too, to make directors personally liable for the
acts of corporations almost completely broke down. During World War I, the
entire program was, to all intents and purposes, suspended; through ensuing
Republican administrations, the legislation was seldom invoked. When the
National Recovery Act of 1933 was placed on the statute book in an effort to
rescue the country from a great depression those laws were expressly waived
for as long as the emergency legislation should remain in force. This period
of suspension proved, however, of only two years' duration, and thereupon
the laws came back into at least nominal operation. Presently, too, as the New
Deal administration shifted its economic ground some new vigor was placed
behind their enforcement. In 1938, a former professor of law at Yale University, Thurman W. Arnold, was placed in charge of the antitrust division of the
Department of Justice and forthwith became the most assiduous "trust-buster"
that the country had known, instituting in five years 44 percent of all proceedings started under the antitrust laws between 1890 and his retirement in 1943.
There was, however, some shift from the old idea of trust-busting as an object
in itself to that of defending a free market in the necessities of modern life.
With this broader social end in view, prosecutions were directed primarily
against private groups that had established themselves in strategic positions of
control—against "bottle-necks of business" that blocked the distribution of
products anywhere along the line from the raw-material stage to purchase
by the ultimate consumer. In 1938, also, at President Franklin D. Roosevelt's
instigation, Congress provided for a Temporary National Economic Committee charged with looking deeply into the entire problem of concentration of
wealth and economic control, and the effects of it on American life.

---

held or construed to be illegal combinations or conspiracies in restraint of trade, under
the antitrust laws." Although hailed by the AFL leader Samuel Gompers as "labor's
charter of freedom," this part of the law proved disappointing to organized labor because of the manner in which the courts interpreted and applied it in specific cases, e.g.,
United Mine Workers *v.* Coronado Coal Co., 259 U. S. 344 (1921). Early in 1950,
indeed, a coal-miners' strike inspired introduction in the Senate of a bill (not passed)
making the antitrust laws fully applicable to "the monopoly power of national labor
unions."

The
situation
during
World
War II

World War II broke out in Europe just as the committee was concluding its studies.[47] Soon the United States was involved and once more the anti-monopoly campaign was slowed down. The government sought more benevolent relations with the larger corporations in order to encourage armament production. President Roosevelt announced in 1942 that, while every effort would be made to protect the public interest, with no violation of law escaping ultimate punishment, prosecutions would be postponed whenever it could be shown that they would tend to interfere with production of materials for war use. In the same year, indeed, Congress expressly exempted from prosecution at any time any acts or omissions "deemed in the public interest" and approved by the chairman of the War Production Board after consultation with the attorney general. There was not complete cessation of antitrust activity, for in 1944 the "largest antitrust suit in history" was filed against the Association of American Railroads and various individual railroad companies and investment banking houses, aimed at breaking an alleged rate-making monopoly in the transportation field. In general, however, the war years were a period of slackened effort.

More
recent
develop-
ments

After the war President Truman showed concern, and indeed during the campaign of 1948 made a great deal of political capital out of attacks on "big business," special interests, trusts, and Wall Street. After the election, moreover, Administration forces launched a twofold program, on the one hand a vigorous drive for antitrust law enforcement, and on the other a more cooperative approach aimed at clarifying for business the many ambiguities of existing law and drawing sharper lines between what the government considered legal and what illegal combinations and practices. The period from 1948-1952 was another period of vigorous enforcement. In 1950, the Antitrust Division of the Attorney General's Office received the largest appropriation in its history, $3,800,000. In 1950, also the Clayton Act was amended (Antimerger Act of 1950) to prohibit not only the acquisition of stock of a competing corporation but also of its assets where competition was lessened by such action.[48] Suits were started or activated against some of the largest enter-

[47] *Final Report and Recommendations of the Temporary National Economic Committee,* 77th Cong., 1st Sess., Sen. Doc. No. 35 (Washington, 1941). A full analysis of the testimony presented before the committee will be found in D. Lynch, *The Concentration of Economic Power* (New York, 1946). More recent information on the same general subject is contained in a report of the Federal Trade Commission, "The Present Trends of Corporate Mergers and Acquisitions," 80th Cong., 1st Sess., Sen. Doc. No. 17 (1947).

[48] On the other hand, the Congress in 1952 moved in a different direction when it strengthened a law of 1937 exempting "fair-trade" price agreements between manufacturers and retailers from the antitrust laws. The act of 1952 legalized such agreements and authorized states with fair-trade laws to make price agreements binding even on nonsigners. The action followed a Supreme Court decision [Schwegmann Bros. *v.* Calvert Distillers Corp., 341 U. S. 384 (1951)] which had weakened most state laws and had resulted in an epidemic of price "wars" among New York merchants. A later decision of the Court, however, Eli Lilly & Co. *v.* Sav-On-Drugs Inc., 366 U. S. 276 (1961) further weakened state laws on the subject. Furthermore such laws have been held unconstitutional in whole or in part in 24 states. Presidents Kennedy and Johnson announced their opposition to proposals to strengthen further the national law.

prises in the nation: the "Big Four" meat packers (Swift, Armour, Wilson, and Cudahy), du Pont, American Telephone and Telegraph, the A & P grocery chain, Aluminum Company of America, the leading motion picture distributors, the three large farm machinery manufacturers (International Harvester, Deere, and Case), and many others. The Supreme Court, meanwhile, enunciated interpretations more friendly to the antimonopolists. It reversed an earlier position taken in the case of the U. S. Steel Corporation,[49] and held in the case of the Aluminum Company [50] that size alone could be objectionable. In the American Tobacco Company case,[51] the Court held that the power to raise prices or to exclude competition is an abuse whether these things have been done or not.

The Eisenhower administration from 1952-1960 abated, somewhat, the aggressiveness of the campaign against monopoly. Attorney General Brownell announced his policy as primarily one of promoting competition rather than attacking bigness and stated that criminal prosecution would rarely be used. A large number of new suits were, nevertheless, started and numerous pending cases were terminated by agreement. The major emphasis seemed to be to halt mergers rather than attack existing combinations. The Kennedy approach was to concentrate on fewer suits but to select those of economic significance and strong efforts were especially made in cases of alleged price fixing.

The results of the activities of the past two decades are mixed. The Aluminum Company was ordered to divest itself of its Canadian properties. The A & P Company was fined $175,000 and ordered to divest itself of a subsidiary wholesale operation, the Atlantic Commission Company. It successfully resisted efforts to break it up into seven retail divisions. The du Pont case, dismissed by the district court after months of argument, was carried to the Supreme Court by the government and the company was ordered to divest itself of its stock in the General Motors Corp. This position was reaffirmed vigorously after the government again appealed a district court order calling only for limited divestiture.[52] The case against A. T. and T. was settled by consent decree before adjudication was complete and while the company was ordered to license a large number of its patents free to all applicants and others for a reasonable charge, it was not required to divest itself of Western Electric, its chief supplier of telephone equipment. International Business Machines agreed by a similar procedure to offer for sale as well as rental its tabulating and computing machines and to license a number of its patents free or on a "reasonable" royalty basis. A proposed merger of Youngstown Sheet and Tube Company with the Bethlehem Steel Company was halted by injunction requested by the government in 1958. Perhaps the most damaging attacks

[49] 251 U. S. 417 (1920).
[50] 322 U. S. 716 (1945).
[51] 328 U. S. 781 (1946).
[52] See United States v. E. I. DuPont Co., 353 U. S. 586 (1957) and United States v. E. I. du Pont Co. (1961).

were those against the largest manufacturers in the electrical industry including Westinghouse and General Electric. Charged in late 1960 with a price-fixing conspiracy on heavy electrical equipment, the major defendants pleaded guilty and several officials were actually sent to jail.[53] The acquisition of the Rome Cable Company by Aluminum Company of America was nullified by the Supreme Court in 1964.[54] Price-fixing suits were also entered against the major steel companies and several drug firms in 1963 and against the major flour mill companies in 1964. The Supreme Court broadened further the antitrust powers of the government by vetoing the proposed purchase by a leading manufacturer of metal containers of a leading manufacturer of glass containers on the grounds that the competition to be preserved is that in the whole market.[55]

A continuing dilemma   Over a 75-year stretch, frontal attack on monopoly through the Department of Justice has yielded mixed and not highly impressive results. A limited number of large concerns, for example, the Standard Oil Company and the American Tobacco Company, have been broken up; others have been brought to book and penalized; many minor punishments have been inflicted along the way. Large obstacles, however, remain, and by their nature can never be wholly overcome. Among them is the dependence of the laws for vigorous enforcement upon the economic predispositions, and personal inclinations of successive Presidents, attorneys general, and other high officials concerned. A second impediment is recurring uncertainties, despite all the legislation and court decisions, as to what, in many situations, actually constitutes "unfair competition," "unreasonable" restraint of trade, and the like. A third is the sometimes wavering support given by the courts. A fourth is the processes used —the criminal provisions have not always been effectual. And the most obstructive of all is divided opinion, with resultant hesitation, springing from the circumstance that large-scale production and merchandising, requiring large-scale organization, make for economies, and therefore often for more and cheaper goods and services for the consuming public. Big business it is argued is performing economic miracles for our society and now is acting more and more from a sense of social responsibility.[56] It is also argued that bigness in industry is offset and held in check by bigness in labor organizations and bigness in government.[57] There is, furthermore, some evidence that the era of concentration of corporate power may be passing. There has been a rapid increase in the number of firms during the postwar years and the huge corporations are not expanding as rapidly as the smaller ones.[58] On the other hand,

---

[53] See J. Jerling, *The Great Price Conspiracy* (Washington, 1962).

[54] U. S. *v.* Aluminum Co. of America, 377 U. S. 271.

[55] U. S. *v.* Continental Can Co., 378 U. S. 441 (1964).

[56] See D. E. Lilienthal, *Big Business; A New Era* (New York, 1953).

[57] See J. K. Galbraith, *American Capitalism: the Concept of Countervailing Power* (New York, 1952).

[58] See J. F. Watson, *The Role of Mergers in the Growth of Large Firms* (Berkeley, Calif., 1953) and A. D. H. Kaplan, *Small Business; Its Role and Its Problems*, Brookings Institution (Washington, 1953). Recent studies of our antitrust policies in-

there have been many mergers in the postwar period. A number of our larger industries are dominated by three or four huge firms rather than one and operate under what has been called administered rather than competitive prices. They compete on many levels, but not in pricing.

THE FEDERAL TRADE COMMISSION AND POLICING BUSINESS PRACTICES

The Sherman Act, as we have observed, depends for enforcement almost entirely upon the antitrust division of the Department of Justice. The Clayton and Federal Trade Commission Acts of 1914 directed at dishonest and unfair, as well as monopolistic, business practices provided a new independent establishment in the form of the Federal Trade Commission, consisting of five members appointed by the President and confirmed by the Senate for seven-year terms with not more than three drawn from any one party. No clear jurisdictional line between the two enforcing agencies was established at first; both were intended to curb the formation of trusts and the growth of monopolies. The entire development of the Federal Trade Commission, however, has been rather in the direction of defining fair and prosecuting unfair trade practices of whatever business organizations and establishments happened to exist at any given time. In other words the Commission has sought to maintain "fair" competition rather than to attack monopolies. In pursuance of this purpose it enforces not only the Acts of 1914 as amended but also: (1) the Anti-discrimination (Robinson-Patman) Act of 1938, designed to clarify price-discrimination provisions of the Clayton Act, and aimed at preventing sellers from arbitrarily giving advantages to some buyers as against others through disguises such as advertising allowances and brokerage fees;[59] (2) a Truth-in-Advertising (Wheeler-Lea) Act of 1938, applying especially to the food, drug, and cosmetics businesses; (3) a Wool Products Labeling Act of 1940, which seeks to protect producers, manufacturers, and consumers against the

1. Functions

---

clude: S. M. Whitney, *Antitrust Policies: American Experience in Twenty Industries* (New York, 1958); A. G. Papandreou and J. T. Wheeler, *Competition and its Regulation* (New York, 1954); W. Adams and H. M. Gray, *Monopoly in America; the Government as Promoter* (New York, 1955); E. S. Mason, *Economic Concentration and the Monopoly Problem* (Cambridge, Mass., 1957); G. C. Means, *Pricing Power and the Public Interest; A Study Based on Steel* (New York, 1962).

[59] Under this measure, it is unlawful for any person or firm engaged in interstate commerce "to discriminate in price between different purchasers of commodities of like grade and quality, where such commodities are sold for use, consumption, or resale . . . and where the effect of such discrimination may be substantially to lessen competition, or tends to create a monopoly in any line of commerce." The measure was both defended and opposed in Congress as a means of protecting "independent" merchants against the competition of chain stores, and often is referred to as the "Chain-Store Act." See W. Patman, *The Robinson-Patman Act* (New York, 1938); B. Werne [ed.] *Business and the Robinson-Patman Law* (New York, 1938); and G. H. Montague, *The Robinson-Patman Act and Its Administration* (Chicago, 1945). See also, C. D. Edwards, *The Price Discrimination Law: A Review of Experience* (Washington, 1959).

presence of unrevealed substitutes and mixtures in wool products; (4) the Export Trade (Webb-Pomerene) Act of 1918, amending the Clayton Act by permitting exporters to form and operate associations more or less in the nature of cartels (which otherwise would be illegal), so long as approved by the Commission as not "substantially" lessening competition in the domestic market; (5) the Fur Products Labeling Act of 1951 which seeks to protect consumers and manufacturers against misleading labeling of furs and fur products; and, (6) the Textile Fiber Products Identification Act of 1958 which seeks to protect consumers against mislabeling of various yarns and cloths.

2. Activities

In pursuance of its many duties, the Commission: (1) enforces the laws against unfair competitive practices on the part of corporate and other businesses participating in interstate commerce (except banks, common carriers, broadcasting companies, and other enterprises regulated through different channels); (2) works out lists of unfair practices and holds conferences in which representatives of industry are encouraged to agree to avoid such practices (although the line between lawful and unlawful agreements is not always easy to fix); (3) issues "cease-and-desist" orders when violations of law are discovered and the violators are not disposed to desist of their own accord; (4) requires corporations to submit reports covering aspects of their business on which the Commission desires information; (5) advises with corporations on organizational and other matters with a view to helping them avoid running afoul of the law; (6) guards against unlawful acquisitions of stock by corporations and against prohibited interlocking directorates; (7) investigates trade conditions and practices in and with foreign countries where combinations or practices may affect the foreign commerce of the United States; and (8) recommends to Congress new legislation calculated to uphold the principle of fair competition in the interest of both business itself and the public.

3. Procedures

In enforcing the laws against unfair and fraudulent practices, the Commission may act in response to a complaint received, or by direction of the President or of Congress, or at the suggestion or request of the attorney general.[60] As a rule, however, action starts with a complaint lodged by some individual, group, firm, or corporation having a grievance against a specified business concern because of some practice which it is alleged to be pursuing. Hundreds of such complaints are filed every year. If, upon preliminary investigation, the Commission finds a complaint groundless or trivial, or relating to something over which the Commission has no jurisdiction, or not affecting the public interest (mere private controversies have no status under the law), nothing happens. If, however, the protest is believed to have merit, the offender is called upon to explain—often with the result (since 1925) that all parties consent amicably to a "stipulation," or agreement, that the practice complained of shall be abandoned. If, finally, the concern under attack is not

---

[60] Attorney General Kennedy invoked a long-neglected provision of the FTC act by requesting the Commission, in 1961, to check up on the way a number of antitrust decrees are being carried out.

prepared to yield so readily, and if after hearings the Commission finds it clearly in the wrong, a cease-and-desist order will command the offender to discontinue the objectionable practice or practices within 60 days. If there is failure to comply, the Commission may ask the appropriate court of appeals to affirm its order, which, if done, subjects the offender, in case of continued disobedience, to action for contempt of court.[61]

The Commission has a mixed record of achievement. Some of its diffi- *4. Diffi-* culties grow out of the obscurities of the law. It has not always had adequate *culties en-* financial support from Congress; its members have been shifted rapidly, and *countered* often have been selected primarily on political grounds. Although supposed, too, to be final judge of the facts in a case, it frequently has found the courts insisting upon making their own inquiries, and many times has seen its cease-and-desist orders overthrown. Further, the cease-and-desist system, dependent as it is upon protracted litigation for its enforcement, is greatly weakened by long delays between issuance and final determination. The process was speeded somewhat by an Act of 1958 aimed at expediting court consideration. President Kennedy in 1961 urged additional legislation aimed at the same problem. While it has played an insignificant part in curbing monopoly, by preventing misleading advertising, deception, fraud, and misrepresentation, and by otherwise policing the business world, the Commission has done much to raise the standards of American business.[62]

REGULATION OF FINANCIAL INSTITUTIONS

Because of its responsibility for the monetary system and because the *1. Bank-* credit structure of the economy is so intimately tied to the system of banking, *ing* the national government has long evinced great interest and exercised special authority in this field. Under the leadership of the Federalists and over the strenuous objections of the Jeffersonians, the government first chartered a Bank of the United States to serve as the principal fiscal agent of the government and as the main regulator of private financial institutions. The Supreme Court in the celebrated case of McCulloch v. Maryland (1819) triumphantly affirmed the Federalist position and a government bank served the nation until

[61] This mode of enforcement applies to cases arising under the Clayton Act, as a majority do. For those arising under the Federal Trade Commission Act, there is a slightly different procedure involving fines for noncompliance.

[62] E. P. Herring, "Politics, Personalities, and the Federal Trade Commission," *Amer. Polit. Sci. Rev.,* XXVIII, 1016-1029 (Dec., 1934), and XXIX, 21-35 (Feb., 1935), is an illuminating analysis of the "atmosphere" in which the Commission carries on its work. Cf. the same author's *Federal Commissioners; A Study of Their Careers and Qualifications* (Cambridge, Mass., 1936). An excellent account of the Commission's tasks, methods, problems, and shortcomings will be found in M. Fainsod, L. Gordon, and J. C. Palamountain, Jr., *Government and the American Economy* (3rd ed., New York, 1959), Chap. XVI.

The Hoover Commission was critical of the operation of the Commission. See its *Task Force Report on Regulatory Commissions* (Washington, 1949), 119-125.

1836. When Andrew Jackson finally strangled this "monster," as he called it, the control of banking devolved entirely on the states. The chaotic situation which resulted with "wild cat" banks, unsupported currency, special charters, and many other abuses was not brought under control until 1863. The necessities of Civil War finance stimulated the Congress to find a better method of controlling currency and also of marketing its bonds. The result was a system of national banks and a confiscatory tax on state bank notes.

National banks

Under the national banking system, privately owned banking firms could be chartered as national banks with the right to issue paper money and with the obligation to accept national regulation of their fiscal practices including audit of their accounts. State banks continued to exist, as they do today, but most of the large firms became and have remained national banks and are closely supervised by the comptroller of the currency in the Treasury Department.

The federal reserve system:

Originally, national banks were entirely separate establishments, with no more means of coming to one another's relief in time of stress than railroads or merchandising enterprises. From the ups and downs of business during recurring cycles of prosperity and depression flowed embarrassments and failures which often might have been mitigated. To remedy this situation by linking up all national banks in an integrated series and imparting greater elasticity to their operations, Congress in 1913 created an independent establishment known as the Federal Reserve System which ever since has been a principal feature of our national banking arrangements.

a. Organization

First of all, the country is divided into 12 Federal Reserve districts, in each of which is located a Federal Reserve bank, usually in the district's principal city.[63] In each case, all or nearly all stock is subscribed by the member banks within the district, and control is vested in a board of nine directors, three named by the general management of the reserve system in Washington, six by the member banks.[64] The general management referred to consists of a board of governors (the Federal Reserve Board) of seven members appointed for 14-year terms by the President and confirmed by the Senate, with due regard for both geographical distribution and representation of financial, agricultural, industrial, and commercial interests. This board, endowed with broad supervisory and regulatory powers, bears full responsibility for formulating monetary policies and exercising general direction of the system. All national banks must belong to and hold stock in the Federal Reserve bank of their dis-

[63] The federal reserve cities—well distributed for business purposes—are Boston, New York, Philadelphia, Richmond, Atlanta, Cleveland, Chicago, St. Louis, Minneapolis, Kansas City, Dallas, and San Francisco.

[64] Of the six directors chosen locally, three directly represent the member banks, but the others must be nonbankers and actively engaged in commerce, agriculture, or industry. The chief executive of each district bank—known as the president (formerly the governor)—is chosen by the board of directors for a five-year term, is eligibile for reappointment, and must be approved by the central board of governors.

trict; state banks may do so if they meet the requirements and find membership to their advantage—as most of them do.

The Federal Reserve banks—often referred to as "bankers' banks"—do not carry on a general banking business with individuals and corporations, but instead perform services, directly at least, only for the national government and for the member banks of their respective districts. Services to the government are many and various. Proceeds of revenue collections are deposited with them, and in general they have custody of government funds which in earlier days were left idle in subtreasuries; they make transfers of such funds according to instructions; and they serve as fiscal agents in selling securities and paying government checks and coupons. For member banks, they act as clearing houses for the handling of checks and other financial instruments, serve as depositories for surplus funds, and, more important, provide rediscounting facilities enabling the needs of customers to be met and a greater volume of business to be done. *b. Workings*

What happens in this latter connection can be explained briefly. A national or state bank loans money to individuals and corporations, taking the borrowers' notes—"discounting" them, as the phrase goes. If demand is heavy, the bank may reach a point where it has no more money at its disposal; and in the old days that would end matters—the bank would simply have to refuse further applicants. Nowadays, however, what a bank in this situation almost invariably does is to transmit at least a substantial part of its accumulated "commercial paper" (which may include mortgages and various forms of collateral) to the Federal Reserve bank to which it belongs and get it "rediscounted," that is, borrow money on it just as the original borrower did; and with this money it can make new loans and of course earn new profits. But this is not all. On the basis of the commercial paper thus pouring in with also backing of gold certificates based on the government's stock of gold, the Reserve bank can issue paper money with which to perform its rediscounting operations (the national banks themselves no longer can do this). In this way arise the Federal Reserve notes which, as we have seen, constitute by far the largest part of the paper currency circulating in the country today.

One of the ways in which the Federal Reserve Board seeks to stabilize the credit structure of the country and control cyclical tendencies to alternating prosperity and depression is by expanding or contracting the credit facilities of commercial banks by lowering or raising the rediscount rate. A lower rate will give the commercial banks easier access to funds and encourage them to help business by lending at moderate interest rates, a higher rate of course, for example that ordered in 1965, having the opposite effect. Stabilization is sought also through the open-market buying and selling of commercial paper and of government bonds and other securities by the reserve banks— large purchases of commercial paper naturally having the effect of supplying member banks with more free funds and, in the case of government bonds, strengthening the market and keeping up prices—both of which may prove *c. Stabilization of the credit structure* desirable in depression-time. The Board also determines the reserves required by banks against their deposits and by raising or lowering these amounts can influence the interest rate and the amount of credit available.

The banking crisis of 1933 and some remedial measures

As set up under the legislation of 1913, the Federal Reserve System served useful purposes and indeed seemed to have solved our major banking problems. Certainly it helped greatly to carry the country through the expansion and later contraction of its economy incident to World War I. In the "roaring twenties," with their gross overextension of credit, however, it failed to furnish a sufficient brake. After the stock-market crash of 1929, our banks proved unable to weather the storm in any such fashion as did those of Great Britain, Canada, and some other countries. It became necessary for President Roosevelt, immediately upon taking office in 1933, to bring into play a half-forgotten wartime grant of Presidential power and temporarily close every bank in the land. A stop-gap Emergency Banking Act was rushed through Congress liberalizing the conditions under which Reserve banks might issue notes, and applying other remedies. In a short time banks able to demonstrate their soundness were permitted to reopen, with others—provided with additional capital by the Reconstruction Finance Corporation—eventually reopening also. The experience however, was harrowing, and it is small wonder that a good deal of remedial banking legislation of permanent character (too complicated and technical to be reviewed here) was enacted in the next two years. In a Banking Act of 1935 the Federal Reserve System was given its first systematic overhauling and placed in the general situation already described. Speculative temptations to which large numbers of banks had succumbed in the past were at least partially removed by requiring that thenceforth banking establishments should not engage in both commercial, that is, general, banking and "investment" banking. If they insisted upon continuing the latter, they had to give up the former. In the hope that if depositors could be assured that their money would be safe in banks, they would be willing to leave it there, thus averting bank "runs" and resulting bank closings, a plan of governmental guaranty of bank deposits was introduced, temporarily in 1933 and permanently in 1935. Deposits in all banks included within the Federal Reserve System, nationally authorized trust companies, and all nonmember state banks applying and meeting certain specifications—in all, some 13,400 institutions—are now insured through a Federal Deposit Insurance Corporation (an independent establishment which the Hoover Commission recommended transferring to the Treasury Department) with a maximum protection of $10,000 on each separate deposit. The insurance, of course, is purchased by the participants by premiums paid on their deposits.

In the recent recessions of 1957-1958 and 1960-1961 the Federal Reserve System has played an important and much-debated role. Under the Eisenhower administration, the Board on several occasions acted to tighten credit in order to halt inflation—as it did again in 1965—and was vigorously urged to ease it to combat the fall-off in business activities and the spread of unemployment in 1958 and in 1960. The Board, on occasion under Truman and later, came into conflict with the Treasury Department over the question of the influence of its decisions on the interest rate and marketability of government bonds. Widespread disagreement still exists over the proper role of the Board and the proper policies for combatting inflation or recession.[65] President Johnson disagreed with the interest-raise policy of 1965.

The stock-market crash of 1929 which signaled the beginning of the depression led not only to an overhauling of the government's system of controlling banking. It stimulated national concern with abuses in the management of stock exchanges and in the sale of stocks and bonds. State action having been tried for a generation in the form of "blue-sky laws" regulating securities vendors was found inadequate to the task of protecting the interest of the millions of shareholders. Congress under the spur of President Roosevelt assumed regulatory authority in this field with the passage of a Securities Act in 1933 and a Securities Exchange Act in 1934. *2. Securities*

The primary purpose of these two interlocked pieces of legislation is to protect investors against every sort of fraudulent practice in the issuing and handling of securities offered for sale in interstate commerce. To this end, the act of 1933 requires all issues of stocks, bonds, or other securities (with certain exceptions indicated below), if to be offered in interstate commerce or by mail, to be registered with (originally the Federal Trade Commission) the Securities and Exchange Commission (SEC) set up in 1934.[66] Every such registration must be accompanied by a "registration statement" containing full financial and other information, and also by the "prospectus" intended to be used in soliciting purchases by the public, and containing all information which an investor ought to have when making a decision. Selling or offering to sell to the public in interstate commerce or through the mails any security not properly registered with the Commission is made a penal offense. Not only so, but heavy civil liability is laid upon any corporation, including its directors and principal financial officers, for any untrue or only partly true declaration of a material fact in a registration statement or prospectus. It is not the business of the Commission, any more than that of a state securities commissioner, to pass *The Securities Act of 1933*

[65] A good recent discussion of some of these issues will be found in the report of the Commission on Money and Credit, *Money and Credit; Their Influence on Jobs, Prices, and Growth,* Committee on Economic Development, printed in *The New York Times,* June 25, 1961.

[66] This Commission consists of five members appointed by the President and confirmed by the Senate for staggered five-year terms, and operates through three divisions, or branches, with regional offices in about a dozen principal cities. Excepted from the provisions of the act are securities issued by the national, state, and local governments, by national and state banks, by religious, educational, and other corporations not organized for profit, by raliroads and other common carriers, and by building and loan associations. The constitutionality of the Securities Act was upheld by the Supreme Court in Electric Bond and Share Co. *v.* Sec. and Exch. Commission, 303 U. S. 419 (1938). It may be added that the states continue to maintain regulatory agencies in this field, but usually focus their attention upon issues of less than $100,000—the level at which national regulation begins.

upon the inherent value of securities issued or upon the outlook for prosperity of the corporation issuing them. No action by the Commission is to be construed as a recommendation of any security to potential purchasers. The agency's only function, up to this point, is to see that complete information concerning a security is made available to the public, that this information is accurate, and that no fraud is practiced in connection with sales.

3. The Securities Exchange Act of 1934

To aid in promoting this general end, the Securities and Exchange Act of 1934 went an important step farther. A large proportion—doubtless the major part—of the securities registered with the Commission are bought and sold on stock exchanges found in 20 or more of our principal cities, the largest and best known being that in New York. Formerly, however, transactions in securities in these markets were subject to little regulation beyond the few restrictions which the exchanges themselves saw fit to impose upon their members. These provided little protection for the investing public. All manner of unsavory and dishonest practices grew up—"wash sales," matched orders, "rigging the market," "jiggles," pools, and other manipulations—by which prices were pushed up or forced down for the benefit of insiders, while innocent investors were fleeced. Speculation "on margin," too,—that is, paying only a certain percentage in cash for what is bought—reached scandalous proportions, notably in the frenzied market operations shortly preceding the crash of 1929, and threatened to precipitate the entire national credit structure into chaos.

To remedy this situation, the transactions of all exchanges engaged in interstate commerce (as every one is) are declared by the act of 1934 to be "affected with a national public interest" which makes it necessary to provide for their regulation and control "in order to protect interstate commerce, the national credit, the national taxing power, to make more effective the national banking system and the federal reserve system, and to insure the maintenance of fair and honest markets in such transactions." Annual and other reports are required to be filed with the exchanges and the Commission by all corporations or companies having securities listed, and any deviations from material fact constitute grounds for suspending or withdrawing a given security from trading. Various provisions outlaw objectionable practices of the past, and, all in all, the measure seeks to make the exchanges fair and open market-places for investors rather than mere rendezvous for conspiring speculators. One will not be so naive as to suppose that all stock-market operations have since been, or will in future be, beyond reproach.[67]

[67] The powers of the Securities and Exchange Commission have been enlarged by successive acts of Congress, until it now (1965) administers four important statutes in addition to the two hitherto mentioned: the Public Utility Holding Company Act of 1935, the Trust Indenture Act of 1939, the Investment Company Act of 1940, and the Investment Advisers Act of 1940; and persons dissatisfied with its decisions under any of these measures have recourse to an appropriate court. In addition, the Commission advises district courts under the bankruptcy laws in connection with reorganization proceedings for debtor corporations.

A major review of the effectiveness of the regulating procedures govern- *Review*
ing the securities market was completed by a special study group of the SEC, *of the*
in 1963 and a number of technical changes in the law were enacted in 1964 *program*
as a result of the shortcomings revealed by the study. Most of the changes
tightened extant procedures by closing loopholes that had been found. The
authority of the SEC was extended to certain persons, institutions, and securities not previously covered and the "self-regulating" programs of the exchange
managements were expanded.[68]

In the depression years particular attention was invited to the question- *4. Public*
able character of certain corporations whose major function was to own the *utility*
stock of operating utilities. The towering structure of the Insull empire, which *holding*
pyramided these holding companies on top of each other until it had gained *companies*
control over a major sector of the gas, light, and water supply businesses of
the Midwest, came crashing down in the depression spreading injury to many
innocent persons. The securities regulations did not quite get to the heart of
this related problem. Congress, therefore, attempted to regulate these holding
corporations. It passed in 1935 a Public Utility Holding Company Act giving
the Securities and Exchange Commission jurisdiction over all holding companies concerned with the production of gas or electricity and either participating in interstate commerce or making use of the United States mails.
Regulation of rates, services, and general business practices of such companies
was vested in the same act in a Federal Power Commission already in existence since 1920. The same agency has control over security issues, mergers,
and sales of property by *operating* gas and electric companies engaged in inter-
stae commerce. But, aside from rates and services, practically all aspects of
gas and electric *holding* companies fall under Securities and Exchange Commission regulation. Every such company (unless holding less than 10 percent
of the stock of any subsidiary) must register with the Commission, file full
information concerning itself and its subsidiaries, and receive Commission approval, without which it has not even any right to exist. The issuance and sale
of such companies' securities, and all proposals for mergers and sales, must
likewise have Commission endorsement. Loans of operating companies to
holding companies are forbidden as also are the payment of "excessive" divi-
dends. All accounts must be supervised by the SEC and full financial reports
made to it. Corporate members of holding companies may make no political
contributions and if engaging in lobbying must report on all such activities.

DIRECT PARTICIPATION IN BUSINESS

Although no government in this country, whether national, state, or local, *Various*
has entered the field of business like some governments abroad, most people *forms*
would be surprised by a full account of how far our various governments *taken*

[68] For texts of the major studies see *The New York Times,* April 4, 1963, July 18,
1963, and August 9, 1963.

nevertheless have gone. More or less incidental to its strictly governmental functions, every one of the states not only buys supplies but sells products; a state university, for example, marketing livestock and foodstuffs produced on the experimental farms of its agricultural college is as truly engaged in business as any private purveyor of such commodities. Numerous municipalities, too, own and operate waterworks, electric-light plants, gas works, street railway or bus lines, airports, bridges, tunnels, and other utilities. From the earliest days, the national government also has been in business. A survey in 1949 revealed that it owned or was financially interested in no fewer than 100 important business enterprises, representing a direct investment of more than $20 billion.[69] The forms taken are various, and only a few can be mentioned here. (1) To begin with, through General Services Administration (created in 1949 and superseding a former Bureau of Federal Supply in the Treasury Department), the government purchases general supplies in almost incredible quantities, and through the Commodity Credit Corporation in the Department of Agriculture huge stocks of farm products in connection with the price-support program. (2) It also sells, e.g., electric power, fertilizers, farm products, and since 1945 industrial plants and great quantities of supplies representing surpluses left over from war. (3) It manufactures munitions, currency, fertilizers, and many other things, constructs ships, erects buildings, and operates the largest printing establishment in the world. (4) It owns and operates the Alaska Railroad and the Panama Canal. (5) On the list, too, are the largest hydroelectric enterprises in the country—Boulder Canyon (Hoover Dam), the Columbia River Power System (Bonneville Dam, Grand Coulee Dam), and the Tennessee Valley Authority, besides many lesser ones. (6) More than 30 different national establishments are engaged in lending, guaranteeing, or insuring money in fields as diverse as agriculture, banking, housing, veterans' aid, Indian affairs, and public health, not to mention the huge items of foreign loans. (7) In the postal system, taken over in 1789 from the old Confederation, and therefore representing the earliest venture in the field, the government today operates one of the largest business enterprises known. Some of these steadily multiplying undertakings are carried on directly by regular departments (like the Post Office), by branches thereof (like the Bureau of the Mint in the Treasury Department), or by independent establishments (like the Export-Import Bank of Washington). An increasing proportion are managed by government-owned corporations.[70]

[69] (Hoover) Commission on the Organization of the Executive Branch of the Government, *Federal Business Enterprises* (Washington, 1949), 1. The second Hoover Commission in 1955 found more than 1000 additional government business enterprises. Commission on the Organization of the Executive Branch of the Government, *Business Enterprises* (Washington, 1955).

[70] During World War I, the national government took over temporarily the management of all railroads and telegraph and telephone systems, and at various times during World War II coal mines and even certain mercantile establishments. Coal mines have been taken over also (as in 1946) during peacetime strikes.

One national monopoly is the postal service, about which a word may be added. So intimate is the connection between the postal service and commerce that, had the Constitution been entirely silent on postal matters, Congress easily might have established a postal system under powers implied in the commerce clause. One finds, however, in the list of powers expressly conferred that of establishing "postoffices and postroads." The only serious constitutional issue which has ever arisen in connection with the subject has been that of whether, as strict constructionists for a good while contended, the power conferred extended only to designating which of existing routes should be used for transmission of the mails, or whether, as broad constructionists argue, it included the right to build and operate roads especially designed for the purpose. As has usually happened, the more liberal interpretation prevailed; and in later decades the improvement of the postal service has repeatedly been employed as a justification for national aid to highway construction and development of airlines, even within individual states. The postal power belongs exclusively to Congress, and the postal service that has arisen under it is, in the strictest sense, a government monopoly. *The postal service: 1. Constitutional basis*

Anyone desiring to convey some impression of the amazing development of the United States in the past 180 years could hardly do so more effectively than in terms of the growth of the postal system. He could cite the 33,600 post offices and 31,000 rural delivery routes in operation in 1965; the receipts of $4.5 billion in the same year, compared with $280,000 in 1800; and the more than 71 billion pieces of mail of all kinds handled. But even more striking would be the panorama of expanding functions and activities which have made the Post Office an agency close to the great mass of the people. High points in the exhibit would be the introduction of the registration system in 1855, the beginning of urban free delivery in 1863, the establishment of the money-order system in 1864, the starting of "special delivery" service in 1885, the initiation of rural free delivery in 1896, the introduction of the postal-savings system in 1911, the starting of the parcel-post system in 1913, and the launching of air-mail service (operated largely under contracts with private aviation companies) in 1918. Traditionally, one of the strongest arguments made by the opponents of governmental business enterprises has been the fact that the service has paid its way in only some 17 years out of the last 100. There are many contributing factors to this situation; the basic one is that although it is conducted as a business, the people to whom it ministers (including those in rural areas where costs necessarily exceed returns) and those who conduct their business by mail (publishers of periodicals, direct-mail advertisers, book publishers), demand facilities which cannot be supplied on the simple dollars-and-cents, income-outgo, pattern of a chain store or a motor plant and their wants are reflected in Congressional control of post-office finances. *2. Growth and functions*

References

1. GENERAL

M. E. Dimock, *Business and Government* (New York, 1953), Chaps. I-VIII, XVI-XXVI.

M. Fainsod, L. Gordon, and J. L. Palamountain, Jr., *Government and the American Economy* (3rd ed., New York, 1959), Chaps. I-V, IX-XX, XXI, XXIV, XXVI.

V. A. Mund, *Government and Business* (New York, 1950), Chaps. VI-XX.

F. P. Hall, *Government and Business* (3rd ed., New York, 1949), Chaps. VI-X, XVII-XXVII.

J. T. Adams, *Big Business in a Democracy* (New York, 1945).

T. C. Blaisdell, Jr., *Economic Power and Political Pressures,* Temporary Nat. Econ. Committee, Monograph No. 26 (Washington, 1941).

————, *American Democracy Under Pressure* (New York, 1957).

National Resources Committee, *The Structure of the American Economy* (Washington, 1939).

L. S. Lyon, M. W. Watkins, V. Abramson, *et al., Government and Economic Life; Development and Current Issues of American Public Policy,* 2 vols. (Washington, 1939, 1940).

T. W. Arnold, *Democracy and Free Enterprise* (Norman, Okla., 1942).

C. Wilcox, *Public Policies Toward Business* (Chicago, 1955).

M. Anshen and F. Wormuth, *Private Enterprise and Public Policy* (New York, 1954).

A. A. Berle, Jr., *The Twentieth Century Capitalist Revolution* (New York, 1954).

P. F. Drucker, *The New Society* (New York, 1950).

E. S. Redford and C. B. Hagan, *American Government and the Economy* (New York, 1965).

L. D. Muslof, *Government and the Economy* (Chicago, 1965).

2. NATIONAL ASSISTANCE TO BUSINESS

C. Warren, *Bankruptcy in United States History* (Cambridge, Mass., 1935).

J. A. Dienner, *The United States Patent System* (Cleveland, 1940).

B. Currie [ed.], "The Patent System," *Law and Contemporary Problems,* XII, No. 4 (1947).

U. S. Department of Justice, *Investigation of Government Patent Practices and Policies* (Washington, 1947).

J. P. Dawson, "The Gold Clause Decision," *Mich. Law Rev.,* XXXIII, 647-684 (Mar., 1935).

————, *Gold and the Gold Standard* (New York, 1944).

A. W. Crawford, *Monetary Management Under the New Deal* (Washington, 1940).

G. Greer, "This Business of Monetary Control," *Harper's Mag.*, CLXXI, 169-180 (July, 1935).

C. Warburton, "Monetary Control Under the Federal Reserve Act.," *Polit. Sci. Quar.*, LXI, 505-534 (Dec., 1946).

L. Pasvolsky, *Current Monetary Issues* (Washington, 1934).

G. G. Johnson, *The Treasury and Monetary Policy, 1933-1938* (Cambridge, Mass., 1939).

H. Spero, *Reconstruction Finance Corporation's Loans to Railroads, 1932-1937* (Cambridge, Mass., 1939).

J. D. Larkin, *Trade Agreements; A Study in Democratic Methods* (New York, 1940).

G. Beckett, *The Reciprocal Trade Agreements Program* (New York, 1941).

S. Chase, *Tomorrow's Trade; Problems of Our Foreign Commerce* (New York, 1945).

P. W. Bidwell, *What the Tariff Means to American Industries* (New York, 1956).

A. Maas, *Muddy Waters* (Cambridge, Mass., 1951).

W. Gorter, *United Shipping Policy* (New York, 1956).

R. A. Bauer, I. de S. Pool, and L. A. Dexter, *American Business and Public Policy; the Politics of Foreign Trade* (New York, 1963).

Congressional Quarterly Service, *Special Report. The Trade Expansion Act of 1962* (Washington, 1962).

M. Friedman and A. J. Schwartz, *A Monetary History of the United States, 1867-1960* (Princeton, N.J., 1963).

American Assembly, *United States Monetary Policy* (New York, 1962).

3. National Regulation of Business

F. P. Hall, *The Concept of Business Affected with a Public Interest* (Bloomington, Ind., 1941).

R. E. Cushman, *The Independent Regulatory Commissions* (New York, 1941), Chaps. iii-vi.

H. H. Trachsel, *Public Utility Regulation* (Chicago, 1947), Chaps. ix-xi, xix-xx.

V. M. Barnett, Jr., "The Power to Regulate Commerce," *Amer. Polit. Sci. Rev.*, XLI, 1170-1181 (Dec., 1947).

J. E. Kallenbach, *Federal Co-operation with the States Under the Commerce Clause* (Ann Arbor, Mich., 1942).

C. L. Dearing and W. Owen, *National Transportation Policy* (Washington, 1950). The most recent thorough study.

C. D. Drayton, *Transportation Under Two Masters* (Washington, 1946).

F. Frankfurter, *The Commerce Clause Under Marshall, Taney, and Waite* (Chapel Hill, N. C., 1937).

E. W. Williams, "The I.C.C. and Regulation of Intercarrier Competition," *Harvard Law Rev.*, LXIII, 1349-1372 (June, 1950).

H. Koontz and R. Gable, *Public Control of Economic Enterprise* (New York, 1956).

M. H. Bernstein, *Regulating Business by Independent Commission* (Princeton, N.J., 1955).

R. E. Westmeyer, *Economics of Transportation* (New York, 1952).

G. Goodman, *Government Policy Toward Commercial Aviation* (New York, 1944).

W. Beard, *The Regulation of Pipe Lines as Common Carriers* (New York, 1941).

C. J. Friedrich and E. Sternberg, "Congress and the Control of Radio-Broadcasting," *Amer. Polit. Sci. Rev.*, XXXVII, 797-818, 999-1013 (Oct. and Dec., 1943).

M. Edelman, *The Licensing of Radio Services in the United States, 1927 to 1947; A Study in Administrative Formulation of Policy* (Urbana, Ill., 1950).

S. Krislov and L. D. Muslof (ed.), *The Politics of Regulation—A Reader* (New York, 1964).

J. E. Anderson, *The Emergence of the Modern Regulatory State* (Washington, 1962).

H. J. Friendly, *The Federal Administrative Agencies: The Need for Better Definition of Standards* (Cambridge, Mass., 1962).

4. Regulation of Business Combinations

W. Hamilton and I. Till, *Antitrust in Action,* Temporary Nat. Econ. Committee, Monograph No. 16 (Washington, 1941).

D. Lynch, *The Concentration of Economic Power* (New York, 1946).

E. S. Mason, "The Current Status of the Monopoly Problem in the United States," *Harvard Law Rev.*, LXII, 1265-1285 (June, 1949).

E. V. Rostow, "Monopoly Under the Sherman Act; Power or Purpose?," *Ill. Law Rev.*, XLIII, 745-793 (Jan.-Feb., 1949).

L. I. Wood, "Patent Combinations and the Anti-Trust Laws," *Geo. Washington Law Rev.*, XVII, 59-96 (Dec., 1948).

W. Adams and H. M. Gray, *Monopoly in America* (New York, 1955).

Mason, E. S., *Economic Concentration and the Monopoly Problem* (Cambridge, Mass., 1957).

G. W. Stocking and M. W. Watkins, *Monopoly and Free Enterprise* (New York, 1952).

H. B. Thorelli, *The Federal Antitrust Policy* (Baltimore, 1956).

S. N. Whitney, *Antitrust Policies: American Experience in Twenty Industries* (New York, 1958).

Dirlam, J. B. and A. E. Kahn, *Fair Competition: The Law and the Economics of Antitrust Policy* (Cornell, 1954).

E. W. Kintner, *An Anti-Trust Primer* (New York, 1963).

5. Regulation of Financial Institutions

E. W. Kemmerer, *The A B C of the Federal Reserve System* (11th ed., Princeton, N.J., 1938).

————, *The A B C of Inflation* (New York, 1942).

P. M. Warburg, *The Federal Reserve System; Its Origin and Growth* (New York, 1930).

G. L. Bach, *Federal Reserve Policy-Making* (New York, 1950).

The Federal Reserve System; Its Purposes and Functions (2nd ed., Washington, 1947). Published by the Federal Reserve System.

L. Loss, *Securities Regulation* (Boston, 1951).

E. Stein, *Government and the Investor* (New York, 1941).

E. T. McCormick, *Understanding the Securities Act and the S. E. C.* (1948).

M. D. Regan, "The Political Structure of the Federal Reserve System," *Amer. Pol. Sci. Rev.*, LV, No. 1 (Mar., 1961).

6. Direct Participation in Business

H. Seidman, "The Theory of the Autonomous Corporation," *Public Admin. Rev.*, 89-96 (Spring, 1952).

★ 19 ★

Government and Labor

Labor in the national scene

THE DEVELOPMENT OF a labor interest in our society is a product of the Industrial Revolution in which small handicraft industries were replaced by large mass-production factories and in which management was separated from daily contacts with employees. In the early years of our history, the laboring men did not participate in political processes. Voting and officeholding were considered the prerogative of property owners. The democratization of the suffrage paved the way for labor interests to be represented. Before the rapid industrialization of the nation after the Civil War, the laboring multitudes seemed to accept the idea that cheap land and low taxes were the most useful public policies to serve their needs. Only after the victorious Northern Republicans swung the full weight of the national government behind the rapid development of industry did the industrial worker emerge as a strong claimant for governmental protection. The emergence of labor as a powerful interest in modern politics, furthermore, has followed closely upon the organization of this interest in the economic sphere through unionization. At first, labor sought to achieve better conditions, higher pay, and shorter hours by purely economic procedures. Only as governmental power and prestige were repeatedly thrown into the struggle on the side of employers did labor come to appreciate that political power was also essential to its ambitions.

The development of unions

Even before 1800 mechanics and artisans in a few of the larger cities began drawing together in unions. As industry expanded and workers multiplied, consciousness of a weak bargaining position without organization, combined with growing desire for improvement of labor conditions in other respects, led to unionization on a steadily increasing scale. Employers did not like what was going on; public opinion was skeptical; and in pursuance of old common-law doctrine, the courts long looked askance at unions as constituting, or threatening, criminal conspiracy. In spite of numerous obstacles, the movement began to take root and after about 1870 went steadily forward. In time local unions began drawing together in regional, or even nation-wide, federations. In 1881, a Federation of Organized Trades and Labor Unions became the common voice of organized labor. In 1886, the present name of American Federation of Labor (AFL) was adopted and for another half-century this organization held the field almost alone. In 1935, however, a militant rival, the Congress (until 1938 Committee) of Industrial Organiza-

500

tions (CIO) was created by the secession of several unions from the parent body. Outside of these over the years grew the powerful Railroad Brotherhoods and numerous minor independent organizations. In 1955, the CIO and AFL unions were reunited into one grand federation. One of the largest unions, the Teamsters, was expelled by the Executive Council of the AFL-CIO in 1957 for corrupt management and continues as an independent union.

Throughout the period 1880-1932, the growth of labor unions was stubbornly and bitterly, sometimes violently, contested by the managerial interests. "Freedom of contract" and "criminal conspiracy" doctrines were asserted by business and enunciated by courts to justify fine and imprisonment for the leaders of strikes and boycotts, labor's principal weapons in the economic sphere. The Sherman Antitrust Law of 1890, designed as we have observed to halt the consolidation of corporate power, was applied with devastating effect to certain labor union activities.[1] Congressional sympathy for the aims of organized labor, expressed in the Clayton Act's apparent exemption of labor from the antitrust laws, was overcome by judicial hostility and virtually all of the alleged protection was repealed by judicial interpretation.[2] The courts, furthermore, fell increasingly into the habit of granting injunctive relief to business concerns harassed by labor disputes, actual or threatened, and in so doing prohibited the use of many of labor's most effective economic weapons. In spite of this hostility the AFL slowly grew in numbers and influence, but by 1932 it still counted only 3,000,000 members and had little real strength in most of the large industries (steel, textiles, automobiles, rubber). It is only since 1932 that organized labor has deployed upon the national scene as one of the great economic interests of modern America. With a drastic change in governmental attitude from a suspicious pseudo-neutrality to benevolent protection, labor unions have flourished as never before. Their membership has steadily advanced reaching a peak in 1959. They now speak for about 22 percent of all persons gainfully employed in the United States and for 30 percent of non-agricultural wage earners.

Hostility of business and the courts

Throughout most of its history, organized labor in America has eschewed any attempt to build its own political party. Several nineteenth-century efforts to do so, beginning with the Working Men's Party of 1828, were not conspicuously successful. Marxism, around which so many European labor parties were built, has never strongly appealed to the American laborer. Labor's political doctrine was largely supplied by Samuel Gompers, leader of the AFL. He preached abstention from independent party organization and participation in the American two-party system by supporting friendly candidates in either party and by appealing to both parties for favorable platform declara-

Labor in politics

---

[1] See Loewe *v.* Lawlor, 208 U. S. 274 (1908), and Gompers *v.* Buck Stove and Range Co., 221 U. S. 418 (1911).

[2] In the Duplex Printing Company Case, 254 U. S. 443, 469 (1921), the Supreme Court said that nothing in the Clayton Act authorized any activity by labor unions or their leaders which was previously held to be unlawful.

UNION MEMBERSHIP, 1869-1962

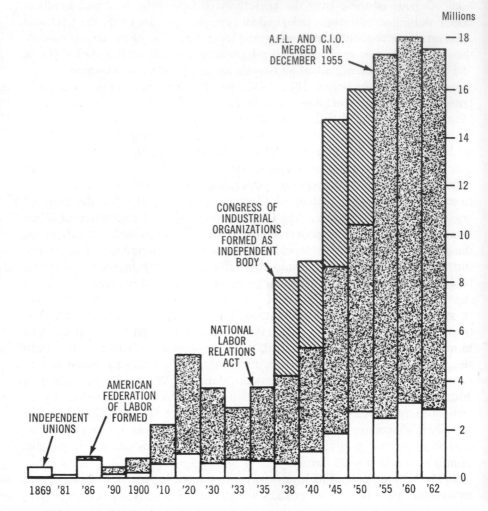

tions and for benevolent legislation. Labor's main weapons, he felt, were economic, not political.[3] Lip service is still paid to the Gompers policy, but the large federation of unions has swung more and more heavily toward active intervention in political campaigns, usually in behalf of Northern Democrats and of Democratic Presidential candidates.[4] Through generously financed subsidiaries like the CIO Political Action Committee and Labor's League for Political Education of the AFL, and now the Committee on Political Educa-

---

[3] It was, however, quite by exception that the AFL in 1924 openly and officially endorsed the LaFollette Progressive Party.

[4] For some case studies of labor in politics see F. Calkins, *The C.I.O. and the Democratic Party* (Chicago, 1952).

tion of the AFL-CIO, labor has sought to sway the electorate in behalf, usually, of Democratic candidates. In New York City a powerful independent labor party has been organized by local trade unions and their party (the Liberal Party) has held the balance of power in many municipal and state elections. Labor is in politics to stay and its influence, especially in the Democratic Party, has been growing steadily in the large industrial cities of the North and Midwest. In fact, labor recorded perhaps its most spectacular success of the post war period in the national elections of 1964.

NATIONAL PROTECTION OF LABORERS

As industrialization rapidly spread throughout the nation in the latter *State* half of the nineteenth century, laboring men increasingly demanded protection *regulation* from unhealthy and dangerous working conditions, from competition on the job market from children and immigrants, from long hours and low pay, and from many other abuses of mechanized manufacturing and corporate management. Much of their effort was directed to state legislatures in the belief that the national government had no power to regulate the conditions of mining and manufacturing. State action, and there was a great deal of sympathetic legislation in the period of 1880-1932, was always embarrassed by the fear that any particular state would place its own industry at a competitive disadvantage with that of other states if it imposed costly standards of safety, health, and welfare. Despite this difficulty, labor won important gains from state after state in the fields of industrial safety, child labor, improved factory conditions. In fact, much of the legislation protecting labor interests at present on the law books is still state law, and the states continue to play an important role in regulating industry benevolently toward working men and women.

Although national regulation of industry in behalf of workers is largely *Early* a product of the New Deal period, the national government had never been *efforts at* completely indifferent to labor interests. As far back as 1840, the government *national* adopted the policy of setting a standard for private employers in its treatment *protection* of its own employees. At that time, President Van Buren prescribed by executive order a 10-hour day for national civil servants. Congress in 1868 prescribed an 8-hour day for laborers on the government's payrolls and this privilege was gradually extended throughout the service. The movement to restrict immigration, especially of contract laborers, which began in 1882 and which has been described in an earlier chapter was largely motivated by a desire to protect the job security of American workers. Unlike workers in industry, those engaged in transportation early looked to the national government for protection and after prolonged agitation an Hours of Service Act in 1907 limited to 16 the hours of consecutive employment of train crews. In 1916, and at the behest of the by now strongly organized railway brotherhoods, the Congress passed an 8-hour-day law for all trainmen. Coincident with state action to protect workers against industrial accidents, the Congress in 1908 passed an Employers' Liability Act for the protection of workers in interstate commerce. This act drastically amended the old common-law rules of "contributory negligence" and "assumption of the risks of employment" which up to this time had substantially allowed employers to escape liability for the injury or death of workmen while performing their duties. The Seaman's (LaFollette) Act of 1915 surrounded employment in the merchant marine with guarantees of proper conditions, hours, food, and wages. In 1920, the benefits of the Employers' Liability Act were extended to sailors. So rapidly did national interest in the plight of the workingman unfold in this century that by 1913 the Congress was persuaded to establish a separate Department of Labor of cabinet rank by breaking up the Department of Commerce and Labor created in 1903. This new agency was designed "to foster, promote, and develop" the welfare of wage earners in the United States, to improve their working conditions, and to advance their opportunities for profitable employment. It should be added, however, that the methods selected by Congress for the achievement of these goals were largely educational and noncoercive.

Unsuccessful efforts to expand national protection

Not all of the early national efforts in behalf of labor were successful. When, in 1916, Congress undertook to restrict child labor in factories and mines by excluding from interstate commerce the products of such labor, the Supreme Court held the law invalid as regulating manufacturing rather than commerce.[5] In 1919, an effort to achieve the same object by using the taxing power was also invalidated by the highest court.[6] An attempt in 1918 to fix minimum wages for women and children employed in the District of Columbia was also set aside on the grounds that women were being unconstitutionally denied freedom to contract for their employment at whatever wages they would accept.[7]

As the nation entered the depression, the national government had already thrown its protective mantle around certain laboring groups (railroad workers and sailors) but was still largely restrained from interceding for the great mass of laborers by narrow judicial construction of its commerce and taxing powers. Impressed with the plea that the descending spiral of economic activity could only be reversed by placing more purchasing power in the hands of consumers (labor), the New Deal early addressed itself to improving the wages and working conditions of the great mass of industrial wage earners.

The National Recovery Administration

The first major effort in this direction was embodied in the National Recovery Act of 1933 which, among many other specifications, provided that codes of fair competition be drawn for similar industries by joint labor-industry-government teams and that these codes should set minimum wage levels, fix maximum hours, eliminate child labor, and spread available employment. These codes, which were also to include provisions governing competitive trade prac-

[5] Hammer v. Dagenhart, 247 U. S. 251 (1918).
[6] Bailey v. Drexel Furniture Co., 259 U. S. 20 (1922).
[7] Adkins v. Children's Hospital, 261 U. S. 525 (1923).

tices, would then be enforced upon the industries concerned by the national government. Codes were rapidly drafted and put into operation under the National Recovery Administration and minimal conditions of employment imposed upon a large sector of American industry. In 1935, however, the entire procedure was called into question by litigation and the Supreme Court invalidated the core of the Recovery Act, mainly on the grounds that the code procedure constituted an invalid delegation of legislative power to an administrative agency.[8]

Operating within the prevailing conception of constitutional power, Congress next sought to establish standards of employment for all those firms supplying the government by contract. The Public Contracts Labor (Walsh-Healey) Act of 1936 prescribed the payment of prevailing minimum wages, limited hours of employment to 40 per week, outlawed child and convict labor, and prescribed minimum standards of health and safety for the employees of all businesses holding government supply contracts in excess of $10,000. These prescriptions were made a part of every appropriate government supply contract.

Establishment of labor standards for public contractors

Incidental to the attempt of President Roosevelt to reconstitute the Supreme Court, a series of decisions issued in 1936 and 1937 indicated the Court had revised its views on the extent of national power to protect industrial wage earners and that it no longer found any constitutional barriers to national legislation regulating manufacturing and mining benevolently toward labor. With its sweeping triumph at the polls in 1936, the Roosevelt administration promptly moved to occupy the new ground opened to it; in 1938, in a Fair Labor Standards Act a large proportion of workingmen were placed under the protection of the United States government.

As amended in 1949, 1950, 1961 and 1963 the Fair Labor Standards Act extends to about 27.5 million wage earners of both sexes "engaged in interstate commerce, or in the production of goods for interstate commerce," including workers in occupations "directly essential" to this production, the benefits of minimum standards of employment. A minimum wage of $1.25 an hour (originally 25 cents) for all covered employees is established, and a maximum work week of 40 hours (originally 44 hours). For all hours worked in excess of the maximum, overtime at the rate of one and one-half times the base pay is required, except that by collective bargaining agreements in certain industries the work week may be extended. The employment of children under 16 is forbidden in manufacturing, mining, transportation, and commerce and under 18 in occupations declared by the Bureau of Labor Standards in the Department of Labor to be "particularly hazardous . . . or detrimental to their health and well being." In other occupations and businesses covered by the law, children of 14 or 15 may be employed in periods not interfering with their schooling and under beneficent working conditions. This general prohibition of child labor, incidentally, makes the passage of the pending child

The establishment of labor standards for industry generally

[8] Schechter *v.* United States, 295 U. S. 495 (1935).

labor amendment largely an academic question. In 1963, the scope of the act was further extended to require covered employers to pay the sexes equally for equal work. Challenged before the courts soon after its passage, this bold effort to provide a nation-wide floor below which the conditions of employment in industry might not sink was sustained unanimously by the Supreme Court.[9]

Enforce-ment   The enforcement of labor standards on covered industries and governmental contractors is the responsibility of the Wage and Hour and Public Contracts Division of the Department of Labor. Violators may be subjected to injunctive proceedings, criminal prosecutions, and employee suits (to recover unpaid minimum wages). Different and less exacting standards are imposed by the same law on industry in Puerto Rico, the Virgin Islands, and Samoa.

NATIONAL PROTECTION OF LABOR UNIONS

Throughout the period of developing governmental concern with the plight of labor, there has always been an impressive argument made by some that elaborate legislative and administrative efforts to protect labor from exploitation are both unnecessary and unwise. Let the government, it is argued, encourage the unionization of employees or at least do nothing judicially or otherwise to discourage such unionization and the unions will take care of wages, hours, and working conditions. It was not, however, until the depression of the thirties that this point of view won wide, although never universal, acceptance. As the national economy rapidly plummeted, the arguments of the labor leaders and their friends gained increasing support. Here again was an opportunity to sustain consumer purchasing power and to spread employment by the actions of unions.

Anti-Injunction Act of 1932   The first target of the labor unionists was their ancient enemy, the injunction. The broadening concept of corporate property rights which characterized the decisions of the national bench from 1875 to 1936 and which embraced as property such nebulous values as "good will" and "going-concern value" suggested to able members of the bar a device for thwarting the spread of unions. Strikes, picketing, and boycotts, the central weapons of the labor movement, could normally be shown to a sympathetic court as threatening irreparable damages to corporate property thus broadly defined. The writ of injunction, an old equity process issued by courts of equity on proper plea and in circumstances in which only one side is normally heard, was designed, they said, exactly to ward off such damages. From about 1890 onward courts fell into the habit of granting injunctions against union leaders and members, ordering them to continue work or to refrain from actions which might

---

[9] United States *v.* Darby Lumber Co., 312 U. S. 100 (1941)—completely repudiating the conceptualism of Hammer *v.* Dagenhart, 247 U. S. 251 (1918). Cf. H. A. L., "Constitutional Aspect of the Fair Labor Standards Act of 1938," *Univ. of Pa. Law Rev.,* LXXXVII, 91-105 (Nov., 1938).

threaten property loss. Violation of such an order placed a unionist in contempt of court and subjected him to summary (without jury trial) punishment. In the decade of the twenties these injunctions became more and more sweeping in their prohibition of all the traditional methods of union agitation. An effort to prohibit injunctions in labor controversies embodied in the Clayton Antitrust Act of 1914 met the same fate as the provision of that law ostensibly exempting labor from antitrust prosecution. It was interpreted out of existence by the courts. Thus many union leaders and sympathetic legislators felt, as we entered the depression, that the greatest service to the spread of labor unionism would be done by removing the injunction from among the employer's weapons. The Anti-Injunction (Norris-LaGuardia) Act of 1932 represents the first successful national effort to foster trade unionism in the United States and marks the turning point in the attitude of the government. This act surrounded the injunction procedure in the national courts with so many safeguards to protect labor union interests that the injunction became largely useless as a device by which employers could break existing unions or thwart their organizational efforts. This act also declared the "yellow-dog" [10] contract as contrary to public policy and unenforceable in national courts.

The New Deal's National Recovery Act of 1933 carried governmental benevolence to unions one step farther. Bent upon leaving no stone unturned and no theory of depression-beating untried, the act not only provided for the labor standards already mentioned but required in famous Section 7(a) each industrial code to include a provision recognizing the right of employees "to organize and bargain collectively through representatives of their own choosing." It also provided for the codes to carry a prohibition against forcing membership in a company union or forcing anyone to agree not to join a union as a condition of his employment. Thus the company-dominated unions of the twenties were outlawed. A National Labor Relations Board was set up within the NRA to administer these provisions of the law and to conduct employee elections where the question of representation in collective bargaining arguments was at issue. *The NRA and labor unions*

Congress and the President moved swiftly to salvage the policy of labor union protection from the wreckage of the Supreme Court's decision condemning the NRA. The National Labor Relations (Wagner) Act of 1935 represents the fruit of this effort. This act proclaims as the policy of the national government the fostering of collective bargaining between employees and employers through unions and surrounds the process with safeguards for unionization which substantially deprive the employer of several of his traditional weapons. Using the Federal Trade Commission Act as its guide, the act specifies a number of "unfair labor practices" and prohibits them to employers. Company-dominated unions are outlawed; employers are forbidden to coerce *The National Labor Relations Act of 1935*

[10] A "yellow-dog" contract is one in which a prospective employee binds himself as a condition of his employment never to join a labor organization.

or restrain employees in the exercise of their rights to become members of a union and to bargain through such organization; employers may not hire or fire employees in such a way as to discriminate against union members or officers; employers are required to bargain with the proper representatives of their employees. A National Labor Relations Board (originally of three but now of five members) was established independently of any existing agency and authorized to enforce the new law upon employers engaged in industries "affecting" commerce. Through a network of regional offices the board was empowered to discharge its responsibilities by: (1) ascertaining by election procedures or otherwise who are the bona fide representatives of the employees in covered industries or plants; and (2) determining on complaint of an employee or his representative, if an employer is engaging in an "unfair practice." Should the Board, after proper hearing, find an employer to be violating the law, it may issue a "cease-and-desist" order against him which may be enforced by a proper national court.

The act's constitutionality upheld

This legislation, with its strong deterrents to employer interference in the unionization of his employees, has ever since been regarded as the Magna Carta of the labor union movement. It represents the greatest gain in governmental benevolence ever achieved by organized labor. And, by staying the hands of management, it contributed in no small way to the tremendous increase in union membership which followed upon its enactment. It was not to be expected that the business community would allow such a sweeping reinterpretation of national authority as this act entailed to go unchallenged. The major cases reached the Supreme Court shortly after it had revised its position on minimum-wage legislation and thus shortly after the bitter legislative contest over President Roosevelt's efforts to reconstitute the court. The Court by five-to-four decisions sustained the administration's argument that the national power to regulate interstate "commerce" embraced the power to regulate the labor relations of concerns whose raw materials or finished products were shipped across state lines even though the firms were not themselves directly engaged in commerce.[11] More than any other decision of this period, this pronouncement celebrated the change in the Court's attitude toward national power to regulate business.

Attacks upon the act

From its inception, the National Labor Relations Act has been the target of a large segment of business community. The theory of this act, the business interests argued, is that employers and employers alone are to blame for the plight of the working mass and for spreading industrial unrest. Only employers can commit unfair labor practices. Unions can coerce employees into becoming members without penalty under the law. Special safeguards are provided for "closed-shop" agreements (agreements which require an employee

---

[11] National Labor Relations Board *v.* Jones & Laughlin Steel Corp., 301 U. S. 1 (1937); National Labor Relations Board *v.* Fruehauf Trailer Co., 301 U. S. 49 (1937); and National Labor Relations Board *v.* Friedman-Harry Marks Clothing Co., 301 U. S. 58 (1937).

to belong to the union in order to be employed) and all forms of company unions are proscribed. Labor responded that employers still have ample legal sanctions for dealing with unlawful behavior by union leaders and agents. Nothing in this law authorizes unions to commit violence or modifies existing limitations on picketing or boycotting. During World War II, the controversy over national policy toward unions abated. It broke out with renewed vigor in the postwar era, however, and led finally to a new policy of governmental regulation of unions as well as of management.

While the sentiment in favor of unions was running at high tide, the Congress added another important law favorable to them. In 1936, Congress, in the Strike-Breakers Act, forbade the transportation in interstate commerce of "any person with intent to employ such person to obstruct or interfere . . . with peaceful picketing during any labor controversy."

Strike-Breakers Act of 1936

THE PROMOTION OF INDUSTRIAL PEACE; REGULATION OF UNIONS

Much as some groups have argued in behalf of a governmental policy of hands-off economic questions like the relations of labor and management, and much as the government has in the past few decades sought to relieve itself of some of the burden of regulating industry by strengthening the hands of the unions, the government has never been able wholly to turn its back upon the combats between labor and management. As unions have grown in size and power, their controversies with the great corporate combinations have threatened not only local and sporadic violence as of old but also national economic paralysis. The strike or collective work stoppage is the oldest and strongest bargaining device the unions have, and when they are able to shut down the entire steel industry or coal industry or railroad system the national economy must grind slowly to a complete halt. There has developed, in other words, a public interest different from that of either labor or management in a particular industry which demands that this paralysis never be allowed to creep through the whole of society. The government's interest in promoting industrial peace has grown steadily as unions and corporations have grown and is, perhaps, at the present time its paramount interest in the field of labor relations. In times of war or of war-emergency there has been no question of the transcendent necessity for maintaining full production, but even in "peace" the government must prevent economic collapse.

The public interest and industrial peace

Prior to the Anti-Injunction Act of 1932, the national policy toward labor disputes was that labor was largely to blame for them and that its leaders must be closely restrained whenever serious property damage or obstruction to the free flow of commerce was threatened. In prosecuting the leaders of the Pullman Strike of 1894, the Cleveland administration invoked the national power to prevent interference with the mail to justify its actions in moving into

National power to deal with disputes

Illinois against the wishes of Governor Altgeld of Illinois.[12] Subsequently, as was mentioned earlier, the Sherman Antitrust Act was invoked time and again to punish the participants in strikes and boycotts and to re-establish peaceful relations in various industries. The injunctions granted by national courts were also widely used to stop strikes and thus to terminate industrial unrest. From all of this it is plain that there has never been a serious question of the power of the national government to intervene in many types of labor disputes and that its intervention until well into this century was largely repressive and punitive, especially in regard to labor. A very large share of the responsibility for fostering industrial peace was, nevertheless, left to the states so long as the disputes were largely local in their scope and effect.

Mediation procedures established for railroads

The shortcomings of these wholly negative procedures for dealing with labor disputes were first clearly realized by the national government in the field of transportation. In this field also the power of the government to experiment with other procedures was unquestioned. Starting with legislation dating from as early as 1888 and culminating in the Railway Labor Act of 1926 (strengthened in 1934), a scheme for handling disputes in that field was developed which for several years was hailed as the best achievement of its kind in our experience. The machinery employed is based on the principle of one mediating agency taking over when another fails. In event of a dispute between a railroad company (or an express or Pullman company, or an airline company —for the system applies also to these) and its employees, either party may invoke the services of a National Mediation Board of three members appointed by the President and confirmed by the Senate; or the Board may step into the picture by volunteering its good offices.[13] In any case, it will endeavor to get the parties into conference and bring about a settlement. If the Board is unsuccessful, it is obliged to recommend that that dispute be arbitrated. If this is refused, the President may at his discretion start negotiations afresh by referring the controversy to an "emergency board" of his own choosing, whose findings and recommendations, it is true, will have no binding effect, but may be received with such public approval as to leave the contenders little practical alternative to accepting them.

The emergency board procedure has become almost standard in the bitter rail disputes of the postwar era. Mediation has frequently failed to budge the parties, each of which—but particularly labor—hopes to do better in the heady atmosphere of Presidential politics. The government, acting under wartime powers, had to take over the roads in 1946, 1948, and 1950 to avoid difficult and perhaps paralyzing strikes, and in 1963 the first peacetime compulsory arbitration procedure was imposed by Congress to resolve the long controversy over the employment of firemen on diesel engines and the man-

---

[12] *In re* Debs., 158 U. S. 564 (1895).

[13] Grievances of railroad employees are handled through a separate agency, the National Railroad Adjustment Board, which has representatives of both sides and meets in panels.

ning of train crews. In 1964, President Johnson had to use all the force of his personality and position to get a settlement at the eleventh hour from the stubborn contestants.

When the Department of Labor was separately organized in 1913, Congress authorized it to act as a mediator in labor disputes. Through a Conciliation Service thereafter established, agents of the government offered their good offices in thousands of controversies and, without any coercive authority of any kind, nevertheless contributed to the peaceful adjustment of a large number of them. The service proved unable, however, to cope effectively with the great strikes of the post-World War II era. Its location in the Department of Labor lent some slight color to the charge of its critics that it was biased in favor of labor. In 1947, amidst the general reorienting of governmental policy toward unions and industrial peace, the mediation functions were withdrawn from the Department of Labor and independently organized as the Federal Mediation and Conciliation Service. This service, through its regional offices, continues to promote peaceful settlement of labor disputes by lending to the parties its trained conciliators. In a typical year it will be involved in 18-20 thousand disputes and is likely to contribute to the settlement of a very high percentage of them.

National mediation in disputes of all types

As governmental policy toward labor and labor unions was sharply changed in the thirties, great reliance came to be placed on first the NRA and then the National Labor Relations Board for heading off industrial conflict. Under the theory that most violence and intransigence in labor disputes was employer-directed rather than union-stimulated, it was supposed that the protection of the bargaining rights of workers would contribute to industrial peace. The entrance of the United States in World War II brought a new dimension to the government's interest in industrial peace and a new urgency for finding more compelling procedures for dealing with strikes and strike threats in coal and steel and other essential industries. A determined Congress in 1943 passed over a Presidential veto a War Labor Disputes (Smith-Connally) Act which imposed strong deterrents to work stoppages. The President was empowered to take possession of and operate any plant, mine, or facility in which a labor disturbance threatened the production of materials needed for the war effort. As long as governmental operation continued, any interference in production by strike, lockout, slowdown, or any other tactic was illegal. Labor disturbances were not completely halted by this act, but certainly they were markedly reduced for this and other reasons. Coincident with the expiration of this act (at the end of World War II) a new rash of strikes swept the country and stimulated bitter debate over the proper method of dealing with them. In the absence of effective legal sanction, the President personally intervened on many occasions to bring the stoppage to a halt by the power of public opinion and his own prestige. In those parts of the economy still under wartime price controls, wage settlement boards and committees threw their energies into peaceful amelioration of the swelling tide of unrest as unions

World War II and industrial peace

sought desperately to keep wages up to the rising spiral of inflationary prices.

*Changing
attitudes
toward
unions*
The election in 1946 of a Republican Congress brought to Washington a group of legislators (including also many Democrats) determined to remake the whole governmental policy and machinery for dealing with labor disputes and with labor-management relations. By this time a large segment of articulate opinion was convinced that the major fault for the dreaded paralysis of industry-wide strikes lay with the unions. Swollen by increased employment and governmental benevolence, it was argued, they had become too powerful and their leaders too arrogant. The public interest in resisting inflation and in stopping the hardships of prolonged strikes in key industries demanded that these new giants of economic power be brought under governmental control. Such was the setting for the passage of the Labor-Management Relations (Taft-Hartley) Act of 1947. Seldom has feeling on proposed legislation—pro and con, inside and outside of Congress—run as high as when this bill was pending; seldom has a piece of legislation, once on the statute book, evoked warmer attack and defense. Although on record for labor-law revision, President Truman thought the measure much too drastic. His sharply worded veto charged that if placed on the statute book it would encumber collective bargaining with "bureaucratic procedures," promote labor-management friction, and discriminate against workers "in a consistent pattern of inequality." Pronouncing the act "extreme," "vindictive," "a slave bill," labor leaders agreed, as did also a majority of Democrats. In other quarters (mainly, although by no means exclusively, industrial and Republican), the measure as passed—while conceded to be imperfect and subject to amendment as experience with it was gained—was commended for making employees as well as employers answerable for unfair practices, for guaranteeing new and needed protection for union minorities, for giving workers assurance of being able to pursue their trades whether they join unions or not, for putting an end to allegedly arbitrary and prejudiced procedures of the Labor Relations Board, and, in general, for imposing for the first time upon labor unions, with their swollen powers, responsibilities commensurate with those powers.

*The
Labor-
Manage-
ment Act
of 1947:*
In form, the Labor-Management Act of 1947 is an amendment to the National Labor Relations Act of 1935 and thus preserves for labor all of the basic guarantees of the earlier law. The general principle of unionized labor is accepted as axiomatic. At the same time, the right of every worker to "refrain from . . . concerted activities," that is, to identify himself with no union, if he

*1. Rights
and duties
of unions*
so prefers, is expressly recognized and protected. Every union desiring to be in a position to avail itself of the services of the Labor Relations Board in defense of its bargaining and other interests is required to keep on file with that agency full information on its membership, officers, finances, rules and regulations.

*2. Closed
and union
shops*
When the act was passed, 30 percent of all organized employees (notably in the printing industry and the building trades) worked in closed shops, that is, in establishments in which one must be a union member even to be hired; and more than that proportion were under union shop rules requiring every

worker in an establishment to become a union member, if not already such, within 30 days after taking employment. Under the Act of 1947, the closed shop is completely banned, and union shop may be maintained only if a majority of all workers in a plant eligible to vote on the question so demand,[14] and only under other restrictions aimed at protecting employer interests.

The basic rights and procedures of collective bargaining guaranteed in the legislation of 1935 are reaffirmed, with full freedom for both employers and employees to choose the agents who will represent them at the bargaining table. But whereas previously only employers were compelled to bargain, employees now are equally forbidden to refuse to do so; and whereas formerly employers might not, in the course of bargaining or otherwise, make even noncoercive statements to their employees or others without risk of having what they said adduced as evidence of unfair practice, now they may do this with impunity. A ban on "industry-wide" bargaining—bargaining on the basis of an industry (like coal-mining) as a whole—was voted by the House but deleted in the Senate. Notwithstanding that three months before the act was passed, one of the most bitterly contested disputes in recent labor-management-relations history was supposedly settled when the Supreme Court in effect ruled that unions of foremen and supervisors, linked up in a Foremen's Association of America, were covered by the act of 1935 and that employers must bargain with them on that basis,[15] the new law denies such unions (on the ground of being managerial rather than labor) any bargaining rights. *3. Collective bargaining*

The new law added to the unfair practices of employers several unfair practices sometimes engaged in by unions. Employees, for example, may not be coerced to join unions; members in a union shop may not be required to pay excessive initiation fees or dues; employers may not, under the practice popularly known as "featherbedding," be required to pay for services not rendered, for example, to pay a textile worker for operating a single machine when he could just as well operate four or five, or, in the case of a radio station using records, to hire "live" musicians. Secondary boycotts (in which one party refuses to deal with another unless the other will, in turn, refuse to deal with a third) and jurisdictional strikes (arising, for instance, out of conflicts between AFL and CIO unions, or between any such and independent unions) are forbidden. For all of the practices named, unions are made liable to suit. *4. Unfair practices*

The act attempts to strengthen the traditional governmental procedures for dealing with strikes. In general, the right to strike when other measures fail is fully recognized. However, certain kinds of strikes, for example, jurisdictional strikes and strikes against the national government (for which the penalty is instant dismissal) are absolutely prohibited; and for situations threatening strikes in themselves legitimate, procedures are ordained in con- *5. Labor disputes*

[14] The need for a prior election for each union shop agreement was repealed in 1951.

[15] Foremen's Association of America *v.* L. A. Young Spring and Wire Corp. *et al.*, 333 U. S. 837 (1947).

nection with the new Federal Mediation and Conciliation Service designed to give the parties a chance to "cool off" and mediation an opportunity to achieve its purpose before overt action occurs. A special procedure is established for dealing with industry-wide strikes or those threatening a serious economic breakdown. The President, when he finds such a strike or lockout threatens national health or safety, may appoint a board of inquiry to examine into the causes. On receipt of a report from this board, the executive may request an injunction to stop this strike or lockout. If the proper court finds such a dispute is industry-wide and if continued will threaten national health or safety, it may issue the injunction regardless of the provisions of the earlier act limiting such orders. The parties are then required to continue to seek agreement with the aid of the conciliation service and the inquiry board for at least 60 days. Then the inquiry board's final report is made public and a secret ballot of the employees must be taken by the Labor Relations Board in 15 days to see if they will accept the board's terms. At the end of this process the injunction is lifted, and if no settlement has yet been reached the strike may proceed.

6. Political provisions   There also are provisions of political import. Benefit of National Labor Board procedures, for example, hearing and deciding complaints against employers, cannot be claimed by any union having any officer who refuses to declare under oath that he is not a member of the Communist Party and that he does not favor the forceful or unconstitutional overthrow of the government.[16] The Federal Corrupt Practices Act of 1925 is amended to bracket labor unions with corporations by forbidding them to make any contributions or incur any expenditures from union funds in connection with any election [17] to any national political office. No feature of the law stirred hotter controversy than the latter, and labor has strongly resented it, while at the same time finding means through auxiliary organizations (like the Committee on Political Education) of circumventing it.[18]

7. Administrative arrangements   Finally, the National Labor Relations Board was increased from three to five members, and its activities confined largely to adjudication. This was done to meet the criticism that formerly the board was at the same time "investigator, prosecutor, judge, and jury." All work of investigation and prosecution is devolved upon a new official, the "general counsel," appointed

[16] An amendment to the act in 1951 waived this provision as well as that requiring annual reports on officers and finances insofar as the AFL-CIO headquarters are concerned.

[17] Construed to include primaries, caucuses, and conventions.

[18] Labor leaders widely attacked this provision as violating the free speech guarantees of the First Amendment. In a number of cases, the Court, although modifying somewhat the most rigorous interpretation of the prohibition, has thus far avoided the central constitutional question. In U. S. v. CIO 335 U. S. 106 (1948) the Court declared that supporting a candidate in a labor newspaper is not a violation of the law. There is also involved the question of spending union dues for political purposes not approved by the members. In its most recent consideration of this matter, the Court held that a worker compelled to join a union under a union shop agreement may prevent the union from spending his dues for political purposes if he files a formal protest with the union. Int.'l. Assoc. of Mach. et al. v. Street, et al., 367 U. S. 740 (1961).

by the President and confirmed by the Senate for four years, and with full supervision over 20 regional offices and their field staffs.[19]

This act thus clearly marks a new phase in governmental policy toward labor and toward disputes. Labor unions are regulated nationally for the first time and peace is to be achieved by adjudicatory determination of the rights and grievances of both parties. Crippling strikes may be halted for a time by injunction and executive intervention in disputes is supported by law.

WORK STOPPAGES, 1946-1963

	Number	Workers Involved	Man-Days Idle
1946	4,985	4,600,000	116,000,000
1947	3,693	2,170,000	34,600,000
1948	3,419	1,960,000	34,100,000
1949	3,606	3,030,000	50,500,000
1950	4,843	2,410,000	38,800,000
1951	4,737	2,220,000	22,900,000
1952	5,117	3,540,000	59,100,000
1953	5,091	2,400,000	28,300,000
1954	3,468	1,530,000	22,600,000
1955	4,320	2,650,000	28,200,000
1956	3,825	1,900,000	33,100,000
1957	3,673	1,390,000	16,500,000
1958	3,694	2,060,000	23,900,000
1959	3,708	1,880,000	69,000,000
1960	3,333	1,320,000	19,100,000
1961	3,367	1,450,000	16,300,000
1962	3,614	1,230,000	18,600,000
1963	3,362	941,000	16,100,000

Almost two decades have now elapsed since the government sharply changed its policy toward labor unions and sought to promote industrial peace by a different approach. Has the new policy been successful? There is little agreement on this question. Labor has yielded little in its demand for outright repeal of the new policy, and business has steadfastly supported the act. In the campaigns of 1948, 1952, and 1956 the Democratic Presidential candidates pledged their party to repeal while the Republican candidates, especially General Eisenhower, pledged only to seek modifications. Congress has sternly refused to modify the law in any important respects although a few changes

Experience under the new policy

[19] A Presidential reorganization plan of 1950 abolishing the office of general counsel and returning its functions directly to the board—a plan favored unanimously by the board, but not by the incumbent general counsel, Robert N. Denham, and not recommended by the Hoover Commission—failed because of Senate objection. Another plan of 1961, which aimed at expediting the work of the Board by eliminating compulsory full-board review of many cases, was also rejected.

were made in 1951 and in 1959. Experience thus far under the new law indicates that its effects were not wholly anticipated by either side. The unions have not grown appreciably in membership since 1947 despite an increase of 13.5 million in the industrial labor force. Many factors may account for this, for the experience has not been different in earlier boom periods. Industrial peace has certainly not been completely achieved. While no year since 1946 has been as bad from the point of view of strikes, in 1949, 1952 and 1959 more than 50 million man-days of idleness were created by labor disputes. This record is worse than that of any year since 1900 except, again, 1946. However, relatively few of the disputes since 1946 have been crippling. The inquiry board and injunction procedure have been used about 25 times. The most successful uses were those halting longshoremen's strikes in 1953, 1956, 1961 and 1965. Several strikes in coal and other industries were not halted. The steel strikes of 1952 and 1959 presented the most severe challenges to the Act of 1947. President Truman refused to use the procedure in 1952 and referred the issue to the Federal Wage Stabilization Board set up during the Korean emergency. When this failed to bring settlement he attempted unsuccessfully to take over the steel plants. In the prolonged strike of 1959, the injunctive procedure was challenged by the union on the grounds that there was no real emergency and that the courts were being made part of the executive branch contrary to constitutional theory. Although the Supreme Court upheld the use of the injunction as proper,[20] the strike was not settled by the inquiry board or by injunction but rather by the mediation of the Secretary of Labor (Mitchell) strongly supported behind the scenes by Vice-President Nixon. The effort to outlaw the closed shop and to place the union shop under more rigid control has had mixed results. More plants now have some form of union security agreements than before but the unions have been less able to discipline their own members, since expulsion from the union no longer carries with it loss of the job.[21] However, state "right-to-work" laws which place even more severe restrictions on union shops have been spreading (19 states now have them in some form) and the Act of 1947 provides that state regulations of this matter may take precedence over the national rules.[22] Labor, with the aid of President Johnson, in 1965 launched an all-out assault to repeal this feature of the Act and thus weaken the effectiveness of the state acts.

Controversy over the wisdom and effectiveness of the Act of 1947 continues but it is presently overshadowed by new issues of public policy raised by the revelations of corruption, racketeering, association of union officials with "crime rings," and other union abuses by the investigations in 1957-1958

[20] United Steelworkers *v.* United States, 361 U. S. 39 (1959).

[21] See E. E. Witte, "Taft-Hartley Law After Five Years," *The Milwaukee Journal,* June 8, 1952 and D. B. Straus, "Laws Won't Stop Strikes," *Harper's,* July, 1952.

[22] In the railroad industry, where union shop agreements are authorized by the Railway Labor Act, the Supreme Court ruled that state laws aimed at preventing such agreements are invalid. Railway Employees Dept. *v.* Hanson, 351 U. S. 225 (1956).

of a Senate Select Committee headed by Senator McClellan (Arkansas). These investigations, directed by Robert Kennedy (later Attorney General and now Senator from New York) and dealing largely with the Teamsters' Union, brought the union movement and its leaders once again under a cloud of public suspicion and paved the way for greater and more detailed national regulation of unions. The upshot of this new controversy was the passage of the Labor-Management Reporting and Disclosure Act of 1959.

This act seeks in the first place to protect the rights of individual members of labor organizations by guaranteeing them: (1) equal rights and privileges to participate in elections and meetings; (2) freedom of speech and assembly to discuss the conduct of union officers; (3) secret balloting in the determination of dues, fees, or other assessments; (4) the right to take legal action against officers; and (5) protection against arbitrary or improper suspension, expulsion, or other disciplinary action. Labor unions are, further, required to adopt constitutions and by-laws and file with the Secretary of Labor copies of these together with other detailed information on such matters as the rules governing admission, dues, audits of funds, selection of officers, and strike votes. They are also required to file annually complete financial reports. Officers are required to disclose to the Secretary financial transactions of their own with employers. Employers are also required to report certain payments to union officials or to union members or to personnel consultants. Private personnel consultants are also required to report any agreements involving union matters which they may undertake in behalf of employers. Trusteeship agreements by which one labor union controls or influences another are also regulated. The selection of union officers is carefully regulated and maximum terms are prescribed as well as secret ballots and some effort is made to keep the nominating procedure open and competitive.[23] The fiduciary responsibility of union officers managing labor funds is spelled out in more detail with various safeguards provided and convicted criminals are disqualified from holding union positions. The act also tightens the prohibitions against secondary boycotts of the Act of 1947 and adds to its unfair labor practices, picketing aimed at forcing recognition of a union not supported by the employees. Finally, the confused controversy over the relative extent of the jurisdiction of the NLRB and of state labor boards is partly resolved by authorizing the NLRB to refuse to accept jurisdiction in many types of "small" cases.

The Labor-Management Reporting Act of 1959

DEPARTMENT OF LABOR

Although many agencies of the executive branch are charged with functions relating to labor, the central agency for presenting the situation of labor

Smallest executive department

[23] The provision of the act which makes it a crime for a Communist to hold office in a labor union was invalidated by the Suprme Court on the grounds that it constituted a bill of attainder. U. S. v. Brown, 85 S. Ct. 1707 (1965).

to the Congress and to the President is the Department of Labor. Since its creation in 1913, the department has experienced a checkered history. Its earliest responsibilities were largely fact-finding and hortatory. During the New Deal period of benevolent labor legislation few of the new functions were assigned to it and, in fact, it was gradually deprived of some of its traditional functions. President Truman attempted to strengthen it by reassigning some of its old functions and granting to it some new ones, and President Eisenhower continued the effort. It is still, however, the smallest of the executive departments.

Major divisions   The main divisions of the department administer: (1) workmen's compensation for employees of the national government—Bureau of Employees' Compensation and the Employees Compensation Appeal Board; (2) apprentice training programs for skilled workers in industry, largely by co-operation with state labor agencies—Bureau of Apprenticeship and Training; (3) public employment offices now in the various states and state unemployment insurance programs—Bureau of Employment Security; (4) standards of industrial safety and child labor, the latter functions largely by cooperation with state agencies—Bureau of Labor Standards; (5) the collection of timely data on the cost of living, manpower, cost trends, and other data on labor economics—Bureau of Labor Statistics; (6) research on automation and its consequences and on retraining programs—Office of Manpower, Automation, and Training; (7) fair labor standards—Wage and Hour Division; (8) the promotion of standards for health and welfare of women in industry—Women's Bureau; and (9) reporting requirements for labor unions and officers—Labor-Management Services Administration.

References

M. Fainsod, L. Gordon, and J. C. Palamountain Jr., *Government and the American Economy* (3rd ed., New York, 1959), Chap. VII.

M. E. Dimock, *Business and Government* (rev. ed., New York, 1953), Chaps. IX-XI.

H. R. Northrup and G. F. Bloom, *Government and Labor* (Homewood, Ill., 1963).

J. H. Leek, *Government and Labor in the United States* (New York, 1952).

G. W. Miller, *American Labor and the Government* (New York, 1948).

G. W. Taylor, *Government Regulation of Industrial Relations* (New York, 1948).

D. H. Wollett, *Labor Relations and Federal Law* (Seattle, Wash., 1949).

A. K. McAdams, *Power and Politics in Labor Legislation* (New York, 1964). Deals with the passage of the Labor-Management Reporting and Disclosure Act of 1959.

H. U. Faulkner and M. Starr, *Labor in America* (New York, 1945).

H. W. Metz, *Labor Policy of the Federal Government* (Washington, 1945).

—— and M. Jacobstein, *A National Labor Policy* (Washington, 1947).

C. O. Gregory, *Labor and the Law* (New York, 1946).

E. E. Cummins and F. T. DeVyver, *The Labor Problem in the United States* (3rd ed., New York, 1947).

S. H. Slichter, *The Challenge of Industrial Relations* (Ithaca, N.Y., 1947).

N. W. Chamberlain, *Collective Bargaining Procedures* (Washington, 1944).

W. E. Moore, *Industrial Relations and the Social Order* (New York, 1946).

E. E. Witte, "An Appraisal of the Taft-Hartley Act," *Amer. Econ. Rev.*, XXXVIII, (May, 1948), 368-382.

F. A. Hartley, Jr., *Our New National Labor Policy* (New York, 1948).

H. A. Millis and E. C. Brown, *From the Wagner Act to Taft-Hartley: A Study of National Labor Policy and Labor Relations* (Chicago, 1950).

C. Eaton *et al.*, "Labor Relations and Labor Law," *Univ. of Chicago Law Rev.*, XIV (Apr., 1947), 331-454.

F. Tannenbaum, "The Social Function of Trade Unionism," *Polit.-Sci. Quar.*, LXII (June, 1947), 161-194.

W. H. Leiserson, *American Trade Union Democracy* (New York, 1959).

S. Lens, *The Crisis of American Labor* (New York, 1959).

K. Braun, *The Settlement of Industrial Disputes* (Philadelphia, 1944).

H. Harris, *Labor's Civil War* (New York, 1940).

P. S. Foner, *History of the Labor Movement in the United States* (New York, 1947). Covers the subject to about 1880.

P. Jacobs, *The State of the Unions* (New York, 1963).

J. Lombardi, *Labor's Voice in the Cabinet: A History of the Department of Labor from its Origin to 1921* (New York, 1942).

K. C. McGuiness, *The New Frontier NLRB* (Washington, 1963).

Labor Research Association, *Labor Fact Book 9* (New York, 1949).

Annual reports of the Secretary of Labor, National Labor Relations Board, etc.

★ 20 ★

Government and Agriculture

Agriculture
the
favored
interest

THE SEAL OF the United States Department of Agriculture declares, "Agriculture is the foundation of manufacturing and commerce." This motto expresses a view, widely held in the life of the American nation, that agriculture is the backbone of our society. Cities, industry, and commerce may all be swallowed up in the maw of war or pestilence and life would still be possible; if the soil or those skilled in making it yield its bounty were to be destroyed, all life would disappear. Furthermore, in this view, rural life is demonstrably superior to urban life on every significant count: it is healthier, better for raising the young, and spiritually stronger. It produces a self-reliant, independent, vigorous, and healthy people. Trade and manufacturing produce the urban swarm, dependent, frail, neurotic, materialistic, and fearful. These convictions are properly described as agricultural fundamentalism and have played an important part in shaping the policy of the government toward agriculture. That these views have not been decisive on all occasions of national controversy is due, in part, to the fact that they have been sharply contested by another view which holds that agriculture, like every other economic interest, should find its proper place in the national economy through competition. If the calculus of the market place decrees that manufacturing should rise and farming decline, so be it. Agricultural fundamentalism, however, has been sufficiently impressive in the national scene that the government has usually been disposed to grant to the agricultural interest whatever that interest was agreed upon. The rural interest has been bolstered also by the fact that our political institutions are not geared perfectly to represent majority opinion. Having once been a majority, the rural interest has steadfastly clung to institutional arrangements which give it political strength disproportionate to its numerical strength in the population. The United States Senate, to a lesser extent the House of Representatives, and dozens of state legislative chambers award to rural America many more representatives than a strict population accounting would require. Because of these arrangements and because of the appeal of the fundamentalists' creed, it would not be unfair to say that agriculture has been treated benevolently by the government more consistently than any of the other great economic interests. Despite the faith of the fundamentalists and the bounty of a sympathetic government, the place of agriculture in American life has slowly but certainly declined. The court-ordered reapportionment of state legislatures and Congressional districts is likely to hasten the reduction of rural influence. This decline and the conflict of ideologies about it provide the setting for most of the modern controversies surrounding the determination of national agricultural policy.

The position of agriculture in modern America has been determined largely by the tremendous revolution in agricultural technology which has been occurring since about 1850. This revolution, although obscured from the view of the city-dweller by the blinding light of the industrial revolution, has been just as sweeping in its impact. The continuing application of scientific methods and power-driven machinery have been pushing the output per farmer and per acre to unimagined heights. In 1830, for example, it took about three farm families to produce enough food and fiber beyond their own needs to feed and clothe one city family. In 1960, one farm family could feed and clothe more than six urban families and two more persons abroad. Production per worker has increased more than 250 percent in 100 years. The improvement in productivity has been striking in just the last twenty years. Wheat yields were about 17 bushels to the acre in 1945 and 26.2 bushels in 1964; corn yields rose from 32.7 bushels to 61.1 bushels per acre in the same period. The story for many other crops is similar. Stated another way, the revolution in agriculture has meant that a constantly increasing share of agricultural produce is for sale rather than subsistence—90 percent in 1960. Agriculture has become a great "business" venture and is no longer simply a way of life. Even so, about 78 percent of the farms in 1960 produced little more than subsistence

PRODUCTIVITY IN AGRICULTURE
(PER MAN HOUR)

1830
HAND METHODS

1896
EARLY MACHINES

1950
MODERN MACHINES

Each symbol represents 40 lbs. of wheat produced

for their owners or operators. The income of these farmers was greater from working in nearby cities than from their farming. The tremendous outpouring of agricultural products thus comes from one-fourth of the farm population. In fact, the most productive 10 percent of the farms produce more than half of the agricultural output measured in terms of dollars.

The decline of the farm population

Fewer and fewer farmers are producing more and more crops, and whereas in 1860 the United States was 80 percent rural, today fewer than 7 percent of our people are actually on farms. The farm population has been declining relative to the city population since 1790 but it has been declining absolutely since 1916. The farm population of 15.6 million in 1960 is about the same as it was in 1864. The farmer's share of the national income has also been falling: it was less than 7 percent in 1960. It is well known, further, that even the present reduced farm population can, with the aid of modern technology, produce of many crops much more than the nation has been able to consume or to export and that this excess seems to be increasing. The American farmer has turned Malthus right around: in the United States, the food supply is pressing on the (farm) population.

Rural blight

The faith of the fundamentalists, sorely tested by these developments, is being challenged further by the persistence and spread of rural blight. The argument for the superiority of rural ways could, in the past, be bolstered by reference to the statistics of infant mortality, disease, death, crime and other symptoms of social ills. In all of these respects and with minimal governmental efforts, the rural areas were superior to the urban ones. In each year that passes, however, the difference is narrowing. In infant deaths and in many diseases, the urban areas are now ahead of the rural ones. Even the urban birth rate—one of the best indications of strong family life—closely rivalled the rural rate in the past fifteen years. There are some cities, in fact, that are superior in every one of these respects to the rural areas. Underlying these developments is not only aggressive urban governmental attack on the problem but also subsidence in the rural economy. More than one-fifth of all acreage now tilled is so eroded and its fertility so depleted that it ought not to be cultivated any longer. One-crop agriculture produces surpluses and eats up the soil. The operation of farms by tenants rose sharply from 1880 to 1930—from 26 percent of all farms to 42 percent—and has only been declining during the recent war and postwar periods of farm prosperity. Among that half of the farm population which produces little above subsistence, living standards, real income, and per capita wealth are all quite low. In fact, much of the most desperate poverty in the United States is on the farm, and rural slums rival the worst that our large cities can produce. If the national government were to withdraw its benevolent hand and capacious pocketbook from agriculture, it seems clear that the misery, disease, crime, and suffering in rural America would compare with the worst that our great cities have ever produced.

The farmers in politics

The farm interest, like that of business and of labor, relies heavily today on its great associations to press its claims before Congress, the executive branch, party committees, and state governments. The strongest of these, described in an earlier chapter, are well financed, competently led, and frequently effective. Unlike the business or the labor interests, the farmers are not so solidly dedicated to one party. They are influential in both parties and are more inclined to shift loyalty from one party to the other if harassed by economic distress or assuaged by promises of benevolence. The farm vote appeared to be influential, for example, in the victory of Truman in 1948 after having aided the Republicans to gain control of Congress in 1946. The farmers, furthermore, unlike business and labor, have historically provided the basis for several strong third parties: Republican, Greenback, Populist, and Non-Partisan League, for example. Farmer-supported minor parties have captured control at various times of several state governments. No labor party has ever achieved as much success. Economic distress in agriculture has produced as much home-grown radicalism in both economics and politics as has distress in any other segment of the economy. This has been articulated through party platforms and campaigns as frequently as for any other interest. The alleged conservatism of the farm interest cannot be supported historically.

DECLINE OF AMERICAN AGRICULTURE

Year	Farm Population (1000)	% of Total Pop.	No. of Farms (1000)	Ave. Size of Farms (Acres)
1935	32.161	25.3	6.812	Not Available
1945	24.420	17.5	5.859	194.8
1950	23.048	15.3	5.382	215.3
1954	19.019	11.8	4.782	242.2
1959	16.592	9.4	3.704	302.4
1960	15.635	8.7	N.A.	N.A.
1964	12.954	6.8	N.A.	N.A.

SOURCE: *Statistical Abstract of the U.S., 1965*

Any discussion of the farm interest in American politics is predicated to some degree on a myth. Like the business interest, the farm interest is nothing like as homogeneous as it is frequently made to appear. Cash crop farming is frequently at odds with subsistence farming. Truck crop farming is not as dependent on world economic conditions as export crop farming. Southern cotton agriculture is usually at loggerheads with Midwestern dairy farming because of the rivalry between cotton-seed oil and butterfat. Tenant farmers oppose absentee landlord farmers. Small operators battle large operators. On few questions of public policy is the farming population agreed. Most farmers accept the tenets of agricultural fundamentalism, but beyond this there is little agreement. Even the fundamentalists are likely to export their children to the urban-industrial areas of America.

Unity of farm interests?

THE IMPROVEMENT OF AGRICULTURAL PRODUCTION

Although by nature and tradition the most highly individualistic form of enterprise, agriculture long ago turned to government for encouragement and assistance. And from the earliest days, local governments have provided roads for the movement of farm products to market, have supported land title registration and surveys to insure the rights of ownership, have financed fairs and exhibitions to encourage better breeding of plants and animals, and in numerous other ways have aided the farmer in his struggle against nature. The states too have responded to the farmers' claims by providing programs of research and education designed to supplement local efforts. The farmers turned to the national government with some reluctance and only after they became convinced that state and local efforts were not adequate to their needs. Out of its power to spend money, to regulate commerce, to provide post roads, the Congress has found constitutional authority to support an everwidening array of programs for the benefit of American agriculture.

The distribution of the public domain

Virtually everything the national government does effects agriculture in one way or another: its tax policies, tariff program, international dealings, defense program, regulation of business, and all the other policies it has undertaken impinge on the farmer. We are concerned here, however, only with those programs which are of direct and immediate benefit to the farmer and are largely designed for him alone. Among these the oldest and perhaps the most persistently pursued through the years has been the improvement of production. Until about 1890, one of the major methods used by the national government to achieve greater output of food and fiber was its program for the distribution of the huge public domain. More and more land was thus brought under cultivation and the priceless heritage of the American people was distributed among those who undertook to cultivate it. Until the Civil War the policy for the distribution of land was determined by statesmen with one eye on the Treasury, but the Republican Party pledged itself to give away the national domain as quickly and as cheaply as possible.[1] By 1890, the last usable land had been placed under cultivation and the frontier was gone.

Provision of scientific research

A more enduring method of national assistance to agricultural production has been the provision of scientific research. The first appropriation for agriculture was made by the Congress in 1839 in the amount of $1000 for seed collection and distribution and for agricultural investigations. The first full-time employee devoting himself to agricultural problems was a chemist. When the Department of Agriculture was created in 1862 as a separate agency under a commissioner, one of the major functions assigned to it was the collection of information about agriculture by the conduct of "practical and scientific experiments." From these modest beginnings the research program of the De-

---

[1] Notably under the Homestead Act of 1862, by terms of which any person could acquire 160 acres of the public domain by paying a modest registration fee and actually occupying the "homestead" for at least five years.

partment of Agriculture has grown by mighty leaps until it is the most comprehensive of its kind in the world and the department one of the greatest research establishments. Within the department, the Agricultural Research Service coordinates the work of numerous bureaus, branches, and divisions, each of which specializes in some particular phase of agricultural production or distribution. From this service each year flow hundreds of bulletins describing the results of the experiments and investigations. Chemists, engineers, economists, bacteriologists, geneticists, management experts, nutritionists, horticulturists, and scores of other experts labor daily at the task of showing the American farmer how to wrest larger yields, larger profits, greater leisure, and higher standards of living from nature. This research is carried on not only in the departmental laboratories and at the great 12,000 acre Agricultural Research Center at Beltsville, Maryland, but also in hundreds of state and territorial experiment stations and state college laboratories. Beginning in 1887, the agricultural experiment station program has been supported by national grants to state agricultural colleges. An Office of Experiment Stations within the Research Service supervises and coordinates the state and territorial programs. The states and territories, on their parts, appropriate matching and supplementary funds to the colleges and stations, altogether more than doubling the total annual investment in agricultural research. This comprehensive attack on farm problems has throughout the years contributed importantly to the revolution in agricultural technology which has done so much to shape the modern American economy.

Improvement of agricultural education

Underlying the great program of discovering new knowledge beneficial to agriculture has been a powerful national effort to improve agricultural education. Scientific farming requires scientific farmers and these require institutions dedicated to instruction in agricultural arts and science. It is not coincidence that the same Congress which created the first Department of Agriculture also created the first national-state program of agricultural colleges. The Land Grant College (Morrill) Act of 1862 granted millions of acres of the public domain to the states for the support of state colleges of agriculture, engineering, and home economics. Out of this program grew the great state universities and agricultural colleges of modern America. Since 1890, national money grants have replaced the land grants, and state appropriations have grown to exceed many times over the national gifts. Through the national grants, of course, the national government exercises a continuing influence over the programs of the agricultural colleges.

The development of Agricultural Extension Service

The colleges, however, can work directly with only a small portion of the agricultural population. A new program designed to carry the knowledge and skills of the colleges and the experiment stations to the farmers' backyards was inaugurated in 1914. The Co-operative Agricultural Extension (Smith-Kerr) Act of that year provided the basis for the modern extension service. Through county agricultural agents supported by national, state, and county governments, the accumulating knowledge about agriculture is today carried into the farmyard and there adapted to the needs of the individual farmer. The Extension Service unites the levels of government in a unique way to produce an itinerant encyclopedia of farm science at the beck of virtually every farmer in the land. With this triumvirate of college, experiment station, and extension agent under the mild, generous, and beneficent hand of the national department, the American farmer is the recipient of more solicitous concern, expert advice, and improving instruction than any other sizable group in the population.

IMPROVING THE ECONOMIC POSITION OF THE FARMER

The problem of surpluses

Unlike factories, farms cannot close down when the supply of agricultural products creates a glut on the market. The only recourse to a farmer in a period of falling farm prices is to try to increase his output. This is especially true of highly specialized, one-crop, staple agriculture. The great technological advance in agriculture, stimulated partly by the determined efforts of government scientists to improve productivity, has helped to produce in this century a new and unusual farm problem—surpluses. Two world wars added new urgency to the expansion of agricultural production as European cultivation was halted by the guns of opposing armies. The restoration of European production, the exhaustion of foreign purchasing power, and the growing restrictions on international trade combined in the postwar eras to reduce the export market for American staples and to leave the greatly expanded output of American farms without markets to absorb the yield.

Early aids to marketing

The farmer's interest in improving the marketing and distribution of his crops is, of course, not new. The long battle of the Midwestern, Southern, and Plains farmers in the 1870's and 1880's against the railroads and the grain elevators represented a determined effort to improve distribution and to gain for the farmers a larger share of the ultimate price to the consumer of their products. Until the New Deal era, however, the demands of agriculture for governmental aid in distribution were largely met by: (1) inaugurating an elaborate system of collecting and disseminating timely data on crop prospects and market prices; (2) establishing and maintaining by state cooperation uniform grades and standards for commodities shipped to out-of-state markets; (3) regulating bonded warehouses, stockyards, commission merchants, brokers, and commodity exchanges in the interests of fair play for the producers. All of these programs, directed for the most part by the Agricultural Marketing Service, have been strengthened with the years and are still key activities of the national department. However, they all fell short of striking decisively at the heart of the farmers' problem after World War I.

Farm problems in the twenties

Industrial prosperity in the twenties masked real distress among the staple farmers, and their leaders battled vainly against the stubborn determination of Calvin Coolidge in one Congress after another to rescue the farm economy by the resources of the United States Treasury.[2] In 1929, a compromise was worked out between Congressional farm leaders and President Hoover: a Federal Farm Board was created to promote producer cooperatives in agriculture and to assist in better marketing of farm products both at home and abroad. The board program virtually disintegrated in the depression. The collapse of industrial prosperity after 1929 destroyed a good share of the domestic market for agricultural products and forced the economy of agriculture to its lowest point in generations. Farm prices fell in three years more than 50 percent and farm income more than 70 percent while industrial prices fell only 32 percent in the same period. This widening disparity between industry and agriculture became a major national problem.

The Roosevelt administration faced in 1933 a deep and disastrous drop in industrial activity. It faced a situation in agriculture which had been aggravating since 1922 and which was bankrupting the great agricultural regions of the nation. Borrowing the ideas of the Farm bloc of the twenties, the New Deal struck boldly at the heart of the problem. In the Agricultural Adjustment Act of 1933 it sought to increase farm income by raising farm prices and to raise farm prices by curtailing production and subsidizing the farmer for the curtailment. The price level on farm products sought was one which would restore the purchasing power of farm products obtaining in the relatively favorable period of 1909-1914.[3] To achieve this goal the act aimed to reduce production to the extent necessary to bring agricultural prices up to the relative level of industrial prices. For this curtailment, the farmer was to be paid out of the proceeds of a tax levied on "processors" of the commodities for which curtailment was directed. This tax would, of course, be passed on to the consumer in the form of higher prices. Originally the act extended to only seven commodities: wheat, cotton, corn, rice, tobacco, hogs, and milk. Later, beef, dairy cattle, peanuts, barley, flax, sorghums, sugar beets, sugar cane, and potatoes were added. The Secretary of Agriculture was charged with administering the program through voluntary agreements with farmers to reduce acreage, plow under a portion of crops already planted, kill surplus animals, and by other means to produce less in consideration of a cash subsidy. Within one year, 40 million acres were withdrawn from cultivaton and farm income,

The first Agricultural Adjustment Act

---

[2] It was in this era that the Farm bloc came into existence in the Congress. Uniting partisans of both groups, it sponsored one (McNary-Haugen) bill after another designed to raise farm prices by government purchase of surplus and disposition of it abroad. The successes achieved by the bloc were largely in improvements in farm credit which will be discussed later in this chapter.

[3] This objective is popularly referred to as "farm parity" and represents an attempt to bring agriculture prices into a more favorable relationship with industrial prices. A period is selected in which these price relationships were favorable to agriculture and then both sets of prices in this period are indexed at 100. The price situation at any time after the base period can then be measured in terms of the base and farm prices pegged so that the change from the base will be the same for both farm prices and industrial prices. What, in fact, constitutes parity prices for farm products must, under this scheme, be constantly recomputed on the basis of changes in industrial prices relative to the base period.

including the subsidy, had increased 39 percent. The Secretary was also given broad power to eliminate unfair trade practices in the marketing and distribution of all kinds of agricultural commodities.[4] In 1936, this much-debated effort to improve the relative position of American agriculture was swept away by the Supreme Court.[5] The Court held the processing taxes which financed the subsidy program to be unconstitutional. These are not taxes in a real sense, said the Court, but levies upon one group of people for the benefit of another. The field of agricultural production, further said the Court, is reserved to the states and may not be the object of national regulation thinly disguised as taxation.[6] Actually the plan had cost almost twice as much as the tax had yielded.

Produc-
tion-
control
tied to
soil con-
servation

The objectives of the farm policy of the New Deal were partly aided by the devastation of drought, dust storms, and floods in 1934. While helping to keep production down, these disasters also spread new distress among the farmers of the Plains, driving them in large numbers from their homes and onto the highways as itinerant farm laborers. The catastrophes also convinced the nation's leaders that they had some obligation to preserve the nation's resources. The combination of ideas and events suggested to the Congress a way out of the predicament created by the Court decision. In the Soil Conservation and Domestic Allotment Act of 1936, production control was made incidental to soil conservation. Restoration of 1910-1914 farmer purchasing power was now sought by benefit payments to farmers for soil conservation practices which also reduced production of basic commodities. By shifting land from soil-depleting crops (corn, tobacco, wheat, cotton, etc.) to soil-building crops (clover, alfalfa, pasture grasses, etc.), the farmers were stimulated to reduce surpluses of staple crops and save the soil at the same time. No special tax was levied this time: the whole program was financed out of general receipts.

The
second
Agricul-
tural Ad-
justment
Act (1938)

The curtailment in production under the new program was not adequate and, when 1937 and 1938 proved exceptionally good crop years, the old vicious spiral of commodity surpluses and sharply declining prices set in again.

[4] By fixing prices, establishing quotas for producers, providing rules of fair competition, and setting up boards of control, marketing agreements under the act brought into existence a far greater amount of cooperative marketing than previously existed; and the great growth of farm cooperatives in this country (now over 8500) dates from this point. The Department of Agriculture is now required by law to encourage the formation of such cooperatives, and money is lent by the government to supply necessary capital.

[5] United States *v.* Butler, 297 U. S. 1 (often referred to as the Hoosac Mills case). The case arose out of the refusal of the receivers of a bankrupt New Hampshire textile establishment to pay taxes still due on the processing of cotton. A national district court had ordered them to pay the sum; a circuit court of appeals had told them not to pay it because the levy was unconstitutional; and the government had taken the case to the Supreme Court.

[6] The marketing provisions of the law were not affected by the decision, and Congress promptly re-enacted them. But the production features, centered in the processing taxes, went out of the window.

Accordingly, in the latter year, Congress passed a new Agricultural Adjustment Act, scrupulously avoiding processing taxes and any other devices likely
to encounter judicial disapproval, but nevertheless contemplating, like the ill-
fated measure of 1933, direct control of agricultural production. Without
abandoning the conservation tie-up of 1936, the new law sought to achieve the
desired control by supplementary arrangements briefly as follows: (1) if in any
year the production of wheat, corn, cotton, rice, or tobacco threatened to
create a surplus that would break the price, the new Agricultural Adjustment
Administration (AAA) now set up (absorbed in 1945 into the present Production and Marketing Administration) should take a referendum among the
producers of a given crop on the desirability of imposing limitations for the
next crop year; [7] (2) if two-thirds voted favorably, the AAA, operating
through state committees, should allot to each producing county for that year,
on the basis of the average acreage seeded during the preceding 10 years, the
number of acres that might be planted to the given crop; (3) within each
county, and with the cooperation of democratically elected local farmer committees, an allotment should be made, in turn, to each producing farmer (again
on a basis of past average production) of a maximum acreage from which he
might market his product without restriction; (4) a farmer suffering a reduction in income under his allotment should be compensated by a government
subsidy; (5) on the other hand, he might raise more acres of the crop if he

PARITY: INDUSTRIAL AND AGRICULTURAL PRICES

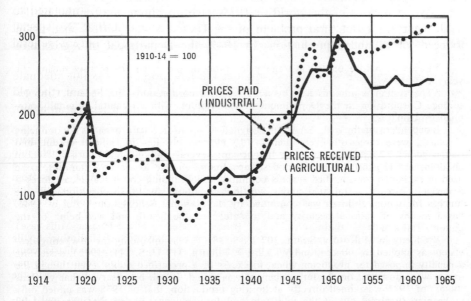

7 L. V. Howard, "The Agricultural Referendum," *Pub. Admin. Rev.,* II, 9-26 (Winter, 1942).

wished, but if marketing products from excess acreage during a period of surplus, he should be subject to fine; (6) on surplus crops so produced, he might, nevertheless, receive loans from the Commodity Credit Corporation in the Department of Agriculture in amounts calculated according to parity prices; [8] (7) such surplus crops should be stored under government seal in elevators or warehouses until a time of scarcity, when the farmer might sell them at the parity price and repay his loans—such sales operating to prevent the market price from ever rising far above parity; and (8) when the price of a given stored commodity should fall below parity, the producer should be entitled to receive from the government payments sufficient to make up the deficiency. In short, surplus crops were to be stored in years of superabundance, without the farmer being left short of cash, and then would be available to be thrown on the market in years of shortage from drought or other cause.

To this system of an "ever-normal granary"—keeping part of the supply out of the market so that what remains will bring a "just" price—were added arrangements for crop insurance, starting tentatively with wheat in 1938 and later extended to cotton and flax. The idea of the insurance program was to protect producers against losses from depleted yields caused by drought, flood, *The new* hail, insect infestation, and plant diseases. Insurance costs (i.e., premiums) *program* were made payable by the insured to the government either in cash or in *found* surplus wheat (or other products), the latter becoming an additional reserve *constitu-* of the ever-normal granary.[9] The revamped farm program was sustained as *tional* constitutional by a now reconstructed Supreme Court [10] and it has formed the basis of all subsequent legislation in this field.

Agricul- As the nations of the world in 1939 gave up diplomacy for the battle-
ture in field, the main agricultural problem of the United States shifted once again
World to need for expanded production. In 1942, the Department of Agriculture
War II

[8] Based as before on the average price ratio of the given commodity during the years 1909-1914.

[9] The system is administered by a government corporation—the Federal Crop Insurance Corporation in the Department of Agriculture, with all capital originally supplied by Congress.

Independent of the new AAA but designed to re-enforce its provisions for reducing surpluses, were three other expedients: (1) export subsidies for wheat, cotton, and cotton goods; (2) provision of free lunches for several million undernourished school children; and (3) distribution of food stamps among eligible low-income families, to be used in exchange for specified surplus commodities (including cotton) at local stores— a device, however, terminated under wartime conditions in 1943. Provision for free lunches for school children was continued by the National School Lunch Act of 1946, "as a means of national security and to safeguard the health and well-being of the nation's children."

[10] Chiefly in Mulford v. Smith, 307 U. S. 38 (1939), upholding the marketing provisions as applied to tobacco, and Wickard v. Filburn, 317 U. S. 111 (1942), sustaining a penalty imposed for producing wheat in excess of a prescribed quota, even though the excess was consumed on the farm where it was raised. It will be observed that whereas the act of 1933 was aimed directly at limiting production, that of 1938 was aimed only at keeping surpluses out of the interstate and foreign markets, and that therefore the Court had to test the latter statute only in terms of interstate and foreign commerce— which made full acceptance of it a matter of no particular difficulty.

announced its goal as "the largest production in the history of American agriculture." The farmers, with bitter memories of the twenties still alive, were, however, reluctant to expand their production facilities without governmental assurance of protection against the inevitable drop in exports at the close of the war. A sympathetic Congress promised (the Stabilization Act of 1942) that the government would support prices of the staple agricultural products (cotton, corn, wheat, rice, tobacco, and peanuts) at not less than 90 percent of parity for the two years after the emergency ended. A benevolent government also made every effort to raise farm income during the difficult periods of wage and price controls and rationing. The result was that American agriculture entered the postwar period in what was probably the strongest financial position it had ever known.[11]

President Truman declared the war emergency at an end in December, 1946. The postwar recession in the national economy and especially the precipitous decline in markets for agricultural products predicted by most of those charged with plotting national policy did not occur immediately. Pent-up consumer demand in the United States and the Marshall Plan of aid to shattered economies abroad sustained a lively demand. And when price and wage controls were abandoned by a government bent on returning to normalcy, agricultural prices led a headstrong upsurge in prices which in a few short years drove the American cost of living to dizzy heights. As the time approached in 1948 for the expiration of the price-support guarantees, a Republican Congress began to hammer out a new farm program in the light of the intoxicating farm prosperity of the forties. Farm groups, however, fearful that the bubble would collapse, leaving them with high production costs and expanded facilities, continued to demand governmental price supports. A bitter wrangle, lasting until the hour of adjournment, developed between the supporters of rigid price supports for the staples at 90 percent of parity and the supporters of a more flexible support program (60-90 percent) by which production might gradually be readjusted to consumption.[12] In the end, the Agriculture (Hope-Aiken) Act of 1948 provided for a temporary continuance of rigid, 90 percent, supports until 1950 and then a long-term program of flexible supports. The old 1910-1914 base period for determining parity with industrial prices was abandoned—as it had been in fact during the emergency —and was replaced with a new formula using prices of the war and postwar

Postwar price-support program

[11] M. R. Benedict, *Farm Policies of the United States 1790-1950,* Twentieth Century Fund (New York, 1953), 459.

[12] It was in this controversy that a new agricultural program was tentatively put forth by Secretary of Agriculture Brannan. This plan figured largely in the campaign of 1948 and was championed by urban Democrats and by the Farmers Union. It was bitterly opposed by the Farm Bureau, the Grange, the southern Democrats, and most Republicans. Brannan's plan briefly was to allow agricultural prices to find their own levels in a free market, thus passing on the savings from mechanization to the consumer and then to subsidize the farmer directly for any losses to him that this program entailed. Although much debated, the plan has never been given serious Congressional consideration.

periods. Since this meant a decline in a few staple prices (wheat, notably), the act provided a transitional period in which the new lower level of prices would gradually be achieved. The support program, although intended for the staples, was authorized for many other crops at the discretion of the Secretary of Agriculture if trouble developed in marketing those commodities at "fair" prices.

The Agri-
cultural
Act of
1949

The repudiation of the Republican record in the election of 1948 was taken by many Democrats as an authorization to abandon the "flexible" features of the Act of 1948. The Agricultural Act of 1949 was largely a victory for the high, rigid, price-support program as against the flexible program. Although provision was made for adjusting support for most types of agricultural products to the market situation, the basic staples which had been the center of the difficulty through the years were virtually assured of a high level of support. The parity formula was once again revised to take account of the high postwar wages of farm labor and the wartime subsidy payments to farmers designed to hold consumer prices down.

The Republican victory of 1952 paved the way for a reconsideration of the whole program. The Eisenhower administration confronted a changed situation in agriculture. The world markets had fallen away as after World War I, and even the Korean episode, and the high level of industrial activity which it stimulated could not bridge the growing gap between production and consumption. The government warehouses, elevators, bins, cribs, and refrigerators were bursting with the protected commodities bought up by the Commodity Credit Corporation in keeping with the high level price-support mandate of the Act of 1949. The Corporation, for example, had in storage in March of 1953:

103,000,000	lbs.	butter	188,000,000	lbs.	linseed oil
96,000,000	lbs.	peanuts	110,000,000	bu.	wheat
52,000,000	lbs.	cheddar cheese	135,000,000	lbs.	resin
257,000,000	bu.	corn	455,000,000	lbs.	cottonseed oil
525,000,000	gal.	turpentine	7,900,000	lbs.	wool
148,000,000	lbs.	dried milk	4,315,000	lbs.	tobacco
236,000,000	bales	cotton	1,600,000,000	lbs.	beans

The Agri-
cultural
Act of
1954

The new administration finally unveiled its farm program in 1954 after a panel of farm representatives had reviewed the matter for several months. The result was a new Agricultural Act which conformed in broad outlines to the recommendations of President Eisenhower and his Secretary of Agriculture, Benson. This act: (1) directed the Commodity Credit Corporation to "set aside" from its inventories large quantities [13] of wheat, cotton, cottonseed

[13] wheat	400-500 million bu.
cotton	3-4 million bales
cottonseed oil	500 million lbs.
butter	200 million lbs.
milk solids	300 million lbs.
cheese	150 million lbs.

oil, butter, milk solids, and cheese which, subject to Presidential direction, might be donated for disaster relief, school lunches, or research purposes, bartered with foreign nations, transferred to the national stockpile of strategic materials, or sold on the market at not less than 105 percent of the parity prices of the commodities; (2) provided for the "basic" or staple commodities a system of flexible price supports at 82½ to 90 percent of parity prices and for dairy products at 75 to 90 percent of parity prices; (3) directed the Veterans Administration and the Defense Department to accept supplies of milk, butter and cheese from the Commodity Corporation from its stocks; (4) expanded the national program for eliminating brucellosis from dairy cattle; (5) tightened the provisions aimed at preventing expansion of staple production into new areas; (6) established agricultural attachés to be located in diplomatic missions abroad for the purpose of promoting the marketing of American agricultural products.

The Soil Bank

To this program was added in 1956, on the recommendation of the President, a "soil bank" arrangement aimed at permanently reducing by voluntary and compensated effort the acreage planted to the protected crops—mainly, corn, wheat, cotton, and rice. Farmers could retire acres from cultivation, putting them into pasture, trees, or grasses and receive payments for the loss of production involved. Under this program 28 million acres were retired from cultivation from 1956 to 1960.

The Kennedy Program

Meanwhile the Democrats recaptured control of the Congress in 1954 and held it through Eisenhower's second term. Efforts to restore rigid price support programs were turned back in 1956 and in 1958 by Presidential veto. Although committed to improving farm income, President Kennedy was urban-consumer minded and thus anxious to hold prices of food down and also to reduce the cost of agricultural programs in order to finance new urban reforms without increasing the overall budget. The farm program unveiled in 1961-1962 recommended much greater flexibility in supply management. Heretofore, the major production control system had been acreage allotments, and as more and more crops were being harvested from the same acres the control was not effective. The Kennedy program sought to combine market controls with acreage allotments and also to reduce the acreage whenever feasible. Congress, on the whole, refused to give the Secretary of Agriculture the kind of flexible authority requested and refused seriously to curtail acreage except by paid and temporary retirement of land from cultivation. A patched-up law, passed late in 1962, was satisfactory to no one, and in 1963, for the first time in 30 years a production control referenda among wheat farmers was defeated.

Johnson shifts emphasis

President Johnson attempted in 1964, and even more so in 1965, to shift the emphasis from price supports to general improvement of rural life, linking his efforts to maintain farm income with his general attack on poverty. Subsidies to cotton textile mills to compensate for the artificially high prices of domestic cotton were introduced into the legislation in 1964 and a two-price (one for domestic and one for export and feed grain sales) system for wheat introduced in 1963 was continued through 1964 and 1965. Programs for long-term removal of acreage from staple crop production were started on a small scale in 1965. New and increased diversion of surplus crops to the needy at home (food stamp plans and school lunch programs) and abroad (the food-for-peace program) were authorized.

The Commodity Credit Corporation

The heart of the modern effort to sustain a relatively high level of farm prosperity is the purchase by the government of the excess yields of farm products. The chief instrument for its accomplishment is the Commodity Credit Corporation in the Department of Agriculture. This Corporation, created in 1933 and assigned to the Department of Agriculture in 1939, is governed, under the general supervision of the Secretary, by a board of directors of six members appointed by the President with the consent of the Senate. It is authorized to borrow $14.5 billion to carry out its missions. The Corporation's typical method of operation is to loan to eligible farmers the full value of their harvest at the supported price with the harvest as security. If the farmer cannot dispose of his crop on more favorable terms, he simply allows the Corporation to possess the crop. Commodities are also purchased in the open market at the support price. During World War II, the Corporation gradually disposed of its holdings, usually at a profit, but the modern era of falling exports has forced the corporation to take on more and more commodities. Its inventories had grown to $3.5 billion by June, 1953, and were $7.4 billion by June of 1961, and $4.3 billion in June, 1965.

Every effort by the experts of the Department of Agriculture to promote the diversification of agriculture in the great staple producing areas, to improve marketing practices, to find new uses for the staple crops, to reduce acreage devoted to price-supported commodities, to dispose of surpluses to needy children and to barter surpluses abroad has thus far fallen short of bringing production into line with demand. The supporters of a flexible price program believe it offers the only feasible hope for gradually adjusting production to effective consumption. Those favoring "high" supports cite the distress of the twenties, the pledges of the government during World War II, the importance of the great staple producing areas in the nation, the value of the family farm, and the amount of rural poverty as justification for heavy and continuing annual subsidies to the producers. There is not on the horizon a politically acceptable program looking toward the return of a free market for agricultural production. In an imperfect world, it is, of course, better to be troubled by glut than by famine.

PROVISION OF FARM CREDIT

A growing need

When, in earlier days of more diversified agriculture, a farmer wanted to acquire additional land, make improvements, or perhaps carry over a crop in the hope of a better market, he normally turned for funds to a commercial bank. And a considerable amount of such borrowing still goes on. Commercial banks, however, have always been interested primarily in serving the needs of industry and commerce, and, if loaning money at all to farmers and stock raisers (regarded as greater risks), have been likely to do so only on less favorable terms, including higher rates of interest. Moreover, in recent decades a steadily increasing proportion of agriculture has ceased to be diversified and become specialized. Cotton farmers there always were, but now we have, in addition, wheat farmers, corn and hog farmers, dairy farmers, fruit farmers, ranchers, and what not. While some of these, especially dairy farmers, may have proceeds coming in more or less all of the time, it is characteristic of most of them to have little income except at one or two periods of the year when cash crops or herds are ready for marketing. To normal farmer needs for credit on favorable terms are therefore added special demands arising from this new situation. Furthermore, the farmers complained persistently for several generations about the heavy exactions on farm income made by Eastern financial institutions.

The result has been the building up, over the past 50 years, of a country-wide system of credit institutions—a network of banks and other agencies authorized, supported, and regulated by the national government, and operated exclusively for service to the farmer. The development started in 1916, when, after commissions appointed by Presidents Taft and Wilson had looked into the needs existing even in that day, Congress passed the first piece of farm credit legislation in our history, a Federal Farm Loan Act. Some quarters viewed it as dubiously "radical," yet both major parties had warmly endorsed such a program in the last previous Presidential campaign. A Federal Farm Loan Board was set up in the Treasury Department as manager, and in a leading city of each of 12 districts was established a federal land bank, with capital originally subscribed mainly by the national government, and endowed with power to issue tax-exempt bonds to raise money with which to make long-term loans secured by first mortgages on landed property. These land banks lend money, however, not directly to individual farmers, but to groups of 10 or more organized voluntarily in what are known as national farm loan associations. An association receives applications from its members, approves or rejects them, takes and endorses mortgages on approved applicants' property, and, on the basis of these, secures from the appropriate bank funds which it passes out in the form of loans to its members.[14] To broaden the service, the same act of 1916 also authorized the formation of joint-stock land banks, with capital stock subscribed by private individuals, and enjoying about the same privileges and performing the same functions as the federal land banks. And to complete the structure, an Agricultural Credits Act of 1923 instituted a series of 12 intermediate credit banks designed particularly

A farm loan system instituted

[14] R. J. Bulkley, "The Federal Farm Loan Act," *Jour. of Polit. Econ.,* XXV, 129-147 (Feb., 1917); G. E. Putnam, "The Federal Farm Loan Act," *Amer. Econ. Rev.,* VI, 770-789 (Dec., 1916). The Federal land bank system is organized on the cooperative principle, and all of the stock of the 12 banks is now owned by the national farm loan associations and a few direct borrowers.

to serve the farmer who wanted not long-term credit but loans for a few months or a year, and loans secured not on land but on livestock, corn, wheat, or other commodities.

After the depression of the thirties harassed the country for some time, with little promise of abating, it became apparent that still ampler credit facilities would have to be provided. By 1933, a tenth of the country's farms had been sold at public auction to satisfy creditors, and the number of such sales was steadily rising.[15] The act creating the Reconstruction Finance Corporation in 1932 had, it is true, empowered that agency to organize regional agricultural credit corporations in the 12 federal land-bank districts, with capital in each case of not less than $3 million subscribed by the Corporation; and loans made by these institutions had helped. Need remained; and additional legislation providing various new borrowing facilities was introduced. An Emergency Farm Mortgage Act of 1933 (constituting a section of the Agricultural Adjustment Act of that year) opened up ways for the farmer to borrow directly from a fund of $200 million administered by a farm-loan commissioner (later land-bank commissioner) in a Farm Credit Administration now superseding the Federal Farm Loan Board, and in particular made borrowings available for the redemption or repurchase of farm property lost under foreclosure proceedings during the previous two years. A Farm Credit Act of the same year (*a*) set up 12 production credit corporations, one in each city having a federal land bank, to provide short-term credit for all types of farm and ranch operations; and (*b*) instituted a system of banks to serve 12,000 or more cooperative buying and selling associations among farmers of the country—a central bank for cooperatives and regional banks operating in the same 12 cities. The Commodity Credit Corporation mentioned above was brought into existence by executive order of 1933, with power to buy, hold, sell, lend upon, or otherwise deal in such agricultural commodities as might be designated from time to time by the President. And a Federal Farm Mortgage Corporation, created by Congress in 1934 in an act amplifying the Emergency Farm Mortgage Act of the previous year, was empowered to issue tax-exempt bonds (guaranteed by the government) which might be exchanged for others held or issued by federal land banks, thereby increasing the resources of those banks available for the refinancing of farm mortgages.[16]

The outcome of the somewhat complicated series of measures reviewed is a gigantic credit structure with the following present principal features:

[15] Most farms thus sold passed into the possession of banks, insurance companies, mortgage companies, and other financial institutions. In Iowa, for example, one-tenth of all farm land was by 1935 held by corporations.

[16] After one act of Congress providing for moratoria on the foreclosure of farm mortgages was pronounced unconstitutional by the Supreme Court in 1935 (Louisville Joint-Stock Land Bank *v.* Radford, 295 U. S. 555), another on somewhat different lines was upheld (Wright *v.* Vinton Branch Mountain Trust Bank, 300 U. S. 440) in 1937. As a result, large numbers of farmers were enabled to procure adjustments with their creditors and retain their land.

(1) a federal land bank in a principal city of each of 12 farm credit districts, such banks making mortgage-secured 5 percent loans through local farmer associations to individual members for purchasing land, equipment, or livestock, improving land, constructing buildings, or liquidating debt; (2) a federal intermediate credit bank in each district, making loans to production credit associations, banks for cooperatives, livestock loan companies, and similar financing institutions; (3) a production credit corporation in each district serving the farmer who wants not long-term credit but loans for a few months or a year, and secured not on land but on livestock, corn, wheat, or other commodities; and (4) a bank for cooperatives in each district, providing a permanent source of credit on a sound business basis for the multiplying farmers' cooperative associations.

In all cases, capital was supplied originally by the national government. Borrowers, however, were required to purchase stock, with a view to the banks eventually passing completely under cooperative ownership. As a result of wartime and postwar agricultural prosperity, most of the government's capital has now been retired. All of the different layers of credit institutions, too, are coordinated within a district by a farm credit board composed of the directors of the four banks, and nationally by a Farm Credit Administration—an establishment which in performing its functions has become one of the principal banking institutions of the country.

The Farm Credit Administration (FCA) was created in 1939 by gathering together the autonomous and Treasury-directed loan agencies of the time and placing them in the Department of Agriculture. The move to bring these heretofore conservatively managed credit programs under the direction of the reforming zeal of Secretary Wallace was strongly opposed at the time by the Farm Bureau and the Grange. A Republican Congress in 1953 finally responded to the wishes of these farm associations and detached the FCA from the Department and gave it independent status in the executive branch. Under the Farm Credit Act of 1953, the governing body prescribed for FCA is now a Federal Farm Credit Board of 13 members, one from each of the 12 credit districts, appointed by the President with the consent of the Senate and with the advice of the local farm loan association members, and one appointed by the Secretary of Agriculture. A governor appointed by the Board is the chief executive officer of the system. A Farmers Home Administration, which supplies credit for the purchase or repair of family-size farm units, remains in the department as does the Federal Crop Insurance Corporation. Some conception of the magnitude of these credit operations may be gathered from the fact that in 1965 there were more than $4 billion of loans outstanding among these various agencies.[17]

Farm Credit Adminis- tration

[17] See the *Report of the Commission on Organization of the Executive Branch of the Government* entitled "Lending, Guaranteeing and Insurance Activities" (Washington, 1955) for a review of the farm credit program and recommendations for reducing the government influence in the area of farm credit.

IMPROVEMENT OF RURAL LIFE

Throughout the years and especially in the periods 1933-1940 and 1963-1965, the national government has supplemented its concern for production and distribution with programs aimed at improving the human, or social, aspects of farming. Impelled to do this by rural backwardness and distress brought sharply to view by the depression of the thirties, and by the continued exodus from farm to city, the Department of Agriculture, with a good deal of backing from Congress, now regards as part of its task the systematic promotion of better living conditions on the farm and in rural communities.[18] Only a few outstanding services of this nature can, however, be mentioned here.

1. Relief for farm tenants

The agricultural credit institutions described above are designed primarily to benefit farmers who own, or have an ownership interest in, the land they cultivate. There is another large agricultural element that cannot avail itself of these agencies, for the reason that those belonging to it own no land and little, if any, other property that might serve as security for loans. These less fortunate people—commonly excluded also from wage and hour provisions, unemployment insurance, and workmen's compensation—are the tenant farmers, sharecroppers, and farm laborers, who from 1880 until 1945 steadily increased in proportion to the number of farm owners, and now comprise at least one-third of the total number tilling the soil. They (or many of them) are the people who give rise to what is called the farm tenancy problem; and the areas where large numbers of them live, notably the southern and southwestern states, form our "rural slums." Following a penetrating, and fairly startling, report in 1937 on the conditions and outlook of these submerged groups, submitted by a committee on farm tenancy appointed by President Franklin D. Roosevelt, Congress in the same year passed the Farm Tenant (Bankhead-Jones) Act, under which the government, operating through state and local machinery terminating in county committees of farmers, offers 40-year loans (at 5 percent and up to $12,000) to farm tenants, farm laborers, and sharecroppers (with preference for veterans) to enable them to acquire homes and lands of their own; and likewise "rehabilitation loans" (at 5 percent and to a maximum of $5,000) for the purchase of livestock, seed, fertilizers, and farm equipment, for refinancing indebtedness, and for family subsistence, including medical care. Mortgages on loans for similar purposes made by private lenders also are insured. Under the direction of a Farmers Home Administration set up in the Department of Agriculture in 1946 (and of a previous Farm Security Administration), more than $3 billion had been loaned directly or insured up

[18] This function it shares, of course, with establishments such as the Department of Labor, the Public Health Service, and the Office of Education; and all have drawn inspiration and guidance from private agencies such as the Country Life Commission appointed by President Theodore Roosevelt some 55 years ago. For a broad treatment of the subject, see J. M. Gaus and L. Wolcott, *Public Administration and the Department of Agriculture* (Chicago, 1940), Chap. XI.

to 1965. Loans (made through offices commonly located in county-seat towns) are not confined to the categories of persons mentioned, but are extended also to better situated "family-type" farmers who for some reason cannot get the credit they need elsewhere, at all events on favorable terms.[19]

Until three decades ago, the United States lagged behind several other *2. Rural* countries in bringing electrical energy within the reach of rural populations, *electrifi-* and even today some 2.5 percent of the nation's more than 3.7 million farms *cation* still are without electric light and power. In 1936, however (when only 10 percent of farms were electrified), Congress passed a Rural Electrification (Norris-Rayburn) Act launching a long-term program under which large progress has been made toward providing farms with cheap light and power, relieving the drudgery of the farmer and his wife, and adding to the farm's income-producing equipment. Management of the undertaking is vested in a Rural Electrification Administration (REA), at first independent, but since 1939 a unit within the Department of Agriculture. Such management consists principally in making long-term, self-liquidating, 2 percent loans up to 100 percent of cost (1) to associations (usually farmer cooperatives organized for the purpose), corporations, or local-government bodies, to enable them to build transmission lines and buy generators for furnishing electrical energy to people in rural areas for whom central-station services are not available, and (2) to individuals or firms engaged in wiring farm buildings and installing electrical and plumbing appliances and equipment—no loans being extended directly to consumers. Down to June 30, 1965, funds to a total of $4.72 billion (usually borrowed by the REA from the Reconstruction Finance Corporation) were loaned to 1105 cooperative or corporate borrowers in 47 states and the Virgin Islands—making possible more than 1.5 million miles of line, serving more than 5.4 million farms and rural dwellings. Private utility companies also have, of course, been expanding their services in rural areas— sometimes, it is charged, deliberately to discourage government-financed undertakings from being started. Fifty-seven percent of all farms electrified since 1936, however, get their power through systems developed by REA.[20]

The government's task of rural electrification is expected to start taper- *3. Rural* ing off and to be completed in a few years. In 1949, however, Congress decided *telephone* to move also into the field of rural communications and passed an act author- *service* izing the REA to begin making 2 percent loans to independent telephone companies (of which there are 5762 in the country), farm cooperatives, and nonprofit mutual associations to establish and extend telephone services for the 58 percent of the nation's farms still without such conveniences. Critics of

---

[19] *Report of the President's Committee* [on farm tenancy], published by the National Resources Committee at Washington, in 1937; R. B. Vance, "Farmers Without Land," *Pub. Affairs Pamphlets,* No. 12 (New York, 1937); *Law and Contemporary Problems,* IV, 423-575 (Oct., 1937), series of articles on farm tenancy. A congressional joint subcommittee made a new study of the low-income farmer in 1949-1950.

[20] For a full account see H. H. Trachsel, *Public Utility Regulation* (Chicago, 1947), Chap. XXI.

the plan objected that it would inflict unfair competition upon private companies, that the telephone might become obsolete, leaving the government with a useless investment, and that the undertaking might prove an entering wedge for government control of all communications and for curtailment of freedom of speech. But such arguments did not prevail and by mid-1965 the REA had loaned $1.2 billion for telephone service extensions.

References

M. Fainsod, L. Gordon, and J. Palamountain, *Government and the American Economy* (3rd ed., New York, 1959), Chap. VI.

E. S. Redford and C. B. Hagan, *American Government and the Economy* (New York, 1965), Chap. XXII.

S. C. Wallace, *The New Deal in Action* (New York, 1934), Chaps. IX-XV.

B. Rausch, *The History of the New Deal, 1933-1938* (New York, 1944), Chaps. XI, XIV.

D. C. Blaisdell, *Government and Agriculture: The Growth of Federal Farm Aid* (New York, 1940).

A. L. Meyers, *Agriculture and the National Economy,* Temporary Nat. Econ. Committee, Monograph No. 23 (Washington, 1940).

J. M. Gaus and L. O. Wolcott, *Public Administration and the Department of Agriculture* (Chicago, 1940).

C. R. Ball, *Federal, State, and Local Administrative Relationships, in Agriculture,* 2 vols. (Berkeley, Calif., 1938).

A. C. True, *A History of Agricultural Experimentation and Research in the United States, 1607-1925* (Washington, 1937).

T. S. Harding, *Two Blades of Grass: A History of Scientific Development in the United States Department of Agriculture* (Norman, Okla., 1947).

G. Baker, *The County Agent* (Chicago, 1939).

C. B. Smith and M. C. Wilson, *The Agricultural Extension System of the United States* (New York, 1930).

E. S. Sparks, *History and Theory of Agricultural Credit in the United States* (New York, 1932).

E. L. Butz, *The Production Credit System for Farmers* (Washington, 1944).

J. C. Clendenin, *Federal Crop Insurance in Operation* (Palo Alto, Calif., 1942).

W. H. Clark, *Farms and Farmers: The Story of American Agriculture* (Boston, 1945).

W. McCune, *The Farm Bloc* (Garden City, N.Y., 1943).

A. F. Oehman, "The Agricultural Adjustment Act of 1938," *Georgetown Law Jour.,* XXVI (Mar., 1938), 680-694.

Congressional Quarterly Service, *U. S. Agricultural Policy in the Postwar Years: 1945-63* (Washington, 1963).

E. G. Nourse *et al., Three Years of the Agricultural Adjustment Administration* (Washington, 1937).

J. D. Lewis, "Democratic Planning in Agriculture," *Amer. Polit. Sci. Rev.*, XXXV, (Apr. and June, 1941), 232-249, 454-469.

E. Higbee, *Farms and Farmers in an Urban Age* (New York, 1963).

D. E. Hadwiger and R. B. Talbot, *Pressure and Protests: the Kennedy Farm Program and the Wheat Referendum of 1963* (San Francisco, 1965).

W. Gee, *The Social Economics of Agriculture* (New York, 1932).

F. M. Muller, *Public Rural Electrification* (Washington, 1944).

M. R. Benedict, *Farm Policies of the United States, 1790-1950,* Twentieth Century Fund (New York, 1953).

R. M. Christensen, *The Brannan Plan: Farm Politics and Policy* (Ann Arbor, Mich., 1959).

Dept. of Agriculture, *After a Hundred Years: The Yearbook of Agriculture, 1962* (Washington, 1962).

Annual reports of the Secretary of Agriculture, the administrator of the Farm Credit Administration, the administrator of the Farmers Home Administration, the administrator of the Rural Electrification Administration, etc.

★ 21 ★

Conserving the Nation's Resources

PERHAPS IT IS inevitable that an energetic and growing people taking over a virgin continental expanse richly endowed by nature should be guilty of extravagance and waste. So, at all events, it has been in the United States, where for 100 years good land was so abundant, and forest, mineral, and other resources so apparently inexhaustible, that no generation felt much concern about economical use in its own time or possible shortages later on. On the theory that the quickest and surest way to develop the country was to get its resources into the hands of people who would settle new areas, promote new industries, and expand national production, the national government (state governments also within their more restricted spheres) prodigally sold or gave away agricultural land, mineral lands, forest lands, and whatever else was available, to substantially any private individuals, corporations, or other interests desiring them. When good grass land was put to the plough and exposed to ruinous soil erosion, or noble forests were devastated by rapacious lumber companies, or petroleum, gas, coal, and other mineral deposits were wastefully used, there were few to protest.[1]

Toward the close of the nineteenth century, however, warnings began to be sounded, not only that the supply of available public land was fast diminishing, but that continued heedless exploitation of forests, minerals, and other natural wealth would one day leave the country impoverished. Sharing this apprehension were President Theodore Roosevelt and a group of close associates; and measures for protecting and developing the country's resources became one of that chief executive's principal concerns. A new gospel of conservation was preached with crusading zeal; a national commission was set to work surveying conditions and needs; the governors of the states were called into conference at the White House; and for the first time the nation became to some degree "conservation conscious." The entire idea, however, ran sharply counter to a century-old tradition, and not only did powerful interests with something to lose resist it, but people generally had difficulty divesting

---

[1] "It was once said by Henry A. Wallace . . . that 'no civilization has ever builded in so short a time what our forefathers builded in America'; but it may equally well be suggested that no civilization has in so short a time consumed and destroyed so much of the resources of the earth." H. Finer, *The T.V.A.: Lessons for International Application* (Montreal, 1944), 3.

themselves of the notion that there was plenty of everything and that future generations would take care of themselves. During the next half-century, the fact was gradually brought home that—with greater needs in prospect as population grew and standards of living improved—we already had used up more than half of our known petroleum supply, the larger part (it was reported) of our natural gas, more than a third of our high-grade coal, most of our best iron, an alarming share of our copper, lead, and zinc, and an amazingly large proportion of our forest reserves (to say nothing of having exhausted millions of acres of our soil). During this half-century, laws were passed, agencies of enforcement and supervision set up, and land, forests, minerals, water supply, and water-power sites here and there given moderately effective protection. The earliest efforts were directed almost exclusively at the resources of the publicly owned parts of the country. But gradually it became clear that if the nation was to benefit from the conservation on the scale required for its future well-being, controls would have to be extended, so far as constitutionally possible, to privately owned areas as well. Spurred by the depression of the thirties, by the recurring droughts, dust storms, floods, and other disasters of the same period, and eventually by the necessity for maximum utilization of our resources (the "sinews and muscles of our defense machinery") for national defense and war—such broadening of scope became one of the major themes of the New Deal era.

In the course of this development, the concept of conservation underwent significant expansion. At the outset, it was limited to maintaining in adequate supply resources like forests which, as used, could be renewed, and to eliminating avoidable waste of others, such as oil and gas, not capable of replenishment. It still includes these things, but in addition extends to many kinds of resources not originally embraced. To this somewhat negative emphasis on simple replacement or avoidable depletion has been added the idea of conservation as a positive policy of maximum utilization of resources for the satisfaction of maximum social needs. As the Department of the Interior put it in a report of three decades ago, conservation now means "the management and wise use of the natural assets to prevent their depletion and at the same time *to produce wealth.*" [2] It has come to mean not only preventing

What conservation means

[2] *Why a Department of Conservation,* 75th Cong., 3rd Sess., Sen. Doc. No. 142 (1938), 3. How appropriately the Interior Department (dating from 1849) might be renamed "Department of Conservation," or of "Natural Resources"—as often suggested —is indicated by the following list of its major bureaus and other divisions: (1) Bureau of Land Management; (2) Bureau of Reclamation; (3) Geological Survey; (4) Bureau of Mines; (5) Fish and Wildlife Service; (6) Bureau of Indian Affairs; (7) National Park Service; (8) Bureau of Outdoor Recreation; (9) Bonneville Power Administration; (10) Southwestern Power Administration; (11) Southeastern Power Administration; and (12) Office of Territories. With three members urging a new "Department of Natural Resources," a majority of the Hoover Commission of 1948-1949 nevertheless thought the present Interior Department (with considerable reorganization) and the present name sufficiently satisfactory to be retained. Transfers recommended included the Bureau of Indian Affairs to a proposed new Department of Social Welfare and the Bureau of Land Management to the Department of Agriculture, and of Flood Control and Rivers and

existing farms from being ruined by soil erosion, but making new farms available through provision of water for irrigation; not only protecting existing forests from devastation, but developing means for their prudent use, with additions meanwhile from lands too worn out or otherwise marginal to be worth much for other purposes; not only keeping oil and gas from burning in the fields, but restricting general output in the interest of coming generations. Broadly, as stated by two writers, it means adjusting the entire natural environment—forbidding here, restricting there, developing yonder—to human requirements and achieving a reasonable balance between the present and future needs of society.[3]

National-state relations

From every point of view, conservation is an appropriate field for governmental action, and indeed quite dependent upon it. The rugged individualists who developed the country in pioneering days proceeded on the principle of taking and using what they found; and, left to themselves, their more sophisticated but hardly less acquisitive descendants probably would have not much more regard for the interests of posterity. Moreover, the tasks involved (including planning) are of such magnitude, geographically and otherwise, that only governments can undertake them. Like so many others of our public enterprises, however, the work of conservation is considerably complicated by our federal system. Up to a point, it is true, the national government has free scope. As we shall see, more than one-fifth of the country (mainly but by no means exclusively west of the Mississippi) is owned outright by the nation as a whole; and on this "public domain" the national government, as proprietor, can lease grazing lands, restrict access to minerals, regulate the use of forests and plant new ones, control the exploitation of water power, protect wildlife, and, speaking broadly, do anything else that it likes, with no constitutional questions raised. Here is where conservation activities have been pursued most vigorously and effectively. The greater part of the country's resources, however, are in areas over which the national government has no control as owner; and in these it falls to the states and their subdivisions to do much of whatever is done. The results are very uneven. Some states have well-developed programs covering forest protection and extension, control over water resources, regulation of oil and gas production, promotion of drainage and irrigation projects, and protection of fish and other wildlife, according as such activities are appropriate to particular states. Other states are lax; some

---

Harbors Improvement from the Department of the Army to that of the Interior. *The Department of the Interior* (Washington, D.C., 1949). Two major conservation agencies —the Soil Conservation Service and the Forest Service—were to be left where they still are, i.e., in the Department of Agriculture. No one of the transfers mentioned has as yet been made.

[3] M. Fainsod and L. Gordon, *Government and the National Economy* (rev. ed., New York, 1948), 735. The conservation problem is world-wide, with great barren stretches of China affording perhaps the best illustration of what happens to a country where resources are consumed without control or replacement. Two books in which the subject is interestingly treated in its world setting are F. Osborn, *Our Plundered Planet* (Boston, 1948), and W Vogt, *Road to Survival* (New York, 1948).

do not even have a department of conservation, planning board, or other such agency. In any event, plenty of room is left for national authorities to help out—which indeed they must do if there is to be any approach to effective conservation the country over.

In spite of constitutional limitations, means for such participation have been discovered. Through discussion and published information, the national government can educate the people on the subject; through grants-in-aid, it can join with the states in financing and controlling conservation activities; its commerce power can be invoked in regulating the development and use of navigable streams, the sale of commodities and services, for example, hydroelectric energy, and the interstate transmission of oil and gas, and its treaty-making power in protecting migratory wildlife; through voluntary arrangements carried out in conjunction with states, it can enlist farmers in programs of soil conservation, and from these in turn derive means of controlling crop production. All of these things not only can be, but are being, done; and it is reasonable to expect that as time goes on, conservation, like many other activities cutting across national-state lines, will more and more be nationalized.

LAND AND LAND USE

National conservation activities have to do, first of all, with the most *Public* basic of natural resources, that is, land, and in two principal ways—safeguard- *land* ing the public domain and protecting the soil of arable land wherever threatened by depletion through erosion. Of the total 2.2 billion acres contained in the United States today, upwards of 1.8 billion acres, or 80 percent, have at one time or another been "public land," land nationally owned. Of this, more than a billion acres have been sold or given away, leaving a present national domain of somewhat over 770 million acres or more than one-fifth of the total national area. Five states, Nevada, Idaho, Alaska, Oregon, and Utah, contain more public land than private land. Of lands disposed of, vast quantities were in earlier times granted to the states for sale in aid of education and internal improvements; later on, much was bestowed upon transcontinental railroads; a great deal was allotted to veterans; large tracts were sold to speculating land companies; and under terms of the Homestead Act of 1862—offering 160 acres to anyone who would pay a registration fee of $10 and perform a limited amount of work on his holding during a period of five years—millions upon millions of acres were parcelled out among pioneering home-seekers.[4] Prodigality and fraud often went hand in hand; yet vast areas passed into the possession of thrifty populations and helped make the country what it is today.[5]

With the national domain shrinking, however, to something approaching

[4] In 1909, homestead grants in arid and semiarid areas were increased to 320 acres; and in 1916 grants in other areas to 640 acres, in the interest of stock-raising.

[5] On public land history and policy, see B. H. Hibbard, *A History of Public Land Policies* (New York, 1924); R. S. Yard, *Our Federal Lands: A Romance of National Development* (New York, 1928); and R. M. Robbins, *Our Landed Heritage: The Public Domain, 1776-1936* (Princeton, N. J., 1942).

its present proportions, and with the newer idea of conservation developing, the government 40 or 50 years ago grew less lavish. Restrictions were imposed on free entry; large areas were set off as permanent national holdings; and finally, after a decade of virtual suspension, allotments were entirely stopped in 1935. In 1946, President Truman, by executive order, reopened certain remaining lands to entry (except any containing deposits of thorium, uranium, or other "fissionable materials for the release of atomic energy") under carefully guarded conditions. With the government also acquiring land by purchase, condemnation, cession, or gift, from private (or sometimes even public) holders, and adding it to public forests or utilizing it for park development, water-power development, or other purposes, the expectation is that henceforth there will be little net loss of acreage in the public domain. Land acquisitions sometimes raise fiscal problems for the states affected. Once the title to land is vested in the national government, such land becomes immune from state and local taxation. In response to demands for recompense, Congress has enacted legislation requiring some of the national undertakings to make contributions to units of government most affected, in lieu of taxes.[6]

Bureau of Land Management

A large part of the public domain—180 million acres in continental U.S. and 290 million acres in Alaska—is today administered by the Bureau of Land Management of the Department of Interior. This Bureau was created in 1946 by a consolidation of the General Land Office and the Grazing Service. The Bureau is responsible for leasing mineral rights on public lands, for granting permits to livestock growers for grazing privileges on the national ranges, and for the protection and care of the lands under its control. The Bureau is one of the few governmental agencies that regularly earns more income than it spends. The grazing program which it administers on about 170 million acres of the national domain is a good illustration of modern conservation policies. In 1934, President Roosevelt, largely under the authority of the Taylor Grazing Act of that year, closed off large sections of the public domain to further entry but provided for national management of these lands as grazing areas for the cattle and sheep herders who had been theretofore overusing them. Under this law, the bureau attempts to control grazing and also charges a fee for the use of the areas for these purposes. These fees have increased several times since the original imposition.

Project 2012

Late in 1960, the bureau proposed to the Congress a long-range program, called Project 2012, for managing the public domain. This plan was aimed at transferring into private ownership lands that might be valuable for urban or suburban development and at classifying all public lands with a view to improving their usability. The proposals came late in the session and many Congressmen were critical of land sales that would allow substantial private

---

[6] Contributions within its area are made, for example, by the Tennessee Valley Authority. In lieu of taxes on national forests lands, the national government turns over 25 percent of its receipts from such lands to the states in which they are situated; and in the case of mineral lands, 37.5 percent of all royalties received.

development profits. However, in the Public Land Administration Act of that year, the bureau was given broad authority to investigate land areas and to enter cooperative agreements for more effective management of the land. The Kennedy administration indicated it would not support sales of public lands where parties other than the government receive windfall profits, but it approved classification and improved multi-purpose utilization. It also promulgated the policy that the lands would no longer be open to settlement except under unusual circumstances. President Johnson has also endorsed these policies and supported the creation of a Public Land Law Review Commission by Congress in 1964 to reconsider the entire policy of public land administration.

Large stretches of the earlier public domain, located chiefly in the western states, were arid or semiarid—much of the land fertile enough, but unproductive unless supplied with water. Since 1902, a Bureau of Reclamation in the Interior Department has been charged with conservation and distribution of limited water resources in 17 Rocky Mountain, Southwestern, and Pacific Coast states and Alaska—largely by construction of dams, reservoirs, aqueducts, pumping stations, and the like. In 1965, 92 completed projects or divisions of projects were serving with water more than eight million acres, producing crops worth more than $1 billion. The primary objective is, of course, the transformation of dry lands into permanently productive farms and the maintenance of production on lands threatened with drying up because of shortages of water supplies from other systems. Bracketed with these purposes are drainage, flood control, municipal water supply, sometimes navigation, and more and more frequently, the generation of hydroelectric power. The bureau was in 1965 operating 40 power plants with 5.7 million kilowatts of installed capacity. The most spectacular of its reclamation projects is the

Reclamation

EXTENT OF EROSION IN THE UNITED STATES

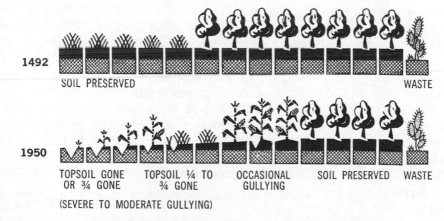

1492

SOIL PRESERVED   WASTE

1950

TOPSOIL GONE   TOPSOIL ¼ TO   OCCASIONAL   SOIL PRESERVED   WASTE
OR ¾ GONE   ¾ GONE   GULLYING

(SEVERE TO MODERATE GULLYING)

EACH BLOCK REPRESENTS 135 MILLION ACRES

Colorado River development, which features Hoover Dam. By irrigating lands and opening up farms, the government tends to aggravate its already serious problem of agricultural overproduction. But it also meets a strong demand for cultivable land. Three-fourths or more of the national funds expended are recovered from water uses and power sales; and, in any case, pressure of western sentiment for such improvements is too strong to be resisted. Throughout its history, in fact, reclamation has been a fruitful source of sectionalism in politics. In efforts to meet the growing criticism of the huge demands on our water resources from irrigation and of the use of such programs to swell crop surpluses, Congress began writing into some of the reclamation authorizations prohibitions against using irrigated land for crops in surplus supply and also encouraging the bureau to consider municipal and industrial uses for its stored water capacity.

Soil con-
servation
For a good while before an unprecedented plague of devastating floods and dust storms prompted Congress, in 1935, to pass the Soil Conservation Act mentioned earlier,[7] it had been realized by agricultural experts that the country's most precious resource of all (apart from water), soil, was being depleted in almost every area where land was ploughed, and in great regions of the West and Southwest with startling rapidity. Yellowed rivulets and turbid major streams alike, after every rain, testified mutely—as did also clouds of powdery dust borne eastward across the country by air currents in periods of drought—to the irrecoverable wealth that was being lost; fields once productive grew barren and useless; farm after farm went to ruin. Starting its work under the new legislation mentioned, a Soil Conservation Service in the Department of Agriculture reported in 1936 that, throughout the country as a whole, a total of 735 million acres of land (enough to make 20 states the size of Illinois), once well adapted to cultivation, grazing, or forest culture, had been seriously impaired or totally destroyed by either water or wind erosion, or both. Ten years later, the same authority still was obliged to say that 500,000 acres were being ruined by erosion every year, at a direct and indirect cost to the country of $3 billion. Even yet there is alarming wastage, 3 billion tons of top matter, we are told, being washed or blown annually from our fields, many of which ought never to have been ploughed. The worst dust storms in history occurred in 1954 and damaged 13.2 million acres of crop land. But the Soil Conservation Service now cooperates vigorously with states, localities, and individual farmers in bringing about physical adjustments in land and introducing soil conservation methods (contouring, strip-cropping, terracing, crop rotation, farm drainage, and the like). The vehicle selected by the Congress to achieve soil conservation on farms was the specially created Soil Conservation district rather than the traditional Agricultural Extension system. Every state

[7] The act declared it "the policy of Congress to provide permanently for the control and prevention of soil erosion and thereby to preserve natural resources, control floods, prevent impairment of reservoirs, maintain the navigation of rivers and harbors, protect public health and public lands, and to relieve unemployment." See M. S. Steward, "Saving Our Soil," *Publ. Affairs Pamphlets,* No. 14 (New York, 1947).

and major territory has now enacted laws under which soil-conservation districts (often coinciding with counties) may be set up for carrying out the program under direction of a state soil-conservation committee and of locally elected farmer committees. By 1964 a total of 2971 such districts, embracing more than two-thirds of all the farms in the country, have been organized.[8] Individual landowners within any district have a right to help and guidance from field offices of the Conservation Service, or from county agents, in planning "layouts" adapted to the particular needs and productive capacities of their farms or ranches. The service undertakes to send technicians to advise and work directly with anyone in need of them. A farmer may participate in the plan or not as he chooses; there is no compulsion, either national or state. Under related legislation in 1936 subsidies have been made available, mainly for lime and fertilizer, to those employing soil-conservation practices. The soil-bank program begun in 1956 has added a new stimulus to the retirement of overworked, staple-producing crop land and, as we have observed in the preceding chapter, 28 million acres have been taken out of cultivation.[9]

In 1944, a new responsibility for watershed protection and flood control was given to the service. Under legislation in 1954 that greatly expanded this area of activity, the service now aids in planning and developing projects to prevent floods, halt erosion, and conserve water resources—mainly but not exclusively, on small watersheds. Grants and loans are used, usually on a matching basis, to finance state or local projects.

FORESTS AND WILDLIFE

As a positive program deliberately adopted, conservation in this country *Forests* really had its beginning 60 years ago as an effort to preserve and extend the nation's forests. Theodore Roosevelt not only perceived the immense value to the people of forests yielding lumber, stabilizing the distribution of moisture, preventing soil waste, fostering wildlife, and furnishing recreational facilities, but deplored the rapidity with which forest wealth was disappearing at the hands of lumber companies and other private exploiters. Under legislation dating from 1891, he and later Presidents set aside generous portions of the public domain as national forests. Envisaging a forest program for the entire country, Congress in 1911 provided for extensive purchases of forests on the

[8] H. Walker and W. R. Parks, "Soil Conservation Districts; Local Democracy in a National Program," *Jour. of Politics,* VIII, 538-549 (Nov., 1946).

[9] Additional large-scale special undertakings for which the service has been mainly responsible include (1) efforts—not particularly successful—to stop erosion in the "Dust Bowl" (western Oklahoma and Kansas, eastern Colorado, etc.) by planting cover grasses; (2) protecting areas somewhat eastward by planting 217 million "shelterbelt" trees along a general axis, 1000 miles in length, from North Dakota to the Texas Panhandle; and, (3) administering a special Great Plains Conservation program, enacted in 1956, of aid and advice to farmers in the Dust Bowl.

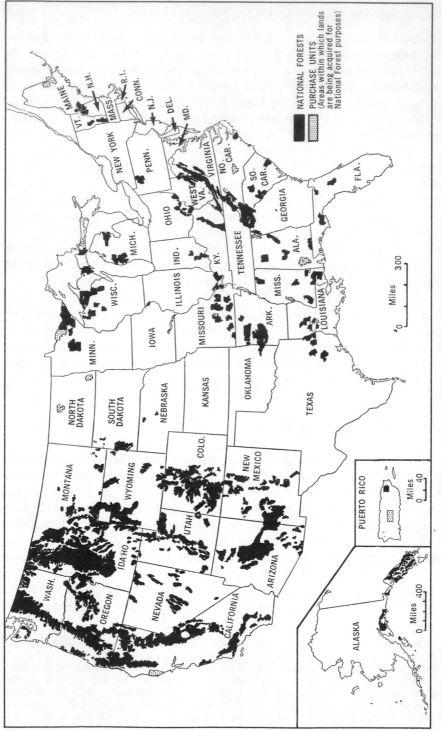

NATIONAL FORESTS

PURCHASE UNITS
(Areas within which lands
are being acquired for
National Forest purposes)

NATIONAL FORESTS OF THE UNITED STATES

Miles
0   300

PUERTO RICO

Miles
0   40

ALASKA

Miles
0   400

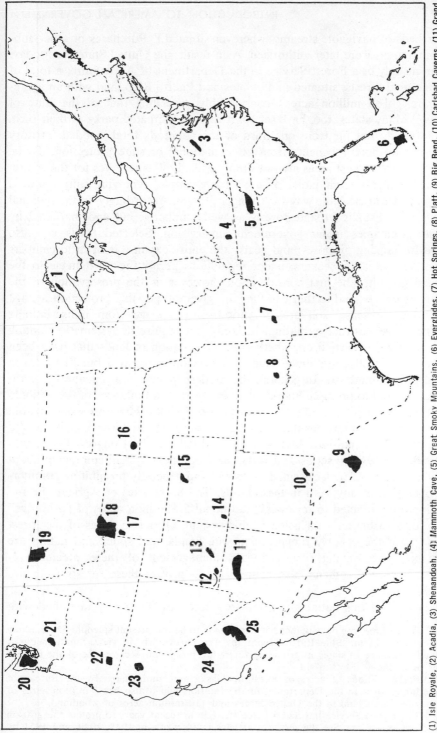

MAJOR NATIONAL PARKS IN THE UNITED STATES

(1) Isle Royale, (2) Acadia, (3) Shenandoah, (4) Mammoth Cave, (5) Great Smoky Mountains, (6) Everglades, (7) Hot Springs, (8) Platt, (9) Big Bend, (10) Carlsbad Caverns, (11) Grand Canyon, (12) Zion, (13) Bryce, (14) Mesa Verde, (15) Rocky Mountain, (16) Wind Cave, (17) Grand Teton, (18) Yellowstone, (19) Glacier, (20) Olympic, (21) Mount Rainier, (22) Crater Lake, (23) Lassen, (24) Yosemite, (25) Sequoia.

watersheds of navigable streams, wherever situated.[10] Purchases of other sub-marginal areas were later authorized. As a result, the United States has today, under custody of a Forest Service in the Department of Agriculture, a total of 152 national forests, situated in 42 states and Puerto Rico, and with an aggregate area (186 million acres) considerably exceeding that of the state of Texas.[11] Many states, too, have set apart forests or created parks of their own, and in reality not far from one-third of the country's total wooded territory (630 million acres) benefits from direct national or state protection. To be sure, the public forest areas are not simply walled off as reserves for the future. A forest benefits from judicious use—for example, removing fully matured trees in order to clear the way for younger growth. Accordingly, in the national forests (and usually in state forests as well) timber is cut and marketed by private companies under government supervision. Selected tracts are also leased for grazing purposes; and nearly the entire expanse is open to campers and other recreation-seekers, under regulations permitting no damage to the wooded growth. The first consideration, however, is the preservation of the forests as *forests*; and to that end they are given all possible protection against fire, insects, disease, soil erosion, flood, and damage from indiscriminate grazing [12] and destructive cutting. In areas that require it, systematic planting of young trees is carried on, whether as reforestation of lands that have been denuded or as afforestation of lands not previously wooded but likely to be useful only if made so. In general, the modern policy is to encourage recreational use and to promote lumbering operations, and both uses of the national forests have sharply increased in the last two decades. However, conservation interests have been anxious that some part of our forested heritage be preserved in its primitive condition. After a prolonged debate, the Congress finally was persuaded in 1964 to set aside a National Wilderness System embracing about 9 million acres of lands classified as "wild" and generally prohibiting commercial operation of any kind in these lands. The Secretaries of Agriculture and Interior were directed to review an additional 5.4 million acres of "primitive" areas for possible later inclusion in this system. Over two-thirds of the forest resources of the country remain in private hands, and states and nation are constantly encouraging sustained-yield management of these precious resources. The governments also collaborate to protect these forests from fire and disease.

The national parks   Not all of this nation's precious resources are so closely identified with

[10] At the time, the development of what came to be the present splendid Shenandoah National Park in the Blue Ridge Mountains was particularly in view. Simultaneously, national assistance to states in providing forest-fire protection became one of the earliest forms of national grants-in-aid.

[11] Forty millions of acres of forest in Alaska are administered by the Bureau of Land Management in the Department of the Interior, which also has 5 million acres of commercial forest land in the United States and 110 million acres of woodland.

[12] The Forest Service has had a fierce struggle in recent years to protect the grazing areas from excess use. See the series of articles in *Harper's*, in 1948, 1949, and 1951 by B. DeVoto.

material well-being as are soil, timber, water power, and minerals. Conservation to many of our people embraces also the preservation of scenic beauty, of spectacular natural phenomena, of historic spots, of areas which may remind us of the land before the white man came. The enjoyment of these things should also be passed on to our children's children. Although this phase of conservation has been the least adequately supported by "practical" statesmen, through the years the nation has set aside from its own lands or acquired from private owners 25.8 million acres in 44 states and one territory, in 31 national parks and 152 historic and other areas. Yellowstone was the first of these areas, set aside by the Congress in 1871. A National Park Service, created in the Department of the Interior in 1916, now administers Yosemite, Grand Canyon, Smoky Mountains, Grand Teton, Yellowstone, Mount Rainier, Glacier, and the other parks and historic areas. Much of the cost is borne out of income from concession privileges and admission or other charges. Appropriations for maintenance, however, fell far behind the demands created by the millions of touring Americans who are now using the parks. To meet this problem, the Park Service in 1956 launched a 10-year program (Mission 66) to bring its facilities to the level necessary to care for the 83 million persons estimated to become park-users by 1966. Actually, 94 million people visited these areas in 1964. In general, the Congress has responded favorably to the needs for added expenditures.

Well before the close of the nineteenth century, Congress recognized the value of the country's fish and game, not only to the sportsman, but to the people generally as a source of food and an otherwise productive element in the national economy. An office of Commissioner of Fish and Fisheries (becoming in 1903 a bureau of fisheries in the Department of Commerce and Labor) was created in 1871, with a biological survey established in 1885 in the Department of Agriculture becoming in 1905 a regular bureau. In 1940, these and other agencies entering the field as the conservation movement gained momentum were gathered into the present Fish and Wildlife Service in the Department of the Interior. Here again, as in the case of forests, there must be a division of labor with the states. Throughout the public domain, the national service is free to regulate fishing and hunting as it likes, to maintain fish hatcheries and stock streams and lakes, to correlate wildlife protection with forest control. It administers and enforces, too, the laws relating to marine fishing, and even operates the fur seal industry of the Pribilof Islands of Alaska, selling the product to private traders. Outside of the public domain, it cooperates with states and their subdivisions, and indeed with private agencies and organizations, in much that relates to the development, protection, rearing, and stocking of all desirable species of wildlife. It carries on research, helps plan useful regulations, provides wildlife refuges (more than 280 have been established), administers grants-in-aid,[13] helps enforce local

Fish and wildlife

[13] A statute of 1937 earmarks the proceeds of national excise taxes on firearms, shells, and cartridges for apportionment among the states in aid of wildlife conservation.

game laws, and generally provides a spearhead for conservational work in this field. Congressional power over interstate and foreign commerce is available for direct control of the program. As long ago as 1900, it became a national offense to ship out of a state game of any sort taken in violation of state law. To meet a situation created by the passage back and forth every year of wild fowl between nesting places north of the border and winter refuges in the southern states, Mexico, and Caribbean countries, agreements for protection have been entered into under a Migratory Bird Treaty Act of 1918 [14] with both Canada and Mexico. Our own states are forbidden to make or sanction any less rigorous rules concerning killing such birds than those laid down nationally.

MINERALS—PETROLEUM

Minerals   Top soil, when lost, can be replaced only very slowly and precariously; when minerals disappear, they are irreplaceable—except in geological time. Originally, the United States was richly endowed with mineral wealth; and compared with many other countries, it still is so. Nevertheless, for 100 years there have been heavy use and wastage, and in the last 30 or 40 a machine civilization and mechanized warfare have taken terrific toll of supplies once lightly viewed as virtually inexhaustible. In 1950, the American economy consumed about 2.5 tons of ore per person. The list of minerals still abundant has grown surprisingly short. On the present scale of consumption, we are told we still have enough bituminous coal for 1000 years and enough anthracite for 175 years. With oil and gas already cutting sharply into demand, and civilian uses of atomic energy at hand, not all of the underground stocks may ever be needed. We still have long-range supplies of iron (at any rate lower-grade ores), oil, gas, phosphate, and molybdenum. But unmined supplies of gold, copper, zinc, and bauxite (from which aluminum is extracted) are said to be good for only about 20 more years, and of lead, manganese, and vanadium for only 10; while stocks of platinum, antimony, mercury, tungsten, chromium, nickel, tin, mica, graphite, asbestos, diamonds, and quartz crystals are—in proportion to the uses we make of such materials—negligible. As we quickly discovered during the two world wars, we are, with respect to many strategic minerals indispensable to our economy, a "have-not" nation. Each year we are importing a larger proportion of our raw materials. Recognizing that new discoveries and inventions may improve the situation at various points, one nevertheless understands why, in the present-day conservation program, minerals hold a high place.[15]

[14] The legislation passed by Congress in support of this treaty, sustained by the Supreme Court in Missouri v. Holland, 252 U. S. 416 (1920), is frequently cited in the contemporary controversy over the curtailment of the treaty-making power.

[15] For an excellent summary of the situation in respect to minerals and other natural resources, see J. F. Dewhurst and Associates, *America's Needs and Resources* (New York, 1955), Chapter xxi.

The task of identifying, locating, investigating, and mapping mineral resources falls principally to the Geological Survey in the Interior Department; and prolonged researches of this agency, with aid from the former General Land Office (now absorbed into the Bureau of Land Management), have resulted in detailed classifications and descriptions of all mineral-producing lands. The bulk of the country's minerals of primary concern to industry and defense—coal, iron, oil—are located in areas outside of the public domain; and governmental policies looking to preventing their wastage have to be more or less indirect, for example, in the case of oil and gas, through regulation of interstate and foreign commerce. Mineral deposits on the public domain also, however, are important; and here systematic protection is afforded under a policy of the past 40 years by which (a) when such land is alienated to private persons or corporations, the government reserves all mineral wealth contained, to be kept intact or exploited only under such terms as the government may impose, and (b) when land remaining publicly owned is leased for any purpose, no mineral rights pass with it except such as the government specifies, and with royalties on any minerals extracted paid into the Treasury and in part passed on to the appropriate states.

Only 2 percent of the oil produced in the United States today comes from *Petroleum* the public domain. Although the amount produced on state-owned lands is larger, the great bulk of the annual output is yielded by lands that have passed into private ownership—which means that whatever is undertaken by government in the interest of conservation must, by and large, proceed by public regulation rather than by management of a resource still in public possession. Until within the last 30 years, not much was accomplished, and wastefulness ran riot. Under the "law of capture," any landowner in an oil-producing area was at liberty to drill as many wells on his property as he liked, tapping pools under it and drawing off oil from underneath neighboring properties as well. Many another dubious device calculated to speed up the flow of riches from "black gold" was freely invoked. Beginning with Oklahoma in 1915, some states sought to curb extravagance and keep prices high by regulating the distance between wells, forbidding oil and gas to be left flowing and burning in fields, and even assigning production quotas through an administrative agency. Results were not happy. Yet only after discovery of the rich eastern Texas fields in 1930-1931, augmenting output and shattering prices, were two lines of action started which in time led to the restrictive system that we now have—(1) interstate agreement and (2) national control through the commerce power.

The first of these did not begin auspiciously. In 1931-1932, Texas, Okla- *Present* homa and Kansas tried, by agreement, to discourage overproduction and price *controls* demoralization by forbidding shipments exceeding fixed quotas from the respective states. In spite of all that they could do "hot oil" streamed into other parts of the country, production continued at extravagant levels, and chaos prevailed, especially after the Supreme Court held that governors of states might not resort to martial law in order to police production controls. But the excess oil was shipped in interstate commerce; and this gave the national government an opening. In the National Industrial Recovery Act of 1933, the President was authorized, with a view to helping the states out of their dilemma, to prohibit the transportation in interstate or foreign commerce of any petroleum or its products produced or withdrawn from storage in excess of amounts permitted by state law or regulation. A code for the oil industry, with the Secretary of the Interior as administrator, was duly put into operation. Here again, however, there was discouraging experience. Tested in the courts, the arrangement collapsed: in "hot oil" cases of 1935, the Supreme Court ruled that Congress had exceeded in constitutional authority by delegating to the chief executive power which by its nature was tantamount to making laws.[16] The damage, nevertheless, was not irreparable.

Congress followed the Court rebuff by passing the hot oil (Connally) Act of 1935, forbidding the shipment in interstate or foreign commerce of oil in violation of state laws and regulation. This act was extended in 1937 and 1939 and made permanent in 1942. The major oil-producing states then got together and agreed, by compact, to enact and enforce laws aimed at wasteful production practices. They also agreed to plan coordinated production controls through an Interstate Oil Compact Commission, but this feature of the program has never been particularly effective. The compact was approved by Congress and in the years since that time has been repeatedly extended and approved. It now embraces 30 states and has been approved through 1967.[17]

WATER AND WATER POWER

Bases of national authority

In most parts of the country, water is something that is there when and where it is needed, and people simply take it for granted. But for city-dwellers at least, it is there only because government has provided for its capture, storage, purification, and distribution. For the nation as a whole, water raises problems as serious as does any other resource. From early times, towns and cities have been concerned with providing water for their inhabitants; and states, counties, and specially organized districts have had to do with protection against floods and with drainage projects, pollution abatement, power development, and irrigation. Almost from the beginning, the national government likewise has been involved. Important rivers commonly border or flow through a number of states; drainage basins cut widely across state lines; areas requiring water storage and irrigation know no state limits. And constitutional authority to operate in this field is ample. First of all, there is full power over

[16] Panama Refining Co. *v.* Ryan, 293 U. S. 388 (1935).
[17] Lack of space forbids treatment here of the more or less parallel problem of conserving natural gas. The main regulatory statute is the Natural Gas Act of 1938; the subject will be found fully covered in F. F. Blachly and M. E. Oatman, *Natural Gas and the Public Interest* (Washington, 1947).

the water resources of the public domain, in whatever states located. In the second place, there is authority to improve and regulate the use of navigable streams as avenues of interstate commerce; and the Supreme Court has said that "navigability . . . is but a part of this whole (authority). Flood protection, watershed development, recovery of the cost of improvement through utilization of power, are likewise parts of commerce control." [18]

Aside from the navigability of streams, entailing chiefly the removal of natural obstructions, the regulation of artificial ones such as bridges and dams, and the control of water-power development, the national government's role in connection with water resources presents itself in four main phases: (1) the adjustment of situations in which there is danger of too much water; (2) the conservation and use of meager supplies in areas naturally semiarid or especially subject to drought; (3) the development of hydroelectric power from installations designed to promote irrigation, navigation, or flood control; and (4) the promotion and financing of programs to eliminate pollution. *General water program*

While looking to states and localities to bear primary responsibility for providing levees and other forms of local flood protection, the national government has for three-quarters of a century stood ready to lend financial assistance, especially at times of unusual disaster. More significantly, however, as the concept of conservation has broadened, and as destructive floods have multiplied in the basins of the Mississippi, Ohio, Missouri, Colorado, Columbia, and other rivers, it has extended its activities to include permanent programs of flood prevention, in collaboration with state and local authorities. On public works connected with such programs it already has spent, since the serious Mississippi Valley flood of 1927, considerably more than $3 billion, with further liberal outlays authorized. The states, of course, are not absolved from continued responsibility for their own protection. Congress, in 1936, authorized any two or more of them to enter into flood-control compacts, and four New England states promptly signed an agreement for flood control in the valleys of the Connecticut and Merrimac; Minnesota and the Dakotas followed with a compact for similar control in the valley of the Red River of the North; and other compacts covering the Yellowstone River, Arkansas River, Pecos River and many others have followed in recent years. The same comprehensive Flood Control Act, however, which authorized such interstate arrangements virtually accepted flood control as in general a national function, with states and localities obligated only to provide necessary land and rights of way and even this obligation has since been considerably relaxed. *Flood control*

New Flood Control Acts in 1944 and 1946 and a Watershed Protection and Flood Prevention Act in 1954 have considerably expanded the national program. The Soil Conservation Service, working through local soil-conservation or flood-control districts, has entered the field in an important way promoting watershed protection, small dams, and on-the-farm water control measures with loans, technical advice, surveys, and grants. The Corps of

[18] United States v. Appalachian Electric Power, 311 U. S. 377 (1940).

THE DUST BOWL

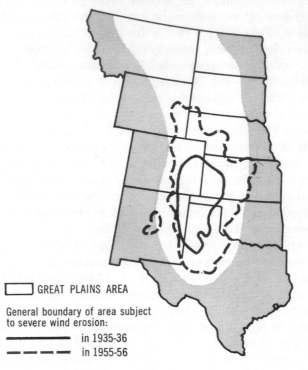

GREAT PLAINS AREA

General boundary of area subject
to severe wind erosion:

———————— in 1935-36

— — — — in 1955-56

Engineers of the Department of the Army, long charged with planning and constructing public works on navigable rivers, has also enlarged its flood-prevention activities.

Water scarcity   Apart from the irrigation needs of portions of 17 western states met by the Bureau of Reclamation, scarcity of water, until a decade or two ago, presented no problems sufficiently serious to evoke wide public concern. Destructive droughts and devastating sandstorms occurring in the summers of 1934, 1936, and again in 1953 and 1954, however, dramatically stressed the need for conserving and enlarging the water resources of the Dust Bowl. Surveys of that stricken territory revealed that a chronically serious condition had been growing worse. Large stretches of once fertile land were being turned into desert by unscientific farming (overgrazing and ploughing of grass land); and ironically, good rainfall, far from being a blessing, might only add to the area's impoverishment by carrying away still more of the topsoil. Realization of the situation prompted cooperative efforts by state and national governments to minimize the effects of droughts, if not actually to prevent them. An act of Congress in 1937 authorized the Department of Agriculture to promote in arid areas the construction and maintenance of reservoirs, ponds, wells, dams, and pumping facilities, while another in 1939 provided especially for water conservation in districts where farmers were too distressed to assume repayment obligations under the general reclamation laws. In 1954, the responsibilities of the Department of Agriculture for water conservation were extended by the Congress to all areas "arid" or not. Another large area presenting an especially acute problem of water conservation and redistribution is the interior of California, where the Sacramento and San Joaquin Valley join to form the Great Central Valley, now benefiting from a tremendous "Central Valley Project" conserving and distributing run-off water from mountains to the north and east.

The water problem of the United States, however, is by no means confined to the arid and now irrigated areas of the West and Southwest. Currently, our people use about 250 billion gallons of water a day but by 1980 the daily consumption is estimated at 600 billion gallons. We have this much water but not necessarily in the right places. Whereas, for many decades the farm was the major user of water, industry is now surpassing it and this use combined with the consumption of our urban citizens is likely to present in the future the most serious of water problems. Much of the water available for municipal and industrial use is water of poor quality (polluted by industrial and human wastes) and can only be made usable by extensive and expensive treatment. While many industries that use water for cooling purposes can use polluted water, others cannot. A great outpouring of wealth and energy is necessary if treatment is to be provided on a scale correlative to the problem. Congress in 1956 began a program of grants to communities on a matching basis for construction of facilities and for the development of pollution-control programs. Efforts to increase national participation were resisted by the Eisenhower administration. The Kennedy administration proposed and Congress approved increased appropriations for these purposes. A new Federal Water Pollution Control Administration in the Department of Health, Education, and Welfare was created in 1965 to spearhead the national drive against pollution. *Water pollution*

Other attacks being made on this problem include renewed experimentation in converting salt water to human use; efforts to procure more stringent enforcement of antipollution laws as well as the adoption of more effective laws; and research programs aimed at better utilization of water and easier removal of contaminating elements.

The great river systems of the United States afford almost limitless opportunities for harnessing and utilizing water power. From the conservation standpoint, the use of this power of falling water to drive the wheels of industry and to ease the burdens of homemaking is vastly superior to the use of irreplaceable natural resources like coal and oil for these purposes. Industrial development is dependent in great measure on the availability of cheap sources of power. The South and West have lagged behind the East in industry partly because of the difficulty in extracting power profitably from their main resource, water. The extensive development by the national government of dams for flood control, irrigation, or navigation improvement has made it feasible to *Hydro-electric power* extract power from these same projects at favorable cost rates so long as the major installation costs are charged to the other uses of the project. Amidst fierce and continuing controversy over publicly-supplied versus privately-supplied power and over the proper allocation of costs in multipurpose projects, the national government has moved, at first cautiously then strongly, into the field of power generation and distribution.

National regulation of water power

Earlier in this century the main national interest in water power was the regulation of private exploitation of water resources in the public domain and on navigable rivers. Citing its constitutional authority over navigable rivers, over the public domain, and over the interstate transmission of electric energy, the Congress in 1920 created a Federal Power Commission of three cabinet members to license the construction of power plants in sites under national jurisdiction, to control interstate wholesale electricity rates and to regulate the security issues of private utilities engaged in interstate commerce.[19] Ten years later, a full-time commission of five members replaced the cabinet committee. The Flood Control Act of 1936 extended the commission's jurisdiction to include multipurpose river-basin planning, and the development of electric power at government-constructed dams. The Natural Gas Act of 1938 added further to the Commission's authority the power to regulate the interstate transportation and sale of natural gas.

The national development of power projects

In recent years, the major governmental concern in water power has been the development of power resources rather than the regulation of private developments. Beginning with the Tennessee Valley Authority (TVA) and Hoover Dam on the Colorado River and largely under New Deal leadership, the Corps of Engineers, the Department of the Interior, and independent government corporations have steadily increased the amount of public power generated on government projects. In virtually all cases, power production has been bracketed with conservation, flood control, irrigation, navigation, or national defense in great multipurpose dams. Opposition to these developments has also steadily mounted in intensity. Eastern industry, coal producers and unions, and private power interests have bitterly opposed using their tax payments to create competition in the South and West. The Republican administration elected in 1952 slowed down, but did not halt, the spread of public power and attempted to stimulate more private development of water power.[20]

[19] This Federal Water Power Act was upheld as constitutional in 1940 in United States *v.* Appalachian Power Co., 311 U. S. 377. The Court's extremely generous interpretation in this decision of what constitutes a navigable stream—and of the activities which national control over navigable streams can be stretched to include—operated to expand the government's jurisdiction over water power even beyond that clearly envisaged in the statute itself. Not only was the New River (in Virginia and West Virginia), concerning which the case arose, not actually navigable; there were not even plans for making it so. The Court nevertheless held it "navigable" simply because *potentially* it could be made so.

[20] The Dixon-Yates contract controversy of 1954-1955 illustrates the attitude of the Eisenhower administration. This contract, sponsored by the Bureau of the Budget, was made by the Atomic Energy Commission with a private syndicate to construct power

The Kennedy administration announced that the "no new projects" policy of the previous administration would be abandoned and that new public power projects would be undertaken in the light of available financing.[21] Johnson has not changed his predecessor's program.

In addition to the great dams of the Tennessee Valley Authority which now have a capacity of more than 6 million kilowatts, the government projects include: the Columbia River program begun in 1937, administered by the Bonneville Power Administration with a capacity of 7.0 million kilowatts installed by mid-1965; the Southeastern Power Administration created in 1950 operating throughout 10 southeastern states with a capacity of 1.6 million kilowatts at 14 installations; the Southwestern Power Administration, created in 1943, operating in Arkansas, Louisiana, and parts of Kansas, Missouri, Oklahoma, and Texas, with a capacity of 1.0 million kilowatts already installed and a few projects still to be completed; the Bureau of Reclamation with many installations including those in the Central Valley of California, on the Colorado River, and in the Missouri basin with a total installed capacity of 5 million kilowatts; the Corps of Engineers with dozens of installations and with a total capacity in 1965 of 7.3 million kilowatts.[22]

REGIONAL CONSERVATION—THE TENNESSEE VALLEY AUTHORITY

Conservation as practiced in this country draws heavily upon science and technology; it operates through legislation and administration; it sometimes gets into politics; and its pattern is fixed largely by geography, both physical and political. Physically, the pattern follows the distribution of resources to be protected—land and water everywhere, forests in eastern and western wooded areas, power where the main rivers are, oil and gas in the richly endowed fields of the South and Southwest. Politically, its planning and management are conditioned by the distinction between publicly and privately owned land, by the principle of federalism, by the allocation of constitutional powers, and by the framework of governmental and administrative units—states, counties, dis-

The regional approach

projects supplementary to those available to it from the Tennessee Valley Authority. The hold-over members of the TVA opposed such a contract vigorously and the Democratic 84th Congress tried to block the administration from proceeding. Ultimately the administration gave in and cancelled the contract.

[21] See President Kennedy's "Special Message to the Congress on Natural Resources," *The New York Times,* Feb. 24, 1961, for this policy as well as for other policy announcements affecting natural resource conservation.

[22] Surveys of national hydroelectric power developments will be found in H. H. Trachsel, *Public Utility Regulation* (Chicago, 1947), Chap. xxii; *A Water Policy for the American People,* The President's Water Resources Policy Commission (Washington, 1950), 1, Chap. xv; and J. H. Scattergood, *et al., Electric Power and Government Policy* (New York, 1948).

tricts. Historically different forms of conservation, whether nation-wide like soil conservation or more localized like the maintenance of forests and parks, have been developed separately. We still have largely independent land, forest, wildlife, mineral, oil, gas, water-power, and other laws, authorities, and services, with dispersion aggravated by allotment of administrative responsibilities to many different departments and regulatory agencies. Another approach, would be to bring together most or all of the various activities under a unified management functioning for a group of states or parts of states having common problems. We now have one outstanding example of this procedure in the Tennessee Valley Authority. As a regional area for such treatment, the valley of a large river is logical and convenient. Serving often as political boundaries, rivers commonly are thought of primarily as dividing lines. In reality, however, they usually unite rather than divide; their watersheds, to right and left, generally are alike physically, homogeneous socially and economically, and in need of the same protection for soil and forests and the same power and other services.

The Ten-
nessee
Valley
Authority:

1. Origin
and
purpose

Construction of works at Muscle Shoals on the middle Tennessee River during World War I for extraction of nitrogen from the air, to be used in manufacturing explosives, left the national government the possessor of 2300 acres of land, two nitrate plants, a power house, and Wilson Dam. Postwar years saw much controversy over the use, if any, to be made of this property. Senator George W. Norris of Nebraska, an ardent advocate of public power development, launched a tireless campaign for enlarging the property and basing upon it a broad program of public ownership and development throughout the river valley. Two measures looking in that direction were killed by vetoes of Presidents Coolidge and Hoover. But President Franklin D. Roosevelt became enamored of the idea. Spurred by him, Congress in 1933 passed a Tennessee Valley Authority Act aimed at improving the navigability and promoting flood control of the Tennessee, providing for reforestation and proper use of marginal lands in the Tennessee Valley, encouraging the Valley's agricultural and industrial development, assisting national defense by operating government-owned nitrate plants, and indeed pointed toward other objectives not fully specified. Over a potentially rich and productive area of almost 41,000 square miles (four-fifths the size of England), embracing portions of seven states, and having a present population of more than 5 million, agriculture and industry were to be reconstructed, forests restored, soil erosion checked, mineral resources developed, cheap power and chemical fertilizers produced, and the inhabitants assured the benefits of a "more abundant life." To carry out the plan, the Tennessee Valley Authority was created as a government corporation under a board of three directors appointed by the President with the consent of the Senate and operating with funds supplied by Congress, supplemented by the proceeds of bonds which the authority might issue in limited amounts and eventually by sales of surplus power. As envisaged by President Roosevelt and by the TVA itself, the project was a significant undertaking

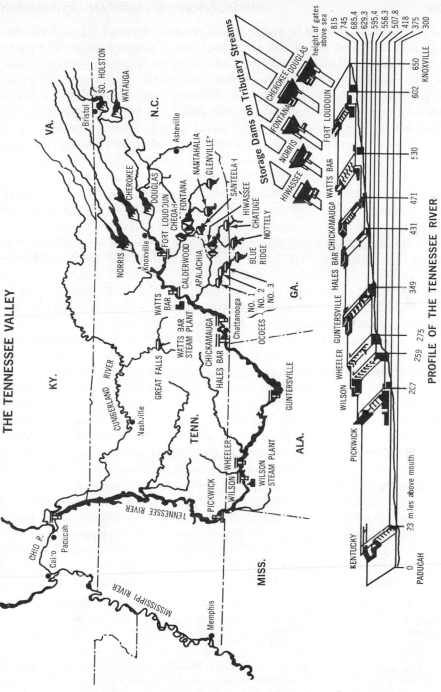

THE TENNESSEE VALLEY

Storage Dams on Tributary Streams

PROFILE OF THE TENNESSEE RIVER

in democratic management and in the relatively new art of regional planning, blazing the way, it was hoped, for enterprises of similar nature and scope in other suitable sections of the country. As viewed by people of contrary opinion, it constituted a venture in subsidized governmental competition with private utility and other business which would be unfair, uneconomical, and a flagrant abuse of national powers; and the two points of view still are encountered wherever TVA affairs come up for discussion, in Congress or outside.[23]

2. Activities and achievements   From its inception, TVA was characteristically a multiple-purpose enterprise. Throughout its history it has been concerned with flood control, improvement of navigation, soil conservation, production of chemical fertilizers, reforestation, and development of power. It carries out directly enterprises like building dams, but, in the case of activities like soil conservation, it rather provides funds and centralizes planning, with administration decentralized, so that the area's people themselves and their governments may bear an active share in what is done.[24] Although by no means overlooking other objectives, the authority has (especially during its first 20 years) focused its efforts mainly upon taming the unruly Tennessee River, thereby promoting navigability, reducing flood hazards, and, in particular, providing great quantities of electric power. Twenty-seven major dams on the main stream or its larger tributaries have been built or acquired; others are contemplated; and arrangements have been made for selling surplus power to counties, cities, cooperative associations, and larger private industries (though not to individual consumers), with a view not only to recovering some portion of the huge expenses incurred, but also to providing a long-desired "yardstick" for measuring the fairness of rates charged consumers by private producers. Agreements entered into with leading private power companies, too, have enabled the authority to extend its market considerably beyond its own immediate area. Several private utility properties have been purchased outright; and TVA is now the largest producer of electric energy in the country. In meeting the urgent need for increased resources to vitalize our defense and war industries after 1940, the authority proved an important asset, particularly helpful being the production of chemicals and fertilizers at Muscle Shoals and the stepping up of power production at the various dams. While an object of much continuing criticism and attack, partisan and otherwise, the experiment is to be regarded as having justified itself, for purposes of peace as well as of war. In cases decided in 1936

[23] C. H. Pritchett, "The Development of the Tennessee Valley Authority Act," *Tenn. Law Rev.*, XV, 128-141 (Feb., 1938). Indispensable to any study of the project's documentary history is A. M. Norwood [comp.], *Congressional Hearings, Reports, and Documents Relating to T.V.A., 1933-1946* (Knoxville, Tenn., 1946), a full chronological check-list of materials.

[24] M. H. Satterfield, "T.V.A.—State-Local Relationships," *Amer. Polit. Sci. Rev.*, XL, 935-949 (Oct., 1946), and "Intergovernmental Co-operation in the Tennessee Valley," *Jour. of Politics*, IX, 31-58 (Feb., 1947); J. M. Ray, "The Influence of the Tennessee Valley Authority on Government in the South," *Amer. Polit. Sci. Rev.*, XLIII, 922-932 (Oct., 1949).

and 1939,[25] the Supreme Court sustained all essential features of the underlying legislation.[26]

In President Roosevelt and others of like mind, TVA inspired a vision of a country refurbished throughout its length and breadth by similar enterprises undertaken in suitable areas. Congress has for more than two decades been deluged with proposals relating to particular valley regions. In 1937, President Roosevelt himself advocated TVA types of undertakings in the Arkansas and Columbia basins; in 1944, he called for a Missouri Valley Authority, to develop the water and other resources of parts or all of 10 or 11 western states comprising nearly one-fourth of the better crop land of the country; in 1949, President Truman urged both a Missouri Valley Authority and a Columbia Valley Authority. The valley authority system for resource development and conservation has gained increasing support also from the unseemly quarrels and frustrations growing out of the dispersion of authority among the Soil Conservation Service, Forest Service, Bureau of Reclamation, Bureau of Land Management, Power Administrations and Corps of Engineers. Each of these, however, has managed to protect its present jurisdiction. Thus far, all efforts to achieve a more logical allocation of functions among the departments or to achieve it regionally by valley authorities have been unsuccessful. The first Hoover Commission recommended that virtually all land management programs be consolidated in the Department of Agriculture and water resource programs in the Department of the Interior. It did not support the valley authority idea.[27] The Bureau of Land Management resisted transfer from Interior and the Corps of Engineers from the Army and the recommendations got nowhere. Much of the present controversy centers around development of the Missouri Basin, with the Corps of Engineers and the Department of Interior and Agriculture each presenting a separate plan.[28] Early in 1961 a

Other proposed "valley authorities"

[25] Ashwander *et al. v.* T.V.A., 297 U. S. 288 (1936), and Tennessee Electric Power Co. *et al. v.* T.V.A., 306 U. S. 118 (1939).

[26] Good brief discussion of T.V.A. will be found in H. H. Trachsel, *Public Utility Regulation* (Chicago, 1947), Chap. XXIII.

[27] The "Department of the Interior," *Report of the Commission on Organization of the Executive Branch of the Government* (Washington, 1949). The second Hoover Commission contented itself with suggesting that the president appoint a committee to study rural land programs. "Real Property Management," *Report of the Commission on Organization of the Executive Branch of the Government* (Washington, 1955).

[28] In August, 1950, Secretary of Agriculture Charles F. Brannan asked Congress to authorize a 30-year, $8.5 billion agricultural program for the Missouri Valley, to tie in with a Pick-Sloan $5.5 billion plan (already under way) for flood control, irrigation, navigation, and power development—somewhat over half of the cost to be borne by landowners and operators, $3.063 billion by the national government, and the remainder by states and localities. Cf. W. C. Clark, "Proposed 'Valley Authority' Legislation," *Amer. Polit. Sci. Rev.*, XL, 62-70 (Feb., 1946); R. Terral, *The Missouri Valley* (New Haven, 1947); H. C. Hart, "Valley Development and Valley Administration in the Missouri Basin," *Pub. Admin. Rev.*, VIII, 1-11 (Winter, 1948); C. McKinley, "The Valley Authority and Its Alternatives," *Amer. Polit. Sci. Rev.*, XLIV, 607-631 (Sept., 1950).

Senate Select Committee on National Water Resources urged the development in cooperation with the states of comprehensive river-basin plans for the major rivers of America by 1970. The Kennedy administration unsuccessfully urged Congress to authorize the establishment of planning agencies for all river basins where no coordinated program exists.

RESOURCES PLANNING

A chapter cut short

Soil conservation, forest conservation, flood control, conservation of water, oil, and natural gas, and the development of hydroelectric power sites present a series, not of isolated but of closely interrelated and overlapping problems affecting the entire country. For many informed persons, adequate solution of them is conditioned upon planning on a nation-wide scale. The leadership of the New Deal was mainly aware of this and, starting with the establishment of a National Planning Board in July, 1933, comprehensive studies of land use, stream use, mineral resources, and related matters were carried on over a period of a decade. Virtually all of the states were also influenced or induced, on their part, to set up planning boards or commissions for similar work. From the Planning Board evolved, in 1939, a National Resources Planning Board (in the Executive Office of the President), with three members appointed by the President with the consent of the Senate. In promoting the ensuing defense and war effort, this board cooperated actively with the Office of Production Management, the War Production Board, and other agencies on studies related to the location of war industries, and with state planning boards and defense councils on special community problems. It also devoted much attention to the postwar period, with a view to developing plans for necessary readjustments, and in 1942-1943 presented to the President two illuminating reports (climaxing a lengthy list of earlier publications)—one entitled *National Resources Development Report for 1943,* in which were outlined some of the major problems to be faced and some of the steps which would need to be taken in effecting an orderly transition from war to peace and for the longer-range development of an expanded economy; and the other bearing the challenging title of *Security, Work, and Relief.* The latter document received considerable attention from the press and public, but both encountered frigid reception in Congress. Moved by political animus against an activity regarded as pre-eminently "New Dealish," Congress not only terminated the Board in 1943 by cutting off its funds, but barred the President from utilizing any substitute for it by specifying that the functions previously exercised should not be transferred to any other agency or performed "except as hereafter provided by law." Fortunately, the great amount of useful material assembled and published after 1933 by the board and its forerunners remains available to those, including Congress itself, who, after all, cannot escape wrestling with many of the very problems to which the board thoughtfully addressed itself.[29]

Resources planning did not stop when the board came to an end. No single central establishment is nowadays responsible for guiding it. But a score of agencies—the Forest Service, the Bureau of Reclamation, the Soil Conservation Service, the Bureau of Land Management, the TVA, and others—necessarily plan within their respective provinces even as they execute. The difficulty in the present situation is, of course, the lack of adequate coordination among the various agencies working on resource plans. President Kennedy early in 1961 moved to re-establish central coordination by assigning the duty of studying and reporting on resource programs and national needs to the Council of Economic Advisors. He also established under the council an advisory committee on natural resources on which the interested agencies were represented.[30]

References

M. Fainsod, L. Gordon, and J. C. Palamountain, Jr., *Government and the American Economy* (3rd ed., New York, 1959), Chap. XXIII.

R. M. Highsmith, J. G. Jensen, R. D. Rudd, *Conservation in the United States* (New York, 1962).

G. Pinchot, *Breaking New Ground* (New York, 1947). An account of the growth of the conservation movement by one of its principal leaders.

J. F. Dewhurst *et al., America's Needs and Resources* (New York, 1955).

A. F. Gustafson *et al., Conservation in the United States* (Ithaca, N.Y., 1944).

II. E. Flynn and F. E. Perkins, *Conservation of the Nation's Resources* (New York, 1941).

G. T. Renner, *Conservation of National Resources: An Educational Approach to the Problem* (New York, 1942).

B. Lyons, *Tomorrow's Birthright: A Political and Economic Interpretation of Our Natural Resources* (New York, 1955).

---

[29] C. E. Merriam, "The National Resources Planning Board; A Chapter in American Planning Experience," *Amer. Polit. Sci. Rev.,* XXXVIII, 1075-1088 (Dec., 1944). On the general subject, see G. B. Galloway [ed.], *Planning for America* (New York, 1941); J. W. Van Sickle, *Planning for the South; An Inquiry into the Economics of Regionalism* (Nashville, Tenn., 1943); "A Symposium on Regional Planning," *Iowa Law Rev.,* XXXII, 193-406 (Jan., 1947); and for a more popular treatment, S. Chase, *Goals for America* (New York, 1942). A discussion of "national economic planning" in the broadest sense will be found in M. E. Dimock, *Business and Government* (New York, 1949), Chap. XXVI. The National Planning Association (800 21st St., N.W. Washington) issues *Planning Pamphlets* and other useful publications.

[30] See President's "Special Message on Natural Resources," *op. cit.*

D. C. Coyle, *Conservation: An American Story of Conflct and Accomplishment* (New Brunswick, N.J., 1957).

R. M. Robbins, *Our Landed Heritage; The Public Domain, 1776-1936* (Princeton, N.J., 1942).

R. L. Parson, *Conserving American Resources,* 2d ed. (Englewood Cliffs, N.J., 1964).

E. G. Cheyney and T. Schantz-Hanzen, *This is our Land: the Story of Conservation in the United States* (St. Paul, Minn., 1940).

J. Cameron, *The Development of Governmental Forest Control in the United States* (Baltimore, 1936).

S. W. Holbrook, *Burning an Empire: The Story of American Forest Fires* (New York, 1943).

V. W. Breever, *Forestry Activities of the Federal Government* (Washington, 1946).

F. Sweeney, *The Changing Forest Situation* (New York, 1950).

E. H. Graham, *The Land and Wildlife* (New York, 1948).

E. V. Rostow, *A National Policy for the Oil Industry* (New Haven, 1948).

L. M. Fanning (ed.), *Our Oil Resources* (New York, 1945).

F. F. Blachly and M. E. Oatman, *Natural Gas and the Public Interest* (Washington, 1947).

B. Frank and A. Netboy, *Water, Land, and People* (New York, 1950).

J. W. Fesler (ed.), "Government and Water Resources: A Symposium," *Amer. Polit. Sci. Rev.,* XLIV (Sept. 1950), 575-649.

State Government, XIX (Sept. 1946), 215-240, "Managing Our Rivers." A series of articles.

P. L. Kleinsorge, *The Boulder Canyon Project: History and Economic Aspects* (Palo Alto, Calif., 1941).

C. M. Hardin, *The Politics of Agriculture: Soil Conservation and the Struggle for Power in Rural America* (Chicago, 1952).

R. L. Duffus and C. Krutch, *The Valley and Its People: A Portrait of T.V.A.* (New York, 1944).

M. Clawson and B. Held, *The Federal Lands: Their Use and Management* (Baltimore, 1955).

D. E. Lilienthal, *T.V.A.—Democracy on the March* (New York, 1944).

C. H. Pritchett, *The Tennessee Valley Authority: A Study in Public Administration* (Chapel Hill, N.C., 1943).

H. Finer, *The T.V.A.: Lessons for International Application* (Montreal, 1944).

G. R. Clapp, *The T.V.A.: An Approach to the Development of a Region* (Chicago, 1955).

P. Selznick, *T.V.A. and the Grass Roots* (Berkeley, Calif., 1949).

W. V. Howard, *Authority in T.V.A. Land* (Kansas City, Mo., 1948). A highly unfavorable view.

J. Bauer, *Public Organization of Electric Power: Conditions, Policies, and Program* (New York, 1949).

D. E. Mann, *The Politics of Water in Arizona* (Tucson, Ariz., 1963).

G. H. Smith (ed.), *Conservation of Natural Resources* (New York, 1958).

J. D. Millett, *The Process and Organization of Government Planning* (New York, 1947).

Report of the President's Water Resources Policy Commission (Washington, 1950-51), 3 vols.

A. Maass, *Muddy Waters; The Army Engineers and the Nation's Rivers* (Cambridge, Mass., 1951).

M. W. Straus, *National Resources Development: Administration and Execution* (New York, 1952).

C. McKinley, *Uncle Sam in the Pacific Northwest* (New York, 1952).

A. H. Carhart, *The National Forests* (New York, 1959).

National Geographic Book Service, *America's Wonderlands: The Scenic National Parks and Monuments of the United States* (Washington, 1959).

W. G. Hoyt and W. M. Langbein, *Floods* (Princeton, N.J., 1955).

J. Ise, *Our National Park Policy: a Critical History* (Baltimore, 1957).

P. O. Foss, *Politics and Grass* (Seattle, Wash., 1957).

Annual reports of the Secretary of the Interior (1946 report entitled "National Resource Problems") the Tennessee Valley Authority, etc.

★ 22 ★

Promoting Public Health and Welfare

The welfare function

AN IDEAL SOCIETY would be one in which every individual had enough to eat and wear, adequate shelter, protection for health and safety, a chance for a good education, and an opportunity to earn a living by moderate toil, with safeguards against worry and want in old age. Such a society never existed, and some people would say that in the troubled world in which we live there is no use dreaming of one. Doubtless the United States has come nearest to realizing something of the kind, but not even our rich resources and technical competence have availed to prevent much poverty, misfortune, and insecurity. It has been necessary from earliest days for the more fortunate to help the disadvantaged through private agencies and through government on all levels. The promotion of public well-being has been a primary responsibility of government for generations. In a sense, everything that government does is intended to advance the people's well-being. Public activities contributing to health, morals, rehabilitation, poor relief, and social insurance are aimed at that objective most directly. These are the important elements in modern public welfare programs.

Local and state welfare activities

The earliest welfare activity on record (using the term in the specialized sense in which it will be employed here) was care of the poor. In England, this responsibility, insofar as not discharged by relatives or other private benefactors, early fell to the church parish. Even before the American colonies were founded, however, parliamentary legislation authorized taxation for this purpose, and the colonies inherited the concept of poor relief as a public, tax-supported function. In New England and some of the Middle Colonies, the town became the relief agency; farther south, the parish—soon replaced, however, by the county. To this day, towns and counties throughout the country raise and spend much revenue for this purpose. More than 100 years ago, the states also entered the field—establishing hospitals and asylums for special classes of unfortunates such as the feeble-minded, the insane, hardened criminals, and the blind; setting up boards and other authorities to administer such institutions; organizing departments of welfare; and in some cases supervising local services. In times of stress, programs of public succor sometimes proved pitifully inadequate. On the other hand, deficiencies were met to some extent by the private charities for which our people have traditionally had a commendable record. Early in the present century, states began helping their local governments extend financial aid to persons outside of institutions, chiefly the aged, the blind, and needy mothers. Meanwhile, too, states and localities were contributing to welfare in the broader sense by developing health services, introducing safety requirements in transportation and industry, building up educational systems, providing highways, fostering agriculture, protecting natural resources, regulating working conditions for women and children, fixing hours and minimum wages in industry, enacting workmen's compensation laws, encouraging good housing, and in many other ways.

From early days, the national government likewise had a good deal to do with welfare in the broader meaning of the term. In the case of the states, broad constitutional authority flowed from reserved powers; in that of the national government, such authority was ample also, not only because specific powers like that of regulating interstate and foreign commerce could be drawn upon, but especially because of the blanket grant of power to raise money "to provide for the . . . general welfare of the United States." And through the years— particularly after 1900—national welfare activities took such forms as: (1) humanizing the conditions attending immigration, (2) curbing the transmission of diseases and the distribution of impure food and drugs, (3) maintaining hospitals for certain classes of the ill and injured; (4) conducting research on problems of health and creating a public health service to cooperate with and assist state health services; (5) imposing safety regulations on railroads, air and water carriers, and mines; (6) taxing out of existence injurious forms of manufacturing, for example, making matches from white phosphorus; (7) curbing and controlling traffic in narcotics; (8) prohibiting the circulation of immoral matter through the mails and the interstate transportation of persons for immoral purposes; (9) matching state contributions for support of vocational rehabilitation; (10) promoting the well being of Indians on reservations; and (11) caring for veterans. Until the Great Depression, however, the national government largely left to the states the task of caring for the poor, the sick, and the unfortunate. In 1912, a Children's Bureau was established in the then existing Department of Commerce and Labor, to encourage the states to enact remedial legislation on child labor. In 1918, small grants to the states were initiated for combating venereal diseases, and in 1920 for encouraging vocational rehabilitation. In 1921 a Maternity (Sheppard-Towner) Act gave the states limited funds for five years for promoting the well-being of mothers and infants. Although judicially sustained when challenged,[1] this measure was allowed to lapse at the end of its period. Not until after 1930 was anything further added to the record.

The national government and welfare

[1] Frothingham *v.* Mellon and Massachusetts *v.* Mellon, 262 U. S. 447.

FROM RELIEF TO SOCIAL SECURITY, 1929-35

The shock of depression

During the relatively prosperous decade of the twenties, local and state welfare services expanded only slightly and along traditional lines despite the fact that there was considerable poverty. National programs remained as before. The nation, thus, entered the depression firmly attached to a system of public care for the unfortunate which emphasized local responsibility and which was supported mainly by local taxes. In its main contours the American system of poor relief had been designed in Elizabethan England. The swelling tide of unemployment spreading want, fear, and despair over the face of the land soon engulfed the private charities and the town, parish, and county poorhouses and dole systems. The states attempted to bolster the local units with grants and loans and work programs but they too were soon swamped by falling income and inadequate machinery. Still unemployment mounted, to 10, then to 13 millions, and private charity, local units, and state governments looked to the national government for help.

The first national efforts took the form of loans by the Reconstruction Finance Corporation to state and local governments for public works construction to give employment and for direct cash relief. These units soon exhausted their credit as the "natural" recovery hoped for by the Hoover administration failed to materialize. And to the ensuing Roosevelt administration it fell to attack the problem with fresh determination and a new philosophy. The policy of the new regime was to put vast new resources at the disposal of the states and local units and also to act directly, on many different fronts, to create employment and provide relief. Most of the major steps taken have been touched upon at various points in preceding chapters of this book, and need not be reviewed here. Suffice it to say that billions of dollars were appropriated, piling up a national debt considered extraordinary until dwarfed by that incurred during the later years of defense effort and war. Through a Federal Emergency Relief Administration, a Public Works Administration, a Civil Works Administration, a Works Progress Administration, and other huge agencies that came and went, vast programs of employment and relief were carried forward by direct action of national agencies and through grants to states, counties, and cities. Novel measures like the National Industrial Recovery Act of 1933 and the Agricultural Adjustment Acts of 1933 and 1938 were placed on the statute book (even though in some instances judicially invalidated).

The Social Security Act (1935)

Down to 1934-1935, thought and effort were centered largely upon breaking the back of the depression. Huge outlays for relief, for employment on public works and vast loans and gifts to states and localities, however, could not go on forever, even though the conditions currently requiring them easily might recur. Moreover, there ought to be ways not only of cushioning the impact of "hard times" when encountered, but of giving large masses of people a new sense of security against hazards of both bad times and good. The interest of those having to do with making national policy now turned, therefore, to tapering off the national government's public works expenditures and devising ways by which the states, with the help of insurance systems and relatively modest grants-in-aid, could be brought back into the center of the welfare picture. National spending on employment-making public works and on other forms of relief went on to some extent until after the economic situation was sharply reversed by the defense and war effort starting in 1940. In 1935, however, and after careful studies of the social insurance systems in Europe, and of the question of a permanent program for this country,[2] Congress, by heavy majorities, passed an omnibus Social Security Act representing the first concerted nation-wide attack involving all levels of government on the problem of economic security for wage earners and their families. Conceding that the measure as enacted did not provide complete protection against "the hazards and vicissitudes of life," President Roosevelt, at all stages a vigorous sponsor, nevertheless characterized it as "the most useful and fundamental single piece of legislation ever enacted in the interest of the American wage earner." As now operating after several expansions of coverage, the program furnishes impressive testimony to the accepted responsibility of government on all levels for assuring all people in all parts of the country a reasonable degree of economic and social well-being.

SOCIAL INSURANCE

Towering above all else in the general scheme provided by the act of 1935 are two plans of social *insurance:* (1) unemployment; and (2) old age and survivors. These two insurance programs represent efforts to provide long-term solutions to the central problems of social security.

1. Unemployment compensation: a. The national-state basis

Loss of their jobs by millions of workers during the great depression sharply emphasized the hazards of layoff and dismissal confronting industrial workers. A major objective of the legislation of 1935 was to encourage the states to soften the impact of such disasters by providing benefit payments from which employees, usually with meager savings, could, when laid off or dismissed, keep themselves and their families going for at least a limited period

[2] Principally by a special Committee on Economic Security appointed by President Roosevelt in 1934, by the National Resources Committee (forerunner of the later National Resources Planning Board), and by the Brookings Institution. See a publication of the Committee on Economic Security entitled *Social Security in America* (Washington, 1937), and one by the National Resources Committee entitled *The Problems of a Changing Population* (Washington, 1938).

As was to be expected, fantastic schemes were advanced from various quarters, e.g., the Townsend Plan (which still has numerous adherents), in its original form calling for payment of $200 a month to all persons over 60 on condition only that they stop work and spend their pensions as fast as received; and the Lundeen Plan, calling for weekly payments of not less than $10 to all unemployed persons 18 years of age or over. Cf. M. S. Stewart, "Pensions After Sixty," *Pub. Affairs Pamphlets,* No. 46 (New York, 1940); N. Roosevelt, *The Townsend Plan* (New York, 1939); and S. Downey, *Pensions or Penury* (New York, 1939).

without turning to public relief. Virtually every state already had workmen's compensation laws under which employers were required to carry insurance to enable them to pay benefits to employees kept from work by industrial accidents or occupational disease. This had become an accepted part of the cost of production and was passed on to the consumer in the price of goods produced. To this was now added benefits for employees kept from work, not by accident or illness, but by lack of employment. The cost was to be part of the legitimate expense of doing business and passed on to consumers. Like the President's Committee on Economic Security, whose recommendations were largely followed, Congress weighed the desirability of a straight national system of unemployment insurance, uniformly compulsory and nationally administered. Fearing, however, that such a scheme would be held unconstitutional, and considering it desirable not to dictate any one of the many different forms that such insurance might take, the two houses agreed upon a plan offering the states substantial inducements (including subsidies to cover costs of administration) to devise and set up unemployment compensation systems of their own. If any state failed to do so, the minimum system prescribed in the law would be applied to the industries of that state by the national government. With this type of sanction, every state promptly established its own program. Speaking strictly, therefore, under existing law there is no national system of unemployment compensation, but only a variety of state systems operating under national standards and with national supervision.

b. Finan-cial ar-range-ments
The heart of the plan is the arrangement for financing the insurance from payroll taxes paid by employers. In the first place, the national government levies a 3.1 percent tax upon the payrolls of all employers of at least four persons during at least 20 weeks of a calendar year. The taxable payrolls are so computed, however, as not to include anything paid to any employee in excess of $3000 a year. In the second place, each state levies its own payroll tax, for support of its own unemployment compensation system, set up and operated under its own law. The state tax may apply only to those liable to the national tax or it may be, and in many states is, applied to more employers. In the third place, when an employer pays his national tax, he is allowed an offset for the amount he is paying his state; in other words, he actually pays the national government a payroll tax of 0.4 percent. A state therefore can tax an employer at the rate of 2.7 percent without imposing any additional burden, because anything up to that amount will be deducted when the national tax is paid. In all but six states (Alaska, California, Maryland, Massachusetts, Pennsylvania, and Wyoming), 2.7 percent is the maximum rate of state tax. However most states have established systems of "merit" or "experience" rating by which employers with good records for steady employment may reduce their state tax liability without increasing their national taxes. The average rate of tax is, therefore, somewhat less than 2.7 percent of covered payrolls (2.2 percent in 1964). Should any state elect to remain out of the system, its employers still

would be liable for the national tax, the proceeds of which in such a case would be retained in full by the national government and used nationally. All funds assessed by the states go into an unemployment trust fund in the national treasury (held, however, in separate state accounts), and are invested in national bonds, subject, of course, to requisition by the states as needed for benefit payments. The relatively high levels of employment of the postwar decades have resulted in the piling up of a reserve of more than $7.2 billion by 1965 in the unemployment trust fund. The continuing drag of unemployment more recently, however, has meant annual benefit payments in excess of $2.5 billion and the reserves of several states are woefully inadequate. During the recessions of 1958 and 1960-1961, unemployment rose rapidly and thousands of covered employees exhausted their benefits while still out of work. Congress on both occasions provided for a temporary extension of payments to these persons for an additional 13 weeks. In the first instance (1958), 17 states that had exhausted their own reserves were authorized to borrow from the national reserve to make the payments. The second effort was also financed by advances out of the reserve, but the national payroll tax was raised from 0.3 to 0.4 percent in 1960, to .8 percent for 1962, and then to 0.65 percent for 1963 in order to replenish the national reserve.

To participate, a state must meet certain requirements. It must, of course, set up an unemployment compensation system, levy the necessary tax, and provide for administration through a regular industrial commission, a special unemployment commission, or some other suitable agency. It must arrange to have all benefits paid through public employment offices or other approved agencies. It must agree that funds withdrawn from its treasury account in Washington shall be used solely for payment of benefits. There are also restrictions upon its liberty to withhold benefits under special circumstances arising from industrial disputes. Apart from these restrictions, a state is free to adopt any particular type or scheme of compensation preferred, to determine the categories of unemployment to be covered, and to fix the scale of benefits to be paid. Under these conditions—with every state, and the District of Columbia participating since 1939 and Puerto Rico since 1960—there are many differences from state to state. The tendency over the years has been for the various state systems to become more and more similar. Nine states started by taxing employees as well as employers, but now only New Jersey, Alabama and Alaska do this. Nearly all states follow the national act in excluding from coverage self-employed persons, agricultural workers, domestic employees, and employees of nonprofit agencies and institutions. Almost half of the states, however, cover smaller firms than the national act.

c. State patterns

Altogether about 48 million workers are covered by the system out of a labor force of 75 million. The only major changes in coverage since 1935 have been: (1) the extension of coverage to employees of the national government in 1954; (2) extension to smaller firms beginning in 1956; (3) removal of

d. Changes since 1935

railway employees in 1938 and provision for them by a separate system; (4) addition of maritime workers in 1946; and (5) inauguration of a special coverage for ex-servicemen in 1958.

Inflation in the postwar era has markedly reduced the real value of the benefit payments despite the fact that most states have been increasing their maximum weekly rates. The most recent tabulations (1964) show the average weekly payment for the entire United States at $36. Benefits are paid during any one year for not more than 26 weeks in most states. Eligibility for benefits is computed according to somewhat varying wage-credit formulae, in which length of employment and taxable wages received are principal factors. Many students of the subject consider that the maximum weekly payment ought in no case to be less than $45 nor the maximum period less than 26 weeks. Except, however, for the large number of workers not covered and the diminished value of benefits resulting from inflated living costs, existing arrangements have, in the past at least, yielded generally good results. The system, however, is designed only for short-run or seasonal unemployment. It is not geared to take care of prolonged economic depression. It has not been adjusted to the modern level of unemployment nor to the constant pressure of automation. Several states have nearly exhausted their reserves. President Kennedy in 1961 and 1963 asked Congress for extensive reconstruction of the system designed to: (1) increase the numbers of workers covered; (2) increase the amount of annual wages covered; (3) increase the benefits paid; (4) make greater provision for long-range unemployment; (5) expand national responsibility by inaugurating equalization grants for states and industries hard hit by unemployment. President Johnson added his voice in support of these proposals in 1964 and 1965. Finally, it should be clearly understood that this system is designed to take care of those who are ready, willing, and able to work. It is not for the disabled, the sick, the infirm, or the aged. To receive benefits a worker is obliged to register at the nearest public employment office, operated by the state in conjunction with the unemployment insurance program and he must accept "suitable" employment if offered to him.[3]

National responsibility for unemployment compensation is now discharged by the Bureau of Employment Security in the Department of Labor (prior to 1953 in the Federal Security Agency). This Bureau administers grants to the states for administrative costs for unemployment insurance and for public employment offices. It also regulates payments to the states from the insurance reserve fund and inspects state systems for compliance with national standards.

e. Benefits

2. Old age, survivors, and disability insurance:

The other insurance plan provided by the Social Security Act of 1935

---

[3] The definition of "suitable" employment varies from state to state. Many states, for example, do not expect an employee to accept work in a firm where a labor dispute is in progress. Many states do not expect an employee to accept work which is below his present skill. These and many other similar questions growing out of suitable employment are the center of much contemporary controversy.

was designed especially for the aged. The problems of the nation's senior citizens were brought into sharp focus by the depression. Layoffs had been especially heavy among workers over 50. The mechanization of industrial production and the introduction of assembly-line techniques had made it difficult for the older workers to keep up with their younger rivals. The great improvements in this century in private and public health had produced a rapid increase in the percentage of our population over 60. The urban family unit, unlike the rural family, was not equipped by living space or income to take care of its overaged dependents. The result: a disproportionate share of those in distress were in the older age group. Public works programs, the preferred method of the Roosevelt administration, did not greatly aid those who were past their prime and thus unable to do heavy labor. Everywhere in the nation the older citizens were demanding special attention—many of them through the Townsend movement for old-age pensions.

In essence, the system established in 1935 is a nation-wide joint contributory retirement system under which annuities or pensions, graduated in amount on the basis of earnings and duration of employment, are payable at age 65

a. Outline of system

POPULATION CHANGES BY AGE GROUP, 1940-1960

POPULATION (in millions)	AGE (in years)	PERCENT CHANGE
1940 TOTAL 131.7 / 1960 TOTAL 179.3		
9.0 / 16.5	65 and over	+45.5
10.6 / 15.6	55-64	+32.1
15.5 / 20.5	45-54	+24.4
18.3 / 24.1	35-44	+24.0
33.0 / 33.6	20-34	+1.8
24.1 / 30.0	10-19	+19.7
21.2 / 39.0	0-9	+45.6

from a fund built up from money paid in equally by employers and employees. The national government was intended to make no financial contribution beyond meeting the costs of administration. It does bear undivided responsibility for operating the system and plays the combined roles of collector, bookkeeper, and manager. The states and their subdivisions have no part in the undertaking. On the employee's side, the plan is one for compulsory savings—in other words, for spreading wages over his adult lifetime rather than over merely his wage-earning years, so that after retirement he may have a resource on which to draw for a living. And on the theory that the employer (not to mention the taxpaying public), has a stake in fostering employee saving and in keeping his employees from eventually going on relief, he is required to give his workers, in effect, a premium for their industry, and in so doing to help make the plan workable, as a scheme of "cooperative thrift," by sharing in creating and maintaining the fund. Under the system, more than 18 million retired workers already are drawing benefits, while other millions still on the job are building up potential rights to future old-age income.

b. Coverage   At the outset, old-age insurance applied to substantially the same workers as unemployment compensation, with approximately the same groups, for example, self-employed persons, agricultural workers and domestic employees, excluded. Whereas, however, the coverage of unemployment insurance never has been expanded on any large scale, that of old-age insurance has been greatly broadened. In 1939, 1.5 million workers not previously reached were brought in, the name was changed to "old age and survivors" insurance, and coverage was further widened to include protection not only for the worker but for his family, through provision for monthly benefits for aged wives and young children of retired workers, and for widows, orphans, and aged parents of workers dying before retirement. After prolonged agitation, an amending act of 1950 brought under the system, in addition, 4.7 million self-employed nonfarm workers, 1.45 million employees of state and local governments, a million household servants, 750 thousand regularly employed farm workers, and certain smaller groups—an aggregate of some 10 million. In 1954, another 10 million workers were potentially added to the system, including public employees in all jurisdictions desiring it, farm laborers, and members of many professions. In 1956, a system of disability insurance was made available to covered workers. More than 90 percent of the country's entire labor force is now covered by the system.

c. Financing   Contributions made by employees and employers alike started at 1 percent each of the wages received or paid in 1937, and under the original law would, by stages, have reached a maximum of 3 percent each by 1949. Because, however, huge reserves were necessarily built up in anticipation of future claims, Congress, from year to year, and usually over Presidential objection, "froze" the tax at 1 percent. Beginning in 1950, however, the levy was allowed to rise to meet the costs of increased benefits, lower retirement ages, medical care benefits, and greater allowances for widows and dependents.

The original schedule was modified and the tax now, in 1965, is 3.6 percent and is scheduled to rise to 5.65 percent by 1987. In the beginning the tax was paid on the first $3000 of annual wages; then on the first $4800 and now in 1966 on the first $6600. Thus the maximum annual payment is expected to reach $373 each for the employee and his employers.[4]

Accompanying the tax increases in the postwar years has been a general increase in benefits paid out by the system. Under the original act, average monthly payments of $20-$25 were typical, with lower payments to surviving widows and higher payments to families with children. Increases granted at various times have raised the average monthly benefits to $70-$75 for retired workers and to $130 for a worker and his aged wife. Each rise in the benefit schedule has also been accompanied by rises in the allowable earnings of retired beneficiaries. The reserve created against future claims had by 1965 reached the staggering total of $22 billion and the annual payments to beneficiaries had mounted to $16 billion.

d. Benefits

There has been a good deal of controversy, first and last, about whether this system is actuarially sound and solvent. The long delay by Congress in raising the tax rates as originally planned gave a good deal of support to those who argued that ultimately deficit financing by Congressional appropriation would be required.[5] A special review of the program in the light of the charges of the 1950's, conducted in 1958 by an Advisory Council for the board of trustees of the O.A.S.I. trust fund, pronounced the present system reasonably sound.[6] Annual reports of the trustees, thereafter, have reiterated these views.

Inevitably, the Social Security Act of 1935 was attacked at many points on constitutional grounds, and amidst confusing decisions of lower courts a good deal of doubt arose as to how much of it would ultimately be sustained. In a series of notable decisions handed down on May 24, 1937,[7] however, the Supreme Court—although by narrow margins of five to four—took a more liberal view than in earlier decisions and upheld every vital feature of the basic law. The Court discovered at last, as someone has remarked, "a method for implementing nationalism." Minority justices looked upon the unemployment compensation (and some other) provisions of the legislation as invading the powers guaranteed to the states by the Tenth Amendment, and therefore as unconstitutional. But the majority considered that the states had been lax

e. The system sustained by the Supreme Court 1937

[4] Employee contributions are ordinarily collected by the employer and paid to the Internal Revenue Service. Self-employed persons make their payment, at a slightly higher rate, at the time they pay income taxes.

[5] The Chamber of Commerce of the United States proposed in 1953 the ultimate liquidation of the reserve, the extension of benefits to all persons 65 or over not already covered, the continuation indefinitely of the 2 percent tax rate, the abolition of the companion old-age-assistance program and the placement of all old-age payments on a pay-as-you-go basis.

[6] See "Introduction and Conclusions by Advisory Council on Social Security," *The New York Times,* Jan. 2, 1959.

[7] Carmichael *et al. v.* Southern Coal and Coke Co., 301 U. S. 495; Charles S. Steward Machine Co. *v.* Davis, 301 U. S. 548; Helvering *et al. v.* Davis, 301 U. S. 619.

about social security matters, that meanwhile the problem had become national in scope and dimensions, and that therefore Congress was justified in what it had done. "It is too late today," said Justice Cardozo, "for the argument to be heard with tolerance that in a crisis so extreme the use of moneys of the nation to relieve the unemployed and their dependents is a use for any purpose narrower than the promotion of the general welfare"—adding that what constitutes the general welfare is for Congress to determine.

f. Medical cost insurance added

After almost 20 years of controversy amidst drastic changes in the scope, character, and costs of medical care and increasing evidence of the effect on the aged and their families of attempts to meet these costs, Congress under the leadership of President Johnson finally, in 1965, added a program of medical care insurance to the insurance programs for the aged described above. For those now retired and receiving O.A.S.D.I. payments and for those who will hereafter retire, the new program will pay most of the costs of hospital, nursing-home, and posthospital home-care visits for each illness. The payroll levies were increased to the levels described to pay for this program. A voluntary program of insurance of the costs of doctors, medical technicians and specialists, and various health services was also made available. The government agreed to match the monthly premium payments of those who elected to receive this further coverage.

g. Results

The nation has now therefore insured its people against most of the hazards of age. Each worker is guaranteed a minimum retirement income when he or she reaches age 65 (62 in some cases) and, if he should die or become disabled prior to that time, his family is assured support. A substantial share of the costs of illness after retirement will hereafter be borne by the system. With these measures we have taken a long and overdue step toward eliminating the concern of our people about their declining years.

PUBLIC ASSISTANCE

Categorical assistance:

The two insurance systems established in 1935 were designed to make long-range provision for the aged and the temporarily unemployed. Neither scheme was intended to relieve immediate distress. The Social Security Act of 1935, therefore, provided a program of immediate and continuing assistance to certain needy individuals. In examining the types and conditions of persons who needed help at that time and would be likely to need it in the foreseeable future, the Congress selected certain categories of such persons for whose welfare the national government ought to assume continuing responsibility. The sponsors of the *categorical assistance* program expected that responsibility for virtually all other classes of unfortunates would, henceforth, fall wholly on the states and local communities.

1. Old age assistance

The first group for whom the act established a continuing program of succor were the needy aged. Obviously no insurance program would help those at or near retirement age at the time, and, as we have noted, thousands and thousands of such persons were destitute in the mid-thirties. The pattern selected for aiding those needy aged was one which had been tested in some of the states. A few states had experimented with old-age pensions as early as 1923 and 25 states had some kind of system in operation in 1935. In most cases, however, the state systems were inadequate as to both coverage and benefits. Using the familiar grant-in-aid technique, the Act of 1935 created a joint national-state program of old-age assistance. National money was appropriated to any state which qualified by meeting the minimum national standards. These standards were: (1) that aid to be paid on the basis of need; (2) that aid be extended beginning at age 65; (3) that the program cover the entire state; (4) that a single state agency administer the state's part of the program; (5) that the state pay a portion of the cost of the assistance; and, (6) that all personnel—state or local—engaged in administering the program be selected on a merit basis. To states with approved programs, the national government agreed to pay 50 percent of all administrative costs and, originally, about 50 percent of the assistance grants up to $50 per month for any single beneficiary. Most states quickly enacted laws qualifying them for participation and today every state, Puerto Rico, Guam, the Virgin Islands, and the District of Columbia participate in the old-age-assistance program. There are, of course, many variations in practice from state to state. Since the amount of actual benefit depends upon need and need is determined in each case by state or local public welfare workers, standards of assistance show wide regional variations. Eligibility for aid is also based upon varying requirements as to residence, responsibility of relatives, and citizenship. The state's programs vary also in the amounts they are willing to put into the program. Many states, for example, have higher maximum monthly grants than the national formula entails. The average monthly payments, in fact, vary from $10 to $90. Modifications in the formula for national grants have been made in the ensuing years in the direction of increasing the national contribution. At present, the national government pays 64 percent of the total cost of old-age assistance. During 1964, approximately 2.1 million persons received an average of $79 a month under this program.

In 1960, a supplementary medical assistance program (Kerr-Mills) was introduced under which the national government undertook to aid in defraying the costs of medical care for the aged who were not poor enough to qualify for old-age assistance but too poor to pay for adequate medical care. The sponsors, in part, hoped to avoid a major new medical cost-insurance program by adding this new feature to categorical public assistance. One-third of the states, however, refused to participate in this new program and it delayed rather than obviated the major medical insurance ultimately adopted in 1965. In the enactment of 1965, however, the medical assistance program was extended to the other categories of assistance (blind, dependent children, disabled), the amount of national participation in financing was increased, and more flexible "means" tests for eligibility were required.

2. Special medical aid

It might well be asked at this point why the old-age-insurance system has not after twenty-five years eliminated the need for old-age assistance. In the first place, the insurance program did not until 1950 include several million workers. As the coverage has been extended (in 1950, 1954, and 1958), the need for old-age assistance has been declining, but it will be another decade before those newly brought into the system can be supported more or less adequately by it. There are also some persons still not included in the insurance program. Secondly, the benefits paid under the insurance program are in some instances not adequate to maintain a decent level of subsistence and must be supplemented by grants of assistance. Thirdly, the continued rise in longevity accompanied by major increases in medical care costs have made it necessary to use assistance grants for medical purposes. It is anticipated that as insurance benefits are enlarged, coverage extended, and the major costs of medical care provided under the newly enacted program, the need for old-age assistance will gradually diminish. In numbers of recipients, the peak of 2,789,000 was reached in 1950 and the case load has been declining slowly since that time.

3. Aid to the blind

The second category of needy persons selected by the Congress in 1935 for a continuing national-state program of assistance was the blind. In general, the standards required for state participation were the same as those for the aged, except that payments were to be made beginning at age 16 or 18 to persons whose deficiencies of eyesight incapacitated them for normal work. All of the states and territories participating in old-age assistance now also participate in assistance to the blind. In 1964, 96 thousand persons (a little more than one-third of the blind population) received an average grant of $86 per month of which the national government paid 48 percent.

4. Aid to dependent children

Many dependent children are cared for (in a fashion) in privately or publicly supported asylums, orphans' homes, and foster homes. With a view, however, to salvaging the advantages of home care wherever possible, numerous states, even before 1935, enacted laws providing pensions or other forms of aid for needy mothers having children in their charge. The Social Security Act undertook to generalize this type of beneficence by instituting grants-in-aid for its support. State-operated systems vary, but in virtually all instances assistance is available only in behalf of children under 16 years of age (18 if in school), only if financial need is shown, and only if living with a parent or relative, although some provision is now made for children in foster homes. All states now receive subsidies for this purpose and the program has been repeatedly liberalized since 1935. Aid payments may now be made for needy parents as well as children, and even for both parents if the father is unemployed. In 1964, children and parents' aid went to upwards of 4.2 million at a total cost of some $1.6 billion, of which the national government paid 57 percent. A special addition—for one year only—to the program for dependent children was enacted in 1961, authorizing payments for children of the needy unemployed.

A fourth category of needy beneficiary of national grant was added to the original three by the amendments of 1950: the totally and permanently disabled. National grants were, thereafter, made available to acceptable state programs which made provision for grants to persons 18 or over who were totally and permanently incapacitated and who were not mentally ill or tubercular. In 1964, 527 thousand persons received grants averaging $80 per month at a total cost of $495 million of which the national government paid 57 percent. One state, however, has not yet put this program into operation. *5. Aid to the totally and permanently disabled*

The administration of the national aids, including supervision of state systems for compliance with standards, is now the responsibility of the Welfare Administration of the Department of Health, Education, and Welfare. *Administration*

Under the categorical aids program the national government has undertaken a continuing indefinite commitment to pay a share of the costs of providing assistance to all persons found to be eligible by state and local agencies. In this respect, the assistance aids differ from all other types of grant-in-aid programs operated by the national government. With need and eligibility determined locally or by the state and with national, state, and, in some cases, local contributions to the total costs, a pattern of assistance has been worked out which unites all of the levels of government. Each level meets that portion of the responsibility for which it is best suited. Controversy continues mainly over the share of the cost which should be borne by each level, the effort which can or should be expended to keep people off the relief rolls in the first place, and the amount and character of supervision which the national government should exercise over the states.[8]

CHILD HEALTH AND WELFARE SERVICES

For a few years in the twenties (1921-1928), the nation had aided state programs for improving maternity care and child welfare. The Social Security Act re-established a child health and welfare service program. Under it grants-in-aid are now made to the states and some territories for general support of appropriate state activities. As operated in 1964, $90 million is distributed annually among the states and territories for these programs. The grants are made in proportion to demonstrated need and on condition that standards are met and matching funds appropriated by the state.

To share in maternal and child health grants, a state must not only have a health department but within such department a maternal and child health division with a physician in charge. The function of the division must be *1. Maternal and child health services*

[8] A recent controversy, for example, occurred between the state legislature of Indiana and the national authorities over the provision of the Act of 1935 requiring that the confidential character of state and local assistance records be maintained. Indiana, in 1951, defied the rule and opened its assistance records to public inspection. The national administrators then ordered a withdrawal of national grants. The Congress, after some delay, amended the law so as to authorize the Indiana practice. Many state laws were, thereafter, amended to open the relief rolls to public inspection.

principally to help county health departments develop and operate health services for children from birth through school age and for mothers before and after childbirth. With emphasis on prevention rather than treatment, prenatal clinics are held, child health conferences organized, school children given medical and dental examinations, immunization precautions taken against communicable child diseases, and nutritional information imparted. In both quantity and quality, national-state-county services of these kinds vary greatly from state to state, and even from community to community. That they have more than proved their worth is indicated by a decline of mothers' deaths in connection with childbirth from 58 to 3.5 per 10,000 during the first 30 years of the system's operation, and of infant deaths, on the same numerical basis, from 560 to 250.

2. Services for crippled children

Grants are also made, as provided by the law, to "extend and improve [especially in rural areas and in areas suffering from severe economic distress] . . . services for locating crippled children, and for providing medical, surgical, corrective, and other services and care, and facilities for diagnosis, hospitalization, and after care, for children who are crippled or who are suffering from conditions which lead to crippling." The emphasis on rural areas was later abandoned. In 1964, more than 750 thousand crippled children were registered in the various states, many of them receiving help. Every state except Arizona participates in the program, but in few areas are the funds sufficient to finance an adequate state-wide service for all those suffering physical handicaps. Over the years increasing emphasis has been given to research into causes and cures and to demonstration projects of various kinds.

3. Child welfare services

Dependent children may stand in need of help beyond that of a financial nature; and many not classified as "dependent" require assistance also. They may suffer from neglect, abuse, physical or mental deficiency, the stigma of illegitimacy, or tendencies to delinquency. The national government's yearly grant in their behalf is designed to assist state child welfare agencies in supervising and aiding local services in arranging for foster-home or institutional care, protecting against mistreatment, conducting clinics, encouraging neighborhood activities tending to curb juvenile delinquency, assisting schools and courts in handling children's cases, and other such activities. Originally, the national effort was largely confined to rural areas but this limitation was removed in 1958. State matching requirements were also introduced at that time. Special programs to provide day-care centers for children of working mothers have been emphasized in recent years. In no state is this work all that it should be, but in 1964 more than 450,000 children were receiving aid.

Administration

The maternal and child health and welfare programs established under the Act of 1935 and enlarged in recent years are administered by the Children's Bureau now lodged in the Welfare Administration of the Department of Health, Education, and Welfare. Regrettably, a keen rivalry continues between this Bureau and its program and the Bureau of Family Services with its program of aid to dependent children. In most states and local units these two programs for children continue to be separately organized and administered.

GENERAL PUBLIC HEALTH SERVICES

The Social Security Act of 1935, a landmark in the development of a coordinated national program for the care of the needy and the handicapped, also marked the beginning of a growing national-state public health program. Public health grants to the states, abandoned in the twenties after a brief history, were re-established on a broader scale than ever before. The earlier grants for venereal disease control (1918-1925) and child and maternal hygiene (1922-1929) had been swept away by economy-minded statesmen. When the nation turned its attention to the enduring causes of widespread suffering, it found that illness was a major contributor to loss of job, family breakdown, and individual destitution. Concern for the health of our citizens was not wholly a new responsibility of the national government. A United States Public Health Service of trained scientists and physicians had been in operation in the Treasury Department almost since the founding of the nation. Founded for the care of ailing sailors by the Congress in 1798, a Marine Hospital Service had slowly acquired new functions—controlling epidemics, aiding states in the development and enforcement of quarantine regulations at ports of entry, investigating the causes, methods of transmission and cures of communicable diseases, regulating the interstate sale of biologics, loaning trained medical scientists to the armed services and to other agencies—and by 1912 it had become the modern Public Health Service. To this service the Act of 1935 assigned responsibility for directing a new grant-in-aid program to assist states in improving their general public health services, including vital statistics gathering, communicable disease control, public nurse services, and many others. The original appropriation for these purposes of $8 million has now grown to $96 million.

Early national health efforts

The thirties brought a new frankness to discussions of sex problems in American society and thus opened the way to a concerted drive on one of the nation's greatest health problems: venereal diseases.[9] Led by Surgeon General Parran, a campaign against these dread scourges was launched. In 1938, Congress enacted the Venereal Disease Control Act which revived the grant-in-aid procedure of 1918 and made national funds available for approved state programs of education, treatment, and case-finding. Aided by the discovery of penicillin and other antibiotics during and after World War II, the national-state programs helped markedly to reduce the incidence of venereal diseases and reported cases dropped steadily until 1958. Since that time, the incidence has been increasing gradually, seriously, it is asserted, among young

Venereal disease program

[9] When the venereal disease program started in 1938, 16 persons out of 100,000 died annually from syphilis alone. By 1952, this toll had been reduced to 3.7 and by 1962 to 1.5.

THE TEN LEADING CAUSES OF DEATH IN THE U.S.
1900 AND 1960

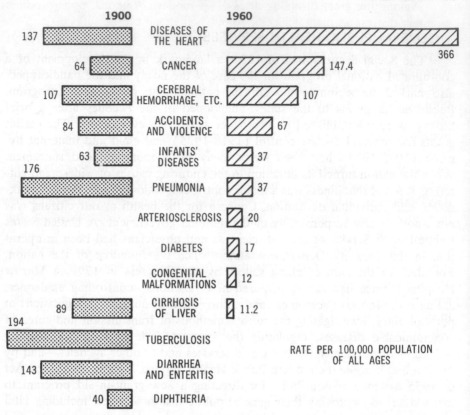

RATE PER 100,000 POPULATION
OF ALL AGES

people. From a peak annual appropriation to the states of $3 million, the national program had dropped to $700 thousand but has now climbed again to $10 million.

From contagious diseases to degenerative ones

Success in the battle against venereal disease, followed in the fifties by the break-through against poliomyelitis, marked some of the last major episodes in the attack upon communicable disease that had begun with Pasteur's great discoveries in the late nineteenth century. To be sure, much suffering and death were and are caused by tuberculosis, and a new aid program to assist states in case-finding and treatment was inaugurated in the Public Health Service Act of 1944. Also, rheumatic fever, scarlet fever, and others continue to cause incapacitation. The mortality tables of the fifties and sixties reveal, however, that cancer and heart and circulatory diseases are now the chief causes of death. The modern killers and disablers do not respond to the techniques developed to combat the contagious diseases. The emphasis in public health work has, therefore, been gradually shifting to: (1) research to discover causes and cures; (2) education on proper living; (3) improved environment; and (4) early diagnosis.

Among the great disabling diseases of modern America, none produces as much distress as mental illness. About half of all the hospital beds in the United States are occupied by mentally ill patients. During World War II, 12 percent of all men ages 18-37 examined for induction into the armed forces were rejected because of mental and personality disorders. The Metropolitan Life Insurance Company has estimated that one out of every twenty persons born alive in this country will at some time have to be hospitalized for mental disorders.[10] Responsibility for the care of the mentally ill has traditionally belonged to the states. The National Mental Health Act of 1946 marks the beginning of a national program in this field. Grants are now made to state mental health agencies for community programs, research efforts, and demonstration projects. The main thrust of the national effort is in promoting the development of diagnostic and treatment facilities in local communities and in connection with community hospitals, rather than the improvement of state asylums or hospitals. *Mental illness*

Grants to the states to engage in research and to promote diagnostic procedures and educational services relating to cancer were begun in 1947 and to heart diseases in 1948. Local programs for the improvement of our environment by reducing pollution of air and water have also been launched in the last two decades. Grants are made to states for pollution control projects, for research, and demonstration. Regulatory efforts in these areas were also expanded, for example, by the Clean Air Act of 1963 which provided a series of legal steps which community, state, and nation might take to halt air pollution.

The major effort of the United States Public Health Service in the fields of chronic illness and death-causing disorders is research. The older National Institute (now Institutes) of Health has been greatly expanded and now includes a Cancer Institute dating from 1937, Mental Health Institute created by the act of 1946, a Heart Institute, a Dental Institute, a Microbiology Institute created in 1948, an Institute for Arthritis and Metabolic Diseases and one for Neurological Diseases and Blindness created in 1950, an Institute for Allergy and Infectious Diseases created in 1955, and an Institute of General Medical Sciences and one of Child Health and Human Development created in 1962. These institutes carry on their programs in a Clinical Center established in 1953 and in other facilities of the service at Bethesda, Maryland. Grants are made to medical schools, universities, laboratories, and public and private hospitals for research projects. Fellowships for work in the national facilities are awarded and conferences of scientists and doctors are sponsored. More than $1 billion annually is now poured into this stupendous research program. *Research*

[10] The figures in this paragraph on mental illness are from J. F. Dewhurst and Associates, *America's Needs and Resources: A New Survey* (New York, 1955), 304.

Grants for hospital construction and for medical training facilities

One of the key problems in the postwar era in improving the health of the American people has been the shortage of hospital, clinical laboratory and medical training facilities. With a larger and larger portion of available hospital beds occupied by sufferers from protracted and chronic illness, and with construction and operating costs climbing beyond the capacities of local private organizations, the national government moved in to give the states a lift. The Hospital Survey and Construction Act of 1946 inaugurated a new grant-in-aid program by which national funds are now made available to states to pay a portion of the construction costs for public and private hospitals, public health centers, and other health facilities. An additional annual subsidy for construction of nursing homes, research facilities, diagnostic and treatment centers, and rehabilitation centers was made available beginning in 1955. Grants for medical schools and for facilities for training nurses and technicians were begun in 1963 and greatly expanded in 1965.

The efforts to reduce smoking

One of the most contentious areas of public health activity in recent years has been the efforts of the Public Health Service to establish the relationship between smoking and lung cancer. After some years of agitation based on statistical studies showing a high correlation between heavy smoking and the incidence of lung cancer, emphysema, chronic bronchitis, and arteriosclerotic heart disease, a report prepared by an advising committee to the Service and issued in 1964 concluded that smoking was unquestionably injurious to health and that heavy cigarette smokers had much higher death rates from heart and lung diseases than nonsmokers. The Federal Trade Commission then announced it would require a health warning on cigarette packages and in all cigarette advertising. Congress, by legislation in 1965, required the warning on cigarette packages but suspended for four years the effective date of the FTC requirement of a warning in all cigarette advertising.

PUBLIC HOUSING

Beginnings of a major problem

The acute housing shortage experienced by the country during and after World War II focused attention upon a problem really as old as our present industrial society. Rural housing often is far from what it should be. But when our population dwelt almost entirely on farms or in villages and small towns, most people had reasonably good homes, even though frequently with primitive equipment; and there was not much for public authorities to do about the matter. With the rise of great industrial centers, however, the situation changed, and decidedly for the worse. Rising land values produced building congestion; detached houses gave way to drab tenements; high rents forced families into pitifully inadequate quarters; immigrant workers congregated in teeming ghettos, "Little Italy's," and the like. The slum—dreary, crowded, and dangerous alike to health and morals—became a blot upon an otherwise fair social economy. Aside from some control over fire hazards and structural safety, the first serious attention given to housing by public authorities was directed to ameliorating the condition of low-income groups in slum areas.

Even in the third quarter of the nineteenth century, a few cities bestirred *Slow development of local and state action* themselves to some extent about the matter, enacting local codes prescribing building regulations and sanitary standards. The effects, nevertheless, were slight, and in time people concerned turned with more hope to the legislatures of the states. From this source in certain of the more highly industrialized sections did indeed come measures fixing standards with beneficial results. At best, however, the laws merely imposed regulations on private owners of existing housing or upon private construction, without directly bringing new and better housing into existence. New York, it is true, went farther by enacting measures calculated to encourage private enterprise to undertake a good grade of building for people of low incomes, and even by setting up a state housing board charged with planning and promoting slum clearance in the crowded districts of the metropolis and with supervising the construction of "model tenements." But for a long time no other state emulated the example thus set. Principal ways in which states and localities eventually contributed to housing betterment included municipal building codes and zoning regulations, rent regulation, loans for home construction and repair, tax exemptions for newly-constructed dwellings, and redevelopment corporations for undertaking slum clearance and new building. But in nearly all states these ameliorations came late and slowly.

Aside from some provision for the housing of war workers during World *The national government enters the field* War I, the national government kept almost completely out of the field until the depression of the thirties. From that time, however, it has been continuously involved, in many different ways and through the medium of legislation and administrative machinery so complicated, and so frequently changed, as to bewilder almost any one except a professional student of the subject. The first form of national effort, undertaken at a time when large numbers of people were losing their homes through mortgage foreclosures, was aimed not particularly at increasing or improving housing but at enabling hard-pressed homeowners to avoid being dispossessed. The method consisted in setting up (in 1932) a series of home loan banks (under a Federal Home Loan Bank Administration) to provide credit for local institutions engaged in home-financing and in addition a Home Owners' Loan Corporation (in 1933) to make direct long-term mortgage loans out of national funds and at low interest rates to distressed homeowners who for one reason or another could not borrow through other channels. Almost simultaneously, however, encouragement of new low-cost building and of renovation of run-down residential properties was undertaken through a Federal Housing Administration, authorized not only to insure lending institutions against possible losses on loans made for the purposes indicated, but itself to make loans to these institutions to be employed in promoting low-rent dwellings. To this point, the objectives had been primarily to enable people to save their homes and to stimulate employment in home building and modernization. Growing concern with the social values of good housing, however, to say nothing of the financial saving in terms of fire hazards, disease, delinquency, and crime, was reflected in a

United States Housing ("Wagner-Steagall") Act of 1937, setting up a United States Housing Authority charged with making long-term loans (up to 80 percent of the costs involved) to state or local housing authorities for the construction of low-rent housing and for slum clearance. The national agency was not to engage directly in the work of construction or demolition, but merely to make construction loans and annual operating grants; municipal or other local authorities directly concerned were to plan projects, furnish such additional funds as might be needed, and execute the different enterprises. Within four years after the legislation was enacted, all but nine of the states qualified for aid by setting up the requisite authorities—sometimes with jurisdiction confined to one or two cities, but often extending to all cities and towns and even to rural areas.

Housing and World War II

The plan outlined had only limited opportunity for operation before the national defense effort launched in 1940, together with the ensuing war, gave the housing problem a new slant and emphasis. With the rapid expansion of shipyards and of plants for manufacturing airplanes, explosives, and other war materials, the building of new plants for such purposes, and the construction of military camps and training quarters, hundreds of thousands of workers and their families flocked to localities not equipped to house them; and, partly in order to meet this situation, partly because of scarcity of labor and materials, and partly because Congress virtually cut off supporting appropriations, the general program of civilian construction and slum clearance came almost to a stop. Indeed, under legislation of 1940 national housing activities were substantially restricted to such as had to do with taking care of the armed forces and of war-plant workers; and between 1940 and the close of 1944, nearly 1.5 million war-housing units were constructed or reconstructed, about half of the number publicly and about half privately.

The postwar problem

Almost complete cessation of civilian building for five or six years (on top of heavily reduced building during the preceding depression decade), an unexpected increase of population in the meantime, return from overseas of millions of servicemen looking for homes, and continued deterioration of a great deal of housing long obsolescent—these and other factors produced a severe shortage for several years after World War II. In the steady advance of our people toward material well-being, housing had lagged: working hours had been reduced by a third to a half; food consumption had increased; education and recreation had progressed; social security had been initiated; even the average span of life had been lengthened. But millions in the low-income groups still lived in slums (both urban and rural), and other millions in homes more or less substandard.[11]

[11] A survey made in connection with the census of 1940 showed one-third of the country's population to be ill-housed and another third only fairly well provided for; and competent authorities estimated that even if all existing housing were put in good condition, 3 million new units were needed—a figure stepped up in 1945 to 6 million. See E. E. Wood, *Introduction to Housing; Facts and Principles* (Washington, 1940), 9.

After the war, the record of achievement had its bright spots, yet hardly was one to stir enthusiasm. The program under the United States Housing Act of 1937 came back into practical operation and by 1950 some 192,000 new dwelling units in 268 localities had been provided under it. In a limited way, the program was extended to rural areas. A chaotic administrative situation was improved in 1947 by establishment of the Public Housing Administration under a new co-ordinating Housing and Home Finance Agency.

NONFARM HOUSING, 1945-1965
Units Started

Public Housing	682,000
Insured by F.H.A.	5,008,000
Guaranteed by V.A.	2,737,000
Private	19,434,000
Total	27,861,000

What the situation seemed to require was a coherent long-term program under which the government would not merely *loan* but also *spend,* and with some liberality; and as early as 1945, a measure of this purport known as the National Housing (Taft-Ellender-Wagner) Bill made its appearance in Congress and passed the Senate. For almost four years, however, the project, bitterly fought by real estate and building lobbies, languished in the House of Representatives, and only in the early summer of 1949 was it found possible, after bitter contention in the two houses, to get an act of the kind, amending and extending the legislation of 1937, on the statute book. Party lines were broken but most of the votes were cast by Democrats. Under the new law— aimed particularly at urban and rural slum clearance and redevelopment—a total of 810,000 new housing units (separate houses or small apartments, but only for low-income families) was aimed at over a period of six years. All projects were to be developed, owned, and operated by local housing authorities (usually municipal) established under state statutes. While the national government was to expedite construction by loans in individual instances where needed (a total of $1 billion was made available for the purpose), local authorities were expected usually to provide for costs by sales of nationally-supported, tax-free bonds to private investors. To supplement contributions by local governments, the national government was to subsidize the system to a maximum of $100 million a year for five years to help make up the difference between the "economic rent" (based on annual operating costs and debt service) and the rent families of the low-income group could afford to pay, estimated at not over $30 a month.

The National Housing Act of 1949

The fighting in Korea (1950-1953) and the renewed emphasis it induced on national defense resulted in redirecting national housing interest into housing for defense plants and military installations. The Defense Housing and Community Facilities and Services Act of 1951 reflects this shift in emphasis

Developments in public housing 1950-1960

in the public housing program. The Eisenhower administration, although pledged to reduce national programs competing with private enterprise, revealed deep sympathy for the public housing program. In a message to the Congress early in 1954, the President called for a broadening of the objectives of the national public housing program to include urban redevelopment as well as slum clearance. In this way cities might salvage declining neighborhoods and stop others from deterioration and not have to await the appearance of the slum for national help. He also asked the Congress to extend the low-rent public housing program of the Act of 1949, although at a reduced rate of 35,000 new units per year for the next four years. The Housing Act of 1954 substantially met the President's request except that it limited the commitment on public housing units to one year. The President again in 1955 asked for a broader program of public housing and finally wrested authority for 45,000 more units from a reluctant Congress. Returning to the attack in 1956, the President got Congressional approval for 35,000 more units for 1956 and an equal number for 1957. No units were authorized in 1958. In 1959, the Congress twice passed housing bills providing for a renewed and expanded low-cost housing construction program but the President vetoed each. Authorization for 37,000 new units was finally approved. The Housing Act of 1959 also launched a new loan program aimed at promoting private construction of facilities specially designed for elderly persons and expanded somewhat the loans and grants for urban renewal programs.[12] Metropolitan regional planning through state or regional agencies was also promoted by grants-in-aid.

Kennedy emphasizes program for cities

President Kennedy, shortly after his inauguration, called for a much expanded housing and community rebuilding program, and Congress responded with a Housing Act of 1961 that: (1) removed the statutory prohibitions on the yet unbuilt 100,000 low-cost housing units contemplated by the original act of 1949; (2) expanded the loans available for college housing, housing for the elderly, and farm housing; (3) increased the monies available for grants for urban planning and for urban renewal projects; (4) authorized new loans to improve urban transportation facilities and utilities; and (5) authorized new grants for community purchase and development of "open" adjacent areas for recreational or conservation purposes. In an effort to strengthen and dramatize the modern program of national aid to cities, Kennedy also proposed the creation of a new department of Urban Affairs to include the various housing agencies. This proposal the Congress vetoed in accordance with the reorganization act and it also refused to create the department by statute.

Congress approves rent subsidies and new department

In 1965, President Johnson returned to these themes and gave them vigorous and effective support. A new Housing and Urban Development Act inaugurated rent subsidies for needy families to help pay for housing when

12 Special encouragement was provided for renewal projects in urban areas including colleges or universities. College student housing was also to be financed by loans at favorable interest rates.

suitable accommodations could not be obtained for 25 percent of their income. The program was confined to housing provided in public or government-insured housing. The new act also: (1) expanded the FHA program of low-interest home financing for low and modest income families and for veterans; (2) authorized local public housing agencies to lease units in private housing for occupancy by needy families; (3) expanded the urban renewal programs to embrace areas closely related to those previously eligible for renewal; (4) extended the low-rent public housing programs until 1969 at a level of 60,000 new units per year; (5) expanded loans for college housing; (6) authorized grants to local units for various types of public facilities including water works, sewer systems, health and recreation centers; (7) inaugurated grants to local units for acquisition of open areas and for urban beautification. Johnson also proposed the creation of a Department of Housing and Urban Development and the Congress endorsed his request.

THE NATIONAL GOVERNMENT AND EDUCATION

The mounting controversy in the last two decades over national aid to public education may have obscured the fact that the national government was already deeply involved by subsidy and direct expenditures. In earlier chapters we have described the programs of national assistance for agricultural education at the college level and through the Extension Service. A new program (National Defense Education Act) of aid to university students and staff was begun in 1958, renewed in 1961, and greatly expanded in 1964. In 1917, a broad program of national grants to the states for vocational education, largely at the high school level, was inaugurated. Expanded greatly in the past four decades, this program now provides national funds for and national supervision over training of young men and women in skilled trades, distributive occupations, industrial techniques, home economics, nursing (practical), and agriculture. Funds are also granted for preparing teachers in these subjects to staff the vocational schools. Many states have been stimulated by the national grants (some had them before the national grants began) to establish a system of vocational schools under the supervision of a state agency and to appropriate funds for the purpose of providing such education. Related programs of vocational training to help workers displaced by automation were established, beginning in 1962, under the Manpower Development and Training Act. In many cases these training efforts are carried on by the vocational school system. These programs were considerably enlarged in 1964 and 1965. To this program of education aids was added—beginning in 1920, greatly expanded in 1954 and again in 1964—aids for vocational rehabilitation for training the physically handicapped for useful employment.

During the depression numerous grants, loans, and direct national expenditures were made for school construction, remodeling, and equipment. Thousands of local school districts benefited from these temporary measures.

Aid to vocational education

Temporary grants during depression and war

Beginning in World War II and continuing to the present, substantial grants have been made for school construction in areas heavily burdened by military or defense facilities and for the establishment of child-care centers, nursery schools, and other educational facilities. Grants were also made to aid school districts obliged suddenly to make provision for large numbers of children whose parents were stationed at military installations. A huge subsidy to education has been made by the national government in the past two decades by means of the veterans' aid program, inaugurated in the GI Bill of 1944 and continued for Korean veterans and others.

Aid for school construction

Through continuing grants for school lunches for needy children and for aid to the large numbers of school districts affected by national installations, the national government has made and is still making important contributions to public primary and secondary education in the United States. All of this did not, however, set at rest the urgent demand for national grants for general public education aimed at helping localities deal with the great flood of school-going children and at placing a floor below which, regardless of local revenues, educational programs may not fall. President Eisenhower in 1955 asked Congress to inaugurate a new program of national assistance to local school districts for building construction loans at low interest and for grants for especially needy districts. He renewed his proposal on several subsequent occasions. President Kennedy entered the fray in 1961 by proposing a three-year program of aids for teachers' salaries and for school construction. He suggested a minimum grant of $15 per pupil and a general formula for distribution that would take account of the local effort and resources. As with all previous efforts, the Kennedy program foundered on the two great shoals of education legislation: (1) the religious issue—Catholics generally oppose general aid programs if parochial schools are not somehow taken care of; (2) the racial issue—many Northern Congressmen feel that aid must not be given to segregated schools.

General aid to education adopted

It remained for President Johnson to find a path through this legislative maze. He did so in 1965 in which year the first general aid program to primary-secondary education was established. The Johnson proposal tied school aids to help for the needy in order to avoid some of the constitutional and emotional problems of race and religion. The national grants are to be given to states on the basis of a formula which includes the amount spent per child in the state school program and the number of children from families with incomes under $2000 in each school district. The aids are to be given by the state to the school districts and may be spent as the districts wish, subject to approval by state and national authorities. Grants are also made available for the purchase of library materials and textbooks for children in public and private schools, but private school materials must be the same as those approved for public schools and may not include religious literature. Additional grants are also made to the state for: (1) community-wide educational services not provided by individual schools and (2) strengthening and improving state departments of education. All together more than $1 billion annually is authorized under the Act of 1965.

References

M. Fainsod, L. Gordon, and J. C. Palamountain, Jr., *Government and the American Economy* (3rd ed., New York, 1959), Chap. XXV.

L. Meriam, *Relief and Social Security* (Washington, 1946).

———— et al., *The Cost and Financing of Social Security* (Washington, 1950).

Ross, M., *Social Security in the United States* (Washington, 1948). A Federal Security Agency publication.

G. Abbott, *From Relief to Social Security* (Chicago, 1942).

E. M. Burns, *The American Social Security System* (Boston, 1949).

D. Gagliardo, *American Social Insurance* (New York, 1949).

Committee on Economic Security, *Social Security in America* (Washington, 1937).

J. E. Hughes, *The Federal Social Security Tax* (Chicago, 1941).

J. S. Parker, *Social Security Reserves* (Washington, 1942).

T. Lansdale et al., *The Administration of Old-Age Assistance* (Chicago, 1939).

R. Atkinson, *The Federal Role in Unemployment Administration* (Washington, 1941).

H. A. Gray, *Should State Unemployment Insurance Be Federalized?* (New York, 1946).

A. J. Altmeyer, "Unemployment Insurance: Federal or State Responsibility?" *Nat. Mun. Rev.,* XXXII (May, 1943), 237-242.

P. A. Rauschenbush, "Unemployment Compensation: Federal-State Cooperation," *ibid.,* XXXII (Sept. 1943), 423-431. A reply to the preceding article.

Council of State Governments, *Unemployment Compensation in the Postwar Period* (Chicago, 1944).

C. Abrams, *The Future of Housing* (New York, 1946).

————, *Man's Struggle for Shelter in an Urbanizing World* (Cambridge, Mass., 1964).

D. Schaffter, *State Housing Agencies* (New York, 1942).

M. L. Colean et al., *American Housing: Problems and Prospects* (New York, 1944).

R. B. Vance and G. W. Blackwell, *New Farm Homes for Old: A Study of Rural Public Housing in the South* (University, Ala., 1946).

E. R. Latty (ed.), "Housing" (Symposium), *Law and Contemporary Problems,* XII (Winter, 1947), 1-208.

M. B. Schnapper (comp.), *Public Housing in America* (New York, 1939).

Social Security Bulletin (monthly) and *Social Security Yearbook*. Issued by the Department of Health, Education, and Welfare.

A. M. Rivlin, *The Role of the Federal Government in Financing Higher Education* (Washington, 1961).

H. D. Babbidge, Jr. and R. M. Rosenzweig, *The Federal Interest in Higher Education* (New York, 1963).

F. J. Munger and R. F. Fenno, *National Politics and Federal Aid to Education* (Syracuse, N.Y., 1963).

S. C. Suprin, *Issues in Federal Aid to Education* (Syracuse, N.Y., 1963).

M. Anderson, *The Federal Bulldozer: A Critical Analysis of Urban Renewal, 1949-1962* (Cambridge, Mass., 1964).

E. May, *The Wasted Americans: Cost of Our Welfare Dilemma* (New York, 1964).

E. E. Witte, *The Development of the Social Security Act* (Madison, Wis., 1962).

★ 23 ★

Conducting Foreign Affairs

IF THE FATHERS and grandfathers of the statesmen of modern America were to revisit the scenes of their earthly endeavors, nothing, perhaps, would surprise them quite so much as the prominence now given to foreign affairs. For generations our people worked out their various destinies largely indifferent to the aspirations of the peoples of the rest of the world. In fact, they were determined not to allow the quarrels or feuds, the wretchedness or splendor, of other peoples or nations to entice their notice away from the main show of building a free and prosperous nation out of a wilderness. Separated by broad oceans from nations powerful enough to menace their national independence, selected by immigration from among those most dissatisfied with the societies from which they came, confident of the virtues of a political system built upon freedom, the American people felt they had little to fear and nothing to learn from Europe and Asia. Occasionally their idealism and their wealth might be enlisted in behalf of the starving Chinese or the struggling Armenians and then they would applaud the statesmen who lectured the "power hungry" and "cynical" politicians of Europe on their bad behavior. Mainly, however, America had few important ties abroad and wanted none. "Why," in the language of Washington's Farewell Address, "by interweaving our destiny with that of any part of Europe, entangle our peace and prosperity in the toils of European ambition, rivalship, interest, humor, or caprice?"

> *The transcendent importance of foreign affairs in the modern world*

Today it is quite different. The United States is tied to half of the world by military alliance, its troops march under the flag thousands of miles from this continent in fulfillment of commitments solemnly undertaken, its treasure has been exported in billions of dollars to bolster the defenses and the economies of friendly powers, its sons by the thousands have died and are dying in battles far from home. Its newspapers and airways are filled daily with the comings and goings and sayings of diplomats and statesmen from the entire world, its legislative halls resound with the clash of tongues on the conduct of affairs in Seoul, in Vietnam, in Geneva, Bandung, Laos, and Bonn—places the average American had never even heard of until the day before yesterday —and the utterances of its statesmen are awaited with respect and perhaps with awe by the leaders of every nation on earth. The earth has shrunk; technology has annihilated space. Our distant neighbors of yesterday are just across the street today. What is more, science has at last handed to men the power to destroy themselves completely. Failure in the conduct of foreign policy can well mean destruction for us all. The conduct of American foreign affairs has thus become the dominant concern of our government.

THE CONSTITUTIONAL BASIS

Exclusive national control and its basis

We have the word of the Supreme Court for it that, even if no authority could be found granted in the Constitution, nor indeed any clauses from which it could be deduced, the conduct of foreign relations would still be a proper and necessary function of our national government as "a necessary concomitant of nationality." [1] There is, however, no lack of expressly conferred power. Nowhere, it is true, is there a single blanket grant, or even any mention of "foreign relations" as such. But the President is authorized to "appoint ambassadors, other public ministers and consuls," to make treaties and to "receive ambassadors and other public ministers." The Senate is allotted a share in treaty-making, as well as in appointments, and Congress is given power to regulate foreign commerce and to declare war. Furthermore, national control in this field is made exclusive by clauses forbidding the states to "enter into any treaty, alliance, or confederation"—or into *any* agreement or compact with . . . a foreign power" except with the consent of Congress, or to engage in war unless actually invaded. By discriminating against alien residents in their land-ownership or other laws, or by failing to do justice when aliens suffer from mob violence, the states may raise difficult international problems for the national government. But that government has the sole right and power to handle such matters internationally. If we are to believe the Supreme Court, it has *all* power (not actually prohibited, as for example by the Bill of Rights) to act for us in the international field, with or without constitutional authorization, express or implied.

National responsibility diffused

The conduct of foreign relations is an executive function in many countries. In the United States, too, it is such a function primarily, yet one also shared heavily with other branches of the government. As chief executive, the President unquestionably is the supreme director of our official international intercourse. Nowhere in the Constitution, however, is he expressly assigned such primacy. On the contrary, he is merely given certain powers, the Senate is given others and Congress as a whole still others. And while we must allow him the center of the stage, it should be clearly understood that what we have in this area of our government is a responsibility shared by the executive and legislative (and, in matters of interpretation and enforcement, even the

---

[1] United States *v.* Curtiss-Wright Export Corporation, 299 U. S. 304 (1936). This case turned on the validity of a Presidential embargo on the sale of arms to two warring Latin-American nations, Bolivia and Paraguay, in pursuance of a joint resolution of Congress (1934) conferring such power. Cf. C. P. Patterson, "*In re* The United States *v.* the Curtiss-Wright Corporation," *Tex. Law Rev.,* XXII, 286-308, 445-470 (Apr. and June, 1944). The same view as that taken by the Court is expounded in E. S. Corwin, *The Constitution and World Organization* (Princeton, N. J., 1944).

judicial) branches—a responsibility considerably more diffused than that prevailing in the corresponding field in any other important country. For this product of our constitutional heritage—this "invitation to struggle for the privilege of directing American foreign policy"—we often pay a price in terms of unpredictability, delay, confusion, and frustration. And yet as the conduct of foreign affairs has become uppermost in importance among the functions of the national government, the Congress has insisted that it be taken into full partnership in determining what our policy should be. If we must vote huge funds and call up our manpower for military service, says the legislature, we should participate in the decisions that make these steps necessary.

An appreciation of the complexities and difficulties in the way of conducting foreign affairs within the governmental structure prescribed by the Constitution may, perhaps, best be obtained by a consideration of how particular powers and responsibilities are discharged by the President and Congress. *The President's powers:*

Basic to everything else is the maintenance of day-to-day intercourse with foreign governments. For this the President (utilizing the facilities of the State Department) is the official channel. On the one hand, subject to the Senate's right of confirmation, he appoints all ambassadors and ministers to foreign countries, and all foreign service officers (including consuls) stationed therein, with of course the full power of direction and removal which the appointing power entails. Indeed, in the belief that more can be accomplished by informal contacts than can be achieved through the formal channels of diplomacy, he may employ "special," "secret," or "personal" agents abroad, who, not being technically public officers, require no Senatorial confirmation, and who commonly receive their pay, if any, out of a Presidential "contingent fund." [2] Conversely, he receives, on his own responsibility, all foreign ambassadors and other public ministers, with power also, if occasion requires, to break off dealings with them and in effect send them home. Through the State Department, he carries on correspondence abroad, obtaining information, declaring policy, pressing claims, offering settlements, and replying to all manner of inquiries and proposals. Congress, on its part, may not address any foreign power or receive any communication from one. Any private citizen or corporation undertaking, "directly or indirectly, . . . to carry on verbal or written *1. Carrying on foreign intercourse*

[2] The diplomatic or semidiplomatic activities of such agents, may on occasion be quite as important as those of regular ambassadors and ministers, as, for example, were those of Nicholas Trist in negotiating peace with Mexico in 1848, of Commodore Perry in getting our first treaty with Japan in 1854, and of Colonel E. M. House as a roving special emissary of President Wilson in Europe during World War I. From 1940 onwards, Myron C. Taylor appeared intermittently at the Vatican (with which the United States does not maintain regular diplomatic relations) as special representative of Presidents Roosevelt and Truman charged with promoting the interests of peace; and from 1945 to 1947, General George C. Marshall was occupied in China as a special agent of President Truman in what proved a futile effort to bring about a reconciliation between Chiang Kai-shek and the communists. See H. M. Wriston, "The Special Envoy," *Foreign Affairs,* XXXVIII, No. 2 (Jan., 1960) for an analysis and justification of the use of "personal" agents.

correspondence or intercourse with any foreign government or its officers or agents (without express authority from the President) designed to influence the measures or conduct of any foreign government . . . in relation to any disputes or controversies with the United States or to defeat the measures of the government of the United States," becomes liable to penalty.[3] While normally using the State Department as his channel, to such a degree that even foreign governments must ordinarily address the White House through the Department, the President may nevertheless go as far as he likes in handling matters directly and personally—even to the extent of managing the country's foreign relations from his own desk, as did President Wilson during World War I and President Franklin D. Roosevelt at intervals during World War II. He may go abroad to lead in the negotiation of a great international settlement, as did Wilson when peace was to be made in 1919, or to meet with representatives of foreign governments at any places (in either hemisphere) selected for the purpose, as Roosevelt repeatedly met and conferred with Prime Minister Churchill and Marshal Stalin (and on one occasion with President Chiang Kai-shek) during World War II and as Truman, Eisenhower, Kennedy and Johnson have on occasions too numerous to record.

2. Recognition
From authority to speak for the nation in its dealings abroad springs a second significant Presidential function, that of determining the attitude to be taken by our government toward newly risen states or newly risen political regimes in existing states. As to who is to decide whether we shall officially recognize and have dealings with such states and regimes, the Constitution is silent. At various times it has been argued that Congress is entitled to participate along with the President. International usage recognizes the function as executive and the power to appoint and receive envoys would certainly make it such in the United States. Precedent, backed by judicial opinion,[4] places it wholly in the President's hands, subject only to the discretion of the Senate in confirming diplomatic appointments and assenting to treaties, and to that of both houses in voting foreign service appropriations. Recognition may take the form of welcoming into the family of nations (so far as we can do it by our own action) a state that has lately asserted its independence—as President Monroe, after 1817, recognized a number of newly risen Latin American republics, or as President Theodore Roosevelt in 1903 recognized the republic of Panama, thereby paving the way for the construction of the Panama Canal. The usual method in such instances is to send and receive diplomatic repre-

[3] This provision relating to private activities is quoted from the Logan Act of 1799 (U. S. Code, Title 18, Sec. 5), and was prompted by unauthorized efforts in Paris of a certain Dr. Logan of Philadelphia to avert threatened war between Napoleon and the United States.

[4] In United States v. Belmont, 301 U. S. 324 (1937) the Court went so far as to say that the President was the "sole organ of the federal government in the field of international relations." This case grew out of the procedure by which President Roosevelt in 1933 had extended recognition to the Soviet regime. This view was emphasized again in a more recent case growing out of the same situation, United States v. Pink, 315 U. S. 203 (1942).

sentatives. Or recognition may take the form of instituting official relations with a new political regime that has taken over in a given country, as when, in 1928, President Coolidge recognized the Nationalist government set up by the Kuomintang in China by concluding a treaty with it; or when, after the U.S.S.R. had waited 16 years for American recognition, President Roosevelt, in 1933, invited President Kalinin, of the All-Union Central Executive Committee at Moscow, to send a representative to Washington for conference, and followed by concluding an agreement with the emissary, Foreign Commissar Litvinov. A recent, and perhaps melancholy example, is the recognition rather quickly and easily accorded the Castro regime in Cuba only six days after the flight of the former dictator, Batista.[5] The power to recognize carries with it also the power to refuse to recognize. Students of our diplomatic history will recall how President Wilson, in 1915, became primarily responsible for the downfall of the revolutionary president Huerta in Mexico by declining to have dealings with the regime which he headed.[6] Presidents Hoover and Roosevelt steadfastly refused to recognize the new "state" of Manchukuo established under Japanese auspices on Chinese soil in 1932; and President Truman, in 1945-1946, refused to recognize Communist-dominated governments in Bulgaria, Romania, and Yugoslavia, established in defiance of decisions reached at the Yalta Conference, even though later developments forced him to open diplomatic relations with them. The United States, too, has never recognized Russia's acquisition of the Baltic countries in 1940 and has not, in spite of the British example, recognized Communist China.[7]

"Under our system of government," the courts have declared, "the citizen abroad is as much entitled to protection as the citizen at home." [8] The President, as chief executive and director of our foreign relations, is expected to see that such protection is duly extended, whether on the basis of treaty provisions usually covering such matters or otherwise. If an American sojourning in a foreign land or traveling on the high seas is mistreated and cannot obtain justice, the President, acting through the State Department, may make demands in his behalf, and may go to any length short of a declaration of war to obtain

3. Protection of citizens abroad and of alien residents

[5] Still another form of recognition presents itself when, an insurrection having arisen in a country, the President officially acknowledges the insurgency, or even the belligerency, of the insurrectionists by giving them (so far as the United States is concerned) certain rights which they would not have as mere rebels. President Cleveland thus recognized a state of insurgency in Cuba in 1895.

[6] Moved by a desire to consolidate an Anti-Communist front in the Western Hemisphere, the United States proposed at a Bogotá conference of 1948 that American nations agree to maintain diplomatic relations with any government on this side of the Atlantic, irrespective of the methods by which it had come into power. The only apparent effect, however, was to give the green light to organizers of military coups in Venezuela, Peru, and El Salvador.

[7] The United States did, however, participate in 1954 in a conference at Geneva on Indo-China (now Vietnam, Laos and Cambodia) with representatives of the Chinese Communist regime. Secretary Dulles announced, however, that this did not constitute recognition.

[8] Durand *v.* Hollins, Fed. Case No. 4186 (1860).

redress for him.[9] Similarly, it is the President's duty—up to the limits of national authority—to see that protection is extended to aliens legally domiciled in the United States. He must execute all provisions of the Constitution, the national laws, and treaties bearing on their rights; and while he has no way of compelling state authorities to guarantee equal treatment in matters, like land ownership, outside the scope of national jurisdiction, he may admonish them to be mindful of alien rights and may instruct district attorneys to lend aliens needed legal aid. In time of war abroad, he may be of assistance to both aliens and citizens by issuing a proclamation of neutrality calling attention to rules of international law and to statutes forbidding various unneutral acts. When the United States itself is at war, however, the rights of aliens of enemy nationality resident in the country become merely such as international law recognizes in situations of the kind. The President is not obligated beyond that point.

INTERNATIONAL AGREEMENTS

He [the President] shall have power, by and with the advice and consent of the Senate, to make treaties, provided two thirds of the Senators present concur. . . . ART. II, Sec. 2, cl. 2

The most sensitive aspect of foreign dealings with regard to the respective powers and duties of the President and Congress is the matter of international commitments. Who can and should commit this nation to a course of action by agreement with one or more foreign states?

4. Making international commitments: a. Treaties

One of the main instrumentalities for regulating and stabilizing international relations is treaties. Under the Articles of Confederation, Congress made treaties; and the framers of the Constitution at first thought of giving the power to the Senate. As, however, the concept of the Presidency grew in their minds, the view developed that it would be better to assign treaty-making, along with the general management of the country's foreign relations, to the chief executive, associating with him the Senate as an advising and restraining council. The House of Representatives was deliberately omitted from the plan in the interest of "secrecy and dispatch." Assent to treaties by two-thirds, rather than simple majority, of the Senate was specified, not primarily in deference to any general policy or theory, but mainly to protect important interests of certain sections of the country from being "sold out" by bare Senate majorities.[10]

Scope of the treaty power

So far as they went, these arrangements for treaty-making were simple and obvious enough. But they left open one fundamental question on which

[9] E. M. Borchard, *The Diplomatic Protection of Citizens Abroad* (new ed., New York, 1927).

[10] The South and West feared lest navigation rights on the Mississippi be lightly waived by treaty, and New England was similarly apprehensive about fishing rights. See R. E. McClendon, "Origin of the Two-Thirds Rule in Senate Action on Treaties," *Amer. Hist. Rev.*, XXXVI, 768-782 (July, 1931).

sharp differences of opinion soon arose: how far, under a system of limited powers, was the treaty power to be regarded as extending? Could treaties deal with matters outside of those constitutionally committed to the national government? And, with legislation often required for making treaty provisions effective, could a treaty open a way for Congress to exercise legislative powers not otherwise possessed? Approaching the matter from his strict-construction, states'-rights viewpoint, Thomas Jefferson sought to establish the view (1) that the Constitution's provisions on treaty-making merely set forth a procedure for exercising granted powers and are not themselves a substantive grant; (2) that the President and Senate have no right to employ treaties as means of evading constitutional restrictions generally applicable to the government; and (3) that treaties entailing extraconstitutional legislation should not be negotiated. Throughout most of our history, however, and especially in the last half-century, a different view has prevailed. The Supreme Court has recognized the treaty power as extending to "all proper subjects of negotiation between this government and those of other nations," regardless of the Constitution.[11]

When, in 1918, Congress, in pursuance of a treaty with Great Britain authorizing agreements between the United States and Canada for the protection of migratory birds, enacted a stringent measure on the subject, the Supreme Court fully sustained the law,[12] on the ground (1) that while control of bird-life is, of course, not a power which is expressly conferred upon Congress, it is a proper subject for treaty agreement, and (2) that treaty-making is one of the many powers which the "necessary and proper" clause authorizes Congress to implement by legislation. Significantly, in order to be supreme law of the land, acts of Congress must be "made in pursuance" of the Constitution, but treaties simply, and more broadly, "under the authority of the United States." This does not exempt them from judicial invalidation because of unconstitutional provisions, though none has ever been overthrown in this way. And this suggests virtually the only definite limitation upon the treaty-making power that can be discovered today.

Jefferson's doubts about the validity and wisdom of a treaty power so broadly defined have found staunch modern advocates. In the period since World War II, this issue has reappeared in national politics with an unexpected vigor. Participation by the United States in numerous international organizations has involved us in negotiations looking toward the conclusion of treaties or conventions on a wide variety of subjects. Among the subjects, human rights appears to have awakened the gravest concern that the treaty process might be used to confer power on the national government which has heretofore been regarded as reserved to the states. Led by Senator Bricker, Republican of Ohio, a nation-wide campaign was carried on for several years (1950-1954) in favor of an amendment to the Constitution which would restrict the treaty power to

The Bricker amendment debate

[11] Holmes v. Jennison, 14 Peters 540, 569 (1843).
[12] State of Missouri v. Holland, 252 U. S. 416 (1920). Without treaty support, Congress previously had been unable to get a similar act past the courts.

those subjects on which the national government has express authority. This campaign, largely supported by Republicans, appears to have reached its peak in 1954 with a determined effort by the Bricker group to drive an amendment through the United States Senate. Senator Bricker was able to find 62 other Senatorial sponsors for his proposal when he introduced it after the Republican election victory of 1952. Numerous versions of an amendment which might achieve the stated purpose were fashioned in an effort to compromise disagreements. The Eisenhower administration gave little aid or comfort to the Bricker plan and Democratic Senators, in general, lined up against it. The Senate debated the matter for weeks early in 1954 but when the matter finally came to a vote the language had been so modified that little of the original proposal was left.[13] The final vote was one short of the necessary two-thirds. The Democrats in control of the Senate since 1955 have shown no interest in reviving the matter. The Bricker proposal, it should be added, was aimed also at alleged abuse of the executive agreement, about which more will be said later. One result of the Bricker amendment debate was the declaration by Secretary of State Dulles that the administration had no intention of agreeing to the proposed international covenant on human rights and would, therefore, not submit it to the Senate. The Bricker amendment debate illustrates the strong determination by some groups in the Congress to strengthen the hands of the legislature in the field of foreign affairs. President Eisenhower, on his part, declared that as originally proposed the amendment would shackle the hands of the executive in the conduct of foreign policy.

Presidential initiative in treaty-making

The language of the Constitution seems to associate the Senate with the President throughout the entire process of concluding and ratifying a treaty. Passages in *The Federalist* indicate that this is what the framers had in mind, and President Washington actually began his treaty-making (with certain tribes of Southern Indians in 1789) on that assumption, several times visiting the

[13] The text of the "Bricker" amendment which came to the Senate floor from the Committee was:

Section 1. A provision of a treaty which conflicts with this Constitution shall not be of any force or effect.

Section 2. A treaty shall become effective as internal law in the United States only through legislation which would be valid in absence of treaty.

Section 3. Congress shall have power to regulate all executive and other agreements with any foreign power or international organization. All such agreements shall be subject to the limitations imposed on treaties by this article.

Section 4. The Congress shall have power to enforce the article by appropriate legislation.

Section 5. This article shall be inoperative unless it shall have been ratified as an amendment to the Constitution by the legislatures of three-fourths of the several states within seven years from the date of its submission.

The final vote was taken on the following text of the key articles proposed by Senator George, Democrat of Georgia:

Section 1. A provision of a treaty or other international agreement which conflicts with this Constitution shall not be of any force or effect.

Section 2. An international agreement other than a treaty shall become effective as internal law in the United States only by an act of the Congress.

Senate chamber for the purpose. A year or two of experience demonstrated, however, that it was more practical and expeditious for the President to negotiate the treaty and to seek the Senate's "advice and consent" only afterwards —such consent being simply to a final act of ratification to be performed by the President and making the instrument effective so far as our own government is concerned.[14] To be sure, either branch of Congress, or the two concurrently, may by resolution advise or request that a given treaty, or series of treaties, be negotiated; and the President (or Secretary of State acting for him) may, and usually will, in advance or during the course of a negotiation, consult with individual Senators.[15] Unless the chief executive chooses to set the necessary machinery in motion, no negotiation can be started; he can begin a negotiation regardless of the desire (and even without the knowledge) of either branch of Congress; and rarely indeed is the Senate as a body given any chance to express itself on a proposed treaty until the completed instrument is transmitted to it. Short of flatly withholding assent to ratification, the most that the Senators can then do by way of registering disapproval is to attach amendments making it necessary for the President to renew negotiations with a view to securing the foreign government's acceptance of the proposed changes; or, in the case of a great multilateral agreement on which negotiations could not well be reopened, to assent to ratification but attach reservations designating various features of the agreement as not to be held binding on the United States. In exercising his powers of initiative and direction, the President may work through the regular diplomatic representative accredited to the foreign government concerned; or he may appoint a special plenipotentiary or commission to go abroad for the purpose; again, he may cause the negotiations to be carried on in Washington through the Secretary of State; or, finally, he may undertake, or at least participate in, the negotiations himself, as did President Wilson in connection with the Treaty of Versailles in 1919. When the treaty is completed, he has full freedom to submit it to the Senate, return it to the negotiators for revision, or drop

[14] On the way in which our treaty-making authority "split into two authorities," see E. S. Corwin, in J. B. Whitton [ed.], *The Second Chance; America and the Peace* (Princeton, N. J., 1944), 143-150.

[15] In only about a dozen instances since Washington's day has the opinion of the Senate as a whole been sought. As a matter of expediency, the President and Secretary of State usually keep in close touch with the Senate committee on foreign relations when an important negotiation is in progress, sounding out sentiment on pending proposals and ascertaining how far it is safe or wise to go in this direction or that—a precaution the more necessary because, under the two-thirds rule, a treaty will usually have to enlist the support of members of both political parties if it is to be approved. The President may, indeed, make one or more Senators members of a negotiating commission, and this has several times been done; although the policy has been criticized, both in the Senate and outside, on the ground that it puts the senatorial negotiators in the position of helping formulate proposals which they will be expected to pass upon later as members of a separate branch of the government, and also on the ground that it is incompatible with at least the spirit of the constitutional provision that "no person holding any office under the United States shall be a member of either house during his continuance in office" (Art. I, Sec. 6, cl. 2) although membership in an international conference can be, and is, construed as not properly an "office."

it altogether. He may hold it back because he considers it unsatisfactory, or because he recognizes that submission of it to the Senate would be useless. Indeed, even after the Senate has given its consent, a treaty still may be held up. It remains for the President to ratify it, and, upon being apprised of ratification by the other government (or governments), to promulgate it; and he has the option of refusing to take these last necessary steps, although clearly he will do so only under very unusual circumstances.

The role
of the
Senate

"A treaty entering the Senate," wrote John Hay after six years of experience as Secretary of State, "is like a bull going into the arena; no one can say just how or when the final blow will fall—but one thing is certain—it will never leave the arena alive." [16] This statement is much too strong, as is evidenced by two or three major facts: (1) no treaty was rejected outright by the Senate until 1824; (2) the total number so rejected throughout the history of the country to 1935 is only 14; and (3) while in about 150 other cases to the date mentioned the Senate either failed to act or insisted on amendments or reservations of such character that either our own government or the other party (or parties) chose not to go ahead with the project, it unconditionally approved some 900 treaties, or more than four-fifths of the entire number presented to it.[17] Quite a number of treaties slip through with no opposition at all. None has been rejected since 1935. Those that stir controversy, however, encounter a genuine hurdle in the two-thirds rule. It must be admitted that of the treaties that have come to grief in this way a large proportion have been of first-rate importance, for example, the treaty for the annexation of Texas in 1844, the Olney-Pauncefote, Hay, and Taft-Knox arbitration treaties of 1897, 1904, and 1911-1912, respectively, the Treaty of Versailles in 1920, the St. Lawrence Waterway Treaty of 1934, and the protocol for adherence to the Permanent Court of International Justice (World Court) in 1926 and 1935. Many which finally emerge unscathed do so only after a great parliamentary battle, calling into play every sort of pressure from the White House. During and after World War II, however, with the United States undertaking the most extensive treaty commitments in its history, the Senate has consistently approved without serious difficulty.

Criticism
of treaty
procedure

For 50 years prior to the Bricker amendment campaign the chief criti-

[16] W. R. Thayer, *Life and Letters of John Hay* (Boston, 1920). Under Senate Rule XXXVII, a treaty received from the President is given a first reading, referred to a committee (typically that on foreign relations) reported back with or without amendments, considered in committee of the whole (as pointed out elsewhere, this is now the only use made of committee of the whole in Senate practice), reported from committee of the whole to the Senate with or without amendment, and brought to a final vote in the form of a resolution assenting to ratification. Until 1929, the entire procedure was shrouded in secrecy, but since then it has been not at all unusual for treaties (by Senate decision) to be discussed with the galleries open to the press and public. In any case, a treaty is considered only in *executive* session, whether open or closed.

[17] D. F. Fleming, "The Role of the Senate in Treaty-Making," *Amer. Polit. Sci. Rev.*, XXVIII, 583 (Aug., 1934). Congressional Quarterly Service, *Weekly Report*, Aug. 2, 1963, pp. 1350-1351.

cisms of the treaty-making procedures were aimed at easing the path for international agreements by eliminating the two-thirds rule or at strengthening the role of the House of Representatives by giving it a share in the ratification. The refusal of the Senate to support American adherence to the League of Nations after World War I stimulated much of the dissatisfaction with the present procedure. The ease with which the President obtained approval for our participation in the United Nations and for the tradition-shattering military alliances of the "stop Russia" epoch have largely obviated these criticisms. The attack, nowadays, as we have noted, has been on the latitude of the treaty power and on the commanding position of the President in foreign affairs.

Once duly ratified by the governments concerned and proclaimed by the President, a treaty becomes, from the international point of view, a contract between the United States and the nation (or nations) constituting the other party, and from the domestic point of view, an extension of the law of the land, supreme and enforceable like any other portion of the law. Both national and state courts must give it full effect. Of course not all treaties are, or are intended to be, permanent. Some expressly provide for their own expiration; some are terminated by war; some are replaced by new agreements; some are abrogated by being "denounced" by one or more of the parties. When it is desired in this country to dispense with a treaty, or some portion thereof, our government is likely to seek an agreement to that end with any nation or nations concerned. In default of such agreement, however, the President may, on his own authority, simply proclaim the treaty at an end; or he may take such action with the support of a joint resolution of Congress; or Congress itself may make any of the treaty's provisions of no legal effect by enacting legislation inconsistent with them. Although treaties are "law of the land," the Supreme Court has said that they are no more truly such than are acts passed by Congress. Invariably the Court has been reluctant to construe a statute as in violation of a treaty; but when there is manifest conflict, the later in date prevails.[18] Neither a Court decision nor a statute can, however, abrogate a treaty as an international contract. Although thus rendered unenforceable at home, it preserves its international status until revoked by executive action. In the meantime the foreign power concerned may construe a crippling judicial decision or statute as a breach of contract entitling it to reparation through an international proceeding.

Execution and termination of treaties

Treaties can be ratified and become operative only with the advice and consent of the Senate. But not every agreement entered into with a foreign government takes the form of a treaty. A great many, in this century especially, are "executive agreements," for which—notwithstanding that there is no mention of them in the Constitution, and that as a rule they are to all intents and purposes treaties—consent of a two-thirds Senatorial majority is neither sought

b. Executive agreements

[18] Chinese Exclusion Cases, 130 U. S. 581 (1889).

nor obtained.[19] In some instances, for example, postal conventions and trade agreements (the lend-lease agreements of the World War II period also), such agreements rest upon authority conferred in advance by blanket act of Congress. Others, however, are concluded by the President (directly or through agents) without such authorization—sometimes in pursuance of a treaty, sometimes as commander-in-chief of the armed forces, and occasionally simply as chief executive and supreme representative of the country in its dealings with foreign states. If they are submitted on Capitol Hill at all (as some are), it is not to the Senate alone, as in the case of a treaty, but to the two houses for approval by majority vote in each. Furthermore, such agreements may be upheld by the courts as "supreme law of the land," [20] and the limits to which the President may carry them are nowhere defined.[21] Many agreements deal with minor matters which, by their nature, do not call for a treaty—for example, pecuniary claims of American citizens against foreign governments. Others relate to affairs of considerable importance.[22] Indeed, an executive agreement

[19] In his *International Executive Agreements* (New York, 1941) W. McClure computes that the total of executive agreements entered into by our government between 1789 and February, 1941, was "well over 1250—a third more than the number of treaties." From 1929, the texts of such agreements were published in the State Department's *Executive Agreement Series* until 1946, when this Series was merged with a similar *Treaty Series* in the present *Treaties and Other International Acts Series*. Not all agreements, however, immediately become matters of public record. Promises may be made and understandings reached, fully tantamount to agreements, without any knowledge (at least until long afterwards) on the part of either Congress or the public. A classic example is President Theodore Roosevelt's agreement with Japan on Far Eastern policy at the close of the Russo-Japanese war, first brought to light 20 years afterwards when the Roosevelt papers in the Library of Congress were explored. See T. Dennett, *Roosevelt and the Russo-Japanese War* (Garden City, N. Y., 1925), 112-114. More recent examples would include many agreements entered into by President Franklin D. Roosevelt both early and late during the course of World War II especially those at Yalta and Teheran and unknown, outside of perhaps a small select circle, until later years.

[20] As in United States *v.* Belmont, 301 U. S. 324 (1937), and United States *v.* Pink, 315 U. S. 203 (1946). These cases grew out of the agreement with Litvinoff in 1933 by which recognition was extended to Soviet Russia. They were cited constantly by the proponents of the Bricker effort to limit Presidential power to enter executive agreements which might supersede domestic law.

[21] As a result, when the chief executive wants a settlement of some situation with a foreign power, he commonly has a three-way choice: to negotiate a treaty and then submit it to the Senate, to secure advance consent of Congress to an executive agreement, or to procure an executive agreement independently, afterwards submitting it to Congress if its nature so requires. His decision upon which course to follow, at least when the matter at stake is important, will be influenced by the political situation at the time and perhaps by other considerations. But, in general, all three methods are constitutional and valid.

[22] Examples include the Hay Open-Door notes of 1899; the Boxer protocol with China in 1901; the "Gentleman's Agreement" of 1907 with Japan terminating the immigration of Japanese laborers; the Root-Takahira notes of 1908 on the Open Door in China; the agreement with Panama in 1914 for enforcing the neutrality of the Panama Canal; the somewhat unfortunate Lansing-Ishii agreement with Japan in 1917; the armistice of 1918 with Germany; the agreement entered into by President Franklin D. Roosevelt with the British government in 1940 under which the United States turned over to Britain 50 overage destroyers in return for 99-year leases of sites in British possessions on

may become frankly a means of evading—temporarily at any rate—the necessity of going to the Senate with a treaty. In 1905, President Theodore Roosevelt worked out a treaty with Santo Domingo specifying that the United States should guarantee the security of that republic and take over the collection of its customs duties with a view to settling foreign claims and warding off European intervention. The Senate refused to consent to the treaty; whereupon the President entered into a *modus vivendi* with the Dominican government on the desired lines; and for two years the protectorate was maintained on this basis. In 1907, a treaty making the arrangement regular was at last assented to and ratified. In 1911, President Taft entered into a similar agreement with Nicaragua, not replaced by a treaty until 1916.

So far, indeed, was the power of executive agreement formerly carried *Congress* that in 1941 a responsible State Department official could seriously argue not *and* only that the two-thirds rule in the Senate was "a peril to the national wel- *executive* fare," but that anything that can be done by treaty can also be done (and the *agree-* implication was *should* be) by executive agreement.[23] The war years then *ments* dawning, however, saw an uprising on the matter in a quarter where it was most to be expected—the Senate. Executive agreements of 1940 under which the United States secured from Great Britain long-term leases of sites in the Atlantic for naval development, and from Denmark the right to take various precautionary measures in Greenland and Iceland, were so obviously germane to the President's function as commander-in-chief that they stirred little protest. When, however, in pursuance of power conferred in the Lend-Lease Act of 1941, the State Department, under Presidential direction, began concluding agreements with Great Britain, the U.S.S.R., China, and other nations involving a network of long-term commitments running into billions of dollars, dissatisfaction manifested itself. And when, in 1943, it was learned that a United Nations Relief and Rehabilitation Convention was to be treated as an executive agreement and not referred to the Senate, notwithstanding that it entailed "practically illimitable obligations for the United States practically in perpetuity," the State Department was vigorously challenged. Controversy ensued in which the Secretary of State was threatened with an official investigaton, and in the end a compromise was forced under which, while UNRRA itself was entered into as a matter of executive-legislative action only, and

---

this side of the Atlantic for the development of American naval bases; the agreements with Denmark's government-in-exile in April and July, 1941, under which the United States acquired the right, in the one case, to establish air bases and other military and naval facilities in Greenland and, in the other, to undertake a naval occupation of Iceland, both aimed at curbing or forestalling German armed operations in the North Atlantic; numerous agreements with allied nations under the Lend-Lease Act of 1941 and the United Nations Relief and Rehabilitation Agreement of 1943-1944; and the loan of $3.75 billion to Great Britain in 1945. The Rush-Bagot convention of 1817 with Great Britain for the limitation of naval forces on the Great Lakes, and from which developed the policy of the unfortified border between the United States and Canada, was originally an executive agreement, although in the following year it was given a treaty basis.

[23] W. McClure, *op. cit.*

without a treaty, the executive branch promised in future to be more circumspect about observing "constitutional processes." In anticipation, too, of efforts already started to build up a world organization for the preservation of peace, both branches of Congress, in the year mentioned, passed resolutions asserting that American participation must be by such "constitutional processes," which, in Senate phraseology, were expressly defined as meaning Senate approval by regular two-thirds majority. In 1945, the Charter of the United Nations was duly submitted to and approved by that body—as were also the Marshall Plan for aid to Europe in 1947, the North Atlantic Pact in 1949, the agreements with West Germany re-establishing its independence in 1955, and the "Pacific Area" alliances. The understandings entered into by President Roosevelt with Stalin and Churchill at Teheran and Yalta have frequently been attacked on the grounds that the Senate was never asked to consent to them.

The rapid extension of the executive agreement procedure during the last few decades has been appreciably slowed down by opposition in the Senate. Pointed up again in the debate over the Bricker amendment, Congressional hostility to the procedure has made the Truman, Eisenhower, Kennedy and Johnson administrations much more cautious. No important financial commitment or agreement affecting foreign policy directly in the past several years has been entered into by the executive alone without Congressional or, at least, Senatorial approval.[24] In general, these agreements are now used: (1) to implement such legislation as the reciprocal trade agreements and foreign-aid statutes; (2) to provide U. S. membership in certain technical types of international organizations—these are usually submitted for approval to both houses of Congress; and, (3) to achieve military arrangements such as armistices, treatment of American troops and, most recently, the installation of a "hot" teletype line between the White House and the Kremlin.

c. Joint resolutions

A third recognized method of achieving international settlements takes the form of a joint resolution passed by simple majorities in the two branches of Congress and approved by the President. When initiated by the chief executive to implement some international agreement which he favors, and duly enacted by Congress, the procedure of joint resolution is hardly distinguishable from that followed when an executive agreement is negotiated and submitted. In the case of a joint resolution, however, Congress itself may take the initiative—though in any event action at the White House, as in the case of a bill, is a necessary final step. More than once in our history, a joint resolution, requiring mere Congressional majorities, has been resorted to when the

---

[24] The fullest treatment of the general subject, although not covering recent developments, is W. McClure, *International Executive Agreements*, previously cited. Cf. K. Colegrove, *The American Senate and World Peace*, Chap. v; H. M. Caturdal, "Executive Agreements; A Supplement to the Treaty-Making Procedure," *Geo. Washington Law Rev.*, X, 653-669 (Apr., 1942); Q. Wright, "The United States and International Agreements," *Amer. Jour. of Internat. Law*, XXXVIII, 341-355 (July, 1944); and E. M. Borchard, "Treaties and Executive Agreements," *Amer. Polit. Sci. Rev.*, XL, 729-739 (Aug,. 1946).

treaty-making process, calling for two-thirds in the Senate, broke down. Under such circumstances, Texas was annexed in 1845 and Hawaii in 1898; probably the Philippines would have been annexed in 1898 in the same way if the Senate had not at the last, and by a narrow vòte, decided not to reject the annexation clause of the Treaty of Paris. It was by joint resolution, too, that war with the Central Powers was terminated in 1921, after the Treaty of Versailles had failed of ratification, and that in 1934 President Roosevelt was authorized to accede to Part III of the Versailles Treaty establishing the International Labor Office. From time to time, the device has been proposed, and even employed, in still more recent years; and as it grows in favor, the trend toward increased control of Congress over foreign relations at the expense of the Senate acting singly receives fresh impetus.

The extensive costs of and the large commitments undertaken in connection with our modern foreign policy have raised the problem of the proper roles of Congress and the President in its most acute form. Senatorial balking at the executive agreement system, the Bricker amendment, the demands of the House for a more important voice in foreign affairs, all are symptoms of the modern struggle over who is going to shape foreign policy. The President, meanwhile, has continued to assert his pre-eminence in this field and has given little, in any formal sense, away to his Congressional critics. The very fact, however, that successful defense of the national interest abroad seems to demand huge expenditures has given Congress a new strength in the procedure that it did not possess to the same degree in earlier epochs.

FORMULATING AND CONTROLLING FOREIGN POLICY

The foreign policy of a nation has been defined as "the courses of action undertaken by authority of the United States in pursuit of national objectives beyond the span of jurisdiction of the United States." [25] Every action taken by our government in dealing with other governments presumably reflects a policy. The sum of these actions at any given time is our foreign policy. This definition distinguishes the policy from the *objectives* sought by the government and from the *principles* which may underlie the objectives and policies. Disturbed by the shifts and turns that have characterized the dealings of the United States with other nations over the years, some people have charged that the country really follows no consistent principles, but merely zigzags from position to position as the rough winds of international politics toss the ship of state about. Undoubtedly it is true that our physical isolation in times past, our traditional aloofness from European affairs, and our preference for avoiding long-term commitments seemed for generations to manifest a rather negative attitude on many matters of concern to other nations. Undoubtedly it is true, too, that officers and agencies engaged in managing our dealings with foreign governments have been prone to feel their way through situa-

Has the United States a foreign policy?

[25] C. B. Marshall, *Department of State Bulletin,* Vol. 26 (1952), 915.

tions as they arose, to make choices and decisions as they went, and to leave behind them records of performance not always remarkable for continuity and consistency. Even aloofness, however, and preference for meeting situations as they arise, constitute policies; and actually we have had not only various broad overall objectives of our foreign policies in different periods in our national history, but plenty of generally recognized and often cogently asserted aims toward particular countries and situations.

Compli-
cating
factors

The entire matter of foreign policy is, indeed, one of the most perplexing that students of our government—to say nothing of our public officials—encounter. First of all, there is the extensive array of other nations, large and small, near and far, with which, singly and collectively, relations must be sustained. Then there are the bewilderingly numerous and complex factors— geographical, economic, technological, military, psychological, and ideological —that have to be taken into account. Further, there is the circumstance that, while certain primary axioms or principles may and do govern, there is, and can be, no single, all-embracing, global policy, but instead must be actions and objectives of many sorts, on many different subjects—threads, perhaps, in a skein, but of different color and texture. Still further is the complicating fact that foreign and domestic affairs are not two separate and independent national concerns, but on the contrary are always intermingled. "External affairs" may sound like something remote. Usually a little examination will reveal them to be closely connected with interests and objectives that we have at home, and attitudes and policies concerning them to be dictated, or at least colored, by such interest and objectives. The world scene, too, is constantly changing, at times very rapidly; far from remaining static, foreign policies must change with it; and this adds to the complexities which the student of the subject must be prepared to meet. Finally, from the time when the Federalists favored the quasi-war with France in 1798-1801 and the Jeffersonian Republicans opposed it, political parties more often than not have disagreed on the aims of foreign policy. The rather remarkable record for interparty cooperation in this field achieved at Washington since 1945 has been exceptional rather than typical.[26]

Who
makes
foreign
policy?

Under our American system, the determination of the objects of our foreign policy is not the function of any single branch or department of government, or even exclusively of government at all, since public opinion (with the press, the radio and television, churches and other organizations, playing significant parts) has much to do with it. Within the government itself, the Department of State naturally plays a major role. It provides much of the information and advice on which all policy-making in this field rests. The Department of Defense has contributed actively, occasionally even fashioning policy in particular situations independently. The Treasury, Commerce, Agri-

[26] B. Bolles, "Bipartisanship in American Foreign Policy," *Foreign Policy Reports,* XXIV, No. 16 (Jan. 1, 1949), and H. B. Westerfield, *Foreign Policy and Party Politics: Pearl Harbor to Korea* (New Haven, 1955).

culture, and Interior Departments—not to mention independent establishments like the United States Tariff Commission, the Maritime Board, the Export-Import Bank, and the Atomic Energy Commission—also make contributions. Needless to say, Congress, on its part, takes a hand—enacting legislation, voting appropriations, declaring war—not to mention, of course, the role of the Senate in connection with foreign service appointments and treaty-making. Indeed, it would be difficult to mention many agencies in Washington that do not, at some time or other, in one way or another, directly or indirectly, have at least some modest share in providing the information, supplying the incentives, or formulating the plans lying back of one phase or another of the foreign policies developed.

The supreme architect of foreign policy is, however, the President. Even when he is not the actual author of a given policy, he commonly becomes such to all intents and purposes by declaring it to the world and taking the necessary steps to carry it into effect. When Washington proclaimed American neutrality in 1793, and in his Farewell Address warned his countrymen against political entanglements with Europe, he started the country on a course of "isolation" from which for several decades only the most extraordinary emergencies ever availed to swerve it. Monroe, in 1823, voiced in a message to Congress certain principles concerning foreign political activities in the Western Hemisphere which, under the name of the Monroe Doctrine, developed into one of the most enduring and important of all our foreign policies. When, in 1844, President Tyler's Secretary of State, Daniel Webster, instructed Caleb Cushing as our first emissary to China to see to it that the United States received assurance of equal economic opportunity in that country, he inaugurated a line of policy which, under the more familiar name of Open Door, became, and long remained, the cornerstone of all American dealings with the Far East. Theodore Roosevelt, Taft, and Wilson brought a number of Caribbean republics under United States supervision and, for better or worse, left us a policy of maintaining Latin American financial protectorates. This only two decades later gave way to the Good Neighbor policy instituted by President Hoover and amplified by his successors. Wilson in 1915 and Hoover in 1932, through their respective Secretaries of State, Bryan and Stimson, made it American policy to withhold recognition from international agreements and actions in the Far East interfering with the territorial or administrative integrity of China or with equal opportunity for trade and other enterprise in that country. During the earlier stages of World War II, President Franklin D. Roosevelt led in formulating and carrying out the national policy under which the United States first severely strained and later frankly abandoned its neutral position in order to give aid to Great Britain and other fighting nations which, in the chief executive's opinion, must at all costs be kept from going down. Similarly, he bore full responsibility for the government's unyielding opposition to Japan's proposed "New Order" in Eastern Asia, bringing the two countries to the brink of war by 1941 and precipitating them into actual combat before the year

The role of the President

ended. In the Atlantic Charter of 1941, he joined with Prime Minister Churchill in proclaiming broad postwar international policies to which the United States was solemnly committed on his sole responsibility. Usually without consultation with Congress, policies were further determined and declared throughout the war, frequently as a sequel of conferences with spokesmen of allied states, as at Teheran, Cairo, and Yalta; and step by step, with the President leading, the way was prepared for emergence of the present United Nations. Early in 1947, President Truman enunciated the Truman Doctrine calling for aid to nations threatened by Soviet aggression. In 1948, he committed the United States to military assistance for Western European states; and in his 1949 inaugural he announced the Point Four program for technical help for underdeveloped areas. President Truman also, on his own responsibility, ordered American troops to aid the United Nations in resisting aggression in Korea in 1950. The policy of sharing atomic materials with other nations for peaceful purposes was announced by President Eisenhower on behalf of this nation in 1954. President Kennedy assumed major responsibility for the naval blockade of Cuba in 1962 and the war preparations associated with it. The decision to "escalate" American military efforts in behalf of South Vietnam in 1964-1965 and to intervene militarily in the "revolution" in the Dominican Republic in 1965 was made by President Johnson.

When a foreign complication arises, or a new international problem presents itself, it is the President (speaking directly or through his Secretary of State) who has the first opportunity to say what the attitude of the nation shall be. By the stand that he takes he can so put the country on record that it will be next to impossible for Congress, or even a later President, to change the course that he has set. As we shall see, he may even lead the nation into war; for although he cannot declare war, he can adopt an attitude or create a situation, for example, by refusing to yield in a controversy with a foreign government, that may make war unavoidable.

Congressional limitations and controls

Nevertheless, the President does not play a lone hand, or always have his own way. Rarely can the policies which he formulates or sponsors achieve their purposes unless accepted and perhaps financially implemented by Congress; and they may be completely thwarted by lack of Congressional support. A zealous Congress forced upon a reluctant Chief Executive the War of 1812, and likewise the intervention in Cuba in 1898 which led to the war with Spain, the annexation of the Philippines, and a long train of other momentous consequences. An unconvinced Senate balked President John Quincy Adams in his Pan-American policy, Pierce in his Cuban policy, Grant in his Dominican policy, Cleveland in his Hawaiian policy, and Wilson in his endeavor to put the United States into the League of Nations. One of the vigorous and important standing committees in each of the two branches is the Committee on Foreign Relations,[27] in which, in connection with proposed legislation (and, in the Senate committee, with foreign service appointments and treaties) prob-

[27] "Foreign affairs" in the case of the House of Representatives.

lems of foreign policy receive extended discussion, sometimes supplemented by lively public hearings. Other standing committees—too—Appropriations, Banking and Currency, Agriculture—touch foreign policy at various points; and special committees may be set up to investigate phases or consequences of Presidential policy-making. From any of these directions may come criticisms or recommendations eventuating in decisions making it necessary for lines of policy to be abandoned or sharply altered. Finally, too, whatever funds may be required for carrying Presidential policies into operation are obtainable only through appropriations voted by Congress. For example, in 1947 President Truman would have been unable even to start doing anything very tangible about fending off the spread of Russian domination in Europe and the Near East unless Congress had been willing to appropriate the $400 million requested for aid to Greece and Turkey as the first step in the program —followed by the vastly larger authorizations required under the Marshall plan. The Senate is particularly conscious of its special role in the conduct and planning of American foreign policy and its leaders have played an increasingly important part in the great decisions of this generation.[28]

Back of both President and Congress stand the people. Although the backward state of popular information on and interest in the affairs of distant nations reflects an older, perhaps happier, era, in the last analysis no long-term program of foreign policy can be carried out that lacks the support of the voters. "No matter," ex-Secretary of State Hull once remarked, "how brilliant and desirable any course may seem, it is wholly impracticable and impossible unless it is a course which finds basic acceptance . . . by the people of this country." Here, as in other areas of planning and action, the Chief Executive and leaders in Congress must ascertain, study, and assess public opinion; failing to do so, they may easily be betrayed into embarking upon a course of action leading straight to humiliating frustration at the hands of the people or their elected representatives. Not infrequently, cross-currents of opinion make it difficult to discern what the nation really thinks and wants with respect to a given situation or problem; considerations of self-interest and altruism often are bewilderingly intermingled, and economic, ethnic, or other interest groups, such as business, labor, and religious bodies, may pull in diametrically opposite directions. There does appear, however, to be a growing awareness in our people of the demands of modern foreign policy and an increasing willingness to make the sacrifices necessary to support huge military and foreign aid expenditures. There is also some diminution in the influence of ethnic groups in policy decisions—an influence which plagued the professional policy-makers for years. Perhaps, there is also an abatement of some of the sharp regional differences in foreign policy objectives. The portion of the public prepared to

The role of public opinion

---

[28] For a more thorough discussion of this subject see R. Dahl, *Congress and Foreign Policy* (New York, 1950); G. B. Galloway, *The Legislative Process in Congress* (New York, 1953), Chap. VII; H. N. Carroll, *The House of Representatives and Foreign Affairs* (Pittsburgh, Pa., 1958); and H. H. Humphrey, "The Senate in Foreign Policy," *Foreign Affairs*, XLVIII, No. 4 (July, 1959).

take an active, continuing, and responsible interest in foreign policy, although still quite small, appears to be growing.[29]

FOREIGN POLICIES: PAST AND PRESENT

The signal features of American policy today are our involvement in different forms of international organization aimed at collective security, and our efforts to curb Communist expansion. An appreciation of just what an extraordinary turn of affairs this is may be gained by a brief review of five stages through which our basic world attitude has passed—stages commonly characterized as (1) continentalism, (2) hemispheric security, (3) imperial expansion, (4) isolationism, (5) collective security (through interhemispheric organization) combined with regional alliances aimed at battling the spread of communism.

1. Conti-
nentalism
The American nation got its start with the aid of an alliance with France, narrowly escaped a shooting war with that country during John Adams' administration, and was drawn into the first of a series of international armed conflicts as early as 1812. Nevertheless, for a generation or more its basic policy was one of political self-containment within its Western continental homeland—a policy persuasively enunciated by Washington in his Neutrality Proclamation of 1793, and particularly in the Farewell Address of 1796 in which he reminded his countrymen that Europe had "a set of primary interests" of little or no concern to America, inquired why Americans should quit their own and "stand on foreign ground," and asserted the "true policy" of the rising young nation to be "to steer clear of permanent alliances with any portion of the foreign world." There was no disposition to close our doors against foreign intercourse. On the contrary, the nation stood ready to accept its obligations under international law, to extend traditional international courtesies, to send and receive diplomats and make treaties, and even to enter into special temporary international understandings and engagements when clearly to its interest to do so; above all, it wanted the benefits of overseas commerce. But for a few decades our government was animated chiefly by the ideal of a nation busy with its own development at home and free from relationships and commitments abroad that might get it into trouble or limit its freedom of action.

2. Hemi-
spheric
security
In time, however, the course of world events—particularly in the other Americas—inspired some new conceptions of our national interest and

[29] G. A. Almond, *The American People and Foreign Policy* (New York, 1960), Introduction to Second Edition. See also L. H. Chamberlain and R. C. Snyder, *American Foreign Policy* (New York, 1947), Chaps. XII-XIII; V. M. Dean, "U. S. Foreign Policy and the Voter," *Foreign Policy Reports*, XX, No. 13 (Sept. 15, 1944); K. Colegrove, "The Role of Congress and Public Opinion in Formulating Foreign Policy," *Amer. Polit. Sci. Rev.*, XXXVIII, 956-969 (Oct., 1944); W. Johnson, *The Battle Against Isolation* (Chicago, 1944); and M. Beloff, *Foreign Policy and the Democratic Process* (Baltimore, 1955).

prompted a significant reorientation of our foreign policy. Between 1815 and 1830, a wave of revolution swept over Latin America, leaving in its wake a dozen or more republics newly risen on the wreckage of the old Spanish and Portuguese empires. When some prospect arose of efforts by reactionary European powers to help the dispossessed nations recover their lost territories and trade monopolies, such possibility was viewed by our government as a threat, not only to our own commercial and other interests, but to the rightful freedoms and immunities of an entire hemisphere. The upshot was the famous message of President Monroe in 1823 serving notice that, while we had no intention of interfering with any existing European colony or dependency on this side of the Atlantic, or of taking any part in Europe's wars, any move for recovery or control of newly liberated states or for extension of the "European system" to the Western hemisphere (as by new colonization) would be looked upon by us as "a manifestation of an unfriendly disposition toward the United States." Initiated under these circumstances and cordially supported by Great Britain as being in her interest also, the Monroe Doctrine became, and long remained, one of our primary foreign policies. Sentimental regard for the newborn neighboring republics had some influence. The objective primarily in mind, however, was security for the United States, now visualized as predicated upon security for the entire hemisphere of which the United States was a part. And as time went on, many new interpretations and applications were aimed at protecting the hemisphere against actions from abroad which might have the effect of strengthening external controls within its wide reaches.

For two generations, the point of view of our policy-makers remained essentially hemispheric. Of course we developed policies relating to more distant parts of the world—for example, that of equal opportunity in China, voiced in our very first treaty with that country in 1844. But in general we were content with our role as the leading power on our side of the Atlantic, and beyond that—being still occupied mainly with developing our own territories and resources—aspired merely to function unostentatiously as a respected member of the family of nations. Toward the close of the nineteenth century, however, a new spirit manifested itself. The entire country had been occupied and the beckoning frontier was gone. Agriculture was producing more than our own people could consume. Industry had developed and needed wider markets. The nation, it was felt, had "grown up," "come of age," and was ready for new ventures. Nor was it difficult for those impressed with these things to figure out the direction which such new ventures should take. For a generation, ambitious European powers had been carving out colonies and protectorates in Africa, Asia, and the islands of the seas, and making them outposts of trade and empire. The United States, it was now contended, should get into the game before it was too late—not so much with a view to annexing foreign territory (of which little was still available) as rather to acquiring strategic locations for naval bases and good vantage points for trade, developing sea power, and raising the nation's sights generally as a participant in world

3. Imperial expansion and "world power"

affairs. Moral misgivings could be partially overcome by arguing that it was our bounden duty to reach out into the world and help civilize and Christianize backward peoples. Those who still doubted could be assured that, in any event, for a nation that had grown from small beginnings by expansion, still more expansion was only "manifest destiny."

The outcome was a succession of developments which require little elaboration. (1) The Monroe Doctrine was stretched (principally by Secretary Olney during the Venezuelan crisis of 1895) so as to ban any restrictions by a European power upon the self-government of an American nation with a view to enforcing debt or other obligations. A corollary was laid down by President Theodore Roosevelt in 1904 that since the United States would not permit a European power to intervene in an American country to protect the interests of its own nationals, the United States must itself see that such interests were safeguarded, and by any means found necessary. (2) With this as a starting point, our government embarked upon a systematic policy of intervention in restless Latin American countries (mainly in the Caribbean, and including Cuba)—a policy not unnaturally evoking sharp criticism of the Monroe Doctrine among our southern neighbors as truly enough protecting the hemisphere against aggressions from Europe, but leaving the way wide open for acquisitive and repressive actions by the United States. (3) The policy of equal opportunity, or Open Door, in China was restated and urged upon the trading nations in 1899. Our growing hand in Far Eastern affairs was further shown by an active role shortly afterwards in helping to liquidate the results of China's Boxer Rebellion and by Theodore Roosevelt's part in bringing the Russo-Japanese War to a close in the Treaty of Portsmouth. More startling (4), the United States now for the first time became the possessor of an overseas colonial empire. Starting in 1889 with a protectorate in Samoa (shared with Great Britain and Germany), we acquired Hawaii in 1898 and, as a result of the war with Spain, the tropical islands of Puerto Rico, Guam, and the Philippines, with also a protectorate over Cuba; control over the Panama Canal Zone followed, in 1904. Strongly tinged with imperialism, the foreign policy of the period brought the country for the first time into the position of a recognized world power.

4. Isola-
tionism   In time, however, the confidence and buoyancy with which the nation embraced its new global responsibilities declined, and a different mood developed. The overseas possessions proved less valuable than had been expected, and not only so, but a source of a good many embarrassments and troubles. The anticipated upsurge of foreign trade (especially in the Far East) did not materialize. Our farmers and laborers complained of the new competition from Philippine commodities and immigrant workers. Things went badly in Cuba. Altogether the experience, deplored by many people from the beginning, was disillusioning. In an atmosphere of growing doubt but nevertheless of continued confidence in the desirability of our position as a great world power, we entered World War I. We held out against involvement as long as we could,

and from the outset made it clear that we neither expected nor wanted any new territory or other material gain as a result of it. As sponsor of the plan for the League of Nations, President Wilson sought to commit us at its close to permanent cooperation with other nations in the earliest system of world-wide collective security ever suggested by high authority in this country. Disillusionment and doubt spread throughout the nation and Wilson's leadership was repudiated. Although there probably was as much public sentiment for our playing a part with the other powers in this new venture as against it, we never did more than cautiously cooperate with the League on a few occasions and share in the work of certain of its investigative and regulative agencies. Although the term has sometimes been construed too literally, our official policy for the better part of two decades thereafter is fairly to be described as one of isolation. The high point of this epoch came in the mid-thirties during the Presidency of Franklin Roosevelt. Congress, in 1934, passed and the White House approved a Debt Default (Johnson) Act forbidding loans to foreign nations in arrears on their debts (chiefly war debts to the United States), and in 1935, a Neutrality Act, subsequently renewed and amended, prohibiting the sale of munitions to belligerents, banning the export of such to any country except by license, and authorizing the President, during any future war, to warn American citizens that travel on belligerent ships would be at their own risk. In 1934, the Philippines were given qualified independence, to become absolute in 1946. A treaty with Cuba somewhat later terminated our treaty right to intervene in that island to preserve order and uphold independence. Finally, we went the whole distance on this path by repudiating "dollar diplomacy" and joining in a Pan-American convention denying to every participating state any right to intervene in either the internal or external affairs of any other state. All of these actions may have been motivated primarily by other considerations, but they evidenced a disposition to curtail political commitments and activities beyond our borders and to keep out of every future European conflict.

Once more, however, the current of foreign policy shifted its course— this time very sharply. During our period of aloofness, the democratic world moved steadily toward disaster. Dictatorships mounted to power in Europe and planned subjugation of their neighbors; democracies faltered and fell; Japanese war lords mapped out a new order calculated to make all Eastern Asia tributary to Tokyo. World War II began in 1939, with France quickly overwhelmed, Great Britain thrown into jeopardy, and totalitarianism threatening the earth; soon the greatest armed conflagration in history was raging in three continents. For the United States, this tragic course of events was a source of rapidly deepening apprehension. Our interests and policies in Europe and Asia were flouted; the spectacle of one free people after another going down was sickening; we too might be within the plans of the conquerors, and intervening oceans which had failed to save us from involvement in 1917-1918 assuredly could not be depended upon now. Eventually, in 1941, we were borne directly into the maelstrom. The attack upon us by Japan was surely the consequence

5. Collective security

of one of our policies—our unswerving insistence that the Japanese stop their aggressions in China. If this had not served, the war probably would have come to us anyway as a result of another policy, namely, our frankly unneutral course in repealing our embargo on the export of munitions in order that we might sell to the nations at war with the Axis, followed early in 1941 by the Lend-Lease Act in which we virtually underwrote the war effort of all such nations. Despite assurances in the campaign of 1940 that the country would be kept out of war, by these policies President Roosevelt involved the nation more and more deeply in the great struggle abroad.

Accept-
ance of
inter-
national
organi-
zation

The President then led the country in the direction of another foreign policy, namely, that of abandoning the isolationism which so palpably had broken down and substituting the principle of world-wide, internationally organized collective security for which Woodrow Wilson had vainly fought.[30] Although, at Roosevelt's insistence, the Atlantic Charter of 1941 made no mention of any international *organization,* some system of collective security was clearly envisaged. In the Washington Agreement of January, 1942, instituting the United Nations in its original purely military form, an organization was more than hinted at; and in the Moscow Declaration and other American-British-Russian-Chinese pronouncements of 1943, it became a prime objective. Meanwhile, with determined isolationists holding back, or at all events skeptical, the idea captured support in Congress and the country. In 1943, Congressional sponsorship was added to Presidential when (1) the House of Representatives overwhelmingly passed the Fulbright Resolution declaring for American participation in "appropriate international machinery with power adequate to establish and to maintain a just and lasting peace among the nations of the world"; and (2) the Senate, on its part, almost unanimously adopted the Connally Resolution, carefully worded to preserve the right of that body to pass upon any agreement committing us to such an arrangement, but also endorsing American membership in an association of free nations with power "to prevent aggression and preserve the peace of the world." In these earlier stages, no blueprints for a future international organization were furnished by either President or Congress; those came later, as plans for the present United Nations developed. Long before the war was over, the country was thus as solemnly committed to a share in such an organization as President and Congress could contrive; and the commitment was backed by a great body of anxious public opinion. There were people who objected in principle, and others who doubted whether anything useful would come of it all. But in any case the nation had moved out of one period of foreign policy into another. The rationale of the new policy might be described as follows: (1) technological changes have brought all parts of the world extremely close

---

[30] After having earlier advocated American membership in the League of Nations, President Roosevelt changed his attitude by 1932; and, aside from sending up an ineffectual "trial balloon" in a memorable speech at Chicago in 1937 calling upon peace-loving nations to join in "quarantining" aggressor nations, he thereafter kept clear of any commitment on international organization until 1942.

together, whether they like it or not; (2) aggressions and war occurring anywhere are of vital concern to peoples everywhere; (3) the United States no
longer can enjoy security standing alone; and (4) therefore our only hope lies
in associating ourselves with all nations of good intent in an organization prepared to uphold peace and order by collective action. Moreover, when we
actively led in instituting the present United Nations (UN) in 1945, followed
by two regional organizations within its framework—based in one case on the
Inter-American Defense Pact of 1947 and in the other on the North Atlantic
Pact of 1949—it was demonstrated that we had indeed shifted our grounds,
in action as well as in words.

*6. Defen-
sive
military
alliances*

The United Nations system was made dependent for its effective functioning on reasonable harmony among the five great powers—Britain, France,
China, Russia, and the United States. When the harmony evaporated before
Russian intransigence soon after victory, and the capture of the Chinese government by the Communists, disillusionment once again spread widely among
the American people. In any event, the United States has found it necessary to
supplement its attachment to the UN by regional military alliances with friendly
powers to halt communist expansion. This era of "Cold War" between the
United States and its allies and Russia and China and their satellites has produced another modification in our policy. Officially, however, our dedication
to the UN is as firm as ever.

Contemporary American foreign policy is thus largely built around two
objectives: (1) preservation of a system of international collective security
through the UN, and (2) resistance to the spread of communism. Both of
these require more elaborate analysis.

PARTICIPATION IN INTERNATIONAL ORGANIZATION

*Miscella-
neous
multi-
lateral
relation-
ships*

The foreign relations of the United States have never been entirely confined to direct and separate dealings with other nations individually. To begin
with, they have been operated within a framework of international law, which,
although often honored in the breach rather than the observance, is at all
events a matter of more or less general international acceptance and agreement. It clearly is not a creation of the United States or of any two or three
nations alone. In the second place, many international agreements in the past
have been multilateral, that is, shared by a considerable number of states:
for example, the Versailles Treaty at the close of World War I (which we
failed to ratify), the Washington treaties of 1922 relating to China, and the
London Treaty of 1930 on the limitation of naval armaments. Such treaties
or conventions have on several occasions been concluded at diplomatic meetings or conferences in which the United States was represented along with
other states. As world affairs have grown more complex, the number and importance of such meetings have increased. There are also numerous international bureaus, commissions, councils, unions, and other establishments to

which the United States has become a party, often in pursuance of some multi-lateral convention or agreement. Even before a new galaxy of such agencies sprang from World War II and the United Nations, official government manuals listed 70 such international bodies in which the United States was participating or to which it was giving financial support. These ranged from an International Hydrographic Bureau, an International Bureau of Weights and Measures, and a Universal Postal Union to the International Labor Organization created as an autonomous part of the League of Nations at the close of World War I and the Organization of American States (more commonly known by the name of its secretariat as the Pan American Union), dating from 1890 and linking up 21 republics of the Western Hemisphere for purposes of friendly cooperation. Organizations of the kind come and go; but the United States still bears some responsibility for more than 75 international organizations of various types, many within the orbit of UN but others quite independent.[31]

The League of Nations

Agencies of the sorts mentioned are specialized forms of international organization. Of a different order, however, is international organization as represented by the now defunct League of Nations and by the more recently established United Nations. With the relations of the United States to the ill-fated League, most people are now familiar. Organized on a pattern largely devised by President Wilson, the intended universal association of states for the preservation of peace was probably foredoomed by the refusal of our Senate to assent to the United States becoming a member. After a checkered career of 20 years it collapsed under the weight of a global war which it had been powerless to prevent. Even though outside, the United States could never hold completely aloof from the League's activities. We employed observers at Geneva, participated in many conferences held under League auspices, ratified various conventions of League origin, took part in the work of several technical and other commissions performing League functions, and eventually (1934) joined the League-sponsored International Labor Organization, although persistently refusing to adhere to the Permanent Court of International Justice (World Court), which the League set up.

THE UNITED NATIONS

1. Origin and nature

The most significant participation of the United States in international organization has come as a result of the challenging experiences of the 1940's. After one of the most extraordinary reversals of national attitude and policy on record, the country now finds itself in many respects the key member of the most imposing international association or union known to history, namely, the United Nations. With the idea of such an organization growing in sharpness

[31] For a full list at a current date, see latest edition of the *United States Government Organization Manual*. Descriptions of listed organizations may be found in *United States Contributions to International Organization, Fiscal Year 1961* (House Doc. #460).

UNITED NATIONS STRUCTURE: THE PATTERN OF THE ORGANIZATION

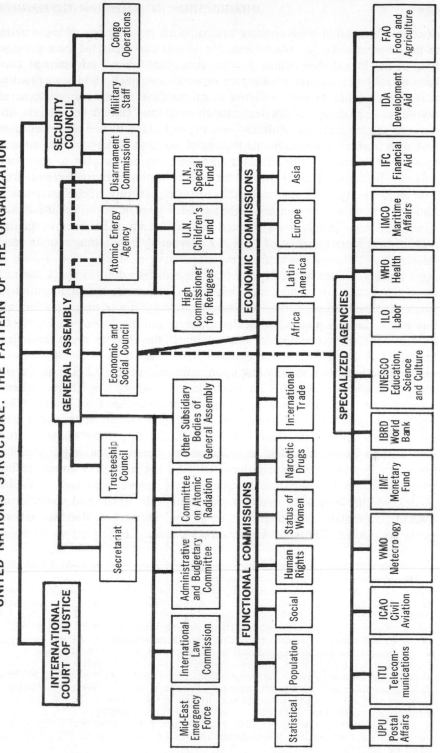

of conception and in public interest and support, preparations went on quietly in government circles at Washington for almost two years before representatives of the four leading Allied powers were gathered in conference at Dumbarton Oaks (an historic Washington estate) in August, 1944, to draw up a plan. Two months of work resulted in proposals stirring wide and generally favorable discussion, but leaving difficult problems still to be settled. After some of the most thorny of these—relating especially to voting procedures—had been freshly canvassed by the leaders of the "Big Three" at the Yalta conference of February, 1945, responsibility for carrying the plan to completion was devolved upon a more general international conference convened at San Francisco on April 25, 1945. In this historic gathering, the Charter of the United Nations was written and signed by delegates of 50 different nations.[32] There had been, in a sense, a "United Nations" from as far back as January, 1942, when representatives of 26 nations, meeting in Washington, adopted a "declaration" binding their states to cooperative military action against the Axis powers. Basically the United Nations subscribed to in the Charter by these same states and others was designed to perpetuate that association into times of peace and convert its function from waging war to preventing it. In any event, the new plan was quickly accepted and implemented. Transmitted by President Truman almost as soon as signed, the Charter swept through the Senate (July 28, 1945) by the extraordinary vote of 89 to 2. Other governments acted with such alacrity that upon adherence of the U.S.S.R. in October, the American Secretary of State was able to announce the Charter adopted; and the first UN instrumentality brought into operation, the General Assembly, began functioning at London early in 1946.[33] Doubts about the constitutional competence of the treaty-making authority to put the country into an organization of the kind had troubled many Senators and other people in 1919. But in 1945 constitutional problems did not seem very important.[34]

2. Organization

There were people, when the Charter was framed, who would have been glad to see the traditional national-state system discarded and some form of "world government" instituted. A step as revolutionary as that was not seriously considered. The new organization, like the League before it, became

[32] The text (with full commentary) will be found in the work by L. M. Goodrich and E. Hambro listed at the end of the chapter.

[33] American membership was finally and officially validated in a United Nations Participation Act of December 20, 1945. By a vote of 60 to 2, the Senate on August 2, 1946, also accepted for the United States compulsory jurisdiction of the UN's International Court of Justice, although qualifying by excepting disputes on matters regarded by the United States as "essentially" within its own jurisdiction.

[34] One of the major constitutional questions in 1919 had been the power of the President and Senate to enter into an agreement which might require us to make war when the Constitution gives to the Congress this power to declare war. See E. S. Corwin, *The Constitution and World Organization* (Princeton, N. J., 1944), published while plans for UN were being formulated, and attributing full power to the national government in the matter and in the field of foreign relations generally.

The UN Participation Act of 1945 did, however, contemplate that Congress would share with the President the determination of when armed forces of the United States might be employed.

legally only a voluntary contractual arrangement among states retaining virtual equality and exempt from any international intervention in matters within their several separate jurisdictions. Originally, there were 51 such states; later admissions have brought the roll to a total of 113. The major outsiders in 1965 are Communist China, Germany (East and West), Indonesia and Switzerland.

It is possible here to merely list the principal organs through which the UN operates: (1) a deliberative and advisory General Assembly—a "Town Meeting of the World"—embracing all of the member states each with from one to five delegates but only one vote,[35] and meeting in regular session every September, with special sessions as needed; (2) a Security Council, charged with primary responsibility for maintaining international peace and security, composed of five permanent members—noncommunist China, France, the U.S.S.R., Great Britain, and the United States—and ten nonpermanent members elected by the General Assembly for two-year terms, and in session almost continuously;[36] (3) an Economic and Social Council, reflecting the organization's concern with world-wide economic and social conditions and problems (especially as related, even potentially, to the causes of war), and composed of 27 (originally 18) member-states—now including the United States—chosen by the General Assembly for three-year terms;[37] (4) a Trusteeship Council, charged with supervising the administration of trust territories (including some formerly League mandates), and composed of 7 trustee member-states (including the United States) and 7 nontrustee states, either permanent or elective; (5) an International Court of Justice, similar to the now displaced League World Court, composed of 15 judges elected by the General Assembly on recommendation of the Security Council, sitting in the Peace Palace at The Hague, and with all UN members (and other states so desiring) parties to the organizing "statute"; and finally (6) a Secretariat, servicing the principal organs (except the International Court) and the specialized agencies through some 4000 employees drawn from all over the world, headed by a secretary general, and forming, to all intents and purposes, an international civil service.

[35] Two constituent states of the U.S.S.R. (Ukraine and Byelorussia), however, have separate votes, as do the various units composing the British Commonwealth of Nations.

[36] Originally, the Security Council had been composed of 11 members but was enlarged by amendment approved in 1965. Here is where the famous "veto power" is encountered; on "substantive," as distinguished from "procedural" matters, no decisions can be taken except with the concurrence of 9 (originally 7) members, *including all five permanent members.* As one of the permanent members, the United States is no less in a position to block any UN policy or action considered objectionable than is the member whose vetoes have caused so much trouble, i.e., the U.S.S.R.

[37] A dozen or more "operating arms" of UN and attached to this Council have added to the ever-lengthening list of specialized unions, commissions, "organizations," and the like referred to earlier in this chapter. Some (such as the Universal Postal Union and the International Labor Organization) antedate the UN, but several (such as the Food and Agricultural Organization, the World Health Organization, and the United Nations Educational, Scientific, and Cultural Organization, or UNESCO), have made their appearance along with it.

MEMBER STATES OF THE UNITED NATIONS 1965

Western Bloc

Australia	Luxembourg
Austria	Malta
Belgium	Netherlands
Canada	New Zealand
China (Formosa)	Norway
Denmark	Portugal
Finland	Spain
France	Sweden
Greece	Union of
Iceland	South Africa
Ireland	United Kingdom
Italy	United States
Jamaica	

Latin-American Group

Argentina	Haiti
Bolivia	Honduras
Brazil	Mexico
Chile	Nicaragua
Colombia	Panama
Costa Rica	Paraguay
Cuba	Peru
Dominican	Trinidad and
Republic	Tobago
Ecuador	Uruguay
El Salvador	Venezuela
Guatemala	

Asian and Middle Eastern Group

Afghanstan	Kuwait
Algeria	Laos
Burma	Lebanon
Cambodia	Nepal
Ceylon	Pakistan
Cyprus	Philippines
Malaysia	Saudi Arabia
India	Singapore
Iran	Syria
Iraq	Thailand
Japan	Yemen
Jordan	

African Group

Burundi	Malawi
Cameroon	Mali Fed.
Central	Mauritania
African Rep.	Morocco
Chad	Niger
Congo (for-	Nigeria
merly Belg.)	Rwanda
Congo (for-	Senegal
merly French)	Sierra Leone
Dahomey	Somalia
Ethiopia	Sudan
Gabon	Tanzania
Ghana	Togo
Guinea	Tunisia
Ivory Coast	Uganda
Kenya	United Arab Rep.
Liberia	Upper Volta
Libya	Zambia
Malagasy Rep.	

Soviet & Satellites

Albania	Mongolia
Bulgaria	Poland
Byelorussia	Rumania
Czechoslovakia	Ukraine
Hungary	U.S.S.R.

Others

Israel
Yugoslavia

The United Nations, essentially, provides a framework within which a nation carries on foreign relations with other nations through collective channels instead of in the traditionally nation-by-nation manner. Of course, direct and independent diplomatic relations between nation and nation on an individual basis continue—as do various unattached international commissions, bureaus, and the like. Although the theory is that virtually everything pertaining to the interests of world peace will be channeled through UN, there still are quite independent international discussions and agreements of the highest importance, yet affecting peace—for example, those culminating in the North Atlantic Pact of 1949. Indeed there not only is overlapping between two spheres of action—nation-by-nation and international organization—but possibility of confusion and conflict. The present point, however, is that a member-state's dealings within UN *are* foreign relations, to be carried on subject in general to the same constitutional checks and political limitations applying in the case of international dealings outside of the UN orbit.

3. U.S. agencies for UN participation: a. A matter of foreign relations

This being the case, it is natural that the agency within our government primarily responsible for UN relations should be the Department of State. So broad, it is true, is the range of UN functions and activities that hardly a department or establishment in our government fails to have interests involved. Representatives of departments like Agriculture, Commerce, and Labor, and of establishments like the National Security Council and the United States Tariff Commission constantly advise State Department officers and representatives at UN meetings, with upwards of a dozen interdepartmental committees functioning similarly. It is on the State Department chiefly that responsibility falls; and there is where one must look for the machinery through which our UN relations are officially carried on. The first agency set up for the purpose was a rather casually created Office of Special Political Affairs. In 1948, however, this was replaced by a Bureau of United Nations Affairs (now called Bureau of International Organization Affairs), since developed into a main unit under its own Assistant Secretary of State and organized in four offices functioning on lines indicated by their names—(1) United Nations Political and Security Affairs (concerned broadly with affairs of the General Assembly); (2) International Economic and Social Affairs (having to do particularly with the interest of the Council of that name); (3) International Administration; and (4) International Conferences. As the Department's focal agency for UN relations, the Bureau of International Organization Affairs and its branches are expected to serve as the main channel between the Department of State and UN organs and agencies, to keep informed on all UN business and on the general state of international affairs, to make information available to all branches of the government concerned and to the general public, to review UN procedures and offer suggestions for improving them, and in general promote the development of United States policies and programs pertaining to the peaceful settlement of international controversies. It is hardly necessary to add that, like all Department operations, these and

b. Bureau of International Organization Affairs

other functions are performed in the name of, and subject to control by, the President.

For purposes of representation at UN headquarters in New York City, there is—as in the case of most other member-nations—a permanent mission, which with us consists chiefly of a representative or chief of mission [38] and a deputy to him, a deputy representative to the Security Council, and representatives to the Economic and Social Council, the Trusteeship Council, and other organs and agencies, the whole staffed with a secretary general, certain advisers, and a secretariat equipped for year-round service. Delegations to the General Assembly, however, do not belong to the mission, but are separately appointed (five delegates and five alternates, with the Secretary of State serving as senior representative) for each meeting. Under the terms of the United Nations Participation Act of 1945, the President reports to Congress every year on UN activities and on United States participation therein.

In a world polarized into hostile blocs, each burdened with huge and increasing armaments and each competing for the favorable opinion of the unaligned states and the newly emerging societies and over all hanging the dread specter of nuclear war, the United Nations still stands as a symbol of hope. The early, and perhaps too optimistic, expectations of our people in its capabilities have given way to more sober realization of its limitations. Its peace-keeping functions are based largely upon the concert of victors and cannot easily be discharged if the victors fall out among themselves or if the disputes are between the "great" powers. Its machinery for the imposition of military sanctions has never been fully developed. The great expansion in membership of the Assembly from among the newly emerging nations has meant a shift in emphasis in that body. Although the UN has been able to achieve little relaxation of the armaments race or of the tensions among the Soviet, Chinese, and the Western blocs, it nevertheless has earnestly addressed itself to many serious international problems. It has successfully isolated and dealt with potentially dangerous outbreaks in Iran, Kashmir, Palestine, Korea, Cyprus, the Congo, and Pakistan-India. Through the specialized agencies dealing with health, food, and economic development, it has fostered many and valuable enterprises for the less fortunate areas and peoples of the world. Our government continues to express its faith in the UN and to give it loyal and largely bipartisan support.

In a speech to the UN in June, 1965, celebrating its twentieth anniversary, President Johnson said: "I came to raise a voice of confidence in both the future of these United Nations and the fate of the human race . . . there can be no doubt that the United Nations has taken root in human needs and has established a shape and a purpose and a meaning of its own." On the other hand, we no longer place our sole, perhaps not even our major, reliance

---

[38] Under Eisenhower, Kennedy and Johnson with Henry Cabot Lodge, Adlai Stevenson, and Arthur Goldberg successively occupying this post, it has come to be virtually a Cabinet position.

on the UN to preserve peace, security, or freedom. We plan and carry out, independent of it, measures to strengthen the "free world" and to aid developing nations.

RESISTANCE TO COMMUNIST AGGRESSION: "COLD WAR" WITH THE U.S.S.R.

Amid the bitter experience of World War II, many thinking people, impressed with the technological annihilation of distance and the resulting close interrelation of activity, and even community of interest, of peoples everywhere, became enamored of the concept of a future in which there would be but one world, and a world so knit together by moral, economic, and even political ties that thenceforth the follies and disasters of the past could be completely avoided.[39] To a considerable extent, United Nations, as planned, reflected such aspiration. The unhappy outcome has instead been a profound cleavage among three worlds: the world of the Western bloc including the restive Americas; the world of the U.S.S.R., its satellites and the aggressive Chinese and their puppet regimes; and the world of the "neutrals"—mainly the newly organized states of Africa, and Southern Asia and the Middle East. To the United States, this situation has presented the most acute challenges in our history and has resulted in major and continuing readjustments in our foreign policies.

Not "one world," but three

When the U.S.S.R. absorbed the Baltic states in 1940, there were misgivings in this country; and, as indicated above, our government never has recognized those annexations. But for more than three years the Soviet Union fought as one of the Allies against the Axis powers. It participated actively in planning and establishing UN and became a leading member. From Anglo-American-Russian agreements, notably at the Yalta Conference of 1945, it achieved recognition of its important status in the world and acceptance of many of its traditional ambitions. Hardly was the war over, however, before the former ally shifted to a policy of intransigence and aggression. Remaining in UN, it repeatedly blocked needed action by use of the veto in the Security Council,[40] many times has "walked out" when displeased, as for example early in 1950 in protest against continued representation of Nationalist China and has on several occasions boycotted the meetings of the Council, Assembly, or specialized agencies. It has communized Poland, Hungary, Romania, Bulgaria, Albania, and Czechoslovakia, contrary in most instances to agreements made at Yalta, and has established satellite governments in all of these states. For a time it seriously threatened Greece, Iran, and other Near Eastern states by supporting uprisings by Communists against the established governments.

U.S.S.R. aggression and intransigence

[39] The idea gained vogue from a widely read and discussed book, *One World* (New York, 1943), written by Wendell Willkie after extensive world travel.

[40] The Soviet Union has used the veto more than fifty times since 1945, many times on matters not directly concerned with peace or security.

It has brought border Asiatic areas under its control and supported the communizing of almost all of China. Unquestionably it encouraged and assisted the North Korean assault on the (South) Korean Republic in 1950. To many it has seemed that the Soviet Union is bent upon the ideological if not physical conquest of Southeast Asia, India, all Western Europe, and perhaps, the world.

The fall of China   Perhaps the greatest setback to American hopes, however, was the successful Communist revolution in China (1947-1949) which toppled the Nationalist regime, drove it from the mainland, and established effective Red domination of this vast and storied land. Aided and encouraged by the Soviet Union, the Reds soon emerged as a powerful force in Asiatic affairs and began pressing all the Western positions there. They intervened in Korea forcing a stalemate, supported the uprising against the French in Indo-China, and the subsequent establishment of the Communist-dominated state of North Vietnam, conquered Tibet, pushed back the northeastern frontiers of India, allied themselves with Indonesia in putting pressure on Malaysia, and are continuing to support revolutionary forces in Laos and South Vietnam. The loss of China and the resultant decline of Western influence in Asia precipitated angry and bitter controversy in the United States with charges hurled across the political battle lines of "softness," ineptitude, and downright disloyalty. Countering Chinese pressure, we have used the procedures developed to contain Communist expansion in Europe. A major split in 1962-1963 between the Asiatic and European communists largely over the peaceful coexistence aims of the Soviet leaders revealed that the Chinese Reds are, at present, much the most aggressively anti-Western and anti-American of the Communist states.

The rise of new nations   The emergence of the neutrals—unaligned states as they prefer to be called—has also shaken the foundations of the one-world concept and introduced striking changes in the nature and objectives of the UN. One by one the former colonies of the Western bloc—mainly those of England, France, and the Netherlands—have successfully shaken off their colonial fetters and have deployed on the world stage as new nations. All are seeking rapid industrialization, improved living standards, and national identification. For the most part this has been or is now being accomplished without major violence but in India, Algeria, Indo-China, and the Congo the blood-letting preceding or accompanying independence was prolonged, expensive, and constantly threatened world-wide conflagration. In several cases, some of the burden and much of the obloquy for supporting colonial regimes fell upon the United States as it tried to aid its European allies or to support pro-Western elements among the emerging states. More often, the United States has sought to aid economic development and to counter the pressures for continued chaos from the Communist world. In any event, these new states, many with strong anti-Western feelings, present challenges to our position which cannot be ignored.

Significance for American foreign policy   For the United States, as for many other nations, all this has forced a painful reorientation of policies. Our statesmen and people have come to the conclusion that American and world security can be won only by strong methods, namely, by augmenting our own military might, by preparing for atomic warfare if it cannot be averted, by developing UN's hitherto latent military potentialities,[41] by building supplementary regional defense systems—in short, by mobilizing the moral, economic, and military resources of the free world with sufficient vigor and effectiveness to "contain" Communist power, that is, to prevent it from overflowing its existing bounds and extinguishing Western institutions and culture and subjugating the millions of Asia and Africa. To this difficult and costly objective the overall foreign (and much domestic) policy of our government in the past seventeen years has been directed. A few of the measures invoked—in addition to the rearmament program outlined in the next chapter—must be mentioned.

The turning point in American-Soviet relations came in 1947. The Moscow Conference of foreign ministers of the Big Four early in that year achieved not a single important agreement and ended all hope of the "friendly" cooperation for which we had been striving since 1945. Even while the conference was in progress, President Truman took the first large step to curb Russian expansion. In a message to Congress on March 12, 1947, he called attention to northern Greece, where protracted guerrilla operations under encouragement from Moscow were threatening a coup overthrowing the Greek government and delivering the country to communism. Such a coup if successful would put Russia on the Mediterranean and place Turkey and the strategic Dardanelles in an impossible position. To avert such a disaster, he proposed that the United States at once bolster local resistance by giving both Greece and Turkey liberal aid in the form of money, goods, military supplies, and military counsel.[42] During vigorous and prolonged discussion in Congress and outside, it was objected that by such independent action the United States would be by-passing the organization ostensibly existing for dealing with such threats to world peace and order, the UN. The President replied that the need was too urgent to permit of waiting for UN to organize measures, that the harassed countries had no place to turn except the United States, and that it was no disservice to UN for a powerful individual member to act unilaterally to maintain or create conditions favorable to the organization's ultimate mastery in the international field. Under an act approved May 22, 1947, the United States launched a program of assistance (an initial appropriation of $400 million was voted) to the two countries which has continued. Regimes friendly to the West were stabilized and the threatened subversion thwarted.

Hardly had the new idea of employing material aid to bolster war-torn

Expedients for containing Russian power: 1. Aid to Greece and Turkey

2. The Marshall Plan:

[41] Under Art. 43 of the Charter, member-states are required to place armed forces and facilities at the disposal of the UN Security Council for use in maintaining peace. Until the Korean war of 1950, no state did this. The Council's appeals at that time, although not under Article 43, elicited no very impressive practical response except from the United States. Great Britain, the British dominions, and a few other states did, however, contribute naval and air assistance, and in certain instances limited ground forces.

[42] In the course of his address President Truman enunciated the policy of the United States "to support free peoples who are resisting attempted subjugation by armed minorities or by outside pressure." This is now known as the Truman Doctrine.

nations against Soviet seduction been inaugurated before a vastly broader field

a. Origin and purpose

opened for applying it. While Congress was still debating assistance to Greece and Turkey, the State Department published a significant study under the title of *The Development of the Foreign Reconstruction Policy of the United States*. A few weeks later (June 5, 1947) Secretary of State George C. Marshall dramatized the document in a commencement address at Harvard University, outlining an ambitious scheme for cooperative but mainly American assistance in a general rehabilitation of the sagging national economies of Western Europe. At the outset, the plan was not avowedly anti-Russian; on the contrary, the U.S.S.R. and its satellites were invited to participate in it. When, however, the invitation met with flat refusal, the project—promptly named by journalists the "Marshall Plan"—was fast reoriented as a phase of the Truman program for employing American resources and power to contain, or block, the Soviet Union's aspirations. The rationale of this program was that if tired, impoverished, and despondent Western peoples could be helped to their feet and given a vision of better things under a revived economy, the strong Communist parties then operating in many nations would lose their appeal. In response to a request from Washington, 16 European governments conferred on the extent of their needs and on what they and their peoples could themselves do toward meeting them, arriving in the end at a four-year rehabilitation

b. Adoption

program under which the United States (mainly) was to be asked to supply goods, money, and credit to a total for the period of $22.44 billion. Warmly supporting the project, President Truman passed it on—under the name of the European Recovery Program (ERP)—to Congress, convoked in special session. After debates carrying over into the following year, he was able, on April 3, 1948, to affix his signature to a Foreign Assistance Act, so named because embracing aid for countries outside of the 16 (e.g., China), but with the major Title I designated as the Economic Cooperation Act. Congress was unwilling, however, to commit the Treasury for the full period of four years and the legislation was limited to a single year. To keep the project going, later continuing and amending measures were necessary. To manage the enterprise, too, an independent establishment, the Economic Cooperation Administration (ECA) was set up under an administrator appointed by the President and Senate, and with "economic missions" stationed in each cooperating country.[43]

Foreign aid embraces military aid and then development assistance (Point Four)

Strictly speaking, the Marshall Plan program ended about 1952 having largely succeeded in rehabilitating the economies of many Western European nations. Before it had done so, it was to some extent overshadowed by a new outpouring of funds to aid in the rearmament of our European and Asiatic allies linked with us in a series of defensive alliances hereafter described.

[43] The term "cooperating" is used advisedly, because in return for American aid the participating countries agreed not only to exert themselves to the utmost in behalf of their own economies, but also not to do certain things, e.g., not to use donated commodities in manufacturing or processing products for sale in the U.S.S.R. or satellite countries.

U. S. FOREIGN AID, 1945-1964
(Millions of Dollars)

Region	Total	Economic Aid	Military Aid
1. Europe	$41.421	$25.555	$15.886
2. Far East	24.806	13.880	10.926
3. Latin America	5.867	4.976	.891
4. Near East-South Asia	19.370	13.762	5.608
5. Africa	2.019	1.862	.157
6. Nonregional	2.512	2.119	.393
Sub Total	95.993	62.152	33.841
7. International Financial Inst.	1.290	1.290	
Total	$97.283	$63.442	$33.841

SOURCE: *Statistical Abstract of the U. S., 1965.*

Military considerations tended for most of the decade of the fifties to dominate foreign-aid policies. Gradually, attention focused on the desperate plight of the emerging states and underdeveloped areas of the world.

In a notable "Point Four," of his inaugural address in 1949, President Truman had first called for a bold new program for making the benefits of our scientific advances and industrial progress available for the improvement and growth of underdeveloped areas. A modest program of technical assistance was inaugurated both unilaterally by America and multilaterally through the UN. As Russian and Chinese efforts to spread communism among the newly emerging forces seeking independence and national identity in Asia and Africa increased so American assistance soon went beyond technical aid to financial aid and the purpose of our aid program shifted away from rearmament to development assistance. Finally, in 1961 Congress, at the urging of President Kennedy, dropped the mutual security framework for our aid program and assigned major responsibility for foreign-aid (technical and financial) administration to a new Agency for International Development (AID) affiliated with the Department of State and placed the military aspects with the Department of Defense. During the most recent decade, development aid has also been given indirectly through American support for such multinational efforts as the World Bank, International Development Association, and the Organization for Economic Cooperation and Development. In some of these and in our own Development Loan Fund, loans both "hard" and "soft" have been and are being used more extensively than before to substitute for or supplement outright grants for economic progress.

If we include the postwar relief and rehabilitation grants which preceded the establishment of our foreign-aid program, almost $100 billion has been

LARGEST RECIPIENTS OF U. S. FOREIGN AID, 1964
(Millions of Dollars)

India	$864	Korea	$157
Pakistan	377	Turkey	126
Vietnam	221	Chile	96
Brazil	212	Yugoslavia	91
Egypt	194		

SOURCE: *Statistical Abstract of the U. S., 1965.*

Congress and foreign aid

spent or committed on aid to foreign peoples for 1945 to 1965. We are still spending at the rate of $3-$4 billion yearly. To maintain this continuing flow of treasure each President, Truman, Eisenhower, Kennedy, and Johnson, has faced stern Congressional critics and has had to battle vigorously for the level of support he felt essential. Rarely has he received as much as he requested or as much flexibility in administration as he thought desirable.[44] Several changes in administrative arrangements have accompanied or followed the shifts in emphasis in the program and much of the time it has been criticized for slack administration, extravagance, and inadequate coordination with other aspects of American diplomacy through the embassies or ministries. Throughout much of its history foreign aid has been regarded as a temporary expedient aimed at a limited goal and annual extension of authority and funds have been necessary to keep it alive. With prime emphasis now on development aid, it begins to look as if aid at some level is an aspect of our foreign policy that is going to be with us for many years to come.[45]

The Peace Corps

A special and new form of technical aid to developing nations was created in 1961 by Congress on the strong recommendation of President Kennedy: the "Peace Corps." A semiautonomous agency was created in the

[44] Some of the major controversies have been over: (1) whether aid could or should be authorized for avowedly Communist but not completely Soviet-dominated countries such as Poland and Yugoslavia or for leftist-leaning countries such as Ghana and Indonesia; (2) whether aid should be given to support "Socialist" enterprises, i.e., to countries to nationalize industries or services; (3) what kind of strings should be attached to aid-requirements to buy American products with American cash or to refrain from selling to or trading certain materials with Cuba, Russia, China, or North Vietnam; (4) how much of our surplus farm commodity stockpile might be supplied in lieu of dollars; (5) how much influence military considerations should play in grants.

[45] The necessity and desirability of foreign economic aid is supported by the Report of the President's Committee to Study United States Military Assistance Programs, *The New York Times*, Mar. 18, 1959, by Committee for Economic Development, *Economic Development Assistance* (New York, 1957), by H. Feis, *Foreign Aid and Foreign Policy* (New York, 1964) and by F. M. Coffin, *Witness for Aid* (New York, 1964). See also, J. D. Montgomery, *The Politics of Foreign Aid: American Experience in Southeast Asia* (New York, 1962), H. J. P. Arnold, *Aid for Developing Countries* (London, 1962), G. Liska, *The New Statecraft: Foreign Aid in American Foreign Policy* (Chicago, 1960); E. S. Mason, *Foreign Aid and Foreign Policy* (New York, 1964); J. A. Rubin, *Your Hundred Billion Dollars: The Complete Story of American Foreign Aid* (New York, 1965).

Department of State to recruit, train, and make available to underdeveloped nations for agreed upon projects a cadre of young men and women trained in various specialties (teaching, agricultural sciences, medicine, etc.), and in the language and culture of the nation to which they are assigned. These young people are to offer on the spot technical help and thus compensate for grave shortages of trained people in the new nations. In so far as possible these are to be dedicated young people who will live among the people they are to help without uniforms, or high pay, or special perquisites and who will serve tours of duty not to exceed five years. By 1965, the Corps had an authorized strength of 14,000 and was engaged in projects in 46 nations. It had captured the idealism and enthusiasm of many young citizens and had established a favorable position in the international scene.

The Communist coup in Czechoslovakia in 1948, transforming that unhappy country into a satellite of the U.S.S.R., convinced the leading statesmen of Western Europe that Russia would not be content simply to consolidate its gains of World War II but was bent on continued expansion. Great Britain, France, the Netherlands, Belgium, and Luxembourg meeting at Brussels in March of 1948 joined together in a fifty-year mutual military alliance against aggression. American support was essential if the Western bloc was to constitute an effective barrier against Russian advance. President Truman spoke out bluntly to Congress calling for American support and enlarging on the Russian menace. Led by Senator Vandenberg (Republican of Michigan), the Senate adopted by a vote of 64 to 4 a resolution declaring that this country should by constitutional processes seek peace and security by the "progressive development of regional . . . arrangements for . . . collective self-defense." Early in 1949, the President submitted for Senate ratification a North Atlantic Pact uniting the five nations of the Brussels Pact with seven other nations of the "Atlantic community" in a defensive military alliance. Apart from the Inter-American Pact of 1947 uniting the nations of the Western Hemisphere in resisting aggression, this was the first peacetime alliance of its kind seriously considered by the United States for more than a century. After extended hearings and debates the Senate approved American adherence by a vote of 82 to 13. The North Atlantic Treaty remains the cornerstone of contemporary American foreign policy in Europe. By this pact the twelve nations agreed that an armed attack on any one of them in Europe or North America is to be regarded as an armed attack against all; and if such an attack occurs, they will take action, including the use of armed force, necessary to maintain the security of the North Atlantic area.[46] Greece and Turkey acceded to the treaty in 1952 and were added to the allied states.

The North Atlantic Treaty provides for continuing consultation among

3. The Atlantic Alliance

Strengthening the defense of Western Europe

[46] For the text of the North Atlantic Pact, see 81st Cong., 1st Sess., Sen. Doc. Exec. L (1950). The difficult legal problem of the power of Congress to declare war is evaded by the treaty through language which stipulates that the provisions are to be carried out by the signers in accordance with their various constitutional processes.

the signatories to develop ways and means, mainly military, for making the alliance formidable. A Council of Foreign Ministers of the participating nations and a Defense Committee of the Defense Ministers were specifically established in the treaty. In the fall of 1949, these organs formally began their work under the general title of North Atlantic Treaty Organization (NATO) and they have continued to meet regularly since that time. In 1951, General Eisenhower took command of headquarters established near Paris from which it was hoped to build a coordinated armed force of the units dedicated to NATO by the various allies. The military forces which the United States might contribute to the joint endeavor became the subject of a lengthy debate in the Congress, largely over the question of the proper way in which the Congress ought to be involved in such a determination. The Senate, by resolution, in 1951 finally approved an increase of American divisions stationed in Western Europe from two to six, but suggested that Congressional consent should be obtained by the President to the sending of any more. In general, the U.S. has held to this decision and has kept the six divisions in Western Europe. The substantial forces which NATO military planners had envisioned as ultimately being dedicated to the common task by the member states have not, however, materialized. In the meeting of Defense Ministers in 1965 it was agreed that these "fictitious and unrealistic" goals would be replaced by more appropriate (smaller) ones.

The
problem
of
Germany

One of the most difficult problems confronting the Western allies has been the role to be accorded friendly West Germany. The United States strongly urged the rearmament of the Germans and the inclusion of German divisions in the armed forces of the Allies. The European victims of German aggression in World War II were, on the other hand, as frightened by a rearmed Germany as by an aggressive Russia. To America, the attempt to defend industrial Western Europe against a Russian advance with a hostile or possibly indifferent Germany seemed unthinkable. The leaders of NATO finally in 1952 after months of negotiations worked out a series of treaties and agreements creating a European Defense Community under which would be organized a single European military force including German units. To this force would be added under NATO, American and British armed forces as well as those of the other members not partners in EDC. France, however, refused in 1954 to accede to the arrangements despite heavy American pressure and a new set of arrangements were then hammered out late in that same year. The new agreements: (1) invited West Germany to become a member of NATO, (2) provided that Italy and West Germany would be invited to accede to the Brussels Treaty of 1948; (3) created a new organization of the Brussels Pact states called a Western European Union and endowed this new organization with power to control the armaments dedicated to support of the Union; (4) provided for the restoration of full sovereignty to and an end of the occupation of West Germany; (5) provided for a substantial military contribution to NATO by West Germany but with the size and character

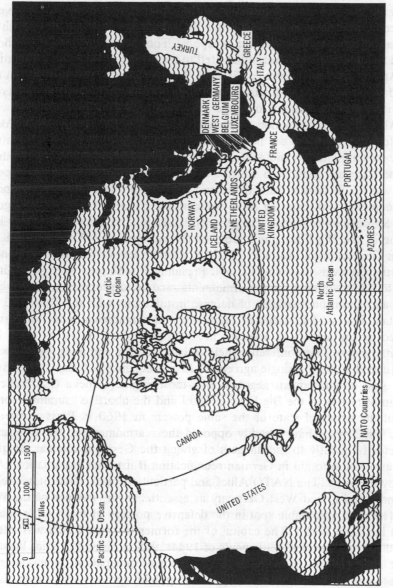

THE NORTH ATLANTIC ALLIANCE

NATO Countries

Miles

0   500   1000   1500

Pacific Ocean

UNITED STATES

CANADA

Arctic Ocean

NORWAY

ICELAND

NETHERLANDS

UNITED KINGDOM

North Atlantic Ocean

FRANCE

PORTUGAL

AZORES

ITALY

GREECE

TURKEY

DENMARK
WEST GERMANY
BELGIUM
LUXEMBOURG

of this contribution carefully limited in deference to French anxiety over a rearmed Germany; (6) provided that West Germany renounce the right to manufacture atomic and nuclear weapons. Those agreements to which the United States was a party were submitted to the Senate late in 1954 and ratified by it April 2, 1955, by a vote of 76 to 2. The other nations, in their turn, also ratified the pacts, France finally acceding after another set of agreements between it and West Germany over the Saar were fashioned.

Russian attitude changes

Although the completion of the network of agreements uniting the Atlantic states in a solid bloc did not of itself create the strong military forces ultimately contemplated by the Allies, it did present the Soviet with a strong front and the Russian attitude in Europe began to change perceptibly. A peace treaty was finally concluded with Austria by the Allies in March, 1955, ending the occupation and restoring its sovereignty after years of frustrating negotiations. So conciliatory grew the tone of Russian diplomacy that a top-level meeting of the Big Four reminiscent of the late years of World War II was held in Geneva in mid-summer of 1955. At the Geneva meeting, the tone of all participants was most conciliatory. President Eisenhower went so far in an effort to find a solution for the armaments race as to propose swapping blueprints and aerial photographs of defense installations with the Russians. The important issues—the status of Germany and armaments reductions—were referred by the leaders to a conference of their foreign ministers to be held later at Geneva. This conference, held in late October and early November of 1955, ended without a single agreement of consequence between the East and West. And all subsequent negotiations—those of the Geneva Conference of Foreign Ministers of the Big Four in 1959 and the abortive "summit" conference of the heads of state of the same powers in 1960 in Paris—have also failed. The Soviets have steadily opposed the rearmament of West Germany and refer frequently to the dangers of giving the Germans nuclear weapons. They also refuse to aid in German reunification if it means domination of the state by the West. The NATO Allies and particularly the United States regard a friendly and armed West Germany as essential to the defense of the West.

Berlin: the "Achilles Heel"

The most vulnerable spot in the defensive posture of the NATO alliance is and has been Berlin. The capital of the former German Reich was left, by the military and political settlements of 1944-1945, an island of joint Western-Soviet responsibility in the midst of the Soviet occupation zone—later the Soviet dominated German Democratic Republic, the eastern sector. Large sections of the city were assigned to each of the four powers and in those under Western authority a large measure of self-government with free elections was soon established. All land access to this bastion of Western strength, however, must be across territory controlled by the Soviet Union. The Russians struck quickly after the collapse of the wartime alliance and sealed off the city in 1949. The Western position and that of the citizens of West Berlin were saved only by a mammoth air-lift organized by the West. Late in 1958, after efforts to weaken NATO and prevent the rearming of West Germany had failed,

BERLIN AND THE TWO GERMANYS — 1965

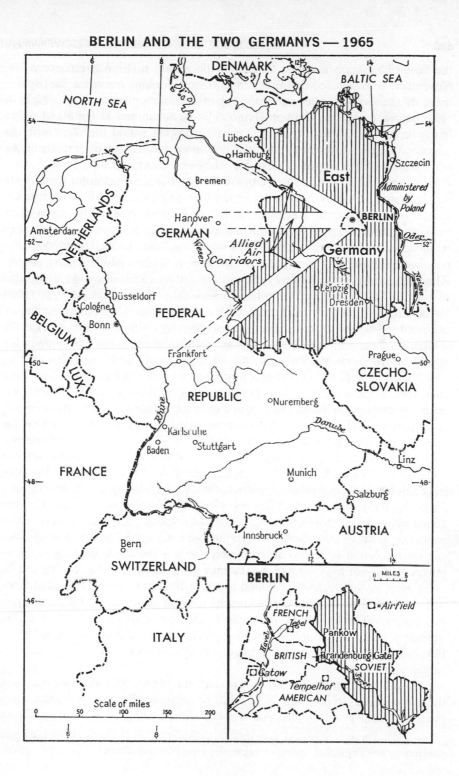

the Soviet Union again sought to exploit this chink in the Western armor. In November, it announced that unless negotiations looking toward a final settlement of the German question were begun in six months, it would make a separate peace with the German Democratic Republic and assign all its rights in Berlin to this satellite state. The Western powers would then be forced to negotiate with East Germany for their continued position in Berlin. The Russians indicated that in case of "trouble" they would support their puppet state. Khrushchev, the Soviet premier, apparently wanted a new summit conference on Germany. Instead, a conference of the foreign ministers of Britain, France, Russia, and the United States assembled in Geneva in mid-1959 and after prolonged discussions of the conflicting proposals for a German peace settlement adjourned without agreement. For a year, the Soviet Union pounded away at the West in soft and friendly and then in strident and belligerent tones. Khrushchev visited the United States in the fall of 1959, disavowed any ultimatum on Berlin, spoke of his hopes for amicable relationships, and promoted his country and his plan for a new summit conference. The conference finally occurred in May of 1960 in Paris and was dissolved almost before it began by a vigorous Russian attack on the United States and President Eisenhower for spying on the Soviet Union by means of high-flying planes, the U-2, one of which was unhappily captured just prior to the conference meeting. The Russians then began to step up their pressure for a Berlin settlement on their own terms. A meeting in June, 1961 with President Kennedy in Vienna achieved no apparent results, and the Russians increased their pressure. Kennedy announced that the Soviet aim was to dislodge the Western powers from Berlin. He ordered an increase in troop strength in the threatened city and asked for larger defense expenditures. The denouement in August of 1961 was the construction by the Communists of a fence, then a wall, sealing off the Soviet zone from the Western zones and halting virtually all movement of people and goods between the zones. Pressure did not subside at once, however, and menacing gestures continued throughout 1962. Congress on its part by concurrent resolution in that year expressed its view that "this country is determined to prevent by whatever means may be necessary, including the use of arms" any Soviet violation of Allied rights in Berlin. In 1963, President Kennedy himself visited Berlin to reassure the inhabitants of our continued interest and support. The Soviets in 1964 finally did sign a treaty of friendship and support with East Germany but the pact recognized Soviet commitments in Berlin and was not the separate peace agreement which the leaders had repeatedly threatened.

4. Military aid to friendly nations

Apart from an allusion to mutual aid, the North Atlantic Pact obligates the United States to no program of military assistance.[47] Such assistance, however, had been given Greece and Turkey since 1947 and Nationalist China

[47] Senator Robert Taft attempted unsuccessfully to attach a reservation to the treaty disclaiming any obligation, moral or legal, to rearm Western Europe.

over a longer period. No one ever doubted that American aid would be required by the more needy Atlantic Pact states if they were to rebuild their armies. No sooner, indeed, was the pact assured than a comprehensive and coordinated program of American assistance long in preparation was placed before Congress. President Truman was able to sign a Mutual Defense Assistance Act in October, 1949, carrying an appropriation of $1.314 billion mainly for the Atlantic Pact states, but also in relatively small amounts for Greece, Turkey, Iran, Korea, the Philippines, and the "general area" of China. Thus was launched the third great program of bolstering friendly nations against Communist subversion or attack with American money. In the years since 1949, the program of military assistance has been expanded to include many other friendly nations. For a time (1952-1960), military aid was more important than economic assistance. Aimed originally at strengthening our European allies, our military aid has been repeatedly broadened to include our Asiatic friends as well, notably South Korea, China (Taiwan), Thailand, India, when threatened by the Chinese Reds, Pakistan, and Vietnam. To 1964, more than $33 billion had been advanced to rebuild armies of our allies all over the world. Several shifts in administrative responsibility for the program have occurred—similar to those characterizing the economic-aid program. The Defense Department now has virtually complete charge of it as a result of the reorganizations of 1955 and 1961.

The Marshall Plan helped make Western Europe prosperous: military assistance helped make it formidable. The first great "entangling" alliance of the United States, a solid pillar of its modern foreign policy, is nevertheless in deep trouble as it approaches its twentieth anniversary. Its troubles are perhaps the consequence of its success. Soviet adventure in Western Europe is no longer feared. Repeated probings have revealed few signs of American withdrawal or refusal to defend the position of its allies. Nuclear power has reached a kind of stalemate. Great gains have been made economically, especially by France and West Germany. Heavy commitments of the French in Indo-China and Algeria have finally been liquidated and blood and treasure are being spared. The movement for European unity which proceeded at a good pace with the formation of the Coal and Steel Community and the Common Market, both supported strongly by the United States, has slowed down to a crawl. France, led by de Gaulle has determined to reduce Anglo-American influence on the continent, to gain its own nuclear weapons and thus abandon its reliance upon ours, to regulate the nature and scope of German participation, and to develop a purely European policy for dealing with the Soviet Union. In furtherance of these aims, France has vetoed the membership of the United Kingdom in the Common Market (1963) and refused to join the American-proposed, multilateral submarine force armed with Polaris missiles with nuclear warheads (approved by England and the United States in the Nassau Agreement of 1962) as a method of equipping NATO with nuclear weapons.

NATO in the Sixties

England is anxious to reduce its military commitments on the continent and West Germany wants reunification with East Germany and access to nuclear power. The Allies are thus sharply divided.[48]

5. Armed resistance in Korea:

In one area thus far, namely Korea, Communist containment has involved the United States—as also the United Nations for the first time—in actual war. During World War II, the United States, Great Britain, China, and near the close the U.S.S.R., agreed that after the country's liberation from Japanese rule, Korea should again become a free and independent nation. When Japan accepted defeat, it became a matter of convenience for Russian authorities to receive the surrender of Japanese forces in the Korean north and American authorities that of forces in the south; and for the purpose, an arbitrary dividing line was fixed at the 38th parallel. Before long, it became apparent that, quite contrary to American intention, the U.S.S.R. proposed to regard the division as permanent. Although Russian troops were alleged to have been withdrawn from the northern zone in 1948, every effort of the United States, supported by associates in the recent war, to bring about the creation of a free government for a united Korea was frustrated. In the north, a well-armed puppet Communist regime—the Democratic People's Republic of Korea—arose under encouragement from Moscow. In the south, a Republic of Korea was established as an independent nation in 1948 after a free election held under the auspices of the United Nations—a republic promptly recognized by the United States and 31 other UN members, although barred by Soviet veto from membership on its own part. With the northern Communist regime from the first claiming jurisdiction over the entire country, there always was danger that it would attempt by force to make its asserted authority good. On June 25, 1950, a military assault across the 38th parallel was launched with that end in view. A seven-man United Nations commission concluding investigations in the country at the time testified—as was well known from other sources—that the attack was entirely unprovoked and unjustified. At the request of the United States the UN Security Council instantly took notice of it, insisting upon an immediate cessation of hostilities, requesting all UN members to refrain from aiding the aggressors, and, as the situation grew worse, calling upon all to assist in repelling the invasion. Fifty-three of the 60 UN members joined in condemning the North Koreans' action, and in time more than 30 pledged material assistance in stopping it.[49]

a. The UN moves to halt aggression

b. The role of the United States

The military operations that ensued proved decidedly more prolonged, difficult, and costly than originally expected. With encouragement and assistance from both the U.S.S.R. and Communist China, the invaders overran

[48] See T. W. Stanley, *N.A.T.O. in Transition: the Future of the Atlantic Alliance* (New York, 1965); H. A. Kissinger, *The Troubled Partnership: A Reappraisal of the Atlantic Alliance* (New York, 1965); and, R. E. Osgood, *N.A.T.O., The Entangling Alliance* (Chicago, 1962).

[49] For documentary sources, see two publications of the Department of State: "Korea 1945-1948" (Pub. 3305, Washington, 1949), and "United States Policy in the Korean Crisis" (Pub. 3922, Washington, 1950).

almost the whole of the South Korean territory. For a time, poorly armed Koreans and handfuls of American occupation troops brought over from Japan could fight only delaying actions, with danger of being pushed into the sea. Calls of United Nations upon its members brought wide moral support and appreciable naval and air, with some ground, assistance. The bulk of the armed forces were supplied by the United States and with UN authorization were quickly thrown into action. By late autumn, a successful conclusion of the operation seemed in sight—when suddenly the entire picture was changed by the entrance of Communist China into the conflict; for a time gravely threatening total defeat for UN forces. The UN forces finally succeeded in driving the Chinese back north of the 38th parallel and there the battle lines were stabilized. Meanwhile, too, conviction that the Korean assault marked a new stage in the East-West tension of later years, a possible beginning of attempted systematic Communist conquest of the free world, stirred the United States not only to new measures for seeing the Korean war to a successful conclusion, but, as described elsewhere, to a general and expensive program of rearmament.

As the Korean struggle settled into a stalemate approximately along the 38th parallel a growing rift between the Truman administration and General MacArthur, the Commander of UN forces in Korea, burst into the open. The issue concerned the character and scope of American policy toward Red China. The General was anxious to push forward to complete victory in Korea by bringing military pressure on the Chinese in Manchuria and China if necessary even at the risk of an all-out war with China and perhaps with its ally, Russia. The administration, under grave pressure from its Atlantic Pact allies, was unwilling to push China too far. It feared that plunging our armies into a huge effort against the unlimited Chinese manpower would open Western Europe to the Russians. On April 11, 1951, President Truman relieved MacArthur of his commands in the Far East. The General returned somewhat in the style of a conquering hero, plunging the nation and the Congress into a violent debate over the administration's Korean policy. Truman held firm in the face of the bitter controversy and the Congressional efforts of his critics ended inconclusively. Persuaded by a Russian hint and by an earnest desire to have done with the Korean "police action," the United States agreed to open armistice negotiations under the UN banner with the North Korean leaders in July of 1951. One train of patient negotiators after another debated over the table first at Kaesong and later at Panmunjom for month after weary month. By early 1952, agreement had been reached on all points save one—the repatriation of prisoners of war. There the truce talks bogged down for nearly a year. A new President, Eisenhower, in fulfillment of a campaign pledge visited Korea to try to end deadlock. In general, he supported the position of his predecessor but perhaps added a threat of extending the conflict. In April of 1953, the talks were resumed and, after a difficult period with the head of the South Korean Republic, Syngman Rhee, final agreements were concluded in

c. The armistice

July of 1953. A cease-fire accompanied by a withdrawal of the armies two kilometers from the battle-line and a voluntary repatriation of prisoners were the highlights of the settlement. A commission of neutral states was created to enforce the arrangements. A meeting of the South Koreans and their UN defenders with the North Koreans, Chinese, and Russians in Geneva in 1954 failed to find a more permanent solution and the armistice continues. Both Chinese and UN forces, however, have been withdrawn in large numbers from the wartorn peninsula.

6. Formation of Pacific alliances:

Korea turned American attention more forcefully than ever westward to the Pacific. The Communist success in China had undone years of patient efforts by the United States in behalf of this strife-ridden and war-beset country. The Chinese Communists immediately formed a close alliance with their Russian sponsors and began to push their influence in Manchuria, Korea, and later Indo-China and Tibet. The remnants of the defeated Chinese Nationalists took refuge on the island of Formosa which with American help was transformed into a bastion against the advancing Reds. The Republicans seized on the loss of China to berate the Truman administration and every single act of omission or commission was scrutinized and analyzed to show ignorance and incompetence if not willful treachery by a group which had always been "soft," as the extremists put it, toward communism. No issue in recent years has lit such an emotional bonfire or produced such hysterical oratory as this. The MacArthur dismissal was, perhaps, the high point of the controversy, but the campaign of 1952 was filled with angry words. The election of President Eisenhower did not quiet the debate, for he soon felt obliged to part company with some of the staunchest critics of the Truman policies, including Senator Knowland, floor leader of the Republican Party in the Senate. The issues in this controversy were complex but one of the major ones has been whether the gravest threat to American interests is in Europe, as the Truman administration seemed to believe, or in Asia as the Republican critics declared. In any event, no one thought Asia could be ignored or that the Communist influence could be allowed to spread throughout the peoples of this area unchallenged.

a. Japan

The first major move in the Pacific, after the fighting began in Korea, was to strengthen Japan as a friendly fortress against the Soviet-Chinese advance. A peace treaty bringing to an end the enemy status of Japan was negotiated throughout much of 1950 and 1951 by John Foster Dulles, later to become Republican Secretary of State, in collaboration with most of our allies of World War II. At a conference in San Francisco in September, 1951, the treaty was formally approved by more than 40 nations invited to participate. Russia attended the conference but refused to sign the treaty when its proposals for amendments were rejected. The treaty imposed no unusual disabilities on the Japanese except for loss of outlying possessions which had been anticipated. Sovereignty was restored to the nation but a Security Treaty signed at the same time with the United States permitted our armed forces to remain in

Japan to help maintain the peace in the Far East and the security of Japan. This right was to continue as long as necessary. Both treaties were appropriately ratified and Japan attained formal sovereignty on April 28, 1952. The next major step in the build-up of the Japanese came in 1954 when the United States concluded a mutual defense agreement with Japan providing for the progressive rearmament of Japan with American aid. The Japanese promised in return to make the full contribution permitted by their resources to the defense of the free world. Economic and military aid began thereafter to flow from the United States to Japan.

In 1960, the United States negotiated a new mutual security treaty with Japan to replace that of 1952. Under its terms, United States armed forces could continue to use Japanese facilities, but in accompanying notes, it was made clear that the Japanese would be consulted before any major shift in their deployment, or change in their equipment (nuclear weapons) or before they would be used in combat operations.[50] Although this treaty was more favorable to the Japanese than the one it replaced, its ratification was accomplished in the Japanese Diet only after a prolonged crisis including riots. So grave and menacing was the crisis that the Japanese government was forced to ask President Eisenhower to cancel his proposed visit.[51] Prime Minister Ikeda attempted by a visit to President Kennedy in 1961 to repair some of the wounded feelings in this country and although American administration in Okinawa and our resistance to Japanese efforts to establish closer relations with Red China are not widely applauded in Japan, the two countries are nevertheless still bound by close ties.

Some of the victims of Japanese attacks in World War II were not anxious to build up this aggressive nation. To alleviate this anxiety the United States concluded with Australia and New Zealand a mutual defense pact. This pact, negotiated just prior to the Japanese Peace Treaty, provides (Article IV) that "an armed attack in the Pacific area on any of the parties" would be regarded by each party as "dangerous to its own peace and safety" and each party promises to "act to meet the common danger in accordance with its constitutional processes." [52] A similar treaty was also concluded with the Philippines at the same time. South Korea demanded similar guarantees as a price for accepting the armistice and early in 1954 such a treaty was ratified by the Senate.

b. Australia, New Zealand, Philippines, and Korea

The Red drive, stopped at the 38th parallel in Korea, now shifted to French Indo-China and particularly to the state of Vietnam, and after months of hostilities between Communist-led northerners and French-supported southerners, this state, like Korea, was divided by international agreement at

c. Southeast Asia

[50] The text of the treaty and the accompanying notes may be found in the *Congressional Record,* Senate, 12513-12521, June 21, 1960.

[51] For an analysis of the affair see E. O. Reischauer, "The Broken Dialogue with Japan," *Foreign Affairs,* XXXIX, No. 1 (Oct., 1960).

[52] It should be noted that this language does not impose nearly so clear an obligation to go to war as does the Atlantic Pact.

Geneva in the summer of 1954. The American Secretary of State, Mr. Dulles, now sought to create in the whole Southern Pacific area a concert of powers and resources similar to NATO. Led by India, however, a major portion of the peoples of this area, including those of Indonesia and Burma, were determined to remain neutral in the Communist-West conflict. The best that could be achieved was a union of Pakistan and Thailand with the Philippines, Britain, France, Australia, New Zealand, and the United States. A Southeast Asia Defense Treaty was worked out by these states at Manila in September, 1954. This treaty dealt with aggression against the territory of the signatories in about the same way as had the other Pacific mutual defense treaties. It extended the area of concern, however, to include the Indo-Chinese states of Laos, Cambodia, and South Vietnam. It also attempted to deal with aggression by internal subversion. Threat of subversion from inside of any of the participating states is agreed to be a matter of concern for all and they promise in such a case to "consult together immediately" to agree on measures for common action. A Council (SEATO) and other appropriate implementing agencies are established to concert energies, resources, and policies. The United States Senate ratified the Southeast Asia Collective Defense Treaty in the spring of 1955.

Laos
Crisis
1960-61

Communist pressure in Southeast Asia, halted for a time by the Geneva settlement of 1954, resumed in mid-1960. Infiltrating Laos from Communist-held North Vietnam and supported by Russian equipment, the Reds by late 1961 controlled a substantial part of the northeastern area of the country. The SEATO states, assembled in Bangkok in March, 1961, pressed for a negotiated settlement. The United States believed that a cease-fire should precede negotiations and asserted that it would agree to a neutral and independent state. Negotiations among 14 interested states and regimes begun at Geneva in 1961 reached agreement in mid-1962 on a neutralized Laos from which all foreign troops were required to withdraw. The negotiations were aided by the creation in Laos of a coalition government in which three warring factions, including the Communists, were represented. Settlement was also influenced, perhaps, by the landing of American troops in Thailand in May, 1962, under SEATO agreements to strengthen its defenses should Laos crumble. Within a year, however, the Communists withdrew from the coalition and strife broke out anew. The situation has continued to be dangerous and confusing. The United States has actively aided the anti-Communists and the Chinese and North Vietnamese have aided the Reds.

Vietnam
Crisis
1963-

In 1963, the Reds of China and Hanoi (North Vietnam) stepped up their pressure on the weak and unstable regime of South Vietnam and through the Viet Cong (local Communist organization) gradually extended their hold on the villages and countryside. The United States gave increasingly heavy assistance, economic and military, to the recognized government in an effort to bolster its will and capacity to resist subversion. In August, 1964, our own forces struck at Hanoi by air in retaliation for torpedo-boat attacks on Ameri-

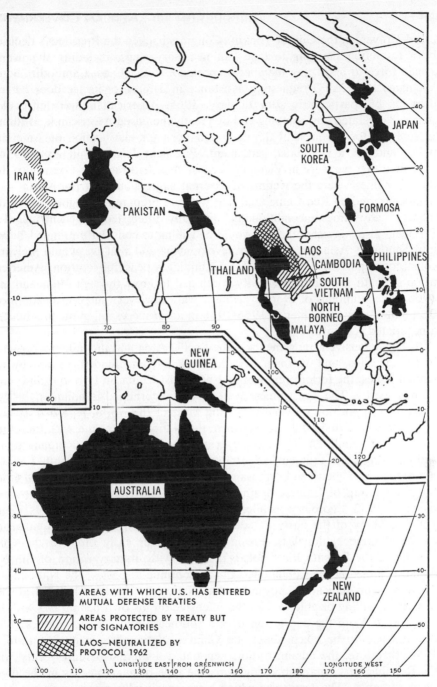

ASIATIC DEFENSIVE TREATY ARRANGEMENTS OF THE U.S.

Iraq and Iran are indirectly affiliated with the United States defensive treaty arrangements.

can destroyers in the Gulf of Tonkin: Congress backed the President's decision by a resolution pledging to take "all necessary steps, including the use of armed force to assist any member or protocol state (Laos, Cambodia, South Vietnam) of SEATO requesting assistance in defense of its freedom." From then on, but particularly after January, 1965, American military effort was sharply "escalated" by bombing and by greatly increased American land forces. In replying to a request by 17 neutral nations for clarification of American policy and for a negotiated settlement, President Johnson, in April, 1965, explained that we were in Vietnam because they had requested our help, that the Vietnamese were the victims of external aggression led from North Vietnam supported by Red China, and that we were prepared to negotiate a settlement at any time unconditionally with any interested governments. The President also suggested that we would be willing to consider putting $1 billion into Southeast Asia for economic development and that we would welcome constructive participation by the UN in finding a peaceful solution. American troop strength and military activity continued to grow through 1965 and into 1966. The bombing of North Vietnam was, however, suspended for more than a month in the winter of 1965-1966 in an unsuccessful effort to stimulate a negotiated settlement.

d. Nationalist China   The defensive arrangements in the Pacific Area and the military activities in Korea, Laos, and Vietnam left unsettled and undefended, except by the United States, the forlorn remnant of Nationalist China on Formosa and other islands nearby. The Red Chinese were clearly determined to conquer this last outpost of opposition on what they, and most of the world, regarded as Chinese territory. Britain did not recognize the Nationalist regime and, therefore, could not or would not agree to aid in its defense. During the Korean "police action," President Truman had ordered the United States Seventh Fleet to patrol the waters between Formosa and the mainland to prevent military action by either group of Chinese against the other. The Republicans in the campaign of 1952 vigorously assailed the Truman administration for its China policies. Many of the party's leaders demanded stronger measures in behalf of the Chinese Nationalists. President Eisenhower early directed the commander of the Seventh Fleet not to interfere with military action of the Nationalists aimed at the Communists but to continue to protect the Nationalists. There was no indication, however, that Nationalist leader Chiang Kai-shek was either willing or able to take the offensive on his own behalf and with his own forces. With the conclusion of the Southeast Asia Treaty some kind of decision had to be taken about the Chinese Nationalist territories. Late in 1954, therefore, the administration negotiated a mutual defense treaty with the Republic of China embodying the same type of guarantee as in the other Pacific treaties. The territories which were specifically recognized as within the scope of the commitments were the islands of Formosa and the Pescadores. Several Nationalist-held islands just off the mainland of China, including Quemoy and Matsu, were not expressly included. The United States was given the right to station its armed forces in and around the protected islands. The Chinese treaty was ratified by the Senate early in 1955.

During Senate consideration of the Chinese Treaty, the Chinese Communists began making menacing gestures toward the offshore, Nationalist-held islands of Quemoy and Matsu. They also reaffirmed in belligerent tones their intentions of conquering Formosa. This was a bold stroke aimed at the territories whose situation was not covered by American guarantees. Unwilling to announce the intention of the government in advance, certain that we could not count on our European allies, especially Britain, uncertain of the real direction of the Communist policy, and yet anxious to avoid a Korea which might be charged to him alone (the Republicans had designated Korea "Truman's War"), President Eisenhower went to Congress. He proposed a resolution by which Congress would authorize him to use armed forces in accordance with the pending treaty and to include the "protection of such related positions and territories" now in friendly hands as he felt the defense of Formosa and the Pescadores justified. Only three dissenting votes were cast in each house against the resolution. A sort of armed truce has been in effect in the Formosa Straits since these actions. The Reds in 1958 and occasionally since then have fired on the islands but, in general, the area has been relatively quiescent.

The Formosa Resolution

The Red Chinese have not confined their military and propaganda offensive entirely to efforts to dislodge Western power in South Asia. Neutralist India has also been pressured strongly. Late in 1962, the Chinese opened attacks on the northeastern frontier to force recognition of Chinese claims to disputed territory in that area. The attack pushed the Indian forces back several miles and sent thousands of refugees streaming out of the area. The United States and Britain rushed arms to the Nehru government. A peace committee organized among the neutrals sought a negotiated settlement and although no formal agreement was reached the fighting was halted. When in 1965, an effort to resolve the fate of disputed Kashmir resulted in war between India and Pakistan, the Chinese now allied to Pakistan made several more menacing gestures, including the delivery of a virtual ultimatum to India. A fragile armistice was pieced together under UN auspices later strengthened by a bilateral agreement between the belligerents engineered by the Soviet Union in Tashkent in January, 1966 and the Chinese ceased for a time their belligerent gestures.

Chinese attack on India

The critical theater of the struggle of East and West in the mid-1950's was undoubtedly the Middle East. A resurgent Arab nationalism led by Nasser, dictator of Egypt and supported, for a time at least, by the Russians aimed its gathering strength against the remnants of European colonialism. France had been pouring out treasure and troops it could ill afford to remain dominant in Algeria. The drains and stresses of this struggle brought down the Fourth Republic, introduced Charles DeGaulle as president of a reconstructed political system, and are continuing to promote division even after

The Middle East

negotiated settlement in 1962 granted Algeria independence. The Suez Canal was seized by Egypt in advance of the date that the extant agreements called for its transfer. Syria and Iraq experienced upheavals which unseated governments friendly to the Western powers, and Jordan and Lebanon were saved by American and British troops landed in 1958 to bolster tottering regimes.

American policy in this area was tentative and uncertain. We had encouraged but not joined mutual defense arrangements among Turkey, Iraq, Iran, Pakistan, and Great Britain concluded in 1955 at Baghdad. Despite our joining in the military planning of the Baghdad states in 1958, the bloc was rent by the pro-Nasser revolution in Iraq of that same year. We had turned against our European allies, France and Britain, when in 1956 they had sought by force to recapture the Suez and then had to join them in 1958 by landing troops in Lebanon while the British landed troops in Jordan.

Middle East Resolution of 1957

As in the Formosa crisis of 1955, the Eisenhower administration sought advance approval from Congress for its movement of troops into this troubled area. Early in 1957, the President appeared before Congress and asked for a resolution authorizing him to furnish military or other aid to any nation in the general area of the Middle East threatened by Communist aggression. After several weeks of debate, the Congress approved by large majorities a resolution announcing that the "United States regards as vital to the national interest and world peace the preservation of the independence and integrity of the nations of the Middle East." The President was authorized, on his own determination of necessity, to use armed force to assist any nation requesting it against armed aggression from any Communist-controlled country. However, the Congress insisted that it be allowed to terminate the commitment by concurrent (not subject to veto) resolution when it saw fit. This resolution was cited in 1958 to support moving troops temporarily into Lebanon.

Despite these actions, we have rather consistently sought to strengthen the role of the UN in mediating disputes in this area. At the time of the troop movements, the President appeared before the General Assembly and pled for a UN protective force and offered to withdraw our soldiers if such a force should be organized to stop raids from Nasser-held states into pro-Western territories.

Cuba and Latin America

The grim realities of the cold war came closer to the American continent than ever before on July 10, 1960 when Khrushchev warned the United States that if we should attempt intervention in Cuba, the Russians would use rockets if necessary to support the regime of Fidel Castro. Until that time, most of our people supposed that Red pressure was still comfortably remote in Korea, Laos, or Tibet. True, a Communist-like regime had been established briefly in Guatemala in 1954 but had rather easily been ousted without threat of American military intervention. Further signs that all was not well with our Good Neighbor Policy were available: the stoning of Vice-President Nixon's car in Caracas in 1958; the increasingly anti-American character of Castro's revolutionary government; the growing discontent with régimes like that of Trujillo in the Dominican Republic. These were noticed by the experts, however. Congress and the administration made no determined effort to reorient our policies and increase our assistance until Russia seemed ready to perch on our very doorstep. In keeping with our various Latin American professions, the immediate reaction to the Castro revolution in 1959 was friendly and only as its anti-American aims became increasingly manifest did we take alarm. The situation in 1960 deteriorated rapidly. Agreements were negotiated between Castro and the Soviets for economic aid and for trade; Czech armaments began to appear in Cuba; with Congressional authority we began to clamp down on sugar imports; we also stopped all economic aid; the Cubans nationalized large American private holdings and made menacing gestures toward our great naval base in Guantanamo Bay. Our efforts to get support from the other American republics at San José in order to resist the establishment of a Communist-dominated state in this hemisphere revealed the widespread discontent among our southern neighbors. The situation became worse in 1961 when we facilitated an invasion of Cuba by an army of Cuban refugees at the Bay of Pigs organized and equipped with our aid. The attack was a complete failure and the Castro regime became more admittedly pro-Russian than before. Not since the Civil War has the Monroe Doctrine been so firmly questioned and vigorously restated as in 1961.[53] In the late fall of 1962, we were in fact carried to the very brink of nuclear war. Aerial photography revealed the presence in Cuba of new missile bases equipped by Russia to fire nuclear rockets into the very heart of the United States. President Kennedy imposed a naval blockade of the island designed to halt all armaments shipments into it and declared these would be continued until the bases were dismantled. He further declared it to be our policy to regard any nuclear missile launched from Cuba as an attack on this hemisphere by the Soviet Union. Congress had earlier by resolution authorized the use of force, if necessary, to contain the Cuban regime or to prevent the use of Cuba as a base threatening the security of the United States. It had, also, in response to a Presidential request, authorized calling up certain portions of the Ready Reserve. In case the blockade should not be immediately effective, the President ordered preparation for invasion. Under this threat the Russians agreed to withdraw missiles and jet bombers and dismantle the bases. Russian military "aides" remain in Cuba, however, and several Senators continue to criticize the administration's acceptance of Soviet troops in the Western Hemisphere.

Anxious, some charged overanxious, to avoid another Cuban problem when revolt flared in the Dominican Republic in the Spring of 1965, President Johnson quickly rushed troops into the island avowedly to protect American lives and property and to prevent Communist take-over of the revolutionary

Dominican intervention

[53] President Kennedy in his inaugural address said: "And let every other power know that this hemisphere intends to remain the master of its own house." Mr. Khrushchev at a news conference, July 12, 1960, said: the Monroe Doctrine had "outlived its time" and "should best be buried."

forces. In doing so we reversed suddenly a policy of nonintervention to which we had adhered since the Hoover administration. American troops were soon replaced, however, by forces supplied by other Latin American nations under the direction of the Organization of American States (OAS). An uneasy truce was enforced between the warring elements and a new moderate regime established by agreement among the contending leaders.

In an effort to recoup our declining position in Latin America, a new and substantial program of economic aid was launched by the Kennedy-Johnson administrations under the title of Alliance for Progress.

ADMINISTRATION OF FOREIGN AFFAIRS:
THE DEPARTMENT OF STATE

The policies and objectives just described can be achieved only through an effective administrative organization. It is appropriate, therefore, to conclude this chapter with a description of the executive agencies which handle our foreign affairs. Many departments and agencies are concerned but none is so clearly in the center as the Department of State.

1. Beginnings

After experimenting with first a "Committee on Secret Correspondence" and afterwards a "Committee of Foreign Affairs," the Continental Congress projected, and early in 1781 the Congress of the Confederation created, a "Department of Foreign Affairs"; and in 1789 this establishment became the first of three to be taken over as a unit of the new government under the Constitution. Finding it useful to assign the department various duties having little or no connection with foreign relations, Congress within two months reorganized it as the Department of State. This more general name it has ever since retained—although "home" functions have since, in virtually every instance, been reassigned elsewhere (the last surviving important ones to the newly established General Services Administration in 1949).

2. Functions

Subject always to Presidential direction and control, the Secretary of State and his subordinates perform tasks falling into four major categories. First comes the gathering of all information necessary to enable the President primarily, but also other officials, Congress, and even to some extent press and public, to keep abreast of national policies and international situations throughout the world. Means employed to this end are many and varied, but with heaviest reliance upon our diplomats abroad and foreign diplomats stationed in Washington. Second comes service as the principal executive agency, under the President, for formulating and implementing our own foreign policies, and for handling essential matters like extradition, passports and visas, communications and records. A third is representing the United States abroad through the Foreign Service, carrying on negotiations with other governments individually, bilaterally, and in international organizations like the United Nations, negotiating treaties and trade agreements, and protecting the life, property, and asserted or established rights of American citizens beyond our borders. And fourth is the increasingly important function of interpreting American institutions, conditions, and policies to governments and peoples abroad. This function has grown tremendously in significance in the last two decades. Through a United States Information Agency (USIA), a semi-autonomous agency associated with the State Department, a steady stream of words and pictures is spread over the globe countering hostile propaganda here, demonstrating sympathy with the aspirations of other peoples there, and generally presenting America, its culture, art, and ideology, in the most favorable light possible. The State Department must stand ready at all times, in peace or war, to formulate (with the President) any policies which the protection or promotion of American rights and interests abroad requires, and to employ all of its resources in carrying them out. Foreign governments and their representatives normally communicate with our government, and in turn receive its communications, only through the Department of State.

The Department of State is not a large agency in terms of personnel but in the geographic sweep of its activities, it is the most extensive of all. It is indeed the long arm by which the government reaches out to and deals with matters large and small, in countries far and near, in every quarter of the globe. So completely and uniquely, too, is it an agency of the White House that requests made of it by Congress are regarded as made of the President himself. At the Department's helm is the Secretary of State, commonly the most conspicuous Cabinet officer and in any event endowed with a certain primacy by statutory recognition as first in line among the department heads in succession to the Presidency. His is the oldest department, with functions of a more delicate nature than those of any other; and usually he sustains more intimate relations with his chief in the White House than does any other department head. Not all Secretaries of State have been great men or able administrators, and comparatively few have, like Jefferson and Hay, brought to the office actual experience in diplomacy. The roster of incumbents since 1789 has, however, been adorned with enough honored names—Jefferson, John Marshall, Madison, John Quincy Adams, Clay, Webster, Calhoun, Seward, Blaine, Hay, Root, Hughes, Stimson, Hull, George C. Marshall—to have invested the Secretaryship, like the Presidency itself, with a lofty tradition. *3. The Secretary of State*

Many circumstances combine to render the internal organization of the Department exceptionally fluid, and a detailed description probably would not long hold true. The most recent of numerous reorganizations in late years was started in 1949 in pursuance of recommendations offered by the Hoover Commission,[54] and has since been going forward intermittently under wide discretionary authority granted the department head. Principal features of the structure in 1965 are: (1) an Undersecretary of State (ranking next to the Secretary in importance and authority); (2) an Undersecretary of State for *4. Departmental organization*

[54] *Foreign Affairs; A Report to the Congress* (Washington, 1949), 28-68. A statutory basis for the resulting reorganization was supplied by an act of Congress approved May 26, 1949.

Political Affairs; (3) deputy Undersecretaries for political affairs and for administration; (4) a Director of Intelligence and Research; (5) 11 assistant Secretaries of State heading main branches—five organized geographically (Inter-American Affairs, African Affairs, European Affairs, etc.) and six organized functionally (Congressional relations, public information, international organizations, etc.); (6) under each Assistant Secretary a number of offices either geographic or functional; and (7) under each geographical office a number of "country desks," one for each main nation. The department also includes the separately organized Agency for International Development and the Peace Corps alluded to earlier in the chapter.[55]

5. The Foreign Service: a. Status

Department machinery thus far outlined is localized in the national capital. Operations are carried on, however, over the entire world; and the agency through which this distant work is performed is the Foreign Service. Traditionally, and as regulated under a comprehensive Foreign Service Act of 1946, the service—while auxiliary to the department—was largely autonomous under its own director general, advised by a board representing four of the executive departments. As the Hoover Commission observed, however, relations between the service and the department suffered seriously from jealousies inspired by salary differentials, social distinctions, and other inequalities. Following the Commission's recommendation, the Congressional Act of 1949 providing for State Department reorganization made the service an integral part of the department, administered by the Deputy Under Secretary for Administration under direct responsibility to the Secretary of State, and with the former Director General now merely a staff member and adviser. In earlier times, too, the service, instead of being a single establishment as it now is, was really two: diplomatic and consular. Each had not only its own functions but its own personnel, its own salary scales, and transfers between the two were rare. For many years the feeling grew that the wall separating the two ought to be broken down, and after numerous proposals had fallen by the wayside, the Rogers Act of 1924 accomplished the desired reform. Diplomatic and consular services

[55] The best account of the history and earlier organization of the Department is G. Hunt, *The Department of State of the United States* (New Haven, 1914). On the Department in more recent times, see L. H. Chamberlain and R. C. Snyder, *American Foreign Policy* (New York, 1947), Chap. VII, the work of G. H. Stuart cited at the end of this chapter and D. K. Price (ed.), *The Secretary of State* (Englewood Cliffs, N.J., 1960). The management of foreign relations by Secretaries of State down to and including Charles E. Hughes is dealt with by various writers in S. F. Bemis (ed.), *The American Secretaries of State and Their Diplomacy,* 10 vols. (New York, 1927-1929); and by those from Hay to Dulles by various writers in N. A. Graebner (ed.), *An Uncertain Tradition: American Secretaries of State in the Twentieth Century* (New York, 1961).

The Department carries on an extensive program of publication. First of all, there is a weekly *Department of State Bulletin,* containing press releases, articles of current interest, texts of documents, and much miscellaneous material. There are serial publications embracing large numbers of bulletins, articles, addresses, and reports. Numerous volumes in the series *Foreign Relations of the United States* present selected official papers covering the period from 1861 to the point reached at any given time in the compilation. In addition, there are special collections, notably on World War I and II, the Paris Peace Conference, Russian relations, and Japan. Full lists are obtainable from the Department.

were consolidated in a common field force known as the Foreign Service of the United States. The diplomatic and consular branches of this Service were put on an interchangeable basis, so that transfers might be made from one to the other; and provision was made for assignment of recruits to either branch of the service in which they happened at the time to be needed.

Ambassadors, ministers, and foreign service officers are appointed by the President with the consent of the Senate; other employees and consular agents by the Secretary of State; and alien clerks and employees are chosen in the field subject to the Secretary's approval. Like other government establishments, the diplomatic and consular services of earlier days suffered from the spoils system. Men of ability and experience sometimes were carefully selected for given positions, especially more responsible ones, but by and large appointments were likely to reflect mere personal or political favoritism. In 1895, President Cleveland introduced the rudiments of a merit system in the consular service, and in 1906 President Theodore Roosevelt instituted a plan of competitive examinations and efficiency ratings for the appointment and promotion of consuls of all grades, including consuls general. In 1909, President Taft started a scheme of competitive examinations in the lower grades of the diplomatic service, with provisions for efficiency records as a basis for promotion. Later legislation carried the reforms farther and now many foreign service staff officers are included among those admitted by examination and protected in tenure.

b. Examinations and appointments

A very important place in the system is occupied by the foreign service officer; and a word may be added concerning the manner of his selection. To begin with, the examinations which he must take are of such a nature that only well-trained college graduates, or persons of equivalent attainments, can hope to pass them. As a rule, the written tests, covering four general and three special fields, and conducted by the Civil Service Commission for the Foreign Service's board of examiners, are held throughout the country, are taken by several hundred young men and women, and are successfully passed by several score. Among the successful at this stage half may be eliminated by the rigorous orals held later in Washington and stressing character, personality, experience, and proficiency in modern languages as well as loyalty. Candidates must be between the ages of 21 and 30, citizens of the United States, and previously designated by the board of examiners for a particular examination. Women are eligible, and since 1922 a few not only have met the tests imposed but later have received appointment. All successful candidates are recommended by the examiners for appointment to the lowest class in the foreign-service-officer bracket. The usual routine is for an appointee to be given a preliminary or preparatory term of a few months as salaried vice-consul at some nearby post (e.g., Mexico City or Ottawa), then to receive some months of intensive instruction in a Foreign Service Institute operated in the State Department at Washington, and only afterwards to be given regular assignment as a fully ordained foreign service officer.

c. Foreign service officers

As throughout the past, ambassadors and ministers are appointed by the President with the consent of the Senate on grounds in which political and personal considerations, for example, reward for party service and for contributing generously to campaign funds, may weigh heavily. Tenure, too, is uncertain, and sometimes brief, especially if the party to which the incumbent belongs soon goes out of power. To be sure, the Rogers Act and the more recent Foreign Service Act of 1946 have as one of their objectives the encouragement of young men of ambition and talent to make the foreign service a career; to that end, both statutes require the Secretary of State to give the President from time to time the names of members of the service who have demonstrated their fitness for promotion to the grade of ministers. In recent years a gratifying number of such promotions have been made. Until of late, an obstacle of considerable seriousness arose from restrictions on salaries that placed numerous posts beyond the reach of persons not of independent means. Several increases in pay and perquisites have improved the situation but not entirely removed the problem.

Conduct of the modern foreign relations of the United States has long since spilled out far beyond the organizational arrangements, traditions, and practices of the Department of State. The brief review earlier in this chapter of the modern policies and aims of the United States in international relations indicates that we are conducting affairs abroad with our money, our goods, our soldiers, our engineers, our technicians, and our publicists as well as with our diplomats. The Defense Department is as concerned with our international commitments as the State Department. The Central Intelligence Agency under the National Security Council is deeply involved in gathering data and in attempting to influence the course of affairs throughout the world. The Treasury is involved in a vast array of international fiscal agencies and agreements. Commerce and Agriculture seek markets abroad, give technical counsel to friendly foreign states, and in many other ways implement our determined effort to build a strong free world. The Justice Department controls immigration. Various independent establishments have administered part or all of our postwar programs of economic, technical, and military assistance to Europe and Asia. The Hoover Commission in 1949 found no less than 46 executive agencies to be more or less concerned with foreign affairs. All of this development has raised grave problems of coordination, of multiple and thus confusing representations to foreign powers, of adjusting our policies to our military capabilities or vice versa, and of making the authority and responsibility of the President effective. Several new coordinating devices have been attempted in recent years—interdepartmental committees of many varieties, advisory councils, added staff assistance for the President. The most important of the new devices is surely the National Security Council created by the National Security Act of 1949 in the Office of the President to integrate diplomatic and military strategy. This agency is essentially a Cabinet committee to advise the President, aided by a small staff, and its operation will be described in the next chapter. None of the devices has been completely satisfactory and the search for improvement still continues. In general, the present policy seems to be to enlarge the State Department by bringing into it or associating with it other major agencies concerned with foreign affairs.[56]

References

1. FORMULATION AND DIRECTION

E. Plischke, *Conduct of American Diplomacy* (Princeton, N.J., 1961).

J. L. McCamy, *The Administration of American Foreign Affairs* (New York, 1950).

G. H. Stuart, *American Diplomatic and Consular Practice* (New York, 1936).

———, *The Department of State: A History of its Organization, Procedure, and Personnel* (New York, 1949).

D. S. Cheever and H. F. Haviland, Jr., *American Foreign Policy and the Separation of Powers* (Cambridge, Mass., 1952).

J. R. Childs, *American Foreign Service* (New York, 1948).

S. D. Kertesz and M. A. Fitzsimmons (eds.), *Diplomacy in a Changing World* (South Bend, Ind., 1960).

E. R. Elder, *The Policy Machine: the Department of State and American Foreign Policy* (Syracuse, N.Y., 1960).

Don K. Price (ed.), *The Secretary of State* (Englewood Cliffs, N.J., 1960).

B. C. Cohen, *The Political Process and Foreign Policy: the Making of the Japanese Peace Settlement* (Princeton, N.J., 1957).

———, *The Press and Foreign Policy* (Princeton, N.J., 1963).

W. F. Ilchman, *Professional Diplomacy in the United States, 1779-1939* (Chicago, 1961).

56 This whole subject is ably treated in J. L. McCamy, *The Administration of American Foreign Affairs* (New York, 1950). He suggests that coordination can only occur at the level of the President and, therefore, the President's staff should be enlarged to provide for it. A. W. MacMahon, *Administration in Foreign Affairs* (Tuscaloosa, Ala., 1953), recommends a greatly enlarged and reorganized State Department entitled Department of Foreign Affairs, and given major responsibility over all aspects of foreign relations. J. J. McCloy, *The Challenge to American Foreign Policy* (Cambridge, Mass., 1953), is sharply critical of the State Department and believes that new civilian leadership of the military agencies must be given a more important role in foreign policy. The Brookings Institution, *Administration of Foreign Affairs and Overseas Operations* (Washington, 1951) deals also with these problems in a report prepared for the Bureau of the Budget, and in a later report prepared in 1960 for the Senate Foreign Relations Committee as do the paper prepared for the Jackson subcommittee of the Senate Committee on Government Operations—Sen. H. M. Jackson (ed.), *The Secretary of State and the Ambassador* (New York, 1964).

W. P. Dizard, *The Strategy of Truth: the Story of the U. S. Information Service* (Washington, 1961).

K. London, *How Foreign Policy Is Made* (New York, 1949).

R. A. Dahl, *Congress and Foreign Policy* (New York, 1950).

L. Markel et al., *Public Opinion and Foreign Policy* (New York, 1949).

G. A. Almond, *The American People and Foreign Policy* (New York, 1950).

J. A. Robinson, *Congress and Foreign Policy* (Homewood, Illinois, 1960).

E. W. Spaulding, *Ambassadors Ordinary and Extraordinary* (Washington, 1961).

A. De Conde, *The American Secretary of State* (New York, 1962).

2. AMERICAN FOREIGN POLICY—GENERAL

G. Kennan, *American Diplomacy, 1900-1950* (Chicago, 1950).

———, *Realities of American Foreign Policy* (Princeton, N.J., 1954).

B. H. Williams, *American Diplomacy; Policies and Practice* (New York, 1936), Chaps. XXI-XXIV. Also Chaps. I-XX for an excellent analysis of American Foreign policies to 1935.

L. H. Chamberlain and R. C. Snyder, *American Foreign Policy* (New York, 1947).

R. J. Bartlett (ed.), *The Record of American Diplomacy: Documents and Readings in the History of American Foreign Relations* (New York, 1947).

W. Lippmann, *United States Foreign Policy: Shield of the Republic* (New York, 1943).

W. Johnson, *The Battle Against Isolation* (Chicago, 1944).

L. Pasvolsky et al., *Major Problems of United States Foreign Policy* (new ed., Washington, 1950).

H. Agar, *The Price of Power* (Chicago, 1957).

J. Grange, *American Foreign Relations: Permanent Problems and Changing Policies* (New York, 1959).

N. M. Blake and O. T. Barck, Jr., *The United States in Its World Relations* (New York, 1958).

H. J. Morgenthau, *The Purpose of American Politics* (New York, 1960).

W. W. Rostow, *The United States in the World Arena* (New York, 1960).

W. A. Williams, *The Tragedy of American Diplomacy* (New York, 1959).

L. J. Halle, *Dream and Reality; Aspects of American Foreign Policy* (New York, 1959).

A. A. Berle, Jr., *Tides of Crisis* (New York, 1957).

C. O. Lerche, Jr., *The Foreign Policy of the American People* (Englewood Cliffs, N.J., 1958).

K. W. Thompson, *Political Realism and the Crisis of World Politics: An American Approach to Foreign Policy* (Princeton, N.J., 1960).

V. M. Dean, *Foreign Policy Without Fear* (New York, 1953).

M. W. Graham, *American Diplomacy in the International Community* (Baltimore, 1948).

D. Perkins, *The Evolution of American Foreign Policy* (New York, 1948).

J. W. Pratt, *A History of United States Foreign Policy* (New York, 1955).

Q. Wright (ed.), *A Foreign Policy for the United States* (Chicago, 1957).

E. A. Mowrer, *The Nightmare of American Foreign Policy* (New York, 1948).

S. F. Bemis, *The United States as a World Power* (New York, 1950).

W. G. Carleton, *The Revolution in American Foreign Policy* (New York, 1963).

J. W. Fulbright, *Old Myths and New Realities* (New York, 1964).

R. E. Osgood, *Ideals and Self-Interest in America's Foreign Relations: the Great Transformation of the Twentieth Century* (Chicago, 1964).

C. V. Crabb, Jr., *American Foreign Policy in the Nuclear Age* (New York, 1965).

J. D. Spanier, *American Foreign Policy Since World War II* (New York, 1962).

3. PARTICULAR POLICIES AND PROCEDURES

a. *The United Nations*

L. M. Goodrich and E. Hambro, *The Charter of the United Nations; Commentary and Documents* (Boston, 1946).

N. Bentwich and A. Martin, *A Commentary on the Charter of the United Nations* (New York, 1950).

H. V. Evatt, *The United Nations* (New York, 1948).

E. P. Chase, *The United Nations in Action* (New York, 1950).

L. P. Bloomfield, *The U.N. and U.S. Foreign Policy* (Boston, 1960).

C. M. Eichelberger, *U.N.: the First Fifteen Years* (New York, 1960).

H. F. Armstrong, "U.N. on Trial," *Foreign Affairs*, XXXIX, No. 3 (April, 1961).

R. E. Asher, W. M. Kotsching *et al.*, *The United Nations and Promotion of the General Welfare* (Washington, 1957).

W. H. C. Laves and C. A. Thomson, *UNESCO: Purpose, Progress, Prospects* (Bloomington, Ind., 1957).

F. O. Wilcox and C. M. Marcy, *Proposals for Changes in the United Nations* (Washington, 1955).

A. N. Holcombe, *Organizing Peace in the Nuclear Age* (New York, 1959).

Commission to Study the Organization of Peace, *Strengthening the United Nations* (New York, 1957).

R. W. Gardner, *In Pursuit of World Order* (New York, 1965).

E. A. Gross, *The United Nations: Studies for Peace* (New York, 1962).

F. O. Wilcox and H. F. Haviland (ed.), *The United States and the United Nations* (Baltimore, 1961).

B. V. Cohen, *The United Nations: Constitutional Developments Growth and Possibilities* (Cambridge, Mass., 1961).

b. Foreign Aid

F. M. Coffin, *Witness for Aid* (Boston, 1964).

J. A. Rubin, *Your Hundred Billion Dollars: the Complete Story of American Foreign Aid* (Philadelphia, 1965).

E. S. Mason, *Foreign Aid and Foreign Policy* (New York, 1965).

Barhard W. Jackson, "Foreign Aid: Strategy or Stopgap?" *Foreign Affairs,* Vol. 41, No. 1, Oct. 1962.

H. Feis, *Foreign Aid and Foreign Policy* (New York, 1964).

J. D. Montgomery, *The Politics of Foreign Aid; American Experience in Southeast Asia* (New York, 1962).

c. Europe

J. A. Krout (ed.), "The United States and the Atlantic Community," *Proceedings of Acad. of Polit. Sci.,* XXIII (New York, 1949).

H. L. Hoskins, *The Atlantic Pact* (Washington, 1949).

G. F. Kennan, *Russia, the Atom and the West* (New York, 1958).

D. Acheson, *Power and Diplomacy* (Cambridge, Mass., 1958).

H. A. Kissinger, *The Necessity for Choice: Prospects of American Foreign Policy* (New York, 1961).

————, *The Troubled Partnership: A Reappraisal of the Atlantic Alliance* (New York, 1965).

A. Wolfers (ed.), *Alliance Policy in the Cold War* (Baltimore, 1960).

H. L. Roberts, *Russia and America: Dangers and Prospects* (New York, 1956).

R. Steel, *The End of Alliance: America and the Future of Europe* (London, 1964).

A. J. Cottrell and J. E. Dougherty, *The Atlantic Alliance* (London, 1964).

R. Kleiman, *Atlantic Crisis: American Diplomacy Confronts a Resurgent Europe* (London, 1965).

R. Osgood, *NATO: the Entangling Alliance* (Chicago, 1962).

d. Asia

H. Feis, *The China Tangle* (New York, 1954).

K. S. Latourette, *The American Record in the Far East, 1945-1951* (New York, 1952).

E. O. Reischauer, *Wanted: An Asian Policy* (New York, 1955).

W. W. Rostow and R. W. Hatch, *An American Policy in Asia* (New York, 1955).

D. E. Kenedy, *The Security of Southern Asia* (London, 1965).

R. G. Boyd, *Communist China's Foreign Policy* (New York, 1962).

R. E. Mosely, "The Chinese-Soviet Rift; Origins and Portents," *Foreign Affairs,* Vol. 42, No. 1, Oct., 1963.

B. B. Fall, *The Two Vietnams* (London, 1964).

M. W. Brown, *The New Face of War* (New York, 1965).

A. J. Donimeu, *Conflict in Laos* (London, 1965).

G. F. Kennan, "Japanese Security and American Policy," *Foreign Affairs,* Vol. 43, No. 1, 1964.

e. Other areas

D. M. Dozer, *Are We Good Neighbors?: Three Decades of Inter-American Relations, 1930-1960* (Gainesville, Fla., 1960).

G. Lenczowski, *The Middle East in World Affairs* (Ithaca, N.Y., 1952).

American Assembly, *The United States and Latin America* (New York, 1959).

T. Draper, *Castroism: Theory and Practice* (New York, 1965).

C. G. Fenwick, *The Organization of American States* (Washington, 1963).

D. L. Larson (ed.), *The Cuban Crisis of 1962: Selected Documents and Chronology* (New York, 1963).

★ 24 ★

Defending the Nation
Against Attack

Once a casual. interest EARLY RESOLUTION to keep out of Europe's wars did not save us as a nation from a threatened conflict with France in 1800 or an actual one with Great Britain in 1812. Nevertheless, by acquiring Louisiana and Florida we soon eliminated France and Spain as potential trouble-makers on our borders. After the final defeat of Napoleon, affairs abroad took a more peaceful turn; and for over 100 years we enjoyed a comfortable sense of national isolation and security. Wars with Mexico and Spain carried no serious threat; and although in 1917 we were drawn into the greatest armed conflict that the world to that time had known, we came off still effectively sheltered, as we thought, by our geographical location. In days which older persons can well remember, our Army numbered only 150,000, our Navy was better developed but not top-flight, and the national temper so averse to militarism that impressive defenses hardly could be maintained at all.

Now a paramount concern Then dawned a period of great change. International turmoil gripped the world; technological developments robbed us of the protection of broad oceans; mechanized global war advanced in our direction and finally in 1941 overtook us; by rapid stages, defense, long a matter of only sporadic interest, became our paramount national concern—and defense no longer confined to prudent preparedness, but actualized in deadly combat on land and sea and in the air in every quarter of the globe. And this time there was no lapsing back into an easy feeling of security after the fighting was over, even though new international machinery was set up to prevent such things happening again. Before long, in fact, an ominous "cold" war set in with the world's other principal power, the U.S.S.R. The new "absolute weapon" of nuclear fission and the new and spectacular thrust of rockets and missiles might presently be turned against us. In wars of the future, distance would mean little or nothing. In short, in spite of the great victory of 1945, the country had never been in so exposed a position, or so much in need of measures for protecting itself. In this situation, defense remained a paramount concern. When, in 1950, a Communist assault upon the Korean Republic brought upon us undeclared but difficult and costly war, we soon found ourselves back in the atmosphere

662

of 1940-1941—tripling military appropriations, increasing taxes, conscripting troops, imposing economic controls, and otherwise girding for an all-out international conflict which only extreme good fortune could avert. Even after a truce was patched up in Korea, the government continued to devote $35-$50 billion yearly to national security, the draft of young men for military service continued, and three million men stood under arms. Then with the Russian launching of the first space satellite in October, 1957, we learned how well equipped our rivals were and the dangers became even more acute. These alarms were followed by the Soviet effort to plant missiles in Cuba and by heavy commitment of our men and arms to bolster Vietnam. All indications are that for a good while to come, defense, under a war or semiwar economy, linked to diplomacy, will be paramount among our national interests.

SOME CONSTITUTIONAL PRINCIPLES

During the Revolution and the ensuing Confederation period, lack of power of Congress to mobilize the fighting strength and material resources of the country with full effectiveness, and to deal promptly and decisively with domestic disorders, gravely imperiled the beginnings of the nation. The experience put the makers of the Constitution in a frame of mind to apply strong remedies. Into the new fundamental law they therefore wrote upwards of a dozen provisions which, taken together, provided every power at that time deemed necessary for defending the country, whether against Indian depredations, domestic uprising, or foreign attack. Three principles of the resulting defense system require mention at the outset.

To start with, full responsibility for defense was placed where it remains today, in the national government. The states may and do maintain militia for use in enforcing their own proper authority. But unless Congress gives permission, they may not "keep troops or ships of war in time of peace . . . or engage in war unless actually invaded or in such imminent danger as will not admit of delay." Even the state militia may be called into the service of the United States, thereupon passing under supreme command of the President; and, as explained presently, the military establishments of the states have in later times, as the National Guard, become an integral part of the war machine of the nation. In time of defense emergency, and especially of war, states, counties, cities and other jurisdictions collaborate with the national government in a multitude of ways. Their efforts, however, are merely phases of an overall national effort; and full responsibility for that effort rests with the government at Washington. *1. Defense a national responsibility*

A second principle is equally fundamental. While solicitous about providing for defense, the framers of the Constitution had no desire to open a way for an overweening military establishment, or for the rise of military dictatorship. True, they did not expressly enjoin in the document—as is done in all of the state constitutions except that of New York—that the military *2. Civil authority supreme over military* establishment should in all matters be subject to civil control. But they achieved the same end by so defining the defense and war powers of Congress and the President (civil branches of the government) as to set up safeguards against military domination. Congress alone can raise and support armies, make rules for governing them, and declare war; the President is commander-in-chief of all armed forces, whether in peace or in war. The principle has been buttressed by custom and by statutory elaboration. The Secretary of Defense must by law be a civilian; [1] and firmly established practice makes the same requirement of the heads of the now subordinate Army, Navy, and Air Force Departments.[2]

3. Constitutional limitations fully applicable

Finally, defense, like every other national function, must be kept within bounds constitutionally determined. Powers granted the President and Congress are broad and under stress of war tend to be stretched to their limits, if not sometimes a bit beyond. Moreover, Presidents Lincoln and Franklin D. Roosevelt plainly viewed the war power as something over and above any particular power conferred, or in fact all such powers combined. Despite occasional appearances to the contrary, however, the Constitution is not suspended in wartime. The President, as commander-in-chief, is no more entitled to disregard its restrictions then than in days of peace.

DEFENSE POWERS AND FUNCTIONS OF CONGRESS

1. Providing for the armed services

To begin with, Congress has sole power to "raise and support armies" and to "provide and maintain a navy." These things it does by specifying the number and kinds of troops to be enlisted, prescribing the method of recruitment, fixing scales of pay, authorizing the building and manning of war craft, providing for auxiliary equipment such as forts, arsenals, and dockyards, and of course by raising and appropriating money for the maintenance of military, naval, and air establishments, subject to the constitutional restriction that no appropriation for raising and supporting armies may be made for a longer period than two years. There is no lack of power to take any steps considered necessary (including conscription) to safeguard the nation in time of peace

[1] The National Security Act of 1947 expressly prohibits the appointment as Secretary of Defense of any commissioned officer who has been in active military service within 10 years. When, however, in September, 1950, President Truman dismissed Louis A. Johnson from the post and wished to appoint General George C. Marshall—a professional soldier, chief-of-staff of the Army during World War II, and currently a general of the Army—Congress cleared the way by amending legislation sanctioning the appointment but definitely waiving the general rule for the one occasion only.

[2] Under Secretaries and Assistant Secretaries in the department also invariably are civilians. The President may have had military experience; several incumbents, indeed (e.g., Washington, Jackson, Taylor, Grant, and Eisenhower), had previously attained the rank of general. When President, however, all have been civilians. When refusing, in January, 1948, to sanction use of his name as a candidate for the Presidency, General Dwight D. Eisenhower gave notable expression to the principle of civilian supremacy which ought to govern in a democracy. See *The New York Times,* Jan. 24, 1948. Cf. L. Smith, *American Democracy and Military Power* (Chicago, 1951).

and to insure vigorous and effective prosecution of hostilities in time of war.

In the second place, Congress has unrestricted authority to make "rules for the government and regulation of the land and naval forces," and also "rules concerning captures on land and water." Resulting Articles of War for the Army and Articles for the Government of the Navy long were separate and subject to criticism not only for their lack of uniformity but for harsh features of the system of military justice for which they provided. Experience during World War II led to a general revision by a special committee of experts. In 1949, Congress enacted a new consolidated code, uniform for all of the armed services, and entitled Military Laws of the United States.

2. Enacting military and naval regulations

Congress may provide for as large a standing army as it sees fit. Nothing is more certain than that the world situation will in future require a considerably larger one than in the past. Our earlier traditions, however, in common with those of English-speaking peoples everywhere, were opposed to any formidable army in time of peace, inclining rather, as a safeguard of freedom, to a volunteer citizen militia in each state with only such modest training and equipment as would enable it to cope with domestic disorder and to meet other relatively minor needs. All states have such militia, even though nowadays linked up, in a manner that would have shocked our ancestors, with the national defense establishment and bearing the significant name of National Guard.[3] State contingents of the National Guard still are primarily state instrumentalities, with (so long as not drawn into national service) appointment of their officers and provision for their training expressly reserved to state authorities. Congress nevertheless is authorized to "provide for arming and disciplining the militia," to provide for calling into national service any and all portions of it required for executing the national laws, for suppressing insurrections, or for repelling invasions, and to make rules for governing such forces when "employed in the service of the United States." In pursuance of these broad powers, Congress in an Army Organization Act of 1920, gave the President permanent authority to make use of the National Guard for emergency purposes, and has enacted numerous regulations aimed at increasing the establishment's effectiveness and coordinating its organization, training, and equipment with that of the Regular Army—in addition, of course, to contributing heavily to its financial support. When, as a phase of the national defense program launched in 1940, the entire National Guard was drawn into national service and placed in cantonments for training, Congress specified that it might be used only in the Western Hemisphere and in United States territories and possessions, including the Philippines. After war came, however, the restriction was removed, and Guard units, or at any rate the men who

3. Regulating the National Guard

[3] Speaking strictly, the militia includes, under terms of a statute of 1898, all able-bodied male citizens (and aliens who have declared their intention to be naturalized) between the ages of 18 and 45; and all such are "liable to perform military duty in the service of the United States." In ordinary usage, however, the term denotes only the armed establishments maintained by the states, i.e., the organized and trained portion of the militia embraced in the National Guard.

had composed them, were sent to all overseas theaters of operation. National Guard units again were called into national overseas service in 1950 in connection with our military operations in Korea, in 1961 in connection with the Berlin crisis, and such use was foreshadowed by Congressional resolution in the Cuba crisis of 1962.

4. Declaring war

Constitutionally, Congress alone can declare war. Hostilities may, of course, begin without a formal declaration, as in the instance of the Spanish-American War of 1898. Indeed, as illustrated by the war with Japan, Germany, and Italy starting in December, 1941, they may be forced upon us, and with an element of surprise, by aggressive action of a foreign power, leaving us no alternative. Even in such situations a declaration will promptly be adopted by the two houses, as a means (if for no other purpose) of fixing, for the benefit of neutrals, an exact date from which the rights and liabilities incident to war are to be reckoned. The usual method is a joint resolution, requested and afterwards signed by the President. Many times it has been proposed by people anxious to keep the United States out of war that, except when the nation is directly attacked, the question of going to war shall in all cases be put to a country-wide popular vote. Unless the Constitution were amended, however, the decision must finally rest with Congress; and it is not clear that anything would be gained from the suggested procedure. With events moving as rapidly as they usually do, a plebiscite might not be practical; and momentary passions might make it even dangerous. The discretion of Congress in declaring war often is more theoretical than actual, not only because war may be forced upon us in spite of anything we can do, but also because the President, in conducting foreign relations, may bring the country to a point where no honorable alternative to war remains. Indeed, he may independently take steps leading to actual combat, as when President Roosevelt in 1940-1941 (before Pearl Harbor) supplied naval escorts for merchant ships carrying lend-lease materials to Great Britain and other countries, resulting in armed clashes between American destroyers and German submarines. On the other hand, if Congress can declare war, it also can take measures designed to avert it, a good illustration being the Neutrality Act of 1935 (later renewed and expanded) making it unlawful, with war in progress between two or more foreign states, to ship arms and munitions to the belligerents, as entailing risk of the United States being drawn into the hostilities.[4]

New aspects from international commitments

From 1950 to 1953, the United States was engaged in an armed conflict in Korea of sufficient proportions to disturb the entire national economy, yet

[4] Congressional power to declare war is matched by power to terminate it. At the close of World War I, there was discussion of whether the President may take such action independently by proclamation; but eventually (in July, 1921) the usual method was invoked, i.e., a joint resolution of Senate and House, duly signed by the chief executive. In the case of World War II, "hostilities" were officially ended for the United States by Presidential proclamation of December 31, 1946. Treaties subsequently concluded, especially with Japan and West Germany, brought the struggle to an end technically.

with no war "declared" by Congress. We came into the operation entirely through (1) the President bringing the Communist invasion of South Korea officially to the attention of the UN Security Council, (2) the latter calling upon all UN members to assist in repelling the invaders, and (3) decision by our own executive branch to comply by military means on any necessary scale.[5] Article 43 of the UN Charter, requiring UN members to place armed forces at the organization's disposal for maintaining peace, already had created the possibility that if such forces actually were raised and used, the United States might some day find itself in a war not declared by Congress. The Korean eruption produced precisely such a situation. To be sure, no UN forces had as yet been organized. But to stop a Communist aggression, the UN Security Council asked member-states to join in military resistance. Recognizing both our interest and our moral, if not strictly legal, obligation, the President (as agent for implementing our UN relations) put us instantly into action. In doing so he consulted with Congressional leaders but never formally asked the approval of Congress. This procedure allowed Republican statesmen, notably Senator Taft, to charge executive usurpation and to refer to Korea as "Truman's War." As long, moreover, as UN serves the purpose for which it was created, the experience is not unlikely to be repeated. To this extent, the control of Congress over war by "declaring" it has been greatly reduced. In general, however, Congressmen are jealous of their constitutional prerogatives in the matter and, as we noted in the last chapter, all of the great regional defense pacts to which the United States is a party, while requiring signatories, in case of attack upon any of their number, to consult and to take individual or collective action, have been so drawn as to leave the United States (and every other signatory) free to follow the constitutional procedure.

There was a time when, except in case of invasion, war was of no great concern to the general mass of the people. Armies were volunteer, taxes indirect, supplies bought in the open market, sacrifice and morale demanded chiefly of the forces in the field. The vast scale on which the mechanized wars of today are waged, however, makes them of hardly less civilian than military concern. When war comes or is imminently threatened, it is, as President Wilson remarked in 1917, "not an army that we must shape and train; it is a nation." Experience gained during both world wars revealed in startling manner the lengths to which Congress may go in reorganizing and regimenting the national life for purposes of successful prosecution of, or even simply preparation for, war under twentieth-century conditions. As commander-in-chief of the armed forces, the President independently possesses war powers of impressive magnitude. To Congress, however, it falls, not only to provide the necessary men and money—by conscription acts, revenue acts, and appropriation acts—but to endow the chief executive with all the broad authority required for mobilizing industry, commerce, transportation, and even science

5. Mobilizing the nation for war effort

[5] *United States Policy in the Korean Crisis,* Dept. of State Pub. No. 3922 (Washington, 1950).

and education. The method commonly is that of legislation delegating specified powers for the duration of the war (or other designated period), either with or without creation by Congress of new machinery for exercising them. In each field covered, the resulting system of controls is organized and administered by the executive branch. The underlying authority comes from Congress. While the courts often have looked with disfavor upon delegations of power by one branch of the government to another, developments during the two world wars indicate that under wartime stress and excitement Congress can go almost as far as it likes with such grants. Sometimes grants are made with little hesitation; at other times, only over strong opposition and at urgent Presidential request. Occasionally, indeed—as, for example, when in 1944 President Roosevelt asked for power to conscript labor—they are refused.

6. Regulating wartime civil liberties

Except for the provision for suspension of the writ of habeas corpus, the Constitution recognizes no distinction between civil rights in peacetime and in wartime. War, however, brings not only an intensity of military activity but a tenseness of the public mind, stimulating restrictions that would not be undertaken or tolerated in time of peace. And such restrictions, as we observed in an earlier chapter, may be imposed by the President (commonly through the Department of Justice), either under his powers as commander-in-chief or in pursuance of authority delegated to him by Congress. Congress itself may impose them directly by legislative act—going, indeed, to undefined lengths in restraining speech, press, assembly, and other normal rights.

7. Caring for veterans

Inheriting the practice from English and colonial usage, Congress not only has provided regular pay for soldiers and sailors, but has bestowed land, money pensions, civil service preferences, or other special benefits upon the demobilized forces after every war in which the United States has engaged from the Revolution onwards. The particularly hazardous nature of the service rendered the country by those who bear arms in its defense has always been given recognition. Persons actually incapacitated, together with their dependents, have usually been conceded to have an indisputable claim to the nation's care. However, powerful political pressure brought to bear upon Congressmen by veterans' organizations often has led to grants where the obligation was considerably less clear. So generous, indeed, has been Congress where veterans are concerned that between 1792 and 1930 national outlays on money pensions alone, regardless of land allotments in earlier days and of later heavy costs of hospitalization and medical treatment, reached a total of $15 billion. Today (1965), as part of the aftercost of World War II, Korea, and Vietnam, the annual expenditure for veterans exceeds $5 billion. Benefits bestowed on veterans of the recent wars in addition to the operation of regular pension, rehabilitation, and hospitalization systems, have included government aid in carrying protection originating in in-service war-risk insurance; opportunity to acquire on favorable terms surplus war property disposed of by the government; increased preferential eligibility for employment in the civil service; continued monthly payments for a period after honorable discharge; terminal leave pay for all wartime furlough periods not actually used; generous support for high school, collegiate, and professional education; and assistance in acquiring a home, business, or farm. The entire national program of veterans benefits is now administered by one of the largest independent establishments in the Executive branch, the Veterans Administration.

DEFENSE POWERS AND FUNCTIONS OF THE PRESIDENT

The President as the central figure

The authority of Congress manifestly underlies our entire system of national defense. Without it there would be no army or navy, no money, and only imperfect means of mobilizing the nation for a defense or war effort. The central figure in defense, and especially in the conduct of war, is nevertheless the President. During its three great wars of the last hundred years, the nation had in the White House chief executives—Lincoln, Wilson, and Franklin D. Roosevelt—who would have loomed large in history in any event. All gained stature, however, from guiding the country's destinies amid a supreme war effort. Each of these men also added something to the concept of the office of the Presidency, partly in each case as an outgrowth of ideas of the defense powers.

Sources of his defense powers

Whether in peace or in war, every President, however, has significant defense powers and functions, accruing from (1) his constitutional status as chief executive, (2) his constitutional role as commander-in-chief, and (3) grants, or delegations, by Congress. In all that he does, even under stress of war, a President is presumed to keep within limits of authority coming to him from one or more of these sources. But he does not always have to be prepared to justify an action by citing any particular one of them. President Franklin D. Roosevelt rarely considered it necessary to indicate in other than very broad terms the basis of specific war powers as he exercised them, leaving it rather to others to speculate, if they chose, upon whether, in the case of any given act or order, he was relying principally upon his permanent peacetime powers as chief executive, or upon his status as commander-in-chief, or upon statutory grants; and if perchance he made allusion to the latter, he was likely not to cite chapter and verse, but merely to invoke "the statutes."

The powers of the President in relation to national defense were explored in an earlier chapter. There remains, however, the difficult and highly controversial subject of committing the nation to war to be elaborated here.

The President and the beginning of war

In his conduct of foreign relations the President may create a situation making war virtually inevitable. In the course of stormy negotiations with Mexico in 1846, President Polk ordered American troops to advance into territory then in dispute with that country. The Mexican authorities had made it plain that such a step would be regarded as an act of war, and the soldiers were promptly fired upon. Polk then said that war existed by act of Mexico, and Congress proceeded to a formal declaration. President McKinley ordered the battleship *Maine* to Havana harbor in 1898, notwithstanding that the

Spaniards were certain to regard the act as unfriendly. The vessel blew up and the Spanish-American War followed. By his handling of relations with Berlin after the sinking of the *Lusitania* in 1915, President Wilson brought the United States to a situation where the only alternative to a declaration of war upon Germany would have been national stultification. And later, the whole course of policy and action which, over a period of years, led the United States straight to involvement in World War II, while sustained by increasing evidences of broad national support, was projected and carried forward under the sole ultimate responsibility of President Franklin D. Roosevelt. Congress could, if it liked, declare a war to which the President was opposed, and he could attempt to avert it by interposing a veto. With the possible exception of the War of 1812, however, all of our wars have been declared at Presidential request.

The nature of Congressional participation

The extensive moral and legal obligations of the United States arising from its participation in the UN and from the numerous mutual defense treaties to which it is a party and the large armed forces constantly available for deployment around the world have added a new dimension to this problem of taking the nation into war. Congress, as we observed in the previous chapter, is demanding a larger share in Presidential decision-making in the area of international military undertakings. The debate over the Korean police action and over the "Troops for Europe" Resolution in connection with NATO revealed Congressional discontent with what it called growing executive domination in these matters. The most recent effort to shape an appropriate relationship between Congress and the President in committing the United States to a position which might easily result in war began with the Formosa Resolution of 1955, described in the previous chapter. In the course of the Congressional debate over the resolution requested by President Eisenhower, a number of the Democratic leaders took the position that legally the resolution was unnecessary. The President, they said, already had the power to command the armed forces to defend Formosa or the offshore islands of Quemoy and Matsu. The resolution they regarded simply as a means of showing the Chinese Communists that the nation was united in its determination to prevent their further expansion. Many other Congressmen, mainly Republicans, took the position, however, that by requesting this resolution the President was acknowledging his obligation to consult Congress on such a momentous decision and was, thus, reversing the pattern of several decades. The President's message and the reports of the committees which considered the resolution evaded this explosive question. The resolution [6] itself, however, left

---

[6] The text of the resolution was as follows:

"*Resolved, etc.,* That the President of the United States be and he hereby is authorized to employ the Armed Forces of the United States as he deems necessary for the specific purpose of securing and protecting Formosa and the Pescadores against armed attack, this authority to include the securing and protection of such related positions and territories of that area now in friendly hands and the taking of such other measures as he judges to be required or appropriate in assuring the defense of Formosa and the Pescadores.

the President a free hand to use force or not to defend the Nationalist-held islands. In the Middle-East crisis of 1957, the same procedure was followed. In this case the Congressional resolution left the President free to determine when or where troops might be used. The Congress, however, reserved the right to terminate the commitment by its own action. In the Berlin crisis of 1961, while announcing his policy and securing Congressional approval for calling up Reserve units, the President did not seek a resolution of this type authorizing him to use troops to protect West Berlin. However, in the fall of 1962 as the Cuban situation grew menacing, the Republican leaders of Congress proposed a resolution authorizing the use of force to prevent the spread of Castro's influence. The President countered by asking Congress for standby authority to call up a part of the Ready Reserve in order to "permit prompt and effective responses, as necessary, to challenges which may be presented in any part of the free world." Congress acceded to the President's wishes but then on its own adopted a separate resolution on Cuba and another stating the determination of the United States to meet its commitments in Berlin. In the Vietnam situation in 1965, after American retaliatory air strikes and heavy increases in troop strength in the area, President Johnson asked for and got a Congressional resolution approving the use of force in this area.[7]

In time of peace, the President performs the normal functions of chief executive in connection with defense interests and activities substantially as in relation to other government services. It is when war comes that he rises to the full stature implicit in the sources and forms of authority above described. Subject to restrictions by Congress (which almost certainly would not be imposed in the midst of conflict), he can send all branches of the armed forces anywhere that he chooses, and use them as he desires.[8] He can take as

The President in wartime

"This resolution shall expire when the President shall determine that the peace and security of the area is reasonably assured by international conditions created by action of the United Nations or otherwise, and shall so report to the Congress."

[7] The text of the Southeast Asia Resolution is as follows:

Resolved, etc., *Sec. 1.* That the Congress approves and supports the determination of the President, as Commander-in-Chief, to take all necessary measures to repel any armed attack against the forces of the United States and to prevent further aggression.

Sec. 2. The United States regards as vital to its national interest and to world peace the maintenance of international peace and security in Southeast Asia. Consonant with the Constitution of the United States and the Charter of the United Nations and in accordance with its obligations under the Southeast Asia Collective Defense Treaty, the United States is, therefore, prepared, as the President determines, to take all necessary steps, including the use of armed force, to assist any member or protocol state of the Southeast Asia Collective Defense Treaty requesting assistance in defense of its freedom.

Sec. 3. This resolution shall expire when the President shall determine that the peace and security of the area is reasonably assured by international conditions created by action of the United Nations or otherwise, except that it may be terminated earlier by concurrent resolution of the Congress.

[8] During World War I, the power to send troops abroad before the country was actually invaded was challenged, but in the Selective Draft Law Cases, 245 U.S. 366, 369 (1918), the Supreme Court fully sustained it, asserting that in his capacity as commander-in-chief the President may (in the absence of restrictions imposed by Congress) dispatch forces to any part of the world in which he considers their services needed.

much part as he likes in mapping out strategy and directing campaigns; [9] indeed there is nothing to prevent him from taking the field in person if he so desires. Modern communication technology has, in fact, made it possible for Presidents to talk directly with field commanders and combat leaders and President Johnson is reported to be doing just that in Vietnam. Like any other supreme commander, he can terminate hostilities by agreeing to an armistice. He can set up military governments in conquered territory, and, directly or through appointed agents, exercise all executive powers there, and all legislative powers as well until Congress makes different arrangements. Meanwhile, availing himself of broad grants of emergency authority already on the statute book, or voted by Congress in response to White House requests unfailingly made, he can carry out sweeping programs of armed recruitment, civilian mobilization, and economic controls, authorize or issue multitudes of administrative regulations, reorganize governmental agencies and create new ones, take over plants in which labor stoppages are interfering with war production or the railroads if transportation difficulties are impeding the war effort, and do such a multitude of other things that the sum total of authority amassed and exercised almost defies comprehension. Indeed, the object in modern war being to discover and make effective all national potentialities as speedily as possible, and at the same time to break down the enemy's power of resistance, control over the use of the armed forces inevitably broadens into the general function of taking whatever measures may be found necessary to those ends. As a former Secretary of War phrased it, the commander-in-chief's duty is nothing less than to prosecute a war "to the fullest extent." In discharging this responsibility, he, of course, must not violate the Constitution or the laws; and, to a degree, he must work in cooperation with Congress, from which much of his high authority has come and to which at least some of it will return. Outside of these limitations, however, he and his advisers, civil and military, have, and must have, virtually a free hand.[10]

---

[9] More than most Presidents in wartime, President Roosevelt shared, and even led, in planning military and naval strategy and operations during World War II. In the summer of 1942, there was some complaint that he and Prime Minister Churchill were trying to exercise too much personal direction. In a later "fireside chat," the President freely conceded the wisdom of leaving military decisions to military men, although without suggesting any relinquishing of his own ultimate power to make them in so far as he chose. It was primarily by the President's decision that the liberation of Europe was given priority over the subjugation of Japan, and that Europe was invaded across the English Channel.

[10] The best compact analysis of the President's war powers, especially as commander-in-chief, is E. S. Corwin, *The President: Office and Powers* (4th ed., New York, 1957), Chap. VI. Cf. E. P. Herring, *The Impact of War* (New York, 1941), Chap. VI; C. Rossiter, *The Supreme Court and the Commander-in-Chief* (Ithaca, N. Y., 1951); and E. R. May, *The Ultimate Decision: The President as Commander-in-Chief* (New York, 1960).

ORGANIZATION FOR NATIONAL SECURITY

Until after World War II, defense organization in the United States was *Former* notoriously lacking in integration. At the top, the President as chief executive *separate* and commander-in-chief supplied a measure of unity. But the War (later *defense* Army) and Navy Departments were entirely separate; the armed services *administrations* whose affairs they managed were not only separate but often uncooperative *and* and even antagonistic. In making appropriations and enacting defense legisla- *services* tion, Congress rarely considered Army and Navy needs at the same time or in much relation to each other.[11] In earlier and simpler days, the disadvantages of such disunity often were apparent but usually not serious, and little was done toward overcoming them. We emerged from our wars successfully, and the country was satisfied. Even World War I brought no significant change. World War II, however, was different. In the first place, its magnitude and complexity were unprecedented. Secondly, it demonstrated that for the attainment of objectives in such a conflict there must be a wholly new type of collaboration between land, sea, and air forces. Finally, shortly after it ended we were confronted with a world situation making it indispensable that we permanently maintain an armed establishment far larger than ever before in peacetime and organized and integrated for a maximum of efficiency at a minimum of what must in any case be stupendous cost.

From far back, there had been intermittent proposals to merge the War *National* and Navy Departments into some form of defense department. Later the rapid *Security* development of air warfare led some people to suggest moving in the opposite *Acts of* direction and setting up a separate department of military (and perhaps *1947 and* civilian) aviation. World War II at last drove home the idea that basic re- *1949* organization must no longer be delayed and that it must be in the direction of all-around integration. After two or three years of lively bickering between the Army and the Navy, each of which had a plan of its own, and with the Truman administration sturdily urging action, Congress eventually, in 1947, passed a comprehensive National Security Act following the Navy plan in broad outline and providing for a defense reorganization outstripping any in all our previous history. The defense setup about to be outlined rests principally upon that piece of legislation, as amended in the direction of further coordination by two enactments: (1) the National Security Act Amendments of 1949 stemming largely from recommendations of the Hoover Commission;[12] and (2) the Defense Reorganization Act of 1958. President Eisenhower made some further changes in the structure by a reorganization order in 1953.

---

[11] Until the Legislative Reorganization Act of 1946 substituted in each house a consolidated committee on the armed services, there were separate military and naval committees in each.

[12] *The National Security Organization* (Washington, 1949).

ORGANIZATION FOR NATIONAL SECURITY

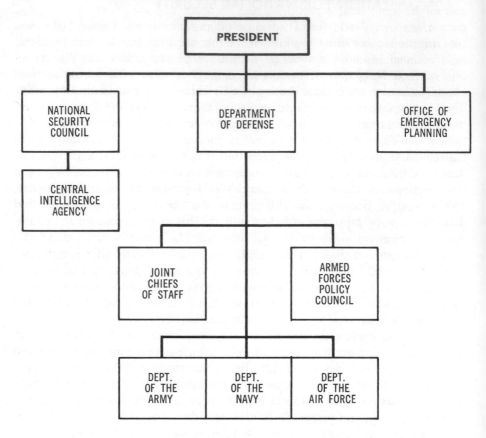

1. The Department of Defense

In pursuance of the announced objective of "integrated policies and procedures for the departments, agencies, and functions of the government relating to the national security," the Act of 1947 undertook to gather substantially everything into an administrative and advisory structure known as the National Security Organization, with a National Military Establishment as its core and a National Security Council and a National Security Resources Board on the periphery. The National Military Establishment represented a major innovation, because its creation marked the first time that the previously separate War and Navy Departments were joined under any directive authority other than that of the President. Since, however, the departments named (with the War Department rechristened Department of the Army, and with a new Department of the Air Force added) retained most of their previous autonomy, the change was more apparent than real. An entirely new official—a Secretary of Defense, appointed by the President and confirmed by the Senate, and with only civilians eligible—was introduced and charged with (1) establishing general policies and programs for the National Military Establishment and for all component departments and agencies, (2) exercising "general direction, authority, and control" over such departments and agencies, (3) discovering and eliminating unnecessary duplication or overlapping in their activities, and (4) advising with the departments and agencies in the preparation of their budgets and formulating a single unified military budget for consideration by the Budget Bureau, the President, and eventually Congress. The "Establishment" (largely a paper affair) did not have the true character of an executive department and the Secretary of Defense, although seated in the Cabinet—as the heads of the three service departments were not—found himself possessed of prestige but very little else. Combined with the service departments' characteristic love of autonomy, the old traditional fear lest one man be given too much power in military matters had operated to cause the Secretary to be given too little. In practice, the "general" authority over the department given him very nearly evaporated. He could not appoint or dismiss (except within his own very limited staff); he could not enforce orders; he could not reorganize; even his control over budgets proved merely nominal.

The principal objective of the amending act of 1949 was to remedy this unhappy situation. The ethereal National Military Establishment was discarded, and in its place was put a single full-orbed executive department, the present Department of Defense, officially ranking second only to the Department of State. In line with this, the Secretary was given powers commensurate with those of other department heads—his principal limitations being that he may not abolish any of the established functions of the Army, Navy, or Air Force or merge any portions of the armed services. Logically enough, the act also transferred the National Security Council and the National Security Resources Board to the Executive Office of the President.

Changes in 1949

Demand for even greater subordination of the three services to the Secretary of Defense was a by-product of general dissatisfaction with American progress in missiles, rockets, and space exploration. Failure to keep pace with the Russians was blamed, in part, on continuing interservice rivalries and the lack of clear-cut assignments of responsibility for development of the new weapons to any service. President Eisenhower strongly urged Congress in 1958 to entrust greater authority to the Secretary of Defense, to strengthen the Joint Chiefs of Staff as professional advisors to the Secretary, and to facilitate unified command in the field. Congress responded half-heartedly. The Defense Reorganization Act of 1958 gave the Secretary power to transfer, abolish, or reassign defense functions, but an order to do any of these things was made subject to Congressional veto. The Secretary was given clear and specific power to assign new weapons or weapons systems among the various services and a new Director of Defense Research and Engineering was established in the Department of Defense. Power to merge any of the military departments or services or to establish a single military chief-of-staff was expressly withheld. In later spelling out the assignments of each of the services, Secretary

Defense Reorganization Act of 1958

of Defense McElroy made no major changes and avoided any resolution of the continuing controversies over their respective roles in missile development and space exploration. Major criticism of these arrangements, especially of the lack of clear decision by the joint chiefs, continues to be voiced by the Army leaders and, to some degree, by those of the Air Force. Under the direction of Robert McNamara centralization of control under the Secretary of Defense has proceeded energetically since 1961. Central agencies for intelligence, supply, organization, and management have been created and the staff of the joint chiefs has been enlarged at the expense of the staffs of the three services. Many of these moves have been strongly criticized by some members of Congress and by some military officers. An effort in 1963 by certain service leaders to make the joint chiefs less dependent on the favor of President and Secretary by prescribing four-year terms for the official members was successfully resisted.[13]

The "military departments" The legislation of 1949 definitely reduced the Departments of the Army, Navy, and Air Force to their present status of so-called "military departments." The Department of the Army is charged with responsibility for organizing, training, maintaining, and equipping the United States Army, and with various subsidiary functions such as directing the Corps of Engineers in improving waterways, formulating and executing plans for flood control, constructing national monuments and memorials, and operating the Panama Canal. When it shall have divested itself (as now intended) of all insular administration, the Navy Department will have no functions not directly connected with the Navy itself. Taking over most aeronautical functions from the War Department, the relatively new Department of the Air Force already has developed extensive machinery concerned with substantially everything relating to not only the Regular Air Force, but to an Air Reserve, and Air National Guard, and an Air Reserve Officers Training Corps. All three departments undergo occasional organizational changes, but in general operate on lines not widely different from those familiar in the War and Navy establishments before 1947. All have the basic task of maintaining firm central and civilian control while promoting the military capacities and energies for which the respective—and still separate—armed forces under them exist.[14]

Staff agencies At the top level, the Defense Department is rounded out by two staff agencies designed for planning and policy determination: (1) the Armed

[13] A good review of the defense reorganization problems and the debates over them may be found in W. Millis, H. C. Mansfield, and H. Stein, *Arms and the State: Civil-Military Elements in National Policy* (New York, 1958). A critique, to some degree from the Army standpoint is W. R. Kintner with J. I. Coffey and R. J. Albright, *Forging a New Sword: A Study of the Department of Defense* (New York, 1958). McNamara sets forth his own philosophy in "McNamara Defines His Job," *New York Times Magazine,* April 26, 1964.

[14] That many of the economies anticipated from integrating the management of the armed forces have not been achieved was demonstrated by the second look taken by the second Hoover Commission. See the Reports on *Business Organization of the Department of Defense* (Washington, 1955) and *Depot Utilization* (Washington, 1955).

Forces Policy Council [15] (replacing a former War Council), advising the Secretary of Defense on broad policy matters and rarely used; (2) the Joint
Chiefs-of-Staff,[16] originating during World War II and having as its province
all matters pertaining to military strategy. The joint chiefs-of-staff are also military advisers of the President as well as of the Secretary of Defense. The joint
chiefs arrangement has survived the various reorganizations and has been
shored up by the development of a substantial staff under it and separate,
therefore, from the various services. It has, however, been the object of continuing criticism for its alleged failure to provide genuine, coordinated planning either in strategy or in budgeting and many internal disagreements have
been carried to the Secretary, to the President, to Congress, and even to the
public.[17] The Munitions Board and the Research and Development Board
originally provided were discarded in 1953.

With the secretary of defense supplying the principal point of contact, the
Department of Defense is the arm of the President for purposes of national
security in its military, naval, and aeronautical aspects. To provide broader
basis for decisions involving defense the National Security Act of 1947 introduced two other major agencies already mentioned, the National Security
Council and the National Security Resources Board, both placed in 1949 in the
Executive Office of the President. Only the first of these has survived. Its task
is nothing less than to formulate for the President the collective advice of all
appropriate officers and agencies of the executive branch on the integration of
domestic, foreign, and military policies in any manner touching the national
security. In addition to the President as chairman, the members include the
Vice-President, the Secretaries of State and Defense, and the director of the
Office of Emergency Planning, who from their different official environments
can bring together foreign-policy, military, and economic viewpoints, with
indeed the financial also contributed by the Secretary of the Treasury sitting,
not as a member, but as a regular participant by Presidential invitation. Meeting normally twice a month (with the President usually absenting himself in
the interest of freer discussion), the Council is intended to thrash out large
questions of national security and through its secretariat keep the chief executive currently informed on all its discussions and decisions. Under the direction of the Council is a Central Intelligence Agency (CIA) to coordinate
the intelligence activities of the various defense agencies and to supply the
Council and the President with information necessary to their decisions. The
Council does not itself determine policy. That is for the President to do, on

2. The National Security Council

[15] Composed of the top military and civilian officials of the three component departments.

[16] Composed of a chairman, the chiefs of staff of the Army and the Air Force, the
Chief of Naval Operations, and the Commandant of the Marine Corps (the latter added
in 1952 for certain types of decisions). The chairmanship has been held, in turn, by
representatives of each of the services.

[17] A slashing attack on the Joint Chiefs may be found in Gen. M. D. Taylor, *The
Uncertain Trumpet* (New York, 1960). Gen. Taylor was a close military advisor to
President Kennedy and is now advisor to President Johnson.

the basis of Council advice, which, however, he is free to accept or reject, in whole or in part. If it is possible in our system—and some doubt it—to achieve high level correlation of the nation's foreign objectives, commitments, and risks with its military and economic capacities, this is the agency designed to do so. Like the Joint Chiefs, however, it has not escaped severe censure when crises arise [18]—as in Korea with the entrance into the fray of the Chinese and in Cuba with the abortive effort to overthrow Castro and in the lag in rocketry and missile development—for which it has not seemed to be prepared and for dealing with which its advice has not seemed clear or persuasive. It must be emphasized, however, that the final responsibility for coordination and decision falls upon just one man, the President of the United States.

Office of Emergency Planning

Success in war depends heavily upon a nation's economic preparedness, or at any rate upon the speed and effectiveness with which the economy can be converted to war production. Deeply impressed by World War II experience at this point, the authors of the Security Act of 1947 provided a National Security Resources Board to investigate and plan correlating foreign and military policy with natural resources and economic capacity. The board was replaced in 1953 with an Office of Defense Mobilization.

The greatly increased possibilities of breaching American defenses from the air, combined with the perfection of weapons of awesome destructive power, encouraged the President and later the Congress to create a new agency of government to prepare our industrial areas for attack. The Federal Civil Defense Administration was established in 1950 first in the Office of Emergency Management in the Executive Office and later by Congress as an independent executive agency. This agency is charged with developing, in cooperation with state and local authorities, plans for the protection of our civilian population in case of enemy air attacks. Grants are made to states for equipment and materials for approved projects. Since 1953, this agency has also been assigned responsibilities for administering national disaster relief programs of certain types. In 1958, this agency and the Office of Defense Mobilization were merged by an executive reorganization plan into the Office of Civil and Defense Mobilization. The civil defense responsibilities were largely

---

[18] The surprise communist attack on South Korea in June, 1950, brought criticism upon the Central Intelligence Agency, on the ground that, with its facilities, it should have been able to give authorities at Washington some idea of what was coming. In fact, there was dissatisfaction with the Security Council itself, which had recommended the withdrawal of American troops from Korea as carried out in 1949. The criticisms of CIA in connection with the failure of the Cuban expedition in 1961 were even more vigorous and led to some decentralization of intelligence to the military services as well as to a change in the leadership of CIA.

President Eisenhower added to the secretariat of the Council a special assistant to the president in charge of security matters. This post has been continued by Presidents Kennedy and Johnson. In the reorganization of 1953 the President also created an Operations Coordinating Board made up of the deputies to the leading cabinet participants plus the head of CIA to implement Council decisions within the various departments concerned. This latter agency was abolished by President Kennedy and the chief responsibility for implementing Council decisions placed by him on the Secretary of State.

shifted to the Department of Defense in 1961 and the office retitled the Office of Emergency Planning.

THE ARMED FORCES

Creating an effective military force has always been a troublesome problem for democratic countries whose peoples have been suspicious of the military and of militarism. It has been especially difficult for the United States. We have normally disavowed aggressive aims against our neighbors and, sheltered behind broad oceans, have felt no need for large or expensive forces to protect our safety. We have been unwilling to create a peacetime army of conscripts as the Europeans have preferred, but rather have relied on volunteers in peace and conscripts in war. Volunteering has proved effective only when very small forces are to be staffed. After mobilizing our people and resources for combat on a large scale in the two great wars of this century, we have demobilized them after victory as rapidly as possible. The development of nuclear weapons and of unmanned missiles to carry them, the collapse of the concert of victors after World War II, the spread of Communist influence, the rise of Soviet Russia, and the emergence of new states from European colonial territories have all contributed to an international situation to which most of our military traditions are inappropriate. The last three decades, therefore, have witnessed not only a complete turnabout of our old military policies, and the maintenance of huge armed forces in "peace"time backed by great stockpiles of strategic materials and armaments, but also constant changes in emphasis among the types of forces and weapons systems on which we should place our major reliance. During this period we have also become intimately involved in the deployments of our allies and have had to appraise the importance of the rapid technological developments of our potential enemies.

Change in defense policies after World War II

At the close of World War II, despite the warnings of some of our statesmen and several of our allies, under the spell of our well-established traditions we dismantled our war machine about as fast as we could and thus made it impossible to oppose Soviet adventure except by all-out war and remobilization. Deterioration of our relations with the Soviet and the loss of China to the Reds spread deep concern in high Washington circles but did not and perhaps could not at that time have convinced our people to reassemble our armed might and reverse our traditional peacetime military posture. We knew only war—full-scale with all our resources mobilized—or peace with an army deployed for Indian fighting and a Navy to patrol our shores and protect the Panama Canal. Korea offered the occasion and the justification for rearmament short of total mobilization. Comfortable in our superiority in atomic weapons, no longer, unfortunately, a monopoly, we then felt that we must in concert with our European allies organize ground and sea forces large enough to halt or to delay the overwhelming ground strength of Russia. Two

Rearmament after Korea

major policies ensued: (1) a call for Universal Military Training in the United States to supply a pool of partially trained reserves; and (2) the organization of substantial Western European armies including those of West Germany. Both of these called for heavier peacetime military expenditures and heavier demands on the services of our young men than we had ever believed to be bearable. They also assumed that given our air and atomic bomb superiority the Soviets would probably attack in Europe with their own superior ground forces.

The nuclear deterrent

The economic burden of these policies on the American taxpayer was a matter of grave concern to those elected to office in 1952 who feared the collapse of our economic strength upon which our military effectiveness must inevitably rest. Universal Military Training like fighting in Korea and rearmament was widely unpopular and was never fully implemented by Congress. Furthermore, it could legitimately be argued that any attack in Europe would have to be halted there by the troops on hand. We would not be given time to mobilize reserves in the earlier fashion and then bring them into action months after the start of hostilities. Korea and its demand for ground forces was ended by armistice. With these concerns we decided to reduce our reliance on traditional forces and to depend henceforth largely on nuclear weapons delivered from manned bombers to break up or to prevent Soviet aggression. We brandished our nuclear warheads, talked of "massive retaliation," and curtailed ground and sea forces. The risk of these policies, as several critics pointed out, notably General Taylor, was that we might leave ourselves unable to deal with new Koreas, Quemoys, Suez Canals, or Congo revolutions except by a nuclear holocaust.

The new emphasis on conventional arms

Sputnik, in 1957, virtually spelled the end of this era. Soviet technology having opened the secrets of the atom in 1949 and produced a hydrogen bomb in 1954, had now caught up and perhaps passed our own in rocketry and missiles. Russia was no longer dependent upon its ground superiority. It could now threaten, not only Europe on the ground, but also America from the air and our airplanes could not certainly stop their rockets and perhaps could not even survive a first strike in sufficient numbers to launch a counterattack. We were thus obliged to catch up in rockets and missiles at any cost. Assuming that a balance of deterrent power existed, we came back to the earlier policy of strengthening our conventional forces to deal with "crises" and to allow us to limit their spread. This has proved, of course, the most costly of all our postwar military policies and seems likely to commit us to a very highlevel of expenditure for many years to come. Our statesmen are still wrestling with these difficult decisions. Few believe that our present posture is wholly satisfactory.[19] Some feel that we already have superior nuclear armaments and that so long as this is true no attack will be started against us and we should act on this basis. Others, that we cannot hope to match Russian or Chinese

[19] See S. P. Huntington, "Strategic Planning and the Political Process," *Foreign Affairs,* Vol. 38, No. 2, January, 1960.

manpower in traditional warfare at or near their homelands and that we should place little reliance on conventional forces.

In the democratic system, shifts in emphasis and changes in direction are rarely clean cut. Many of the dispositions, institutional arrangements, statutory authorizations, and expenditure patterns of each phase are carried on— perhaps slightly modified—into the new phase. We have, at present, therefore, a complex and not wholly consistent set of military policies and procedures on the basis of which our armed forces are recruited, trained, equipped and deployed. We are now spending for these forces between $50 and $55 billion annually compared to $12 billion in 1948 and to $35 to $40 billion in 1953 to 1957. We have 2.7 million men under arms in various forces backed up by another 950 thousand reserves in various conditions of training and readiness. These are organized into 16 army and 3 marine divisions, 88 air combat wings, 135 air combat support squadrons, and 873 commissioned warships. While we do not have a full-fledged system of universal military training, we do have peacetime conscription under which young men register at age 18 and are called up for service as needed for periods up to two years. The reserve apparatus, including the National Guard, has been reorganized—mainly in 1955—and tightened to maintain more effective control over the preparation of those in the "Ready" or immediate reserve components. Missiles of various types are rolling off production lines and numerous sites have been "hardened." We maintain a string of bases—air and missile—in various friendly countries around the defense perimeter of the West and have missile-firing submarines patrolling the oceans.

Present military posture

NATIONAL CONTROLS IN WARTIME

Half a dozen clauses of the Constitution suggest that for carrying on a war Congress may tax, borrow, raise troops, and build ships practically without restraint, with the President exercising the broad and undefined functions accruing to him as chief executive and commander-in-chief. But they convey little idea of what this may mean either for the machinery and processes of government or for the national economy—industry, transportation, communications, labor, prices, manpower, and daily civilian life. To visualize these things, one has rather to recall what happened during two world wars, during the Korean struggle, and, in part at least, continuing right up to the present. No two wars are alike; certainly an atomic war would differ from any we have known. Up to now, however, war's impact on government and economy can best be apprehended in terms of World War II; and a word on that chapter of our experience will be in order.

Fundamentally, wartime controls are exercised by the regular peacetime authorities. Congress stays in session and broadens and deepens its regulations as needs require, with little, under the circumstances, to fear from the courts. As chief executive, and particularly as commander-in-chief, the President

Expansion of powers and agencies

mounts from peak to peak of directing authority, reading more and more power into his constitutional prerogatives and drawing almost equally from delegations by Congress. The executive departments and independent establishments intensify their activities in all that relates to the war effort. With new and vast specialized tasks developing, however, need arises for additional machinery, created directly by Congress or more frequently by executive order implementing some broad Congressional grant. Even before we entered World War I, a top-level Council of National Defense was set up; and during that conflict a War Industries Board furnished a nucleus for new regulatory and administrative agencies. Again, the defense effort of 1940 called into existence, a year and a half before Pearl Harbor, an Office of Emergency Management, lodged in the Executive Office of the President and becoming a framework under whose broad roof were later gathered 15 major establishments concerned with wartime control, administration, and research. These agencies and others, in turn, provided hooks from which were suspended, as time went on, a maze of additional offices, boards, commissions, and the like, so numerous and so frequently reshuffled as to bewilder even the near-at-hand observer in Washington. Under stress of war, a government already big inevitably grows bigger.

Some areas of control: 1. Military service

    The principle is clear that the government may, insofar as it finds need, draft into its armed services able-bodied men of all ages and conditions, and women too for duties appropriate to them. Conscription was resorted to (for the first time) not only during the Civil War, but on a vast scale during World Wars I and II—in the latter instance, indeed, at a stage when war merely seemed probable. When raising forces in this way, Congress fixes age limits for men liable to induction, specifies or authorizes classifications and priorities in terms of number of dependents and occupational usefulness for war purposes, and determines exemptions. Room is left for volunteering, especially by women. But, within bounds of reason, expediency, and humanity, the government always can dig as deeply into the reservoir of potential combat and auxiliary forces as circumstances seem to it to require.

2. Industrial production

    Aside from a steady stream of trained men, the prime necessity in present-day war is abundant munitions and supplies. With a view to assuring ample production of these, the government may build plants (operating them directly or more often through private corporations under contract), finance the establishment or expansion of others, require plants to be turned to war production, take over and operate establishments crippled or threatened by labor difficulties, curb or suspend production of nonessential consumer goods, build stockpiles of necessary raw materials, and establish priorities for funneling materials to war industries most in need of them. Largely through a major agency known as the War Production Board, all of these things actually were done during World War II. At the beginning of hostilities in 1941, some people considered that any and all industry producing articles likely to be needed should forthwith be taken over. Far from adopting this idea, the government held steadily to the policy of relying principally upon industry privately operated. There was no drawing back, however, from drastic controls; and undoubtedly more industrial potential would have been taken over if the results of private operation had proved less satisfactory.

In line with the same objective of all-out effort in prosecuting a war, the government may take any needful measures for maximum utilization of the nation's civilian manpower and womanpower, even to the extent of registering all able-bodied personnel of both sexes, imposing a "work or fight" rule, and assigning people to jobs. Although urged in some quarters to do so, Congress did not go this far during World War II. But almost immediately after Pearl Harbor the draft as already operating was broadened to require all men up to the age of 64 to register for conscription in the armed forces or for noncombatant duty; and throughout the conflict a War Manpower Commission, although without authority actually to compel men and women to work at particular jobs in particular places, promoted maximum use of personnel by measures calculated to keep people employed in jobs and places where they were most needed and to discourage moving around in quest of more congenial and better-paying positions. Strikes in industry and transportation never were expressly outlawed, and many occurred. But the conditions under which they could legally be declared and carried on were circumscribed, and heavy penalties were imposed upon labor leaders fomenting them. *3. Civilian*

A war of any proportions instantly starts a chain of dislocations in the national economy. An upsurge of government expenditures, re-enforced by augmented employment, produces a rise of prices; higher prices push up wages; higher wages, more spending power, and increasing scarcity of consumer goods stimulate further price rises. Unless brakes are applied, the spiral ends in heavy inflation, particularly devastating for people of fixed incomes but eventually disastrous for the entire economy. Speaking broadly, whatever checks are imposed must come from government; and, with various wage and price controls during World War I as precedents, an Office of Economic Stabilization early in World War II fixed wage ceilings for different industries, while an Office of Price Administration placed and kept under some restraint prices of commodities (rents also) likely to be most affected by prevailing scarcities. In connection with price controls, the OPA also rationed among consumers, the country over, long lists of commodities (automobiles, tires, gasoline, fuel oil, farm machinery, shoes, coffee, sugar, meats, and many other things), demand for which was out of proportion to supply.[20] Proposals at the beginning of the war that wages and prices be frozen all around never were adopted. At the end, the country was left with a considerable heritage of inflation. Matters, however, would have been far worse without the wartime stabilizations achieved. *4. Wages, prices, and distribution of goods*

[20] P. M. O'Leary, "Rationing and Governmental Organization," *Amer. Polit. Sci. Rev.*, XXXIX, 1089-1106 (Dec., 1945); E. S. Redford, *Field Administration of Wartime Rationing* (Washington, 1947).

5. Trans-
portation

Almost as vital as the production of war materials is the transportation of them (and of troops) to places where they are needed; and here the government, with full power over interstate and foreign commerce, has especially free scope. During World War I, the railroads were taken over and operated. During World War II, no need for such a course arose. But, within the framework of pre-existing transportation controls exercised by the Interstate Commerce Commission and allied agencies, an Office of Defense Transportation correlated the services of railways, inland waterways, air transport, motor transport, coastwise shipping, and pipelines in the interest of maximum contribution to the war effort.[21] When neighbors took to group-riding to relieve carriers and save tires and gasoline, they were acting in the spirit of ODT requests.

6. Com-
munica-
tions

War is waged not only with men, munitions, and materials, but also with ideas. Every wartime government (at any rate in a democratic country) must concern itself not only with getting to the people the information it wants them to have and with cultivating a public opinion favorable to the war effort, but also with keeping from the enemy information useful to him and with preventing both the enemy and enemy sympathizers from damaging the national morale through open or secret propaganda. Both tasks present difficulties; and the second, raising complicated questions of free speech, free press, and the like, not only is difficult, but also delicate. The story of our government's efforts during World Wars I and II—in the first instance through a Committee on Public Information and in the second through an Office of War Information—to keep the nation (and friendly peoples abroad) discreetly informed on war aims and developments would reveal a good deal of fumbling, yet reasonable attainment of the ends sought. During World War II, responsibility for guarding against dissemination of information or opinion in ways injurious to our cause was intrusted to an Office of Censorship set up almost as soon as hostilities started. Here, too, the record of achievement was generally good. On the one hand, there was literal and positive censorship, in the sense that all mail, cablegrams, long-distance telephone calls, radio messages, and other communications going out of (or in the case of mail coming into) the United States were minutely inspected, with objectionable passages deleted or even the entire message intercepted. In the case, on the other hand, of domestic publications and radio broadcasting, the milder method was employed of relying upon voluntary compliance of the press and the broadcasting companies with "codes of wartime practices," telling them what they must not print or put on the air—although, of course, with no lack of power to compel obedience where not otherwise forthcoming. Closely related in wartime are, of course, laws and enforcing agencies designed to repress espionage, sabotage, and sedition, and especially to protect the armed forces against subversive influences.

7. Civilian
defense

The conduct of war is definitely a national function, but collaboration by

---

[21] The Office of Defense Transportation was maintained until July 6, 1949, when its surviving duties were transferred to the Interstate Commerce Commission.

state and local governments, and by voluntary citizen groups as well, is essential to solidarity of effort. During World War II, state and local machinery was employed in operating the Selective Service System, the rationing system, and to some extent the system of price control. Civilian defense—aimed chiefly at protecting people and property against the hazards of air raids, but later principally at promoting morale and encouraging productiveness—was organized also largely on a state and local basis. Every state eventually set up a defense council; several thousand cities and counties did likewise: and, in all, millions of men and women rendered various voluntary services. National encouragement and supervision were supplied by an Office of Civilian Defense established in 1941, with power only to advise, suggest, and exhort, but not to compel local agencies.

Greatly amplified after war came, the system of controls described had its beginning in 1940-1941, during days of nominal peace; and 10 years later, with the country also technically at peace, although engaged in military action in Korea, a new defense effort brought such controls again into the picture. With resolution formed in government circles to embark upon a major program of military preparedness, and with Congress and the country won to full support, President Truman, in September, 1950, stressed as three great requisites: (1) production of the materials and equipment required, (2) new taxation to meet the costs involved, and (3) prevention of inflation. A special revenue act of September marked the first stage of the heavier taxation contemplated; and powers for pursuing the other objectives were supplied in a Defense Production Act conveying authority to control wages and prices and to introduce rationing; and authority also (for a year longer) to requisition materials and plants necessary to rearmament, to allocate goods in short supply, and to advance money for encouraging output. Most of the controls were discontinued after 1953 as a result of armistice in Korea and of the election of an administration pledged to reduce restrictions on the private economy. Many of the powers, however, remain in the statute books ready to be invoked should a new emergency occur.

A new program of controls instituted in 1950

ATOMIC WEAPONS

On August 6, 1945, the first atomic bomb was dropped upon Hiroshima, Japan, by the United States armed forces, killing 78,000 and wounding 150,000 more and introducing a new technique of destruction unparalleled in the history of the world. It is appropriate that we conclude this discussion of national defense with some notice of the consequences of this new and terrible threat to the continued existence of life on this planet.

As the result of a suggestion by Albert Einstein, President Roosevelt put scientists to work early in the war to discover if the power of the atom could be unlocked for military purposes. Thousands of scientists—American, Canadian, and British—worked in this secret project for more than four years and

Efforts to achieve international control of atomic weapons

finally achieved an explosive with the force of 20,000 tons of TNT. A successful explosion was set off at Los Alamos, New Mexico, in the summer of 1945 and, when Japan rejected the surrender ultimatum issued by the Allies at Potsdam on July 26, President Truman decided to drop the bomb.[22] The Japanese surrender came within a few hours of the dropping of the second bomb on Nagasaki on August 9. Guided by the group of scientists, statesmen, and soldiers who had directed the successful research, the government now faced the problem of the future use of this dread weapon. Certain that they could not keep the secrets of its composition and manufacture indefinitely, fearful of the holocaust which might result from widespread use of the bomb in war, confident that peaceful uses of atomic energy of great benefit to mankind might be discovered by energetic application of many scientists, the three nations concerned, Great Britain, Canada, and the United States, proposed that the UN establish a commission to study and recommend a program for the control of atomic weapons and for the peaceful exploitation of the energy potential unloosed for the first time in man's history.[23]

The UN created such a commission and before it the United States submitted a plan for the international control of atomic energy with an international agency equipped with inspectorial authority to enforce such controls upon the nations of the world. When and if such an agency should be established, the manufacture of atomic weapons should be prohibited. The Russians countered with a proposal for the outlawing of such weapons immediately, the prohibition of their manufacture in the future, and the destruction of all those in existence at the time. They would not agree to any procedure which involved inspection of their industrial operations by outsiders. Months of subsequent negotiations failed to move either major power from its central position.

Atomic Energy Act of 1946

Meanwhile, in the United States, President Truman seeking a more permanent arrangement for the domestic control of atomic energy research and weapons manufacture, proposed to the Congress, in late 1945, that a civilian commission be created in the executive branch for this purpose. And the Congress passed in 1946 an Atomic Energy Act creating an independent five-man commission to exercise complete control over the production of atomic energy and the research program associated with it. The commission was assigned full ownership of all domestic uranium and other materials essential for the production of the bomb. The principal battle of civilian versus military control of atomic energy was thus largely resolved in favor of the civilians. A special Division of Military Application was created to handle military aspects and to deal with research agencies created in the Defense

---

[22] An excellent statement on this decision written by Henry L. Stimson, then Secretary of War, will be found in *Harper's*, Feb., 1947. The statement by President Truman after the first bomb was dropped may be found in *The New York Times*, August 7, 1945. See also: L. Giovanitti and F. Fried, *The Decision to Drop the Bomb* (New York, 1965) and A. Alpervitz, *Atomic Diplomacy: Hiroshima and Potsdam* (New York, 1965).

[23] The text of the allied proposal may be found in the *New York Times*, Nov. 16, 1945.

Department for experiments with various military uses of atomic power. To this was added in 1949 a Military Liaison Committee consisting of representatives of the armed services and headed by a chairman appointed by the President. Extremely rigid security regulations, since made even more rigid, were enacted to control virtually all phases of the commission's operations. Many scientists have since contended that the "secrecy" requirements have inhibited effective private scientific inquiries and have thus limited the search for peaceful and constructive application of the scientific knowledge of the Commission's experts. The fact that the measure gave to a government agency complete ownership and control over a source of power which might some day replace other energy sources both at home and abroad did not at that time precipitate much controversy. Later, however, growing criticism of the atomic program on the grounds that private enterprise ought to have a larger share in the exploitation of the peaceful possibilities and that too much emphasis was placed on the military phases by the commission paved the way for a new Atomic Energy Act of 1954. This act opened the way for private industry to construct atomic furnaces and to carry on experiments of many kinds, under commission supervision. A Joint Committee of the Congress on Atomic Energy established by the Act of 1946 provides continuing legislative oversight of the commission's program.

The Atomic Energy Commission (AEC) over the years has become one of the most expensive of the executive branch agencies. It now spends about $2.5 billion annually. The major production facilities of the AEC are at Oak Ridge, Tennessee and Richland, Washington, the major research centers are the Argonne National Laboratory at Chicago, the Brookhaven National Laboratory at Upton, N. Y., and the laboratories at Schenectady, N. Y., Ames, Iowa, and Berkeley, Cal. The domestic proving grounds are at Los Alamos, N. M., and Las Vegas, Nev., and the testing areas at sea are in the Eniwetok atoll in the Marshall Archipelago. The commission carries on numerous research tests and studies by contract with college, university, and industrial scientists. *Atomic Energy Commission*

On the international scene, the problem of control of atomic weapons has become more and more acute in the years since 1946. The Soviet Union, in part at least through a clever spy ring and with the help of some captured scientists, acquired the secret of the bomb—an atomic explosion occurred in Russia in 1949—much sooner than the Anglo-American allies anticipated. The AEC scientists—after some bitter internal controversy—produced the hydrogen bomb, a weapon more deadly than the atom bomb and carried their researches to the very threshold of a bomb that would wipe out the entire human race.[24] The Russians, on their part, produced a hydrogen weapon also. *The hydrogen bomb*

[24] In the test explosion of a hydrogen bomb at Eniwetok in March, 1954, an area of 7000 square miles was contaminated to the point that only prompt rescue would have saved any of the inhabitants. See Report issued by the AEC in *The New York Times*, Feb. 16, 1955.

Thus the very real possibility that a war between the two great powers would result in extermination of life over much of the earth's surface has for more than a decade faced the nations of the world. Hoping to realize some of the constructive benefits, President Eisenhower in December, 1953, proposed to the UN an international pool of atomic energy resources and offered to make an American contribution to such a pool. An international conference on peaceful uses of atomic energy held in Geneva in 1955 helped to pave the way for the creation in 1957 of an International Energy Agency supported by 80 nations. American participation, including the donation of fissionable materials, was approved by the Senate and the implementing statute by the Congress.

Nuclear
test bans

Throughout these developments, the AEC scientists continued by test explosions to study the effects of various types of nuclear weapons and the administration continued to seek agreement on international control that would include inspectorial enforcement. Adlai Stevenson, in the campaign of 1956, reflected the view of a growing body of scientific opinion that fallout of radioactive particles from the test explosions was sufficiently dangerous to life and health that testing should be halted and that America should take the lead in this matter.[25] Our position remained, however, that until or unless international agreement could be reached containing "adequate" guarantees we must keep perfecting our knowledge. Just as we were about to launch a new series of tests early in 1958, Russia announced that it was suspending its testing and would continue to do so if the Western powers would stop also. After the completion of our test series, we also halted further testing and continued to press for international agreement. Negotiations for a permanent test ban continued thereafter for month after weary month—the Americans insisting that available long-range detecting devices were not completely reliable and that we must have neutral inspection—the Russians that inspection was a facade for Western spying. The test suspension as a year-to-year policy continued,[26] however, until 1961 when as an outgrowth of the Berlin crisis of that year, the Russians announced the resumption of testing and launched a series of new tests. President Kennedy then announced that in self-defense we must resume our tests and a new series of test explosions began in April 1962 and continued in the summer and fall. Russia then also announced a new series of tests.[27]

[25] On the question of dangers from the fallout from testing see National Academy of Science, Genetics Committee Report, "Biological Effects of Atomic Radiation," reprinted in *The New York Times,* June 13, 1956; Albert Schweitzer, "A Declaration of Conscience," *The Saturday Review,* May 18, 1957; Report of the United Nations Scientific Committee on the Effects of Atomic Radiation, reprinted in *The New York Times,* Aug. 11, 1958; and Report of the Congressional Joint Committee on Atomic Energy, "Fallout from Nuclear Weapons Tests," reprinted, in part, in *The New York Times,* Aug. 24, 1959.

[26] Prior to 1961, the gravest threat to mutual but informal test suspension was the tests conducted by France after de Gaulle took power.

[27] The Soviet statement on the resumption of testing may be found in *The New York Times,* Aug. 31, 1961. The American statement on resumption is in *The New York Times,* Sept. 16, 1961 and the Allied proposal for agreement on underground testing only is in *The New York Times,* Sept. 4, 1961.

Perhaps stimulated by a threatened rupture with its Chinese allies over Soviet cold war strategy, the Soviet leadership began in mid-1963 to take a more conciliatory tone in disarmament negotiations at Geneva. These had been going on for many months under continuing pressure from the UN General Assembly. President Kennedy announced in June a suspension of tests pending the outcome of negotiations to be started in Moscow among Britain, Russia, and ourselves. A limited Test-Ban Treaty was finally agreed upon by these powers on July 25, 1964. This treaty prohibits the signatories from conducting nuclear tests in the atmosphere, in outer space, or on the seas. It does not apply to tests underground. Other nations are invited to subscribe to these terms and each party reserves the right to terminate its commitment if it decides that "extraordinary events . . . have jeopardized the supreme interest of its country." The treaty was approved by the Senate in September by 80-19 and signed by the President. More than 100 nations (excluding France and Red China) later accepted and signed the treaty. *The Test-Ban Treaty*

The friendly atmosphere of the test-ban negotiations led to other proposals for reducing cold war tensions. The Russians called for an East-West nonaggression pact, a mutual reduction of military forces in Berlin and a freeze on military budgets. The United States responded that it would not make any agreement which constitutes recognition of East Germany or in any way reduces its rights in Berlin. Nothing had come of these overtures when, in early fall of 1964, the Chinese Communists achieved an atomic explosion and thus entered the select circle of nuclear powers. Little further progress in control of nuclear weapons has been achieved. An Arms Control and Disarmament Agency created at the request of President Kennedy in 1961 and extended to 1969 at the request of President Johnson continues its search for American policies and programs which may facilitate agreement at the continuing disarmament conference in Geneva.[28]

SPACE SATELLITES

American complacency in our military superiority based on our advanced nuclear research, our ready fleet of great bombers, our network of bases in NATO countries, and in our scientific and technological superiority was suddenly and devastatingly shattered in October, 1957. The Soviet Union launched the first artificial earth satellite. Scientists and military leaders appreciated that rockets with a thrust capable of hurling a 184-pound (later a 1120- and then a 2925-pound) device hundreds of miles into space might also hurl nuclear warheads upon Pittsburgh or Chicago with little chance of interception by man-driven airplanes. The Soviets then followed this by a successful moon- *"Sputnik"*

[28] The whole subject of arms control and disarmament is explored in a growing body of literature. See A. T. Hadley, *The Nation's Safety and Arms Control* (New York, 1961); T. C. Schelling and M. H. Halperin, *Strategy and Arms Control* (New York, 1961); D. G. Brennan (ed.), *Arms Control, Disarmament, and National Security* (New York, 1961); American Assembly, *Arms Control: Issues For the Public* (New York, 1961).

shot in 1959 and by two manned space flights in 1961. The Soviet Union thus demonstrated that it had the capability of leaping over our protective bases and striking directly at the United States.

The lag in American rocketry

The American rocket and missile program, it appeared on subsequent investigation, had languished for some years—a victim of budgetary economies, interservice rivalries, and unwarranted satisfaction with our air-bomb retaliatory power. Congress assembled in 1958 in a mood to spare no pains and no expense to catch up scientifically and militarily to the Russians in missiles, rockets, and space explorations, if indeed we were behind. The Army finally thrust a 31-pound satellite into orbit in January, 1958. This has been followed by several breathtaking thrusts into outer space and by manned space flights in 1961, followed by longer flights of several days duration and flights involving exits from the space capsule by astronauts and in 1965 by the spectacular Gemini series in which two capsules met in space. The administrative arrangements both inside and outside the Department of Defense have been changed several times. We are now spending more on rockets than on the atomic bomb; we have shifted our military arrangements to lesser dependence on airpower and have increased our missile bases and rocket capabilities and have undoubtedly overhauled and probably surpassed the Russians in this new weapons system and perhaps even in penetration of outer space.

Debate over military policy

A related development has been the increasing amount of discussion of our whole military program and policies. For some time, the emphasis on nuclear striking power had been criticized—mainly by Army leaders—as forcing us into a position that we could fight no other kind of war. It was also argued that nuclear weapons alone could not accomplish the likely objectives of the nation, conventional forces would still be necessary to meet and deal with the enemy. Soviet pressure, it was claimed, would normally stop short of all-out attack, but would confront us with "brush-fire" wars at the danger points—Laos, Berlin, Cuba, Suez, Vietnam. These we could not handle with nuclear bombs dropped from high-flying planes or Polaris missiles hurled from submarines under the sea. We must in every international situation have a choice of responses. Now that we are clearly vulnerable, said many, we must recast our thinking.[29]

A third development has been the growing emphasis on exploration of outer space. A new Aeronautics and Space Administration created in 1958 spearheads the nonmilitary research and experimentation aimed at probing the universe. It is surely a wondrous new world when the President of the United States soberly tells the Congress that we intend to reach the moon by 1970.

[29] Military policy, nuclear weapons, and their relation to foreign policy are considered in such works as: H. A. Kissinger, *Nuclear Weapons and Foreign Policy* (New York, 1957); and his, *The Necessity for Choice: Prospects of American Foreign Policy* (New York, 1961). See also, H. Kahn, *On Thermonuclear War* (Princeton, N. J., 1960) and W. W. Kaufmann (ed.), *Military Policy and National Security* (Princeton, N. J., 1956).

References

E. P. Herring, *The Impact of War; Our American Democracy Under Arms* (New York, 1941), Chaps. III-IX.

E. S. Corwin, *Total War and the Constitution* (New York, 1947), Chaps. I-III.

C. C. Tansill, "War Powers of the President of the United States, with Special Reference to the Beginning of Hostilities," *Polit. Sci. Quar.*, XLV, 1-55 (Mar., 1930).

L. W. Koenig, *The Presidency and the Crisis* (New York, 1944), Chaps. III-V.

R. E. Cushman, "The Impact of War on the Constitution," in R. E. Cushman *et al., The Impact of War on America* (Ithaca, N.Y., 1942), Chap. I.

E. Huzar, *The Purse and the Sword; Control of the Army by Congress Through Military Appropriations, 1933-1950* (Ithaca, N.Y., 1950).

B. Bolles, "Military Establishment of the United States," *Foreign Policy Reports,* XXV, No. 8 (Sept. 1, 1949).

H. and M. Sprout, *Toward a New Order of Sea Power* (Princeton, N.J., 1940). Carries to 1918 the naval history begun in an earlier volume.

——, *America's Problem Of National Defense* (Princeton, N.J., 1939).

A. Westcott [ed.], *American Sea Power Since 1775* (Philadelphia, 1947).

N. J. Padelford, *The Panama Canal in Peace and War* (New York, 1942).

B. Brodie [ed.], *The Absolute Weapon; Atomic Power and World Order* (New York, 1946).

F. Pratt, *A Short History of the Army and Navy* (Washington, 1944).

A. P. deSeversky, *Air Power; Key to Survival* (New York, 1950).

J. C. Duggan, *The Legislative and Statutory Development of the Federal Concept of Conscription for Military Service* (Washington, 1946).

J. A. Krout (ed.), "The Defense of the Free World," *Proceedings of Acad. of Polit. Sci.*, XXIV, No. 2 (Jan., 1951).

H. L. Hoskins, *The Atlantic Pact* (Washington, 1949).

F. S. Dunn, *War and the Minds of Men* (New York, 1950).

J. R. Neuman and B. S. Miller, *The Control of Atomic Energy; a Study of its Social, Economic, and Political Implication* (New York, 1948).

H. D. Smyth, *Atomic Energy for Military Purposes* (Princeton, N.J., 1945).

G. Dean, *Report on the Atom* (New York, 1953).

R. E. Lapp, *The New Force* (New York, 1953).

Committee on Government Operations, United States Senate, Subcommittee on National Policy Machinery, *Hearings and Reports on Organizing for National Security*, 86th Congress, 2nd Session (Washington, 1960); also, *A Bibliography* prepared for the Subcommittee (Washington, 1959).

Bulletin of the Atomic Scientists, published monthly by the University of Chicago Press.

P. Y. Hammond, *Organizing for Defense: the American Military Establishment in the Twentieth Century* (Princeton, N.J., 1961).

W. Millis, H. C. Mansfield, and H. Stein, *Arms and the State: Civil-Military Elements in National Policy* (New York, 1958).

H. D. Kissinger, *Nuclear Weapons and Foreign Policy* (New York, 1957).

———, *The Necessity for Choice: Prospects of American Foreign Policy* (New York, 1961).

S. P. Huntington, *The Common Defense: Strategic Programs in National Politics* (New York, 1961).

———, *The Soldier and the State: the Theory and Politics of Civil-Military Relations* (Cambridge, Mass., 1957).

A. Herzog, *The War-Peace Establishment* (New York, 1963).

R. A. Goldwin (ed.), *America Armed: Essays on United States Military Policy* (Chicago, 1961).

E. Fogelman (ed.), *Hiroshima: the Decision to Use the A-Bomb* (New York, 1964).

W. W. Kaufmann, *The McNamara Strategy* (New York, 1964).

J. C. Ries, *The Management of Defense: Organization and Control of the U. S. Armed Services* (Baltimore, 1964).

M. R. Laird, *A House Divided* (New York, 1963).

A. Griffith, *The National Aeronautics and Space Act* (Washington, 1962).

V. Van Dyke, *Pride and Power: the Rationale of the Space Program* (Urbana, Ill., 1964).

C. FINANCES

★ 25 ★

Financing the National Government

THE RESPONSIBILITIES of the national government, described in the preceding chapters, are heavy and the demands of the people for services are great. Sooner or later all discussions of public affairs must come to grips with the costs involved and the resources available to pay them. We, too, must turn now to the melancholy subject of paying the bills for the services the government performs. The complex structure of the national government, described in an earlier section, is obviously a costly one to sustain, and courts, Congress, and executive require millions of dollars for their effective functioning in the modern world. These costs are, however, but trifles compared with the billions required to equip and maintain our great military establishment, to aid our allies, to uphold the economy of the farmers, to sustain the poor, the aged, and the unfortunate, to care for the veteran, to reclaim wasteland, to harness the power of our great rivers and to conquer outer space. Measurable changes—up or down—in our national budget result largely from changes in the services rendered and all the structural tinkering conceivable would effect the costs of government but slightly.

THE SPENDING POWER

The Congress shall have power to lay and collect taxes, duties, imposts and excises, to pay the debts and provide for the common defense and general welfare of the United States; . . . ART. I, Sec. 8, cl. 1

The Constitution has more to say directly about raising revenue than about spending it. A government, however, that could not spend would be no government at all; and in the case of the national government, power to spend not only is expressly granted but is clearly implied in numerous provisions conferring authority to do things which could not possibly be done without spending money, for example, raise and support armies, provide and maintain a navy, establish post offices and post roads, and maintain a system of courts. If necessary, spending power could probably be deduced also from the granted powers to tax and borrow, since manifestly there would be no

Constitutional basis

point to raising money if it could not be used. Only three specific restrictions are imposed: (1) that appropriations for the support of the Army shall not be "for a longer term than two years"; (2) that "no money shall be drawn from the Treasury but in consequence of appropriations made by law"; and (3) that "a regular statement and account of the receipts and expenditures of all public money shall be published from time to time."

Some broad interpretations

Nevertheless, throughout much of our national history the spending power of Congress has been a prolific source of constitutional controversy. Primarily, the question has been whether the power to spend is restricted to purposes connected with the exercise of *other* powers delegated in the Constitution, or whether it is a power independent of, and in addition to, other powers and properly to be exercised for *any* purpose so long as having to do with "common defense and general welfare." In early days, strict constructionists like Madison took the first view, loose constructionists like Hamilton the second. The more liberal interpretation eventually prevailed, with Congress falling into the habit of regarding its spending power as properly extending to any and all objectives rationally associated with defense or welfare. Nay, more: no appropriation made on this assumption was ever—simply as an act of spending—successfully challenged in the courts. And not only so, but in its memorable decision of 1936 invalidating the Agricultural Adjustment Act of 1933,[1] the Supreme Court—while condemning the processing taxes for which that measure provided—went out of its way to assert that "the power of Congress to authorize the expenditure of public moneys [or to tax] for public purposes is not limited by the direct grants of legislative power found in the Constitution," and further that such expenditure is constitutionally legitimate so long as the welfare at which it is aimed can be plausibly represented as national rather than local, with Congress the judge, subject only to judicial veto if discretion is exercised arbitrarily or unreasonably.[2]

The matter of grants-in-aid

A good while before these principles were so securely established judicially, the spending power was brought into significant controversy by the rise of grants-in-aid. With Congress appropriating funds to states for promoting agricultural education, building roads, protecting natural resources, maintaining employment offices, and performing other functions traditionally regarded as state rather than national, taxpayers sometimes objected to diversion of their contributions to such purposes. In 1923, the Supreme Court was confronted with a case brought by a taxpayer, and also one brought by the state of Massachusetts, challenging the constitutionality of a measure of 1921 appropriating money to aid states in reducing maternal and infant mortality on the

---

[1] United States *v.* Butler, 297 U. S. 1, 66 (1936).

[2] For general discussions, see E. S. Corwin, "The Spending Power of Congress," *Harvard Law Rev.,* XXXVI, 548-582 (May, 1923), and R. L. Post, "The Constitutionality of Spending for the General Welfare," *Va. Law Rev.,* XXII, 1-30 (Nov., 1935). In our time, Congress even spends for the welfare of underdeveloped areas in other continents—the justification presumably being that our own well-being (including security) is promoted by raising the welfare level of the rest of the world.

ground that the act was serving purposes not national but only local, and invading the sphere of self-government reserved to the states under the Tenth Amendment. No direct affirmation of the act's constitutionality resulted. But in a consolidated decision of the two cases the Court (1) brushed aside the contention of Massachusetts by pointing out that under the law no state was obliged to accept the grant unless it chose, and (2) set aside the taxpayers' protest on the ground that her share of the funds granted under terms of the legislation was too inconsequential to give her reasonable ground for suit.[3] And from that day, the swelling stream of national funds flowing into the states and localities in the form of grants-in-aid has found sanction in these considerations—reinforced by the Court's later ruling that Congress has power to appropriate money for any purpose comprehended within "common defense and general [i.e., national] welfare." For a good while, national officials were fearful lest such undertakings as slum clearance and other housing activities be regarded judicially as "out of bounds"; but a decision of 1945 allayed such apprehension. So long, therefore, as a general-welfare purpose can be shown (and this usually offers little difficulty), the way for grants to states and their subdivisions seems wide open. Nor is it essential that grants be matched with state funds; and as for the regulatory power commonly going along with grants, the Supreme Court has said that it is natural and proper for the government "to regulate that which it subsidizes." [4]

PLANNING AND CONTROLLING EXPENDITURES: THE BUDGET SYSTEM

The role of Congress

Not a dollar of money can be expended legally except in pursuance of authorization, direct or indirect, by Congress. Voting the great appropriations becomes one of the most laborious but important tasks of the two houses at every regular session. In appropriation acts, Congress in effect instructs the Treasury to supply the executive departments and other spending agencies with stipulated sums, according to specifications set forth in considerable detail. Indeed, one of the chief means by which Congress exercises control over administration is this minute and itemized allocation of money, cutting off an activity here by leaving it without funds, adding an activity or agency there by making the necessary financial provision, and in these and other ways predetermining—not always to the satisfaction of the President, of other authorities, or even of the people—the lines on which the government's work shall be carried on.

Loose methods of appropriation before 1921

For many years before the adoption of a budget system in 1921, appropriation bills were drafted and introduced by no fewer than nine separate House committees—the bills themselves commonly numbering 14—and in the Senate were handled by as many as 15 different committees. Based upon

[3] Massachusetts v. Mellon and Frothingham v. Mellon, 262 U. S. 447 (1923).
[4] Wickard v. Filburn, 317 U. S. 111, 131 (1942).

requests made by the various spending agencies, and merely swept together and transmitted to Congress in an undigested mass by the Secretary of the Treasury, these bills were not only framed, but considered and reported by the several committees, in little or no relation to one another—and, what was worse, in little or no relation to the condition of the Treasury or to the outlook for revenue. With no single guiding hand to exercise restraint, they were likely to emerge in even more swollen form than when they first made their appearance. Although the President might, if he chose, warn and admonish, he as a rule could do nothing in the end except affix his signature, since to do otherwise might mean halting essential government activities. Under such division of responsibility, log-rolling became a fine art, the "pork-barrel" an inexhaustible resource.

The Budget and Accounting Act of 1921

In the days when expenditures were relatively modest and revenues usually adequate to meet them, criticism of such haphazard procedures had little or no effect. The startling upswing of national outlays during World War I, however, lent new force to a growing demand for reform; and in 1921 a national budget system, long talked about, became a reality. The essence of a sound budget system consists in careful planning of the expenditures of a given fiscal period (usually a year) in relation to anticipated income, by a single authority, which not only will correlate income and outgo, but see that all reasonable economies are practiced. While the plan introduced by the Budget and Accounting Act of 1921 left, and still leaves, a good deal to be desired, it in general meets this basic specification.

The Bureau of the Budget

The planning and coordinating agency set up by the act is the Bureau of the Budget, originally attached loosely to the Treasury Department, although in effect an independent establishment. As supreme director of national administration, the President is, however, the logical authority to bear primary responsibility for preparing integrated programs of spending and revenue-raisings. After Franklin D. Roosevelt became chief executive, the bureau was drawn into closer relations with the White House, until eventually, under authority conferred in the Reorganization Act of 1939, it was definitely placed in the new Executive Office of the President. It thereupon became the chief executive's largest and most important staff agency—his arm for all contacts and dealings with the financial side of the government.[5]

Its expanded role

Moreover, with the passage of time there has been a remarkable expansion of functions. From an agency concerned with coordinating requests for funds in relation to anticipated revenues and putting them into coherent shape for transmission to Congress, the bureau has developed into a principal aid to the President in planning and guiding the operations of the entire executive branch of the government. Conceptions of the budgetary process itself have been broadened to include not only the formulation of well-defined financial programs for the various departments and establishments, but also supervision

[5] The director is appointed by the President alone, for an indefinite term; and Bureau personnel numbers some 480.

of and control over the execution of such programs, including continuous study of problems of administrative organization and business methods. Resulting in part from the enlargement of governmental activities in fighting the depression of the thirties, the bureau's new role arose to an even larger extent from situations created by the defense effort and war.

Such service the bureau is able to render through the broad power given the director to "assemble, correlate, revise, reduce, or increase" the estimates of the several departments and agencies—a power from which flows wide discretion over the substance of department programs, not only in the planning stage but also later. After the programs have received bureau approval, and after Congress has voted the necessary appropriations, the departments and establishments still must obtain the bureau's approval for their financial procedures in carrying out their programs, including the periodic (usually monthly) allotment of funds and the maintenance of reasonable reserves for contingencies. In addition, since 1939 a division of legislative reference in the bureau has examined and reported upon all measures pending in Congress which, if enacted, would impose a charge upon the public treasury or otherwise affect the President's fiscal policy, the purpose being to determine the relation of such measures to the "financial program of the President"; indeed, if the bureau does not think well of a measure passed, it may, and sometimes does, prepare a veto message and advise the President to sign it. The legislative division also acts as a central clearing house for all legislative recommendations emanating from the executive branch. All bills proposed by anyone in the executive establishments must be checked by the bureau to see if they conform to Presidential policy.

Although the government's tax year, the year for which taxable income *Preparing* is computed and in which most taxes are paid, corresponds to the calendar *a budget* year, and therefore starts on January 1, its fiscal year, the year for which expenditures are planned and accounts made up, opens on July 1.[6] A fiscal year hardly begins before systematic work on the financial arrangements for the ensuing year is started. First of all, every spending agency is asked by the Budget Bureau to compile detailed estimates of the funds that it will need in the next fiscal year and to submit such estimates not later than September 15. In larger agencies, this is done by special budget officers, in lesser ones by members of the staff detailed for the purpose. For many weeks conferences go on between these or other agency representatives on the one hand and Budget Bureau officials on the other—the former commonly pressing for as generous allotments as they can hope to get, the latter raising questions, offering objections, and seeking to whittle down requests regarded as extravagant or at any rate impracticable. On larger matters, the budget director is brought into the discussions; and, subject only to reversal by the President, his word

[6] A fiscal year, therefore, runs from July 1 to the following June 30, and is designated by the year in which the last six months fall. Thus "fiscal 1951" is the period from July 1, 1950, to June 30, 1951.

is law for every department, bureau, board, and commission as to what expenditures (and in what amounts) shall be recommended to Congress and what ones shall not. Meanwhile, the Treasury Department, on its part, has been asked not only for data concerning interest charges on the national debt, but also for detailed estimates of the revenues that may be expected in the period, together with proposals for increasing such revenues in case they promise (as nowadays they almost always do) to be insufficient. Since 1947, the Council of Economic Advisors may also, at this stage, be asked for information on the impact of spending, borrowing, and taxation on the national economy. With all of the estimates and other information finally in hand (ordinarily by December 1), bureau officials total up the amounts, arrange data in logical order, and work the whole into a volume of 1200 pages or more—the "budget"—which, by the close of the calendar year, is placed on the desk of the President. The President is then free to revise or strike out items. Usually he has already assented to most of them. Congress comes into regular session normally on January 3, and his budget message is due within the first fifteen days. In this message, the President presents his fiscal plan covering not only appropriations but revenues and, if necessary, proposals for deficit financing or for new taxes.[7]

A budget before Congress

In 1920, with the adoption of a budget system imminent, the House of Representatives prepared for the new order of things by enlarging its appropriations committee to 35 (now 50) members, giving it jurisdiction over all appropriation proposals, and authorizing it to employ as many as 15 subcommittees (the present number is 21) for handling proposals relating to particular departments or agencies.[8] Received in the House, a budget's revenue proposals are turned over at once to the Committee on Ways and Means, and its far bulkier proposals for expenditure to the Appropriations Committee. With a view to more coordination of the two committees, the Legislative Reorganization Act of 1946 interposed a new procedural stage by requiring that, upon the President's proposals for a given fiscal year being received, the House Committees on Ways and Means and Appropriations and the corresponding Senate committees (on Finance and Appropriations), or duly authorized subcommittees thereof, should form themselves into a joint committee and, with

[7] If unanticipated necessity arises, supplementary and deficiency estimates may be presented to Congress after submission, or even after adoption, of the regular budget; and "deficiency" appropriation bills are passed at every session.

The workings of the Budget Bureau are discussed at first hand by a former director, Harold D. Smith, in his *The Management of Your Government* (New York, 1945). Other accounts will be found in N. M. Pearson, "The Budget Bureau; From Routine Business to General Staff," *Pub. Admin. Rev.*, III, 126-149 (Spring, 1943); F. Morstein Marx, "The Bureau of the Budget: Its Evolution and Present Role," *Amer. Polit. Sci. Rev.*, XXXIX, 653-684, 869-898 (Aug. and Oct., 1945); J. Burkhead, *Governmental Budgeting* (New York, 1956); and, A. Smithies, *The Budgetary Process in the United States* (New York, 1955).

[8] A general appropriations committee had been maintained since 1865, when the duties of the committee on ways and means were divided; but from 1885 to 1921, many appropriation proposals, as indicated above, were actually handled by other committees.

the President's recommendations before them, work out a legislative budget, fixing ceilings for expenditures and providing for any necessary borrowing, and report the results to the two houses by February 15 (or later date agreed upon) as recommendations for adoption. As tested in sessions of 1948 and 1949, however, this plan almost totally failed to yield the expected economies; "ceilings" tentatively established in legislative budgets were afterwards largely ignored; and in 1950 the experiment was abandoned.

Whether adhering to the President's recommendations or striking out on more or less independent lines, appropriations subcommittees in the House evolve 10 or 12 separate appropriation bills providing for departments and establishments, singly or in groups. After being approved by the main committee and passed by the House, these several measures are transmitted to the Senate. The Senate Appropriations Committee usually confines its activity to reviewing changes made in the President's requests by the House. Thus, the major weight in Congressional review of spending is clearly in the House. Conference committees ordinarily reconcile the conflicting views of the two houses and as the session nears its end the bills go to the President. In 1950, a "single-package" plan was introduced under which, before appropriations finally were voted, all major ones were brought together in one bill, after the manner of the single great annual appropriation bill in the British Parliament, and also of consolidated appropriation bills encountered in some of the American states. By decision of the House Appropriations Committee, however, the device—although warmly supported by many members of both branches as in the interest of unity and economy—was abandoned after one trial. In almost every session since 1950 supporters of the consolidated appropriation bill and of the Joint Committee on the Budget have introduced legislation to re-establish, with some modifications, the procedures recommended in the Legislative Reorganization Act of 1946. While support for some or all of these innovations has been strong at times, the two houses have failed thus far to agree on a new procedure.[9]

Framing and adopting appropriation bills

During the 45 years since the budget system went into operation, it has abundantly proved its worth. Even though we have had many years of deficit financing, no one would dream of returning to the earlier procedure. The

Some benefits realized

[9] As presented to the House of Representatives in March, 1950, the general appropriation bill of fiscal 1951 (allocating some $29 billion) was 431 pages long, accompanied by a report 337 pages long, and backed by 25 large volumes of testimony taken in hearings. As approved by the President the following September 6, it appropriated $36.154 billion.

Appropriation measures, like others, are of course subject to veto. Even when applying only to particular departments or groups of agencies, however, they rarely can be disapproved without risk of disrupting essential government services; and a consolidated bill like that of 1950 would be even more immune, regardless of how many provisions it might contain to which the chief executive objected. As we have seen, there is no item veto.

A review of the various reforms aimed at improving Congressional handling of the budget may be found in R. A. Wallace, *Congressional Control of Federal Spending* (Detroit, 1959).

system has imparted unity and responsibility to the spending program which otherwise would have been lacking. It opens a way for thorough and impartial review of the estimates of all spending agencies, and for reduction of those found questionable, before they are sent to Capitol Hill, and enables Congress to act with fuller information concerning spending proposals, the state of the country's finances, and the state of the national economy.

Possible further improve- ments

There is, however, room for improvement. While general appropriation bills are no longer introduced except by the regular Appropriations Commit- tee, Representatives and Senators freely exercise their privilege of presenting bills calling for the expenditure of money for particular projects—building a post office, constructing a dam, dredging a harbor, or "improving" a river—in which they (at any rate the voters back home) are interested. Some of these are usually approved and the expenditure totals thus increased without, in most instances, providing any additional revenues. Furthermore, the enactment of a dozen or more major appropriation bills each year at different times makes it very difficult to keep the Congressional eye on the revenues which might be needed. The legislative budget provided for by the Legislative Reorganiza- tion Act of 1946 was based on a good idea, but has proved abortive. Many experts believe that Congress should emulate the example of the British Parliament, and, as a matter of regular practice, refrain from voting money for any purposes, or in any amounts, not specified in the carefully considered plans of the executive. Others propose that by constitutional amendment, the President be given power to veto separate items of appropriation bills as gov- ernors in all but nine states have been authorized to do.

A "per- formance budget"

In one of its 1949 reports,[10] the Hoover Commission sharply criticized the budget as "an inadequate document, poorly organized and improperly de- signed to serve its major purpose, which is to present an understandable and workable financial plan for the expenditure of the government." Two main improvements were urged: (1) clear separation of capital outlays, for ex- ample, on public buildings, from current operating expenditures, and (2) presentation of the latter, not in terms simply of who is to get how much, department by department and bureau by bureau, but in terms rather of func- tions, services, and activities—in other words, of "performance." Both recom- mendations found ready acceptance. Congress at once passed a resolution requiring the new performance principle to be applied to budgeting for the military department. The President requested all other spending departments and agencies to follow the same pattern; and the general budget for fiscal 1951, presented in January, 1950, embodied, as far as possible, the first effort at a "performance budget" in our history.[11] Moreover, a Budget and Accounting

[10] *Budgeting and Accounting* (Washington, 1949), 7.
[11] A simultaneous innovation was publication by the government of a 40-page "budget for the layman," reducing to easily comprehensible form the essential data con- tained in the regular 1000-page document.

Procedures Act of 1950 made the new type of budget a permanent statutory requirement. The second Hoover Commission reaffirmed the performance system for presenting budgetary data and urged continued experimentation to spread its use and to improve its effectiveness. The Congress, in 1958, accepted one suggestion originating with the commission and attempted by statute to modify its method of handling, in each appropriation, obligations arising under previous legislation. The House Appropriations Committee, however, has not thus far elected to follow the procedure suggested in the law.[12]

In its report of 1937, the President's Committee on Administrative Management criticized the Budget Bureau for concentrating too much upon the preparation of budgets and not giving enough attention to "supervision over the execution of the budget by the spending agencies." As the committee was frank to recognize, the bureau had never up to that time been given sufficient staff or money to enable it to perform this added task. The situation has now been measurably corrected; and much is done by way of checking up on the use actually made of funds voted and supervising the transfer of funds from one agency to another. There is need for such work, notwithstanding the existence of another establishment—the General Accounting Office. This office was created by the same act of 1921 which brought the Budget Bureau into existence, and by the Legislative Reorganization Act of 1946 is expressly declared a part of the legislative branch. In addition to auditing the accounts of spending agencies and prescribing their form, this large independent agency —particularly independent because its head, the Comptroller General, is appointed by the President and confirmed by the Senate for a 15-year term and is removable only by impeachment or, for cause, by joint resolution of Congress—has as a main function the validation of payments for services, supplies, and so on, as a means of seeing that all such outlays fall within the purposes and limits of appropriations made by Congress. Without the Comptroller General's approval, money for such purposes cannot be drawn from the Treasury, or, if drawn and paid over, must be refunded. After 1933, the General Accounting Office became a focus of vigorous controversy, partly because the then Comptroller General, personally hostile to the New Deal, held up numerous payments in connection with New Deal enterprises as lacking proper authorization in Congressional appropriations. In 1937, the President's Committee made recommendation, warmly supported by the President himself, looking to abolition of the office, transfer of "pre-audits" to the Treasury Department, and retention of post-audits in a new agency to be headed by an

Executing the budget —the General Accounting Office

[12] *Budget and Accounting* (Washington, 1955), 11-17. A detailed review of the development of budget legislation, the fate of the Hoover Commission proposals, and the controversies over accrued annual accounting rather than cash-outlay accounting may be found in Committee on Government Operations, United States Senate, *Financial Management in the Federal Government,* 86th Congress, 2nd Session (Washington, 1961).

auditor general. Sharply clashing views developed, however, and no action resulted. Reverting to the subject in 1949, the Hoover Commission proposed retention of the General Accounting Office (as an agent of Congress) for purposes of post-auditing, but urged the introduction of a chief accounting officer in the Treasury Department (as an agent of the executive) with the title of accountant general of the United States, to take over the administrative work of pre-auditing expenditures and of prescribing and enforcing day-by-day administrative accounting methods in all departments and agencies with a view to a single system of fiscal accounts, elimination of duplications, and a degree of uniformity then lacking. The Budget and Accounting Procedures Act of 1950, while it gave departments and agencies fuller accounting functions than before, nevertheless continued the system of dispersed responsibility. It directed the Treasury, Budget Bureau, and General Accounting Office to collaborate in prescribing accounting systems but left principal authority in the latter office. The Second Hoover Commission in 1955 suggested that the Budget Bureau ought to develop its accounting services for other agencies and did not grapple with the thorny problem of where ultimate authority ought to reside. The basic issue here is between the Congress and the President with the Congress reluctant to curtail the authority of its own agency.

THE GROWTH AND PRESENT PATTERN
OF NATIONAL EXPENDITURES

The tables and charts here and elsewhere in this volume tell better than words the astounding story of the growth of the expenditures of the national government since the founding of our nation. A few observations are justified. In the first place, the shift in public expenditures among the various levels of government has been pronounced. Prior to the depression of the thirties, the national government accounted for about 35 percent of the total governmental expenditures in the United States, the states about 15 percent, and the local units about 50 percent. Today, the national government spends about 70 percent, the states about 12, and the local units 18. In the second place, national governmental income has equaled or exceeded outgo only about half the time in our national history. Presidents Lincoln, Grant, Hayes, Garfield, Arthur, Franklin Roosevelt and Kennedy never experienced one year of balanced budgets during their tenures of office; and Madison, Van Buren, Tyler, McKinley, Wilson, Truman, and Eisenhower had more years of deficits than of balances. Thus far, Johnson has had only deficits. In only five years since 1930 has the government lived within its income. In the third place, the towering costs of modern government at the national level are attributable, as a noted Senator has said, to the "warfare" world rather than to the "welfare" state. More than 75 percent of our national expenditures have, since 1942, steadily gone into war, its aftermath, its conduct or preparation for it. The total national budget as outlined by the President and reported in the news ordinarily does not include a substantial part of the actual income and outgo. It is now referred to as the administrative budget. All payments into and out of trust funds like those for OASI, the long-range highway programs and others are not included and receipts of large government enterprises like the Post Office and TVA are counted only in the "cash flow" or "national income account" methods of reporting national expenditures. Finally, the mere size of the present national budget has overborne the laudable efforts described earlier to develop a rational procedure in the executive branch and in Congress for handling the annual tax and expenditure programs.

THE GROWTH OF NATIONAL EXPENDITURES
ADMINISTRATIVE BUDGET
(In Millions of Dollars)

Period	Yearly Average
1789-1800	5.7
1801-1810	9.1
1811-1820	23.9
1821-1830	16.2
1831-1840	24.5
1841-1850	34.1
1851-1860	60.2
1861-1865	683.8
1866-1870	377.6
1871-1875	287.5
1876-1880	255.6
1881-1885	257.7
1886-1890	279.1
1891-1895	363.6
1896-1900	457.5
1901-1905	535.6
1906-1910	639.2
1911-1915	720.3
1916-1920	8,065.3
1921-1925	3,579.0
1926-1930	3,182.8
1931-1935	5,214.9
1936-1940	8,267.2
1941-1945	64,242.5
1946-1950	42,801.4
1951-1955	63,332.3
1956-1960	73,088.0
1960-1965	91,422.0

Adapted from *Statistical Abstract of the United States, 1965.*

PATTERN OF EXPENDITURES
NATIONAL GOVERNMENT—FISCAL, 1965
(In Millions of Dollars)

Major National Security	52.2
International Affairs and Finance	4.0
Space Research and Technology	4.9
Veterans Services and Benefits	5.4
Labor & Welfare	6.2
Agriculture and Agricultural Resources	4.5
Natural Resources	2.7
Commerce, Housing	3.4
Education	1.5
General Government	2.4
Interest	11.3
Adjustment for Interfund Transactions	1.
Subtotal Administrative Budget	97.5

Additional Items Not Ordinarily Summarized

Payments to Trust Funds—Social Insurance, Highways, Veterans Insurance, etc.	39.0
Earnings Spent by Government Enterprises, Post Office Receipts, Power Sales, etc.	15.2
Grand Total	141.7

SOURCES OF NATIONAL FUNDS

1. Loans

Governments on all levels habitually live partly on borrowed money. In a given year, they may take in as much as they spend and thus have the comfort of a "balanced budget." But hardly ever are they out of debt; and in periods of stress their borrowings may mount to disturbing totals. Borrowings are not revenue. A man borrowing $1000 from a bank may have the money in his pocket, but he is not taxed on it as income; for of course it is *not* income. At some specified rate of interest, he may have the use of it for a while. But he will have to pay it back. Nevertheless, borrowing is a source from which for a good many years, even in peacetime, our national government has been deriving a considerable part of its current operating funds.

2. Nontax revenue

Most of the actual revenue commonly comes from taxes. There is, however, a good deal of nontax revenue. To begin with, the government carries on business, or quasi-business, enterprises and pockets the receipts from them as any private business man or corporation would do. One thinks instantly of the postal service, from which in 1965 the government drew more than $4.4 billion—not *profit* certainly, but that is beside the present point. There are receipts also from the mints, the Government Printing Office, the Tennessee Valley Authority, the Alaska Railroad, the Panama Canal, the various power installations, and other such diversified sources. In the second place, there is income from fees charged for services or privileges, as when a patent is applied for, a book copyrighted, or a lawyer admitted to practice before the Supreme Court. Third, there are fines levied in the courts, penalties for non-payment of taxes, and forfeitures of property taken from transgressors, for example, liquor or tobacco on which the required excise taxes have not been paid, or liquor, jewelry, perfumes, and the like confiscated from smugglers or from importers and travelers making fraudulent declarations. There are sales of property, too—public land or surplus war equipment. There are rentals from grazing lands and irrigated areas. There is interest on loans to farmers and to homeowners. There are even gifts, as the National Gallery of Art in Washington (presented by the Mellon estate) eloquently testifies. Relatively, the national government enjoys less nontax revenue than do many of the states, especially with their heavy national subsidies in the form of grants-in-aid.

Nevertheless, the national government lives principally from taxes. A *3. Taxes* major difference between the government under the Articles of Confederation and that under our present Constitution is that, whereas the former could raise money (aside from borrowings) only by making requisitions upon more or less reluctant and negligent states, the latter can reach down past the state governments to the individual citizen, levy on his business transactions, income, inheritances, and the like, and enforce payment, if necessary, by seizing and selling his possessions. Very appropriately, the long list of powers given Congress in the eighth section of the Constitution's first article starts off with the power "to lay and collect taxes, duties, imposts, and excises." Nor was it simply by chance that the Constitution's framers employed all of these different terms. To them, "taxes" meant primarily levies, like poll taxes and land taxes, falling *directly* on persons or property, and with the burden impossible to shift to other shoulders; "duties" and "imposts" denoted levies on imports and exports, respectively (what we commonly call tariff or customs duties [13]); and "excises" were levies on the production, distribution, or use of commodities—"internal revenue," as we early fell into the habit of terming this form of tax in distinction from revenue derived from foreign trade and collected at the ports. Moreover, in contrast with taxes, duties, imposts, and excises are *indirect,* in that, they can be, and commonly are, passed on to the consumer in the form of higher prices for goods, so that it really is he who pays the duty or excise, even though he may not realize that he is doing so. The various terms employed in the taxing clause are therefore not without significance, even though in everyday

---

[13] Although (in the clause cited) using terms broad enough to include national levies on exports, the Constitution elsewhere forbids any such to be laid.

RECEIPTS OF THE NATIONAL GOVERNMENT
FISCAL, 1965
(In Millions of Dollars)

Individual Income Taxes		47.0
Corporate Income Taxes		25.6
Excise Taxes		10.7
Alcoholic Beverage	3.7	
Tobacco	2.1	
Manufacturer's (Gasoline, Oil, Autos)	2.7	
Retailers (Jewelry, Furs, Cosmetics)	.5	
Misc.	1.7	
Estate and Gift Taxes		2.8
Customs Duties		1.4
Misc.		4.4
Interfund Adjustments		−.7
Total Administrative Budget Receipts		91.2
Trust Fund Receipts		
Employment Taxes	16.6	
Highway Excise Taxes	3.6	
Interest	1.7	
Misc.	8.6	
Total		30.5
Enterprise Receipts		15.2
Grand Total		136.9

usage it is customary to lump all of the different levies together under the general heading of taxes—which, indeed, we shall do in the present chapter.

A tax (in the broad sense indicated) is, of course, a levy or charge imposed normally to raise money for public purposes [14]—"an exaction," the Supreme Court has said, "for the support of the government." [15] It may be assessed upon individuals or upon corporations or other groups. It may take any one of many forms (not all employed by the national government)—property taxes, income taxes, excise taxes, sales taxes, license taxes, inheritance taxes, poll taxes, tariff duties, and still others. It may be direct or indirect. Always, however, a tax is compulsory; one may choose whether to pay rent or wages or prices, but not whether to pay taxes. Furthermore, while justified solely as a contribution in return for government service rendered (in at least some broad sense), tax burdens necessarily are apportioned among payers according to their property, income, business transactions, and the like, and not at all on the basis of benefits individually received. It may be presumed,

[14] The qualified form of statement is made necessary by the circumstance that, as we shall see, taxes are occasionally designed primarily for regulative purposes and only incidentally to raise revenue.

[15] United States v. Butler, 297 U. S. 1 (1936), 61.

however, that when tax money is employed for police or military protection, for example, the big taxpayer has more to be protected and in that sense gets service in some proportion to what he pays.

THE TAXING POWER

Under the Constitution's taxing clause, Congress has general freedom to tax persons and objects within the national jurisdiction, and with nothing said about the rates that may be imposed. If the people at large think themselves taxed oppressively, they will find remedy, not in the courts, but in electing a Congress—perchance also a President—pledged, or at least predisposed, to a different tax policy. Comprehensive, however, as the taxing power is, it can be exercised only in accordance with certain express or implied restrictions. *Restrictions:*

To begin with, Congress is not free to levy taxes for any conceivable purpose whatsoever, but only (as the Constitution plainly says) "to pay the debts and provide for the common defense and general welfare of the United States." "Debts" and "defense" are sufficiently definite terms. "General welfare," however, is so broad that there always have been differences of opinion as to what activities and objectives may be read into it. It no longer, however, offers much of a hurdle for tax- and spending-planners to surmount. *1. Purpose*

Down to World War I, the largest part of the national revenue always came from indirect taxes; and, as we shall see, a large share is still derived from that source. In laying taxes of this kind, Congress, however, is bound by the constitutional provision that "all duties, imposts, and excises shall be uniform throughout the United States." The requirement does not prevent tobacco excises, for example, from falling more heavily upon regions where tobacco products are manufactured extensively than upon others where there is little industry of the kind; it means merely that, in general, all cigars or cigarettes of a given kind or condition must be taxed at the same rate in all parts of the country. A tax may fall with very different weight on different areas, on different businesses, or on different classes of people. But—save as qualified with respect to tariff duties—it must bear with the same weight on the same objects of taxation wherever found. *2. Uniformity of indirect taxes*

To reinforce this principle, the Constitution further enjoins that in regulating commerce Congress shall not authorize customs duties to be collected at one rate at one port and at a different rate at another, or to be computed at different ports according to different rules. At one time, this meant absolute uniformity at all ports for any given kind or class of imports, whatever their place of origin. Under Supreme Court decisions since 1901, however, rates on commodities coming from the insular dependencies may differ from those on imports from other areas; and under the trade agreement system instituted in 1934 there is much additional variation, according to the foreign country from which given commodities are received. The constitutional re- *3. Uniformity among ports of entry* striction mentioned, however, is fully preserved; the duty on a box of cigars from Puerto Rico may differ from that on a box from Brazil, but each will be uniform at all ports.

4. Other express restrictions

The taxing power is further limited (1) by a constitutional provision forbidding duties to be imposed on exports, although Congress is authorized to regulate export trade in every way other than by taxation; and (2) by a requirement that direct taxes shall be apportioned among the several states according to population. As interpreted in earlier days, to include only poll or capitation taxes and taxes on land (and at one time slaves), direct taxes have been laid by Congress only four times in our history, most recently in 1861.[16] Taxes on incomes laid in 1862 were held by the Supreme Court to be excise, not direct, levies. When, however, the validity of a new income tax law was challenged in the last decade of the century, the Court ruled differently.[17] Ultimately the obvious impossibility of taxing incomes in accordance with any mathematical apportionment among the states led in 1913 to adoption of the Sixteenth Amendment, brushing aside the entire question of whether income taxes are or are not direct taxes and expressly authorizing Congress to "lay and collect taxes on incomes, from whatever source derived," without apportionment.

5. Implied restrictions

Finally may be mentioned restrictions nowhere specified but up to now regarded, with judicial support, as implicit in the nature of the federal union: restraints from taxing (a) the property or essential functions of state governments or their subdivisions, and (b) securities issued by such jurisdictions or incomes derived therefrom. As observed elsewhere, the restriction relating to securities probably will in time be abrogated by Congress, with Supreme Court sanction, as a similar one on the taxation of state and local salaries already has been.

Taxation not primarily for revenue

Most laws imposing taxation can readily be classed as revenue measures, that is, measures in which the primary, if not sole, purpose is to produce income for the government. As intimated above, some measures are tax laws in form but intended mainly or entirely for regulative purposes and, if yielding revenue at all, do so only incidentally. A good example is tariff schedules planned for the protection of American industries against foreign competition. Insofar as goods affected find their way to our ports notwithstanding heavy duties payable on them, revenue results. But high productiveness is not expected. Indeed, Congress has at times gone so far as to impose taxes with the avowed purpose of destroying a business enterprise altogether—taxing it out of existence and thereby rendering it wholly unproductive. A case in point is the act of 1865—in form a tax measure pure and simple—imposing so onerous a levy on notes issued by state banks that, as was the intention, it became unprofitable to issue them and their issuance ceased. In general,

[16] C. J. Bullock, "The Origin, Purpose, and Effect of the Direct-Tax Clause in the Federal Constitution," *Polit. Sci. Quar.*, XV, 217-239, 452-484 (Sept. and June, 1900).
[17] Pollock v. Farmers' Loan and Trust Co., 158 U. S. 601 (1895).

measures of the kind have been sustained whenever the courts considered that the taxing power was being used in pursuit of a purpose expressly or impliedly within the scope of Congressional authority. Protective tariffs, however, have commonly been upheld, quite apart from the taxing power, on the basis of power to regulate foreign commerce.

Is a tax constitutional when not clearly either a revenue measure or a device for rendering effective some delegated or implied power, but rather is aimed principally or solely at promoting the general welfare of which we have spoken? This question was raised pointedly by laws of 1886 and later laying burdensome excise taxes on wholesale and retail sales of oleomargarine colored to resemble butter; by an act of 1912 taxing the manufacture of poisonous white phosphorous matches (and almost completely ending the industry); by laws of 1914 and 1919 imposing taxes on registered dealers in narcotic drugs; by the child labor law of 1919 laying a special tax on the profits of industrial establishments employing children under the age of 16; and by the Agricultural Adjustment Act of 1933 imposing levies on processors of grains, meat, cotton, and other commodities as a means of raising money for a program of curtailing agricultural production. In cases coming before it at different times, the Supreme Court upheld the oleomargarine and narcotics laws as revenue measures, refusing to inquire into the legislative intent behind them; [18] and the constitutionality of the phosphorous match law has never been judicially tested. When, however, the child labor law was challenged, the Court fixed attention on the motive animating Congress and held the measure invalid for the reason that the tax imposed had as its sole purpose an objective—the regulation of child labor—regarded by the justices then sitting as a function reserved to the states.[19] Similarly, the Agricultural Adjustment Act was overthrown not only because, said the justices, the processing taxes for which it provided were not true taxes in the sense of levies for general support of the government, but also because these taxes, too, were being employed to extend the national regulating arm into a field—the control of agricultural production —belonging to the states.[20] In other words, the taxing power might not properly be invoked, even for the sake of the general welfare, when the effect would be to project national authority beyond limits constitutionally fixed, and as understood by the judges.

Since these decisions were rendered, however, there have been changes. A Court with different personnel and viewpoints has broadened its concept of national power (especially under the commerce clause) as illustrated by the

Taxation and "general welfare"

A changed attitude

---

[18] McCray v. United States, 195 U. S. 27 (1904); United States v. Doremus, 249 U. S. 86 (1919); Nigro v. United States, 276 U. S. 332 (1928). Over vigorous opposition from dairy interests, all oleomargarine taxes were repealed in 1950, with, however, numerous state taxes and other restrictions remaining.

[19] Bailey v. Drexel Furniture Co., 259 U. S. 20 (1922).

[20] United States v. Butler, 297 U. S. 1 (1936). Cf. Carter v. Carter Coal Co., 298 U. S. 238 (1936), in which a tax on producers of bituminous coal was similarly invalidated.

justices' approval of the Social Security taxes introduced in 1935.[21] General welfare now can be promoted by levies which once would hardly have escaped judicial condemnation; and the presumption is that to the many occasions on which the national taxing power already has been used in advancing social and economic ends, with considerations of revenue wholly incidental, will in future be added still others of major significance. When the question is one of justifying taxing or spending on the basis of welfare, not only Congress itself but the Supreme Court as now constituted is rather more easily satisfied than before. In much of our pre-World War II income and inheritance taxation, indeed, the purpose of curbing "swollen fortunes" can be discerned almost as clearly as that of obtaining revenue. In messages to Congress in 1935 and on other occasions, President Franklin D. Roosevelt, pushing farther ideas advanced by President Theodore Roosevelt, Wilson, and Hoover, warmly advocated such a policy, with a view to more equitable distribution of wealth and economic power. Since 1940, the problem has very nearly been taken care of automatically by tax schedules drawn to meet the heaviest demands for revenue in the country's history.

THE ENACTMENT OF TAX MEASURES

Origins and frequency of tax legislation

Appropriations are usually made for some specified and limited period, most commonly a year, and consequently a sheaf of appropriation bills must be passed every 12 months, with deficiency measures interspersed as needed. Measures imposing or readjusting taxation, on the other hand, are usually without time limits; a given tax once levied, or a given rate once established, continues operative as long as not repealed or amended. It is true, however, that in recent years Congress has exhibited a tendency to enact temporary or "emergency" taxes. Every annual budget transmitted to Congress by the President contains estimates of the revenue to be anticipated from existing sources. Along with these commonly will be submitted proposals for increasing the inflow by new or amended taxation if the yield does not promise to be sufficient, or for decreasing it if it promises to exceed needs, or perchance for maintaining the yield but redistributing tax burdens. On its part, Congress, too, may—as in the case of two tax-reduction bills killed by Presidential veto in 1947 and one passed over a veto in 1948—initiate revenue measures wholly outside of the executive's budget plans and even conflicting with them. Accordingly, tax legislation (if not in the form of a comprehensive overall revenue act, at least in that of a more or less significant amending measure) is to be anticipated with substantially the same yearly regularity as appropriation acts.

The handling of revenue bills

All measures for raising national revenue are required by the Constitution to originate in the House of Representatives. All portions of the President's annual budget message relating to the subject are immediately referred

---

[21] The object of these taxes was not to raise money, but to induce the states to establish employment insurance systems.

to the Ways and Means Committee of that body; and to this group it falls to whip into shape a tax bill, sometimes following closely, sometimes less so, the plans and recommendations of the chief executive and his budget director. Working for weeks, through subcommittees when necessary, and with help from conferences with the chief executive, budget director, Treasury officials, bankers, businessmen, and others, the committee finally emerges with a measure which for further weeks absorbs much of the time and energy of the House. Passed by that body, the bill goes to the Senate, where, notwithstanding that the House was originally intended to enjoy substantial primacy in controlling the national purse, most revenue measures are more or less drastically altered, either in the Finance Committee or on the floor. There is, indeed, nothing to prevent the Senate from amending a House revenue bill by striking out all parts after the enacting clause and inserting an entirely new bill; and something of the sort has happened on several occasions. It is even possible for a bill which in effect, and almost in technical form, is a bill to raise revenue to be passed in the Senate before the House has taken any action at all. In any event, a major tax bill, after passing in both branches, will certainly have to "go to conference." Commonly it is in the form in which it emerges from conference that the two houses finally enact it and the President signs it.[22] Throughout the entire procedure, the country—especially the business element—watches with interest, and even anxiety, to see what new taxes will be decided upon, and what increases or other changes will be made in existing ones.

THE PATTERN OF TAXATION

On the basis of "incidence," that is, the point where the actual burden falls, taxes may be classified as direct and indirect—the former assessed upon and paid (as in the case of land taxes and poll taxes) by persons who cannot shift the impact to other shoulders; the latter imposed and collected commonly at some stage of production or distribution, and afterwards passed on (in the form of higher prices for commodities) to consumers. Back in the eighteenth century, the national government started off by relying almost entirely on indirect levies, principally duties on imports designed to shelter the country's developing industries as well as to yield revenue. So satisfactorily were tax

Earlier situation

---

[22] Until 1947, the only Presidential veto of a general revenue bill in the nation's history was President Franklin D. Roosevelt's strongly worded disapproval, February 22, 1944, of a measure providing for hardly more than one-fifth of the additional revenue of $10.5 billion urgently requested by the administration—a bill objectionable to the President also on other grounds. In both houses, the veto was overridden by heavy majorities. In June and July, 1947, President Truman successfully vetoed two major revenue bills (differing only in dates for taking effect)—both providing for a substantial lowering of income tax rates, and both framed and introduced in a Republican Congress over strong Presidential objection. In April, 1948, he vetoed another such bill, but this time unsuccessfully.

needs met in this way that until the Civil War direct taxes were invoked only three times, and even excise taxes (indirect) only in two brief early periods. The exigencies of the conflict between the states, however, not only forced a temporary reversion to direct taxation, but brought excise taxes once more into use; and from then on these had a place in the tax structure. Tariff duties were, however, dominant for a good many years. Sometimes the point was made that people would be more tax-conscious, and therefore more concerned about economy and efficiency in government, if taxation were less disguised. But politicians always considered it good strategy to keep the tax burden well concealed.

Later changes   Throughout a long period of our history, the country's tax structure was thus relatively stable: state and local governments lived principally from the proceeds of the general property tax, the national government principally from the yield of customs duties. The past 60 years, however, have brought changes greatly complicating the tax picture. Mounting expenditures, increasing inadequacy of the general property tax, tempting new resources for revenue like motor cars and gasoline, and newer tax ideas and objectives, have attracted the states to numerous forms of taxation rarely or never employed before. On its part, the national government has revolutionized its tax pattern, with customs duties relegated to an insignificant position and reliance now placed mainly upon levies on incomes, on the production and consumption of goods, and on inheritances. The shift in the national sphere came shortly before World War I, when, with the idea growing that the nation's principal tax should be based on ability to pay as measured in terms of individual and corporate incomes, this newer (although not wholly untried) form of levy, validated by the Sixteenth Amendment, established itself promptly and firmly in our system.[23] One of the advantages of income taxation is its flexibility—the ease with which, by juggling a few rates and brackets, it can be made to yield vastly more or vastly less as desired. Under the impact of the then unparalleled wartime expenditures of 1917-1918, the national revenue from this source rose to first place—a position which it consistently maintained until 1933. With depression conditions deepening in the early thirties, taxes on personal and corporate incomes yielded steadily diminishing returns. Once more the bulk of national revenue began to come from customs duties and excises, even though languishing commerce and slackened business caused these also to produce less than formerly. Some measure of prosperity, however, having been regained, the income tax stream began rising again in 1937; and under wartime tax legislation after 1941 it became a torrent, quite transcending all other tax sources.[24]

1. Income taxes: The largest single source of revenue of the national government today

[23] State taxation of incomes started slightly earlier—in Wisconsin in 1911.

[24] The national government has never imposed a general sales tax, although proposals to do so received attention during the Civil War, in 1917-22, in 1932-33, in 1942-43, and in 1951.

is the individual income tax. As enacted in 1913, this tax fell upon only 2 or 3 million persons and at a graduated rate beginning at 4 percent on net taxable income in excess of $5500 for a married man. Under the pressure of war emergencies the rates have been revised upward quite sharply and the deductions and exemptions downward, so that more than 70 million persons now file returns. In other words, all but a small handful of the wage earners of the United States pay a tax on their incomes to the national government. A large proportion of modern income tax payers pay their taxes "painlessly" through a scheme introduced in 1943 of employer withholding of a portion of their wages each pay period and transmitting the deducted portion to the government. A reckoning, of course, still occurs on April 15 (until 1955, March 15) when each taxpayer computes his tax liability for the previous year and pays any amount still owing or, perchance, files a claim for a refund from the total already paid for him by his employer. *a. Individual*

The modern income tax is a tax on "net" income rather than on total receipts. From the total earnings from all taxable sources, there may be subtracted: (1) personal allowance of $600 for each person dependent on the taxpayer including the taxpayer himself; (2) expenses incurred by self-employed, professional, and wage-earning taxpayers in earning the income; (3) privileged personal expenses, for example, donations for religious, charitable, or educational purposes, abnormal medical expenses, interest paid on loans, and taxes of many kinds paid to other governmental units. On the balance of the income after these allowances and deductions are taken, a graduated tax is imposed. The rate of this tax in 1965 was 14 percent on the first $500, advancing by steps to 70 percent on net income in excess of $200,000. The graduation or "progressivity" in the tax rates is designed to make larger incomes pay a proportionately larger tax on the theory that the higher the income the greater the ability of the taxpayer to support his government.

A tax is also imposed on the annual net income of corporations and this ranks next to the individual income tax in the size and importance of its yield to the national government. This is undoubtedly the most complex tax used by the national government. Most of its complexities arise from an earnest effort of lawmakers to have the tax fall on the "net" income of corporations after allowances are made for legitimate expenses in earning the income. The rate of tax on corporate net income is 22 percent on the first $25,000 and 48 percent on the remainder.[25] During World War II and from 1951 to 1953, the corporation income tax was supplemented by an "excess" profits tax designed, in theory at least, to levy on the swollen corporate earnings of wartime so as to recapture as much of the abnormal profit as possible. In general and with numerous exceptions, the tax fell on the difference between "normal" earnings and those of the years in which the tax was imposed. The most recent excess profits tax, associated with the Korean combat and rearmament was fixed at *b. Corporate*

[25] The basic 22 percent rate is referred to in the law as a "normal" tax and the extra 26 percent on the amount over $25,000 is referred to as a surtax.

30 percent of the abnormal earnings, but the combined corporate income and excess profits taxes could not exceed 70 percent of the net income.

2. Estate and gift taxes

On a number of occasions from the Civil War onwards, the national government imposed some form of tax on estates of deceased persons or on inheritances of portions thereof. Since 1916, an estate tax has been a regular feature of the national tax pattern. Formerly, exemptions ran as high as $100,-000, and rates in lower brackets were relatively moderate, although high in upper ones. Naturally, under wartime taxation, exemptions were reduced (to $60,000) and rates stiffened. In order to reach wealth that might escape estate taxation by being given away by the possessor with that end in view, a gift tax (on a graduated scale approximately three-fourths as heavy as estate taxation) was introduced in 1924, repealed in 1926, and reimposed in 1932. In order to protect existing state inheritance taxes, a credit of 25 percent against national tax liability for taxes paid to a state was inaugurated in 1924. It was increased to 80 percent in 1926. The Revenue Act of 1954 substantially reduced this credit. Estate tax rates were increased during World War II. The present rate is 3 percent on the first $5000 above the $60,000 exemption, graduated to 77 percent on estates of more than $10 million. Combined with "progressive" income taxes, estate and gift taxes now operate powerfully to check the growth and transmission of large fortunes.

3. Excise taxes

Everybody pays national taxes, although many people do so without realizing it. Even persons of means too modest to be reached by the income tax make their contributions when they buy articles like a package of cigarettes, priced so as to cover the excise tax due the government from the manufacturer or distributor. Traditionally, excise, or "consumption," taxes have been planned to fall principally on luxury goods, and therefore to be paid chiefly by the comparatively well-to-do. The theory, however, never was completely adhered to in practice; and excises were progressively broadened during World War II until long lists of articles were covered which, for many people at all events, were everyday necessities. In 1947, existing heavy rates on tobacco, liquor, motor fuel, theater admissions, cosmetics, and scores of other articles were continued indefinitely by Congress. By 1950, however, popular demand for relief reached a point where both President and Congress became agreeable to a readjustment (the President on condition that lost revenue be made up in some other way). The Korean crisis, however, quickly turned the government's concern from remitting taxes to increasing them. It was not until 1954 that a Republican Congress was able to make a general reduction in excise taxes. A few more reductions were made in 1959 and substantial reductions were achieved in 1965.

4. Payroll taxes

A special form of excise is a tax imposed upon employers for support of state systems of unemployment insurance under the Social Security program. Levied by the national government, the tax differs from others in that its proceeds are not for general government purposes; only about 10 percent of the yield actually accrues to the national government at all, the remainder being simply held by the Treasury for requisitions by the states for paying benefits. Even the 10 percent is employed in meeting administrative costs of the system. Of similar nature (although without the states involved) are payroll taxes on both employers and employees for support of the old age and survivors insurance system.

SOME QUESTIONS OF TAX POLICY

The close of World War II and later of the Korean conflict naturally left the country vitally concerned about reduction of the extraordinarily heavy tax burden carried over from the war years. Despite some lowering of income and excise taxes, such concern is still deeply felt. No one, however, pretending to any understanding of the current world situation and of America's relation to it, or of the financial implications entailed, looks forward to any very significant curtailment of taxes in the foreseeable future. Cold war with the U.S.S.R., preparations for eventualities if cold war should suddenly break into armed conflict, assistance to nations we hope to have on our side in such a situation, a huge debt largely incurred in past war, to say nothing of mounting costs of Social Security and other domestic services—indicate a continuance of high levels of taxation. Barring unexpected developments, such as a Russian collapse, people and politicians will for a good while be most concerned about tax programs in terms of an immediate crisis.

Long before World War II, however, criticisms of our tax methods, policies, and objectives suggested need for general reconsideration and overhauling of our system. A few of the older long-term issues may at least be called to mind. Should any new forms of taxation be introduced, for example, taxation of income from state and local securities, or fees for licenses, certificates, and other papers now issued gratis? Should the income tax base be broadened by terminating exemptions now enjoyed by a lengthy list of interests and enterprises, such as farm and consumer cooperatives, mutual insurance companies, rural electrification undertakings, surplus funds of labor unions, and even philanthropic and educational organizations in so far as engaged in business enterprises? Should the taxation of incomes be deliberately kept at levels, in the higher brackets, making accumulation of wealth difficult or impossible? How can adequate revenue be raised without unduly impairing the volume of production and the general level of national income? And what about the time-honored issue of duplicating, or "double," taxation? A word here on this last-mentioned matter is perhaps in order.

1. Readjustment of national taxation

With both nation and states reaching out in recent decades for new sources of revenue, it has come about that frequently they are found taxing the same objects. In recent years, indeed, no less than 90 percent of national and state receipts came from the same sources. To be sure, the national government leaves the general property tax entirely to the states (principally for

2. "Double taxation"

local use) and, as we have seen, relies for the major part of its revenue upon personal and corporate income taxes, estate and inheritance taxes, and consumption taxes of different kinds. But nearly all of the objects affected are taxed by some or all of the states as well. Indeed, apart from the general property tax and customs duties, there are few if any important forms of taxation not claimed by both national and state governments, each without much regard to the other. Often (indeed almost invariably in these days) the sums collected by the national government within a state from a given tax exceed the amounts collected from that tax by the state itself. Persons finding their salaries or the gasoline they buy taxed twice sometimes harbor an idea that such double imposition is unconstitutional. In this, they are wrong. The Constitution has nothing to say against double taxation; it in effect presupposes it by leaving broad and general taxing powers to two largely independent governments, both resting directly upon the people. Even though not unconstitutional, however, the existing situation imposes handicaps on business and industry and sometimes excessive burdens on individual taxpayers, and one will not be surprised to learn that a good deal of thought has been devoted to it not only by tax experts but by business organizations, taxpayer associations, and state officials. Sometimes it is suggested that the national government withdraw from gasoline taxation (a field which it entered only in 1932), while the states give up taxing tobacco and its products; or that, in return for a monopoly of taxing liquor, the states give up taxing incomes. Often it is urged that the national government stop competing with states and localities by taxing amusements, local telephone calls, retail electrical energy, and other things. The issue is further entangled in the complexities of the grant-in-aid controversy. Those who propose the abandonment of some national aids to states, of course, expect the national government to abandon some taxes so the states can take up the burden more easily. A recent extensive staff study in the Treasury Department, however, stops short of any definite recommendations on these or related lines, as does the study of President Eisenhower's Commission on Intergovernmental Relations. In a period when all governments instinctively shy away from proposals looking to drying up sources of revenue, solutions are not in sight.[26]

[26] On the general subject, see W. Kilpatrick, "Neglected Aspects of Intergovernmental Fiscal Relations," *Amer. Polit. Sci. Rev.*, XLI, 452-462 (June, 1947); also three articles by J. W. Martin: "The Problems of Duplicating Federal and State Taxes," *State Government*, XVII, 287-289 (Mar., 1944); "Functions of Intergovernmental Administrative Co-operation in Taxation," *ibid.*, XVII, 327-332 (May, 1944); and "Federal-State Tax Co-operation," *Nat. Mun. Rev.*, XXXIV, 21-26 (Jan., 1945). In February, 1933, an interstate commission on conflicting taxation was set up by the Interstate Legislative Assembly of the American Legislators' Association, and in 1935 it published at Chicago a volume entitled *Conflicting Taxation*. This, however, is now largely superseded by the Treasury Department study mentioned (Division of Tax Research, Treasury Department, *Federal-State Tax Co-ordination*, mimeo., Washington, 1947). See also, the *Report of the Commission on Intergovernmental Relations* (Washington, 1955), Chap. IV; J. A. Maxwell, *The Fiscal Impact of Federalism in the United States* (Cambridge, Mass., 1946).

BORROWING MONEY: THE NATIONAL DEBT

When expenditures and revenues are approximately equal, a government *The bor-* is said to have a balanced budget. If, on the other hand, expenditures exceed *rowing* receipts, there is a deficit, and the budget is said to be out of balance. In *power* ordinary times, and for ordinary purposes, income derived from taxation, supplemented by receipts from nontax sources, ought to be, and much of the time has been, sufficient to meet the government's needs. In time of war or threat of war, however, or other unusual strain, for example, a depression, or to meet the cost of some special undertaking like the Panama Canal or a Marshall Plan, the government must borrow. The accumulated obligations thus incurred give rise to the national debt. Power to borrow not only is expressly conferred in the Constitution, but is one of the very few powers entirely unencumbered by restrictions—with the result that Congress may borrow from any lenders, for any purposes, in any amounts, on any terms, and with or without provision for the repayment of loans, with or without interest.[27]

Borrowing may take any one of several forms. By authority of Congress, *Methods* the Treasury may sell notes or certificates attractive to banks and other institu- *of bor-* tions; and this is constantly done. To accelerate tax receipts, it may issue "tax *rowing* anticipation" notes to large taxpayers, to be turned in by the corporation or individual at tax time at face value plus interest received on what has been in effect a loan. It may and does, in effect, borrow from itself; that is to say, it may arrange for interest-bearing loans out of funds accumulated and held for specific purposes by national agencies, for example, old-age, unemployment, veterans, and bank deposit insurance funds and postal savings deposits. Of far greater importance, however, is the sale of long-term interest-bearing bonds in large denominations to banks, insurance companies, administrators of trust funds, and the like, and in smaller denominations (down to $25 savings bonds) to individual savers and investors. For some years now there has been a continuing controversy between the Treasury and Congress over the statutory ceiling (4.25 percent) on interest on new long-term government bonds. The Treasury has argued that this has forced it to place too much of the debt (80 percent in 1961) in relatively short-term securities with more marketable interest rates. The Congress has taken the position that removing the ceiling will stimulate a general rise in interest rates.[28] The position of banks is such that

[27] The United States operates under no *constitutional* debt limit, such as is fixed for many of the states in their constitutions and such as states commonly establish for counties and cities. Since 1917, however, a debt limit has been maintained by act of Congress, the figure being raised by stages during World War II to $300 billion (March, 1945), later lowered to $275 billion (June, 1946) and then raised to $285 billion (June, 1959). Beginning in 1953 temporary rises in the authorized debt ceiling have been made by Congress and in 1965 the temporary ceiling stood at $328 billion. A critical study of the ceiling system for debt management is M. A. Robinson, *The National Debt Ceiling: An Experiment in Fiscal Policy* (Washington, 1959).

[28] When conditions become favorable, the government may, however, refund a loan, i.e., retire it and substitute another at lower interest rates.

THE NATIONAL DEBT
Selected Years, 1791-1965

Year	Gross Debt in Millions of Dollars
1791	75
1801	83
1816	127
1821	90
1831	39
1840	3.5
1851	68
1861	91
1866	2,755
1871	2,322
1881	2,019
1891	1,005
1901	1,221
1911	1,154
1919	25,482
1931	16,801
1941	48,961
1946	269,422
1951	255,222
1961	289,211
1965	316,545

they can virtually be compelled to purchase. In the case of private individuals, if in time of special need the investment motive, reinforced by patriotic appeals and high-pressure salesmanship, fails to bring about voluntary purchases in sufficient amounts, the government may force them by "deferred-savings" devices of one kind or another.[29]

The problem of liqui- dation

During the past half-century, the United States has been added to the long list of countries laboring under a huge national debt. The national government, after three decades of deficit financing, now owes $1600 for each man, woman, and child in the United States. People who think seriously about such matters are by no means of one mind on how a debt of such proportions might be expected to affect the country's future. Some, comforted by the circumstance that we "owed the debt to ourselves" and not to foreign lenders,[30] thought that,

[29] During the Civil War, there was borrowing even by inflating the currency. The government issued "greenbacks" covered by no adequate reserve of gold or silver, and then used them in paying for goods and services; anyone accepting them in effect held simply government promises to pay, supported merely by a good reputation for integrity.

[30] The "owners" of the debt today consist of individuals (about 27 percent), banks (about 26 percent), corporations, institutions, insurance companies, state and local governments, and other American investors, all of whom have a stake in everything pertaining to the way in which the debt is handled.

with moderate national prosperity, the burden could be carried and the debt itself gradually reduced with no perceptible lowering of living standards. Others could not see how owing the debt to ourselves made any great amount of difference (we still *owed* it), or how the dead weight of so stupendous an obligation could fail to retard economic and social progress over a long period of years. Certain it was that generations as yet unborn would feel the impact of debt burdens which we in our time had improvidently piled up. Certain it was also that the least that this generation could decently do, for its own good as well as that of succeeding ones, was to whittle down the burden as rapidly as possible by scrupulously meeting all interest charges as they fell due and paying off principal whenever the national income permitted. Favored by a very high level of national prosperity, as well as by a combination of fiscal circumstances too complicated to be explained here, the government actually did contrive to shave off about $25 billion from the peak debt at the end of World War II. Rearmament, Korea, and the cold war, however, renewed deficit spending and the debt has now climbed past the height reached in 1946. If the nation cannot tax itself sufficiently to pay the going expenses of the government during a period of unprecedented prosperity and high standards of living, the outlook for any significant lowering of the debt is dark indeed.

There is a school of opinion holding that we ought not to expect in our day to do much more than simply "maintain" the debt, paying interest scrupulously, but not making much effort to reduce principal, with the country meanwhile "growing up" to the debt by attaining such population and wealth that, proportionally, the burden would in time be materially reduced. Such rationalization of our current lack of progress with debt reduction (almost as fantastic in one direction as it is, in another, to expect the country ever to be literally debt-free) certainly does not appeal to many thoughtful people.[31]

References

1. NATIONAL EXPENDITURES: THE BUDGET SYSTEM

R. Young, *This Is Congress* (New York, 1943), Chap. VII.

C. S. Hyneman, *Bureaucracy in a Democracy* (New York, 1950), Chaps. XVII-XVIII.

D. T. Selko, *The Federal Financial System* (Washington, 1940), Chaps. IV-X, XXIII-XXIX.

——, *The Administration of Federal Finances* (Washington, 1937).

[31] See, for example, J. M. Buchanan, *Principles of Public Debt: A Defense and Restatement* (Homewood, Ill., 1958).

H. M. Groves, *Financing Government* (6th ed., New York, 1964), Chaps. XXI-XXIV.

W. Withers, *Public Finance* (New York, 1949), Pt. III.

A. E. Buck, *The Budget in Government of Today* (New York, 1934).

H. D. Smith, *The Management of Your Government* (New York, 1945).

E. E. Naylor, *The Federal Budget System in Operation* (Washington, 1941).

R. H. Rawson, "The Foundation of the Federal Budget," in C. J. Friedrich and E. S. Mason [eds.], *Public Policy* (Cambridge, Mass., 1941), Chap. IV.

F. Morstein Marx, "The Bureau of the Budget; Its Evolution and Present Role," *Amer. Polit. Sci. Rev.*, XXXIX, 653-684, 868-898 (Aug. and Oct., 1945).

L. Wilmerding, *The Spending Power; A History of the Efforts of Congress to Control Expenditures* (New Haven, Conn., 1943).

F. C. Mosher, *Program Budgeting* (Chicago, 1954).

A. Smithies, *The Budgetary Process in the United States* (New York, 1955).

V. J. Brownie, *The Control of the Public Budget* (Public Affairs Press, 1949).

G. Colm with M. Young, *The Federal Budget and the National Economy: How to Make the Federal Budget a Better Tool of Fiscal Policy* (Washington, 1955).

H. C. Mansfield, *The Comptroller-General; A Study in the Law and Practice of Financial Administration* (New Haven, Conn., 1939).

Annual Report of the Secretary of the Treasury on the State of the Finances.

F. B. Bator, *The Question of Government Spending: Public Needs and Private Wants* (New York, 1960).

R. A. Wallace, *Congressional Control of Federal Spending* (Detroit, 1960).

A. Williams, *Public Finance and Budgetary Policy* (New York, 1963).

A. Wildavsky, *The Politics of the Budgetary Process* (Boston, 1964).

D. S. Ott and A. F. Ott, *Federal Budget Policy* (Washington, 1965).

F. C. Mosher and O. F. Poland, *The Costs of American Government: Facts, Trends, and Myths* (New York, 1964).

2. NATIONAL REVENUES: THE TAX SYSTEM

D. T. Selko, *The Federal Financial System* (Washington, 1940), Chaps. I-III, XI-XXII.

H. M. Groves, *Financing Government* (6th ed., New York, 1964), Chaps. VII-XIV, XVI-XVIII.

W. Withers, *Public Finance* (New York, 1949), Pt. II.

R. G. and G. C. Blakey, *The Federal Income Tax* (New York, 1940).

P. J. Strayer, *Taxation of Small Incomes* (New York, 1939).

R. E. Manning, *Federal Excise Taxes* (Washington, 1949).

S. Ratner, *American Taxation; Its History as a Social Force in Democracy* (New York, 1942).

L. H. Kimmel, *Taxes and Economic Incentives* (Washington, 1950).

———, *Governmental Costs and Tax Levels* (Washington, 1948).

P. Studenski [ed.], *Taxation and Public Policy* (New York, 1936).

M. S. Eccles *et al.*, *Curbing Inflation Through Taxation* (New York, 1944).

R. Blough, *The Federal Taxing Process* (New York, 1952).

W. J. Shulz and C. L. Harris, *American Public Finance* (New York, 1954), Chaps. VII-XXII.

R. E. Paul, *Taxation in the United States* (Boston, 1956).

H. Stein and J. A. Pechman, *Essays in Federal Taxation,* Prepared for the Committee on Ways and Means (New York, 1959).

"Should Legislation Be Enacted by Congress Taxing State and Municipal Securities?" [Symposium], *Cong. Digest,* XXI, 69-96 (Mar., 1942).

"Federal, State, and Local Government Fiscal Relations; A Report by a Special Committee Designated to Conduct a Study on Intergovernmental Fiscal Relations in the United States," 78th Cong., 1st Sess., Sen. Doc. No. 69 (Washington, 1943).

Taxes: The Tax Magazine. Published monthly by the Commerce Clearing House, Inc., Chicago.

E. R. Rolph and G. F. Break, *Public Finance* (New York, 1961).

R. Goode, *The Individual Income Tax* (Washington, 1964).

National Bureau of Economic Research, *Public Finances: Needs, Sources, and Utilization* (Princeton, N.J., 1961).

J. J. Maxwell, *Tax Credits and Intergovernmental Fiscal Relations* (Washington, 1962).

3. Borrowing: The National Debt

H. M. Lutz, *Public Finance* (4th ed., New York, 1947), Chap. XXXII.

W. Withers, *Public Finance* (New York, 1949), Pt. v.

———, *The Public Debt* (New York, 1945).

S. E. Harris, *The National Debt and the New Economics* (New York, 1947), Chaps. I-III, XIII, XVII-XXIV.

C. C. Abbott, *Management of the Federal Debt* (New York, 1946).

H. G. Moulton, *The New Philosophy of Public Debt* (Washington, 1944).

Committee on Public Debt Policy, *Our National Debt; Its History and Its Meaning Today* (New York, 1949).

Part III

STATE GOVERNMENT

★ 26 ★

The Constitutional Basis of
State Government

THE ROLE OF THE STATES

ROBERT E. LEE, confronted in 1861 with a choice between serving the central *Are the* government and serving his state of Virginia, chose Virginia. Such a decision *states* by a major figure in public life today would be unthinkable. The United States *sovereign?* is today one people. All of the fierce loyalties of nationalism center around our government in Washington, D. C., and our institutions of production, distribution, communication, religion, and entertainment which transcend state lines. The division of governmental responsibilities between the nation and the states, although rooted in historical necessities, is continued by habit and convenience. The state is a regional unit of government performing highly important functions in the American system but it is not now and is not likely to become a self-contained, politically conscious community in the sense that Belgium or Holland are such communities. No time-worn cliché of American politics is more misleading about the realities of American life than that which refers to the "sovereign" states. Under the American federal system, it is true, the states are endowed with vast and uncharted reserved powers and in some —but a declining number of—areas of public policy the decisions of state officials may not be reviewed or countermanded by any superior. However, as we have observed in Chapter 3, the national authority has, through grants-in-aid and judicial review, established its right to review state policies and procedures in many of the important areas of public affairs.

Schools of regional writers remind us that our national "oneness" em- *Regional* braces many smaller cultures within the national whole. The patterns of *differences* thought and of politics differ widely among New England, the Plains, the Old *among* South, the Middle West. The economic base and the cluster of organized in- *the states* terests associated with it also vary considerably from region to region. In so far as the states have any identifiable diversities, they arise from these regional affiliations. Probably the most determined loyalties are those of the Old South: here is the stronghold of "states' rights" and of regional autonomy. Regional boundaries are far from precise, however, and many states have no clear regional affinity. Some embrace more than one region and several are micro-

725

cosms of the nation rather than of a particular region. In general, however, our state governments are best understood in terms of the cultural and economic regions within which they are located.

Many efforts have been and will continue to be made to make each state government the focus of a homogeneous local ideology different in some important way from the national culture. School children are, in some cases, required to study the history of their state; local historical societies try to perpetuate "state" traditions; state advertising campaigns designed to attract tourists or industrial facilities describe the "unique" qualities of a state's environment; national political campaign etiquette requires candidates to celebrate the separate traditions or characters of the various states. Few of these efforts are really achieving anything substantial in the way of creating unique systems of law, government, literature, art, or ideology in each of the 50 states. All of them are overborne by the growing impact of national institutions of culture and communication.

The states as national instrumentalities

The American state is indeed a peculiar institution. If it is an institution which tends to perpetuate and, perhaps, even exaggerate, regional loyalties, it is also an institution of national solidarity. In its name, Senators are elected to the national Congress, electors are chosen to attest to the selection of the chief executive, delegates and committeemen are chosen to sit in national political conventions and conferences, and amendments to the national Constitution are submitted for ratification to its officials. Many interest groups and economic institutions such as chambers of commerce, labor unions, and trade associations which operate nationally are organized by states and our largest industrial corporations are legal "persons" of one or more states. Under the growing grant-in-aid programs of the national government, states are the major administrative units through which program goals are achieved. State labor and industrial departments, public welfare agencies, public health departments, and highway commissions have close and continuing administrative relations with agencies of the national executive. Furthermore, like the national government itself, the states act as softeners and reconcilers of economic, educational, social, and religious antagonisms. Few states are predominantly one class, one culture, or one system of production and conflicts of interests occur within states as well as within the central organs of power.

The states as supervisors of local units

The American state also acts in *loco parentis* to thousands of units of local government. It provides legal authority, funds, advice, commandments for, as well as resolute restraint upon, cities great and small, counties, boroughs, villages, townships, parishes, and school districts. There is a body of opinion and of practice in the United States that supports the idea that our federal system is a three-level affair rather than a two-level one. The local units—primarily cities and counties—are regarded as largely independent of state authority. In many areas local pride is stronger than state loyalty. State legislative apportionment systems in which counties are considered units for representative purposes reflect this attitude. "Home rule" provisions in several state constitutions conferring or attempting to confer autonomy upon cities are also examples of this view. The widespread practice of popular election of the officials of these units contributes mightily to their political independence of state officialdom. Thus, there is, in fact, a large measure of power exercised at the local level which cannot easily be reviewed or countermanded by the state government. However, the predominant legal theory is that local units are creatures of the state and must look to its constitution and laws for authority for their every action. Even where home rule has been conferred by constitutional amendment, courts have construed narrowly the power actually granted to the local governments. A substantial and growing volume of local transactions are strongly influenced, if not dominated, by the state governments through the use of grants-in-aid and shared-tax procedures aimed at state support of local functions. The local policy areas of education, welfare, health, and highways are heavily underwritten by the state treasury. State financing normally and inevitably involves state supervision.

INTERSTATE RELATIONS

The states also conduct various relations with one another. They make agreements, extradite fugitives from justice, and participate together in regional and national conferences. If at first view, it should appear that in this aspect of their practice the states resemble sovereign nations, we must remember that these relations are controlled by the Constitution of the United States and to a large degree are regulated by Congressional enactment.

The Constitution authorizes interstate agreements or compacts [1] provided Congress gives its consent. This device for regulating matters of interest to neighboring states, to states in a single region, or to many states with a common interest has proved increasingly popular. The ever-mounting demand for national action on various problems has been allayed somewhat by the growing use of the interstate agreement. In earlier days the agreement procedure was largely confined to the settlement of boundary disputes but in this century a growing number of uses have been discovered. More than 100 are now in existence and the device is serving a steadily widening range of interests. Compacts are now used for: (1) the development, exploitation, and conservation of interstate water resources; (2) the stabilization and conservation of other natural resources such as petroleum, wildlife, or fish; (3) the control of floods; (4) the development of interstate toll highways; (5) the coordination of higher educational facilities; (6) mutual protection against forest fires; (7) the coordination of civil defense measures; (8) the reciprocal supervision of

Interstate compacts

[1] For detailed study of the spread of the compact system see F. L. Zimmerman and M. Wadell, *The Interstate Compact Since 1925* (Chicago, 1951) and *The Law and Use of Interstate Compacts* (Chicago, 1961); R. H. Leach and R. S. Sugg, Jr., *The Administration of Interstate Compacts* (Baton Rouge, La., 1959), and biennial articles in the *Book of the States* (Chicago).

probationers and parolees; (9) the coordination of welfare and institutional programs; (10) the administration of particular functions in interstate metropolitan areas; and, (11) the resolution of interstate tax conflicts, notably in the area of motor licenses receipts and gasoline taxes.

As the compact has become increasingly popular, if not as yet effective in many controversial areas of public policy, the nature and extent of Congressional interest and authority over it has become a matter of growing concern.

National power over compacts

The Constitution appears to require that all compacts be approved by Congress. In practice, however, compacts have been entered into without express approval and the courts have held [2] that Congressional consent is required only of agreements "tending to increase the political power of the states, which may encroach upon . . . the just supremacy of the United States." Consent need not, furthermore, be given expressly for each agreement. On several occasions, notably in the fields of conservation and highway safety, the Congress has given blanket approval in advance. In recent years, however, the Congress seems to be growing more apprehensive about the effect on its power of the spread of the compact arrangement. On several occasions in the past few years it has inserted into actions approving particular agreements restrictions on the use of supplementary agreements or of amendments not expressly approved by Congress. It has also sought to limit the powers of interstate commissions created by compacts to those within the purpose of the original agreement. All of these practices had heretofore been fairly common and unchallenged. In 1960, the Judiciary Committee of the House of Representatives undertook an investigation of the Port of New York Authority (created by compact between New York and New Jersey in 1921) and demanded the production of certain Authority records. The director, acting under instructions from his commission and from the governors of the two states involved, refused to comply with the Committee order in part because the Authority did not come under the lawful powers of Congress. The House promptly voted to cite him for contempt. Although the constitutional question was skillfully avoided by the Court of Appeals in dismissing the contempt action, the Court did say that Congressional power over compacts was not plenary.[3]

The participation of the national government as a partner in the compact for the development of the Delaware River Basin (1961) may also establish a new pattern of national participation in areas covered by compacts.

Interstate rendition of fugitives

"A person charged in any state with treason, felony, or other crime," says the Constitution, "who shall flee from justice, and be found in another state, shall, on demand of the executive authority of the state from which he fled, be delivered up, to be removed to the state having jurisdiction of the

[2] Virginia *v.* Tennessee, 148 U.S. 503 (1893).
[3] U. S. *v.* Tobin, 306 F. 2d 270 (1962). The Supreme Court refused to review the case. 371 U.S. 902 (1962).

crime." The object is, of course, to prevent criminals from "beating the law" by taking refuge on soil over which the states from which they have fled have no jurisdiction on which they can execute no processes. An act of Congress specifies that after the accused has been properly indicted, the demand for his return shall be addressed to the executive of the state into which he has fled and by which he has been captured. The governor, if he chooses to honor the request, then returns the fugitive to the police officers of the state making the request. Governors, however, in practice, have not always elected to honor such requests. The reasons advanced for the occasional refusals are that the individual has become a law abiding citizen of his new state in the meanwhile, or that (in case of Negroes demanded by Southern states) he may not expect a fair trial in the state making the request, or that there is not sufficient evidence against him. Despite the mandatory language of the Constitution and the laws of Congress, there is no legal way to compel a reluctant governor to act.[4]

Acting with Congressional authorization, more than 40 states have, since 1936, entered into an interstate compact for the mutual rendition of witnesses needed in criminal proceedings and have thus effectively enlarged the scope of their obligations. The Supreme Court has held this arrangement to be valid asserting that the "Constitution did not purport to exhaust imagination and resourcefulness in devising fruitful interstate relationship." [5]

OBLIGATIONS OF THE STATES TO ONE ANOTHER

The Constitution of the United States imposes certain further obligations on the states in their dealings with one another. "Full faith and credit," says the Constitution, "shall be given in each state to the public acts, records, and judicial proceedings of every other state." This means that transactions of government and commerce which are authenticated by valid legal instruments must be recognized and accepted everywhere in the land, regardless of the state in which they originated. Of course, these legal instruments must be duly authenticated according to forms prescribed by Congress. Thus, the courts in Illinois, for example, must recognize and carry out a decision made by a court in Michigan if invited to do so under proper circumstances. Contracts entered into in New York may be enforced in Florida. Corporations chartered in Delaware, and many of them are, must in general be admitted to do business in North Dakota. It is not possible to evade legal obligation by the simple expedi-

1. Recognition of legal processes and acts

---

[4] "The words 'it shall be the duty,'" declared Chief Justice Taney, "were not used as mandatory and compulsory, but as declaratory of the moral duty which this command created, when Congress had provided the mode of carrying it into execution. The act does not provide any means to compel the execution of this duty, nor inflict any punishment for neglect or refusal on the part of the executive of the state; nor is there any clause or provision in the constitution which arms the government of the United States with this power." Kentucky v. Dennison, 24 Howard 66 (1861).

[5] New York v. O'Neill, 359 U.S. 1 (1959).

ent of moving out of one state into another. Although the effort to make state laws on commercial transactions more uniform throughout the nation has been gaining headway, there is still a large variation from state to state in these matters, and the effect of the constitutional obligation is to require a state to recognize actions properly taken in other states regardless of the fact that such actions may be out of line with the practice in that state.

Divorce decrees
          One aspect of this obligation has, in recent years, proved troublesome: what recognition must be granted by strict states to divorce decrees granted in states like Nevada? Two cases in recent years have arisen over the obligation, or lack of it, of North Carolina to recognize Nevada divorce decrees for a couple who took up temporary residence in Reno to obtain the decrees, then married and returned to their home state of North Carolina. The Supreme Court at first held that North Carolina must necessarily recognize the decree, then later said that the parties had not established a bona fide domicile in Nevada and the Nevada court had, therefore, no jurisdiction over them.[6] The latter decision opened the door for states to challenge the validity of divorces granted by other states where the decree had been preceded by only temporary residence on the part of one or both parties. Although in subsequent cases, the Court has appeared somewhat more disposed to enforce Nevada decrees,[7] new decisions involving alimony payments and the custody of children have added to a complex and confused situation.[8] Some groups are proposing a Constitutional amendment to resolve the matter.[9]

2. Inter state citizenship
          The framers of the Constitution rightly thought that no state should be allowed to discriminate, in favor of its own citizens, against persons coming within its jurisdiction from other states. To do so would jeopardize basic rights common to all of the people and seriously interfere with national unity. Hence it is provided (in a clause carried over almost literally from the Articles of Confederation) that "the citizens of each state shall be entitled to all privileges and immunities of citizens in the several states." In general, this means that citizens of any state may move freely about the country and settle where they like, with the assurance that as newcomers they will not be subjected to discriminative taxation, that they will be permitted to carry on lawful occupations under the same conditions as older residents, and that they will not be prevented from acquiring and using property, or denied the equal protection of the laws, or refused access to the courts. It does not mean that privileges of a political nature, for example, those of voting and holding office,

[6] Williams *v.* No. Carolina, 317 U.S. 287 (1942) and Williams *v.* No. Carolina, 325 U.S. 226 (1945).

[7] Sherrer *v.* Sherrer, 334 U.S. 343 (1948). This case involved a Florida decree challenged in Massachusetts but the decision set at rest most of the uneasiness created by the Nevada decree cases. See also, Coe *v.* Coe, 324 U.S. 378 (1948).

[8] Kovacs *v.* Brewer, 336 U.S. 604 (1948) and Vanderbilt *v.* Vanderbilt, 354 U.S 416 (1957).

[9] For conveniently assembled data on marriage and divorce laws of all the states, see National Institute of Municipal Clerks, *Marriage and Divorce* (Chicago, 1957).

must be extended forthwith. Nor is a state prevented from imposing quarantine or other police regulations which will have the effect of denying free admission or the right to move property in or out. But such restrictions must be justified by provable public necessity. Furthermore, they must be so framed as to fall alike upon the citizens of the given state and those of all other states. It is hardly necessary to add that a citizen of New York, migrating to Pennsylvania, does not carry with him the rights which he enjoyed in New York. The point is rather that he becomes entitled to such rights as the citizens of Pennsylvania enjoy.

3. Peaceful settlement of interstate disputes

The history of the Confederation was filled with controversies between states regarding boundaries, commercial regulations, and other matters; and the makers of the Constitution were not so naive as to suppose that under the new frame of government the members of the Union would always live in perfect accord. Among sovereign nations, disputes have traditionally been settled by (1) direct agreements reached through negotiation, (2) arbitration undertaken by some neutral ruler or similar authority, (3) adjudication in an international court, or (4) in the last resort, war. The states of the Union are not supposed to make war on one another—although they did so in 1861-1865. They may, and do, reach agreements through direct negotiation. But the method of settlement chiefly contemplated by the Constitution's authors was that of judicial determination. In pursuance of this intent, the judicial power of the United States is extended to all "controversies between two or more states," with the further provision that in all cases in which a state is a party (regardless of the identity of the opposing party) the Supreme Court shall have original jurisdiction. The road to amicable adjustment of interstate differences by regular judicial process is thus always open, and many troublesome disputes over boundaries, water diversions, fishing rights, and other matters have been cleared up by resorting to it. A good illustration of this is the 1963 decision of the Court in the 40-year-old dispute between Arizona and California over the distribution of water from the lower Colorado River Basin under the terms of the Boulder Canyon Project Act of 1928. Years of effort to resolve the matter through interstate compact had failed. The Court decision upheld the distribution under the Act of 1928 but opened the door for subsequent modification by Congress.[10]

FRAMEWORK OF STATE GOVERNMENT: THE STATE CONSTITUTION

Similarities among the states

To a student of political institutions, the most striking thing about the American states is not their regional peculiarities but their great and abiding uniformities. The government of every one of the 50 states is based upon a written constitution and these are strikingly similar. The first written instru-

[10] Arizona v. California, 373 U.S. 546 (1963). See also J. B. Scott, *Judicial Settlement of Controversies Between States of the American Union* (New York, 1918).

ments of government in this country were established at the time of independence by the original 13 states. The national Constitution leans heavily on those of New York and Massachusetts. The constitutions later enacted by the other 37 states closely parallel the national document and those of the original states.[11] The frame of government provided by these fundamental laws in every case follows the American pattern of limited, representative government organized around three separated and mutually restraining organs of power. Every state constitution contains a Bill of Rights guaranteeing to the inhabitants the basic American freedoms in much the same language and to much the same purpose as those added to the national Constitution and discussed in an earlier chapter. Major differences center around the character of the guarantees of separation of church and state and the protection, or lack of it, afforded to Negroes, Mexicans, and other minority groups. Every state has a single chief executive, the governor, elected by popular vote and a representative legislature also directly elected and, in every state but one (Nebraska), composed of two equal bodies. An elaborate system of courts is also characteristic of the states. Many of the judges of these tribunals are, however, elected. Each of these main branches of government is endowed with some power to check or restrain the other two, much as they are in the national government. Unlike the national Constitution which makes no important provisions for the organs of state government, the state constitutions universally provide in some detail for a system of local governments and an assignment of powers to the various types. The states also impose numerous and detailed restraints upon the lawmaking powers of their legislatures arising from a long history of abuses and not duplicated in the national Constitution by any comparable restraints upon the powers of Congress. Furthermore, the politics of the states center around contests within and between the two major political parties. Every state also has numerous organized interest groups which seek to influence the conduct of public affairs at the state and local levels. In every state but one (Louisiana) the whole system of civil and criminal law is based on the English common law brought here by our forefathers.

State v. national Constitution

There has probably been no more extensive exercise in making constitutions in the history of self-government than that represented by the 50 American states. Considering this experience one can only be deeply impressed with the skill of the framers of the Constitution of the United States. Together, the states have installed more than 130 constitutions and have amended the 50 now in effect more than 3000 times. Almost every state has scrapped one or

[11] Another modest influence in the direction of uniformity is a "model state constitution" prepared by the National Municipal League's committee on state government and published originally in 1921. Issued in six successive editions (the most recent dating from 1963), this interesting document represents the considered opinion of several of the country's ablest students of state government; and while no state ever was expected to adopt the "model" in its entirety, its influence often can be detected in current amendments and revisions. National Municipal League, *Model State Constitution* (6th ed., New York, 1963).

GENERAL STATUS OF STATE CONSTITUTIONS
1964

State	No. of Const.	Effective Date of Present Const.	No. of Amendments Proposed	Approved
Alabama	6	1901	367	212
Alaska	1	1959	—	—
Arizona	1	1912	108	50
Arkansas	5	1874	(Not available)	59
California	2	1879	600	350
Colorado	1	1876	(Not available)	64
Conn.*	2	1965	—	—
Delaware	4	1897	(Not available)	80
Florida	5	1887	176	117
Georgia	8	1945	85	26
Hawaii	1	1959	8	5
Idaho	1	1890	102	68
Illinois	3	1870	30	13
Indiana	2	1851	47	20
Iowa	2	1857	(Not available)	21
Kansas	1	1861	73	45
Kentucky	4	1891	40	18
Louisiana	10	1921	566	439
Maine	1	1820	107	89
Maryland	4	1867	133	108
Mass.	1	1780	98	81
Michigan	4	1964	—	—
Minnesota	1	1858	178	90
Mississippi	4	1890	104	35
Missouri	4	1945	26	13
Montana	1	1889	46	30
Nebraska	2	1875	147	94
Nevada	1	1864	97	56
New Hamp.	2	1784	105	41
New Jersey	3	1947	9	6
New Mexico	1	1912	130	55
New York	6	1894	174	133
North Car.	2	1868	(Not available)	(Not available)
North Dak.	1	1889	(Not available)	76
Ohio	2	1851	162	88
Oklahoma	1	1907	135	49
Oregon	1	1859	249	111
Pennsylvania	4	1873	92	62
Rhode Island	1	1843	70	36
South Car.	6	1895	364	251

State	No. of Const.	Effective Date of Present Const.	No. of Amendments Proposed	Approved
South Dak.	1	1889	132	71
Tennessee	3	1870	24	10
Texas	5	1876	247	154
Utah	1	1896	(Not available)	33
Vermont	3	1793	193	44
Virginia	5	1902	98	92
Washington	1	1889	(Not available)	39
West Virginia	2	1872	61	36
Wisconsin	1	1848	99	66
Wyoming	1	1890	48	25

SOURCE: Council of State Governments, *Book of the States 1964-65* (Chicago, 1964) 12.
 * Connecticut adopted a new constitution in December 1965.

two constitutions since 1789, frequently after amending them many times. Only 2 states are now operating under constitutions of the late eighteenth century and these have been extensively altered.

Contents of a typical constitution   The typical state constitution is divided into articles and like the national Constitution contains: (1) a Bill of Rights; (2) a section on the organization, powers, and duties of the legislature; (3) a section on the mode of selection and the powers of the governor and other executive officers; (4) a section on the court system and (5) a section on the amending process. Unlike the national document, in addition to these features, many state constitutions provide sections dealing with: (1) the structure and powers of local units of government; (2) the organization and financing of the state system of public education; (3) the qualifications for voting and the conduct of elections; (4) the procedures governing and the regulations imposed upon the chartering of corporations; (5) the organization and operation of programs of public health and welfare; and (6) the levying of taxes and the conduct of the state's fiscal affairs. Partly in consequence of this last list of provisions, most state constitutions are considerably longer than the national Constitution. Partly, however, this is due to the greater penchant of state politicians and voters to load up the fundamental law with details of state policy, such as highway location or the rate of a particular tax. Frustrated by state executive or legislative inaction, interested citizens in several states are able to rush into the constitution by popular initiative, details of policy and administration which later prove to be wholly inappropriate and new amendments have to be drafted to get rid of them. Legislatures, too, are prone to solidify into constitutional prescription public policies which they hope to place thereafter beyond legislative tinkering. State politicians have been generally unable or unwilling to follow the path of the national framers and avoid "minutious wisdom." The constitution of

Florida, for example, not only provides for a two-cent-per-gallon gasoline tax but specifies in detail the formula by which the proceeds are to be distributed. Texas levies a property tax for the benefit of certain public colleges and specifies to the fifth decimal place how much each is to receive. Louisiana, in a constitution of 200,000 words declares Huey Long's birthday a legal holiday forever and names two bridges after him!

The national Constitution is a grant of power to a new central government; the state constitutions, by contrast, are largely restraints upon power. Rarely is the allegedly broad authority of the state spelled out. Since we live in an age of mounting governmental activities, constitutional prescriptions of restraints are likely to prove more fragile than the reverse.

MAKING AND REVISING THE CONSTITUTION

No serious effort has been made since 1787 completely to rewrite the national Constitution although it prescribes a procedure by which this might be done. No comparable myth of sanctity surrounds our state constitutions and in most states they have been rewritten two or three times.[12] All but 12 of the present state constitutions prescribe the assembling of a special convention for this purpose and in seven of the twelve, by judicial or legislative determination, the power to do so has been established. It is generally supposed that regardless of constitutional prescription the power to rewrite it by convention is inherent in the people.

The first formal step toward holding a convention is, generally, a decision by the legislature to submit to the voters the question of whether they want one.[13] In a few states this question may be placed on the ballot by popular initiative petition. Several state constitutions require the periodical submission of this question to the voters: in New Hampshire every seven years; in Alaska and Iowa every 10 years; in Michigan every 16 years; and in Maryland, Missouri, New York, Ohio, and Oklahoma every 20 years.[14] In most of these states but not all, the question may also be submitted at other times. After popular approval has been gained—in several states this is made difficult by requiring extraordinary popular majorities [15]—the legislature by statutes fixes

Calling a convention

[12] The most recent constitutional revisions have been in: Missouri (1945); Georgia (1945); New Jersey (1947); Michigan (1964), and Conn. (1965). A Rhode Island convention assembled in 1964 was still deliberating in November, 1965. A limited convention met in Tennessee in November, 1965.

[13] Only Alaska, Georgia, and Maine do not require a popular referendum on the question but authorize the legislature to go ahead on its own initiative. The most recent example of popular approval of a convention is that of New York where the voters in November 1965 approved a convention to be held in 1967.

[14] This type of provision is not always obeyed. The gist of judicial opinion at present is that there is no valid way to force legislative compliance.

[15] Six states require the approval of a majority of those voting in the election to approve a convention. Typically, many fewer votes are cast on the referendum question than for the major public offices and thus most of those who participate in the election and yet ignore the referendum are counted as if they voted no.

the time, place, and delegate apportionment of the convention.[16] The convention is thus likely to be a mirror of the legislature and at least up to this decade, to reflect the lack of equality as between the urban and the rural and small-town populations. Once assembled, the convention normally functions very much like a legislature with officers, committees, hearings, and debate.

There is a growing disposition to provide technical assistance to conventions through advance preparation of materials on the major questions confronting them. This work is usually done by specialists in these fields. The convention for Illinois in 1920-1922 was aided by 15 bulletins prepared for its consideration; 12 volumes were prepared for the New York convention of 1938; 30 monographs were prepared for the New Jersey convention of 1947; and several studies were made for the Alaska convention (1955-1956). In many cases the advance staff work is done under the direction of an advisory or preparatory commission appointed by the governor or by the legislature for this purpose.

Growing use of preparatory commissions

There is also a developing trend to use preparatory commissions to inquire into whether and to what extent constitutions need revising and even to prepare drafts of proposed new sections for consideration by a convention or by the legislature and electorate if it is decided to attempt amendment rather than revision. Such commissions have been recently established in Florida (1955, 1958, and 1965), Kentucky (1957 and 1964), North Carolina (1957), Pennsylvania (1957), Texas (1957), West Virginia (1957), Wisconsin (1960), Kansas (1957 and 1961), Maine (1961), Oregon (1961), Massachusetts (1962), Georgia (1963), California (1963), Idaho (1965). Those commissions which have proposed amendments have had some success. Those proposing a convention or wholesale revision by amendments have not as yet made much headway. These commissions are easier to establish, less expensive to assemble, and better prepared to analyze and consider various proposals than most conventions are likely to be. The trend toward their use as a substitute for conventions will probably continue.

The power of constitutional conventions

Constitutional conventions have the primary function of drafting new fundamental laws or formulating amendments to existing ones. Some conventions like that in Illinois in 1862, have gone farther and assumed actual management of the state government, displacing existing officers, substituting others chosen by the convention, and attempting to supersede the legislature in various respects. Occasionally the legislature, in making provision for the meeting of a convention, has attempted to impose limitations upon its work which the convention has wholly or in part disregarded. Several times, conflicts have resulted as to the proper powers of a convention; and out of them three theories have developed. According to the first, the legislature is supreme, and in the act of calling the convention may limit the powers of that body by

---

[16] Usually delegates are elected by legislative districts and under the general primary and election laws of the states. Massachusetts, however, provides for nonpartisan election of delegates.

excluding from its consideration amendments to certain sections of the constitution, by requiring it to propose amendments to certain other sections, by prescribing the manner in which its work shall be submitted to popular vote, and by various other ways. Those who take this view hold that the convention has no right to disregard or to deviate from any of these statutory restrictions. According to a second theory, the convention has all the sovereign powers of the people, and accordingly, is during its period of existence, the supreme body in the state. It is superior to the legislature and to all other branches of the state government, and may disregard any or all limitations which the legislature seeks to impose upon its activity, and may, indeed, legally exercise whatever governmental functions it cares to assume—as the Illinois convention of 1862 tried to do.

Prevalent view of convention powers

Each of these two theories has some support in convention precedents and judicial opinion. But the view now most generally held is that a convention is neither sovereign nor wholly subject to the legislature—that, on the contrary, the two are coordinate bodies, each supreme within its proper sphere and bound by the provisions of the existing constitution and statutes. If the constitution authorizes the legislature to impose restrictions on the convention, the latter is bound to respect such limitations; on the other hand, if such authorization is lacking, the legislature cannot bind the convention as to what shall be placed in the revised constitution, or lay other restrictions upon it. The convention, furthermore, may neither supersede any existing organs or agents of state government nor exercise any of the powers assigned to them. Its functions are limited to proposing a new constitution or amendments to the existing one. In practice, however, several conventions, notably that of New Jersey in 1947, have accepted limitations imposed by the legislature on the apportionment system of the legislative seats.

Ratification of a convention's work

Although a minority of state constitutions require it, the almost universal practice among the states is to submit the results of the convention's deliberations to the voters for approval.[17] The vote required for approval is typically a majority of those voting on the question but several states require approval by a majority of those voting in the election.

Method of submitting convention proposals

A convention may submit its work in one of three different forms. It may, for example, present it as a series of specific amendments to be voted on separately, as was done in New York in 1938, in Tennessee in 1953 and in Connecticut in 1965. This is practicable only when a comparatively small number of amendments are proposed. Or it may submit a complete new or revised constitution, to be accepted or rejected as a whole, as in Illinois in 1922, in Georgia and Missouri in 1945, in New Jersey in 1947, and in Michigan in 1964. This method has the disadvantage of compelling articles or clauses not widely opposed to suffer the same fate as others stirring controversy. Opposi-

---

[17] The constitutions of Virginia (1902) and Louisiana (1921) were not submitted to popular vote.

tion to some change in the system of taxation, for example, may be so strong that, rather than see a proposal of the kind adopted, its opponents will vote against the entire document, although everything else may be satisfactory. The sum total of such fractional opposition may mean the entire constitution's defeat. In this cumulative fashion, the proposed new constitution for New York was wrecked in 1915, that for Illinois in 1922, and that for Florida in 1958.

The third method is a compromise between the two mentioned. A substantially complete revision may be submitted for ratification or rejection as a whole, with at the same time one or more especially controversial articles or sections submitted separately, thus enabling the electorate, if so inclined to approve the convention's work in general while yet disapproving specific features.

CONSTITUTIONAL AMENDMENT

Amendment by legislative proposal

The constitutional convention is a drastic method for up-dating constitutions. It is, however, responsible for relatively few alterations. By far the most common method of state constitutional revision is simple amendment. Every state constitution provides a procedure by which particular provisions may be changed. In every state amendments may be proposed by the state legislature.[18] In 36, affirmative action may be taken at one legislative sitting. However, a majority of these states require an unusual majority vote to do so —a two-thirds vote in 19 states and a three-fifths vote in 8 states. In the remaining states (14), affirmative action by two distinct sessions of the legislature is required.[19] In Delaware the action of two legislatures completes the process but in all the other states, an amendment proposed by the legislature must be placed before the voters for ratification.[20] Typically, legislatures may propose any number of amendments at any time but a few states, where the framers were so taken with their product that they wanted it modified only slightly if at all, limit the legislature to two or three amendments at a time— Arkansas, Kansas, Kentucky, and Montana, for example. Vermont's constitution may not be amended at all except at 10-year intervals. Occasionally legislatures have proposed wholesale revision rather than isolated amendment. The New Jersey legislature did this in 1944 on the authority of a referendum but its handiwork was rejected by the voters. An attempt in 1911 by the Indiana legislature to do this was invalidated by the courts.

Proposing amendments by popular initiative

An alternative method of laying amendments before the voters is now

[18] New Hampshire until 1964 was the one state in which the legislature could not initiate amendments but the constitution was modified to permit it in that year.

[19] New Jersey has an unusual provision that requires a three-fifths vote of approval of the membership of one legislative session or a simple majority vote in two successive sessions. Hawaii has a similar arrangement requiring a two-thirds vote in one session.

[20] In South Carolina, voter approval must be obtained between the first and second legislative approvals which are required to complete the process.

authorized in 14 states.[21] This is the popular initiative which originated in Oregon in 1902 and rapidly gained favor over the next two decades. It has attracted little favorable notice since 1920. By this procedure a proposal may be drafted by any person or group and then if a sufficient [22] number of voters' signatures can be obtained on a petition demanding it, the proposal must be placed before the voters for ratification at an early election. Support for the popular initiative stemmed from distrust of or disgust with the behavior of state legislatures in blocking reforms. Experience with it suggests that the only effective alternative over the long run to a corrupt or incompetent legislature is to elect a better legislature.[23] Little is really gained, except increased voter weariness, by running to the electorate with new duties every time a legislature misbehaves.

In the vast majority of states, the popular vote required to ratify a proposed amendment is a majority of those voting on the question. Several of the state constitutions,[24] however, make approval exceedingly difficult to obtain by requiring a majority of those voting in the election. Experience indicates that rarely do more than 60 percent of those who participate in an election pay any attention to referred proposals which may appear on the ballot. Thus a large portion of those who do not vote on the question at all are, in effect, counted as if they voted "no." [25] Other requirements of unusual majorities are imposed in a few states.[26]

Popular vote on amendments

[21] Arizona, Arkansas, California, Colorado, Idaho, Massachusetts, Michigan, Missouri, Nebraska, Nevada, North Dakota, Ohio, Oklahoma, and Oregon. In Massachusetts the initiative is limited to certain provisions and must be filtered through the legislature before it can get to the people. The Idaho provision does not appear to be operative. A recent state supreme court decision (1960) in Nevada prescribes that the Nevada constitution may be amended by an initiative petition without a popular referendum provided the legislature approves the amendment petitioned for.

[22] The number of signatures required varies widely among the states using this procedure. A common requirement is 10 percent of the number voting for governor at the last election.

[23] In three states no amendments have been added to the constitution by this procedure. In several of the other states, more amendments initiated popularly have been rejected than have those proposed by the legislatures.

[24] For example, those of Illinois, Minnesota, Michigan, Mississippi, New Jersey, and Oklahoma.

[25] Of 12 proposed amendments which from 1922 to 1949 failed of ratification in Illinois, 10 received more favorable than unfavorable votes, but not enough to constitute a majority of the total number cast. See K. C. Sears, "Constitutional Revision in Illinois," *Ill. Law Rev.*, XXXIII, 2-14 (May 1938); C. V. Laughlin, "A Study in Constitutional Rigidity," *Univ. of Chicago Law Rev.*, X, 142-176 (Jan., 1943). A "gateway" amendment placed before Illinois voters in November, 1950, on a separate blue ballot to attract attention, was aimed at enabling future amendments to be adopted either by a majority of those voting at the election (as theretofore) or by two-thirds of those voting on the proposition, whichever was less; and the proposal prevailed. On the situation in Minnesota, see W. Anderson, "The Need for Constitutional Revision in Minnesota," *Minn. Law Rev.*, XI, 189-226 (Feb., 1927). For many years, a rule similar to that recently discarded in Illinois prevailed in Indiana, but in 1935 the state supreme court held that a majority of votes cast on each amendment was sufficient for adoption. *In re* Todd, 208 Ind. 168 (1935).

[26] A few states, Hawaii, for example, require the majority approving the amendment to equal at least 35 percent of the total number of voters in the election.

*Elabora-
tion of
constitu-
tions by
other
means*

The frequent use of the amending and revising processes in order to keep state governments abreast of the times does not mean that state constitutions are not elaborated, embellished, and greatly modified by legislation, executive order, judicial construction, and unwritten custom. Just as in Washington, every act of officials in state capitals subtly interprets, enlarges, supplements, or changes the basic framework of government provided by the constitutions. Furthermore, many institutions of American political life have grown up and flourished outside the constitutional prescriptions. The whole system of political parties, the activities of organized interest groups, the character of voter participation, and many other practices and institutions are rarely mentioned in state constitutions.

*State con-
stitutions
too
detailed*

Constitutions which are frequently amended or revised lose much of their value and a great deal of their prestige. The principles underlying our system of government are few and can be set forth in a few carefully written paragraphs. The statesmen of one generation are rarely successful in compelling their successors to achieve these ends only by certain well defined paths. State political leaders and jurists have shown rare ingenuity in circumventing constitutional provisions which they could not or would not alter. The world will not stand still despite the perfection it may be thought to have reached in one moment of time. If, as some fear, the central government may come ultimately so to dominate our polity that the states are no longer significant, our failure to apply in the states the constitutional wisdom of the nation may bear part of the blame. A national commission appointed in 1953 to examine our modern federal system and, if possible, to halt the trend toward centralization reported: ". . . most states would benefit from a fundamental review and revision of their constitutions to make sure that they provide for vigorous and responsible government, not forbid it." [27]

References

Role of the States and Interstate Relations

W. B. Graves, *American Intergovernmental Relations* (New York, 1964).

W. Anderson, *The Nation and the States, Rivals or Partners?* (Minneapolis, 1955).

A. W. MacMohen (ed.), *Federalism: Mature and Emergent* (New York, 1955).

Council of State Governments, *Interstate Compacts, 1783-1956* (Chicago, 1956).

R. C. Martin, *Federalism and Regionalism* (Houston, Texas, 1957).

R. H. Jackson, *Full Faith and Credit: the Lawyer's Clause of the Constitution* (New York, 1945).

K. H. Nadilmann, "Full Faith and Credit to Judgments and Public Acts," *Michigan Law Review*, LVL, 33-88 (Nov., 1957).

[27] The Commission on Intergovernmental Relations, *A Report to the President* (Washington, 1955), p. 56.

R. H. Leach and R. S. Sugg, Jr., *The Administration of Interstate Compacts* (Baton Rouge, La., 1959).

STATE CONSTITUTIONS

1. General

National Municipal League, *A Model State Constitution* (6th ed., New York, 1963).

J. A. Burdine, "Basic Materials for the Study of State Constitutions and Constitutional Development," *American Pol. Sci. Rev.* (Dec., 1954), pp. 1140-1152.

W. A. Edwards, ed., *Index Digest of State Constitutions* (New York, 1959).

J. P. Keith, *Methods of Constitutional Revision,* Bureau of Municipal Research, Univ. of Texas (Austin, 1949).

A. L. Sturm, *Methods of State Constitutional Reform* (Ann Arbor, Mich., 1954).

R. Uhl, *Constitutional Conventions; Organization, Powers, Functions, and Procedures,* Bureau of Public Administration, Univ. of So. Carolina (Columbia, 1951).

J. P. Wheeler, *Salient Issues of Constitutional Revision* (New York, 1961).

W. B. Graves (ed.), *Major Problems in State Constitutional Revision* (Chicago, 1960).

R. B. Dishman, *State Constitutions: the Shape of the Document* (New York, 1960).

Council of State Governments, *The Book of States* (Chicago) Sec. I. Published biennially and containing comparative tables on state constitutional matters as well as summaries of developments during the year.

2. Particular States

R. N. Blaisden, *Charter for New Jersey: The New Jersey Constitutional Convention of 1947,* State Dept. of Education (Trenton, 1952).

M. L. Faust, *Five Years Under the New Missouri Constitution* (Jefferson City, Mo., 1959).

V. A. O'Rourke and D. W. Campbell, *Constitution Making in a Democracy: Theory and Practice in New York* (Baltimore, 1943).

W. A. Egan, "The Constitution of the New State of Alaska," *State Government,* (Autumn, 1958), pp. 209-214.

House of Representatives, 86th Cong., 1st Sess., *Report No. 32* (Washington, 1959). Includes a copy of the Constitution of the new state of Hawaii.

R. K. Gooch, "The Recent Limited Constitutional Convention in Virginia." *Va. Law Rev.,* XXXI, 708-726 (June, 1945).

A. L. Sturm, *Constitution-Making in Michigan, 1961-1962* (Ann Arbor, Mich., 1963).

J. K. Pollock, *Making Michigan's New Constitution* (Ann Arbor, Mich., 1963).

R. L. Branning, *Pennsylvania Constitutional Development* (Pittsburgh, 1963).

★ 27 ★

The State Legislature

THE MAJOR CENTER of democratic policy-making at the state level in the United States is the state legislature. It occupies a position in both structure and ideology closely akin to that of Congress at the national level. Many of the conflicts of the body politic are here resolved and the entire machinery of state government provided with purpose and method. Unlike the Congress vis-à-vis the states, the state legislature exercises a wide control over the structures and policies of local governments. State political interest groups concentrate their energies on efforts to influence the legislative process. For all of the activities within the scope of their concern, the legislatures of the states are the main centers of decision.

*The de-
cline of
the state
legislature*

In the beginning of our national history the state legislatures were the major centers of political power in the nation and they remained so until well into the nineteenth century. Their importance and prestige, however, suffered several sharp declines and today they are nowhere near as important as they once were. The first major setback to the power of the state legislature was, of course, the Constitution of 1787. It was designed to restrict the power of state legislatures and was drafted by men who were deeply disturbed by the policies and personnel of the state assemblies. During the Jeffersonian era, however, the national power was in the hands of men friendly to state power and some of the ground was recaptured. The more serious decline in state legislative power and influence was a product of the American industrial revolution. The development of a national economy linking farm and factory by means of the railroads created problems with which the state legislators were unable to cope. Caught up in the ruthless push of greedy land speculators, railroad promoters, currency manipulators and corporate minions, the lawmakers succumbed to temptation or fought vainly against wealth and power which were too big to be contained. Scandal after scandal rocked one state capitol after another as legislatures buckled beneath the irresistible forces of industrialization. Public confidence in the honesty and wisdom of the legislators sagged sharply. The solution to this state of affairs (typically American) was to prevent evil doing by restraining the powers of the doer. If a public body is restrained from evil, it is usually at the same time restrained from doing good and to the humiliation of lack of confidence was added the frustration of lack of valid power. Into state constitutions from 1865 onward for two or three generations were written a growing list of inhibitions and restrictions on state legislative power under which most legislatures labor even today. Meanwhile, the growth of a genuinely national economy effectively placed beyond the competence of states a large number of problems which have required national attention in this century. It is ironic to observe that many of those who have complained so bitterly over the "unwarranted" rise of the power and prestige of the national government have also helped to forge the fetters which constrain the states.

There are some signs, increased pay and more frequent sessions, for example, that public confidence in our state lawmakers is slowing rising. Most of the state assemblies, however, bear the scars of the blows rained upon them in the last half of the nineteenth century.

FUNCTIONS OF STATE LEGISLATURES

Like the national Congress, the state legislatures perform a wide variety of functions. Many of these are not, strictly speaking, legislative. In the first place, the legislature of every state is the major, if not the sole, originator of constitutional amendments as described in the previous chapter. The upper houses of our state legislatures also universally share the appointing power of the governor. The scope of the executive power is, typically, more limited at the state than at the national level because of the widespread practice of electing several of the major state administrative officials. In a few states and for a few officers, state Senators are relatively more powerful than their counterparts in Washington because of their participation in the governor's removal power.[1] In a few states, also the legislature has some independent appointing power: judges, for example, are named by the legislatures in Connecticut, South Carolina, Vermont, and Virginia. State legislatures, like the Congress, also have an important hand in supervising state administration. They create administrative machinery, prescribe the procedures to be followed, and review the conduct of the executive branch in connection with appropriation enactments. They may and do conduct investigations of administrative behavior much as the Congress does. In a few states, legislative control over administration is limited by unnecessarily detailed constitutional prescriptions of administrative structure and procedures.

Functions: 1. Constituent

2. Executive

The lower house of virtually every state is endowed with impeachment authority over state officials and the upper house with the power to try impeached officers.[2] Several states authorize their legislatures to oust judges by a procedure which does not involve a trial but may require a special vote of the two houses.

3. Judicial

The state legislator first and last spends a good part of his time, just like

4. Representative

[1] In Wisconsin, for example, the Senate must concur in any removal of the State Auditor before his term expires.

[2] Oregon is the only state which requires malfeasance in office to be tried in a regular court, and, therefore, forbids impeachment by the legislature.

the Congressmen, in representing his constituents before administrative agencies and intervening, if he can, in their behalf.

5. Legislative

The typical activity of the state legislature, however, is lawmaking and to it lawmakers devote most of their time and energy. Apart from the vast differences of power as between the state and the nation, the most significant legislative difference arises from the time and attention which state lawmakers must give to the problems, structures, powers, and procedures of the thousands of local and special units of government which they must regulate. Congress, although exercising a profound influence upon states through the grant-in-aid procedure, does not enact the comprehensive and detailed prescriptions for the states that the states do for their local subdivisions.

STATE LEGISLATIVE POWER

Powers are residual and un-enumerated

Speaking broadly, a state legislature has the power to enact laws relating to any aspect of our society unless it is forbidden by the Constitution of the United States expressly or by implication, or by the constitution of the state. Under the American federal system, the states are entrusted with all the residue of powers not specifically delegated to the nation and, therefore, a precise delineation of the scope of state legislative power is impossible. A casual perusal of the statute books of an American state reveals that legislatures deal with a vast array of topics of wide social concern. The most important of these are: elections, natural resources, education, veterans' benefits, crime and correctional administration, health, welfare, local government powers and structures, highways, bridges, and airports, agriculture, weights and measures, trade practices, industrial safety, labor-management relations, aeronautics, banking, interest, sales, partnerships, corporations, real estate, domestic relations, judicial organization and procedure, inheritance, trusts, and professions. In almost every matter, however, state legislative authority is confined and restricted in various ways.

Limitations on state power arising from the federal system:

One significant source of limitation on the power of the states is, of course, the federal system. The delegation of power to the national government has placed many subjects beyond the power of state officials and the Congress and courts have broadened and deepened these restraints.

1. Foreign and inter-state relations

The national government is plainly intended to conduct all official relations with foreign nations and the states are consequently forbidden to enter any "treaty, alliance, or confederation." A state may enter into a "compact or agreement" with a foreign state with the consent of Congress, but only if the agreement does not create a political relationship such as an alliance. Except for an agreement between New York and Canada concerning an international bridge, no such agreements have been concluded.

2. Defense

In general, defense, like foreign relations, is a national rather than a state function. Without the consent of Congress no state may keep troops or ships of war, or "engage in war unless actually invaded or in such imminent danger as will not admit of delay." The restriction, however, does not preclude the states from maintaining organized militia for use primarily in repressing domestic disorder. Such militia have, however, long since been assimilated to the armed establishment of the nation. The governors are still fairly free to direct their use inside the state boundaries.

The most important limitation imposed on the power of the states by the Constitution, excluding only the Fourteenth Amendment, is the grant of power to Congress to regulate commerce among the states. In the first place, the national courts have defined "commerce" to include virtually every type of movement of persons or things and every type of communication or negotiation whether for business purposes or not. They have defined "interstate" to embrace any such movement across state lines at any stage of a transaction. They have defined the total regulatory power of Congress to embrace any operation or transaction which might affect the "commerce" they have so broadly defined. There are, in consequence, relatively few business transactions in modern America which do not come within the purview of Congressional power. Furthermore, all of the navigable or potentially navigable rivers of the country come under national authority by a series of interpretations. *3. Commerce*

The power of the states to levy and collect taxes for revenue or regulatory purposes is limited expressly by the Constitution and also by judicial inference from its provisions. In order to assure uniform national impositions on interstate and foreign trade, the Constitution forbids any state, without the consent of Congress, to levy any duty on imports [3] or exports, except for the purpose of financing inspection at terminals or harbors. Such duties, if laid by a state, are subject to validation, revision, or control by the Congress and net proceeds must be turned over to the national Treasury. State duties of this type, while collected for a time in the early days of the nation, are now virtually unused. States are also forbidden without Congressional approval to levy "tonnage duties," that is, taxes on the cargo or carrying capacity of ships. *4. Taxation: a. Export and import duties*

b. Tonnage duties

State taxing power is also bound by the general limitations on states such as those forbidding them to impair the obligation of contracts or to deprive any person of property without due process of law, or to deny to anyone the equal protection of the laws. *c. General limitations*

One of the most significant limitations on state taxing power stems from a decision of the Supreme Court in 1819 written by Chief Justice Marshall in which he asserted that a state could not levy a tax on a national instrumentality. The power to tax, he said, involves the power to destroy, and the federal sys- *d. Exemption of "instrumentalities"*

---

[3] When a commodity ceases to be an import and, therefore, becomes properly subject to state taxation has been a troublesome question for many decades. In a recent decision, Youngstown Sheet & Tube Co. *v.* Bowers, 358 U. S. 534 (1959), Justice Whittaker, speaking for the majority, said that an import loses its distinctive character when: (1) the importer sells it; (2) the original package in which it arrived is broken up; or, (3) the goods are used for the purpose for which they are imported.

tem prescribed by the Constitution did not intend the states to be able to hamper the national government by burdening its agents or functions.[4] Under this general doctrine, the property of the national government has been immune from any type of state or local taxation. In some instances this is true even though the property may be leased to private interests for profitable purposes, but the Court has recently been narrowing the exemption of goods in private possession.[5] This policy has worked some hardship in areas where national holdings are vast, such as the Tennessee Valley. Congress has, therefore, on occasion authorized cash contributions by national agencies to local units of government in lieu of tax revenues lost to the unit by national ownership.[6] The doctrine of national tax immunity also shelters fiscal institutions chartered by Congress and their shares, unless Congress authorizes state or local taxation. Congress has so authorized the taxation of national bank stock and bank property but only under conditions which it imposes. For a time, the Marshall doctrine was construed as protecting the salaries of national employees from state income taxation, but the Congress in 1939 authorized such taxation and the Supreme Court reversed its earlier position and concurred.[7] The income from national securities, even when issued to finance farm or busi-

[4] In 1818, the state of Maryland imposed a stamp tax on the circulating notes of all banks or branches thereof located in the state and not chartered by the legislature. The Baltimore branch of the United States Bank refused to pay the tax. Suit was brought against the cashier, McCulloch, and the state court rendered judgment against him; whereupon the case was taken to the national Supreme Court. Pronouncing the law imposing the tax unconstitutional, Marshall declared (in a decision cited later as helping to establish the doctrine of implied powers), that, otherwise unlimited as is the power of a state to tax objects within its jurisdiction, that power does not "extend to those means which are employed by Congress to carry into execution powers conferred on that body by the people of the United States . . . powers . . . given . . . to a government whose laws . . . are declared to be supreme." McCulloch v. Maryland, 4 Wheaton 316 (1819). National-bank stock and the physical property of national banks are now taxable; but this is not only because such property is private rather than public, but also on the theory that, falling on property rather than on operations, such taxes do not impair the capacity of the banks to serve the national government according to the intent of the laws establishing them.

[5] A major case in which property leased for profitable purposes was held exempt is City of Springfield v. U. S., 306 U. S. 650 (1939). Cases in which government property was not exempted when in private hands by lease, permit, or other arrangement are: U. S. v. Township of Muskegon, 355 U. S. 484 (1958); U. S. v. Detroit, 355 U. S. 466 (1958); and Detroit v. Murray Corp., 355 U. S. 489 (1958).

[6] A. T. Edelman, "Public Ownership and Tax Replacement by the T.V.A.," Amer. Polit. Sci. Rev., XXXV, 727-737 (Aug., 1941). In the special situation of the District of Columbia, the substantial national contribution made annually to the cost of operating the local government is explained primarily by the vast amount of tax-exempt property located in Washington and its environs. The share of total costs thus assumed has, however, been declining.

[7] Graves v. People of the State of New York ex rel. O'Keefe, 306 U. S. 466 (1939). Cf. State Tax Commission of Utah v. Van Cott, 306 U. S. 511 (1939). The point to these decisions was not that national and state governments may tax each other, but only that the taxing by either of salaries paid by the other imposes no burden upon any government, merely one upon the persons who pay the tax.

ness loans, is still exempt from state taxation despite several recent efforts to procure Congressional authorization for such taxation.

The states, it should be added, long enjoyed a similar, but not identical, immunity for their instrumentalities from national taxation. Congress and the courts have, however, been steadily narrowing the allowable exemptions from national taxes. And the national government may now tax salaries of state and local employees, state or local property when used for business purposes, and many other state activities. The Court still insists that some immunity remains to the states, but it is not nearly so broad as that remaining to the national government. *State immunity from national taxation*

One of the advantages the framers hoped to derive from the Union was a common currency system. Hence the Constitution gives the national government full control over the country's currency and forbids the states to coin money, to emit bills of credit (any evidences of indebtedness intended to circulate as money), or to "make anything but gold and silver coin a tender in payment of debts." Under their reserved powers, the states can charter banks; and banking institutions so created exist beside and compete with national banks in all of the states. Furthermore, the states can authorize these banks and banking associations to issue notes for circulation as currency, although not as legal tender. In 1865, however, this latter power was stripped of all practical significance by an act of Congress laying taxes up to 10 percent on such notes and thereby making it unprofitable to issue them. The Supreme Court upheld the measure,[8] and as a result state bank currency has passed entirely out of existence. *5. Currency*

Frightened by Shays' Rebellion and by the continuing threat to creditor interests of the agrarian-debtor-dominated state legislatures, the framers were determined to place the sanctity of contracts beyond the power of states to diminish. The Constitution, in consequence, forbids any state to pass any law impairing the obligation of contracts. This clause has been almost from its inception one of the most fruitful in litigation and in pleas for the Supreme Court to overturn state legislation. Early in our history, in two celebrated cases, the Court held that the contracts protected by the Constitution included public grants of land or privilege, including charters or franchises granted to corporations.[9] The effect of this broad interpretation has been mitigated subsequently by judicial exclusion of charters to public corporations such as municipalities, by state legislation reserving the right to alter or amend charters granted by the state, and by judicial acceptance of the idea that the needs of public health, safety, and welfare may override the sanctity of some types of contractual relations. Since 1900, there has been a growing area of judicially accepted state power over contracts and a consequent diminution in the pro- *6. Contracts*

[8] Veazie Bank *v.* Fenno, 8 Wallace 533 (1869).
[9] Fletcher *v.* Peck, 6 Crandall 87 (1810), and Trustees of Dartmouth College *v.* Woodward, 4 Wheaton 518 (1819).

tection to vested interests prescribed by this constitutional prohibition. Even creditor-debtor relations have been invaded by state legislation during the depression of the 1930's—with the approval of the Court.[10] The clause, nevertheless, continues to provide a basis for judicial review of the justification for the exercise of state power. It also stands as a strong bulwark protecting many rights of creditors.

7. Privileges of citizens of the United States

The Fourteenth Amendment forbids any state to make or enforce any law abridging the privileges and immunities of citizens of the United States. Designed to protect the freed Negroes against discriminatory treatment by Southern state governments, this clause was early construed to add little or nothing to the existent system of protection of personal rights.[11] The Supreme Court has stated that the privileges here protected are only those expressly conferred by the Constitution and laws, and are manifestly attributes of national rather than state citizenship. This particular provision of the Constitution has not, thus, imposed any serious limitation on state power.

Limitations arising from guarantees of civil rights

A second source of limitation on state power is the American dedication to constitutionally recognized civil rights. In considering the American system of rights in Chapter 4, we noted that the "due process" and "equal protection" clauses of the Fourteenth Amendment provide the legal foundation for a national system of rights, uniformly applied and judicially enforced upon the states and their officers and agencies. The Constitution of the United States also expressly prohibits states from passing ex post facto laws or bills of attainder, from impairing the obligations of contract, and from depriving citizens of the vote on account of race, color, sex, or failure to pay a tax. Every state constitution also guarantees certain rights to its citizens and restrains legislatures, executives, and courts from impairing or infringing these guarantees. Every person in this country is, therefore, protected in the exercise of certain rights and from arbitrary governmental procedures by a double guarantee in state and nation. However, there are many variations from state to state in the detailed guarantees of state constitutions. For example, several state constitutions define religious freedom so as to prohibit state appropriations for parochial or seminary instruction. The Supreme Court of the United States does not so define the religious freedom guaranteed by the Fourteenth Amendment nor do the constitutions of several other states. Some state constitutions, further, forbid imprisonment for debt, some forbid distinctions as to property rights between citizens and aliens, and many do not now require indictment by grand jury nor unanimity of decision by trial juries in all cases. Even where guarantees are cast in identical language, "due process of law," for example, courts in different states have given various meanings to these words. The rights of citizens are, therefore, somewhat differently stated and applied in the states.

Limitations imposed by states on themselves

A third group of limitations on state legislative power was imposed by

[10] Home Buildings and Loan Assoc. *v.* Blaisdell *et al.,* 290 U. S. 398 (1934), and East New York Savings Bank *v.* Hahn, 326 U. S. 230 (1945).
[11] Slaughterhouse Cases, 16 Wallace, 36, 71, 77-79 (1873).

the voters or by the legislators themselves and accompanied the decline in legislative prestige in the period 1860-1910. Hundreds of constitutional changes were adopted in this period which confined legislative authority. These may be summarized under a few main headings. One large class of restrictions has to do with special, local, or private laws. Many state legislatures are forbidden to pass such enactments dealing with one or more of the following subjects: municipal corporation charters; business corporation charters particularly in the fields of banking and public utilities; divorce; county government structure and powers; location of seats of local government. There is no doubt that legislative efforts to deal with problems peculiar to one person, corporation, city, or county were frequently incompetent, occasionally corrupt, and rarely discriminating. The prohibitions, strictly applied however, have prevented wise action also in cases where account must be taken of unique circumstances. Moreover, clever lawmakers find ingenious methods of evading the spirit if not the letter of the constitution. A common method in dealing with cities, for example, is to classify them according to size making quite sure that the larger are each in a class by themselves. Classification schemes are subject to court review of their "reasonableness" in the light of the object sought. While many have been overthrown, few judges have ever thought that putting New York, Chicago, Pittsburgh, Cleveland, or San Francisco each in a class by itself was "unreasonable." An even more ingenious evasion is to word a statute, ostensibly applicable generally, in such a way that in reality it fits only one or two cases. In many situations, it must be said, these evasions are both wise and desirable. Large cities, particular associations, or corporations do have peculiar problems and it is highly desirable on occasion to deal with them without disturbing all the cities, associations, or corporations.

1. Prohibition of local and private laws

Another group of constitutional restrictions deals with legislative sessions and procedure. Among such are requirements that: (1) all bills be printed in advance of final action; (2) statutes not be amended by cross reference but that all amended portions be included in full; (3) all bills be given three readings; (4) roll call votes be taken on final passage; (5) sessions of the legislature not last longer than a specified time—usually 60 days. Legislatures have found ways of living with these rules although there are few that are not evaded or ignored on occasion. The attempt to get short sessions by constitutional fiat is little short of absurd in these days of growing government.

2. Regulations of legislative procedure and sessions

Still another category of restrictions on legislative authority are those dealing with taxes, appropriations, and debts. Most states forbid the loan or pledge of public credit to private ventures or to local units of government. Many forbid appropriations except for a "public purpose." Many forbid extra compensation for public officers or contractors. Many states are required to tax property only at a uniform rate based on valuation. In some, like Illinois, such a clause has been interpreted to forbid a graduated income tax. A large number but not a majority forbid borrowing except to suppress insurrection

3. Restrictions on taxes, loans, and appropriations

or repel invasion. Another large number require popular approval by referendum on each borrowing operation proposed by the legislature.

Implied or resulting limitations

To restrictions expressly imposed by constitutions have been added others evolved by state courts: such principles as (1) that any clause empowering the legislature to act in a particular manner is to be regarded as a denial of its rights to act in any other manner; and (2) that every pertinent provision of a constitution is to be construed as limiting legislative power *to the greatest possible extent*. In several states, the upshot of these remarkable interpretations is that, whereas in theory the legislature has all legislative power not denied to it by terms of the national and state constitutions, in practice it has tended to become a body with delegated powers. Few factors have contributed more to deaden popular interest in the work of the legislature, and to deprive the state of the services of its best citizens, than the shriveling of legislative power under express constitutional restrictions, reinforced by narrow judicial canons of interpretation.[12]

THE STATUTORY INITIATIVE AND REFERENDUM

Of all the restrictions upon legislative freedom enacted in the period of popular distrust of state lawmakers none was more sweeping than the statutory initiative and referendum. These two devices, usually associated, are designed, in part at least, to vest lawmaking directly in the hands of the electorate. The referendum allows the voters to disallow laws passed by the legislature and the initiative allows them to place on the statute books measures which the legislature has been unable or unwilling to enact. Starting in South Dakota in 1898, the movement for popular legislation swept through the nation but made most headway in the Plains states and in the Far West. In the next two decades, constitutions were amended to provide for the initiative and referendum in 18 states and for the referendum only in two other states (Maryland and New Mexico).[13] Then the movement came to an abrupt halt and has made no converts since that time.

Forms of the referendum

Initiative and referendum arrangements although varied in detail are similar in essentials. One form, the optional referendum, takes place when the legislature, desiring an expression of popular sentiment upon an act that it has passed, specifies that the measure shall not go into effect until it shall have been approved by the voters at an election. The legislature may also leave districts

---

[12] On legislative powers as affected by judicial canons of construction, see *Ill. Const. Conv. Bull.*, No. 8 (1920), "The Legislative Department," 578-587; E. Freund, "The Problems of Adequate Legislative Power Under State Constitutions," *Acad. of Polit. Sci. Proceedings*, V, 98-126 (1914); and W. F. Dodd, "The Functions of a State Constitution," *Polit. Sci. Quar.*, XXX, 201-221 (July, 1945).

[13] The list, in chronological sequence, is as follows: South Dakota (1898), Utah (1900, 1917), Oregon (1902), Nevada (1904), Montana (1906), Oklahoma (1907), Maine (1908), Missouri (1908), Michigan (1908), Arkansas (1910), Colorado (1910), California (1911), New Mexico (1911), Arizona (1911), Idaho (1912, 1933), Ohio (1912), Nebraska (1912), Washington (1912), North Dakota (1914), Maryland (1915), and Massachusetts (1918).

or counties to determine, each for itself, whether a certain law (licensing of liquor sales for example) shall apply to them. In this form, referenda may be and are used all over the nation. The referendum under consideration, however, is the mandatory type, and independent of the legislature. Where it prevails, provision is usually made for suspending all general legislative enactments for a certain period (usually 90 days) in order to give the people of the state an opportunity to pass judgment on the work of their lawmakers.[14] If during the interval a prescribed number or percentage of the voters (most commonly 5 percent) decide that a given measure is undesirable, they can, by filing a petition, prevent it from taking effect until it has been submitted at the polls and approved by the electorate.

Procedure under the initiative

The initiative may be invoked whenever any considerable number of people believe that the legislature has failed to enact necessary or desirable laws. A citizen or group of citizens, usually a political-interest group, may then, draw up a bill. This done, the next step is to obtain the signatures of a specified proportion of the voters (usually 5 or 10 percent of the number of votes cast at the last preceding election for governor or some other specified office) to a petition requesting that the bill be enacted into law. The petition is filed with the secretary of state and then either of two courses may be taken, as the law prescribes. One is called the direct initiative; the other, the indirect. Under the direct form, the measure is submitted to the people at the next regular election or at a special election, with the popular verdict final and the legislature entirely passive. Under the indirect form, the bill must be submitted to the legislature at its next session; and if that body acts upon it favorably, it becomes law without any popular vote. If, however, the legislature fails to act favorably, the bill is referred to the people and becomes law if approved by the required majority. In most states, the legislature is not permitted to amend any bill originating under the popular initiative. In some, it may put before the people a rival or substitute measure. The governor may in no case veto a measure enacted by initiative and referendum.

Results

Popular lawmaking has not accomplished most of the ambitions of its sponsors. In some states it has rarely, if ever, been used. In others, notably those on the west coast, it has been used excessively. Where it is used, voters in large numbers have shown a great lack of interest in the propositions placed before them. In a few cases laws which were difficult to administer and impossible to finance have been placed on the statute books. In one case (Missouri in 1921-1922) the devices were used by a minority party to prevent laws enacted by the majority from taking effect. Interest groups, some of whose ambitions the devices were designed to thwart, have been as effective in "selling" the people as the legislators. There is little evidence that the legislative process has been improved by inviting the voters to take a direct hand in the matter.[15]

[14] In some cases, measures designated as "emergency measures" may be exempted.
[15] For information on the use of the initiative and referendum see W. W. Crouch, *The Initiative and Referendum in California* (Los Angeles, 1943) and J. K. Pollock, *The Initiative and Referendum in Michigan* (Ann Arbor, Mich., 1940).

STRUCTURE OF STATE LEGISLATURES

The two-house legislature   The states are firmly wedded to a two-house legislature. Nebraska enjoyed a moment of national fame in 1937 when it established a single-chambered body after a vigorous and stirring campaign led by the late Senator George Norris. None of the disasters pictured by the supporters of the old two-house system have occurred but neither have some of the glowing hopes of the proponents been realized. For a time, the question of one house or two was debated up and down the land and the Model State Constitution continues to recommend the one-house system,[16] but interest has subsided and nowhere is this "reform" getting serious consideration. There is really no compelling reason for two houses in the state legislature such as that which created the Senate and the House in Washington. Local governments are not like states in any legal sense. They had no separate existence before, during, or after the Revolution and there was not then and is not now any good reason for representing them as such. Our continued use of the two-house system in states indicates how much we are influenced by habit and tradition. It also indicates that there is nothing so bad about the bicameral plan as to encourage vigorous efforts to change it.

Differences between the two houses   In most states, the major differences between the two houses are: (1) the upper house member serves a longer term than the lower house member—usually 4 years to 2 years; (2) the upper houses are smaller and, therefore, the constituencies of the members are larger—usually from two to three times as large; (3) in one house greater weight has been given to area considerations in fixing the district boundaries than in the other; and (4) the terms of members of upper houses are usually staggered so they do not expire at the same time. The same electorate selects the membership of both houses.

Basis of representation   The major controversy over the structure of legislatures today is that dealing with the basis of representation. Should legislatures represent people.[17] counting each as one or should they also represent area or predetermined units of government? Or should people be represented in one house and area or governmental unit in the other? In most states the legislature itself determines how large each house will be and draws the district boundary lines for the seats. In many, however, this decision is controlled, or at least influenced,

---

[16] The "model state constitution" proposed by the National Municipal League provides for a unicameral legislature, with its members chosen by the single-member district system. While conceding that most of the state legislatures will continue to be bicameral, the committee which prepared the latest (1963) edition of this document preferred the original recommendation. For a defense of the two-house system, see F. E. Horack, "Bicameral Legislatures Are Effective," *State Government*, XIV, 79-80, 96 (Apr., 1941).

[17] Every state requires that people be represented as such in at least one house. It is not always the *total* population, however, that is taken as the basis of representation. Oregon, for example, includes only the white population; Indiana counts only the adult male inhabitants; Maine, New York, and North Carolina exclude all aliens, and California excludes aliens not eligible to become citizens; Massachusetts and Tennessee (for the Senate) base representation upon the number of qualified or legal voters.

by constitutional prescriptions of three types: (1) those fixing an upper limit on the size of one or both houses; (2) those requiring the districts to be redrawn after each census; (3) those modifying a strict population basis for representation by requiring, for example, that each county have at least one member in one of the houses or by forbidding one county to have more than a specified proportion of the total seats in one house or by prescribing equal representation of towns or counties.

The result of past legislative and constitutional decisions is that in virtually every state the sparsely populated regions have been overrepresented and the growing urban and suburban areas underrepresented in the legislature. Typically, the rapidly growing great metropolitan areas of the United States are discriminated against in state systems of apportioning legislative seats. Just as in Congress many districts are also gerrymandered for partisan advantage. Why is this so? In the first place, the national example suggests to many people that population should be recognized as a basis of representation in only one house and governmental jurisdictions (counties mainly) regardless of size should be represented in the other. This argument would have greater weight if the jurisdictions had any recognizable separate identity but most of them were created by and remain creatures of the state legislature. Secondly, adjusting districts to population requires that legislators in stable or declining areas give up seats and this they are usually reluctant to do. Thirdly, our great cities have on many occasions been dominated by highly organized, corrupt, and ruthless machines which the rural and small town people fear and despise. Then too in many large cities organized labor is quite powerful if not decisive politically and the merchants, bankers and farmers of the rural areas and small towns are implacably opposed to increasing its influence. In many cases also, one party (usually the Democratic) is in power in the city and another (usually the Republican) in the small towns and farming areas. Since for a century the flow of people has been from farm to small town to city, the burden of change is on the city people and inertia or deadlock serves the cause of the overrepresented. Finally, there is some evidence to suggest that the city voters do not take their representation in the state legislature seriously. Many political posts —councilman, magistrate, mayor—in our cities are more lucrative and more honorific than the post of legislator. In the country-side, the legislator is relatively more important and the post more widely sought. Our state legislatures, in consequence, have been commonly dominated by the outlook—economic, political, and social—of the small town while our society is metropolitan. The typical state legislator is a county seat lawyer, a prosperous farmer, or a small town merchant.[18] Frustrated in the state legislature, powerful urban groups like organized labor carry their demands to Washington and lend support to the growing influence of the central government.[19]

Urban under-represen-tation

[18] For the occupations of state legislators see B. Zeller (ed.), *American State Legislatures* (New York, 1944), p. 71.

[19] This point was strongly made by the Commission on Intergovernmental Relations, *Report to the President* (Washington, June, 1955) p. 39. See also, M. E. Jewell, *The Politics of Reapportionment* (Englewood Cliffs, N.J., 1962).

A few states have tried to remove reapportionment from the legislative arena by entrusting all or part of the responsibility for adjusting districts to changing population patterns to some other agency. In Arizona, the secretary of state certifies to each county the number of members of the lower house it is entitled to elect. This certification occurs every two years on the basis of the vote cast for governor. California has a reapportionment commission consisting of the lieutenant governor, attorney general, secretary of state, controller, and superintendent of education. These officers are charged with reapportioning if the legislature fails to do its duty. Similar bodies with slightly different powers and members are provided in South Dakota, Texas, and Ohio. Missouri, in the constitution of 1945, provided a commission of 10 members selected by the governor from lists submitted by the central organs of the two major parties. This body is charged with redistricting the Senate and if it should fail to do so in good time the whole Senate must be elected at-large. The secretary of state reapportions the lower house in Missouri on the basis of a formula expressly provided in the constitution. Illinois for a time had a system for both houses much like the Missouri system. Hawaii and Alaska entrust the responsibility to the governor with the help of an advisory board and allow any voter to seek a court order to compel the governor to act properly. Michigan, in its new constitution, provides for a reapportionment agency made up of eight legislators named by their parties—two each from four regions into which the state is divided.

Since inequalities in systems of apportioning seats are in many instances contrary to the letter and spirit of state constitutional prescriptions, state courts have been invited on numerous occasions to intervene. Typically, they have refused to do so and have justified their position on the grounds of want of effective power to compel another branch of the government to act.[20] Until 1962, the Supreme Court of the Uinted States also declined to intervene. However, in one of the most controversial and epoch-making decisions in its history, it held in May, 1962, that the system of allocating seats in state legislatures could and would be reviewed by national courts for compliance with the "equal protection" clause of the Fourteenth Amendment.[21] Failure of the state (Tennessee) to reapportion for 61 years, the Court held, was a justiciable action worthy of being adjudicated on its merits and in the light of the possible debasement of voting rights arising from unequal representation. This decision encouraged challenges to the apportionment system of most of the states and the Court was finally brought to declare that the equal protection

---

[20] Attempts to force a reapportionment have broken down at this point in Wisconsin (1946), Oklahoma (1946), Illinois (1947), and various other states. In 1953, however, the court did reinstall in Wisconsin a reapportionment which the legislature had enacted but subsequently repealed. It did this by declaring a constitutional amendment requiring some attention to area as well as to population in representation invalid on technical and procedural grounds.

[21] Baker *v.* Carr, 369 U.S. 186 (1962).

clause requires both houses of state legislatures to be apportioned on a population basis so that in so far as possible each voter equals every other—"one man—one vote." [22] Since that decision 25 states have adopted new apportionment plans, some of which are still under attack before the courts. Thirteen others have been ordered to prepare new districts before the next election or are now preparing them voluntarily. Five states had already reapportioned on a population basis before the decision. The systems of three states are now before the courts and in the four remaining states no litigation has as yet begun.[23] The case law on what constitutes "equality" is developing very rapidly in view of the wide variety of practices under review and it is, therefore, not possible to state precisely what amount of deviation from strict mathematical equality will be tolerated. It is clear, however, that some will.[24] Meanwhile, several groups have organized a concerted drive to halt or reverse the trend toward judicially imposed equality in districting. Some are pushing for an amendment to the Constitution to deprive the national courts of jurisdiction in state legislative apportionment cases. Others, led by Senator Dirksen of Illinois, for an amendment which would authorize the states to apportion one house of a bicameral legislature on the basis of factors other than population if such an apportionment was approved by the state voters in a referendum. The Dirksen proposal was narrowly defeated in the Senate in mid-1965 but is far from dead.

State legislatures are not addicted to the single-member district system of representation—a system widely believed to be closely tied to our two-party system. A majority of states use multimember districts to some extent and several (Washington, Maryland, and Illinois, for example) use it exclusively for their lower houses. In fact, until the latest round of reapportionments very nearly half of all members of lower houses were elected in districts assigned two or more representatives. In Illinois, the multimember district system in the lower house has been geared to a unique system of cumulative voting which assigns each voter three votes to assign as he wishes among the candidates for the three seats in each district. This system is intended to guarantee minority representation and it apparently has done so.[25] In the other states the multimember district system has resulted from other but related considerations.[26]

Single-member district system

[22] Reynolds *et al. v.* Sims *et al.* 377 U.S. 364 (1964). See also, H. D. Hamilton (ed.), *Legislative Apportionment: Key to Power* (New York, 1964).

[23] See "National Summary: Apportionment Activity," *National Civic Review,* LIV, No. 8 (Sept., 1965).

[24] See R. G. Dixon, Jr., "Reapportionment Perspectives: What Is Fair Representation?" *American Bar Association Journal* (April, 1965), and G. Schubert and C. Piers, "Measuring Malapportionment," *Amer. Pol. Sci. Rev.,* LVIII, No. 2 (June, 1964).

[25] See G. S. Blair, "Cumulative Voting: Patterns of Party Allegiance and Rational Choice in Illinois State Legislative Contests," *Am. Pol. Sci. Rev.,* LII, No. 1 (Mar., 1958).

[26] See M. Klain, "A New Look at the Constituencies: The Need for a Recount and a Reappraisal," *Am. Pol. Sci. Rev.,* XLIX, No. 4 (Dec., 1955).

STATE LEGISLATURES
SIZE, TERM, AND SESSIONS
(as of July 1, 1963)

State	LOWER HOUSE Size	Term (Years)	UPPER HOUSE Size	Term (Years)	Frequency of Regular Sessions
Alabama	106	4	35	4	Biennial
Alaska	40	2	20	4	Annual
Arizona	80	2	28	2	A
Arkansas	100	2	35	4	A
California	80	2	40	4	A
Colorado	65	2	35	4	A
Connecticut	294	2	36	2	B
Delaware	35	2	17	4	A
Florida	124	2	45	4	B
Georgia	205	2	54	2	A
Hawaii	51	2	25	4	A
Idaho	63	2	44	2	B
Illinois	177	2	58	4	B
Indiana	100	2	50	4	B
Iowa	108	2	50	4	B
Kansas	125	2	40	4	A
Kentucky	100	2	38	4	B
Louisiana	105	4	39	4	A
Maine	151	2	34	2	B
Maryland	142	4	29	4	A
Massachusetts	240	2	40	2	A
Michigan	110	2	38	4	A
Minnesota	135	2	67	4	B
Mississippi	122	4	52	4	B
Missouri	163	2	34	4	B
Montana	94	2	56	4	B
Nebraska	—	—	43	4	B
Nevada	37	2	17	4	B
New Hampshire	400	2	24	2	B
New Jersey	60	2	21	4	A
New Mexico	66	2	32	4	A
New York	150	2	58	2	A
North Carolina	120	2	50	2	B
North Dakota	113	2	49	4	B
Ohio	137	2	33	4	B
Oklahoma	121	2	44	4	B
Oregon	60	2	30	4	B
Pennsylvania	210	2	50	4	A
Rhode Island	100	2	46	2	A
South Carolina	124	2	46	4	A
South Dakota	75	2	35	2	A
Tennessee	99	2	33	2	B
Texas	150	2	31	4	B
Utah	64	2	25	4	B
Vermont	246	2	30	2	B
Virginia	100	2	40	4	B
Washington	99	2	49	4	B
West Virginia	100	2	32	4	A
Wisconsin	100	2	33	4	B
Wyoming	56	2	27	4	B

SOURCE: Council of State Governments, *Book of the States*, 1964-1965 (Chicago, 1964) pp. 43, 44-45.

ORGANIZATION OF THE LEGISLATURE

The officers, committees, rules, and party apparatus of state legislatures are, without major exception, patterned very closely after those of Congress. Leadership is provided through the party system; the real work is done largely in the standing committees; the rules are based largely on Jefferson's Manual modified by constitutional prescription; the lobby is filled with energetic spokesmen for the major economic, religious, and social groups of our society. Let us, therefore, concentrate our gaze upon significant differences from the national pattern.

Officers

The speakership in the lower house of state legislatures is nearly everywhere relatively more powerful than his counterpart in Washington. In the vast majority of states, the speaker appoints the members of the standing committees, as he did in Congress until 1910. Further, his control over the procedure is not shared, typically, with a powerful Rules Committee. In some states where the Rules Committee is powerful the Speaker is likely to be its chairman. Since the body he dominates is usually much smaller than that in the Congress his dealings with his colleagues are more direct, personal, and informal than is possible in Washington. Only the majority floor leader closely approaches him in ability to shape the product of his branch of the legislature.

A number of states have abandoned the office of lieutenant governor and replaced it, in part, by a presiding officer elected by the Senate itself. Where this has occurred, this official resembles the Speaker in power and influence rather than the Vice-President. In some states where the national scheme of electing a president *pro tempore* is used, this official appoints the standing committees. In many, however, a small Committee on Committees elected by the Senate does this job.

Committees

Standing committees in each house in every state act very much like those in the Congress. In general, however, it is safe to say that the committees do not constitute as important or as independent sources of influence over the legislative product as their counterparts in Washington. Sessions are shorter and less frequent, turnover is somewhat higher, and seniority is not quite so rigidly adhered to. Thus expertness is less readily acquired by the state legislators.[27] In an effort to avoid the duplications and deadlocks of the two-house system, several states make much greater use of joint committees (including members of both houses) than is done in Washington. Massachusetts, Connecticut, and Maine conduct most of the legislative business through joint committees and several states outside New England use joint committees to shape appropriation and taxation measures. Many observers and students of the legislative process believe the joint-committee system has real advantages over the traditional arrangements.

Interim Committees

State legislatures also make use of special committees meeting between

[27] See M. G. Jewell, *The State Legislature: Politics and Practice* (New York, 1962) Chap. 4.

sessions to conduct studies, carry on investigations, and shape legislation for the future. Whereas in Congress the trend has been to have more investigating and research done by the regular standing committees and to rely relatively less often on special or select committees, in the state capitols the trend is toward consolidating special *interim* committees, into one grand legislative council or research commission supervising all *interim* inquiries and generally preparing a program of legislation for the next session. Little investigating or systematic research is performed by standing committees of state legislatures. Typically, only the major *interim* study commissions or councils are equipped with expert staff assistants. Few regular committees at the state level have anything more than clerical aid. California has been developing a staff of budget analysts for its appropriations committee but elsewhere the Congressional staffing program has not been imitated by the states.

Congressional reorganization in 1946 of its committee system reducing the number of committees and of assignments has stimulated many of the states to do the same and the average number of such committees has dropped from 39 to 22 in lower houses and from 31 to 20 in Senates. Still the typical legislature has far too many standing committees and the typical legislator too many committee assignments.[28]

Secrecy In a great many states the committees' activities are neither reported nor recorded and the rules and traditions encourage a great amount of secrecy in the legislative process. In a few, however, the process is surrounded by an openness unknown even in Washington. Wisconsin, for example, requires committee meetings to be open to the public, requires that due advance notice be given of hearings on proposed bills, requires that all bills be reported out of the committees before the session ends, and in other ways attempts to open its deliberations to public view. Part of the problem everywhere stems from the fact that legislative sessions are not nearly so well nor so expertly covered by reporters as are the sessions of Congress.

Rules Every state legislative body has developed an elaborate and complex set of rules. There are among these many thousands of rare and exotic specimens. In the main, however, the states follow the Congressional precedents. Typically, debate is not quite so closely limited as in the House of Representatives nor so open to filibuster as in the Senate. A two-thirds majority in either house can usually ride roughshod over the normal procedure but this is rarely obtained by any faction or party. Most of the states have made little effort to modernize their rules or to adjust them to the growing volume of legislative business. In this respect, however, they are aping Washington quite skillfully. The most striking thing about state legislative procedure is the almost complete lack of documentation. Only a handful of states [29] keep any kind of

---

[28] For a complete tabulation of state legislative committees, see Council of State Governments, *The Book of the States, 1964-1965* (Chicago, 1964), p. 51.

[29] Connecticut, Maine, New York, North Dakota, Pennsylvania, Tennessee, and West Virginia keep a stenographic or sound-recorded report of debates but these are not always published.

record of the debate either in committee or on the floor. A journal or record of votes and actions taken is about all the record available to a student of the legislative process. There is thus little guidance for the courts in determining legislative intent or for the citizen trying to understand either the process or the result.

In the states as in Congress the two major political parties claim the loyalties of an overwhelming majority of all the legislators. Party affiliation produces also an informal structure of leadership operating through caucuses, floor leaders, and policy committees. This structure is, in general, extremely important in determining committee assignments, in determining the holders of the official positions of speaker and president of the Senate and in determining the nature of the output. The patterns of party politics in the states, however, differ so strikingly one from another that few generalizations about the party in the legislature can safely be attempted. There are, in the first place, a large group of states (perhaps as many as 14, including most of those in the Old South and some in New England) where one party so completely dominates the state government that its influence in the legislative process is impossible to assess. In these states, factions within the dominant party vie with one another for control of the elected officers and influence on the conduct of the government. These factions act very much as parties act elsewhere except that they are much less formal in organization and much less stable and enduring. Party caucuses and formally designated leaders are virtually unknown in most of these one-party states. There is another smaller group of states where one party normally has a majority in both houses but where the other party has some representation. In these also, factionalism in the majority party is quite common and the institutions of party government in the legislature are not highly developed. The closest parallel to the situation in Congress exists in those remaining states (perhaps 23 including most of the large states like New Jersey, Ohio, Pennsylvania, Illinois, California) where the two parties are more closely matched and engage in vigorous and continuing competition. Even in some of these, however, the party is less influential than the interest group in legislative decision-making. In many of the two-party states the instrumentalities of party government are more active than in Congress. In several the caucus meets every day that the legislature is in session and considers all the major matters on the calendar. Less reliance is thus placed on the floor leaders and speakers for carrying out party policy. In many of the states also one or another of the parties may consistently control at least one house, but the governorship tends to be captured by one party and then by another. In these states, party influence through the governor's office is an important factor in the legislative process.

The party apparatus

Finally, in two states, Nebraska and Minnesota, party affiliation is prohibited by law to members of the state legislature. All of them are elected on a nonpartisan ballot. In these, factions tend to form and to act like parties do in the other states. This effort to rid the legislature of the "evils" of party politics has not, thus far, been imitated elsewhere.

In summary it appears that the influence of party affiliation on state legislative decision-making is clearly related to the state party patterns. It is greater where genuine two-party competition exists. Nowhere, not even in Congress, is it decisive. It should be noted further, that the party organizations in many of the states take less interest in the selection and financing of state legislators than they do in Congressmen and that even the successful candidates are unlikely to feel so strong an obligation to the state party.

THE LEGISLATIVE PROCESS

One of the great differences between state legislative and national legislative operations arises from the limits placed by many states on the amount of time the legislature may be in session. Most state legislatures meet regularly only once every two years. About half the state constitutions limit even these sessions to a specified number of days (36, 40, 60, 90 or 120 days with 60 the most common) or limit the number of days for which legislators may be paid.

The effect of limited sessions

Congress meets each year for as long as its leaders feel is necessary to realize the possibilities of that session. The national procedure is, therefore, relatively deliberate and even leisurely. State legislatures faced with several hundred bills and resolutions in a session of 60 days every other year must abandon deliberation and the chance of careful second thoughts. Since legislative business is growing increasingly complex and voluminous, artificial time limitations play havoc with the careful, studied, and unhurried processes contemplated by the rules and traditions of American legislative bodies.[30] Initiative in legislation passes to state executives, dominant interest groups or powerful party leaders and measures are either passed or defeated. There is little time for debate, amendment, conference or research.

"End of the session rush"

One particular manifestation of efforts by law or custom to restrict legislative activities is the "end of the session rush." In many states, the last few days of a session are confused and hectic with hundreds of bills taken up and passed or rejected in a few short hours. On occasion no member nor any presiding officer or floor leader is fully in command of the proceedings and certain as to what has been done and what left undone. In part this has been traced to the legislative habit of beginning each session in the leisurely and deliberate manner specified by the rules and then sprinting to the finish under the lash of the constitutional deadline, a determined governor, and the majority leaders. Various states have experimented, as Congress has not, with devices for abating the storm. Several forbid new measures to be introduced after a certain period without the support of an unusual majority or the scrutiny of a special committee for the purpose. A few have tried the "split session." In the first part of the session bills are introduced and referred to committees for study then after a recess the bills are debated and decisions on them reached. California

---

[30] State legislatures in the 1960's considered in a typical biennium more than 10,000 bills and enacted one-third of them.

made the most use of this plan but finally dropped it in 1959. West Virginia and New Mexico tried it and abandoned it. Massachusetts is authorized by its constitution to use it but has never done so.[31] A great many states have sought to expedite the consideration of measures by the use of electronic voting devices by which roll calls can be completed and votes recorded in a few seconds as compared to the time taken in Congress for this purpose.

Massachusetts has perhaps done as much as any state to improve the uneven flow of legislative traffic. The joint-committee system already described, has helped materially. Committees are required, with some exceptions, to report all matters referred to them not later than early March and in many cases within three days of their receipt.[32] None of these has been wholly successful in helping legislatures avoid the confusion of the last few days of the session.

The imprint of the activities of political interest groups on the state legislative process has been deep and continuous for several generations. Public *Lobbying* concern was earlier attracted to the problems at the state level and has been more widely aroused for a longer period than at the national level. In many states the result of this concern has been to fasten shackles on the legislature so that it can do less harm if corrupted by the "interests." A few have grappled directly with lobbying and the lobbyist and have tried to bring the practice and the practitioner under regulation. In fact some of the experience of these states was incorporated in the national effort at regulation. Outstanding efforts have been made by California, New York, Wisconsin, and Massachusetts. The general pattern of regulation now widespread among the states includes: (1) requiring all lobbyists to register with a state official their names, employers, and the scope and character of their legislative interests; (2) requiring lobbyists to file at intervals or at the close of the session a statement of their expenditures for lobbying purposes; (3) forbidding employment of lobbyists on a contingent fee basis. Where honestly and capably administered, these regulations have made it possible to publicize the extent and character of lobbying and have accomplished little else. Wisconsin, in 1957, took the latest and most drastic step to "purify" the lobby by forbidding any lobbyist to buy or give any legislator anything of value (meal, drink, or even cigar).

The "enemy" in all of these efforts is the paid lobbyist acting directly on the legislature. Few laws deal with the interest group itself and fewer still with

[31] On West Virginia's experience, see M. L. Faust, "Results of the Split Session System of the West Virginia Legislature," *Amer. Polit. Sci. Rev.,* XXII, 109-121 (Feb., 1928). In California, opinion on the merits of the plan is divided. V. J. West, "Our Legislative Mills: California, the Home of the Split Session," *Nat. Mun. Rev.,* XII, 369-376 (July, 1923), presents a generally favorable view; T. S. Barclay, "The Split Session of the California Legislature," *Calif. Law Rev.,* XX, 43-59 (Nov., 1931), shows that in practice the plan did not measure up to its theory.

[32] A good appraisal of the Massachusetts system may be found in J. Hunt, "How Our State Legislatures Can Be Improved," *State Government,* XVII, 400-403 (Sept., 1944).

efforts to influence public opinion (indirect lobbying) or to bring indirect
pressure on legislators or administrators.[33]

Uniform
state laws

Americans are, on the whole, proud of the diversity of methods and
policies for dealing with the problems of our society that 50 separate state
governments encourage. There are some areas of state legislative interest, not
as yet controlled or standardized by national programs, which invite if they do
not require greater uniformity of treament, state to state, than results from our
federal pattern. Many examples could be cited in the field of commercial law,
crime, highway rules and others. Since 1892 a National Conference of Commissioners of Uniform State Laws has been actively promoting such uniformity.
This voluntary agency composed of representative lawyers and professors of
law from each state designs and recommends such laws to each state for
adoption. More than 115 of these have been prepared and offered to the states
on such subjects as: negotiable instruments, bills of lading, declaratory judgments, narcotics, criminal extradition, rules of criminal procedure, divorce,
reciprocal enforcement of support. Thirty or more have been adopted in a vast
majority of states, several more in a sizable number of states, and many in a
few states.[34]

TECHNICAL ASSISTANCE FOR LEGISLATORS

One of the most notable changes of the past decades in the state
legislative process has been the growth of technical and expert aid for the
legislators. Few subjects demanding the attention of modern legislators can be
dealt with intelligently without knowledge of the problems or without aid in
casting the proposed solutions into appropriate legal language. The movement
from pioneer frontier to complex urban industrial environment has increased
the difficulty of legislative problem-solving many times over. The hearing
given to bills might be supposed to elicit all the relevant data needed by the
legislator to make a wise decision, but unfortunately this is not always the case.
Much of the testimony is special pleading and large segments of the public,
although concerned, may be inarticulate.

One of the oldest and most useful aids is the legislative reference bureau.
Such an adjunct was first introduced in New York and Massachusetts in 1890
as a function of the central state library and in Wisconsin in 1901 as a permanent agency and nowadays, under some form or name, is found in virtually

1. Legis-
lative
reference
bureaus

[33] For detailed studies of efforts at regulation see B. Zeller, "Pressure Groups and
our State Legislatures," *State Government*, XI, 121-122 *ff.*, 144-147 (July and Aug.,
1938), and "State Regulation of Lobbying," in Council of State Governments, *The Book
of the States*, 1948-49 (Chicago, 1948), 124-130; E. W. Kilpatrick, "Bay State Lobbyists
Toe Mark," *Nat. Mun. Rev.*, XXXIV, 536-539 (Dec., 1945); R. A. Collings, Jr., "California's New Lobby Control Act," *Calif. Law Rev.*, XXXVIII, 478-497 (Aug., 1950);
B. Zeller (ed.), *American State Legislatures* (New York, 1954), Chap. XIII.

[34] For a complete and up to date tabulation of the status of all Uniform Laws see
Council of State Governments, *The Book of the States, 1964-1965* (Chicago, 1964)
pp. 103-109.

every state. Two main purposes are served: (1) assembling, shelving or filing, and indexing for ready use the statutes of the various states, judicial decisions interpreting and applying such statutes in concrete cases, administrative reports and other materials throwing light on the workings of various laws, governors' messages, and a wealth of miscellaneous materials on all manner of subjects—taxation, transportation, labor, public utilities, insurance, pensions, agriculture, corporations, and education—likely to come up during a session; and (2) providing special research service to legislators to compile in ready form information on any selected topic.

Originally, many of the reference bureaus also provided bill drafting assistance to help legislators put their ideas into proper statutory form. A few continue to do so. Generally, however, the bill drafting function has been detached and separately organized. In many states, it has been joined to the long-standing function of statutory revision—continuous revision of the state laws to eliminate with legislative approval, anachronistic, contradictory and inconsistent provisions.

Beginning in Kansas in 1933 a movement for central, bipartisan research *2. Legis-* commissions spread through the nation. These agencies are usually called *lative* legislative councils and, in general, are designed to aid legislatures by making *Councils* extensive studies of the major state problems and by developing suggested legislation for dealing with these problems. Many of the councils or commissions do most of their work in the interim between sessions and are aided by research assistants regularly employed in the staff of the council. The hope of the sponsors of this development that a self-produced program of major legislation might be prepared at leisure by the leaders of the legislature and that by this method some of the leadership in legislation lost to the executive branch might be recaptured has not been fully realized in most of the states that have created such agencies. A few have been outstandingly successful. Many councils, however, have been obliged to spread their efforts over too many subjects, or have been denied funds to hire competent staff, or have become embroiled in party or factional contests. Several have aroused the animosity and suspicion of the members of the legislature not selected to participate in their deliberations.

The growth of state expenditures in recent years has stimulated increasing *3. Fiscal* legislative concern for more effective fiscal review and postaudit practices. In *review* the past decades, several states have created and staffed agencies responsible *agencies* solely to the legislature which conduct continuous review either of executive agency spending proposals and practices or of the actual expenditures made. The California Joint Legislative Budget Committee established in 1941 is the best and one of the earliest examples of this type of legislative service agency.[35]

[35] For a complete tabulation of state legislative service agencies and a biennial review of developments in this field consult *The Book of the States* published by the Council of State Governments. For example, *The Book of the States, 1964-1965* (Chicago, 1964) pp. 67-86.

References

1. GENERAL

Council of State Governments, *Our State Legislatures* (Chicago, 1946).

B. Zeller (ed.), *American State Legislatures* (New York, 1954).

R. Luce, *Legislative Procedure* (Boston, 1922).

——, *Legislative Assemblies* (Boston, 1924).

——, *Legislative Problems* (Boston, 1935).

J. P. Chamberlain, *Legislative Processes; National and State* (New York, 1936).

H. Walker, *The Legislative Process* (New York, 1948).

T. V. Smith, *The Legislative Way of Life* (Chicago, 1949).

A. E. Buck, *Modernizing Our State Legislatures* (Pamphlet, Philadelphia, 1956).

A. B. Coigne, *Statute Making* (New York, 1948).

J. C. Wahlke and H. Eulau (eds.), *Legislative Behavior* (Glencoe, Ill., 1959).

C. Wahlke, H. Eulau, W. Buchanan, and L. C. Ferguson, *The Legislative System: Explorations in Legislative Behavior* (New York, 1962).

M. G. Jewell, *The State Legislature: Politics and Practice* (New York, 1962).

W. J. Keefe and M. S. Ogul, *The American Legislative Process: Congress and the States* (Englewood Cliffs, N.J., 1964).

T. R. Dye, "State Legislative Politics," in H. Jacob and K. N. Vines (eds.), *Politics in the American States—A Comparative Analysis* (Boston, 1965).

2. PARTICULAR STATES

H. Farmer, *The Legislative Process in Alabama* (University, Ala., 1949).

C. C. Young *et al.*, *The Legislature of California, Its Membership, Procedure, and Work* (San Francisco, 1943).

F. H. Guild and C. F. Snider, *Legislative Procedure in Kansas* (Topeka, Kans., 1946).

J. W. Plaisted, *Legislative Procedure in the General Court of Massachusetts* (Boston, 1948).

S. K. Gove and G. Y. Steiner, *The Illinois Legislative Process* (Urbana, Ill., 1954).

E. E. Witte, "Statute Lawmaking in Wisconsin," *Wisconsin Blue Book, 1947* (Madison, Wis.).

F. S. Sorauf, *Party and Representation: Legislative Politics in Pennsylvania* (New York, 1963).

W. Buchanan, *Legislative Partisanship: the Deviant Cast of California* (Berkeley, Calif., 1963).

W. C. Howard and L. P. Bath, *The Politics of Mis-Representation: Rural-Urban Conflict in the Florida Legislature* (Baton Rouge, La., 1962).

3. PARTICULAR PROBLEMS

C. W. Shull, *American Experience with Unicameral Legislatures* (Pamphlet, Detroit, 1937).

"Unicameral Legislatures" (Symposium), *Cong. Digest,* XVI, 203-224 (Aug. and Sept., 1937).

H. J. Morgenthau, "Constitutional Reform in Missouri," *Univ. of Kansas City Law Rev.,* XI, 1-64 (Dec., 1942). Contains a symposium on unicameralism, with special reference to state legislatures.

A. W. Johnson, *The Unicameral Legislature* (Minneapolis, 1938).

W. A. Schnader, "The Constitution and the Legislatures," *Annals of Amer. Acad. of Polit. and Soc. Sci.,* CLXXXI, 39-49 (Sept., 1935).

C. G. Haines, "Judicial Review of Legislation in the United States and the Doctrine of Implied Limitations on Legislatures," *Tex. Law Rev.,* II, 257-290, 387-421 (Apr. and June, 1924), III, 1-43 (Dec., 1924).

W. F. Dodd, "Extra-Constitutional Limitations on Legislative Power," *Yale Law Jour.,* XL, 1188-1218 (Jan., 1931).

———, "Judicially Non-Enforceable Provisions of Constitutions," *Univ. of Pa. Law Rev.,* LXXX, 54-93 (Nov., 1931).

C. S. Hyneman, "Tenure and Turnover of the Indiana General Assembly," *Amer. Polit. Sci. Rev.,* XXXII, 51-67, 311-331 (Feb. and Apr., 1938).

C. I. Winslow, "State Legislative Committees; A Study in Procedure," *Johns Hopkins Univ. Studies in Hist. and Polit. Sci.,* XLIX, 150-291 (Baltimore, 1931).

E. E. Sparlin, "Experts for the Lawmakers" (in Missouri), *Nat. Mun. Rev.,* XXXVII, 299-302, 314 (June, 1948).

Interim Report of the New York State Joint Legislative Committee on Legislative Methods, Practices, Procedures, and Expenditures, Legislative Doc. No. 35 (Albany, 1945). *Final Report,* etc., Legislative Doc. No. 31 (Albany, 1946).

O. D. Weeks, *Research in the American State Legislative Process* (Ann Arbor, Mich., 1947).

Oklahoma State Legislative Council, *Constitutional Study* No. 4, "Strengthening the Legislative Process"; No. 7, "Legislative Organization and Procedure" (Oklahoma City, 1948).

C. O. Johnson, "The Adoption of the Initiative and Referendum in Washington," *Pacific Northwest Quar.,* XXXV, 291-303 (Oct., 1944), and "The Initiative and Referendum in Washington," *ibid.,* XXXVI, 29-53 (Jan., 1945).

H. W. Davey, "The Legislative Council Movement in the United States, 1933-1953," *Amer. Pol. Sci. Rev.,* XLVII, 785-797 (Sept., 1953).

E. C. Lee, *The Presiding Officer and Rules Committee in Legislatures of the United States* (Berkeley, Calif., 1952).

W. J. Siffrin, *The Legislative Council in the American States* (Bloomington, Ind., 1959).

★ 28 ★

The Governor and the

Executive Branch

*Impor-
tance of
the office* THE PRINCIPAL POLITICAL OFFICER of each state is the governor. He is also
the chief executive, a major law-maker, an important party leader and the
ceremonial head of the commonwealth. His major task is to devise a program
for the conduct of the affairs of his state and then to seek appropriate legislation, necessary financing, and popular support to carry it out. To the public he
is the state and they expect him to find a remedy for every ill of the body
politic. He is rarely, however, able to work his will by command. Exhortation
is his most widely used method and close bargaining with those whom he cannot dominate his daily exercise. The governorship in America is a miniature
Presidency but without many of the President's most powerful tools. Unlike
the Presidency, however, the governorship is not the summit of a public career
but rather a small hill on which to learn the art of mountain climbing. The
governor's office is the testing grounds for statesmen and many of the men
who occupy it expect to go on to the Senate, the Cabinet, or the Presidency.

Term   In every state the governor is today elected by popular vote on a partisan
ballot for a term of two or four years. The office was not originally so conceived. In only two colonies (Connecticut and Rhode Island) was the governor
chosen by the people and in 11 of the 13 original states he was selected by the
legislature. Popular election gradually won its way during the early half of the
past century and prepared the ground for the emergence of the popular and
powerful leader of the present era. The general trend has been toward lengthening the governor's term and whereas several decades ago two years was
typical now the governor serves four years in all but 11 states.[1] Fear of unrestricted tenure, as in the case of the Presidency, has led in a number of states
to constitutional restrictions on continued eligibility. In 14 states, the governor
may not succeed himself [2] and in 9 states he may serve no more than two con-

---

[1] Arizona, Arkansas, Iowa, Kansas, New Hampshire, New Mexico, Rhode Island,
South Dakota, Texas, Vermont, and Wisconsin.
[2] Alabama, Florida, Georgia, Indiana, Kentucky, Louisiana, Mississippi, No. Carolina, Oklahoma, Pennsylvania, So. Carolina, Tennessee, Virginia, and West Virginia.

secutive terms.[3] Many of the great industrial states which have produced so many strong Presidential aspirants (*e.g.,* Ohio, Illinois, California, New York) have four-year terms without restrictions of this type. New York, for example, has had only six different governors in four decades. In these states, furthermore, party competition is unusually keen. Many of those with eligibility restrictions are one-party states. In summary, the trend everywhere is toward creating a more powerful position manned by more experienced leaders.

In every state the governorship is now selected under party auspices in a partisan election. In a few states candidates for the major parties are nominated by state-wide conventions (*e.g.* New York) of locally-elected delegates. The typical method is by popular voice in state-wide direct primaries. In several of the states where primaries are used, however, the party seeks through official conventions or semiofficial and informal caucuses and conventions to present to the voters aspirants bearing the approval of the organization. In most of the Southern states, the primary is more important than the election since Democratic nominees virtually always win in November. In an effort to secure majority choice, many of these states have two primaries with the two candidates finishing at the top in the first heat contesting in a second or "run-off" primary election. Three states for many years used a modified electoral college system weighted somewhat in favor of the rural and small town populations in connection with the gubernatorial election. In Mississippi a legislative-district, electoral-vote system was used in the election and the winner had to obtain both popular and electoral majorities. In Georgia and Maryland a system based on counties was used in the nominating procedure but not in the final election. These systems were held invalid by the Supreme Court of the United States as violating the equal protection clause in so far as they tend to deny equality of voting rights.[4] The character of the procedure for entering the gubernatorial sweepstakes is to a large degree influenced by the existence of real two-party competition. In general, the more competitive the parties the more nearly the process resembles that for the Presidency. But in the numerous one-party states the contest is really an intraparty affair and many kinds of informal organizational and campaign patterns exist.[5] Whatever the method of reaching this high office, in every state there are numerous practices, customs, and traditions which influence selection and are collectively of greater consequence than the qualifications as to age and length of residency written into the constitutions.[6]

The governor, as well as other major state officials, may be removed by

Nomination and election

Removal

[3] Alaska, Delaware, Maine, Maryland, New Jersey, New Mexico, Ohio, Oregon, and South Dakota.

[4] See, for example, Gray *v.* Sanders, 372 U.S. 368 (1963).

[5] For a suggestive analysis of the variations in practice arising from the intensity or lack of it of party competition see: V. O. Key, *American State Politics: An Introduction* (New York, 1956). Chaps. IV and V.

[6] See J. A. Schlesinger, *How They Became Governor: A Study of Comparative State Politics, 1870-1959* (East Lansing, Mich., 1957).

impeachment and conviction on the national pattern in every state except Oregon. As in Washington, this procedure is rarely used: only 13 governors have ever been impeached and of these only 6 were convicted and removed from office.[7] In a dozen states governors may be recalled by popular petition and vote. Only one governor—Frazier of North Dakota in 1921—has been ousted by this method. Typically, the lieutenant governor succeeds to the office on the death, resignation, or removal of the governor. Several states without this office, place the secretary of state, president of the Senate, or Speaker of the lower house next in line.

THE GOVERNOR AND LEGISLATION

Constitu-
tional
position
and
powers:

The modern governor invests a large part of his energy in procuring the legislation and fiscal resources to carry out his program. Popular election, the organization of political parties, and partisan campaigning have all contributed to the emergence, in most states, of the governor as a major influence in law-making. This development closely parallels that of the office of President and is supported in large measure by factors outside the formal constitutional assignment of powers and duties. Many of the newer state constitutions and amendments, however, reflect the increasing importance of executive leadership in the legislative process and provide to the governors a more extensive and more compelling set of legislative powers than the President can command.

1. Special
sessions

State legislatures, typically, meet less frequently than does Congress and the sessions are, in many states, rigidly limited as to length. The power of the governor to call the legislature into special session is relatively of greater importance, therefore, than that of the President. Typically, the governor by declaring the purposes of the session, may bar consideration of other subjects.[8] Of course, the governor cannot compel the legislature to agree with his proposals.

2. Mes-
sages

Like the President, the governor is obliged by constitutional prescription to inform the legislature on the condition of the state's affairs. Ordinarily the major message which opens the regular session is delivered orally and attracts a wide audience. This "state of the state" message is commonly followed by numerous messages on particular subjects from time to time during the session. Bills exactly designed to achieve the governor's suggestions also flow from the

[7] The most recent impeachments of governors include Sulzer of New York in 1913, Ferguson of Texas in 1917, Walton and Johnson of Oklahoma in 1923 and 1929—all of these were convicted. Huey Long of Louisiana was impeached in 1929 but the trial was never completed. Governor Moodie of North Dakota was impeached in 1935 but never tried.

[8] In a few states, the governor may enlarge the agenda from time to time during the special session. In a few others, the legislature may itself by extraordinary vote enlarge the scope of the session. Also in a half-dozen states, the legislature itself may force a call for a session.

executive office in a steady stream. In many of our large and influential states his is the principal initiative in lawmaking.

Year in and year out the most important set of executive recommenda- *3. Budget* tions are those embraced in the budget. Virtually every state has since 1910 *proposals* adopted the executive budget system which places the governor in the leading role in preparing and recommending a fiscal program for his state. In discharging this responsibility, the governor gains, probably, his greatest influence over the conduct of the state administration and, at the same time, initiates the most important bill or set of bills in each regular legislative session.

Originally the states bestowed the veto power grudgingly or not at all *4. Veto* (Massachusetts and South Carolina made the only provision for it among the *power* original thirteen states). As popular election gradually freed the governor from his early dependence on the legislature, the veto became an important adjunct to his position. It is authorized in every state except North Carolina. Furthermore, in all but a handful of states,[9] the veto extends to items in appropriation bills (a power for which several recent Presidents have pled vainly). In Washington the item veto extends to all measures and in Oregon to bills declaring an emergency. The item veto equips the governor with power to deal with riders and with expenditures outside his budget suggestions and tends to enhance his influence in legislation. In a few states, Massachusetts, Tennessee, Pennsylvania and California, for example, the item veto has been construed to permit the governor not only to strike out particular appropriations but to reduce the amounts. This places him in an even more powerful position to determine the character and scope of the state's fiscal commitments. It also may encourage legislative extravagance and irresponsibility. The legislators rely on the governor to whittle the appropriations back down to the limit of the state's income and, of course, to accept whatever onus attaches to this procedure.

Like the Congress, state legislatures may override a veto but the vote necessary to do so varies from a mere majority in a few states to two-thirds of the full membership in each house in almost half of the states. Most states allow the governor five days to consider a bill after he receives it when the legislature is in session. After adjournment, many states give the governor more time. Some give him a pocket veto but in others he must actually veto the bill to prevent its becoming law. New Jersey provided in its new constitution for a practice which, in fact, had been used increasingly in several states of reassembling the legislature at a specified time after adjournment to consider the governor's vetoes of measures passed in the closing days of the session. This has the effect of eliminating the "pocket" veto—*i.e.* vetoing a bill by inaction.[10]

[9] Indiana, Iowa, Maine, Nevada, New Hampshire, Rhode Island, Vermont and West Virginia have no item veto.

[10] For a tabulation of the governor's veto authorization in the 50 states, see Council of State Governments, *The Book of the States, 1964-1965* (Chicago, 1964), 58-59.

All things considered, the typical governor has a stronger and more effective negative on legislation than does the President. At both levels of government, however, vetoes are rarely overridden and largely occur after the legislature has adjourned.[11] At best, however, the veto is a negative influence and can be transformed into positive leadership only by skillful bargaining.

The governor's influence over legislation, and it is usually considerable, really arises like that of the President from his position as the leader of his party, his superior ability to gain public interest and support for his program, his near monopoly on the creation of statehouse news, his ability to dispense favors large and small to legislators who follow his lead, and his power to punish by veto, refusal of appointment, or publicity those who obstruct his programs.

THE GOVERNOR AS EXECUTIVE

Weaker than the President in:

If as legislator, party leader, and popular hero, the modern governor closely resembles the modern President, as an executive and as manager of the administrative machinery the two are poles apart. The President's towering and lonely position as director of a huge and complex administrative apparatus, as commander of great military forces, and as deviser of the foreign relations of the nation is unmatched at the state level.

1. Constitutional power

In the first place, few state constitutions assign executive authority to governors in clear and unambiguous terms. Some say that he shall take care that the laws be faithfully executed but rarely is he assigned any agencies of law enforcement under his direct control. Some say that he shall be chief executive but on several occasions state courts have held that this endows him with little or no inherent executive authority. Many grant to him certain power of appointment and removal but this too is in many states hedged around with inhibitions.

2. Control over departments

Further, in every state one or more officials of the state administration are directly elected by the voters and are in no sense subordinates to the chief executive. Most commonly, the offices of attorney general, secretary of state, treasurer, auditor, and superintendent of public instruction are filled in this way. Each presides over an important agency which is thus largely removed from oversight by the governor. In many of the newer constitutions, notably those of New Jersey and Alaska, this group of independently elected state executives is either sharply reduced or eliminated. In many states, other major

---

[11] For case study of the veto see M. N. McGeary, "The Governor's Veto in Pennsylvania," *Amer. Polit. Sci. Rev.*, XLI, 941-946 (Oct., 1947) and Wisconsin Legis. Ref. Library, *The Operation of the Executive Veto in Wisconsin, 1937-55, with Special Reference to the Partial Veto*. Information Bulletin, Madison (Jan., 1957).

departments or agencies are controlled by lay boards appointed for long and staggered terms. Such boards usually select the executive officer of the department and serve as screens between him and the chief executive. These arrangements blur, if they do not obliterate, any sense of subordination by the agency directors. A movement inaugurated in Illinois in 1920 by Governor Lowden and subsequently spreading to many other states has sought to sweep away the board system of department management and, to some extent, the elected department head system and replace it with single, governor-appointed heads along the lines of the national executive branch. Several of the largest and most important states have adopted what has come to be called "the strong executive" plan but a large number cling to the system described earlier in this paragraph.

The Presidents appointing and, by inference, his directing authority is limited, as we have noted earlier, by the spread of the civil service merit system throughout the national administration. The same thing on a smaller scale has happened in the state houses. In general, however, the "merit" system has made relatively less progress among state employees and thus executive patronage is somewhat more extensive. It may be argued that "patronage" strengthens the governor's hand in party affairs and in dealing with the legislature; it does not improve his position as an effective state executive.

As in Washington, executive appointments, typically, must be confirmed by the upper houses of the state legislatures. In a few states, notably North Carolina, Massachusetts, New Hampshire, and Maine, some appointing authority is shared with an executive council or council of state.[12]   *3. Requirements of confirmation*

Finally, the state executive everywhere must rely heavily for law enforcement and the provision of some state services on locally elected and locally controlled officials such as mayors, sheriffs, prosecuting attorneys and assessors. Except that the governor is empowered in several states to remove these officials for sufficient cause, they are largely beyond the reach of his direction and owe him no particular loyalty or deference. Presidents, as a result of the decision made in 1787-1788 suffer no comparable disadvantage in discharging their responsibilities.   *4. Reliance on local officials*

It is apparent that few governors are in as commanding positions over their state administrations as the President is over his. The trend everywhere is to improve the governor's position in this regard. The movements for the four-year term, the elimination of many independent agencies, the reduction of the number of elected administrators, the substitution of governor-appointed department heads for boards or commissions, the executive budget system all are designed to achieve this end. In many of our great states giant steps have already been taken and some steps have been taken in almost every state but the typical governor is still not a powerful executive.

12 On the role of the executive council in Maine see C. E. Vose, *The Executive Council of Maine in Decline* (Brunswick, Me., 1959).

"WEAK" EXECUTIVE TYPE OF STATE ADMINISTRATIVE ORGANIZATION

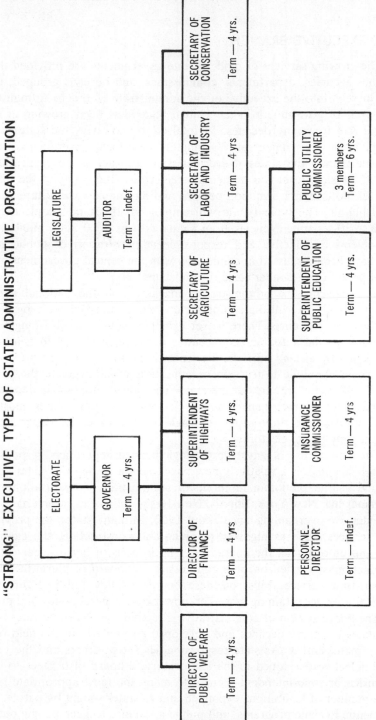

"STRONG" EXECUTIVE TYPE OF STATE ADMINISTRATIVE ORGANIZATION

LEGISLATURE

ELECTORATE

AUDITOR
Term — indef.

GOVERNOR
Term — 4 yrs.

SECRETARY OF CONSERVATION
Term — 4 yrs.

SECRETARY OF LABOR AND INDUSTRY
Term — 4 yrs

SECRETARY OF AGRICULTURE
Term — 4 yrs

SUPERINTENDENT OF HIGHWAYS
Term — 4 yrs.

DIRECTOR OF FINANCE
Term — 4 yrs

DIRECTOR OF PUBLIC WELFARE
Term — 4 yrs.

PUBLIC UTILITY COMMISSIONER
3 members
Term — 6 yrs.

SUPERINTENDENT OF PUBLIC EDUCATION
Term — 4 yrs.

INSURANCE COMMISSIONER
Term — 4 yrs

PERSONNEL DIRECTOR
Term — indef.

THE EXECUTIVE BRANCH

Importance of administration

The growing services of modern state governments are provided through numerous agencies, departments, commissions, and bureaus grouped, usually rather loosely, into the executive or the administrative branch. Administration at all levels of government in the United States has been growing at a phenomenal rate for many decades. In total effort, however, the states are still far behind the government at Washington. Our local governments, in fact, spend more than the states. Nevertheless, administering governmental programs at the state level is a tremendous enterprise and occupies the time and energy of more than 1.8 million persons and an annual expenditure in excess of $40 billion. The typical state will employ 90 thousand people organized into 20 to 30 separate agencies at an annual cost of $700-$800 million. All of the problems of effective and responsible administration of public policies which have been discussed in connection with the central government are also present, albeit on a smaller scale, in the states.

Organization:

In comparing the administrative machinery at the national and state levels, it is well to recall the comparatively feeble sweep of the typical governor's directing influence. There is, for example, nothing at Washington quite comparable to the autonomous executive departments found in nearly every state headed by elected officials. The most important of these by far are the departments of public instruction or education which regulate the provision of public education throughout the state. The other autonomous departments, treasury, state, attorney general's are relatively less important in most states but nevertheless constitute separate, single-headed, executive departments responsible only to the electorate.

1. The use of autonomous departments

2. The use of single-headed departments

The general use of any type of single-headed department responsible to the chief executive is a relatively new phenomenon among the states and may be found as the predominant mode of administrative organization only in those states like New York, Illinois, New Jersey, Michigan, which have undergone extensive overhauling since about 1920. In many states, the provision of major services, such as highway planning and construction, the care of the needy and unfortunate, the operation of institutions of healing, correction, or rehabilitation, is carried on by a commission, or board of plural membership and part-time service. Most of these boards employ full-time directors to manage the service retaining, however, power over general policy and program.

3. Continued reliance on boards and commissions

The board system of administrative direction was the preferred system in most states for many decades and developed particularly in the field of institutional management. As state responsibilities for prisoners and the mentally ill and defective developed in the last century, a board of trustees to oversee the warden or superintendent seemed to many the most appropriate method. As the number of institutions expanded and as states sought by parole, probation, mental hygiene programs, and public assistance to keep people out of the institutions, the board system became cumbersome and inappropriate and demands for its abolition became more insistent and gradually more compelling. The board system, however, was never confined to institutional management and has been and is being widely used for the regulation of agriculture, the conservation of resources, the promotion of business, the administration of labor laws and many other purposes.

In the delicate area of regulation of the rates and profits of public utilities the states have almost uniformly followed the national pattern of adjudication through the independent regulatory commission. In general, these are staffed by full-time, relatively well-paid, commissioners appointed by the governor and serving staggered terms of 6 to 9 years. In more than a dozen states, however, the public utility or railroad commission members are elected by popular vote and, in at least one state (North Carolina) are selected by the legislature. It is not uncommon to require that members on such commissions be drawn from more than one political party. *4. The regulatory commission*

The government corporation or authority may also be found in several states but nowhere is it used as extensively as in the national government. The most widely used state-corporations are those for the administration of toll roads or turnpikes, liquor stores, building construction, and power distribution. Commonly the state corporations have relatively greater freedom to arrange their finances than do the other types of agencies. *5. The corporation*

Modern state administration is characterized by the rapid growth of management services. In fact many services such as central purchasing, consolidated budgeting, pre- and postauditing, maintaining buildings, and procuring personnel were tried out initially in state and city governments. The success there attained commended them to other state capitals and city halls, and to the central government in Washington. Whereas in Washington, all of these management agencies are ultimately responsible to a single executive head, the President, in many, if not most, states this is not the case. Almost everywhere, for example, legal advisement is provided to the departments or agencies and to the governor by the attorney general's department and this official is separately elected in all but a handful of states. Auditors, treasurers, and controllers charged with prescribing systems of accounts, keeping track of cash, and reviewing fiscal transactions either before or after the incurring of the obligation are also almost universally elected in the states. Typically, purchasing, building construction and maintenance, budget preparation, and central printing are closely associated with the executive office and, therefore, more directly subject to executive authority but there are numerous exceptions among the 50 states. In several states, administrators of service functions are insulated against executive direction by long terms or merit selection with tenure. *Growth of management services*

As in Washington, the growth of centralized management services has accompanied the demand for more efficiency and economy in governmental administration. The controls exercised by such agencies arose, however, in

*Manage-
ment
services in
weak-
executive
states*

response to charges of "spoils" and "boodle." The problems of responsibility for the accomplishment of public policies raised by the growth of management services are many and have been discussed in connection with the national government. A different and additional set of difficulties characterizes the growth of these services in states without strong executive direction and without a coordinated executive branch. In many cases, the purchasers, auditors, accountants, legal advisors, printers, engineers, architects, and personnel administrators may, in fact, be responsible to no one in the entire executive establishment. On the other hand, governors lacking direct and specific directional authority over state departments and agencies have on many occasions sought to achieve influence through the management services attached to their offices or under their direction. When this has occurred, the management services have become instruments of control and direction over state affairs in a way that may also threaten the position of the line administrators. The most sweeping moves in the direction of strengthening the executive through management controls have occurred in Minnesota, Wisconsin, Alaska, and a few other states where the major management functions have been gathered into Departments of Administration and placed directly under the governor.

*Continuing
efforts at
reorgani-
zation*

The administrative apparatus of the states like that in Washington, can never be fully and finally organized. New services, new methods, new ideas make change both inevitable and necessary. Reorganization is, therefore, a continuing concern in the states. Initiated in this century largely by Governor Lowden of Illinois and Governor Smith of New York sweeping changes have been made in the direction of strengthening the governorship and streamlining a hodgepodge of agencies and services. No sooner had this set of reforms swept through many states than new demands for change occurred. The Hoover Commission, for example, stimulated many states to follow the national lead and from 1949 to the present one state after the other has established study commissions—in some cases several—to review administrative organization and procedure and to make suitable recommendations for reform. It would be hard to picture the net impact of all these studies. Many have been abortive and without substantial result; others have led to far-reaching changes. In general, the greater changes seem to have been made in states that had avoided or resisted the reforms of the twenties.[13] Most state legislatures have proved unwilling to go as far as the Congress in implementing reorganization studies by endowing the executive with the authority to make changes by executive order subject to legislative veto. New Hampshire in 1949, Michigan in 1958 and Oregon in 1959 are the only states that have, with various limitations, endowed their governors with this power.[14] The new state of Alaska grants this authority in its constitution. In many states, also, administrative organiza-

---

[13] For descriptions of administrative reform efforts in the various states see the articles on this subject in each biennial edition of the Council of State Governments, *Book of the States.*

[14] Pennsylvania in 1955 gave its governor a very limited reorganizing authority applicable only within bureaus or similar units.

tion is prescribed for part or all of the executive branch in the state constitution and effective reorganization may require changing the constitution as well as the statutes. The principal beneficiary of most of the studies and most of the successful reform efforts has been the governor and thus reorganization efforts may be classed with other developments already described as part of a general movement to strengthen the governor as chief executive of the state.

STATE PERSONNEL ADMINISTRATION

No administrative organization can be very much better than the quality of the people who service it. To the states the problem of recruiting and maintaining an able body of public servants is one of continuing importance and difficulty. The civil service reform movement which led to the growth of the merit system of personnel administration in the national executive branch also sought comparable results in the state houses. A few states, notably Wisconsin in 1905, adopted sweeping merit system laws and a few others (New York in 1833, Massachusetts in 1844, *e.g.*) adopted merit systems for some employees but most resisted the removal of partisan appointment and by the mid-thirties only a small minority of states had very effective merit systems for a majority of their employees. The great expansion in state merit systems occurred after 1936 as a result of the requirement of the Social Security Act of that year that states participating in national grants under that law must install merit system selection and protection for employees in the various assistance, insurance, and health programs. Thus by national compulsion a large number of state employees in every state were brought under an approved merit system. Since that time gains have been made in Indiana, Oregon, North Carolina, Vermont, Montana, Nevada, Oklahoma, Kentucky, Alaska, Hawaii, and a few other states. There remain, however, a large minority of states without state-wide merit systems of personnel administration.[15]

The adoption of the merit system has by no means solved all the personnel problems of the states. There is a persistent tendency for merit systems to become routine, mechanical, and unimaginatively directed. Much more positive efforts at recruiting talent, maintaining attractive wage and benefit schedules, encouraging public careers, and overcoming the undue rigidities of classification schemes are necessary even in states most widely committed to merit selection. The three-man civil service commission, so widely used for enforcing merit rules, have scores of critics. Many reorganization studies have suggested single-headed personnel departments as more appropriate under modern conditions and many have sought to enlarge the power of the governor to influence personnel administration. In general, states without extensive merit systems, however, continue to lag far behind the others in the national search for talent to man the services of the states.

*Impor-
tance of
personnel
policies*

*Spread of
state
"merit"
systems*

*Continuing
state per-
sonnel
problems*

[15] The latest tabulation of state personnel systems showing coverage and type of administrative organization may be found in Council of State Governments, *Book of the States, 1964-65* (Chicago, 1964), pp. 178-181.

References

1. THE GOVERNOR

L. Lipson, *The American Governor: From Figurehead to Leader* (Chicago, 1939).

J. A. Fairlie, "The Executive Power in the State Constitution," *Annals of Amer. Acad. of Polit. and Soc. Sci.,* CLXXXI, 59-73 (Sept., 1935).

M. L. Faust, *Manual of the Executive Article for the Missouri Constitutional Convention of 1943* (Columbia, Mo., 1943).

C. J. Rohr, "The Governor of Maryland: A Constitutional Study," *Johns Hopkins Univ. Studies in Hist. and Polit. Sci.,* L, 303-475 (1931).

C. Jensen, *The Pardoning Power in the American States* (Chicago, 1922).

J. A. Perkins, *The Role of the Governor of Michigan in the Enactment of Appropriations* (Ann Arbor, Mich., 1943).

P. J. Collins, "The Executive Council in State Government," *State Government,* XX, 269-274 (Oct., 1947).

W. J. Kohler, Jr., "The Governor's Office," *Wisconsin Magazine of History* (Summer, 1952).

J. A. Friedman, *The Impeachment of Governor William Sulzer* (New York, 1939).

C. A. M. Ewing, "Southern Governors," *Jour. of Politics,* X, 385-409 (May, 1948).

C. B. Ransome, Jr., *The Office of Governor in the South* (University, Ala., 1951).

———, *The Office of Governor in the United States* (University, Ala., 1956).

J. A. Schlesinger, "The Politics of the Executive," in H. Jacob and K. Vines, *Politics in the American States: A Comparative Analysis* (Boston, 1965).

J. S. Allen, *New Governor in Indiana: the Challenges of Executive Power* (Bloomington, Ind., 1965).

D. Lockert, *The Politics of State and Local Government* (New York, 1963), Chaps. 12-13.

Autobiographical writing of ex-governors like Theodore Roosevelt, Robert M. LaFollette, and Alfred E. Smith.

2. ADMINISTRATIVE ORGANIZATION

K. H. Porter, *State Administration* (New York, 1938), Chaps. I-IX.

A. E. Buck, *The Reorganization of State Governments in the United States* (New York, 1938).

J. C. Bollens, *Administrative Reorganization in the States Since 1939* (Berkeley, Calif., 1947).

L. K. Caldwell, "Perfecting State Administration," *Pub. Admin. Rev.*, VII, 25-36 (Winter, 1947).

J. W. Fesler, *The Independence of State Regulatory Agencies* (Chicago, 1942).

O. G. Stahl, *Public Personnel Administration* (5th ed., New York, 1962).

Civil Service Assembly of the United States and Canada, *A Digest of State Civil Service Laws* (Chicago, 1939).

———, *Civil Service Agencies in the United States: A 1940 Census* (Chicago, 1940).

National Civil Service League, *Model State Civil Service Law* (New York, 1946).

Good Government, LXVII, 36-41 (Sept.-Oct., 1950), "Removals in the Civil Service."

G. C. S. Benson, *The Administration of the Civil Service in Massachusetts* (Cambridge, Mass., 1935).

O. P. Field, *Civil Service Law* (Minneapolis, 1939).

J. K. Coleman, *State Administration in South Carolina* (New York, 1935).

R. L. Carleton, *et al.*, *Reorganization and Consolidation of State Administration in Louisiana* (Baton Rouge, La., 1937).

State Budget Office and Bureau of Government, University of Michigan, *A Manual of State Government in Michigan* (Ann Arbor, Mich., 1949).

New York State Department of Commerce, *A Guide to State Services* (in New York) (Albany, N.Y., 1946).

Brookings Institution, *Organization and Administration of Oklahoma* (Oklahoma City, Okla., 1936).

Keesling Committee, "Report on State Reorganization Plan" (in California), *Tax Digest*, XIX, 156-159, 170-176 (May, 1941).

Council of State Governments, *Reorganizing State Government* (Chicago, 1950).

W. V. Holloway, *Personnel Administration in the States* (Oklahoma City, 1948).

New York State Civil Service Commission, *Civil Service Administration in the Empire State* (Albany, 1949).

Y. Wilbern, "Administration in State Governments," in American Assembly, *The Forty-eight States* (New York, 1955).

State Functions and Services

RECALLING FOR A MOMENT the enormous array of national services and controls, we might well ask if there is anything left for the states to do. The answer is: a great deal. States have never been so active, spent so much money, or provided such comprehensive services as they do today. There is scarcely an aspect of our society untouched by the state. The states and their local government units are the primary protectors of life and property; they are deeply engaged in regulating and stimulating economic activities inside their boundaries; they provide the most extensive system of public education for their young people ever known; they succor, rehabilitate, and care for the sick, the poor, the handicapped, the veteran, the neglected, the criminal, the aged; they engage in many kinds of internal improvements including particularly the most complex and elaborate system of highways and airports in the world; they act to protect consumers, preserve resources and manage elections. The list could be extended for several pages. More than two-thirds of the states' fiscal resources, however, are expended on three programs: public education; highway construction and maintenance; and public health and welfare.

PUBLIC EDUCATION

The greatest single public enterprise of the states and their local subdivisions is the provision of education to the youth of the nation. In the numbers of persons involved and, probably, in social consequences this is the greatest public effort at any level. It is topped in dollars spent only by the huge national defense effort of the nuclear age and the cold war. In 1964, more than 41 million pupils attended public primary and secondary educational facilities; they were taught by more than 1.6 million teachers; and the expenditures on their behalf exceeded $18 billion.

From the earliest days of this nation the provision of free public education has been considered a cornerstone of the American way of life. Even before the adoption of our present Constitution, the Congress had required that public lands in the territories be set aside for the support of schools (Northwest Ordinance of 1787). Throughout our history, however, education has been regarded as a state rather than a national responsibility. Certainly, throughout the last century the national government was concerned only slightly and mainly at the college level. In the states the main burden of building, staffing, and managing the schools was carried for generations by the localities with the state governments concerned largely with providing a legal framework for the local discharge of these responsibilities. Administratively and financially the state involvement was modest. Largely to avoid partisan, political influences on the school system, separate units of local government— the school districts—have been the principal agencies for managing education. These districts—usually coterminous with some other local political unit— were operated by elected boards and were financed almost exclusively by levies on property.

At the turn of the century, the typical rural school district operated one school building with one teacher and offered instruction through 6 or occasionally 8 grades to 15-20 pupils. City school systems had already widely substituted the multiple-teacher platoon system or the grade and subject specialist system for the one teacher per school arrangement. The high school was also becoming increasingly common in the cities. About 17 million young people were enrolled in 1900 and the typical American youth might average 6-8 years of schooling at public expense. *The schools in 1900*

As this century progressed the demand for educational services and opportunities grew rapidly. The high school became well-nigh universal, kindergartens and nursery schools reached pre-school-aged children, vocational courses were developed on a large scale both inside and outside the regular school organization, recreational programs during and after school hours were begun, libraries in the schools and in the communities were established, evening classes for adults were started, efforts were made to reach out to the handicapped, the abnormal, and other categories of children unsuited to the normal classroom situation. By 1945, the school systems were reaching more than 23 million young people and more than 60 percent of those of high school age were actually in school. All of these developments added greatly to the costs of education and brought sharply into focus the remarkably unequal abilities of local school units to finance these programs from levies on local property. During this period, therefore, the state governments came to play an increasingly active role in financing and supervising the school program. State educational departments, heretofore largely hortatory in method and limited in function, were professionalized and given more active supervisory responsibilities. One state after another: (1) established minimum standards of teacher training, curriculum coverage, and adequacy of physical facilities below which impecunious or incompetent local management might not sink; (2) brought to the aid of hard pressed local units fiscal resources gathered from a broader tax base; (3) developed public teacher training institutions to supply the growing need for competent teachers; (4) assumed full responsibility for special educational programs for handicapped, neglected or abnormal children; (5) expanded the coverage and stiffened the *Rapid expansion of educational programs* *State responsibilities* enforcement of compulsory school attendance laws; and (6) during the depression made numerous special grants to succor distressed districts and to aid school construction.

Impact of birth rate rise on schools

The postwar period has brought greater demands on the school system than ever before. The rapid rise in the birth rate—from 18.4 per 1000 in 1936 to 27.0 per 1000 in 1947—launched a period of unprecedented growth in school enrollments. First the elementary schools were flooded; then the high schools and now the colleges. Enrollments have been growing at the rate of almost 1 million a year for over a decade. Second, the heavy migration of population from farm to city and from central city to suburb has left many old schools without pupils and brought together hundreds of thousands of children without adequate schools. Third, the continuation of early trends toward lengthening schooling has kept these new millions of youngsters in school longer than their fathers. Fourth, the tremendous scientific and technological advances of the past few decades have sharply increased the need for competent instruction while many of the potential instructors have been lured into industry, government and institutions of higher learning by better pay and greater social recognition.

The upshot of all of this is that the states are more deeply involved—legislatively, financially, and administratively—in the provision of schooling from kindergarten through university than ever before. The major controversy today is the extent to which the national government now that it has entered the field of public education in 1965 and brought its vast tax resources to the aid of the states should seek to exercise control over public education.

School district reorganization

A major effort of modern educational statesmanship, despite the growing power and influence of the state governments and the nation, has been to strengthen the local district by vastly enlarging its size so that it might through a broad enough tax base and a large enough child population be able efficiently to provide an adequate educational program. The number of districts has declined from 127,000 in 1932 to 37,000 in 1962. A dozen states have made the county the smallest unit for school administration and one state (Delaware) has a state-wide school unit. The number of one-teacher schools has fallen from 149,000 in 1930 to 26,000 in 1959. Nevertheless, many experts believe there is much yet to be done. They cite the 4100 districts which operate no schools at all, the 17,000 districts with fewer than 50 pupils, and the continued sharp discrepancy in the burden of taxes required to support adequate programs. On the other hand some of the great metropolitan systems have become such giants that effective management is well-nigh out of the question. No doubt these developments have strengthened many local districts that have survived reorganization and consolidation. They have been achieved, however, largely by stern state control and by heavy commitments from the state treasury. Perhaps the most difficult and most important of the remaining problems of district organization is the small high school. Most experts believe that it is financially prohibitive and administratively wasteful to attempt to offer modern education in a school of fewer than 450-500 pupils.[1] Nevertheless, of the 25,000 high schools in America only 4,000 are as large or larger. Almost one-third of the nation's high school pupils attend schools of inadequate size, and therefore, of inadequate depth or breadth of subject matter. The high school, however, is the center of the social life of many small communities; without one the possibilities of growth are thought to be small. The residents, therefore, tend to cling to these outworn facilities with desperate and bitter determination.

The major source of continuing and expanding state influence in American education is the growing reliance on the states' fiscal resources to finance it. In 1930, about 16 percent of the cost of public education through high school was provided from state tax funds and virtually all the rest from locally assessed taxes on property. Today (1964) more than 39 percent comes from state taxes, another 4 percent from the national government and only 57 percent from local sources. The major aim of state participation is, of course, to equalize educational opportunities by supplementing inadequate local means. However, the state appropriations are also widely used to encourage consolidation, for example, by paying a large share of the costs of bus transportation essential to the enlargement of the pupil-service area. As has been true of the national grant-in-aid system, state grants have typically increased the regulatory and supervisory power of state departments of education. Typically, money is distributed to local districts on the basis of formulae established by law. These commonly take into account: (1) local ability to pay measured by the value of taxable property per pupil or per school unit; (2) the number of pupils in attendance or the number of teacher-pupil units; (3) the amount of tax actually levied. Compliance with certain minimal standards is usually required of units receiving state money. These may relate to number of days or hours of schooling, the qualification, pay, and tenure of teachers, the variety of the courses offered, and the characteristics of the physical plant. State subsidies are also used to stimulate the development of special services such as libraries, medical and dental services, vocational guidance or to finance school lunch programs, special services to handicapped children and building planning. *States' heavy fiscal commitments*

The chief battleground in the development of state educational policy is the legislature. Here the whole pattern of state aids has been hammered out in countless long and difficult sessions. Virtually the whole code of laws governing the provision of public education has, of course, been enacted and revised by the legislature. All local school units are, legally, creatures of the state and their organization, management, powers, and functions are spelled out in the state law in considerable detail. Underlying the state's school program is in every state a compulsory school attendance law requiring, typically, *The state legislature and education*

[1] For example, J. B. Conant, *The American High School Today* (New York, 1959). This booklet is the summary of the widely discussed report on the quality of American education made by the former President of Harvard University.

young people from age 6-16 to be in regular attendance at some school and authorizing employment for youths 14 or over only under carefully regulated conditions. The movement for consolidation, the elimination of the one-room school, the attack on the small high schools, the demand for better paid and more broadly trained teachers; these and many other struggles occur in the legislative halls of every state and at every session. Taxpayer groups, chambers of commerce, labor unions, and educational associations of every type may be found pressing their respective and differing views on state legislatures throughout the nation.

State edu-
cational
adminis-
tration

The administration of the state's growing educational commitments is entrusted everywhere to a department of education or instruction insulated in most cases from gubernatorial influence. In most states today and in nearly all of them a few decades ago the chief of this department (commissioner or superintendent) is or was elected by the voters for 2 or 4 years and in many cases on a nonpartisan ballot. In the past few years, however, a movement to replace popular election by selection by a state board of education has gained momentum and this is now the mode of selection in 24 states. All but a handful of states, now, associate a board of education with the chief educational officer. Typically these boards are appointed by the governor, although in some of the states the members are elected and in a few states are selected by the legislature.[2] The state board commonly has broad policy-making functions and, in some cases, authority to utter detailed rules and regulations governing various aspects of school administration. However selected, the chief educational officer presides over a department with professional and clerical assistants and through them administers school aids, inspects facilities and curricula to enforce state standards, certifies as teachers properly qualified persons, collects and correlates statistical material on expenditures, teachers, attendance, and in other ways discharges state responsibilities.

Vocational
education

The concentration of the early high schools on college preparatory courses not entirely suited to the 90 percent of the graduates who did not attend college, the demands for skilled workers caused by rapid technological advances, and the stimulus of national subsidy begun in 1917 combined to foster the development in every state of a more or less elaborate system of vocational education at the high school and post-high school level. In most states vocational programs and schools are managed at the local level through the regular school organization. At the state level, however, it is not uncommon to find vocational and adult education separately organized and financed. There may be, as in Wisconsin, a state board of vocational education with a subordinate director and staff administering state aids and exercising supervision or there may be separate bureaus or offices within the state department of education. Commonly there is a pattern of financing and a code of laws

[2] For a detailed presentation of the term and method of selection of chief state school officers and boards of education see Council of State Governments, *Book of the States, 1964-65* (Chicago, 1964), 336.

unique to the vocational system. Until quite recently, in fact, state supervision of vocational education was more detailed and more elaborate than that for the regular schools. The increase of college-going among young people and the demands of the business community for more highly trained people have combined to reduce the relative importance of vocational training for the young and many of these schools are now emphasizing adult and special training programs.

Virtually every state maintains a state library or libraries serving the *State* needs of lawyers, historians, legislators and citizens at the capital and in many *library* instances providing some state-wide library services. A growing number of *services* states—29 in 1963—now also provide financial aids to local public libraries. Usually these aids are based on population or area or both served by the library and involve some imposition of standards of library management. Congress, since 1956, has also been appropriating national grants to states for library services largely in the rural areas and this has stimulated greater state participation in the development of local library programs.

Every state now includes as part of its system of education one or more *State col-* institutions of higher learning supported in large measure by public funds. *leges and* Although there were a few public colleges and universities—mainly in the *universities* Midwest—established prior to 1862, the famous Land Grant College (Morrill) Act of that year marks the beginning of the era of rapid growth of public colleges. This famous law set aside public lands for each state, the proceeds from the sale of which were to be used to endow and maintain at least one college in each state for the purpose of providing instruction particularly in agriculture and mechanical arts. A few states (Massachusetts, New York, New Jersey, and Pennsylvania) arranged for existing private institutions to carry out this purpose of the law but all the rest established or assigned to existing public institutions the responsibilities indicated. Thus grew our great American land-grant or public universities. In the Midwest, Plains, Far-West, and South these are in most states the major institution of higher learning. State legislatures subsequently matched many times over the national grants and the state universities and colleges gradually expanded to their present importance. To these, most states subsequently added normal schools for teacher training and these then grew into teachers colleges and finally into general colleges with diverse curricula. In recent years, as the demand for college education has grown, locally sponsored junior or community colleges have been added to the school systems of several states. These, although locally managed, are, typically, heavily supported by state aids.

The famous GI Bill which sent veterans of World War II to college at *Rise of* government expense coupled with the rising demand for more and more tech- *college* nical and professional training have in the postwar era started a trend toward *enroll-* college-going of surprising dimensions. Whereas in 1920 perhaps one high *ments* school graduate in ten went on to college, today more than a third do so (5 out of 10 in California). This rise in the proportion of 18-year-olds seeking further education and the sharp upturn in the birth rate described above are flooding our colleges (public and private) and causing heavier and heavier demands upon state financial resources. Although originally it was hoped that the public institutions would be free to natives of the various states, the great pressure for adequate income has caused most states to impose higher and higher tuition charges on the public university student. The state schools have also, over the years, greatly expanded their research programs not only in the fields of agriculture and engineering but throughout the subject-matter disciplines. Led by Wisconsin, they have also undertaken wide programs of service to the citizens of the states bringing to farm, factory, union meeting hall, professional office, governmental headquarters, and private home the knowledge and technical competence developed on the various campuses. In this decade the national government has moved in with research contracts, fellowships, facilities grants and dormitory loans to augment greatly the aids long provided to the colleges. The national treasury has thus become a growing source of support for the public—and private—institutions of the land.

Government of public colleges
Public institutions of higher learning are almost universally governed by lay boards of trustees appointed by the governor, elected by the voters, or, in a few cases, selected by the legislature. Usually there is one board for each institution but a few states (Oklahoma, New York, New Mexico, and Oregon, for example) have placed all or most of the institutions under a single governing body. These boards select the president, deans, and other administrative officers and through them direct the institution. In many states, Michigan and Minnesota are good examples, the government of the state university is provided for in the constitution and the institution occupies a position of administrative and fiscal autonomy somewhat different from the typical state department.

PUBLIC HEALTH AND WELFARE

The attack on communicable disease
In the long struggle against contagion, plague, and infectious diseases, a struggle which has wiped out one after another of the death-dealing epidemics, the states and their local subdivisions have borne the major responsibilities. By the support of local hospitals, the administration of vaccination, the distribution of sera, the imposition of quarantine, the purification of water, the regulation of food handling, the administration of tests and check-ups and countless other procedures local officials have helped to eradicate the great scourges of the past. The states began to assume responsibilities for disease control in the last quarter of the nineteenth century. Massachusetts created the first state department of health in 1869 and within 50 years every state followed suit. State activities were early designed to supplement and strengthen the local programs by the distribution of aids, the imposition of standards, the stimulation of lagging areas, and by the financing of institutional care for certain illnesses, mainly tuberculosis. Although ceaseless vigilance and the

maintenance of support for preventive inoculations are still essential, the major battle against contagion has been largely won in the United States. To be sure, some of the germ-caused diseases continue to resist efforts to suppress them. Tuberculosis continues to require state and local diagnostic programs and the maintenance of sanatoria. The death toll, however, has been gradually falling and many states find their facilities only half used. Venereal diseases also present continuing problems. After a sharp decline from 1937-1953, the incidence is once again on the rise. Rheumatic fever continues to take its toll but a major effort has yet to be made to deal with this crippler. The major health problems of modern Americans, however, are of a far different sort. The chronic and degenerative diseases are the great killers and cripplers of the mid-twentieth century.

As was noted in discussing the national health programs, cancer and heart and circulatory disorders are the leading causes of death today and chronic disabilities such as arthritis, mental illness, cerebral palsy, epilepsy, and muscular dystrophy are the main incapacitators. None of these respond to the methods used to fight germs. State programs, thus far, are largely, educational and are designed to promote early diagnosis, better diet, and proper living habits. A few successes have been achieved, for example in the early detection of uterine cancer by the widespread administration of the Papanicolaou testing procedure. In general, however, major advances must await the discoveries by research scientists of causes and then perhaps of cures. Meanwhile, every state carries a heavy load of institutional care and relief grants for the poverty-stricken disabled. *The attack on degenerative diseases*

Of all the chronic cripplers none presents the states with more baffling and more expensive responsibilities than mental illness. Every state maintains one or more institutions for the custody and treatment of the mentally disturbed and in four states (New Jersey, Wisconsin, Iowa and Michigan) these are supplemented by county hospitals or asylums.[3] On the average, more than 500,000 patients occupy these facilities at an annual cost of nearly $1 billion. For decades the major concern of the states was to protect and preserve family and community welfare by the removal and incarceration of those who were dangerous or unmanageable. The story of the long struggle to free these hopeless sufferers from chains, strait jackets, rocking chairs, and cells, not to say the occasional brutality of their keepers has been well told.[4] Staggering problems remain however. Despite the widespread provision for voluntary admission and the growing emphasis on prompt diagnosis and intensive treatment, far too many people come to the state hospitals only in advanced stages of mental breakdown when rehabilitation has become nearly hopeless. Every effort at accelerated and intensive treatment has been embarrassed by the very *Mental illness*

[3] Wisconsin is unique in this respect in that more mentally ill are cared for in the county institutions than in the state institutions.

[4] See, for example, A. Deutsch, *The Mentally Ill in America* (New York, 1949), and *The Shame of the States* (New York, 1948).

short supply of qualified psychiatrists and by the inability or unwillingness of the states to offer sufficiently attractive financial rewards. A growing number of senile persons (accompanying the lengthening life span of our people) for whose illness there is little hope, is filling the beds of the state institutions. Enormous obstacles remain to recruiting and maintaining an adequate staff of nurses and attendants. There is still much to be learned about the types, causes, and pathologies of mental diseases. The modern state efforts, therefore, are directed to: (1) formation of community clinics and local hospital programs aimed at early diagnosis and prompt treatment; (2) encouragement of specialized facilities for the senile, the emotionally disturbed child, the violent, and other categories; (3) development of more widespread public understanding of the nature and symptoms of mental breakdown; and (4) in collaboration with the national government, stimulation of research. Of course, many states have a long way to go to bring their institutions up to the level of those in the more progressive states.

Mental deficiency

The institutional care offered by the states also includes facilities for those who are born hopelessly, and, in the state of present knowledge, incurably defective. About 126 thousand mentally retarded children are born every year. Modern practice is to encourage the early and lifelong institutionalization of those who are hopelessly defective rather than to leave them amidst family and community. The result of this and of the higher birth rate has been to throw an increasing load on the already hard-pressed facilities in most states. Also, the effectiveness of the antibiotics in curing germ diseases has kept these unfortunates alive longer. Most state institutions for the mentally defective or retarded provide training in simple laboring skills for those able to profit by it and are likely thus to release some into gainful employment.

The care of the aged

The rapid rise in the number of persons over 65 in our society [5] has had far-reaching implications. Not the least of these is the increasing numbers of persons suffering from the degenerative ills of age and for whom public assistance or old-age insurance payments are scarcely adequate to pay for protracted medical care. In most states, old-age assistance payments have continued to rise to help cover these costs and Congress has had to increase sharply the medical benefit payments under the old-age and survivors insurance programs. Many states also are introducing licensing, regulation, and inspection for the growing number of private nursing homes catering to these aging citizens. Colorado is experimenting in state-provided homes for the aged. Connecticut, New Jersey, New York, Massachusetts, and Minnesota are encouraging local construction of low-rent housing projects designed particularly for the aged. A White House Conference on Aging held in 1961 sponsored by Congress encouraged the states to reconsider their programs to give priority to constructing special geriatric institutions, to encourage more community housing projects, to seek wider employment opportunities, to

[5] In 1900, there were 3 million persons in America over 65; in 1960 there were 16 million and it is expected that in 1970 there will be 20 million.

improve home-nursing services and, in other ways, to bring the best knowledge and experience to the aid of those in the sunset of life.

The health department through which most of these programs are carried on is, in most states, headed by a director or health officer appointed by the governor. Usually a lay board of health is associated with the director for policy-making and in a dozen states this board appoints the health officer. In most states, these departments are woefully understaffed due, in part, to the acute shortage of qualified doctors, nurses, and technicians available for public employment. It is not uncommon for states to separate the administration of institutions, such as those for the mentally ill, from the educational and regulatory health functions and to provide a separate agency, board, or department for institutional management. Typically, state health programs are largely achieved through local health offices and departments, especially in the cities, and the state staff provides technical aid and assistance. In addition to the more costly programs already described, state health services commonly include: (1) collection, analysis, and publication of vital statistics; (2) regulation and testing of public and private water supplies and administration of controls over pollution and sewage disposal; (3) inspection of food handling and food processing; (4) development and promulgation of regulations aimed at improving industrial hygiene and at alleviating disability arising from poisonous, noxious, or disease-causing industrial processes; (5) promoting better maternal and infant hygiene; (6) administration of national and state grants for hospital construction; (7) provision of laboratory diagnostic services to physicians and hospitals not serviced by local facilities; and (8) in a few states, development of controls over air pollution. *Health administration*

Although illness or disability may be a big factor in producing poverty, improvements in the nation's health have not eliminated, as yet at least, the need for elaborate programs for the care of the needy. We have noted that beginning in 1935 the national government has played a major role in financing public assistance and that state responsibility has thus been greatly diminished from the days of the poorhouse and the soup kitchen. Nevertheless the principal burden of administration and a substantial part of the financing still falls upon the states and their local units. In general the determination of who is to receive aid and, within broad limits, the amount of aid each is to receive is determined by local welfare agencies through professionally trained social workers. The state welfare departments keep the books, prescribe standards, coordinate local efforts, and assist local units that cannot carry their part of the financing. Everywhere, under the present national-state-local arrangements, the states and the local units are jointly or separately wholly responsible for the relief of all those who cannot qualify for categorical assistance or whose payments under the national programs are inadequate to the exigencies of their situations. This "general relief" responsibility embraced in 1964, more than 350,000 persons. *Public assistance*

Despite the heavy emphasis in modern public assistance on cash grants *"Indoor relief"* to individuals, there remains a large residue of "indoor" or institutional care provided, mainly by counties, to the unfortunate. County poorhouses, homes for the aged, and hospitals for the infirm continue to serve those who are unable to look after themselves in the community. Many states, in fact, are encouraging by aids or grants the expansion of county or city institutional facilities especially for the aged who require nursing care.

The care of offenders

It is not uncommon for states to include among the responsibilities of departments of public welfare, the incarceration and rehabilitation of offenders against the criminal laws of society. Some states, of course, organize this function separately in a department of correction. Modern penology is based on the idea that criminals are largely so because they are sick or poor or underprivileged and that correctional programs should place greater stress on treatment, education, and rehabilitation than upon discipline and isolation. For this reason many of the procedures and policies suited to care of the mentally ill, relief of the poverty-stricken, and education of the neglected are, with appropriate modifications, the basis of correctional programs and are administered by agencies with these other responsibilities.

Developing role of the state

The role of the state in correctional administration has been a slowly developing one. Counties and cities had in the beginning the major responsibility for keeping in their jails or lockups those convicted of criminal offenses. Early in the nineteenth century, movements for prison reform swept through much of Europe, the British Isles, and the United States. The reformers demanded, among other things, that hardened or habitual offenders and those convicted of grave offenses be removed from local facilities where, mixed with those awaiting trial, witnesses, and minor offenders of all ages, they tended to spread their malevolent influence and to require costly security measures not suited or needed by the other occupants. States began to build penitentiaries where those guilty of felonies—as distinguished from misdemeanors—would be guarded and cared for at state expense. Later as studies revealed the desirability of further classification of offenders, states built and operated separate institutions for female offenders, for juveniles, and for those not really requiring maximum security incarceration. By the end of the century most of the states operated several correctional institutions. In many cases each was directed by a warden and a separate board of trustees.

State programs in this century

In this century, dissatisfaction with the results of penitentiary administration continued arising from: (1) high rates of recidivism; (2) high costs of construction and management of maximum security programs; (3) continued high incidence of crime; and (4) the belief that in some way as yet scarcely tried, a large number of criminals could be made socially useful citizens. Further classification of offenders was proposed and the supervision of a large portion of the prison population in medium and minimum security camps, farms, and training schools was widely adopted. Parole was introduced as a method for supervising the return of the offender to society, cushioning the shock of freedom, and restoring to useful labor those who should no longer be locked up. Under the same kind of extramural supervision by welfare agents, systems of probation were developed for those who might be harmed rather than helped by incarceration, provided, of course, the dangers to society from their freedom were minimal. Within the institutions greater and greater stress has been placed on vocational training, regular education for those who had not received much schooling on the outside, and physical and psychological therapy based on prompt and extensive physical and mental examinations. Working more and more with the courts, state correctional agents have sought more flexible sentencing—relating the sentence to the needs of the criminal rather than to the nature of the crime—more supervision before and after and even in lieu of incarceration.

No one is yet entirely satisfied with results. The states vary widely in the degree to which they have accepted and put into practice the theories of modern penologists. Although most of the newer programs such as probation and parole are considerably cheaper per offender than immuration in a maximum security penitentiary, the penitentiaries are still used and appropriations for correctional programs are everywhere rising. There are still not enough specialized minimum security installations in most states according to the experts and the case loads of parole and probation agents are usually excessive. Juvenile and sex offenders continue to present troubling problems. Putting prisoners at useful labor, especially, manufacturing, has everywhere attracted the opposition of organized labor. Few states are able or willing to afford the kind of medical and psychiatric attention for prisoners that some experts demand. The century-long debate over the value of capital punishment continues almost unabated especially in the 37 states that have not abolished it. In 1964, there were more than 194,000 prisoners in state institutions.

HIGHWAY CONSTRUCTION AND MAINTENANCE

Every state must, of course, provide itself with public buildings, a capitol, a state office building, university and other educational structures, hospitals, asylums. Most have built airports; a few have constructed harbor works (as at San Francisco, New Orleans, and Mobile); and New York State built, owned, and operated the Erie Canal. Dams and reservoirs have been constructed for flood control; and parks and forest preserves have been laid out and provided with suitable buildings and other facilities. By all odds the most important public works with which any state has to do, however, are highways. These are increasingly the life blood of the state economy, bringing food and fibers from farm to market and supporting village industry and merchandising everywhere. There is no more persistent drive for larger and larger state expenditures in any field of state service than that for wider, thicker, smoother highways.

The record of highway construction, financing, and administration in this country is a story of progressive shifting of activities from smaller areas

States as builders

Highways become a state concern

to larger ones, until finally the states came to occupy a predominant role. Originally, roads were built and repaired wholly by towns, townships, villages, and cities. With the advent of the automobile and the resultant demand for paved roads linking up various mercantile and manufacturing centers, the county became involved. Finally, in the early nineties, Massachusetts and New Jersey led the way to substantial management by the state. Legislatures began giving financial aid to local highway authorities to be expended under state supervision and with the advice and assistance of state officials. Then they started taking over main roads, often to the great advantage of counties financially unable to provide the thoroughfares everywhere demanded by the modern motorist. With the advent of national subsidy in 1916, state authority was increased and systems of state trunk highways were established linked up by national influence into a system of interregional roads for the whole nation. Typically, however, no unit ever completely abandoned its interest in or control over some portion of the highways. Today we find township roads administered, frequently with state aid, by townships, village and city streets maintained by those units, county trunks, and state highways.

The highway situation today   County and township roads still comprise some 75 percent (2.3 million miles) of the country's total highway mileage. The city motorist usually tries to avoid them, because only about two-thirds of this mileage has hard surfacing and most of this is gravel or crushed stone. Altogether they carry less than 15 percent of the nation's total traffic. As farm-to-market roads and as feeders to the state system, they, however, are indispensable. Farm-to-market roads are controlled in some states mainly by towns or townships, in others by counties; while roads of a little more importance, often described as "secondary" and linking up county seats and other such centers, usually are chiefly county-controlled. Heavily traveled main thoroughfares are everywhere parts of the state system and in many states most of the feeder roads are also. Thus: (1) Four states—Delaware, Virginia, West Virginia, and North Carolina—have centralized the management and financing of *all* roads in the state government; (2) four New England states divide responsibility for farm-to-market and secondary roads between the state and the towns; (3) 27 states divide it between the state and the counties; and (4) the remaining states apportion it three ways: among state, counties, and towns or townships. In all cases in which local units function, funds come in considerable measure as aids from the state treasury. "Primary" roads, comprising the *state* system, constitute only a quarter of total mileage (600 thousand miles), but link up the principal cities, usually are well paved, and carry 85 percent of the traffic. All primary and some secondary roads are heavily subsidized by the national government and are built and maintained in close cooperation with the supervising Public Roads Administration in the Department of Commerce at Washington. Particularly significant is a trunk-line network of some 40,000 miles constituting a National Interstate Highway System planned during World War II and postwar years by state highway departments and the Public Roads

Administration, and linking up 42 of the 50 state capitals and indeed all but a few of the country's cities of over 50,000 population. On this system more than 70 percent of the current aids paid to states is being spent.

All states administer their highway programs through either a separate highway department or a highway division of a public works department, usually the former (by national requirement they must have one or the other if they are to qualify for grants-in-aid). In more than one-third of the number, the department head is a full-time, salaried highway commissioner or a director of highways; in the remainder, a part-time highway commission of from three to seven members, functions through a director. They are commonly appointed by the governor, although in some instances they are elected. In counties, highway functions sometimes are kept immediately in the hands of the county board or one of its committees but often are entrusted to an appointive or elective highway commissioner or supervisor. In New York, New Jersey, and Pennsylvania, and in 22 other states one or more state roads have been placed in the charge of a turnpike or toll-road authority. The toll-road authority has been a popular device for constructing very expensive, multilaned, grade-separated, limited-access superhighways for through traffic and levying a special charge on that traffic for these unusual facilities. In this way, the state highway income is reserved for providing less adequate but more widely distributed highway service to the state motorists. The standards of construction on the new national interstate system are so closely parallel to those of the toll roads that it is doubtful if new roads in any numbers will hereafter be built by this procedure.

Administrative arrangements

If the simple and rather straightforward description of state highway developments set forth in the previous paragraphs suggests that all is going smoothly in highway matters, such is far from the case. We now have almost 86 million motor vehicles registered in the United States traveling more than 800 million miles per year. In addition to the increasing rate of obsolescence of our highways which the rapid growth of vehicular traffic and the vastly increased driving speeds have brought about, there are 40,000 persons killed annually in auto accidents and perhaps 1,500,000 seriously injured. By 1955, in fact the number of persons killed on our highways in this century surpassed the numbers killed in all of the wars thus far fought by our soldiers. This terrible and continuing toll of life and limb has meant increased costs of insurance and increased costs of safety enforcement programs. A growing portion of our uniformed police forces, state, county, and municipal is assigned to regulating traffic and is not available for protection of persons and property against criminals. Then too there is the question of who should pay for the highways and streets and the relative contribution of each: the abutting property owner, the municipal resident, the passenger car operator, the trucker, the farmer, the merchant. In general, the abutting property owner in municipalities pays on the front-foot basis for original paving and for curbs and gutters. The property-tax payer pays for much of the cost of maintenance and reconstruction of most city streets, and some town roads. The state and national treasuries pay from gas tax or other taxes on autos or drivers for through streets connecting state trunks, state and many county trunks. Many experts feel that the trucking industry pays less than its share of the cost of the highways since trucks cause much serious maintenance and reconstruction costs. Urban residents feel that they get too small a share of highway user taxes in view of the fact that such a large part of the vehicular mileage is on city streets. The farmers feel that urban interests are the major beneficiaries of the state and national road systems. The railroad owners and workers, of course, argue that the highway program is subsidizing their demise. Finally, there are the troublesome questions of highway planning: which roads should be surfaced and when; what kinds of surfacing should be used; what controls should be exercised over the development of signs, taverns, and other commercial enterprises along the roads; what course should main highways follow —through towns or around them?

PROMOTION AND REGULATION OF PRIMARY ECONOMIC INTERESTS

1. BUSINESS

Basis of state control

By virtue of its police power, a state is entitled to regulate all business activities within its borders except those instituted by the national government or those involving transactions in or those affecting foreign or interstate commerce. A good while ago, the courts developed a category of businesses, including public utilities, banks, and insurance companies, regarded as of particular concern to the public, and hence specially "affected with a public interest." These have been held to require more intensive regulation than business in general.[6] Few forms of business, however, are not now of concern to the public in one way or another. While the public-interest concept has by no means been discarded, the present tendency is to look upon all businesses as subject to whatever regulation may be required for protecting public health, safety, morals, and welfare—so long as there is no deprivation of life, liberty, or property without due process of law, or denial of equal protection of the laws.

Corporations: 1. Status

Many people engage in business (usually on a modest scale) requiring no government authorization. Most medium-sized and larger businesses, however, are carried on by partnerships or corporations fully subject to state control. The formation and dissolution of partnerships and the rights and liabilities of partners are amply covered by state law. A corporation cannot operate, or even exist, without a charter issued by a government. Certain

---

[6] This doctrine, clearly enunciated in Munn v. Illinois, 94 U. S. 113, 126 (1877), is fully treated in F. P. Hall, *The Concept of a Business Affected with a Public Interest* (Bloomington, Ind., 1940).

corporations, for example, national banks, are chartered under Congressional authority but the overwhelming majority of business corporations are chartered by the states. Originally, corporations were chartered individually by special legislative act. From this, however, arose so much favoritism and corruption that even before the Civil War most states substituted a general corporation statute under which any responsible group of persons desiring to incorporate may do so by meeting prescribed conditions and applying to the proper administrative authority, usually the secretary of state. Today nearly all state constitutions either forbid incorporation by special act or severely restrict it. A corporation chartered in one state may do business in other states, but only as a "foreign corporation" subject not only to the same regulations as "home" corporations, but also to any special requirements that may be imposed upon it or its class.

With charters easy to obtain and operation under them commonly advantageous, the corporate method of doing business has become general. The most comprehensive regulation of the business community as a whole arises in most states, thus, in connection with the initial granting of corporate charters. Certain types of business operations, however, have been selected for special attention by state legislatures. Among these are financial institutions (banks, savings and loan companies, small-loan companies, insurance companies), utilities, stock brokers, milk distributors, and manufacturers. Certain practices of the business community have also been subjected to regulation, for example, monopolistic price fixing. *2. Regulation*

Early in the history of corporate enterprise, concern was stirred by the rise of business combinations prone to squeeze or drive out competitors, control prices, and indulge in other monopolistic practices. Much legislation aimed at curbing "trusts" was enacted. With business, however, taking on an increasingly interstate aspect, the problem outgrew the capacities of the states; and in 1890 the Sherman Antitrust Act started a long and even yet by no means wholly effective program of national action. Virtually all the states, however, still have copious antitrust laws (applicable, of course, only to strictly intrastate situations and actions) and codes of fair business practices similar, within their spheres, to the national laws enforced by the Federal Trade Commission. As on the national level, enforcement is, typically, left to the attorney general who has neither the means nor time to do much. A few states have launched successful suits against undertaking combines, gasoline dealers, milk distributors and other local enterprises. On the whole, the state record in this field is, if anything, less successful than that of the national government. Furthermore, in recent years several states have partially reversed the traditional concepts of competitive enterprise and have authorized price-fixing agreements of certain types between manufacturers and dealers. These acts have been underwritten by a national law of 1937 (amended in 1952) authorizing such price agreements wherever state laws support them. All but a handful of states have enacted these Fair Trade Acts, but the highest state *Antimonopoly regulations* courts in 21 states have declared all or part of such laws unconstitutional. The fair trade program is, therefore, in decline.

Two commercial banking systems exist side by side in the United States —national and state. National banks, of course, are chartered and regulated by the national government, but state banks by the several states. State control, within its field, extends to bank organization and management, capital stock, liabilities of stockholders and directors, assets and investments, loans, reserves, other forms of protection for depositors and customers, and arrangements for periodic inspections of records and accounts by representatives of the state banking department or other designated agency. Trust companies, building and loan associations, and similar financial institutions are regulated in the same general manner. Any bank or other such concern becoming insolvent or otherwise embarrassed may be taken over by state authorities and operated until it can either be put on its feet or liquidated. Most state banks are, however, members of the Federal Reserve System and this brings them under the scrutiny of the Federal Reserve Board and all savings institutions are members of and inspected by the Federal Deposit Insurance Corporation. A large amount of needless duplication of examining of banks and savings institutions is avoided in many states only by administrative arrangements among the national and state examiners. Small-loan companies and pawnbrokers continue to be regulated, more or less effectively, by the states alone.

Every state also regulates all forms of insurance, with a view to protecting the public against exorbitant rates, requiring companies to honor valid claims for insured losses, and, in the case of life insurance, maintaining the security of invested savings. General laws prescribe the conditions which a corporation must meet in order to engage in insurance business in the state. Usually each company and all of its agents must be licensed by an insurance department or other authority; detailed regulations cover forms of policies, reasonableness of rates, types of securities in which funds may be invested, and volume of reserves that must be held for covering policies as they become payable; and full provision always is made for periodic reports and for official inspections as in the case of banks. As pointed out earlier, the Supreme Court, in 1944, reversed an earlier ruling by holding that insurance is interstate commerce. While this opened a way for national regulation under the commerce clause, Congress has thus far been content to leave the matter to the states. Many states in late years have been strengthening their regulatory statutes in the hope of staving off such intervention.[7] A few states, such as Wisconsin, have actually entered the business of providing some types of insurance in competition with private companies. In recent years also a few states, led by New York, have expanded the scope of their state insurance agencies to embrace inspection of labor-union welfare and pension funds.

[7] See E. W. Sawyer, *Insurance as Interstate Commerce* (New York, 1945); Council of State Governments, *Revision of State Systems for Insurance Regulation* (Chicago, 1946); L. B. Orfield, "Improving State Regulation of Insurance," *Minn. Law Rev.,* XXXII, 219-261 (Feb., 1948).

The most stringent, steady, and effective state regulation is reserved for *Regulation* public utilities—businesses which although as a rule owned and operated by *of public* private persons and concerns, are preeminently "affected with a public inter- *utilities* est," enjoy special privileges (such as the use of streets and highways and the right of eminent domain), and either are or tend to become "natural monop- olies." Included are all public transportation facilities such as railroads, street railways, air transport, bus and cab lines, and all enterprises providing electric light and power, water, gas, and telephone and telegraph services. All of these are subject to state (and in varying degrees also local) control, except that the interstate aspects fall within the jurisdiction of the Interstate Commerce Commission, the Federal Communications Commission, and the Federal Power Commission. State regulation, under a multitude of laws, and in every state except Delaware through a public utilities commission (or its equiva- lent), touches such matters as permits and franchises, financial structures, securities issues, accounting and reporting, quality of services, rates, and gen- eral safety and convenience for the public. Since 1900, too, the basis of action has largely shifted from municipal franchise regulation under the contract power to direct state regulation under the police power.

All of the states' interests in the business community are not repressive *Promotion* and regulatory. Many states spend generously to promote industrial develop- *of business* ment within their boundaries. Departments of Commerce, Bureaus of Indus- trial Development, Planning and Development Commissions have been spring- ing up all over the nation in the past two decades and each of them is dedicated to attracting more industry and to facilitating expansion of the industry already established. One business, apart from those identified with agriculture, has been selected for special support through state advertising in many states, that is the resort business.

2. LABOR

For many years regulatory legislation to protect factory workers from the abuses of industrialization was left almost entirely to the states. But as the national economy continued expanding, with more and more employment connected in some way with interstate and foreign commerce, inadequacies of state control stimulated national activity. As shown in an earlier chapter, labor legislation and the enforcement of labor regulations have developed, especially since 1933, into one of the principal functional sectors of our national govern- ment. Even yet, nevertheless, millions of workers labor only in intrastate activities, and accordingly, as workers, are subject only, or at least primarily, to state authority. Half a dozen ways in which states meet their obligations may be mentioned.

Springing in part from pressures exerted by organized labor, in part from *1. Health* voluntary legislative recognition of the obligation to promote general well- *and safety* being, laws protecting health and safety of workers—in some instances dating back 60 or 70 years—have multiplied on state statute books. Aimed especially at health are, for example, laws restricting the hours of continuous work for women in industries, stores, and hotels, forbidding employment of women in mines, regulating the labor of children not covered by the national Fair Labor Standards Act, requiring proper heating, lighting, and ventilation and the removal of dust and noxious fumes in factories, and fixing standards of sanitation. Directed at safety are measures designed to avert or mitigate the effects of industrial accidents and diseases by requiring safeguards for dangerous machinery, exits, fire escapes, equipment of street cars and local trains with safety appliances, and by providing for the safety of laborers on buildings, bridges, and other public works, together with periodic inspection of factories, workshops, and mines. Laws in this comprehensive category often are necessarily rather broad and general, with appropriate administrative authorities, usually commissioners, left to prescribe more detailed rules and regulations. Undoubtedly the frequency and severity of industrial accidents have been reduced by these state efforts.

2. Workmen's compensation

Closely related to safety and health regulations are the elaborate systems of workmen's compensation insurance established by the states. Occupational accidents are, by these programs now treated as a proper charge upon industry. Some of the systems are compulsory and some optional; some apply to all accidents of the kind and others only to those in the more hazardous occupations. Most grant compensation for some or all occupational diseases. Employers in every state are required to procure insurance either from the state or from private firms providing coverage for their employees in case of on-the-job accidents. State agencies of various types closely supervise the program to assure prompt and adequate recompense to the injured worker. Coverage, however, is almost everywhere confined to manufacturing. Construction, transportation and agricultural workers are not protected. Benefit schedules also have hardly kept pace with postwar inflation. With the related problem of sickness among wage-earners, little has been done, although New York has pioneered in the development of a state program of insurance for nonoccupational illness. Since Congress passed the Vocational Rehabilitation Act of 1920, state and national governments have cooperated in restoring to self-supporting capacity persons who have been disabled in industry, or in any legitimate occupation, or by disease; and thousands have been refitted to earn a livelihood.

3. Labor standards and relations

Much of the early effort of several progressive states in establishing by law standards of employment, including maximum hours, minimum wages, and special protection and prohibitions for working women and children, has now been overshadowed by the national effort in these fields. The national laws, however, still leave a numerous working population over whom the states may and do claim jurisdiction. Most states, therefore, have some kind of regulating agency in these fields. The touchy and controversial field of labor-management relations is also characterized by state activity. Most of the states which have enacted labor relations laws have done so in the past

20 years and most of their laws follow rather closely the National Labor Management (Taft-Hartley) Act of 1947 rather than the earlier act of 1935. They impose restrictions on unions as well as on employers. A growing stream of state legislation in the past decade has been directed against the practices of labor unions and their leaders. Much of it is aimed at the "closed" or "union" shops, boycotting, jurisdictional disputes, and work stoppages in public utilities. So-called "right to work" laws aimed at outlawing the closed or union shop have been passed by 20 states in recent years. The jurisdiction of state labor-management agencies is not yet completely settled but on any definition of national power, some workers and employers are under control of the state. The Eisenhower administration attempted with some success to narrow the national activities in the field and to allow state agencies to operate in borderline cases.

Little more need to be added ot the earlier discussion of the elaborate state programs of public employment service and unemployment compensation which have been established under national supervision since 1935. *4. Unemployment compensation*

Presidential efforts to secure a national fair-employment-practices law were successfully resisted by Southern and other elements in the Congress until 1964. A number of state legislatures, meanwhile, declared discrimination against Negroes and other minority groups in matters of employment to be contrary to public policy. A few states also provided educational agencies and conciliatory procedures to achieve this policy, for example, Colorado, Indiana, Kansas, and Wisconsin. Since World War II four (those of New York and New Jersey in 1945, Massachusetts in 1946, and Connecticut in 1947) have gone even farther by enacting penal statutes forbidding any employer of more than six persons (five in Connecticut) to refuse to hire any applicant, or to discharge or discriminate against any employee, because of race, creed, color, or national origin, and also forbidding labor unions to exclude, expel, or discriminate against any person for such reasons. New Mexico, Oregon, Rhode Island, and Washington more recently have enacted compulsory laws of this type. There were in 1964, twenty-six states with mandatory antidiscrimination laws. In the first two and one-half years of New York's experience, the fair-employment-practices commission set up for purposes of enforcement was able to dispose of over 1000 complaints received without resorting in a single instance ot criminal proceedings, or even to formal hearings. *5. Fair employment practices*

3. AGRICULTURE AND CONSERVATION

Agriculture and natural resources arc important in thc economy of every state and, in most instances, basic. Furthermore, the rural members have dominated a large number of state legislatures. Every state, therefore, has an active and well-supported program of benevolent aid to farmers and farming. Ample constitutional authority is supplied both by the police power and by the power to levy taxes and spend money for general-welfare purposes.

1.
Research and education

Every state maintains at least one agricultural college and in connection therewith an agricultural experiment station and an agricultural extension service. In these institutions scientific studies are carried on relating to soils and fertilizers, land use, the breeding and care of plants and live stock, agricultural marketing, and indeed every resource, operation, and activity of concern to the farmer. Bracketed with research also is education in the form not only of agricultural training at the college level in classrooms and laboratories, but wide circulation of bulletins and reports, extension courses bringing new ideas to people on the farm, and counseling and demonstration work carried on by county agricultural agents and (for the benefit of the farmer's wife) home demonstration agents as well. All of this, as we have observed, is supported in part by national subsidy.

2.
Suppression of diseases and pests

Aside from bad weather and adverse marketing conditions, the principal agricultural hazard is a legion of plant and animal diseases and pests—bollweevil, corn borer, Mexican fruit fly, Japanese beetle, and other insects in the case of plants; hoof-and-mouth disease, hog cholera, brucellosis, bovine tuberculosis, and the like, in animals. In every state, means of eradicating or curbing the ravages of these scourges are objects of study; and inspections, quarantines, and other controls are provided both through legislation and by administrative action. Weed-eradication receives attention also; and in sparsely-settled western areas, protection of flocks and herds against predatory animals.

3.
Marketing

Because so largely interstate, agriculture marketing falls mainly within national jurisdiction. Room remains, however, for state (1) regulation of the grading, packaging, and labeling of products, (2) control of marketing through commission merchants, (3) encouragement of farm cooperatives (for buying as well as selling and shipping), (4) assistance to state and local agricultural fairs, and (5) country-wide advertising of the state's products—the citrus fruits of Florida, the dairy products of Wisconsin, the wines of California, Washington apples, and Idaho potatoes.

4.
Conservation

Closely related to promotion of agriculture is the mapping, development, and conservation of natural resources. On the legal theory that wildlife is owned by the state and held in trust for the people, virtually every state licenses and otherwise controls hunting and fishing, and also carries on propagation activities at game farms and fish hatcheries. Forest lands are protected against fire; private owners are encouraged and aided in forest development, in some states by "forest crop laws" deferring taxation of growing timber; three-fourths of the states maintain state forests; and others (notably Wisconsin) develop and protect county or other local forests for both conservational and recreational purposes. For 60 years, states having important oil and gas resources have combatted waste, first with regulations designed to prevent unchecked flow and to control the spacing of wells. More recently also, and chiefly, in the case of oil, with production quotas fixed and enforced by some administrative agency and operated in a large group of states in accordance with a significant interstate compact on the subject. Of particularly wide concern, too, is soil conservation, carried on in conjunction with the national government in soil conservation districts, established in the several states under supervision in each case of a state soil conservation committee and operated by district boards of supervisors or directors in part locally chosen.

References

1. GENERAL

L. W. Lancaster, *Government in Rural America* (New York, 1937), Chaps.VII-XIV.

K. H. Porter, *State Administration* (New York, 1938).

G. A. Graham and H. Reining, Jr. (eds.), *Regulatory Administration* (New York, 1943).

C. H. Chatters, *An Inventory of Governmental Activities in the United States* (Chicago, 1947).

N.Y. State Department of Commerce, *A Guide to State Services* (Albany, N.Y., 1946).

H. Jacob, K. Vines (eds.), *Politics in the American States: A Comparative Analysis* (Boston, 1965), Chaps. 9-11.

Council of State Governments, *State-Local Relations* (Chicago, 1946).

———, *The Book of the States, 1964-65* (Chicago, 1964), 323-575.

———, *State Government* (Chicago). Published quarterly since 1958 and abounding in articles on topics dealt with in the foregoing chapter.

———, *State Government News* (Chicago). Published monthly since 1959.

2. EDUCATION

C. A. DeYoung, *Introduction to American Public Education* (New York, 1942).

D. K. Freudenthal, *State Aid to Local School Systems* (Berkeley, Calif., 1949).

R. L. Moran, *Intergovernmental Relations in Education* (Minneapolis, 1950).

Council of State Governments, *The Forty-eight State School Systems* (Chicago, 1949).

———, *Higher Education in the Forty-eight States* (Chicago, 1952).

P. Smith, *et al., Education in the Forty-eight States* (Washington, 1939).

P. R. Mort and W. C. Reusser, *Public School Finance,* 3rd ed. (New York, 1960).

F. F. Beach and A. H. Gibbs, *The Structure of State Departments of Education* (Washington, 1949).

———, *Functions of State Departments of Education* (Washington, 1950).

L. M. Thurston and W. H. Roe, *State School Administration* (New York, 1957).

F. F. Beach and R. F. Will, *The State and Education: The Structure and Control of Public Education at the State Level* (Washington, 1958).

C. D. Hutchins and L. C. During, *Financing Public School Facilities* (Washington, 1958).

S. Bailey, R. T. Frost, P. E. Marsh, and R. C. Wood, *Schoolmen and Politics: A Study of State Aid to Education in the Northeast* (Syracuse, N.Y., 1962).

N. A. Masters, R. H. Salisbury and T. H. Eliot, *State Politics and the Public Schools* (New York, 1964).

3. PUBLIC HEALTH AND WELFARE

H. S. Mustard, *An Introduction to Public Health* (2nd ed., New York, 1944).

———, *Government in Public Health* (New York, 1945).

B. J. Stern, *Medical Services by Government: Local, State, and Federal* (New York, 1946).

J. W. Mountain and E. Flook, *Guide to Health Organization in the United States* (Washington, 1947).

W. G. Smillie, *Public Health Administration in the United States* (3rd ed., New York, 1947).

Council of State Governments, *The Mental Health Programs of the Forty-eight States* (Chicago, 1950).

A. Deutsch, *The Shame of the States* (New York, 1949).

A. P. Miles, *An Introduction to Public Welfare* (Boston, 1949).

A. W. James, *The State Becomes a Social Worker; An Administrative Interpretation* (Richmond, Va., 1942).

G. Abbott, *From Relief to Social Security* (Chicago, 1941).

A. C. Millspaugh, *Public Welfare Organization* (Washington, 1935).

R. C. White, *Administration of Public Welfare* (Cincinnati, 1940).

M. Stevenson and A. McDonald, *State and Local Public Welfare Agencies* (Chicago, 1939).

B. Y. Landis, *Rural Welfare Services* (New York, 1949).

C. R. White, *Administration of Public Welfare* (2nd ed., New York, 1950).

D. Schaffter, *State Housing Agencies* (New York, 1942).

L. A. Fietz, *The Role of the States in Recreation* (Berkeley, Calif., 1947).

Russell Sage Foundation, *Social Work Year Book* (New York). Published biennially.

W. Vasey, *Government and Social Welfare: Roles of Federal, State, and Local Governments in Administering Welfare Services* (New York, 1958).

4. PUBLIC HIGHWAYS

R. A. Gomez, *Intergovernmental Relations in Highways* (Minneapolis, 1950).

C. L. Dearing, *American Highway Policy* (Washington, 1942).

W. Owen, *Automotive Transportation* (Washington, 1949).

Public Roads Administration, *Highway Practice in the United States of America* (Washington, 1949).

J. Labatut and W. J. Lane (eds.), *Highways* (Princeton, N.J., 1950).

L. I. Hewes, *American Highway Practice* (New York, 1942).

Committee for Economic Development, *Modernizing the Nation's Highways* (New York, 1956).

P. H. Burch, *Highway Revenue and Expenditure Policy in the United States* (New Brunswick, N.J., 1962).

5. BUSINESS

J. M. Edelman, *Securities Regulation in the 48 States* (Chicago, 1942).

H. H. Trachsel, *Public Utility Regulation* (Chicago, 1947).

L. B. Orfield, "Improving State Regulation of Insurance," *Minn. Law Rev.*, XXXII, 219-261 (Feb., 1948).

Council of State Governments, *Occupational Licensing Legislation in the States* (Chicago, 1952).

6. LABOR

C. C. Killingsworth, *State Labor Relations Acts* (Chicago, 1948).

E. F. Staniford, *Recent State Labor Legislation* (Berkeley, Calif., 1949).

W. F. Dodd, *Administration of Workmen's Compensation Laws* (New York, 1937).

F. Lang, *Workmen's Compensation Insurance* (Chicago, 1947).

L. Manning and N. Diamond, *State Child Labor Standards* (Washington, 1949).

H. M. and A. R. Somers, *Workmen's Compensation: Prevention, Insurance, and Rehabilitation of Occupational Disability* (New York, 1954).

7. AGRICULTURE AND CONSERVATION

S. Chase, *Rich Land, Poor Land* (New York, 1936).

H. H. Bennett, *Soil Conservation* (New York, 1939).

C. J. Hynning, *State Conservation of Resources* (Washington, 1939).

L. M. Fanning (ed.), *Our Oil Resources* (New York, 1945).

I. N. Gabrielson, *Wildlife Conservation* (New York, 1941).

L. L. Durisch and H. L. Macon, *Upon Its Own Resources; Conservation and State Administration* (University, Ala., 1951).

★ 30 ★

Financing State Government

ALL OF THE SERVICES, regulatory programs, and administrative organizations described in the last chapter cost money. Each passing year, in fact, they seem to cost more than they did the year before. Rare indeed is the state legislature which is not bedeviled every session by financial problems of the most difficult kind. With the public demanding more and more services, the growing resistance to tax increases, the heavy exactions of the national government on the one hand and the urgent pleas for aid from the local governments on the other, to maintain the solvency of state government requires the highest caliber of statesmanship. Given these exigencies of modern life, the miracle is that many states are as well off as they are. It is not at all surprising that some are in desperate straits.

Limitations on state independence The states are not in as strong a position to cope with this situation as might be imagined. Constitutionally, it is true, the federal system permits them a great deal of leeway. Under their reserved powers, they can tax almost anything except national property and income from national securities, spend at least as freely as the national government, and borrow at will. Practically, however, there are limitations. From considerations of prudence, most states have tied their own hands with constitutional provisions severely restricting state borrowing, or even in some instances forbidding it altogether. Nearly everything of importance, except general property, which states undertake to tax—incomes, inheritances, gifts, motor fuel, liquor, tobacco, and what not—is already taxed heavily by the national government. At best the states can merely share in the overall proceeds. Urgently needing more tax revenue, all have watched the national government steadily moving in on them with tax programs and rates siphoning off most of what the people believe they can afford to pay for government's support. In the foreseeable future no more favorable situation can be envisaged. The two great areas of pressure for state spending—education and welfare—reflect the high birth rate, the increase in longevity, and the increased demand for more and more education already alluded to at several places in earlier chapters. National activities and commitments are not likely to diminish; national pressures for tax money will hardly abate. In terms of expendable funds, the balance may be, and to considerable extent already is, redressed by multiplied and augmented national subsidies. But grants-in-aid are supported by tax money which the states otherwise might raise for themselves; they certainly do not contribute to state and local financial independence. More than one leading student of intergovernmental relations is urging that current trends be reversed by giving state and local governments exclusive access to more tax sources, for example, motor fuels, and in this way discouraging the habit of depending on the national treasury. The table indicates better than words what is happening to the costs of state government in this century. To be sure, post-World War II inflation caused a sharp upturn in expenditures without proportionate increases in the services rendered. It should be observed also that grants from the national Treasury make up an increasing part of the income supporting the outlays listed. Many of the payments to local units, for example, are simply passed through the state treasuries on their way from Washington to city hall and county courthouse.

GROWTH OF STATE EXPENDITURES
Selected Years, 1902-1964

Function	TOTAL EXPENDITURE (IN MILLIONS)					
	1902	1932	1942	1952	1960*	1964*
Payment to local governments	$ 52	$ 801	$1,780	$ 5,044	$7,521	$11,620
Education	17	272	391	1,494	3,557	5,711
Highways	4	843	790	2,556	6,070	7,850
Welfare	10	74	523	1,410	3,704	2,796
Health and Hospitals	32	215	299	1,132	2,072	2,464
Police	—	15	40	106	251	315
Natural Resources	9	119	159	539	862	1,185
General Government	23	114	164	361	663	871
Interest on Debt	10	114	122	144	536	765
Veteran's services	—	—	1	142	112	—**
Employment security	—	—	59	177	313	426
Correction	14	87	80	223	433	586
Other	15	106	181	369	1,133	1,790
Liquor stores	2	—	288	723	907	1,117
Insurance trust (retirement and unemployment compensation)	—	63	505	1,413	3,461	5,094
	$188	$2,829	$5,342	$15,833	$31,595	$42,600

SOURCE: Bureau of the Census, *Historical Statistics on State and Local Government Finances*, 1902-1953 (Washington, D.C., 1955); and Bureau of the Census, *Governmental Finances in 1963-64* (Washington, 1965).
  * Includes Hawaii and Alaska
 ** Included in *Other*

METHODS OF APPROPRIATION—BUDGET SYSTEMS

*Earlier
appro-
priation
methods*

One factor that has added immeasurably to the burden of state legislatures in dealing with their fiscal problems has been the pitiful inadequacies of state budget and appropriation methods. Prior to about 1913, it was impossible in virtually every state either to make comprehensive plans for the distribution of public revenues among the state's direct activities and state-aided local enterprises or to control, in any strict and effective way, the use of state money or property. With demands often pouring in from 100 or more state agencies and institutions, and with no method of balancing claims upon the treasury against one another, and of distributing appropriations on the basis of a full consideration of the state's requirements, unseemly scrambles for funds invariably took place whenever the legislature came into session. The departmental and institutional estimates were either merely "compiled" by some officer, such as the treasurer or auditor, and transmitted by him to the legislature, or presented directly and independently to the appropriations committees by heads of departments and institutions themselves. No administrative officer acquainted with the entire business of the state reviewed such estimates, compared them, cut them down to actual necessities, measured them against estimated revenues, and laid before the legislature a carefully prepared financial program. Furthermore, every member of the legislature was at liberty to introduce as many bills as he chose carrying charges upon the treasury. When the legislature adjourned, no one pretended to know, even approximately, how much money had been appropriated.

Meanwhile, without any knowledge of what the total of authorized expenditures for the next fiscal period would be when the governor had finished vetoing bills and items, the legislature would pass revenue bills prepared by separate committees with little or no relation to the work of the committees in charge of appropriations. Neither the governor nor the legislature could be held to a proper degree of accountability by the citizens of the state who had to foot the bills.

*Adoption
of budget
systems*

Relief from these conditions became imperative as the cost of government mounted. It has been found, in greater or lesser degree, in plans of budgetary procedure introduced by statute, or in a few instances by constitutional amendment, in all of the states after Wisconsin and California set the example in 1911—ten years before a budget system was adopted for the national government.

The states have adopted a wide variety of budget systems differing in detail and in fundamentals. Most important among points of variation is the budget-making agency—in other words, the location of responsibility for formulating the budget or program of expenditures in relation to anticipated revenues. On this basis, the systems fall into three fairly distinct classes. (1) In one state, Arkansas, the budget is "legislative," prepared and submitted to the legislature by the Legislative Council. In recent years, however, the council has been assisted by a budget division in a recently created Department of Finance and Administration. California and Texas have established legislative budget agencies in recent years which serve the legislature only. Formally, however, the budget in both states is prepared by the governor. (2) Six states [1] have budgetary boards or commissions, consisting usually of the governor and one or two other executive officers and a few members of the legislature, or made up solely of the principal executive officers. (3) The remaining states have what is called the executive type of budget.[2] In some of these, the governor is made directly responsible for formulating the program of state expenditures; in the others, budget-making is in the hands of a comptroller, a budget director, a budget bureau, or some other official or agency whose work is performed, at least nominally, under the governor's supervision. Concentrating responsibility in the executive officer best situated to be informed on the financial needs of all branches of the state government, the executive type is generally regarded as best.[3]

Various state budget systems

Some states have budget systems which concentrate power in the executive to a greater degree even than that of the national government. In New York, Maryland, West Virginia, and Nevada, for example, the legislature may reduce or strike out any item in the budget, but may not (with slight exceptions) increase any amounts requested or insert new items.[4] Elsewhere, however, amounts may be increased and new items inserted.

Still room for improvement

Some of the requisites of a sound budget system for a state—many of them still lacking in too many states are: (1) Each department, office, or institution should be required to submit to a central budget-making agency, two or three months before the legislature meets, an estimate of its financial needs for the ensuing fiscal period, upon uniform sheets having items arranged in accordance with some uniform system of classification; (2) the central budget-making agency under the supervision of the governor should then make a careful review, revision, and compilation of the estimates submitted; and to aid in this work, it should be given a staff to conduct investigations and make reports; (3) at some time within the first few days of the legislative session, this budget-making agency should submit a complete budget, that is, a comprehensive program of recommended expenditures and estimated revenues, and accompanied by a balance sheet, a debt statement, and a statement

Essentials of a sound budget system

---

[1] Florida, Indiana, Mississippi, North Dakota, South Carolina, and West Virginia.

[2] New Hampshire and Rhode Island are included in this third group, although their budgetary systems show important variations from the true executive type budget.

[3] A tabulation of state budgetary provisions is presented in Council of State Governments, *The Book of the States, 1964-65* (Chicago, 1964), 159-163.

[4] In New York, the legislature may not increase items already in the budget, but may add items separate and distinct from the original ones, each such addition being for a single specified object or purpose.

of the financial condition of the state for each year covered by the budget; (4) all appropriations should be consolidated in a single appropriation bill; [5] (5) as far as possible the budget should state the services or programs to be financed by the proposed expenditures; (6) the legislative committees should forthwith proceed to a consideration of the budget proposals, and should report their appropriation bills in ample time to allow full debate, criticism, and amendment, so that the bills may be passed well before the close of the session; (7) no supplementary or special appropriation measures should be enacted until after the final passage of the budget bills. Even if made effective on all of these lines, a state budget system would not serve all of its purposes unless accompanied by such ancillary reforms as (1) concentration of the handling of all appropriation measures in a joint committee of the two houses; and (2) a grant to the governor (where he does not already have it) of the power to veto items.

SOURCES OF STATE REVENUE

Over the years there has been a decided change in the tax and revenue program of the states. We have already noted how national grants-in-aid have multiplied in the twentieth century to the point where state expenditure programs are heavily dependent upon the national treasury. These subsidies today constitute the largest single source of state income. This fact alone is a compelling cause of the continuance of the grant-in-aid program at a high level. A second striking change in the state revenue picture has been the gradual abandonment by the states of the property tax as a source of income. As recently as 1902 the general property tax produced more than half of the tax revenues of the states and throughout most of the nineteenth century it was almost the sole revenue source. Virtually all of the states have, however, in this century relinquished this revenue source to their local units. It now yields less than 10 percent of the states' total income. There has been an increase in this century also in the receipts from state-operated enterprises, the most important of these being: (1) the liquor stores operated by several states after repeal of the prohibition amendment; (2) the turnpike and tollroad authorities; and (3) the sale of power in a few states. New Hampshire in 1963 inaugurated a new source of state income which may start a new trend in state finances: it established a state-operated sweepstakes lottery with chances sold through state liquor stores and at the two state-regulated racing tracks. The automobile and the elaborate highway programs accompanying its introduction have also drastically altered state tax practice. Since 1920, the gasoline tax and motor license fees have become one of the largest sources cf state receipts.

[5] Constitutional obstacles to this exist in many states where segregated funds are required or officers' salaries must be separately appropriated.

THE GENERAL PROPERTY TAX

Although the property tax is no longer an important source of state income, nevertheless many states continue to concern themselves in its administration and to seek methods of overcoming its limitations. It remains, furthermore, the very heart of local government financing. Looking at the tax program of the United States as a whole it is one of the two or three most important supports of our governmental system.

In its broadest meaning, the general property tax is a tax on the estimated *Nature* exchange value of property, levied at a common rate for all property in the *and basis* same taxing area. It is thus universal and uniform; it is imposed on the property where it is located; and it is paid by the owner. Taking, of course, a multitude of forms, property nevertheless falls broadly into two categories:

COMPOSITE PATTERN OF STATE INCOME—1964
All States

Source	Amount in Millions of dollars
TAXES	
General Sales	$ 6,084
Motor fuels	4,059
Liquor and beer	864
Tobacco	1,196
Other sales and gross receipts	1,754
Motor vehicle licenses	1,783
Liquor	125
Corporation—miscellaneous licenses	1,155
Individual income	5,415
Corporate income	1,695
Property	722
Death and gift	658
Severance	489
Miscellaneous taxes	244
PAYMENTS FROM OTHER GOVERNMENTS	
National	9,046
Local	417
RECEIPTS FROM STATE SERVICES AND ENTERPRISES	3,942
PAYMENTS FOR INSURANCE AND TRUST FUNDS	
Employee retirement	2,369
Unemployment Insurance	3,250
Workman's Compensation	706
BORROWING	2,793
	$46,765

SOURCE: Bureau of the Census, *Government Finances in 1963-64* (Washington, 1965).

(1) real estate, consisting of land, buildings, and permanent fixtures, and (2) personal property—the one immovable, the other movable. Personal property, in turn, may be either tangible, for example, livestock, grain, merchandise, household furniture, machinery, and automobiles, or intangible, as stocks, bonds, promissory notes, mortgages, and bank deposits. Where the general property tax is really general, these distinctions are, at least in theory, of no great significance; all property of equal value is supposed to pay the same tax regardless of classification. In the majority of states, however, some categories of property are set apart for special (usually lower) rates of taxation, or indeed are exempted altogether; so that the term *general property tax* must often be taken in an approximate rather than a strictly literal sense.

The "tax calendar"   Although numerous, complicated, and varying somewhat from state to state, the stages or steps involved in administering the property tax—the "tax calendar" of which the experts speak—may be summarized as follows. (1) First comes the tax levy, the competent authority (usually the legislative body) of each unit of government, including the state itself where sharing in the proceeds, determines the amount of revenue that must be raised from this source and then imposes it as the year's tax burden, so to speak, on the property concerned. (2) The property is valued by local (county, township, or city) assessors in order to determine the valuation on which the owners' tax obligations shall be computed. Personal property is assessed annually, real estate also annually in about half of the states, but in other states at longer intervals ranging from two to four years; and all assessments are supposed to indicate value on a certain day. (3) Valuations determined by local assessors are far from uniform, and property-owners often raise objections. Hence a third step involves inspection of the assessments, with adjustment of inequalities and injustices, by a county, city, or township board of review.

Equalization   (4) A fourth step is "central assessment or equalization." Along with the locality, the county, and in many instances the state, makes a property-tax levy. Each taxing jurisdiction might, of course, set up its own separate assessment machinery. But this would involve expensive duplication, and what happens is that each takes the locally-made assessments as a starting point and on the basis of them makes such equalizations and other adjustments as boards of equalization employed for the purpose may decide upon. Sometimes the work is performed on the state level by a board of equalization consisting of certain elective state officers serving ex officiis, but often it is in the hands of a specially appointed body known as the tax commission. This commission is likely to have the important functions of (*a*) issuing instructions to assessors and other tax officials regarding the proper performance of their duties, including methods of procedure, accounting, and recording, and (*b*) making the original assessments of certain kinds of property which are difficult to assess locally, especially railroads, telegraph and telephone systems, express and sleeping-car services, and other public utilities. Incidentally, it would, of course, be possible to let the state do *all* of the assessing; and this would make for considerably greater uniformity than even assiduous equalization authorities can hope to achieve. Local assessors, however, are supposed to have the advantage of familiarity with local property; and, although yielding grudgingly on many other forms of centralization, local jealousy of state authority has been at this point difficult to break down. (5) Once the results of assessment and equalization, the state over, are known, taxes can be apportioned and rates determined. In the city, township, or other local assessment district, the clerk or other proper official has only to figure out how many cents on the dollar, or dollars on the hundred, will be necessary to produce the revenue required locally. From the county will come similar information for purposes of county revenue, and finally also from the state for its purposes, except, of course, where the state no longer shares in the proceeds of the tax. Adding to the local rate the rates certified to him by the overlying units, the local official arrives at the total tax rate; and tax bills are made out and sent to property-owners accordingly.

Completing the tax calendar are three further stages which for present purposes require only to be mentioned: (6) collection of the taxes as levied, commonly by a local collector or treasurer, who forwards the county and state shares to the proper officials; (7) efforts to collect taxes that become delinquent; and (8) appeals from dissatisfied taxpayers or tax districts, first to the state tax commission, and afterwards, if desired, to the courts.

Advantages of the tax

For 150 years, the general property tax has been a cardinal feature of the American fiscal system. Notwithstanding its many and serious faults, there are many points in its favor. Property receives protection from government, and may logically be asked to contribute to government's support. Lending itself particularly well to local use, the tax is in keeping with the persisting spirit of home rule. Its easy elasticity—the facility with which its yield can be moved up or down by simple manipulation of the tax rate—fits it to meet varying needs after other sources of income have been exhausted.

Disadvantages:

1. Concealment of personal property

Nevertheless, the tax has some serious defects. First may be mentioned the unfairness arising from frequent concealment of intangible personal property, resulting in complete escape from taxation. In early times, nearly all property was in the form of real estate or of tangibles such as livestock, furniture, merchandise, farm implements, and grain. Nearly everything could be located and its value determined by the tax assessor, and little, if any, taxable property failed to pay its just share. From this relatively simple situation, we have moved to one in which the value of stocks, bonds, mortgages, bank deposits, and other intangibles often exceeds that of real estate and tangibles. Furthermore, it has become virtually impossible for tax assessors actually to see and appraise all tangible personal property, to say nothing of intangibles. The common practice is to require taxpayers themselves to make out sworn statements of their personal property and simply hand them to the assessors —a method which amounts to self-assessment. Still further, while real estate and personal tangibles are usually immune from national taxation, intangibles (or at all events the income derived from them) are taxed so heavily from Washington that when national taxes and state taxes are added together, they amount to onerous exactions, at least in the eyes of many who pay them. Under these circumstances, vast amounts of property which the tax assessor has no chance to see are never reported to him—the portion actually reported depending almost entirely upon the personal honesty of the taxpayer in the given case. Responding to these and other difficulties, legislatures have exempted many kinds of personalty from taxation. In general, the effort to tax intangible personal property is everywhere being abandoned. Tangible personalty, however, forms such a considerable portion of the tax base (15 to 20 percent) that eliminating it presents serious difficulties. Most states are struggling along with it but it is under heavy attack everywhere.

2. Defective assessments

A second main defect of the general property tax arises from faulty assessment of property actually reached. The reasons for such deficiency are numerous, but doubtless the chief one is that a substantial proportion of the thousands of assessors functioning particularly in the rural areas and small towns throughout the country are part-time elective officials, with little training qualifying them to weigh the many factors entering into the determination of property values; "much of what they do is mere guesswork." There are architects' tables, land-value maps, and other equipment which would be of assistance; but only rarely are they used. Directions from the state tax commission and readjustments made by equalization boards help considerably, but not enough to assure satisfactory results. In the outcome, what purports to be a uniform general property tax is in many states neither uniform nor general, and of course not equitable. Real property usually bears more than its fair share; and often there is glaring inequality in the valuations placed upon real estate located in different parts of the same state, and even within the same county. Personal property, on the one hand, either is shockingly undervalued or, because of being easily concealed, escapes taxation altogether.

Modes of improvement:

1. Classification for tax purposes

Problems connected with these and other defects of the property tax have received much study, and in a good many states improvements, although certainly not full solutions, have resulted. Most important among changes undertaken has been the abandonment of constitutional or other requirements of uniformity, in order that property may be thrown into different classes for taxation at different rates. Approximately two-thirds of the states, in fact, have adopted classification at least in principle, and in half or more some classification has been carried out. Here and there, as in Minnesota, classification has been sufficiently extensive to admit of quite a number of rate levels. In most instances, however, it has not gone beyond differentiating intangibles from tangibles, on the theory that lower rates on the former will lessen the incentive for concealing them and draw them out of hiding. Gains undoubtedly have been realized; although concealment of intangibles is still common and yields sometimes have actually been smaller than before classification was undertaken. Because of the inequities referred to, several states are moving toward the abolition of personal property taxes.

Two or three other approaches to improvement have commanded attention. One relates to the quality of assessments. The need is to get away from untrained, part-time, popularly elected local assessors, and substitute a plan under which assessors would become state or local civil servants, appointed on a merit basis by the tax commission or other central authority.[6] A second improvement well might have to do with county and other boards of review or equalization, now composed commonly of members serving ex officiis and, for obvious reasons, hardly better equipped than the assessors themselves. If there is virtue in having assessors appointed by the state tax commission, the same arrangement well might be applied to members of equalization boards. Any plan tending to obviate the tug-of-war between members representing rural and urban taxing districts would be a clear gain. *2. Appointive assessors and reviewers*

Still another step in advance would be to place on the tax rolls a great deal of real estate now exempted—nearly one-sixth throughout the country as a whole. Real estate used for religious, educational, and philanthropic purposes long has been immune, on the ground that the institutions owning it are run, not for profit, but for performing essential community services. Presumably this is justifiable. But some states go farther—for example by partly or entirely exempting property of veterans, manufacturing plants, farm implements, growing crops, and (in more than a dozen instances) homesteads, that is, urban or rural dwellings occupied by the owner, with the sites on which they stand. All such exemptions narrow the tax base and increase the tax rates on remaining taxable property. With heavy pressure for augmented public revenues promising to continue through the years, we are likely to see determined efforts to bring on the tax rolls much property now exempted, even though perhaps at reduced rates or valuations. *3. Reduced exemptions*

PRINCIPAL STATE TAXES TODAY

The general property tax has been crowded out of the state tax picture—and even on the local level is of diminished importance—partly as a result of distress of property-owners during the depression of the thirties, partly through taxpayer efforts to curb mounting public expenditures by influencing legislators and constitution-makers to surround property taxation with new restraints, but in large measure also because of the discovery of newer tax sources having the merits of liberal yield and easier and surer collection. If, for

[6] Short of this, a great many states are doing remarkably well in improving assessments by: (1) developing training courses and manuals for assessors; (2) completely reassessing local units by state experts on request of the local unit; (3) penalizing jurisdictions whose assessments deviate by more than some stipulated percentage from the state norm as in Arkansas; (4) consolidating local assessment at the county level as in Minnesota although on a voluntary basis.

example, intangibles cannot be reached for taxation directly, they still may be made to contribute their share by taxing income derived from them, and also the transmission of them by inheritance. For local purposes, the general property tax still is indispensable; for state purposes, however, it no longer appears necessary. Several forms of taxation have, in most states, largely or wholly superseded it for state purposes. Each of six such taxes have of late yielded the states more revenue than the property tax: (1) general sales, gross receipts, and use taxes, (2) motor fuel taxes, (3) income taxes, (4) motor vehicle license taxes, (5) liquor taxes, and (6) tobacco taxes.[7]

1. General sales and use taxes

State as well as national taxes on sales of particular commodities, for example, liquor, tobacco, and motor fuel, long have been familiar. Desperate fiscal needs during the depression of the thirties led one state after another, however, to carry the principle farther by instituting *general* sales taxes. In terms of yield such taxes (along with related gross receipts and use taxes) have now taken top place in the overall state tax picture. Beginning with West Virginia in 1921—somewhat before the depression indeed—a total of 37 states introduced the general sales tax in one form or another, most of them between 1933 and 1936 and several more in the 1950's. In some instances, the step was inspired, at least partly, by fear of inability, in the lack of such a tax, to meet the obligations imposed by the new social security system at a time when state revenues were sagging. In most cases, indeed, the tax was adopted as a supposedly temporary or emergency measure. The early unpopularity of the general sales tax because of its "regressive" character, bearing with greatest proportional weight upon consumers least able to pay, has largely given way before the compelling needs of the states for large and stable sources of income. Thirty-six states, located in all sections of the country, now rely heavily on this tax. Typically, the tax is imposed on retail sales only, but in some instances on sales by manufacturers and wholesalers as well. In most of the sales-tax states a compensating "use" tax is laid on the use, storage, or consumption of commodities that would have been subject to the sales tax if bought in the state instead of brought in from outside.[8]

Yield

Wherever tried, the sales tax has been highly productive, and it is difficult to see how some states could have avoided bankruptcy without it. The rate of the tax is now, typically, 3 percent and the yield exceeds $6.0 billion to the states that levy it. This is more than from *any* other source except grants-in-aid.[9] Whether, as a matter of social policy, it is justifiable to deflect tax

---

[7] Payroll taxes for support of the unemployment compensation program are not included, because, while yielding heavily, and indeed rating second only to the sales group, their proceeds are not available for general state purposes.

[8] The object of the use tax is, of course, to help eliminate tax evasion arising from crossing a state line to buy in a "taxless" state. As a rule, no attempt is made to apply the tax to purchases in petty amounts.

[9] Local sales taxes, also, are found in 17 states and are used in New York City, New Orleans, and no fewer than 120 other cities, mostly in California and Illinois. Gross receipts taxes are used by more than 200 cities including Philadelphia.

burdens in such degree from property and incomes to the mass of the people as consumers may be, and is, warmly debated. In some states the impact is alleviated by exempting food and other necessities; and in any event urgency for revenues seems likely to continue to overbear all scruples on the point in many states.

The first significant chapter in the history of income taxation in this country was written on the national level (starting in 1861), and culminated in the Sixteenth Amendment and the income tax law of 1913. In the states, there were a few earlier unsatisfactory experiments, but the first permanent and effective law was passed in Wisconsin in 1911. Two years later, Massachusetts, Delaware, Missouri, and Mississippi enacted similar legislation; in 1915, New York and North Dakota joined the growing list. Thereafter the movement spread until at present (1965), 39 states have income taxes applicable to either individuals or corporations, and usually to both. In aggregate yield the income is the fourth most important source of state tax income. But in a few states, notably New York, Oregon, and Wisconsin, it is the main support of the state government. Though differing in details from state to state, the principal features of the tax are: (1) taxation of net income only; (2) exemption of specified amounts (usually from $500 to $1000) for single persons and of larger amounts (commonly $2000 or $2500) for a married couple, with allowances ranging from $200 to $400 for dependents; (3) a scale of rates rising from commonly 1 percent on the first $1000 of taxable personal income to usually 5, 6, or 7—but in a few instances as high as 10 percent in the highest bracket; (4) a "normal" rate sometimes supplemented by surtaxes (general or for specific purposes such as education) after a certain point is reached; (5) usually a flat, but sometimes a progressive, rate on incomes of corporations; and frequently (6) review and collection, not by local officials, but—as started in Wisconsin in 1911—through the state tax commission and a force of civil service employees. In the state as in the national field, the graduated, or progressive, income tax is widely regarded as the most equitable tax form. However, the possibility of realizing more from it is sharply restricted by the extremely heavy (and increasing) taxation of both personal and corporate incomes by the national government.[10]

2. Income taxes

Until comparatively recent times, highways and streets were financed almost entirely from the general property tax. The advent of the motor vehicle to almost universal use led, however, to demand for more and better roads, and prompted the idea that the highways, rural and urban, used by the insatiable motorist should be paid for and kept up by him. The result has been the development of the country's present remarkable network of hard-surfaced thoroughfares and the rise to great prominence of a newer group of tax levies,

3. Motor fuel and vehicle taxes

[10] The income-tax field has also been entered by municipalities. Cities like Philadelphia are imposing a tax as a flat percent of wages and are applying it to wages earned in the city by nonresidents.

essentially in the nature of privilege or service charges, and often referred to as the "motor vehicle tax family." Chief among the members of this family are: (1) the motor vehicle license, which in essence is an annual charge for the privilege of operating a motor vehicle on the highways, and whose yield exceeds the yield of state income taxes paid by either individuals or corporations; and (2) the motor fuel tax, starting as simply a gasoline tax in Oregon in 1919,[11] and now employed in every state. Currently the rates range from five to eight cents a gallon and the average is about seven cents. Over the protest of rural and road-building interests, not to mention automobile associations, varying portions of motor vehicle and motor fuel proceeds were, in depression years of financial stress, diverted, in two-thirds of the states, to education, welfare, and other state purposes. Efforts to halt such diversions have been successful in a large number of states. At the same time, even with no such diversion, proceeds throughout the country as a whole have never sufficed (except during wartime suspension of construction) to meet the full outlay on roads and streets. The property tax still supplies a good share of the costs of local streets. Both motor vehicle and motor fuel taxes have the great merits of being highly productive and easy to administer.

4. Liquor and tobacco taxes

Prior to the prohibition era, the states, while making license charges in connection with the liquor traffic, left excise taxation of liquor to the national government. Subsequently, however, they, too, entered the excise field. Combined with license fees on dealers when there is no state monopoly and on bars and taverns almost everywhere, the taxes on liquor yield about half as much as do state income taxes. In the more than a dozen states where the traffic is a state monopoly, income from licenses is replaced by profits from the operation of dispensaries. Like excises on liquor, taxes on tobacco and tobacco products represent a more recently developed source of state revenue; as in the case of liquor, also, dealers usually are licensed and the commodity itself taxed. Nearly all states tax cigarettes (most commonly at about six cents a package), and several tax tobacco also in other forms. Like liquor, tobacco is subject also to heavy national taxation. Few taxes are as popular as those on liquor and tobacco for by them the state can encourage virtuous living and raise revenue at the same time. The only limits to these taxes would appear to be those fixed by rising enforcement costs.[12]

---

[11] In most states, the tax is now more than a gasoline tax because of applying, in addition, to diesel fuel, liquefied gases, and other such fuels.

[12] Other state taxes of varying importance, but necessarily passed here with bare mention, include—in addition to the payroll taxes referred to above—(1) a wide variety of often rather complicated business taxes (including gross receipts taxes), (2) estate and inheritance taxes (together known as death taxes), (3) gift taxes, (4) severance taxes on the extraction of natural resources, and (5) poll taxes, authorized (for either state or local purposes) in about three-fourths of the states, but employed on the state level in only a few states, mainly in the South.

TAX ADMINISTRATION:
THE COLLECTION AND CUSTODY OF FUNDS

In times when nearly all state revenue was derived from the general *Tax*
property tax, the state financial authorities had little to do except receive the *collection*
money passed along after being locally collected. Nowadays, the situation is
different, because the taxes on which the state depends have become highly
diversified, and many are collected by officers or other representatives of the
state itself. The general property tax is still gathered by local collectors or
treasurers, county or city, with the proceeds apportioned among the various
taxing units (including the state where it shares) according to the different
rates that have been imposed. A difficulty often presented is that of tax
delinquency, which became serious indeed during the depression of three
decades ago, with often as high as 30, 40, or even 50 to 60, percent of the
amounts due in individual taxing districts going unpaid. With considerable
uniformity, the states provide for (1) a regular payment period (on the basis
of payment either at a single time or, in about half of the states, in instalments), and (2) an additional period during which, if payment is not made,
accrued interest must be included, with often the amount of the tax somewhat
increased also by way of further penalty. Procedures in cases of persistent
delinquency vary, but in most states there are "tax sales" enabling the taxing
authorities to get their money, and giving private purchasers ownership of,
or at least an interest in, the properties involved.

Local collection of virtually all other forms of state revenue is not eco- *Local vs.*
nomical, the expense entailed often consuming a large share of the sums *central*
gathered. Centralized collection has therefore grown in favor, especially in *collection*
connection with income, estate, inheritance, motor vehicle, and business taxes.
In Wisconsin, the founder of the modern income tax, taxes on incomes are
collected by income-tax assessors, selected according to merit principles and
each functioning in one of four districts, where their duties are performed
under direction of the state tax commissioner. This is an exact reversal of
procedure in the case of the property tax, in that most of the proceeds of the
income tax in that state, is turned over to counties and other local areas.
All other states employing income taxes have substantially similar arrangements, at least for collection and several (12) of them also share the proceeds
with local governments. Revenues gathered by state agencies and retained for
the state do not always, however, go into the state general fund. Fees collected
by the secretary of state or the insurance commissioner, for example, frequently are used to pay the expenses of the office collecting them, only the
surplus, if any, being turned for general state use. Much of the money paid
directly into the treasury is earmarked for particular purposes, for example,
education, highways, and conservation, making it necessary for the fiscal
officers to maintain an accounting system permitting of separate accounts for

various funds. Among experienced persons, sentiment is growing in favor of concentrating all state tax administration in the state tax commission or some other single department and all state revenues in a single, general, all-purpose fund.[13]

The care
of funds

In some states, all state funds are kept in the state's vaults, with no interest received. Elsewhere the practice is to deposit such money in banks located in different parts of the state and designated as depositories. Of course the latter plan opens a way for favoritism and collusion in selecting the banks, and for losses arising from bank failures. After unhappy experiences at these points, most states, however, have protected themselves, at least against loss, by requiring depository banks to furnish adequate guarantees of security; and some profit to the state usually accrues from interest at a modest rate on deposits made.

STATE CONTROL OVER LOCAL FINANCES

It must be apparent at this point that the finances of a state and of its political subdivisions are so intermingled that neither can be understood in isolation from the other. For the ordinary taxpayer, the finances of his local governments (there almost always are more than one) are, in fact, more important than those of his state. Such governments, in the aggregate, spend more than do the 50 state governments combined. These local governments, however, raise by no means all of this money by their own efforts; and this leads, first of all, to a word about the sources from which local revenues are derived.

Sources
of local
revenue:

1. Local
taxes

(1) First among these (mentioning only the most important) is locally imposed taxes, supplemented by many kinds of license and other fees. On this matter, little need be said. The one universally employed and chiefly important local tax is the general property tax already described. The great bulk of the proceeds of this tax (in many states all of them) goes for local needs; and it is difficult to see how the tax, with all its faults, could be replaced by any other. (2) Next may be mentioned the proceeds of "shared taxes." These are taxes (like several we have mentioned) which, although imposed, and usually collected, by the state, are by law so administered that some agreed proportion of the yield is automatically turned over to counties and other local units. Technically, the general property tax is not such a tax, because although the taxpayer gets a single tax bill, he is really paying, by a single transaction, two or more property taxes—county, city, state—included in one bill for purposes of convenience. A taxing unit on any taxing level can

2. Shared
taxes

[13] Every state except Florida now has a tax commission or similar agency. About 20 states have a commission of from three to seven members (usually three), and some 13 others concentrate the functions in a single tax commissioner, sometimes with the assistance of a board of tax appeals. Under either plan, tax commissioners are commonly appointed by the governor, for terms most frequently of six years.

put into the composite bill whatever proportion it desires.[14] The truly "shared" tax is *one* tax, state levied, and with the locality having no part in it except to receive such percentage of the yield as has been allocated to it by law. Good examples in different states are motor vehicle license taxes, motor fuel taxes, and in varying numbers of states, income taxes, liquor taxes, and general sales taxes.

(3) Finally, there are grants-in-aid—extended almost as generously by state governments to localities as by the national government to the states. For the year 1964 the states extended $11.6 billion (including shared taxes) to their local subdivisions. However, a share of this originated in the national Treasury and the state acted only as intermediary in the transaction. Aids may be distinguished from shared taxes in that, whereas under the shared tax the state automatically hands over to the localities from year to year such proportion of the proceeds of a given tax as has been fixed by law, under the grant-in-aid system the state bestows on the localities such amounts, for such purposes, and on such conditions, as it may choose. In the one case, the amount distributed is dependent on the yield of a particular tax; and·usually the distribution is such as to return the money to the communities where it was collected. In the other case, a fixed amount for a given year, from general funds, is distributed by appropriation and commonly on some basis of demonstrated need. Funds received by localities from shared taxes may usually be expended for any purposes whatsoever, but those from grants-in-aid only for purposes expressly indicated in the grant. Both shared taxes and grants-in-aid have attained their present proportions fundamentally because of (a) the greatly superior taxing means and powers (as well as borrowing facilities) of the state governments as compared with local governments, and (b) the general trend in later times toward centralization, expressing itself in fiscal relationships as well as in other ways.

3. Grants-in-aid

Even in imposing their own taxes, local units are likely to be subject to constitutional or state statutory restrictions, for example, as to the maximum tax rate they may employ. In any case, local assessments are likely to come under the scrutiny of the state tax commission or other equalization agency, which may readjust them or even (usually on appeal from taxpayers) cause reassessments to be made. In spending their funds, too, local governments are under some state controls. (1) Grants-in-aid are received on condition that the services for which they are earmarked are kept on a satisfactory level of efficiency. The states have a good deal to do with establishing such levels and, through inspection and direction, seeing that they are maintained. (2) Local budgets often are subject to review by state authorities, who may protest items which they consider excessive or otherwise unjustified. Deficiency appropriations and transfers from one fund to another also may come under the critical eye of a state auditor, board of accounts, or other agency. (3) Local finance officers often are required to use uniform systems of records and accounting;

Forms of state control

[14] Except as restricted by general constitutional or statutory limitations.

and in any event, in nearly all states, representatives of a state finance officer or department pay annual (usually unannounced) visits to spending officers of local governments, look over their accounts, require carelessness to be corrected, and cause embezzlers to be brought to justice. (4) Debt limits commonly are imposed. While borrowing within these limits usually may proceed without intervention from the outside, a county board or city council proposing to issue bonds to build a highway, develop a park, or construct a court house or city hall may find a group of taxpayers arguing before a competent state authority that the outlay is unnecesary, extravagant, or ill-advised at the particular time, and may be obliged to convince state examiners that the proposal is sound, on penalty of seeing it vetoed at the state capital. In protest against all of these forms of state intervention, many people cry out that the sacred principle of home rule is being violated, and that the officials who impose and enforce the restraints are too far away to know the needs and conditions involved. In some states, however, large sums have been saved by protection given in these ways against the looseness and waste occasionally characterizing the local administration of affairs by inexperienced, careless, partisan, or even corrupt, public officials.[15]

STATE AND LOCAL DEBTS

State debt

A final phase of state and local finance requiring a word of comment is borrowing and indebtedness. Unlike the national government, which can borrow without restraint,[16] the governments of all but three states (New Hampshire, Vermont, and Connecticut) are restricted by constitutional provisions designed to prevent a recurrence of the reckless piling up of debts which marred the work of many state legislatures before the Civil War and during the Reconstruction period. Despite these limitations, state borrowing has increased many fold in this century. Today every state carries some debt, even though in some states the debt is not a charge on the general resources and in several others this debt is quite small. As of 1964, the total long-term debt of the 50 states was $24.4 billion. Some of this was covered by accumulated sinking funds.

Local debt

Debt burdens incurred by counties, cities, and other local units weighed heavily on taxpayers during the great depression, and in 1934 Congress came to the relief of embarrassed local governments by passing a Municipal Bankruptcy Act under which any of them unable to service their debts could voluntarily go into a bankruptcy court and get plans approved for readjusting

15 A thorough discussion of the fiscal relations of state and local governments will be found in Council of State Governments, *State-Local Relations* (Chicago, 1947), Pts. III-IV; and cf. L. L. Pelletier, *Financing Local Government* (Hallowell, Me., 1948).

16 Except of course, the statutory limit on the national debt which may be amended or repealed at any time by act of Congress.

their obligations.[17] After 1940, the wartime economic upsurge enabled local governments of all kinds to reduce indebtedness, but in the postwar years the trend has reversed and local debts are again increasing. The main pressure on local income nowadays is in the field of education. In order to house the flood tide of new children, school building is pushing on the debt limits of local units almost everywhere in the country. As of 1964 the outstanding debt of local governments in the United States exceeded $63 billion.

State and local governments borrow money ordinarily by issuing interest-bearing bonds running for periods of from 10 to perhaps 20 years, and taking the form of either sinking-fund issues or serial issues. Under the sinking-fund plan, all bonds of a given issue mature at one time, and a definite sum is set aside each year from current revenues to meet principal and interest in full when the date arrives. Serial bonds, on the other hand, mature in instalments or series, thus enabling a definite proportion of a given debt to be extinguished every year, or at other stated intervals, by payments from current revenues which, under the other system, would go into the sinking fund. Serial bond issues have grown rapidly in popular favor in the past three decades and are fast supplanting the earlier sinking-fund system.

Methods of borrowing

References

H. M. Groves, *Financing Government* (6th ed., New York, 1964).

H. L. Lutz, *Public Finance* (4th ed., New York, 1947).

W. J. Shultz and C. L. Harris, *American Public Finance* (New York, 1954).

W. Kilpatrick, *State Supervision of Local Budgeting* (New York, 1940).

———, *State Supervision of Local Finance* (Chicago, 1941).

———, "Neglected Aspects of Intergovernmental Fiscal Relations," *Amer. Polit. Sci. Rev.*, XLI, 452-462 (June, 1947).

A. H. Hansen and H. S. Perloff, *State and Local Finance in the National Economy* (New York, 1944).

M. Ermarth and G. H. Watson, *Recent Trends in State Revenue* (Chicago, 1943).

J. D. Silverherz, *The Assessment of Real Property in the United States* (Albany, N.Y., 1936). [New York] State Tax Commission, Special Report No. 10.

C. E. Rightor and I. A. Applebee, *Property Taxation: 1941*. Bureau of the Census, State and Local Government Special Study No. 22 (Washington, 1942).

[17] Declared unconstitutional by the Supreme Court in 1936, this measure was replaced by another in 1937 providing for somewhat different procedures and with the Court later fully approving. United States *v.* Bekins, 304 U. S. 27 (1938).

R. G. Blakey and V. Johnson, *State Income Taxes* (Chicago, 1942).

R. G. and G. C. Blakey, *Sales Taxes and Other Excises* (Chicago, 1945).

R. M. Haig and C. Shoup, *The Sales Tax in the American States* (New York, 1934).

N. H. Jacoby, *Retail Sales Taxation* (Chicago, 1938).

M. Criz, *The Use Tax; Its History, Administration, and Economic Effects* (Chicago, 1941).

J. F. Due, *Sales Taxation* (Urbana, Illinois, 1960).

F. G. Crawford, *The Gasoline Tax in the United States* (Syracuse, N.Y., 1939).

R. G. Hutchinson, *State-Administered Locally-Shared Taxes* (New York, 1931).

L. D. Woodworth, *Shared Taxes* (Chicago, 1944).

L. H. Kimmel, *Taxes and Economic Incentives* (Washington, 1950).

A. E. Buck, *The Budget in Governments Today* (New York, 1935).

M. L. Faust, *The Security of Public Deposits* (Chicago, 1936).

B. U. Ratchford, *American State Debts* (Durham, N.C., 1941).

C. H. Chatters and A. M. Hillhouse, *Local Government Debt Administration* (New York, 1939).

C. Penniman and W. Heller, *State Income Tax Administration* (Chicago, 1959).

C. Penniman, "The Politics of State Taxation," in H. Jacob and K. Vines, *Politics in the American States—A Comparative Analysis* (Boston, 1965).

J. F. Due, *State Sales Tax Administration* (Chicago, 1963).

U. S. Bureau of the Census, *Summary of State Government Finances* (Washington). Published annually.

————, *Historical Statistics on State and Local Government Finances, 1902-1953* (Washington, 1955).

Council of State Governments, *Grants-in-Aid and Other Federal Expenditures Within the States* (rev. ed., Chicago, 1947).

————, *Federal Grants-in-Aid* (Chicago, 1949).

————, *State-Local Relations* (Chicago, 1947).

————, *Postwar State Taxation and Finance* (Chicago, 1947).

————, *Sources of State Tax Revenue, 1940-49* (Chicago, 1960).

————, *The Book of the States, 1964-1965* (Chicago, 1964).

Federation of Tax Administrators, *Recent Trends in State Finance* (Chicago, 1948).

Tax Foundation, *Recent Trends in Major State Taxes, 1941-1947* (New York, 1948).

————, *Recent Trends in State Expenditures, 1942-1947* (New York, 1948).

F. C. Mosher and O. F. Poland, *The Costs of American Government; Facts, Trends, Myths* (New York, 1964).

★ 31 ★

The State Judiciary

ROUNDING OUT the government of every state is a system of courts providing *Functions* means for (1) adjusting disputes between private parties, and between such parties and state or local governments; (2) determining the guilt or innocence of persons accused of violating the state's criminal laws; (3) protecting the constitutional rights of individuals and corporations; (4) keeping the executive and legislative branches of government within the bounds fixed for them by the state constitution; and (5) promoting adjustments of sundry kinds, including the settlement of estates of deceased persons.[1]

Three cardinal features of these state courts require emphasis at the outset. First, the "state judicial system" embraces not only tribunals operating on a state-wide basis (of such, in fact, there are few), but those functioning in counties, cities, and other local areas as well. From justice of the peace and police court to supreme court—and regardless of whether created by the state constitution or established and regulated only by legislative act—all of the courts on all levels form parts of a single pattern, even though not completely integrated. Second, and contrary to a common popular impression, the state judicial system is in no way subordinate to the national system. The two sets of courts are separately rooted and mount through their successive grades on parallel lines, each with its own field of jurisdiction and operating independently within it. Any case, it is true, originating in a state court, but involving determination of a right claimed under the national Constitution, laws, or treaties may be removed or carried on appeal to a proper national court. The great majority of cases coming before the state courts do not, however, raise any such "federal question," but involve simply the adjudication of rights claimed under the state constitution, the state statutes, or the common law when not modified by state legislation. Nearly all judicial actions started in a state court are completed there with just as much finality as if there were no national courts at all. A third fact is that, while many suits may be instituted in either a state or a national court, and while the dockets of national

Some general features:

1. Scope

2. Status

---

[1] In addition to purely judicial functions, duties of a more or less administrative nature sometimes are imposed on intermediate courts, esepcially in connection with receiverships, elections, management of certain county affairs, appointment of school boards, and granting of various licenses. On the other hand, functions of a quasi-judicial nature frequently are exercised by state administrative agencies, such as public utility and railway commissions, civil service commissions, and tax commissions.

3. Jurisdiction

courts are nearly always crowded, the great bulk of judicial business the country over—probably nine-tenths of it—is transacted in the courts of the states. Under the principle of delegated powers, the national courts have only such jurisdiction as the national Constitution expressly gives them, and in general are confined to administering national law. Under the principle of reserved powers, the state courts have everything else, the state law which they administer covering not only a wider and more indeterminate range of matters, but matters often peculiarly provocative of legislation, and consequently of litigation. Much of the time, state courts and their decisions do not attract as much attention as those in the national sphere. Nevertheless, here it is, rather than in the national courts, that most people, as plaintiffs, defendants, jurors, or witnesses, have their contacts (if any) with the judicial process.

THE SYSTEM OF COURTS

Regulated partly by the constitution and partly by statute, the court structure in almost every state has some individual features. In general, however, differences are minor and the court systems of the states tend to follow a standard pattern as follows: (1) justices of the peace and other courts of petty jurisdiction, (2) special courts of limited jurisdiction, (3) courts of general trial jurisdiction, (4) appellate courts, and (5) a supreme court.

1. The lowest courts: a. Justices of the peace

At the bottom of the scale stand tribunals of purely local character, consisting of justices of the peace, municipal magistrates, or other officers of similar grade. Originally, justices of the peace functioned in rural and urban areas alike, and some still are found in cities of considerable size. The tendency, however, has been to displace them in urban centers by other magistrates, and today they are largely confined to rural communities. As a rule, justices are chosen by popular vote in townships or other subdivisions of the county, and for short terms (usually two years); although in a few states they are appointed by the governor. In any case, their jurisdiction commonly extends throughout an entire county, and includes both petty civil suits (involving up to perhaps $100) and breaches of the peace and other minor infractions of law. They may also issue warrants for the arrest of persons charged with more serious offenses, may hold preliminary hearings, and if the evidence warrants may bind over a suspect to await action by a grand jury or prosecutor. In

b. Municipal or police courts

contrast with other state and local courts, the justice courts have no official seal, no clerk, and keep no permanent official record of their proceedings. Accordingly, they are not "courts of record," as are most of the others. Furthermore, they may render final decisions in only the most petty misdemeanor and civil cases. In all others, appeal lies to the next higher court, which, however, ordinarily will consider an appealed case *de novo,* without reference to what has taken place in the justice's court.

In most incorporated places of appreciable size, the functions elsewhere performed by justices of the peace are assigned to one or more minor tribunals variously known as municipal courts, police courts, or magistrates' courts, with jurisdiction confined to the given municipality. Sometimes the judges of these courts are elected by the people, sometimes they are appointed by the mayor or even by the governor. In any event, their handling of the multitude of petty cases coming before them too often is inept if not actually corrupt. Unhappy experience with such tribunals, especially where two or more were found operating in the same jurisdiction, has led most large cities, for example, New York, Chicago, Philadelphia, Detroit, Boston, and Baltimore, to co-ordinate and integrate all work of the kind in a single municipal court. Of necessity such a tribunal must parcel out its tasks among sections or branches dealing with cases in particular fields such as traffic, juvenile offenses, domestic relations, small claims, and the like. The jurisdiction of courts of this nature usually transcends that of justices of the peace.[2]

In many states, the next level above the justice and municipal courts is occupied by courts of general trial jurisdiction in which most important litigation originates and most persons accused of crime are tried. In others, however, there are courts intermediate between these tribunals and the justices, organized frequently on a county basis and with jurisdiction limited and defined so that a plaintiff may choose whether to sue before a justice or in an intermediate court.

2. Special courts of limited jurisdiction

Even where such intermediate courts exist, however, greater importance attaches to the courts of general trial jurisdiction on a somewhat higher level. In many states, a tribunal of this grade is called the county or superior court, and there is a single judge in each county. More often, however, two or three counties are grouped for the purpose, with a district or circuit court serving each group, and with usually a single judge except in urban or other areas where the volume of work requires more. In any case, a "trial" court session is held at least once a year in virtually every county, either by the county court judge or by a district or circuit judge making his rounds in accordance with a regular schedule. It is in these court sittings that trial juries are most extensively employed.[3] In 34 states, all county, district, or circuit judges are chosen by popular vote, and for terms most commonly of four years. On this level and above, too, all judges may be assumed to be men of legal training.

3. General trial (county, district, or circuit) courts: a. Organization

b. Jurisdiction

Whether held by a local county or superior judge or by a district or

---

[2] Formerly, California had 768 inferior courts of eight different types below the superior (county) courts, several types often existing in the same community and handling the same kinds of cases. A constitutional amendment adopted in November, 1950, prepared the way for a simplification by dividing each county into judicial districts and giving each district only one court. All inferior courts were consolidated into two types: municipal in districts with more than 40,000 population, and justice courts in all others.

[3] In some New England states, there are no county, district, or circuit judges of the types mentioned, but instead the several judges of the superior (or supreme) court hold court in the different counties throughout the state, in addition to serving collectively as an appellate court. There are, however, special probate districts, each with an elective probate judge.

circuit judge making periodic visitations, county courts regularly have both criminal and civil, and also both original and appellate, jurisdiction. On the criminal side, they handle all cases except those of a petty nature taken care of by the justices of the peace or magistrates or by an intermediate court. Ordinarily their decisions are final insofar as questions of fact are concerned, although if disputed matters of law are involved, a case may usually be carried on appeal to a higher tribunal. Jurisdiction in civil cases is commonly unlimited, although in a few states restricted to actions involving less than $1,000 or some other stated amount. Here again most cases have their first hearing, although some are brought up on appeal from decisions of justices of the peace or magistrates. In populous counties, the settlement of the estates of deceased persons and the discharge of functions relating to the property, custody, and welfare of minor children and other persons under guardianship are in the hands of a separate probate, surrogate, or orphans' court. Elsewhere, however, these duties commonly devolve upon the regular judges, who also, in several states, have important administrative duties in connection with the enforcement of certain state laws and with specified phases of county government, for example, poor relief.

4. Appellate courts   Above these general trial courts, and with a view to relieving congestion in the supreme court, about one-fourth of the more populous states have placed one or more appellate courts. The judges are sometimes appointed but usually elected from a few large judicial districts into which the state is divided for the purpose and sit in "benches" of three or more, with decisions reached by the majority.[4] Limited original jurisdiction is occasionally conferred by the legislature, but most of the time of these courts is devoted to hearing appeals from the general trial courts and rendering decisions which in many classes of cases are final. As a rule, only questions of law are involved, with juries therefore not employed.

5. Supreme courts: a. Structure   The highest state court is usually called the supreme court and consists of either five or seven judges (including a "chief justice") sitting together when hearing cases. In at least one-third of the states it is permissible to sit in sections. In any event, a majority of the whole number of members of the court or section must concur in any decision rendered. The judges are nearly always elective, most often on a state-wide nonpartisan ticket, although in a few states by districts. There are instances in which nominations are made in districts, but with election by the voters of the state at large. Ranging all the way from two years in Vermont to 15 and 21 years in Maryland and Pennsylvania, respectively, and "good behavior" in Massachusetts, New Hampshire, and Rhode Island, the term of office is most often six years (in 18 states). Salaries vary from $10,500 in Vermont to $39,000 in New York.[5]

4 New York somewhat perversely calls its appellate court of this grade the "supreme court." The tribunal, however, is not supreme, because above it stands a higher one, the "court of appeals."

5 For a complete tabulation of salaries, see Council of State Governments, *The Book of the States, 1964-65* (Chicago, 1964), 128.

The work of the supreme court consists almost entirely in hearing and *b. Func-* deciding appeals on questions of law coming up from the lower trial courts *tions* or appellate courts where they exist. In most states the court may also issue certain writs, and in a few others it may give first hearing to cases of one or two types, for example, those in which the state is a party. In performing its appellate functions, the court not only adjudicates cases, but becomes—like the Supreme Court of the United States within its sphere—the highest interpreter of the constitution and laws. Its decisions and interpretations, too, are final, except for those which may be carried to the national Supreme Court.[6]

STRUCTURAL DEFECTS AND REMEDIES

The system of courts outlined is far from uniform in detail from state to state and undergoes frequent minor changes in any particular state. Viewed in the large, however, it is deeply rooted in American practice. This being the case, a general overhauling such as virtually all experts agree to be needed is difficult to bring about.

Of structural faults challenging attention, the first centers in the layer of *Principal* courts closest to the people and handling more cases than all other tribunals *faults:* combined: the courts of the justices of the peace. Usually these leave a good *1. The* deal to be desired. To begin with, the justices themselves are invariably *outmoded* devoid of legal education, with the justice which they administer likely to be *justice of* of a more or less rough-and-ready sort. Of course there are handbooks of law *the peace* for them to consult. On the elementary level on which they operate, lack of formal training may be offset by a good stock of common sense. Nevertheless, if they are to be continued, some surer guarantee of competence is highly desirable. Equally serious is the circumstance that, with only modest salaries or none at all attached to the office, the justice normally must look for his compensation to such fees as he can collect. In the great majority of instances, he derives but little from this source—perhaps a few hundred dollars a year, perhaps less. There have been instances, however, in which favorably located justices pocketed thousands of dollars a year. A system of justice which puts a premium on drumming up business and squeezing the utmost out of every offender is hardly to be commended. Too often, it has been marred by fee-splitting with conniving constables, "speed-trap" abuses on public highways, and other forms of chicanery and extortion. In the early history of the country, when travel to the county seat (where the higher courts dispensed justice at infrequent intervals) was difficult and time-consuming, rural justices of the peace performed useful, if not indispensable, functions as tribunals near at

[6] Decisions of the State supreme courts (including "concurring" and "dissenting" opinions) are published regularly in volumes known as *Illinois Reports, Indiana Reports,* etc., prepared under the editorial supervision of a reporter of decisions appointed by the court. In most states, the decisions of appellate courts are published also, but in separate volumes. For many years (through 1949), state supreme court decisions were reviewed annually in the August issue of the *American Political Science Review.*

hand for adjusting minor differences between members of the same community. With the greatly improved means of travel and communication existing today, such usefulness has largely disappeared.

2. Lack of judicial articulation

A recent thoughtful writer has ventured the observation that the most serious weaknesses growing out of existing state judicial organization are (1) lack of specialization, (2) inequalities in the distribution of work, and (3) lack of uniformity in interpretation and administration of the law. And he goes on to comment as follows: [7]

> By and large, the organization of our courts on a geographical rather than a functional basis prevents any substantial degree of specialization. Each court usually serves a city, county, district, circuit, or some other geographic area, and handles all types of cases therein. Hence it is practically impossible for a judge to become a specialist in any particular kind of cases, such as criminal, equity, or domestic relations. Moreover, under the geographic basis of organization the dockets of some courts are crowded while those of others are light, and no adequate provision is made for transferring judges temporarily from courts having little to do to those that are overworked. Finally, in the absence of central supervision, judicial administration is far from uniform, especially in the field of criminal law. Considerable discretion is commonly vested in the courts with respect to criminal penalties to be imposed, with the result that a given offense is likely to draw widely different penalties at different places in the same state, depending upon the attitude of the particular judge before whom the case is tried.

In our study of state administration, we saw how disadvantageous is the usual lack of unified supervision and control over the many separate administrative officers and agencies. Unhappily, the same lack too often interferes with the most effective functioning of the state's judicial machinery. It seems self-evident that all of the courts belonging to the so-called *judicial system* should be closely articulated with one another, and that there should be some chief justice or other authority in a position to coordinate the work of the several courts, devise plans for a useful division of labor among them, transfer cases, assign judges, and do other things needed to promote speed and efficiency. Instead of this, however, we find in the majority of states "a jumble of disconnected and disjointed courts, each pursuing its own way, with little regard to any other"—a "heterogeneous assortment of miscellaneous courts of miscellaneous and often overlapping jurisdiction." In earlier and simpler days, there was some unity and coherence; but so much new machinery has been tacked on without regard to system that any former articulation has almost disappeared.

Likewise, in the case of any particular court, it seems manifest that efficiency calls for a chief justice or effective head clothed with authority to

[7] C. F. Snider, *American State and Local Government* (New York, 1950), 281.

supervise the work of all judges belonging to that court, to require them to make periodic reports showing the state of business on their dockets, to admonish the careless and indolent, to relieve the overworked, and to keep all reasonably busy. As matters stand, however, in nearly every part of the country the judges in the same court are elected independently of one another and seldom are made subject to any actual directing or supervisory control. Each judge can hold court when he pleases, for as few hours a day as he pleases, and hear cases on such calendars as he pleases. Whatever cooperation, teamwork, or division of labor exists depends almost entirely upon voluntary cooperation of the judges constituting the court.

With so loose organization, or lack thereof, it is not surprising that there are few reliable statistics showing what our different state courts are doing or how much they are costing the taxpayers. Of most of our states it may truly be said that "the judiciary is the one department which publishes no data bearing upon the efficiency of its work"—though without such data there is no adequate basis for judging how well it is performing its duties or what changes are needed to increase its efficiency. *3. Inadequate reporting*

For many years, crime commissions and other analysts of judicial administration have urged abolition, state by state, of the entire justice-of-the-peace system. The obstacles are great—and not merely tradition and inertia, but the necessity (in most states) of constitutional amendment, and also the influence of existing justices with local electorates. In a few states—Missouri (1945), New Jersey (1947), Connecticut (1959), North Carolina (1962) and Colorado (1962)—the system has been suppressed outright. In some half-dozen others, however, the essential purpose has been wholly or partially attained by constitutional or legislative action stripping justices of their power to try cases, even though leaving them authority, for example, to issue warrants and subpoenas and perform marriages. Thus Virginia, in 1934, supplanted former justices for purely judicial purposes by salaried "trial justices" appointed for each county by the circuit court, and supervised by it; Tennessee had replaced justices in certain counties by salaried "general sessions" courts and in 1961 replaced those in most of the remaining counties; North Carolina in 1937, and Indiana in 1939, empowered counties (only more populous ones in Indiana under an amendment of 1941) to create courts with appointive and salaried judges handling most cases formerly tried by justices; Maryland in 1939 made such courts state-wide. Missouri in 1945 replaced justices altogether by magistrate's courts, at least one in each county; and New Jersey in 1947 replaced them by district and municipal courts under appointive magistrates. California in 1951 replaced them with district courts in the most populous areas of the state. Hawaii and Alaska entered the union without justice courts. Justices have been dispensed with also in a number of cities, for example, Chicago in 1905 and Milwaukee in 1945. New Mexico has provided a system of state supervision of their finances and Idaho and Wyoming have eliminated their constitutional status. *Some limited improvements: 1. Justices of the peace abolished or partly superseded*

NEW JERSEY'S COURT SYSTEM
UNDER THE CONSTITUTION OF 1947

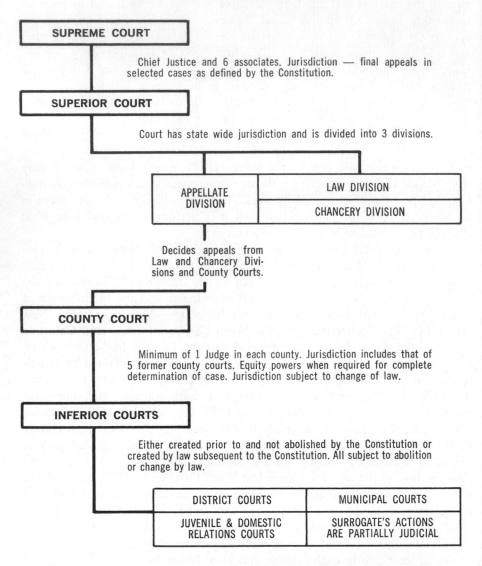

SUPREME COURT

Chief Justice and 6 associates. Jurisdiction — final appeals in selected cases as defined by the Constitution.

SUPERIOR COURT

Court has state wide jurisdiction and is divided into 3 divisions.

APPELLATE DIVISION	LAW DIVISION
	CHANCERY DIVISION

Decides appeals from Law and Chancery Divisions and County Courts.

COUNTY COURT

Minimum of 1 Judge in each county. Jurisdiction includes that of 5 former county courts. Equity powers when required for complete determination of case. Jurisdiction subject to change of law.

INFERIOR COURTS

Either created prior to and not abolished by the Constitution or created by law subsequent to the Constitution. All subject to abolition or change by law.

DISTRICT COURTS	MUNICIPAL COURTS
JUVENILE & DOMESTIC RELATIONS COURTS	SURROGATE'S ACTIONS ARE PARTIALLY JUDICIAL

All judges appointed by Governor with approval of Senate except Municipal Judges, who are appointed by governing body excepting where serving in two or more municipalities and then appointed by the Governor. Surrogates are elected.

An important aid to the efficient functioning of our state courts would be a state department of justice, charged with exercising general supervision over the administration of both criminal and civil justice, and also with collecting and publishing judicial statistics covering the entire state—an agency performing for the state courts functions analogous to those now performed for the national courts by the Department of Justice and the Administrative Office of the United States Courts at Washington. A few have provided themselves with such a department but in no one of the number does the establishment appear to be working effectively as an agency for imparting vigor and uniformity to the administration of criminal justice. In addition, about one-fourth of the states have conferred upon the attorney general limited power to supervise the work of county or other local prosecuting attorneys. Here again results have not proved impressive. Undoubtedly the attorney general's office might be made a nucleus around which to develop an effective state department of justice, as envisaged in California under a constitutional amendment adopted in 1934. *2. Coordination through state departments of justice*

In about a dozen states, including Wisconsin, Missouri, and Louisiana, the constitution vests in the supreme court "a general superintending control" over all inferior courts. Until recently, however, the contemplated authority was rarely employed to bring about any notable measure of unification and coordination. The court reform programs of a number of states have included strengthening the supervisory and administrative powers of the Supreme Court. The constitution of Michigan is a good illustration of this development. More significant has been the establishment, in approximately three-quarters of the states, of investigative and advisory judicial councils charged with collecting and studying judicial statistics, formulating rules for the equalization and more efficient handling of court business (with power in California and a few other states to put them into operation), and recommending to the legislature desirable changes in the laws governing court organization and procedure.[8] In these states, as elsewhere, however, many desirable improvements remain to be made, with often the adoption of a constitutional amendment a necessary first step. *3. Judicial councils*

Impressed by the efficiency of a highly integrated judicial system in Great Britain, the authors of the National Municipal League's "model state constitution" provide in their plan for a "general court of justice," or unified state court; and many bar associations and other interested groups have en- *4. Unified state courts*

[8] Most such councils include both judges and members of the bar; a few are composed of judges alone; and some also include state officials, members of law school faculties, and even representatives of the general public. The New York, Ohio, and Michigan judicial councils have been especially active; and the device marks one of the more important developments in connection with state courts during the past 30 years. See P. S. Sikes, "The Work of Judicial Councils," *Amer. Polit. Sci. Rev.*, XXIX, 456-472 (June, 1935); E. R. Sunderland, "The Judicial Council as an Aid to the Administration of Justice," *ibid.*, XXXV, 925-933 (Oct., 1941); and G. R. Winters, "Silver Anniversary of the Judicial Council Movement," *Jour. of Amer. Judic. Soc.*, XXXIII, 43-49, 79-84 (Aug. and Oct., 1949).

dorsed it. The proposal is (1) that in each state all courts of the various grades (at least those having civil jurisdiction) be merged into a single state-wide tribunal, organized in branches or divisions (with probably subdivisions) permitting judicial business to be distributed more logically and judges to develop more specialized experience and talent than now; (2) that all judges be members of this unified court and subject to service at any point in the state where needed; (3) that the court be headed by an elective chief justice, perhaps with power to appoint all other judges from panels presented by the judicial council; and (4) that the chief justice, acting singly or in conjunction with the judicial council under his chairmanship, be vested with broad supervisory powers, including assigning judges to the various branches, transferring them from courts with light dockets to others with heavy ones, requiring systematic reports, and imposing rules designed to speed up business and promote uniformity of action. Plans of court organization based on similar principles have yielded good results within the narrower limits of several of our larger cities. With adoption on the state level manifestly promising large gains, it is significant that Missouri, in her revised constitution of 1945, went a considerable distance by empowering her supreme court to make rules for all courts and to transfer judges from court to court; and that New Jersey in 1947 went farther (also in a revised constitution) by boldly adopting the unified state court system in all of its essentials. Both Hawaii and Alaska provide for a completely unified system of state courts in their new constitutions. Wisconsin in 1959, Colorado and Illinois in 1962, Michigan in 1963 and New York, Idaho, North Carolina, New Hampshire, and Connecticut in 1962-1963 have all carried out extensive court reorganizations. Judicial reformers hope and expect that as other constitutions are rewritten or amended, similar advances will be made.

JUDICIAL PERSONNEL: SELECTION AND REMOVAL

Prevalence of popular election

In most foreign countries (except the U.S.S.R.), and in our own national government, judges are appointive rather than elective. And so they were in all of our earlier states, with appointments made either by the governor and council or by the legislature. In 1812, Georgia, and in 1832, Mississippi, made judges of certain courts popularly elective. In this, they stood alone until near the middle of the century. Then, however, general change set in, reflecting somewhat belatedly the democratic impulses associated with the rise of the West and with the equalitarian philosophy of the Jacksonian era. Curiously, it was an Eastern state that led off—New York in 1847. But New York was strongly infected with the democratic spirit; and most of the middle states were borne along on a current of judicial popularization which by 1860 engulfed everything west of the Alleghenies. After that time every new state admitted came in with the elective plan until Hawaii came in with an appointive system and Alaska with a combination of an appointive and elective system. Today in 34 states judges are elected by popular vote; about half in partisan elections.[9]

Long experience has disclosed two inherent weaknesses in the elective system. The first is that it is no more likely to result in the choice of persons qualified to perform the highly technical work required of the judiciary than it is to secure the selection of experts in other branches of state government or in the field of municipal administration. As an early writer remarks: [10]

Defects

> A judge, in addition to any other qualifications, must possess certain technical knowledge and experience. However high his character, however sound his general intellectual equipment, however wide his acquaintance with business or public affairs, he must also possess a technical knowledge of the law and of legal procedure. To ask the public at large to pass upon a question of technical fitness in the case of a lawyer is as inappropriate as it would be to ask for a similar judgment regarding the technical fitness of an engineer, or a doctor, or a musician . . . the determination of technical fitness is obviously a task in which only a comparatively few persons can helpfully take part.

A second defect of popular election, too, is that what passes under that name often is only a fiction, being in reality nothing more than a method of appointment by partisans who succeed in putting their judicial "slates" through so-called nonpartisan primaries, or through party primaries, or through nominating conventions. All that is generally left for the voter on election day is to endorse one or the other of two judicial tickets thus submitted by persons not interested primarily in the efficient administration of justice, and therefore quite unlikely to pick candidates having the qualities most needed in a judge, namely, unquestioned integrity, dignity, independence, judicial temperament, and adequate legal training for highly technical duties.

It is not to be inferred that results under popular election are invariably bad. Our state judiciary, the country over, contains plenty of judges deficient both in learning and in ability, but also many who measure up exceedingly well both in learning and in other qualifications. In a good many states (notably New York, Pennsylvania, Maryland, Michigan, Wisconsin, Minnesota, and Iowa) the elective system has proved at least moderately satisfactory partly because of a strong local tradition in favor of re-electing incumbents. All in all, nevertheless, the plan's shortcomings usually outweigh its advantages—in some states very heavily. A great many people are now prepared to concede that a different one well might prove superior. So firmly

Some partial remedies

[9] The other systems in current use are: (1) selection by the legislature of some or all state judges in 5 states; (2) appointment by the governor with senatorial or council confirmation in 6 states; and (3) original appointment by the governor and then nonpartisan popular vote on incumbents at intervals thereafter in 5 states. See Council of State Governments, *Book of the States, 1964-65* (Chicago, 1964), 126.

[10] W. MacDonald, *A New Constitution for a New America* (New York, 1921), 182-183.

entrenched, however, is the system where it prevails, and so warmly would state and local leaders resist abandoning it, that most proposals for reform do not go beyond devices aimed at securing better choices with popular election still operating. One such device—subject to discount because of the manner in which politicians frequently manipulate it—is the choice of judges on non-partisan ballots; and this method is employed in 18 states. Another, aimed also at minimizing partisanship, is the holding of judicial elections separately from others. And a third, utilized to advantage in a few states, takes the form of nomination of candidates for higher judicial posts, not in the usual primaries or conventions, but by the state bar association, as a body presumed to have special knowledge of the qualifications to be sought and of the fitness of persons aspiring to judicial preferment.[11]

Three notable plans: 1. California

Three plans of judicial selection, however, which are attracting increasingly favorable attention are those operating in California, Alaska, and Missouri. They combine the better features of appointment and popular election and at the same time provide safeguards not offered by either of those methods alone. In 1934, the voters of California approved a constitutional amendment under which (1) a judge of the supreme court or of a district court of appeals may, as the end of his term approaches, declare his candidacy to succeed himself, and the people at the ensuing election simply vote for or against him; (2) if an incumbent chooses not to seek another term, the governor nominates someone for the post, and he similarly is voted on without any opposing candidate; (3) if in either case the popular vote is unfavorable, or if a judicial vacancy occurs otherwise, the governor makes a temporary appointment until the next general election, when the voters approve or disapprove of the person appointed, with a defeated candidate, however, ineligible for appointment to another judicial vacancy; and (4) as a further check upon the governor, all judicial appointments must be approved by a majority of a commission consisting of the chief justice of the supreme court, the presiding justice of the appellate court of the district involved, and the attorney general. The plan is not expressly made applicable to superior (county) court judges; instead, each county is left free to employ it or not as the voters choose. The system has several significant advantages. In the first place, judges are nominated by intelligent and responsible agents, while the ultimate selection nevertheless remains in the hands of the people. Secondly, a nominee is not running against somebody, but on his own record as a judge or as a lawyer, thus greatly diminishing the likelihood that irrelevant considerations will influence the voters. Finally, sitting judges are relieved of the necessity of devoting a large amount of their time to political activity in order to retain their positions; all

11 On a similar plan in Chicago, see E. M. Martin, "The Selection of Judges in Chicago and the Role of the Local Bar Therein," *Amer. Polit. Sci. Rev.*, XXX, 315-323 (Apr., 1936); H. A. Gardner *et al.*, "The Selection of Judges for Cook County: The Chicago Bar Association Plan," *Ill. Law Rev.*, XXXI, 893-906 (Mar., 1937).

they need do is fortify the judicial record on which they will appeal to the electorate.[12]

The Missouri plan, adopted by popularly initiated constitutional amendment in 1940 and continued with little change by the constitution of 1945, is so similar that only two differences (neither fundamental) need be mentioned. (1) When temporarily filling a higher judicial vacancy, the governor must appoint one of three persons nominated by a nonpartisan commission consisting of the chief justice of the supreme court as chairman, three lawyers named by the organized bar, and three laymen named by the governor. (2) On lower levels, the plan is applied to circuit and probate judges in the city of St. Louis and Jackson County (Kansas City) and to judges of such judicial circuits elsewhere as may adopt it by popular vote. In these cases, nominations to the governor are made by a local five-member commission in the judicial circuit concerned. Under the new arrangements, we are told by the chief justice of Missouri's supreme court, the state judiciary is being gradually improved, with partisanship completely eliminated and judges, freed from primary and election campaigning, able at last to bring their dockets up to date—to "keep their minds on the next case and not the next election." [13] Iowa, Kansas, and Nebraska now use the Missouri plan for selecting some of their judges. Alaska's new constitution provides still a third plan. Under it the governor appoints to vacancies on the supreme or superior court benches from nominations made by the judicial council. Three or more years (ultimately every 10 years for supreme court justices and every 6 years for a superior court justice) thereafter the justice must run for election on a nonpartisan ballot and on his record.

2. Missouri

3. Alaska

In the national judicial system, judges retain their posts during good behavior, and the only method of removing them is impeachment. Even in times when state judges were largely or wholly appointive, there was a tendency to give them only limited terms. With the spread of the elective system, the practice became general, so that today "life" tenure survives only in Massachusetts, New Hampshire (until the age of seventy), and Rhode Island. As a rule, however, terms, in the higher courts, are relatively lengthy (4, 6, 8, 10, 15, in Pennsylvania even 21, years [14]). How to retire incumbents proving incompetent or otherwise unworthy of public confidence presents a problem as yet not solved satisfactorily. A fully acceptable method must be one which can be put into operation without undue delay, and one which at the same time insures for the judge whose removal is sought a fair hearing before a tribunal free from partisan bias and not subject to the influence of

Removal of judges a difficult problem

[12] C. Aiken, "A New Method of Selecting Judges in California," *Amer. Polit. Sci. Rev.*, XXIX, 472-475 (June, 1935).

[13] L. M. Hyde, "Choosing Judges in Missouri," *Nat. Mun. Rev.*, XXXVIII, 491-493, 503 (Nov., 1949).

[14] For a tabulation of terms see Council of State Governments, *Book of the States, 1964-65* (Chicago, 1964), 125.

waves of popular passion. Three or four principal methods now in use in the different states fail, in varying degrees, to meet these standards.

Methods in use:

1. Failure to renominate or re-elect

A judge sitting by popular election may, of course, be retired by failure to secure renomination, either because his character or work is considered unsatisfactory or because party leaders want his position for some one else. Even though he wins renomination, the people may retire him by failing to vote for him in sufficient numbers at the election. Popular choice, however, is almost as likely to bring wrong results as right ones, for often it happens that a judge whose work has been beyond reproach is defeated for renomination or re-election by circumstances wholly unrelated to his record as judge, perhaps because some overshadowing issue in state or national politics, wholly unconnected with the judicial election, has swept down to defeat the entire party ticket on which his name appeared. Furthermore (apart from the recall), a popular election furnishes a means of retiring an unworthy judge only at a given time, at the expiration of his term of office. The public has also shown a very strong disposition everywhere to re-elect incumbent judges, even those who have become superannuated.

2. Impeachment or legislative removal or address

In most states, judges may be removed before the close of their term only by impeachment proceedings begun in the lower house of the legislature and tried before the senate, a two-thirds vote of the latter usually being required for conviction and removal. The constitutions of about half of the states, however, provide also for removal (without trial) by the legislature (or by the governor in pursuance of legislative action) upon "address," that is, concurrent resolution, of the legislature, after the English manner. Neither impeachment nor legislative removal is without serious defects. Under either method, there is much delay; and partisan considerations are likely to exert undue influence. Furthermore, evidence sufficient to convince two-thirds of the senate may be difficult to obtain; and the dereliction may not be grave enough to seem to merit extreme measures, yet sufficiently serious to warrant public condemnation and impair the judge's usefulness. In practice, it has been found that impeachment and legislative removal do not really work, and that unfit judges sometimes remain on the bench because no other modes of removal are available.[15]

3. Recall election

This experience has led eight states [16] to adopt the seemingly drastic policy of authorizing special elections at which the voters may recall judges whose removal is desired. Thus far, however, the plan has proved drastic only on paper. In no instance has the recall been invoked against a judge of a superior or supreme court, and instances of its use against judges on lower levels have been negligible. At one time it was predicted that fear of recall

[15] A recent impeachment and conviction of a state judge in Tennessee will be found reported in *The New York Times,* July 12, 1958. An impeachment trial of a supreme court judge in Oklahoma is reported in *The New York Times,* May 11, 1965.

[16] Arizona, California, Colorado, Kansas, Nevada, North Dakota, Oregon, and Wisconsin.

would place judges under unfair pressure and even impair judicial independence; but no ground for such apprehension has thus far appeared.[17]

THE JUDICIAL PROCESS

Nature and regulation

In handling a case of any kind, a court of any grade has three essential things to do. First, it must inform itself as fully as possible on the facts involved. At the lower levels, for example, in a justice's or magistrate's court, this may entail little more than hearing a police officer's charges against the defendant and giving the latter a chance to reply and explain. Farther up the scale, it is likely to entail, in civil cases, hearing the different versions of the two parties, with evidence introduced through witnesses or in other ways, and perhaps with final determination by a jury. In criminal actions there is, typically, a hearing of the case as presented by the prosecution, the defense as offered by the defendant and his counsel, with almost certainly witnesses heard on both sides and other evidence weighed, and with nearly always a jury striking the balance and declaring whether the facts as brought out establish the defendant's guilt and in what degree. In the absence of a jury, whether the case be civil or criminal, facts are determined by the judge. In any event, the remaining two steps necessary to complete the process fall to that official. Of these, the first is to decide what provisions of law are applicable in the particular situation; and the second, to apply these provisions in terms of a specific judgment or verdict. All of these stages, furthermore, are governed by elaborate and often highly technical rules of procedure covering such matters as the rights of the accused, the admissibility of evidence, the selection of jurors, the privileges and limitations of counsel, the role of the judge, and many others. The promptness and quality of justice are greatly affected by the spirit and terms of such regulations.

Except insofar as predetermined by occasional constitutional provision, procedural rules were in earlier days made almost entirely by the courts themselves. At present, however, not only do constitution-framers write them more freely into their documents, but legislatures often enact them in such detail in statutes that residuary powers of the courts to supply whatever is needed but not otherwise furnished amount to little. Students of judicial administration, including many judges and lawyers, regard this development as unfortunate, not only because legislatures have neither the time nor the technical competence to perform the task satisfactorily, but because they sometimes are not above amending given rules at the behest of influential litigants hoping to gain some advantage in a particular case.

[17] It may be added that more than half of the states have constitutional or statutory provisions permitting the retirement of judges on account of age or physical infirmity, although only four (Louisiana, Maine, New Hampshire, and New York) have a compulsory retirement age. The retirement systems of the several states are tabulated in Council of State Governments, *The Book of the States, 1964-65* (Chicago, 1964), 129.

The heart of the judicial process consists in applying the law in each particular case after the facts have been established. This, of course, involves determining what law is applicable. In our American situation any one or more of several different bodies of law may be relevant. First of all is national law—the Constitution, acts of Congress, treaties, and regulations of executive or administrative authorities having the force of law. Although most litigation in state courts turns on state law, national law is the "supreme law of the land," and the judges in every state are bound by it, "anything in the constitution or laws of any state to the contrary notwithstanding." Second comes state law, also constitutional, statutory, or regulatory. Even local law in the form of city and county charters, ordinances, and regulations sometimes must be taken into account, especially in lower courts. And supplementary to all else is the common law operating in the state. Classified differently, the law that may be applicable in a given case is (1) constitutional, (2) statutory, (3) regulatory or administrative, and (4) common. In descending order of priority, the judge must be guided by (1) the national "supreme" law, (2) state constitutional and statutory law, which, however, he can declare to be no law at all if found in conflict with national law, (3) state and local ordinances and regulations, which also he can hold invalid under either national or state constitutions or statutes, and finally (4) the common law.

With national law always latent in the background, the law invoked in the great majority of cases tried in state courts is state law—constitutional, statutory, or common, with the third resorted to only when, and insofar as, the others do not cover a given situation. Constitutions and statutes are, of course, *enacted* law—written, and in the case of statutes often gathered into systematic codes kept up to date by periodic revisions. Common law, on the other hand, is law originally built up by the decisions and procedures of judges in mediaeval England, brought to America by the colonists, carried over and gradually modified to fit the American scene (to some extent even the localized needs of particular states) after the country became independent, and operating today in all of the states except Louisiana. There, as a result of early French influence, Continental "civil law" is followed instead.[18] In the sense that judges developed it by selecting among earlier decisions those to be followed as precedents, and by incorporating principles and rules deduced from general custom where precedents failed, common law is essentially *judge-made* law. In their use of it, as well as in their interpretation of constitutions and statutes, judges still add to and otherwise "make" law. A frequent popular conception of common law as *unwritten* law is, however, inaccurate—first, because every element of it will be found set forth, here or there, in written decisions and opinions published in court reports, and sec-

[18] G. A. Pope, "How Real Is the Difference Today Between the Law of Louisiana and That of the Other Forty-seven States?" *Geo. Washington Law Rev.,* XVII, 186-198 (Feb., 1949).

ond, because in many states important portions of it have been reduced to formal codes. Suggestions for complete codification, however, have been generally opposed by jurists on the ground that this would destroy the flexibility and capacity for adaptation which always have been among the common law's principal virtues. Important as is the common law in our legal system, it applies only insofar as not modified or superseded by constitutional provision or statute.[19]

In general, cases tried in state courts fall into two broad categories— *Types of* civil and criminal. The essential aspect of a civil case is that it turns on a *cases* dispute between private parties—a plaintiff and a defendant—over possession *tried:* or use of property, payment of a claim or debt, execution of a contract, a *1. Civil* wrong [20] (or "tort") for which damages are sought, the validity of a will, an action for divorce, or any one of many other possible things. The method is that of a suit in a proper court by one party against the other. Except when (usually only with its own consent) a state or one of its subdivisions is one of the parties,[21] no government is involved, save in the sense of having made or authorized the law under which the action is brought and of having provided the judicial machinery through which a settlement may be reached.

Criminal cases are quite different. From petty misdemeanors up the *2.* scale to felonies, offenses coming under the criminal laws, although they *Criminal* usually involve personal or property damage, are regarded as injuries done to society; and their perpetrators are prosecuted by *public* officers, not in the name of individuals who may have suffered, but in that of "the people of the state of" New York, Ohio, or Texas, as the case may be. The object of the court action which follows is to determine whether the accused is guilty; if so, of what, and in what degree; and what penalty should be assessed. And when the verdict is in, if guilt is found, the state, which started the proceeding in the first place, finishes it by seeing that the penalty is enforced.

Long before the American colonies were founded, the right of an accused *The jury* person to be tried by a jury of his peers was a bulwark of English liberty. *system:* On this side of the Atlantic it has been equally treasured. In the national

[19] One hears also of a branch of law known as "equity"; and it has importance. Like the common law itself, to which it is supplementary, equity is of English origin, being a body of jurisprudence gradually built up to provide remedies in situations to which the common law did not apply (or if applied, worked *inequity*), and in these days often employed, through the use of injunctions, to prevent wrongs from being committed, as contrasted with correcting them afterwards, which usually is all that the common law is able to do. In half a dozen states (including Delaware, Tennessee, and Mississippi), there are separate equity courts; in others, the same courts handle both law and equity cases, but by different procedures; in still others, even procedural differences have disappeared.

[20] Such as libel, slander, assault, abduction, trespass, nuisance, and injury through negligence.

[21] About half of the states have general laws making themselves liable to suit in certain types of cases (most often involving contracts), but with trial commonly in a special "court of claims."

sphere, all persons accused of crime are guaranteed the right to "a speedy and public trial by an impartial jury," and (with certain exceptions) no one may be proceeded against on a capital charge unless "on a presentment or an indictment of a grand jury." State constitutions and statutes everywhere abound in provisions of similar nature. Coming straight out of English common law, the jury in this country thus presents itself in two characteristic forms—the grand jury, which brings indictments against suspected persons, and the trial or petit jury, which (in addition to functioning in civil cases) determines their guilt or innocence. Both are important, and both are sharply criticized. They are important adjuncts of the judicial machinery of courts and prosecutors described above.[22]

1. The grand jury

With the county, typically, as its area of operation, and with criminal, rather than civil, proceedings as its field, a grand jury is a body of normally from 13 to 23 persons, chosen by lot or by some other prescribed procedure, convening at regular intervals, and charged with bringing indictments on its own initiative against persons who in its opinion have transgressed state laws and should be held for trial. More commonly it considers such indictments after examining the evidence against persons brought to its attention as suspected transgressors by a justice of the peace or by the county or district prosecuting attorney. If, in the latter situation, the jury considers the evidence sufficiently incriminating, it endorses on the draft indictment prepared by the prosecutor the words, "A true bill"; the foreman attaches his signature; and the accused person is held for trial. If, on the other hand, the jury is not satisfied that a "prima facie case" has been made out, it instructs its foreman to inscribe on the draft indictment, "This bill not found," and the accused is discharged. Indictments found are duly reported to the county court, and the county or district attorney proceeds to prosecute.

The alternative device of "information"

Indictment by grand jury is cumbersome and expensive, and the tendency nowadays is to get away from it. In England, the land of its origin, it has been almost completely abandoned. While in the United States it cannot be dispensed with in national practice as long as the Constitution's clause on the subject stands unchanged, in the states the device is gradually breaking down. In about half of the number, grand-jury procedures still are required when felonies are involved, but optional in the case of lesser charges. In several states, the legislature is constitutionally empowered to do away with grand juries altogether. The procedure everywhere substituted is a simpler and more direct one known as "information," under which the prosecuting attorney, on his own initiative, merely files with the appropriate court a formal charge in which, upon his oath of office, he "gives said court to understand and be

---

[22] Trial juries rarely are employed in courts of petty jurisdiction below the county court, and never in supreme and other higher courts concerned only with applying law and not with determining facts.

informed" that the offense described therein has been committed by the person named.[23]

At common law, the trial or petit jury consisted of twelve impartial men chosen from the community. Its function was to judge of the facts in a case, the court itself passing upon all questions of law. Verdicts could be rendered only by unanimous vote. All criminal, and substantially all civil, cases called for jury procedure. Fundamentally, this is still the situation. Many states, however, have introduced significant modifications. (1) Whereas through long centuries it would have been inconceivable that jurors be other than men, 45 states now (1965) permit women to serve, and others probably will be added to the list. (2) In a few states, for example, Maryland and Illinois, juries serve as judges of both law and facts. (3) The constitutions of 22 states now authorize civil trials by juries of less than twelve persons (most commonly six), and eight states have similarly relaxed the old rule for criminal trials except in capital cases (involving a death penalty). (4) More than half of the states, including New York, now authorize verdicts by something less than unanimous vote (usually three-fourths) in civil cases, and eight have similarly modified the old rule for criminal (but not including capital) cases.[24] (5) Nearly all states allow jury trial to be waived altogether in civil cases if both parties are willing; and a large majority permit similar waiver in criminal cases as well if the offense is a minor one and the accused person agrees—about a third, indeed, extending the option also to cases of a more serious nature, although in no instance to capital cases.

2. The trial or petit jury

The grand jury has proved so defective, or at any rate superfluous, that it is being widely discarded. No such fate would appear in store for the trial jury, even though, as indicated, it too is not so uniformly employed as formerly. But one has only to read newspapers and law journals, or even hear lawyers and judges talk, to realize that all is not entirely well with the trial-jury system. To start with, the caliber of jurors could be improved. Jury service is supposed to be one of the primary obligations of the citizen, with the jury itself representing a cross-section of the community. Many occupational groups, however, including persons in public employment, are usually exempted by statute; business and professional people rarely are called upon to serve; and the elements from which jurymen are actually drawn are neither entirely representative nor usually of the experience and capacity that might

Short-comings

[23] California was one of the first states to authorize (1879) the prosecution of felony cases by information instead of indictment. In a murder case, it was contended that the new procedure violated the due process clause of the Fourteenth Amendment; but in *Hurtado v. California*, 110 U. S. 516 (1884), the Supreme Court held to the contrary. For a full discussion of grand-jury problems, see L. B. Orfield, *Criminal Procedure from Arrest to Appeal* (New York, 1947), Chaps. IV-V.

[24] Three-fourths is the required majority in 11 states, but five-sixths in six, two-thirds in three, and nine- or ten-twelfths in eight. Six permit majority verdicts only with consent of the parties, and two only after a jury has deliberated for a given number of hours without arriving at unanimity. See chart in Council of State Governments. *The Book of the States, 1950-51* (Chicago, 1950), 515.

be desired.[25] Legal exemptions ought to be cut down and the practice of letting useful people off merely because they are otherwise occupied should be tightened up. Another criticism, often heard from judicial experts, is that whereas in national practice judges are expected, and indeed required, to assist juries in understanding and evaluating evidence, state judges usually are without such authority; and that, in the absence of such help, juries often flounder and waste time, occasionally bringing in verdicts influenced by serious misconceptions. Finally may be mentioned the problem of making the lot of the juror more tolerable also by greater courtesy from court officials than sometimes is shown, and by curbing the verbosity and dilatoriness with which lawyers often draw out proceedings to inordinate length.[26]

Judicial review

Lower state courts confine themselves to the function for which all courts exist primarily, that is, deciding cases. Like higher national courts, however, state supreme courts, in addition, look into the constitutionality of laws and executive actions, refusing to enforce any found contrary to a national or state constitutional provision. In ten states, "advisory opinions" on constitutional questions will be given in advance to the governor if requested, and in seven of these to the legislature also.[27] But elsewhere, judgment on such questions will be rendered only in deciding actual cases. The power of judicial review has been exercised almost from the beginning of the nation's history, but with increasing frequency in later decades (especially since about 1890), and for reasons closely associated with the overloading of state constitutions in this last half-century with subject matter, and with detailed specifications, which ought to have been left to legislative discretion. A great deal of criticism has been stirred, particularly by the frequency with which statutes, or portions thereof, are invalidated (sometimes by narrow margins of four to three or three to two) on the ground of taking property or denying liberty without due process of law. Dislike of such control over public policy in virtual defiance of the people's elected representatives in the legislative branch has encouraged

---

[25] C. N. Callender, *The Selection of Jurors* (Philadelphia, 1924); J. A. C. Grant, "Methods of Jury Selection," *Amer. Polit. Sci. Rev.,* XXIV, 117-133 (Feb., 1930).

[26] I. Stalmaster, *What Price Jury Trials?* (Boston, 1931); R. S. Sutcliffe, *Impressions of an Average Juryman* (Cleveland, 1932); A. S. Osborne, *The Mind of the Juror* (Albany, N. Y., 1937). For varied viewpoints, see J. E. Johnsen [comp.], *The Jury System* (New York, 1928). See also C. Boh, "The Jury System in America," *Annals of the American Academy of Political and Social Science* (May, 1953), for a sympathetic view of the jury system.

[27] In Massachusetts, Maine, New Hampshire, Rhode Island, and Colorado, the constitution requires such opinions to be given to the governor or to the legislature; in Florida and South Dakota, to the governor only. In Alabama, statute requires like assistance to either governor or legislature, in Delaware to the governor only; while in North Carolina it is extended to both simply as a matter of usage. Such opinions, regarded as mere personal expressions by the justices individually, do not bind the court if and when later confronted with the same questions in deciding cases. Recent studies include O. P. Field, "The Advisory Opinion—An Analysis," *Ind. Law. Jour.,* XXIV, 203-230 (Winter, 1949), surveying the experience of five states; and P. W. Edsall, "The Advisory Opinion in North Carolina." *N. C. Law Rev.,* XXVII, 297-344 (Apr., 1949).

(a) a dozen states to adopt the popular initiative for constitutional amendments as a means of circumventing obstructive courts; (b) three states (Ohio, North Dakota, and Nebraska) to change their constitutions so as to require something more than a bare majority for declaring a law null and void; and (c) some people even to propose that due-process clauses be deleted from state constitutions, leaving all protection of private rights, when involving due process, to the national courts. Unless expunged by the legislature, a measure judicially invalidated remains, of course, on the statute books; it simply can no longer be invoked against anyone violating it.[28]

PREVENTIVE JUSTICE

For a long time our state judicial establishments largely confined their activities to the redress of wrongs already committed, and agencies of "preventive justice" remained almost entirely undeveloped. Only within very narrow limits was it possible to clear up in advance of hostile litigation any doubt as to the legal status of persons, the title to property, or the meaning of a contract. In the last three or four decades, however, the view has gained favor that "a system of law that will not prevent the doing of a wrong, but only affords redress after the wrong is committed, is not a complete system, and is inadequate to the present needs of society; that whenever a person's legal rights are so uncertain as to cause him potential loss or disturbance, the state ought to provide instrumentalities of preventive relief to remove the uncertainty before a loss or injury has been sustained." And in pursuance of these considerations, more than 40 states, beginning with New Jersey in 1915, have authorized their courts, on proper application, to define or declare disputed rights and duties before any suit involving them has been fought through the courts. In 1934, too, the national courts were authorized to render similar "declaratory judgments." [29]

Declaratory judgments

The courts always have favored the settlement of legal disputes by arbitration, or compromise, after a trial has commenced; and almost contemporaneously with the adoption of declaratory-judgment laws, legislation appeared authorizing less formal, time-consuming, and expensive methods of adjusting legal disputes than prevail in ordinary judicial proceedings. Small-claims courts have become common, especially in cities; and special courts of conciliation and arbitration have been set up, or existing courts have been empowered to adopt rules providing for such procedures. Conciliation takes place when parties to a dispute reach a settlement through the mediation of a third party called a conciliator. An agreement of the kind, however, is not

Conciliation and arbitration

---

[28] Cf. O. P. Field, *Judicial Review of Legislation in Ten Selected States* (Bloomington, Ind., 1943).

[29] *Harvard Law Rev.*, LXII, 787-885 (Mar., 1949), "Developments in the Law of Declaratory Judgments, 1941-1949." The principal work on the subject is that of E. M. Borchard, cited at the end of this chapter.

legally enforceable in the courts if either party fails to abide by it. In arbitration proceedings, on the other hand, the parties submit their controversy to a third party, called the arbitrator, and agree in advance to be bound by his decision; and his award is enforceable by either side like the judgment of a regular court. Not the least among merits of these newer judicial agencies and practices is the way in which they tend to encourage a spirit of good-will between parties to a dispute, thereby lessening or averting the animosity and rancor usually attending hostile litigation.

References

F. R. Aumann, *The Changing American Legal System* (Columbus, O., 1940).

W. E. Hannan and M. B. Csontos, *State Court Systems* (Chicago, 1940).

J. Frank, *Courts on Trial: Myth and Reality in American Justice* (Princeton, N.J., 1949).

H. T. Lummus, *The Trial Judge* (Chicago, 1937).

G. Warren, *Traffic Courts* (Boston, 1942).

Convention Committee, "New Judicial System Adopted in New Jersey," *Jour. Amer. Judic. Soc.,* 138-144 (Feb., 1948).

Report of the Commission on the Administration of Justice in New York State (Albany, N.Y., 1934).

E. Haynes, *The Selection and Tenure of Judges* (Nat. Conf. of Judic. Councils, 1944).

C. N. Callender, *American Courts—Their Organization and Procedure* (New York, 1927).

E. R. Sunderland, "Study of Justices of the Peace and Other Minor Courts," in *Fifteenth Annual Report,* Judicial Council of Michigan (1946).

C. S. Davis, *Judicial Selection in West Virginia* (Morgantown, W. Va., 1959).

R. Pound, *Organization of Courts* (Boston, 1940).

———, *Criminal Justice in America* (Cambridge, Mass., 1945).

E. M. Martin, *The Role of the Bar in Electing the Bench in Chicago* (Chicago, 1936).

R. Moley, *Politics and Criminal Prosecution* (New York, 1929).

———, *Our Criminal Courts* (New York, 1930).

———, *Tribunes of the People* (New Haven, Conn., 1932).

A. T. Vanderbilt, *Minimum Standards of Judicial Administration* (New York, 1949).

————, *Judges and Jurors: Their Functions, Qualifications and Selection* (Boston, 1956).

S. D. Elliott, *Improving Our Courts: Collected Essays on Judicial Administration* (New York, 1960).

L. Mayers, *The American Legal System* (New York, 1955).

J. W. Hurst, *The Growth of American Law: The Law Makers* (Boston, 1950).

L. B. Orfield, *Criminal Procedure from Arrest to Appeal* (New York, 1947).

A. Lepawsky, *The Judicial System of Metropolitan Chicago* (Chicago, 1932).

R. H. Smith, *Justice and the Poor* (3rd ed., New York, 1934).

"Legal Service Offices for Persons of Moderate Means," *Jour. Amer. Judic. Soc.,* XXXI, 37-47 (Aug., 1947).

E. M. Borchard, *Declaratory Judgments* (2nd ed., Cleveland, 1941).

Council of State Governments, *The Book of the States* (Chicago). Section on "Judicial Systems and Legal Procedures" in successive issues.

————, *State Court Systems* (Chicago, 1962).

————, *Courts of Last Resort in the Forty-eight States* (Chicago, 1950).

————, *Trial Courts of General Jurisdiction in the Forty-eight States* (Chicago, 1951).

K. N. Vines, "Courts as Political and Governmental Agencies," in H. Jacob and K. Vines, *Politics in the American States—A Comparative Analysis* (Boston, 1965), Chap. 7.

H. Jacob, *Justice in America* (Boston, 1965).

S. Schulman, *Toward Judicial Reform in Pennsylvania* (Philadelphia, 1962).

Part IV

LOCAL GOVERNMENT AND

ADMINISTRATION

★ 32 ★

Local Government Pattern
and Legal Basis

FROM SEVENTEENTH-CENTURY ENGLAND early Americans inherited a strong liking for managing their own affairs. With the ideas of limited government and popular sovereignty and the practice of representative government, the English tradition of local self-government was transplanted to America. The institutions and offices that embodied this tradition—the county, the town, the borough, the coroner, the sheriff, and others—remain with us to this day. Though adapted somewhat to the needs of the new environment and later to the growth and industrialization of the country, they have shown remarkable resistance to change. More so than any other part of our governmental system. There are many reasons for this endurance. Foremost among these is the importance of the functions they perform. Next our theories of local government have strengthened them. Lastly is the importance to the political parties of their organizations in the local units.

By tradition, local governments have responsibility for many of the basic functions of government. They have the primary responsibility for protecting buildings from fire and persons and property from robbery, theft, and criminal violence. In urban areas, the necessity for maintaining a pure water supply and a sanitary environment puts a large burden for public health protection on the local units. In a democratic society, education is ranked with protection as a government duty; and here again, the local units have the basic responsibility.[1]

Impor-tance of local government

Granted that the functions of local government are important, why are they administered locally? Tradition has always been an important element in the creation of local units. The English colonists brought with them a devotion to local autonomy which has continued throughout our history. The image of the New England town meeting as the archetype of "true" democracy is firmly fixed in American political philosophy. It is commonly called "grass roots"

Theories of local self-government

[1] This importance can be expressed in other ways too. For instance, in 1962, 53.2 per cent of all public employees worked for local governments. Of these 27.8 percent worked for school districts. The balance of public employment was divided 17.5 percent for the states and 29.3 percent for the national government. From the *Census of Governments 1962, Compendium of Public Employment* (Washington, 1963).

849

democracy. It means both that the existence of many small units of government gives people a chance to practice democracy at the grass roots or home
level where the issues are easily understood and the necessary knowledge upon
which to base judgments is available and that the closer a political unit can
approximate the conditions of the New England town with its town meeting,
the purer the democracy will be that is practiced. Essentially, government in
small units is personal government. The individual can identify himself more
easily with this kind of government, even when it no longer represents a social
community whose members have common interests. Grass roots democracy
holds a special attractiveness for the suburbanite, partly, because it provides
a rationale for his "separateness" from the city, but partly also because the
suburban environment recalls the simpler patterns of life that were the base
of the theory.[2]

*Local
political
organi-
zation*

Our local governments are training grounds for party leaders. The roots
of party organization are here. In the county government, especially, is usually
found the base of the state organization. In these units are the strongholds of
Jackson's legacy—the spoils system, the amateur in public office, many elected
officials, and short terms of office. Local governments, therefore, are of paramount importance to the political parties.

TYPES AND NUMBERS OF LOCAL GOVERNMENTS

*Rural
forms*

The general picture of local government in rural America is: towns in
New England; counties in every state except Rhode Island, Connecticut, and
Alaska; and, townships in sixteen states in a broad northern belt from New
York westward to the Great Plains. In colonial New England the town was
dominant and the county played a minor role. This is true today. In the old
South, the county was dominant and no towns or townships existed.[3] Because

[2] S. Elkins and E. McKitrick in "A Meaning for Turner's Frontier" suggest that many
suburban communities, being new, resemble the conditions of an earlier time. This is an
idea with interesting implications. *Pol. Sci. Quarterly,* LXIX, 321-353 and 565-602 (Sept.
and Dec., 1954).

For a critique of "grass roots" democracy as the ideal local government see R. C.
Wood, "Metropolitan Government, 1975: An Extrapolation of Trends," *Am. Pol. Sci.
Rev.,* LII, 108-122 (Mar., 1958).

For the difficulties faced by local units in trying to govern themselves with their own
resources see W. Anderson, *The Nation and the States, Rivals or Partners?* (Minneapolis,
1955), Chap. IX.

[3] These terms are used interchangeably. In New York and Wisconsin the term *town*
is used as in New England, but this is of historical significance only. Elsewhere the term
township is used. The New England town was a self-contained area with a population
bound together by community tradition and as such not wholly adaptable to broad regions
with more scattered populations. In the meantime, the township was introduced. The
Northwest Ordinance introduced a scheme of "survey" townships, each six miles square,
in order to pave the way for the disposal of public lands recently ceded to the United
States. This plan was later extended geographically. These townships were not governments but there arose "civil" townships, often covering the same area, that were and still
are such units. Today towns and townships have enough common features to be treated
together.

westward migration was largely along parallels of latitude, we find today that
the county system is used throughout the South and West. There are no towns
or townships south of the Mason-Dixon Line and few west of the Rockies.[4]
In Illinois, Nebraska, and Missouri, where two lines of migration met, there
are townships in some counties but not in all. In the Middle Atlantic states
a mixed system prevailed and this was carried westward also. Local government in these states in general follows the New England pattern of township
importance; however, the county tends to be dominant in border states such
as Ohio, Indiana, Kansas, and Missouri. As a rule, civil townships are created
and their boundaries may be changed by the board of supervisors or commissioners of the county in which they are situated.[5]

Urban centers, both large and relatively small, are set apart and in-   *Urban*
forms

GOVERNMENTAL COMPLEXITY

TAXING AND CHARGING JURISDICTIONS
IN A TYPICAL METROPOLITAN AREA

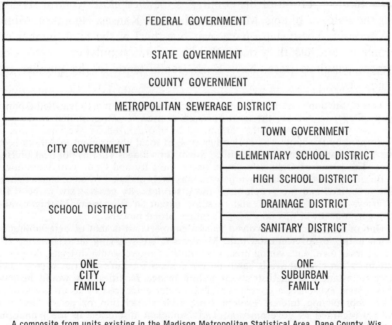

A composite from units existing in the Madison Metropolitan Statistical Area, Dane County, Wis.

Total local units in the urbanized area — 129
Total local units in the county — 212
County population in 1960 — 222,095

[4] Washington has two counties with township governments.

[5] On the earlier development of local government throughout the country see K. H.
Porter, *County and Township Government in the United States* (New York, 1922)
Chaps. III-IV; J. A. Fairlie and C. M. Kneier, *County Government and Administration*
(New York, 1930), Chaps. I-III.

corporated as cities with their own governments. Less populous places, desiring some of the powers and services of cities, may be similarly incorporated as villages or boroughs.[6] Some boroughs and villages are larger than some cities, but in general the opposite is the case. These units are termed "municipalities" because they are incorporated. Any unit as it increases in population may progress from a town or township to a village or city by using procedures prescribed by the state in which it lies.[7]

Other units

Numerous artificially constructed areas, mostly small, and seldom coinciding geographically with any of the subdivisions thus far mentioned, have been erected into school, fire protection, sanitary, and other units called "special districts."

Numbers of local government units

The variety of local governmental units so far described has been the result of historical development. The same can be said for the large numbers of them. The number of units in any given region does not often correspond to population. Until of late, no one—not even the Bureau of the Census—could have indicated the number for the country as a whole. Even now, all that one can say is that the figure is in the neighborhood of 91,000.[8] The most highly saturated portion of the country is the west north central section containing the states of Illinois, Michigan, Missouri, Kansas, Nebraska, Minnesota, and Wisconsin. These states have over one-third of the total number of local governments but less than one-fifth of the total population (1960 Census). The most populous state, New York, ranks tenth in the number of local governments.

[6] This distinction is nominal. In some states a small urban area is called a borough, in others a village. In Alaska, the term *borough* is used for an area that is similar to the county elsewhere. It may be either organized or unorganized. In the latter case, services are performed by the state. The only other type of local government in Alaska is the city. Hawaii, on the other hand, has no cities, towns, or villages (*i.e.* as political units)—only counties. The island of Oahu is a single unit—the City and County of Honolulu.

[7] But it does not have to. Town powers may be broadened by state legislation as areas become more urbanized and the people need more services. By general law in New England, New Jersey, and Pennsylvania, and to some extent in Wisconsin, Michigan, and New York, towns and townships may assume rather broad powers.

[8] One of the difficulties involved in any enumeration is that of determining what is, and what is not, a governmental unit. Manifestly, areas having no governmental organization of their own, e.g., voting precincts, wards, Congressional districts, do not qualify. The enumeration cited above is based on the Census Bureau's criteria: a geographic area (in special instances as in districts providing bridge facilities this would be modified) that has a legal existence; a governmental character evidenced by its ability to levy taxes or issue debt paying interest exempt from federal taxation or performing a service commonly regarded as governmental; and "sufficient discretion in the management of its own affairs" to distinguish it as separate from any other unit.

The first complete enumeration and analysis of American governmental units appeared in W. Anderson, *The Units of Government in the United States* (Chicago, 1934) reprinted with new appendices in 1945 and 1949. The Census Bureau now makes periodical inventories of units, the most recent being that of 1962 cited in the table. See also the annual editions of *The Municipal Year Book,* published by the International City Managers' Assoc. (Chicago), which reports the findings of regular and special counts by the Bureau of the Census and other national government agencies.

LOCAL GOVERNMENTAL UNITS IN THE
UNITED STATES
1962

Counties	3,043
Municipalities	17,997
Townships	17,144
School Districts	34,678
Special Districts	18,323
Total	91,186

SOURCE: U. S. Bureau of the Census, *Census of Governments—1962* (Washington, 1963), Vol. I, p. 1.

LOCAL GOVERNMENT REFORM

Fixed in a rural environment and before the development of rapid transportation, the local government pattern is one of too many and too small units for the management of local affairs. Our two newest states have entered the union with a distinct advantage over the older ones in this regard. Determined to profit from the experience in the older states, Alaska expressed its philosophy of local government in its constitution—namely, "to provide for maximum local government with a minimum of local government units, and to prevent duplication of tax levying jurisdictions" (Art. X, Sec. 1). In Hawaii, the legislature may create subdivisions in addition to the county but has not done so.[9] Elsewhere, however, people live under several layers of government, overlapping in intricate patterns.

General need

The first effect of this is that the average voter is confused and the result is all too often a lessening of democratic control of the political process rather than the better control the advocates of grass roots democracy hope for. In addition, many citizens reside and work under different jurisdictions. When this is the case, they are disfranchised from having a voice in decisions that are taken by the municipality where they work. Only indirectly can they influence these. The second effect is an inefficient duplication of activities. The American people have shown a willingness to pay for this inefficiency, considering other less mundane goals more worthy. However, the recent spectacular population growth has aggravated the situation so acutely in urban areas that many concerned citizens have joined students of the subject in urging disentanglement and simplification. The most important aspect of this phenomenon is the shift of the urban population from the more crowded central cities to the less crowded suburbs and beyond to rural areas. This has brought problems to areas ill-equipped governmentally to handle them. Para-

[9] For the evolution of the Hawaiian system, see N. Meller, "Centralization in Hawaii: Retrospect and Prospect," *Am. Pol. Sci. Rev.*, LII, 98-107 (Mar., 1958).

doxically, the first response of the people affected has been to *increase* the numbers of local units. Special districts have been created to provide urban services and townships or parts of them have incorporated for the same reason.[10]

*Suburbani-
zation
in detail*   Cities in the United States have been growing at their peripheries for a century, but before 1920, the central cities grew more rapidly than the outlying parts. The reverse did not become a widespread pattern until after World War I though it was evident earlier in the older and more densely populated cities.[11] Since World War II, this trend has accelerated. The following figures show the trend:

	Percent of Increase	
	1940-1950	*1950-1960*
U. S. TOTAL	14.5	19.
Metropolitan Areas [12]—		
total	22.	26.4
Central Cities	13.9	10.6
Outlying parts	35.6	49.

From 1940 to 1950, the oldest and largest central cities increased but slightly in population and from 1950 to 1960, many of them actually declined.[13] The bald fact seems to be that given the means and the opportunity people no

[10] The number of special districts increased from 12,340 in 1952 to 18,323 in 1962 and the number of new municipal incorporations increased by 1,100 in the same period. *Census of Governments, 1962,* Vol. 1, No. 1, Bureau of the Census (Washington, 1963).

[11] L. F. Schnore, "Metropolitan Growth and Decentralization," *The Amer. Journal of Sociology,* LXIII, 171-180 (Sept., 1957).

[12] These are the 212 Standard Metropolitan Statistical Areas. As defined by the Bureau of the Census, an SMSA is a "county or group of contiguous counties which contains at least one city of 50,000 inhabitants or more or 'twin cities' with a combined population of at least 50,000. In addition to the county or counties containing such a city or cities, contiguous counties are included in an SMSA if, according to certain criteria, they are essentially metropolitan in character and are socially and economically integrated with the central city." The 'certain criteria' include incorporated contiguous places with populations of 2,500 or more and areas with a certain density of population. Metropolitan character is also shown by whether the county is the residence or place of work for concentrations of nonagricultural workers. In New England, the city or town is used as the base reporting area instead of the county. Whenever metropolitan areas are mentioned hereafter in the text, it will be these Census areas that are being referred to.

Figures on population for 1940-1950 are from *The Municipal Year Book, 1959, op. cit.,* 37; and for 1950-1960 from U. S. Bureau of the Census, *Statistical Abstract of the United States,* 1961, 14 (Washington, 1961).

[13] Of the ten largest cities only Los Angeles and Houston, Texas, increased in population during the '50's. Boston fell from 10th place to 13th and Pittsburgh from 12th to 16th. Thirty-five cities, most of them in the east, lost population. Cities in metropolitan complexes lost population along with their larger neighbors; for instance, Camden followed Philadelphia's decline and Newark and Jersey City suffered losses similar to New York City's.

longer find the city attractive as a place in which to live. The increased use of the private automobile, postwar prosperity, and national government inducements to home ownership have combined with other factors to produce a suburban spread over the landscape.[14]

In 1962, there were 18,442 local governments in the 212 Standard Metropolitan Statistical Areas of that year. Most of them were incorporated municipalities, special districts, and school districts. The surprising number of townships reflects the suburban spread.[15] The leaders of most metropolitan areas are conscious of the disparity between modern urban living and this inherited governmental pattern that is expected to facilitate it. In almost every recent year a study of local problems has been started in some metropolitan area. The recommendations proposed in these studies are many and various but the difficulties and problems uncovered are markedly alike. The common problems reported are that: the multiplicity of governments is a serious impediment to the administration of government services; many units are so small and financial resources vary so widely that there is an inadequacy or even absence of certain services. The main problem fields are: *(the right margin note: Problems posed by the multiplicity of units in metropolitan areas)*

(1) *Transportation.* Traffic congestion and frustration is ubiquitous. An integrated system of local streets, major arterials, and mass transit is necessary for the efficient movement of people and goods. Perhaps this is an ideal impossible to achieve in the larger urban areas, but it is clear that the problem cannot even be attacked without an area-wide approach.

(2) *Disposal of sanitary and industrial wastes, storm water drainage, and provision for a water supply.* Adequate and equitable provision for these is virtually impossible or excessively costly on an individual basis. The result of individual effort in too many cases is water pollution, flooding of streets and basements, and mutual recrimination.

(3) *Land use planning.* Competition among units for industrial, business, and "desirable" residential development in order to bolster local finances widens the gap between units in their relative ability to provide services. Typically, too, a unit that secures a new industry does not consider the effect of this on the rest of the area—the changed traffic pattern and the new residents who find homes in other places with their needs for schools and other governmental services. In addition, it is difficult for small governments to obtain or set aside the large areas needed for parks and playing fields by an urban population.[16]

All of these problems are particularly troublesome in rural areas that are

[14] A most readable account is *The Exploding Metropolis* by the Editors of *Fortune Magazine* (New York, 1958).

[15] There were in these 212 metropolitan areas 310 counties, 4,142 municipalities, 2,575 townships, 6,004 school districts and 5,411 special districts.

[16] A succinct summation of governmental inadequacy in metropolitan areas is given by L. Gulick in W. Owen, *Cities in the Motor Age*, 115-117 (New York, 1959). See also Commission on Intergovernmental Relations, *Report*, 47-55 (Washington, 1955).

in the process of becoming urbanized. In some instances, the needed services and controls are not provided to the detriment of other areas.[17] Since the solutions proposed hinge on the powers and finances of the individual governments, discussion of them will be postponed until a later chapter.

LEGAL BASIS OF COUNTIES AND MUNICIPALITIES

Local units as public corporations   All units of local government are public corporations, created by, or under authority of, state law to provide services more appropriately furnished in this way than through private effort. As such, they have continuous existence, regardless of population changes, as long as the state does not revoke them; as such, also, they enjoy all customary corporate rights, such as those of suing and being sued, making contracts, acquiring, holding, and disposing of property, and exercising every power conferred. All, however, are not of quite the same nature and function. One category, known as municipal corporations proper, includes those at least presumed to have been created primarily in response to local initiative based on desire for local management of affairs. Cities, villages, boroughs, and incorporated towns are of this sort. A second category, termed quasi-municipal corporations, consists rather of units created by the state (or the county as agent of the state) on its own initiative, regardless of local opinion, and for carrying on locally state-wide activities such as enforcement of law, assessment and collection of taxes, and educational and public health services. Counties, towns, townships, school districts, and numerous other kinds of special districts are here included. Legally, the distinction is significant; practically, it is not.[18] Units of both types serve at the same time as organs of self-government and as areas for state administration. Many townships, counties, and special districts have also been created because the people in the area wished or asked for them. The distinction is thus one of *primary* purpose only, but it assumes some importance when broad grants of power are contemplated for counties and special districts to enable them to provide more urban-type services.

[17] The difficulties encountered when a county tried to remedy such a deficiency were reported by the Public Administration Service in its study of the Miami metropolitan area. The county (Dade) had tried to give urban services to the unincorporated area within the county but with each new incorporation this area was reduced though its nominal jurisdiction and its ability to levy taxes continued to encompass the whole area. See *The Government of Metropolitan Miami,* Public Administration Service (Chicago, 1954).

[18] For example, in determining whether a unit is liable for personal or property damage arising from acts performed by its officers or employees. The general principle is that quasi-corporations share the immunity of the state itself unless made responsible by statute; while corporations proper are liable for acts of persons representing them in their *corporate* capacity, *i.e.,* as units of local government, but not for those performed on behalf of the state at large (again unless made so by statute). Though regarded as quasi-corporations, New England towns are held liable. It must be added that governmental immunity from suit for the torts of its employees is everywhere under attack and has been abandoned or greatly restricted in several states, *e.g.* New York, Wisconsin, Washington, Arizona, Alaska, Hawaii, Tennessee.

From the fact that all local-government units are created by, or on authority of, the state in which they are situated, and by it are endowed, expressly or by fair implication, with whatever functions and powers they possess, it follows that the relation between the state and its subdivisions is totally different from that existing, in the reverse direction, between the state and the United States. In the latter case, the state is not a division existing for the use and convenience of the national government; on the contrary, it is, within limits, a separate and independent area of government, in several respects on a footing of equality with the nation itself. Whether counties, towns, townships, or districts, created primarily for state purposes, or cities, villages, or boroughs, organized primarily to meet the demand for local control of local affairs, local units exist by no original or inherent right and have no reserved or residual powers. On the contrary, all (at least broadly) are instrumentalities of the state, employed by it in the enforcement of its laws, the collection of its revenues, and the performance of others of its functions. In short, the United States is organized on a federal basis, but the governmental system of each state is formally speaking unitary. *Local units as state instrumentalities*

Every city has as its fundamental law a charter (its own separately, or one shared with other cities through the medium of a code) establishing its boundaries, defining its powers, outlining its system of government, prescribing the method of electing its council and choosing its mayor and other officials, assigning to some or all such officials their respective duties, and fixing with varying degrees of precision the relations of officials with one another. City charters (or at any rate the right to frame them) come from the legislature; and since charters or charter laws differ in no essential respect from other acts of the legislature, that body has authority to grant, withhold, suspend, alter, or revoke them at will, even against the expressed wishes of the people of any city concerned. In practice, such legal autocracy is tempered by considerations of political expediency, by moral inhibitions where charters have been made locally under express legislative grant of authority, and of course by such restrictions upon state legislative power as may be found in the national or the state constitution. *Legal position of the city— the charter*

Counties are created and their boundaries fixed by act of the legislature, with, however, constitutional provisions protecting them in most states against extinction or loss of territory unless assented to by the voters concerned. Once established, they become quasi-corporations. As such, they generally have less broad powers to deal with matters of local concern and have more duties to fulfill in matters of state-wide concern. Their forms of organization, the officers they shall have, and the powers they may exercise are prescribed by state laws and constitutions. Whereas, most provisions for the organization and powers of municipalities are found in the statutes, constitutional provisions relating to county government are more numerous. For this reason, the framework of county government is more rigid than that under which municipalities operate. *Legal position of the county*

State methods of prescribing for local governments:

1. Special laws

Some state legislatures grant charters and pass laws governing counties and municipalities by special act (as well as by general law). This is the practice in New England (except Massachusetts) and in parts of the South. Under this system, there may be as many varieties of city and of county government as there are cities and counties. Varying local conditions can be taken into account and change is sometimes more easily accomplished when only one unit is involved; but, since the system also lends itself to flagrant abuse, it came into disrepute during the latter nineteenth century—a time when local and state governments were notably corrupt. The constitutions of the rest of the states were changed to prohibit such special legislation. General laws only can be enacted in these states.

2. General laws and classification systems

General laws limit factious and arbitrary interference in local affairs on the part of the state legislature but the local governmental framework suffers from too much uniformity. The difficulty of prescribing for all cities or all counties the same powers, duties, and forms of organization, regardless of differences in size, character, or need is obvious. The result is a compromise —the classification system. The most popular and the most practicable method is to classify by population.[19] Thus we find that cities of over 25,000 people and less than 50,000 will have a different set of rights and duties or a different form of government than cities of more than 50,000. The usual number of classes is four or five. Classification *systems* are more commonly created for cities than for counties. Though several states have set up four or five classes of county government, two is more common—one for the largest county, if it contains a metropolis, and one for the rest of the state's counties.[20] Like most compromises, the plan has not been very satisfactory for cities. As they grow in population, they may be forced to change their form of government or assume burdens against their will. Two other and newer methods of prescribing for local governments are receiving more attention today—the home rule and the optional charter plans.

3. Home rule charters

All the above methods of providing the legal framework within which local governments operate are vulnerable from the standpoint of local initiative

---

[19] And the one most apt to be sustained by the courts. Classification done by statute, instead of by constitutional change is, of course, subject to judicial review. The main legal question is whether the classification is special legislation in disguise. In this regard, the courts have been surprisingly tolerant. For instance, California succeeded in putting each of its counties in a different classification for purposes of salary schedules. J. C. Bollens and S. Scott, *Local Government in California,* 71 (Berkeley, 1951). Given in C. F. Snyder, *Local Government in Rural Areas,* 74 (New York, 1957).

[20] For instance in Wisconsin: the state constitution prescribes one form of county government that is modified by law for Milwaukee county. However, in prescribing *powers* (as distinguished from *form*) of government for counties, the Wisconsin legislature has used elaborate classifications, often with confusing results. In 1957 there were 188 different sections of the statutes that classified counties in some way, setting up 46 differing categories. Bureau of Government, University of Wisconsin, *County Government and the Problems of Urban Expansion,* Report to the Wisconsin County Boards Assoc. (Madison, Mar. 2, 1959), 48.

and local desires for self-determination and control of their own governmental destinies. The fundamental idea of home rule is that the people directly affected by their local government should have the right to draft their own charter and embody therein whatever plan of government they prefer, as well as to exercise under it all powers not inconsistent with the constitution and laws of the state and nation. The home rule method of charter drafting has been constitutionally authorized for cities in half the states and in eight additional ones the legislature has granted broad authority to some or all cities to amend their charters or adopt new ones.[21] More than 600 cities and villages are now operating under home rule charters including most of the thirty largest ones. County home rule is currently widely discussed for urban counties. Though the number of counties with home rule is small, the movement is spreading.[22] The chief difficulty with framing county home rule charters is the frequent provision that separate majorities be obtained—one in the city and one in the rest of the county—to ratify them. More proposals have thus been defeated than have been adopted.[23]

The home rule plan has a number of manifest merits. First, it enables the people of a city or county to have whatever form of government they consider best adapted to their needs and to formulate it locally rather than have it handed down to them by the legislature. In determining, too, what is best adapted, they are free to experiment and thus to assist local governments everywhere. Secondly, home rule stimulates greater interest of citizens in

Home rule appraised

---

[21] Ordinarily the home rule provision is applicable only to cities of specified population. In a few states, the constitutional grant is not self-executing but must await subsequent action by the legislature; which has by now been given in every instance, though sometimes for one city only (for instance, in Pennsylvania, it has only been extended to Philadelphia). Sometimes, even where the grant is self-executing, only one city in the state will take advantage of it or succeed in adopting a charter. For instance, in Maryland, only Baltimore actually has home rule.

In other states, e.g., Ohio, the authority conferred has been considerably restricted by judicial interpretation. For the Ohio situation, see H. Walker, "Let Cities Manage Themselves," Nat. Mun. Rev., XXXVI, 625-630 (Dec., 1947).

There are different modes for framing home rule charters, but as a rule the voters elect a sizable board of freeholders, or a charter commission, which drafts the instrument and submits it for popular ratification. In nearly all instances, the charter must receive final enactment at the hands of the legislature, but this is likely to be merely a matter of form. Amendments are usually initiated by petition and made effective simply by popular ratification.

[22] Starting with California in 1911, nine states have now authorized county home rule. The number of home rule counties is 22, ten of which are in California. The others are Montgomery County, Maryland (near the Washington, metropolitan area and indeed part of it), 1948; Baltimore County, Maryland, 1956; St. Louis County, Missouri, 1951; Dade County (Miami), Florida, 1957; Erie County (Buffalo), New York, 1959; Anne Arundel and Wicomico, Maryland (1964), and Hood River, Oregon (1964).

[23] Like counties, towns do not ordinarily possess charters—home rule or other kinds. A case study of an urban town's struggles to obtain a charter may be found in: C. E. Vose and K. E. Carpenter, "Municipal Charters in Maine: The Case of Brunswick," Bowdoin College Bulletin, No. 331 (Dec., 1958).

their own local government. When the charter is being framed and adopted local citizen interest and participation in governmental affairs reaches a peak. Finally, the plan would seem to benefit the state legislature by relieving it of the necessity for considering a multitude of local questions that it is poorly prepared to answer intelligently, even if it had unlimited time which it doesn't. Actually, this has not happened to anything like the degree anticipated by its sponsors. No system, however, completely frees the municipality or county from state domination. Locally-made charters are subject to the general state laws and state laws take precedence over local ordinances in most states. This is as it should be. A city or county is part of the state and is inextricably interlocked with the state in its interests and responsibilities. Even if the legislature is disposed to leave a city entirely free to deal with purely local matters as it desires,[24] there is no clear line of demarcation today between things that are wholly local and those that, while perhaps primarily local, transcend city boundaries and concern the people of other portions of the state. As a method, therefore, for carving out a sphere of local autonomy for cities into which no higher level of government ought to intrude, home rule has lost much of its pristine attractiveness.[25] Our society has grown too interdependent. However, as a method for reforming county government and equipping it to meet the needs of an urban population where this is necessary and for distinguishing these urban counties from the vast majority of rural ones, home rule is extremely useful.

4. Optional charters and permissive legislation

In recent years, an alternative method for providing local charters has been growing in popularity. This is the optional charter system. Over half the states now employ it for cities, including 15 home rule states, and several states provide alternative forms of county government. Noteworthy among the latter are New York, Virginia, North Carolina and North Dakota.[26] The optional charter system was designed to avoid both the disadvantages of uniform local government codes and the special law system. Like classification it permits variety within a standard framework but unlike the classification system it is not used to define local powers and responsibilities. Optional charters prescribe alternative *forms* of local government only. In effect, this system introduces a sort of *à la carte* charter service by incorporating into the general law of the state several standard types of charter providing for different forms of government—for cities the commission form, the council-manager plan, and sundry varieties of the mayor-council type; for counties alternative forms that may be used to replace the existing one. The county options all have

[24] Some states have given cities a good deal of local autonomy; *e.g.,* Minnesota, California, Michigan, Wisconsin, and Texas.

[25] For appraisals, see L. S. Lyon (ed.), *Modernizing City Government: A Report of the Chicago Home Rule Commission* (Univ. of Chicago Press, 1954) and H. Walker, *op cit.*

[26] Michigan's new constitution of 1964 provides a charter system for counties but it is not self-executive and appropriate legislation has not as yet been passed.

features of reform; for instance, they usually include provisions that would consolidate offices or provide for a county executive, manager, or administrator. Each local unit can select for itself a form of government from the menu thus provided.

Permissive legislation is the same sort of menu service. Grants of authority to local units or to classes of them to perform certain functions if and when they so desire are given by the state. The desires of the local units for self-determination are more or less satisfied and questions of what is and what is not solely a matter of local concern are avoided. For these reasons, among others, permissive legislation combined with the optional charter system has worked as well as, if not better than, formal home rule.

The main object of all of these different plans of charter-framing, except the special-charter system, is to reduce state interference with local autonomy. While this effort has been pursued energetically and with some success, a contrary trend of almost irresistible force has been taking place: the development of administrative supervision over certain local activities by state officers or boards. Thus in New York, Massachusetts, and Ohio, the state civil service board is authorized to exercise direct supervision over the work of local civil service commissions. In order to check local abuses, several states have placed supervision of the enforcement of their election laws in the hands of a state official or board. Similarly, state boards of health or education, state finance departments or commissions, and state public utilities or public service commissions have, in a number of states, taken over in recent years many of the functions previously performed by the state legislature. A number of states go so far as to provide for state auditing of local accounts, and require the adoption of a uniform system of bookkeeping and submission of regular financial reports in a specified form to the state auditor or some other state authority. Whenever, also, a public service problem transcends the boundaries of several adjacent municipalities, there is a tendency to invoke state administrative control. Under circumstances of this kind one is likely to find a state-established park, sewerage, or police board such as now exercise authority throughout the metropolitan district of Boston. As a rule, state administrative supervision has proved more beneficial to local units directly affected than has legislative supervision.[27] With a view, indeed, to unifying and harmonizing such supervision it has been advocated that every state create an agency concerned only with local affairs—as did Pennsylvania in 1919, when a state bureau of municipalities was set up. Small cities in particular, might be helped by such an agency.[28]

5. State administrative supervision

[27] The underrepresentation of the urban population in state legislatures has often resulted in discriminatory treatment of cities. This may be one reason why administrative supervision is more palatable than legislative to cities and probably why it is more common over cities than over counties.

[28] Council of State Governments, *Report of Committee on State-Local Relations,* 50 (Chicago, 1946).

References

For details on points discussed in this and in the following chapters, the student is referred to the following texts:

C. F. Snider, *American State and Local Government* (New York, 1950).

————, *Local Government in Rural America* (New York, 1957).

C. M. Kneier, *City Government in the United States* (3rd ed., New York, 1957).

C. R. Adrian, *Governing Urban America* (2nd ed., New York, 1961).

A. F. Macdonald, *American City Government and Administration* (6th ed., New York, 1956).

B. Baker, *Urban Government* (Princeton, N.J., 1957).

A. W. Bromage, *Introduction to Municipal Government and Administration* (2nd ed., New York, 1957).

J. C. Phillips, *Municipal Government and Administration in America* (New York, 1961).

S. A. MacCorkle, *American Municipal Government and Administration* (Boston, 1948).

H. Zink, *Government of Cities in the United States* (rev. ed., New York, 1948).

J. E. Pate, *Local Government and Administration* (New York, 1954).

M. J. Fisher and D. G. Bishop, *Municipal Government and Politics* (New York, 1950).

H. F. Alderfer, *American Local Government and Administration* (New York, 1956).

D. Lockard, *The Politics of State and Local Government* (New York, 1963).

D. R. Grant and H. C. Nixon, *State and Local Government in America* (Boston, 1963).

L. W. Lancaster, *Government in Rural America* (rev. ed., New York, 1952).

C. M. Kneier and G. Fox, *Readings in Municipal Government* (New York, 1953).

P. W. Wager (ed.), *County Government Across the Nation* (Chapel Hill, N.C., 1950).

E. F. Nolting and D. S. Arnold (eds.), *The Municipal Year Book* (Chicago). Published annually by the International City Managers' Association.

1. ADDITIONAL REFERENCES

R. L. Mott, *Home Rule for American Cities* (Chicago, 1949).

————, "Strengthening Home Rule," *Nat. Mun. Rev.*, XXXIX, 172-177 (April, 1950).

J. R. Kerstetter, "Municipal Home Rule," *The Municipal Year Book, 1956,* 256-266 (Chicago, 1957).

J. P. Keith, "County Home Rule for Michigan," *The County Officer,* XVII, 234-240, 245, 252 (Aug., 1952).

A. M. Schlesinger, *The Rise of the City, 1878-1898* (New York, 1933).

E. S. Griffith, *History of American City Government* (New York, 1933).

National Resources Planning Board, *Our Cities—Their Role in the National Economy* (Washington, 1937).

L. Mumford, *The Culture of Cities* (New York, 1938).

———, *The City in History* (New York, 1961).

A. H. Hawley, *Human Ecology: A Theory of Community Structure* (New York, 1950).

A. Maass (ed.), *Area and Power—a Theory of Local Government* (Glencoe, Ill., 1959).

M. M. Gaffney, "Urban Expansion—Will It Ever Stop," *U. S. Yearbook of Agriculture* (Washington, 1958).

C. Press, *When One-Third of a City Moves to the Suburbs* (E. Lansing, 1959). Pamph.

C. Bauer, "First Job: Control New City Sprawl," *Architectural Forum,* CV (Sept., 1956).

★ 33 ★

Rural Local Government

THE COUNTY

The county's compli- cated role

FROM PREVIOUS COMMENT on the nature and position of the county, one would infer that the role played by that local unit in our governmental system is difficult to evaluate; and so indeed it is. In the first place, it is not the same in all parts of the country. In New England, the county has no great importance except as a judicial unit; in the South and Far West, it controls justice, education, public health, public works, welfare, highways, and many other things; in the Middle and Midwestern states, it holds an intermediate position, frequently sharing many local functions with the township. In the second place, the county is at the same time an area for purposes of its own locally-controlled government and an area for carrying on state administrative and judicial activities. In fact, it is an area for the performance of a few functions promoted by the national government as well. In many instances the powers and duties entailed overlap and can be disentangled only by one willing to spend patient hours grubbing in the laws, records, and accounts stored up in the court house. Observing the steady transfer of functions from county to state in later years—to say nothing of the ever-advancing hand of the national government—some people have been puzzled about what the role of the county really is, and even have predicted that, whatever it is, it is doomed to extinction. Such observers fail to perceive that if the county as a self-governing unit is losing, it also is gaining—that, indeed, the number of functions passing under state or national control is counterbalanced by the number of new ones acquired as activities on all government levels continue to multiply. Judged, in fact, by the variety of functions performed (for the county itself or by it for state or nation), the number of employees on its payroll, and the amounts of money expended, the county is today, on the whole, a more vital part of our governmental system than at any time past.[1] County employees, other than those in education, have increased from 455,-000 in 1957 to 784,000 in 1962.

Confusing variety

To the governmental organization of counties, very little thought appears

[1] See M. H. Satterfield, "The Growth of County Functions Since 1930," *Jour. of Politics,* III, 76-88 (Feb., 1941); E. A. Mauck, "County Pattern for the Future," *Nat. Mun. Rev.,* XXXVI, 83-88 (Feb., 1947); and B. F. Hillenbrand, "Urban Counties in 1964," *The Municipal Year Book, 1965,* 68-71 (Chicago, 1965).

to have been given by constitutional conventions, state legislatures, or the general public—at any rate in comparison with the amount of attention bestowed on the government of states and cities. On this account and on account of their position as creatures of the state, the governments of counties not only differ from state to state, but sometimes even from county to county within the same state. City governments are of different types, for example, mayor-council, commission, council-manager; but, speaking broadly, all city governments of the same type are much alike, allowing only for differences of population and physical environment. County governments, however, classify in no such convenient fashion. There are officers, boards, and commissions, but no standardized nomenclature; some are elected by the people, others are appointed, still others are ex officio; each often occupies a little island of separate power, with hardly a trace of supervision or coordination; there are deputies, assistants, and employees—sometimes small armies of them. The overall impression gained by anyone seeking to penetrate the labyrinth is that of jumble. Amid the disorder, however, arises one agency—the county board —which comes closest to being a central governing body.

Although under different names, a county board is found in all states except Rhode Island and Connecticut where there is no county government at all. With a few exceptions (mainly in the South), it is everywhere elective, with the term two years in one-fourth and four years in nearly half, of the counties. Structurally, there are two main types. One is a board made large by allotting one or more representatives (locally elected as supervisors) to every town or township and to every city ward within the county; and such a board of supervisors (found chiefly in New York, New Jersey, Virginia, Michigan, and Wisconsin, and in parts of Kentucky, Tennessee, and Louisiana) often has 40 or 50 members—in Dane County (Madison), Wisconsin, 87 and in Wayne County (Detroit), Michigan, 97. In many counties the city has been under-represented in terms of population on the board in comparison with the out-lying towns and villages. These arrangements, attacked under the one-man, one-vote doctrine of the modern Supreme Court, were successfully overthrown in Wisconsin by the Wisconsin Supreme Court in 1965 and are under assault in Michigan and a few other states.[2] The other type is a board consisting rather of a few—commonly three, but sometimes five, seven, or more—"commissioners" elected (usually) by the voters of the county at large, and known as a board of commissioners. At least 70 percent of all counties have a board of this nature. Insofar as the board is a legislative body, the broader representation provided by a large membership seems appropriate; and in many localities the constituent areas of the county cling resolutely to it. In practice, however, the board's functions are far more administrative than legislative; and for purposes of administration the small board is clearly preferable. Large boards

County board 1. Structure

[2] W. S. Boyd (ed.). "One-Man, One-Vote for Local Units, Too," *National Civic Review,* Vol. LIV, No. 2 (Feb., 1965).

must do most of their work through more or less autonomous committees,[3] are often scenes of petty log-rolling among members owing primary allegiance to their townships, and are more expensive. If counties were adequately organized, with an integrated administrative branch and the board simply a policy-determining agency, a board of intermediate size probably would be desirable. Given the typical administrative organization, the large board is rarely or never advantageous.

2. Organization

In some states, the county judge or some other designated official serves as ex officio chairman of the board. In a few instances, for example, Cook County, Illinois, a chairman is elected by the people. In the great majority of cases, the position is filled by the board members themselves. In any event, with occasional exceptions, the incumbent has little if any more power (except for appointing committees) than his associates. As indicated, large boards work chiefly through committees, with general meetings occurring about once a month. With committees less practicable, small boards commonly meet more frequently.

3. Powers and functions

In powers and functions, as in other respects, the county board is purely a creature of the state. All powers conferred upon the county and not delegated by law to any other authority are regarded as belonging to the board. One important field of authority is finance. The board levies taxes for county purposes; equalizes the assessment of taxes among the different townships and cities in the county; borrows money; fixes the salaries or other compensation of minor county officials and employees; and appropriates money for various county purposes. Highways are also a major area of board concern and in recent years regulatory activities such as zoning have been undertaken. The county board also supervises elections and administers state, national, and county programs in welfare and public assistance. In populous counties, the board is likely to have power to fill a very large number of positions on the county payroll, and appointments frequently show the spoils system at its worst. Fourteen states, however, have merit laws applying either to all counties or to more populous ones, and in more than 300 counties some effort has been made to supplant spoils by competitive civil service examinations.

Other county officers

Besides the county board, counties, typically, have six or more elective officers, all largely independent of one another, of the county board, and usually of the officers of the state as well. Titles and duties vary widely, but the officers of chief importance are always the sheriff and the prosecuting attorney.

1. Sheriff:

Historically descended from the old Saxon *shire-reeve,* the sheriff is found

---

[3] These usually are appointed by the chairman of the board, and not infrequently are made up on a strictly partisan basis, with the chairmen appointed under a seniority rule which may leave the best qualified men in positions of little or no influence. The committees look after various branches of the county administration and make their reports and recommendations to the full board, which generally accepts and approves the action of a committee in a perfunctory manner. If the board as a whole attempts to consider in detail any phase of county work, it soon degenerates into a debating society.

in nearly every state.[4] Usually, he is elected. In Rhode Island he is appointed by the governor, and in New York City a single sheriff for the five counties is appointed by the mayor.[5] His term is usually two years, although three-year and four-year terms are not uncommon. In a number of states the constitution unwisely makes him ineligible for immediate re-election. Included among his prerogatives is that of appointing almost any number of deputies, whose powers become the same as his own, but with himself responsible for any official acts performed by them. In most states he is a salaried official; but sometimes both he and his deputies receive much (if not all) of their compensation in the form of fees, which, in very populous counties, sometimes amount to tens of thousands of dollars a year.

a. Police duties

The duties most commonly assigned to the sheriff fall into two main groups: those relating to the preservation of the public peace, sometimes called police duties, and those connected with the operation of the courts. On paper, the sheriff's police duties are impressive, including as they do management of the county jail, arrest and safe-keeping of persons charged with crimes or misdemeanors, and enforcement of statutes against gambling, vice, and liquor-selling. Except, however, in some of the more sparsely settled portions of the country, they actually are quite limited. No county police, corresponding to a city police force, is at the sheriff's command,[6] and as a rule neither town and village constables nor city police units are in any way subject to his control. In time of public disorder, therefore, the sheriff is likely to be obliged to summon to his aid the *posse comitatus* (such able-bodied men of the county as he may select), or even to call upon the governor for assistance from the state militia (National Guard) or—where such a force exists—the state police.

b. Court duties

The greater portion of the sheriff's time is consumed in the performance of his duties as executive agent of the courts. He attends court sessions; he serves the various writs and other processes in connection with civil suits, and also warrants for the arrest of persons accused of crime and subpoenas for the attendance of witnesses; he carries out the judgments of the courts in civil cases (for example, seizing and selling property to satisfy judgments), and executes court sentences upon persons convicted of crimes or misdemeanors.[7] These activities are more lucrative than tracking down criminals, and thus

[4] New Orleans has two sheriffs, one to deal with crime and one to deal with civil actions.

[5] In Connecticut, the abolition of the counties by statute and the transfer of the custody of the county jails to a "jail administrator" appointed by the state prison board left the sheriffs without duties. (Constitutional offices, such as the sheriff's cannot be abolished by statute and in some states it is doubtful if their duties that are known to the common law can be taken from them.) The new jail administrator said he would appoint the sheriffs as his deputy jailers. See *The New York Times*, Aug. 28, 1960.

[6] Exceptions are found in Los Angeles County, California, St. Louis County, Missouri, and in a few other urban counties, where the sheriff has direct command of a uniformed, trained, and equipped police force of several hundred men.

[7] In addition, he is, in some states, ex officio tax collector.

they often are the ones to which the sheriff devotes himself most assiduously.

Although sheriffs are elected locally, they are, in law, agents of the state; and many, if not most, of their functions have to do with the enforcement of state laws. In very few states, however, do the higher state officials exercise effective control over them. In New York, Michigan, and Wisconsin, the governor may remove a sheriff for cause; and in Illinois, he must remove a sheriff who allows a prisoner to be taken from his custody by a mob.

2. Prose-cuting attorney: Of considerably greater importance is the prosecuting attorney—known in different states as state's attorney, district attorney, or county solicitor. Generally such an official is elected in each county; but in some states he is (or may be) chosen in a district containing more than one county, in which case his jurisdiction extends throughout his district. In a very few states, the attorney is appointed by the governor, as in Florida, or by the judges of some court. Selected in most instances county by county, and by popular election, such attorneys inevitably vary greatly in character and ability. They are likely to reflect the dominant sentiment of their communities toward law enforcement, a fact which partly explains the unfortunate lack of uniformity sometimes found in different parts of the same state in the enforcement of laws against gambling, vice, illicit liquor-selling, and other offenses. However chosen and supervised, the prosecuting attorney is paid a salary in a number of states, and in others is recompensed with fees. The tendency is to substitute salaries for the fee system.

a. Civil duties In most states, the prosecuting attorney has important civil duties: he is the legal adviser to most, if not all, of the county officials; he draws up and passes upon the validity of county contracts; he institutes and conducts suits brought by the county and defends those brought against the county, or against any officer thereof in his official capacity; he prosecutes all cases of forfeited official or bail bonds; and he cooperates with the attorney general of the state in the handling of important cases affecting the county.

b. Law enforce-ment But the prosecuting attorney's most conspicuous duties, as his title implies, relate to the enforcement of criminal statutes; and the extent to which crime is repressed depends largely on his ability, judgment, and energy. He investigates crimes which come to his attention through the public press, the police, or on complaint of private citizens; he institutes proceedings for the arrest and detention of persons accused or suspected of crime and the detention of important witnesses who otherwise might leave the state; he commences criminal actions where in his judgment the facts warrant doing so, either by filing an "information" with the proper court or by drawing up indictments and submitting evidence in support of them to a grand jury; and, either in person or by deputy, he conducts the trial of criminal cases.[8] Recommenda-

---

[8] To the end that poor persons charged with crimes or misdemeanors may have honest legal advice and competent aid when tried, the office of public defender has been created in some parts of the country, notably in Los Angeles County, California. More than 150 communities in the country, indeed, have organizations prepared to furnish counsel to persons unable to afford the services of a lawyer. On the most noted of such

tions which he makes concerning the fixing of bail, the discontinuance or nol-prossing of criminal actions, and the severity of sentences are usually given serious consideration by the courts. It is often his duty, also, to bring to trial public officers accused of official misconduct.

The office is truly one of great responsibility and invested with ample possibilities for good or evil. Control of it in counties containing large cities is a political prize of the first magnitude for both the law-abiding classes and the criminal and vicious elements interested in lax law-enforcement and a "wide-open town." It should invariably go to a lawyer of unquestioned ability, a citizen of the highest character, a man forceful and fearless in the discharge of duty, and one who is above suspicion of being controlled by, or under obligations to, any corrupt organization. Courageous and efficient prosecuting attorneys often have won distinction and political advancement. The governor's chair has been attained by many. *c. Demands of the office*

The office of coroner is of nearly the same antiquity as that of sheriff, although considerably less important. Almost everywhere the incumbent is popularly elected, for two or four years, although in six or seven states he is appointed by the county board or by the judges of one of the higher courts; in Rhode Island, he is appointed by the town council, and therefore is not a county official at all. As set forth in a New York statute, the coroner's main function is to investigate the circumstances under which any person has died "from criminal violence or by casualty, or suddenly when in apparent health, or when unattended by a physician, or in prison, or in any suspicious or unusual manner." When holding an inquest to determine the cause of a death, a coroner acts both as a medical examiner and as a magistrate, with authority in the latter role to conduct a hearing and examine witnesses; and he may act singly or may (in some states must) enlist the assistance of a jury, usually of six, selected from bystanders or other people of the neighborhood. A verdict of natural death, accidental death, or suicide usually ends the matter. If, however, reason appears for believing some person or persons to have been criminally responsible, the district attorney or police are supposed to start work on the case, with the coroner himself empowered to issue a warrant for the arrest of any suspected person whose identity is known. In many counties the coroner's office is little more than a booby prize awarded to some insignificant adherent of the dominant political machine, with most incumbents having neither the medical nor legal qualifications presumed. A far better situation exists in five New England and two Southern states,[9] where the coroner has *3. Coroner*

---

organizations (almost a century old), see M. V. Callagy, "The Legal Aid Society in the City of New York," *N. Y. Univ. Law Quar. Rev.,* XXIV, 356-371 (Apr., 1949). On the public defender, see D. Freeman, "The Public Defender System," *Jour. Amer. Judic. Soc.,* XXXII, 74-78 (Oct., 1948), and other articles in the same periodical during 1948-49.

[9] Massachusetts, New Hampshire, Rhode Island, Vermont, Maine, Virginia, and Maryland. Some additional states have authorized counties to adopt the plan or some features of it and elsewhere individual counties have been authorized to use it; *e.g.,* Milwaukee County, Wis., and New York City have medical examiners.

been supplanted by an appointive "medical examiner" (full-time in larger cities) required to have competence as a physician or pathologist, and with all legal aspects of the work left to the prosecuting attorney.[10] The coroner well may be on his way out along with the justice of the peace.[11]

4. Clerk   In about half of the states, there is a county clerk, nearly always popularly elected, and for two or four years. Duties vary widely, but as a rule they include (1) serving as secretary to the county board; (2) making formal records of ordinances, resolutions, and other board actions; (3) performing the duties of an auditor or comptroller where no such officer exists; [12] and (4) issuing marriage licenses, hunting and fishing licenses, and other licenses and permits. Not infrequently, too, the clerk has electoral duties, such as registering voters, receiving nomination petitions, and supervising the preparation of ballots. In other words, he is a sort of clearing house for county business. In one or two states, for example, Wisconsin, he somewhat approaches the character of a county chief executive.[13]

5. Other offices and boards   This outline of county offices might be continued at wearisome length. For the rest, it must, however, serve merely to enumerate the most important ever found in some counties. The general nature of the duties attached will be apparent from the name: (1) one or more court clerks; (2) a treasurer; (3) an auditor or comptroller; (4) a recorder or register of deeds; (5) a superintendent of schools; (6) a surveyor; (7) a highway superintendent; (8) an assessor; (9) a county agricultural agent; (10) a female home demonstration agent; (11) a health officer; (12) a welfare superintendent; (13) a purchasing officer; and (14) a veterinarian; and of boards, (1) a board of (tax assessment) review; (2) a board of education; (3) a library board; (4) an election board; and (5) a planning commission. In total officers and employees, about 800 thousand persons serve county governments in this country.

THE PROBLEM OF COUNTY REFORM

Belated recognition of a bad situation   Fifty years ago, a challenging book was published under the title of *The County; The Dark Continent of American Politics.*[14] What the author had in mind was that county government was a labyrinth whose intricate windings were known to very few people except practical politicians, and that even professional students of government had paid scant attention to it in comparison with the governments of nation, state, and city. To a considerable extent, this unfortunate situation still exists. In the interval, however, an increasing number of disinterested explorers have penetrated the jungle in

[10] In Virginia the name of coroner is retained, but not the former office.

[11] R. S. Childs, "Rubbing Out the Coronets," *Nat. Mun. Rev.*, XXXIX, 494-496 (Nov., 1950).

[12] Reciprocally, the auditor often serves as secretary to the board where there is no county clerk.

[13] L. H. Adolfson, "The County Clerk as 'Manager'" [in Wisconsin], *Nat. Mun. Rev.*, XXXIV, 125-128 (Mar., 1945).

[14] The author was H. S. Gilbertson and the place and date were New York, 1917.

different states (notably New York, New Jersey, Illinois, Minnesota, North Carolina, and Virginia), afterwards reporting significantly on what they found. And all accounts agree that in general the county has been largely untouched by reform movements which have yielded remarkable improvements in states and especially in cities; that, almost everywhere,[15] cumbersome machinery and antiquated methods persist, along with divided authority and responsibility—defects which, until the depression of three decades ago, went almost unchallenged.[16]

Troubles associated with that hard experience did what scattered reformers never had succeeded in doing; they convinced public officials and taxpayers alike that there was more ground for criticism than they had been wont to admit. Even yet, changes for the better have been only sporadic and most have occurred in urban counties, which comprise only one-tenth of the total number. The first need is the recognition that there are two main kinds of counties, urban and rural and subtypes within these. What this involves in state law and what has been done in this line has been discussed in the last chapter. The particular problems of urban counties will be discussed in Chapter 36. These involve extending county powers and making the county boards representative bodies. The main shortcoming of the rural counties is that there are too many of them. Common to both types is the need for internal reorganization. A closer look at these is in order.

Governmental shortcomings and suggested remedies:

With rare exceptions, county governments are not departmentalized and correlated but are aggregations of scattered and almost independent offices and boards.[17] In particular, too many county officers are elected. This results in: (1) lengthening the ballot and confusing the voter on election day; (2) preventing overall direction of these officials by a responsible superior; and (3) preventing the making and administering of a comprehensive county budget.

1. Internal reorganization—the need for central control of county functions:

As most counties now are organized, the most serious shortcoming, however, is the lack of any chief executive. Any administrative reorganization would fall short unless some such apex, as in city, state, and nation, were provided. In a few scattered counties, something approaching such a unifying

a. Too many elective offices

---

[15] As mentioned before, our two newest state constitutions have sought to prevent comparable situations.

[16] "In county governments, we have generally had about the poorest kind of government. . . . Politics has been exploited to the highest degree. Nepotism has been practiced to the limit. Patronage has been rampant. Supervisory officials, as well as elected officers, have been compelled to give far too much time to the consideration of patronage. Incompetency of subordinates and waste have been the rule rather than the exception. Corruption, too, has found its place in the wake of spoils." H. E. Kaplan, in *Nat. Mun. Rev.,* XXV, 597 (Oct., 1936). In every one of our larger states, one or more counties probably could be found in which all of these charges could easily be substantiated; while one or more of the number would hold true in virtually every county in any state.

[17] Counties are not alone in this, as seen in the discussion of state administration. One reason for the county situation is that whenever a new function is contemplated, its proponents dislike having it come under any older county office which they regard as using antiquated methods or be dependent any more than is necessary on the existing county political set-up. Cities also share the difficulty of having too many boards and commissions; however, both the states and the cities have made more progress in integrating functions under unified departments.

b. Need for a chief executive

authority has been supplied. Since 1900 Hudson and Essex Counties in New Jersey have had an elective executive somewhat like a weak mayor.[18] Since the mid-thirties, Nassau and Westchester Counties in New York have had an elective executive with powers of appointment, removal, supervision and veto.[19] An elective chief executive with powers generally similar to those of a mayor in a strong-mayor city also serves in Cook County (Chicago), Illinois and in Milwaukee County, Wisconsin. The home-rule charters adopted in St. Louis County, Missouri, and Baltimore County, Maryland (in 1950 and 1956, respectively) provide for a similar head.

The county managership

Another type of executive which is finding favor is the county manager, patterned after the city manager now found in so many municipalities. Some counties (for example, in Georgia, North Carolina, and Wisconsin [20]) have taken hesitant steps in the direction of a managership under authority to vest limited duties of a managerial character in some one of the older county officials—the chairman of the county board, the county clerk, or the auditor. In some counties in other states, an appointive executive will have varying degrees of administrative responsibility but without having all the duties associated with true managership. Noteworthy among these are California's "chief administrative" officers.[21] Other counties with modified manager plans are: Cuyhoga County (Cleveland), Ohio; Hamilton County (Chattanooga), Tennessee; Clark County (Las Vegas), Nevada; and Charleston County, South Carolina.[22] Where true managership exists, a full-time salaried manager is appointed by the county board, for no fixed term, and presumably without reference to politics or local residence. To him is assigned, under responsibility to the board and through it to the electorate, the entire task of coordinating and directing county administration. The board continues to levy taxes, borrow and appropriate money, enact ordinances, and determine the nature and extent of county services. It is supposed to leave the conduct of administration entirely to the manager and the higher officials appointed by and responsible to him. He should be operating through the integrated departments that almost of necessity go along with the system. If the board does not approve the way in which things are done, its proper course is to change managers rather than to interfere with and embarrass the existing one.

Its outlook

Authorization, constitutional or statutory, for the manager system in a

[18] J. M. Collier, *County Government in New Jersey* (New Brunswick, N.J., Rutgers University Press, 1952), 16-17, and "Elected County Chief Executives in New Jersey," *The County Officer,* XX, 47-48 (Feb., 1955).

[19] H. W. Robertson, "Westchester Likes Executive," *Nat. Mun. Rev.,* XXXVIII, 219-223 (May, 1949).

[20] L. H. Adolfson, *op. cit.*

[21] See J. C. Bollens, *Appointed Executive Local Government: The California Experience* (Haynes Foundation, Los Angeles, Calif., 1952) and A. Holtzman, *Los Angeles County Chief Administrative Officer: Ten Years' Experience* (Uni. of Calif., Bur. of Govt. Res., Los Angeles, Calif., 1948).

[22] For a typical description see Cleveland Bur. of Govt. Res., *Development of the Administrative Officer in Cuyahoga County: A Report to the Board of County Commissioners of Cuyahoga County, Ohio* (Cleveland, Ohio, 1955).

few states, followed by actual adoption in 35 scattered counties (17 in North Carolina) by 1965,[23] undoubtedly may be regarded as the most significant advance recently recorded in the field of county government. Many obstacles are encountered: tradition, which perhaps is nowhere stronger than in local government; popular fear of "one-man rule"; and constitutional impediments, as for example, in Nebraska, where an optional county-manager act of 1933 was overthrown as incompatible with a constitutional requirement that all county officers be elected. In any state authorizing county home-rule, however, the plan may be adopted by any county to which the privilege applies; in other states, it usually is constitutionally possible for the legislature to approve the system for a particular county. With testimony almost universal, where the scheme has been tried, that it yields good results, further progress may be confidently predicted. The one qualification to be added is that experience thus far has been almost entirely in populous, urbanized counties, and that it is there, rather than in sparsely inhabited counties with comparatively few activities, that one would expect the system's benefits to be greatest. In strictly rural counties of small population, the advantages might be less demonstrable, although from the one such county in the present list (Petroleum County, Montana, with a population in 1950 of less than one per square mile) come no less impressive reports of successful operation.[24]

COUNTIES CLASSIFIED BY POPULATION
1960

Size	No. of Counties
Over 250,000	108
100,000-249,999	169
50,000-99,999	283
25,000-49,999	584
10,000-24,999	1,081
5,000-9,999	544
Under 5,000	272
Total	3,043

[23] A list of county managers may be found in the directory of approved manager cities in *The Municipal Year Book, 1965* (Chicago, 1965), 521-553.

[24] See "Petroleum County Thrives with Manager," *Nat. Mun. Rev.*, XLIII, 250-251 (May, 1954), reprinted from *Montana Taxpayer* (March, 1954).

For additional references on the county managership, see R. C. Houston, "County Manager Government in California," *Nat. Mun. Rev.*, XXVIII, 128-133 (Feb., 1939); R. B. Highsaw, "City and County Manager Plans in the South," *Jour. of Politics*, XI, 497-517 (Aug., 1949); G. W. Spicer "Manager Counties Evaluated," *Nat. Mun. Rev.*, XLII, 331-337 (July, 1953); W. E. Weller and C. M. Smith, "Sixteen Years of Progress" (Manager Government in Monroe County, N.Y.), *Nat. Mun. Rev.*, XLII, 393-397 (Sept., 1953); A. W. Stewart, "Well-Managed Counties," *National Civic Review*, LIV, No. 10, Nov. 1965.

In early days, when travel was mainly by horse, a large number of counties in a state was required if the county seat was to be within a day's round-trip from all parts of the county. Today, despite the railroad, the automobile, and the telephone, the number of counties remains about what it formerly was, seven states having 100 or more. With the country's population shifting from section to section, and even within the same section, in response to changing economic conditions, many counties have come to be sparsely inhabited.[25] All, however, are required by rigid constitutional or statutory provisions to maintain the same forms of government as more favored ones. All must also meet the costs of improved highways and of the multiplied social services now so conspicuously added to the older county functions—with the result that numerous small and poor counties are unable to finance themselves out of local resources.[26] In most states the number of counties could be reduced by a third, or even half, without harm to the principle of local self-government. This could be done by (1) consolidations, (2) deorganization by local action, or (3) abolition by the state. Consolidations have been authorized in several states, but only two have been accomplished.[27] Authorizations for counties to deorganize (go out of existence) exist in many states. This requires local voter approval. The best statutes on this subject are in the Dakotas. The record in this type of reform is virtually *nil*. Connecticut and Rhode Island have abolished their counties as we have seen, but they are our most densely populated states rather than the reverse. Rural local government has been largely untouched by this movement to reduce the number of counties as it has been largely untouched by the other reforms. Local pride, opposition of county officeholders and county-seat tradesmen, and reluctance of legislatures to force the matter, joined to constitutional obstacles, have combined to keep the number of counties constant.

Ultimate need for constitutional amendment

An aroused public opinion might compel a county board to adopt a sort

[25] In numerous counties scattered over the country, and especially in the northern portions of Michigan, Wisconsin, and Minnesota, timber resources have been depleted, farm lands are unproductive, population has dwindled, and in many sections slum conditions prevail. The problems raised are being solved in part by rural zoning measures empowering counties to designate areas suitable for cultivation, for forestry, and for recreation, and also to relocate occupants barely eking out an existence on cut-over lands. See L. A. Salter, Jr., "County Zoning and Postwar Problems," *State Government*, XVIII, 187-189 (Oct., 1945); G. S. Wehrwein, "The Administration of Rural Zoning," *Journ. of Land and Pub. Utility Econ.*, XIX, 264-291 (Aug., 1943); and E. D. Solberg, *Rural Zoning in the United States* (U. S. Dept. of Agri., Washington, 1952) though this latter publication contains information on county zoning for suburban land uses also.

[26] Though the trend has been to give counties more functions to perform, North Carolina and West Virginia (which contains a depressed soft coal area) have been taking over county activities. As for the use of the county as an agent of the state the trend has been in the opposite direction as evidenced by the practice of state departments to set up district offices of their own organizations rather than to add to county duties.

[27] In 1919, Tennessee consolidated two counties and in 1932, Georgia consolidated two small ones with a larger one. In both cases, a major city was within the consolidated area—Chattanooga and Atlanta respectively.

Consolidations of counties with cities is discussed in Chapter 36.

of self-denying ordinance and introduce the managership into the existing government, without waiting for special authorization from the legislature. A progressive county board might also, within limits, consolidate offices, or at least introduce more businesslike methods in them. Probably no legislature is without power to provide for a thorough survey of county government, to authorize the employment of county managers, to abolish the fee system as some states have done, or to remedy loose financial methods by state supervision, audit, or inspection of accounts [28] and the requirement of uniform systems of accounting and budgeting.[29] A legislature might also enact county civil service laws, such as California did in 1939 and New York in 1941, abolish any unnecessary county offices created by statute and reassign their functions, or convert statutory elective offices into appointive ones.

In most states, however, "The roots of county government are imbedded in the legal granite of the state constitution and can be removed only by blasting them out with a constitutional amendment." Even the most intelligent and sympathetic legislature is limited, under existing powers, in what it may do to promote better county government and county boards are even more limited in what they can do on their own. There are constitutional provisions making all offices elective, frequent provisions imposing a uniform type of government upon all counties, and others. Nothing less, therefore, than a series of constitutional amendments in most states, will clear the way for the simplification and unification of county organization essential to effective local government. Reform proposals on such drastic lines, however, are likely to encounter sturdy opposition. The county commonly is the most important unit of "grass-roots" party organization and county government the chief reservoir of party resources in local political contests.[30]

THE NEW ENGLAND TOWN

The New England town is usually a rural trade center. There are towns with populations running into the thousands, but the majority of the 1400 or more are not urban.

The principal organ of government is a primary assembly composed of *The town* the town's qualified voters, and known as the town meeting. Substantially all *meeting*

[28] In New York, Ohio, Minnesota, and Iowa, for example.

[29] Iowa, New York, Nebraska, and a number of other states prescribe uniform systems of accounting for all counties and California, North Carolina, Florida, and half a dozen others require counties to follow a uniform budget system.

New Jersey has a division of local government in the state treasury department vested with broad powers of supervision and control over the fiscal affairs of all local units.

[30] H. P. Jones, "Constitutional Barriers to Improvements in County Government," *Nat. Mun. Rev.*, XXI, Supp., 523-542 (Aug., 1932); M. H. Satterfield, "County Government and Constitutional Revision in Tennessee," *Tenn. Law Rev.*, XIX, 707-717 (Feb., 1947).

of the town's powers are exercised by this body directly or through committees or officers acting as its agents. The town meeting is convoked in the town hall once every year (in October in Connecticut, but elsewhere during the spring months), with special meetings called if needed. For every meeting an itemized list of matters to be taken up is prepared and circulated by the "selectmen," with ordinarily no topic permitted to be considered unless it appears on the list. Among items enumerated will certainly be appropriations for all of the town's supported activities (including schools), a tax-rate designed to produce the necessary funds, and provisions for borrowing if any are required. Among them, too, are likely to be proposed by-laws relating to public buildings, water supply, gas or electric lighting, highways, upkeep of cemeteries, and indeed anything else within the town's range of authority, including, of course, local police. Any voter present at a meeting is entitled not only to vote but also to speak; indeed even nonvoters usually may attend and sometimes may participate. Many times the proceedings, as carried on under the guidance of an elected moderator, are stereotyped and dull. But occasionally issues arise which provoke wide differences of opinion, and even divide the townsfolk into hostile camps; and when this happens, meetings may become lively, with much of the wire-pulling, speech-making, and excitement ordinarily associated with political conventions. In smaller towns, where town-meeting day takes on the aspect of a neighborhood holiday, there still is, as a rule, good attendance and plenty of action, even though to an outsider many of the matters discussed might seem ridiculously trivial. In larger places, attendance is likely to be more scant and business to be pretty much of the cut-and-dried variety. Sometimes, in fact, the moderator simply appoints a committee which brings in recommendations on the various items and the voters approve them with little or no discussion.[31]

"Representative" town meeting   As towns grow in population, a mass meeting is likely to be found ill-adapted to satisfactory handling of business, and one of two remedies may be adopted: (1) a standing advisory budget committee of from 10 to 40 members may be set up to expedite the work of the general meeting; or (2) a "limited town meeting" may be substituted with all voters still privileged to attend, but only 200 or 300 chosen representatives entitled to vote. The latter course has been taken thus far largely in Massachusetts. The effect is to convert the meeting, somewhat clumsily, from a primary assembly according to the original design into a rather crude *ad hoc* representative body. Sooner or later, however, an overgrown town may take the logical course of giving up the town-meeting idea altogether and applying for incorporation as a city or bor-

[31] J. Gould, *New England Town Meeting; Safeguard of Democracy* (Brattleboro, Vt., 1940); M. R. White, *The Connecticut Town Meeting* (Storrs, Conn., 1949), a handbook for moderators and other town officers; E. Tidyman, "Self-Government in Maine," *Nat. Mun. Rev.,* XXXVIII, 101-103 (Feb., 1949); L. H. Robbins, "Democracy Town Meeting Style" [in Wolfeboro, N. H.], *New York Times,* Mar. 23, 1947. Cf. *ibid.,* Mar. 21, 1948; L. Smith, "Town Meeting Government," *Soc. Sci.,* XXX, 174-185 (June, 1955).

ough.[32] A good many larger towns have done this. Usually there is reluctance to abandon the old usages, and many towns hold off from doing so until long after they have outgrown the homogeneity of population and the neighborliness of spirit that make government by meeting feasible.

No mayor or other chief executive exists.[33] Instead there is the board of selectmen (called town council in Rhode Island) already mentioned—a group of three, five, or sometimes as many as nine, persons chosen to serve as an executive committee of the town meeting and as such to act for that body during the long intervals between its sessions. Usually the term is one year, but in many Massachusetts towns it is three years; and in any event re-elections frequently assure fairly extended periods of service. As an executive committee, the selectmen have authority only to enforce the orders of the meeting and carry on such of the town's affairs that do not fall in the province of some different agency. They do not act as executives by wielding centralized control over other town officials because they do not appoint them. In smaller towns, purely minor officials are likely to be appointed by the selectmen, but aside from this, officials and boards are chosen by the voters—not on the floor of the town meeting as such, but by balloting carried on while a meeting is in progress, and sometimes prolonged for a day or two after it adjourns [34] or, in a few towns, on a different date. The town selectmen may, however, grant licenses, lay out highways, care for town property, award contracts, and arrange for town meetings and elections.

Selectmen

TOWNSHIPS

From a reading of the laws, one might deduce that the township meeting required by statute in the civil townships of eight states (confined to the northernmost tier across the central portions of the country) would look and act very much like the New England town meeting on which it is modeled.

The township meeting

[32] A similar effect is accomplished in Maine by a town's acquiring a charter. Nineteen Maine towns operate under charters. In these, legislative powers are wielded by councils elected from districts and operating essentially like city councils. Representative town meetings can be used in Maine by special act of the legislature but their basic weakness was revealed by the case of Sanford which had difficulties getting a quorum present for an important action. See C. E. Vose and K. E. Carpenter, "Municipal Charters in Maine," *Bowdoin College Bulletin*, No. 331 (Dec., 1958).

[33] Town managers, however, are authorized in all the New England states and the number of these officials is increasing. (There were more than 155 in 1965.) Maine accounts for the vast majority of these. See L. Pelletier, "New England Pioneers Again," *Nat. Mun. Rev.*, XXXVIII, 79-84 (Feb., 1949).

[34] Of the other officials, the most important is the town clerk, elected annually, but often continued in office year after year until he becomes the acknowledged authority on town history, precedents, and genealogy. There is always a town treasurer, sometimes an auditor, at least one constable. There is also an elected school committee, which in most New England states has direct control over the town schools. Usually, too, in larger towns there is a board of health and a board of overseers of the poor. Minor officials (who often receive no pay) may include justices of the peace, road surveyors, sealers of weights and measures, library trustees, almshouse custodians, and park commissioners.

All qualified voters are entitled to participate; the body has an annual spring meeting in the town hall, with special meetings as required; an elected moderator presides; and functions include electing township officers, levying taxes, making appropriations, and enacting by-laws. Almost everywhere, however, the township meeting, if kept up at all, is only a pale image of the usually well attended and reasonably vigorous New England gathering. Interest is lax and attendance scant; often there are not enough persons present to prevent the officers from completely dominating the perfunctory proceedings. In New York, experience has been so unhappy that the meeting has been abolished; and altogether, as a recent writer has observed, "the spirit of town-meeting government has failed to take root in most . . . townships in which the meeting system has been established by law." [35]

The township board

Whatever the township meeting may amount to in states employing it, every township state provides by law for a governing board in each township, variously termed board of supervisors or trustees, advisory board, or board of auditors, but (whatever called) usually consisting of three members, all elective, all ex officio, or partly both. Functions, both of the board as such and of individual members, vary widely. They are more important where there is no township meeting; for in that situation the board may become the nearest

DISTRIBUTION OF TOWNSHIPS BY STATE*, 1962

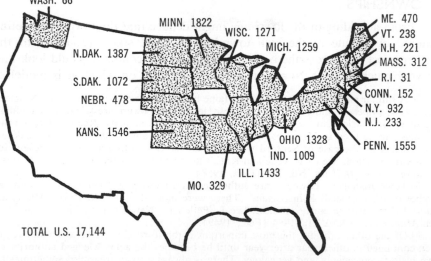

WASH. 66

MINN. 1822

WISC. 1271

MICH. 1259

ME. 470

VT. 238

N.H. 221

MASS. 312

N.DAK. 1387

R.I. 31

S.DAK. 1072

CONN. 152

NEBR. 478

N.Y. 932

N.J. 233

KANS. 1546

OHIO 1328

PENN. 1555

IND. 1009

ILL. 1433

MO. 329

TOTAL U.S. 17,144

*States not shown have no townships (or towns)

[35] C. F. Snider, *American State and Local Government* (New York, 1950), 357. One reason is the relative preponderance of the county as compared with that unit in New England, and another is the weaker ties of tradition than in the New England town, at least of earlier times.

approach to a general governing authority, with usually the elective, financial, and regulatory powers that the meeting would exercise if there were one. In any case, the board frequently is charged with responsibility for any township affairs not expressly assigned to some other agency.

In about half of the township states (whether with or without town meetings), management of affairs, however, centers rather in a single elective officer known in New York, Michigan, and Illinois as supervisor, in Indiana, Kansas, and Missouri as trustee, and in Wisconsin as town chairman. Where such an officer exists, the function of the township board becomes mainly that of advising and checking him. In Indiana, where this chief officer's functions attain their peak, the trustee serves the township—not only in its general civil capacity but as a school township as well—as ex officio clerk and treasurer, with responsibility for the care of property, the administration of poor relief, the preparation of civil and school budgets, and even the selection of teachers for rural schools, though not for taxing, appropriating, or borrowing, which remain functions of the township board. In other states, duties are much the same, although usually do not include school affairs. *The supervisor or trustee*

Where the chief township officer does not serve as ex officio clerk and treasurer, there are likely to be separate officers bearing those names; and where tax assessment and collection have not been transferred to the county, an assessor also and perhaps a separate collector. An overseer of the poor and a highway commissioner will likely exist in addition unless the duties are otherwise provided for. Almost invariably there will be two or more elective justices of the peace, with an equal number of elective constables charged with tasks, within the smaller area, similar to those of the county sheriff.[36] *Other officers*

Most authorities agree that, under modern conditions of travel and communication, the township, where and as it exists, is an institution which well might be discarded. In several states, upwards of a fourth of all townships contain fewer than 400 people living outside any village or city, and in any case the area is bound to be very small—commonly only 36 square miles. In more than half of the states the township as a unit of government has never existed at all. Principal township activities usually relate to law enforcement, poor relief, and highway maintenance. All of these are at the same time functions of the county. Ordinarily, much would be gained, in both economy and efficiency, if the township were simply eliminated, with everything left to the county, or in some cases to county and city. Some progress in this direction is being made. Under a statute giving county boards the necessary power, some 90 townships in northern Minnesota have been dissolved since 1933; all those of Oklahoma (about 900) were, for all practical purposes, abolished in the same year by withdrawal of their power to levy taxes, followed by transfer of their tax-supported functions to counties.[37] Iowa townships have also ceased *Township abolition*

[36] Twelve New Jersey townships and 38 Pennsylvania (first class) ones have managers. Usually, these are suburbs of large cities.
[37] L. D. Melton, "The Elimination of Township Government in Oklahoma," *Nat. Mun. Rev.*, XXVII, 405-407 (Aug., 1938).

to exist for all practical purposes since 1952. In Maine and Vermont in areas classed as "wild lands," townships have been deorganized by the state legislatures and their functions assumed by the states. Approximately three-fourths of the states have laws under which local units can be deorganized by local action and in North Dakota more than a score of townships have disappeared in this way, when their corporate existence proved too expensive to maintain. In this state, the functions of a deorganized unit are performed by a neighboring unit of the same level.

References

1. Counties

G. S. Blair, *American Local Government* (New York, 1964).

W. S. Carpenter, *Problems in Service Levels* (Princeton, N.J., 1940).

E. W. Weidner, *The American County—Patchwork of Boards* (New York, 1946).

―――, "The Confused County Picture," *Nat. Mun. Rev.*, XXXV, 166-171 (Apr., 1946), 228-232 (May, 1946), 288-294 (June, 1946).

―――, "County Reform Run-Around" [in Wisconsin], *ibid.*, XXXIV, 386-392 (Sept., 1945).

―――, "A Review of the Controversy Over County Executives," *Pub. Admin. Rev.*, VIII, 18-28 (Winter, 1948).

M. H. Satterfield, "Counties in a Strait Jacket," *Nat. Mun. Rev.*, 81-85, 124 (Feb., 1948).

U. S. Bureau of the Census, *County Boards and Commissions* (Washington, 1947).

G. W. Spicer, *Fifteen Years of County Manager Government in Virginia* (Univ. of Va. Extension, 1951).

J. C. Bollens, P. W. Langdell, and R. W. Binkley, Jr., *County Government Organization in California*, Mimeo. (Berkeley, Calif., 1947).

M. Rohrer, *County Manager Government in California*, Mimeo. (Berkeley, Calif., 1950).

National Municipal League, *Model County Charter* (New York, 1956).

―――, *The County Manager Plan* (new ed., New York, 1950).

―――, *Digest of County Manager Charters and Laws* (New York, 1950).

Nebraska Legislative Council, *Report of the Committee on Reorganization of County Government* (Lincoln, Neb., 1950).

W. W. Crane, Jr., "Reflections of a County Board Member," *The County Officer*, XXI, 202-204 (Sept., 1956).

L. M. Holland, "Legislative Authority of County Government in Georgia," *The County Officer*, XX, 16-18 (Jan., 1955).

J. Wood, and C. L. Ringgenberg, *Terms of Office of Elective County Officials in the 48 States* (Iowa County Officers Assoc., 1954).

J. C. Bollens, "Administrative Integration in California Counties," *Pub. Admin. Rev.,* XI, 26-34 (Winter, 1951).

E. E. Sparlin, "Missouri Counties Streamlined," *Nat. Mun. Rev.,* XXXV, 337-343 (July, 1946).

W. L. Bradshaw, *County Government Manual for the Missouri Constitutional Convention of 1943* (Columbia, Mo., 1943).

C. F. Snider and I. Howards, *County Government in Illinois* (Carbondale, Ill., 1960).

————, "County and Township Government in 1935-36," *Amer. Pol. Sci. Rev.,* XXXI, 884-912 (Oct., 1937); and similar surveys annually thereafter until 1949 by the same author (in later years in collaboration with N. F. Garvey) in the same journal (usually the December issue).

————, "American County Government: A Mid-Century Review," *Am. Pol. Sci. Rev.,* XLVI, 66-80 (Mar., 1952).

New York State, *Fourth Interim Report of the Temporary State Commission to Study . . . and Make Uniform Existing Laws Relating to Counties,* Legislative Doc. No. 37 (Albany, N.Y., 1948).

National Association of County Officials, *The County Officer* (Washington), edited by B. F. Hillenbrand.

2. Towns and Townships

C. L. Fry, *American Villagers* (New York, 1926).

C. J. Rohr et al., *Local Government in Massachusetts* (Amherst, Mass., 1941).

J. Gould, *New England Town Meetings; Safeguard of Democracy* (Brattleboro, Vt. ,1940).

State Planning Board, *Towns of South Carolina. . . .* (rev. ed., Columbia, S.C., 1943).

C. R. Tharp, *A Manual of Township Government in Michigan* (Ann Arbor, Mich., 1948).

L. H. Robbins, "Democracy, Town Meeting Style," *The New York Times,* Mar. 23, 1947.

M. R. White and S. Raissi, *Forms of Town Government in Connecticut* (Storrs, Univ. of Conn. Inst. of Public Service, 1952).

L. Smith, "Political Leadership in a New England Community," *Review of Politics,* XVII, 392-409 (July, 1955).

————, "Town Meeting Government," *Social Science,* XXX, 174-185 (June, 1955). Also "Leadership in Local Government—the New England Town," *ibid.,* XXIX, 147-157 (June, 1954).

A. Lincoln, "Some Notes on Representative Town Meetings," *Mass. Law Quarterly,* XXXIII, 30-46 (April, 1948).

G. E. McLaughlin, "Town Manager," *Vermont Life,* VIII, No. 3, 19-24 (Spring, 1954).

R. P. Bolan, *Handbook for Massachusetts Selectmen* (Amherst, Univ. of Mass., Bur. of Govt. Res., 1956).

M. L. Corr, "The Small Town under Big Pressure," *The New York Times Magazine,* 20-22, 24 (Feb. 24, 1952).

W. B. Guitteau, *Ohio's Townships; The Grassroots of Democracy* (Toledo, O., 1949).

C. F. Snider, "The Twilight of the Township," *Nat. Mun. Rev.,* XLI, 390-396 (Sept., 1952).

A. E. Nuquist, *Town Government in Vermont* (Burlington, Vt., 1964).

T. F. Hady and C. J. Hein, "Congressional Townships as Incorporated Municipalities," *Midwest Jour. of Pol. Sci.,* Vol. VIII, No. 4 (November, 1964).

Urban Government and Politics

CITY GOVERNMENT

THE FORM OF GOVERNMENT for American cities has been much less static than that for counties and, in many instances, a city government has a more progressive form than the state in which it lies. The impact of the industrial revolution has fallen directly on the cities. By necessity, they have had to adapt their governmental forms and methods to a more rapid tempo of life and a more complex society. Two basic forms have been invented in this century and new ones are being experimented with to meet the challenges that are constantly appearing. Urban government, therefore, is characterized by change and diversity. Amidst this diversity, however, three patterns stand out: mayor-council, commission, and council-manager.

The mayor-council form, once monopolizing the field, is still found in about one-half of all municipalities of over 5000 population and in all but four of the nation's large cities (over 500,000 population).[1] Something resembling it is found also in villages, boroughs, and a few incorporated towns. Based on the historic principle of separation of powers, its most distinguishing characteristic is a division of authority between an elective council and an elective chief executive, or mayor.

The Mayor-Council Form

Municipal councils of earlier days, especially in larger cities, consisted almost invariably of two branches or houses. A pattern borrowed from the state and nation served no useful purpose, however, and many practical disadvantages developed, with the result that municipal bicameralism has now been very widely abandoned. Only a few cities of over 5000 retain it.[2] No municipality that has once discarded it has ever gone back to it. Except in Illinois and a few other states, where the number of council members is by law graduated according to population, there usually is little correspondence between population and the council's size. New York City has a council of 35 members; Cleveland one of 33, and Chicago one of 50; elsewhere the number

1. The council: a. Structure

---

[1] *The Municipal Year Book, 1965,* 114 (Chicago, 1965). The manager cities are Cincinnati, Dallas, San Antonio, and San Diego.

[2] Waterville, Maine, and Everett, Massachusetts. New York had a powerful board of estimate acting as a kind of second chamber until 1963 when a charter revision substantially reduced the legislative power of the board.

FORMS OF CITY GOVERNMENT

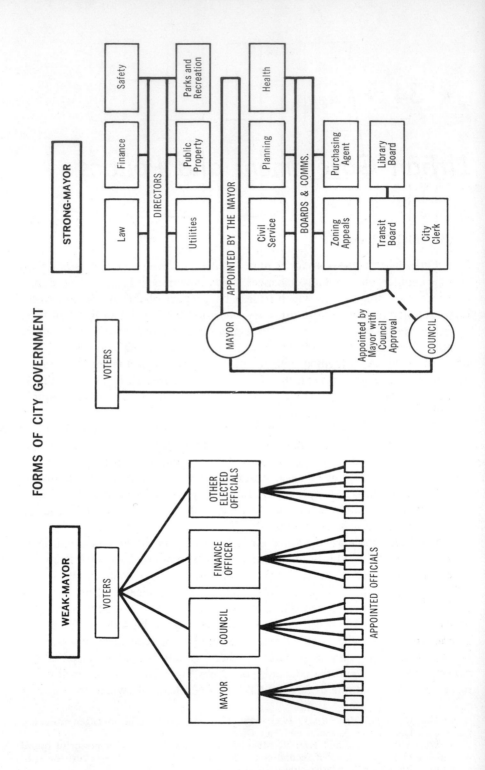

STRONG-MAYOR

VOTERS

MAYOR

COUNCIL

DIRECTORS

APPOINTED BY THE MAYOR

Law | Finance | Safety

Utilities | Public Property | Parks and Recreation

BOARDS & COMMS.

Civil Service | Planning | Health

Zoning Appeals | Purchasing Agent

Transit Board | Library Board

City Clerk

Appointed by Mayor with Council Approval

WEAK-MAYOR

VOTERS

MAYOR | COUNCIL | FINANCE OFFICER | OTHER ELECTED OFFICIALS

APPOINTED OFFICIALS

FORMS OF CITY GOVERNMENT

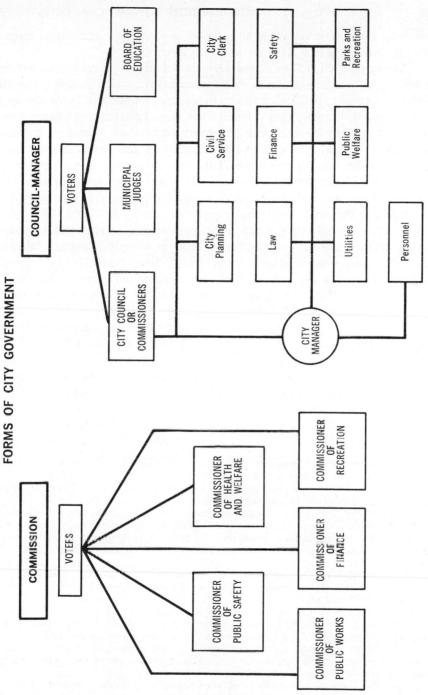

runs from 20 to 30 downwards all the way to nine, even in cities as large as Detroit, Denver, Seattle, Boston, and Pittsburgh.

b. Method
of election

At one time, council members were chosen almost invariably by districts, or wards, each returning one or two representatives. This still is a common method. Generally speaking, it results in a larger council and often one larger than is needed. Furthermore, it lends itself to gerrymandering.[3] Many places (including virtually all with manager governments) have discarded it, substituting election on a general city-wide ticket giving every voter a voice in the selection of the entire membership. This latter plan, too, has disadvantages, especially in cities of considerable size; and in not a few instances some combination of the two systems is found: a small proportion of the councilmen are elected by the city at large; the majority are chosen by wards.[4] Six municipalities elect not only by general ticket, but under a system of proportional representation.[5] The term of members is more commonly two years, but more progressive places are gradually going over to four. Formerly on a partisan basis, elections now are at least nominally nonpartisan in more than half of the cities of over 5000 population—more commonly places with commission or council-manager than with mayor-council government.[6]

c. Func-
tions

To the council it falls chiefly (1) to adopt the yearly municipal budget, levy taxes, borrow money, and allocate funds to the spending offices and services; (2) to grant franchises to lighting, telephone, street railway, and other public service corporations; and (3) to serve as the municipal legislature for enacting, amending, and repealing local laws, known as ordinances, on a great variety of subjects and commonly implementing one phase or another of the police power. In the state municipal code, or in individual charters, the scope of the ordinance power is always set forth in more or less detail, and no coun-

[3] City wards divided unequally may be and have been challenged as violating the "one-man, one-vote" concept of the equal protection clause of the Fourteenth Amendment. See *The New York Times,* July 10, 1965, for a ruling by the Court of Appeals on the council districts of Binghamton, N.Y.

[4] In 1965, of 1516 cities with the mayor-council form of government, 43 percent elected the council at large, 32 percent from wards, and 25 percent from a combination of the two procedures. In commission cities almost all councilmen are elected at large and in 76 percent of the council-manager cities the same is true. *The Municipal Year Book, 1965,* 118.

[5] Cambridge, Lowell, and Worcester, Massachusetts, Hamilton, Ohio, Hopkins, Minnesota, and Oak Ridge, Tennessee. After a ten-year trial, New York City abandoned the plan in 1947 and after 32 years of "P.R.," Cincinnati abandoned it in 1957. New York City, since 1963, has two councilmen from each borough elected at large. Each party is limited to nominating one candidate, and each elector to one vote for these seats. Limited voting has the same objective as "P.R."—minority representation.

[6] Candidates run under a party label in 52 percent of the mayor-council cities, but in only 36 percent of the commission cities and in 16 percent of the council-manager ones. *The Municipal Year Book, 1965, op. cit.,* 118.

The case for nonpartisanship is ably presented in Editorial, "Revolt of the 'Independents,' " *Nat. Mun. Rev.,* XL, 564-565 (Dec., 1951). For the case against see, C. A. Beard, "Politics and City Government," *Nat. Mun. Rev.,* VI, 201-205 (Mar., 1917). For the situation in the big cities, see C. R. Adrian, "Some General Characteristics of Non-Partisan Elections," *Am. Pol. Sci. Rev.,* XLVI, 766-776 (Sept., 1952).

cil enactment is valid and enforceable unless clearly authorized in, or properly inferred from, some code or charter provision—and, of course, unless consistent with all statutes and all provisions of the state and national constitutions. More and more, however, American city government has become a matter of administration rather than legislation—with corresponding decline of the council in relative importance.[7]

In earlier days, when popular suspicion of strong executives still lingered, municipalities endowed the mayor with comparatively little authority. He could make few appointments, and only with council approval; if he had a veto at all, it could be overridden rather easily; and management of the municipal services was largely in the hands of departments, boards, or commissions subject to little mayoral control. Under this "weak-mayor" plan, the city's chief executive was in very much the position in which the governor still is found in many states—and with the same bad effects upon unity, economy, and efficiency. In more than half of all mayor-council cities (mostly smaller ones, but including such large ones as Chicago and Los Angeles), this weak-mayor arrangement persists. In others, however, the mayor has been given considerably more authority; and some, for example, Boston and Cleveland have gone over unreservedly to a "strong-mayor" type, in which power of appointment and removal is substantially increased, the veto power strengthened, and control over administration expanded and integrated. Although numerous other municipalities still present only varying compromises between weak-mayor and strong-mayor types, the office has been distinctly on the upgrade. In cities retaining the mayor-council form, reform movements have been aimed principally at making the mayor actual as well as nominal head of the city government, and responsible for unified management of affairs.

2. The mayor— "weak" and "strong":

American mayors are uniformly chosen by direct popular vote—not by the council, as in Europe—sometimes on a partisan ballot and sometimes otherwise. Terms vary from one year in some smaller cities, especially in New England, to six years; in larger places, it is typically four years; elsewhere it most commonly is two. Salaries vary also from mere nominal sums in smaller places to $50,000 in New York. The mayors of our largest cities get as much as or more than the governors of the states in which the cities are located.

a. Election and term

[7] Moreover, the legislative authority of a city is not vested exclusively in the council. Certain administrative bodies, such as the board of health and the fire department—even single officers—often are empowered to prescribe rules within their respective fields of jurisdiction. Such rules are called "regulations," in order to distinguish them from ordinances. But they are generally of the same legal force as ordinances, subject to the same restrictions, and no less binding upon all citizens.

Regular meetings of the city council are held monthly or even weekly in larger places, with the mayor or a specially chosen chairman presiding; and unless the body is very small, there will be a good deal of use of committees. Experiences and impressions of a university professor serving on the council of a midwestern city are presented in A. W. Bromage, *On the City Council* (Ann Arbor, Mich., 1950). *Cf.* S. A. MacCorkle in *Nat. Mun. Rev.,* XL, 76-80 (Feb., 1951).

**b. Powers
and duties**

From what has been said about the varying and transitional position of the mayor in our mayor-council governments, it is obvious that no single generalized statement of powers and duties is possible. A few broad facts, however, may be indicated. Everywhere it falls to the mayor to represent the city in its dealings with other municipalities and on ceremonial occasions. Everywhere he is expected to enforce the council's ordinances, to maintain order, and in general to cooperate with the law-enforcing authorities of county, state, and nation. Everywhere, too, as chief executive, he is supposed to exercise some supervision over the work of the various city departments. How effectively he can do this, however, depends on the actual authority with which he has been endowed, and especially on his power of appointment and removal. The tendency has been to confer more independent power at these latter points. Nevertheless, in the great majority of cities' appointments (and often removals also) still are contingent on approval by the council; and where removals cannot be made independently, the effect is to lessen responsibility for efficient conduct of administration.[8]

Considerable growth of mayoral authority has come also in connection with budget-making. In earlier times, this function commonly belonged to the council exclusively, and in some cities it still does. In Boston and an increasing number of other cities, however, it has been vested in the mayor alone. Finally, may be mentioned the mayor's relation to municipal legislation, that is, ordinance-making. In most cities he presides over council meetings and convokes special sessions. Everywhere he transmits recommendations (by formal message or otherwise), along with reports of department heads or of other officials. In approximately two-thirds of all mayor-council cities he has power of veto (sometimes extending to veto of items). A veto usually may be overridden in the council by a two-thirds vote—increased in some strong-mayor cities to three-fourths, or even five-sixths.

**3. Advan-
tages of
the mayor-
council
system**

The mayor-council system has been criticized because legislative and administrative authority is often clumsily diffused and responsibility scattered. This criticism—insofar as the troubles come from a separation of powers—is less valid, the larger the electorate concerned. The larger cities cling to the traditional mayor-council form while many smaller places have successfully instituted forms in which legislative and administrative authority is either com-

---

[8] The same effect occurs also when other officials besides the mayor are elected. Other principal municipal officers usually include a clerk, a treasurer, and a city attorney, often serving on a part-time basis in smaller places, but in larger ones full time and with staffs of subordinates. Charged with keeping records, issuing licenses and permits, and sometimes with managing elections, the clerk is in some places elected by the council, in others by the voters. Collecting, caring for, and disbursing city funds, the city treasurer is usually either popularly elected or appointed by the mayor. As law officer, the city attorney advises the council, mayor, and other officials on legal matters, represents the city in the courts, drafts ordinances, prepares contracts or approves them for form, and in some cities, prosecutes violators of local ordinances. In many larger places, he is appointed by the mayor; in smaller ones, he is likely to be chosen by the council or by the voters.

bined or sharply separated. The advantages of executive control of the administration can be realized to the degree in which the mayor is made "strong." The political advantages of the mayor-council system are, however, sometimes paramount. The commission and the council-manager forms seem to work best in a nonpolitical atmosphere and in a homogeneous community with more rather than less agreement on fundamental goals. The larger a city, the more complex the social groupings within it and the more diverse the social and economic goals of these groups. There is a need in these places to represent these groups, even if a large council results, and to mediate among them. (The council-manager and commission forms typically have small councils.) There is also a need, especially in the larger cities, for political leadership and for arousing the voter to action and organizing sentiment for the public good. This the mayor—an elected executive—can do and be held politically responsible for his program. Therefore, especially in the larger cities and where the office of mayor has been strengthened,[9] the mayor-council form is still widely preferred.

An increasingly popular practice that furthers good municipal administration is the appointment of a professional administrator to serve under and at the direction of the mayor. The usual title for this post is chief administrative officer.[10] This official differs from a city manager. He is appointed by the mayor and is responsible to him, not to the council. The mayor is still ultimately responsible for the conduct of the city's affairs. The creation of this post with adequate staff frees the mayor for policy-making and leadership. Though designed for large cities, smaller places find it useful to provide the mayor with an administrative assistant, which is a version of the same idea.

4. The public administrator

A number of cities have instituted forms in which executive and legislative powers are combined in one body. The first experiment in this line was the commission form of city government instituted first in Galveston, Texas, in 1900. This reform captured the imagination of many municipal reformers in the period 1900 to 1920. About 500 cities of all sizes, though mostly small or of intermediate size, adopted it in this period. Since that time, the commission system has lost favor and in 1965 only 237 cities of 5000 or more population still clung to it. The best known are Memphis, Portland, St. Paul, and Tulsa.

The Commission Plan

The commission plan is remarkably simple. Instead of a large and un-

1. Essential features

[9] Administration has also been improved in quite a few cities by streamlining the organization in the same manner that state administration has been improved—with related functions grouped together under single-headed departments. These reforms are not limited, of course, to any one form of city government. Similarly merit systems have been on the increase. In 1965, of 1170 reporting cities, 83 percent had some degree of formal civil service; of these about half covered substantially all employees and about half covered only police and firemen. *The Municipal Year Book, 1965, op. cit.,* 205.

[10] He differs from the California "chief administrative officers" described earlier. Except for San Francisco, the "CAO's" in California are more like "semimanagers," *i.e.,* they are appointed by and report to councils but have less authority than regular managers. Among the cities with strong mayors and professional administrators are San Francisco, Philadelphia, Boston, New Orleans (parish and city), and Newark. New York City, where the idea started, has two.

wieldy council, one finds a small commission, consisting usually of five full-time salaried members elected on a general ticket. All other elective municipal offices are eliminated. In this commission are concentrated all of the legislative, and most of the administrative, authority of the city government. Each commissioner serves as a legislator, fixing the tax rate and passing ordinances, and as the head of one of the five departments—such as public safety—into which the administrative work is divided.

2. Incidental features The foregoing constitute the *essential* features of the system. In addition, certain incidental features almost invariably appear. The ward system has almost everywhere been abolished. The commissioners are elected from the entire city.[11] Moreover, candidates are generally nominated either by petition or by nonpartisan primary, and are voted for on election day on a nonpartisan ballot. With such extensive powers vested in a small group, it is wise, too, for the public to retain means of direct and prompt control; and to this end, provision is made in most commission-governed cities (outside of Pennsylvania) for the recall of an unsatisfactory commissioner in a special election held before expiration of his term of office. Another common safeguard is the initiative and referendum in connection with ordinances. In varying degrees, all of these devices have contributed to the improved civic conditions which usually have followed adoption of the commission plan. None is either essential or peculiar to commission government, and any mayor-council city can make use of any or all, as some do, without adopting the commission plan.[12]

[11] The ward system is usually regarded as resulting in less eminent councilmen than the at-large system. Whether or not this is provable, election by wards is essentially area representation. This has a bad connotation when used to elect members of the lower house of state legislatures because it generally discriminates against urban populations there. However, given the patterns of city land use development that have resulted in territorial separations of ethnic and racial groups and income levels and the use of unicameralism, the ward system does give some representation to minority groups. The need to represent various sections of a city is most pronounced in the larger places. Of the cities over 500,000 population, 25 percent elect councilmen by wards and another 35 percent by a combination of wards and at-large. New York City elects councilmen from state senatorial districts. In the 10,000 to 25,000 population class, 62 percent of the cities elect at-large (general ticket). *Municipal Year Book, 1965, op. cit.,* 118. See also, M. Grodzins, "Metropolitan Segregation," *Scientific American,* Vol. 197, No. 4, 33-41 (October, 1957); and O. D. and B. Duncan, "Residential Distribution by Occupational Stratification," *The Amer. Journ. of Soc.,* LX, 493-503 (March, 1955).

[12] The initiative, referendum, and recall—also nonpartisan election—were grafted on the system by the Iowa law under which Des Moines adopted the plan. All fitted in with the "progressive" idea of popular rule which was then sweeping the country, and the Des Moines pattern, with these features, gained great vogue. Interestingly enough, after serving for 40 years as a model of commission government, Des Moines in 1949 went over to the council-manager plan.

The New York charter of 1938 provides for the initiative and referendum, although restricted to charter amendments and other fundamental measures. *Cf.* W. W. Crouch, "The Initiative and Referendum in Cities," *Amer. Polit. Sci. Rev.,* XXXVII, 491-504 (June, 1943); J. M. Selig, "San Francisco Voters Prove Sound 'Lawmakers,'" *Nat. Mun. Rev.,* XXXII, 486-492 (Oct., 1943). This city had a less happy experience with the recall. See J. M. Selig, "San Francisco Upholds Mayor," *Nat. Mun. Rev.,* XXXV, 465-470 (Oct., 1946) and *Time* (July 15, 1946). These are digested in C. R. Adrian, *Governing Urban America,* 90-91 (New York, 1955).

In almost all cases, a mayor is still provided for, and as a rule elected directly to the office by popular vote, although in a few cities the commissioner who receives the highest popular vote automatically becomes mayor. In New Jersey and Nebraska, the commissioners select a mayor from their own number. In any event, the commission-government mayor is traditionally little more than first among equals. Commonly he wields no veto power; usually he has no appointing power *as mayor;* and almost never does he have any general power of removal. To be sure, he is the nominal head of the city government, and on ceremonial occasions he acts as such. But of real authority he usually has little or none beyond that of his colleagues.

3. The mayor under the commission form

There is no doubt that at first it revitalized city government. How much of the improvement came from the commission system's inherent virtues and how much rather from the awakened civil consciousness that accompanied the plan's adoption was never easy to say. Certain advantages of the plan are obvious. It is simple. Theoretically it provides unified governmental policies. However, in practice, administration may be divided, each commissioner going his own way. Neither is anyone responsible for the city as a whole. In addition, the elected commissioners are (at least at first) each an amateur in the department assigned to him. If the city can hire professional technical staffs, things may go not too badly, but the essentials of good administration so necessary in a city are largely unprovided. There is no apex to the administration to insure unity, teamwork, and the proper gradation of authority. Reversions to the mayor-council form have occurred in Buffalo, Oakland, Newark, New Orleans, and Omaha. Changes from the commission form to the newer council-manager system are more numerous but have usually been by smaller cities.

4. Decline of the plan

A more enduring pattern of municipal government designed to meet the defects in the mayor-council system and also invented in this century is the council-manager system. Introduced first in any sizable city in Dayton, Ohio, in 1914, this plan has won converts steadily in the years that have followed. In fact there have been more adoptions of it in the last two decades than at any other period in its history. Its popularity has never waned. In 1965, more than 40 percent (1202) of all cities with more than 5000 population as well as a large number of smaller places were governed under the manager system.[13] The plan has been especially popular in cities of 25,000 to 100,000 population.

The council-manager system

Under the council-manager form, there continues to be an elective council, but always a small one. In about three-fourths of the manager cities, its members number five, and where the number is larger, it rarely exceeds seven, eight or nine. Furthermore, the council has, in general, the functions of the council in the mayor-council system except in the domain of administration—

Essential features: 1. The council

[13] There were 1995 manager-governed cities and 32 counties as of Jan. 1, 1965. *The Municipal Year Book, 1965,* 114, 521-554 (Chicago, 1965). The best known of the manager cities are: Cincinnati, Dallas, Fort Worth, Kansas City, Missouri, Long Beach, Oakland, Rochester, San Antonio, San Diego, and Toledo. All the cities of Alaska employ the council-manager system. Honolulu, however, has a strong mayor.

and except also for the very important function of choosing the manager. It enacts ordinances and regulations, levies taxes, votes appropriation, authorizes borrowing, grants franchises, creates and abolishes departments, investigates the financial transactions or official acts of any officer or department—in short, serves as the supreme policy-determining and general supervisory authority of the city. Restricted, however, to these functions, it devotes only limited time to the city's affairs (rarely meeting more than once a week, and frequently not oftener than once in two or three weeks). Its members are paid only nominal sums for their services. Councilors usually are elected on nonpartisan tickets, and their work may be subject to checks imposed by the initiative, referendum, and recall. They are also, typically, elected at-large rather than by wards.

2. The manager

The really distinctive feature of the system arises in connection with administration. Under the mayor-council plan, administration is carried on in departments subordinate to the mayor, but with control considerably diffused between that official and the council and in the "weak-mayor" system among numerous elected administrators. Under the commission plan, it is vested in the commission and exercised through departments distributed among the commissioners. Under the council-manager plan, on the other hand, the entire job of administrative management is concentrated in the hands of a single well-paid official—the manager—chosen by the council and fully responsible to it, but picked as a professional administrator and presumed to be divorced from all political connections and motivations. The council has only to determine larger matters of policy, find the necessary money, and keep a watchful eye on what goes on. Day-to-day operations of the police, fire, public works, and other departments, are not its concern. The plan is thus essentially like that of a business corporation, with the electorate corresponding to the stockholders, the council corresponding to the board of directors, chosen by the stockholders and charged with general responsibility for the conduct of the business, and with the city manager corresponding to the superintendent, president, or general manager, chosen by the board of directors, responsible to it, and charged with looking after all the details of the business.[14]

The manager's functions

As the most conspicuous official in the city government and the one around whom all administration revolves, the manager has many and exacting duties. (1) With the exception of the city auditor or comptroller, the city attorney, and sometimes the city clerk (all usually chosen by the council, or even by the people), he appoints city officials—heads of departments and usually higher subordinates—and (within broad lines marked out by the

[14] Often under this plan there still is a mayor, who may be chosen by the council or by the voters, or may be the councillor who polled the heaviest popular vote, but who in any event is always simply some member of the council bearing the title. As under the commission plan, the office serves no purpose except to provide the city with some one to represent and speak for it on ceremonial occasions.

council) assigns them their duties, with no power in the council to confirm or reject, although of course with due regard for whatever civil service regulations the city may maintain. The manager also can independently suspend or remove. (2) As the city's chief executive, he sees to the enforcement of all local ordinances and likewise of such state laws as the city is expected to administer. (3) He supervises, and insofar as necessary directs, all administrative work carried on in the various departments, issuing instructions, receiving reports, advising and guiding. (4) Only the council, representing the taxpayers, can adopt the municipal budget. But it is the business of the manager not only to keep the council informed on financial conditions and needs, but also to prepare the budget for council consideration and to explain the significance of its various items. Finally, (5) as the connecting link between the legislative and administrative branches of the city government, and the person knowing the city's affairs most intimately, the manager not only must attend council meetings (taking part in discussions, although of course not voting), but stand at all times ready to assist with information and advice. Members of the council are expected to refrain from meddling with administrative activities and from attempting to influence the manager in selecting department heads, awarding contracts, and the like. This they do not always do, and in many places sound traditions as to the proper sphere of the council under the system remain to be established. Properly the council's functions are exhausted when it has picked a good man for the manager's job, set up adequate machinery with which he may work, laid down any broad lines of policy that it wants to see followed, provided the necessary funds, and placed itself in a position to keep informed on what the manager is doing and to avail itself of the information and advice that he can give.[15]

The foregoing enumeration of managerial functions and duties carries obvious implications as to the qualifications that a city manager should have. In all cities employing the plan, the council makes the selection. Appointment usually is for no definite term, the understanding being that an incumbent will be retained as long as he gives satisfaction. The salary is fixed by the council, usually at whatever figure it becomes necessary to pay in order to obtain the person desired. Manifestly, the manager must be a man of energy and of demonstrated executive ability; he must be skillful in dealing with people, yet interested in administration rather than in politics.[16] It is desirable that he shall have had previous experience as a manager, presumably in some smaller city, or at all events as a mayor, council member, or other municipal official. He need not be an expert in any one branch of municipal activity, for example, public works or public health, but he must have at least some

Qualifications and selection of managers

[15] "The City Manager's Relations with the Council," *Public Management*, XXIV, 39-45 (Feb., 1942); *Ibid.*, XXVII, 71-74 (Mar., 1946).

[16] The city managership long was a failure in Kansas City because the people persisted in electing a machine-dominated council, which in turn appointed politician managers. Since 1940, the situation has been corrected. See K. Detzer, "Everything's Changed Now," *Nat. Mun. Rev.*, XXXVIII, 320-323, 338 (July, 1949).

acquaintance with all branches and an intelligent appreciation of the importance and interrelations of all. City managership is now a profession followed
by many hundreds of experienced people.[17]

Results
achieved

The steadily lengthening list of council-manager cities suggests that the
manager plan has come to stay. Eighty cities that have tried it have, it is true,
given it up (sixteen of them later went back to it). The most conspicuous
abandonment was that of Cleveland. Sometimes partisan politics has been
allowed to scuttle the system, or it has been abandoned for other reasons not
reflecting on the plan's intrinsic merits. In scores of cities, administrative personnel has been improved, better business methods have been introduced
(especially with respect to purchasing, accounting, and awarding of contracts),
budget-making has been placed on a more scientific basis, debts have been
reduced and expenditures held within the limits of revenues, partisan politics
has been eliminated from administrative planning and operation, and general
administrative efficiency has been promoted. Not all of the credit should go to
the plan as such; some of it is due the awakened civic interest which led to
adoption of the plan in the first place. Unquestionably the managership has in
plenty of places demonstrated its very great merits.

Impedi-
ments and
problems

There is, however, no golden road to efficient, economical, and completely
satisfactory municipal government, and the council-manager plan has its obstacles and problems as does any other. The initial high hurdle is the selection
of the manager himself. The manager is the key figure in the system, and unless
he is the right man, things will not go well. A second problem is that of the
proper functioning of the council under the system, often aggravated by the
almost incurable inclination of legislative bodies to dabble in administrative
matters about which they know little. If, as is true, the average tenure of city
managers is brief (perhaps four or five years) a main reason—apart from
resignations to accept better positions—is the tendency of councils to interfere
with their work and make good relations impossible. Some councils go to the
opposite extreme, taking the road of least resistance, thinking *all* of their
responsibilities are discharged when the manager is selected, abdicating even
their role of policy formulation.

The man-
ager as
civic
leader

There is also the question of the extent to which the manager shall assume
an active leadership in municipal life and affairs. The earlier idea was that he
should be a strictly professional and almost impersonal administrator, leaving
it entirely to the council not only to shape policy but to set the pace and fix
the tone of municipal public life. Indeed, the professional organization of the
craft—the International City Managers' Association—once expressly advised
its members not to try to assume leadership in their city's general affairs.

[17] An evidence of this is the International City Managers' Association, dating from
1924 and maintaining headquarters in Chicago. One of this organization's publishing
enterprises is the *Municipal Year Book* frequently cited in these pages.

In past experience, more managers have been drawn from engineering than from any
other one profession. But in the present roster law, accounting, merchandising, public
administration, and many other fields are represented.

Leadership by a council or any other collective agency is likely, however, to be rather colorless; people like to see leadership dramatized in some conspicuous personality. Reports from many council-manager cities indicate a present tendency of the manager to emerge in the role of community leader, in the sense at least of giving primary public expression to municipal aims, aspirations, and objectives. Such a role involves hazards. The council may take offense, and there is danger of being drawn into politics. More and more managers are finding, however, that the risks must be taken. For leadership of a more or less personalized character there must be. If not supplied from within the city's government, it will arise outside, where it is likely to become a source of embarrassment. Leadership, however, is not dictatorship; a manager obviously will be well advised to respect public opinion and keep within the limits of what it will support.[18]

VILLAGES

When a portion of a New England town, or of a Western township, or of a county that does not have township government, becomes more thickly settled than the rest and begins to take on a semi-urban aspect, its inhabitants are quite certain to demand more public services, such as fire protection, street paving and lighting, water supply, and sewerage facilities, than the town, township, or county authorities will be willing to provide. Sooner or later such communities are likely to be incorporated as villages or boroughs.[19] State law often requires that a community seeking incorporation as a village shall meet certain standards of area and population, and that the question of incorporation be submitted to a popular vote. In Illinois, for example, any area of not more than two square miles, with at least 100 inhabitants, if not already within a village or city, may become a village by a vote of the people at a special election. It then remains a village until it has 1000 inhabitants, when it may (but is not obliged to) change to a city government. Incorporation

Status

[18] For case studies on manager leadership see, C. R. Adrian, "A Study of Three Communities," *Pub. Admin. Rev.*, XVIII, 208-213 (Summer, 1958). See also, G. M. Kammerer, C. D. Farris, J. M. Degrove, A. B. Cluboh, *City Managers in Politics: An Analysis of Manager Tenure and Termination* (Gainesville, Fla., 1962).

The necessity for having a civic leader induces some communities to retain the elective mayor: *e.g.*, the home rule charter adopted by Anchorage, Alaska, in 1960 provides for both a mayor and a city manager. The relation between the manager system and the size and political characteristics of the city is ably explored in J. H. Kessel, "Governmental Structure and Political Environment: A Statistical Note About American Cities," *Amer. Pol. Sci. Rev.*, LVI, No. 3 (Sept., 1962). See also R. R. Alford and H. M. Scoble, "Political and Socio-Economic Characteristics of Cities," in *Municipal Yearbook, 1965* (Chicago, 1965).

[19] In Alaska, boroughs are unique local units designed to serve purposes elsewhere served by counties and also purposes served by urban units. The constitution provided for boroughs but the legislature in 1963 required all areas outside municipal limits to organize as boroughs. See, S. K. Gore, "Alaskan Boroughs Establish Roles," *National Civic Review*, Vol. LIV, No. 7 (July, 1965).

gives a village power to undertake community services of the kinds referred to above, to levy taxes and borrow money to support them, and to have its own village government, distinct from the governments of township and county. There are more than 10,000 such incorporated villages in the United States, and they are found in all parts of the country, including New England and the Southern and Western states—although by far the greater number are in the North-Central section, where Illinois alone has some 800.

Govern-
ment

The government of villages is a comparatively simple affair. In some states, notably New York, there is a village meeting, much like the town or township meeting. In most states, however, there is no meeting, and control of most matters is left to certain elected officials. In such cases, the main governing authority is likely to be a village board of from three to nine members, called by various names: trustees (New York), assessors (Maine), commissioners (New Hampshire), burgesses (Connecticut), or the village council. Other village officers include a mayor or president or chief burgess, who is the village chief executive, with sometimes a veto upon the acts of the village board; also a clerk, a treasurer, a marshal or police officer, and a police magistrate with functions similar to those of a justice of the peace. Thus, in structure and functions, the government of villages resembles that of cities, except that it is on a smaller scale. However, as a village increases in size and urbanization, it need not become a city in order to operate on a larger scale. State legislatures have heeded the desires of village residents to keep their village governments by passing permissive legislation and providing alternative forms of government. By taking advantage of these laws villages can provide essentially "city" services and modernize their governmental machinery in line with the best management practices in the same way cities can.[20]

Villages as
suburbs

Though the distinction in law between cities and villages (or boroughs) is disappearing, real differences in character exist when the latter are suburbs, especially dormitory ones.[21] The first difference is psychological. The term, "village," is appealing to some suburbanites. It connotes a cohesive community with the old-fashioned rural virtue of neighborliness. They are, therefore, apt to cling to a village form of government even though the city form might be more advantageous. (As it is, for instance, in Wisconsin where cities have more representatives on county boards than villages do.) The second type of

[20] *E.g.*, the Minnesota legislature in 1949 authorized three optional plans of village government, including a council-manager form.

Suburban governments are particularly quick to take advantage of such laws. *E.g.*, of the boroughs in the Pittsburgh metropolitan area, an overwhelming majority have managers. The same cannot be said of nonmetropolitan areas. It is interesting to note that in the same state, the enabling legislation for small cities (3rd class) to modernize their governments is so recent that very few have done so.

[21] These terms—"suburbs," "satellites," "dormitory suburbs," "employing suburbs," "independent cities," etc.—are found in the literature on urban ecology. See especially: V. Jones and A. Collver, "Economic Classification of Cities and Metropolitan Areas," *The Municipal Year Book, 1960,* 69-79 (Chicago, 1960); L. F. Schnore, "Satellites and Suburbs," *Social Forces,* XXXVI, No. 2, 121-127 (Dec., 1957).

difference is social and economic. The residents in dormitory suburbs tend on the whole to have higher income levels than central city residents and to be employed in white collar, professional, and executive occupations rather than in the labor force.[22] Lastly, these differences exhibit themselves in political behavior of a distinctly suburban flavor. In the dormitory suburb [23] (and most suburbs are of this variety), there is a high regard for nonpartisanship in local elections, independent political thinking, and citizen participation in government. There is a corresponding reliance on amateurs. The volunteer fire company performs not only a governmental function but a social one as well. Their politics, too, are apt to be run by political amateurs who need neither office nor patronage and are usually free from the pressures of the tightly organized groups that play so prominent a part in the politics of the city. In national elections, the suburbs often return a Republican vote (*i.e.* in the North) while the city returns a Democratic one.[24]

Altogether, these characteristics result in a bifurcation of patterns of thought and behavior and of political aims that makes a meeting of minds between a central metropolis and its suburbs difficult. When any metropolitan area tries to achieve solutions to problems that cover the entire area, a *modus operandi* that brings these diverging elements together is essential.

References

R. C. Wood, *Suburbia; Its People and Their Politics* (Boston, 1959). An excellent presentation in a new field.

W. C. Hallenbeck, *American Urban Communities* (New York, 1951).

D. W. Hoan, *City Government: The Record of the Milwaukee Experiment* (New York, 1936).

J. C. Bollens and J. R. McKinley, *California City Government* (Berkeley, 1948). Pamph.

G. R. Sherill, *Municipal Government in South Carolina* (Columbia, 1950).

F. Shaw, *The History of the New York City Legislature* (New York, 1954).

[22] For documentation, see O. D. Duncan and A. J. Reiss, Jr., *Social Characteristics of Urban and Rural Communities, 1950* (New York, 1956). Some of the material from this book is reprinted along with other urban studies in W. Dobriner, Ed., *The Suburban Community* (New York, 1958). The student is urged to be on the lookout for similar analyses based on the 1960 Census of Population.

[23] The "employing" suburbs are more like the central city in their social, economic, and political characteristics than they are like other suburbs.

[24] *E.g.*, see E. C. Banfield, "The Politics of Metropolitan Area Organization," *Midwest Journal of Political Science*, Vol. 1, No. 1, 77-91 (May, 1957).

F. M. Stewart, *A Half Century of Municipal Reform* (Berkeley and Los Angeles, 1950). A history of the National Municipal League.

R. S. Allen (ed.), *Our Fair City* (New York, 1947). On politics and corruption in leading cities.

R. S. Childs, *Civic Victories* (New York, 1952).

J. Reichley, *The Art of Government: Reform and Organization Politics in Philadelphia* (The Fund for the Republic, New York, 1959).

R. H. Salisbury, "The Dynamics of Reform: Charter Politics in St. Louis," *Midwest Journ. of Pol. Sci.,* V, No. 3, 260-275 (Aug., 1961).

W. S. Sayre and H. Kaufmann, *Governing New York City* (Russell Sage Foundation, New York, 1960).

A. W. Bromage, *On the City Council* (Ann Arbor, Mich., 1950).

International City Managers' Association, *City Management—A Growing Profession* (Chicago, 1957). Pamph.

H. A. Stone, *City-Manager Government in the United States: A Review After Twenty-five Years* (Chicago, 1940). Covers 50 cities.

National Municipal League, *The Story of the Council-Manager Plan* (rev. ed., New York, 1958). Pamph.

C. F. Lee-Decker, *Manager Government in Pennsylvania Municipalities* (State College, Pa., 1946).

W. S. Sayre, "The General Manager Idea for Large Cities," *Public Admin. Rev.,* XIV, 253-258 (Autumn, 1954).

H. Stein (ed.), "The Cambridge City Manager," *Public Administration and Policy Development: A Case Book,* 573-620 (New York, 1952).

C. E. Ridley, *The Role of the City Manager in Policy Formulation* (Chicago, 1958).

Bureau of the Census, *Local Government Structure* (Washington, 1957).

T. H. and D. D. Reed, *The Government of Cincinnati, 1924-1944; An Appraisal* (Cincinnati, 1944).

R. A. Straetz, *PR Politics in Cincinnati: Thirty-two Years of City Government Through Proportional Representation* (New York, 1958).

E. C. Lee, *The Politics of Nonpartisanship* (Berkeley, Calif., 1961).

H. J. Nelson, "The Vernon Area, California: A Study of the Political Factor in Urban Geography," *Annals of the Assoc. of Amer. Geographers,* XLII, 177-191 (June, 1952).

E. C. Banfield and J. Q. Wilson, *City Politics* (Cambridge, Mass., 1963).

T. J. Lowie, *At the Pleasure of the Mayor* (New York, 1964).

National Municipal League, *Forms of Municipal Government: How Have They Worked?* (New York, 1963).

———, *Model City Charters,* 6th ed. (New York, 1964).

★ 35 ★

Municipal Services and Functions

A CITY is fundamentally a physical place that is the work, indeed the achievement of man. Characterized by its built-up nature, this environment is very difficult to make and keep livable. Most of the activities of our city governments have as their prime objective the mitigation of the effects of congestion on people. Their greatest contributions to human welfare, for instance, in public health, have been made with this goal in mind. The outstanding city problems today can be traced back to shortcomings in this environment that have not yet been adequately resolved. Hardly an activity of our city governments is uninfluenced by the physical form of the city. The density pattern influences the kind and amount of police and fire protection that is needed and the kinds of streets and highways that are laid. The size of a city affects the kind of sewage disposal system that will be adequate and virtually determines what water supply sources will be required. The fact that city land is used for different purposes in different areas of the city, such as residential, industrial, and commercial areas and subclasses within these, makes simple movement a prime concern and the city government is called upon to *add to* the city's physical plant in order to facilitate it. In fact, many city governmental activities revolve around providing physical facilities that in rural areas are privately provided or virtually nonexistent—from playgrounds to garbage incinerators—because "built-up-ness" devours the open land. Lastly, like all physical things, cities decay and we find our city governments today assuming new functions like urban renewal.[1]

Influence of the physical environment

The services of city government that are closely related to its physical form are often called by the generic term, urban services, for as the built-up area expands, the same service needs are brought to other local governments outside the city proper. The prior experiences of our cities and older boroughs

---

[1] Many of these problems are most intense in the most crowded sections. Whether high density is necessary or inherent in city form is one of the concurrent issues in urban economic and planning theory. For the factors influencing concentration and dispersion of economic activity, the student is referred to the works of Raymond Vernon. See also S. Scott, R. R. Boyce, and R. L. Brown, *Two Notes on Metropolitan Research* (The Maxwell Graduate School of Citizenship and Public Affairs, June, 1961), Chap. II. For two differing planning theorists, he is referred to Mumford and Corbusier. However, even extreme dispersal is unlikely to do away with the need for a healthful environment.

899

and other municipalities in providing these services should be invaluable to
the people in these areas that are newly becoming urbanized.[2]

PUBLIC SAFETY

The police
depart-
ment

    In a municipality of any size a police chief is the head of a department
organized on quasi-military lines into specialized divisions: patrol, detective,
traffic control, vice, juvenile and women's, and housekeeping (records, etc.).
The backbone of the force is the patrol division, upon whose efficiency largely
depends the quality of the whole establishment. The patrolmen are the most
numerous of the department's personnel and perform its most important function—patrolling the streets, day and night, on foot, on motorcycles, and in
one-man or two-man "prowl cars," for the detection and prevention of crime.
They also arrest offenders, gather and preserve evidence, and are usually called
upon to handle street traffic and exceptional throngs of people. The detection
and apprehension of criminals whose identity, or at least whereabouts, are
unknown is the responsibility of detectives and plain-clothesmen who in the
larger cities are organized in a highly specialized bureau or division of criminal
investigation. Crime prevention is also a function of the department. Since
juvenile delinquency is a major urban problem, women are often used since
they are peculiarly qualified to work with children, advise parents, watch dance
halls and other places where youth congregate, and maintain helpful contacts
with social-service and recreational agencies.

Police
effective-
ness

    The increase in criminality [3] that has continued since the end of World
War II has been blamed on the war's aftermath, the restlessness of the young
in a time of cold war and an uncertain future, and on police inability to keep
pace with changing conditions. The last is our present concern and is as difficult to document as the first two. Some facts and figures do, however, emerge.
Our police are the best equipped in the world but our crime rate is consistently
higher than Europe's. Our police are most successful against crimes of violence, less successful against crimes against property, and least successful in
enforcing those laws not supported by public sentiment.[4] The American public

    [2] Some problems are called "urban" mainly because most people live in cities. Cases
in point are public welfare and public housing for which the national government is
taking increasing responsibility.

    [3] Crime rates (number per 100,000 population) have increased in the last five years
as follows: forcible rape, 12 percent; aggravated assault, 3 percent; burglary (breaking
and entering), with intent to commit a felony, 13 percent; larceny (over $50), 16
percent; and auto theft, 11 percent. From 1950 to 1960, the absolute increase in all
major crimes was 98 percent while the population increase was 18 percent. U.S. Department of Justice, F.B.I., *Uniform Crime Reports* (Sept., 1960). From 1958 to 1964 crime
increased almost six times faster than population. *Uniform Crime Reports, July, 1964*
(Washington, 1965).

    [4] Offenses cleared by arrest in 1964 per 100 known to the police were as follows:
murder and nonnegligent manslaughter, 49; manslaughter by negligence, 86; forcible
rape, 67; aggravated assault, 74; robbery (theft by force or threat of violence), 37;
burglary, 25; larceny (simple theft), 19; auto theft, 26. *Uniform Crime Reports, 1964*.
These figures should be interpreted with caution because of the human tendency of
police chiefs to make reports "look good."

is curiously apathetic about loss by theft, for instance, probably thinking that the "insurance will pay for it." The public is less tolerant when crimes against the person (violence) are involved. Public apathy, however, is not the only reason for the generally acknowledged poor record of our police departments. Public distrust and false economies instituted to "save the taxpayers' money" are also factors. Both probably go far in explaining the relatively small number of policemen employed by our cities as compared to European practice and the generally low salaries paid them.[5] The number of police employees has increased gradually over the last ten years and has approximated the increase in total population but has not nearly kept pace with the rise in crime. Meanwhile, more of the force has been employed in traffic duties.

Across the nation the work of the police is complicated by the large number of units of government. The tradition of localism means many local police forces and uncoordinated activity that favors the extremely mobile criminal. Also the spread of urbanism has tended to bring urban crime into more areas. The inherent weaknesses of small police establishments and amateur forces in these areas has led to the establishment of state and county professional forces, that, however, where they exist, usually supplement rather than replace the traditional sheriffs, deputies, and town constables. There are vast interstate networks for radio and teletype communication. The states and the federal government have also established laboratories for the scientific examination of evidence, helped train recruits, and in other ways improved police administration and coordinated local activities without abandoning the tradition of local responsibility.

Police protection outside the city limits

No branch of municipal administration offers more opportunities for corrupt influences to make themselves felt than does the police force of a large city. In virtually every startling revelation of corruption connected with city government the police have been more or less implicated.[6] It may be stated categorically that organized vice on any scale is impossible in an American city without the connivance of the police department. Temptation to favoritism, collusion, and graft besets the department's personnel on all levels; every

The problem of police integrity

---

[5] The median number of police employees in cities over 10,000 population in 1959 ranged from 1.50 per 1000 population to 2.63 gradually increasing with city size. *The Municipal Year Book, 1965,* 444. Over half of the nation's police force is concentrated in the 50 largest cities.

Entrance salaries of patrolmen ranged in 1965 from $4740 to $5515, also increasing with city size. *The Municipal Year Book, 1965.* Virtually the only way for a patrolman to increase his salary is by promotion, a strictly limited procedure.

Crime rates also increase with city size. Typical rates (number per 100,000 population) range from 2.3 in cities under 10,000 population to 6.9 in cities over 250,000 for murder and nonnegligent manslaughter; from 71.8 to 361.9 for auto theft. *Uniform Crime Reports, 1964.*

[6] The spectacularly televised hearings of the Kefauver Committee brought these revelations into millions of living rooms. Stunned as many people were by them, no great improvements have been discernible. Even the recommendations of the Committee were mild. See *Hearings before the Special Committee to Investigate Organized Crime in Interstate Commerce* and the three *Interim Reports* and *Final Report of the Special Committee* (Washington, 1951).

lawless element deriving profit from its activities is prepared to share its ill-gotten gains with the police in return for immunity from prosecution. The possibilities of misconduct become especially grave when the police are expected to enforce laws not supported by the moral standards in the community, as frequently happens in the case of laws against the sale of liquor, gambling, and prostitution. However, even in cities where the citizenry and the police both have the will to stamp out the rackets, they do not always have the means. A gang driven from a central city merely moves to a sympathetic suburb or county area.

Traffic regulation and control

The duty of police departments to regulate vehicular traffic deserves special consideration. The objective in traffic control is safety. Automobiles cause approximately 40 percent of the total number of accidents. The duties of the police (in the largest cities a special force) are: regulating traffic flow, enforcing traffic laws and ordinances, and educating the public on traffic safety and changes in the regulations. An increasing number of cities is separating from departments of public works and streets, duties relevant to traffic engineering and putting them under a professional traffic engineer. He needs to work closely with the police but he is usually not part of their establishment. Typically, the traffic engineer designates the locations for stop and caution signs, the intersections for signals, and the locations for curb loading zones. He also often engages in planning for off-street parking, conducts mass transit surveys, and reviews plans for street layouts in new subdivisions. These specialized city activities, plus the work of highway engineers in designing safer highways, are still unable to prevent annual increases in the number of motor vehicle deaths. The death and accident rate in relation to the number of miles travelled on the nation's roads, streets, and highways is not quite so disturbing.[7]

Fire departments and forces

A few decades ago, paid professional fire departments existed in only the largest cities, with fire-fighting left elsewhere to unpaid volunteer bands of citizens armed only with leather hose, buckets, and hand pumps. Now all is changed; any city, large or small, without a professional, paid, adequately equipped fire department is regarded as decidedly backward. Except in places of 25,000 or less, the basic pattern is a system of fire districts or precincts covering the city, each with a fire company operating, with full equipment, from a fire station serving as headquarters, and in large places with company commanders usually grouped under subchiefs. Like police protection, fire protection must be available around the clock, and consequently the force operates in platoons, or shifts, most commonly two, each with one day on duty and one day off, but sometimes three, each serving eight hours a day.

Fire department functions:

1. Fire-fighting

The primary function of a fire department is, of course, to fight, check and extinguish fires when they break out. For doing this American firemen have at their command equipment and facilities far surpassing any ordinarily to be found in European cities. Huge pumpers (a pumper company is the

[7] J. M. Stein, "Traffic Administration," *The Municipal Year Book, 1965*, 456-458 (Chicago, 1965).

basic fire-fighting unit), ladders extensible to great heights by mechanical power, water-tower trucks, turret pipes, "fog trucks" carrying equipment for smothering fire with fine spray, asbestos clothing, two-way radio communication, special high-pressure water mains serving areas containing tall buildings are only parts of the apparatus available in large cities. Even in small ones there has been great advance since the old horse-drawn "fire engine" used to go clanging down the street.

Despite all this, the annual fire loss in the United States is shockingly heavy—an estimated 11,900 deaths, twice as many serious injuries, and in terms of money, more than $1.67 billion. With inferior facilities for fighting conflagrations, Europe suffers far less from them (in peacetime), partly because less inflammable building materials are used, but partly also because of other precautionary measures. American cities in the past two or three decades have been waking up to the need for fire prevention. Through their National Board of Fire Underwriters, insurance companies look anxiously into the facilities of cities for fire fighting and programs of prevention and advise with the proper authorities. City councils now fix areas within which inflammable buildings may not be erected and prohibit structural arrangements favorable to the spread of fire. Since more fires occur in private dwellings and the main causes are children playing with matches and careless smoking, fire departments are increasing their educational activities, especially in the public schools. Faulty electric equipment and wiring and other substandard building practices also contribute greatly to the nation's fire losses. These can be uncovered only by inspection and fire department personnel are engaging in this more and more. When private dwellings are inspected by firemen with the homeowner present and cooperating, public education in fire prevention can be furthered at the same time. Since the increase in manufacturing and mercantile building fires has been much lower than that for dwelling fires, monetary loss has not increased proportionately. The results of fire prevention activities are, therefore, mixed, but a good deal more attention and concern is required, for the last decade showed more loss of life than the previous one.

2. Fire prevention

PUBLIC HEALTH AND SANITATION

Where, as in the modern city, large numbers of people are massed within relatively small areas, much is required not only to promote safety but also to safeguard health. To do this cities own and operate water supply and distribution systems to provide pure drinking water. They own and operate facilities to dispose of unsanitary and other wastes. And direct health services are provided by a department that may regulate personal conduct in the interests of the public health and in other ways provide a healthy environment for the people of the city.

The head of a municipal health department is usually a professionally trained public health administrator. In large places, he typically heads a more

Health departments

or less elaborate and specialized administration with medical officers, sanitarians, nurses, inspectors, and other employees. Smaller places, considering that they cannot afford such a setup, frequently leave public health matters to be attended to by a designated physician devoting most of his time to private practice. In such situations what is done may leave a good deal to be desired.[8]

Health department activities and current problems

In times past, municipal health departments concerned themselves almost wholly with discovering and abating nuisances, fighting epidemics, and controlling communicable diseases. Nowadays, effort is focused far more upon preventive measures made possible by advancing medical and sanitary science. Vital statistics are gathered and compiled to afford a continuous picture of the state of the community's health; inspections of water and milk supply, and of every establishment and operation (often in both production and distribution) through which articles of food reach the consumer are carried on; campaigns of health education are carried into homes, schools, and factories; and, of course, the battle against contagion still goes on with health departments enforcing quarantines, supervising immunization, and administering isolation centers. Tuberculosis is still a threat, especially in some metropolitan areas where the mortality rate is comparable to what it was in the general population 20 years ago. Nor does the infant mortality rate seem to be declining as it should in some metropolitan areas. Whether or not the influx of migrants from cultures that usually experience a higher infant mortality rate is the cause,[9] population movements do not make public health work any easier. Port cities usually have to be particularly careful. This is pointed up in the annual surveys of the American Public Health Association which reveal that suburban expansion is one of the major current problems of public health leaders. The others ironically reflect public health and private medicine successes and our industrial progress of which we are so proud. They are: aging, chronic disease, radiological health, mental health, air pollution, rehabilitation, and accident prevention.

Waste collection and disposal:

The collection and disposal of wastes is everywhere an important municipal activity, although the job is done a good deal more effectively in some

[8] A standard of at least 50,000 people has been set by the American Public Health Association as the population necessary to support a *specialized* department. If local health administration were the responsibility of the counties instead of the cities and villages, more places could support specialized departments. Where state boards and departments of health establish district offices of their own instead of using the county, the movement to increase county health functions is hindered. However, some progress in consolidating local health services has been made. Michigan, for example, provides that when any city fails to maintain a full-time health officer, its health activities automatically are transferred to the county. In some states, counties may contract with local units to take over their public health work. This practice has made most headway in California. Occasionally, two or more small places have combined to employ a full-time health officer and to develop a joint health administration to the advantage of each community concerned.

[9] The ability of staphylococci to mutate into strains resistant to antibiotics has also been cited as a cause.

cities than in others. Few people appreciate the fact that, counting all kinds—ashes, inorganic rubbish, street sweepings, garbage, and sewage—a city's wastes exceed a ton a day per capita. In every city of size, the task of collecting and disposing of this is, therefore, immense and involves thousands of dollars and hundreds of functionaries. Collection does not pose any particular problems by now but disposal is literally as well as figuratively a mounting problem.

How can a city dispose of the garbage and inorganic refuse after it is collected? The older methods of dumping garbage in a convenient stream or burning it with other combustible refuse in an open dump are no longer acceptable. River and lake water can cleanse itself of organic waste matter but this ability is lost when the amount dumped into it is too great—a situation that exists in many areas today. Open dumping grounds can no longer be found within an economically feasible distance without the fumes from them discommoding neighboring towns. The sanitary landfill method is, therefore, becoming more popular. In addition to its health advantages, economies result. The collection of garbage and trash can be combined (and the ubiquitous tin can added) and otherwise unusable land can be reclaimed for public parks or sold for private development, thereby adding either to the amenities or to the tax base. Where land is not available, cities are turning to incinerators as the second best method. Some localities, though, resist the added expense unless forced. When the public health is affected, a state can intervene. New Jersey, for instance, prohibits the open dump as a means of municipal refuse disposal.

1. Garbage and refuse

Sewage consists primarily of waterborne human effluvia from dwellings and wastes from many industrial plants such as laundries and slaughterhouses. More than other forms of waste, this bears the germs of disease; and proper collection and disposal have urgent importance for the health of the community. A prime municipal engineering activity is, therefore, the installation, operation, and maintenance of an adequate sewerage system consisting of trunk lines, lateral branches, and connections for every building used as a dwelling or for commercial or industrial purposes. The problem is not solved with the construction of a sewerage system, the chief purpose of which is to collect sewage and carry it off; there remains the question of final disposal. In cities on an ocean or a large lake or river, the matter may find ready, even if not ideal, solution. Where, however, the same lake or river serves as the source of water supply for nearby communities, different methods of disposal have to be found, or the sewage must be subjected to chemical treatment before it is turned into the lake or stream in question.

2. Sewage

The contamination of the water in and about most of our cities has progressed to the point where only drastic action can restore our streams to acceptable [10] conditions. Of the significant sources of pollution, half were

Water pollution

[10] Pristine purity is recognized as an impossible goal for many areas.

municipal sewerage systems in the early 1950's.[11] Both the state and the national government have laws prohibiting stream pollution. The basic Water Pollution Act of the national government was passed in 1948, amended in 1956, 1961, and 1965. A separate division of the United States Public Health Service has been created to implement this law. The service issued its first enforcing order against a municipality in 1959. Prohibiting pollution may not be enough unless municipalities are also aided in constructing treatment plants. To this end, the same act in 1956 authorized $500 million and in 1961 an additional $570 million for matching grants to the states for municipal plant construction and other state antipollution activities. By 1965, over 6,000 projects have been completed or were under construction under this program. Preferences under the 1956 authorization were given to small plants; therefore, the situation in metropolitan areas was not particularly alleviated. Though providing that one-half of the aid should go to communities of less than 125,000 people, the 1961 amendments raised the ceiling for individual projects to $600,000 and projects that would serve more than one community could receive aid up to $2.4 million for each one. In 1965, the ceiling was raised to $1.2 million for a simple community project and $4.8 million for multicommunity projects and the overall appropriation increased to $150 million annually. Furthermore, the power of the national government and states to prevent pollution as well as to halt it once begun was expanded.

Sewerage districts   One approach that is finding increasing favor is the sewerage district. These districts are independent units of government established usually by the voters of the area under state enabling acts. A sewerage district can be created to serve an entire metropolitan area—the central city and its suburbs—or any portion of it where the need is greatest. Once created, these districts enjoy financial and administrative autonomy under state law. They are governed by boards appointed by the governor or other state official (such as a judge) or by local officials in the areas they serve. Sometimes part of a board membership is elected by the voters of the area but very rarely do the voters elect an entire board.[12] These boards employ professional staffs, which are usually technically proficient. One of the oldest is the Metropolitan Sanitary District of Greater Chicago.

Water supply   Though water for domestic uses is only a very small part of the amount used in cities, the necessity for keeping it pure for drinking purposes makes its supply and distribution a public health concern. American urban communities use at least 100 gallons a day per capita, but a municipality has to be able to provide more than its average need. Demands for water fluctuate and

[11] R. Eliassen, "Stream Pollution," *Scientific American,* Vol. 186, No. 3, 17-21 (Mar., 1952). This article also presents in lay language the other causes, the types of pollution, and their effects.

[12] Sometimes all or part of a board consists of local officials serving *ex officio.* For details on methods of selecting board members in special districts see A. W. Bromage, "Political Representation in Metropolitan Areas," *Amer. Pol. Sci. Rev.,* 413-418 (June, 1958).

on a maximum day 50 percent more than the average consumption may be needed and the maximum hourly demand may be two or three times the hourly average. The needs of domestic users and industry are making increasing demands. Population growth, technological advances that depend on water (such as air-conditioning and home garbage disposal units) and new industrial processes that need a lot of water (such as the manufacturing of synthetic fibers) are depleting ground water levels and burdening surface sources. The American Waterworks Association reported in 1959 that $400 million is needed every year just to keep up with increasing population and expanding uses and that one out of every five public systems is deficient in supply.[13] However, some recent studies have abated somewhat the alarms of the decade by pointing out that the nation is not in danger of running out of fresh water. The supplies will be available, however, only if wisely managed. The National Water Resources Act of 1964 is intended to step up the efforts of scientists to aid in water resource management.[14] Sources are being found farther and farther away from the cities and sources formerly bypassed are being reconsidered. Fortunately, purification advances have made some of these relatively economical. The need to conserve this vital natural resource is leading to some interesting experiments. For instance, Oceanside, California, has adopted a program of reclaiming its entire sewage flow for reuse by industry, for irrigation, or for ground-water recharging.

A new assault was also launched in 1963 on the growing increase in air pollution. The Clean Air Act of that year, building upon an earlier law of 1955, provides national funds for research and for grants for local projects. A growing number of cities are adopting and more vigorously enforcing smoke abatement and air-pollution control ordinances.

Air pollution control

TRANSPORTATION

About one-third of all the land in an average city is occupied by its streets and parking facilities. Though these streets comprise only 10 percent of the three million and more miles of highways in the United States, they carry one-half of the nation's traffic.

One of the major advances in street and highway design during the last few decades has been classification according to use. Streets and highways are now classified as: local and residential streets, secondary thoroughfares, major boulevards and expressways, and limited access highways and freeways. Paving, width, and other elements of design should differ for each type, and the pattern of a city's arterials and access streets should be planned not only for present but for expected future use. Although breaks in paving occur because of poor drainage and extremes of weather, street paving does not often get a

Streets: 1. Types

13 *The Municipal Year Book, 1960,* 343.
14 *The Municipal Year Book, 1965,* 370.

chance to wear out. Obsolescence is usually caused by traffic patterns that put streets to uses heavier than the ones for which they were intended.

2. Cost and financing

Constructing and maintaining streets is extremely costly. Concrete paving runs as high as $6 a squard *yard,* including gutters and curbs. Construction costs of municipal streets amount to approximately $4.2 billion a year and this does not include the costs associated with land acquisition, demolition, and moving of utility lines. Maintenance has amounted to $1.2 billion annually in recent years. Not all this is financed from local sources, though most of it is. The states follow different patterns of help including direct state construction of city streets that are part of the state trunk system, financial aids, and shared motor fuel or other taxes. However, local dissatisfaction with rurally dominated state legislatures and highway administrations has led city officials to Washington. Since 1944, urban extensions of the primary and secondary federal aid system have been specifically provided for in national grants (even though the grants are still channelled through the states). A major portion of the System of Interstate and Defense Highways authorized in 1956 is being built in urban areas. It will carry not only long distance traffic but a large number of urban and suburban commuters.

3. Problems

Though all this money is being spent on city streets, traffic congestion, as most people are aware, continues to plague the urban resident. This problem arises mainly because the effect of streets on other land uses has not always been taken into account. For instance, an improved or new street is supposed to relieve congestion by moving traffic faster; but if commercial activity is intensified along its length (which usually happens), more people are brought into an area and congestion is increased. Each year more cities are taking a critical look at their streets and traffic patterns in order to plan them as part of an overall land-use plan and to relate them to other public programs that are also changers of land use, for example, slum clearance, urban renewal, and recreational facilities.[15]

Rapid transit

In the opinion of most experts, the decaying cores of our large cities can not be saved without dependence on transportation facilities that are more efficient carriers of persons and goods than the private automobile. One bus can carry 30 to 50 people, takes up only a little more street room, and rests in a terminal. Vehicles that run on tracks are even more efficient users of space. However, many privately owned and operated transit systems are losing

---

[15] In this connection it may also be mentioned that slum clearance, urban renewal, *and* expressway construction dispossess people who move on, creating new slums by overcrowding other neighborhoods unless all public programs are planned together. It is expressway construction that has too often been planned in a vacuum. It is not mandatory for a local government to relocate people and businesses in this instance. Also a new expressway that slashes through existing developments may destroy more community values than it creates in the absence of overall planning.

The national Bureau of Public Roads has established an Urban, Secondary, and Analyses Divsion to facilitate coordination of urban highway and street development with urban land-use planning and quite a few states have urban divisions within their highway departments with similiar goals. The first responsibility, however, is local.

money. Deficits have been attacked by raising fares and letting facilities deteriorate; then fewer people use them. Threats of abandonment have brought city officials increasingly into the picture. Municipal ownership is one solution. In 1965, more than 60 cities owned transit systems, either directly or through authorities created for the purpose as in Pittsburgh and Dallas.[16] Other cities are considering buying or leasing private systems but there is less enthusiasm for this solution than formerly. More cities and states are experimenting with tax reductions and direct subsidies designed to alleviate the financial plight of the privately owned and operated systems. Revitalizing central business districts by relieving traffic congestion is not the only goal of these cities and states. Many commuters are dependent on this form of transportation.[17] The Urban Mass Transportation Act of 1964 brings the national government into the picture with grants for acquisition.

CONSTRUCTION AND IMPROVEMENT OF TRANSPORT FACILITIES

Many cities own and operate terminal facilities, usually through a business agency such as a municipal utility. The two most common are airports and parking facilities for private automobiles. The situation in airports has been characterized succinctly in the phrase—everyone wants one for his city but not near his home. The national government has encouraged even small cities to build airports with financial aid for construction. Few cities are breaking even on the operation of their airports. Of the 7000 cities and towns with airports in 1965, fewer than 750 were served by commercial airlines.

Terminal facilities: 1. Airports

Parking a private automobile is sometimes a desperate undertaking. Most cities of any size meter curb space, provide municipal lots, or do both.[18] More off-street parking facilities are being provided each year at a high cost for land acquisition in high value areas and a subsequent loss of tax base. Proportionately more parking spaces are provided by middle-sized cities. Each city

2. Parking

---

16 The Philadelphia Plan, which is being watched with interest, seems to be passing the experimental stage. A nonprofit Passenger Service Improvement Corporation has been formed with the Philadelphia Transportation Company (publicly owned and privately operated subway and elevated lines) and two commuter railroads and their connecting bus lines. In return for better and more service at reduced fares, the city subsidizes the operation; $500,000 was appropriated in 1960 by the city. A significant drop in the number of cars entering the city has been reported. *Encyclopedia Britannica Book of the Year,* 1961, 463.

The National Housing Act of 1961 makes loans available to improve urban transport facilities.

17 Special district governments also engage in this type of public enterprise. The best known and largest of these is probably the Port of New York Authority, which has bus and truck terminals, marine terminals, airports, bridges, and tunnels under its jurisdiction.

18 Enforcing parking regulations is the duty of the police. An increasing number of cities with metered space are relieving the police of this chore by employing women ("meter maids").

must decide for itself whether it is better to discourage private cars from entering central business districts or encourage this by improving parking facilities.[19]

A properly coordinated metropolitan transportation system that integrates mass transit facilities with streets and highways and parking facilities is recognized as a most important present need. Studies and plans of this kind are under way in the metropolitan areas of Washington, Pittsburgh and Allegheny County, St. Louis, New York, San Francisco, and many other cities.

EDUCATION

Indepen-
dent status
In the great majority of cities, education is not administered by the regular city government. While many school districts are coterminous (or substantially so) with cities of various sizes, schools are usually in charge of a popularly elected school board endowed with independent power to levy taxes and appropriate school funds subject only to the requirements of state law.[20] The objective in removing school affairs from the regular city government has always been to "keep the schools out of politics." Some also fear that city school systems would come off with diminished financial support. Educational activities are invariably the ones on which most money is spent whether the schools are an integral part of the city government or not. Much of the discussion is philosophical and no change has been made either way for many years. Most schools are well run by competent staffs and high-minded officials.

Expansion
of educa-
tional
activities
The last 50 years have seen a remarkable expansion of educational activities in American cities. These now include—over and above the regular work of instruction through the familiar 12-year gradation—medical, dental, and psychological examination of school children; operation of low-priced or free lunch-rooms; special classes for children found mentally or physically

---

[19] A bitting comment is given on New York City's proposal to build midtown garages by Lewis Mumford in "The Sky Line," *The New Yorker Magazine,* Sept. 3, 1960, 95-105.

On the other hand Detroit officials attribute a reversal of a fifteen-year drop in downtown retail trade to the city's urban renewal and expressway programs, but especially to the completion in 1959 of an underground downtown garage. *The Municipal Year Book, 1960,* 337.

[20] In 29 states, the independent school district is the only system. Most of these are in the Middle West. Dependent districts operated by state, county, city, or New England towns are more numerous than independent districts in Connecticut, Maine, Massachusetts, Tennessee, Vermont, Alaska, and Mississippi. Only four states (Hawaii, Maryland, Rhode Island, North Carolina and Virginia) have no independent districts (*The Municipal Year Book, 1965,* p. 14). Some city school systems classed as dependent enjoy administrative autonomy under an elective board, going to city councils only for approval of their tax levies and expenditures. Even in places where the school board is an integral part of the city government, education may enjoy a good deal of autonomy.

defective; evening classes for immigrants and illiterates; vocational preparation, including manual training, domestic science, skilled trades, and commercial courses; sometimes provision of junior colleges, or even of regular four-year collegiate institutions; and numerous other services—including training in the driving of motor cars. In hundreds of cities, schoolhouses are made available for evening lectures and entertainments and as centers of neighborhood sociability. Many school yards, too, have been enlarged and transformed into general public playgrounds equipped with special apparatus, with children of the neighborhood not only permitted, but encouraged, to resort to them outside of school hours. Hundreds of schoolhouses throughout the country, also, are now used as polling-places on Election Day, and even some so-called conservative New England communities permit public meetings to be held in them, including political gatherings during electoral campaigns.[21]

The last decades have been serious ones for public education. It has been an era of desegregation, Sputnik and the resulting re-examination of educational goals, and the decade of suburban expansion. The American Society of Planning Officials has estimated that 100 new families in a community means four new teachers and four new classrooms. For fast-growing communities this has meant a new school every year. The most difficult problems are in secondary education and they are in the critical stage now when the postwar "baby boom" is in the high school years. A community that can support an adequate grade school at present standards may find that it is not large enough to support a high school.[22] Many suburbanites are caught in a vise when and if city school systems or districts reverse their past practices of admitting tuition pupils. As enrollments mount, more schools (and they are usually high schools) have had to close their doors to nonresidents. In the last decade, school enrollment in the United States rose by one million pupils every year and the forecast for the late sixties and seventies is two million more each year with the greatest growth expected in the high schools.

Current problems

Under state school district organization laws, a district large enough for a modern high school can be formed by merging or consolidating smaller

---

[21] Public libraries had their beginning in this country with a New York law of 1835 authorizing school districts to levy a tax for provision of libraries for school and community use; and by 1900 a few other states took similar steps. The public library as we now know it—as a municipal enterprise—began, however, with the Boston Public Library, authorized by the Massachusetts legislature in 1848; and the characteristic method of administering such institutions, *i.e.*, through a small board chosen by the council or mayor, or both, started at the same time. Municipal libraries in some large cities, *e.g.*, Boston, Detroit, and St. Louis, now are incorporated and have significant independent powers.

[22] The recommended standard for a high school is that it be large enough to have a graduating class of 100. [J. B. Conant, *The American High School Today* (New York, 1959)]. Though there is no definite standard on the population required to accomplish this, for urban areas, it is probably in the neighborhood of 10,000 to 12,000 people, depending on assessed valuations and others factors. By contrast a grade school can be based on as few as 2000 people.

districts. Sometimes grade school districts are combined. Sometimes grade school districts join others that give instruction in the full twelve years. Where popular consent is required in the individual districts, mergers are exceedingly difficult to accomplish. Wealthier districts do not wish to merge with poorer ones, and vice versa, each certain that taxes will be raised. If a new building is required, each district wants it in its own area. If an existing building is abandoned, the district owning its objects. These difficulties are not confined to high school organization but are more intense there, for the high school more than the grade school is the center of community activities. Nor are these difficulties confined to suburban areas, but they are intensified here if cleavages between old and new residents occur, the new residents wanting the "best of everything" and the former residents hurt and bewildered that what they have been proud of is not considered good enough. Only in those few states where the county is the unit for school administration are these problems somewhat alleviated. In many current discussions on increasing county functions, education is not included.

PUBLIC WELFARE

Because of the development of programs by the nation and the states, the city's welfare responsibility has become simply that of providing general assistance or relief (indoor and outdoor) for persons not sufficiently provided for by the state, nation, and community chests. Such relief is usually financed in part by state grants-in-aid. Numerous other activities varying from city to city and frequently related to public health are also carried on, such as vocational guidance clinics, free legal aid for the poor, day care centers for children of working mothers, visiting nurse services, public baths, race relations advisement, and many other activities aimed at advancing people's physical, moral, and economic well-being.

PARKS AND RECREATION

Although considered by many part of the welfare program, recreational activities are becoming so important they deserve separate consideration. The shorter work week has given adults more leisure. The vacant lot for children's play has disappeared and the streets are no longer safe for them. The recognition of the relation between delinquency and idleness has stimulated a demand for more recreational activities. The old-time remedy, work, is no longer a cure-all. Compulsory school attendance laws and prohibitions of child employment have closed this door. The greatest need in this field is the need for space. The community that has enough park acreage available and has been able to keep its parks inviolate from through-traffic or has managed to acquire open land ahead of development is either lucky or unusually foresighted.[23]

HOUSING AND URBAN RENEWAL

This is, typically, a city not a suburban activity. The national program provides financial assistance to local authorities for low-rent public housing and urban renewal and redevelopment projects. The keystone of the city government's responsibilities is urban renewal. By participating in this program, cities may acquire, clear, and prepare blighted areas for new construction and rehabilitation. Cleared land may be used for public housing or resold to private builders for redevelopment. To be eligible for aid, a city has to commit itself to the following program: adequate building and housing codes, effectively enforced; a comprehensive planning division; [24] analysis of its blighted neighborhoods; assumption of responsibility for relocating displaced families; provisions for citizen participation in the program; and ability to finance its part and administer the program. These commitments are approved by the Housing and Home Finance Agency and are recertified annually. After the project is planned, it too must be approved. The objective of urban renewal is not only to clear hopelessly blighted neighborhoods and reverse incipient blight but to rebuild in such a way that future blight is prevented. By the end of 1965, more than 2000 renewal projects had been approved in more than 425 different communities. In meeting project standards, cities have had the most difficulty with relocating families and businesses displaced by the projects. A special type of mortgage insurance (FHA) is available to assist communities and private builders to provide new housing or rehabilitate existing housing to ac-

Slum clearance

[23] A readable account on the need for land is E. Higbee, *The Squeeze: Cities Without Space* (New York, 1960).

The National Housing Act of 1961 made grants available for the purchase and development of "open" adjacent areas for recreational purposes and conservation. Methods for *reserving* private land for anticipated public use are limited in law and in practice. For the recent English experience in this field see P. Self, *Cities in Flood* (London, 1957). In the United States, the Urban Land Institute has recommended acquisition of easements, through which the owner's right to develop would be surrendered. New York and California have recently authorized municipalities to acquire these. See also, A. L. Strong, "A Time to Experiment," *National Civic Review*, LIV, No. 9 (Oct. 1965).

[24] This agency prepares a comprehensive land-use plan which usually consist of maps, charts, etc., showing: (1) the appropriate distribution, location and extent of housing, industry, business, and recreational and open spaces, buildings and facilities for education, streets, and other categories of public and private land use; (2) the identification of neighborhoods that are planned to minimize through traffic and to provide service centers for commercial activities and public facilities that are used by the residents on a daily basis; (3) distribution of sites for employment and service centers throughout the area planned to minimize the time and effort involved in the daily journey to work and in the movement of goods and supplies; (4) density and development standards.

See also R. A. Walker, *The Planning Function in Urban Government* (rev. ed., Chicago, 1951).

commodate people displaced by this program and other governmental action. However, some cities have had to undertake public housing projects they had previously shied away from and others have had to expand their public housing programs. The displaced families are not usually able to afford private housing that meets standards, either FHA or municipal.

Housing conserva- tion

It has been estimated that it would take the entire national product for one year to replace all the substandard buildings in the United States. The impossibility of such a task makes rehabilitation of existing housing necessary. Such rehabilitation also serves to reverse incipient blight. Municipal responsibility in this field is mainly discharged by the enforcement of various codes that set up building standards—health and sanitation codes, building codes, plumbing codes, fire codes, etc. The newest addition to this roster is the housing code. Unlike the older ones that mostly govern structural and material requirements, a housing code sets up occupancy standards. These are usually persons per dwelling unit, persons per bedroom, or floor area or combinations of these. This type of code tries to reach directly the basic cause of deterioration, which is the crowding of more people into a building than it was intended to house. Building codes have been subject, however, to severe criticism. The most common criticisms are: outmoded structural requirements, uncoordinated enforcement, unnecessarily elaborate procedures for notification of violations and repair orders, costly and time-consuming court cases in the last resort, and fines too low to act as a deterrent. Needed repairs and alterations are either not made or are delayed while blight spreads through a neighborhood. Most cities could do more in this field, especially where relatively small areas of blight threaten otherwise good neighborhoods.[25]

FINANCING THE SERVICES

Expendi- tures

Besides having to find the money to meet the new needs caused by the growth of our urban areas and the demands for better and more service by a prosperous citizenry, our cities have been hit by the high cost of living as has every other enterprise. School construction costs, for example, continue to rise (a half a point a *month*), construction costs for streets and other public works increased 50 percent from 1950 to 1959 and advanced more than 6 percent 1960-1965, municipal employment increased 16 percent from 1953 to 1959 but payrolls rose 49 percent and have continued to climb into the mid-sixties.[26]

Across the nation cities and suburbs alike have been feeling the pinch. The cities have suffered a loss of income from the movement out of their

[25] Milwaukee and Baltimore have successfully passed ordinances to enlarge the city's powers to rehabilitate substandard housing. If a landlord doesn't comply with an order to repair, the city may do it and assess the cost against the property.

[26] Because of variations in the division of responsibility between local governmental units from one state to another and even within states, it is best to consider all local expenditures together when comparing services.

jurisdiction of the very people best able to pay—manufacturing and retail trade and the middle-income group. At the same time, cities have been under increasing obligations to provide streets and other services for nonresidents, and to rebuild an aging physical plant. The suburbs have the opposite difficulty. They have been building an entire physical plant in one generation, and at inflated prices. The suburbs for their part are not able to take advantage of large-scale economies and they pay the costs of independence in other ways, too—in duplication of services and inexperienced administration. In 1963, the expenditures of all local governments [27] totaled over $48 billion.

Local revenue comes from sources falling into a half dozen very unequal *Revenue* categories. At the top of the list, by a very wide margin, is the general property tax. In 1962, the property tax accounted for 44 percent of all revenue received by municipal governments. Before 1950, the main nonproperty tax resource of municipal governments was the gross receipts tax levied on public utilities. (Counties and school districts were still virtually limited to the property tax.) Since then, more local units have adopted general local sales taxes. By 1963, over a thousand municipal, county, and school sales taxes were being levied. Most of them were in Illinois and California. In some municipalities —virtually all in Pennsylvania and Ohio—income taxes, personal or both personal and corporate are levied. Besides relieving the property tax, both these taxes reach the nonresident and force him to contribute to a government whose services he uses. Of the two, the sales tax is the most popular though both are regressive as used by local governments. Somewhat similar to taxes, but not of general application, are special assessments levied against benefiting property owners to meet part or all of the cost of pavements, gutters, sidewalks, or water and sewer mains which tend to improve property values in the neighborhood. Usually there also will be income from water rates and other utilities, such as street railways or electricity distributing plants. Charges for other services, such as care in municipal hospitals or extra street sprinkling have been common in the past also. Because of the sheer inadequacy of the property tax to support municipal services today, more places are resorting to these direct charges. The most common is the sewer rental charge. Municipalities also charge for services to outlying areas.[28] Licenses and permit fees are extracted from a multitude of enterprises and pursuits, many of which are regulated, such as dance halls. Finally, and more important than anything else except taxes, are the proceeds of state-collected locally-shared taxes and grants-in-aid, the latter bringing cities substantial sums not only from the state treasury

[27] City government expenses have been rising from six to eight percent annually, in recent years. The most complete coverage of local government finances is made in connection with the Census of Governments referred to earlier; the last was made in 1962 and is published by the Bureau of the Census in the volumes repeatedly referred to.

[28] Most of the charges and taxes levied by local governments are based on the theory that those who benefit most should pay the most. For a cogent criticism of this theory see, M. Walker, "Fiscal Aspects of Metropolitan Regional Development," *Univ. of Penna. Law Rev.*, Vol. 105, No. 4, 489-503 (Feb., 1957).

but, for certain purposes, for example, airports and highways, from the national Treasury as well. In 1963, state and national money returned to local units accounted for 27 percent of all local revenue.

Financial resources in metropolitan areas
Because a metropolitan area is not a legal entity, it is composed of many taxing and charging jurisdictions of unequal financial resources. These inequalities are intensified by local property assessment because it provides a means by which units can compete for desirable development, thus increasing a comparative advantage. However, equalizing assessments as described earlier would not remove all the inequalities.[29] Reliance on the property tax as the main source of revenue in itself creates situations that have adverse effects on other parts of the area. In the first place, the temptation for a unit to seek industry or to zone for large lots only on the theory that these types of land development can best pay for increased school enrollments and other services is almost irresistible. Such activities can result in premature or ill-advised land use that increases sewer, water, and transportation costs for other units also. In the second place, if most or all of a community's tax base consists of low value property, the burden on it becomes intolerable. Inequality of financial resources is inevitable as long as separate taxing jurisdictions remain, but when services are provided on an unequal basis because of it, a situation exists that demands attention. We still do not have an acceptable theory of local taxation that takes into account the metropolitan complex. Within a city, the ability to support services differs from one neighborhood to another, yet police and fire protection are not allocated on this basis. The resources of the whole city are pooled. The only way at present that the resources of an entire metropolitan area can be tapped to provide a minimum standard of service throughout the area is the indirect one of state aid and shared taxes and national aid. State aids and shared taxes are often criticized, however, for their maldistribution. Income taxes are usually distributed according to the residence of the taxpayer, which intensifies service inequalities. It has been urged that they be distributed on the basis of need. State aids are supposedly distributed on this basis but often the formulae used assume that cities are wealthy places of high property values that need less, and that municipalities generally do not need aid to give a minimum standard of service, which is the main concern of the state. Neither of these assumptions is borne out by the facts in many metropolitan areas. For this reason and the fact that metropolitan areas sometimes cross state lines and because of the national interest in so many urban activities, national aid is becoming an increasingly important revenue source for units in metropolitan areas.[30]

Borrowing
Local government debts have been increasing from the same causes as expenditures. From a low of $13 billion in 1946, the local debt outstanding

[29] An argument *against* abolishing tax differentials is ably presented in H. A. Simon, *Fiscal Aspects of Metropolitan Consolidation* (Berkeley, Calif., 1943).

[30] See also Commission on Intergovernmental Relations, *Advisory Committee Report on Local Government,* 24-26 (Wash., June, 1955).

today is over $63 billion. In authorizing new indebtedness, a local governing body usually operates under certain restraints. In the first place, many charters or state laws require popular approval in a referendum before new bonds can be issued; in the second place, in nearly all states, a ceiling is fixed by the constitution or a statute. The effect of these restrictions has often been adverse. Rather than producing local economy they have put local governments in a straitjacket to find ways to finance needed improvements. Enterprises that pay their own way from their own revenues commonly finance their extensions by issuing revenue bonds that need neither voter approval nor are they subject to ceilings. The popularity of special districts for providing services such as water supply and sewage disposal and many others is in part traceable to this, for they finance their capital programs this way. (And, incidentally, often charge for their services directly instead of relying on property taxes for their operations.) Commonly too, debt limits take no cognizance of overlapping debt. Consolidation of units is hindered if the combined debt limit is lower than the sum of the separate units. This sometimes occurs in school district reorganization. Because debt limits are stated in terms not of a fixed amount, but of some percentage of the jurisdiction's assessed valuation, they are not applied uniformly over an area because assessment ratios vary. This results in the same inequalities in resources that resulted from the local assessments in the first place (*i.e.,* for taxation). For these reasons, and the fact that today needs are increasing faster than assessments, especially for schools, a different approach seems called for. One proposed suggestion is to use the total financial resources of the local government as the basis for a ceiling. Another is the approach used by North Carolina. A state administrative agency is authorized to handle each situation on its merits and to approve local debt with broad discretion.

References

1. GENERAL

T. H. Reed, *Municipal Management* (New York, 1941).

H. S. Churchill, *The City Is the People* (New York, 1945).

Mayor's Committee on Management Survey, *Modern Management for the City of New York,* I (New York, 1953).

E. B. Schulz, *American City Government: Its Machinery and Processes* (New York, 1949).

U. S. Conference of Mayors, *City Problems* (Washington). Annual publication.

R. M. Fisher (ed.), *The Metropolis in Modern Life* (New York, 1955).

"Metropolis in Ferment," *The Annals of the Amer. Academy of Polit. and Soc. Sci.,* Vol. 314 (Nov., 1957). Entire issue.

Le Corbusier (C. E. J.-G.), *Concerning Town Planning* (New Haven, Conn., 1948).

E. Saarinen, *The City: Its Growth, Its Decay, Its Future* (New York, 1943).

L. Rodwin (ed.), *The Future Metropolis* (New York, 1961).

R. A. Futterman, *The Future of Our Cities* (New York, 1961).

R. Vernon, *Metropolis, 1985* (Cambridge, Mass., 1960). A synthesis of the New York Metropolitan Region Study by its director.

R. C. Martin, F. J. Munger, *et al., Decisions in Syracuse* (Bloomington, Ind., 1961).

J. Gottmann, *Megalopolis* (New York, 1961).

C. S. Stein, *Toward New Towns for America* (New York, 1957).

2. PUBLIC SAFETY

O. W. Wilson, *Police Administration* (2d ed., New York, 1963).

B. Smith, *Police Systems in the United States* (rev. ed., New York, 1949).

"New Goals in Police Management," *The Annals of the Amer. Academy of Polit. and Soc. Sci.,* Vol. 291 (Jan., 1954). Entire issue.

D. R. Taft, *Criminology* (New York, 1950).

The Police Year Book (Chicago). Published annually by the Assoc. of Chiefs of Police.

President's Conference on Fire Prevention, *Report of Committee* (Washington, 1947).

R. S. Moulton (ed.), *Handbook of Fire Protection* (National Fire Protection Assoc., Boston, 1954).

W. Y. Kimball, "Manpower and Effective Fire Fighting," *Public Management,* XLI, 183-187 (Aug., 1959).

Report of Project East River (Assoc. Univ., Inc., New York, 1952). A study of civil defense.

J. C. Ingraham, *Modern Traffic Control* (New York, 1955).

3. PUBLIC HEALTH

W. G. Smillie, *Public Health Administration in the United States* (3rd ed., New York, 1947).

American Public Health Association, *Local Health Units for the Nation* (New York, 1945). Report by H. Emerson, M.D.

National Health Council, *Urban Sprawl and Health* (New York, 1959).

"A Critique of Community Public Health Service," *Amer. Journ. of Public Health,* XLVII, No. 11, pt. 2 (Nov., 1957).

M. N. Baker, *Water for the Cities: A History of the Urban Water Supply Problem in the United States* (Syracuse, N.Y., 1956).

V. Ostrom, *Water and Politics: A Study of Water Policies and Administration in the Development of Los Angeles* (Los Angeles, 1953).

4. Transportation

W. Owen, *Cities in the Motor Age* (New York, 1959).

————, *The Metropolitan Transportation Problem* (Washington, 1956).

Public Administration Service, *Better Transportation for Your City* (Chicago, 1958).

J. D. Carroll, Jr., "The Future of the Central Business District," *Public Management,* XXXV, 150-153 (July, 1953).

J. Rannells, *The Core of the City* (New York, 1956).

R. Vernon, *The Changing Economic Function of the Central City* (Committee for Economic Development, New York, 1959).

R. B. Mitchell and C. Rapkind, *Urban Traffic, a Function of Land Use* (New York, 1954).

H. Bartholomew, *Land Uses in American Cities* (Cambridge, Mass., 1955).

F. S. Chapin, Jr., *Urban Land Use Planning* (New York, 1957).

N. Hebden and W. S. Smith, *State-City Relations in Highway Affairs* (New Haven, Conn., 1950).

L. C. Fitch and Assoc., *Urban Transportation and Public Policy* (San Francisco, 1964).

5. Education, Welfare, and Recreation

National Education Association, *Your School District* (Washington, 1948).

J. C. Bollens, *Special District Governments in the United States* (Berkeley and Los Angeles, 1957). Chap. VI.

E. E. Engelbert, "Education a Thing Apart?", *Nat. Mun. Rev.,* XLII (Feb., 1953). The pros and cons of independent school districts.

E. Rose, *The Public Library in American Life* (New York, 1954).

R. Raup, *Intergovernmental Relations in Social Welfare* (Minneapolis, 1952).

G. D. Butler, *Introduction to Community Recreation* (New York, 1959).

6. Urban Renewal and Housing

C. Woodbury (ed.), *The Future of Cities and Urban Redevelopment* (Chicago, 1953).

E. C. Banfield and M. Grodzins, *Government and Housing in Metropolitan Areas* (New York, 1958). Chaps. IV, V, VII.

M. C. McFarland, *The Challenge of Urban Renewal* (Washington, 1958).

"Redevelopment," *Journal of Housing,* XIV, No. 9 (October, 1957). Entire issue.

"Rehabilitation," *Journal of Housing,* XVI, No. 5 (May, 1959). Entire issue.

J. Jacobs, *The Death and Life of Great American Cities* (New York, 1961).

K. Kaflan, *Urban Renewal Politics: Slum Clearance in Newark* (New York, 1963).

C. Abrams, *Man's Struggle for Shelter in an Urbanizing World* (Cambridge, Mass., 1964).

7. FINANCE

A. M. Hillhouse and M. Magelssen, *Where Cities Get Their Money* (Chicago, 1946). 1949 supplement by A. M. Hillhouse. 1951 supplement by M. B. Phillips. 1956 supplement by H. F. Alderfer and R. L. Funk.

New Jersey Commission on State Tax Policy, *The General Property Tax in New Jersey* (Trenton, 1953).

C. F. Snider, "What Can Cities Tax Next?" *Nat. Mun. Rev.,* XXXVII, 212-218 (May, 1949).

R. A. Sigafoos, *The Municipal Income Tax: Its History and Problems* (Public Admin. Service, Chicago, 1956).

Municipal Finance Officers Association, "Municipal Sales Taxes in the United States and Canada," *Municipal Finance* (Feb., 1956). Entire issue.

————, "Metropolitan Area Financial Problems," *Municipal Finance* (Nov., 1956). Entire issue.

W. O. Winter, *The Special Assessment Today* (Ann Arbor, Mich., 1952).

J. A. Vieg, *et al., California Local Finance* (Stanford, 1960).

J. S. Floud, Jr., *Effects of Taxation on Industrial Location* (Chapel Hill, N.C., 1952).

H. E. Brazer, *City Expenditures in the United States* (New York, 1959). A statistical study of the effects of city size, density, and other factors on per capita expenditures.

W. Anderson, *Intergovernmental Fiscal Relations* (Minneapolis, 1956).

State Government, XVIII, 55-72 (April, 1945). Series of articles on "States and Cities."

Tax Institute, *Financing Metropolitan Government* (Princeton, N.J., 1955).

Cleveland Metropolitan Services Commission, *A Fiscal Profile* (Cleveland, 1958).

J. A. Vieg, H. C. Armstrong, F. Farnes, G. N. Rostvold, J. P. Shelton, P. Thomson, *California Local Finance* (Palo Alto, Calif., 1964).

G. Y. Steiner, *Municipal Tax Referenda and the Political Process* (Urbana, Ill., 1953).

★ 36 ★

Government in Metropolitan Areas

THE BAFFLING THING about government in metropolitan areas is that there is none. Though a majority of these areas are contained within a single county, in no area is there a local government with authority to provide all the needed services for the entire area. There are cities that provide these for parts of areas; there are special districts that provide one or two services for an entire area. There are all sorts of combinations of service and area between these two. The results as we have seen are: governmental complexity, unequal financial resources, unequal and inadequate provision of services, and lack of citizen control and political accountability. The ideal form for a metropolitan government would be a general purpose one with jurisdiction geographically corresponding to the metropolitan community. Under such a government there would be no duplication of services. There would be one tax system. And the government would receive its support from and be accountable to the people of the entire area. Most of the older methods for preventing or overcoming governmental deficiencies in urbanized areas assume that the city is the appropriate form to accomplish these ends. These methods include: (1) extraterritorial jurisdiction and services by which a municipality provides services to or extends its controls over adjacent areas; (2) annexation by which a city physically extends its boundaries and, therefore, its jurisdiction; (3) city-county consolidation by which the area of the county is put under the city government for the provision of municipal-type services; and (4) city-county separation by which the urban area is separated from the rural area and consolidated under the city government. Today the problems are more complex and extend beyond the city's ability to encompass them. The methods most discussed today are: (1) federating all the units in a metropolitan area into a supergovernment; (2) making the county an urban government with municipal powers to provide urban services; (3) setting up special districts; and (4) providing services jointly.

EXTRATERRITORIAL JURISDICTION AND SERVICES

In most states, municipalities may extend their jurisdictions and services beyond their boundaries in a radius of from one to five miles. The most common types of jurisdiction extended are regulatory and involve the control of land use, such as extension of a city's zoning, planning, subdivision controls, and licensure of dance halls and places of business into unincorporated territory. This helps control the fringe problem and assure that developments won't occur contiguous to the city that would put an unnecessary burden or

METROPOLIS — 1960 STYLE

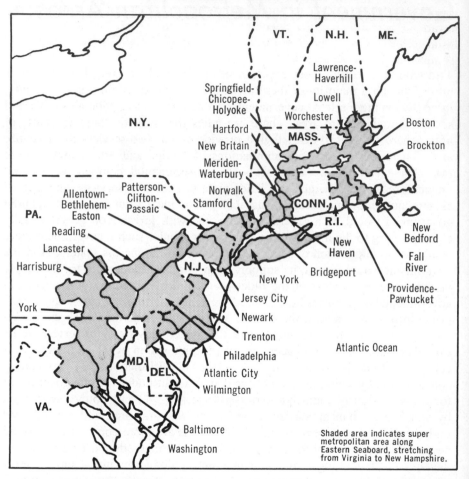

future responsibility on the city that it would not be able or wish to assume.[1] Another type of extraterritorial jurisdiction is the ownership of land by a city outside its limits for parks, airports, water supply, and the like. This is sometimes objected to by the residents of the area but the city's interest is limited to that of a proprietor and anyone may use its facilities equally.

[1] The following states do not give municipalities this power: Rhode Island, Connecticut, Delaware, Massachusetts, Michigan, Missouri, New Jersey, New York, Pennsylvania, and Washington. In Delaware, Michigan, New Jersey, New York, Pennsylvania, and Washington, control of subdividing (the process by which land is divided into lots for urban development) is vested in the county.

Services are provided for areas outside a city by the city's selling particular ones. Some are sold to persons directly but the common practice is for the city to sell the service to another municipality which in turn bills the ultimate user. Sewage disposal and water distribution are the most common services sold. These practices may ease the pressure on the suburbs to find other methods for solving common problems. On the other hand, the city can use its services as a lever to obtain return advantages, such as eventual annexation.[2] Sometimes a city is compelled to sell a service by the state. For instance, New York City must furnish water to the suburbs in the vicinity of its aqueduct in Westchester County.

ANNEXATION

In the latter part of the nineteenth century when the urban population was expanding with the new industrialization, American cities engaged in frequent and large scale annexations. A typical example is Pittsburgh, which grew from half a square mile to 28 square miles by 1900. City boundaries kept pace with and indeed often went beyond the urban area. From then until 1945-1948, annexations were fewer and fewer in number and in the amount of territory taken in.[3] Since the end of the Second World War, the pace has accelerated but the amount of annexed territory is still small. The average amount taken in in 1948 was less than half a square mile. In 1964 the total number of square miles annexed annually had increased to 514, but the average amount had not increased so rapidly. Many cities must make many separate annexations to acquire even a small amount of territory. For instance, Rockford, Ill., had to complete 53 separate actions to gain less than one and a half square miles.[4] The use of this device is increasingly falling behind urbanization. The main reasons for this are that: (1) Many areas now contain numerous incorporated municipalities adjacent to the central city that resist annexation. (Some, like Minneapolis, Minn., are completely ringed. In older areas even incorporated suburbs are surrounded.) (2) Metropolitan areas have grown beyond state and county lines. (3) State laws are too cumbersome to apply, too stringent, and frequently unworkable.[5] Most of the recent sizable

Current use

[2] Exchanges can be made that are not only mutually advantageous but that cover related problems. See B. Tableman, "How Cities Can Lick the Fringe Problem," *Public Management* (March, 1952).

[3] For an historical summary see A. H. Hawley, "The Incorporation Trend in Metropolitan Areas, 1900-1950," *Journal of the American Institute of Planners*, XXV, No. 1, 41-45 (Feb., 1959).

[4] Annexations are reported annually in *The Municipal Year Book*.

[5] Delaware, Maryland, and the New England States have no general annexation laws. It is done by special act of the legislature. Rhode Island prohibits annexation. In the other New England states, since representation in the legislature is based on the towns, annexation is in practice, unavailable.

An example of a complicated law is given in V. Jones, "Local Government Organization in Metropolitan Areas," *The Future of Cities and Urban Redevelopment*, C. Woodbury (ed.), 559 (Chicago, 1953).

annexations have taken place in small, medium-sized, or fast-growing communities—mostly in Wisconsin, and in the South and Southwest, notably in Virginia, California, and Texas. The greatest legal difficulty is the requirement of most states that the residents of territory to be annexed must approve the action in an election. Even in the states with the most liberal annexation laws, voters in incorporated municipalities have this separate and controlling vote. It is noteworthy that none of the recent large annexations (of 10 square miles or more) has been of incorporated territory and none has required this separate vote. Most of them have been accomplished under one of the following five types of legal authorization: (1) The city council of the annexing city passed an ordinance. (2) The people of the city undertaking the annexation voted in favor of the proposal. (3) The election results in the city and the area to be annexed were counted together. (4) A state legislature passed a special law. (5) A court rendered a decision favorable to the annexation. Since the problems of metropolitan areas have the most effect on municipalities, most students feel that their ability to annex should be encouraged, that state laws should be liberalized, but that safeguards should exist to protect the public interest in the area as a whole.

State responsibility for local boundary changes

The experience of Texas, which has very liberal annexation laws and where the most amount of territory has been taken into the cities, points up the difficulties in purely local determinations of the wisdom and expediency of annexations. It also shows the relationship of annexation to incorporation. In Texas, any home-rule city may write into its charter the procedure by which it will acquire additional territory that, however, must be unincorporated at the time of the proposed annexation.[6] Most of them have taken advantage of this to write charters that permit them to annex such territory without the consent of the people in the area involved. This unilateral action has resulted in competitive actions by municipalities to acquire territory considered desirable while other areas have been neglected. It has also resulted in relay races of new incorporations to forestall annexation and premature annexation proposals to forestall new incorporations.[7] In 1963, Texas wrote a strong law inhibiting new incorporations within a five-mile zone around each city of 100,000 population or more.

The states are beginning to modify the relevant laws to facilitate annexation but to limit incorporations in outlying parts of urban areas. When an area has a choice between annexing or incorporating, it is as doubtful if the merits of either can be decided in an election as it is that the local governing body can decide it. The broader aspects of local boundary changes should be considered by some procedure that takes into account the effects of the

[6] Missouri cities have similar powers. There home rule cities may annex territory by simply amending their charters.

[7] To forestall an incorporation, a city may simply file an intention to annex.

Incorporation *per se* is not invariably disadvantageous. For instance, three nationally dominated communities in 1958-1959 successfully completed incorporations to set up their own local governments; namely, Richland, Wash. and Oak Ridge, Tenn., the sites of the nation's two major atomic installations, and Boulder City, Nev.

changes on the area as a whole. In Ohio, this is accomplished by having the county governing body consider proposals. In New Mexico, boards of arbitration consisting of city and fringe-area residents consider proposals. The best alternatives, however, include the establishment of standards in state law and this is the current trend. In North Carolina, for example, a city council may annex territory on its own determination but has to follow certain legal standards and its action may be appealed. The application of standards by a state agency, however, is the preferred method. Virginia has been following this procedure for years and in this state annexation has had the most sustained use, possibly because of it. In Virginia, special annexation courts hear proposals that have been instituted by a city or by the governing body or residents in the area of the proposed annexation. The standards applied by the court are written into state law and include such items as the need of the city for this territory for its orderly growth and development, the need of the area under consideration for services, the financial ability of the annexing city, and the existence of a community of interest between the two. The city council may accept or reject an affirmative finding of the court and any decision may be appealed. The chief criticism of the Virginia system has been that special courts do not accumulate and use a sustained body of information and knowledge. It is also dubious whether the adversary system is applicable to the weighing of issues and policies involved in this type of action.[8] For this reason, the creation of state administrative agencies to pass on the merits of each proposal is receiving more attention. Besides being able to consider the impact of a proposal on the area as a whole, in the light of public policy, such an agency can initiate actions and consider alternative proposals. Minnesota and Wisconsin, to take two examples, have similar agencies that consider annexations, incorporations, and consolidations.[9] In Alaska, a Local Boundary Commission has been created in the executive branch of the state that will consider proposed boundary changes and establish procedures for adjustments. In addition, Alaskan boroughs (counties) may not create service districts in an area that

---

[8] To set up the Virginia system might require constitutional change in some states for it might be regarded as an unconstitutional delegation of legislative power. However, the courts are increasingly being brought into deciding questions of land use. In equity, they are open for injunctions against annexation actions; in law, they hear zoning decisions and annexation orders on appeal. For an analysis of this role of the courts see, C. M. Haar, "Regionalism and Realism in Land-Use Planning," *Univ. of Penna. Law Rev.*, Vol. 105, No. 4, 515-537 (Feb., 1957).

[9] In Wisconsin, the state agency has more power in incorporations than in annexations. A petition to incorporate is first reviewed by the Superior Court which applies nondiscretionary standards. It then goes to the division of planning which may accept, reject, or change the boundaries. The standards applied by it are: present and potential tax resources of the area; the level of governmental services to be offered compared to the level available from a contiguous municipality, the impact on the remainder of the town from which the territory is to be taken, and the effect upon the future rendering of services both inside the proposed municipality and elsewhere within the metropolitan community. Proposed consolidations are also subject to review and approval and certain types of proposed annexations receive advisory review. The agency reports affirmative findings to the Circuit Court which then orders a referendum. A finding against may be appealed. *Wisc. Statutes 1959*, Sec. 66.013-66.018.

can be served by an existing one, by becoming a city, or by annexing to one.

Regardless of changes in annexation laws and better procedures, many areas will be unaided. In the first place, quite a few cities are unable to assume additional burdens. (It has been estimated that a newly annexed area will not "pay its way" for ten years.) In the second place, annexations are limited to adjacent and as mentioned above, in practice, to unincorporated territory. Even cities that have annexed considerable territory still comprise only part of their metropolitan areas. For example, Dallas, Texas, which has annexed over 80 square miles in recent years, still includes much less than one-half of its metropolitan area. Other solutions are also necessary to reach an entire metropolitan area.

CITY-COUNTY CONSOLIDATION

Charac-
teristics
and
difficulties

Next to annexation, the preferred method for reorganizing government in metropolitan areas was for many years city-county consolidation. This reform eliminates one level of government by combining the city and the county and is accomplished by extending the city's territory to the county boundaries and transferring county functions to the city. Not all city-counties are exactly coterminous in area with their respective counties and not all, or identical functions, have been consolidated. The county retains its identity and certain officials such as the coroner are commonly retained.[10] The administration of justice usually continues to be a county function. But the pattern of consolidation is different in each case. In the nineteenth century, Boston, Philadelphia, New Orleans, and New York City were merged with their counties. The only city-county consolidations instituted in the twentieth century have been that of the City of Baton Rouge and the Parish of East Baton Rouge, La. and of Nashville-Davidson County in 1962. The following characteristics of the early consolidations are of special importance: (1) Except for the New York City consolidation, only one county was involved in each. (2) All were accomplished by state legislation. (3) Other units existing in the county were merged with the new unit. (4) Though the city area was expanded at the time of the consolidation, city-counties have been unable subsequently to enlarge. None of these city-counties now contains as much as one-fifth of its respective metropolitan area. Consolidation is still useful for small areas that embrace only one county and do not cross state lines but two main differences from the earlier situations limit its chances of success today. First, existing municipalities other than the city have commonly been retained

---

[10] For the efforts of Philadelphia to bring all county officers into the consolidated government see: J. D. Crumlish, *A City Finds Itself: The Philadelphia Home Rule Charter Movement* (Detroit, 1959) and *National Municipal Review*, "Court Decision Delays Philadelphia Merger," XLIV, 210 (April, 1955). Since 1955, transfer of functions and administrative consolidations are being made gradually. Additional legislative authority has also been conferred.

in recent proposals. If they continue to be part of the county and, therefore, contribute to its support, they would in effect be relinquishing autonomy.[11] Secondly, there are many more incorporated municipalities now in urban counties and to protect them state legislation today usually requires local referenda on proposals, the results of which are often counted separately in the city and in the county.[12] At least 18 proposals for consolidations have been defeated at some stage in the twentieth century. The fact that other proposals for metropolitan reorganization have also been defeated in most of these areas [13] shows that the common requirement of separate majorities in local referenda is the greatest single stumbling block. The Baton Rouge consolidation was accomplished by a single overall vote. The Nashville plan, after an earlier defeat, did gain a majority outside and one inside the city. Most of the negative votes occur in the suburban and rural areas. These areas with some justification feel their taxes will be raised to provide municipal services they either do not need or desire. There is a real difficulty in adjusting financial support for different levels of service in the hinterland outside the central city. The creation of service districts within the county with different tax rates obviates this difficulty and is one of the most promising recent developments. Since this is applicable to other forms of metropolitan reorganization, a closer look at the Baton Rouge consolidation plan which includes this device is in order.

The City of Baton Rouge and the Parish (county) of East Baton Rouge were consolidated in 1949 pursuant to a 1946 constitutional amendment. The legal identities of the parish and the city are maintained and each has its own budget. The parish provides for the administration of justice and highways and bridges for the area. Certain parish officials are retained   the assessor, sheriff, coroner, district attorney, tax collector, and clerk of court. Functions not common to the two units are supported separately. (Schools are administered by a separate unit and welfare is a state responsibility.) The city and county are under one executive, an elective mayor-president, and the city council of seven members elected at-large serves as the parish council with the addition of two members elected from the rural area. At the time of

Baton Rouge

---

[11] The Public Administration Service rejected city-county consolidation for Dade County and the City of Miami for this reason among others. See its report, *The Government of Metropolitan Miami* (Chicago, 1954).

[12] In 1925 and 1936, proposals to consolidate Cuyahoga County and Cleveland, Ohio, were locally defeated. The 1936 proposal required *four* separate majorities: (1) in the county as a whole; (2) in the central city; (3) in the county area outside the central city; and (4) in all the municipalities. All majorities failed. A 1929 charter for consolidation of Allegheny County and Pittsburgh, needed a *two-thirds* majority in a majority of the municipalities. Surprisingly enough this proposal almost passed.

[13] Only two counties successfully reorganized subsequently—Fulton County (Atlanta), Ga., and Dade County (Miami), Fla. City-county consolidations have been defeated in Houston, Fort Worth, Salt Lake City, Macon, Cleveland, Portland, Durham, Birmingham, Seattle, the Hampton Roads area, Miami, Atlanta, Pittsburgh, Knoxville, St. Louis, Nashville, San Francisco, and Albuquerque.

the consolidation, the boundaries of Baton Rouge were extended, almost tripling the size of the city, but a town and village were left undisturbed. Further incorporations are prohibited. To provide for the differences in service needs in the urban and rural territory, the parish is divided into three districts:

(1) The *urban service district,* in which the highest tax rate is paid. In this area, services are supplied by the city and include police and fire protection, garbage and refuse collection and disposal, street lighting, traffic regulation, and inspectional services.

(2) The *rural service district,* in which a minimum level of service is supplied at a lower tax rate by the parish. The only "urban" service is police protection. Other municipal-type services may be provided by the parish as need arises but only by creating taxing districts for them.

(3) The *industrial service district* where no residences are permitted in which municipal services are provided by the industries at their own expense. Additional ones may be provided by creating tax districts for them on petition of 90 percent of the property owners of the area.[14] The successful Nashville plan also established two service areas—one urban and one not.

Urban and rural service districts   One drawback apparent in the Baton Rouge division of the area into service and taxing districts is that changing land uses would make difficult readjustments necessary. In areas of mixed uses, drawing boundaries would be so complicated as to make the plan unworkable. However, since this is one of the better ways to secure voter approval of reorganization proposals, it deserves serious consideration where applicable. The more common proposal is the creation of only two districts—a general one that would cover all the territory of the area and in which the common services at a minimum level would be provided, such as general police and fire protection, schools, parks, and recreation; and an urban service area or areas for extended services such as water and sewer mains, increased police and fire protection, street lighting, refuse and garbage collection. California, Alaska, Connecticut, Virginia, and Kentucky, for example, have authorized local governments to create these different taxing districts.[15]

---

[14] For a more detailed description see T. H. Reed, "Progress in Metropolitan Integration," *Public Admin. Rev.,* IX, 7-10 (Winter, 1949). See also, J. C. Bollens and H. J. Schmandt, *The Metropolis: Its People, Politics, and Economic Life* (New York, 1965), 427-434.

[15] See M. R. White, "Town and City Consolidation in Connecticut," *Amer. Polit. Sci. Rev.,* XXXVI, 492-502 (June, 1942).

Most of the other laws are too new for passing judgments in their operations; however, a few such areas have been set up in California under its County Service Area Law passed in 1953. Difficulties there have been experienced in defining "extended" urban services and in financing capital improvements from taxation (no provisions were made for debt financing). See J. C. Bollens, *Special District Governments in the United States,* 238-240 (Berkeley and Los Angeles, 1957).

It should be mentioned here that these service districts are *not* the *special districts* that are independent units of government (such as school, sewage disposal, etc. districts) as defined by the Census, which are the main concern of Professor Bollens' analysis.

CITY-COUNTY SEPARATION

Separation of a city from its county and the formation of the remainder of the county into a new or reconstituted county has been urged on different occasions as a means for city residents to avoid paying county taxes. There is something parochial about separation. The main benefit, a financial one, accrues to the city. City-county separation does not solve problems common to a whole area or provide an adequate answer on how to provide a minimum level of services throughout an area. It is not often urged today by students of the subject [16] and two of the cities that were separated from their counties in the nineteenth century have since examined and tried to institute other forms of governmental organization.[17] As in the case of the consolidated city-counties, these separated cities were given land at the time of the separation but have been unable to annex any since. Denver is the only one that has annexed land and it still comprises only a small part of its metropolitan area. *Limited use*

In Virginia a different situation exists. In that state separation is automatic for any city of 5000 or more population and is complete for cities of 10,000 or more inhabitants. Virginia cities have been able to expand because of their judicial system of annexation described above [18] and so have avoided some of the problems of urban expansion experienced by other cities.[19] In that state, however, the question of what happens to the remainder of the county if it becomes too small to give adequate services has not been solved. This has happened in Henrico County.[20] *City-County separation in Virginia*

The 1952 reorganization of the City of Atlanta and Fulton County, Georgia, has elements of city-county separation, consolidation, and annexation. As such, it is hoped that most of the knotty problems resulting from one *The Atlanta-Fulton County plan of improvement*

[16] However, see J. A. Rush, *The City-County Consolidated* (Los Angeles, 1941), which is a plea for separation.

[17] San Francisco (separated in 1856) and St. Louis (separated in 1876) have since tried to consolidate with their adjacent counties and St. Louis has also tried to set up a multipurpose metropolitan district government. The latter was defeated in 1959. On efforts to consolidate San Francisco and San Mateo County see J. C. Bollens, "They All Want To Stay Out," *Nat. Mun. Rev.*, XXXVIII, 309-314 (June, 1948).

Besides the cities in Virginia, Baltimore was separated in 1851 and Denver in 1912.

[18] See R. B. Pinchbeck, "City-County Separations in Virginia," *Nat. Mun. Rev.*, XXIX, 476-472 (July, 1940).

[19] But not all, as witness the history of the Hampton Roads area. In 1950, a proposed consolidation of the cities of Newport News and Hampton with the town of Phoebus and two counties, Warwick and Elizabeth City, failed. To prevent Newport News from annexing, the county of Warwick incorporated as a city in 1952. Elizabeth City County incorporated with the city of Hampton and the town of Phoebus as the City of Hampton. See J. E. Pate, "Virginia Counties Turn Cities," *Nat. Mun. Rev.*, LXI, 387-9 (Sept., 1952). In 1958, the cities of Newport News and Warwick consolidated.

[20] See Report of the Commission to Study Urban Growth to the Governor and the General Assembly of Virginia, *Adjustment of the Boundaries of Virginia Municipalities and Adjacent Counties* (Richmond, 1951).

In 1961, the state passed a new county optional charter plan for use in urban areas that included, among other provisions, protection against new internal incorporations.

or the other of these methods will be mitigated. At the time of the reorganization, 82 square miles of territory, mostly urban, were added to the city and in the following year 10 more square miles were annexed. The county was excluded from performing municipal functions. The city provides water, sewage disposal, parks and recreation, and traffic engineering throughout the area. The county performs consolidated area-wide services such as public health and rural services. Certain management functions have been merged, such as tax assessment and collection. The city health department was abolished and the county fire protection, airport, refuse collection, parks and recreation were transferred to the city. Incorporated units other than Atlanta were left untouched and some functions still overlap; for instance, schools, law enforcement, and public works are performed by both governments, but the plan has been considered a distinct step forward in improving metropolitan relationships.[21]

FEDERATION

Advantages and present use

The obvious parallel between metropolitan areas with their sectional interests and established governments and the national government with its states has made the idea of metropolitan federation most intriguing to students of the subject. Under this type of reorganization the individual local units are retained to provide local services and meet diverse needs and a new metropolitan "federal" government is created to provide area-wide services. Citizen control of governmental decisions that affected people where they work and also where they live would be enhanced. A means would be provided for flexibility in meeting future problems. The financial resources of the entire area would be pooled to provide a minimum level of service throughout the area and an area-wide approach to common problems would be possible. Though the home rule enjoyed by the individual units would be diminished, the area as a whole would find increased ability to stand on its own feet.

There are two types of federation possible: (1) the borough plan, the prototype of which is London with its County Council, which provides common functions, and its 28 boroughs and the city, which take care of more local affairs; [22] and (2) the district plan. The only example of a metropolitan feder-

---

[21] PAS, *The Government of Metropolitan Miami, op. cit.*, 78.

For details, see Local Government Commission of Fulton County, Georgia, *Plan of Improvement for the Governments of Atlanta and Fulton County* (1950).

[22] At present the London County Council does not have jurisdiction over the entire metropolitan area and some functions are performed by special authorities or by the nation directly.

New York City has been regarded by some as a federated city because its five boroughs have retained their identity and their elected presidents sit on the Board of Estimate. However, the city operates under a unitary system. The boroughs have been administrative units but under a revised charter, highway and sewer works are transferred to city-wide departments, and the local legislative powers of the Board of Estimate reduced.

ation in North America is Toronto. In 1953, the legislature of Ontario created a supergovernment for this area that is six times the size of the city. County functions were transferred to it and this metropolitan government was given responsibility to provide the basic area-wide services. Local services remain the responsibility of the local units—the city of Toronto and the suburban cities and townships. The legislative body of 25 members is a metropolitan council composed of the 12 heads of the suburban governments, 12 officials from the city, and a chairman appointed by the provincial government.[23] The basic weakness of this plan is this system of representation.[24] In the first place, it is based on political units not on population. Each suburban unit has one representative regardless of size and the representation is weighted in favor of the city since the most rapidly growing areas are on the outskirts. In the second place, the representatives have dual responsibilities—a legislative one to the metropolitan government and an administrative and executive one to their localities.[25] For these reasons, recent proposals for federation in the United States have recommended the district system of representation.

Because concessions are made to the local units, proposals for federation have the most chance of lasting success and it would seem also of local approval. Such, however, has not been the case. More proposals have been defeated locally at the polls than at any other stage.[26] A constitutional amendment is usually required before a local charter can be drafted but this is usually secured. The only exceptions have been one for Cleveland that was defeated by the voters of Ohio in 1958 and one for the St. Louis area that

Obstacles to federation

---

[23] See E. Hardy, "Metropolitan Area Merges," *Nat. Mun. Rev.,* XLII, 326-330 (July, 1953); and W. W. Crouch, "Metropolitan Government in Toronto," *Public Admin. Rev.,* XIV, 85-95 (Spring, 1954).

[24] However, the Metropolitan Toronto Commission of Inquiry reported to the Lieutenant Governor of Ontario in 1958 that the plan was basically sound in both organization and operation. See *The Municipal Yearbook, 1959,* p. 48 (Chicago, 1959).

[25] These criticisms can be found, among other places, in C. Adrian, *Governing Urban America,* 252 (New York, 1955) and PAS, *The Government of Metropolitan Miami, op. cit.,* 83, 84.

For Miami, PAS recommended a federated metropolitan government, nevertheless, because of its advantages, but with representation on the governing body partly elected by the people directly from districts and partly consisting of *ex officio* local government representatives. *Ibid.,* 84. Their recommendations were changed by the Florida legislature to the urban county approach.

In Nashville, the charter drafters also rejected the "borough" plan because it would have had a tendency to divide the loyalties of community leadership at times when unity would be needed. Their charter would have replaced the existing city and county with a single metropolitan government which would have had an elective mayor and a 21 member council, 15 to be elected from districts and six to be elected at-large. It would also have created general and urban service taxing districts. For more details of this plan, which was defeated in June, 1958 by the voters of the area, see Public Administration Service (PAS), *Metropolitan Surveys: A Digest* (Chicago, 1958).

[26] Defeats have thus been suffered by proponents of federation in the Alameda, Sacramento, and San Francisco areas in California and in Cleveland and Pittsburgh. Proposals for multidistrict metropolitan governments with "federal" aspects have also been defeated in the St. Louis and Seattle areas as recently as 1959 and 1958.

was defeated in Missouri in 1930. Some of the reasons for local charter defeats are the same as those for defeats of other types of reorganization—fear of raises in taxes, fear of big government, fear of loss of independence, and public apathy. In addition, proposals for federation need to have more details worked out than do other types of metropolitan reform. Decisions have to be made on the distribution of powers among the units involved and the method of representation on, and composition of, the governing body. The result is a long and complicated charter difficult to understand.

A
federated
county—
Dade

The nearest approach to a federal system of metropolitan government in the United States is the one established in 1957 in Dade County (Miami) Florida. Following a constitutional amendment adopted in 1956 permitting Dade County to draft a home rule charter, a Metropolitan Charter Board appointed by the governor drew up a charter which was submitted to the voters and approved.[27] The charter provides for a reorganized county government with a manager and the abolition of certain constitutional offices, such as the sheriff and coroner. The county is a union of 26 municipalities and Metro, which is the name given the reorganized county. Functions are being transferred to the county very gradually, though the charter gives the county control over sewage disposal, water supply, transportation, traffic, central planning, and other municipal functions to which area-wide control may be applicable. All other municipal powers are reserved to the cities. The county may set minimum standards that the municipalities may raise, for instance, in zoning and subdivision regulation. The municipalities will retain responsibility for local services such as local streets. Difficulties were experienced from the outset in allocating these functions but Metro is still in existence and has received four distinct votes of confidence from the people.[28] The governing body is a board of eleven commissioners (reduced to nine in 1963), five elected at-large, five from districts, and one from the city of Miami. Other cities may have a representative when they reach 60,000 population.

THE URBAN COUNTY

Reasons
for use of
the county
as a
metropoli-
tan gov-
ernment

The failure at the polls and the inadequacies of so many proposals for metropolitan reorganization have led to a reconsideration of the role of counties in urban areas. Over half of the metropolitan areas consist of one

[27] For a discussion of probable reasons why this vote was successful see E. Sofen, "Problems of Metropolitan Leadership: The Miami Experience," *Midwest Journal of Pol. Sci.*, Vol. V, No. 1 (Feb., 1961).

[28] Reasons for the difficulties experienced are also examined in E. Sofen, *supra* and in E. Sofen, *The Miami Metropolitan Experiment* (Bloomington, Ind., 1963). So far several Miami city functions have been transferred to the county, for instance, traffic engineering. The county operates the seaport and the airport, which it had before, and has created an urban renewal agency. The voters were called to the polls to vote on Metro a fifth time in Oct., 1961. See *The New York Times*, Oct. 22, 1961, 54.

county and in quite a few others it is a major portion of the area. It is the only existing general purpose local government that approaches the area-wide criterion for a metropolitan government. In addition, many counties in urban areas are already assuming functions that are in effect municipal. Though reorganizing county governments so they would be equipped to deal with urban problems more extensively is difficult, it would be easier than trying to abolish or bypass them.[29]

At present most urban counties are not in a position to assume additional responsibilities. To transform a county into an efficient unit of government capable of performing urban functions requires first the internal reorganization outlined in Chapter 34. Urban counties need, in addition, as we have mentioned, reconsideration of (1) their roles as agencies of their state governments and (2) the composition of their governing bodies. Counties are not municipal corporations in law. Though they are becoming more so in practice, the courts are still able to distinguish their powers from municipal ones.[30] In some states, counties may adopt home-rule charters and a few have done so. It is difficult to see how a county can perform urban functions without municipal and ordinance making powers. In some areas, however, there are also nonlegal objections to extending county powers.[31] The greatest benefit so far in this county activity has accrued to suburban residents in unincorporated areas and city residents do not particularly enjoy paying through their county governments for services for others that they provide for themselves in their

Prerequisite—county reform

[29] For places where the county does not embrace the whole area, this approach is, of course, limited in its usefulness. In fact, counties in these areas that have reorganized to perform urban functions may stand in the way of proposals that would include the entire area. For instance, the county adjacent to the (separated) city of St. Louis, Mo., adopted a home rule charter in 1950. This county (St. Louis County), which is suburban in character, may assume the functions of any governmental unit within it except school districts on the approval of the local voters. In 1954, a county police department was organized and by 1956, the county was furnishing health services to more than one-half of its municipalities. Whether or not this was a factor in the defeat of a 1959 proposal for a multipurpose metropolitan district government, which would have included the city area, one cannot say, but it is possible. Neither can the effect of the adoption in 1956 of a home-rule charter in Baltimore County (adjacent to the separated city) on solving area-wide problems be judged. But as a means for solving suburban problems, it cannot help but reduce the pressure for area-wide governmental mechanisms.

[30] The Ohio Supreme Court made this distinction in striking down a county charter for Cuyahoga County (Cleveland) in 1936. See V. Jones in C. Woodbury (ed.), *op. cit.,* 594, 5. This area has had more trouble in trying to establish a metropolitan form of government. City-county consolidation has been defeated twice and county home-rule charters were defeated in 1950 and 1959.

[31] For instance, in California where the counties have been the most active, the League of California Cities has opposed municipalization of the county. See V. Jones, *supra.,* 547 and 593.

The Atlanta-Fulton County plan was introduced to *prevent* the county from becoming a municipal unit. For their reasons see *Local Government Commission of Fulton County, op. cit.* See also M. C. Hughes, "Annexation and Reallocation of Functions" *Public Management,* XXXIV, 26-30 (Feb., 1952).

own units.[32] To meet this criticism separate taxing and service districts could be used.[33]

When county services are extended to *municipalities* in its area, an additional set of considerations arise. The composition of the county governing body becomes important. Central cities, in particular, are commonly underrepresented on county boards.[34] If the county is to extend its operations to cities (in order to eliminate duplication and provide area-wide approaches to problems), it should be more representative. County governing bodies could be organized on a federated basis and many of them are by having township supervisors sit with city and other municipal representatives. This usually results in too large a board and has the same drawbacks as the borough plan of federation. A small board, such as has been advocated for rural areas, is not appropriate either. Urban counties are not homogeneous and sectional interests need representation just as they do on city councils. This could be secured by district representation (Milwaukee County is an example) combined with election at-large if that is desired (such as is in use in Dade County, Fla.). This can have the added advantage of relating representation to population.

Methods for increasing county functions

When sweeping proposals have been submitted to the voters to reorganize counties and give them power to act as urban governments, they are usually defeated.[35] The most common method for reaching this goal is the *gradual* transference of municipal activities (with or without previous reorganization). Authorizations for this can usually be given by state enabling acts (instead of constitutional amendment) and can be accomplished then by contract between the units without voter approval. Each year additional states pass laws permitting counties to contract with municipalities to perform services for them. The actual use of this method has progressed furthest in California.[36] A survey by the National Association of County Officials in 1958 revealed a pattern to this activity across the country. Only a very small number of urban counties reported no cooperative activity. Most formal agreements (*i.e.* contracts) were with cities. Functional consolidations accounted for the greatest number of these and the most common were in public health, prisoner care, and elections. Informal agreements were most common in police and fire

[32] *E.g.,* R. Graves, "Fringe Areas Should Pay Their Own Way," *Public Management,* XXXIV (Feb., 1952).

[33] The cities' objection to county "municipal" activity in California was resolved in this way.

[34] The one-man, one-vote, rule of the U. S. Supreme Court has, however, brought this situation under challenge in a few states and this discrepancy may well disappear.

[35] As was the 1959 Cuyahoga County (Cleveland) home rule charter. For details see *The Municipal Yearbook, 1960, op. cit.,* 61, 49.

[36] The enabling legislation in that state dates from 1891 and 1921 and by the mid-1950's over 17,000 transfers had taken place. They have occurred in virtually all the counties of the state and in a large share of its unincorporated area. Most of them are in metropolitan areas and Los Angeles County accounts for approximately two-fifths of the total. See Los Angeles County Chief Administrative Office, *Services Provided by the County of Los Angeles to Cities in Los Angeles County* (Los Angeles, 1955).

protection. In the majority of agreements, fees were charged. The most common services provided free but under contract were public health services and tax assessment and collection.[37] (Fees are not usually charged when the service is provided on an informal basis.)

The increasing use of the county to solve urban problems testifies to the popularity of this method. However, this should not be confused with metropolitan *government*. It represents rather an indication of an *emerging* metropolitan government in some areas. Although the list of urban county activities is long, it is not so impressive when compared with the problems still remaining.

SPECIAL PURPOSE DISTRICTS

The most widely-used device for dealing with metropolitan problems has been the special-purpose district, a quasi-municipal corporation [38] established for the performance, usually, of a single governmental function. Created because older units have been or are inadequate for the purpose contemplated or because other proposals to meet urban problems have failed to get approval, urged by those who are concerned with (to them) an overwhelming need in one particular area,[39] popular with the general public (by analogy with the familiar school district, they are considered to be "out of politics"), appealing to some groups because of their business methods and engineering proficiency, these special purpose districts are almost universally frowned on by the experts in political science. However, they have advantages that are generally recognized. These are as follows: (1) A special district can be organized to include an area covering one or more local governmental units. All the devices studied so far are intracounty (with the exception of the consolidation that created New York City) either in conception or in practice and the legal and practical difficulties involved in using any of the other devices in interstate areas are or seem to be insurmountable.[40] Special districts need not

Advantages

[37] B. F. Hillenbrand, "Urban Counties in 1958," *The Municipal Yearbook, 1959*, 60-62.

See also J. J. Carrell, "Learning to Work Together," *Nat. Mun. Rev.*, XLIII, 526-533 (Nov., 1954) and J. C. Bollens, "Administrative Integration in California Counties," *Public Admin. Rev.*, XI (Winter, 1951).

[38] This discussion of special districts is concerned only with those that are independent units of government that perform urban services for the whole or a part of a metropolitan area. School districts are, therefore, not included, nor are rural districts such as soil conservation districts, nor are the dependent districts, such as housing authorities, which do not enjoy administrative or fiscal autonomy. Most special districts in the country are school or rural districts. Most of those we are concerned with in this chapter operate in the fields of port facilities, sewage disposal, and parks.

[39] *E.g.*, see J. Bauer, *Postwar Planning for Metropolitan Utilities* (New York, National Municipal League, 1945).

[40] For instance, L. Gulick, not an advocate of this approach in general, has, however, recommended two more districts for the New York area—one for transportation and one for water supply and waste disposal. See his *Metropolis in the Making* (New York Regional Planning Assoc., New York, 1955).

be limited to one county operation and they can be set up by interstate compact and international agreement. (2) These special districts can be established relatively easily compared to the other methods. They are authorized by state law, not by constitutional amendment. If local approval is needed, one overall vote is all that is usually required. (3) Once established, they have a flexible structure that can often be changed by amendment of state law without local approval, or amendment of an interstate compact, which would not require local approval in any case. In expanding their boundaries, they also enjoy flexibility. Such action can sometimes be taken under a simple court order, sometimes on petition of a small percentage of the voters or property owners in the area, sometimes by the district governing body acting alone. In a few states, expansion of the area is impossible or limited, but this is not the usual practice. (4) Their establishment does not disrupt or change the established governmental structure or affect local office holders. (5) They do not usually suffer the financial restrictions imposed by state law on the other units that were discussed earlier. (6) In their relationships with the state legislature, they do not seem to labor under the antagonism cities do. (7) They can provide an area-wide approach to an area-wide problem. (8) Finally, the wide variety existing in their uses and organizational practices makes a tailor-made plan not only possible but probable. It is not surprising, therefore, that the numbers of special districts have increased rapidly since 1942 when rapid growth of urban areas has produced so many service needs.[41] This has led to the suggestion that the uses of special districts could be increased and their functions expanded, but this necessitates an examination of their disadvantages and inadequacies.

Inade-quacies   The criticisms of the special district as a solution to problems in metropolitan areas revolve around their relationships with the other units of government in the area, the limitations on their activities, and their remoteness from the general public. The creation of a special district means that the number of units in an area is increased; local government is made more complex; and intergovernmental cooperation and planning is decreased by the withdrawal of a function from the responsibility of the general purpose governments.[42] Of equal importance, when an expanded use of special districts is contemplated, are the limitations on their functions that result from their lack of general legislative power and their methods of finance.[43] The types of districts

All the metropolitan areas that contain over one million inhabitants embrace more than one county; five are interstate; one is international (Detroit).

[41] The number of districts has increased from 8300 in 1942 to 18,323 in 1962.

[42] A special district could be regarded as a form of practical cooperation. Once organized, however, the district has autonomy and the initial cooperation is usually not continued. Special districts have a reputation for going their own ways. In the survey of county cooperation mentioned above (B. F. Hillenbrand, *op. cit.*), the services of counties to districts were mostly administrative (p. 63).

[43] See W. Miller, "Legal and Constitutional Problems," *Univ. of Penna. Law Rev.,* Vol. 105, No. 4 (Feb., 1957).

we have been discussing in general have no ordinance-making power and there is no move apparent to increase this power as there is for counties. This usually debars them from regulatory activities and limits them to service functions. Their methods of finance—commonly special assessments, charges, rates, and rents—limit them to self-supporting activities. The effect of both these limitations so far has been that in suburban areas especially, water supply and sewage disposal are usually more adequately provided for than police and fire protection.

The most serious criticism of the special-purpose district, however, is its remoteness from the general public. This occurs because of one or more of the following practices: (1) Many of their governing bodies are appointed in whole or in part by state judges or governors. In the case of interstate districts, they are appointed by the respective governors. (2) Sometimes a district is organized in such a complicated fashion that the typical voter does not know what it is let alone what it does.[44] (3) Often the governing bodies are not directly elected by the people, either in whole or in part, and in some instances franchise depends on property qualifications—a voting restriction virtually abandoned for other electoral processes.[45] All these practices place the voter at one or more removes from the district government and lessen political accountability.

It has been suggested by many observers of the metropolitan scene that special-purpose districts might be transformed or evolve into multipurpose ones. In this case a very useful metropolitan government would result—always provided that these districts could be made more responsive to the public. This would involve decisions on the composition and methods of selection of their governing bodies comparable to those encountered in plans for federation. It is not likely that many present single-purpose districts will evolve into many-purpose ones. Most districts at present are single purpose; a few provide related services such as sewage disposal and storm water drainage, but, even when a district is permitted by state law to give other services, the practice has been for districts not to expand their activities.[46] Neither have these districts shown any inclination to *seek* authority to add to their responsibilities. The creation anew of a multipurpose district to serve as a metropolitan govern-

Can the special district be retooled?

44 The Milwaukee Metropolitan Sewerage District has two governing bodies, one for the city and one for the metropolitan area it covers. The city commission has five members appointed by the mayor and the metropolitan commission has three appointed by the governor. Each has different responsibilities.

45 A district with almost unbelievably complicated organization and voting procedures is the Southern California Metropolitan Water District. See J. C. Bollens, *Special District Governments in the United States,* 90, *supra.*

46 Enabling laws for multipurpose districts are not common. Connecticut, South Carolina, Michigan, Colorado, California have such and the number of states authorizing these is increasing. The areas that have utilized these laws are usually urban fringes—mainly to avoid annexation. In California, the districts that have been established have not taken advantage of the enabling legislation (the Community Services District Law, passed in 1951) to expand. See J. C. Bollens, *supra.,* 110, 111.

ment seems even more difficult to achieve than the other forms of metropolitan reorganization.[47]

JOINT AGENCIES AND COOPERATIVE ACTIVITY

The conclusions on the possibilities of metropolitan government reached by many are that local units are incapable of creating broader mechanisms of government to solve the urban problems of an expanding population. Though more special-purpose districts will be created and more urban counties will undertake additional functions, other proposals have little chance of success. The stake of the national government in the economic and social vitality of our great metropolises and the legal responsibility of the states mean that they will undoubtedly participate more and more in solving metropolitan problems.[48] On their own endeavors, however, the local units have made progress in cooperative arrangements. Sanitation, health, fire protection, water supply, airports, and library services are among the functions that with increasing frequency are being turned over by individual governmental units to joint agencies. Minnesota, Louisiana, Missouri, Georgia, New Jersey, and California are among the states that permit local units to perform jointly any function they may perform separately. The Municipal Authorities in Pennsylvania are an outstanding example of joint activity.[49] The advantage of this form of endeavor is that it can be intercounty [50] and interstate. The latest addition to cooperative activity among local units is metropolitan councils. These are associations of local officials who study the problems of their areas (with the help of professional staffs). They may make plans for their areas and recommend lines of action to their local units. The largest is the Metropolitan

[47] No instance exists of a success. Three such proposals have been defeated in recent years—one for Nashville in 1958; one for Seattle in 1958 and one for St. Louis in 1959. A 1959 proposition for Seattle that limited the district to sewage disposal and decreased its territorial size was approved.

[48] A new national department of urban affairs sponsored by the Kennedy administration was in fact created in 1965.

There is a need for considering the impact of national activities on urban areas, coordinating them, studying urban problems, and advising and assisting local units. The Advisory Commission on Intergovernmental Relations was made permanent by Congress in 1959. It consists of private citizens and national, state, municipal, and county officials. Some regard it as obviating the need for a department.

Though slow to recognize their responsibilities, a growing interest in metropolitan problems is being shown by state governments. Each year more states create local government agencies to expedite the availability of state services to local units, coordinate activities and services of the states, encourage and assist cooperative efforts, advise and make studies on local problems, etc. The particular interest of the states in metropolitan problems is shown by the increasing number of legislative committees and governors' commissions studying them and making recommendations for their solutions.

[49] For the creation, functions, and pros and cons of the uses of these authorities see J. C. Bollens, *op. cit.,* 240-246.

[50] For recent examples of inter-county cooperation see B. F. Hillenbrand, *op. cit.,* 62.

Regional Council for the New York area.[51] Similar agencies are also functioning in Denver, Washington, and Wichita, Kansas. Of less broad scope are regional planning commissions such as those operating in the Twin Cities (Minneapolis and St. Paul), the Northeastern Illinois, and Detroit areas. Though many avenues of approach can and should be taken simultaneously by the largest areas, probably the only all-inclusive methods possible for them on local government terms (short of the creation of "city states") are these councils and commissions for discussion, study, and planning.

References

V. Jones, *Metropolitan Government* (Chicago, 1942).

J. C. Bollens, *The States and the Metropolitan Problem,* Report to the Governors' Conference of the Council of State Governments (Chicago, 1956).

―――, *Special District Governments in the United States* (Berkeley and Los Angeles, 1957). Chaps. I-V, VIII.

―――, "Metropolitan and Fringe Area Developments," *The Municipal Year Book.* Annual article.

B. Tableman, *Governmental Organization in Metropolitan Areas* (Ann Arbor, Mich., 1951).

E. C. Banfield and M. Grodzins, *Government and Housing in Metropolitan Areas* (New York, 1958). Chaps. II, III, VI-IX.

R. H. Connery, *The Federal Government and Metropolitan Areas* (Cambridge, Mass., 1960).

"A Symposium on Metropolitan Regionalism: Developing Governmental Concepts," *Univ. of Penna. Law Rev.,* Vol. 105, No. 4 (Feb., 1957). Entire issue.

R. C. Wood, *Metropolis Against Itself* (Committee for Economic Development, New York, 1959).

G. S. Birkhead, "Metropolitan Areas Demand Attention," *Nat. Mun. Rev.,* XLII (July, 1953).

J. C. Bollens and J. C. Schmandt, *The Metropolis: Its People, Politics, and Economic Life* (New York, 1965).

E. Sofen, *The Miami Metropolitan Experiment* (Bloomington, Ind., 1963).

R. C. Martin, *Metropolis in Transition: Local Government Adaptation to Changing Needs* (Washington, 1963).

Y. Wilbern, *The Withering Away of the City* (Birmingham, Ala., 1964).

[51] The text of the report urging full legal status for this council may be found in *The New York Times,* January 9, 1959, 16.

Creation of these councils has been advocated by L. Gulick. See his *Metro: Changing Problems and Lines of Attack* (Washington, Government Affairs Institute, 1957).

S. Greer, *Metropolitics, a Study of Political Culture* (New York, 1963).

W. S. Fiser, *Mastery of the Metropolis* (Englewood Cliffs, N.J., 1962).

G. E. Baker, *Rural vs. Urban Political Power* (New York, 1955).

Toronto Civic Advisory Council: Committee on Metropolitan Problems, *Final Report* (Toronto, 1951).

Cleveland Metropolitan Services Commission, *Prologue to Progress* (Cleveland, 1959).

————, *Governmental Organization for Metropolitan Cleveland* (Cleveland, 1959).

Cleveland Bureau of Governmental Research, *Metropolitan Follow Up: A Continuing Research Program for Metropolitan Cleveland* (Cleveland, 1959).

New York Metropolitan Region Study (Cambridge, Mass., 1958-1960). Ten volumes. The following are especially appropriate:
R. C. Woods, *1400 Governments.*
E. M. Hoover and R. Vernon, *Anatomy of a Metropolis.*
R. Vernon, *Metropolis: 1985.*

Conference on Metropolitan Area Problems, *Metropolitan Surveys Now in Progress* (New York, 1960).

Charter Study Commission of San Mateo County, *Report* (Redwood City, Calif., 1959).

Metropolitan Community Studies, Inc., *Metropolitan Challenge* (Dayton, Ohio, 1959).

St. Louis, Mo., Metropolitan Survey, *Background for Action* (1957).

————, *Path of Progress for Metropolitan St. Louis* (St. Louis, 1957).

Joint Congressional Committee on Washington Metropolitan Problems, *Meeting the Problems of Metropolitan Growth in the National Capital Region* (Washington, 1958).

"Seeking Solutions of the Metropolitan Problem," *State Government* (Nov., 1956). Entire issue.

J. C. Bollens, "Annexation of Fringe Areas," *Public Management* (April, 1949).

R. E. Fryer, *Analysis of Annexation in Michigan* (Bur. of Govt. Univ. of Mich., Ann Arbor, 1951).

S. Scott and L. Keller, *Annexation? Incorporation?: A Guide for Community Action* (Univ. of Calif., Bur. of Public Admin., Berkeley, 1959).

H. Stein (ed.), "Gotham in the Air Age," *Public Administration and Policy Development: A Case Book,* 143-196 (New York, 1952). On the Port of New York Authority.

W. G. Thrombley, *Special Districts and Authorities in Texas* (Austin, 1959).

J. R. Donoghue, "County Government and Urban Growth," *Wis. Law Rev.,* 30-54 (Jan., 1959).

Metropolitan Study Commission of Allegheny County, *An Urban Home Rule Charter for Allegheny County* (Pittsburgh, 1955).

National Association of County Officials, *The Urban County Congress* (Washington, 1959).

G. Serino, *Miami's Metropolitan Experiment* (Gainesville, Fla., 1958).

Public Administration Service, *The Government of Metropolitan Miami* (Chicago, 1954).

E. H. Denton, *Extension of Municipal Services to Fringe Areas* (Univ. of Kansas Govt'l. Research Center, Lawrence, 1959). Pamph.

Appendix

THE CONSTITUTION OF THE UNITED STATES OF AMERICA

WE, THE PEOPLE OF THE UNITED STATES, in order to form a more perfect union, establish justice, insure domestic tranquility, provide for the common defense, promote the general welfare, and secure the blessings of liberty to ourselves and our posterity, do ordain and establish this Constitution for the United States of America.

ARTICLE I

Section I

All legislative powers herein granted shall be vested in a Congress of the United States, which shall consist of a Senate and House of Representatives.

Section II

The House of Representatives shall be composed of members chosen every second year by the people of the several States, and the electors in each State shall have the qualifications requisite for electors of the most numerous branch of the State legislature.

No person shall be a Representative who shall not have attained to the age of twenty-five years, and been seven years a citizen of the United States, and who shall not, when elected, be an inhabitant of that State in which he shall be chosen.

Representatives and direct taxes shall be apportioned among the several States which may be included within this Union, according to their respective numbers, which shall be determined by adding to the whole number of free persons, including those bound to service for a term of years,[1] and excluding Indians not taxed, three fifths of all other persons.[2] The actual enumeration shall be made within three years after the first meeting of the Congress of the United States, and within every subsequent term of ten years, in such manner as they shall by law direct. The number of Representatives shall not exceed one for every thirty thousand, but each State shall have at least one Representative; and until such enumeration shall be made, the State of New Hampshire shall be entitled to choose three, Massachusetts eight, Rhode Island and Providence Plantations one, Connecticut five,

[1] Altered by the Fourteenth Amendment.
[2] Rescinded by the Fourteenth Amendment.

New York six, New Jersey four, Pennsylvania eight, Delaware one, Maryland six, Virginia ten, North Carolina five, South Carolina five, and Georgia three.[3]

When vacancies happen in the representation from any State, the executive authority thereof shall issue writs of election to fill such vacancies.

The House of Representatives shall choose their Speaker and other officers, and shall have the sole power of impeachment.

Section III

The Senate of the United States shall be composed of two Senators from each State, chosen by the legislature thereof,[4] for six years; and each Senator shall have one vote.

Immediately after they shall be assembled in consequence of the first election, they shall be divided as equally as may be into three classes. The seats of the Senators of the first class shall be vacated at the expiration of the second year, of the second class at the expiration of the fourth year, and of the third class at the expiration of the sixth year, so that one third may be chosen every second year; and if vacancies happen by resignation or otherwise during the recess of the legislature of any State the executive thereof may make temporary appointments until the next meeting of the legislature, which shall then fill such vacancies.[5]

No person shall be a Senator who shall not have attained to the age of thirty years, and been nine years a citizen of the United States, and who shall not, when elected, be an inhabitant of that State for which he shall be chosen.

The Vice-President of the United States shall be President of the Senate, but shall have no vote, unless they be equally divided.

The Senate shall choose their other officers, and also a President *pro tempore* in the absence of the Vice-President, or when he shall exercise the office of the President of the United States.

The Senate shall have the sole power to try all impeachments. When sitting for that purpose, they shall be on oath or affirmation. When the President of the United States is tried, the Chief Justice shall preside; and no person shall be convicted without the concurrence of two thirds of the members present.

Judgment in cases of impeachment shall not extend further than to removal from office, and disqualification to hold and enjoy any office of honor, trust, or profit under the United States; but the party convicted shall, nevertheless, be liable and subject to indictment, trial, judgment, and punishment, according to law.

Section IV

The times, places, and manner of holding elections for Senators and Representatives shall be prescribed in each State by the legislature thereof; but the Congress

[3] Temporary provision.
[4] Modified by the Seventeenth Amendment.
[5] Modified by the Seventeenth Amendment.

may at any time by law make or alter such regulations, except as to the places of choosing Senators.

The Congress shall assemble at least once in every year, and such meeting shall be on the first Monday in December, unless they shall by law appoint a different day.[6]

Section V

Each house shall be the judge of the elections, returns, and qualifications of its own members, and a majority of each shall constitute a quorum to do business; but a smaller number may adjourn from day to day, and may be authorized to compel the attendance of absent members, in such manner, and under such penalties, as each house may provide.

Each house may determine the rules of its proceedings, punish its members for disorderly behavior, and with the concurrence of two thirds, expel a member.

Each house shall keep a journal of its proceedings, and from time to time publish the same, excepting such parts as may in their judgment require secrecy, and the yeas and nays of the members of either house on any question shall, at the desire of one fifth of those present, be entered on the journal.

Neither house, during the session of Congress, shall, without the consent of the other, adjourn for more than three days, nor to any other place than that in which the two houses shall be sitting.

Section VI

The Senators and Representatives shall receive a compensation for their services, to be ascertained by law and paid out of the Treasury of the United States. They shall, in all cases except treason, felony, and breach of the peace, be privileged from arrest during their attendance at the session of their respective houses, and in going to and returning from the same; and for any speech or debate in either house they shall not be questioned in any other place.

No Senator or Representative shall, during the time for which he was elected, be appointed to any civil office under the authority of the United States, which shall have been created, or the emoluments whereof shall have been increased, during such time; and no person holding any office under the United States shall be a member of either house during his continuance in office.

Section VII

All bills for raising revenue shall originate in the House of Representatives; but the Senate may propose or concur with amendments as on other bills.

Every bill which shall have passed the House of Representatives and the Senate shall, before it become a law, be presented to the President of the United States; if he approves he shall sign it, but if not he shall return it, with his objections, to that house in which it shall have originated, who shall enter the objections at

---

[6] Superseded by the Twentieth Amendment.

large on their journal and proceed to reconsider it. If after such reconsideration two thirds of that house shall agree to pass the bill, it shall be sent, together with the objections, to the other house, by which it shall likewise be reconsidered, and if approved by two thirds of that house it shall become a law. But in all such cases the votes of both houses shall be determined by yeas and nays, and the names of the persons voting for and against the bill shall be entered on the journal of each house respectively. If any bill shall not be returned by the President within ten days (Sundays excepted) after it shall have been presented to him, the same shall be a law, in like manner as if he had signed it, unless the Congress by their adjournment prevent its return, in which case it shall not be a law.

Every order, resolution, or vote to which the concurrence of the Senate and House of Representatives may be necessary (except on a question of adjournment) shall be presented to the President of the United States; and before the same shall take effect, shall be approved by him, or being disapproved by him, shall be repassed by two thirds of the Senate and House of Representatives, according to the rules and limitations prescribed in the case of a bill.

Section VIII

The Congress shall have power to lay and collect taxes, duties, imposts, and excises, to pay the debts and provide for the common defense and general welfare of the United States; but all duties, imposts, and excises shall be uniform throughout the United States;

To borrow money on the credit of the United States;

To regulate commerce with foreign nations and among the several States, and with the Indian tribes;

To establish an uniform rule of naturalization, and uniform laws on the subject of bankruptcies throughout the United States;

To coin money, regulate the value thereof, and of foreign coin, and fix the standard of weights and measures;

To provide for the punishment of counterfeiting the securities and current coin of the United States;

To establish post-offices and post-roads;

To promote the progress of science and useful arts by securing for limited times to authors and inventors the exclusive right to their respective writings and discoveries;

To constitute tribunals inferior to the Supreme Court;

To define and punish piracies and felonies committed on the high seas and offenses against the law of nations;

To declare war, grant letters of marque and reprisal, and make rules concerning captures on land and water;

To raise and support armies, but no appropriation of money to that use shall be for a longer term than two years;

To provide and maintain a navy;

To make rules for the government and regulation of the land and naval forces;

To provide for calling forth the militia to execute the laws of the Union, suppress insurrections, and repel invasions;

To provide for organizing, arming, and disciplining the militia, and for governing such part of them as may be employed in the service of the United States, reserving to the States respectively the appointment of the officers, and the authority of training the militia according to the discipline prescribed by Congress;

To exercise exclusive legislation in all cases whatsoever over such district (not exceeding ten miles square) as may, by cession of particular States and the acceptance of Congress, become the seat of the Government of the United States, and to exercise like authority over all places purchased by the consent of the legislature of the State in which the same shall be, for the erection of forts, magazines, arsenals, dockyards, and other needful buildings; and

To make all laws which shall be necessary and proper for carrying into execution the foregoing powers, and all other powers vested by this Constitution in the Government of the United States, or in any department or officer thereof.

Section IX

The migration or importation of such persons as any of the States now existing shall think proper to admit shall not be prohibited by the Congress prior to the year one thousand eight hundred and eight, but a tax or duty may be imposed on such importation, not exceeding ten dollars for each person.[7]

The privilege of the writ of *habeas corpus* shall not be suspended, unless when in cases of rebellion or invasion the public safety may require it.

No bill of attainder or *ex post facto* law shall be passed.

No capitation or other direct tax shall be laid, unless in proportion to the census or enumeration hereinbefore directed to be taken.

No tax or duty shall be laid on articles exported from any State.

No preference shall be given by any regulation of commerce or revenue to the ports of one State over those of another; nor shall vessels bound to or from one State be obliged to enter, clear, or pay duties in another.

No money shall be drawn from the Treasury but in consequence of appropriations made by law; and a regular statement and account of the receipts and expenditures of all public money shall be published from time to time.

No title of nobility shall be granted by the United States; and no person holding any office of profit or trust under them shall, without the consent of the Congress, accept of any present, emolument, office, or title, of any kind whatever, from any king, prince, or foreign State.

Section X

No State shall enter into any treaty, alliance, or confederation; grant letters of marque and reprisal; coin money; emit bills of credit; make anything but gold and silver coin a tender in payment of debts; pass any bill of attainder, *ex post facto* law, or law impairing the obligation of contracts, or grant any title of nobility.

No State shall, without the consent of Congress, lay any imposts or duties on imports or exports, except what may be absolutely necessary for executing its inspection laws; and the net produce of all duties and imposts, laid by any State

[7] Temporary provision.

on imports or exports, shall be for the use of the Treasury of the United States; and all such laws shall be subject to the revision and control of the Congress.

No State shall, without the consent of Congress, lay any duty of tonnage, keep troops or ships of war in time of peace, enter into any agreement or compact with another State or with a foreign power, or engage in war, unless actually invaded or in such imminent danger as will not admit of delay.

ARTICLE II

Section 1

The executive power shall be vested in a President of the United States of America. He shall hold his office during the term of four years,[8] and together with the Vice-President, chosen for the same term, be elected as follows:

Each State shall appoint, in such manner as the legislature thereof may direct, a number of electors, equal to the whole number of Senators and Representatives to which the State may be entitled in the Congress; but no Senator or Representative, or person holding an office of trust or profit under the United States, shall be appointed an elector.

The electors shall meet in their respective States and vote by ballot for two persons, of whom one at least shall not be an inhabitant of the same State with themselves. And they shall make a list of all the persons voted for, and of the number of votes for each; which list they shall sign and certify, and transmit sealed to the seat of government of the United States, directed to the President of the Senate. The President of the Senate shall, in the presence of the Senate and House of Representatives, open all the certificates, and the votes shall then be counted. The person having the greatest number of votes shall be the President, if such number be a majority of the whole number of electors appointed; and if there be more than one who have such a majority, and have an equal number of votes, then the House of Representatives shall immediately choose by ballot one of them for President; and if no person have a majority, then from the five highest on the list the said House shall in like manner choose the President. But in choosing the President the votes shall be taken by States, the representation from each State having one vote; a quorum for this purpose shall consist of a member or members from two thirds of the States, and a majority of all the States shall be necessary to a choice. In every case, after the choice of the President, the person having the greatest number of votes of the electors shall be the Vice-President. But if there should remain two or more who have equal votes, the Senate shall choose from them by ballot the Vice-President.[9]

---

[8] Modified by the Twenty-second Amendment.
[9] Superseded by the Twelfth Amendment.

The Congress may determine the time of choosing the electors and the day on which they shall give their votes, which day shall be the same throughout the United States.

No person except a natural-born citizen, or a citizen of the United States at the time of the adoption of this Constitution, shall be eligible to the office of President; neither shall any person be eligible to that office who shall not have attained to the age of thirty-five years, and been fourteen years a resident of the United States.

In case of the removal of the President from office, or of his death, resignation, or inability to discharge the powers and duties of the said office, the same shall devolve on the Vice-President, and the Congress may by law provide for the case of removal, death, resignation, or inability, both of the President and Vice-President, declaring what officer shall then act as President, and such officer shall act accordingly until the disability be removed or a President shall be elected.

The President shall, at stated times, receive for his services a compensation, which shall neither be increased nor diminished during the period for which he may have been elected, and he shall not receive within that period any other emolument from the United States or any of them.

Before he enter on the execution of his office he shall take the following oath or affirmation:

"I do solemnly swear (or affirm) that I will faithfully execute the office of President of the United States, and will to the best of my ability preserve, protect, and defend the Constitution of the United States."

Section II

The President shall be commander-in-chief of the army and navy of the United States, and of the militia of the several States when called into the actual service of the United States; he may require the opinion, in writing, of the principal officer in each of the executive departments, upon any subject relating to the duties of their respective offices, and he shall have power to grant reprieves and pardons for offenses against the United States, except in cases of impeachment.

He shall have power, by and with the advice and consent of the Senate, to make treaties, provided two thirds of the Senators present concur; and he shall nominate, and, by and with the advice and consent of the Senate, shall appoint ambassadors, other public ministers and consuls, judges of the Supreme Court, and all other officers of the United States, whose appointments are not herein otherwise provided for, and which shall be established by law; but the Congress may by law vest the appointment of such inferior officers, as they think proper, in the President alone, in the courts of law, or in the heads of departments.

The President shall have power to fill up all vacancies that may happen during the recess of the Senate, by granting commissions which shall expire at the end of their next session.

Section III

He shall from time to time give to the Congress information of the state of the Union, and recommend to their consideration such measures as he shall judge necessary and expedient; he may, on extraordinary occasions, convene both houses, or either of them, and in case of disagreement between them with respect to the time of adjournment, he may adjourn them to such time as he shall think proper; he shall receive ambassadors and other public ministers; he shall take care that the laws be faithfully executed, and shall commission all the officers of the United States.

Section IV

The President, Vice-President, and all civil officers of the United States shall be removed from office on impeachment for and conviction of treason, bribery, or other high crimes and misdemeanors.

ARTICLE III

Section I

The judicial power of the United States shall be vested in one Supreme Court, and in such inferior courts as the Congress may from time to time ordain and establish. The judges, both of the supreme and inferior courts, shall hold their offices during good behavior, and shall, at stated times, receive for their services a compensation which shall not be diminished during their continuance in office.

Section II

The judicial power shall extend to all cases, in law and equity, arising under this Constitution, the laws of the United States, and the treaties made, or which shall be made, under their authority;—to all cases affecting ambassadors, other public ministers, and consuls;—to all cases of admiralty and maritime jurisdiction;—to controversies to which the United States shall be a party;—to controversies between two or more States;—between a State and citizens of another State,[10]—between citizens of different States;—between citizens of the same State claiming lands under grants of different States, and between a State, or the citizens thereof, and foreign States, citizens, or subjects.[10]

In all cases affecting ambassadors, other public ministers, and consuls, and those in which a State shall be a party, the Supreme Court shall have original jurisdiction. In all the other cases before mentioned the Supreme Court shall have appellate jurisdiction, both as to law and fact, with such exceptions and under such regulations as the Congress shall make.

The trial of all crimes, except in cases of impeachment, shall be by jury; and such trial shall be held in the State where the said crimes shall have been committed; but when not committed within any State, the trial shall be at such place or places as the Congress may by law have directed.

Section III

Treason against the United States shall consist only in levying war against them, or in adhering to their enemies, giving them aid and comfort. No person shall be

[10] Restricted by the Eleventh Amendment.

convicted of treason unless on the testimony of two witnesses to the same overt act, or on confession in open court.

The Congress shall have power to declare the punishment of treason, but no attainder of treason shall work corruption of blood or forfeiture except during the life of the person attainted.

ARTICLE IV

Section I

Full faith and credit shall be given in each State to the public acts, records, and judicial proceedings of every other State. And the Congress may by general laws prescribe the manner in which such acts, records, and proceedings shall be proved, and the effect thereof.

Section II

The citizens of each State shall be entitled to all privileges and immunities of citizens in the several States.[11]

A person charged in any State with treason, felony, or other crime, who shall flee from justice, and be found in another State shall, on demand of the executive authority of the State from which he fled, be delivered up, to be removed to the State having jurisdiction of the crime.

No person held to service or labor in one State, under the laws thereof, escaping into another, shall, in consequence of any law or regulation therein, be discharged from such service or labor, but shall be delivered up on claim of the party to whom such service or labor may be due.[12]

Section III

New States may be admitted by the Congress into this Union; but no new State shall be formed or erected within the jurisdiction of any other State; nor any State be formed by the junction of two or more States or parts of States, without the consent of the legislatures of the States concerned as well as of the Congress.

The Congress shall have power to dispose of and make all needful rules and regulations respecting the territory or other property belonging to the United States; and nothing in this Constitution shall be so construed as to prejudice any claims of the United States or any particular State.

Section IV

The United States shall guarantee to every State in this Union a republican form of government, and shall protect each of them against invasion, and on application

---

11 Made more explicit by the Fourteenth Amendment.
12 Superseded by the Thirteenth Amendment in so far as pertaining to slaves.

of the legislature, or of the executive (when the legislature cannot be convened), against domestic violence.

ARTICLE V

The Congress, whenever two thirds of both houses shall deem it necessary, shall propose amendments to this Constitution, or, on the application of the legisatures of two thirds of the several States, shall call a convention for proposing amendments, which in either case shall be valid to all intents and purposes as part of this Constitution, when ratified by the legislatures of three fourths of the several States, or by conventions in three fourths thereof, as the one or the other mode of ratification may be proposed by the Congress, provided that no amendments which may be made prior to the year one thousand eight hundred and eight shall in any manner affect the first and fourth clauses in the ninth section of the first article,[13] and that no State, without its consent, shall be deprived of its equal suffrage in the Senate.

ARTICLE VI

All debts contracted and engagements entered into, before the adoption of this Constitution, shall be as valid against the United States under this Constitution as under the confederation.[14]

This Constitution, and the laws of the United States, which shall be made in pursuance thereof, and all treaties made, or which shall be made, under the authority of the United States, shall be the supreme law of the land; and the judges in every State shall be bound thereby, anything in the Constitution or laws of any State to the contrary notwithstanding.

The Senators and Representatives before mentioned, and the members of the several State legislatures, and all executive and judicial officers both of the United States and of the several States, shall be bound by oath or affirmation to support this Constitution; but no religious test shall ever be required as a qualification to any office or public trust under the United States.

ARTICLE VII

The ratification of the conventions of nine States shall be sufficient for the establishment of this Constitution between the States so ratifying the same.

Done in convention by the unanimous consent of the States present, the seventeenth day of September, in the year of our Lord one thousand seven hundred and eighty-seven, and of the independence of the United States of America the twelfth. In witness whereof, we have hereunto subscribed our names.

[Signed by] [15]

---

[13] Temporary clause.
[14] Extended by the Fourteenth Amendment.
[15] The signatures are omitted here.

ARTICLES IN ADDITION TO, AND AMENDMENT OF, THE CONSTI-
TUTION OF THE UNITED STATES OF AMERICA, PROPOSED BY CON-
GRESS, AND RATIFIED BY THE LEGISLATURES OF THE SEVERAL
STATES [OR CONVENTIONS THEREIN] PURSUANT TO THE FIFTH
ARTICLE OF THE ORIGINAL CONSTITUTION:

Article I. Congress shall make no law respecting an establishment of religion,
or prohibiting the free exercise thereof; or abridging the freedom of speech or of
the press; or the right of the people peaceably to assemble, and to petition the government for a redress of grievances.

Article II. A well-regulated militia being necessary to the security of a free
state, the right of the people to keep and bear arms shall not be infringed.

Article III. No soldier shall, in time of peace, be quartered in any house without the consent of the owner, nor in time of war, but in a manner to be prescribed
by law.

Article IV. The right of the people to be secure in their persons, houses, papers,
and effects, against unreasonable searches and seizures, shall not be violated, and
no warrants shall issue but upon probable cause, supported by oath or affirmation,
and particularly describing the place to be searched, and the person or things to be
seized.

Article V. No person shall be held to answer for a capital or otherwise infamous crime, unless on a presentment or indictment of a grand jury, except in cases
arising in the land or naval forces, or in the militia, when in actual service in time
of war or public danger; nor shall any person be subject for the same offense to be
twice put in jeopardy of life or limb; nor shall be compelled in any criminal case
to be a witness against himself, nor be deprived of life, liberty, or property, without due process of law; nor shall private property be taken for public use without
just compensation.

Article VI. In all criminal prosecutions the accused shall enjoy the right to a
speedy and public trial, by an impartial jury of the State and district where in the
crime shall have been committed, which district shall have been previously ascertained by law, and to be informed of the nature and cause of the accusation; to be
confronted with the witnesses against him; to have compulsory process for obtaining witnesses in his favor, and to have the assistance of counsel for his defense.

Article VII. In suits at common law, where the value in controversy shall exceed
twenty dollars, the right of trial by jury shall be preserved, and no fact tried by
a jury shall be otherwise re-examined in any court of the United States, than according to the rules of the common law.

Article VIII. Excessive bail shall not be required, nor excessive fines imposed,
nor cruel and unusual punishments inflicted.

Article IX. The enumeration in the Constitution of certain rights shall not be
construed to deny or disparage others retained by the people.

Article X.[16] The powers not delegated to the United States by the Constitution,

16 The first ten amendments took effect December 15, 1791.

nor prohibited by it to the States, are reserved to the States respectively, or to the people.

Article XI.[17] The judicial power of the United States shall not be construed to extend to any suit in law or equity, commenced or prosecuted against one of the United States by citizens of another State, or by citizens or subjects of any foreign State.

Article XII.[18] The electors shall meet in their respective States [19] and vote by ballot for President and Vice-President, one of whom, at least, shall not be an inhabitant of the same State with themselves; they shall name in their ballots the person voted for as President, and in distinct ballots the person voted for as Vice-President, and they shall make distinct lists of all persons voted for as President and of all persons voted for as Vice-President, and of the number of votes for each; which lists they shall sign and certify, and transmit sealed to the seat of the government of the United States, directed to the President of the Senate. The President of the Senate shall, in the presence of the Senate and House of Representatives, open all the certificates and the votes shall then be counted. The person having the greatest number of votes for President shall be the President, if such a number be a majority of the whole number of electors appointed; and if no person have such a majority, then from the persons having the highest numbers not exceeding three on the list of those voted for as President, the House of Representatives shall choose immediately, by ballot, the President. But in choosing the President the votes shall be taken by States, the representation from each State having one vote; a quorum for this purpose shall consist of a member or members from two thirds of the States, and a majority of all States shall be necessary to a choice. And if the House of Representatives shall not choose a President whenever the right of choice shall devolve upon them, before the fourth day of March [20] next following, then the Vice-President shall act as President, as in the case of the death or other constitutional disability of the President.

The person having the greatest number of votes as Vice-President shall be the Vice-President, if such number be a majority of the whole number of electors appointed; and if no person have a majority, then from the two highest numbers on the list the Senate shall choose the Vice-President: a quorum for the purpose shall consist of two thirds of the whole number of Senators, and a majority of the whole number shall be necessary to a choice. But no person constitutionally ineligible to the office of President shall be eligible to that of Vice-President of the United States.

Article XIII.[21] *Section* 1. Neither slavery nor involuntary servitude, except as a punishment for crime whereof the party shall have been duly convicted, shall exist within the United States or any place subject to their jurisdiction.

Section 2. Congress shall have power to enforce this article by appropriate legislation.

Article XIV.[22] *Section* 1. All persons born or naturalized in the United States,

[17] Proclaimed January 8, 1798.
[18] Proclaimed September 25, 1804.
[19] Modified by the Twenty-third Amendment.
[20] Superseded by the Twentieth Amendment.
[21] Proclaimed December 18, 1865.
[22] Proclaimed July 28, 1868.

and subject to the jurisdiction thereof, are citizens of the United States and of the State wherein they reside. No State shall make or enforce any law which shall abridge the privileges or immunities of citizens of the United States; nor shall any State deprive any person of life, liberty, or property, without due process of law; nor deny to any person within its jurisdiction the equal protection of the laws.

Section 2. Representatives shall be apportioned among the several States according to their respective numbers, counting the whole number of persons in each State, excluding Indians not taxed. But when the right to vote at any election for the choice of electors for President and Vice-President of the United States, Representatives in Congress, the executive and judicial officers of a State, or the members of the legislature thereof, is denied to any of the male inhabitants of such State, being twenty-one years of age, and citizens of the United States, or in any way abridged, except for participation in rebellion, or other crime, the basis of representation therein shall be reduced in the proportion which the number of such male citizens shall bear to the whole number of male citizens twenty-one years of age in such State.

Section 3. No person shall be a Senator or Representative in Congress, or elector of President and Vice-President, or hold any office, civil or military, under the United States or under any State, who, having previously taken an oath as a member of Congress, or as an officer of the United States, or as a member of any State legislature, or as an executive or judicial officer of any State, to support the Constitution of the United States, shall have engaged in insurrection or rebellion against the same, or given aid or comfort to the enemies thereof. But Congress may, by a vote of two thirds of each house, remove such disability.

Section 4. The validity of the public debt of the United States, authorized by law, including debts incurred for payment of pensions and bounties for services in suppressing insurrection or rebellion, shall not be questioned. But neither the United States nor any State shall assume or pay any debt or obligation incurred in aid of insurrection or rebellion against the United States, or any claim for the loss or emancipation of any slave; but all such debts, obligations, and claims shall be held illegal and void.

Section 5. The Congress shall have power to enforce, by appropriate legislation, the provisions of this article.

Article XV.[23] *Section* 1. The right of citizens of the United States to vote shall not be denied or abridged by the United States or by any State on account of race, color, or previous condition of servitude.

Section 2. The Congress shall have power to enforce this article by appropriate legislation.

Article XVI.[24] The Congress shall have power to lay and collect taxes on incomes, from whatever source derived, without apportionment among the several States and without regard to any census or enumeration.

Article XVII.[25] The Senate of the United States shall be composed of two Senators from each State, elected by the people thereof, for six years; and each

[23] Proclaimed March 30, 1870.
[24] Proclaimed February 25, 1912.
[25] Proclaimed May 31, 1913.

Senator shall have one vote. The electors in each State shall have the qualifications requisite for electors of the most numerous branch of the State legislature.

When vacancies happen in the representation of any State in the Senate, the executive authority of such State shall issue writs of election to fill such vacancies: *Provided,* That the legislature of any State may empower the executive thereof to make temporary appointments until the people fill the vacancies by election as the legislature may direct.

This amendment shall not be so construed as to affect the election or term of any Senator chosen before it becomes valid as part of the Constitution.

Article XVIII.[26] *Section* 1. After one year from the ratification of this article the manufacture, sale, or transportation of intoxicating liquors within, the importation thereof into, or the exportation thereof from the United States and all territory subject to the jurisdiction thereof for beverage purposes is hereby prohibited.

Section 2. The Congress and the several States shall have concurrent power to enforce this article by appropriate legislation.

Section 3. This article shall be inoperative unless it shall have been ratified as an amendment to the Constitution by the legislatures of the several States, as provided in the Constitution, within seven years from the date of the submission hereof to the States by the Congress.[27]

Article XIX.[28] *Section* 1. The right of citizens of the United States to vote shall not be denied or abridged by the United States or by any State on account of sex.

Section 2. Congress shall have power to enforce this article by appropriate legislation.

Article XX.[29] *Section* 1. The terms of the President and Vice-President shall end at noon on the 20th day of January, and the terms of Senators and Representatives at noon on the 3rd day of January, of the years in which such terms would have ended if this article had not been ratified; and the terms of their successors shall then begin.

Section 2. The Congress shall assemble at least once in every year, and such meeting shall begin at noon on the 3rd day of January, unless they shall by law appoint a different day.

Section 3. If at the time fixed for the beginning of the term of the President, the President-elect shall have died, the Vice-President-elect shall become President. If a President shall not have been chosen before the time fixed for the beginning of his term, or if the President-elect shall have failed to qualify, then the Vice-President-elect shall act as President until a President shall have qualified, and the Congress may by law provide for the case wherein neither a President-elect nor a Vice-President-elect shall have qualified, declaring who shall then act as President, or the manner in which one who is to act shall be selected, and such person shall act accordingly until a President or Vice-President shall have qualified.

[26] Proclaimed January 29, 1919.
[27] Rescinded by the Twenty-first Amendment.
[28] Proclaimed August 26, 1920.
[29] Proclaimed February 6, 1933.

Section 4. The Congress may by law provide for the case of the death of any of the persons from whom the House of Representatives may choose a President whenever the right of choice shall have devolved upon them, and for the case of the death of any of the persons from whom the Senate may choose a Vice-President whenever the right of choice shall have devolved upon them.

Section 5. Sections 1 and 2 shall take effect on the 15th day of October following the ratification of this article.

Section 6. This article shall be inoperative unless it shall have been ratified as an amendment to the Constitution by the legislatures of three-fourths of the several States within seven years from the date of its submission.

Article XXI.[30] *Section* 1. The Eighteenth article of amendment to the Constitution of the United States is hereby repealed.

Section 2. The transportation or importation into any State, territory, or possession of the United States for delivery or use therein of intoxicating liquors, in violation of the laws thereof, is hereby prohibited.

Section 3. This article shall be inoperative unless it shall have been ratified as an amendment to the Constitution by conventions in the several States as provided in the Constitution, within seven years from the date of the submission hereof to the States by the Congress.

Article XXII.[31] *Section* 1. No person shall be elected to the office of the President more than twice, and no person who has held the office of President, or acted as President, for more than two years of a term to which some other person was elected President shall be elected to the office of the President more than once. But this Article shall not apply to any person holding the office of President when this Article was proposed by the Congress, and shall not prevent any person who may be holding the office of President, or acting as President, during the term within which this Article becomes operative from holding the office of President or acting as President during the remainder of such term.

Section 2. This article shall be inoperative unless it shall have been ratified as an amendment to the Constitution by the legislatures of three-fourths of the several States within seven years from the date of its submission to the States by the Congress.

Article XXIII.[32] *Section* 1. The District constituting the seat of Government of the United States shall appoint in such manner as the Congress may direct:

A number of electors of President and Vice-President equal to the whole number of Senators and Representatives in Congress to which the District would be entitled if it were a State, but in no event more than the least populous state; they shall be in addition to those appointed by the states, but they shall be considered, for the purposes of the election of President and Vice-President, to be electors appointed by a state; and they shall meet in the District and perform such duties as provided by the twelfth article of amendment.

Section 2. The Congress shall have power to enforce this article by appropriate legislation.

Article XXIV.[33] *Section* 1. The right of citizens of the United States to vote in

[30] Proclaimed December 5, 1933.
[31] Proclaimed March 1, 1951.
[32] Proclaimed April 3, 1961.
[33] Proclaimed February 4, 1964.

any primary or other election for President or Vice-President, for electors for President or Vice-President, or for Senator or Representative in Congess, shall not be denied or abridged by the United States or any state by reason of failure to pay any poll tax or other tax.

Section 2. The Congress shall have power to enforce this article by appropriate legislation.

ARTICLE OF AMENDMENT BEFORE THE STATES, 1965

Section 1. In case of the removal of the President from office or of his death or resignation, the Vice President shall become President.

Section 2. Whenever there is a vacancy in the office of the Vice President, the President shall nominate a Vice President who shall take office upon confirmation by a majority vote of both Houses of Congress.

Section 3. Whenever the President transmits to the President pro tempore of the Senate and the Speaker of the House of Representatives his written declaration that he is unable to discharge the powers and duties of his office, and until he transmits to them a written declaration to the contrary, such powers and duties shall be discharged by the Vice President as Acting President.

Section 4. Whenever the Vice President and a majority of either the principal officers of the executive departments or of such other body as Congress may by law provide, transmit to the President pro tempore of the Senate and the Speaker of the House of Representatives their written declaration that the President is unable to discharge the powers and duties of his office, the Vice President shall immediately assume the powers and duties of the office as Acting President.

Thereafter, when the President transmits to the President pro tempore of the Senate and the Speaker of the House of Representatives his written declaration that no inability exists, he shall resume the powers and duties of his office unless the Vice President and a majority of either the principal officers of the executive department or of such other body as Congress may by law provide, transmit within four days to the President pro tempore of the Senate and the Speaker of the House of Representatives their written declaration that the President is unable to discharge the powers and duties of his office. Thereupon Congress shall decide the issue, assembling within forty-eight hours for that purpose if not in session. If the Congress, within twenty one days after receipt of the latter written declaration, or, if Congress is not in session, within twenty-one days after Congress is required to assemble, determines by two-thirds vote of both Houses that the President is unable to discharge the powers and duties of his office, the Vice President shall continue to discharge the same as Acting President; otherwise, the President shall resume the powers and duties of his office.

REFERENCES

Department of State, *Documentary History of the Constitution of the United States of America, 1786-1870* (3 vols., Washington, 1894-1900).

The Constitution of the United States of America, Annotated to June 22, 1964, 88th Cong., 1st Sess., Sen. Doc. No. 39.

INDEX